MANUFACTURING PROCESSES AND MATERIALS FOR ENGINEERS

CONTRIBUTING AUTHORS

CARL A. KEYSER
Professor Emeritus of Metallurgical Engineering
University of Massachusetts

JAMES L. LEACH
Professor Emeritus of Mechanical Engineering
University of Illinois

GEORGE F. SCHRADER
Associate Dean
College of Engineering
University of Central Florida

MORSE B. SINGER

THIRD EDITION

MANUFACTURING PROCESSES AND MATERIALS FOR ENGINEERS

LAWRENCE E. DOYLE

Professor Emeritus of Mechanical Engineering
University of Illinois

PRENTICE-HALL, INC., ENGLEWOOD CLIFFS, NEW JERSEY

Library of Congress Cataloging in Publication Data

DOYLE, LAWRENCE E.
  Manufacturing processes and materials for engineers.

  Includes bibliographies and index.
  1. Metal-work. 2. Metals. I. Keyser, Carl A.
II. Title.
TS205.D64 1985   671   84-9766
ISBN 0-13-555921-9

MANUFACTURING PROCESSES
AND MATERIALS FOR ENGINEERS, THIRD EDITION

Lawrence E. Doyle, Carl A. Keyser, James L. Leach, George F. Schrader, Morse B. Singer

Editorial/production supervision: *Mary Carnis and Esther S. Koehn*
Interior design: *Anne T. Bonanno*
Cover design: *Anne T. Bonanno*
Manufacturing buyer: *Anthony Caruso*

Printed in the United States of America

10 9 8

ISBN 0-13-555921-9   01

Prentice-Hall International, Inc., *London*
Prentice-Hall of Australia Pty. Limited, *Sydney*
Editora Prentice-Hall do Brasil, Ltda., *Rio de Janeiro*
Prentice-Hall Canada Inc., *Toronto*
Prentice-Hall of India Private Limited, *New Delhi*
Prentice-Hall of Japan, Inc., *Tokyo*
Prentice-Hall of Southeast Asia Pte. Ltd., *Singapore*
Whitehall Books Limited, *Wellington, New Zealand*

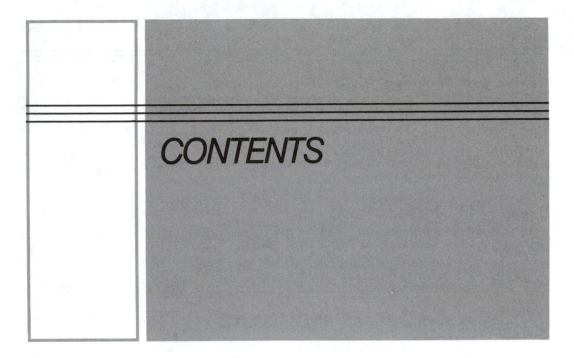

CONTENTS

8 FOUNDRY PROCESSES 120

9 HARD MOLD CASTING PROCESSES 176

10 POWDER METALLURGY 197

15 MEASUREMENT AND INSPECTION   399

16 HOW METALS ARE CUT   452

17 ECONOMICS OF METAL CUTTING   486

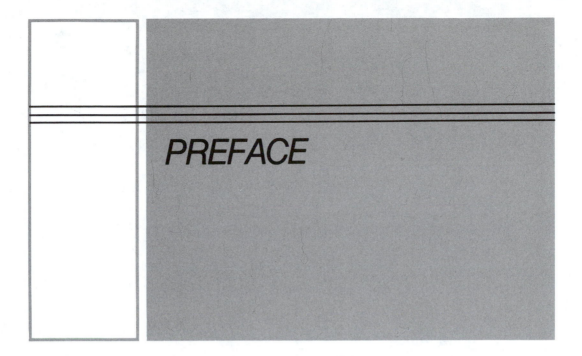

PREFACE

The trend today in engineering education is to emphasize fundamentals and give secondary attention to practices. A major reason for this is that practices rapidly become obsolete and change as knowledge increases. The approach in this text is to emphasize the *principles* on which manufacturing processes are based. Up-to-date processes are described to illustrate the principles.

Manufacturing processes and their efficient utilization are looked on in this book as engineering problems. One aim is to show how scientific and economic principles are applied to evaluate and solve these problems. Then similar problems are given at the ends of the chapters to afford the student exercises in applying engineering principles.

To the many manufacturers of machines and tools who have furnished illustrations and information, credit is extended throughout the book. Their generous cooperation is a mark of their sincere interest in promoting engineering education.

Lawrence E. Doyle

MANUFACTURING PROCESSES AND MATERIALS FOR ENGINEERS

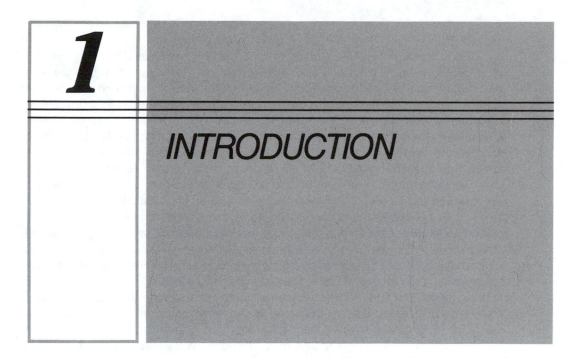

INTRODUCTION

THE PURPOSE OF THIS TEXT

Manufacturing Processes. Manufacture means to make goods and wares by industrial processes. Manufacturing is the largest segment of industry in the United States today and embraces many branches of industry. If we consider only a few, the drug, food, machinery, electrical, and shoe and leather industries, we see that each has its own technology. In the aggregate, all encompass a much larger store of knowledge than could be contained in one textbook. To keep within bounds, this book must be confined to the processes that are basic to all industry.

The derivation of the word *manufacture* reflects its original meaning: to make by hand. Today, however, manufacturing is done largely by machinery. The activity upon which all branches of manufacturing depend is the fabrication and use of machinery. In some areas, such as the machine tool and automobile industries, machinery is the end product as well as the means of manufacture. In those like the textile and furniture industries, machinery is the means of production. On the whole, those processes that produce machinery and hardware are basic to all forms of industry and are the ones treated in this book.

Mechanization of industry started with the industrial revolution during the eighteenth century. Early impetus was given the textile industry in England by the great inventions of machines for spinning and weaving. At the end of that century and the beginning of the next, the basic machines were brought forth in England and Europe for forming, shaping, and cutting metal. At about the same time in the United States, Eli Whitney gave practical effect to the principle of interchangeable manufacture, so that mechanical parts could be assembled without hand fitting. This provided the basis for full utilization of machines to make mechanical parts.

Early in the nineteenth century the rudimentary processes and concepts for producing mechanical parts were known and practiced. The course of events furnished the products upon which the practices were nurtured. Inventions after inventions were made of mechanical devices that men wanted and would buy; sewing machines, repeating guns, locomotives, engines, low-cost watches, and automobiles were among the leaders. Others have followed in the present century. The demand to produce the growing host of industrial and consumers goods gave the impetus to developing and refining the processes, machinery, and systems of manufacturing.

Manufacturing has always been and is today a growing and a changing art. Processes of the present can be expected to change in years ahead. Metal cutting is an example. For a hundred years cutting tools were made of plain hardened high-carbon steel with little alloying. In 1900, Taylor and White introduced high-speed steel containing alloys that enabled tools to operate at red heat and up to several times faster than ever before. Designs of machine tools were appreciably strengthened to get the benefits of the improved tools. Then about 1930 industry was given tools of hard carbides instead of steel. As they became accepted, they were found able to cut metal faster and give better finishes than steel tools. Again metal cutting changed; new machines were needed to drive the tools to their full capacities. Within recent years tools of ceramic and other materials have been discovered able to cut at heretofore fantastic rates. Merely to describe current practices and processes in any area is not enough. In this text the emphasis is placed upon the principles and underlying physical phenomena. The processes are described to illustrate the principles.

Materials.   Manufacturing is dependent upon materials. The main ingredients of mechanical devices are metals because they provide an optimum balance of strength, ductility, hardness, resilience, endurance, dimensional stability, resistance to wear, appearance, and economy for most applications. During this century plastics have become important supplements to metals because they offer corrosion-resistance, pliability, formability, colorability, and lightness in various forms. These are the materials that will be given prime attention.

Costs.   Manufacturing has given us an abundance of goods to satisfy our needs and wants at prices most people can afford to pay. To meet competition, the manufacturer must ever seek the lowest cost for acceptable quality. A meaningful basis for understanding a manufacturing process is in its elements of cost. What determines costs and how the costs of processes can be controlled, estimated, and compared are stressed throughout this text.

Manufacturing is commonly thought to connote large-quantity production. Many products, particularly consumers' goods, are manufactured in large quantities, but many others are made in only small or moderate quantities. Special-purpose machines, experimental or prototype models of aircraft, and huge turbogenerators may be manufactured one or a very few at a time. Railroad locomotives, commercial aircraft, and most machine tools are manufactured in lots of a few dozen to a few hundred. Quantity is the factor that has the most bearing upon the cost of a manufacturing process. A process for a few pieces must have features and a basis of cost quite different from those of a process to produce the same results on millions of parts if the least cost is to be realized in each case. The relationships between quantity and cost are pointed out for processes throughout this text.

Because machinery is essential to manufacturing, almost any manufacturing process requires a sizable investment. To give an appreciation of the relative amounts needed for comparable processes, approximate costs of major units of equipment are stated in the text. It can be expected that such costs will change from year to year with economic conditions, but the relative costs will stay about the same in most cases. The prices given are for the early 1980s. Guides are available for adjusting these costs to any other years, should the reader wish to do so. These guides are the published index numbers of prices of industrial machinery and equipment. Two outstanding ones are the *Wholesale Price Index of the U.S. Bureau of Labor Statistics* and *American Machinist Index of Metalworking Prices*. These offer index numbers for metalworking machinery, general purpose machinery and equipment, electrical machinery, fabricated metal products, and the like.

As an example of how index numbers may be used, consider the case of a machine tool that cost $19,000 in 1978. An index of metalworking machinery stood at 190 in that year and at 230 in 1980. The cost of the same type and size of machine in 1980 was estimated to be at 19,000 (230/190) = $23,000. An index number represents an average of individual prices. However, studies have indicated that most machinery and equipment costs can be estimated in the manner suggested within 10%, and practically all within 20% of actual costs.

PREPARATION FOR MANUFACTURING

Efficient manufacturing methods do not just happen. They are carefully planned. Typical steps taken to plan and coordinate the processes and their elements are depicted in Fig. 1-1. Most of these functions are performed by engineers, and surveys have shown that most engineers are engaged at some stage or other in such work. A knowledge of the principles of manufacturing processes is essential for the majority of engineers.

Planning the Product. The first stage in preparation for manufacturing is the development and design of a salable product, an analysis of its potential sales, and an estimate of the costs of making it. These are steps (1), (2), and (3) in Fig. 1-1.

Product design engineers must select the proper materials, ascertain the proportions and physical properties needed, and design the parts for efficient performance. Design engineers usually encounter two major problems. First, the product must function properly for a reasonable period of time. Second, it must be possible to manufacture the product at a competitive cost to earn a profit. Designers must select material that satisfies the two requirements. They must proportion the parts so they perform satisfactorily and can be made by the processes of lowest cost. As for materials, designers may have to choose from among plain-carbon steel, alloy steel,

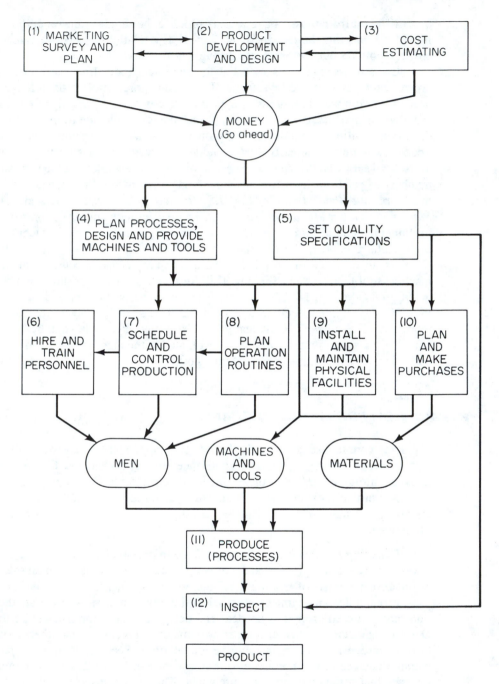

Figure 1-1 Functions that lead to efficient manufacturing.

aluminum, brass, plastics, or others. For processes, they may have to decide from among casting, forging, welding, machining, or a combination. From the standpoint of raw materials, they may have available castings, forgings, plates, standard structural shapes like I-beams, barstock, or others. The judgment and final selection made by designers will be influenced partly by the labor skills, types of machines, and raw materials available. For example, if the base and frame of a machine is to be manufactured, a choice may be presented between casting and welded shape construction. If the plant's principal installation is a foundry, the design may take advantage of the facilities. On the other hand, if welding skills and equipment are on hand and favorably priced rolled steel shapes and plates are readily available, the units may be made advantageously from steel and weld fabricated. In most cases, the alternatives need to be studied carefully for the quantity of output required to find the processes that promise lowest costs. To do that efficiently, design engineers must be acquainted with the fundamentals of manufacturing processes and materials.

Planning for Production. When the management of an enterprise decides on the basis of market surveys and cost estimates that a product as designed can be manufactured profitably, the money is appropriated and budgeted for the project. The first step is to delineate the processes on paper. Common practice is to list the steps or operations for each process on a *routing* or *process sheet,* which usually specifies also the machines, equipment, and tools needed and performance expected. Routings have many forms; one is shown in Fig. 1-2. Commercial machines and equipment are ordered and special tools are designed to conform to the process plan. A number of other forms, such as purchase and design orders, may also enter into the planning procedure. Quality specifications are set as a basis for procuring the gaging equipment and planning for inspection.

On the basis of the process plans, activities are initiated to prepare the physical means for production, as indicated by steps (6) through (10) in Fig. 1-1. Individual operation routines are planned and specified in detail; production schedules are set up; and steps are taken to hire and train the necessary personnel. Orders are issued to purchase machines, tools, and materials. The layout of the plant is planned and physical equipment installed accordingly as soon as available. When all is ready, the elements are brought together to carry out the processes. Certainly those who bear the responsibility for the planning and preparation described must be well acquainted with the principles of manufacturing processes.

The Engineer's Viewpoint. Evidence has been given to show that a knowledge of manufacturing processing is necessary for most engineers to do their work efficiently. There is yet another compelling reason for all engineers to study manufacturing processes. Manufacturing is beset with many challenging engineering problems. A study of processes shows how these problems are solved in realistic ways. Specific instances are pointed out, and many more are evident in this text. It is not proposed that students will apply these solutions to the same problems when they meet them in later years. Rather it is expected that they will improve upon them. On the other hand, an ingenious solution in one area can often be turned to good advantage

SPECIAL MFG. CO.   PRODUCTION AND MACHINE TOOL ROUTING   MIDWEST, IND.

PART NAME __Cover-Gear Housing__   PART NO. __72845__

MATERIAL __Cast Iron__   ROUGH SIZE __As Cast__   ROUGH WEIGHT __3 pounds__   DATE EFFECTIVE __8/15/84__

MODEL __E-33__   QUANTITY PER ASSEMBLY __1__   SHEET NO. __1__ OF __1__

OP NO.	DEPT NO.	OPERATION NAME	MACHINE NAME	MACH NO.	TOOLS & GAGES	TOOL NO.	GROUP NO.	REQ NO.	STD TIME MINS	STD TIME HRS	CAP EACH MACH PER HOUR
	307	Receive	Receiving Dept.		(1) Foundry Insp. Fixture	72845–T–1					
					(1) Cutter Driver	72845–T–2					
					(2) Cutter	72845–T–3					
5	327	Laboratory test	Laboratory Bench		(1) Receiving Insp. Fixture	72845–T–4					
	317	Inspection			(1) Tool Layout	72845–T–5					
	338	Stock	Stock Room		(1) Face Plate Fixture	72845–T–6					
	355	Locate from (3) Foundry pads to 1.3915 ±.005 on edge of flange and on (3) foundry pads on back side of flange. Face end of casting to 3.998 ±.001 dim. from end of casting. Leave 1/32 rad. in corner. Finish face joint face of bolt flange to .829 ±.003 dim. from end of casting. Leave 1/32 rad. in corner. Finish turn pilot to 3.998 ±.001 dia. Leave 1/32 radius in corner.	12" x 5' Leblond Engine Lathe.	777	(1) Tool Bit #DSF–2–NF	Std.			3.60	.06	13.89
					(1) Flush Pin Gage to Check 1.3915 ±.005 dim.	72845–T–7					
					(1) Flush Pin Gage to check .829 ±.003 dim.	72845–T–8					
					(1) 3.998 ±.001 Snap Gage.	Std.					
10	366	Break edges. Final Inspection.	Bench		(1) Flush pin gage to check 1.3915 ±.005 dim.	72845–T–7					
					(1) Flush pin gage to check .829 ±.003 dim.	72845–T–8					
					(1) 3.998 ±.001 snap gage.	Std					

ENGR. GROUP INDEX	ASSEMBLY NO. 93724	WRITTEN BY C.E.M.	TOTALS PER PC		.06
			PER JOB		

REMARKS:

Figure 1-2   Example of a process-planning sheet.

in another. A control system on a machine tool may serve admirably on excavation equipment also, for example. But most of all, a glimpse of the ingenuity, finesse, and good judgment that have been exercised by other engineers can do much to arouse those traits and bolster the self-confidence of young engineers when they come to pit their knowledge of science and economics against the problems of the world.

The International System of Units. There is a definite trend in industry in the United States to convert from the inch-pound (U.S. Customary or English) to the International System (SI) (commonly referred to as the *metric* system) of measurement units. This movement is sanctioned by law. To conform, the present edition of this book is written in SI units with corresponding inch-pound units. The standard practice followed herein is that prescribed by the *Metric Practice Guide E380* of the American Society for Testing and Materials except for practical conventions. For instance, the standard unit for velocity in SI is meters per second, and in this text the velocity of moving or falling bodies is so given for ready incorporation into scientific formulas. However, shop performance, such as cutting speed or linear production rate, is expressed in meters per minute, as generally sanctioned by the ANSI B5.51 M-1979, *Preferred SI Units for Machine Tools*.

2

MAKING IRON,
STEEL,
AND NONFERROUS
METALS

IRON, STEEL, AND POWER

Pig iron, which contains impurities amounting to 7% by weight, is made in a blast furnace by reduction of iron ore. Pig iron is then refined to produce cast iron or steel. The availability of raw materials, particularly fuels, is the major factor in determining the location of blast furnaces and steel mills. The equivalent of about two tons of fuel is required for the manufacture of each ton of hot-rolled steel product. The dilemma of undeveloped countries which lack adequate fuel sources is that it is politically desirable but economically impractical to build steel mills. The same objection can be raised to the agitation for steel mills in New England.

The ability to produce steel is basic to the development of economic, political, and military power. A study of steel production statistics over the last century shows this to be true. The westward expansion of the United States would have been impossible in the absence of tonnage production of the steel needed for the creation of an efficient land transportation system. Exploitation of the West was limited until the middle of the nineteenth century, when economical methods were devised for production of steel on a large scale. Increasingly, modern industrial societies require efficient methods of converting fuel to energy, and for this, machinery made of steel is essential.

IRONMAKING

The raw materials for making 1 ton of pig iron are approximately: 2 tons of ore (or other source of iron), almost 1 ton of coke, nearly $\frac{1}{2}$ ton of limestone, and about $3\frac{1}{2}$ tons of air. Thus the blast furnace produces about 1 ton of principal product for every 7 tons of material which enters it. Although the composition of pig iron is variable, a typical analysis might be: carbon 4%, silicon 1.5%, manganese 1%, sulfur 0.04%, phosphorus 0.4%, and the balance iron. The exact composition will depend upon the composition of the iron source, the flux, and the coke, and upon the operating conditions of the blast furnace.

The major sources of iron in the blast furnace charge or *burden* are ore or agglomerates. Minor sources are scrap, roll scale from hot-rolling operations, and slag. The principal ores used are hematite (Fe_2O_3) and limonite ($Fe_2O_3 \cdot x\,H_2O$). Magnetite (Fe_3O_4) and other ores are less commonly used. Agglomerates are made from naturally fine-particle ores, flue dust, and ore concentrates. Agglomerates are available as sinter, which resembles medium-sized clinkers, or pellets, which are rounded particles less than about 1 in. in diameter. Sinter is made by mixing the iron-bearing fines with high-ash coke and fine particles of limestone flux, and carefully burning the mixture. Pellets are made from very fine particles of iron ore concentrate, fuel, binder (bentonite clay), and water. The mixture is placed in a rotating drum, where it is formed into small pellets. These are then fired to achieve the strength necessary to prevent them from crumbling when placed in the blast furnace. If the solids charged into the blast furnace crumble, they will become so compacted that the air blast is restricted, and effectiveness of the furnace declines. Most ores and sinter contain 50 to 65% iron. Pellets, often made from magnetic fines obtained by processing low-grade taconite rock, contain about 60 to 67% iron. Other ingredients of the iron-source materials are alumina (Al_2O_3), silica (SiO_2), limestone ($CaCO_3$), carbonaceous materials, and chemically combined water.

Limestone ($CaCO_3$) and/or dolomite [$CaMg(CO_3)_2$] are the principal blast furnace fluxes. The function of the *flux* is to react with the principal impurities, such as alumina (Al_2O_3) and silica (SiO_2), forming a low-melting slag. The slag is lighter than the molten iron and floats on the latter in the bottom of the furnace. The composition of the slag is adjusted to assist in lowering the sulfur content of the iron. At temperatures encountered in the blast furnace, calcining takes place: $CaCO_3 \rightarrow CaO + CO_2$. The basic lime (CaO) then reacts with the acidic impurities (Al_2O_3 and SiO_2) to form slag.

The metallurgical coke used in blast furnaces must be strong enough to prevent crumbling and blocking of air passages. Since most of the sulfur in the iron originates in the coke, the sulfur content of the coke should be less than 1.5%, and usually is in the range of 0.4 to 1.2%. Ash and phosphorus contents should also be low. Finally, although the coke should be free from fines, the pieces should not be so large that optimum burning rates are not reached.

The coke serves two functions: (1) it provides heat, necessary for the attainment of desirable chemical equilibria and adequate rates of reaction; and (2) it provides the reducing gas, carbon monoxide (CO), which is largely responsible for reduction of iron oxide. Additional sources of heat include the hot-air blast up to about 1100°C (2000°F) and gaseous fuel injected with the air. A typical energy balance for a furnace with an 8.5-m (28-ft)-diameter hearth producing about 2500 metric tons (2800 tons) of pig iron per day is shown in Table 2-1.

Coke is produced by the destructive distillation, in the absence of air, of special

TABLE 2-1 ENERGY BALANCE FOR A BLAST FURNACE

	MJ/kg of pig iron	Millions Btu/2000 lb of pig iron
Energy input		
Coke	14.9	12.80
Hot-air blast	2.0	1.68
Gaseous fuel	1.1	0.96
Total input	18.0	15.44
Energy consumed: reduction of iron and other oxides, heat lost with hot metal and hot clay	10.6	9.07
Energy output: heat carried away by recoverable top gas	7.4	6.37

Source: Adapted from, *The Making, Shaping, and Treating of Steel*, 9th ed., H. E. McGannon, ed., United States Steel Corporation, 1971., Pittsburgh, Pa., p. 457.

grades of bituminous coal. In addition to metallurgical coke, a large quantity of important by-products is obtained. They consist largely of gas, compounds of ammonia, coal tars, and light oil containing benzene, toluene, naphtha, etc. Thus the steel industry, through coking, is intimately connected to the production of fertilizer, and a host of organic chemical products such as dyes, plastics, solvents, drugs, and explosives. Typical yields from coal are shown in Table 2-2.

In addition to solids which are charged into the furnace at the top, air is blown in at the bottom of the blast furnace. This air is at a temperature between 760 and 1100°C (1400 and 2000°F) and is under pressure. The air is enriched with gaseous fuels, and moisture is added in controlled amounts. These additions to the air blast enable control of flame temperature and produce the extra quantities of reducing gases needed to keep up with the high operating rates developed by the high-temperature operation of modern furnaces. Coke alone in the burden will not produce enough reducing gases for maximum efficiency.

TABLE 2-2 YIELDS FROM COKING

	Per 1000 kg (metric ton) of coal	Per 2000 lb (ton) of coal
Blast furnace coke	600–700 kg	1200–1400 lb
Coke breeze (fines)	50–100 kg	100–200 lb
Coke-oven gas	275–375 kL	9500–11,500 ft^3
Tar	30–50 L	8–12 gal
Ammonium sulfate	10–13 kg	20–25 lb
Ammonia liquor	60–130 L	15–35 gal
Light oil	10–15 L	2.5–4 gal

Source: Adapted from, H. E. McGannon, *The Making, Shaping, and Treating of Steel*, 9th ed., United States Steel Corporation, Pittsburgh, Pa., 1971, p. 105.

THE BLAST FURNACE AND ITS CHEMISTRY

The reactions taking place in the blast furnace can be substantially represented as follows:

$$2C + O_2 \longrightarrow 2CO \qquad \Delta H = -221.1 \text{ kJ} \qquad (2\text{-}1)$$

$$C + H_2O \longrightarrow H_2 + CO \qquad \Delta H = 131.3 \text{ kJ} \qquad (2\text{-}2)$$

$$Fe_2O_3 + 3CO \longrightarrow 2Fe + 3CO_2 \quad \Delta H = -25.5 \text{ kJ} \qquad (2\text{-}3)$$

$$CO_2 + C \longrightarrow 2CO \qquad \Delta H = 172.6 \text{ kJ} \qquad (2\text{-}4)$$

$$Fe_2O_3 + 3H_2 \longrightarrow 2Fe + 3H_2O \quad \Delta H = 97.9 \text{ kJ} \qquad (2\text{-}5)$$

$$H_2O + C \longrightarrow CO + H_2 \qquad \Delta H = 131.3 \text{ kJ} \qquad (2\text{-}6)$$

$$CaCO_3 \longrightarrow CaO + CO_2 \qquad \Delta H = 179.3 \text{ kJ} \qquad (2\text{-}7)$$

$$XCaO + YSiO_2 + ZAl_2O_3 \longrightarrow XCaO \cdot YSiO_2 \cdot ZAl_2O_3 \text{ flux reaction}$$

A minus sign with a ΔH value means that heat is liberated by the reaction.

Essentially the blast furnace is an irregularly shaped cylinder into which solids are fed at the top and enriched air is blown in at the bottom. Liquid slag and metal are tapped from the bottom of the furnace and flue gases and dust escape from the top of the furnace. The furnaces operate continuously for 5 to 7 years and then must be rebuilt. The dimensions and material balance are shown for a typical blast furnace in Fig. 2-1. As the solids in the charge progress downward in the furnace they are heated and expand. At the same time, the gases become cooler as they approach the top of the furnace. In the bosh (see Fig. 2-1) the iron and slag melt and drip from the still solid portion of the charge, thus reducing the solid bulk. The reduction in diameter of the bosh, along with a central pillar of unburned coke, supports the charge. Gas volume increases in the bosh as a result of heating and because of oxidation of coke [see Eqs. (2-1), (2-2), (2-4), and (2-6)]. The initial increase in gas volume is also accommodated by the shape of the bosh.

Special refractories and brick are used in furnaces. At the top of the furnace a super duty, hard-fired brick is used which is resistant to the abrasion of the charge dumped into the furnace. High-temperature resistance is not a factor here. Brick in the inwall zone (see Fig. 2-1) must withstand moderately high temperatures and moderate abrasion from the charge as it moves downward. The brick in the hearth and bosh must withstand very high temperatures as well as erosion and slag attack. Carbon brick is occasionally used in the hearth. The refractory brick in the inwall and bosh are cooled by hollow copper plates fitted between courses of brick. Water is circulated through these plates as well as through the tuyere (air-blast nozzle) linings. A furnace producing about 2600 metric tons (2800 tons) of pig iron per day uses over 38,000 m^3 (10,000,000 gal) of recirculating water for cooling purposes.

The flue gases leaving the top of the furnace are passed through a dust catcher to remove solids and are then burned in stoves used for preheating the air blast. The dust is agglomerated and used in the burden.

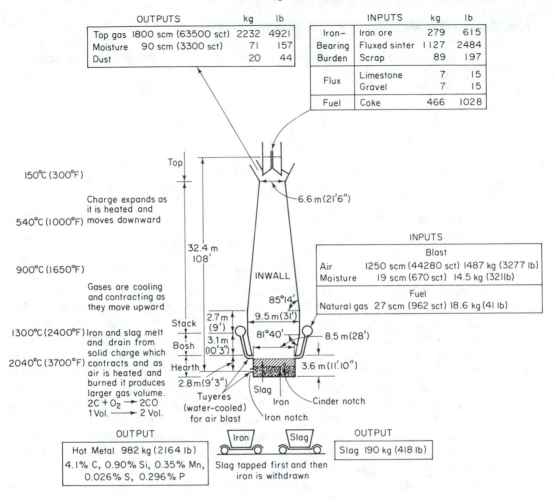

Figure 2-1 Typical blast furnace, showing inputs, outputs, dimensions, and temperatures developed in the furnace. The abbreviations *SCF* and *SCM* refer, respectively, to *standard cubic feet* and *standard cubic meters,* measured at 16°C (60°F) and 762 mm (30 in.) of mercury. (Data from *The Making, Shaping and Treating of Steel,* 9th ed., H. E. McGannon, ed., © United States Steel Corporation, Pittsburgh, Pa., 1971, p. 457.)

STEELMAKING

Steel is made by refining either pig iron or scrap steel or by refining a combination of both materials. Pig iron supplies, by far, most of the steel produced, but scrap steel plays a vital role in steel production. In steel produced from pig iron, the basic problem is to oxidize the impurities present, which are then removed either as a gas (in the case of the major impurity, carbon) or in the slag (in the case of silicon, phosphorus, and sulfur). Oxygen is supplied either by an air blast (as in most of the older methods) or as pure oxygen (in the most modern methods) or by means of oxides (such as iron ore or rusty scrap).

In the last two decades there has been a revolution in the methods used for producing steel. For instance, 80% of production came from basic open hearths in 1963. By 1984 this figure dropped to 7%. More efficient processes have been adopted. Basic oxygen converters currently account for 63%, while 30% is made in electric furnaces. The latter are especially suited for small non-integrated specialty mills known as mini-mills.

STEELMAKING BY THE BASIC OXYGEN PROCESS

The basic oxygen process is a development of the Bessemer process, the first method by which large-scale tonnages of steel were produced. The Bessemer process relied on blowing air from holes in the bottom of the converter through the molten pig iron charge. Oxidation of impurities supplies not only enough heat to keep the charge molten, but also enough to maintain favorable chemical equilibria. In the basic oxygen process, air is replaced by pure oxygen, introduced through a lance whose end is just above the surface of the molten metal.

The most widely used basic oxygen method is known as the L-D process, the name for which derives from the towns of Linz and Donawitz in Austria, where it was first used. A typical furnace is shown in Fig. 2-2. The end of the water-cooled oxygen lance is suspended about 3 ft above the surface of the charge and supplies oxygen at a pressure of 1000 to 1240 kPa (140 to 180 psi). The furnace, a cylindrical vessel about 9 m (30 ft) high with an inside diameter of about 5.5 m (18 ft), has a mouth about 2.75 m (9 ft) in diameter. It is tilted to receive its charge, first scrap and then molten pig iron, after which it is brought to a vertical position under a water-cooled hood. The oxygen lance is lowered and the blow started. The oxygen quickly produces iron oxide in the melt and this, in turn, oxidizes carbon, causing vigorous agitation of the melt as carbon monoxide and carbon dioxide are evolved. Fluxing agents, such as lime and fluorspar, are dropped from a hopper through a chute after the oxygen blow has commenced. The lance is removed after the impurities have been oxidized. Then the furnace is tilted, first to one side to tap the steel through a taphole, and then to the other side to pour off the slag. Final adjustment of the composition is made by ladle additions. The time of blowing varies according to composition and heat size, but about 25 minutes is typical. Gases and slag particles carried along with the gas stream are scrubbed before being exhausted to the atmosphere.

Basic oxygen furnaces vary from 45 to 320 metric tons (50 to 350 tons) capacity. They use from 12 to 30% scrap in the charge, which is below the minimum acceptable for basic open hearths. (Both the basic open hearth and electric furnace can use up to 100% scrap in the charge.) But the basic oxygen furnace can produce steel at the rate of about 360 metric tons (400 tons) per hour per furnace, whereas the basic open hearth could only produce at the rate of about 55 metric tons (60 tons) per hour per furnace. Since each heat from a basic oxygen furnace requires only between one-half

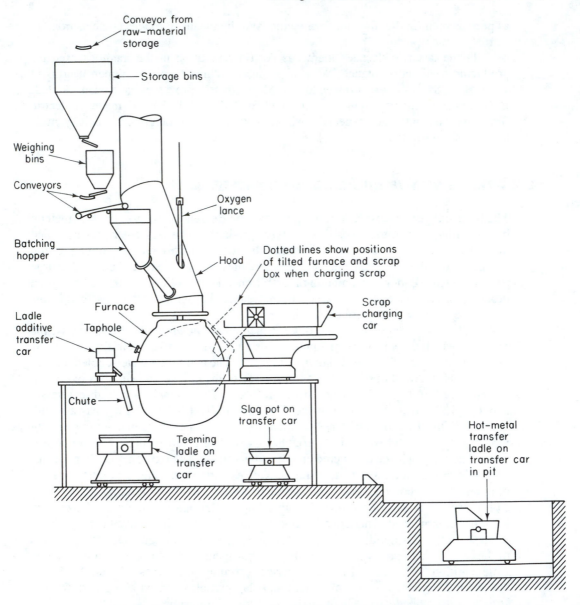

Figure 2-2 Schematic elevation showing the relative locations of various operating units of the basic oxygen process. (From *The Making, Shaping and Treating of Steel,* 9th ed., H. E. McGannon, ed., © United States Steel Corporation, Pittsburgh, Pa., 1971, p. 489.)

and three-fourths of an hour (compared to up to 10 hours per basic open-hearth heats), quick and precise methods of checking composition and computing requirements for adjustment of the charge are essential.

The basic oxygen furnace can be used for the same composition pig iron as the basic open hearth. High-phosphorus (up to 2.0%) pig iron can be refined if a doubleslagging method is used. In this process, the first slag to form is removed and replaced with a fresh slag that removes additional phosphorus.

The same grades of steel are produced in the basic oxygen process as in the basic open-hearth process, and in addition some grades of stainless and higher-alloy steel can also be produced which could not be made in the basic open hearth. The quality of product is as good or better than that of open-hearth steel. Very fluid slags yield a low phosphorus content. Nitrogen content is also low because pure oxygen rather than air is used for the blow. Surprisingly, oxygen content is also low and this reduces requirements for aluminum deoxidizing additions. Sulfur is low because of the avoidance of sulfur-bearing fuels as a heat source. Manganese economies have also been realized because of better control of the process.

About half of the basic oxygen steel produced is used for sheets, plates, and structural steel of welding quality. The other half is used for rimming steel (explained later), from which deep-drawn parts are made, such as automobile body parts.

STEELMAKING BY THE ELECTRIC-FURNACE PROCESS

Most electric-furnace steel produced in the United States is made in furnaces heated by an arc which is formed between electrodes and the metal of the charge. This is the type of furnace whose operation is described below. Some steel is made in electric furnaces in which the heat is radiated to the bath from an arc formed between two electrodes positioned over the charge. A small amount of steel is also made by induction-heated furnaces. Both acid and basic linings are used, depending upon the nature of the charge and the product desired. In general, the highest-quality steels are produced in the electric furnace. Since hydrocarbon fuels are not needed for heat, this source of contamination is eliminated. Better than 30% of all steel made in the United States is produced in electric furnaces.

The procedure followed in making electric-furnace steel depends upon the product being made. If the steel is to contain an appreciable percentage of easily oxidized alloying elements, such as chromium, tungsten, and molybdenum, two slag covers are used during a heat. An oxidizing slag promotes oxidizing and fluxing of carbon, phosphorus, and silicon. The oxidizing slag is then removed and replaced by a reducing slag in which CaO and CaC_2 are important ingredients. This slag blanket helps removal of surfur and oxide impurities and affords protection against oxidation of alloy element additions. In making steel for ordinary castings the second slag is not needed, since the easily oxidized elements found in stainless and tool steels are not present.

An electric arc furnace is shown in Fig. 2-3. Three electrodes, which can be raised and lowered, project through the refractory-lined top. The top can be swung aside when the electrodes are raised so that the charge can be dropped into the furnace. The electrodes are made from petroleum coke, bonded with pitch or tar and shaped to approximate size. The rough electrodes are then heated to 2200°C (4000°F), which converts the coke to graphite. Electrodes up to 76 cm (30 in.) in diameter and 213 cm

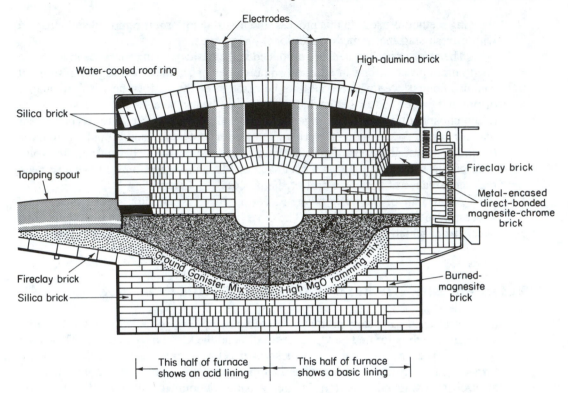

Figure 2-3 Schematic cross section of a Heroult electric furnace. (From *The Making, Shaping and Treating of Steel*, 9th ed., H. E. McGannon, ed., United States Steel Corporation, Pittsburgh, Pa., 1971, p. 551.)

(84 in.) long are available. Furnace capacities vary from 1 to 360 metric tons, (1 to 400 tons), but furnaces in the range 14 to 140 metric tons (15 to 150 tons) are most common. A typical, but by no means universal procedure for operating an electric furnace is described below.

After a heat is tapped, the furnace is inspected for damage and repaired as needed. Selected scrap is charged through the top of the furnace by means of a drop-bottom bucket. If ore is included in the charge, it is added with the solid scrap or after partial or complete melting. Modern practice tends toward use of oxygen to lower carbon content, rather than the use of ore. Some nonoxidizable alloys may be added prior to meltdown. The electrodes are then lowered, the power is turned on, and an arc is struck. As melting proceeds the electrodes burn down through the metal charge and a pool of molten metal forms in the hearth of the furnace. A slag forms from oxidized impurities and by reaction with lime or the furnace lining. After oxidation is complete, this slag is drawn off and replaced by a new slag cover in which the principal ingredients are lime, silica, magnesia, and calcium carbide. As soon as the final analysis of slag and bath have been adjusted to proper levels, necessary alloy additions are made and the furnace is tapped. When the furnace is tilted for tapping, the molten steel remains covered and protected by the slag until the furnace is empty. The time elapsed from charging to tapping is dependent upon the size of the furnace and nature of the product, but about 4 hours is typical.

Although the cost of making steel in an electric furnace is generally higher than for steel made in basic oxygen furnaces, the quality of the product that can be achieved is better. Steel of the lowest possible phosphorus and sulfur contents and having the fewest nonmetallic inclusions is made by the electric-furnace process, and only by this process can high-alloy steels, such as some stainless grades and some tool and die steels, be made. The higher cost of the process is also justified where small-scale, intermittent steel production requirements would not support a blast furnace–basic oxygen furnace installation.

FINISHING AND INGOT TEEMING

After hot metal in the basic oxygen furnace has been brought to the desired composition specifications, it is tapped into a refractory-lined ladle and separated from its oxidizing slag cover. It is now possible, if desired, to add deoxidizing agents such as ferrosilicon, ferrotitanium, and ferroaluminum. If deoxidation had been attempted before separation from the slag cover, phosphorus impurities in the slag would have been reduced and redissolved in the metal.

When steel is made in the electric furnace, the oxidizing slag containing phosphorus impurities is usually removed partway through the refining process and replaced in the furnace by a fresh reducing slag so that return of the phosphorus to the molten metal is not a problem. The steel is then tapped into a ladle.

Pouring the steel from a ladle into ingot molds is known as teeming. If deoxidation is not carried out, the oxygen dissolved in the molten steel reacts to form increasing amounts of carbon monoxide and solid iron oxide as the temperature of the steel in the mold drops. The carbon monoxide is evolved as a gas, whose bubbles are trapped in the solidifying mass. The iron oxides form nonmetallic inclusions which are harmful to the mechanical properties of the finished steel. The control of the amount of carbon monoxide evolved is very important and leads to three kinds of steel: *rimmed, semikilled,* and *killed steel.*

Rimmed steel is essentially not deoxidized, although a small amount of aluminum may be added to the steel in the mold to prevent excessive carbon monoxide evolution. The bubbles of carbon monoxide are trapped below the first surface layers to solidify and near the top of the ingot. The evolution of gas compensates for the shrinkage which normally accompanies solidification and eliminates pipe formation (see Chap. 8). This results in larger yields per ingot, for when pipes occur (see Fig. 2-4) the piped end must be cropped off and remelted as heavy scrap.

The gas bubbles in rimmed ingots are formed by carbon monoxide and are far enough below the rim, or outer skin, of sound steel that they do not become oxidized upon subsequent heating and hot rolling of the ingot. Therefore, they are welded shut. The surface of the rimmed steel ingots is very nearly pure iron, and after hot and cold

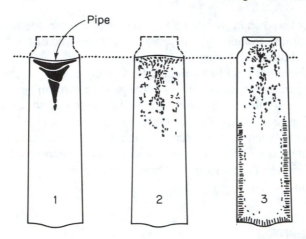

Figure 2-4 Typical ingot sections showing (1) killed steel, (2) semikilled steel, (3) rimmed steel. (Adapted from *The Making, Shaping and Treating of Steel*, 9th ed., H. E. McGannon, ed., © United States Steel Corporation, Pittsburgh, Pa., 1971, p. 587.)

rolling these ingots are well suited for deep-drawing sheet (see Chap. 12), strip, and tin plate. Rimmed steels are low-carbon grades.

Semikilled steel is made by addition of appreciable quantities of aluminum and ferrosilicon in the ladle, but not enough for complete deoxidation (see Fig. 2-4). Semikilled steels provide a compromise between good yield and quality, the quality being suitable for structural steels and heavy plates. Semikilled steels are of intermediate carbon contents.

Killed steel is made by following the treatment for semikilled steel excepting that final quantities of aluminum are added in the mold to deoxidize the steel completely. Since there is no evolution of gas from the freezing mass, the metal lies quietly in the mold and hence is called *killed* steel. Large pipes form in killed steel ingots and large cropping losses result. Killed steel ingots are the soundest since they are free from gas bubbles and have fewer entrapped inclusions. The cleanliness of this steel results in part from the opportunity of the oxide inclusions to rise to the surface as the steel solidifies quietly in the mold. Killed steels are high-carbon grades.

The choice of deoxidizing agent also permits a variation in the quality of the semikilled and killed steels. If ferrosilicon is used as the deoxidant, the grain size of the steel is relatively coarse. If aluminum or ferrotitanium is used, Al_2O_3 or TiO_2 forms as a result of oxidation and remains trapped in the molten and solidified ingot. In low-carbon steel this results in a fine grain size, which is particularly useful for deep-drawing applications. In medium- or high-carbon steel a fine-grained structure results, which has superior toughness when quenched and tempered (see Chap. 5).

SPECIAL TECHNIQUES IN STEEL REFINING

In the quest for steels of higher quality, particularly in regard to lower gas content (dissolved hydrogen, oxygen, and nitrogen) and fewer nonmetallic inclusions (oxides), various vacuum techniques have been developed, and are still developing. These are discussed in Chap. 8 under the heading of vacuum melting. Continuous

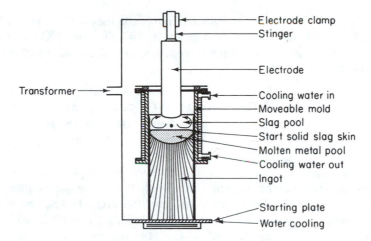

Figure 2-5 Features of a typical electroslag remelting furnace. (From *The Making, Shaping and Treating of Steel,* 9th ed., H. E. McGannon, ed., © United States Steel Corporation, Pittsburgh, Pa., 1971, p. 582.)

casting, described in Chap. 9 accounts 'for more than 30% of the steel made in the United States.

The *electroslag remelting process* (ESR) is basically a method by which an electrode of a given steel composition is remelted and recast under a slag cover to produce a more refined ingot of essentially the same as the starting composition. A refining slag is placed on the baseplate of a water-cooled mold and the electrode to be refined is lowered into this. At first, arcing melts the slag, but eventually the electrical resistance of the molten slag, into which the end of the electrode is immersed, produces enough heat to melt the electrode itself. The water-cooled mold solidifies the refined metal, which rises slowly as more and more refined metal drips from the electrode, and the length of the new ingot grows. Ingots of very high-quality tool steel, bearing steel, high-speed steel, and ultra service steel are produced in this way. They vary in size up to 165 cm (65 in.) in diameter and 5 m (16 ft) long. The ESR process, shown schematically in Fig. 2-5, is a competitor of *vacuum arc remelting* (VAR), which is also known as *consumable electrode melting*. In this process, no slag cover is used, heat is supplied by an arc between the electrode being remelted and the new ingot, and the water-cooled mold is evacuated. Somewhat larger ingots are made by VAR than ESR, but the quality of the steel produced by both is similar. Both processes are used also for refining nonferrous super alloys.

ALUMINUM

One of the most abundant metals on the surface of the earth is aluminum, occuring as an oxide in most clay. However, it is not now economically feasible to concentrate this oxide to the point where it can serve as a source of aluminum. The ore used as a source of aluminum is *bauxite*. Bauxite is essentially hydrated aluminum oxide, $Al_2O_3 \cdot 3H_2O$, but it also contains silica, SiO_2, titania, TiO_2, and iron oxide, Fe_2O_3. After crushing the ore, impurities are removed by treatment with hot sodium hydroxide:

$$2NaOH + Al_2O_3 \cdot 3H_2O \underset{\text{cold}}{\overset{\text{hot}}{\rightleftharpoons}} 2NaAlO_2 + 4H_2O$$

$$\underset{\substack{\text{insoluble in} \\ H_2O}}{} \qquad\qquad \underset{\substack{\text{soluble in} \\ H_2O}}{}$$

Titania and iron oxide do not form soluble compounds with sodium hydroxide, although some of the silica may dissolve to form a complex sodium aluminum silicate. If the solution is filtered while still hot, the TiO_2, Fe_2O_3, and most of the SiO_2 are removed. The concentrated hot sodium aluminate is cooled, seeded with $Al_2O_3 \cdot 3H_2O$ crystals, and precipitation of $Al_2O_3 \cdot 3H_2O$ occurs. The complex sodium aluminum silicate remains in solution and can be filtered away. The pure, hydrated aluminum oxide is heated to form pure alumina:

$$Al_2O_3 \cdot 3H_2O \underset{980\,°C}{\overset{1000°C(1800°F)}{\longrightarrow}} Al_2O_3 + 3H_2O$$

Aluminum oxide is too stable for reduction by carbon monoxide in a blast furnace, and is instead reduced in an electrolytic cell. The purified alumina is dissolved in molten *cryolite*, Na_3AlF_6, to which small amounts (under 10%) of aluminum fluoride and calcium fluoride have been added. The voltage across the cell attracts positively charged Al^{3+} to a negatively charged carbon cathode lining. Molten aluminum with a melting point of 650°C (1200°F) collects on the bottom of the cell, from which it is periodically tapped. Negatively charged oxygen, O^{2-}, is attracted to carbon anodes, where it reacts to form CO. From time to time the alumina is replenished. Carbon anodes are consumed at the rate of about 650 kg/metric ton (1300 lb/ton) of aluminum produced.

COPPER

The sources of copper include native copper, sulfides, oxides, and silicates. In the United States the principal ore contains about 1% copper as a sulfide, and the method described for extracting copper is based on this ore.

Since the copper content of the ore is so low it is necessary to effect a concentration. The ore is first crushed, in gyratory or jaw crushers, and then screened. After ball milling and further screening, it is finally ground wet and mixed with a coating of oil. The oil wets the sulfide particles but not the particles of gangue, which consist of SiO_2, Al_2O_3, $CaCO_3$, etc. The finely ground, oil-coated ore is placed in a tank of water and agitated. The oil-coated sulfide particles pick up small air bubbles and form a froth which is rich in copper and iron sulfides, while the gangue settles out. The froth overflows and is filtered to produce a solid concentrate containing about 40% copper.

Roasting of the concentrate dries and eliminates some sulfur by reactions such as $CuS \rightarrow Cu_2S + S$. This sulfur is oxidized to SO_2. Some of the iron and copper sulfides may be converted to oxides, while arsenic, antimony, selenium, and zinc sulfides are converted to oxides and volatized. Gold and silver, which are valuable by-products, remain with the copper and iron. The product consists mainly of Cu_2S, FeS, and impurities, of which SiO_2 is the major one. Modern roasting furnaces consist of two hearths at the top of a cylindrical furnace. The concentrate is fed to these, where it is dried, preheated, and partially roasted. Rotating rakes work the concentrate toward holes in the hearths and finally the concentrated ore falls through the central part of the furnace where calcination to Cu_2S occurs and some oxidation takes place. The final reactions occur in other hearths at the bottom of the furnace.

Smelting of the roasted ore often takes place in reverberatory furnaces. These are furnaces in which a shallow pool of impure metal and slag is heated by a flame playing over the surface of the charge. A mixture of roasted concentrate and a limestone flux is charged through the top of the furnace at one end. Powdered coal, oil, or gas are introduced at the charging end of the furnace. The charge melts rapidly and separates into two layers. The light slag layer contains most of the gangue, some iron (as iron silicate), and about 4% copper. The slag is sent back through the reverberatory furnace to recover the copper. The heavy layer, called *matte,* consists essentially of sulfides of iron and copper, plus gold and silver. A slag taphole at the end of the furnace allows continuous removal of slag. The matte is tapped periodically through tapholes at the bottom of the furnace. The smelting operations remove some of the iron and most of the other impurities (excepting gold and silver).

The matte (essentially Cu_2S and FeS) is often refined in a converter similar to the L-D basic oxygen converter, except that air nozzles are located in the sides of the converter and air is blown across the bath. Heat is supplied by oxidation of sulfur to sulfur dioxide. The copper sulfide is converted to impure metallic copper and sinks to the bottom of the bath, and the iron sulfide is converted to FeO, reacting with a silica flux or the silica lining to form an iron silicate slag. The converter is tipped to discharge the slag, and the impure copper, containing precious metals and small amounts of Ni, Bi, Se, Te, and S, is cast into pigs for further refining. It is called *blister* copper because it solidifies with evolution of gas and has a porous, blistered surface.

Blister copper is placed into a reverberatory furnace which is operated with an excess of oxygen by blowing air into the charge. This oxidizes sulfur and the oxidizable impurities, which leave as a gas or form a siliceous slag. At the time of slag removal, the bath contains up to about 6% Cu_2O. This is reduced by *poling,* which consists of stirring the bath with green wood poles. These evolve hydrocarbons, reducing the Cu_2O back to Cu. Poling is stopped at an oxygen content of about 0.04%. This amount of oxygen is necessary to prevent impurities from reverting to the copper from the slag. This copper is known as *tough-pitch* copper and is nearly pure copper.

Tough-pitch copper is often electrolytically refined to improve its conductivity, or to recover valuable quantities of precious metals, or both. The electrolytically deposited copper is then remelted and cast into slabs, billets, or bars. This grade of copper cannot contain more than 0.01% of impurities, excluding silver.

The stages of roasting, smelting, and refining copper as described have been practiced in the United States for over a century. In recent years, demands for conservation of energy and the environment have forced changes and improvements in the processes. One improvement has been continuous copper smelting. A typical installation features three stationary furnaces with the molten products flowing by gravity from a smelting furnace to a slag-cleaning furnace to a converting furnace. Stages in the newer processes are not necessarily identical to the older ones. The most undesirable emission from copper smelting and refining is the SO_2 gas. In some installations, electric heating has been adopted to avoid diluting the SO_2 gas with other combustion products, so that the gas can be utilized in acid manufacture. In some cases, sulfide concentrations and oxygen are injected into the furnace and burned to add heat and further concentrate the SO_2 gas. Some smelters have found it necessary to add scrubbers for their exhaust products.

MISCELLANEOUS METALS

There is great similarity between the extractive metallurgy of iron, aluminum, and copper, and the extractive metallurgy of other metals. It is not practical to detail here the methods used for all metals. For the reader who is interested in additional information, attention is called to the references at the end of this chapter. The remaining paragraphs of this chapter outline the general scheme followed for the production of magnesium, zinc, lead, tin, titanium, and tungsten.

Magnesium.   The Dow process was the first commercial method and is still the most important means for production of magnesium. Hydrated $MgCl_2$ is obtained from natural brines by recrystallization. This is dehydrated and mixed with NaCl and KCl to form a mixture which will melt at about 700°C (1300°F). Current is passed through the melt in an electrolytic cell. Magnesium forms at the cathode and floats to the surface, from which it is periodically ladled. Chlorine forms at the anode and is collected as a valuable by-product. Magnesium chloride for electrolysis is also obtained from seawater and magnesite ores.

Zinc.   The ores of zinc usually must be concentrated by flotation methods. Concentrated sulfide ores are converted to the oxide or sulfate by heating in air. Zinc oxide ores, carbonate ores, and the converted zinc sulfate or zinc oxide can be heated with coal. The latter acts not only as a source of heat but provides the reducing medium for reduction to metallic zinc. Since the retorts operate above the boiling point of zinc, the metal passes off as a vapor and is condensed as a liquid near 480°C (900°F). Further purification can be accomplished by redistillation. A small amount of zinc is produced by electrolysis of zinc sulfate solutions. Environmental demands have closed down many zinc smelters in recent years. As these demands become more stringent it is considered likely that the electrolytic process will become the only one feasible in the United States.

Lead.   In the United States, the principal ore is galena or PbS. This is concentrated by a flotation process and is then roasted to convert it to PbO. The lead oxide is charged into a blast furnace with coke and with a flux of lime and iron oxide. Molten lead collects in the bottom of the furnace from which it is tapped at intervals. Impurities are also tapped periodically and treated to recover valuable quantities of other metals. Further refining of the lead is often necessary. This step consists principally of heating the lead in a reverberatory furnace in the presence of air. When so heated, most of the impurities form oxides which pass into the exhaust gases, or into a skin which can be skimmed.

Environmental demands are dictating drastic changes and improvements in the lead refining industry. Measures must be taken to clean stack gases. In one new process, galena concentrates are first oxidized and then reduced in the molten state in a single sealed reactor. The process gases contain 20% SO_2 and are suitable for acid manufacture.

Tin.   Although no significant amount of tin is produced in the United States, this country is the largest consumer of the metal. The principal ore contains the mineral cassiterite, SnO_2, which is often reduced by reaction with coal in a reverberatory furnace. Very high purity tin is obtained by electrolytic refining.

Titanium.   The sources of titanium are ores containing the minerals ilmenite ($FeO \cdot TiO_2$) or rutile (TiO_2). High-carbon ferrotitanium is made in an arc furnace by reducing ilmenite with carbon. Low-carbon ferrotitanium is made by reduction with aluminum. These alloys are used to deoxidize steels and are also used in making some alloy steels. For the manufacture of titanium used in titanium-base alloys, rutile is reduced to TiC in an arc furnace and then converted to $TiCl_4$ by roasting in a chlorine atmosphere. This is then reduced with magnesium at about 760°C (1400°F) to form a mixture of titanium, magnesium, and magnesium chloride. The latter impurities are removed by distillation and leaching, and the sponge titanium is vacuum arc melted to form a compact mass.

Tungsten.   Tungsten has such a high melting point (about 3400°C or 6150°F) that it is not easily converted to the liquid state. Tungsten is mined as an ore containing the minerals wolframite, $FeWO_4$, or scheelite, $CaWO_4$. This is converted to tungstic acid, H_2WO_4, which is reduced to tungsten powder by hot hydrogen. The powder is compressed to form a briquet and sintered in a hydrogen atmosphere at about 1100°C (2000°F) using the techniques of powder metallurgy described in Chap. 10. Following sintering, the dense, solid bar is mechanically worked in order to improve its properties and convert it to wire filaments. Most tungsten is used as an alloying element in steels. For this purpose the ore concentrate is smelted with coal, flux, and iron chips to form a carbonized ferrotungsten.

QUESTIONS AND PROBLEMS

1. What raw materials are required for the production of pig iron?
2. Distinguish between ore and agglomerate.
3. What functions are performed in the blast furnace by (a) limestone? (b) ore? (c) air?
4. (a) Find ΔH for $C + O_2 \rightarrow CO_2$. Is heat absorbed or liberated by the reaction?
   (b) Prove that ΔH for $Fe_2O_3 + 3CO \rightarrow 2Fe + 3CO_2$ is 26 kJ using Eqs. (2-4), (2-5), and (2-6).
5. (a) What are the principal impurities in pig iron which are largely removed when it is converted to steel?
   (b) How are the impurities referred to in part (a) removed?
6. (a) What is the source of heat in the basic oxygen furnace?
   (b) What processes has the basic oxygen process almost entirely replaced.
7. Why are two slag covers needed for production of stainless steels and tool steels produced in the electric furnace?
8. Describe the difference between rimmed, semikilled, and killed steel.
9. (a) What are the reasons for using vacuum-melting techniques in steelmaking?
   (b) What is the difference between vacuum melting and vacuum degassing?
10. (a) How are the principal impurities removed from bauxite to make pure alumina?
    (b) How is aluminum obtained from pure alumina?
11. Describe (a) concentration, (b) roasting, (c) smelting, (d) converting, and (e) refining as applied to the extraction of copper from its ores.
12. Of the metals whose refining is discussed in this chapter, list those whose primary refining is by reduction with coal, coke, hydrocarbons, or hydrogen, and those whose primary refining is by electrolytic action.

REFERENCES

BARKSDALE, J., *Titanium, Its Occurrence, Chemistry, and Technology*, 2nd ed., Ronald Press, New York, 1966.

CAIRNS, J. H., and P. T. GILBERT, *The Technology of Heavy Non-ferrous Metals and Alloys*, George Newnes, London, 1967.

EMLEY, E. F., *Principles of Magnesium Technology*, Pergammon Press, Oxford, 1966.

GILCHRIST, J. D., *Extraction Metallurgy*, 2nd ed., Pergamon Press, Oxford, 1979.

GILL, C. B., *Non-Ferrous Extractive Metallurgy*, Wiley-Interscience, New York, 1980.

McGANNON, H. E., ed., *The Making, Shaping, and Treating of Steel*, 9th ed., United States Steel Corporation, Pittsburgh, Pa., 1971.

SCHLECHTEN, A. W., "Revolutionary Changes in Extractive Metallurgy," *ASM News*, Apr. 1980.

VANHORN, K. R., ed., *Aluminum V*, I–III, American Society for Metals, Metals Park, Ohio, 1967.

VARLEY, P. C., *The Technology of Aluminum and Its Alloys*, George Newnes/Butterworth, London, 1970.

3

TESTING
OF ENGINEERING
MATERIALS

Testing is applied to materials, components, and assemblies. It consists of measurement of fundamental properties or measurement of responses to particular influences such as load, temperature, and corrodants. Inspection is closely related to testing and it also is applied to materials, components, and assemblies. Inspection is concerned with the geometry of objects, detection of internal defects, and examinations for performance, finish, color, and general appearance. This chapter is devoted to testing and to those inspection methods (often loosely called test methods) aimed at detection of internal defects. Other kinds of inspection are discussed in Chap. 15.

Tests and inspection methods may or may not be destructive of the object being examined, and hence, testing is commonly subdivided into two major areas: destructive and nondestructive testing. Tests are also classified as physical, chemical, or mechanical tests. Physical tests include measurement of such quantities as specific gravity, and electric, magnetic, thermal, and optical properties. These are usually performed in scientific laboratories, rather than in engineering laboratories, and are not mentioned further here. Chemical tests, by which chemical properties are determined, are generally in the realm of the scientist rather than the engineer and, with the exception of corrosion testing, are not discussed in this text. Mechanical tests are most often performed in engineering laboratories. These include measurements of properties such as hardness, strength, and toughness, which, along with inspection for internal flaws, are the object of this chapter. These tests require special equipment and techniques.

THE TENSION TEST

The tension test is one of the most widely used of the mechanical tests. There are many variations of this test, specified in detail by the ASTM (American Society for Testing and Materials), to accommodate the widely differing character of materials, such as metals, elastomers, plastics, and glass. The tension testing of metals is described below.

The common round tension test specimen is shown in Fig. 3-1. Its diameter is either 12.5 ± 0.25 mm (SI), or 0.500 ± 0.010 in. (English), with respective gage lengths of 50.00 ± 0.10 mm or 2.000 ± 0.005 in. Additional dimensional details are given in Fig. 3-1.

The specimen is gripped in a machine which can apply loads along the axis of the specimen. If necessary, an extensometer for measuring changes in length can be attached to the specimen. As the specimen is slowly elongated, simultaneous measurements of applied load and length are either noted manually or recorded automatically. It is convenient to convert the loads to *unit loads* or *stresses,* and the changes in length to *unit changes in length,* or *strains.* Stresses are calculated by dividing the load by the cross-sectional area over which the load acts. Strains are found by dividing the change in length by the gage length, i.e., by the original length of the specimen. Stress-strain relationships determined in this way can be applied to speci-

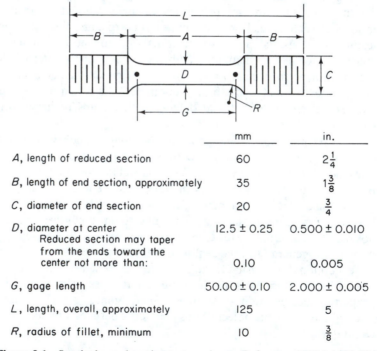

	mm	in.
A, length of reduced section	60	$2\frac{1}{4}$
B, length of end section, approximately	35	$1\frac{3}{8}$
C, diameter of end section	20	$\frac{3}{4}$
D, diameter at center	12.5 ± 0.25	0.500 ± 0.010
Reduced section may taper from the ends toward the center not more than:	0.10	0.005
G, gage length	50.00 ± 0.10	2.000 ± 0.005
L, length, overall, approximately	125	5
R, radius of fillet, minimum	10	$\frac{3}{8}$

Figure 3-1   Standard round tension test specimen. (Reference: ASTM A370-73.)

mens and structural members whose dimensions differ from those of the test specimen. The test is completed when the specimen finally breaks.

Typical load and length data for a mild steel, and their conversion to stress and strain are shown in Table 3-1. A plot of stresses and strains obtained from these data is shown in Fig. 3-2. For most ductile metallic materials, it should be noted, stress and strain are initially proportional to one another. Response of this kind is known as *elastic action*. The constant of proportionality between elastic strain *e* and elastic stress *S* is known as the *modulus of elasticity* or *Young's modulus*, and is denoted by the symbol *E*. Young's modulus is indicative of the property called *stiffness*; small values of *E* indicate flexible materials and large values of *E* reflect stiffness and rigidity. Comparing a spring of steel with one of brass, both having the same dimensions, shows the steel spring to be stiffer than the brass spring. This is as it should be, for brass has a modulus of elasticity of about 110 GPa (16×10^6 psi), while that for steel is about 210 GPa (30×10^6 psi). The modulus of elasticity must be taken into consideration in forming and metal-cutting operations which are discussed in Chaps.

TABLE 3-1 STRESS-STRAIN DATA FOR MILD STEEL

$D_0 = 12.75$ mm (0.502 in.) $A_0 = 127.7$ mm^2 (0.198 in.^{2})
$D_f = 7.47$ mm (0.294 in.) $A_f = 43.8$ mm^2 (0.068 in.^{2})
$L_0 = 50.80$ mm (2.000 in.) $L_f = 68.5$ mm (2.700 in.)

Load		Length		Diameter		Stress		Strain
kN	lb	mm	in.	mm	in.	MPa	ksi[a]	
2.6	590	50.805	2.0002			20.7	3.0	0.0001
5.3	1130	50.810	2.0004			39.3	5.7	0.0002
7.6	1700	50.815	2.0006			59.3	8.6	0.0003
10.6	2380	50.820	2.0008			82.7	12.0	0.0004
12.8	2870	50.825	2.0010			100.0	14.5	0.0005
15.6	3510	50.830	2.0012			122.0	17.7	0.0006
18.5	4160	50.836	2.0014			144.8	21.0	0.0007
20.7	4650	50.841	2.0016			162.0	23.5	0.0008
23.5	5290	50.846	2.0018			184.1	26.7	0.0009
26.4	5940	50.851	2.0020			206.8	30.0	0.0010
28.3	6350	50.856	2.0022			221.0	32.1	0.0011
29.9	6730	50.861	2.0024			234.4	34.0	0.0012
31.7	7120	50.876	2.0030			247.9	36.0	0.0015
32.7	7340	50.902	2.0040			255.5	37.1	0.0020
32.3	7250	50.927	2.0050			252.4	36.6	0.0025
31.6	7110	50.952	2.0060			247.5	35.9	0.0030
32.6	7330	50.978	2.0070			255.1	37.0	0.0035
34.3	7720	51.003	2.0080			268.9	39.0	0.0040
37.2	8370	53.290	2.0980	11.9	0.469	291.3	42.3	0.049
42.3	9500	—	—	—	—	331.0	48.0	—
37.2	8370	65.0	2.56	9.87	0.388	291.3	42.3	0.28
26.1	5870	68.6	2.70	7.47	0.294	204.4	29.7	0.35

[a]1 ksi = 1000 psi.

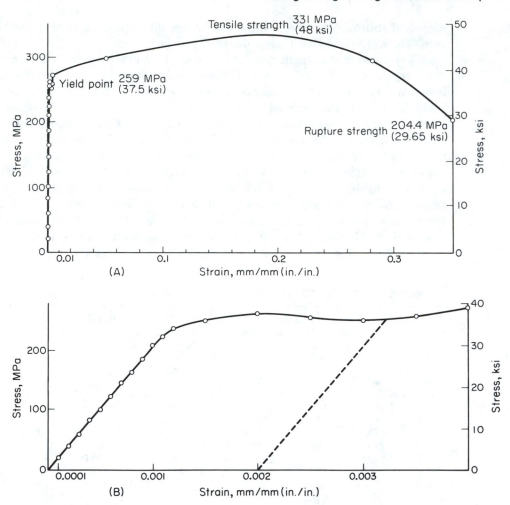

Figure 3-2 (A) Stress-strain curve for a mild steel plotted from data given in Table 3-1; (B) a portion of the same curve as shown in part (A) with the strain axis expanded to permit determination of the yield strength and modulus of elasticity.

13 and 16 through 19. The property of *springback* is a function of the modulus of elasticity and refers to the extent to which metal springs back when an elastic deforming load is removed. If steel and brass wires of the same diameter are to be coiled to make springs of the same diameter, the brass will have to be bent under load to a coil of smaller diameter than the steel, because brass has a lower modulus of elasticity and hence has more springback. (This assumes both the brass and steel have the same yield strength; see below.) In metal cutting, the modulus of elasticity of the workpiece affects its rigidity, and the modulus of elasticity of the cutting tool and the tool holder affect their rigidity. These are major factors in the achievement of dimensional control.

As the stress and strain increase in a tensile test, eventually a point is reached at which stress and strain are no longer directly proportional to one another. The lowest stress at which stress and strain are no longer proportional is known as the *proportional limit*. Beyond the proportional limit, strain increases faster than does stress, and the material is permanently deformed. Permanent deformation or set is known as *inelastic action,* and the first stress at which this occurs is known as the *elastic limit*. Strains below the elastic limit are known as *elastic strains;* elastically strained objects recover their original dimensions upon removal of a load. In mild steels, with increasing strain, a point is reached at which strain increases without further increase in stress. This stress is known as the *yield point*. The yield point is much more readily determined than is the proportional limit or the elastic limit. It is taken as a practical measure of the limit of elastic action, i.e., the stress above which the material is permanently deformed. The practical limit of elastic action is extremely important in manufacturing operations such as rolling, drawing and deep drawing, spinning, etc., for it shows what stresses must be exceeded if permanent deformation is to be achieved (see Chaps. 12 and 13).

Determination of the limit of elastic action in metals and alloys which do not have a yield point depends upon measurement of a limiting value of stress required to produce an arbitrarily selected amount of permanent strain. The selected strain is often 0.2% or 0.002 mm/mm (in./in.) strain. The corresponding stress is called the *yield strength*. Yield strengths, like yield points, are much more easily determined than are elastic limits. Both, of course, indicate practical limits of elastic action. Yield strength measurements for mild steels give essentially the same values as yield points.

If an extensometer is not available for making the strain measurements needed for yield point and yield strength determinations, approximate values can be obtained by coating the surface of the specimen with a brittle lacquer which will flake off at the yield load. If an unmachined, hot-worked, scale-coated rod is tested, yielding causes the scale to pop off, and the corresponding load can be taken as the yield load.

Beyond the limit of elastic action, the tensile specimen at first elongates quite uniformly along its length. Eventually, the elongation tends to become concentrated in one region, and since the volume of the material does not change, this results in development of a constriction. This is called *necking down*. The change in length divided by the original gage length is expressed as a percentage of elongation:

$$\% \text{ elongation} = \frac{L_f - L_0}{L_0} \times 100$$

where L_f is the final length and L_0 is the initial length. The percentage elongation is a factor in the ability of the material to deform inelastically. This ability is called *ductility*. The change in area divided by the original cross section of the specimen is expressed as percentage reduction of area:

$$\% \text{ R.A.} = \frac{A_0 - A_f}{A_0} \times 100$$

where A_0 is the original, and A_f the final, area of cross section. This is also a factor in the ability of the material to deform inelastically. Lack of ductility is known as *brittleness*. Ductility and brittleness are very important in forming operations, for they tend to determine just how severely the material can be deformed without tearing or rupturing. Annealing (see Chap. 5) tends to restore ductility to cold-deformed metallic materials so that forming operations can be continued (see Chaps. 12 and 13). Ductility is related also to metal cutting (Chaps. 16 through 19). Excessive ductility generally tends to be associated in machined parts with development of rough surface finishes and high rates of tool wear.

The tensile stress-strain relationship just described, and for which a curve is plotted in Fig. 3-2, is known as the *apparent stress-strain* or the *engineering stress-strain relationship*. The true, or actual, stress σ at any given instant during the test is greater than the apparent, or engineering, stress S because the actual area $A_{act.}$ over which the load is distributed is smaller than the initial area A_0. Thus, $\sigma = F/A_{act.}$, and $S = F/A_0$, and $\sigma > S$. The difference between the actual and initial areas is negligibly small until the specimen begins to neck down. Likewise, increments of true strain are defined as dL/L where L is the actual gage length at any moment and dL is the incremental change in length caused by an incremental increase in load. The total true strain ϵ at any load l is found from

$$\epsilon = \int_{L_0}^{L_l} \frac{dL}{L} = \ln \frac{L_l}{L_0} \tag{3-1}$$

Since the volume remains constant during straining, then $V_0 = A_0 L_0 = V_l = A_l L_l$, where V_0, A_0, and L_0 are respectively the volume, cross-sectional area, and gage length before a load is applied, and V_l, A_l, and L_l are the same respective values under load l.

$$\epsilon = \ln \frac{A_0}{A_l} \tag{3-2}$$

Since the apparent strain

$$e = \frac{L_l - L_0}{L_0} = \frac{L_l}{L_0} - \frac{L_0}{L_0}$$

then

$$e + 1 = \frac{L_l}{L_0}$$

and

$$\epsilon = \ln(e + 1) \tag{3-3}$$

True stresses and true strains have been calculated from the data of Table 3-1 and tabulated in Table 3-2. Beyond the point of necking down, true strains should not be calculated from Eq. (3-3) which uses apparent strain e. Errors result from such a calculation because the strain is not uniformly distributed over the length of the specimen. This source of error is avoided if Eq. (3-2) is used. However, the true stress calculation is still not exact because of the fact that stress intensification occurs as a

TABLE 3-2 TRUE STRESSES AND TRUE STRAINS AS DETERMINED FROM TABLE 3-1

Load		Diameter		Area, A_l		True Stress, σ		A_0/A_l	True Strain, ϵ $\ln(A_0/A_l)$
kN	lb	mm	in.	mm^2	in.^{2}	MPa	ksi		
37.2	8370	11.9	0.469	111	0.1728	335.1	48.4	1.14	0.131
42.3	9500	—	—	—	—	—	—	—	—
37.2	8370	9.87	0.388	76.5	0.1182	486.2	70.8	1.68	0.519
26.1	5870	7.47	0.294	43.8	0.0679	595.8	86.5	2.92	1.072

Note: Apparent and true values are practically identical for loads up to 34.3 kN (7720 lb) and are not tabulated again. Refer to Table 3-1.

result of the notch which accompanies necking down. Therefore the real stresses are even greater than calculated true stresses. These latter errors do not, however, seriously detract from the value of true stress-true strain relationships calculated as described above. For refined results needed in critical work, tension testing machine–computer systems are available on which the loads, displacement, and specimen responses are continuously measured and analyzed. The conditions of the test are altered as necessary and interpreted to yield a true stress-strain relationship.

A plot of true stress versus true strain in the elastic range yields a straight line identical with the engineering stress-strain curve, since $\sigma = S$ and $\epsilon = e$. See Fig. 3-3 and compare with Fig. 3-2. Similarly, a log-log plot of *elastic* true stress-true strain yields a straight line since

$$\sigma = E\epsilon$$

and

$$\log \sigma = \log E + \log \epsilon$$

This is shown in Fig. 3-4. The value of E can be obtained by extrapolation of the plot to a strain $\epsilon = 1$, for which $\log \epsilon = 0$ and $\log \sigma = \log E$.

A plot of true stress versus true strain in the *plastic* range on linear coordinates deviates from the engineering stress-strain plot, as can be seen from Fig. 3-3. A plot of the true stress-strain data of Table 3-2 on a log-log plot is shown in Fig. 3-4. In the plastic region a straight line is obtained, indicating that

$$\sigma = k\epsilon^m \qquad (3\text{-}4)$$

or

$$\log \sigma = \log k + m \log \epsilon \qquad (3\text{-}5)$$

where m and k are constants. The value of k can be determined by substituting the value for $\log \sigma$ at a strain $\epsilon = 1$, for which $\log \epsilon = 0$. That is, k is the true stress at a true strain $= 1$. Knowing k and substituting corresponding values of $\log \sigma$ and $\log \epsilon$ in Eq. (3-5) yields a value for m. The constant m is a property of the metal or alloy and is known as the *work-hardening coefficient*.

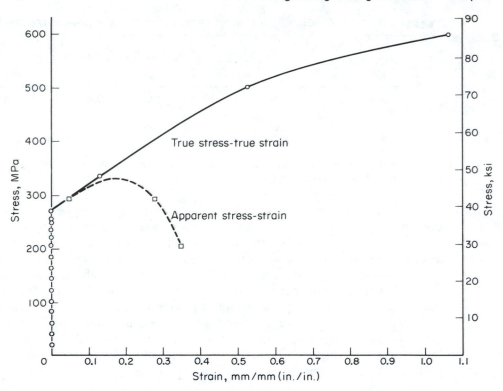

Figure 3-3 Comparison of the true stress–true strain curve with the apparent stress–apparent strain curve (both plotted on a linear scale). The data from which these curves were constructed appears in Tables 3-1 and 3-2.

The engineering tensile strength, or apparent tensile strength (also called ultimate strength), is the figure given in most reference books. It is obtained from

$$S = \frac{F_{ult}}{A_0}$$

where F_{ult} is the maximum or ultimate load sustained by the specimen. The true tensile strength is obtained from

$$\sigma = \frac{F_{rupt}}{A_f}$$

where F_{rupt} is the breaking or rupture load. A comparison of Fig. 3-2 with Fig. 3-3 shows that the true tensile strength is always greater than the engineering tensile strength. The true stress-true strain relationship is important for it shows that metallic materials continue to get stronger as the amount of cold deformation continues, up to the point of rupture. It is for this reason that as drawing and cold work proceed (see Chaps. 12 and 13) the stresses involved become larger. The extent to which a metal or alloy is strengthened by cold work is indicated by the work-hardening coefficient

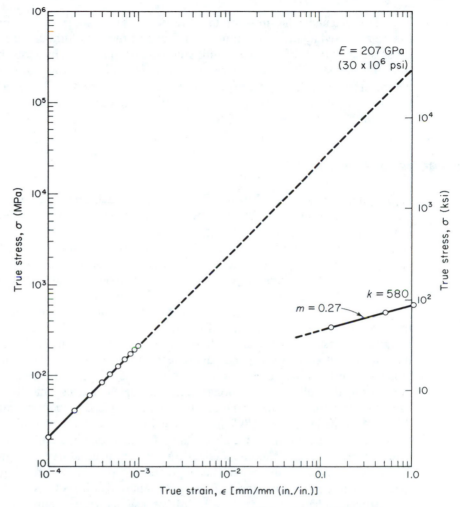

Figure 3-4 True stress–true strain curve for a mild steel, plotted on a log-log scale. The data from which this curve was constructed appears in Tables 3-1 and 3-2.

m. Large values of m show that strength and hardness increase more for a given amount of cold-work than when values of m are small. The value of m is indicated by the slope of the log-log plot of the true stress–true strain curve in the plastic region.

Work hardening affects metal cutting (see Chaps. 16 through 19) because the metal chip becomes more severely deformed before it finally breaks away from the workpiece. The great difficulty of machining austenitic stainless steels can be explained on the basis of the large value of the work-hardening coefficient of these alloys. Since austenitic steels (Chap. 6) are quite ductile, a great deal of work hardening occurs before the point of rupture is reached. This adversely affects power consumption and tool wear.

The area under the stress-strain curve indicates the *toughness,* i.e., energy which can be absorbed by the material up to the point of rupture. Although the engineering stress-strain curve is often used for this computation, a more realistic result is obtained from the true stress-true strain curve. Toughness is expressed as energy absorbed in the material being deformed, expressed in J/cm^3 or in.-lb/in.^{3}. This is obtained from the stress-strain curve by multiplying the ordinate in MPa by the abscissa in mm/mm = m/m, or psi by in./in.

HARDNESS TESTING

Although hardness testing does not directly give as much detailed information as does tensile testing, it is so fast and convenient that it is much more widely used. *Hardness* is usually defined as resistance of a material to penetration. In the most generally accepted tests, an indenter is pressed into the surface of the material by a slowly applied known load, and the extent of the resulting impression is measured mechanically or optically. A large impression for a given load and indenter indicates a soft material, and the opposite is true for a small impression.

Hardness is primarily a function of the elastic limit (i.e., yield strength) of the material, and to a lesser extent a function of the work-hardening coefficient. The modulus of elasticity also exerts a slight effect on hardness. Since for a given metallic material the elastic limit depends upon such factors as the previous history of the material, hardness measurements are useful in determining if processing techniques are meeting their objectives. Among the processing techniques which can be successfully monitored are heat treating (see Chap. 5), casting and foundry processes (Chaps. 8 and 9), forming processes (Chaps. 12 and 13), and welding and joining processes (Chap. 14). In addition since the elastic limit, tensile strength, ductility, and toughness bear a fixed relationship to one another for a given material having a given history, it is possible to deduce these mechanical properties from hardness readings on a given material whose history is known. The most common hardness tests can be classed as macro- or microhardness tests. Macrohardness tests scrutinize a fairly large area of the surface and their impressions are visible to the naked eye. Microhardness test impressions are very small, so that a microscope is required to see them.

The Brinell hardness tester forces a hardened steel or carbide ball having a diameter of 10 mm into a metal by means of a fixed load. A 3000-kg load is used for testing ferrous alloys and alloys of similar hardness. When brass and soft alloys are tested, a 500-kg load is used. The time of loading is specified between 10 and 30 seconds, depending upon the alloy being examined. After the load is removed, the diameter of the impression is measured to the nearest 0.01 mm, by a microscope or by a laser scanner for automatic reading. The hardness, which is actually the load divided by the area of the impression, is read directly from tables for which hardness has been calculated for various diameter impressions.

The Brinell penetration is so large that it results in an averaging effect and is not as sensitive to surface roughness, light scale, or dirt, as are the Rockwell and the microhardness tests. However, specimens must be thicker, successive impressions must be made further apart, and the test is destructive if applied to small components or specimens. Representative Brinell hardness numbers (Bhns) are 425 for white cast iron (very hard), 160 for gray cast iron, and 105 for wrought iron (very soft).

The Rockwell hardness test is probably the most widely used method of hardness testing. Rockwell testers use much smaller penetrators and loads than does the Brinell tester. Four sizes of hard balls from $\frac{1}{16}$ to $\frac{1}{2}$ in. in diameter are available as well as a cone-shaped diamond. For testing metallic materials, the $\frac{1}{16}$-in. ball and the diamond penetrator are most commonly used. The penetrator chuck is mechanically connected to a dial indicator which responds to vertical motion of the penetrator (Fig. 3-5). Since the penetrators are small, the surface of the specimen should be ground smooth and clean. The specimen is placed on the anvil of the machine and the penetrator seated by means of a 10-kg minor load. The dial indicator is zeroed and then a major load of 60, 100, or 150 kg is applied, forcing the penetrator into the specimen. Upon removal of the major load, the indented specimen recovers slightly, and the final depth of penetration is registered directly on the dial indicator as a hardness number. Various combinations of penetrator and major load are used and designated by a series of letters. The two commonest scales are the R_B scale and the R_C scale, respectively standing for the $\frac{1}{16}$-in. ball with the 100-kg major load, and the diamond penetrator with the 150-kg major load. In general, very hard materials are tested with the diamond penetrator. Mild steel might have a R_B reading of 90; hardened alloy steel might have a R_C of 55. These are stated as 90 R_B and 55 R_C.

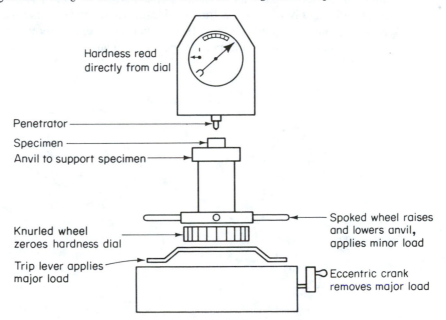

Hardness read directly from dial

Penetrator

Specimen

Anvil to support specimen

Spoked wheel raises and lowers anvil, applies minor load

Knurled wheel zeroes hardness dial

Trip lever applies major load

Eccentric crank removes major load

Figure 3-5   Schematic sketch of Rockwell hardness tester. Weights, not shown, hang from rear of machine.

The impressions made by the Rockwell tester are much smaller than those of the Brinell penetrator. Hence the Rockwell test should not be used on nonhomogeneous alloys such as cast iron, because it is subject to errors from small soft or hard spots, and from small voids. On the other hand, since the impressions are so small, the test is considered nondestructive in many applications. In addition, thinner specimens can be tested by the Rockwell than by the Brinell test. The Rockwell test can be used to test materials over a greater range of hardness because of the many combinations of penetrators and loads which are available. It can be used on plastics as well as on metallic materials.

A series of superficial Rockwell scales are available for testing the hardness of very thin materials or case-hardened steels (see Chap. 5). The superficial Rockwell tester uses a 3-kg minor load and major loads of 15, 30, or 45 kg.

The most frequently used microhardness testers are the Vickers and the Tukon testers. (The Vickers is not always considered to be a microhardness tester.) Both use a diamond penetrator. The Vickers diamond penetrator produces a square-shaped impression; the Knoop penetrator used with the Tukon tester produces a diamond-shaped impression. Impressions formed by both machines are measured by means of microscopes, and the hardness number is obtained from tables listing the load and diagonal measurement of the impression (see Fig. 3-6). The Tukon tester produces the smaller impression of the two, and is a true microhardness tester. It can be used to measure the hardness of alloy components and for measuring the changes in hardness at minute increments below the surface of case-hardened steel. The Tukon tester has been applied to studying metal-cutting operations to measure the hardness over small areas of chip and workpiece surface. Both tests require careful polishing and etching of the specimen surface before measurements are made.

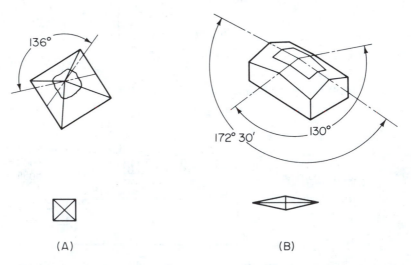

(A)   (B)

Figure 3-6   (A) Vickers diamond penetrator and impression; (B) Knoop diamond penetrator and impression.

A less used hardness tester is the Scleroscope. A diamond-tipped hammer is dropped 10 in. upon the workpiece surface, and the height of its rebound is read on a graduated scale to obtain a hardness number. This device mars the surface the least and can most easily be moved and applied to huge pieces.

NOTCHED-BAR IMPACT TESTING

Contrary to what might be expected from the name, impact testing does not provide a means of studying response of materials to high-velocity loading. The results obtained would not differ greatly if the loads were slowly applied, as in the tensile test. Notched-bar impact testing does provide a quick way of loading and measuring the toughness of a notched bar, i.e., the ability to absorb energy. The results are not directly comparable to the results obtained by integrating the area under the tensile stress-strain curve because of the variable response of materials to the effects of notching. However, the test results are useful in comparing, for a given composition, the effects of prior history on toughness. Of particular interest in this regard is the effect of heat treatment on properties of steel (see Chap. 5). Overheating steel impairs toughness. This can readily be detected by a notched-bar impact test and by examining the appearance of the fractured surface. Another important application is to study the effects of tempering cycles on hardened steels. Certain cycles are harmful to the toughness of some alloy steels, and the notched-bar impact test is useful in detecting these. Still another application is in the determination of embrittling temperatures, particularly for ferrous alloys. Many steel compositions tend to lose toughness as subfreezing temperatures are approached. The notched-bar impact test provides a means of determining the embrittling range for different compositions.

The most common kinds of impact test use notched specimens loaded as beams. The beams may be simply loaded (Charpy test) or loaded as cantilevers (Izod test). The notch is usually a V-notch cut to specifications with a special milling cutter. Other types of notch have been used but they are not popular (see Fig. 3-7).

The specimen is held in a rigid vise or support, and struck a blow by a pendulum traveling at a specified speed; e.g.,5.3 m/s (17.5 fps). The energy input is a function of the height of fall and the weight of the pendulum. The energy remaining after fracture is determined from the height of rise of the pendulum and its weight. The difference between the energy input and the energy remaining represents the energy absorbed by the specimen. Modern machines are equipped with scales and pendulum-actuated pointers, which yield direct readings of energy absorption (see Fig. 3-7).

The function of the notch is to insure that the specimen will break as a result of the impact load to which it is subjected. Without the notch, many alloys would simply bend without breaking, and it would therefore be impossible to determine their ability to absorb energy.

The appearance of the surface of the fractured impact specimen can be correlated with the energy absorbed by a given composition of specimen. Ductile, tough compositions produce fractures with a fine, silky appearance, and evidence of deformation

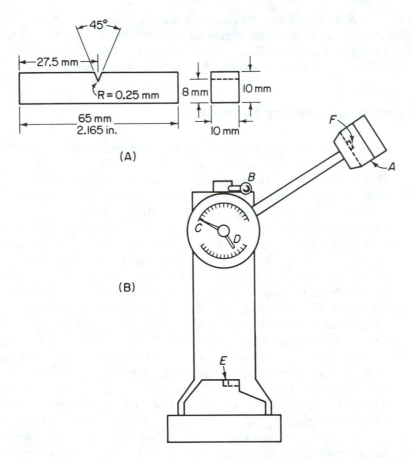

Figure 3-7 (A) Charpy impact specimen; (B) typical impact testing machine. *A*, pendulum; *B*, release and brake lever; *C*, pointer and scale to indicate energy absorbed; *D*, drive arm which pushes pointer around scale; *E*, anvil on which Charpy specimen rests; *F*, striker head.

caused by bending before fracture. Brittle compositions produce a surface which appears coarsely crystalline and shows no evidence of deformation by bending. There are, of course, degrees of brittleness and toughness, and the proportion of surface which is coarse versus silky shows the variations in properties. The transition from ductile to brittle fracture as the temperature is lowered, when such a transition occurs, can be followed by observation of fracture appearance.

BEND TESTS

These multipurpose tests enable determination of maximum fiber stresses, known as *flexure strength*, and modulus of elasticity in materials which are brittle or very hard, and which do not lend themselves to tensile testing. Plastics, glass, cast iron, and concrete are commonly tested as flexed beams. Bending tests are also useful for ductility determinations in sheet and bar stock, and for testing the soundness of welds. These tests often depend upon achieving a certain angle of bend, and tend to be qualitative rather than quantitative.

HIGH-TEMPERATURE TESTS

The kinds of tests described thus far are sometimes conducted at high temperatures. The techniques are similar to those described. However, a furnace (often a vacuum furnace) to heat the specimens before or during the test is provided. High-temperature variations of tensile, hardness, and impact testing would be considered as *short-time tests*. Some special considerations regarding high-temperature testing should be mentioned. Among these are the effects of speed of heating and time at temperature of the test piece before and during test. Since the structure and properties of metallic materials may be significantly altered by high temperatures, as explained in Chaps. 4 and 5, these variables must be controlled. In hot-hardness testing, the effect of the high temperature and atmosphere on the penetrator must be kept in mind. Diamond penetrators will oxidize in the air, and diamond will dissolve in hot steel. Evacuated surroundings or special atmospheres are used to protect against oxidation; sapphire indenters are used to prevent dissolution.

In addition to the short-time high-temperature tests, there are *long-time high-temperature tests* of importance. *Creep testing* aims at relating time, temperature, stress, and strain. Tests may run from a period of days to many years. For each different stress-temperature combination an individual specimen is required. Since each specimen requires its own loading device, and strain measuring and recording equipment, the facilities and space needed are considerable. Some efficiencies can be realized by using multispecimen furnaces. The progress of an ideal creep test is shown in Fig. 3-8 for a fixed stress and temperature. Upon initially loading the specimen, instantaneous strain results which is composed of elastic and plastic components. Following this, the rate of plastic strain declines, during what is known as the *primary stage of creep*, until a steady state is reached. While the rate of creep is constant the specimen is said to be undergoing *secondary creep*. Finally a stage is reached during which small internal cracks form and grow. These act to intensify stress and increase the rate of strain until rupture occurs. The three stages are not always well defined, and the amount of creep occurring in the third or final stage is often variable and unpredictable. Extrapolations to predict behavior beyond the time limits of the test are occasionally made, based on the assumption that the steady state will continue to the time limit for which the extrapolation is made.

Stress-rupture Testing. This technique is also used for long-time high-temperature research. In this type of test the stress, strain rate, and time are such that the amount of strain at rupture is not considered important. Thus only stress and temperature are controlled, and time to rupture is recorded. Strains are not measured. Data for stress-rupture behavior can be obtained from relatively short-time tests which

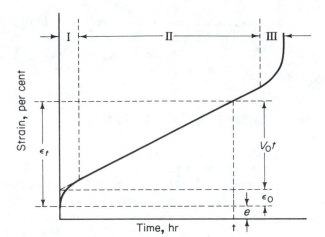

e = instantaneous elastic and plastic strain upon application of load

$e_t = \epsilon_0 + V_0 t$ = total creep at time t

V_0 = steady rate of creep during stage II

ϵ_0 = elementary creep strain

I   Primary stage, creep rate decreasing

II   Secondary stage, creep rate steady

III   Tertiary stage, creep rate increasing

Figure 3-8   Idealized creep curve.

are mathematically manipulated to make predictions of long-time behavior under a variety of stress-temperature combinations.

Creep and stress-rupture tests do not provide information which is relevant to processing methods. However, the high-temperature properties are very important in design applications such as gas and steam turbines, high-pressure steam lines, rocket engines, pressurized nuclear power sources, and chemical-processing equipment which operates at high temperatures and pressures.

FATIGUE TESTING

Probably more metallic components fail by fatigue than by any other mechanical cause. For this reason, fatigue testing and determination of fatigue properties are extremely important.

Fatigue failure occurs as a result of repeated application of small loads which are individually incapable of producing detectable plastic deformation. Eventually, these repeated loads cause a macrocrack to open and spread across the piece. Stress intensification occurs and ultimately a sudden, brittle fracture results. Ferrous metals and alloys have a limiting value of repeated stress which can be applied and reversed for an indefinitely large number of cycles without causing failure. This stress is known as the *fatigue limit*. Nonferrous metals and alloys do not have known limiting stress values below which failure will not occur if the cycle is repeated often enough. For these materials, fatigue strengths are usually given as stresses for which failure can be expected to occur at 10^7, 10^8, or some other specified number of cycles of loading. The results of fatigue tests are usually plotted on semilog plots as shown in Fig. 3-9.

Fatigue tests are most often accomplished using a specimen having a round cross section, loaded at two points as a rotating simple beam, and supported at its ends (see Fig. 3-10). The top surface of such a specimen is always in compression and the

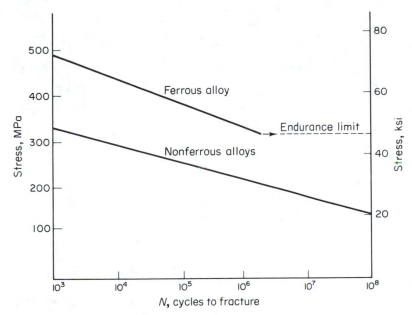

Figure 3-9 Idealized fatigue curves for ferrous and nonferrous alloys. For ferrous alloys an edurance limit, below which stress failure does not occur, is reached near 10^6 to 10^7 cycles. For nonferrous alloys a fatigue limit is not reached, even beyond 10^8 cycles.

bottom surface is always in tension. The maximum stress always occurs at the surface, halfway along the length of the specimen, where the cross section is a minimum. For each complete rotation of the specimen, a point in the surface originally at the top center goes alternately from a maximum in compression to a maximum in tension and then back to the same maximum in compression.

Fatigue failure starts at the point of highest stress. This point may be determined by the shape of a part; for instance, by stress concentrations in a groove. It can also be caused by surface finish, such as tool marks or scratches, and by internal voids such as shrinkage cracks and cooling cracks in castings and weldments (see Chaps. 8, 9, and 14), and by defects introduced during mechanical working (see Chap. 12), and by defects and stresses introduced by electroplating (see Chaps. 30 and 31). It must be remembered that surface and internal defects are stress raisers, and the point of highest actual stress may occur at these rather than at the minimum cross section of highest nominal stress. Thus processing methods are extremely important as they affect fatigue behavior.

Another important characteristic of fatigue behavior, no doubt related to the distribution of defects in metals, is the wide spread in results. Fatigue test data should be subjected to statistical analysis, and it should be remembered that predictions based on tests reflect the probabilities of failure after a certain number of cycles at a particular stress. The fact that, in service, the stress pattern is rarely a regular repeated cycle, but rather a variable cycle, is also a complicating feature.

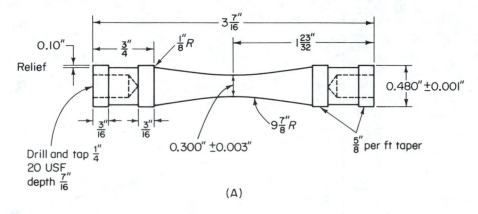

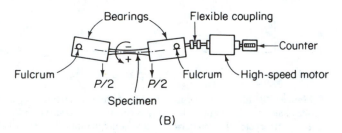

Figure 3-10   (A) Fatigue test specimen; (B) R. R. Moore fatigue-testing machine (schematic). The distance between the fulcrums is 12 in.; between the points of loading and the nearest fulcrums is 4 in.; and the distance between the points of loading is 4 in. In a half-revolution of the specimen, the top fibers go from compression to an equal and opposite tension, and the bottom fibers go from tension to an equal and opposite compression.

Fatigue testing of rubber and plastics is of two types. Static fatigue testing is analogous to creep testing of metals. Dynamic fatigue testing corresponds to fatigue testing of metals.

FRACTURE TOUGHNESS TESTS

These tests are an extension of notched impact tests, and of fatigue and static tensile tests of notched specimens. The technique gives results which are useful in predicting the ability of a material to arrest crack propagation and thus prevent eventual catastrophic failure at stresses below the yield strength. Fracture toughness tests are useful because they permit taking into account the presences of cracks too small to be detected by nondestructive tests, but which are assumed to be present in all components. The tendency for those cracks to grow depends upon the material and its processing history. Studying fracture toughness as a function of processing variables, for instance tempering temperatures or welding techniques (see Chaps. 5 and 14), enables matching of materials and processing for the best performance. Fracture toughness testing has been applied particularly to such components as pressure vessels, rocket motor cases, and high-performance aircraft structural parts.

Fracture toughness tests are carried out on tensile specimens in which small fatigue cracks of controlled and measurable size have been initiated. The results are then mathematically manipulated to obtain a parameter known as the *critical stress intensity factor* or *fracture toughness*. This factor can be applied to design and to predictions of failure based on the assumption that defects of a certain maximum size are present. The end product is then tested by nondestructive means described below to make sure it has no flaws larger than those considered in the design.

NONDESTRUCTIVE TESTING

Most nondestructive test methods are intended to detect internal flaws that are likely to cause fatigue or static load failure. These tests are performed on work in process so that defective parts can be rejected early, thus saving additional expenditure of effort. The tests are also performed on used components during disassembly of equipment which has been in service, in an attempt to detect the start of fatigue cracks. The most common nondestructive test (NDT) methods are briefly described here.

X-ray, gamma ray, and neutron radiography act upon sensitive photographic film or paper. Neutrons first strike a transfer screen to produce a radiation image after they have passed through the material. Radiation is passed, absorbed, and scattered by opaque objects. The thicker and more dense the object, the smaller the proportion of incident radiation which is passed. Thus, if an object, has an internal defect, more radiation will be passed through the defective area than through the sound region, and the defect will show up as a dark area on the film. Unfortunately, scattering tends to obscure the defect, so that small defects may not be detected. Plane defects, such as the surfaces produced by a crack, are not detected by X-rays, but three-dimensional defects, such as gas porosity in a casting, are quite readily discerned. Sand and slag, being much less dense than metal, are also easily found by X-raying of castings.

Although X-ray equipment is available in many sizes and capacities and gives the best results for most applications, other methods are superior in some cases. Gamma-ray sources can be small and convenient to use, say, to inspect from inside a pipe. The short wavelengths of gamma rays are effective for thick material sections. The absorption of neutrons is, figuratively, the reverse of X-rays or gamma rays. For instance, neutrons are more readily absorbed by hydrogen than by lead. Thus neutron radiography can show up conditions not revealed by the others. In all events, care must be taken to avoid the hazards of radiation to human beings.

Magnetic methods for detection of defects are based on the principle that flaws or discontinuities distort a magnetic field induced in a ferrous material. There are several methods for detecting the irregularities. The most common is *magnetic-particle testing* or *Magnafluxing,* which involves dusting the magnetized piece with fine magnetic particles or coating it with a liquid suspension of such particles. The particles are held at leaks in the magnetic field at the edges of cracks. Fluorescent magnetic particles and ultraviolet light serve in a refinement of the process to enhance the appearance of the crack. Magnetic particle testing detects only cracks on or near the surface.

Some *electromagnetic methods* act by inducing eddy currents into a specimen and detecting the forms of or irregularities in the induced currents or in magnetic fields in ferrous materials. In one method, the response is compared to that from a standard piece. These techniques may be applied to detecting flaws (even deep internal ones), separating mixed alloy stock or gaging size, shape, plating or insulation thickness, or depth of case hardening of steel.

Ultrasonic testing can be applied to a wide variety of materials and shapes: metals, plastics, ceramics, glass; laminates, castings, weldments, forgings, etc. An ultrasonic wave is transmitted through a substance and its action is interpreted in three ways to show defects. In the *pulse-echo technique*, waves are reflected back from the far surface and from the internal surfaces of flaws. An oscilloscope trace of the reflections (spikes) indicates the position and sizes of the defects. The sound is passed through the material and picked up on the other side in the *transmission method*. The energy lost in transit because of reflections indicates the sizes and positions of defects. The *resonance technique* applies frequencies over a range. Energy drawn by the transducer increases at the resonant frequency of the specimen. If this frequency is different from that of a standard part of the same size, a defect is indicated. Ultrasonic testing is useful for revealing cracks, voids, and defects far below as well as near the surface. Skill and care is required for its application and interpretation.

Visual inspection methods have been improved by the use of dyes and fluorescent penetrants. The parts are immersed in one of these fluids and then wiped dry of any excess. The absorbed fluid then tends to be drawn from cracks which come to the surface when the member is dusted with an absorbant powder. Dye penetrants can be viewed under ordinary light while fluorescent oils are best seen under ultraviolet light. The method is not restricted to ferrous alloys, but is restricted to detection of thin cracks which intersect the surface.

CORROSION TESTING

The two major areas of corrosion testing are (1) laboratory testing and (2) field testing. Laboratory testing is more formalized and standardized than is field testing.

Laboratory corrosion tests include three major types of test. The first is the total immersion test for stainless steel and nonferrous metals and alloys. The second is the alternate immersion test, which requires cyclic immersion and withdrawal of specimens. Finally, there is the salt spray test, which is carried out in a closed chamber containing a foggy atmosphere of moist salt air. The temperature and composition of the corrodants must be carefully controlled in all three tests.

Fatigue tests may also be conducted under corrosive conditions by placing a wick, immersed in the corrodant, in contact with the specimen. In still another version of this test, the specimen may be immersed in a corrodant which is contained in a leakproof box. Tests of this type are known as corrosion-fatigue tests, and are intended to show the accelerating effect of corrosion on fatigue failure.

Stress-corrosion is a phenomenon in which corrosion, combined with static tensile stresses at the surface of a metallic object, produces cracks. A common way of testing for stress-corrosion is to immerse an elastically bent, flat, bar-type specimen in corrodant. The stresses can be calculated from the dimensions of the specimen and the extent of the bend. A tendency toward stress corrosion may result from residual tensile stresses introduced by cold-forming operations (see Chap. 12).

Field corrosion testing aims at determination of corrosion resistance under environmental conditions which are expected in actual service. Thus, specimens are mounted on insulated racks and exposed to the atmosphere. Tests are commonly conducted in marine atmospheres and industrial atmospheres since these represent very severe conditions. Rack-mounted specimens are commonly immersed in seawater. Specimens are also buried in soil to study long-time resistance. Since soil composition varies greatly, tests from one site may not be useful in predicting behavior at another site. Plant corrosion tests consists of placing small specimens in actual pieces of equipment in the plant.

The progress of corrosion tests is followed by periodic examination of the specimens for weight loss, pitting, depth of pits, length and depth of cracks, or inches of penetration (for uniform attack), as appropriate, for the composition tested and the corrosive medium.

The results of corrosion testing are useful as an aid in the choice of metals and alloys for particular applications, and as a supplement to published data on the chemical activity of metallic materials.

PROBLEMS

1. A certain steel alloy has a yield strength of 372 MPa (54,000 psi) and modulus of elasticity of 210 GPa (30×10^6 psi). A specimen made from this steel has a rectangular cross section of 13×13 mm ($\frac{1}{2} \times \frac{1}{2}$ in.). A gage length of 100 mm (4.000 in.) is marked along the length of the specimen.
   (a) A 45 kN (10,000-lb) load is applied to the specimen and then removed from it. What is the gage length when the load is applied, and what is the gage length after the load is removed?
   (b) What load would produce a stress in the specimen equal to the yield strength? Assume 0.2% offset.
   (c) Under the yield load, what would be the gage length of the specimen?
   (d) After removal of the yield load, what would be the gage length of the specimen?
   (e) Recalculate parts (c) and (d) above, substituting a brass rod having $E = 100$ GPa(15×10^6 psi) and the same yield strength and dimensions as the steel rod.

2. Given a standard tensile specimen made of brass. $D_0 = 0.505$ in., $L_0 = 2.000$ in. Load-length readings were made as follows:

Load (lb)	Length (in.)	Load (lb)	Length (in.)	Load (lb)	Length (in.)	Load (lb)	Length (in.)
320	2.0002	1600	2.0010	2760	2.0018	3220	2.0060
590	2.0004	1880	2.0012	2920	2.0020	7220	2.30
920	2.0006	2270	2.0014	3020	2.0030	8960	3.10
1310	2.0008	2560	2.0016	3080	2.0040	6210	3.32

Ultimate load, 9960 lb; $D_f = 0.2525$ in.; $L_f = 3.32$ in.

Calculate stresses and strains, percent elongation, and percent reduction in area. Plot a stress-strain curve on a scale which will permit accurate determination of the modulus of elasticity and yield strength. Plot a second stress-strain curve showing behavior up to the point of rupture.

3. Given a standard tension test specimen made of brass. $D_0 = 12.50$ mm, $L_0 = 50.00$ mm. Load-length readings were made as follows:

Load (N)	Length (mm)	Load (N)	Length (mm)	Load (N)	Length (mm)	Load (N)	Length (mm)
1,350	50.005	6,760	50.025	11,660	50.045	13,610	50.150
2,495	50.010	7,940	50.030	12,340	50.050	30,510	57.50
3,890	50.015	9,590	50.035	12,760	50.075	37,860	77.50
5,540	50.020	10,820	50.040	13,020	50.100	26,240	83.00

Ultimate load = 42,090 N, $D_f = 6.25$ mm, $L_f = 83.00$ mm. Calculate stresses and strains, percent elongation, and percent reduction in area. Plot a stress-strain curve on a scale which will permit accurate determination of the modulus of elasticity and yield strength. Plot a second stress-strain curve showing behavior up to the point of rupture.

4. In addition to the data presented in Prob. 2, diameter readings were made as follows:

Load (lb)	Diameter (in.)
320–3220	0.505
7220	0.466
8960	0.370
6210	0.2525

Calculate true stress-true strain data and plot elastic and plastic true stress-true strain curves. From these determine the value of the modulus of elasticity E, the work-hardening coefficient m, and the constant k, in $\sigma = k\epsilon^m$.

5. In addition to the data presented in Prob. 3, diameter readings were made as follows:

Load (N)	Diameter (mm)
1350–13,610	12.50
30,510	11.53
37,860	9.16
26,240	6.25

Calculate true-stress strain data and plot elastic and plastic true stress–true strain curves. From these determine the value of the modulus of elasticity E, the work-hardening coefficient m, and the constant k, in $\sigma = k\epsilon^m$.

6. Notched-bar impact test results were obtained on a heat of steel as follows:

Energy absorbed (ft-lb)	T (°F)	Energy absorbed (ft-lb)	T (°F)
126, 119, 111	200	45, 44, 28	40
124, 117	180	32, 20, 20	10
118, 113, 112	160	24, 17, 12	0
114, 113, 108	140	16, 10, 7	−20
115, 112, 108, 104	120	11, 9, 6	−40
108, 93, 89, 78	100	11, 9, 9	−60
81, 60, 51	70	15, 8, 7	−80

Plot the results and determine the approximate critical temperature range over which the steel changes from ductile to brittle. For what purpose can the notched-bar impact test be used?

7. Describe and explain the applications of hardness testing to acceptance and processing of materials.

8. What variables are usually related in long-time high-temperature tensile tests? In short-time high temperature tests?

REFERENCES

ASTM Standards, American Society for Testing and Materials, Philadelphia. Revised at various intervals.

DAVIS, H. E., G. E. TROXELL, and C. W. WISKOCIL, *The Testing and Inspection of Engineering Materials*, 3rd ed., McGraw-Hill, New York, 1964.

FENNER, A. J., *Mechanical Testing of Materials*, George Newnes, London, 1965.

Impact Testing of Metals, Symposium, American Society for Testing and Materials, Philadelphia, 1970.

KEYSER, C. A., *Materials Science and Engineering*, 4th ed., Charles E. Merrill, Columbus, Ohio, 1985.

McGONNAGLE, W. J., *Nondestructive Testing*, 2nd ed., Gordon and Breach, London, 1966.

WILSON, C. R., "Neutron Radiography Complements X-Ray," *Metal Progress*, Aug. 1970, p. 75.

4

METALS AND ALLOYS

Metals have a common set of properties that make them among the most useful of engineering materials. Not all metals have the same properties or properties to the same degree. Most are solid at room temperatures; mercury is an exception. Actually, the melting points of various metals range to over 3300°C (6000°F). Metals are relatively heavy, but densities (mass per unit volume) vary over a wide range. Among the more common metals, aluminum has a density of 2.66 g/cm^3 (0.096 lb/in.^{3}), and tungsten 18.77 g/cm^3 (0.678 lb/in.^{3}). Polished metal surfaces show a high luster, but most oxidize and corrode rapidly.

Strength, hardness, wear resistance, shock resistance, and electrical and thermal conductivity are important metallic properties. Most metals are elastic to a limit; they deform in proportion to stress and return to their original state when the stress is released. At higher stresses they deform plastically. Some metals will accept a great deal of plastic deformation before failure, and others very little.

METAL STRUCTURES

A metal may exist as a plasma, gas, liquid, or crystalline solid. Plasmas and gases exist only at quite high energy levels. The liquid state results from enough free energy to cause the atoms to move at random; their movements are limited only by the container. At no time do the atoms take fixed positions in relation to each other in a liquid.

Unit Cells. The atoms of a metal assume nearly fixed positions relative to each other in the solid state. A solid metal usually is composed of a multitude of crystals.

49

Within any one crystal, the atomic arrangement is repeated by adjacent atoms many times. An imaginary line can be drawn through a string of atoms arranged side by side. In fact, such lines can be drawn in three coordinate directions and form a lattice work called the *space lattice* of the crystal. The space lattice is made up of a small, repeating, three dimensional, geometric pattern having the same symmetry as the crystal and called a *unit cell*. The whole crystal is built up of unit cells stacked together like building blocks.

Crystals are formed out of the atoms of a liquid metal when it freezes. When the free energy level (heat content) at any point in a liquid becomes low enough to be at the freezing point, atoms join together into unit cells. This may occur at many points at the same time. Unit cells that start at different points do not have the same orientation and form different crystals. All unit cells within any one crystal have the same orientation. A crystal grows by taking on atoms to form more unit cells during freezing until it meets other crystals. The crystals are called *grains,* and the orientation changes from one grain to another at the grain boundary (Fig. 4-1).

There are a number of shapes and sizes of unit cells. The three most important in metals are illustrated in Fig. 4-2. The *face-centered-cubic* (FCC) unit cell has an atom at each corner of a cube and an atom in the center of each face of the cube. Note that in the lattice, each atom at the corner of one cube is at the same time in the face of a different cube, and so on. The *body-centered-cubic* (BCC) cell has an atom at each corner of a cube and an atom in the geometric center of the cube. Note that the latter atom is also at the corner of another cube. The *hexagonal-close-packed* (HCP) array has a honeycomb shape. The top and bottom of a cell are parallel hexagons, and halfway between is a triangle with an apex pointing to every other side of the honeycomb walls. Each apex is halfway between the longitudinal center line and a side. An atom is located at every corner of the cell.

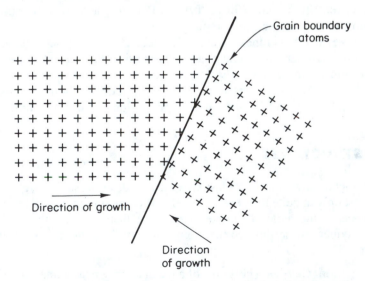

Figure 4-1 Schematic depicting the nature of a grain boundary.

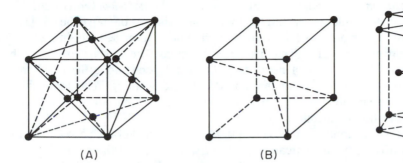

Figure 4-2 Common unit cell structures: (A) face-centered-cubic (FCC), also called cubic-close-packed; (B) body-centered-cubic (BCC); (C) hexagonal-close-packed (HCP).

Changes in Crystal Structure. Any solid metal normally has a definite cell shape and size at a certain energy state, but in some metals the shape as well as the size changes from one energy state to another. The energy state is usually changed by adding or taking away heat. Such a process is called *heat treatment*. A space lattice changes to whatever shape is most stable at each energy level. Such a change is called an *allotropic transformation*. A space lattice is usually stable over a wide range of energy levels, and a metal may have to be heated to high temperatures or cooled to quite low temperatures to make its space lattice change.

An important variation of the BCC structure occurs from the distortion of the space lattice. The atoms of a pure metal are all of the same size and are regularly arranged in positions where the uniform forces from one atom to another are in equilibrium. An atom of foreign material trapped in a cell is of a different size, exerts different forces, and distorts the shape of the cell. Under these conditions the cell is no longer cubic but becomes a body-centered-tetragon with one coordinate axis a little longer than the other two. This does not happen to every unit cell, and BCC and tetragonal unit cells exist side by side in the lattice.

Crystalline Structure and Physical Properties. The type of space lattice and the degree of perfection of the space lattice have much to do with the physical properties of a metal. The face-centered-cubic space lattice is in general more ductile and malleable than the body-centered type. The body-centered type is usually the harder and stronger of the two. The close-packed-hexagonal type lacks ductility and accepts little cold-working without failure. There are exceptions to these rules.

The crystals of a metal change shapes when subjected to stresses and heat. Imperfections in the space lattice help determine the strength of a metal. If a stress is imposed on a crystal, some or all of the atoms are moved from their equilibrium positions, and the crystal is deformed. If the atoms are not moved out of the regions of influence of their neighbors, they return to their original positions after the stress is removed. The deformation is said to be *elastic*. If enough stress is applied to deform the lattice permanently, the atoms do not return to their original positions and the deformation is said to be *plastic*. If this occurs below what is called the *re-*

crystallization temperature, the metal is said to be *cold-worked* (Chap. 12). Cold-working distorts, elongates, and fragments the grains. At or above the recrystallization temperature, the atoms become mobile enough to form new strain-free grains that nucleate from points of high strains in the old grains. The crystals grow until they meet each other. The number of new grains formed depends upon the number of nuclei which in turn depends upon the amount of cold working. The more the metal is strained the smaller are the grains after recrystallization. Each metal has its own recrystallization temperature.

It has been found that the actual stress required to deform a crystal is only a small fraction of what is theoretically necessary to displace all the atoms involved at the same time. Thus it is obvious that all the atoms do not move at the same time but in sequences. Experiments have indicated that these atomic movements emanate from and are affected by imperfections in the crystals.

There are several kinds of crystalline imperfections. The place where an atom should be may be vacant, and that is called a *vacancy*. In another case, a whole plane of extra atoms may appear in a lattice to form an *edge dislocation* as depicted in Fig. 4-3. Part of the planes of a lattice may be offset in a *screw dislocation* represented by Fig. 4-4. Also, space lattice mismatching occurs between crystals at grain boundaries (Fig 4-1). Large or small atoms distort the lattice. Quite small interstitial atoms may bulge the lattice. There are probably other kinds of imperfections not yet recognized; investigations of them is far from complete. The number and distributions of the imperfections have a great effect on the properties of a metal.

Plastic distortion takes place by one part of a crystal sliding on another. It appears that slip occurs between atomic planes in the lattice that are spaced farthest apart and have the highest atomic population. These are called the *glide planes* and are usually not the planes that bound the regular geometric shapes of the cells. As has been pointed out, one plane does not slip over another all at once but glides in a series of movements. This is illustrated by Fig. 4-5. As a shear stress is applied between two planes, a dislocation is strained until it is moved to the next cross plane, and so on. With a myriad of atoms in even a small crystal, there exists a large number of dislocations. Also, some types of dislocations, called *sources,* regenerate and create

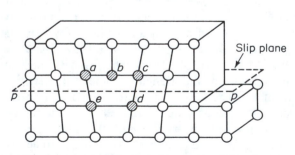

Figure 4-3 Schematic depicting an edge dislocation.

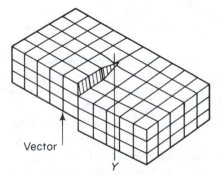

Figure 4-4 Schematic depicting a screw dislocation.

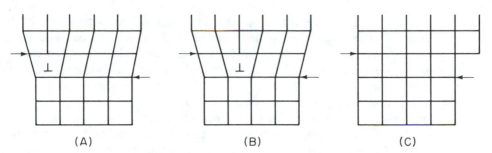

Figure 4-5 How a dislocation travels across a lattice under stress, thus causing displacement of the lattice.

new dislocations. So as stress is continued or raised, more and more dislocations are moved to cause more plastic deformation. Dislocations travel through a crystal on many planes until they reach grain boundaries or imperfections in the lattice that stop them. Other dislocations from behind interact with those stalled ahead, and movement becomes more difficult. The cold-worked metal is said to *work-harden* or *strain-harden* because a higher stress is necessary to move the entangled and crowded dislocations. As dislocations are piled up under higher and higher stress, they are forced to combine into small cracks that ultimately grow to fractures in the metal.

As just indicated, anything that interferes with the flow of dislocations across a grain makes that grain harder. That may be a distortion of the space lattice or the presence of a foreign material. The first is the mechanism in what is called *solid solution hardening*, and the second in *dispersion hardening*. As will be shown, heat treatment is a process often used to control these conditions and, thus, the physical properties of metals. Alloying of metals is another way of controlling lattice conditions. Metals like gold, silver, zinc, tin, and copper are often used in nearly pure states, but most metals are alloyed with others for best utility. The space lattice of an alloy is commonly distorted because atoms of different metals are of different sizes and exert different atomic forces. Added atoms may or may not replace atoms of the parent metal in a space lattice but in any case they do cause lattice distortions. More aspects of alloying will be discussed in connection with equilibrium diagrams.

The sizes and diverse orientations of grains in a metal largely affect its properties. A fine-grained metal is likely to have a better distribution of grains oriented to respond to stresses in any direction than a coarse-grained metal. Of more importance, fine grains present more grain boundaries to inhibit the propagation of dislocations. For these reasons, a fine-grained metal as a rule has a greater yield strength (the level of stress required to start plastic deformation), ultimate strength (the level of stress at failure), hardness, fatigue strength, and resistance to impact.

Grain orientation in a piece of metal becomes more uniformly directed when the metal is cold-worked. The grains in a metal cooled slowly from high temperature have random orientation so that the path of plastic slip has to change direction from one grain to the next one. Those grains favorably oriented to the applied stress are deformed most, but if enough stress is applied, all grains deform to some extent. The slip planes glide over one another, and the corresponding parts of a crystal turn with respect to each other with a tendency to reach orientation in the direction of the stresses. The larger the applied stresses, the more numerous become the grains oriented strongly in directions of the stresses. Under subsequent stresses, the metal shows *directional properties*; that is, it yields more readily if stressed in some directions than in others.

A secondary mode of crystal deformation is called *twinning*, which is a limited and ordered movement of a large block of atoms in a definite section of a crystal. Twinning can account for only small strains and does not occur in some materials but has some importance in that it can reorient atomic planes more favorably for slip.

Fracture.   A piece of metal breaks in one or both of two general ways after deformation by sufficient stress. One mode of fracture is termed *ductile*, and the faces of the break may be described as gray, fibrous, and silky. The parting surfaces are wiped across each other by shear stresses, and the break occurs after a large amount of deformation. Some classify this as mainly fracture through the grains (transgranular). The other kind is *brittle* fracture, called *cleavage*, where the material actually is pulled apart across atomic planes within the crystals or along the grain boundaries. The metal may first deform plastically to some extent until the forces holding it together are overcome. Then it snaps sharply in two, leaving a rough, granular, and rather bright fractured surface.

The relation between ductile and brittle failure is one of degree. Nodular cast iron fails in a ductile manner as compared to gray cast iron but is considered brittle in comparison with steel. Frequently, the two types exist in the same rupture because of progressive hardening as failure takes place. The outside of a break may shear in a ductile manner while the center may fail as a brittle section. Many steels fail by ductile fracture at high temperatures and by cleavage at low temperatures.

FUNDAMENTALS OF METAL ALLOYS

A metal melts if heated to a high enough temperature. If heat is added continuously, the temperature of a piece of metal rises with time as indicated in Fig. 4-6. When melting starts, the temperature does not rise (as shown by the plateau of the diagram) until melting is complete if the liquid is kept well mixed. This is because the liquid exists at a higher state of energy than does the solid. Heat energy added during melting is used to cause a change of state rather than to increase temperature. This energy is called the *latent heat of fusion*. The process is reversible, and the same heat is given off when the metal cools and solidifies.

Another kind of change of state involves a relocation of the atoms in a solid metal. This causes a change in the space lattice and is an allotropic transformation as described in the preceding section. The space lattice changes at a specific temperature for each allotropic metal as heat is added or taken away. The heat given off or absorbed is called the *latent heat of transformation*. If heat is withdrawn rapidly, there may be a small dip in temperature as indicated in Fig. 4-7.

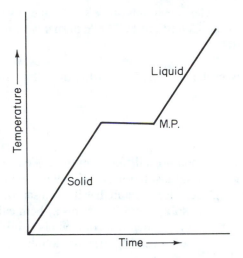

Figure 4-6 Typical time-temperature relationship of a metal being heated.

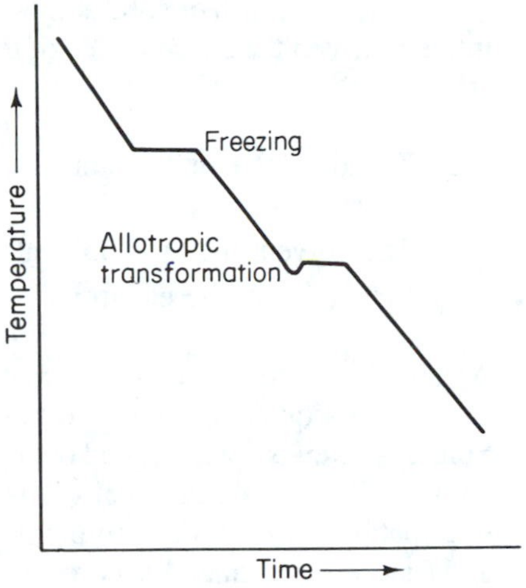

Figure 4-7 Temperature-time relationship of a metal that solidifies and passes through an allotropic transformation as it is cooled from the liquid state.

Metallic Solid Solutions and Compounds.   An alloy consists of two or more metals, or at least one metal and a nonmetal, mixed intimately by fusion or diffusion. *Diffusion* is the movement of atoms of one material among the atoms of another material. This is a well-known action in liquids, such as when sugar or salt dissolves in water. There the atoms or molecules of the solute move around in the liquid solvent. A similar action can occur in the solid state. A material is said to be dissolved in metal in the solid state when the atoms of the solute may move about among the atoms of the solvent when the proper stimulant is applied. A certain resistance exists to the movement of the solute atoms in a solid, and it must be overcome before diffusion can occur. The energy that just overcomes such resistance is called the *activation energy*. More energy just increases the rate of diffusion.

One form of solid solution has each atom of the solute replacing an atom of the solvent in its space lattice. This is a *substitutional solid solution*; conditions favorable to it are:

1. The atoms of solute and solvent differ in diameter by no more than 15%.
2. The space lattices of solvent and solute are similar.
3. The substances are near each other in the electromotive series; otherwise, a chemical or intermetallic compound may form.

This is not to say that a substitutional solid solution cannot form if the foregoing conditions are not strictly met. It may mean only that the amount of solution formed may be limited.

A second form of solid solution occurs when the atoms of the solute take position interstitially in the space lattice of the solvent. Conditions favorable to such a solution are:

1. The diameter of the solute atom is no larger than 59% of the diameter of the solvent atom.
2. The solvent metal is polyvalent.
3. Proximity in the electromotive series.

Again, limited or no solubility may result if conditions differ from these ideals.

As in liquids, more solute can be held in a solid solution at higher temperatures. Solute is likewise precipitated out on cooling. Each temperature has its own saturation amount. When a solute precipitates from a solid solvent, it often forms a chemical or intermetallic compound, commonly with the solvent. Chemical compounds like Fe_3C and Cr_4C and intermetallic compounds, such as $CuAl_2$ and Mg_2Si, have definite lattice structures and are hard and brittle as a rule.

An alloy of a particular composition contains one or more phases. A *phase* is defined as *a physically homogeneous portion of matter*. It cannot be subdivided by mechanical means or resolved into smaller parts by an ordinary optical microscope. As examples, molten iron is a phase and so is solid (pure) copper.

How Alloys Melt. The melting temperature of an alloy depends upon its composition. Consider an alloy of two or more pure metals. There may be one proportion of the constituents that has a lower melting point than any other. In some cases this is lower than the melting temperature of any of the pure metals in the alloy. This composition is known as the *eutectic composition*, and its melting temperature is the *eutectic temperature*.

Figure 4-8 shows the behavior of three alloys as they are heated. Each is a different proportion of the same two pure metals. There is an arrest at T_1 for each; that is the eutectic temperature at which melting begins. The temperature T_2 at which melting is complete is different for each alloy. For each case, there is a phase in excess

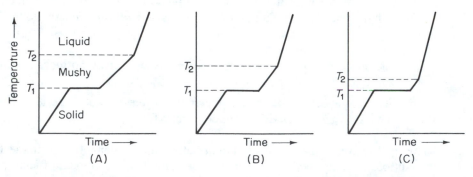

Figure 4-8   Temperature-time curves for three alloys of two pure metals.

of what is needed for the eutectic composition. That excess phase is what is being dissolved between temperatures T_1 and T_2.

Equilibrium Diagrams. A *constitutional equilibrium diagram* is constructed by plotting points T_1 and T_2 (like those in Fig. 4-8) on coordinates of temperature and composition for a number of alloys of the same two or more metals. Lines are then drawn through corresponding points to show changes in phases.

There are three standard types of equilibrium diagrams. Only simple examples of each will be shown and discussed to illustrate principles. The same principles apply to actual alloys and more complicated diagrams.

A *type I equilibrium diagram* as exemplified in Fig. 4-9 depicts alloys of metals soluble in the liquid state but insoluble in the solid state. An explanation of this diagram can be given for the composition of 75%A and 25%B. If these proportions of metals A and B are put in a crucible and heated to any temperature, nothing changes at first except that the materials get hot. At the eutectic temperature (T_1) enough of metal A and metal B combine and melt to form a liquid of eutectic composition. Melting continues without temperature rise until all the metal B is consumed in making the eutectic composition. Some metal A is left over and remains solid. As the temperature is increased, more and more metal A goes into the liquid solution until T_2 is reached. At this temperature all the metal A is dissolved in the liquid. Above T_2 there is no further metallurgical change for this composition.

The process just described is reversible. If the composition under discussion is cooled from the liquid state, some metal A begins to solidify at temperature T_2. More and more metal A freezes from temperature T_2 to T_1, and the composition of the liquid approaches that of the eutectic. Then at T_1 the rest freezes. A eutectic can occur only if there is some lack of solubility in the solid state.

It must be emphasized that the ideal conditions of the diagrams are realized only if heating or cooling is done so slowly as to approach equilibrium conditions closely.

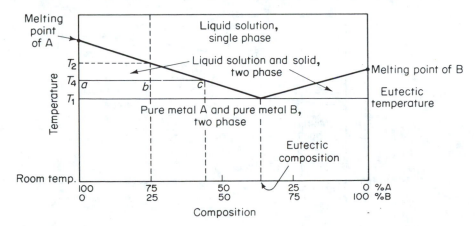

Figure 4-9 Type I equilibrium diagram of metals A and B, which are completely soluble in the liquid state and totally insoluble in the solid state.

A device called the *inverse lever rule* is an aid to obtaining information from equilibrium diagrams. It discloses the relative amount and analysis of each phase present in a two phase area. As an example, consider the 75%A–25%B composition of Fig. 4-9 at temperature T_4. A horizontal line is drawn to represent that temperature from a on the 100%A ordinate to c on the boundary between the liquid and mushy regions. This is the lever. It intersects the 75%A–25%B composition ordinate at b, which is the fulcrum. The amount of each phase present is signified by the inverse end in proportion to the total length of the lever. Specifically in this illustration:

$$\frac{ab}{ac} \times 100 = \text{percent of liquid phase (liquid is approx. 58\%A + 42\%B)}$$

$$= \frac{25}{42} \times 100 = 59.5\%$$

$$\frac{bc}{ac} \times 100 = \text{percent of solid phase (pure A)}$$

$$= \frac{17}{42} \times 100 = 40.5\%$$

Because they are used as ratios, numbers representing ab, bc, and ac can be taken directly from the composition scale without regard to units.

There are definite limits to the use of the lever rule. To gain information about phases, the lever may be used only in a two phase area and must not cross a phase boundary. Subject to these rules, the lever may be used on any equilibrium diagram.

A *type II equilibrium diagram* shows alloys of base metals soluble in both the liquid and solid states. An illustration is given in Fig. 4-10 for a composition of 83% metal C and 17% metal D. No metallurgical change takes place as the solid solution is heated from room temperature until temperature T_1 is reached. The composition is

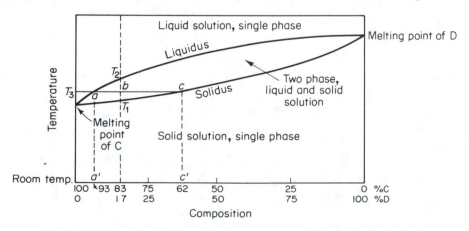

Figure 4-10   Type II equilibrium diagram of metals C and D, which are completely soluble in both liquid and solid states.

the same and entirely liquid above T_2. Gradual melting occurs between T_1 and T_2. In this region there is a continual change in the composition of both liquid and solid phases as temperature is raised or lowered. The compositions and proportion of solid and liquid phases at any temperature in the range can be ascertained by means of the lever rule. Consider the cited composition at temperature T_3 for example. A horizontal line at temperature T_3 intersects the liquidus at a, the composition line at b, and the solidus at c. Point a' represents the composition of liquid, and c' the composition of solid in the crucible at temperature T_3. As for proportions,

$$\frac{ab}{ac} \times 100 = \text{percent of solid phase (composition 62\%C–38\%D)}$$

$$= \frac{10}{31} \times 100 = 32.2\%$$

and

$$\frac{bc}{ac} \times 100 = \text{percent of liquid phase (composition 93\%C–7\%D)}$$

$$= \frac{21}{31} \times 100 = 67.8\%$$

A *type III equilibrium diagram* is for metals completely soluble in the liquid state but only partly soluble in the solid state. An illustration is furnished by Fig. 4-11. This diagram is a composite of type I and type II diagrams. An alloy of 60%G and 40%H acts like a type I alloy. At temperature T_1 and above, it is a liquid solution. At T_2 it is composed of a liquid solution and solid solution. The proportion and compositions of the constituents can be found from the lever *a-b-c*. At T_3, the lever *d-e-f* indicates a mixture of α solid solution and β solid solution. At T_4, the lever *g-h-i* shows the

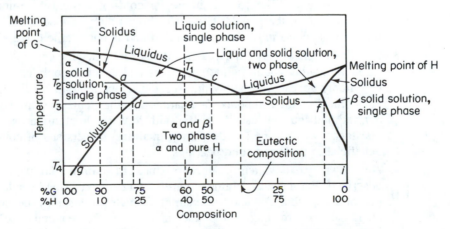

Figure 4-11 Type III equilibrium diagram of metals G and H, which are soluble in the liquid state and partially soluble in the solid state.

proportions of α solid solution and pure metal H at that temperature. The diagram designates that β solid solution does not exist at a temperature as low as T_4.

The alloy of 90%G and 10%H in Fig. 4-11 is comparable to a type II alloy. Only a liquid solution exists at temperatures above the liquidus. This alloy is made up of a mixture of liquid solution and α solid solution at temperatures between the liquidus and solidus lines. The proportions and compositions of each in this region can be ascertained by use of the inverse lever rule. Only the α solid solution exists at temperatures between the solidus and solvus lines labeled in Fig.4-11 and its composition is fixed at the basic composition of the alloy. The lever rule is not applicable in any single-phase region, and thus not in this α region. Below the solvus at T_4, both the α solid solution and pure metal H exist. This is a two-phase area, and the lever rule applies.

Alloys in the Solid State.   Alloys exist in several forms at room temperature after being cooled from the liquid state.

1. An alloy may separate into its original pure metals if they are not soluble in each other at room temperature (type I). Each grain consists of only one of the pure metals, but grains of each metal may exist side by side. In another alloy the grains of one metal may be uniformly distributed through the other metal, or one metal may tend to segregate in groups of grains in the other metal.

2. An alloy may exist as a solid solution of one metal dissolved in another (type II). The solid solution may be saturated or supersaturated. The latter results from rapid (nonequilibrium) cooling in some cases and is not a stable condition but sometimes may continue to exist over a long period of time.

    Controlled decomposition of supersaturated solid solutions is the basis for precipitation hardening of metals described in Chap. 5.

    Solid solutions are relatively ductile, soft, and malleable and have good shock resistance. They are desirable for cold-rolling and deep-drawing operations. Some of the popular brass and bronze alloys are solid solutions. Martensite is a *supersaturated* solid solution and is not ductile (exception).

3. An alloy or phase may exist as a chemical or intermetallic compound. Some are stable at low but not at high temperatures and thus form only on cooling. They commonly appear well below the freezing temperature of an alloy.

    Intermetallic compounds are harder than the elements from which they are derived and thus are usually brittle with low tensile strength and little shock resistance. For hardness and wearing qualities, dispersions of compounds are beneficial in tools and solid bearings.

4. An alloy may exist as a mechanical mixture of two or more of the forms already described. For instance, grains of pure metal may exist side by side with grains of solid solution. As another example, single grains may be composed of chemical or intermetallic compounds in a matrix of pure metal or solid solution. Eutectic alloys with low melting points are desirable for solders. Such alloys

may contain hard particles in a lamellar aggregate that interfere with dislocation movements in the primary phase and impart hardness to the alloy. This accounts for the wearability of some soft bearing materials of eutectic compositions.

Grain Growth.   The way grains form from the atoms of a liquid metal was explained early in this chapter when crystalline structure was described. Molten metal freezes first in contact with the cooler container walls. Heat must flow from inside through the outer layer, and the inside cools at a slower rate.

The shape, size, and composition of the grains in a piece of metal depend partly upon the way it has frozen. Solidification follows a pattern indicated by Fig. 4-12. Metal nuclei form at some points on the surface, and other atoms join to them to build crystalline lattices. As illustrated, nuclei start at such points as *a* or *b* and other atoms attach to them. The solid grows in a stem perpendicular to the surface. Branches grow perpendicular to the original stem. As it solidifies, metal gives up its latent heat to its surroundings, and further freezing is stopped for the moment. When this heat is dissipated, freezing starts again building on the already solid metal. The effect from a curved wall is an elongated grain with a tree-like skeletal form as indicated by Fig. 4-12(B). From a flat surface, the skeleton has a ladder-like or network shape, as in Fig. 4-12(C). These structures are called *dendrites*.

A crystal grows from a nucleus on freezing until it reaches neighboring grains. The size of grains produced thus depends upon the number of nuclei formed. Factors that produce more nuclei are a rough container surface and a fast cooling rate.

The use of the inverse lever rule in the liquid-solid area of an equilibrium diagram shows that the composition of the solid changes as the temperature drops, if the solid formed is a solid solution. This means that the first metal to solidify at the surface has one composition. The next to form on the skeleton has a different composition, and so on. Thus there is a definite segregation of the various compositions formed on freezing. This is said to be *dendritic segregation*. Obviously, there can be no segregation if a pure metal solidifies from the melt.

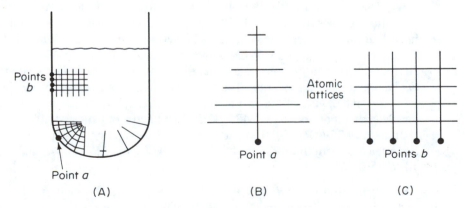

Figure 4-12   Schematic diagrams of the growth of dendritic grains.

METALLURGY OF IRON AND STEEL

Carbon is the basis for the wide range of properties obtainable in iron and steel. It forms different compositions with iron when combined in different ways and amounts. Thus carbon is the primary means for making iron or steel soft and ductile, tough or hard. Most other alloying elements in effect modify or enhance the benefits of carbon.

The fundamental effects of carbon on iron are shown by the iron and iron carbide equilibrium diagram of Fig. 4-13. This is a type III diagram. The carbon commonly appears as iron carbide but not always; e.g., graphite in cast iron. Iron carbide consists of 6.67% carbon and 93.33% iron by weight and has the average formula Fe_3C. It is the hardest constituent in carbon iron and carbon steel and is quite brittle and white in color. It is called *cementite*.

Iron and Iron Carbide Solid Solutions.   The line for zero carbon in Fig. 4-13 shows that pure iron or *ferrite* solidifies at about 1540°C (2800°F). Over a short range of high temperature it has a body-centered-cubic structure called *delta iron*. When cooled to 1400°C (2552°F), the structure changes to face-centered-cubic *gamma iron*. This is the main part of *austenite*, which may dissolve up to 1.7% carbon as iron carbide. Below 910°C (1670°F), ferrite transforms to body-centered-cubic alpha iron. Thus iron is allotropic. It also changes from a nonmagnetic material at high temperatures to a magnetic one somewhat below 800°C (1470°F). Alpha iron dissolves only a small amount of carbide. Ferrite can also hold such elements as nickel, silicon, phosphorus, and sulfur in solution in amounts depending on temperature.

Pearlite.   Steel containing 0.9% carbon is an important iron alloy. It starts to freeze when the molten solution is cooled to about 1480°C (2700°F) and is completely frozen at about 1250°C (2280°F). No change occurs in the austenite until the low temperature of 723°C (1333°F) is reached. This is a minimum in a solid solution comparable to a eutectic in a liquid solution and is called a *eutectoid*. At this point the gamma turns to alpha iron, and the iron carbide is forced out of solution if cooling is slow. The eutectoid alloy increases in volume on transformation, and the resulting formation consists of a series of plates of iron carbide interspersed with plates of ferrite in each grain. This lamellar structure is known as *pearlite* and is illustrated under high magnification in Fig. 4-14. What is shown is *coarse pearlite* produced by quite slow cooling. Faster cooling rates cause closer spacing of the plates in what are known as *medium* and then *fine* pearlite. Hardness increases from coarse to fine pearlite.

The interlayers of the two phases in pearlite reinforce each other. Ferrite has a tensile strength of about 295 MPa (42,500 psi) and elongation of 40%, and cementite a strength of 35 MPa (5000 psi) and negligible elongation. The pearlite combination has a tensile strength of 825 to 860 MPa (120,000 to 125,000 psi) and elongation of 10 to 15%.

Hypoeutectoid and Hypereutectoid Steels.   Steel containing less than 0.9% carbon is called *hypoeutectoid* and with more than 0.9% carbon is *hypereuctectoid*. The first may be exemplified by a steel containing 0.4% carbon on the diagram of Fig. 4-13. This composition starts to freeze at around 1500°C (2730°F). First delta iron is

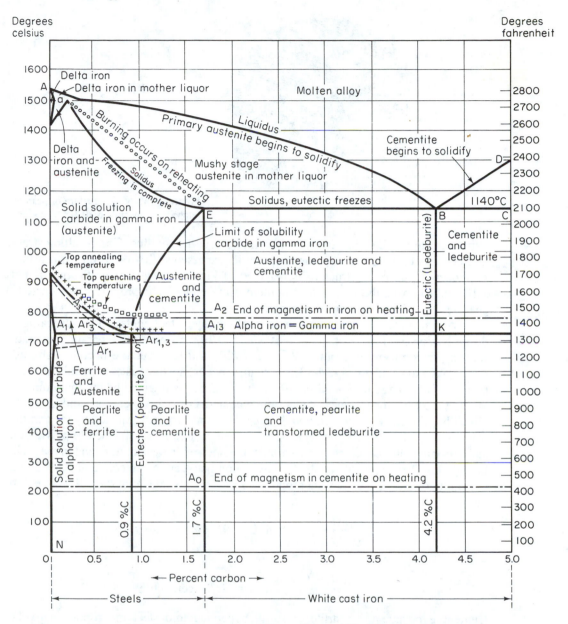

Figure 4-13 Equilibrium diagram of iron and iron carbide. (From *Metal Progress*, Sept. 1980, by permission of the publisher.)

precipitated. Then the delta iron changes to gamma iron, and freezing is complete in austenite at 1400°C (2550°F). No further change occurs with falling temperature until a little above 800°C (1470°F) is reached at the A_3 line. Then ferrite precipitates as the temperature is lowered to 723°C (1333°F), at which point the remaining austenite

Figure 4-14 Microstructure of pearlite (etched and magnified 1000×).

transforms to pearlite. Precipitation is completed at the Ar_1 line. The resulting structure consists of about 55% grains of ferrite interspersed with 45% grains of pearlite. A hypoeutectoid microstructure is depicted in Fig. 4-15. The magnification is not sufficient to reveal the laminations in the pearlite grains. The proportion of ferrite to pearlite depends on the carbon content.

A hypereutectoid alloy may be exemplified by a steel containing 1.4% carbon. Solidification commences at about 1450°C (2640°F) with austenite separating out until freezing is complete at about 1160°C (2120°F), and the structure becomes all austenite. As indicated in Fig. 4-13, no change occurs in the austenite until the temperature falls to about 1040°C (1900°F). Iron carbide is rejected below that point; at 900°C (1650°F), for instance, the austenite contains only 1.1% carbon, and at 800°C (1470°F), a little over 0.9% carbon. The excess iron carbide is rejected by the gamma iron. At 723°C (1333°F), the remainder of the austenite is transformed to pearlite on slow cooling with the rejected iron carbide interspersed in the structure and in the grain boundaries. The lever rule applied to the region between the eutectoid at 0.9%C and cementite of 6.67%C shows the proportions of the constituents of the 1.4%C steel to be

$$\frac{6.67 - 1.4}{5.77} \times 100 = 91.3\% \text{ pearlite}$$

and

$$\frac{1.4 - 0.9}{5.77} \times 100 = 8.7\% \text{ cementite}$$

Cementite outside the pearlite exists in hypereutectoid steel in proportion to the amount of carbon beyond the eutectoid point. Iron containing more than 1.7% carbon is usually not considered to be steel.

Martensite.   The structures considered up to now have been those formed by cooling at a slow rate. Now let the hypoeutectoid steel (Fig. 4-13) be heated from room temperature to above 723°C (1333°F). As the temperature is raised above that point, austenite is formed and dissolves all the carbon. The excess ferrite is dissolved

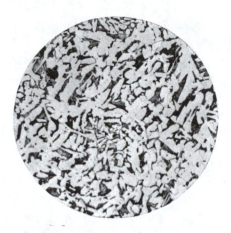

Figure 4-15 Microstructure of a polyhedral hypoeutectoid steel (etched and magnified 100×).

between the A_1 and A_3 lines. At a temperature above the A_3 line, the metal is all austenite and contains all the carbon in an interstitial solution. If the alloy is quenched in water from above the A_3 temperature, it is cooled so quickly that the transformation of gamma to alpha iron does not have time to occur at 723°C (1333°F). Instead, the change is suppressed to some low temperature, say around 200°C (400°F), and there is not enough energy available to cause diffusion of the carbon atoms. They remain in and distort the lattice. This makes a hardened steel called martensite. Its needle-like or acicular microstructure is depicted in Fig. 4-16. The more highly strained layers in the lattices are attacked more readily by the etchant and appear as dark lines. Mar-

Figure 4-16 Microstructure of martensite (etched and magnified 1000×).

tensite is formed and hardening occurs when any steel (hypo- or hypereutectoid) is quenched fast enough from above the critical temperature.

Other Structures of Steel.   Other steel structures may be produced by various heat treatments described in Chap. 5. If instead of being quenched from the austenite region, a steel is cooled slowly and held for a period of time around 700°C (1300°F), the iron carbide will disperse in small spheroidized particles instead of lamellar plates in the ferrite. This is called *spheroidite*. On the other hand, if a steel is not fully quenched, but cooled quickly to and held at a temperature above 230°C (450°F) for a period of time, it is transformed to *bainite*. This is a structure intermediate between fine pearlite and martensite and appears to be a mechanical mixture of ferrite and minute carbide particles.

Practical Aspects of Carbon in Steel.   Steels are selected with specific carbon contents to suit certain purposes. Easily formed sheet steel for cans and automobile fenders and body panels contains 0.1% carbon or less. Tensile strength is about 350 MPa (50,000 psi) and elongation 35% or more. Structural steel, like that in I beams and channels for buildings, has around 0.2% carbon with tensile strength of about 415 MPa (60,000 psi) and elongation 30% or so. Medium carbon steels widely used for machine parts like gears and axles with 0.30 to 0.45% carbon have up to 700 MPa (100,000 psi) tensile strength and 20 to 25% elongation. Steels with carbon contents over 0.30% have the added advantage that they can be hardened, particularly on wearing surfaces, to the extent indicated by Fig. 5-4. A carbon content of 0.70% may be chosen for wear resistance without brittleness, as for railroad rails, for a tensile strength of about 825 MPa (120,000 psi) and elongation of 10%. Higher-carbon steels are used largely for tools and dies. Other alloying elements enhance heat treatment and properties of steel as described in Chaps. 5 and 6.

Grain Size of Steel.   The grain size of a steel nominally refers to the size of the austenitic grains before the steel is cooled to room temperature. This grain size is important because it influences many of the physical properties of steel. Occasionally, the size of the ferrite grains is important, as in deep-drawing sheet steel, and is then definitely specified as the *ferrite grain size*. Actually, the austenitic grain size is not altered much by the rate of cooling to room temperature. Coarse austenitic grains raise hardenability, tensile strength as normalized, and creep strength, and improve rough machinability. Fine grains increase impact toughness, improve machining finishes, and mitigate quenching cracks, distortion in quenching, and surface decarburization.

The grain size of a steel depends upon its method of manufacture, heat treatment, the amount of hot and cold working, and alloying elements. A deoxidizer added to a molten steel when it is made to eliminate dissolved gases and reduce FeO leaves minute oxide particles in the metal. These act as nuclei and, if numerous, promote a fine-grained steel. Steel recrystallizes when heated above the A_1 line (Fig. 4-13). The higher the temperature and the longer the time in the austenitic region, the more the grains grow in size, although the actual amount of growth in any case depends upon the composition of the steel. A highly worked steel starts with many small grains from numerous nuclei when recrystallized. As a rule, alloying elements like vanadium that form carbides or fine oxides tend to increase resistance to grain coarsening. This is thought due to the fact that the carbides and oxides resist solution in the austenite and help fix grain boundaries.

Solidification of Cast Iron.   The changes that occur when cast iron cools will be described for a composition of 3% carbon. Solidification from the liquid occurs at about 1330°C (2425°F) and austenite, with a lower carbon content, separates from the melt. The remaining liquid is enriched with carbon and the last of it reaches the eutectic composition of 4.2% carbon when the temperature has fallen to the solidus at 1140°C (2085°F). At that point the austenite contains 1.7% carbon and the last of the liquid freezes as a eutectic mixture (of austenite and primary carbide) known as *ledeburite*. On further cooling at a rate to prevent breakdown of the carbide, secondary carbide is rejected from the austenite in the mixture. At 723°C (1333°F) the austenite contains 0.9%C and is transformed to pearlite. This includes the austenite in the eutectic mixture (ledeburite), and the resulting mixture of primary cementite and pearlite is called *transformed ledeburite*.

With slow enough cooling or with alloys that reduce the stability of iron carbide, graphite is formed instead of iron carbide. That is, graphite is deposited when the eutectic freezes and is rejected by the austenite on further cooling. At transformation temperature the austenite may be changed to pearlite or partially or wholly to graphite and ferrite. Graphite commonly exists in cast iron in flakes as shown in Fig. 8-48(A) but under certain conditions may appear as nodules as in Fig. 8-48(C). The iron graphite diagram is slightly different from the iron carbide diagram.

Differences in cooling rates, compositions, alloying elements, and subsequent heat treatment produce a variety of cast irons. The main ones are described in Chap. 8.

QUESTIONS

1. Name and describe the three most important types of unit cells in metals.
2. What is the recrystallization temperature and how does it affect the cold-working of metal?
3. How does crystal deformation take place, and what is the role of dislocations in such deformation?
4. What is the mechanism of work or strain hardening and eventual fracture of metals?
5. What are the mechanisms of solid solution hardening and dispersion hardening?
6. Describe the two general modes of fracture.
7. What are the latent heat of fusion and the latent heat of transformation of metals? Do all metals have both?
8. Define an alloy.
9. What are the features of substitutional and interstitial solid solutions?
10. What is a phase of a metal or alloy?
11. What is a eutectic composition?
12. Describe the three standard types of equilibrium diagrams.
13. Describe four forms in which alloys may exist at room temperature.

14. How does freezing affect the shapes, sizes, and compositions of the grains of a piece of solidified metal?
15. Describe the allotropic properties of iron.
16. Define austenite, ferrite, pearlite, cementite, martensite, and bainite.
17. What is a eutectoid composition?
18. What effects does grain size have upon the properties of steel?

PROBLEMS

1. Refer to Fig. 4-9. Find the compositions and proportions of the phases of the following alloys midway between the liquidus and solidus temperatures and just above the solidus temperature. The eutectic point is at 38% A and 62% B.

Alloy designation:	R	S	T	U
Percent A	20	40	70	90
Percent B	80	60	30	10

2. Refer to Fig. 4-10. For the following alloys, specify:
   (a) The composition of the first crystals that separate out of the metal.
   (b) The compositions and proportion of the phases of the mixture halfway between liquidus and solidus lines.
   (c) The composition of the last crystals to form on solidification.

Alloy designation:	K	L	M
Percent C	20	50	70
Percent D	80	50	30

3. Refer to Fig. 4-11. Specify the phases and their proportions and composition for:
   (a) An alloy of 90% G and 10%H at temperatures T_2, T_3, and T_4, at the solidus line, halfway between the solidus and liquidus lines, and at the liquidus line.
   (b) An alloy of 80% G and 20% H at temperatures T_2, T_3, and T_4, halfway between the solidus and liquidus lines, and above the liquidus line.
   (c) An alloy of 75% G and 25% H at temperatures T_2, T_3, and T_4, at the solidus line, halfway between the solidus and liquidus lines, and at the liquidus line.
   (d) An alloy of 60% G and 40% H at temperatures T_2, T_3, and T_4, and at the solidus line.
   (e) An alloy of 25% G and 75% H at temperatures T_2, T_3, and T_4, at the solidus line and halfway between the solidus and liquidus lines.

4. From the iron–iron carbide diagram of Fig. 4-13 ascertain the constituents and their proportions for steels containing the following percentages of carbon: (a) 0.10; (b) 0.50; (c) 0.90; (d) 1.00; (e) 1.30.

REFERENCES

BARRETT, C. S., and T. B. MASSALSKI, *Structure of Metals*, 3rd ed., McGraw-Hill, New York, 1966.

CARTER, G. F., *Principles of Physical and Chemical Metallurgy*, American Society for Metals, Metals Park, Ohio, 1979.

Metals Handbook, 9th ed., American Society for Metals, Metals Park, Ohio, 1980.

HEAT TREATMENT OF METALS

PRINCIPLES OF HEAT TREATMENT

Heat treatment is a major way of changing the strength, hardness, ductility, and other properties of metals. It is effective only with certain alloys because it depends upon one element being soluble in another in the solid state in different amounts under different circumstances. The basic metallurgy of heat treatment has been presented in Chap. 4.

Hardening (or strengthening) is done by heating an alloy to a high enough temperature, depending on the material, and cooling it rapidly. A solid solution of the alloying elements is formed at the high temperature. This becomes supersaturated upon cooling, and desired hardness is obtained by controlling the decomposition of the constituents. Under proper conditions, the solute is dispersed in fine particles in the crystal lattice and serves to block dislocation movements when stresses are applied. The added resistance to stresses makes the metal act stronger and harder.

The amount of hardening that takes place in an alloy depends upon the size, shape, and distribution of the particles and the amount of coherence between the particles and the matrix. The size, shape, and distribution of the particles result largely from the dispersion of the solute in the material, which depends in turn upon the temperature and time of heating. There is an optimum particle size in each case that gives best results. Large particles are imposing obstacles but are far apart, and dislocations pass between them. Particles too small do not greatly hinder the movements of dislocations. The degree of coherence between particles and primary phase has the most influence on hardening. Hardening is enhanced if the boundary between particles and matrix is coherent. This is called *coherency hardening* and is effective because each particle distorts the space lattice of the phase around itself and thereby extends its influence in blocking movements of dislocations. Zones of influence may overlap. *Aggregate hardening* occurs with particles that have incoherent boundaries with the primary phase. Examples are plates (such as in pearlite in steel) or globular particles. Dislocations are impeded only partially by such particles and pass readily between them.

Alloys hardened by heat treatment can be divided into two major classes. One kind is *nonallotropic* and is hardened by age or precipitation treatments. The other is *allotropic* (which means the crystal structure is different at higher than at lower temperatures) and can be hardened by suppressing the decomposition of the structure on cooling. The first class contains mostly nonferrous and only a few ferrous alloys; the second class consists of steels and irons. Some metals, such as certain stainless steels, are heat treated by a combination of the two methods.

The reverse of hardening, which is softening of metals, is done by heating alone or by heating and slow cooling. The effects are to gather together and coarsen the dispersed particles, control grain size, and improve ductility and impact resistance. Common processes of this sort are annealing, normalizing, and tempering. Other purposes of heat treating are to relieve stresses, modify electrical and magnetic properties, increase heat and corrosion resistance, and change the chemical composition of metals (as by carburizing steel).

The processes of hardening and softening metals will be explained in detail in this chapter, and the techniques and equipment for the processes will be described.

HEAT TREATMENT OF NONALLOTROPIC ALLOYS

An alloy that does not change in lattice structure when heated can be hardened if it has a minor phase that is more soluble in the primary phase at higher than at lower temperatures. Such an alloy is raised to a temperature that causes the utmost solution of the solute without melting any phases or causing excessive grain growth. It is then quenched fast enough to prevent immediate separation of the solute and thus retains the solid solution even though solubility is much less at lower temperatures. Next, particles of solute are precipitated in the alloy in what is generally called *precipitation hardening*. In some cases this may occur at room temperature over a period of time and is called *natural aging* or *age hardening*. Other alloys must be heated to bring about or hasten precipitation, in what is called *artificial aging*.

Aluminum-copper alloys are common precipitation hardened alloys. Aluminum and copper combine chemically to form copper aluminide, $CuAl_2$, containing about 54% copper by weight. Copper is soluble in aluminum in the α phase shown in Fig. 5-1(A); some consider the copper aluminide to be in solution. The proportion increases from almost nothing at low temperatures to a maximum at 548°C (1018°F) of about 5.5% copper. At lower temperatures some portion is precipitated out as $CuAl_2$.

2024 aluminum is an important commercial alloy that contains about 4.5% copper. As a first step in hardening, it is given a solution treatment by being heated

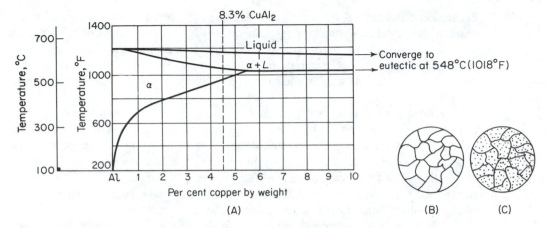

Figure 5-1 (A) Aluminum-rich end of the aluminum-copper equilibrium diagram; (B) sketch of the magnified structure of a 4.5% Cu-Al alloy heated to 490°C (915°F) for solution treatment; (C) the same alloy after quenching and precipitation of particles to induce hardening.

to 490 to 500°C (915 to 930°F). At that temperature most of the copper is in solution in the α phase. For economy, the material is held at solution temperature no longer than necessary to achieve homogeneity. A typical time is 1 hour. It is important that the temperature be kept below that of a eutectic melting temperature [502°C (935°F) in this case] that occurs for an alloy of 33% copper in aluminum. If that temperature is reached, the material is permanently damaged by melting in the grain boundaries.

Solution-treated aluminum is quenched in clean cold water immediately after soaking. The more rapid the quenching rate, the stronger the product and the more it resists corrosion after precipitation. 2024 aluminum ages to practically maximum strength in 24 hours at 20°C (68°F) after quenching. It can be aged to full strength in 2 hours at 175°C (ca. 350°F). Another aluminum alloy (6061) takes 30 days at room temperature to become fully aged. Most aluminum alloys are nearly as formable right after quenching as in the annealed state; some more so. Thus, they are often bent or straightened at that time. Aging may be retarded by refrigeration, and that may be done (as with rivets) to keep material longer in a workable condition.

An advantage of precipitation hardening is that costs are relatively low. Most alloying elements are cheap, temperatures are not high, and procedures are simple. Because temperatures are not high, distortion, scaling, and cracking are minimized. Up to precipitation temperature most hardened alloys retain strength better than alloys not treated.

Precipitation-hardened alloys may be reheated and cooled slowly for softening. Aluminum alloys may be given a *stress relief anneal* or a *full anneal*. In the first instance, the effects of strain hardening may be removed in most cases by heating to about 345°C (650°F). For a full anneal, a coarse and widely spaced precipitate results from soaking for 2 hours at 415 to 440°C (780 to 825°F) followed by slow cooling.

HEAT TREATMENT OF STEELS

Hardening Steel.   Steel is hardenable because carbon is more soluble in the face-centered-cubic structure at high temperatures (austenite) than in the body-centered structure (ferrite) at low temperatures. These regions are shown in Fig. 5-2, which is the steel section of the iron-carbon diagram of Fig. 4-13. If steel is heated to the austenite region and held there until its carbon is dissolved and is then cooled rapidly by quenching, the carbon is not given a chance to escape and is trapped as dispersed atoms or fine particles in a strained low-temperature lattice. That sets up a distorted structure (martensite) that is quite hard and strong but brittle.

The changes that occur when steel is cooled from the austenitic range may be depicted by the *T-T-T diagrams* or *S-curves* like those of Fig. 5-3. These are schematic for one type of steel; each analysis of steel has its own S-curve, and many have been published. These show what takes place in nonequilibrium cooling in contrast to the iron–iron carbide diagram for equilibrium conditions. Any cooling rate can be designated by a line like *AB* or *AD* on a diagram. Figure 5-3(A) shows an *isothermal transformation curve* for steel cooled to below the critical temperature and held there for a period of time while transformation takes place. No change occurs in the area to the left of the S-curve. For example, if the steel is cooled at a rate denoted by *AB* and then held at constant temperature until time *C*, it is transformed from an austenitic to a coarse pearlitic structure. If another sample is cooled rapidly from *A* to *D*, to the left of the nose of the S-curve, no transformation occurs. Then if the sample is held at temperature *D* until time *E*, the structure is transformed to bainite.

A *continuous cooling transformation curve* like Fig. 5-3(B) is a modified S-curve. It shows the changes that occur when austenite is transformed over a range of temperatures rather than at one temperature. The isothermal diagram is drawn in light lines for comparison. The continuous cooling curve is represented by the boundaries of the crosshatched areas. It is seen that the transformation begins later and at lower temperatures when cooling is continuous. The formation of bainite may be disregarded for continuous cooling of carbon steels and some alloy steels. Thus the bainite region is omitted in Fig. 5-3(B). This is not the case for many alloy steels.

Examples of changes when steel is cooled at various rates are given by the lines in Fig. 5-3(B). Steel cooled at the rate depicted by *AF* is all transformed to medium-coarse pearlite. Any steel cooled rapidly along a line to the left of the nose of the curve, such as line *AG*, is kept austenitic until it reaches the M_S temperature. There it starts to transform to martensite, and transformation is complete when the M_f temperature is reached. The line that just passes the nose of the curve represents the *critical cooling rate*. If cooling takes place along a line *AH* in Fig. 5-3(B), the transformation to fine pearlite may be only partially complete by the time the boundary designated (3) is reached. That is where transformation stops. The remaining austenite then is changed to martensite below the M_S temperature. The result is a mixed martensitic and fine pearlitic structure.

The lower the temperature of transformation for a given steel, the harder and

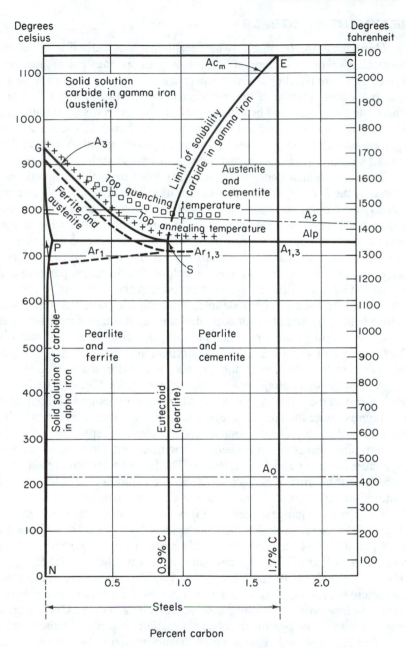

Figure 5-2   Iron–iron carbide diagram for steel.

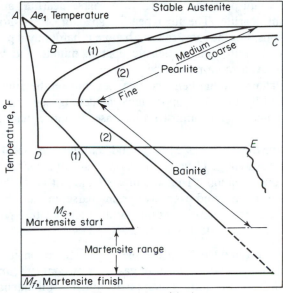

(A)

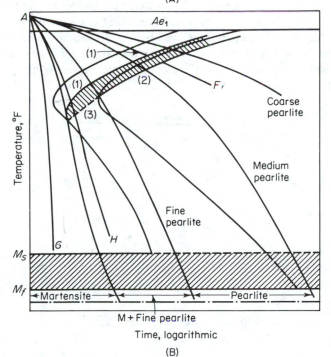

Time, logarithmic

(B)

Figure 5-3 (A) Schematic T-T-T diagram or S-curve for a eutectoid carbon steel; (B) schematic CC curve, which is an S-curve for a eutectoid carbon steel modified for continuous cooling. Symbols: (1) austenite to pearlite transformation begins; (2) transformation complete; (3) decomposition of austenite stops.

stronger the product. Thus medium pearlite is harder than coarse pearlite, and fine pearlite is harder than medium pearlite. The finer pearlite spacing offers more resistance to the flow of dislocations. For the same reason, bainite is harder than pearlite, and martensite is the hardest. Bainite and martensite contain minute and widely dispersed particles that present even more resistance.

The maximum hardness attainable in quenched steel depends on the amount of carbon it contains. As indicated by Fig. 5-4, appreciable hardening does not occur with less than 0.30% carbon, and there is almost no increase for more than 0.60% carbon.

Steel must be heated above the A_3 line of Fig. 5-2 and held there to dissolve the desired amount of carbon for hardening. Usually, no more than 30 to 55°C (50 to 100°F) into the austenite region is enough. Temperatures should not be higher nor soaking time longer than necessary to avoid excessive grain coarsening and burning of the steel. A rough rule is to allow 1 hour of heat time at final temperature per inch of thickness in the heaviest section of a steel workpiece.

Quenching.   Heat may be removed from hot metal by immersion in brine, water, oil, or molten salts or lead, by exposure to air or gases, or by contact with solid metallic masses. Water and oil are the most common media for full quenching. Relative quenching rates of the common methods are indicated by Fig. 5-5. Larger pieces are cooled more slowly with more differences between inside and outside cooling rates than small pieces. The severity of water quenching cracks some parts; oil quenching is less harmful, and air quenching is even better. Oil and air quenching require alloys of higher hardenability to make steel as hard as by water quenching. Synthetic oil-free water-base fluids have been developed in recent years that give quenching results between water and oil.

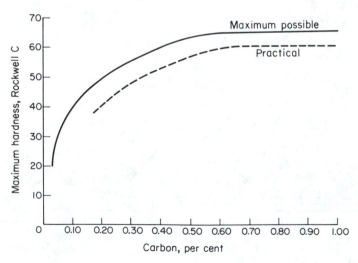

Figure 5-4 Relationship between the hardness and carbon content of quenched carbon steel.

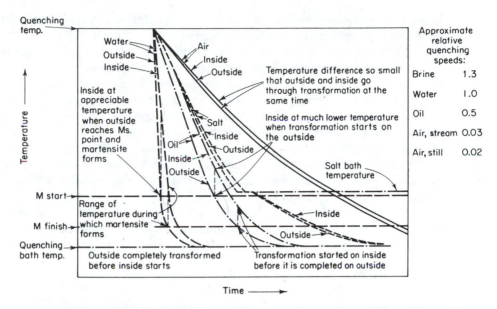

Figure 5-5 Time-temperature cooling curves for several quenching media.

Quenching sets up stresses that warp workpieces, and precautions are necessary to avoid distortion. Slender shafts, thin walls, and thin and thick adjacent sections are particularly vulnerable. A long slender shaft is ordinarily suspended from one end when plunged into a quenching tank. Production parts, such as gears with thin webs, may be *die-quenched*. This means that the piece is clamped firmly in a die in a press while lowered into the quenching medium. The die is made to contact and thus chill selected areas and admit coolant at different rates to various sections to regulate the cooling rate and thus the warpage throughout the part.

Hot workpieces must be moved quickly and safely from the heating device to the quenching medium. This may be done by hand tongs, one piece at a time, for job work. For repetitive production, work may be transported by conveyor, and large pieces by cranes or cars. Small pieces are normally handled in wire baskets or on racks. The coolant is ordinarily agitated or swirled vigorously to achieve uniform cooling and may be circulated through cooling coils.

Ways of Hardening Steel. Direct and full quenching as has been described is the oldest and still common practice. It is economical and gives the highest immediate hardness. The essential structures produced are martensite and retained austenite. Their proportions depend upon carbon and alloy content, austenitizing temperature, quenching medium, and part geometry. The practice of some is to freeze the steel to $-70°C$ ($-95°F$) or lower, to transform the retained austenite. Few parts are left in the as-quenched state because the *fresh martensite* is quite brittle. When the fresh martensite is heated to below the critical temperature, it becomes softer and more ductile, and internal stresses are relieved. Little benefit is obtained below $150°C$ ($300°F$). The initial change is to *tempered martensite*, in the range 150 to 175°C (300 to 350°F) with only slight changes in properties. The second stage, at about 175 to 370°C (350 to 700°F) depending upon the steel, is characterized by transformation of the retained austenite to bainite. Carbon from the martensite appears to become combined into finely dispersed particles of cementite. In the third stage, from about 290 to 700°C (550 to 1300°F), the cementite agglomerates and coalesces. The structure becomes an aggregate of ferrite with cementite in quite fine spheres, referred to as tempered martensite and *tempered bainite*. The structures may become more or less uniformly spheroidized from prolonged heating at the upper end of the range. Reheating after quenching is called *tempering*, but some give the name of *drawing* to reheating below 315°C (600°F). A typical direct hardening and tempering cycle is depicted on the schematic T-T-T diagram in Fig. 5-6(A).

The best combination of strength, hardness, ductility, and toughness for most applications may be obtained by quenching steel to martensite and then tempering as desired. This should be done without delay because martensite can crack, even

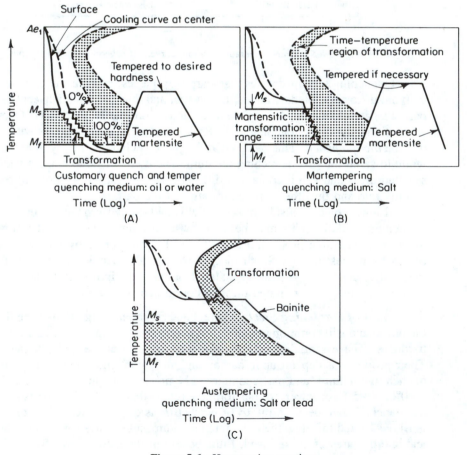

Figure 5-6   Heat-treating practices.

overnight. Tempering softens, but both time and temperature determine the hardness obtained when steel is tempered, as shown in Fig. 5-7. Each analysis of steel has its own set of curves. In this case the same hardness results from heating for 5 hours at 205°C (400°F) or 8 seconds at 370°C (700°F). Recommended practice is to use the lowest possible temperature that gives the required results in a reasonable length of time. Strength usually decreases but may increase at low tempering temperatures as residual stresses are relieved. The higher the tempering temperature, the more the quenching stresses are relieved, but most benefit is obtained at 260 to 315°C (500 to 600°F). As hardness decreases, ductility increases, but toughness does not improve uniformly. After an initial increase as temperature is raised, impact toughness drops off for most steels before it begins to rise again. This low toughness commonly obtained from tempering at 200 to 370°C (400 to 700°F) is called *blue brittleness* or *blue heat phenomenon* because it occurs at temperatures that leave a blue oxide film on the steel. It is ascribed to the precipitation of oxides and nitrides. If impact toughness is desired, tempering must be done at a higher temperature, and a lower hardness must be accepted. The impact toughness of some alloy steels is impaired if they are cooled slowly after tempering in the range of 450 to 600°C (ca. 850 to 1100°F). This is called *temper brittleness*. It may be avoided by quenching from tempering temperature. *Toughening* is the name given to tempering at 540 to 700°C (1000 to 1300°F) when high hardness is not needed. Usually, this gives maximum impact toughness.

Steel is heat treated in other ways besides full quenching and tempering. Much modern practice utilizes interrupted quenching methods that hold the steel for a time at relatively high temperatures to equalize temperatures inside and out. That helps to harden the work uniformly throughout and to eliminate cracking and warpage. The leading methods, martempering and austempering, are described in the following paragraphs.

Martempering or *marquenching* starts with quenching austenitized steel in a molten salt bath as indicated in Fig. 5-6(B). A piece is held in the bath just above the M_S temperature (where martensite starts to form) until its temperature is uniform throughout. Then the piece is cooled in air through the zone of martensite formation.

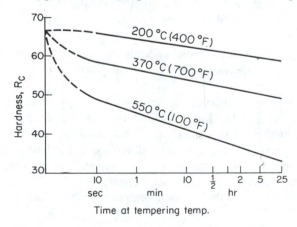

Figure 5-7 How time and temperature of tempering affect hardness of 0.80% carbon steel.

This generally is followed by an ordinary tempering treatment as desired. Mar-tempering is limited to carbon steel sections less than about 6 mm ($\frac{1}{4}$ in.) thick and serves better with alloy steel. That is because the quenching rate of the salt bath is relatively slow, as shown in Fig. 5-5, and does not carry carbon steel readily past the nose of the S-curve.

Steel is quenched in a heated bath at 150 to 425°C (300 to 800°F) for *aus-tempering* as depicted in Fig. 5-6(C). The work is then held in the bath for sufficient time for the austenite to transform to bainite isothermally. Then the piece may be cooled at any rate; no subsequent tempering is needed. A hardness of 45 to 60 R_C may be obtained depending upon carbon content and transformation temperature. A prac-tical range is 50 to 55 R_C with the advantage of more toughness at this hardness than is generally obtained by other methods. Application to carbon steel is limited because of the slow cooling rate of the high-temperature bath.

Hardenability of Steel.   Several steels of different compositions may be hard-ened by quenching in exactly the same way but they will be found to differ in both intensity and depth of hardness. *Hardenability* refers to the degree and depth of hardness obtained in a heat treatment. Any austenite that is transformed to pearlite is lost to the formation of martensite, and hardening is decreased by that amount. Greater hardenability means that more austenite is transformed to martensite and its deriva-tives. The factors that are related to the suppression of pearlite and thus to hard-enability are:

1. All alloying elements that dissolve in austenite (including carbon to 0.9% but not cobalt) push the nose of the S-curve to the right (Fig. 5-3) and make it easier to quench the insides as well as the outsides of parts past the pearlite zone. A comparison of the hardenability of an unalloyed and an alloyed steel is given by Fig. 5-9.

2. A homogeneous austenite structure increases hardenability by holding the S-curve uniform.

3. Coarse austenitic grains push the S-curve to the right and increase hardenability. They may be caused by heating the steel too high or too long before quenching, but coarse grains are not desirable because they reduce the toughness of the hardened steel.

4. Undissolved carbides and nonmetallic inclusions in the austenite decrease hard-enability because they provide nuclei for fine pearlite formation.

The *Jominy end-quench test* holds all factors constant except composition to measure the hardenability of steel. A bar 1 in. in diameter by 3 or 4 in. long is properly austenitized and quenched on the end in a standardized way as illustrated in Fig. 5-8. Heat is removed substantially from the quenched end surface and is thus withdrawn at different rates along any one bar but in the same way along any bars of steel tested. The result is a gradient of hardness along the bar that depends only on the composition of the material. After the piece has cooled to room temperature, two flats are ground

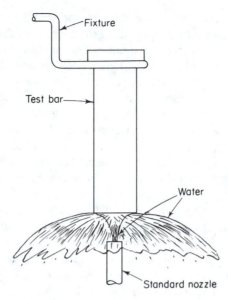

Figure 5-8 Jominy end-quench.

lengthwise on diametrically opposite sides. Rockwell hardness readings are taken along the bar at 1.6-mm ($\frac{1}{16}$-in.) intervals to 25 mm (16/16 in.) and from there at 6.4-mm ($\frac{1}{4}$-in.) intervals to 51 mm (2 in.) and plotted in a manner like that of Fig. 5-9. The hardness illustrated for a plain carbon steel (1040) drops off rapidly a short distance from the end. An alloy steel shows a much smaller rate of decline or none, as the curve for 4340 steel illustrates.

Empirical equations have been developed for calculating the Jominy curves of steels from the carbon and alloy contents. Further calculations can give the hardness of points within round bars and other sections from steel composition and manner of heat treatment.

Annealing of Steel.   *Annealing* in its broadest sense means heating a metal to where a change occurs and then cooling it slowly. A main reason for annealing is to

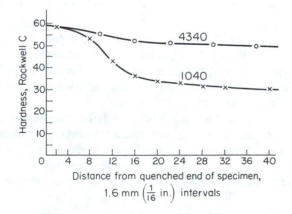

Figure 5-9 Typical Jominy curves for a plain carbon (1040) steel and an alloyed (4340) steel.

soften steel, but it also serves to relieve stresses, drive off gases, alter ductility, toughness, or electrical or magnetic properties, or to refine the grains. The end purpose may be to prepare the steel for further heat treatment or mechanical working or to meet the specifications for the finished product. The role of annealing in heat treatment is illustrated by slow cooling through the upper regions of the S-curve, such as along the path *AF* of Fig. 5-3(B). Since many paths are possible and each gives somewhat different results, there are several ways that annealing is done.

Full annealing consists of heating an iron-base alloy from 30 to 55°C (50 to 100°F) above the critical temperature, holding it there for uniform heating, and cooling at a controlled slow rate to room temperature. The work may be held in a heavily insulated furnace with heat cut off or it may be buried in an insulating material such as ash or asbestos.

Normalizing consists of heating about 55°C (100°F) above the transformation temperature and cooling in still air. The purpose of normalizing a steel is to obtain a homogeneous structure. It usually also imparts moderate hardness and strength. Normalizing is commonly done to restore wrought steel to its near-equilibrium state after cold or hot working or overheating. Steel castings are normalized to modify grain structure and relieve stresses. Thin sections can be cooled rapidly this way and appreciably hardened.

Process or commercial annealing consists of holding iron-base alloys at a temperature a little below the critical for 2 to 4 hours and cooling for desired results. Some softening occurs, but the main benefit is stress relief. The operation is sometimes called *stress relieving*. The advantage of the process is that warpage of thin sections and surface corrosion and scaling are slight because temperatures can be kept low. The process has wide application in preparing steel sheets and wire for drawing or redrawing, for stress relief of weldments and castings, and to remove the embrittling effects of heavy machining and flame cutting (Chap. 14). Large work may be heated locally by a torch; smaller pieces in a furnace.

Cycle annealing is done by cooling austenitized steel at a rate to reach a desired zone on the S-curve. The metal is held at the chosen temperature until transformation is complete. Then the work may be cooled in any way practicable, by quenching or in air, because no more transformation occurs. The main advantage is a short cycle time; 4 to 8 hours as compared to 5 to 30 hours for conventional annealing. The end structure may be pearlite or spheroidite (or a mixture of both) depending upon selections of temperatures and time. *Spheroidizing* is the name given to the process when the carbon is collected into coarse round carbide particles, especially in high-carbon steels. This is a desirable structure to machine because the hard particles in a soft ferrite matrix are readily pushed aside by a cutting tool.

Both wrought and cast steels are annealed in essentially the same ways and for the same reasons. There is one important difference, however. A steel casting solidifies with a coarse dendritic structure and considerable segregation. This structure is not broken up and homogenized as is done by working a wrought steel. The cast structure must be refined by heat treatment. Both full annealing and normalizing are applicable. The first gives maximum softness and ductility; the second provides finer subdivision of the dendritic grains, more homogeneity, and higher strength.

Some work must be annealed two or more times to correct faults (such as gross lack of uniformity) or to get desired results. A typical *double anneal* consists of heating 100 to 150°C (ca. 200 to 300°F) above the A_3 line for thorough diffusion, then air cooling below the critical temperature to inhibit ferrite separation, followed by regular annealing at 30 to 55°C (50 to 100°F) above the line to refine the grains and finally slow cooling.

SURFACE-HARDENING OF STEEL

A principal reason for hardening steel is to retard wear on bearing and rubbing surfaces, but hard steel is brittle and not fatigue and shock resistant. Therefore, for high strength along with durability it is desirable to harden selected outer surfaces of many machine parts for wear and leave their cores soft and ductile for shock resistance. Also, heat treatment can be done at lowest cost when applied only to surfaces where needed. Medium- and high-carbon steels can be surface-hardened by induction- and flame-hardening. Electron beam and laser techniques as well as electric arc methods are modified for surface-hardening. They are primarily welding processes and are described in Chapter 14. All these processes heat only selected surfaces to austenitizing temperatures. The steel is then quenched to harden the surfaces. Surfaces of low-carbon steels may be enriched with carbon by carburizing or case-hardening and then can be hardened. These processes will now be described.

Induction-Hardening. Induction heating is done by passing a high-frequency alternating current through a water-cooled coil or inductor around the workpiece or over a surface. The cyclic magnetic field that is generated induces alternating currents that heat the workpiece, as indicated in Fig. 5-10. The depth of current penetration is $\delta = 1.98\sqrt{\rho/\mu f}$, where ρ is the resistivity, μ is the magnetic permeability ($\mu = 1$ for nonmagnetic materials), and f is the frequency in hertz. The lower the frequency, the deeper the penetration, and vice versa. Actually, the current is not uniform for its full depth but drops off exponentially from the surface and heats the metal accordingly. Magnetic hysteresis adds to the effect for magnetic materials. Steel is less magnetic at higher temperatures and escapes overheating. Induction heating is done to melt metals (Chap. 8), for brazing and soldering (Chap. 14), and to heat stock for forging (Chap. 12) as well as for hardening steel and iron.

A piece may be hardened after induction heating by dropping it into a quenching medium or flooding it with a stream of coolant. A small area on a large piece may be heated quickly and then effectively quenched by the mass of the piece drawing off the heat. The depth of hardening depends upon how deeply the steel is austenitized. That depends upon power input, the time, the heat lost, and the frequency of induction-hardening. Since steel is nonmagnetic at austenitic temperatures, it is sometimes

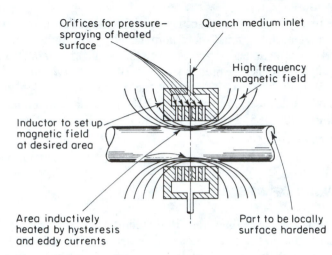

Orifices for pressure–
spraying of heated
surface

Quench medium inlet

High frequency
magnetic field

Inductor to set up
magnetic field
at desired area

Area inductively
heated by hysteresis
and eddy currents

Part to be locally
surface hardened

Figure 5-10 Scheme of
induction-hardening.

economical to heat with low frequencies at low temperatures followed by higher
frequencies at higher temperatures. Motor-generator sets are the usual sources for
frequencies up to 10 kHz and power to 2500 kW. An installation that includes a
100-kW 10-kHz motor-generator unit, heat station with inductor, and quenching fluid
system costs more than $100,000. Spark gap circuits are used for intermediate fre-
quencies, and electronic (vacuum tube) generators for high frequencies (into the
megahertz range).

Flame-Hardening.   The surface of a workpiece may be heated locally or
progressively by a gas flame as depicted in Fig. 5-11. An oxyacetylene or oxy-MAPP
flame, as described for welding in Chap. 14, is preferred for flame-hardening because
heating is most rapid. The torch head is commonly given a shape to match the contour
of the work surface. Hardening results when the austenitized surface is quenched by
the spray (usually water) that follows the flame. Equipment to harden small pieces [up
to 150 mm (6 in.) in diameter] should cost only a few thousand dollars.

Comparison of Methods.   In general, any plain-carbon or alloy steel having
0.40% carbon or more may be induction- or flame-hardened, but the high hardenability of some alloys adds problems. The most usual range is from 0.40 to 0.60%
carbon, and such steels are hardened to 40 to 63 R_C. Examples of work hardened by
these methods are gears, tool drivers, wrist pins, crank shaft bearing journals, cylinder
liners, rail ends, machine tool ways, and pump shafts. Cast iron and steel are hardened
by both methods, and nodular iron and pearlitic malleable iron (described in Chap. 8)
are induction-hardened. Case depths from less than 0.5 to over 5 mm (a few mils to
$\frac{1}{4}$ in.) are rather common.

Each method has certain advantages. Flame-hardening is sometimes more adaptable to surface configuration. For instance, flame heads can be adjusted to heat corners
uniformly with adjacent areas. Induction-hardening is better for a shallow case with
a narrow transition band, and flame-hardening for a deep case. Induction-hardening

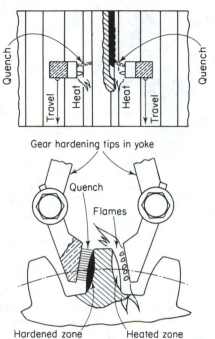

Gear hardening tips in yoke

Quench

Flames

Hardened zone   Heated zone

Figure 5-11 Flame-hardening of gear teeth.

is fast and readily automated and therefore advantageous for large quantity production. Flame-hardening is more suitable for small quantities because it is versatile and equipment cost is less. The selection of these or other methods for surface-hardening depends upon cost in most cases. Electron beam and laser hardening methods are costly and not used extensively. Flame-hardening may be chosen for parts too large for practical furnace heating and immersion quenching. Flame- or induction-hardening may be economical where only some of a part needs to be heated and hardened. On the other hand, a complex part that can be handled in batches and must be heat treated throughout is probably best heat treated in a furnace.

Carburizing to Case-Harden. For a ductile and shock resistant core and a hard surface to resist wear and abrasion, a part may be machined a little oversize from low-carbon plain or alloy steel. It is then carburized to increase the carbon content of the skin and heat treated to bring out the best properties of case and core. The piece is finally ground to size. A cross section of a carburized and hardened surface is shown in Fig. 5-12.

Typical parts that are case-hardened are gears, splines, wrist pins, bearing balls, universal joint spiders, and valve tappets.

Steels for carburizing should have from 0.10 to 0.20% carbon. When a steel is heated to its austenitizing temperature, it absorbs carbon in the presence of CO gas. As much as 1.7% carbon theoretically may dissolve in gamma iron, but in usual carburizing practice, the carbon content seldom exceeds 1.2%. The carbon content decreases from the surface through the case to the core. The "effective case depth" is

Figure 5-12 Carburized and hardened case of gear teeth.

defined in several ways; as the depth to the point of 0.4% carbon, or where the structure is 50% martensite or the hardness is 50 R_c in the hardened part.

The amount of carbon absorbed and the depth of the case depend upon the temperature, time of exposure, the carbon potential of the carburizing medium, and the composition of the original steel. Carburizing temperatures may range from 790°C (1450°F) to 1090°C (2000°F), but usually lie between 900 and 950°C (1650 and 1740°F). The higher the temperature, the more rapid the carbon absorption but also the more furnace deterioration and undesirable grain growth. Case depth increases with the square root of time at any given temperature. Typical conventional practice calls for 12 hours for soaking and carburizing to produce a case 1.5 mm (0.06 in.) deep at 900°C (1650°F). A case may be made as thick as desired, depending on length of exposure, but seldom is over 3 mm ($\frac{1}{8}$ in.). Temperature and time in the austenitic region promote grain growth. Steels with less tendency to coarsen are preferred for carburizing. Where grain growth is excessive, subsequent heat treatment, such as double annealing, may be given to break down grain size.

There are several methods of carburizing steel. *Gas carburizing* is favored for efficient production and consists of heating the work in a furnace with a highly carburizing atmosphere containing largely hydrocarbon gases or vapors. *Pack carburizing* is done by completely surrounding the workpiece with a carbonaceous material in a closed container. The CO gas for carburizing is obtained by heating the packing material. Much mass besides the work must be heated, and that makes the job slower, harder to control, and heat inefficient. On the other hand, pack carburizing has advantages for small lots and for large pieces, particularly because it can be done in almost any furnace. The packing may also serve as insulation to cool the work slowly after carburizing. Carbonaceous material is heated in the furnace but not in contact with the workpiece in *retort carburizing*. *Liquid carburizing* is done by immersing the workpiece in a cyanide bath, as in cyaniding described later. The salt bath composition for liquid carburizing gives a case rich in carbon in contrast to a cyanide case high in nitrogen.

Most carburized parts are hardened by quenching directly from carburizing temperature or after a slight cooling to just above the critical temperature. Some parts are cooled to room temperature and reheated once or twice for quenching. This gives better quality through less distortion, better carbon diffusion, grain refinement, and core toughness. Cooling and reheating may be convenient for parts requiring special handling for quenching, e.g., quenching while held rigidly in a die to control distortion.

Selective carburizing or *hardening* is often required to leave some surfaces soft after heat treatment. One way is to copper plate surfaces initially that are to be left soft. The carbon does not penetrate the copper. Another way is to cool the piece and machine material from the surface to be soft to remove the case before hardening. Also, selected surfaces may be softened by torch heating and slow cooling after the entire part has been heat treated.

Cyaniding. Cyaniding or *liquid carbonitriding* imparts a file-hard and wear-resistant case to steel by immersing it in a molten cyanide salt bath for a time and then quenching it. A cyanide case is seldom over 0.25 mm (0.01 in.) thick, and carburized cases are usually thicker. However, cyaniding requires lower temperatures, usually below 870°C (1600°F), and less time (30 to 60 minutes) than carburizing.

Extreme care must be exercised with cyaniding. The cyanides are fatally poisonous if taken internally and highly toxic in contact with scratches or wounds. When cyanides are brought in contact with acids, fatally poisonous fumes are evolved. Appreciable amounts of cyanide salt are transferred to the quenching liquid and must be neutralized before waste is discharged to the sewer. Sludge accumulates in salt pots and poses a disposal problem.

Carbonitriding, also known as *dry-* or *gas-cyaniding, nicarbing,* and *nicarburizing,* adds both carbon and nitrogen to a shallow case on steel surfaces. It is done in much the same way and with the same equipment as gas carburizing in a carbon- and nitrogen-rich atmosphere. The advantage is that the nitrogen-enriched case can be quenched in oil rather than in water required for unalloyed steels after plain carburizing. The oil quench causes less distortion and cracking.

Nitriding. Steel is gas nitrided in a furnace at 510 to 565°C (950 to 1050°F) with an atmosphere, commonly ammonia, that permeates the surface with nascent nitrogen. The basic process takes a long time; for instance, with SAE 7140 steel at 525°C (975°F) the case depth reaches 0.5 mm (0.02 in.) at 50 hours and 1 mm (0.04 in.) at 200 hours. Liquid nitriding is done also at 510 to 565°C (950 to 1050°F) in a bath of molten salts. Quenching is not needed because the case consists of inherently hard metallic nitrides. For efficient results, nitridable steels alloyed with aluminum, chromium, vanadium, and molybdenum to form stable nitrides are used.

Various modifications of nitriding are practiced to speed up the process. The *Nitemper* process operates at about 575°C (1070°F) with an atmosphere of half endothermic gas and half ammonia. After being heated for only about $1\frac{1}{2}$ hours, the work can be quenched in oil for maximum fatigue strength. Nitempering utilizes a gas mixture that is explosive and must be treated carefully but gives fast results. The case is much thinner than that from regular nitriding but contains an extremely hard complex iron-carbon-nitrogen compound. *Chapmanizing* or *liquid pressure nitriding* entails passing anhydrous ammonia through the nitriding salt bath under pressure while the work is being treated. *Pressure nitriding* is done with the work in a sealed retort holding an ammonia atmosphere under pressure. *Glow discharge nitriding* or *ionitriding* is done with the work as the cathode in an anodic retort. An electric current heats the work and produces a glow discharge that ionizes the nitrogen atmosphere.

Nitriding is more expensive than other hard-case processes but offers several advantages. It is done below the critical temperature without detriment to the strength and other properties of the steel core. The case is quite hard (70 R_C and over) and notably wear, fatigue, and corrosion resistant (except for stainless steel) and stays hard at temperatures up to about 425°C (800°F). Nitriding is applied, for example, to high reliability gears, bushings for conveyor rollers to handle abrasive alkaline materials, antifriction bearings, and gun parts.

HEAT-TREATING FURNACES

Usually, a heat-treating furnace consists of a box-like structure with a steel shell and an access door, a refractory lining, and temperature controls and indicators. Some of these features are lacking or are different in some cases. Furnaces may be classified by the ways the work is handled or by means of heating. For work handling, the basic types are batch furnaces and continuous furnaces. As for fuels, oil and gas predominated at one time, but electricity has gained in popularity. Close process control is easier with electricity. With combustion heating the work must be contained in a separate chamber if it is to be kept from the gases.

Heat-treating furnaces use large quantities of energy. Improvements in furnace design in recent years have been directed toward more efficient processing, improved insulation, more effective combustion control, and recovery of heat from fuel gases that would otherwise be wasted. An example of heat recycling has two facets. Usable sensible heat exhausted by high-temperature furnaces is passed through heat exchangers to furnish about 30% of the needs of the tempering furnaces. Also, radiant heat is collected by steel walls enclosing the furnaces and delivered by circulating air to heat the plant in winter. Each type of furnace has several varieties. The main forms will be described in the following sections. Two major kinds of batch furnaces are hearth furnaces and bath or pot furnaces.

Hearth Furnaces. The *direct fuel-fired furnace* (Fig. 5-13) burns the fuel in the space occupied by the charge. It is of low cost and suitable for all ordinary temperature ranges. This furnace is suitable for rough heating, such as for forging, but may serve for heat treating, particularly at lower temperatures.

The *indirect-fired furnace* has a heating chamber and a muffle which separates the combustion space from the work space. The upper temperature limit for this

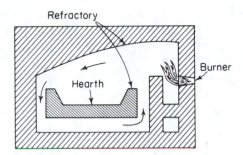

Figure 5-13 Direct fuel-fired furnace.

furnace is approximately 1100°C (2000°F). Reduced scaling and contamination from the fuels are the advantages in its use.

A *recirculation furnace* is indirect-fired but the gases of combustion are circulated through the work space from the combustion area. The hot gases are channeled so the heating will be uniform. Application is mostly below 700°C (1300°F) commonly in ovens for tempering, toughening, and stress relieving.

Muffle and *retort furnaces* are indirect-fired with the work in a protective or carburizing atmosphere and separated from the gases of combustion. The work space of a muffle furnace is surrounded by refractory material sufficiently tight to keep out contaminants. Semimuffle furnaces have a small amount of baffling in the work space to prevent direct impingement of the combustion flame upon the workpiece. A retort furnace takes a heat-resisting retort that is loaded with work outside the furnace, capped and sealed, and then placed in the furnace to be heated. A *radiant-tube furnace* has a tightly encased refractory-lined chamber with the hot gases forced through radiant tubes arranged around the work space.

Electric furnaces look much like other kinds. A common type has resistance heating elements on the refractory wall of the chamber like the one in Fig. 5-14. The heating unit is segregated in some furnaces, and the atmosphere is blown over it into the work chamber. Electric furnaces are more costly to buy and operate than gas furnaces but have the advantages of cleanliness, convenience, controllability, and few environmental restrictions.

Heat is convected better and distributed more thoroughly by circulating the atmosphere in any furnace. The more rapid the circulation, the more the heat is transferred. Pressure in the furnace is commonly kept above that outside to prevent air from entering when the door is opened. Some furnaces have a flame curtain at the door to burn any oxygen that may enter.

A *fluidized-bed- furnace* has the work immersed in a bath of inert (e.g., aluminum oxide) particles in an insulated container. A heated gas mixture flows upward through the beds and holds the particles in suspension. One make operates at temperatures up to 1000°C(1850°F). It has a capacity of 355 mm (14 in.) diameter by 460 mm (18 in.) deep and costs about $30,000.

Batch-type furnaces have a number of shapes. *Box furnaces*, with horizontal chambers, like the one in Fig. 5-14, are made in all sizes. A *pit furnace* has a vertical

Figure 5-14   Electric resistance heated furnace. The heating elements can be seen on the refractory wall.

work chamber with an opening at the top to receive the charge. A *bell furnace* has a box-like cover over the hearth, and the cover is lifted off to remove and place a charge. An *elevator furnace* has a vertical work chamber with an opening at the bottom for charging.

A *car-bottom furnace*, like the one in Fig. 5-15, has a movable hearth like a flat car that is rolled out for unloading and loading. Commonly, the load is stacked on heat-resistant alloy or refractory piers and spacers to facilitate circulation of gases and heat the materials uniformly. In the same family is the *tip-roof furnace*, where the box is raised and tipped to allow work to be inserted. Such a furnace with space of 1.2 × 1.8 × 7.3 m (4 × 6 × 24 ft) capable of taking loads up to about 9 metric tons (10 tons) with a hydraulic manipulator and adjacent quench tanks costs about $500,000.

Vacuum furnaces are necessary for some space-age materials and electronic components and where surface finishes must be preserved on ordinary work. They are made to be tightly sealed and have auxiliary equipment to draw and hold a vacuum like the vacuum melting furnaces of Chap. 8. There are both batch- and continuous-type models. Heat-treating is commonly done by radiant heating in a vacuum.

Rotary Furnaces.   Rotary furnaces are used for both batch and continuous production. One kind is the *rotary-hearth furnace* that is built in a wide range of sizes to heat a few hundred kilograms to 50 Mg (ca. 50 tons) or more per hour. It has a round shell and horizontal hearth that turns slowly. Material is charged through a door and

Figure 5-15 Car-bottom furnace.

may be taken out of the same door or another one. The speed of the hearth is set so that the heating cycle is completed when the hearth makes one turn.

A *rotary-retort furnace* consists of a revolving retort with horizontal axis inside a heating chamber. Small parts are loaded at one end, tumbled, and pushed along by ribs or vanes, and emerge from the other end of the retort. Sizes are available to take loads from about 50 to 700 kg (100 to 1500 lb). Workpieces must be able to withstand a certain amount of rough treatment and cannot be precisely metered out of the furnace for uniform quenching.

Continuous Furnaces. A continuous furnace is the type mostly used for in-line large quantity production. It typically has a horizontal work chamber and a mechanical means of conveying the work from one end to the other. Heating may be electrical or done by burning fuel. Many furnaces have different temperatures precisely controlled in several zones for multistage heat treating.

Some authorities call only those furnaces continuous in which the workpieces all move at the same rate from one end to the other. The name of *cycling* or *semi-continuous furnace* is given when the work is held for a different preset time in each section of the furnace. In either case, small pieces may be carried through in baskets or on trays. Common forms of semi- and fully continuous furnaces are described below.

A motor-driven *belt* or *chain-conveyor furnace* transports the work on an endless hearth of heat-resistant chain or links. An example is given in Fig. 5-16.

In a *roller-hearth furnace* the work rides on driven rollers, one set after another through the length of the furnace. This type is suitable for uniformly sized parts on trays.

The work sits on rollers or skids that are not driven in a *pusher furnace*. Instead, the workpieces or trays are pushed, one against the other, by mechanical, pneumatic, or hydraulic means in a timed cycle.

A *screw-conveyor furnace* has a coarse-pitch powered screw extending through the chamber.

The hearth and work are gradually accelerated forward in a *shuffle-* or *shaker-hearth* or *reciprocating furnace*. Then the hearth is suddenly stopped, and the work slides forward. The motion is not a destructive vibration but is repeated only from time to time. The work is shifted along by beams that rise as they move forward and fall as they move backward in a *walking-beam furnace*.

TABLE 5-1   SPECIFICATIONS FOR A FEW TYPICAL INDUSTRIAL FURNACES

Description	Effective work area: width-height-length [m (ft)]	Energy input	Maximum rated temperature [°C (°F)]	Approximate cost
Box-type, indirect fired, or recirculation hearth furnace for toolroom	$0.6 \times 0.5 \times 0.9$ $(2 \times 1\frac{1}{2} \times 3)$	32 kW (175,000 Btu gas-fired)	680 (1250)	$15,000
Box-type, indirect-fired or recirculation hearth furnace for production	$0.9 \times 0.9 \times 2.4$ $(3 \times 3 \times 8)$	107 kW (640,000 Btu gas-fired)	680 (1250)	35,000
Electric-rod, conveyor-hearth, four-zone hardening furnace plus oil quench tank with discharge flight conveyor	$0.6 \times 0.2 \times 1.7$ $(2 \times \frac{2}{3} \times 12)$	138 kW	900 (1650)	110,000
Electric-globar, mesh belt conveyor hearth, five-zone brazing furnace	$0.6 \times 0.25 \times 2.4$ $(2 \times \frac{5}{6} \times 8)$	130 kW	1150 (2100)	100,000

Furnace Atmospheres.   Metals are subjected to high temperatures for appreciable periods of time during heat treatment. This damages metallic surfaces if they are not protected. Oxygen, carbon dioxide, and water vapor are the most injurious gases, among others, and they are removed in the preparation of furnace atmospheres.

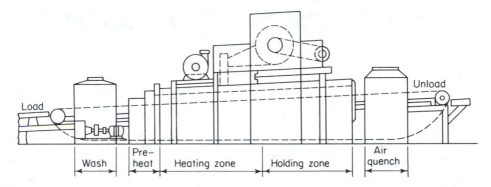

Load

Unload

| Wash | Pre-heat | Heating zone | Holding zone | Air quench |

Figure 5-16 Chain-conveyor furnace for washing, drawing, and cooling hardened gears in large quantities.

Oxygen rusts, corrodes, and scales most metal surfaces and removes carbon from steel; thus it degrades surface finish, impairs size, and keeps surfaces from being hardened. Carbon dioxide scales or decarburizes steel in combination in some ratios with carbon monoxide but is a neutral atmosphere in other ratios and suitable for bright annealing. Water vapor oxidizes iron and steel and is the main agent that turns steel surfaces blue when they are cooled. It combines with carbon in steel to form carbon monoxide and hydrogen.

Some gases that are harmful under certain circumstances serve as protectors when properly utilized. Nitrogen in the molecular state is satisfactory as a furnace atmosphere for bright annealing of low-carbon steel but does decarburize surfaces in the presence of even a trace of moisture. Atomic nitrogen may form hard surface iron nitrides. Hydrogen is absorbed by steel at certain temperatures and causes embrittlement. Dry hydrogen reduces iron oxide and does not cause scale but does decarburize steel under certain conditions. Hydrogen forms undesirable water vapor in reactions with carbon dioxide or oxygen. Hydrocarbons present in a furnace tend to decompose at heat-treating temperatures and to liberate hydrogen and deposit soot.

An atmosphere is generated and induced into a heat-treating furnace to keep from changing the chemistry of and prevent discoloring of the work surface. About a dozen kinds of atmospheres are widely used. The American Gas Association has divided them into six classes, as described in Table 5-2, according to how they are made or what they contain. Each of the six classes may have variants that are designated by numbers added to the second and third digits to the right. For instance, 302 indicates a *rich* endothermic atmosphere, and 501 a *lean* exothermic-endothermic mixture.

Molten Baths for Heat Treating. Metals are often heated or cooled by being immersed in molten salts or lead. Heating is uniform and rapid, temperature can be closely controlled, and the workpiece is shielded from the air. Molten baths are widely used for interrupted quenching, as in martempering and austempering already described, and for surface treatments like cyaniding.

A salt bath protects metal. When a cold piece of metal is placed in fused salts

TABLE 5-2   CLASSES OF ATMOSPHERES FOR HEAT-TREATING

Class	Base	Composition	Uses	Relative cost ($/unit volume)	Note
100	Exothermic	70% or more N_2; remainder CO_2, CO, H_2	Bright annealing	1	Generated by controlled combustion of hydrocarbon; lowest cost
200	Prepared nitrogen	97% N_2	Neutral atmosphere	1.3	Often needs additives; not dependent on natural gas supply
300	Endothermic	40% N_2, 20% CO, 40% H_2	Carburizing, neutral hardening, sintering	1.5	Explosive; not for stainless steel
400	Charcoal	65% N_2, 35% CO	Carburizing, sintering	6	Low equipment cost; for small-scale operations
500	Exothermic-endothermic	70% N_2, 30% CO	General purpose	2	Can be modified to serve in place of most other classes
600	Ammonia	80% N_2, 20% H_2 typical	Bright annealing; sintering, neutral heating	9	Good-quality atmosphere suitable for stainless steel

for the purpose of heating, the salt immediately contacting the piece freezes and clings tightly to the workpiece, thus forming a salt encasement that serves to prevent rapid surface heating and thermal shock. When the temperature reaches equilibrium, the frozen shell disappears, and further heating occurs by conduction. An additional advantage of this method is that the molten salt in direct contact with the workpiece more efficiently transfers heat (four to seven times faster) than would a gaseous atmosphere. Totally immersed, the materials being heated have no contact with the atmosphere and, therefore, compositional changes are avoided (where the salt bath is neutral). At the end of the heating cycle and when the part is removed, a film of molten salt adheres to the part and protects it against atmospheric attack while it is being moved to another bath or to the quenching tank.

Common salts are sodium and potassium chlorides, nitrates, and cyanides. They are mixed in various proportions and with other salts to obtain different melting points for services in various ranges from 160 to 1400°C (325 to 2550°F) and for various purposes. Formulas are given in reference books and handbooks.

Bath Furnaces.   Bath furnaces may be gas- or oil-fired or electrically heated. Bath furnaces are mostly of small and medium size because it is uneconomical to keep a large mass of salt heated for large parts, particularly for intermittent use. *Gas- and oil-fired salt-bath furnaces* have low first and operating costs and are versatile. They can be restarted easily, and pots can be interchanged in one furnace to use a variety of salts. The bath may be heated externally, as in Fig. 5-17, or by immersed radiant tubes, which help keep temperature uniform in the bath.

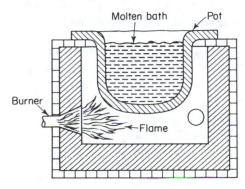

Figure 5-17   Externally heated gas- or oil-fired salt-bath furnace.

There are several kinds of electrically heated salt-bath furnaces. All are surrounded by insulated casing. Heating may be done by resistance elements around the pot in the *externally heated type* depicted in Fig. 5-18. Well-insulated heating elements are put directly in the bath in the *immersion heating-element type* of furnace. Temperatures are usually limited to 600°C (1100°F) for satisfactory resistor life. Higher temperature can be held by passing electricity through the bath between electrodes. The *immersed-electrode salt-bath furnace* has electrodes immersed in a metal pot. The *submerged-electrode furnace* has water-cooled electrodes extending through the sides into a ceramic brick pot. The molten salt penetrates the refractory material until it reaches a zone cool enough to freeze and thus seals the pot. Electrode furnaces use alternating current transformed to low voltages (5 to 15 V) because direct current decomposes the liquid salt. Temperatures are easy to control within 3°C (5°F).

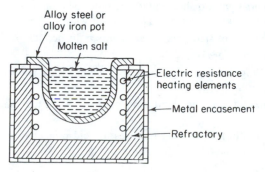

Figure 5-18   Electrically resistance-heated salt-bath furnace.

Electrode furnaces occupy a minimum of floor space but are not easy to restart because the frozen salt is not a conductor and are best for large-quantity continuous production.

Design Considerations for Heat Treatment. Reference books and handbooks specify the properties of materials that may be obtained by heat treatment, as well as specifications for time and temperature, correct hardenability, etc., for each case.

It is important to recognize that most steel mill barstock and forgings have a decarburized skin that must be removed before heat treatment. It will not harden, cannot be carburized properly, and especially in nitriding leaves quite a brittle layer that peels off easily.

Pieces that are long, or large in area and thin, unsymmetrical, or have holes, deep keyways, and grooves are difficult to heat-treat. Troubles arise in nonuniformity, warping, and cracking.

Parts with threads, fine splines, sharp edges, and other thin sections may become faulty from carburizing if their thin sections harden throughout and support of the tough core is lost.

Hardened surfaces are expensive to machine. The bulk of metal removal and forming should take place before hardening. Finishing usually is necessary after hardening to correct unavoidable distortion and must be done by expensive abrasive methods, so it should be confined to essential surfaces and the removal of a minimum amount of stock.

QUESTIONS

1. What is the basic scheme for hardening metals, and why is it effective?
2. What are coherency-hardening and aggregate-hardening, and what are their relative merits?
3. What is the necessary condition for hardening a nonallotropic alloy? How is the condition utilized?
4. How is 2024 aluminum, as an example of a nonallotropic alloy, solution-treated and age- or precipitation-hardened?
5. What is the basic mechanism of hardening of steel?
6. What is a T-T-T diagram or S-curve, and what does it show?
7. Describe three principal ways of hardening steel after heating to austenitic temperature. What results and advantages are obtained from each way?
8. What is the hardenability of steel, and what factors influence it?
9. How is hardenability measured?
10. Describe full annealing, normalizing, process or commercial annealing, and cycle annealing. What does each process do?
11. Describe the processes for surface-hardening of steel. What are their applications and merits?
12. What means are found in heat-treating furnaces to hold protective or carbon-rich atmospheres around the workpieces?

13. What devices are utilized for continuous handling of the work in production heat-treating furnaces?

14. What gases and vapors are detrimental in a heat-treating atmosphere? What gases are mostly utilized for protective atmosphere?

15. What are bath furnaces for heat treating, and what advantages do they offer?

REFERENCES

"A Guide to Surface Hardening," *American Machinist*, Sept. 3, 1973, p. 53.

HUNTRESS, E. A., "Nitrogen: All Purpose Atmosphere," *American Machinist*, Apr. 1980, p. 127.

JATCZAK, C. F., "Determining Hardenability from Composition," *Metal Progress*, Sept. 1971, p. 60.

JUST, E., "New Formulas for Calculating Hardenability Curves," *Metal Progress*, Nov. 1969, p. 87.

KRAUSS, G., *Principles of Heat Treatment of Steel*, American Society of Metals, Metals Park, Ohio, 1980.

Metals Handbook, 8th ed., Vol. 2: *Heat Treating, Cleaning and Finishing*, American Society for Metals, Metals Park, Ohio, 1964.

OSBORN, H. B., JR., "Why Induction Heating?" *Machinery*, June 1972, p. 61.

ROSS, G. A., "New Thoughts on Nitriding," *Manufacturing Engineering and Management*, Sept. 1973, p. 22.

VACCARI, J. A., "Fundamentals of Heat Treating, Special Report 737," *American Machinist*, Sept. 1981, p. 185.

6

STEEL

Strictly speaking, *iron* refers to one of the chemical elements. As used by engineers, *iron* includes commercially pure iron, such as ingot iron, or highly refined iron, such as electrolytic iron and carbonyl iron. These pure irons are used for a few magnetic applications, but otherwise are relatively unimportant. Engineers also apply the term *iron* to the ferrous alloys known as cast iron. These contain fairly large amounts of carbon, usually over 2.5%, and other alloying elements. They are discussed in detail in Chap. 8. The present chapter is devoted mostly to steel. Steels are ferrous-base alloys, containing significant amounts of one or more alloying elements which have been either intentionally added or retained during the refining process.

EFFECTS OF ALLOYING ELEMENTS IN FERROUS ALLOYS

The properties of *all* alloys are determined by the kinds and amounts of phases of which they are composed, by the properties of the phases, and by the way in which these phases are distributed among one another. (See Chap. 4 for a discussion of phases.) Ferrous alloys consist of two or more phases known as ferrite, austenite, carbides, and graphite. The alloying elements in ferrous alloys affect the stability of these phases, the relative amounts of the phases and how the phases are distributed or dispersed throughout one another. The alloying elements also affect the properties of the phases in which the elements exist. Thus the alloying elements achieve control of the properties of ferrous alloys.

   Carbon is probably the most important alloying element found in ferrous alloys. In slowly cooled alloys, containing small amounts of carbon (usually much less than

0.5% carbon) the structure consists of soft, ductile ferrite and hard, brittle carbide phases. Most of the carbon exists in the iron carbide. As the carbon content increases, the amount of iron carbide increases, and these alloys become harder, stronger, and less ductile. When the amount of carbon in slowly cooled alloys increases beyond 2.0%, as in the cast irons, there is an increasing tendency for the carbide phase to decompose into iron and graphite. This reaction is known as *graphitization* and can be represented by

$$Fe_3C \longrightarrow 3Fe + C$$
$$\text{iron carbide} \qquad\qquad \text{graphite}$$

Although increasing the carbon content increases the tendency toward graphitization, carbon content does not alone control the tendency. Since graphite is much softer than iron carbide, cast irons in which graphitization has occurred are softer than those in which it has not occurred. The form and distribution of the graphite phase determine whether these cast irons are ductile or brittle. This is described in more detail in Chap. 8.

The control of graphitization is important in the cast irons and is achieved by a combination of (1) adjustment of cooling rate and (2) alloy content. Slow cooling from the melt favors graphitization; rapid cooling impairs graphitization. Cooling rates can be increased locally by insertion of pieces of metal, known as *chills*, in sand molds (see Chap. 8). These produce areas consisting of hard carbide in castings which elsewhere have a soft, graphitic structure. The alloying elements in ferrous alloys can be classed as carbide formers or as graphitizers. The principal strong graphitizers include silicon, nickel, and, as already mentioned, carbon itself. The strong carbide formers tend to stabilize carbides and resist graphitization. The strongest of these include titanium, vanadium, molybdenum, tungsten, and chromium. The other common alloying elements either have weak graphitizing or weak carbide-forming tendencies, unimportant for most purposes. Cast iron compositions are adjusted, or balanced, to yield either a hard carbide structure, a soft graphitic structure, or an in-between structure in which graphitization is partial but not complete. The strong carbide formers also play an important role in quenched and tempered steels as discussed later.

In steels which are hardened by quenching and tempering, carbon performs at least two functions. All alloying elements (excepting cobalt) when in solution in austenite at the time of quenching tend to shift the T-T-T curve (see Chap. 5) to the right, and thereby increase hardenability. Carbon is no exception to this generalization, although its contribution to hardenability is not great. It must also be kept in mind that carbides which are *not* dissolved in austenite when quenched will detract from hardenability. In alloy steels of higher carbon content it is difficult to achieve complete solution. In addition to its minor contribution to hardenability, carbon is largely responsible for improving the hardness of steel. This is its most important function.

In steels to be hardened by quenching the most important function of the alloying elements is to increase hardenability, i.e., to retard the direct transformation of austenite to a coarse dispersion of ferrite and carbide. The more effective the alloying elements in supressing this transformation, the slower the cooling rate required to attain martensite. Thus, thermal shock and cracking tendencies are minimized and, with a given cooling rate, heavier sections of alloy steels can be transformed to martensite than for carbon steels. In the amounts used, as the percentage of an alloying element is raised, hardenability increases, although the effectiveness and cost of the elements vary. The greatest improvement in hardenability per unit cost of alloying element used is achieved by manganese, followed probably by molybdenum and chromium. Boron is extremely valuable in improving hardenability, but loses its effectiveness when more than 0.004% is present. Manganese is used in amounts up to 1.75%, chromium up to 1.55%, and molybdenum up to about 0.25% for purposes of improving hardenability. Phosphorus is a low-cost element which improves hardenability, but its use is limited by virtue of its embrittling tendencies.

In steels hardened by quenching, a second and important function of alloying elements is to control properties upon tempering. The strong carbide formers are useful because they produce a steel which resists softening when tempered. Titanium, vanadium, molybdenum, tungsten, and chromium are known to impart this quality to steel. In fact, in some tool steels, very large amounts of the strong carbide formers are added because they produce a secondary hardening effect after the initial softening which accompanies tempering. The strong, hard, persistant carbides which are found in tempered steels containing these elements improve wear resistance, abrasion resistance, resistance to creep, and toughness. They permit greater stress relief in steel tempered to a given hardness, because higher tempering temperatures or longer times of tempering can be used without adverse effects.

In slowly cooled steels, the most important effects of alloying elements other than carbon are (1) their tendency to strengthen ferrite *when dissolved in it*, and (2) except for cobalt, their tendency to increase hardenability.

The tendency to strengthen ferrite is important in slowly cooled steels because ferrite is the matrix phase in these steels. An important principle of alloying is that the properties of the alloy tend to be governed by the quality of the matrix. Thus, if the alloy additions strengthen the ferrite, they tend to strengthen the alloy. The alloying elements most commonly used as ferrite strengtheners are phosphorus and silicon. Beryllium and titanium are also potent ferrite strengtheners, but beryllium is far too expensive, and titanium is removed from solution in the ferrite by reaction with always-present carbon to form titanium carbide, and hence cannot strengthen the ferrite. Cobalt is known as a ferrite strengthener at high temperatures. It is used in steels which operate at or near red heat, where hot hardness is required. These steels, however, are quenched and tempered, rather than slowly cooled.

The tendency to increase hardenability in slowly cooled steels is important because it effectively reduces the amount of ferrite in the structure, replacing it with harder, stronger pearlite. The pearlite is also finer, and therefore stronger, than would be the case if the alloying elements were absent. The result of these two effects is a mild steel of improved strength in which there has been a negligible loss of ductility.

Corrosion resistance in stainless steels is obtained from the use of chromium as an alloying element in amounts exceeding 12%. The chromium forms a tenacious oxide film that prevents rusting. In AISI (described later) alloy steels, which usually contain less than a total alloy content of 5%, rust resistance is improved by small amounts of phosphorus, copper, and chromium.

Magnetic characteristics are improved in steels used as temporary or soft magnets for alternating current applications. Pure iron has desirable magnetic qualities but suffers from high eddy-current losses. These are reduced by alloy additions which have a minimal effect on hardening and a maximum effect on increasing the electrical resistance of iron. At the same time the alloy additions should be compatible with fabricating requirements. Silicon is by far the best alloy addition in these respects. The silicon steels used for soft magnets often contain 3.5% silicon, although they may contain up to 5% silicon.

Machinability (see Chaps. 16 and 17) of steel can be improved by several alloy additions. Sulfur improves machinability, but cannot be used in steel unless there is sufficient manganese to combine with it to form manganese sulfide. If manganese is not present, sulfur forms a low-melting iron sulfide network around the austenite grain boundaries. Steel with this structure is very weak and brittle at hot-working temperatures and suffers from what is called *hot shortness*. Manganese sulfide exists as an isolated phase, rather than a network, and acts as an internal lubricant and chip breaker. Internal lubricants reduce friction and wear between tool and workpiece and between tool and chip. Lead, in finely dispersed form, is another element which greatly improves machinability. It is added to ingots in the form of lead shot and is distributed throughout the solidified steel in the free state since it is insoluble in steel. It improves machinability in the same way as does manganese sulfide, acting as a chip breaker and an internal lubricant. Lead is used in carbon steels and AISI steels and does not adversely affect, in the amounts used, the mechanical properties of either unhardened or hardened steels. Selenium is used for the same purpose in some stainless steel compositions.

The toughness of hardened steels is a function of the grain size of the austenite at the time of quenching. Alloying elements which form insoluble particles in the steel tend to minimize austenite grain growth during heating for hardening. Thus, aluminum-killed steels (see Chap. 2) are finer grained and tougher than silicon-killed steels, because the insoluble aluminum oxide particles resulting from deoxidation remain suspended throughout the solidified steel. The strong carbide formers also result in a fine-grained steel. The carbides of these elements are very persistent and difficult to dissolve in austenite and they thus restrict grain growth. Vanadium and molybdenum are particularly noteworthy in this regard. Elements which promote fine-grained steel structures are known as *grain refiners*.

CARBON STEELS

Carbon steels are those in which carbon is the alloying element that essentially controls the properties of the alloys, and in which the amount of manganese cannot exceed 1.65% and the copper and silicon contents must each be less than 0.60%. The carbon steels can be subdivided into those containing between 0.08 and 0.35% carbon, those containing between 0.35 and 0.50% carbon, and those containing more than 0.50% carbon. These are known respectively as *low-carbon*, *medium-carbon*, and *high-carbon steels*. The price of steel depends on whether the steel is in bars, sheets, etc. Prices of typical shapes are quoted in Chap. 12.

Low-carbon steel is relatively soft and ductile and cannot be hardened appreciably by heat treatment. It represents the largest tonnage of all steel produced. It is used for tin plate, automobile body sheet, fencing wire, light and heavy structural members (auto frames, I-beams, etc.), and for hot- and cold-finished bars used for machined parts. Cold finishing improves surface finish, mechanical properties, and machinability of these compositions.

Medium-carbon steel is used for high-strength steel castings and for forgings, such as railroad axles, crankshafts, gears, turbine bucket wheels, and steering arms. Medium-carbon steel can be hardened by heat treatment, but it cannot be through-hardened in sections whose thickness is greater than about $\frac{1}{2}$ in.

High-carbon steel is used for forgings such as wrenches and railroad wheels and for hot-rolled products such as railroad rails and concrete-reinforcing bars. High-strength wire products such as piano wire and suspension bridge cable are made from high-carbon steel. High-carbon steel tools are among the most useful general-purpose tools for applications such as blanking dies, sledges, chisels, and razors.

ALLOY STEELS

Alloy steels contain appreciable quantities of alloying elements in addition to carbon. They include (1) low-alloy, high-strength structural steels; (2) quenched and tempered low-carbon constructional alloy steels; (3) AISI–SAE alloy steels; (4) alloy tool steels; (5) stainless steels; (6) heat-resisting steels; and (7) magnet steels. These seven classes of steel are discussed in the following paragraphs.

Low-alloy, high-strength structural (HSLA) steels contain insufficient carbon and alloying elements to be hardened effectively by quenching to martensite. This is advantageous because it enables them to be welded without becoming brittle (Chap. 14). At the same time, the alloying elements they contain alter the microstructure so that it resembles a higher-carbon steel cooled at moderately fast (air-blast quench) rates. In addition these steels contain slightly more phosphorus and silicon than do the carbon steels, thereby strengthening the ferrite network. These changes in microstructure raise the yield strength about 40 to 50% above that of carbon structural steel. Lighter sections, of lower cost, can therefore carry a given load. Since rust and corrosion become increasingly important as sections sizes become smaller, particularly in unpainted applications, HSLA steels can be made corrosion resistant (as much as eight times more than carbon steel) by proper proportions of phosphorus, copper, silicon, chromium, and molybdenum. In that role, they are sometimes known as *weathering steels*. HSLA steels are typically used for railroad cars, to save weight, and for bridge and building structural members, sometimes to save painting.

A class of low-alloy but high-strength steels is that of the *dual-phase steels*. These have a microstructure of islands of high-carbon martensite-austenite (M-A) in a matrix of much softer ferrite. They are strengthened considerably when worked and offer weight reduction in parts because they provide high strength with less material. Thus dual-phase steels have become important sheet metal materials in the automobile industry.

Quenched and tempered low-carbon constructional alloy steels are also known as *low-carbon martensites*. They are similar to low-alloy, high-strength structural steels, excepting that their alloy content permits quenching to bainite or martensite (see Chap. 5). The low-carbon martensite of these steels retains toughness to $-50°F$, and these compositions produce welded joints fully as strong as the unwelded base-metal. The low-carbon martensites tend to have slightly higher alloy contents than the low-alloy, high-strength structural steels and in addition may contain alloying elements such as B, V, and Mo, all of which contribute to hardenability, and V, Mo, and Ti which form persistent carbides that resist softening upon tempering. These steels are used in the form of plate for the construction of welded pressure vessels and as structural members for large steel structures, mining equipment, and earth-movers.

AISI–SAE alloy steels are steels whose compositions have been standardized by the American Iron and Steel Institute and the Society of Automotive Engineers. A numbering system using as many as five digits designates the composition of the alloy. The nominal carbon content is given in hundredths of a percent by the last two numbers when four digits are used and by the last three numbers when five digits are used. Thus, 4140 and 52100 indicate respective carbon contents of 0.40 and 1.00%. The first two numbers show which alloying elements are present. Thus:

10xx	Plain-carbon steel
11xx	Resulfurized steels for free machining
12xx	Rephosphorized and resulfurized steels
13xx	Manganese steels
2xxx	Nickel steels
3xxx	Nickel-chromium steels
4xxx, 8xxx, 43xx, and 98xx	Steels containing molybdenum alone or in combination with nickel or chromium or both nickel and chromium.
5xxx or 5xxxx	Chromium steels
6xxx	Chromium and vanadium steels
92xx	Manganese and silicon steels

With the exception of the low-carbon, plain-carbon steels, the AISI–SAE steels are always used in the heat-treated condition. Although the low-carbon, plain-carbon steels are sometimes used in the unhardened condition, they are also sometimes surface-hardened by carburizing (see Chap. 5). The low-carbon AISI–SAE alloy steels are used for carburizing if somewhat better core properties and a greater depth of hardening is required. The steels containing more than 0.25% carbon are used in the quenched and tempered condition. Higher carbon contents, up to about 0.60%

carbon, provide tempered martenite of greater hardness. Higher alloy contents serve to increase the depth to which hard martensite will form beneath the surface. In other words, the maximum hardness achievable is a primary function of carbon content, and the proportion of the section which can be hardened is a primary function of alloy content, particularly manganese, molybdenum, chromium, and nickel.

The AISI–SAE steels are used for applications such as carburized or through-hardened gears, steering-mechanism parts, transmissions, shafting, and ordnance parts. The 52000 series are used mainly for ball and roller bearings.

Alloy tool steels represent a small, but extremely important percentage of total steel production, since they are essential to the processing of all other steel and engineering materials. If a tool has a simple shape, does not need to be hardened too deeply (say less than $\frac{1}{4}$ in.), and is to be used near room temperatures, it can be made of carbon tool steel. But when the shape becomes complex, and if hardenability, toughness, wear resistance, hot working, and other requirements become severe, alloy tool steels are needed. The AISI–SAE designations list 13 different classifications of which the major groups are:

Designation	Type
Cold-work steels	
W2–W7	Water-hardening tool steel
O1–O7	Oil-hardening tool steel
A2–A7	Air-hardening tool steel
S1–S5	Shock-resisting tool steel
D1–D7	High-carbon, high-chromium tool steel
F1–F3	Carbon-tungsten tool steel
L1–L7	Low-alloy, special-purpose tool steel
P1–P20, PPT	Low-carbon mold steels
Hot-work steels	
H11–H43	Hot-work tool steels
High-speed steels	
T1–T15	Tungsten high-speed tool steels
M1–M36	Molybdenum high-speed tool steels

The names of the various types of tool steel indicate some of their special properties. All tool steels should be hard, tough, and wear resistant, although the relative importance of these properties varies from application to application.

The *cold-work steels* include the water-, oil-, and air-hardening tool steels (W, O, A steels), all of which have a fairly high carbon content (0.60 to 2.25%) and varying degrees of hardenability, as indicated by their names, and are controlled by the amount and kind of alloying elements they contain. The shock-resisting tool steels (S steels), which can be considered as special cold-work tool steels, have a lower carbon content (0.50%) in order to improve their toughness. It is characteristic of the tool steels that toughness increases with decreasing carbon content, and the shock-resisting tool steels have measurable ductility (needed for toughness, see Chap. 3) even at 60 R_c. The high-carbon high-chromium tool steels (D steels) have large amounts of chromium (12%) and other carbide formers. These alloy additions produce an air-hardening composition with excellent wear resistance, useful for blanking dies, thread-rolling dies, and brick molds. Since the strong carbide formers have such a great affinity for carbon, the carbon content is raised in these steels to assure that there is enough uncombined carbon remaining in the austenite to yield a martensite matrix of adequate hardness upon hardening. The carbon-tungsten tool steels (F steels) are similar to the oil- and water-hardening steels, but they have extra amounts of tungsten, resulting in improved wear resistance because of tungsten carbide particles. The low-alloy, special-purpose tool steels (L steels) are similar to the W steels, but have higher amounts of strong carbide formers for improved wear resistance. The low-carbon mold steels (P steels) have the lowest carbon contents of all the tool steels, and after machining or pressing to shape are carburized for improved wear resistance.

The *hot-work steels* (H steels) contain fairly large amounts of the strong carbide formers, which resist softening at operating temperatures. Chromium, tungsten, molybdenum, and vanadium are found in these compositions. Their carbon contents are below 0.65% carbon so that they exhibit moderately good toughness at high strength levels. They are used for forging dies, extrusion dies, and die-casting dies. One composition has been found useful for structural members in supersonic aircraft, where it resists softening when subjected to temperatures of 550°C (1000°F) or more for long times.

The *high-speed steels* contain either tungsten (T steels) or molybdenum usually with tungsten (M steels) as the principal carbide formers. Both T and M steels contain chromium and vanadium. The high-carbon content is necessary to satisfy the carbide-forming tendencies and produce excellent wear resistance and hardness at red heat. At the same time the carbon content is not so high that toughness is lacking. Since molybdenum is a cheaper alloying element than tungsten and is about twice as effective as tungsten the T steels have been almost entirely replaced by M steels. There is no significant difference between the performance of the two major classes of high-speed steels. Cobalt is used in some compositions because it dissolves in and imparts to the ferrite matrix a specially high strength at red heat. The high-speed steels are used for taps, reamers, milling cutters, broaches, and for heavy-duty high-temperature aircraft bearings. High-speed steel cutting tools are discussed in Chap. 16.

Magnet steels divide into two broad classes: (1) permanent magnets, and (2) temporary magnets. The best permanent magnet materials are not steels, although steel is sometimes used for this application. Permanent magnets are physically hard, and any steel which can be hardened by heat treatment can serve as a permanent magnet. The temporary magnet steels are vastly more important than the steels used for permanent magnets. The temporary magnets are mechanically soft materials, which are readily magnetized and demagnetized by alternating current. The magnetic performance of these steels is impaired by any composition change or treatment which hardens them. This includes even the cold work associated with blanking and stamping, as well as that associated with stacking and clamping laminates. Hardness tends to make the steels more "permanent," that is, more difficult to magnetize and de-magnetize in an alternating current field, resulting in power losses known as *hysteresis losses*. Another source of power losses is by induced eddy currents. This kind of power loss is minimized by using insulated laminates in an assembly, and by increasing the electrical resistance of the laminate material. Two fundamental changes accompanying solid-solution formation are (1) an increase in electrical resistance and (2) an increase in hardness. Therefore, alloying to increase electrical resistance and reduce eddy-current losses is accompanied by an increase in hardness and an increase in hysteresis losses. The alloying element which most effectively increases resistance with a minimum increase in hardness is silicon. The sheet steel used for temporary magnets is a silicon-bearing steel, of very low carbon content. The presence of carbon tends to harden the steel and stabilize austenite (see the discussion of stainless steels, below). Since hardness is undesirable for reasons already mentioned, and austenite is nonferromagnetic, low carbon contents are essential for the highest-quality temporary magnet steels.

Stainless steels rely primarily upon the presence of chromium for the achievement of stainless qualities. In general, the higher the chromium content the more corrosion resistant is the steel. There are three common classes of stainless steel: (1) austenitic, (2) ferritic, and (3) martensitic. The names of these classes reflect the microstructure of which the steel is normally composed. The alloying elements in steel can be classed as austenite stabilizers and ferrite stabilizers. The *austenite stabilizers* of importance are carbon, nickel, nitrogen, and manganese. These elements enhance the retention of austenite as steel is cooled. When 12% or more manganese is present, or when 20% or more nickel is present, it is impossible to cool steel slowly enough to allow austenite to transform to ferrite. Even with much lower nickel and manganese contents the transformation is very sluggish and austenite is stable at room temperature. The *ferrite stabilizers* of importance are chromium and the strong carbide formers. The ferrite stabilizers tend to prevent transformation of steel to austenite upon heating. Whether a steel is austenitic, ferritic, or martensitic depends upon the balance between the amounts of austenite and ferrite stabilizers present, and the heating-cooling cycle to which the steel has been subjected. This is explained in the following paragraphs.

The *austenitic stainless steels* are produced and used in greatest tonnage. Although they all contain nickel, occasionally manganese and nitrogen are used as nickel substitutes. These three elements are responsible for the austenitic structure. The austenitic stainless steels contain, as do all stainless steels, chromium, which is necessary for corrosion resistance. In order for chromium to be effective in imparting corrosion resistance, it must be in solid solution in the austenite. These steels lose their corrosion resistance if the chromium exists in a second phase such as chromium carbide. Chromium tends to precipitate as a carbide from austenite at the grain boundaries when these austenitic stainless steels are cooled from a temperature near 815°C (1500°F). This depletes the grain boundary region of the chromium necessary for corrosion resistance, and renders the grain boundaries susceptible to a form of attack known as *intergranular corrosion*. Corrosion resistance can be restored by heating the steel above 815°C (1500°F), followed by quenching to prevent formation of chromium carbide, thus retaining the chromium in solution in austenite. Welding (see Chap. 14) results in cooling rates near the weld which result in sensitization of austenitic stainless steel to intergranular attack. If the structure does not lend itself to subsequent heating and quenching for restoration of corrosion resistance, special grades of austenitic stainless steels should be used. The simplest modification is a low-carbon grade, in which the maximum permissible carbon content is below 0.03% carbon. There will then be insufficient precipitation of chromium to be harmful. Carbon is also rendered harmless by adding alloying elements which have a greater carbide-forming tendency than does chromium, thus leaving the chromium in the uncombined state. Elements which will achieve this include titanium, columbium, and molybdenum. Austenitic stainless steels containing these elements are known as *stabilized grades*.

The *ferritic stainless steels* contain chromium, no nickel, and tolerate only small amounts of austenite-stabilizing carbon. If the carbon content is increased, the chromium content must be increased in order to maintain balance and a ferritic structure. In this balanced condition these steels can be heated to the melting point without transforming to austenite. Thus it is impossible to harden them by quenching and tempering.

The *martensitic stainless steels* contain balanced amounts of chromium (ferrite stabilizer) and carbon and nickel (austenite stabilizers), so that upon heating the steel becomes austenitic, but upon cooling tends to revert to ferrite. These compositions can be heated to the austenitic range of temperatures and will transform to martensite upon cooling at suitable rates. The carbon content is sufficient to produce a martensitic hardness which is adequate for cutlery and surgical instruments.

Precipitation-hardenable stainless steels have either austenitic, martensitic, or semi-austenitic structures, achieved by adjustment of the amounts of austenite and ferrite stabilizers, principally chromium and nickel. Lowering the chromium/nickel ratio tends to stabilize the austenitic condition; raising it promotes transformation to martensite. Hardening is accomplished by precipitation of titanium or copper from martensitic types, by precipitation of aluminum from semi-austenitic types, and by precipitation of carbide from austenitic types. Precipitation may result from simple heating and aging cycles, perhaps following a subzero treatment or cold-working treatment to transform an austenitic structure to a martensitic one. The precipitation-hardenable steels were developed for applications such as aircraft structural members, where the size and shape of the structure prevented hardening by cold work or by conventional quenching and tempering.

The austenitic stainless steels cost about 10 times as much as ordinary steel and are used where corrosion resistance and high-temperature strength and oxidation resistance are critical. Textile machinery, chemical equipment, food-processing equipment, and architectural trim are examples of austenitic stainless steel applications. The ferritic stainless steels are used in applications where lower strength and corrosion resistance can be tolerated, as in automobile body trim. The martensitic stainless steels cost about seven or eight times as much as carbon steel. They are used where wear resistance is a prime consideration, together with corrosion resistance, as in cutlery, razor blades, and instruments.

AISI type numbers have been assigned to about 40 stainless and heat-resisting steel compositions. These are three-digit numbers (2xx, 3xx, etc.). The second and third digit of a number designates a specific composition. Specifications for standard types are given in reference books and handbooks.

Maraging steels develop martensite upon cooling from the austenitizing temperature, but the martensite formed in these steels is, unlike the martensite of AISI alloy steels, ductile and tough. The ductility and toughness of this martensite result from its low carbon content, which is below 0.03% carbon. In the martensitic condition these steels can be cold-worked and can be hardened by precipitation at temperatures below the austenitizing temperature, e.g., 482°C (900°F). Hardening is believed to result from precipitation of compounds such as Ni_3Mo and Ni_3Ti. The hardened maraging steels have yield strengths up to 2 GPa (300,000 psi) and Charpy V-notch impact strengths well over 15 J (10 ft-lb). The impact strength for maraging steels with about 1.5 GPa (200,000 psi) yield strength is in the range of 65 to 80 J (50 to 60 ft-lb). These steels are particularly useful in the manufacture of large structures having critical strength requirements, such as space-vehicle cases, hydrofoil struts, and extrusion press rams.

QUESTIONS

1. In what ways do alloying elements affect the control of the properties of ferrous alloys?
2. In what forms does carbon exist in ferrous alloys? How does the form in which carbon exists affect the properties of the alloys?
3. What two functions are performed by carbon in steel?
4. How does an increase in carbon content affect the mechanical properties of ferrous alloys which are not hardened by quenching?
5. Is ferrite strengthening a more important function of alloying elements in slowly cooled steels or in quenched steels? Why?
6. How can graphitization be promoted in ferrous alloys?
7. What is the most important function of alloying elements in ferrous alloys which are hardened by quenching?
8. What changes in properties and microstructure accompany the tempering of martensite?
9. How does hardenability differ from hardness?
10. What is secondary hardening? In what types of ferrous alloys does it occur?
11. Why is silicon used as an alloying element in magnet alloys?
12. Explain the effects of lead and sulfur on the machinability of steels.
13. What is the effect of alloying elements on the toughness of hardened steels?
14. Why is low-carbon steel not usually hardened by heat treatment?
15. What are the principal uses for (a) low-carbon, (b) medium-carbon, and (c) high-carbon steels?

16. What functions do the alloying elements performs in the low-alloy, high-strength structural steels?

17. How do the composition and properties of the low-carbon constructional steels differ from those of the low-alloy, high-strength structural steels?

18. In a quenched and tempered piece of steel, upon what does **(a)** the maximum hardness depend, and **(b)** the depth of hardening depend?

19. For what purposes are AISI–SAE steels commonly used?

20. In tool steels what is the relationship between **(a)** carbon content and properties, and **(b)** carbide formers and properties?

21. Correlate the mechanical and magnetic properties of the magnet alloys.

22. What is the effect of the presence of austenite in magnet steels?

23. What determines whether a stainless steel is austenitic, ferritic, or martensitic?

24. What sensitizes stainless steel to intergranular attack, and what steps can be taken to overcome this difficulty?

25. What are common applications for **(a)** austenitic, **(b)** martensitic, **(c)** ferritic, and **(d)** precipitation-hardenable stainless steels?

26. How is hardness achieved in the maraging steels? How does the martensite of maraging steels differ from the martensite of AISI–SAE steels?

REFERENCES

HARVEY, P. D., ed., *Engineering Properties of Steel*, American Society for Metals, Metals Park, Ohio, 1982.

Materials Selector, published annually by *Materials Engineering*, Penton/IPC, Cleveland.

McGANNON, H.E., ed., *The Making, Shaping and Treating of Steel*, 9th ed., United States Steel Corporation, Pittsburgh, Pa., 1971.

Metals Handbook: Irons and Steels, Vol.1, 9th ed., American Society for Metals, Metal Parks, Ohio, 1978.

Steel Products Manual, American Iron and Steel Institute, New York. Published and revised periodically.

NONFERROUS METALS AND ALLOYS

Although pure iron is not of great importance, the same cannot be said of many pure nonferrous metals. The title of this chapter reflects the importance of the nonferrous metals as well as the importance of their alloys. The nonferrous metals are used in pure form because of such superior properties as electrical and thermal conductivity, corrosion resistance, high melting temperature, special electrical properties, special optical properties, and special chemical properties. As in the case of ferrous alloys, alloying the nonferrous metals usually results in improved mechanical properties.

In this chapter the effects of alloying on the properties of pure metals are first discussed. The following metals and their alloys are then considered: the light metals, that is, aluminum, titanium, and magnesium; copper; zinc; and finally, miscellaneous metals.

EFFECTS OF ALLOYING ON PROPERTIES

When any pure metal is alloyed with other metals or nonmetals, some properties are significantly impaired, others are significantly improved, and still others are not greatly altered.

The strongly metallic elements suffer a decrease in electrical and thermal conductivities as a result of alloying. The semiconductor germanium, which is not strongly metallic, shows an increase in conductivity as a result of alloying (or doping). Aluminum, copper, and silver, which are often selected for uses requiring excellent thermal or electrical conductivity, suffer significant decreases in these properties as a result of alloying. For instance, the electrical conductivity of standard copper (taken as 100%) drops to about 93% as a result of only 0.02% aluminum, even though both pure metals are excellent conductors.

The specific gravities of pure metals are raised, lowered, or unchanged by alloying, depending upon the character and amounts of the alloying elements used. When the additions represent about 10% or less of the total weight of alloy, the changes in specific gravity are, for most purposes, insignificant. For instance, pure aluminum has a specific gravity of 2.70, while the 7075 alloy (5.5% Zn, 2.5% Mg, 1.5% Cu, 0.3% Cr) has a specific gravity of 2.80.

The moduli of elasticity of pure metals are not greatly affected by alloying with small amounts of other elements. For instance, annealed nickel has a modulus of elasticity of about 210 GPa (30×10^6 psi), and annealed *Monel* metal, which consists of 34% other elements with the balance nickel, has a modulus of elasticity of about 175 GPa. (26×10^6 psi). It can be reasonably assumed that for most purposes the modulus of elasticity and shear modulus of the alloy have about the same values as for the base metal.

The yield strength, tensile strength, fatigue strength, and high-temperature resistance are generally improved by judicious alloying. Because of this, alloys are much more commonly used than pure metals where mechanical behavior is the primary criterion of performance. In addition, alloying sometimes produces compositions whose mechanical properties can be further enhanced by heat treating. Heat treating is applied to pure metals only to remove the effects of cold work; they cannot be hardened by heat treatment.

Ductility is often reduced by alloying, but an important exception to this is the initial increase in ductility which accompanies the alloying of copper with zinc and other metals.

ALUMINUM

Pure aluminum is known for excellent electrical and thermal conductivity, corrosion resistance, nontoxicity, light reflectivity, low specific gravity, and softness and ductility. The electrical conductivity of EC (electrical conductor) grade aluminum is 61% of the conductivity of standard copper, based on equal cross sections. If equal *weights* of copper and aluminum conductors of a given length are compared it will be found that aluminum conducts 201% as much current as does copper. Since the price of aluminum is generally much lower than that of copper, and since the specific gravity of aluminum is only 2.7 compared to 8.9 for copper, the advantages of aluminum as an electric conductor are obvious. An important limitation of aluminum in this regard is the difficulty of soldering or joining it. This has been overcome by chemically coating aluminum with tin, followed by plating with other metals if necessary. Aluminum can be joined by welding (see Chap. 14). The good thermal conductivity of aluminum has led to its application as a radiator fin material in baseboard heating and in air-conditioning units. Excellent light reflectivity and corrosion resistance account for its use as a sheet metal light reflector and as a coating for high-grade optical reflectors. Its softness and ductility, coupled with its corrosion resistance and its nontoxic nature, have resulted in its use as a foil and packaging material.

ALUMINUM ALLOYS

Aluminum can be hardened by solid-solution hardening, by cold working, and by precipitation hardening. In fact the precipitation hardening of aluminum by copper was the first precipitation-hardenable system investigated, and precipitation-hardenable aluminum alloys were the first ones commercially exploited. Among the elements added to aluminum for precipitation hardening are copper, manganese, nickel, and silicon. However, silicon is used mainly to improve castability. Zinc is used as a solid-solution hardener, and magnesium is added to improve corrosion resistance.

Commercial types of aluminum and its alloys are designated by codes to specify composition and treatment. A wrought material is identified by four digits followed by one or more letters or digits. The first digit signifies the major alloying element; 1 for none (99% or purer aluminum), 2 for copper, 3 for manganese, 4 for silicon, etc. After the alloy designation and a dash, temper is specified by a letter; F as fabricated, O annealed, H strain hardened, W solution treated, and T thermally treated. H and T are followed by digits indicating degree of treatment. Typical designators are 2024-T4 and 7079-W. Designators for casting alloys are somewhat different, as illustrated by a typical one, A357.0. The prefix (A) indicates modification of the original alloy. The first digit signifies the major alloying element, like the first digit for a wrought alloy. The second and third digits are the alloy identification number, and the digit to the right of the decimal point (0) specifies a casting (1 would specify an ingot and 2 a special-composition ingot). Full listings and descriptions of standard aluminum alloys are contained in reference books and handbooks.

The room-temperature mechanical properties of aluminum alloys are, in general, inferior to those of steel, almost equal to those of copper alloys, and superior to those of magnesium alloys. Copper alloys can be used at higher temperatures than aluminum alloys, but neither are known for specially good creep or stress-rupture properties. There is, of course, considerable overlapping of properties among the alloys of the various metals, and reliable references should be used to determine specific properties.

In addition to mechanical properties, several other factors should be kept in mind. One of the most important of these is the specific gravity of aluminum alloys. Dividing the strength values by the specific gravity yields a number known as the *specific strength*. Comparison of specific strengths shows that most, but not all, aluminum alloys are superior to most steel compositions. Specific strengths have an important bearing on payloads and dead weight. When limitations are placed on section size and bulk, steel may be favored over aluminum alloys. When structural rigidity is required, the additional bulk of alluminum alloys is advantageous. Considerations such as the need to develop optimum properties by heat treating, and the need to maintain these after joining are also important in deciding whether steel or aluminum alloys should be used for a specific application.

In addition to specific gravity and specific strength, the cost of aluminum must be considered. On the basis of equal masses, aluminum alloy structural shapes cost about eight times as much as steel. Cost per kilogram (pound) and specific gravity considerations usually favor aluminum alloys over copper alloys and magnesium alloys, but not over steel.

Fabrication of aluminum alloys is rather easily accomplished. These alloys can be cast by any of the casting methods (see Chaps. 8 and 9) including die casting. Major factors in determining the suitability of an alloy for die casting are its melting temperature and the corrosive nature of the molten alloy with respect to the dies and die-casting machine. Aluminum alloys rank in this regard as superior to copper alloys but inferior to zinc-base die castings.

Aluminum alloys, in general, are considered easily machined, though in some cases good surface finish is difficult to obtain. This can be improved by use of cutting fluids (see Chap. 16). Another problem connected with machining of aluminum arises from its relatively large coefficient of thermal expansion, and low modulus of elasticity. These properties are likely to make dimensional control difficult, either because of inadequate cooling or because of excessive deflection of members as a result of cutting forces.

Joining of aluminum alloys (see Chap. 14) is accomplished successfully by a variety of welding and brazing methods. Inert-gas-shielded-arc welding is popular. Soldering is difficult and not generally recommended unless the alloy has been tin coated.

Aluminum alloys are readily mechanically worked, either cold or at elevated temperatures, since they are relatively soft and have good ductility.

Although aluminum alloys can be electroplated, they are more difficult to electroplate than ferrous, copper, and zinc alloys.

TITANIUM

Essentially no high-purity titanium is produced. Commercially pure titanium, sometimes called *unalloyed titanium*, contains up to about 1% of various alloying elements, mainly oxygen, iron, carbon, nitrogen, and hydrogen. This grade of titanium is useful mainly because of its corrosion resistance and specific gravity of 4.5. It is as strong or perhaps slightly stronger than most copper-base and aluminum-base alloys, and low-carbon steels, but is weaker than alloyed titanium. It is, however, the most ductile and the least difficult titanium composition to fabricate. Commercially pure titanium (at about 100 times the cost of carbon steel and about five or six times the cost of stainless steel) is used because of its corrosion resistance in chemical piping, valves, tanks, and prosthetic devices. In the aerospace industry it is used mainly for applications where high-temperature rather than specific strength requirements are of greater importance. These applications include fire walls, tailpipes, and jet engine compressor cases.

TITANIUM ALLOYS

The corrosion resistance and mechanical properties of titanium alloys compare favorably with those of austenitic stainless steel. In general, the titanium alloys are used as substitutes for stainless steel, particularly the austenitic grades, in applications where the lower specific gravity of titanium alloys justifies the much higher cost. About 90% of titanium alloy production is used in aerospace applications. Titanium alloys occur as three different structures: (1) alpha, which has a hexagonal-close-packed structure and cannot be hardened by heat treatment; (2) beta, which has a body-centered-cubic structure and can be age hardened; and (3) alpha-beta mixtures, which also can be hardened by heat treatment. Better than 60% of titanium alloy production is in the form of mixed alpha-beta structures.

Aluminum is a major alloying addition for titanium alloys. It functions as an alpha stabilizer, dissolves in the alpha, and strengthens alpha while in solution. The presence of aluminum is important, for this reason, in alpha or alpha-beta alloys which are to be used at temperatures above 370°C (700°F). Aluminum-free alloys lose strength rapidly when service temperatures rise above 370°C (700°F). Most of the other alloying elements used in titanium alloys are beta stabilizers. The beta phase, containing dissolved elements such as vanadium and chromium, tends to be stronger than the alpha phase. The mixed alpha-beta alloys contain aluminum and beta stabilizers. They can be quenched to a metastable structure containing more than equilibrium amounts of beta. Upon aging, alpha precipitates and the alloys are strengthened.

Fabrication of titanium alloys is much more difficult than for aluminum-base and copper-base alloys. Machinability is about the same as for stainless steels, i.e., difficult. Arc welding can be done only if shielding is provided by helium or argon, since titanium has a great affinity for the oxygen and nitrogen in air. Both oxygen and nitrogen have strong embrittling tendencies. Titanium alloys can be mechanically formed, but frequent annealing is required, and galling and seizing of dies are a problem.

Titanium alloys are used for such applications as aircraft gas turbine compressor blades, forged airframe fittings, missile fuel tanks, and structural parts operating for short times up to 600°C (1100°F), and for autoclaves and process equipment operating up to 480°C (900°F). Low specific gravity, good strength even at high temperatures, and corrosion resistance justify the use of these materials which cost, on a weight basis, about five times as much as ordinary stainless steels.

MAGNESIUM

Pure magnesium is used mainly as an alloy addition to other base metals, as a reagent in the synthesis of organic chemicals, and as an anode material for galvanic protection.

MAGNESIUM ALLOYS

In general, magnesium alloys are weaker, more brittle, and have poorer high-temperature properties than aluminum alloys. The principal alloying additions are aluminum and zinc. Aluminum forms a precipitation-hardenable alloy, and zinc is a solid-solution hardener and improves corrosion resistance. Corrosion resistance is good only in the absence of moisture. The specific gravity of magnesium alloys is the lowest of the light metals at 1.7. Magnesium alloys are among the most machinable of the metallic materials since they have the ideal combination of properties for good machinability, namely softness and brittleness. Their brittleness makes cold mechanical working difficult. However, they are readily hot worked and die cast. Magnesium alloys are used mainly when weight saving is a special requirement such as in ladders, aircraft die castings, and textile spools and machinery. Plates 10 to 75 mm ($\frac{1}{2}$ to 3 in.) thick are quoted at around 20 times the price of carbon steel on the basis of equal masses.

COPPER

Pure unalloyed copper is used for electric wire, bars, and buses, and for tubing and pipe because it has outstanding electric and heat conductivity, corrosion resistance, and solderability.

COPPER ALLOYS

Copper can be hardened and strengthened by cold working, by solid-solution alloying with zinc, tin, aluminum, silicon, manganese, and nickel. It forms a precipitation-hardenable alloy when small amounts of beryllium are present. The ductility of many of the solid-solution alloys is greater than that of copper.

The room-temperature mechanical properties of copper alloys are approximately intermediate between those of aluminum alloys and steel. The elevated-temperature properties, though superior to those of the aluminum alloys, are not outstanding. The copper alloys are known for attractive appearance and corrosion resistance, accounting for large-scale use in hardware, particularly marine hardware. Wide sheets and drawn-ingot copper rods are 12 to 14 times as expensive as equal masses of carbon steel.

Copper-zinc alloys are called brasses. Alpha-phase brass with up to 36% zinc includes ductile, easily worked compositions such as cartridge brass for deep drawing. The beta phase appears with a larger proportion of zinc. It is more brittle and less easily cold worked but more corrosion resistant and machinable. Colors vary in various compositions from red brass to yellow brass. Brass shapes in large quantities cost from 8 to 14 times as much as the same mass of carbon steel.

Most bronzes are alloys of copper with up to 12% tin. The alloys are noted for toughness, wear and corrosion resistance, and good strength. Typical applications are for bearings and worm gears.

Fabrication of copper alloys is readily accomplished by casting, cold work, machining, powder metallurgy, and joining by soldering. The alloys take a variety of finishes and are easily electroplated. Die casting, because of the relatively high melting temperatures, is appreciably more difficult than for aluminum, zinc, and magnesium alloys. The higher melting temperatures result in greater thermal shock to dies and shorten die life. Hot working can be carried out, but some of the alloys are hot short.

The copper-base alloys include some of the most machinable metal compositions. Particularly noteworthy are the leaded, free-machining brasses, in which lead acts as an internal lubricant and chip breaker.

ZINC

The outstanding properties of zinc are its corrosion resistance to ordinary atmospheric conditions and the fact that it is above iron and steel in the galvanic series. Because of these properties the largest use of zinc is as a coating applied to steel wire and sheet.

ZINC ALLOYS

The most important alloy additions for zinc are magnesium and aluminum, which act respectively to improve corrosion resistance and strength in zinc-base die-casting alloys. Copper is sometimes also added to these alloys to stabilize their dimensions. Zinc-base die castings are compared with those of other metals in Chap. 9. Zinc alloys are not widely used in form other than as die castings.

Superplastic zinc alloys containing about 22% aluminum can be formed easily into intricate shapes and then heat treated to increase strength. A typical alloy can be formed with a yield point of 255 MPa (37,000 psi) and then heat-treated to a yield point of 350 MPa (51,000 psi).

THE WHITE METALS

The *white metals* are low-melting alloys in which lead, tin, or antimony predominate. Zinc-, aluminum-, and magnesium-base castings are sometimes erroneously called white-metal castings. The three most important classes of white metals are (1) fusible alloys, (2) type metals, and (3) bearing alloys. Of these, the most important, from an engineering standpoint, are the bearing alloys. These are known as *babbitts*.

True babbitts are tin-base alloys strengthened by the presence of antimony and copper, and occasionally containing lead. Lower-cost lead-base babbitts are also used in place of the true babbitts. The microstructures of all these alloys are similar. They consist of hard primary cube-shaped particles in a soft matrix. If primary particles separate by gravity segregation and sink to the bottom of the casting, a structure of inferior wear resistance results. Segregation is prevented by the use of copper which solidifies first as an interlocking network of spiney crystals. This produces a structure in which the hard, cube-shaped particles are uniformly distributed in the matrix. The babbitt bearing alloys are quite readily cast in the shop.

NICKEL AND ITS ALLOYS

Almost 60% of all the nickel produced is used as an alloying element in steel and iron, particularly the austenitic stainless steels. Nickel plating consumes the second largest quantity of nickel, followed by the high-nickel alloys which account for about 15% of total nickel production. These include the *Monels*, which are essentially nickel-copper alloys. The Monels are quite similar to the stainless steels in corrosion re-sistance, appearance, and properties. They are difficult to machine, but welding does not sensitize them to corrosion, as happens with the austenitic stainless steels. *Nich-rome* is a nickel-base alloy containing chromium or chromium and iron. It is known for high electric resistance and oxidation resistance at red-heat and is therefore used in electrical resistance heater elements. *Inconel* is a nickel-iron-chromium alloy known for high-temperature oxidation resistance. Nickel powder is mixed with car-bide powders, compressed, and sintered to make carbide cutting tools as described in Chaps. 10 and 16. Pure nickel is also used as a catalyst for chemical reactions. Nickel ingots cost about 16 times as much as an equal mass of carbon steel and electrolytic cathodes and alloys about 20 times as much.

REFRACTORY METALS

Tungsten has the highest melting temperature of the metals, (about 3400°C or 6150°F). It is extremely strong, approaching a tensile strength of 3.5 GPa (500,000 psi) in wire of 0.1 mm (0.004 in.) diameter. Pure tungsten is used as the filament wires in incandescent light bulbs. Tungsten is used as an alloying addition to steel and in the form of tungsten carbide in carbide tools. It is also used as the electrode in inert-gas-shielded-arc welding.

Tantalum and molybdenum are also refractory metals, melting respectively at 2996°C (5425°F) and 2620°C (4750°F). Both are used in electronic tubes, as alloying elements in steel, and as carbides in cemented carbides. Tantalum is a *getter*; i.e., it reacts with all but inert gases at temperatures above 300°C (600°F) in electronic tubes. It is also used for surgical implants. Molybdenum is useful as an electrical contact material and as filament supports in light bulbs.

Beryllium is an expensive light metal (specific gravity 1.82); it costs 1200 times as much as carbon steel. It has the highest specific strength of any metal and is used in applications where weight saving is important enough to justify its cost. A few critical rocket motor parts are made from beryllium. Beryllium foil is used for the windows in X-ray and counter tubes, since it has a very low absorption coefficient for short-wavelength radiant energy. It is used in atomic energy installations as a neutron reflector and moderator.

Germanium is a semiconductor and is used in manufacture of rectifiers, transistors, and similar devices. Silicon, however, performs similar functions at a lower cost.

Zirconium is an efficient getter for electronic tubes and, because of its low neutron absorption coefficient and its strength (comparable to low-carbon steel), is used in atomic piles.

PRECIOUS METALS

The most important precious metals are platinum, gold, and silver. *Platinum* is essential to the chemical industry as a catalyst material and to a lesser extent as a highly corrosion-resistant metal from which reaction vessels can be made. *Gold* is used as a lining material for vessels and as a plated coating where corrosion resistance is of extreme importance. *Silver* is the best electrical conductor and is used for this purpose. It is also the basis of the photographic industry in the form of photosensitive silver salts. Like the other noble metals, it has good corrosion resistance.

QUESTIONS

1. What effect does alloying have on the following properties of pure metals? **(a)** modulus of elasticity; **(b)** thermal conductivity; **(c)** electrical conductivity; **(d)** specific gravity; **(e)** high-temperature resistance; **(f)** yield strength; **(g)** fatigue strength.
2. List the outstanding properties of aluminum and some typical applications.
3. What are some of the factors which might be considered in deciding whether a retractible landing gear member for a huge transport plane should be made of an aluminum alloy, H-11 steel, or a maraging steel?
4. Compare the fabricating properties of aluminum, titanium, copper, magnesium, and zinc alloys.
5. What is the function of aluminum used as an alloying element in titanium-base alloys?
6. State some typical applications of unalloyed titanium and titanium alloys. What other alloy do titanium alloys most resemble?
7. Compare the mechanical properties of aluminum-, titanium-, copper-, and magnesium-base alloys.
8. Which is preferred for die-cast automobile hardware: aluminum-, magnesium-, or zinc-base alloys? Why? If the cost of these and copper-base alloy ingots were all the same per unit volume, which would be preferred for making automobile hardware die castings? For aircraft die castings?

9. List an outstanding property and use for each of the following: tantalum, beryllium, molybdenum, zirconium, and germanium.
10. What property is possessed by all the precious metals?

REFERENCES

Aluminum Standards and Data, The Aluminum Association, Washington, D.C., 1982.

CAIRNS, J. H., and P. T. GILBERT, *The Technology of Heavy Non-ferrous Metals and Alloys*, George Newnes, London, 1967.

DONACHIE, JR., M., ed., *Titanium and Titanium Alloys: Source Book*, American Society for Metals, Metals Park, Ohio, 1982.

JAFFEE, R. I., and N. E. PROMISEL, eds., *The Science, Technology and Application of Titanium*, Pergamon Press, Oxford, 1970.

Materials Selector, published annually by *Materials Engineering*, Penton/IPC, Cleveland.

Metals Handbook, 1948 ed., 8th, (1960) ed., and 9th, (1978) ed., American Society for Metals, Metals Park, Ohio.

MORGAN, S. W., *Zinc and its Alloys*, Macdonald and Evans, England, 1977.

SIMONS, E. N., *Guide to Uncommon Metals*, Frederick Muller, London, 1964.

VAN HORN, K. R., ed., *Aluminum V*, I–III, American Society for Metals, Metals Park, Ohio, 1967.

VARLEY, P. C., *The Technology of Aluminum and Its Alloys*, Newnes/Butterworth, London, 1970.

8

FOUNDRY PROCESSES

Chapters 8 and 9 are devoted to the foundry processes and include the common ways of producing castings. The two chapters do not cover the casting of metal in detail but present and illustrate the principles of the more important aspects of the field.

Founding, or *casting*, is the process of forming objects by pouring liquid or viscous material into a prepared mold or form. A *casting* is an object formed by allowing the material to solidify. A *foundry* is a collection of the necessary materials and equipment to produce a casting. Practically all metal is initially cast. The ingot from which a wrought metal is produced is first cast in an ingot mold. A *mold* is the container that has the cavity (or cavities) of the shape to be cast. Liquids may be poured; some liquid and all viscous plastic materials are forced under pressure into molds.

Founding is one of the oldest industries in the metalworking field and dates back to approximately 4000 B.C. Since this early age, many methods have been employed to cast various materials. In this chapter, sand casting and its ramifications receive first attention because they are most used; over 90% of all castings are sand castings. Sand casting is best suited for iron and steel at their high melting temperatures but also predominates for aluminum, brass, bronze, and magnesium. In Chap. 9 other processes of commercial importance are treated, in most cases those for nonferrous metals using permanent molds.

The elements necessary for the production of sound castings are considered throughout this chapter. These include molding materials, molding equipment, tools, patterns, melting equipment, etc. These basic ingredients must be combined in an orderly sequence for the production of a sound casting.

THE PRINCIPLES OF SAND CASTING

Castings have specific important engineering properties; these may be metallurgical, physical, or economic. Castings are often cheaper than forgings or weldments, depending on the quantity, type of material, and cost of patterns as compared to the cost of dies for forging and the cost of jigs and fixtures for weldments. Where this is the case, they are the logical choices for engineering structures and parts.

Some of the characteristics of special interest to be realized from properly designed castings are the following. Properly designed and properly produced castings do not have directional properties. No laminated or segregated structure exists as it does when metal is worked after solidification. This means strength, for instance, is the same in all directions, and this characteristic is especially desirable for some gears, piston rings, engine cylinder liners, etc. The ability of molten metal to flow into thin sections of complicated design is a very desirable characteristic. Cast iron is unique in that it has good dampening characteristics which are desirable in producing bases for machine tools, engine frames, and other applications where it is desirable to minimize vibration.

The Mold.   Good castings cannot be produced without good molds. Because of the importance of the mold, casting processes are often described by the material and method employed for the mold. Thus sand castings may be made in (1) green sand molds, (2) dry sand molds, (3) core sand molds, (4) loam molds, (5) shell molds, and (6) cement-bonded molds. The major methods of making these molds are called (1) bench molding, (2) machine molding, (3) floor molding, and (4) pit molding.

In producing a sand mold, the molder's skill is of great value. He must know how to prepare a mold with the following characteristics:

1. The mold must be strong enough to hold the weight of the metal.
2. The mold must resist the erosive action of the rapidly flowing metal during pouring.
3. The mold must generate a minimum amount of gas when filled with molten metal. Gases contaminate the metal and can disrupt the mold.
4. The mold must be constructed so that any gases formed can pass through the body of the mold itself, rather than penetrate the metal.
5. The mold must be refractory enough to withstand the high temperature of the metal and strip away cleanly from the casting after cooling.
6. The core must collapse enough to permit the casting to contract after solidification.

A *flask* is a wood or metal frame in which a mold is made. It must be strong and rigid so as not to distort when it is handled or when sand is rammed into it. It must also resist the pressure of the molten metal during casting. Pins and fittings align the

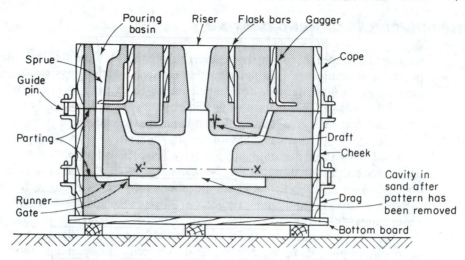

Figure 8-1 Cross-sectional view of a three-part sand mold, with the parts labeled. The line X'-X indicates parting in the pattern.

sections of a flask. They wear in service and must be watched to avoid mismatched or shifted molds.

A flask is made of two principal parts, the *cope* (top section) and the *drag* (bottom section). When more than two sections of a flask are necessary to increase the depth of the cope and/or the drag, intermediate flask sections known as *cheeks* are used.

Figure 8-1 is a diagram of a typical mold and its principal parts. The features and functions of the parts will be explained as they are taken up in the text.

The Behavior of Cast Metal.   When molten metal is poured into a mold, the casting begins to cool inwardly from all bounding surfaces because the heat can flow only outwardly through the mold. The metal on the surface is more or less chilled because at first the mold is relatively cool. If the chilling is severe, the surface may be appreciably hardened. Under usual conditions a fine, close-grained structure occurs near the surface, and coarser grains toward the center where cooling is slower. If a section is thick, enough metal may be withdrawn by contraction from the center before it cools to leave a void or cavity as indicated for the piece on the left in Fig. 8-2. Such a defect in the casting may be avoided by providing a supplementary mass of metal, called a *riser*, adjacent to the casting as on the right in Fig. 8-2. The purpose of the riser is to feed liquid metal by gravity into the body of the casting to keep it full. The riser is cut off after the casting has cooled.

Thin sections cool more rapidly than thick ones. One result is that thin sections benefit more from a "quench effect" and are likely to be stronger and finer grained. This is brought out for one type of material in Fig. 8-3. At the other extreme, if a section is too thin, metal flowing through the narrow passage may be frozen before it has a chance to fill in the wall completely. The practical lower limit of section thickness depends upon the design of the casting and the fluidity of the metal. Iron can

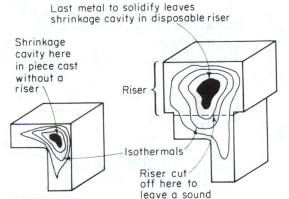

Last metal to solidify leaves shrinkage cavity in disposable riser

Shrinkage cavity here in piece cast without a riser

Riser

Isothermals

Riser cut off here to leave a sound piece

Figure 8-2 Example to illustrate the purpose of a riser on a casting.

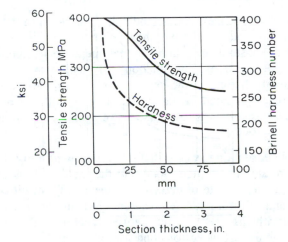

Figure 8-3 Strength and hardness of different thicknesses of a class 40 gray cast iron.

be conveniently handled and cast appreciably above its melting temperature and is commonly cast in sections as thin as 3 mm ($\frac{1}{8}$ in.). Steel melts at a much higher temperature than iron (Chap. 4), and a minimum thickness of 5 mm ($\frac{3}{16}$ in.) is recommended. Phosphorus increases the fluidity but weakens iron, and some foundrymen prefer less phosphorus and higher pouring temperatures. Aluminum may be cast with walls as thin as 3 to 5 mm ($\frac{1}{8}$ to $\frac{3}{16}$ in.).

Sections of different thicknesses cool at different rates. That leads to difficulty if a casting is not designed with uniform sections throughout. Walls that shrink at different rates pull at each other and set up residual stresses. The situation can be eased by providing gradual tapers or changes in thickness where sections of different sizes must meet.

A thick section may be in a casting where it cannot be readily fed by a riser, particularly if it must be fed through thin sections that solidify first, and thus develop voids or tears. Metal concentrations or *hot spots* of this kind are indicated in Fig. 8-4. The correction is in the design of the casting to make the sections uniform. A remedy

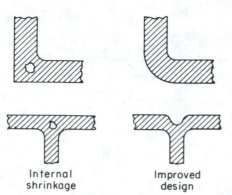

Internal
shrinkage

Improved
design

Figure 8-4 Examples of internal
shrinkage in castings.

may be to chill the metal at the hot spot to make it freeze before the adjoining sections
which can be fed more directly as they cool.

Gates, Risers, and Chills.   Gates, risers, and chills are closely related. The
function of a gating system of a mold is to deliver the liquid metal to the mold cavity.
The function of the riser is to store and supply liquid metal to compensate for
solidification shrinkage in heavy sections. The function of the chill is to cause certain
sections of a casting to solidify before others, often to help distribute properly the
supply of metal from the risers. A good gating system may be nullified by a poor
risering application. Improper use of chills can cause the scrapping of well-gated and
properly fed castings.

Gating.   An example of a gating system in a mold is shown in Fig. 8-5. The
gating system must (1) introduce the molten metal into the mold with as little turbulence as possible, (2) regulate the rate of entry of the metal, (3) permit complete
filling of the mold cavity, and (4) promote a temperature gradient within the casting
to help the metal solidify with the least conflict between sections. The following
principles help achieve the goals just listed for good gating.

The sprue should be tapered with the larger end receiving the metal to act as a
reservoir. Generally speaking, a round sprue is preferred for diameters up to about
20 mm (ca. $\frac{3}{4}$ in.), but larger sprues are often rectangular. There is less turbulence in
a rectangular sprue, but a circular sprue has a minimum surface exposed to cooling
and offers the lowest resistance to flow.

Gating systems having sudden changes in direction cause slower filling of the
mold cavity, are easily eroded, and cause turbulence in the liquid metal resulting in
gas pickup. Right angle turns should be avoided particularly.

A definite relationship must exist between the sizes of the sprue, runners, and
ingates to realize the best conditions for filling the mold. The cross section of a runner
should be reduced in area as each gate is passed, as indicated in Fig. 8-5. This helps
keep the runner full throughout its entire length and promotes uniform flow through
all of the gates. As another consideration, the rate at which metal can flow into the
mold should not exceed the ability of the sprue to keep the entire gating system full
of liquid at all times.

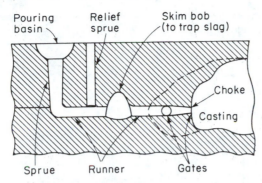

Pouring basin · Relief sprue · Skim bob (to trap slag) · Choke · Casting · Sprue · Runner · Gates

Figure 8-5 Example of a gating system.

The gating system should be formed as part of the pattern whenever possible. This allows the sand to be rammed harder and helps prevent erosion and washing as the metal flows into the mold.

Several ingates rather than one help distribute the metal to the mold and fill the mold quickly, reducing the likelihood of overheating spots in the mold. Ingates should be placed in positions where they will direct the metal into the mold along natural channels. If metal is directed against the mold surface or cores, burning is likely, and loose sand may be washed into the casting. The opening of an ingate into a mold should have as small an area as possible except in cases where the gates are through side risers. An ingate may be reduced in area or "choked" where it enters a mold cavity. This holds back slag and foreign material but must not leave an area at the entrance so small as to cause a shower effect. That may give rise to turbulence resulting in excessive oxidation of the metal.

Types of Gates.   The three main types of gates are (1) parting, (2) top, and (3) bottom gates, illustrated in Fig. 8-6.

The *parting gate* between cope and drag is the easiest and fastest for the molder to make. Its chief disadvantage is that the metal drops into the drag cavity and may cause erosion or washing of the mold. In the case of nonferrous metals, this drop aggravates the dross and entraps air in the metal, which make for inferior castings.

Top gates are at times used for gray iron castings of simple designs but not for nonferrous alloys since they have a tendency to form excessive dross when agitated. An advantage of top gating is that it is conducive to a favorable temperature gradient, but a big disadvantage is that of mold erosion.

A *bottom gate* offers smooth flow with a minimum of mold and core erosion. Its main disadvantage is that it creates an unfavorable temperature gradient. The metal is introduced into the bottom of the mold cavity and rises quietly and evenly. It cools as it rises, and the result is a condition of cold metal and cold mold near the riser and hot metal and hot mold near the gate. The riser should contain the hottest metal in the hottest part of the mold so it can feed metal into the mold until all the casting has solidified.

Gating through side risers should be done wherever possible. Gating directly into the casting results in hot spots, because all the metal enters the casting through the gate

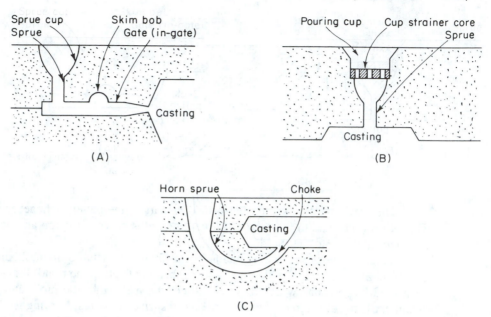

Figure 8-6   Three main types of gates for molds: (A) parting gate; (B) top gate; (C) bottom gate.

and the sand around the gate becomes hot. Cooling in that area is retarded. Unless risers are provided to feed those localities with molten metal, shrinkage cavities or defects result.

Many types of special gates besides those described are used in foundries.

Risers.   In addition to acting as a reservoir, a riser mitigates the hydraulic ram effect of metal entering the mold and vents the mold. It must be the last to solidify, and to serve efficiently must conform to the following principles. The volume of a riser must be large enough to supply all metal needed. The gating system must be designed to establish a temperature gradient toward the riser. The area of the connection of the riser to the casting must be large enough not to freeze too soon. On the other hand, the connection must not be so large that the solid riser is difficult to remove from the casting.

The shape of a riser is an important consideration. Experience has shown that the most effective height of a riser is one and one half times its diameter to produce maximum feeding with a minimum amount of metal. As the area over volume ratio of a molten mass decreases, less chance is offered for the escape of heat, and the solidification rate decreases. What this means for common shapes is shown in Table 8-1. A sphere stays molten longest but is not ideal as a riser; a cylinder is next best and is practical.

Chills.   *Chills* are metal shapes inserted in molds to speed up the solidification of the metal. Examples are given in Fig. 8-7. Two types are external and internal chills. An internal chill becomes part of and should be made of the same metal as the

TABLE 8-1 SOLIDIFICATION TIME FOR VARIOUS CAST SHAPES

Shape	Sphere	Cylinder	Cube	Thick plate	Thin plate
Solidification time (min)	7.2	4.7	3.6	2.7	1.9

Note: All shapes have volume of 1.85 dm³ (113 in.³) and mass of 14.5 kg (32 lb).

casting. An external chill should make enough contact and be large enough not to fuse with the casting. The shape, size, and use of a chill must be proportioned with care to avoid too-rapid cooling, which may cause cracks and defects in a casting.

Vents. *Vents* are small holes made by perforating the sand just short of the pattern in the mold with a wire or vent strip. The function of a vent is to permit escape of gases from the mold cavity to prevent the gases from becoming trapped in the metal or from raising back pressure to oppose the inflow of metal. Vents should serve all high points of the mold and be open to the top. Many small vents are better than a few large ones.

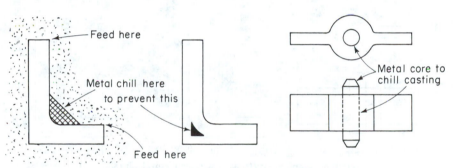

Figure 8-7 Typical forms of chills for castings.

MAKING MOLDS

Hand Tools for Molding. Some of the basic tools used by the molder are shown in Fig. 8-8. Their uses will be shown in the section that describes how a mold is made.

Riddles are used for sifting the sand over the surface of the pattern when starting a mold. The size of the riddle is given by the number of meshes to the inch; a No. 4 riddle has four meshes per inch, etc. Castings with fine surface details require fine sand and a fine riddle.

Making a Mold. A flask is selected larger than the mold cavity it is to contain to allow for risers and the gating system. There must also be enough mold mass over and under the cavity to prevent any breakout of the metal during pouring. Many castings are lost, or require extra cleaning, and many injuries to personnel are caused

Figure 8-8   Hand molding tools: (a) dust bag; (b) rammer; (c) clamps; (d) gate cutter; (e) rapping bar; (f) vent wire; (g) trowel; (h) slick; (i) draw spike; (j) sprue cutter; (k) lifter; (l) swab pot; (m) swab; (n) riddle; (o) bellows; (p) flask; (q) strike bar.

by undersized flasks. A mold cavity may be carved in the sand, but that requires considerable skill for all but the simplest shapes and is seldom done. Normal procedure is to make first an image of the piece to be cast and form the mold around it. That is called the *pattern*. Patterns and pattern making will be discussed more fully later.

Before use, the pattern is checked for cleanliness and the free action of any loose pieces. When a split pattern is used, the drag part of the flask is turned upside down on the ram-up board. The drag pattern is placed with the parting surface down on the ram-up board along with any pieces used for the gating and risering system (Fig. 8-9). Facing sand is then riddled to a depth of about one inch on the pattern and ram-up board as shown in Fig. 8-10. Riddling is absolutely necessary for good reproduction of the pattern. The riddled sand is then tucked into all pockets and sharp corners and hand packed around the pattern.

Figure 8-9 First step in making a mold. The drag pattern is placed with parting surface down on the ram-up board.

Figure 8-10 Facing sand is packed carefully around the pattern.

Backing sand is then put into the flask to cover the facing sand to a depth of 3 to 4 in. and packed with a rammer. The backing should be carefully rammed into any deep pocket as illustrated in Fig. 8-11. The remainder of the mold is filled and then rammed. Care is taken to avoid hitting or coming too close to the pattern. The mold must be rammed uniformly hard in order to obtain a smooth, easily cleaned casting surface and to avoid metal penetration into the sand, swelling of the mold, breakouts, or other casting defects.

The excess sand is struck off, as in Fig. 8-12, by means of a straight edge called a *strike bar*, and the bottom board is placed on the drag. Clamps are applied to hold the drag between the ram-up board and the bottom board. The drag is then inverted, the clamps are removed, and the ram-up board is removed. The mold surface is cleaned and smoothed with a slick in preparation for the cope portion of the pattern and flask.

Parting material is dusted from a bag over the mold joint or parting surface and the pattern. The parting material prevents the sand in the cope from sticking to the sand

Figure 8-11 Backing sand is rammed uniformly in the flask around the pattern.

Figure 8-12 Excess sand is struck off to complete the drag mold.

in the drag. Parting material for large molds is usually fine silica sand and for medium and small molds is finely ground powders such as talc or silica flour.

The cope of the flask is set on top of the drag, seated firmly, and aligned with the aid of flask pins. The cope pattern, riser form, and parts for the gating system are placed in their proper position. Figure 8-13 shows a core being put in place just before setting the cope. In this case sand will be packed around the wires shown to fasten the core to the cope.

Facing sand is riddled over the cope pattern and packed firmly as in the drag. At this time, gaggers (Fig. 8-1) are set in the cope if needed but not close enough to chill the casting. The cope is then filled with sand and rammed as in the drag. It is necessary to ram the sand a little more firmly around the flask in the cope because the sand must remain intact as the cope is removed from the drag. After the ramming is completed, the mold is struck off and vented with a vent wire as depicted in Fig. 8-14. The cope is then removed from the drag, and rolled over to facilitate drawing the cope pattern. All main, gate, sprue, and well patterns are removed at this time. The cutting of ingates is usually done before drawing the pattern.

Figure 8-13 Drag has been inverted and a core is being placed in the pattern.

Figure 8-14 Cope is vented.

When the cope and drag have been properly finished, loose cores should be set into place with care not to damage the mold or core. Figure 8-15 shows the cope with core attached and drag ready for closing.

The mold is closed carefully. Pins guide the cope. After the mold is closed, it is clamped, as shown in Fig. 8-16, and is ready for pouring. Wires from the fixed core are shown bound to the rod on top of the cope. Weights are set on top of some molds to keep them from coming apart due to the hydrostatic pressure of the liquid metal. Pouring of the pump housing is shown in Fig. 8-17, and the pump housing casting obtained is seen in Fig. 8-18.

Several kinds of molding procedures depend upon the sizes of the casting. *Bench molding* applies chiefly to molds small enough to be made on a work bench. *Floor molding* involves molds too large for a bench and made in flasks on the floor of the foundry or on machines standing on the floor. Molds too large to be made entirely in flasks are constructed in pits below the foundry floor. This is called *pit molding*.

Figure 8-15 View of the finished cope and drag with cores in position ready for closing the mold.

Figure 8-16 Closed and clamped mold is ready for pouring.

Figure 8-17 Pouring the metal into the mold.

Figure 8-18(A) Pump housing casting as it comes from the mold with runners, sprues, etc., attached.

Figure 8-18(B) Pump housing casting after cleanup.

Molding Machines. At one time all molding was done by hand but today's labor costs and competition make machine molding mandatory in industry. Molding machines offer higher production rates and better quality casting in addition to less heavy labor and lower costs.

Molding machines serve in two general capacities: (1) to pack sand firmly and uniformly into the mold, and (2) to manipulate the flasks, mold, and pattern. Properly controlled and applied machine ramming is more uniform and dependable and produces more and better molds than hand ramming. Manipulation is done in various degrees on different machines and may include turning over parts or all of the mold and lifting of patterns and flasks. Molding machines are available in a number of makes, models, and sizes and perform the foregoing functions in various combinations and ways. Generally, they fall into one of three classes and will be illustrated by a typical form of each class. These are the jolt-squeeze, jolt-rollover, and sand slinger molding machines.

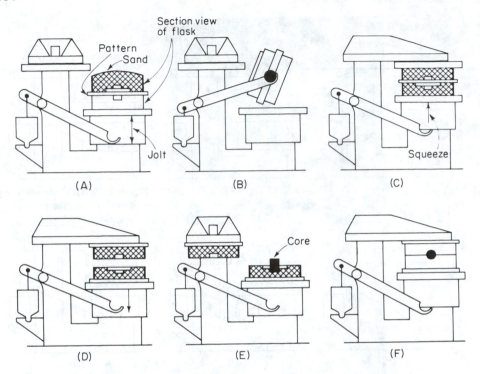

Figure 8-19 Steps in making a mold on a jolt-squeeze-rollover machine: (A) jolting the sand on the pattern in the inverted drag; (B) rolling over the flask to fill the cope; (C) squeezing to pack the sand in the cope; (D) raising the cope to remove the pattern; (E) placing a core; (F) replacing the cope on the completed mold. A medium size machine like this costs around $4500.

Jolt-squeeze Molding Machines.   A jolt-squeezer, shown in Fig. 8-19, consists basically of a table actuated by two pistons in air cylinders, one inside the other. The mold on the table is jolted by the action of the inner piston that raises the table repeatedly and drops it down sharply on a bumper pad. Jolting packs the sand in the lower parts of the flask but not at the top. The larger cylinder pushes the table upward to squeeze the sand in the mold against the squeeze head at the top. Squeezing compresses the top layers of sand in the mold but sometimes does not penetrate effectively to all areas of a pattern. In the case shown, the cope is squeezed so as not to damage the finished drag by jolting. Some machines do simply jolting; others squeezing alone. For high production, one jolt-squeezer may be set up for the drag portion of a mold and another for the cope. A vibrator may be attached to a machine to loosen the pattern to remove it easily without damaging the mold.

Jolt-rollover Pattern-draw Machines.   The machine illustrated in Fig. 8-20 is designed to mold cope or drag. A flask is set over a pattern on a table and is filled with sand and jolted. Excess sand is struck off, and a bottom board is clamped to the flask.

Figure 8-20 Jolt-rollover pattern-draw foundry molding machine. The pattern has just been drawn after the cope and drag of the mold (side by side) have been jolted and rolled over. They then have been swung out to the position shown for unloading.

The machine raises the mold and rolls it over onto a table or conveyor. The flask is freed from the machine. The pattern is vibrated, raised from the mold, and returned to loading position. Similar machines squeeze as well as jolt.

The Sand Slinger. The sand slinger achieves a consistent packing and ramming effect by hurling sand into the mold at a high velocity. Figure 8-21 explains the action. Sand from a hopper is fed by a belt to a high-speed impeller in the head. A common arrangement is to suspend the slinger with counterweights and move it about to direct the stream of sand advantageously into a mold. Mold hardness can be controlled by the operator by changing the speed of the impeller and movement of the impeller head.

Sand slingers can deliver large quantities of sand rapidly and are especially beneficial for ramming big molds. Their only function is to pack the sand into molds, and they are often operated together with pattern-drawing equipment.

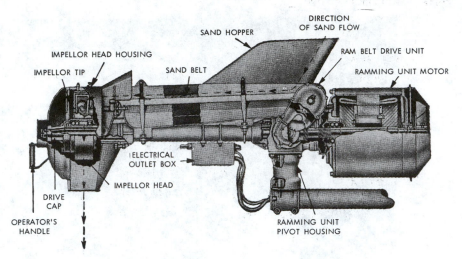

Figure 8-21 View of the mechanism of a sand slinger.

CORES AND COREMAKING

A *core* is a body of material, usually sand, used to produce a cavity in or on a casting. An example of a core in a casting is one forming the water jacket in a water-cooled engine block, and an example of a core on a casting is the one forming the air space between the cooling fins of an air-cooled cylinder. A number of properties are essential for good cores. They are mentioned briefly here but will be discussed in more detail later. A core must have (1) *permeability* (i.e., the ability to allow steam and gases to escape), (2) *refractoriness* (i.e., the ability to withstand high temperature), (3) green strength so that it can be formed, (4) dry strength so that it will not wash away or change size when surrounded by molten metal, (5) *collapsibility* (i.e., the ability to decrease in size as the casting cools and shrinks), (6) *friability* or the ability to crumble and be easily removed from the casting, and (7) a minimal tendency to generate gas.

Core Making.   The tools used in the production of cores are much the same as in making a mold, with the addition of the core box, core driers, and special material and equipment for venting. The core receives its shape from the core box. Driers are special forms or racks used to support complicated cores during baking. Since core driers are quite expensive, they are used only when large numbers of cores are required. Complicated cores can often be made in parts on flat plates and then assembled with paste.

Core making is much like molding except that the core sand is placed in a core box. It can be blown into the box, rammed or packed by hand, or jolted into the box. The excess sand is struck off, and a drier plate is placed over the box. The core box is then inverted, vibrated or rapped, and drawn off the core. The core is then put in a core oven and baked. Cores must be made strong enough to withstand the handling they must endure.

Where the core does not have natural vents, supplementary vents must be provided. For a core made up by pasting parts together, grooves may be cut in the faces to be joined before they are assembled. The vents are continued through to the core prints (Fig. 8-26) so that molten metal will not reach and plug them. If this method cannot be used, wax venting can be done by placing strips of vent wax in the sand before it is baked. If the core is large and rather complicated, the center of the core may be filled with coke, gravel, or other porous material which will give good permeability, good crushability, and good friability. The surfaces of some cores are given a refractory coating.

Several different kinds of cores can be found in the foundry today. *Baked sand* or *dry sand cores* have a binder that must be cured with heat. They are being made less frequently because of energy costs. *Green sand cores* are made of molding sand at the time the mold is made and are relatively cheap and popular. Where they cannot serve adequately, *cold cure cores* are used. They contain a two-part binder that is self-curing or a one-part binder that is cured by passing a gas through the core. There are many such core binders, mostly proprietary, and new ones are introduced each year. They save energy.

Core Shifting. If a core does not stay in just the right place in its mold, the walls of the cavity it produces will not be of proper thickness. Shifting of cores is a major cause of defective castings. A core may be of such a shape that it needs internal support. For that purpose, heavy wire or steel rods may be imbedded in it. *Chaplets* (Fig. 8-22) serve to support cores that tend to sag or sink in inadequate core print seats. A chaplet is usually made of the same metal as, and becomes part of, the casting.

A core is subjected to an appreciable buoyant force when immersed in the liquid metal poured into its mold. An anchor, like the one in Fig. 8-22, prevents the core from rising. Chaplets also serve this purpose.

A core immersed in heavy metal is buoyed up by a force proportional to the difference between its mass and the mass of the metal displaced. As an example, a

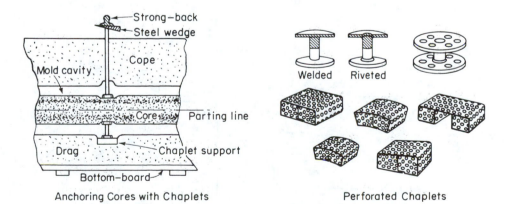

Anchoring Cores with Chaplets   Perforated Chaplets

Figure 8-22 Application of a chaplet and anchor to support a core, and a few examples of chaplets.

sand core with a volume of 1 dm³ has a mass of 1.6 kg. Molten iron has a mass of 7.2 kg/dm³. A force of $(7.2 - 1.6) \times 9.806 = 60$ kN must be resisted to keep the core submerged. The gravitational constant is 9.806. In other units, a sand core with a volume of 1 ft³ weighs about 100 lb, and molten iron 450 lb/ft³. The force acting to raise that core is 350 lb.

Core-making Machines.   Cores of regular shapes and sections may be extruded in a machine like that illustrated in Fig. 8-23 and cut to length. A central vent hole is left by a wire extending from the center of the screw.

Large cores are made like molds in jolt-rollover, sand slinger, and other machines. Small and medium-size irregularly shaped cores may be made by hand but in quantities are produced on a *core blowing machine*. This machine blows sand by compressed air through a core plate with holes arranged to pack the sand evenly and firmly in the core box. Each core box must be designed properly to release the air but retain the sand in a uniformly dense compact form.

Core Baking.   Drying alone is sufficient for many cores, but others (not green sand or cold cured) are bonded by oils and must be baked for ultimate hardness and strength. The purpose of baking is to drive off moisture, oxidize the oil, and polymerize the binder.

A uniform temperature and controlled heating are necessary for baking an oil-bonded sand core. With linseed oil, a major binder as an example, the temperature is raised at a moderate rate, is held at about 200°C (400°F) for about 1 hour, and then is allowed to fall slowly to room conditions. If the same core is baked quickly at 260°C (500°F), it will be overbaked on the surface and underbaked at the center.

The size of a core affects baking. If care is not taken, the outer surface of the core will first bake and attain maximum strength. Then while the inside is curing, the outside will overbake and lose strength. This can be avoided by making the center of

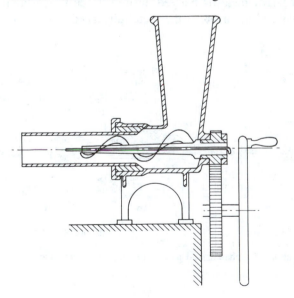

Figure 8-23   Core extrusion machine.

a large core of a porous material such as coke or cinders to allow oxygen to get to the center of the core so that oxidation and polymerization can take place.

PATTERNS

A *pattern* is a form used to prepare and produce a mold cavity. It is another tool in the hands of a foundryman. It has been said that a poor casting may be produced from a good pattern, but a good casting will not be made from a poor pattern.

The designer of a casting must look forward to the pattern to assure economical production. The design should be as simple as possible to make the pattern easy to draw from the sand and avoid more cores than necessary.

Types of Patterns. Many molds are made from *loose patterns*. Such a pattern has essentially the shape of the casting with perhaps forms for sprues, risers, etc., attached. Several examples are given in Fig. 8-24. This is the cheapest pattern to make but the most time consuming to use. A loose pattern may be made in one or more pieces. For instance, a two-piece pattern is normally *split* into cope and drag parts to facilitate molding. For a part difficult to mold, some *loose pieces* may be removable to allow the pattern to collapse for withdrawal from the sand that would otherwise not be possible.

An original casting or an assembly of the pieces of a broken casting may serve in an emergency as a loose pattern. Of course, the part needs to be built up to allow for shrinkage.

Patterns fastened permanently to a board or *match plate* are known as *mounted patterns*. A main advantage is that a mounted pattern is easier than a loose pattern to use and store. Another advantage is that the gating system can be mounted on a match plate, and thus the time required to cut the gating system in the mold can be eliminated. Mounted patterns cost more than loose patterns, but when many castings are

Figure 8-24 Several wood and metal loose patterns.

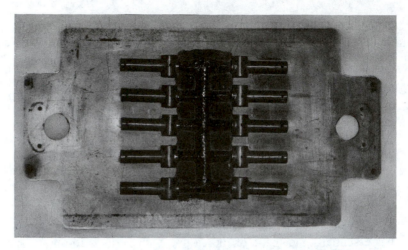

Figure 8-25   Match plate pattern.

to be made from a pattern, the time saved in operation warrants the cost of mounting the pattern. Patterns for a number of pieces may be mounted on one matchplate as shown in Fig. 8-25.

A *core box* is essentially a type of pattern into which sand is rammed or packed to form a core as illustrated in Fig. 8-26.

Symmetrical molds and cores, particularly in large sizes, are sometimes shaped by means of *sweeps* as illustrated in Fig. 8-27. The sweep is a flat board with an outline of the cross section of the part to be made and is revolved around a central axis to clear away excess sand inside the mold.

Pattern Material.   Wood is the most common material for patterns. It is easy to work and readily available. Properly selected and kiln-dried mahogany, walnut, white pine, and sugar pine are often used. Sugar pine is most often used because it

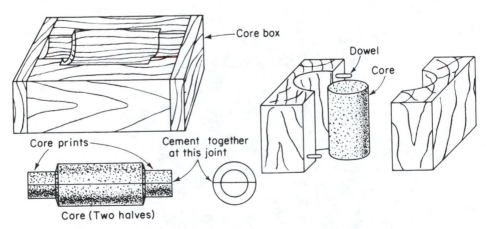

Figure 8-26   Typical core boxes.

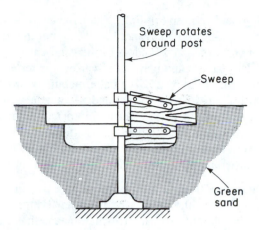

Sweep rotates around post

Sweep

Green sand

Figure 8-27 Sweep pattern.

is easily worked and is generally free from warping and cracking. Moisture in the wood should be about 5 to 6% to avoid warping, shrinking, or expanding of the finished pattern.

Metal patterns may be loose or mounted. If usage warrants a metal pattern, then the pattern probably should be mounted on a plate and include the gating system. Metal is used when a large number of castings are desired from a pattern or when conditions are too severe for wooden patterns. Metal patterns wear well. Another advantage of a metal pattern is freedom from warping in storage. Commonly a metal pattern is itself cast from a master pattern and can be replaced readily if damaged or worn.

Patterns are made of plaster and plastics. Plaster patterns are easy to make; they can be cast where original molds are available. However, plaster is brittle and not suitable for molding large numbers of sand castings. Plaster molds are described in Chap. 9. Plastics serve in several ways for pattern making. Some conventional patterns are made of abrasion-resistant plastics with cost and durability between wood and metal. Another use of certain plastics is to make emergency patterns quickly or to salvage worn or broken patterns. For example, a broken machine part or worn pattern may be built up by layers of fibers and plastic resin to allow for shrinkage. This may serve as a pattern in the sand for a few pieces or to make a plaster mold in which plastic resin is cast for longer life.

The *evaporative casting process* (ECP), also called *full mold*, (FM), *lost foam*, or *lost pattern casting*, utilizes a foamed polystyrene pattern embedded in the sand and vaporized as the molten metal fills the mold. Each pattern is consumed for one casting, and originally the process was confined to producing one or a few castings of a kind. The patterns were carved from polystyrene board stock. Developments have led to the production of automobile cylinder blocks, crankshafts, water pumps, and the like in large quantities. Typically for such work, polystyrene beads mixed with pentane are heated and expanded in a die on a molding press. Sections can be joined to make a complex pattern, and risers, runners, and sprues added. The surface of a pattern is painted with a ceramic slurry to help prevent burning the sand. There are no parting lines and no fins on the casting, and no need for draft, which may save several hundred kilograms (pounds) on a large casting. Fillets do not have to be put in the mold unless required for strength of the part. Cores and binders in the sand can be eliminated.

An indication of the relative costs and benefits of various patterns can be given for the bracket on the middle right of Fig. 8-24. The pattern could be made of foamed plastic for a single casting for about $5 for material and $50 for labor and probably would not need a core. Such a pattern of wood should cost around $250 and be serviceable for 300 pieces. In metal on a match plate, the pattern would cost $425 and serve for 5000 or more pieces. Two such patterns on a match plate with an aluminum core box would cost $600 but would almost double the rate of production.

Pattern Layout.   The *parting line* represents the surface that divides a pattern into the parts that form the cavities of the cope (top) and drag (bottom) of the mold. If at all possible, the parting line should be straight, which means that a simple plane divides the pattern into cope and drag sections. A straight parting line is particularly desirable for a loose piece pattern to enable the sections to lie flat on the molding board. An example is given in Fig. 8-28. A straight parting line is not necessary for a match plate but often makes the pattern easier to fabricate.

Some means are necessary to support and position cores in molds. These are in the forms of extensions, pads, and bosses on the cores and are called *core prints* (Fig. 8-26). A core print must be large enough to support the core. The core weight is carried by the drag, and buoyancy is resisted by the cope.

Pattern Shrinkage Allowance.   As metal solidifies and cools, it shrinks and contracts in size. To compensate for this, a pattern is made larger than the finished casting by an amount called *shrinkage allowance*. Although contraction is volumetric, the correction for it is usually expressed linearly. Dimensions are not shown oversize on a part or pattern drawing to allow for shrinkage, but the patternmaker measures to the finished dimensions with *shrink rules*. Such a rule has a scale that is longer than standard by a definite proportion such as 5, 10, or 15 mm/m ($\frac{1}{16}$, $\frac{1}{8}$, or $\frac{3}{16}$ in./ft). Shrinkage is different for different metals, different shapes of castings of the same metal, and different molding and casting methods. As an example, light- and medium-steel castings of simple design and no cores require an allowance of 20 mm/m ($\frac{1}{4}$ in./ft), and a rule with such a scale is used to make their patterns. In comparison, an allowance of 15 mm/m ($\frac{3}{16}$ in./ft) is adequate for pipes and valves of the same metal because their molds and cores offer considerable resistance to contraction. Typical shrinkage allow-

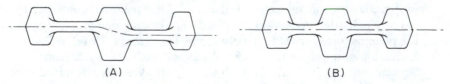

          (A)   (B)

Figure 8-28   The parting line of design (A) is not straight, and the piece is harder to cast than (B).

TABLE 8-2 TYPICAL PATTERN SHRINKAGE ALLOWANCES

Shrinkage allowance	Gray cast iron	Cast steel	Aluminum	Brass	Bronze	Magnesium
mm/m	10	20	13	15	10–20	14
in./ft	$\frac{1}{8}$	$\frac{1}{4}$	$\frac{5}{32}$	$\frac{3}{16}$	$\frac{1}{8}-\frac{1}{4}$	$\frac{11}{64}$

Note: For simple uncored castings with dimensions of not over 610 mm (24 in.).

ances are shown in Table 8-2. A master pattern from which metal patterns are cast must have double shrinkage allowance.

Other Allowances. *Machining allowance* is the amount by which dimensions on a casting are made oversize to provide stock for machining. Dimensions on a pattern drawing include machining allowance. The amount of metal left for machining must be no more than necessary but enough to assure that cutters can get an ample cut beneath and completely remove the hard scale and skin on the surface of the casting. What is sufficient depends upon the kind of metal, the shape of the casting, and the methods of casting, cleaning, and machining. Typical machining allowances are shown in Table 8-3.

TABLE 8-3 TYPICAL MACHINING ALLOWANCES

	Cast iron [mm (in.)]	Cast steel [mm (in.)]	Brass, bronze, and aluminum [mm (in.)]
On outside surfaces	2.5 ($\frac{3}{32}$)	3 ($\frac{1}{8}$)	1.5 ($\frac{1}{16}$)
On inside diameters	3 ($\frac{1}{8}$)	5 ($\frac{3}{16}$)	2.5 ($\frac{3}{32}$)

Note: For finishing surfaces of sand castings with dimensions up to about 300 mm (12 in.). Allowance is in mm (in.) added to the total dimension.

Distortion allowance may be added to dimensions of certain objects such as large flat plates and U-shaped castings that are expected to warp on cooling. The purpose of this allowance is to displace the pattern in such a way that the casting will be of the proper shape and size after it distorts in process.

Draft. *Draft* is the taper or slant placed on the sides of a pattern, outward from the parting line as depicted in Fig. 8-29. This allows the pattern to be removed (drawn) from the mold without damaging the sand surface. Draft may be expressed in mm/m or in./ft on a side or in degrees, and the amount needed in each case may depend upon the shape of the casting, the type of pattern, and the process. For example, draft of 10 mm/m ($\frac{1}{8}$ in./ft) may be required for a certain wood pattern. For the same casting, a metal pattern mounted on a molding machine may need only 5 mm/m ($\frac{1}{16}$ in./ft).

Fillets. A *fillet* is a rounded filling along the convergence of two surfaces of a pattern as indicated in Fig. 8-30. The rounded corner thus produced on the casting

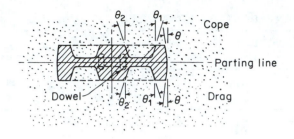

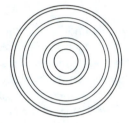

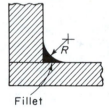

Figure 8-29 Draft on both pieces of a two-piece pattern.

Figure 8-30 Example of a fillet on a pattern.

is also called a fillet. Fillets may be carved in wood patterns but are usually made more inexpensively of wax, plastic, wood coving, or leather. They vary in size from 3 to 25 mm ($\frac{1}{8}$ to 1 in.) radius depending on size, shape, and material of the casting. Fillets obviate sharp angles and corners and thus strengthen both metal patterns and castings. They provide for easier removal of the pattern from the sand, a cleaner mold, freer flow of metal through the mold, less washing of the sand in the mold, and fewer shrinking strains and hot tears between sections as the casting cools.

Locating Pads.   Bosses or pads are commonly added to castings to provide definite and controlled spots for location in machining operations. These *locating* or *foundry pads* are gaged and may be cleaned up by filing to a relationship with the major outline of the workpiece. Care must be taken that such pads do not create too heavy sections and hot spots in a casting.

Color Coding.   All surfaces of a wood pattern are coated with shellac to keep out moisture. Important parts of a pattern may be colored for identification. Some foundries adhere strictly to a color code; others not at all. A widely accepted color code is one adopted by the American Foundrymen's Society (Fig. 8-31).

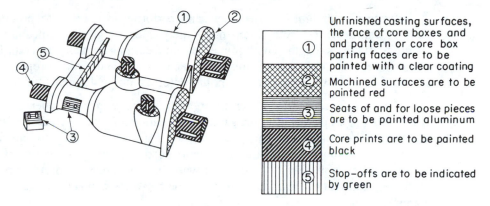

Figure 8-31   Color coding.

SANDS AND OTHER MOLD INGREDIENTS

The primary function of any molding material is to maintain the shape of the mold cavity until the molten metal solidifies. Silica sand is the most widely used molding material, particularly for metals that melt at high temperatures. It serves well because it is readily available, low in cost ($8 to $30 a ton), can be formed easily into complicated shapes, and is able to withstand the molten metal.

The three major parts of a molding sand are (1) the sand grains, which have the necessary refractory properties to withstand the intense heat of the molten metal; (2) a bonding material, which may be natural or added clay, cereal, etc., to hold the grains together; and (3) water to coalesce the grains and binder into a plastic molding material.

Molding Sand.   *Natural sands* contain only the binder mined with them and are used as received with water added. They have the advantages of maintaining moisture content for a long time, having a wide working range for moisture, and permitting easy patching and finishing of molds. Sometimes it is desirable to change the properties of a natural sand by adding bentonite (a clay binder). Such a sand is known as a *semisynthetic sand*.

Synthetic sands are formulated from various ingredients. The base may be a natural sand with some clay content or a washed sand with all clay removed. A binder, such as bentonite, and water are added. The sands have the advantages over natural sands of (1) more uniform grain size, (2) higher refractoriness, (3) moldability with less moisture, (4) requiring less binder, (5) easier control of properties, and (6) the need of less storage space since one kind of sand may suffice for different kinds of castings.

Loam sand is high in clay, as much as 50% or so, and dries hard. *Loam molding* is done by making the mold, usually for a large casting, of brick cemented and lined with loam sand and then dried.

Properties of Sand. The way sand performs in a mold to produce good castings can be tested by and depends largely upon its green permeability, green strength, and dry strength. These properties are determined chiefly by grain fineness, grain shape, clay content, and moisture content of the sand. Other properties of less influence are hot strength, sintering point, deformation, and collapsibility.

Green Permeability. *Permeability* is the porosity from the openings between grains. This gives passage for air, gases, and steam to escape when the molten metal is poured in the mold. Permeability is measured in a common test by passing a definite amount of air through a standard test specimen under specified conditions. The result is expressed by a number $P = 501.2/pt$, where p is the pressure in grams per square centimeter and t is time in minutes. Thus the permeability number is larger as the sand is more porous.

Grain fineness is measured by passing sand through standard sieves, each with a certain number of openings per linear inch. Commercial sands are made up of grains of various sizes. Grain size of a sand is designated by a number that indicates the average size as well as the proportions of smaller or larger grains in the mixture. This is determined by a procedure described in handbooks.

Finer grains in a mold impart a smoother finish to a casting. On the other hand, permeability decreases as the grains and thus the voids between grains become smaller. The same condition results from a large proportion of fine grains in a mixture. The best compromise must be reached. For large castings that require coarse sand for high permeability, the surface of the mold cavity may have a thin layer of fine-grained facing material.

There are two distinct *shapes of sand grains*: angular and rounded, with many degrees of roundness and angularity between the two extremes. Sharp angular grains cannot pack together as closely and consequently give a higher permeability than rounded grains. This is shown in Fig. 8-32.

Both the *type* and the *amount of binder* have a decided effect on the permeability of sand. An illustration of the permeabilities imparted by two common types of clay is given in Fig. 8-33. Over a wide range of moisture content, bentonite was found to give more permeability than fire clay. Permeability may decrease with an increase in clay content, as depicted by the 2% moisture curve for bentonite in Fig. 8-34. The upper curve of 4% moisture content indicates a fairly constant permeability over a wide range of bentonite content. In general, clay content is optimum when present to

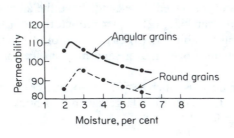

Figure 8-32 Typical relationships of permeability of molding sand to moisture content and grain shape.

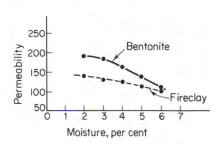

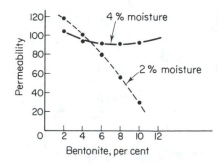

Figure 8-33 Permeability of two kinds of clay for molding sand with various amounts of moisture.

Figure 8-34 How the permeability of a molding sand varies with bentonite content.

the extent of coating the sand particles completely without filling the spaces between the grains.

With a low *moisture content*, fine clay particles clog the spaces between the grains, and permeability is low. More moisture softens and agglutinates the clay around the grains for optimum conditions. An excess of moisture fills the voids and decreases permeability. Peaks of maximum permeability are seen in Fig. 8-32. The optimum moisture content is not the same for all molding sands, although it generally lies between 2 and 8%.

Green Strength. *Green strength* is the strength of a sand ready for molding, and, if the metal is poured immediately, represents the ability of the sand to hold to the shape of the mold. Green strength may be expressed in kilopascals or pounds per square inch required to rupture a standard specimen.

The finer the sand grains, the larger the surface area of a given bulk, and the larger the amount of binder needed to cover the area. The contacts and bonds between grains are more numerous, and thus green strength is higher with finer grains. Figure 8-35 shows that as the grain size becomes larger, the green strength decreases under normal conditions.

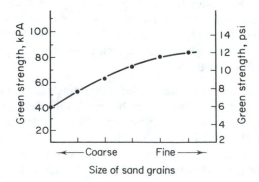

Figure 8-35 Green strength of a molding sand in relation to the sizes of its grains for one set of conditions.

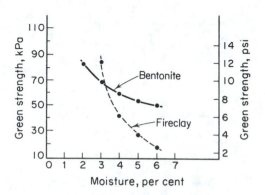

Figure 8-36 Typical relationship of green strength of a molding sand to moisture content and grain shape.

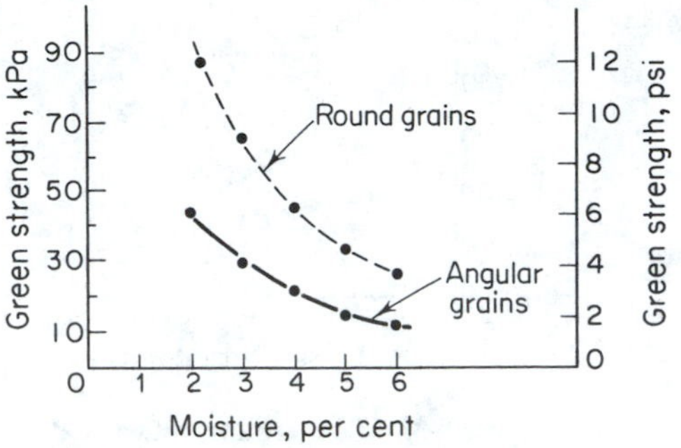

Figure 8-37 Comparison of the green strengths of two samples of molding sand with different clay binders at different moisture levels.

Round grains pack together much more closely than angular grains and as a result are bonded together with a higher green strength than angular grains. A comparison is given for two types of grains in Fig. 8-36.

Some binders provide a higher green strength than others. Comparison of bentonite and fire clay at different moisture levels is given in Fig. 8-37. The green strength increases in proportion to the amount of binder in a molding sand, but, as pointed out earlier, too much binder is detrimental to permeability, and a compromise must be accepted.

The effect of moisture on green strength is similar to the effect on permeability. Green strength increases with the first additions of moisture, reaches a maximum strength, and then starts to decrease as depicted in Fig. 8-38. Also shown is that an excess of moisture has a weakening effect, even nullifying the influence of grain size.

In addition to other factors, mulling or mixing practice affects green strength as will be explained in the section on the preparation of sand.

Dry Strength. *Dry strength* is the strength of sand that has been dried or baked. In general, dry strength varies in the same way as green strength with grain fineness, grain shape, and moisture content. However, different binders can affect dry strength and green strength differently. For example, in contrast to western bentonite, southern bentonite produces a high green strength and a low dry strength, and that is conducive to easy shake out of castings.

Sand Control. Many substances are added to molding sands to impart certain properties or change properties. Many new ones become available each year, particularly substances to minimize heating and save energy. Space is not available here to list many additives, and only the basics are cited. Cereal (such as wheat and corn flour), dextrine, rosin, and similar substances are often added to augment or modify the clay binders. It is important to realize that the action of each additive is somewhat different. Corn flour improves green strength slightly but dry strength markedly.

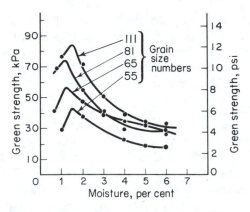

Figure 8-38 How the green strength of molding sand varies for several sizes of grains.

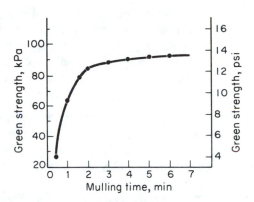

Figure 8-39 Increase in green strength of a molding sand with mulling time.

Wheat flour improves collapsibility. Dextrine binders are a form of sugar and produce a much higher dry strength than do cereal binders but decrease green strength. A rosin-bonded core has a hard surface when baked but absorbs moisture on standing and should be used as soon as possible.

The binder is burned out and the proportion of fine particles is increased when foundry sand is exposed to the heat of molten metal. As a result, green strength and permeability decrease as the sand is reused. By measuring properties periodically with sand-testing equipment, a sand technician is enabled to make appropriate additions to restore the sand before it deteriorates to the point where it must be discarded. Uniform day-to-day properties may be maintained by continuous checks and additions of small amounts of binder.

Sand Preparation. Under a microscope sand grains are seen to exist in clusters of small particles adhering to large particles. This is thought to be the result largely of previous use. Clusters are less refractory and harder to ram than individual particles and need to be broken up, particularly to prepare sand for cores and for facing patterns to make mold linings. Even so, breaking down of the clustered particles is desirable for all sand and is usually done by stirring and kneading it mechanically. A popular machine for that purpose is a *muller* which kneads, shears, slices through, and stirs the sand in a heavy iron pot by means of several revolving rollers and knives. The time needed for mulling depends upon the type of muller and the type and amount of binder. After the optimum length of mixing time in each case, there is no further increase in green strength as shown by the example in Fig. 8-39.

Mulling sand distributes the binder over the grains. Thus less binder is required for satisfactory green strength and permeability is higher than with hand-mixed sand.

Sand is *aerated* to make it fluffy so it flows readily around and takes up the details of the pattern. This is done to some extent in mulling. One device for aeration is a *sand cutter* which hurls the sand from a rapidly moving belt against bars or springs to break the grains apart.

Sands are mixed from the ingredients and by the methods described to many formulas for various metals and purposes. For instance, for steel castings three sands may be prepared: one for the green facing sand, another for the green backing sand, and still another for facing sands that are to be surface dried in the mold by a torch. Formulas for foundry sands are given in reference texts and handbooks.

Core Sand.   Core sand must have much the same properties of permeability, cohesiveness, and refractoriness as molding sand but must also possess collapsibility and friability. *Collapsibility* means that the core gives way easily as the casting cools and shrinks to avoid inducing hot tears and cracks in the metal. *Friability* means that the core crumbles and falls apart when it must be removed from the casting. These properties are imparted by the type and amount of binder, additives to the binder, and by the curing of the cores. For example, if cracks occur in the cored area of a casting, a weaker binder or less binder may be used or a small amount of wood flour may be added to the binder.

Core sand mixes are started with clean dry silica sand. Among various binders used for core sand are corn flour, dextrine, fish oil, raw linseed oil, and commercial core oils. Linseed oil is an ingredient in most proprietary core oils. A long list could be made of binders, each to impart a particular property to the core. As the ingredients are added, the sand is mixed thoroughly in a muller but not excessively, which would cause stickiness.

Oils and other core binders that must be baked have been largely replaced by other substances that require less energy. Popular among these is sodium silicate (water glass) that is mixed with the sand and hardened in the core in a few seconds when exposed to carbon dioxide (CO_2) gas. The core can then be used in the mold immediately. A major disadvantage of sodium silicate and some other no-bake binders is that they must be mixed with the sand only a short time before use because they harden rather soon on exposure to air. Other no-bake binders with longer shelf lives are available and widely used. Among them are plastics materials that can be catalyzed in the core for quick hardening. One in particular is hardened by exposure to sulfur dioxide (SO_2) for a few seconds. New cold-cure substances are being brought out each year and are too numerous for all to be mentioned in an introductory textbook.

MELTING METALS IN THE FOUNDRY

The reduction and melting of iron and steel in blast furnaces, basic oxygen converters, and electric furnaces have been discussed in Chap. 2. Most steel is cast from furnaces of the types already described, but over half of gray iron and malleable iron base for castings is melted in the cupola. Electric furnaces are being used more and more for melting iron. They cost more to operate than cupolas but do not have the pollution control problems and expenses.

The Cupola.   The cupola is simple and economical for melting pig and scrap iron. It is essentially a vertical steel shrouded and refractory-lined furnace. A view of the construction of a typical cupola is in Fig. 8-40. Cupolas are made in many sizes,

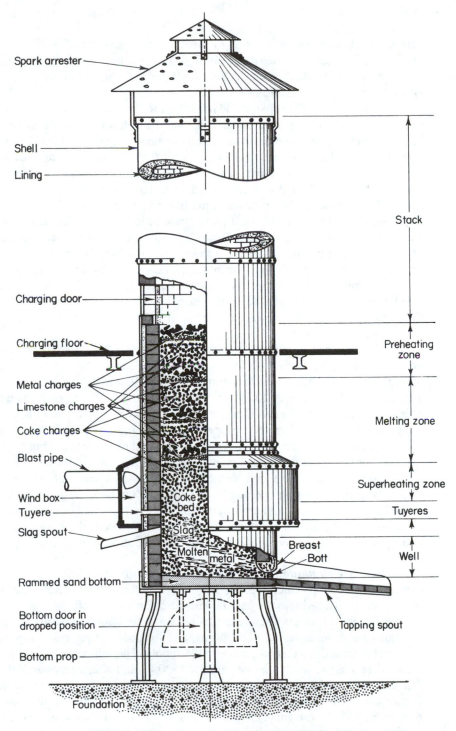

Figure 8-40 External and internal views of a cupola.

commonly about 1 to 2 m (ca. 4 to 7 ft) in outside diameter and 9 to over 12 m (ca. 30 to 40 ft) high. These sizes may turn out 5 to 10 metric tons (ca. 5 to 10 tons) of melted metal per hour. A 4-ft-diameter cupola costs about $100,000 installed with a blower and all auxiliary equipment.

A cupola must be prepared and heated carefully to avoid damage. The refractory lining is repaired or replaced as needed, and the bottom doors are propped shut. A layer of sand sloping toward the tap hole is rammed over the bottom. Excelsior, rags, and wood are placed on the sand to protect it from the initial charge of fuel, which may be a meter or more (several feet) thick, and to ignite the fuel. Materials are charged through a door 4 to 8 m (ca. 15 to 25 ft) above the bottom.

After the initial charge has become hot, alternate layers of fuel and metal with flux are added. The fuel may be a good grade of low sulfur coke, anthracite coal, or carbon briquettes. The flux to help form slag to remove impurities and retard oxidation of metal is usually limestone, but sometimes soda ash, fluorspar, and proprietary substances are added. The proportion of metal to fuel by weight ranges in various practices from about 6:1 to 12:1. A ratio of 10:1, which is common, means that 100 kg of coke are provided to melt 1 metric ton (200 lb of coke for a ton) of iron. Fuel cost is lower with a lower proportion of coke, but the melting and output rates are higher with more coke.

After the charge and cupola have had a chance to become heated uniformly, in an hour or two, the forced draft is started. Air is blown through the wind box and tuyeres around the hearth into the furnace. About 950 m³ of air are required to melt 1 metric ton of iron (about 30,000 ft³/ton). The metal begins to melt. The *tap hole* is plugged with a bott of clay. The molten metal seeps down through the coke and collects at the bottom. Tapping is done by breaking the clay plug in the tap hole. Flow may be permitted at intervals or may be continuous during the melt. For the latter case, the melting rate must be in balance with the capacity of the tap hole. The slag floats on top of the metal. If the molten metal is allowed to accumulate in the hearth, the slag flows off through an opening higher than the tap hole, called the *cinder notch*, in the back of the cupola. Otherwise, the slag may be skimmed off the metal as it flows out of the cupola. When sufficient metal has been melted, the bottom of the cupola is dropped to spill the remaining contents onto the ground to cool.

Cupola Calculations. The cupola does little to refine the metal, and the composition of its product depends largely upon what is put into it. The proportions of the metals charged into the cupola must be calculated carefully to assure a uniform and predictable product. These calculations are based upon knowing the amounts of carbon, silicon, manganese, phosphorus, and sulfur in the pig and scrap iron and the nature of the reactions that take place in the cupola. The following example shows how the calculations are made; in one case for 1500 kg and alternately for 3000 lb of iron fed into the cupola. The typical raw materials available in the storage yard of the foundry are listed in Table 8-4 with their analyses. In other foundries still other materials, such as machinery steel scrap and iron of various analyses, may also be stocked depending upon the sources of supply and the desired product.

TABLE 8-4 COMPOSITIONS OF SOME TYPICAL METALS FOR CUPOLA MELTING (%)

	Carbon	Silicon	Manganese	Phosphorus	Sulfur
No. 1 pig iron	3.5	2.50	0.72	0.18	0.016
No. 2 pig iron	3.5	3.00	0.63	0.12	0.018
Cast-iron scrap	3.4	2.30	0.50	0.20	0.030
Returns (risers, defective castings, etc.)	3.3	2.50	0.65	0.17	0.035

On the basis of current practices and results in this foundry, it is decided to make up the charge of 10% No. 1 pig iron, 20% No. 2 pig iron, 30% new scrap iron, and 40% returns from previous melts. The amount of each element that may be expected in the product can now be ascertained on the basis of the reactions in the cupola.

1. The amount of carbon in the iron remains substantially unchanged during the process. Some carbon is oxidized, but about the same amount is picked up from the fuel. The amount contributed by each ingredient is:

	For 1500 kg of iron:	*For 3000 lb of iron:*
No. 1 pig iron	$1500 \times 0.10 \times 0.035 = 5.25$ kg	$3000 \times 0.10 \times 0.035 = 10.5$ lb
No. 2 pig iron	$1500 \times 0.20 \times 0.035 = 10.5$ kg	$3000 \times 0.20 \times 0.035 = 21.0$ lb
New scrap iron	$1500 \times 0.30 \times 0.034 = 15.3$ kg	$3000 \times 0.30 \times 0.034 = 30.6$ lb
Returns	$1500 \times 0.40 \times 0.033 = 19.8$ kg	$3000 \times 0.40 \times 0.033 = 39.6$ lb
	50.85 kg	101.7 lb

The final percentage of carbon equals

$$\frac{50.85}{1500} \times 100 = 3.39\% = \frac{101.7}{3000} \times 100$$

2. The silicon content can be expected to be reduced 10% by oxidation. The amount of silicon in the charge is:

	For 1500 kg of iron:	*For 3000 lb of iron:*
No. 1 pig iron	$1500 \times 0.10 \times 0.025 = 3.75$ kg	$3000 \times 0.10 \times 0.025 = 7.5$ lb
No. 2 pig iron	$1500 \times 0.20 \times 0.030 = 9.0$ kg	$3000 \times 0.20 \times 0.030 = 18.0$ lb
New scrap iron	$1500 \times 0.30 \times 0.023 = 10.35$ kg	$3000 \times 0.30 \times 0.023 = 20.7$ lb
Returns	$1500 \times 0.40 \times 0.025 = 15.0$ kg	$3000 \times 0.40 \times 0.025 = 30.0$ lb
	38.1 kg	76.2 lb

The final percentage of silicon equals

$$\frac{38.1 \times 0.9}{1500} \times 100 = 2.29\% = \frac{76.2 \times 0.9}{3000} \times 100$$

3. The manganese content is expected to be reduced 20% by oxidation. In the same way as for the other elements, the manganese content is estimated to be 9.12 kg for a 1500-kg charge and 18.24 lb for a 3000-lb charge, and the final percentage of manganese equals

$$\frac{9.12 \times 0.8}{1500} \times 100 = 0.49\% = \frac{18.24 \times 0.8}{3000} \times 100$$

4. Phosphorus losses in the cupola are negligible. In the same way as for the other elements, the amount of phosphorus in the charge is calculated to be 2.55 kg for 1500 kg of iron and 5.10 lb for 3000 lb of iron. From this the final percentage of phosphorus equals

$$\frac{2.55}{1500} \times 100 = 0.17\% = \frac{5.10}{3000} \times 100$$

5. The iron loses almost no sulfur in melting but picks up about 4% of the sulfur in the coke. The quantity of sulfur in the metal charge is calculated to be 0.423 kg for 1500 kg of iron and 0.846 lb for 3000 lb of iron. The iron to coke ratio is to be 8:1, and the sulfur content of the coke is known to be 0.50%. Thus the quantity of sulfur in the coke is $(1500/8)0.005 = 0.9375$ kg, and of that 4% or 0.0375 kg is added to the iron for a 1500-kg charge. Alternatively, the sulfur in the coke is $(3000/8)0.005 = 1.875$ lb, and 0.075 lb is added to a 3000-lb charge. The final sulfur content is estimated to be

$$\frac{(0.423 + 0.0375) \times 100}{1500} = 0.03\% = \frac{(0.846 + 0.075) \times 100}{3000}$$

In summary, the composition of the iron from the cupola is estimated to be carbon 3.39, silicon 2.29, manganese 0.49, phosphorus 0.17, and sulfur 0.03%.

If more or less of any of the elements is wanted, the results can be changed by specifying raw materials in different amounts and of different kinds and by adding ferro alloys of elements to the metal in the ladle after melting. These are less expensive than the pure elements. For instance, if in the example 2.50% silicon is desired, about 2 kg of 50% ferrosilicon can be added to each 500 kg of molten iron. Sometimes elements are added by bubbling gas carriers through the metal in the ladle.

Melting of Nonferrous Metals.   Some nonferrous metal melting is done in almost all types of furnaces. More and more is done in induction furnaces for reasons of convenience, ease of operation, and fewer environmental problems, but oil- and gas-fired crucible furnaces have advantages. Although the fuel cost is about the same for both types of furnaces, an electric furnace may cost 10 to 15 times as much initially as an oil- or gas-fired one. Modern electric furnaces have complicated controls and are costly to service, whereas all a fossil-fuel furnace needs is relining from time to time. On the other hand, oil- and gas-fired furnaces create heat, fumes, and noise problems. A stack is needed, and a baghouse may be required depending upon local environmental regulations. It is difficult to find people to work around hot fumes, particularly in hot weather.

Two types of crucible furnaces are stationary and tilting furnaces. The *stationary type of crucible furnace* requires that the crucible be lifted in and out for pouring. A cross section of this type of furnace is shown in Fig. 8-41. When a stationary furnace is sunk into the floor or deck of a foundry, it is known as a *pit-type furnace*.

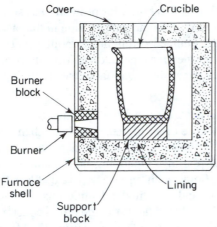

Cover Crucible

Burner block

Burner

Furnace shell

Support block

Lining

Figure 8-41 Cross section of a stationary type crucible furnace. A furnace of this kind with auxiliary equipment and a crucible having a capacity of 250 lb of brass or 120 lb of aluminum costs about $5500.

Figure 8-42 Tilting type crucible furnace. A furnace of this type with a crucible capacity of about 250 lb of brass or 120 lb of aluminum costs about $7500 with auxiliary equipment. (Courtesy Lindberg Engineering Co.)

A *tilting type of crucible furnace*, Fig. 8-42, requires a crucible with a suitable lip for pouring metal when the furnace is tilted.

Most nonferrous metals and alloys oxidize, absorb gases and other substances, and form dross readily when heated. Various practices are followed for each kind of metal to preserve purity and obtain good castings. Space does not permit descriptions of all, and full information may be found in treatises on the subject. The melting of aluminum will be treated in some detail here to point out the nature of the problems and principles.

Aluminum and its alloys have a marked tendency to absorb hydrogen when heated. This gas is released on cooling and causes detrimental pinholes and porosity in castings. Exposure to hydrogen-forming media, such as water vapor, must be avoided. Clean and dry melting stock and crucible are important; a slight excess of air in the furnace atmosphere is desirable.

Molten aluminum reacts readily with oxygen to form a film on the surface. Fortunately the dross serves as a good shield against hydrogen and further oxidation if not broken. Excessive dross may become trapped in the metal, particularly if the metal is agitated, and appear as defects in the final casting. Both the amount of oxidation and the tendency to absorb hydrogen increase with temperature and time. Excessive temperature also causes coarse grains in castings. These considerations dictate the melting procedure for best results. Aluminum should not be heated more than about 50°C (100°F) above the necessary pouring temperature. Temperature is checked with an immersion pyrometer. The melting time should be short with as little agitation as possible.

Aluminum does not ordinarily require as much flux for protection as some other metals because of its oxide film. However, at times the gas or oxide in the metal must be reduced. Chlorine or nitrogen may be bubbled through the molten metal. Solid fluxes, containing aluminum or zinc chloride, may be added. Various proprietary fluxes are commonly used to help dry the surface dross and facilitate skimming it from the metal.

Vacuum Melting.   It has become necessary to develop ways of melting and pouring some metals and alloys in the absence of air to make and keep them pure and clean. This is done in a number of ways. A typical installation is depicted in Fig. 8-43 and represents true vacuum melting and pouring. Operating temperatures with this equipment range up to 1650°C (3000°F). Some such furnaces operate at less than one millionth of normal atmospheric pressure, and most under 10 microns. The metal in the crucible is melted by induction, and the induced field stirs the liquid constantly and aids in the release of gases. This is called *vacuum induction melting* (VIM). Energy for melting is supplied by electron beams (Chap. 14) in some installations. The metal is poured by tilting the crucible; in some cases the whole furnace tilts.

Arrangements like that already described eliminate from the casting process the two contaminating media of air and slag. The third source of impurities, the crucible, is neutralized by the *consumable electrode* method. This utilizes an arc in a vacuum, between an initial charge and an electrode of the metal melted, inside a water-cooled copper crucible. As metal is melted off the electrode by the arc, it is quickly solidified,

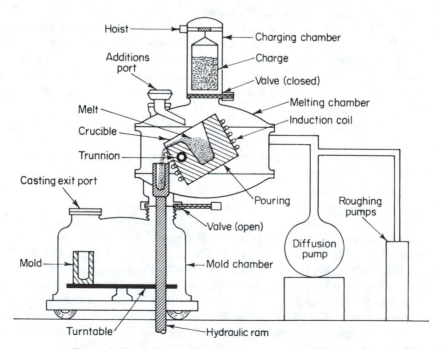

Figure 8-43   Schematic drawing of a vacuum melting furnace.

especially in contact with the cooled crucible. Diffusion between crucible and melt is minimized, and crystalline structure is improved. The process is called *vacuum arc remelting* (VAR) and is commonly a second step after VIM for high-purity alloys.

VADER is a new process that remelts like VAR but is faster and produces smaller grains in the metal. Two ingots to be remelted are held horizontally in line in a vacuum over a mold. An arc is struck between the ingots, and drops of molten metal fall into the mold. All the energy is used for melting, and none to maintain a molten pool. Melting rates at least three times that for VAR are reported.

A process called *degassing* entails pouring only in a vacuum. The metal is melted by conventional means in air. The vacuum need not be extremely high to draw off substantial proportions of hydrogen and other gases. Four common methods are depicted in Fig. 8-44. Stream degassing is done with a ladle of molten steel positioned over an evacuated chamber containing another ladle or ingot mold. When the nozzle is opened, steel pours into the chamber, giving out gas as it falls. Only one ladle is needed for ladle degassing; it is filled with molten steel and placed in the vacuum chamber which is then evacuated. During the operation, continuous stirring, by induction or helium injected at the bottom, constantly brings untreated steel to the

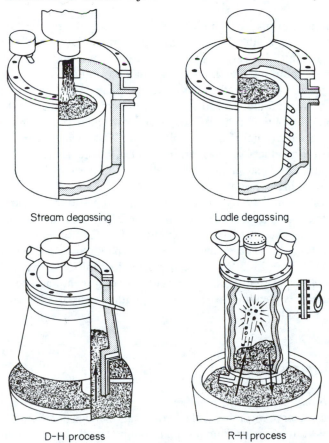

Stream degassing   Ladle degassing

D-H process   R-H process

Figure 8-44 Techniques of vacuum degassing. (From *Metal Progress*, Sept. 1964. ©American Society for Metals.)

surface for degassing. In the D-H and R-H processes increments of molten steel are degassed in small chambers. The D-H chamber (or the ladle) surges up and down; on the first stroke, steel enters the chamber and is degassed, and on the reverse, it sinks back into the ladle. In contrast, the R-H process is continuous. Molten steel, aided by the injection of gas in the up-leg, flows up into the chamber, is degassed, and then drops back down the down-leg.

Uranium, titanium, and alloys with reactive elements can be effectively cast only in a vacuum. In addition, vacuum melting improves the properties of metals, such as steel and aluminum, that can be melted by ordinary means. Raw materials of good grade are, of course, necessary for a superior product. Metals melted and cast in a vacuum can be kept pure because they are not exposed to new contamination and can be further purified because gases are drawn from them. No oxidizers, such as manganese and silicon in steel, are needed, and no slag is formed. In vacuum melting, precise amounts of pure carbon or hydrogen may be added to reduce oxides. As gases are evolved, they are extracted by the pumps, and the reactions driven to completion. The addition of highly reactive elements like zirconium, titanium, and aluminum to an alloy that requires them may be delayed until after the gas content of the melt has been depleted.

Vacuum-melted steel may contain 3 to 20 parts of oxygen per million parts of steel. This is about one-twentieth of the proportion in commercial air-melted steel; and other impurities are reduced to about the same extent. Pure and clean metals are substantially stronger, more ductile, and more resistant to fatigue and corrosion. For instance, the Charpy impact strength at room temperature has been reported to be 298 J (220 ft-lb) for vacuum-melted 430 stainless steel compared to 11 J (8 ft-lb) for air-melted. The benefits obtained have been found particularly desirable for high-temperature alloys, such as nickel and cobalt alloys. Thus vacuum melting is especially in demand for products such as turbine blades, buckets, bearings, and castings, after-burner parts, highest-quality tool steels, and all parts which must serve at high temperatures with high strength.

Vacuum melting is inherently more costly than air melting. Although liquid melts up to 14 metric tons (15 tons) are reported for VIM, most installations are of much smaller capacity because of large equipment costs. Melts of tens of metric tons (tons) are produced by VAR, and as much as several hundred metric tons (tons) by degassing. An 1100-kg (ca. 2500-lb)-capacity production unit of the type illustrated in Fig. 8-43 may cost several million dollars with all equipment and accessories. A 25-kg (ca. 50-lb)-capacity vacuum-melting furnace with accessories for experimental work costs around $50,000.

POURING AND CLEANING CASTINGS

Pouring Methods.   Common practice is to run the molten metal from the cupola or furnace into a large receiving ladle. From that, metal is distributed to smaller pouring ladles. These range in size from ones that can be handled by one man to huge crane ladles holding hundreds of tons. The bottoms of ladles and the sides of large ladles are lined with fire brick. The bottom and sides of a ladle are daubed with an inner coating of fire sand and clay, which is hardened by baking.

Liquid metal may be delivered to a mold in one or more ladles. The important concern is to have sufficient metal to fill the mold, gates, and risers completely. Pouring must be done continuously and at a uniform rate until the mold is full to keep the slag from settling. The metal temperature must be high enough for the fluid to pour easily and rapidly. Slag is always present on molten iron to some degree and must be kept out of the mold to avoid weak slag pockets in the casting. Figure 8-17 gives a view of a hand-pouring operation.

Foundry practices differ in some respects for small quantities from those for large-quantity production. A small quantity may be several pieces up to a few thousand castings of a kind. Low-cost patterns are used with universal handling equipment for a variety of work. Today it is common to have a computerized system guiding the flow of work even with small batches.

It is estimated that over 90% of foundries are automated for large-quantity output. Examples of such systems are given in Figs. 8-45 and 8-46. In common production practice a match plate containing the drag half of a pattern is rigged to a molding machine on which drag halves of a mold are produced continuously. These are placed on an endless conveyor. Cores are set in position as each drag moves along. Cope halves are molded on another machine and placed on the drag halves. The closed molds pass alongside ladles travelling at the same speed on a parallel conveyor and are filled. After the molds cool enough, they are dumped onto a grating to strip out the castings. The flasks return to the molding machines, and the cycle is repeated. The iron pouring system of Fig. 8-46 is operated by two supervisory employees. A typical casting line costs in excess of $500,000.

In a modern high-production process called *no-flask molding*, sand molds are squeezed to shape in a chamber and pushed out of the machine into a line of molds. The molds are set with parting lines vertical and are kept closed and supported by being pressed together back to back in the line. Metal is poured into the molds at about the middle of the line. As each new mold is pushed into place, the line is moved ahead, and a new mold is shoved off onto a conveyor and stripped. This system is depicted in Fig. 8-47(A).

In the *vacuum casting* (V) process, a heated sheet of plastic is fitted over the pattern and placed in a flask. The flask is vibrated while being filled with a fine, dry, binder-free sand. The top of the flask is covered with another sheet of plastic. A vacuum of about 380 mm (15 in.) of mercury is drawn through the sand during pouring and cooling. There is no ramming, jolting, or squeezing, and no wet sand. The mold falls apart when the vacuum is released. The production rate may not be as high as with conventional molding, but smaller tolerance and better surface finish are obtained with some castings.

Cleaning Castings.   After castings have solidified and cooled, they are removed from the sand and cleaned.

Figure 8-45   Car-type mold conveyor (below) and monorail ladle conveyor (above) for production pouring. (Courtesy Link-Belt Co.)

A casting may be separated from the sand in various ways. A rudimentary way for a small casting is to dump the mold assembly upside down, remove the bottom board and flask, and then pull the casting from the sand with a hook bar. After being removed from the sand, the casting is rapped with a hammer to dislodge any clinging material. Essentially the same is done mechanically to castings made in large quantities. The flasks are emptied on a vibrating metal grating. The sand falls through, and the castings are pushed or jolted along to fall off, stripped, at the end onto a conveyor. Sand is reprocessed for future use.

Gates are often broken off gray iron castings by hammers. They are removed from steel and nonferrous castings by sawing or flame cutting. Fins, projections, and other excesses of metal may be ground or chipped away. Finally, clean surfaces are obtained by shot or sand blasting or wire brushing. Small castings may be tumbled with scraps of metal. These processes are described in Chap. 29.

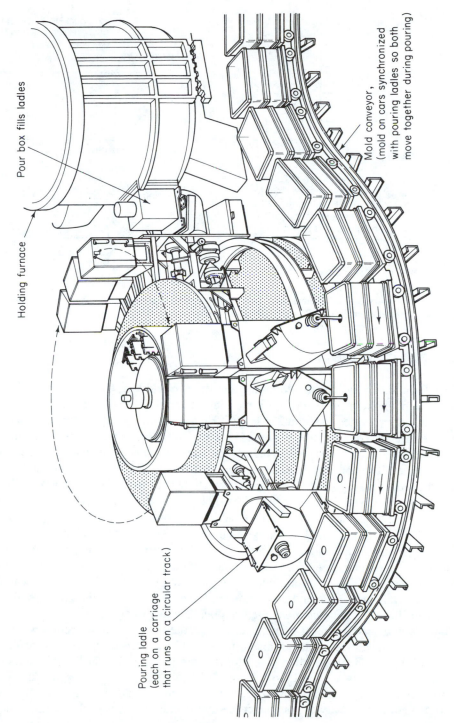

Pour box fills ladles

Holding furnace

Pouring ladle
(each on a carriage
that runs on a circular track)

Mold conveyor,
(mold on cars synchronized
with pouring ladles so both
move together during pouring)

Figure 8-46 Sketch of an automated molding line capable of pouring 110 metric tons (120 tons) of iron per hour.

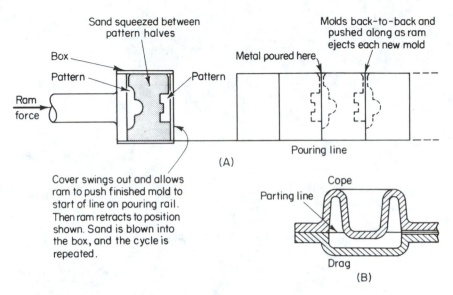

Figure 8-47   Schematics of two modern production sand casting processes: (A) no-flask molding; (B) section of a shell mold.

SHELL MOLD CASTING

Shell mold casting, developed during and since World War II, makes use of fine sand with a phenolic resin binder for a molding material. This mixture is deposited on a metal pattern heated to about 230°C (450°F); a layer around the pattern coalesces, and after a fraction of a minute, the excess is dumped off the pattern. The thickness of the shell depends upon the time the bulk of the material stays on the pattern and is usually from 5 to 10 mm ($\frac{3}{16}$ to $\frac{3}{8}$ in.), as required for the job. The resin is cured, and the shell hardened by baking from 300 to 450°C (600 to 800°F) for a part of a minute. The shell is stripped from the pattern, which is then cleaned and sprayed with a silicone parting compound to prepare it for the next shell.

One method of shell molding is to blow the molding material on the pattern. The material can be deposited uniformly, forced into intricate forms, and controlled in amount. A simpler method consists of placing the heated pattern face down on top of a box partially filled with molding material. The box is turned upside down for the required length of time and then reinverted. The pattern with the green shell is then taken off the box. The *dumping method* does not always produce as accurate shells as the *blowing method* but it is more readily adapted to automatic operation.

Cope and drag shells are made for a mold and joined together as indicated by Fig. 8-47(B). They are often glued together in production, but the thickness of the adhesive film may vary 0.25 to 0.5 mm (0.01 to 0.02 in.), which is not desirable for precision castings. Molds pasted together may be imbedded in sand or shot if reinforcement is necessary to counteract the hydrostatic pressure of the metal. Molds for precision casting are clamped together and, in production, are held in metal backup fixtures, especially for large and heavy castings.

The phenolic resin binder in the shell is mostly burned away, particularly in cores, by the hot metal. The remaining sand is easily stripped from the surface and cleaned from the cavities of the casting by jarring, shaking, and tumbling.

Merits of Shell Molding. Shell molding is more expensive than green sand molding in most cases. This is because the molding material costs four to five times as much as sand alone. Some of this cost, but usually not all, is saved by certain advantages of shell molding. The savings arise because much less sand needs to be worked and handled; the molds are light, easy to handle, and can be made when convenient and stored; gases escape readily through the thin shells and fewer castings are scrapped because of blowholes or pockets; and the process is readily adaptable to mechanization.

The cost of shell molding is justified for the many jobs that it can do better than green sand molding. Complex shapes and intricate parts that cannot be cast at all in green sand can be made by shell molding. Usually, a better finish is obtained and closer tolerances are held by shell molding. Less stock needs to be left for machining castings made to closer tolerances, and often no machining at all is needed. A thin shell does not have the mass chill effect of a thick sand mold. Thus, shell mold castings suffer less from varying cross sections and tend to have softer skins than castings from green sand molds.

METALLURGY OF CASTINGS

Steel castings have low-carbon content and possess essentially the properties attributed to steel in Chaps. 2 and 6. With more carbon, the product is cast iron, with or without appreciable quantities of alloys. Cast iron in its common forms will be discussed in this section.

Cast Iron. The general product cast iron has several commercial forms called gray irons, white cast irons, malleable irons, and nodular cast irons. Also, pig iron, described in Chap. 2, is a form of cast iron. Cast irons contain usually from 2.0 to about 4.5% carbon, and typically their constituents are those represented in that range of the iron-carbon diagram of Fig. 4-13. The various forms of cast iron represent various combinations of the iron and carbon and their compounds, depending upon how the material is cooled and the presence of silicon and other alloys.

Molten cast iron contains much but not all of the carbon in solution as iron carbide. When the iron is cast and cools, its ability to hold the carbide in solution decreases. At moderate cooling rates common in practice, much of the iron carbide decomposes, and the carbon is precipitated out as graphite flakes. As the metal becomes solid, iron carbide, called *cementite*, is restrained from further breakdown and ends up in a pearlitic structure. Pearlite has been defined in Chap. 4. The result is a pearlite matrix with graphite flakes dispersed throughout. A microscopic view of

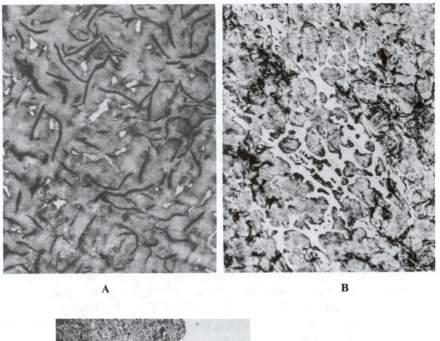

A   B

Figure 8-48 Photomicrographs of (A) gray cast iron (×200); (B) white cast iron (×200) (courtesy R. J. Raudebaugh); (C) nodular cast iron (×500) (from R. W. Lindsay and J. M. Snook, *American Foundryman*, Nov. 1953.)

C

such a structure is shown in Fig. 8-48(A). The edges of the graphite flakes appear as heavy black lines. The flakes have no strength of their own, break up the continuity of the iron, and make the cast iron weak and brittle. The free graphite imparts the nominal coloring to *gray iron*, which usually contains 3 to 4% carbon.

Other forms of cast iron than the gray iron just described result when the metal is cooled at slower or faster rates. Upon slow cooling and particularly with a high silicon and carbon content, considerable ferrite, as well as pearlite, is formed in the matrix because more of the carbon is released. The graphite becomes coarser. The ferrite is softer and not as wearable as pearlite. The product is sometimes called *open* or *soft cast iron*. When the cooling rate is fast, the iron carbide has less chance to decompose before the metal solidifies. Thus more cementite is deposited in the mass than can be accommodated in the pearlite, which must have a definite composition. The presence of cementite makes cast iron hard. When only part of the available carbon appears as dispersed cementite, the product is called *mottled iron* from its appearance. *White cast iron* has its carbon largely as cementite and consequently is extremely hard and brittle. The absence of free carbon is evident in the photomicrograph of Fig. 8-48(B). This condition is caused by very rapid cooling or by additives that stabilize the carbide. It may be desirable to harden certain areas of a casting for wearability. This is achieved by cooling the areas rapidly by means of metal chills in the mold wall, and the product is called *chilled cast iron* in *chilled castings*.

Malleable iron has free carbon in tiny lumps, rather than flakes, in a ferrite matrix, sometimes with pearlite. This makes it ductile, shock resistant, and easily machinable. The structure is obtained by first producing essentially a white iron casting, reheating the casting above the transformation range, and soaking and slowly cooling it. This separates the graphite from the cementite while the metal is solid and prevents the growth of flakes like those that arise when molten metal hardens.

Ductile, *nodular*, or *spheroidal graphite iron* has its graphite in tiny spherulites as depicted by the photomicrograph of Fig. 8-48(C). This form is obtained by adding (just before pouring) minute amounts of magnesium, cerium, or other elements to an iron relatively high in carbon and silicon content. Ductile iron must have a sulfur content below 0.01%.

Elements other than iron and carbon are normally present in cast iron as contamination or additional additives. The properties of cast irons can be varied through wide ranges by adding suitable kinds and amounts of alloying elements. The control of graphitization is an important reason for using alloying elements. Other purposes may be to increase strength or resistance to corrosion, heat, or wear. The principal but not the only alloying elements for cast iron and their purposes are discussed in the following section.

Alloying Elements in Cast Iron.   The most important effect of *silicon* is to promote the decomposition of cementite into ferrite and carbon. The effect increases with the amount of silicon added. Enough should be used for gray iron to decompose all the massive cementite but not the pearlite. Requirements generally range from 0.50 to 3%. A practice of recent years to save energy is to add an excess of silicon to the down sprues in molds to inhibit the formation of hard carbides and avoid the necessity of annealing the castings.

Sulfur exists to some extent in all irons. It comes from pig iron, scrap, and the coke consumed in cupola melting. Sulfur markedly restrains the decomposition of cementite and combines with iron to form iron sulfide, which has a tendency to weaken the grain structure.

Manganese mitigates the effects of sulfur by forming manganese sulfide, which segregates as harmless inclusions. Most irons from American ores contain only 0.06 to 0.12% sulfur, and 0.50 to 0.80% manganese is sufficient. In such amounts, manganese has little effect on the properties of cast iron other than inhibiting the action of the sulfur. In excess, manganese would tend to combine into carbides and make the iron harder.

Phosphorus in most American irons is from 0.1 to 0.90%. Below about 0.50%, phosphorus has little effect upon the properties of the iron. In larger amounts it tends to form brittle iron phosphide which may add some hardness and wearability but weakens the iron and lowers impact strength appreciably. Phosphorus increases the fluidity of molten iron and improves castability in thin sections. Graphite formation is promoted by the increased fluidity.

Nickel acts as a graphitizer but is only about half as effective as silicon. Small amounts help refine the sizes of grains and graphite flakes. Most additions are from 0.25 to 2.0%. Larger amounts, from 14 to 38%, of nickel are found in austenitic gray irons that resist heat and corrosion and have low expansivity.

Chromium acts as a carbide stabilizer in cast iron and itself forms carbides that are more stable than iron carbide. Thus it intensifies chilling of cast iron, increases strength, hardness, and wear resistance, and is conducive to fine-grained structure. Most additions of chromium range from 0.15 to 0.90% with or without other alloying elements. Free carbides that appear with 1% or more chromium make castings hard to machine. With 3% chromium, white cast iron is formed. Special irons to resist corrosion and high temperatures contain as much as 35% chromium.

Molybdenum in amounts from 0.25 to 1.5% is added alone or with other elements to improve tensile strength, hardness, and shock resistance of castings. It is a mild carbide former but also forms a solid solution with ferrite. The presence of molybdenum in cast iron produces fine and highly dispersed particles of graphite and good structural uniformity. This improves toughness, fatigue strength, machinability, hardenability, and high-temperature strength.

Copper, usually from 0.25 to 2.5%, promotes formation of graphite and is a mild strengthener because it helps break up massive cementite and carbide concentrations.

Vanadium is a powerful carbide former and thus stabilizes cementite and restrains graphitization. Its effect in amounts from 0.10 to 0.50% is to increase strength, hardness, and machinability.

Grades of Cast Irons.   A wide variation in the properties of castings is obtainable from the selection of materials put into the melt, control of the rate of cooling, and subsequent heat treatment. A summary of properties is given in Table 8-5.

Gray cast iron produces the cheapest castings and should be considered first when its properties suffice. A classic example of an application that requires a bare minimum of strength is a window weight. For it, cast iron serves adequately at the least cost. Common applications for gray cast iron are guards and frames for machinery, motor frames, motor blocks and cylinder heads, bearing housings, valve housings, fire hydrants, pulley sheaves, and miscellaneous hardware.

TABLE 8-5 TYPICAL PROPERTIES OF FERROUS CASTINGS

Kind of metal	Ultimate tensile strength[a] [MPa (ksi)]	Yield strength[b] [MPa (ksi)]	Hardness (Bhn)	Elongation (%)	Relative sand casting cost[c]
Gray cast iron	135–550 (20–80)	—[d]	150–300	0–3	1
White cast iron	135–620 (20–90)	—[d]	300–600	Nil	1.2
Malleable iron	340–830 (50–120)	205–620 (30–90)	110–285	3–25	1.5
Ductile and nodular iron	410–1100 (60–160)	310–930 (45–135)	190–425	3–25	1.8
Cast steel (plain carbon)	340–690 (50–100)	170–340 (25–50)	110–210	18–27	2
Cast steel (low alloy)	620–1380 (90–200)	410–1380 (60–200)	170–370	9–20	5

[a]Compressive strength of gray cast iron about 550 to 1310 MPa (80 to 190 ksi), of white cast iron over 1380 MPa (200 ksi), and of the others about the same as the tensile strength.

[b]Resistance to dynamic loading nil to low for gray and white cast iron, medium for malleable and ductile irons, and high for steel.

[c]Relative costs can be expected to vary with size and shapes of castings, quality, grade, supplier, market conditions, etc. Typical cost for a 25-kg (55-lb) gray iron casting is about $0.75/kg (ca. $0.35/lb).

[d]Essentially the same as the tensile strength.

Each class of ferrous castings covers a range of properties. As an example, commercial gray irons are graded in the ASTM specification A48 by tensile strength. The range is from class 20 with a minimum tensile strength of 20,000 psi to class 60 with a minimum tensile strength of 60,000 psi. Strength is not always the major criterion for selection of a material. For instance, gray cast irons of the weaker grades have superior qualities for such applications as resistance to heat checking in clutch plates and brake drums, resistance to heat shock in ingot and pig molds, and dampening of vibrations in machine tool members.

White cast iron is brittle but is found on chilled castings to impart wear resisting surfaces to such products as plowshares, rock crushers, and mining equipment. Malleable iron, ductile iron, and steel castings provide various degrees of strength and shock resistance for machinery of all kinds. The tensile properties of ductile iron are specified by a three-number symbol. The first number refers to minimum tensile strength in ksi, the second to minimum yield strength in ksi, and the third to minimum percentage of elongation in a 2-in. gage length. For example, a highly ductile grade is 60-40-18, which is generally annealed for a ferritic matrix. At the other extreme is a high-strength grade, 120-90-02, heat treated to a high but machinable hardness. This represents a remarkable range of properties obtainable in one material.

Nonferrous Cast Alloys. Aluminum, magnesium, brasses, and bronzes are important nonferrous alloys cast in sand. Their main properties have been described in Chap. 7. Except for melting and pouring at lower temperatures, the techniques for sand casting nonferrous metals are much the same as for iron founding. However, nonferrous alloys are also commonly cast by other processes and will be considered in that connection more fully in Chap. 9.

DESIGN OF CASTINGS

An engineer must learn how to design castings that do their jobs adequately and can be made economically. Treatment of the casting process in this chapter has explained the principles that must be observed for good casting design. These principles are summarized as rules for the design of castings in Fig. 8-50. In essence, the rules call for walls and sections that can be kept filled upon cooling, are uniform, do not change abruptly in thickness but blend gradually one into another, and are no more complex than necessary. Sharp corners and angles must be avoided.

Draft. A pattern can be drawn satisfactorily from the sand and a good casting made only if its sides are tapered away from the parting line. In addition, projections such as bosses on the sides of a casting away from the parting line, as indicated in Fig. 8-49, cannot be drawn out of the sand and should be avoided. Cores must be provided for them at extra expense.

Tolerances. Tolerances of ± 1.5 mm ($\pm \frac{1}{16}$ in.) for dimensions up to about 300 mm (ca. 12 in.) are standard commercial practice for sand castings. Tolerances as close as ± 0.8 mm ($\pm \frac{1}{32}$ in.) are held by some foundries but at extra cost that should not be incurred unless necessary. Shell mold castings are made to tolerances of ± 0.50 mm (± 0.020 in.) for steel and nonferrous alloys, ± 0.40 mm (± 0.015 in.) for cast iron, and as small as ± 0.08 mm (± 0.003 in.) in some cases at extra cost.

The smallest tolerances can be held only on dimensions that lie entirely in one part of a mold. Several times as much tolerance must be given to dimensions that extend from one part of a mold to another. That is because a dimension across a parting line is subject to variations from closing the mold, and cores may shift.

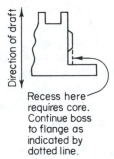

Direction of draft

Recess here requires core. Continue boss to flange as indicated by dotted line.

Figure 8-49 A projection increases the cost of making a casting.

DESIGN FOR CASTING SOUNDNESS

Most metals and alloys shrink when they solidify.

Therefore, design so that all members of the parts increase in dimension progressively to one or more suitable locations where feeder heads can be placed to offset liquid shrinkage.

The illustrations shown portray correct and incorrect methods of design. All of the rules set forth here have been proven in service and <u>assure soundness of section.</u>

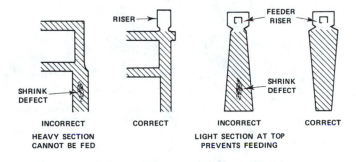

REPLACE SHARP ANGLES AND CORNERS WITH RADII

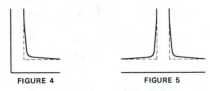

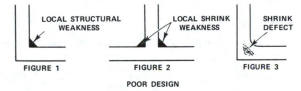

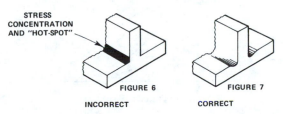

Figure 8-50 Rules for the design of castings.

ALWAYS PRESENT A COOLING SURFACE
AVOID SHARP ANGLES AND CORNERS

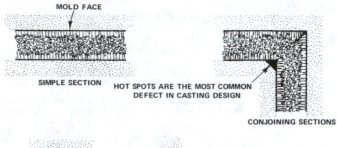

MOLD FACE

SIMPLE SECTION

HOT SPOTS ARE THE MOST COMMON
DEFECT IN CASTING DESIGN

CONJOINING SECTIONS

ILLUSTRATING ADVANTAGES OF ROUNDED CORNERS
TO AVOID LOCAL STRUCTURAL WEAKNESS

METAL STRUCTURE IS AFFECTED BY SHAPE OF CASTING SECTION

Solidification of molten metal always proceeds from the mold face, forming unbalanced crystal grains that penetrate into the mass at right angles to the plane of cooling surface. A simple section presents uniform cooling and greatest freedom from mechanical weakness. When two or more sections conjoin, mechanical weakness is induced at the junction and free cooling is interrupted, creating a "hot-spot."

BRING THE MINIMUM NUMBER OF SECTIONS TOGETHER

FIGURE 1

SOLIDIFIES IN 3 MINUTES

Figure 1 portrays a simple section which cools freely from all surfaces.

FIGURE 2

SOLID IN 3 MINUTES SOLID IN 5 MINUTES

By adding a second section as shown by figure 2, create "hotspots", the area inside circle cools at rate of section 50 percent larger.

FIGURE 3

SOLID IN 3 MINUTES SOLID IN 7 MINUTES

When two sections cross, only material outside circle shown by figure 3, represents true properties. Area inside circle solidifies at the rate of a bar twice its cross-sectional area.

FIGURE 4

SOLID IN 9 MINUTES

Adding too large fillets aggravates defect.

COOLING CURVES SHOWING RATES OF SOLIDIFICATION

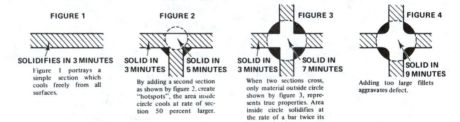

TEMPERATURE °F.

2100

TIME ELEMENT IN MINUTES

COOLING CURVES
AT CENTER OF:
1. BAR NO. 1
2. SINGLE RIGHT
   ANGLE SECTION
3. DOUBLE RIGHT
   ANGLE SECTION
4. TOO LARGE FILLETS

To portray the serious casting problems involved by the joining of an excessive number of members, cooling curves are made by inserting thermocouples at the adjoining sections. The results of these measurements are shown on the graph above.

A WELL DESIGNED CASTING BRINGS THE MINIMUM NUMBER OF SECTIONS TO-GETHER AND AVOIDS ACUTE ANGLES.

Figure 8-50 *(cont.)*

**DESIGN ALL SECTIONS AS NEARLY
UNIFORM IN THICKNESS AS POSSIBLE**

CYLINDER WITH LUGS

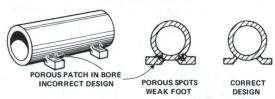

PmmmmmmPOROUS PATCH IN BORE
INCORRECT DESIGN   POROUS SPOTS   CORRECT
                        WEAK FOOT   DESIGN

Design on left caused defects shown. Correct design shown on right. Design all sections as nearly uniform in thickness as possible. Failing this, all heavy sections should be accessible for feeding.

**PROPORTION DIMENSIONS OF INNER
WALL CORRECTLY**

Inner sections of castings, resulting from complex cores, cool much slower than outer sections and cause variations in strength properties. A good rule is to reduce inner sections to 9/10ths of the thickness of the outer wall. Avoid rapid section changes and sharp angles. Wherever complex cores must be used, design for uniformity of section to avoid local heavy masses of metal.

INCORRECT   CORRECT

CYLINDERS AND BUSHINGS

The inside diameter of cylinders and bushings should exceed the wall thickness of casting.

FIGURE 1
CORRECT

RING
RISER

When inside diameter of cylinder is less than the wall thickness of the casting, as shown by Figure 2, it is better to cast solid. Holes can be produced by cheaper and safer methods than by coring.

FIGURE 2
INCORRECT

Figure 8-50   *(cont.)*

DESIGN RIBS AND BRACKETS FOR MAXIMUM EFFECTIVENESS

Ribs have two functions:
(1) to increase stiffness
(2) to reduce weight
If too shallow in depth, or too widely spaced they are ineffectual.

 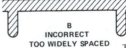

A **INCORRECT** **RIBS TOO SHALLOW**	B **INCORRECT** **TOO WIDELY SPACED**

Thickness of ribs
should approximate
0.8 casting thickness.

Correct rib depth and spacing is a matter of engineering design.

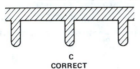

C **CORRECT**	D **INCORRECT**	E **INCORRECT**	F **CORRECT**
	Thin ribs should be avoided when joined to a heavy section. Otherwise, they will lead to high stresses and cracking.	As far as possible, junction between ribs and main casting should prevent any local accumulation of metal.	Ribs should solidify before the casting section they adjoin.

THICKNESS OF RIBS SHOULD EQUAL 80% OF CASTING THICKNESS. SHOULD BE ROUNDED AT EDGE AND CORRECTLY FILLETED.

T AND H SHAPED RIBBED DESIGNS
HAVE THE ADVANTAGE OF UNIFORM
METAL SECTIONS AND HENCE UNI-
FORM COOLING.

Design preference in average design is for ribs to have a greater depth than thickness. Ribs in compression in general offer a greater factor of safety than ribs in tension. How ever, castings having thin ribs or webs in compression may require design changes to give necessary stiffening to avoid buckling.

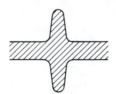 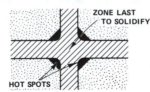 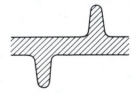

INCORRECT
RIBBING ON BOTH SIDES OF CASTING IS UNDESIRABLE FROM A FOUNDRY VIEWPOINT. IT INCREASES CASTING DEFECTIVES AND COSTS.

THESE CORNERS OF SAND REACH TEMPERATURE OF MOLTEN IRON AND HOLD THIS TEMPERATURE LONG AFTER CASTING IS SOLID.

INCORRECT
CROSS RIBBING CREATES HOT SPOTS, RENDERS FEEDING SOLID DIFFICULT, AND CAUSES LOCAL WEAKNESS AND POROSITY.

CORRECT
CROSS COUPLED RIBS SHOULD PREFERABLY BE DESIGNED AS DOUBLE T FORMS.

Avoid complex ribbing. It simplifies molding procedure, assures more uniform solidification conditions and eliminates "hot spots." Casting stresses and stress distribution favor omission of ribbing if the casting wall itself can be made of ample strength and stiffness.

Figure 8-50 *(cont.)*

BOSSES, LUGS AND PADS SHOULD NOT BE
USED UNLESS ABSOLUTELY NECESSARY

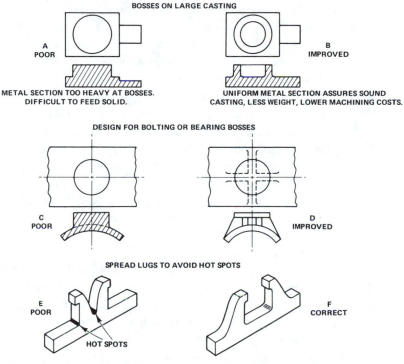

Bosses and pads increase metal thickness, create hot spots and cause open grain or draws. Blend into casting by tapering or flattening the fillets. Bosses should not be included in casting design when the surface to support bolts, etc., may be obtained by milling or countersinking.

A continuous rib instead of a series of bosses permits shifting hole location.

Thickness of bosses and pads should preferably be less than the thickness of the casting section they adjoin, but thick enough to permit machining without touching the casting wall. Where the casting section is light and does not permit use of this rule, then the following minimum recommended heights can serve as a guide.

APPROXIMATE CASTING LENGTH—FEET	HEIGHT OF BOSS—INCHES
Up to 1½	0.25
1½ to 6	0.75
Over 6	1.0

Continuous rib instead of a series of bosses permits shifting hole location.

Figure 8-50   *(cont.)*

QUESTIONS

1. What are the advantages of casting as compared with other processes?
2. What characteristics must a mold have?
3. Draw a sketch of a typical mold and name its principal parts.
4. Explain what happens in a casting when it solidifies and cools.
5. How thick or thin should the sections of a casting be?
6. What elements make a good gating system in a mold?
7. What are the three types of gates and their relative advantages?
8. What principles are conducive to an efficient riser in a mold?
9. What are vents and chills?
10. What are some of the hand tools used by molders?
11. Describe how a typical mold is made.
12. Describe the principles of operation of the three general types of molding machines.
13. What are the seven essential properties of a core?
14. What are chaplets and anchors?
15. Why and how are cores baked?
16. What are the two main types of patterns, and how do they compare?
17. Of what materials are patterns made, and what are the advantages of each material?
18. What is shrinkage allowance, and how is it provided for in a pattern?
19. What is machining allowance, and how is it designated?
20. What is draft on a pattern, and what is its purpose?
21. What are fillets, and what do they do?
22. Why are patterns colored?
23. Why is sand widely used for molding?
24. Describe the three major parts of a molding sand.
25. What are the differences between and relative merits of natural and synthetic molding sands?
26. What are the green permeability, green strength, and dry strength of a molding sand, and how do they determine how the sand performs in a mold?
27. What factors affect the green permeability, green strength, and dry strength of a sand, and how?
28. How is sand restored to its best condition and prepared for use?
29. What properties must core sand have?
30. Describe a cupola and the way it operates.
31. Describe a crucible-type furnace for melting nonferrous metals.
32. What are the difficulties in melting and pouring aluminum, and how are they overcome?
33. Why and how is vacuum melting done?
34. Discuss foundry procedure from the time the mold is made until a finished casting is obtained.
35. How is shell molding done?
36. What are the advantages and disadvantages of shell molding?

37. What are the constituents of cast iron, and how do they vary in gray, white, malleable, and ductile and nodular cast irons?

38. What are the effects on cast iron of (a) silicon? (b) sulfur? (c) phosphorus? (d) manganese? (e) nickel? (f) chromium? (g) molybdenum? (h) copper? (i) vanadium?

39. How do gray iron, malleable iron, and cast steel compare as to properties, costs, and applications?

40. Summarize the principles of design of castings.

PROBLEMS

1. A sand core in a mold has a volume of 1.6 dm³ (100 in.³). What is the buoyant force on the core if the metal poured in the mold is (a) brass or bronze? (b) aluminum? (c) steel? (d) cast iron?

2. In addition to the items listed in Table 8-4, a foundry has in its yard ample supplies of steel scrap that averages 0.30 carbon, 0.05 silicon, 0.50 manganese, 0.05 phosphorus, and 0.05 sulfur, all in percent. Also available is No. 1 machinery scrap that contains 3.5 carbon, 1.9 silicon, 0.6 manganese, 0.405 phosphorus, and 0.085 sulfur, all in percent. The iron to coke ratio is 8:1, with 0.5% sulfur in the coke, of which 5% is picked up by the iron. Calculate the composition of the cast iron resulting from the following charges:
   (a) 60% No. 1 machinery scrap, 25% steel scrap, and 15% No. 1 pig iron in a 1000-kg charge.
   (b) 20% No. 1 machinery scrap, 5% steel scrap, 15% No. 1 pig iron, 10% No. 2 pig iron, 40% cast iron scrap, and 10% returns in a 10,000-lb charge.

REFERENCES

BOESCH, W. J., et al., "Progress in Vacuum Melting: From VIM to VADER," *Metal Progress*, Oct. 1982, p. 49.

FLINN, R. A., and P. K. TROJAN, *Engineering Materials and Their Applications*, Houghton Mifflin, Boston, 1975.

HEINE, R. W., C. R. LOPER, and P. C. ROSENTHAL, *Principles of Metal Casting*, McGraw-Hill, New York, 1982.

Metals Handbook, Vol. 5: *Forging and Casting*, 8th ed., 1970, Vol. 1: *Properties and Selection: Iron and Steels*, 9th ed., 1980, American Society for Metals, Metals Park, Ohio.

Pattern Makers Manual, American Foundrymen's Society, Des Plaines, Ill., 1960.

SCHUYTEN, J., "Ductile Iron: An Overview of Where and How It's Used," *Metal Progress*, Nov. 1975, p. 73.

WEINER, S. A., et al., "Evaporative Casting Process: Some Metallurgical Considerations," *Metal Progress*, Dec. 1982.

9

HARD MOLD
CASTING PROCESSES

Casting in sand molds as described in Chap. 8 gives adequate results at lowest cost in many cases. Other casting processes that produce more uniformly, more precisely, or at lower costs in some cases will be described in this chapter. One group utilizes metal molds that are not destroyed in service as sand molds are, but can be used over and over again. Where metal molds are not suitable, precision casting is done in plaster and ceramic molds. Another group of processes casts metal continuously rather than in individual pieces.

METAL MOLD CASTING PROCESSES

Processes that use metal molds are permanent mold and die casting. Although applied to other kinds of molds also, centrifugal casting is often done with metal molds and is included in this section.

Casting in metal molds is confined practically to metals with low to moderate melting temperatures. Some casting of iron and steel is done in refractory metal molds.

Permanent Mold Casting. When fluid metal is poured into metal molds and subjected only to hydrostatic pressure, the process is called *permanent mold casting*. The mold separates into two or more pieces to release the solidified casting and is clamped together during the operation. Metals commonly cast in this way are lead, zinc, aluminum, and magnesium alloys, certain bronzes, and cast iron. Typical products are refrigerator compressor cylinder blocks, heads, and connecting rods, flat iron sole plates, washing machine gear blanks of cast iron, and automotive pistons and

176

Figure 9-1 Automatic permanent mold casting machine for making pistons. (Courtesy Aluminum Co. of America.)

cylinder heads, kitchenware, and typewriter parts of aluminum. Castings may weigh hundreds of kilograms (lb), but most are under 25 kg (55 lb).

Most permanent molds are made of a close-grained alloy cast iron, such as Meehanite, that is resistant to heat and repeated changes in temperature. Sometimes bronze molds are used for lead, tin, and zinc, and wrought alloy steel molds are used for bronzes. Cores are usually made of alloy steel but may be sand or plaster for severe service. Molds and cores are washed with an adhesive refractory slurry, basically graphite, clay, or whiting. This helps keep the castings from sticking, promotes easy ejection, and prolongs die life. Mold life may run from 3000 to 10,000 iron castings to as many as 100,000 pieces of softer metal.

With sand cores, the process is called *semipermanent mold casting*. Sand cores are cheap and easily removed from irregular holes, but the structure, accuracy, and surface finish of the cored openings are only as good as those of sand castings.

Permanent mold casting is often done manually but is readily adaptable to mechanization. One type of machine is illustrated in Fig. 9-1. A machine generally transfers the molds through several stations for ejection of castings, cleaning and coating the mold, placing of cores, locking, pouring, cooling, and unlocking. Some or all of the functions may be performed automatically as needed. In some variations, called *piercing* and *squeeze casting*, a punch or die is driven into the mold to compress and forge the metal while it congeals.

Low-Pressure Casting. Molten metal is forced by gas pressure upward through a stalk to fill a mold as depicted in Fig. 9-2. The metal cools inwardly in the mold to the stalk and freezes while the pressure is held. Then the pressure is released and the still molten metal in the stalk returns to the pot. The process is used mostly to cast aluminum in plaster, cast iron, and steel molds but has been applied to other metals to a small extent.

Low-pressure casting is at a stage between hydrostatic casting and high-pressure die casting both for sizes and features of castings. It gives moderately thin sections and intermediate accuracy and surface finish, density, and detail. Low-pressure castings are usually the strongest. Equipment and die costs and production rates are in the middle range. For example, operation time for a 2.7-kg (6-lb) aluminum casting is reported to be 1 minute, and for a 30-kg (65-lb) casting is 3 minutes. The process is considered economical for from 500 to 50,000 castings per year.

A form of low-pressure casting is called *vacuum casting* because the metal is pushed upward from the pot by atmospheric pressure as a vacuum is drawn through the mold. Air is drawn from the casting, and porosity is low, finish is good, and walls are more pressure tight. The castings do not blister as some others do when organic coatings are applied later. Tensile strength and hardness are optimum. Because of the lack of an air film in the die, chilling is rapid. Thus it is reported that walls can be cast thinner than, and production rates are comparable to, those of die casting.

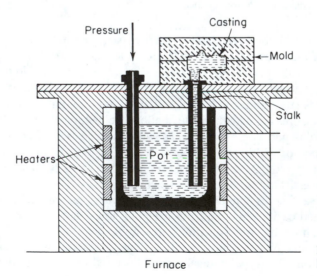

Figure 9-2 Diagram of low-pressure casting.

Slush Casting. Molten metal is poured into a metal mold. After the skin has frozen, the mold is turned upside down or slung to remove the still liquid metal. The thin shell that is left is called a *slush casting*. Toys and ornaments are made in this way from zinc, lead, or tin alloys.

A slush casting is usually bright and well suited for plating but is weaker and takes longer to make than a die casting. Die costs are relatively low for slush castings, and that is an advantage for small quantity production.

Die Casting. Molten metal is forced under considerable pressure into a steel mold or die in the die-casting process. The action that takes place is depicted in a cross section of a die in Fig. 9-3. The molten metal is shot through a runner and gate to fill the die. Vents and overflow wells are provided for escape of air. The metal is pressed into all the crevices of the die, and the pressure is held while the metal freezes to ensure density. Even so because of turbulence and air entrapment, porosity is often a problem, especially with thick sections. In a new *pore-free process* the die is filled with oxygen that reacts with the molten metal to produce insignificant particles of oxides rather than voids. Many dies are water cooled to hasten freezing. After the metal has solidified, the die is pulled open, and the part is ejected by pins actuated by a mechanism in the manner indicated in Fig. 9-3. The product is called a *die casting*.

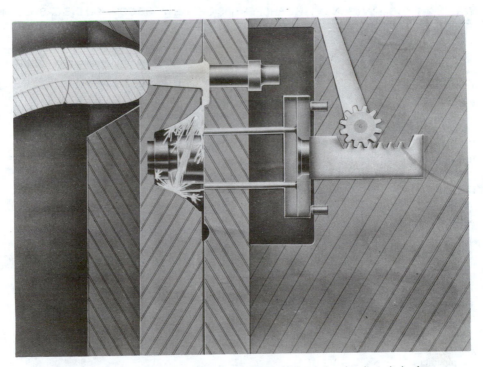

Figure 9-3 Cross section of a die-casting operation, showing how it is done. (Courtesy New Jersey Zinc Co.)

Metals and alloys die cast include zinc, aluminum, magnesium, copper, lead, tin, and even iron and steel in a few cases. First, all metals available and capable of doing the job should be considered for a die casting. For example, zinc or magnesium may suffer from a corrosive atmosphere in service and would be eliminated under such conditions. Lead, tin, or magnesium may not have sufficient rigidity for the product in another case. Factors to be considered include environment resistance, strength, weight, endurance, hardness, and ductility. Then that metal is chosen that gives the lowest total cost on the basis of material, set up, operating (cycle), and tool costs. Pertinent specifications of the most popular die-casting metals in the order of usage are given in Table 9-1.

Zinc alloys serve well for many applications because they have good strength, ductility, and resistance to shock at normal temperatures and a low cost. Zinc is cast at low temperatures, so die, set up, and production (cycle) costs are low. Die life is long. Zinc alloys cost more by volume than aluminum or magnesium, but often can be die cast with less metal in thinner sections, with less draft, and faster and cheaper than the others can. Other metals are used for serviceable properties not furnished by zinc. Notably, zinc alloys have low creep strength [protracted service above 100°C (212°F) is not warranted], become quite brittle at lower temperatures, and corrode

TABLE 9-1   COMPARISON OF THE PROPERTIES OF THE MOST COMMON DIE-CASTING METALS

Property	Units	Alloys of			
		Zinc	Aluminum	Magnesium	Brass, leaded yellow
Tensile strength	MPa	280–330	210–320	230	280–310
	ksi	41–48	30–46	34	40–45
Yield strength 0.5% offset	MPa		110–190	150	100–140
	ksi		16–27	22	14–20
Elongation	%	7–10	1–9	3	15–25
Brinell hardness number		82–91		60	50–75 (500 kg)
Density	g/cm³	6.64	2.657	1.799	8.30
	lb/in.³	0.24	0.096	0.065	0.30
Relative strength to density (strength/weight ratio)		1.9	4.0	5.2	1.4
Minimum wall thickness	mm	0.5–2.0	0.8–2.5	0.8–2.5	1.5–3.0
	in.	0.02–0.08	0.03–0.10	0.03–0.10	0.06–0.12
Approx. relative unit volume cost		180	45	60	400
Relative maximum die life	Number of pieces	10^6	10^5	10^5	10^4
Average die temperature	°C	220	290	260	500
	°F	425	550	500	ca. 950
Average casting temperature	°C	400	660	760	1100
	°F	760	1220	1400	2000

badly from steam and water. Yield and tensile strengths decrease somewhat upon prolonged aging.

Aluminum offers a high strength to density ratio, stability, service at a wide range of operating temperatures, and good resistance to corrosion in die castings. A number of alloys are available with a wide choice of properties. They stand up well in contact with food and fruit acids.

Magnesium alloys are light and fairly corrosion resistant but are badly attacked by humid tropical climate and sea water. The molten metal must be protected by a nonoxidizing atmosphere, and that adds cost to die casting.

Brass alloys have the most strength and wear and corrosion resistance but are not often die cast because their high melting point is damaging to the dies. Thus the cost of brass die castings is relatively high, and they are used only when die castings of other metals are not suitable and where enough can be saved in production and machining costs over sand or plaster castings to make up for the die costs.

Die casting is mainly found in the high-production industries. Intricate parts can be produced, and inserts such as fasteners easily incorporated. Output is fast (100 to 800 pieces/hr), but usually hundreds of thousands of pieces must be made to pay for dies costing thousands of dollars. An automobile may have from 20 to 70 kg (ca. 40 to 150 lb) of die-cast parts: typically, speedometer, windshield wiper motor, and horn parts; carburetor bodies, grill work, and decorations. Also, die-cast parts are found in household appliances, business machines, bathroom hardware, outboard motors, clocks, jewelry, and tools.

Die-Casting Dies. Dies must be massive and strong to withstand the large loads imposed on them by die casting. A die is normally made in two parts like the one in Fig. 9-4. One called the *front cover portion* is mounted on a stationary platen and receives the molten metal from an injection nozzle of the machine. The other is the *ejector portion* and is carried on a movable platen toward and away from the front cover to close and open the die. The two portions are aligned by the machine and by their own dowel pins. The two portions meet at the parting line and are locked together by the machine-locking mechanism when closed.

A die is always made so that the casting shrinks in cooling onto projections and core pins attached to the ejector portion. Thus when the die is opened, the part clings to the movable portion, is drawn away from the front cover and can then be ejected into the opening between the die halves. There it falls clear or is picked up by tongs.

Dies for complicated parts with undercuts, recesses, and angular holes are equipped with slides and movable core pins, like the one in Fig. 9-4. Such construction is expensive but frequently makes possible the production of parts that could not otherwise be die cast. Movable cores and slides are arranged to be withdrawn before the die is opened.

Dies are of single-cavity, multiple-cavity, combination, and unit types. A *single-cavity die* turns out only one casting for each cycle of an operation. For large-quantity production of small and moderate size pieces, a number of cavities may be sunk in a single die and be gated from a common sprue so that several castings are made at once. This is a *multiple-cavity die*. If the cavities are of two or more different

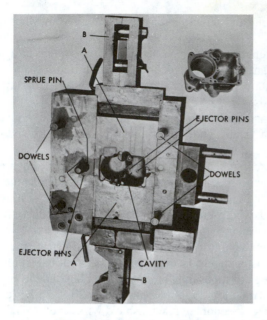
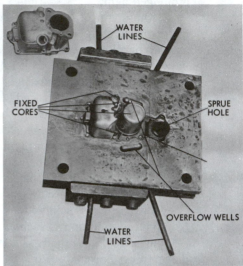

Figure 9-4 Two halves of a die for a zinc alloy carburetor. This complex die has two slides, marked A, to form the side walls and undercuts between the flanges of the part. The slide operating and locking mechanisms are marked B. Severable movable core pins, not readily discernible, are provided for angular holes. (Courtesy New Jersey Zinc Co.)

shapes and produce as many different parts at one time, the die is called a *combination die*. A *unit die* consists of a die holder in which several die elements may be placed and filled at the same time. Any of the units may be blocked off to regulate the quantity cast of each part.

The steel for a die depends mainly upon the material cast, temperature of operation, and quantity of pieces produced. For die-casting zinc alloys at 400 to 425°C (750 to 800°F), ordinary low-alloy steels, moderately heat treated, are satisfactory. Hot-work tool steels (high in nickel, chrome, and/or tungsten) are mostly recommended for high temperatures and large quantity of castings.

Over the years die-casting die design has been largely an art, and dies often have had to be modified to make them work properly. However, intensive research is providing a growing body of knowledge and literature to enable engineers to design dies and control the process more efficiently. Advances in computor technology, programmable controllers (Chap. 34) and many types of instrumentation have been applied steadily to make die casting more efficient.

Die-Casting Machines.   The two basic types of die-casting machines are the *hot chamber* and the *cold chamber* machines. The hot chamber machines may be plunger or air injection operated.

Figure 9-5(A) depicts the method of operation of a typical gooseneck plunger-operated hot chamber die-casting machine for zinc and other low-melting-point alloys. The gooseneck contains a cylinder and curved passageways immersed in a pot of

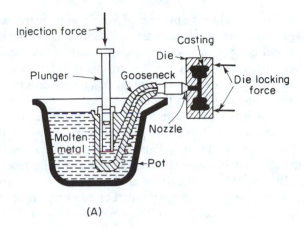

(A)

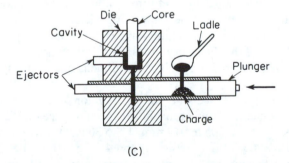

(B)

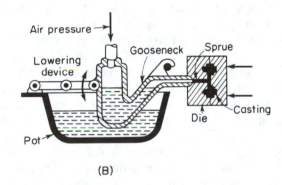

(C)

Figure 9-5 (A) Plunger hot chamber die casting; (B) air injection die casting; (C) cold chamber die casting.

molten metal. When the plunger is retracted, the gooseneck fills with metal. When the die is closed, an air cylinder depresses the plunger and forces the metal through the gooseneck, nozzle, and die passages into the die cavity. Machines like this are more or less automatic and fast and produce from 100 to 800 parts/hr. Zinc alloy can be injected satisfactorily at 10 MPa (ca. 1.5 ksi) and more than 14 MPa (2 ksi) is rarely found necessary.

Molten aluminum attacks iron parts like the plunger of a die-casting machine and in turn becomes contaminated. An air injection die-casting machine, as sketched in Fig. 9-5(B), has a gooseneck that is lowered into the molten aluminum to receive a charge when needed. It is then raised and connects to an air line, which supplies the pressure to inject the metal into the die. Some hot chamber machines for aluminum are made with refractory components exposed to the molten metal.

The metal needed for each shot is ladled from a separate furnace or pot into a cold chamber machine as indicated in Fig. 9-5(C). A plunger is driven by an air or hydraulic cylinder to force the charge into the die. This method avoids having high-melting-point alloys in continuous contact with the working parts of the machine. Pressures are from 20 to 55 MPa (3000 to 8000 psi) for aluminum and from there up to 240 MPa (35,000 psi) for copper alloys. Average production rates are reported up to 175 parts/hr for aluminum alloys, 250 to 300 for magnesium alloys, and 90 for copper-base alloys.

A cold chamber die-casting system called *Acurad* has been developed in recent years to produce complex porosity-free aluminum parts but is adaptable to other metals. A plunger pushes the metal through a large gate in the bottom of the die so that it rises slowly to fill the cavities. Filling rate is 0.3 to 1 second compared to 0.03 seconds by conventional die-casting. The casting is cooled from its extremity to the gate. When a skin is frozen, a small inner plunger in the charging cylinder is pushed forward to raise the pressure in the still-molten metal to about 35 to 100 MPa (ca. 5000 to 15,000 psi). Cooling is efficient, so total operation time is not excessive.

High pressure, depending on the metal, is necessary for dense and true die castings, but pressure alone is not enough. Selection and control of the material, design of the die, and timing and conduct of the operation must be done expertly for best results. An actual operation is usually performed semiautomatically for safety and uniform results. The operator presses a button to start a cycle. The die is closed, and metal is injected. The die is opened after a preset time. Functions are interlocked to avoid spoiling the part, damaging the machine, or spilling metal.

One way of rating a machine is by the locking force (in tons) that keeps the dies closed. The cross-sectional area of the die cavity times the injection pressure must be less than the locking force. Another rating specifies the dimensions of the space for the die.

Die-casting machines range from about 90 kN (10 tons) to over 18 MN (2000 tons) capacity. A 625-ton cold-chamber machine has a die space of 762 by 762 mm (30 by 30 in.) and takes dies from 305 to 914 mm (12 to 36 in.) thick. It can inject 2.2 kg (4.85 lb) of aluminum at 65.5 MPa (9500 psi) and 4.8 kg (10.5 lb) at 29 MPa (4200 psi) normal pressure. Pressures may be increased as much as $3\frac{1}{2}$ times. Operation rates may be as high as 450 cycles per hour. The machine is operated by a 56-kW (75-hp) motor, weighs 28 Mg (62,000 lb), and has a base price of about $200,000. A trim press costs about $30,000, and a 540-kg (1200-lb) melting and holding furnace about $25,000.

Finishing Die Castings. Liquid metal forced into a die cavity under high pressure intrudes into parting face joints, around ejector pins, into overflow wells, and through any cracks. Clearances in dies are held as small as practicable, and the metal in the cracks solidifies into thin and fragile extrusions called *flash*. The flash as well as sprues, runners, etc., must be removed to finish a casting. For small production runs, the excess metal may be broken off by hand and the edges cleaned by filing, buffing, etc. For larger quantities the flash can be removed quickly in a trimming die in a press. Elaborate machines (some called die-casting machine centers) are available that do die casting, trimming, and even drilling, tapping, etc., at successive stations with automatic handling between operations.

Dimensions can be held closely enough by die casting for most purposes, and only a minimum of machining is usually necessary. Some surfaces, like threads in small holes, may be more easily machined than cast. Machining of die castings is no different from machining other objects of the same materials and is governed by the principles presented in the chapters in this book on metal machining.

Centrifugal Casting.   Centrifugal casting is done by pouring molten metal into a revolving mold. Centrifugal force creates pressure far in excess of gravity to cram the metal into the mold. For instance, an aluminum alloy spun at about 2600 rpm is subjected to a pressure of approximately 250 kPa (36 psi) at about 100 mm (4 in.) diameter and more at larger diameters. This is better than feeding a static casting with a head of almost 9 m (30 ft). Centrifugal casting produces good-quality, accurate castings, and saves material. The castings are dense and have a fine grained structure with uniform and high physical properties and are less subject to directional variations than static castings. Metal flows readily into thin sections, and castings come out with fine outside surface detail. Gases and dross are squeezed out of the heavier metal, and the impurities float on the inside surface of the casting from which they can later be cut. Gates and risers are not needed to supply a pressure head and may be almost eliminated. This has been found to mean a saving of 40% and more in metal poured.

All the common metals may be centrifugally cast in either refractory or metal molds. One method is to introduce a ceramic slurry into the rotating flask and centrifuge it into a compact lining before the metal is poured. Rotation about a vertical axis is fast and easy to do. The hole inside the fluid metal rotated in that way becomes shaped like a paraboloid, small at the bottom. For a straight hole, a long piece is rotated about a horizontal axis as depicted in Fig. 9-6. As an example of accuracy, 16-ft-long stainless steel tubes for a proton accelerator are centrifugally cast with a maximum deviation in the inside surface of 0.25 mm (0.01 in.) over the entire tube length.

True centrifugal casting in which a piece is rotated about an axis is best suited for ring- or tube-shaped pieces with straight walls. The outside surfaces may be round, square, hexagonal, etc., and should be concentric with the hole. Round holes may be formed without cores, and that may save appreciable expense for large holes, but holes of other shapes need to be cored. Sometimes bosses may be cast on the perimeter if not too thin or high. Centrifugal castings without holes, like the track wheels in Fig. 9-6, are apt to be porous and weak and contain inclusions at their centers. In the case shown, a hole is later drilled and bored through the center of each part, and the impurities are removed.

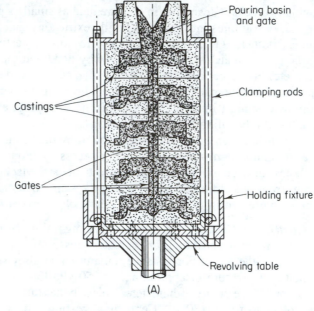

(A)

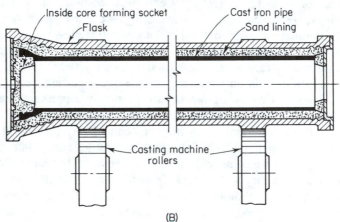

(B)

Figure 9-6 Vertical and horizontal arrangements for centrifugal casting. The vertical setup is for a stack of track wheels; the horizontal for cast-iron pipe. (Courtesy American Cast Iron Pipe Co.)

Parts not symmetrical about any axis of rotation may be cast in a group of molds arranged in a circle to balance each other. The setup is revolved around the center of the circle to induce pressure in the molds. This is called *centrifuge casting*.

Comparison of Metal Mold Casting Methods.   Almost any metal or shape or size of piece, except intricate pieces, can be sand cast, but some cannot be cast in metal molds. Some compositions are too weak at solidifying temperatures or shrink too much and thus crack around the unyielding projections in a metal mold. Some metals melt at temperatures that are damaging to metal molds. Some parts are too complex for metal molds to be practical.

Parts that can be cast in metal molds are stronger, have better surface appearance, can be held to smaller tolerances, can be made with thinner sections, and require less machining than equivalent sand castings. A comparison of the major casting processes in these respects is made in Table 9-2. In general, properties are good in parts cast in metal molds under pressure, but plaster mold and investment casting (described later) are most favored for premium-quality castings. Sometimes only one process gives the required results, but usually a process is selected because it gives the desired results at the lowest costs.

As shown in Table 9-2, tools cost most for die casting and lesser amounts for the other processes. Also, the rate of production decreases and the scrap loss increases

TABLE 9-2 A COMPARISON OF CASTING METHODS

	Type of casting process				
Factor	Sand	Permanent mold	Low pressure	Die	Centrifugal (or centrifuge)
Metals processed	All	Nonferrous and ferrous	Nonferrous[a]	Nonferrous[a]	All
Commercial sizes kg (lb) min. max.	Fractional Largest	0.2 (0.4) 135 (300)	0.2 (0.4) 100 (220)	Minute 50 (110)	0.1 (0.2) Over 23 metric tons (over 25 tons)
Commercial surface finish [μm (μin.)]	8–15 (ca. 300–600)	2–25 (80–1000)	1–4 (50–150)	$\frac{1}{2}$–3 (20–125)	$\frac{1}{2}$–8 (20–300)[b]
Tolerance [mm/25 mm or less (in./first in.)]	1.50 (0.06)	0.40 (0.015)	0.25 (0.01)	0.10 (0.004)	0.25 (0.01)[b]
Tensile strength [MPa (ksi)][c]	130 (19)	160 (23)	170 (25)	200 (30)	170 (25)
Production rate (pieces/hr)[d]	10–15	40–60	50–80	120–150	30–50
Mold or pattern cost ($)[d]	1000	6000	9000	15,000	2000
Scrap loss[e]	5	4	3	2	1

[a]Iron and steel are cast in refractory metal molds but only in a small way.

[b]In metal molds.

[c]For No. 43F aluminum alloy as an example.

[d]Production and total tool cost figures are relative for a 1.5-kg (3-lb) aluminum casting of moderate complexity.

[e]1 lowest to 5 highest.

in much the same order. Sand casting is usually cheapest for a few parts, and the other processes for larger quantities. The actual costs are different for each part. Average experience of one company is depicted in Fig. 9-7. Higher tool costs make die casting more expensive for small quantities, but operation savings more than offset the tool costs for large quantities.

Metal mold castings are even at times competitive with other processes with which sand castings are at a disadvantage. They have been found adequate to replace some forgings and at less cost. They may be cheaper than some drawn parts that require multiple operations. Castings may replace whole assemblies of parts made in other ways. Metal mold castings have even been proven more economical than some parts machined automatically where considerable metal was lost in chips.

Designing Castings for Metal Molds.   The principles that point the way to good castings have been pointed out in Chap. 8 and apply as well to hard mold casting.

Sections may be thinner and less stock needs to be allowed for finishing metal mold castings than for sand castings. From 1 to 3 mm ($\frac{1}{32}$ to $\frac{1}{8}$ in.) stock, depending on the size of the part, is recommended for permanent mold castings. Die castings require little or no machining for most applications. Stock removal should be avoided or minimized because about 1 mm ($\frac{1}{32}$ in.) of the cast surface next to the mold wall is most chilled and thus is the densest part of a metal mold casting.

Metal mold castings must have more draft than sand castings. Inside surfaces must be given about twice as much draft as outside surfaces because they shrink on their cores as they cool.

The parting line is an important factor in the costs of making and operating a metal mold. The line should lie as much as possible in one plane for lowest costs. Flash can be expected to occur along the parting line and can be removed most readily without defacement if the line is located on a bead or along the edge of a flange instead of across a flat surface.

PLASTER MOLD CASTING

Disposable or semipermanent plaster molds or cores for metal molds are made from plaster of paris (gypsum) with added talc, silica flour, asbestos fiber, and other substances to control setting time and expansion. A slurry is poured over a pattern and allowed to harden. The mold is dried to remove water and prevent the formation of steam upon exposure to hot metal. Plaster cores are shown in Fig. 9-8 being assembled into a metal mold for a torque converter casting.

Plaster mold casting was not a success until ways were found to make the plaster permeable so that gases could escape from the mold. Excess water helps because it is driven off when the mold is baked for drying and leaves pores. One form of the process uses a large proportion of sand with only enough gypsum for a binder. The method reputed to give the most porosity is to add the plaster slurry to an agent that is first beaten to a foam. The mold is dried below 200°C (400°F). The walls of the bubbles break as the plaster sets. The proprietary *Shaw process* utilizes two slurries

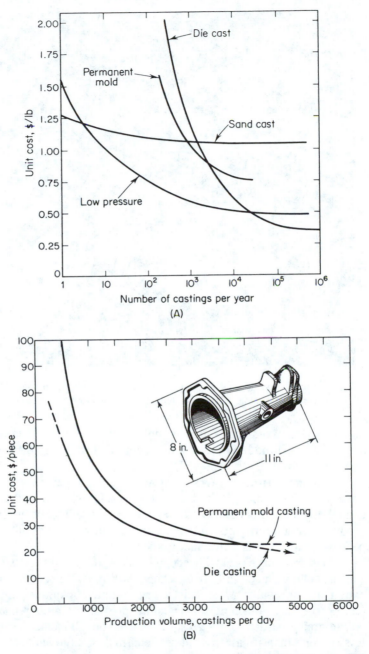

Figure 9-7 Cost comparisons of casting processes. (A) Summary of the experience with average aluminum castings of a large manufacturer. (Reprinted from *Technical Paper 66-523*, courtesy of the Society of Manufacturing Engineers.) (B) Cost comparison for a specific piece. (From *Metals Handbook*, by permission of the American Society for Metals.)

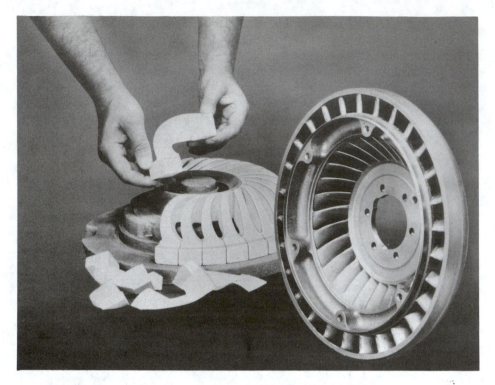

Figure 9-8 Mold being assembled with plaster cores for an aluminum torque converter casting. (Courtesy Aluminum Company of America.)

that gel when mixed and poured at once around a pattern. Volatile agents in the mass are ignited, and the heat leaves a microcrazed structure in the mold, which is finally dried in an oven.

Only nonferrous metals such as aluminum, copper, magnesium, and zinc alloys are cast in plaster molds because most ferrous alloys are poured at temperatures high enough to melt the plaster. Lead is avoided because it reacts with the plaster. Typical products are aircraft parts, plumbing fixture fittings, aluminum pistons, locks, propellers, ornaments, and tire and plastic molds.

Plaster molds have low heat conductivity and provide slow and uniform cooling. Castings can be made in intricate shapes with varying sections and particularly with extremely thin walls. Most satisfactory section thicknesses are from 1.5 to 6 mm (ca. $\frac{1}{16}$ to $\frac{1}{4}$ in.). Inherent slow cooling precludes chilling and is conducive to a coarse-grained structure. As a result, some but not all metals cast in plaster molds have less strength than if cast in sand or metal molds; as much as a 25% loss in strength for some aluminum alloys.

Plaster molding material is yielding enough not to restrain cast metal when it cools and shrinks. On the other hand, plaster may break in thin mold sections and is not favored for large castings because it is weak. Most commercial plaster mold castings weigh from a fraction of a kilogram (pound) to around 10 kg (20 lb), but some have weighed up to 1.8 Mg (4000 lb).

Plaster mold casting yields more accuracy, smoother surfaces, better detail, thinner sections, and more complex shapes than sand or coated permanent mold casting. These advantages often help eliminate costly machining. Tolerances may be held as close as 75 μm (0.003 in.) but common values are $\pm$125 μm ($\pm$0.005 in.) on one side and $\pm$250 μm ($\pm$0.010 in.) across parting lines for dimensions up to 25 mm (1 in.). Surface finish from 0.8 to 3 μm (30 to 125 μin.) can be expected. However, plaster mold casting is on the average about three times as costly as sand casting because patterns and core boxes cost more, and the molds and cores take more time to prepare and must be baked.

Under some conditions plaster mold casting is preferable to metal mold casting; in many cases not. Accuracy and finish produced by the two methods are comparable. Operation cost with plaster molds is generally higher than with metal molds. On the other hand, the patterns for plaster molds may cost less than metal molds, and the overall cost then may be lower for plaster mold casting for small quantities. Plaster mold casting is of particular advantage for the nonferrous metals that melt at higher temperatures and are hard on metal molds. Upkeep may be enough less in such cases to give the cost advantage to plaster mold casting, even for large quantities. This explains why metal mold cores, which are even more exposed to heat than the molds, are often made of plaster.

PRECISION INVESTMENT CASTING

Investment casting, also called the *lost wax process*, is an ancient process that utilizes an expendable pattern of wax or plastic material. The steps in the process are depicted in Fig. 9-9. A pattern may be carved for one or two experimental pieces, but for production it is injected in a prepared die of rubber, plaster, or wood but generally of metal for quantities. Pieces of a pattern may be joined together by heating or by an adhesive. In this way gates, risers, sprues, etc., are added. The patterns for a number of pieces may be joined together in a cluster for economical production. Quite complex parts and even whole assemblies may be fabricated by joining components together in the pattern stage rather than by assembly of finished pieces after casting.

A version called the *Mercast process* starts with a pattern of frozen mercury at $-60°C$ ($-70°F$) or below in a mold. Mercury changes size little on melting and is not as likely to crack a frail mold as is wax or plastic.

A mold is invested around the pattern in the next step. The molding material is basically a refractory silica or zircon sand in a chemical binder such as ethyl silicate, sodium silicate, or colloidal silica to form a slurry. Film forming, wetting, and antifoam agents are also added. One method is to dip the pattern into a series of slurries to build up a layered shell about 3 to 6 mm ($\frac{1}{8}$ to $\frac{1}{4}$ in.) thick of successively coarser grains. Fine grains at the inside surface of the mold impart a smooth surface finish to the casting. The wet coating may be built up by being stuccoed with refractory grains.

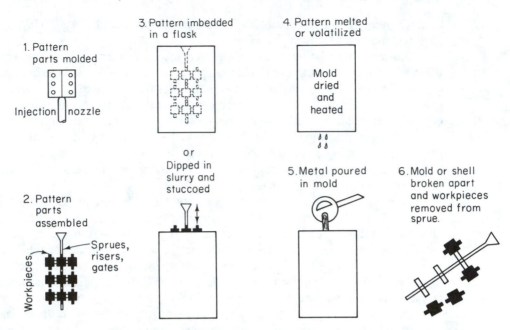

Figure 9-9 Steps in investment casting.

No flask is needed, and the thin shell can be dried in $\frac{1}{2}$ hour or less as compared to hours for a whole mold. Another method is to position the pattern in a flask and pour molding compound around it; usually while vibrating the flask to aid in filling. Sometimes a mold started by the first method is completed by the second; i.e., a shell is formed and then is embedded in a flask.

After the mold has cured for from minutes to hours, depending on the material, it is placed in a furnace at up to 1100°C (2000°F) to bake and to melt or volatilize the wax or plastic pattern. Carefully melted metal is poured into the mold and may be subjected to pressure from compressed air or centrifugal force. One technique is to draw a vacuum from beneath a mold to pull out gases and concentrate atmospheric pressure on the metal. After the casting has cooled, the mold is broken, cores are shaken out, and sprues and irregularities are cut off or ground away.

Merits of Precision Investment Casting.   Many common and uncommon ferrous and nonferrous alloys are investment cast—over 180 according to one authority. The most suitable metals are those with good fluidity, uniform shrinkage or freezing, and chemical inertness because investment casting is usually chosen to get small tolerances, fine details, and thin sections.

A main advantage of investment casting is that the best alloy can be selected for a part. This cannot always be done for machined parts, for instance, because extra hard or tough metals may be too expensive to cut. Most metals can be cast with equal ease, and the material cost of a small part may not affect the final cost much. As an example, a locking cam cast from soft steel (AISI 1020) at $0.26/kg ($0.12/lb) cost $0.05/piece and from a hard Co-Cr-W alloy (CoJ) at $5.30/kg ($2.41/lb) cost only $0.057/piece.

Tolerances as small as ±50 μm (0.002 in.) are held by investment casting, but usually at extra cost. Commercial tolerances normally are at least ±50 μm/cm (±0.005 in./in.). Investment casting has an advantage tolerance-wise because draft may be largely eliminated and the mold does not have a parting face, across which dimensions vary appreciably in other casting processes. Commercial surface finishes range from below 2 to 6 μm (ca. 60 to 220 μin.).

Investment casting is superior to other casting methods in some respects and inferior in others. It is readily automated, particularly for molding and coating the cores, and with many small pieces made and handled in clusters, cost per piece can be quite low. Processors report orders for quantities up to 1 million pieces. However, more steps are required, and investment casting is usually not competitive with sand casting except for small tolerances and fine finishes. As a rule, shell molding is more economical for simpler parts in larger sizes, and investment casting for complex parts, particularly in small sizes. Investment casting can offer no advantage over metal mold and die casting for low melting point alloys except for small quantities or complex parts, for which investment casting tooling costs less. However, it can produce results comparable to those from metal molds but with metals that melt at temperatures too high for metal molds.

Many kinds of parts are investment cast. Most weigh from a fraction of a kilogram (pound) to about 5 kg (11 lb), but some have been made as heavy as 70 kg (ca. 150 lb). Parts are made with sections from 0.75 to 1.5 mm ($\frac{1}{32}$ to $\frac{1}{16}$ in.) but not often over about 25 mm (1 in.) thick. For ages the process has been used for tooth fillings, surgical instruments, and jewelry. Typical products in present-day industry are buckets, vanes, and blades for gas turbines; shuttle eyes for weaving; slides for cloth cutting; pawls and claws for movie cameras and projectors; sights, bolts, triggers, etc., for firearms; cutting tools; and waveguides for radar.

CONTINUOUS CASTING

Continuous casting consists of pouring molten metal into one end of a metal mold open at both ends, cooling rapidly, and extracting the solid product in a continuous length from the other end. This is done with copper, brass, bronze, aluminum, and, to a growing extent, cast iron and steel.

The principle of continuous casting is carried out in a number of ways that differ in details. A typical process for copper-base alloys, called the *Asarco process*, is depicted in Fig. 9-10. Metal flows into a mold or die from below the surface of a charge in a holding furnace to keep out floating slag. The metal flows through a tortuous path in the furnace to protect the mold from sloshing effects during pouring. The lower part of the mold is water jacketed and freezes the metal rapidly. The solidified casting is pulled along at a controlled speed by the withdrawing rolls. The process is started with a dummy bar in the mold upon which the first metal is poured and cooled. Metals like iron and steel that conduct heat comparatively slowly freeze only skin deep while in the mold a practical length of time. They are sprayed with

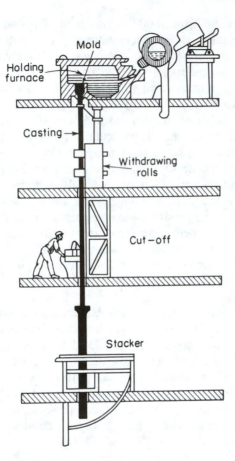

Figure 9-10 Continuous casting process.

water and solidified throughout after leaving the mold. Some systems employ vibrating or reciprocating molds to keep the casting from sticking. Some molds are curved, and the casting veers into a horizontal position where it passes through straightening rolls. Finally, the product is cut to desired lengths by saw or torch.

Continuous casting is done for a number of purposes. It is particularly suitable for any shapes of uniform cross section: round, square, rectangular, hexagonal, fluted, scalloped, gear-toothed, and many other forms; solid or hollow. Shapes from a few millimeters to about 250 mm (10 in.) in diameter and up to 6 m (20 ft) long are offered. A growing use is to produce blooms, billets, and slabs for rolling structural shapes as described in Chap. 12. This is cheaper than rolling from ingots. Copper-base billets 100 mm (4 in.) square and over and steel slabs 150 to 250 mm (6 to 10 in.) thick and 0.8 to 2.2 m (32 to 88 in.) wide are examples. Continuously cast shapes may be cut to lengths and finished by light machining (bushings and pump gears, for instance). Large-diameter and long iron water pipes with flanged ends are cast in a semicontinuous manner with a separate charge of molten metal for each pipe.

Continuous casting offers several advantages. Its yield in rolled shapes is 10% or more over that from ingots. An appreciable amount of the end of each ingot must be cut off and returned to the furnace because it is porous, unsound, and full of impurities. This waste is practically eliminated by the uniformity of continuous castings. Of course, a hollow center occurs from shrinkage in a continuous casting, but it remains pure and is welded shut after four rolling passes. Continuous casting structure is dendritic as in other castings but is more dense and uniform than in individual castings because the whole length receives the same treatment in the same mold. Physical properties and surface finishes are comparable to those obtained in other metal mold processes.

Continuous casting is essentially automatic, and unit labor cost is low. Dies or molds are made of copper or graphite and are simple and inexpensive. Total equipment cost is high, about twice as much as for individual castings. The complete cost of a plant to continuously electrically melt and cast premium alloy steel at the rate of 1.4 Gg (3,000,000 lb) per year is several million dollars.

QUESTIONS

1. What is permanent mold casting, and where does it serve?
2. Describe low-pressure casting.
3. How is die casting done? What are its advantages?
4. What is a hot chamber, what is a cold chamber die-casting machine, and what are the advantages of each?
5. What is centrifugal casting, and what does it offer?
6. How do permanent mold, low-pressure, die, centrifugal, and sand casting compare as to what they can do and as to cost?
7. How much stock should be allowed for finishing metal mold castings?
8. What is essential for satisfactory plaster molds?
9. How is precision investment casting done, and what are its advantages?
10. What is continuous casting, and what advantages does it offer?

PROBLEMS

1. A single gear blank, 200 mm (8 in.) in diameter, is to be die cast from zinc at 14 MPa (2000 psi) pressure. What should be the capacity of the machine in kN (tons) of locking force?
2. When a casting is centrifuged at n rpm around a minimum diameter D, show that the minimum acceleration in gravitational units imposed on the casting is $G = a/g = 1.42 \times 10^{-5} Dn^2$, where a is the centrifugal acceleration of the casting in ft/sec², g is the acceleration of gravity in the same units, and D is in inches. Also, $G = 5.6 \times 10^{-7} Dn^2$ if D is in mm and g is in m/s².
3. Common practice with iron- and copper-base alloys is to centrifuge their castings to impose an acceleration from 40 to 60 gravitational units. This gives good castings without damage to the molds. In one operation the molds are arranged around a 350 mm (ca. 14 in.)

diameter. At what speed should the centrifuge be rotated? Refer to the equations in Prob. 2.

4. A circular disk of unit thickness of molten metal of density γ is rotated around its axis to make a centrifugal casting. Its outside radius is r_2 and its inside radius is r_1. Show that at n rpm the pressure from the centrifugal action at radius r_2 is $P = K\gamma n^2(r_2^2 - r_1^2)$. Also show that for density in lb/in.^{3}, r in in., and P in psi, $K = 1.42 \times 10^{-5}$; or for density in kg/m^3, r in mm, and P in kPa, $K = 5.48 \times 10^{-12}$.

5. Experience has shown that a good centrifugal casting is obtained from aluminum or magnesium if it is rotated at sufficient speed to create a pressure of 200 to 250 kPa (30 to 35 psi) on its periphery. It is assumed the casting is continuous from its center of gravity, around which it is rotated, to its periphery.
   (a) At what speed should a 500-mm (20-in.)-diameter symmetrical aluminum casting be rotated?
   (b) At what speed should a 400-mm (16-in.)-diameter symmetrical magnesium casting be rotated?

6. A 1-m (ca. 36-in.)-diameter cast-iron pipe with a 25-mm (1-in.) wall thickness is centrifugally cast and rotated at sufficient speed to impose an acceleration of 160g on its periphery. At what speed is it rotated? What is the peripheral pressure in the mold in kPa or psi? See the equations of Probs. 2 and 4.

7. A 1.5-kg (ca. 3-lb) aluminum casting for which data are given in Table 9-2 can be made satisfactorily by any of the processes listed in that table. The cost of labor and overhead is $22.50/hr. Assume top production rate and the same setup time and material costs for all processes even though that is not always the case. What process should be selected for each of the following numbers of pieces? (a) 1; (b) 100; (c) 1000; (d) 3000; (e) 5000; (f) 10,000; (g) 20,000; (h) 30,000; (i) 40,000; (j) 50,000; (k) 100,000.

8. For the conditions stated in Prob. 7, what range of production quantities is most economical for each of the following processes? (a) sand casting; (b) permanent mold casting; (c) low-pressure casting; (d) die casting; (e) centrifugal casting (with metal mold).

REFERENCES

BRYSON, F. E., "What's Happening in Centrifugal Casting," *Machine Design*, Oct. 19, 1974, p. 154.

HUNTRESS, E. A., "Spincasting Higher-Temp Alloys," *American Machinist*, Nov. 1980, p. 120.

Metals Handbook, 8th ed., Vol. 1: *Properties and Selection of Metals*, 1961, Vol. 5: *Forging and Casting*, 1970, American Society for Metals, Metals Park, Ohio.

SPROW, E. E., "Low Pressure Casting for High Performance Parts," *Machine Design*, Aug. 5, 1973, p. 122.

WINSHIP, J., "Die Casting Sharpens Its Edge, Special Report 670," *American Machinist*, Nov. 25, 1974, p. 77.

_____, "Diecasting's New Mold, Special Report 735," *American Machinist*, July 1981, p. 129.

10

POWDER METALLURGY

Powder metallurgy is the manufacture of products from finely divided metals and metallic compounds. The powders are loose in some applications and pressed into pieces and parts in others.

Loose powders of metals and their compounds are added to some products. Aluminum and bronze powders are mixed into paints for metallic finishes. Metal powders add strength and wear resistance to plastics. Metals in powder form in fireworks burn with colorful effects.

The most important and growing applications of powder metallurgy in industry are in the manufacture of pieces and parts. As an example, a modern automobile contains about 100 powder metal parts. Powder metallurgy has achieved this status because it excels in several respects, which are explained in the following paragraphs.

Powder metallurgy is the only feasible means of fabricating some materials. The melting points of the refractory metals, such as tungsten (3400°C or 6150°F), tantalum (2996°C or 5425°F), and molybdenum (2620°C or 4750°F), are so high they are hard to work in appreciable quantities with available equipment. Other substances, such as zirconium (mp 1900°C or 3450°F), react strongly with and are contaminated by their surroundings when melted. Powder metallurgy is a practical way of refining and fabricating such metals. It is also the only feasible way to consolidate and form the superhard tool materials, such as cemented carbides and sintered oxides.

Combinations of metals and nonmetals not obtainable economically in other ways can be made by powder metallurgy. This is of particular value to the electrical industry. Motor brushes and contact points must have proper conductivity but be resistant to wear and arcing. Brushes are made from powders of copper, graphite, and sometimes tin and lead; points require combinations like tungsten and copper or silver.

Permanent magnets can be made of densely packed and finely dispersed particles of suitable substances and be held to small tolerances. Other examples are clad or duplexed parts such as rods and slugs for nuclear reactors, bimetallic units for thermostats, and coated welding rods.

A class of materials made possible by powder metallurgy is known as *cermets*. As the name implies, they are combinations of metals and ceramics, with the strengths of the metals or alloys and the abrasion and heat resistances of the metallic compounds, which are the ceramics. One example is Al_2O_3–Cr. Cermets were developed in Germany in World War II for possible jet engine use. That usage was never realized because of their brittleness, but they have found other important applications, such as corrosion-resistant chemical apparatus, nuclear energy equipment, pumps for severe services, and systems for handling rocket fuels.

Metal can be made porous by powder metallurgy. Practical applications are bronze, nickel, and stainless steel filter elements, more shock resistant than ceramic, and bearings, gears, pump rotors, etc., impregnated with lubricants for long, carefree life.

Many machine and structural parts can be made most cheaply by powder metallurgy. This is true of intricate precision parts that can be produced in two quick steps by powder metallurgy instead of by several costly machining operations. Examples are gears, pawls, latches, cams, valve retainers, and brackets. As another example, powder metal preforms make for simple dies and fewer strikes and thus reduce the cost of forging some parts. In some cases higher purity, more variety, and better control of properties can be achieved by powder metallurgy than by melting and casting at fusion temperatures.

Powder metallurgy encompasses the preparation of the powders and their combination into useful articles. Basically, a powder metal is compacted to the shape desired and heated to strengthen the compact. The actual processes are many and differ to suit the materials treated and obtain the properties required in the finished product. The principles of the processes will be discussed.

METAL POWDERS

What a metal powder will produce depends upon its composition and physical characteristics. The most used compositions are the copper-base and iron-base powders; brass, iron, and steel for structural parts, and bronze for bearings. Others of importance, though in lesser amounts, are stainless steel, aluminum, titanium, nickel, tin, tungsten, copper, zirconium, graphite, and metallic oxides and carbides.

Substantially pure metal powders are used for some parts; alloys for others. Alloys may be obtained by alloying a metal before it is powdered or by mixing together powders of the desired ingredients. The first method gives a finer and more uniform alloy. The second is easier to compound but must be sintered with care to assure that the ingredients become diffused.

The physical characteristics of a powder metal are influenced by the way it is made. The chief characteristics are particle shape, size and size distribution, purity, grain structure, density, flow rate, and compressibility. Different powders are commonly mixed together to get desired properties.

Most metal powders are obtained by *reduction* of refined ore, mill scale, or prepared oxides by carbon monoxide or hydrogen. Grains tend to be porous. Particle size can be made quite uniform, which contributes to uniformity in the final product. Crude reduced powder called *sponge iron* is quoted at about $0.64/kg ($0.29/lb) f.o.b.

Metals may be *atomized* in a stream of air, steam, or inert gas. Some may be melted separately and injected through an orifice into the stream; others like iron and stainless steel may be fused in an electric arc (like sprayed metal), and refractory metals in a plasma arc (Chap. 14). As an example, small droplets of titanium freeze to powder after they are flung from the end of a rapidly rotating bar heated by a plasma arc in a helium atmosphere. Atomized particles are somewhat round.

Under controlled conditions metal powder may be *deposited electrolytically*. The material may have to be broken up and is milled or ground for fineness, heated to be annealed and to drive off hydrogen, and sorted and blended. Electrodeposited powders are among the purest and are characteristically dendritic. Cost is about $4.00/kg ($1.82/lb) f.o.b. for electrolytic iron powder.

Milling or *grinding* in ball mills, stampers, crushers, etc., is a means of producing powders of almost any degree of fineness from friable or malleable metals. Tungsten carbide grains are pulverized in this way. Some malleable metals are milled with a lubricant into flakes, which are not suitable for molding but are used in paints and pigments.

Nickel or iron can be made to react with carbon monoxide to form *metal carbonyls* such as $Ni(CO)_4$. These are decomposed to metal powders of high purity, small and uniform grain size, and dense and round particles. Carbonyl powders are costly but easier to work than other forms. For instance, carbonyl iron compacts are as strong and ductile when sintered at only 650°C (1200°F) as other iron compacts sintered at 1100°C (2000°F). They serve well for making continuous strips of powder and for critical electronic components but are mostly added to electrolytic powders to add strength and ductility.

Shotting is the process of dropping molten particles from a small opening through air or an inert gas into water. This produces spherical particles but not the smallest sizes.

Less common methods of making metal powders include ordinary *machining*, *vapor condensation, chemical decomposition, granulation* by stirring vigorously during solidification, and *impacting* of chips and scrap.

FABRICATION PROCESSES

The basic operations of compacting (or pressing) and heating (or sintering) may be combined in a number of ways in processes for fabricating metal powders. Common processes are depicted in Fig. 10-1. In addition, the operations of pressing and

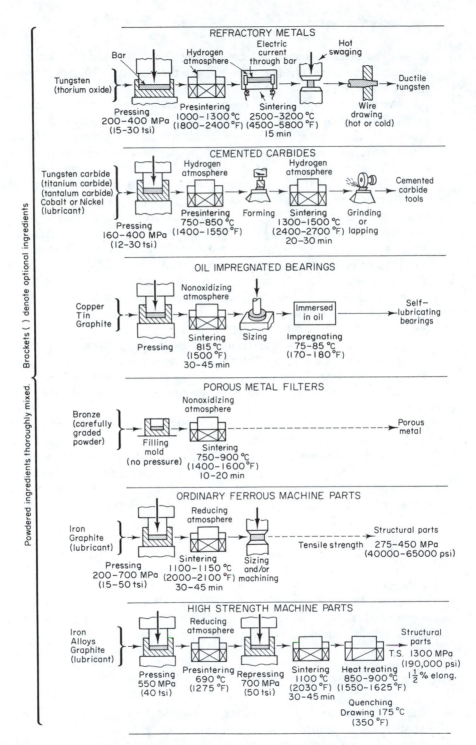

Figure 10-1 Some typical powder metallurgy processes.

sintering are varied and controlled to suit many conditions, and in some cases other operations are added. The basic operations and the principles that govern them will be described in the following sections.

PRESSING

The effect of pressure on powder metal is to squeeze the particles together to lock or key them in place, initiate interatomic bonds, and increase the density of the mass. The pressure applied to a compact determines its ultimate density and strength. A typical case is illustrated in Fig. 10-2. Theoretically if a powder is pressed enough, it will attain 100% of the density and strength of the parent metal, at least on being sintered. This is approached in some parts, in one way by repressing after initial pressing and presintering. High pressures, and particularly additional operations, are expensive and not warranted for parts that do not have to have high strength. On the other end of the density scale, little or no pressure is needed for porous parts.

Most parts are pressed cold. For more density and strength, parts may be subsequently hot pressed or forged (hammered). Hot pressing produces the most accuracy, but forging the most strength and costs more.

Suitable particle shape, size and size distribution, and careful selection and mixing are necessary to obtain a satisfactory pressed part. The best bonds are obtained between jagged particles, but round particles flow better into the mold and under pressure. The way the powder fills the die determines operation speed. Zinc stearate may be added to lubricate the die and the particles to minimize wear and aid in compaction. It volatizes in sintering and helps keep pores connected.

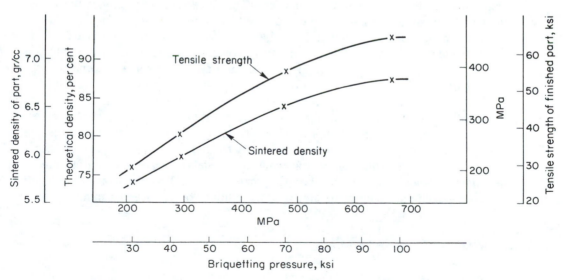

Figure 10-2 Relationships between briqueting pressure and sintered density and tensile strength for a carbon-iron powder sintered at 1110°C (2030°F) for 30 minutes. (As reported by S. R. Crooks.)

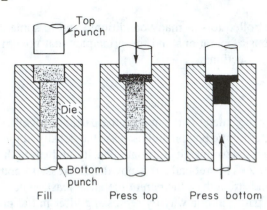

Figure 10-3   Steps in pressing simple powder metal part.

Powder metal is commonly compressed in a die cavity of the shape of the part by one or more punches. Quality depends upon packing the material uniformly. Powder metal does not flow readily around corners and into recesses like a fluid. Friction is high between the particles and walls of the die. Thus, one punch cannot compact any but the simplest parts to a uniform density. Those parts in particular that have steps, thin walls, flanges, etc. must be acted upon by two or more punches to distribute the pressure uniformly through the sections. A simple example is given in Fig. 10-3. The most complex of parts may require as many as two upper and three or four lower punch movements, and even some side core pulling movements supplied by the press. Some parts cannot even be made with available equipment.

Production powder pressing is normally done on presses specifically designed for the purpose. Such a press is rated by the force it can deliver and by the maximum depth of die chamber it can accommodate. The force rating determines the cross-sectional area of the largest part that can be subjected to a given pressure. The depth of die chamber, called the *die fill*, determines how deep a powder filling may be. This limits the length of a pressed part. The ratio of powder depth to compacted part length is from 2:1 to 3:1 for iron and copper and as high as 8:1 for some materials.

Most presses under 1.5 MN (170 tons) force capacity are mechanical for speed. A mechanical press works to uniform size but causes differences in density with variations in conditions such as the amount of charge. A hydraulic press may be set to exert a given pressure for uniform density or to stop at a uniform size. Large hydraulic powder metal presses have ratings up to 25 or more MN (several thousand tons). Presses range from single-stroke hand-fed models for an output of a few pieces per hour, (typically for large pieces in small quantities) to automatic rotary and multiple-punch machines capable of producing hundreds of parts per minute.

OTHER COMPACTING METHODS

Powder metal may be *slip cast* in molds. The powder is dispersed in a liquid containing chemicals to wet the particles to help distribute and then release the mass from the mold. The mold may be porous to absorb free liquid and may be vibrated to densify the compact. Slip-cast parts later sintered have adequate strength for many purposes. Fiber aggregates are used for sound and vibration absorption and as reinforcements for plastics and metals. Mold cost is low, and the method is economical for parts that are complex or made in small quantities. An example is given by a stainless steel part that would have required a $6000 hardened steel die in a 1200-ton press but was slip cast in a mold which cost less than $30. The method is slow and not justified for large quantities.

A method for heavy powders, such as tungsten carbide, is *centrifugal compacting*. The powder is twirled in a mold and packed uniformly with pressures up to 3 MPa (400 psi) on each particle. Parts must have uniform round sections. Equipment cost is not high.

Powder metal is also *injection molded*. A slurry of the powder in water or mixed with a thermoplastic material is squirted into a die. The binder is removed in sintering.

Continuous strips and rods are compacted by *rolling* copper, brass, bronze, Monel, nickel, titanium, or stainless steel powders or fibers. In a typical process, stainless steel powder is fed from a hopper between two rolls in a horizontal plane. The material emerges as a strip with a density of 6 to 6.8 g/cm^3. It is then sintered, rerolled three times, and annealed to a tensile strength of about 745 MPa (108,000 psi) and an elongation of 33%. Another process makes porous sheets for filters; a uniform layer of powder poured on a ceramic tray is sintered and then rolled to the desired density.

A means of applying pressure to obtain uniform density is to enclose powder in a shaped plastic or rubber mold and immerse it in a gas or liquid in a chamber under 70 to 700 MPa (10 to 100 ksi) pressure. This is *isostatic pressing*, sometimes called *hydraulic pressing* in a liquid. Complicated, assymmetrical, and large parts can be pressed more easily than in other ways. Isotropic parts are produced. Metal dies are not needed. For large work, equipment cost is about one-tenth of that for a press.

Powder metal, in metal or ceramic containers, and preforms are subjected to gas pressures as high as 350 MPa (50,000 psi) at temperatures to over 2200°C (4000°F) (but usually less) in *hot isostatic pressing* (HIP). This has been found effective for refractory metals, ceramics, and cermets and spherical powders that do not respond to cold pressing. Close to theoretical densities can be obtained by HIP.

Stainless steel, uranium, and zirconium powders are sealed in cans and compacted by being extruded through dies while protected from contamination. The sheath may be removed to use the base metal or may be left on for further protection, as in the case of uranium reactor rods.

Long tubes can be compacted *magnetically*. Powder metal is poured around a mandrel inside a coaxial conductor. A current of around 1 MA is pulsed through the conductor and sets up the magnetic field that crushes the inner conductor around the compact.

High-energy rate forming (by both presses and explosives—Chap. 13) is capable of compacting powders to nearly theoretical densities with sharp definition of detail and close tolerances. As an example, a 0.33-m (13-in.)-diameter and 9-kg (20-lb) iron powder dish was compacted to a 7.2-g/cm^3 density (7.8 is theoretical) by 270 kJ

(200,000 ft-lb) of energy on a high-energy-rate forging press like that depicted in Fig. 12-18. A 7000-ton hydraulic press would be needed for the same results.

SINTERING

Sintering augments the bonds between the particles and therefore strengthens a powder metal compact. In all cases this occurs because atoms of the particles in contact become intermingled. Generally speaking, this is brought about in one of two ways. In one way, one of the constituents of the compact melts; in the other way, none melts. An example of the first case is the sintering of cemented carbide, which is done above the melting point of the cobalt constituent. The molten cobalt fuses into a pervading matrix but also acts as a medium in which the carbide grains can grow together to form a skeleton throughout the mass. Carbide atoms appear to dissolve into the cobalt at points of high energy levels to build the bridges between the grains. This explains why cemented carbides are harder at high temperatures than high-speed steel that contains isolated carbides held together by a heat-susceptible ferrous matrix.

The second case is characteristic of the sintering of iron, copper, or tungsten powder. It is done usually at 60 to 80% of the melting temperature. The atoms at the spots of contact intermingle and migrate. The reason sintering is done below the melting point is that the process would actually be casting if the metals were melted, and powders would not be needed. Still the temperature must be high enough to excite rapid atomic mobility.

If substantially one constituent is present, as in the sintering of iron powder, a single phase is continuous from one particle to the next after sintering. In compacts of two or more different metals, alloys, or compounds, whether one melts or not, intermediate compounds or phases of the constituents are formed at the points of bonding of the particles. As sintering continues in either case, the bonded areas grow larger, and material more or less fills the voids between the particles. This is depicted in an ideal way in Fig. 10-4 in which particles are assumed round, and metal that enters the voids is shown darkened.

When no melting takes place, atoms must migrate from the solid parent particles to form and enlarge the bonds and fill the voids. The mechanisms believed to have roles in transporting the atoms are *surface diffusion, evaporation and condensation, bulk flow,* and *volume diffusion.* All seem to take place individually, successively, or simultaneously during the sintering process depending on the metal, powder condition, temperature, time, and atmosphere.

Diffusion and movement of atoms on the surfaces of the particles have been found to be the main activities in the early stages of sintering. *Surface tension* is the driving force to reduce the surface area, round and smooth surface irregularities, and segregate the unfilled spaces into fewer but larger pores. The surface area of small particles is large in relation to volume, and the influence of surface diffusion is proportionately great.

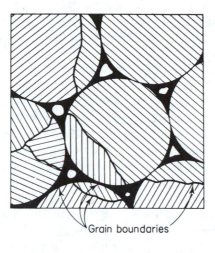

Figure 10-4 Idealized diagram of the arrangement of grains in a metal powder compact. Sections of original particles are depicted as circles.

Grain boundaries

Evaporation and condensation can be expected to have more effect with a molten constituent than with nonvolatile ones. One definite effect seems to be to spheroidize angular voids.

Bulk flow is the movement of solid material under stress. Some stress may be left in the particles after pressing, but most seems to be induced by enveloping surface tension forces, which appear to cause viscous flow of the material within the particles as well as on their surfaces at sintering temperatures.

Volume diffusion originates in the random movements of atoms induced by thermal vibration. Atoms tend to move from a location of high to one of lower concentration. Within metal crystals, atoms migrate from grain boundaries to voids within the lattice structure. There is strong experimental evidence that the major action in the later stages of sintering is a movement of atoms from the grain boundaries to the voids between the particles. Below the recrystallization temperature atoms migrate slowly. Above that temperature the atoms move faster, but the grains grow, and the grain boundaries become fewer. It has been shown that atoms do not rapidly enter and shrink voids no longer connected by grain boundaries. The lower left-hand section of Fig. 10-4 depicts the presence of grain boundaries and diminution of voids. The upper right-hand portion indicates a crystal grown to encompass several grains and the isolated pores within it that do not shrink appreciably.

As atoms leave grain boundaries, their space is filled by the grains moving together. This explains volume shrinkage often evident in sintering. After sufficient grain growth, grain boundaries become insignificant. Then atom migration, volume shrinkage, bond growth between particles, and increase of compact strength practically cease. That explains why there is an optimum time of sintering for each case. Up to that time properties are improved, but beyond that there is little benefit.

All materials do not shrink when sintered; some grow. An example is found in copper-brass compacts in which copper atoms migrate to and zinc atoms from the brass. Vacancies left by atoms from copper appear to be supplied by dislocations and grain boundaries, but zinc atoms leave holes in the brass. Porosity is observed to form on the brass side, and the grains do not shrink. Zinc atoms are added to the copper, and the net result is growth.

Because of its relatively large surface area, a powder metal compact is especially susceptible to oxidation and attack and must be kept clean to coalesce on an atomic scale. Sintering is usually done in a neutral or reducing atmosphere and even in critical cases in a vacuum. Sometimes reactive gases are added to speed the process and purge impurities. Solids are often mixed with powder metals to vaporize and open pores. All such measures must not contaminate the main sintering atmosphere. Precise control of atmospheres and temperature is important. Most sintering is done in semi- or fully continuous furnaces with a mesh belt, a roller hearth, a walking beam, or mechanical pushers and with several chambers for heating and cooling in stages such as preheat and burnoff, high heat, and cooling. Some induction sintering is done; it can be readily controlled and automated for high production rates.

Spark sintering is done by placing loose powder in a die, passing a large current through it, and applying pressure at the same time. An initial surge of current strips the oxide coating from the powder particles to leave clean surfaces that join together. A continuing current heats the mass under pressure. This process has been developed in the aerospace industry for many common and unusual materials and parts. Only one step is required, and the operation is fast.

FINISHING OPERATIONS

These impart specific properties or features to metal parts. They include infiltration, heat treatment, impregnation, sizing, and machining.

Infiltration consists of placing a piece of copper alloy in contact with a pre-sintered iron part and heating to 1150°C (2100°F). The copper melts and is drawn into the pores of the part by capillarity. The same results may be achieved in the sintering stage with copper-filled iron powder. Infiltration increases strength 70 to 100% and may improve machinability but makes the product more brittle. Tolerances cannot be held as closely with infiltration as with other methods, such as double pressing. Infiltration is often more expensive than the other methods such as using higher pressures to get higher density.

Iron parts may have *carbon added* to the original mixture or be *carburized* after sintering. They then are heated, quenched, and tempered like any other high-carbon steel product to a high degree of strength and hardness. An example is given at the bottom of Fig. 10-1.

Impregnation appears in two forms. Sintered compacts such as bearings may be saturated with oil, about 20% by volume, by immersion, or by drawing oil through the compact by vacuum. The oil deposit is withdrawn by heat or pressure as needed in service. Powder metal parts and all kinds of castings such as engine blocks, gear cases, pump bodies, and many more are impregnated to seal pores and prevent leaks in service. This is done with sodium silicate, polyester resins, or anaerobic polymers.

Powder metal parts may be repressed after sintering. This is called *sizing* if done to hold dimensions, and *coining* to increase density. Repressing may be done in compacting presses or in conventional presses like those described in Chap. 13.

METAL COMPOSITES

A new field of metallurgy is that of adding whiskers and fibers for high strengths in metallic parts, particularly at high temperatures. The scheme is similar to that of impregnating fibers with resins for high-strength plastic parts as described in Chap. 11. Aluminum alloys can be increased in strength by 350 to 700 MPa (50 to 100 ksi), with an increase of 50% in the modulus of elasticity, by a 10% addition of alumina whiskers. Nickel alloys with tensile strengths of 135 to 275 MPa (20 to 40 ksi), at 925°C (1700°F) stay at those levels at 1100°C (2000°F) with the addition of alumina whiskers but drop off to one-third as much without whiskers. Composites can attain almost the stiffness of steel with as little as one-third the density but have not been found suitable for some high-temperature applications. Costs are higher than for conventional metals but are expected to decline as the market grows. Ways of making composites include mixing fibers with molten metal, vapor- and electrodeposition of metal on fibers, powder metallurgy techniques, and eutectic solidification of the matrix and whisker constituents.

DESIGN OF POWDER METAL PARTS

Four guides to successful production of powder metal are:

1. Design parts to suit the process, especially if they have been made previously in other ways.
2. Design the tools to conform to the principles of powder metal operations, to compress the powder metal uniformly.
3. Standardize parts as much as possible to be able to use the minimum number of tools on the most parts.
4. Control all operations strictly.

A number of rules must be observed to design parts properly. Keep parts as small as possible. Cylinders, squares, and rectangles are the easiest shapes to press, and flat pieces are best. Steps add difficulty in getting homogeneity (Fig. 10-3). Sharp corners and edges, thin ridges, and deep slots should be avoided because they make tools, preforms, and finished parts weak. A part must not have side recesses that prevent it being pushed out of the die when compacted. Walls that are too thin are difficult to fill. The length of a part should not exceed two to three times its diameter. Thin and thick sections should not be next to each other because they expand differently on heating and cause cracks. Elaborations of these rules are given in handbooks.

Tolerances as small as 10 μm/cm (0.001 in./in.) may be held but are expensive. More practical tolerances are upward of $\pm$20 μm/cm ($\pm$0.002 in./in.) for diameters and $\pm$30 μm/cm ($\pm$0.003 in./in.) lengthwise.

COMPARISONS WITH OTHER PROCESSES

Powder metallurgy stands alone as a means to process some materials and parts and for making porous metal parts. In addition, this process competes successfully with others to produce many machine parts. It does so because it offers simple and fast operations at low cost for the time to make each piece.

The unfavorable costs for powder metallurgy are those for raw materials and tools. Iron powders cost $0.64/kg ($0.29/lb) and up in large quantities as compared with carbon steel billets at $0.37/kg ($0.17/lb) and bars at $0.40/kg ($0.18/lb). Commercial copper powder is quoted at about $2.86/kg ($1.30/lb). The simplest of dies may cost as much as $1000, and a complex die $10,000 or more. However, a die may turn out hundreds of thousands of pieces, and the cost per piece is small if they are all needed.

As a rule, powder metallurgy is not considered competitive for quantities of less than 20,000 pieces. Some cases have been reported where careful designing and planning have made powder metallurgy profitable for lots of even less than 1000 pieces. The capacities of ordinary equipment limit the process to relatively simple parts not over 26 cm^2 (4 in.^{2}) in area across. Parts of 1 to 2 kg (2 to 4 lb) are most common, but some 1.5 m (5 ft) long with a 300-mm (12-in.) diameter and weighing hundreds of kilograms (pounds) have been made.

QUESTIONS

1. What advantages does powder metallurgy offer?
2. How may alloys be obtained in powder metals?
3. What are the important physical characteristics of powder metals?
4. What are the principal ways of obtaining metal powders?
5. Describe the basic operations in powder metallurgy to produce ductile tungsten wire, cemented carbide tools, self-lubricating bearings, porous metal filters, ordinary structural parts, and high-strength machine parts.
6. Why is powder metal pressed? Why is uniformity important, and how is it obtained?
7. What kinds of presses are used for powder metallurgy?
8. What are the benefits of slip casting powder metals?
9. What are isostatic and hydraulic pressing, and what is their main benefit?
10. How are continuous strips made of powder metal?
11. Discuss what takes place to bond powder particles together when they are sintered.
12. What four processes contribute to the movement of atoms to bring about bonding of metal powders?

13. What factors determine the optimum temperature and length of time to sinter a powder metal?

14. Why do some powder metal compacts shrink on sintering? Why do others grow?

15. Why must powder metals be sintered in controlled atmospheres?

16. What is infiltration, and what does it do?

17. What is impregnation, and what is its purpose?

18. What does coining or sizing do to powder metal parts?

19. What precautions must be taken in machining powder metal parts?

20. Describe spark sintering and what it will do.

21. State four guides to successful production of powder metal parts.

22. What helps and what hinders powder metallurgy in competition with other processes?

PROBLEMS

1. A bushing with 40 mm ($1\text{-}\frac{37}{64}$ in.) OD, 25 mm (1 in.) ID, and 32 mm ($1\text{-}\frac{1}{4}$ in.) length is to be made from iron and alloying materials in the manner depicted at the bottom of Fig. 10-1. What force in meganewtons (tons) and what die fill depth in millimeters (inches) must a press be able to provide for the first pressing?

2. The green density of the compact described in Prob. 1 is 7 g/cm^3. What is the approximate density of the powder metal before pressing?

3. A round piece as depicted in Fig. 10-3 has a head 50 mm (2 in.) in diameter and 15 mm (ca. $\frac{1}{2}$ in.) thick. The stem has a 20-mm ($\frac{3}{4}$-in.) diameter and is 18 mm ($\frac{5}{8}$ in.) long. The part is to be made from brass powder. Compacting pressure must be 350 MPa (25 tons/in.^{2}). Estimate the force and die fill the press must provide.

REFERENCES

"The Basics of Modern PM," *American Machinist*, Oct. 1977, p. 124.

BRADBURY, S., "How to Specify Features on Powder Metallurgy Parts," *Machine Design*, Oct. 1, 1970, p. 99.

HUSEBY, R., "P/M—How Parts Are Sintered," *Manufacturing Engineering and Management*, May 1970, p. 27.

KUHN, H. A. and A. LAWLEY, eds., *Powder Metallurgy Processing: New Techniques and Analyses*, Academic Press, New York, 1978.

Metals Handbook, Vol. 4: *Forming*, 8th ed., American Society for Metals, Metals Park, Ohio, 1969.

PRICE, P. E., "Hot Isostatic Pressing in the Aerospace Industry," *Metal Progress*, Feb. 1982, p. 46.

TRUCKS, H. E., *Designing for Economical Production*, Society of Manufacturing Engineers, Dearborn, Mich., 1974.

WEETON, J. W., "Fiber–Metal Matrix Composites," *Machine Design*, Feb. 20, 1969, p. 142.

11

PLASTICS
AND RUBBER

The term *plastic* in its original sense applies to a material that can be made to flow so that it can be molded or modeled. That is true of metals, clay, and other materials, but the name has come to designate specifically a group of organic solids that can readily be made to flow by heat or pressure, or both, into valuable commercial shapes.

Plastics are mostly products of this century. Natural shellac and bitumen have been known for ages. Celluloid was discovered by Hyatt in 1868 in a search for a substitute for ivory for billiard balls. The modern plastic industry started with the development of Bakelite by Baekeland in 1909. Since then growth has been rapid, into more than 30 chemically distinct families of plastics, hundreds of compounds, and thousands of products.

Plastics have been increasingly accepted because they offer unique combinations but yet a wide variety of properties and are particularly fitted for many modern developments. Plastics are light in weight; most weigh less than magnesium. Outside of especially light-foamed plastics, an average specific gravity is about 1.4. This has suited them for trim and accessories in commercial aircraft and has helped lighten many implements held by hand. Plastics are good electrical insulators at low and high frequencies and have important uses in the electrical industry. They are good heat insulators also. Some weather well and are highly resistant to corrosion and chemicals.

The strengths of plastics cover a broad spectrum. Most materials are in the low end of the range, but some have quite high strengths. Their main structural advantage is a high strength-to-weight ratio. The tensile strength of some plastics is only 7 MPa (1000 psi) or so; most range from 35 to 140 MPa (ca. 5000 to 20,000 psi), but some reinforced plastics have strengths all the way to 3 GPa (440,000 psi). As an example of weight advantage, an epoxy reinforced with woven glass fabric, with a tensile strength of 590 MPa (85,000 psi) and a specific gravity of 1.85, has a strength-to-weight ratio of almost twice that for heat-treated alloy steel and only a little less than for heat-treated titanium alloy.

Most mechanical properties of plastics are inferior to those of metals. Plastics are subject to some dimensional instability, with appreciable creep and cold flow at all temperatures, and some are swollen by moisture. Thermal expansion is large compared to metals. Top operating temperatures range from 65°C (150°F) to around 315°C (600°F) for plastics, but most metals serve well above that range. At best, the rigidity and fatigue strength of plastics are well below those of metals.

Manufacture of plastics is economical because most products can be entirely finished by molding and forming without secondary operations. Molding and forming operations are aided by the pliability and heat sensitivity of plastics; for instance, a plastic part can be extricated more easily from a mold than can a metal part. Intricate plastic parts can be molded, and it is not unusual for one plastic molding to take the place of several formed metallic parts.

Probably of most significance, plastics offer a greater range of appeal to the eye than any other class of materials. Molding usually leaves a good surface finish, but a higher luster can be added by a simple solvent treatment or buffing. All colors are available, but not in all plastics. Color is impregnated into an object and is more lasting than paint. Some plastics offer true transparency without the brittleness of glass. Plastic materials are commonly used for coatings for protection and decoration (Chap. 30).

Rubber and synthetic elastomers have some of the same properties as plastics and will be included in this survey.

PLASTIC MATERIALS

The Resins.   Many kinds of materials are called plastics. Most of them are based on some form of synthetic organic resin that is a compound containing carbon as the central element. Other elements such as hydrogen, oxygen, nitrogen, and chlorine are linked to the carbon atoms to form the molecules. The properties of a plastic material depend upon the atoms it contains, the way these atoms are arranged in molecules, and the ways the molecules are arrayed and related in the mass.

An example of an organic compound is methane, one of the simplest. Its formula is written in Fig. 11-1 to designate its structure. Methane is a gas and not a plastic. It is the first of a series of organic chain compounds that are said to be *saturated* because all the valence bonds of the carbon atoms are satisfied. The second compound of the series is ethane; its formula is also given in Fig. 11-1. A compound in which the valence bonds of the carbon atoms are not satisfied is said to be *unsaturated*. The structures of two simple unsaturated compounds, ethylene and acetylene, are indicated in Fig. 11-1. The double and triple lines in the formulas designate the lack of saturation.

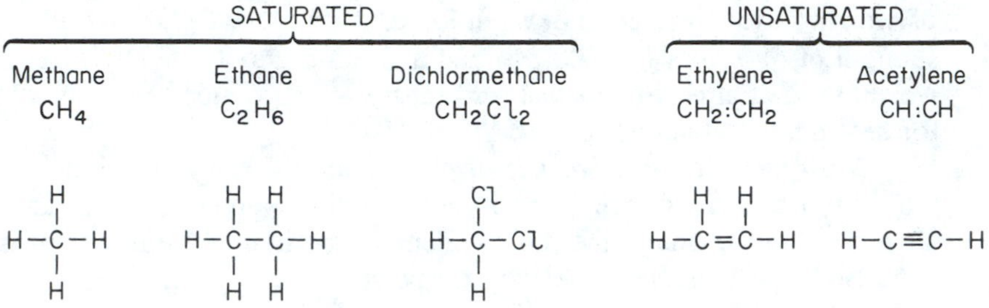

SATURATED			UNSATURATED	
Methane CH_4	Ethane C_2H_6	Dichlormethane CH_2Cl_2	Ethylene $CH_2:CH_2$	Acetylene $CH:CH$

$$H-\underset{\underset{H}{|}}{\overset{\overset{H}{|}}{C}}-H \qquad H-\underset{\underset{H}{|}}{\overset{\overset{H}{|}}{C}}-\underset{\underset{H}{|}}{\overset{\overset{H}{|}}{C}}-H \qquad H-\underset{\underset{H}{|}}{\overset{\overset{Cl}{|}}{C}}-Cl \qquad H-\overset{\overset{H}{|}}{C}=\overset{\overset{H}{|}}{C}-H \qquad H-C\equiv C-H$$

Figure 11-1 Designation of some simple organic compounds.

With proper pressure, temperature, and catalysts, a number of ethylene molecules with unsaturated bonds can be joined together into a long molecule as indicated in Fig. 11-2. A substance composed of basic molecules is a *monomer*. The formation of larger molecules from smaller ones is called *polymerization*. The substance thus formed is a *polymer*. As the molecules grow larger, a gas like ethylene becomes a liquid and ultimately a solid. Polymerization leads to an increase in the boiling point of a liquid and the melting point of a solid.

Polymers are formed in two ways. The first is *linear addition,* as exemplified on the left in Fig. 11-2, and occurs when the final mass of each molecule is the sum of the masses of the original monomers. Some polymers may contain thousands of monomers. Some molecules are chains of one kind of monomer, like the polyethylene illustrated; others contain two or more different kinds. When different monomers are combined, the process is called *copolymerization,* and the product is a *copolymer.* The second way of forming polymers is by *linear condensation,* as exemplified on the right of Fig. 11-2. There the components react, and a by-product, usually water, is cast off.

Various hydrogen atoms in a chain may be replaced by other elements, such as chlorine or fluorine which retard combustion, for instance, or by radicals, such as methyl CH_3. These affixed atoms or radicals denoted by letters R in Fig. 11-3 may be randomly oriented on a chain (*atactic*), all on one side (*isotactic*), or alternately on one side and then the other (*syndiotactic*). Such chains can be more closely packed and have higher melting points in the order of atactic < syndiotactic < isotactic.

One major class of plastics, called the *thermoplastic* materials, is composed of chemically separate long molecules. They are held together by secondary bonds, which are associative attractive forces between the molecules that are weaker than the primary bonds between the atoms within each molecule. When the molecules are

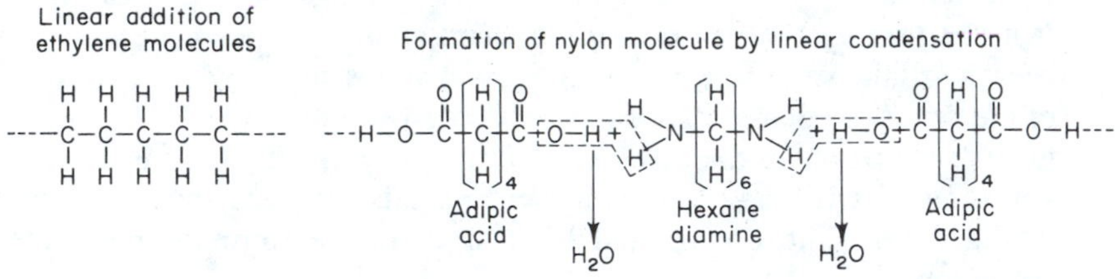

Linear addition of ethylene molecules

Formation of nylon molecule by linear condensation

Figure 11-2 Two examples of polymerization.

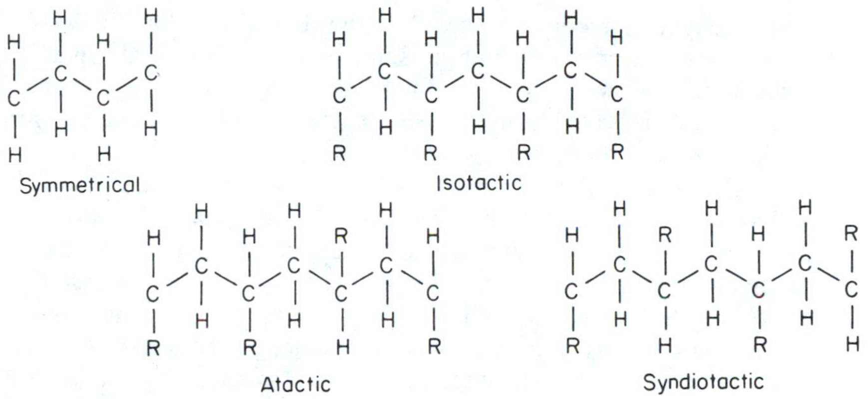

Figure 11-3 Molecular structure of plastics.

activated and separated by heat, the secondary bonds are weakened, and the material softens and ultimately melts.

Most commercial thermoplastics are either amorphous or crystalline. In the amorphous or glassy form, the molecules are intertwined in no apparent order. Examples are polystyrene, polymethyl methacrylate, and polycarbonate. In the crystalline form the long molecules are folded in regular array in small thin crystallites gathered into bundles in larger aggregates called spherulites, which compose the gross internal structure like the grains in metal. The crystallites and spherulites are surrounded by amorphous material but appear to be interconnected by multitudes of links of small fibers of crystalline material. Examples are polyethylene, isostatic polypropylene, acetal, and nylon. A third and less common form is that of rubber-modified-plastics like ABS in which the rubber exists as small round particles well dispersed in a rigid glassy matrix. This toughens a hard and brittle material.

The nature of the molecules as well as the way they are arranged determines the properties of a thermoplastic material. The forces between individual particles depend directly upon the masses and inversely upon a power of the distance between them. Thus long and heavy molecules have strong associative forces and make up strong and tough plastics. Relatively straight molecular chains can be closely packed and form stiff plastics; materials with coiled or branched molecules are more flexible. Substitutional radicals make molecules bipolar and set up a magnetic attraction between molecules. Isostatic molecules, particularly, are strongly bipolar and can be closely packed; they tend to form materials that soften at higher temperatures. Amorphous plastics have fewer associative bonds and soften at lower temperatures while the more crystalline materials have more numerous links and can be made to withstand the highest temperatures that organic substances can endure. Clear plastics are generally amorphous, because crystallites scatter light and make a material translucent.

A second major class of plastics, called *thermosetting* materials, is composed of long molecules linked to each other in three dimensions by primary or valence bonds. They are not broken by heat until the compound is decomposed. An example of the formation of a thermosetting plastic is given by the reaction between phenol and formaldehyde to produce a phenolic resin as indicated in Fig. 11-4. Under proper conditions of temperature and pressure, some of the formaldehyde molecules form links in linear chains, and others form links between the chains of phenol molecules. If the product is heated to an excessive temperature, it chars and decomposes but short of that does not soften once formed.

The thermosetting plastics are generally stronger, harder, more resistant to heat and solvents, and lower in material cost. The secondary bonds of the thermoplastic materials allow deformation and flow under stress. This tends to redistribute stress concentrations under load and makes the material tough. In contrast, the thermosetting plastics are brittle. Because of heat susceptibility, thermoplastics can be molded easily but are found mostly in packaging and consumer goods for uses at room temperatures. Even so the distinctions between the two classes have been fading away as thermoplastics have been developed to be serviceable at 425°C (800°F), well above the top working temperatures of most thermosetting materials.

Another plastic system is that of the *ionomers,* which contain strong metallic polar groups distributed along nonpolar chains (e.g., polyethylene). The polar groups tend to cluster together as much as they can. They inhibit crystalline formation and thus give almost clear plastic. Loss of crystalline strength is more than made up for by the strong polar forces, and the ionomers are tough and highly elastic.

Thermoplastic *superpolymers* have been developed in recent years with service temperatures above 200°C (400°F), in the realm of the thermosets, and exceptional resistances to solvents, oils, corrosive substances, and even burning. Notable among these are the fluoroplastics, polyimides, and polysulfones of Table 11-2. Their usage is limited because their costs are high and they usually are difficult to process.

The forms and properties of polymers depend largely upon how they are prepared. The lengths of the chains, side chains, how the molecules are arrayed, etc. vary with the proportions of ingredients, catalysts, control of temperature and pressure, and commercial processes used. The four general commercial processes are the bulk, emulsion, solution, and suspension methods. A polymer is formed in a mass of the monomers by the bulk method. Other substances are not needed, and impurities are avoided, but high temperatures harmful to the product may be hard to control. The monomer is dispersed or dissolved in another medium, often water, in the emulsion, solution, or suspension methods. Such may be necessary to control the monomer or obtain the product in a certain form, like fine particles rather than lumps.

New materials and methods are appearing in the plastics industry. The realm of plastics is growing beyond the hydrocarbon compounds into that of inorganic polymers. The silicones that are based upon chains of silicon rather than carbon are well established and will be described later. Other series are emerging, built upon such elements as phosphorus and boron. In general, organics cannot stand heat, inorganics cannot stand strain. It is the bridge between the two areas that is being opened by inorganic plastics. In processing, irradiation is used to produce polymers without heat or catalyst, induce cross-links even in thermoplastics, and bring about reactions between polymers and other materials to change properties.

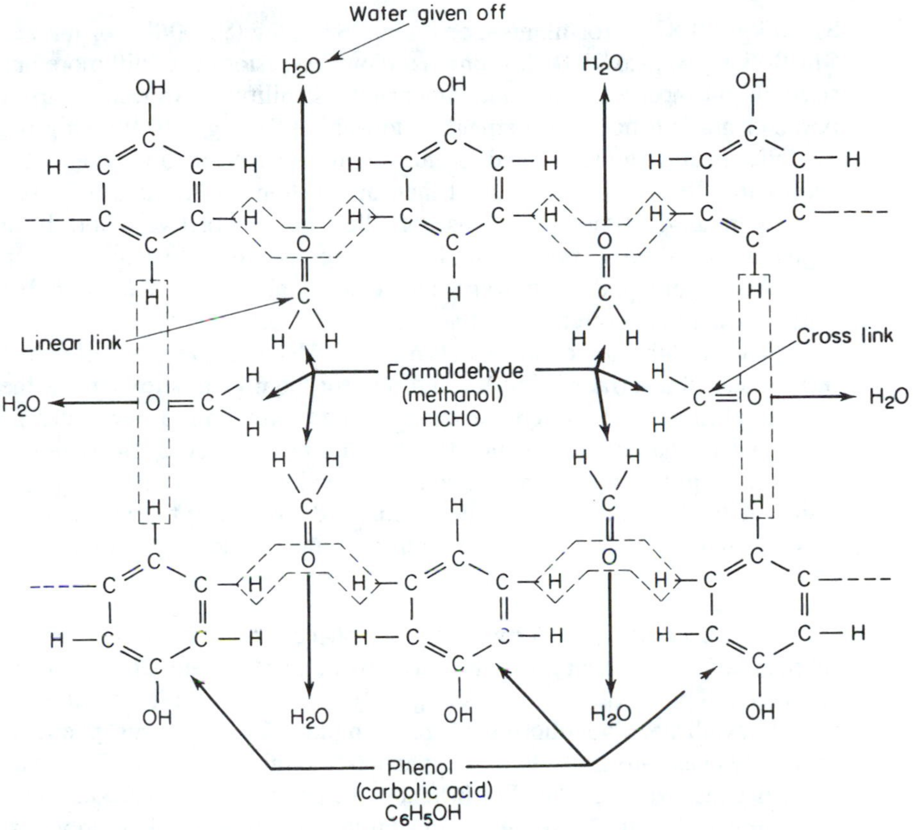

Figure 11-4 Polymerization of a thermosetting phenolic resin.

Other Constituents. The plastic resin in most cases is mixed with other substances to make the final product. The additives may be *fillers, pigments* or *dyes, stabilizers, plasticizers,* or *lubricants.*

Fillers are added to most thermosetting plastics and many thermoplastics. As much as 80% inert material may be put in molded parts. Most commonly earthy materials such as calcium carbonate at $0.10 to $0.45/kg ($0.05 to $0.20/lb), depending upon quality, provide bulk alone. Wood filler for around $0.22/kg ($0.10/lb) gives bulk with some strength and good moldability but tends to absorb moisture. Macerated cloth and fibers at higher prices add more strength. Carbon or silver additives make plastics conductive. Other fillers are used for particular purposes.

Reinforced plastics or *composites* have fibers added to a resin matrix mainly for superior strength. Glass-reinforced plastic (GRP) is the most common. The *aramids* comprise another class of high-strength fibers; Kevlar is a common trade name. Properties depend upon the forms of the materials and processing, but strengths may be increased with glass fibers by a factor of 2 or more. Some typical prices are

$1.80/kg ($0.80/lb) for filament or roving, $2.20/kg ($1.00/lb) for mat, and $6.60 to $11.00/kg ($3.00 to $5.00/lb) for glass cloth. Asbestos costs still more but gives high strength plus heat resistance and dimensional stability. Advanced composites contain boron or graphite fibers or filaments at upward of $22/kg ($10/lb) but provide specific moduli, specific strengths, and fatigue strengths superior to GRP and in some cases surpassing the best metals. As yet their applications are limited by cost.

Normally, neither the resins nor fillers have attractive colors by themselves. Pigments are added to impart color by their presence; dyes to color the resins or fillers.

A solid or liquid plasticizer is intended to make the product more flexible or less brittle. It may help the flow of material in the mold.

Various lubricant or slip agents may be added to aid removal of parts from molds or to make film surfaces slippery and prevent them from sticking together.

A plastic may be in one or more of three forms in the raw material state. First are powders, flakes, or granules for molding plastic pieces. Second are liquids for castings, impregnated laminates, adhesives, paints, and mixed molding compounds. Third are the filaments, films, sheets, rods, and tubes to be fabricated into the finished articles such as by weaving into cloth, cutting and joining into wrappers, or machining.

Plastic Products.   A main purpose of the discussion so far has been to point out the many factors that affect the makeup of a plastic material. Thus a manufacturer can vary the properties of a product greatly, and there is a large variety of different plastics available. Phenolic resins are examples. The two main phenolic resins are nominally phenol-formaldehyde and phenol-furfural compounds. Each maker of these resins has his own formulas. For instance, the phenol may be carbolic acid or any one of a number of related substances. In addition, a variety of fillers in various amounts may be added to the resin. The result is that phenolics are available with a wide range of properties; tensile strength is only one. It may be as low as 35 MPa (5000 psi) in the ordinary run of molded parts but can be made as high as 85 MPa (12,000 psi) where needed. Exceptional properties, of course, cost more, and the attempt of each supplier is to meet his customers' needs at the lowest cost.

Full specifications of the properties of plastics are tabulated in reference texts and handbooks. The chief features of major plastics will be described in this text.

Thermosetting Plastics.   Thermosetting plastics are polymerized when molded or formed. A primary mixture is subjected to heat, pressure, or a catalyst, singly or in combination, over a time to enforce the links within and between the large molecules. The mixture first softens and can be forced into the shape desired but then hardens permanently.

Prices are given for large quantities of plastic materials in this chapter as a basis for comparison. Their purpose is to indicate relative costs. They can be expected to change with economic and other conditions and quantities. Material cost is only part of the cost of the finished product. Processing cost is also a substantial item and is to a large extent based on time. In the case of thermosetting plastics, polymerization takes time, from a fraction of a minute in some molding operations to hours for some castings.

The six principal thermosetting plastic families are described briefly in Table 11-1. The phenolics are the oldest and most used because they serve many purposes at low cost. Other materials offer advantages for particular applications.

Thermoplastic Plastics. Thermoplastics are available as resins and compounds for molding, as sheets, rods, tubes, etc., for fabricating, in textile fabrics, as liquids for paints and adhesives, and as film and foil for packaging. A common way to classify the important commercial plastics is to divide them into families as shown in Table 11-2, but each family has many variations. For instance, one supplier offers over 400 different types of polyethylene. Compounds between different families are common.

Since thermoplastics are available in many grades, varieties, and combinations, the designer using plastic material must select the combination to suit requirements at lowest cost. The desired properties may be physical, mechanical, serviceable, or visual. Some materials have unique qualities. For instance, cellulosics offer high surface gloss; vinyls fluid and wear resistance with unusual flexibility. The polystyrenes are used more than any other for molded articles because of good physical properties and low cost.

Low processing cost is a main advantage of the most used thermoplastics. Studies have indicated for injection molded plastics a ratio of 2 for total cost to material cost; in comparison, for zinc die castings ratios are reported to be from 3 to 5. Processing cost is also important in the choice of a particular plastic. For example, polyethylene costs more in some grades but can be injection-molded faster and more economically than styrenes in some cases.

Elastomers. Elastomers are polymers that in a primary state are tacky and flow readily at room temperatures. To make them useful their molecules are cross-linked at widely separated points (as a quasi-thermoset) into a network. Their molecules tend to curl up in random fashion but when stretched must act in a concerted manner. This property results from vulcanization in natural rubber. Originally, this was done by heating with sulfur, but today selenium, tellurium, and organic sulfur compounds also serve as vulcanizing agents. Other additives to rubber are substances to accelerate vulcanization, activators for the accelerators, antioxidation agents, plasticizers, reinforcing agents, stiffeners, fillers, and pigments or coloring agents to meet specific service conditions.

The main synthetic materials with rubbery properties of commercial importance are described in Table 11-3. Still others are available but less used. Some synthetic rubbers, like isoprene, are chemically and physically much like natural rubber and compete on a price basis. Others have properties that rubber lacks, like oil or temperature resistance, and serve where needed but at higher cost.

TABLE 11-1 MAJOR THERMOSETTING PLASTICS

Class name	Some trade names	Tensile strength [MPa (ksi)]	Max. service temperature [°C (°F)]	Average relative cost [$/kg ($/lb)]	Important properties	Fabrication processes (raw materials)	Typical uses
Alkyds	Durez, Plenco, Plaston	21–62 (3–9)	150 (300)	1.80 (0.80)	Good electrical insulation, dimensional stability, and impact resistance	Molding (powders, liquids, soft sheets, ropes, logs, or slugs)	Electrical equipment
Allylics	Acme, Dapon, Plaskon	28–55 (4–8)	180 (350)	8.60 (3.90)	High moisture and chemical resistance, stability, and dielectric strength	Molding and extrusion, lamination, (powders, liquids, prepregs)	Electronic gear, lenses, laminates
Aminos: (urea- and mela-mine-formalde-hyde)	Bakelite, Beetle, Melmac	34–69 (5–10)	80–100 (170–210)	1.50 (0.70)	Colorful, hard; resist scratches, detergents, and many liquids	Molding and laminating (powders, granules, liquids, foams)	Tableware, distributor caps, counter tops, appliance housings

TABLE 11-1 (cont.)

Class name	Some trade names	Tensile strength [MPa (ksi)]	Max. service temperature [°C (°F)]	Average relative cost [$/kg ($/lb)]	Important properties	Fabrication processes (raw materials)	Typical uses
Epoxies	Durez, Hysol, Polymeric	34–207 (5–30)	260 (500)	2.05 (0.95)	Good electrical and mechanical properties, stable, resist heat and chemicals, strong adhesive	Casting, extrusion, molding, and potting (powders, liquids, foams)	Adhesives, tanks and enclosures, tools, and dies
Phenolics: phenol-formaldehyde and -furfural	Bakelite, Genal, Textolite	34–69 (5–10)	150–260 (300–500)	1.10 (0.50)	Rigid, stable, good electrical and chemical resistance, limited colors	Molding and casting, (powders, pellets, solutions and impregnations)	Electrical gear, appliance parts, laminated panels, grinding wheel bonds
Polyesters	Dacron, Mylar	7–345 (1–50)	65–150 (150–300)	1.10 (0.50)	Make tough reinforcements; resist most solvents, acids, and bases	Molding, casting, laminating (powders, liquids, sheets, rods, and tubes)	Auto body parts, decorations, boats, luggage

TABLE 11-2 MAJOR THERMOPLASTIC PLASTICS

Class name	Some trade names	Tensile strength [MPa (ksi)]	Maximum service [°C (°F)]	Average relative cost [$/kg ($/lb)]
ABS Acrylonitrile-butadiene-styrene	Abson, Cycolac, Marbon, Seilon	28–55 (4–8)	120 (250)	1.40 (0.65)
Acetals: homopolymers, copolymers	Delrin, Celcon	55–69 (8–10)	80–105 (180–220)	2.45 (1.10)
Acrylics: ethyl and methyl-methacrylate	Acrylite, Lucite, Perpex, Plexiglas	42–69 (6–10)	60–110 (140–230)	1.50 (0.70) molding grade
Cellulosics: cellulose acetate (butyrate), cellulose nitrate, cellulose propionate, ethyl cellulose	Ethocel, Lumarith, Tenite	10–59 (1.5–8.5)	50–90 (120–200)	2.20 (1.00)
Fluoroplastics TFE, FEP, PFA fluoro-carbons, ETFE, ECTFE fluoropolymers, CTFE resins, etc.	Fluorthene, Halar, Polyfluoron, Teflon, Tefzel	17–45 (2.5–6.5)	175–290 (350–550)	18.70 (8.50)
Ionomers		14–34 (2–5)	70 (160)	1.90 (0.85)
Phenoxies: phenylene oxide base	Bakelite, Noryl	48–117 (7–17)	75 (170)	3.30 (1.50)
Polyamides	Nylon, Ultramid, Versalon	55–207 (8–30)	120–150 (250–300)	4.30 (1.95)
Polycarbonates	Lexan, Merlon	62–72 (9–10.5)	120 (250)	2.75 (1.25)
Polyesters, polyterephthalates	Celanex, Tenite, Valox	55–121 (8–17.5)	110 (230)	2.20 (1.00)
Polyethylenes	Alathone, Ethylux, Polythene	4–48 (0.5–7)	90 (200)	0.90 (0.40)

Important properties	Fabrication processes (raw materials)	Typical uses
Hard, rigid, and tough; wide range of properties; weather degradable	Extrusion, molding, cold forming, calendering (resin and additives)	Auto trim, impellers, cases, piping, helmets, knobs, grilles, housings
Strong and rigid with good moisture, heat, and chemical resistance; resist most solvents but not strong mineral acids	Extrusion, molding, forming, machining (resins, some with fiberglass and other fillers, and additives)	Gears, sprockets, casters, leaf springs, bearings, levers, fans, piping, valves
Moderate strength, soft, low heat resistance in most grades; good optically, clear to colored; good electrical resistance	Extrusion, molding, casting, machining (molding compounds and cast sheets)	Lenses, signs, nameplates, decorations, display novelties, dials, glazing, bottles, models
Tough, easy to process; good transparency and surface gloss; many colors; moderate resistance to heat and etchants	Extrusion, molding, thermoforming, coating, machining (molding compounds, films, sheets, rods, powders)	Knobs, handles, appliance housings and trim, glazing, packaging, billiard balls, pipe, steering wheels
Outstanding inertness and chemical, electrical, temperature, and weather resistance; low friction; low strength but some reinforceable; tough at low temperatures	Extrusion, molding, coating, forming, dispersion casting, machining (granules, pellets, powders, and dispersions plus fillers, films, sheets)	Bearings, seals, piping, electrical insulation, enamels, nonstick-high-temperature coatings, release surfaces, ablative shields
Light, tough, transparent, and flexible; not stiff and some creep	Extrusion, molding, thermoforming (resins and stabilizers)	Films, toys, containers, trays, wire insulation
Good ductility, stability, and low temperature properties	Extrusion, molding, thermoforming; foamable and some platable (various grades of resins, some reinforced)	Water-flow parts, electronic devices, auto trim, appliance housings and parts
High strength, rigidity, and impact, temperature, electrical, and chemical resistant, absorb water, solvent softened	Extrusion, molding, sintering, forming, casting, coating, machining (solid and liquid resins with fillers and reinforcements)	Cloth, bristles, sutures, tubing, bearings, cams, gears, gaskets, insulation
High strength, ductility, rigidity, and electrical resistance down to $-170°C$ ($-275°F$), transparent	Extrusion, molding, foaming, machining (resins and sheets)	Safety sheets, signs, lenses, covers, sight gages, globes and lighting aides, armor, bearing balls
Good chemical, water, abrasion, and electrical resistance, tough	Extrusion and molding (resins; some reinforced)	Pumps, meters, gears, cams, rollers, electromechanical components
Tough to $-98°C$ ($-145°F$); good chemical, moisture, and electrical resistance; low friction; most used plastic; many grades; flexible to rigid	Worked by all processes (resin with additives)	Housings, piping, ducts, bottles, pails, tanks, insulation, housewares, toys, coatings, films, packaging

TABLE 11-2 *(cont.)*

Class name	Some trade names	Tensile strength [MPa (ksi)]	Maximum service [°C (°F)]	Average relative cost [$/kg ($/lb)]
Polyimides	Gemon, Kapton, Vespel	69–172 (10–25)	315 (600)	26.50 (12.00)
Polypropylenes	Escon, Propylux, Tenite	34–59 (5–8.5)	120 (250)	0.85 (0.39)
Polystyrenes	Cerex, Loralin, Lustron, Styron	14–55 (2–8)	60–80 (140–175)	0.80 (0.36)
Polysulfones	Udel	69 (10)	150–260 (300–500)	7.90 (3.60)
Vinyls: polyvinyl chloride, acetate, etc.	Chemaco, Elvanol, Saran, Vinylite	7–48 (1–7)	60–105 (140–220)	0.90 (0.40)

TABLE 11-3 MAJOR ELASTOMERS

Names	Properties[a]	Average relative cost [$/kg ($/lb)]	Features and particular uses
Natural rubber, natural poly-isoprene, NR	A:R B:20 (3) C:7.5–8.5	1.30 (0.60)	Excellent physical properties; good resistance to cutting, gouging, and abrasion; low heat, ozone, and oil resistance
Isoprene, synthetic poly-isoprene, IR	A:R B:17 (2.5) C:3.0–8.0	1.55 (0.70)	Same as natural rubber but requires less mastication; auto tires, power belts, hoses, gaskets, seals, rollers
GR-S or Buna S, styrene-butadiene, SBR	A:R B:1.7 (0.25) C:4.0–6.0	1.00 (0.45)	Good physical properties when reinforced; excellent abrasion and water resistance; not oil, ozone, or weather resistant
Butyl isobutylene isoprene, IIR	A:R B:18 (2.7) C:7.5–9.0	1.05 (0.70)	Excellent weather and heat resistance; low gas permeability; good chemical, ozone, and age resistance; fair strength and resilience; tire inner tubes, steam hoses, and insulation

[a]Code for designation of properties: A. service: R for no resistance to oils, S for specific resistance to oils, T for prolonged exposure to abnormal temperatures and compounded oils; B. pure gum relative mean tensile strength—MPa (ksi); C. pure gum elongation at rupture, 100%.

Important properties	Fabrication processes (raw materials)	Typical uses
Strong, rigid, and stable with excellent heat, abrasion, creep, and radiation resistance; flexible at $-270°C$ $(-450°F)$	Molding and sintering (powders, coatings, films, solid forms)	Valves, electrical insulation, hundreds of parts in every jet engine
Chemical, moisture, and electrical resistance; special grades for impact strength and high- or low-temperature service	Extrusion, molding, laminating, coating, sintering (resin with additives)	Electrical equipment, hinges, piping, packaging, luggage, auto trim
Good electrical and stain resistance	Extrusion, molding, thermoforming, foaming (resin with additives)	Piping, dials, toys, H.F. insulation, battery boxes, dental plates, dinnerware, auto and appliance parts, lenses
Rigid and ductile to $-100°C$ $(-140°F)$; stable, and electrical resistance	Extrusion, molding, thermoforming (resin with additives)	Auto and electrical parts, housings, piping, cable insulation
Very flexible to rigid; good flame, electrical, chemical, oil, abrasion, and weather resistance in various grades; colorable and attractive; easy to process	Extrusion, molding, calendering, coating, casting, foaming (resin with additives, dispersions, sheets, films)	Floor and wall covering, upholstery, rainwear, house siding, tubing, toys, insulation, phono records, safety glass

TABLE 11-3 *(cont.)*

Names	Properties[a]	Average relative cost [\$/kg (\$/lb)]	Features and particular uses
Chlorobutyl-, chloroisobutylene-isoprene, IIR modified	A:T B:18 (2.7) C:7.5–9.0	1.10 (0.50)	Properties similar to butyl with service temperatures to 200°C (400°F) and good oil resistance when blended; for inner tubes and curing bladders
Polybutadiene, *cis*-4, BR	A:R B:4 (0.6) C:4.0–10.0	1.25 (0.55)	Overall properties like rubber and SBR but better abrasion and weather resistance, low-temperature service and resilience; usually used in blends
Ethylene propylene, EPM (terpolymer EPDM)	A:R B:7 (1.0) max. C:Poor	1.65 (0.80)	Good mechanical properties when reinforced; exceptional sunlight, oxygen, and ozone resistance; good electrical and temperature properties; for insulation, footwear, weather stripping
Neoprene, chloroprene, CR	A:S B:25 (3.5) C:8.0–9.0	2.25 (1.05)	Excellent ozone, heat, weather, and flame resistance and mechanical properties; good oil and chemical resistance; for oil hoses, tank linings, and insulation

TABLE 11-3   *(cont.)*

Names	Properties[a]	Average relative cost [$/kg ($/lb)]	Features and particular uses
Buna N, nitrile, acrylonitrile-butadiene, NBR	A:S B:5 (0.7) C:4.5–7.0	2.50 (1.15)	Excellent oil and good chemical resistance; fair mechanical and poor low-temperature properties; carburetor and gas tank and pump parts, gaskets, printing rolls
Hypalon (HYP), chloro-sulfonated polyethylene, CSM	A:S B:25 (4.0) max. C:max. 6.0	2.45 (1.10)	Excellent ozone, weather, and acid resistance, and color stability; fair oil and low-temperature resistance serviceable to 120°C (250°F); for chemical and petroleum hoses, connectors, etc., shoes, and flooring
Urethane, polyester U, AU, polyether U, EU	A:S B:35 (5.0) and up C:5.4–7.5	5.15 (2.35)	Exceptional abrasion, cut, and tear resistance; high strength, modulus, and hardness; good oxygen, ozone, and sunlight resistance; especially for vibration dampening and sound deadening; low moisture and heat resistance
Silicone rubbers, MQ, PMQ, etc.	A:T B:7 (1.0) C:1.0–5.0	10.50 (4.75)	Temperature −85 to 315°C (−120 to 600°F); high oxygen, ozone, and radiation resistance; high compression set; low strength, wear, and oil resistance; insulation, seals, gaskets
Viton, fluorocarbon elastomers, FKM	A:T B:15 (2.0) and up	38.80 (17.65)	Temperature −40 to 315°C (−40 to 600°F); outstanding oil and chemical resistance, especially at high temperature; good mechanical properties; for aircraft and industrial equipment
Acrylic rubbers, polyacrylate, ACM	A:T B:2 (0.3) C:4.5–7.5	3.45 (1.60)	Excellent ozone and oil resistance; poor water resistance; for seals, gaskets, hose, and O-rings
Thermoplastic elastomers, thermolastic	A:S	3.90 (1.80)	Good elastic and mechanical properties; flexibility at low temperature; processing fast and at low cost; number of kinds with wide ranges of properties

Properties of Elastomers.   The best known feature of elastomers is that they can be stretched to at least twice original length. They usually do not conform to Hooke's law, as indicated by Fig. 11-5, and return only approximately to original length. The loss in size is called *tension set* or *compression set,* according to the mode of loading. This is an indicator of how an elastomer will act in service. *Modulus* is the amount of load required to stretch a test piece to a given elongation. The modulus and the full strength vary with the hardness of an elastomer, as typified in Fig. 11-5. Rubber can respond to flexion repeatedly; this property is needed for gaskets, printing rolls, upholstery, and hoses. The ability to give back energy upon release is *resilience*. The high resilience of natural and some other rubbers is desirable in articles like golf balls. An elastomer of low resilience is used in such a place as a bowling alley backstop. Another feature is impermeability to liquids and gases, in different degrees for different elastomers. This is desirable for rainwear, protective coatings of all kinds, and insulation.

Reinforcing agents such as carbon black improve the strengths of most elastomers. Even so, the strength of rubbers is far below that of metals and many plastics. For high strength, rubber is coated on fabrics, cords, glass fibers, or wire—largely as flexible insulation against friction. Examples are automotive tires and conveyor belts.

The standard to measure the hardness of rubber is the Shore durometer, a simple and widely accepted pocket-size device. It is pressed against the rubber surface to apply an indentor and obtain a hardness reading. There are two scales: Shore A is based on a blunt-end, and Shore D on a needle-point indentor. Readings usually are rounded to 10 point increments. Soft and medium rubbers are gaged on the A scale from 20 (softest) to 100. The D scale is set to 100 on a glass surface; 50 on D roughly is the same as 100 on A.

Commonly, the properties of an elastomer can be varied by compounding and vulcanizing. Hardness is varied in these ways. Fillers and reinforcing agents can produce hardness of 50 to 90 Shore A in vulcanized rubbers. Natural and similar rubbers and neoprene are made harder with more sulfur. The hardest consists of a mixture of natural, styrene-butadiene or acrylonitrile rubbers with 32% sulfur. Other

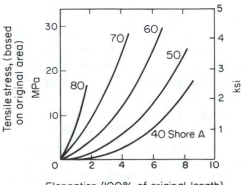

Figure 11-5 Typical stress-strain curves for an elastomer of various grades of hardness designated by Shore durometer numbers.

elastomers, like urethane, are made hard by varying their basic structures. The highest strength of a typical elastomer occurs at a 60 Shore A hardness as shown in Fig. 11-5. Material in this range generally has the best balance of properties (strength, wear resistance, durability) and is commonly chosen for severe service, such as on tire treads.

Standard systems are in use for specifying properties of elastomers and matching them with service requirements. The most common is that of the American Society for Testing Materials (ASTM) and the Society of Automotive Engineers (SAE). By this standard, the properties of each elastomer are described by a line of numbers and letters. Other systems are the AMS specifications for the aircraft industry, the Military Specifications of the armed services, and the RMA standards of the Rubber Manufacturers Association.

Silicones.   The *silicones* are compounds built around a basic silicon-oxygen unit in a manner similar to the way the organic compounds are formed from their basic carbon and hydrogen atoms. The silicone compounds can be polymerized in chains and rings to produce a large number of compounds. They are less active chemically than similar organic compounds and more resistant to heat. They stand temperatures in various applications to 425°C (800°F). Some are molded thermosetting plastics, others are varnishes for high-temperature electrical insulation, and still-others are in the forms of high-temperature greases and oils. They are found in such products as waxes and polishes, paints, cosmetics, antifoaming agents, and dielectric fluids. Some properties of silicone elastomers are given in Table 11-3.

Adhesives.   Adhesives have served to join weak materials like paper, plastics, and wood for many years. Discoveries of new plastics and elastomers have brought forth stronger adhesives, suitable for more materials and applications. This has led to the growing use of adhesives for joining metals to metals and other materials. Certain metal honeycomb structures, for instance, would not be possible without adhesives. Adhesive joints can be made strong enough for many purposes, do not require overheating the work, save weight, are relatively cheap, and can serve as sealers and insulators and add resistance to corrosion, vibration, and fatigue. Screws and rivets form projections on a surface and act as stress raisers; adhesive joints do not have these faults.

An adhesive joint must be designed properly. An adhesive does not act alone but only with the materials it unites. No adhesive can bond anything to everything and stand up under all conditions. Whatever the joint, an adhesive must be selected to suit the materials to be joined and the temperatures, atmospheres, and other conditions under which it must hold. An adhesive joint must be properly sized. An adhesive bond is about one-tenth as strong as brazing on the same area. Thus, a welded, brazed, bolted, or riveted joint of relatively small area cannot be directly replaced by an adhesive. An even larger than proportional area is needed because strength is not uniform over an adhesive interface. A joint should be designed for straight shear or tension, uniform over the whole area to avoid bending and peeling and stress concentrations.

Casein and natural glues are widely used, but thermosetting and thermoplastic plastics and elastomers are becoming more and more important in critical industrial applications. Many formulations are available. Epoxides are popular because they do not shrink much on setting, are stable under a wide range of conditions, and adhere to many materials. Thermoplastics are not used for heavy long-time loading because of creep. Acrylic adhesives offer a matchless combination of clarity and long life. Most contact adhesives are based on neoprene elastomers in a vehicle. Some adhesives are mixtures of different polymers to obtain properties for particular applications. Examples are epoxyphenolics or epoxy nylons that are among adhesives suitable for temperatures to below $-240°C$ ($-400°F$). Silicones and polyimides make adhesives serviceable for short exposures to 480°C (900°F). Brittle ceramic adhesives based on glass frit stand up to about 815°C (1500°F). Adhesives for particular purposes cost upward of several dollars per liter. That usually means a fraction of a cent or little more per square centimeter—a small part of the total cost of the product.

Adhesives harden and develop cohesive strength by chemical curing, drying, or freezing. Chemical reactions to polymerize thermosetting plastics may be brought about by heat or a catalyst. Many plastics and elastomers may be dissolved in water or an organic solvent which is evaporated or diffused for drying. This method wets surfaces well and needs little or no heat. It is popular for bonding fabric to rigid surfaces. Thermoplastics may be heated for application and then cooled to set.

Adhesive joints are made in a number of ways. In any case the surfaces to be joined must be clean. A cleaned surface primed with a thin film of adhesive solvent can be stored a long time until final adhesive application. Liquids or pastes are applied by brush, trowel, dip, flow, gun, or roller. Films cut to size are placed on the surface. Powders may be sifted over an area. A bonding layer 80 to 130 μm (3 to 5 mils) thick is best for most adhesives. Fixtures are commonly used to hold and press parts together while the adhesive dries, is heated, or cures. Heating is commonly done in ovens.

PLASTIC PROCESSING

There are two main steps in the manufacture of plastic products. The first is a chemical process to create the resin. The second is to mix and shape all the material into the finished article or product.

Plastic objects are formed by compression, transfer, and injection molding. Other processes are casting, extrusion and pultrusion, laminating, filament winding, sheet forming, joining, foaming, and machining. Some of these and still others are used for rubber. A reason for a variety of processes is that different materials must be worked in different ways. Also, each method is advantageous for certain kinds of products. The principles of operation and merits of the processes will be discussed.

Compression Molding. In compression molding a proper amount of material in a cavity of a mold is squeezed by a punch, also called a force. The plastic is heated in most cases between 120 and 260°C (250 and 500°F), softens, and flows to fill the space between force and mold. The mold is kept closed for enough time to permit the formed piece to harden. This is done in a press capable of exerting 15 to 55 MPa (2000 to 8000 psi) over the area of the work projected on a plane normal to the ram movement, depending on the design of the part and the material.

Compression molding is mostly for thermosetting plastics which have to be cured by heat in the mold. Other methods are faster for large-quantity production of thermoplastics. Loose molding compound may be fed into a mold, but a cold-pressed tablet or rough shape, called a *preform,* may be prepared for more rapid production. For efficient heat transfer, parts should be simple with walls uniform and preferably not over 3 mm ($\frac{1}{8}$ in.) thick. Even so, it may take several minutes to heat and cure a charge. This time may be reduced as much as 50% by preheating the charge. To speed the process as much as possible, molding presses are usually semi- or fully automatic.

The three basic types of compression molds for plastics are shown in Fig. 11-6. The force fits snugly in the *positive-type mold*. The full pressure of the force is exerted to make the material fill out the mold. The amount of charge must be controlled closely to produce a part of accurate size.

The force is a close fit in a *semipositive-type mold* only within the last millimeter of travel. Full pressure is exerted at the final closing of the mold, but excess material can escape, and the charge does not have to be controlled so closely. This type is considered best for large-quantity production of pieces of quality.

The force does not fit closely but closes a *flash-* or *overflow-type mold* by bearing on a narrow flash ridge or cutoff area. The amount of material does not need to be

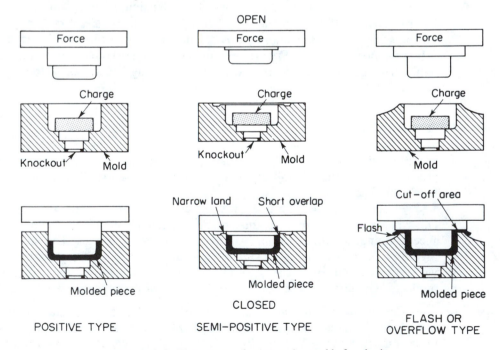

Figure 11-6　Three types of compression molds for plastics.

controlled closely, and the excess is squeezed out around the cavity in a thin flash. Some material is wasted, and all pieces must be trimmed. Full pressure is not impressed on the workpiece. A mold of this kind is usually cheapest to make.

Elaborate molds are used for certain purposes. *Multiple-cavity* or *gang molds* are economical for large-quantity production, of bottle caps for instance. A *sub-cavity gang mold* has a common loading chamber for a number of cavities. A *split-cavity mold* can be opened to remove a piece with undercuts, etc.

Compression molding is mostly done hot, but some *cold molding* is done, particularly for refractory-type compounds, because it is fast. The material is pressed to shape in the mold and then baked in an oven until cured. This method does not control size as well nor give as good a surface finish as hot molding.

Akin to molding of thermosets is *forging* of thermoplastics. A heated preform is placed in a die which is closed to apply pressure to the material and make it fill the cavity. Injection molding described below it preferable for most thermoplastic parts, but forging can be done at lower pressures and with cheaper tooling. It has been found economical for parts with sections thicker than 6 mm ($\frac{1}{4}$ in.), small quantities, and materials that soften at temperatures too high for practical injection.

Transfer Molding.   In transfer molding, also called *extrusion* or *gate molding*, the material is heated and compressed in one chamber and forced through a sprue, runner, and orifice into the mold cavity (Fig. 11-7). The mold is costly, but closer tolerances and more uniform density can be held, time is generally shorter for thick sections, and thick and thin sections and inserts can be molded with less trouble than in other molds. The reason is that the material enters the mold under pressures of 40 to 85 MPa (6000 to 12,000 psi) and acts like a fluid.

Injection Molding.   Ways of injection molding plastic material are sketched in Fig. 11-8. The oldest is the single-stage plunger method. When the plunger is drawn back, raw material falls from the hopper into the chamber. The plunger is driven

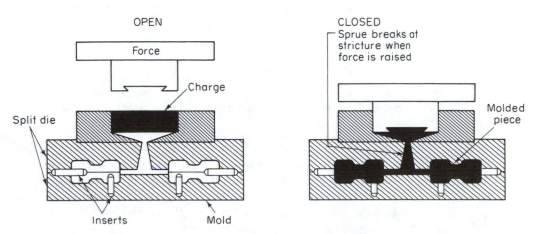

Figure 11-7   Transfer mold.

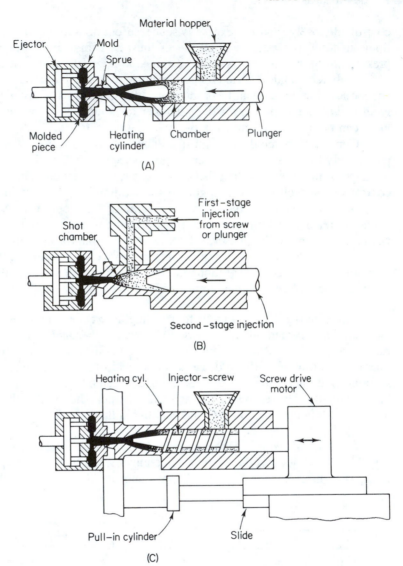

Figure 11-8 Injection molding systems: (A) conventional single-stage plunger type; (B) two-stage plunger or screw-plasticisor types; (C) single-stage reciprocating screw type.

forward to force the material through the heating cylinder where it is softened and squirted under pressure into the mold. The single-stage reciprocating screw system has become more popular because it prepares the material more thoroughly for the mold and is generally faster. As the screw turns, it is pushed backward and crams the charge from the hopper into the heating cylinder. When enough material has been prepared, the screw stops turning and is driven forward as a plunger to ram the charge into the die. In a two-stage system, the material is plasticized in one cylinder, and a definite amount transferred by a plunger or screw into a shot chamber from which a plunger injects it into the mold.

An injection molding machine heats to soften, molds, and cools to harden a thermoplastic material. Operating temperature is generally between 150 and 380°C (300 and 700°F) with full pressure usually over 35 and up to 350 MPa (5000 to 50,000 psi). The mold is water cooled. The molded piece and sprue are withdrawn from the injection side and ejected from the other side when the mold is opened. The mold is then closed and clamped to start another cycle. Thermosetting plastics can be injection molded but have to be polymerized and molded before they set in the machine. This may be done in a reciprocating screw machine where one charge at a time is brought to curing temperature. By another method, sometimes called *jet molding*, preforms are charged one at a time into a single-stage plunger machine.

Machines are available for molding sandwich parts. One cylinder and plunger injects a measured amount of skin material into the die, and then a second cylinder squirts the filler inside the mass. Finally, a final spurt from the first cylinder clears the core material from the sprue. The aim is to produce composites with optimum properties. Either case or core may be foamed.

In liquid reaction molding (LRM), two highly reactive liquids are injected in a mold where they combine to form the plastic product. Pressures are low, and large parts like auto bumpers and body panels can be molded without excessive die forces.

The capacity of an injection molding machine is designated by the maximum amount of material it injects efficiently at each shot and the force it can exert to lock the die. The force tending to open the die is the molding pressure times the projected area of the workpiece. A medium-size reciprocating screw injection molding machine rated at 113 g (4 oz) and 670 kN (75 tons) has a die area of 305 × 508 mm (12 × 20 in.), an injection pressure up to 155 MPa (22,500 psi), a weight of 2840 kg (6250 lb), and a price over $30,000.

Injection molding is a low-cost way of making thermoplastic parts in large quantities. With fully automated equipment, three to six shots a minute are common for moderate-size work. Intricate parts can be made to close tolerance with no need for second operations. Scrap loss should be less than 10%. However, molds cost from about $2000 for a single-cavity die to over $50,000 for quite complex parts in multiple cavities. As few as 500 pieces of a kind have been economically injection molded, but as many as 10,000 are required in some cases for economical operation. Injection molding of thermosets averages 25% faster than compression molding but requires careful attention.

Casting.   Liquid resins are cast in molds of relatively soft materials, such as rubber, plaster, etc. Such molds may be formed around a model easily shaped in wood, plaster, metal, etc. A catalyst is added to polymerize the resin, which is commonly heated in an oven for hours or days at about 65 to 95°C (150 to 200°F) to harden. Equipment cost is low, but the process is slow. Ornaments, prototypes, dies, and encapsulated electrical parts are examples of cast plastic products.

Extrusion and Pultrusion.   Thermoplastics and elastomers are extruded into successive strips of uniform sections, such as rods, tubes, angles, etc., by the intermittent action of a plunger in a cylinder. Also, a continuous method is depicted in Fig. 11-9(A). The material drops from a hopper into a heated cylinder and then is pushed through the die by a screw. This is faster and cheaper than molding. Insulated cable and wire commonly has its covering extruded around it as it is pulled through an extrusion die.

Strong and stiff reinforced thermosets are pultruded as typified in Fig. 11-9(B). Reinforcing material (glass fiber, paper, etc.) is pulled through a resin bath, forming and squeezing rolls, and a long heated die in which the plastic is cured and hardened. A typical pultrusion system is said to process about 16 kg/hr (35 lb/hr) as compared to an average of 90 kg/hr (200 lb/hr) by extrusion because of the time to cure the thermoset.

Foams.   Cellular plastic foams are made by chemically or mechanically expanding resins. Their structure provides thermal insulation, buoyancy, cushioning, and light weight. Strength-to-weight ratios can be two to five times those of conventional structural metals. Cells may be opened or closed and parts may be molded with smooth skins. Plastic foams may be flexible or rigid; dense or open. They may be foamed in place, sprayed on a surface, and then expanded (as on tanks), molded, extruded, or cast, and are available in stock shapes.

Plastics of all classes may be foamed. Depending upon the material, foaming is done by (1) injecting a gas under pressure into a soft plastic mass; (2) adding a low-boiling-point solvent or chemicals and heating to release vapor or gas; (3) me-

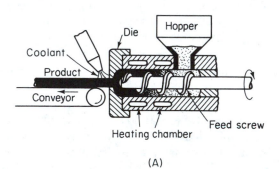

(A)

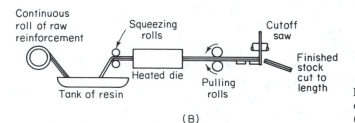

(B)

Figure 11-9 (A) Extrusion
of plastic material;
(B) pultrusion.

chanical aeration or frothing by mixing, stirring, etc.; (4) including chemicals with the components of a plastic to form gas when mixed; and (5) mixing fine metal particles and gas with a plastic mass under pressure to cause bubbles to form on the metal particles when the pressure is released.

Laminates and Reinforced Plastic Moldings. Many thin-walled objects, parts, and structures are made by mixing and laminating plastic resins or films with reinforcing materials. Two kinds of products are (1) *high-pressure laminates*, and (2) *low-pressure* or *reinforced plastic moldings*.

High-pressure laminates are available commercially as sheets, rods, and tubes in standard sizes and are fabricated in special shapes. Several trade names are Formica, Micarta, and Lamicoid. Reinforcement materials include paper, cotton or glass cloth, asbestos, and nylon. The resins ordinarily used for impregnation are phenolics, melamines, silicones, and epoxies. The material is cut to size, arranged in layers, compressed at over 7 MPa (1000 psi), and heated to around 150°C (300°F) to harden the resin. Operations on flat and curved sheets are depicted in Fig. 11-10(A) and (B). Plastic films are laminated to metals in sheets or rolled strips.

Reinforced plastic moldings include such products as storage bins, loudspeaker horns, machinery housings, truck cabs, and aircraft panels. The most common reinforcing material is glass as fabric or fibers, but others are asbestos, boron, cotton, and nylon fibers. Mostly thermosetting, but some thermoplastic resins are used.

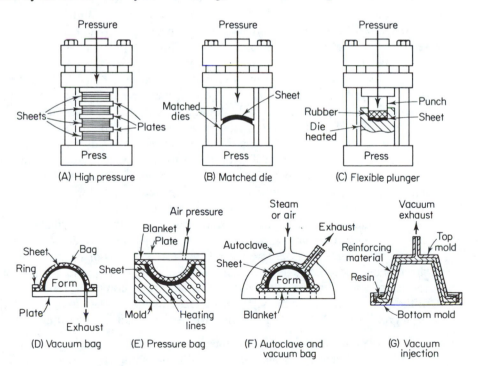

Figure 11-10 Methods of molding laminated and reinforced plastics.

The simplest way of preparing reinforced plastic shapes is by *contact laminating* or *molding*. Layers of reinforcing material are placed by hand over a low-cost form or mold, and resin is brushed or sprayed on each layer. Sheet molding compound (SMC) containing glass fibers and available commercially may also be spread over the form.

For quantities of parts, molding may be done by *preforming* or by *premixing*. To preform, chopped glass roving, plastic resin, and fillers are blown together into a die, mold, form, or screen by a spray gun. Good strength and appearance result because the material is evenly distributed. Structures as large as 5-m (16-ft) boats and swimming pools are fabricated in this way because the only limitation is the size of the form. In contrast to preforming, the resin, fibers, and fillers may be premixed and spread over a form and cured.

After reinforced plastic moldings have been formed, the resin may be catalyzed to harden without heat or pressure or it may be baked, or the molding may be finished in a vacuum bag or matching die operation. Reinforced plastic moldings may be cured under pressure in *vacuum bag* or *pressure bag molding*, as depicted in Fig. 11-10(D) and (E). A workpiece may also be placed between matched dies in a bag. Pressure is applied by exhausting the air from the bag and is limited to atmospheric pressure. Up to about 2.1 MPa (300 psi) may be applied by a pressure bag. Either arrangement may be put in an autoclave with hot air or steam to increase pressure and temperature as indicated in Fig. 11-10(F). These operations are quite slow; some take hours. Tooling cost is low; one estimate is $270 to $430/m^2 ($25 to $40/ft^2) of workpiece area. The methods were developed and are widely used in the aircraft industry for radomes, wing sections, missile noses, and sonar domes. They are not considered economical for more than 1200 to 1500 pieces of a kind.

In the *vacuum injection process*, illustrated in Fig. 11-10(G), reinforcing material is clamped between two matching nonporous molds. The resin is put in a trough around the bottom and is drawn up through the material by a vacuum drawn through the top mold. The saturated molding is held in position until it sets.

Reinforced plastic moldings may be finished by rigid or flexible punches and dies in presses as indicated in Fig. 11-10(B) and (C). Rigid dies are usually heated by steam or electricity to about 120°C (250°F). Pressures may be up to 7 MPa (1000 psi) but usually are much lower. Steel or cast iron dies are fastest and last longest, but cheaper Kirksite dies serve for moderate quantities. The cycle time in a press may be several minutes but in some cases has been reported reduced to a fraction of a minute, depending upon the material and size of the workpiece and the amount of automation. This is still longer than the few seconds to form a part from sheet metals. However, sheet metal dies must be more durable and costly. As an example, tooling for a plastic sports car body is reported to have cost $500,000 as compared to an estimated $4.5 million for a sheet metal body. Some parts are made as plastic moldings in quantities of approximately 100,000 pieces and from sheet metal in larger quantities.

Filament Winding.   Continuous strands of glass roving or other filaments are machine positioned and wound on a mandrel as depicted in Fig. 11-11. The roving may be impregnated before (a *prepreg*), during, or after winding with resin that is

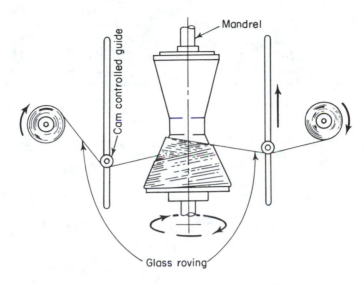

Figure 11-11   Scheme of filament winding.

cured in the final form for a continuous bond. The mandrel is removed (extracted, collapsed, dissolved, or melted) after the material has set.

Filament winding is done to produce lightweight tanks and pressure vessels, rocket tubes, motor cases, exit covers, radomes, and also more complex shapes such as helicopter and wind tunnel blades and leaf springs. Parts have been made from 3 mm to 4.5 m ($\frac{1}{8}$ in. to 28 ft) in diameter. The process is best suited for surfaces of revolution but can be applied wherever tension can be held as with square or triangular sections. Tolerances of ±130 to ±250 μm (±0.005 to ±0.010 in.) on various dimensions are reported practical. Many winding patterns are possible, such as circular, helical, variable, and lengthwise. Good design and procedure orient the filaments as nearly as possible in the directions of the principal tensile stresses and produce a structure of highest strength.

Filament winding is expensive; costs are reported from $4 to over $1000/kg ($2 to over $500/lb) of finished product. The process is a way of fabricating fiber-resin composites and is not competitive except as a means of achieving the advantages of such composites.

Forming Plastic Sheets.   Thermoplastic sheets are softened by heating and *formed* or *thermoformed* into a large variety of thin-walled articles such as display packages, bowls and trays, refrigerator door liners, lighting fixtures, safety helmets, and luggage. The material is held in the desired shape until it cools and becomes rigid. Sheets may be formed by pressing between molds or by mechanical bending as indicated in Fig. 11-12(A). Mechanical pulling or stretching is done in some cases. Another group of methods is based upon blowing or drawing the sheets by air pressure or vacuum. In this way certain shapes may be free formed as exemplified in Fig. 11-12(B). This avoids marring the surface, which is of advantage in such products as

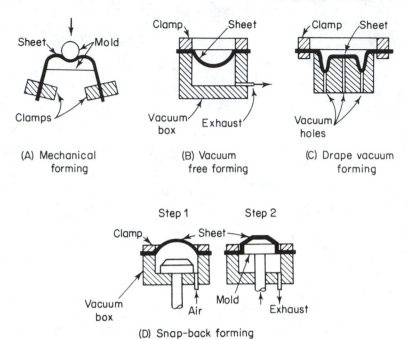

Figure 11-12   Typical methods of forming plastic sheets.

clear windshield canopies for aircraft. Plastic sheets are blown or drawn to shapes against molds in a number of ways basically illustrated by Fig. 11-12(C) and (D).

A major advantage of sheet forming is that the sheets may be predecorated, coated, or preprinted for such effects as wood grain, lettered, or metallic finishes. The formed parts may have quite thin walls or large areas which are difficult to mold in other ways. Sheet forming is not hard on molds, which may be of plastic, wood, plaster, masonite, soft metals, or cast iron. They seldom cost more than a few hundred dollars and can be made up quickly.

Thermoforming is done manually for small quantities (such as prototypes), and that is slow. The process is automated for large-quantity production. One example reported is that of one-piece, double-cavity liners for refrigerators turned out on a four-station machine at the rate of about 35 per hour.

Some plastic material in sheets can be cold-formed rapidly by metal-working methods with suitable modifications. One example is a small container, press-drawn at the rate of 1500 per minute. When injection molded in a 64-cavity die, only 384 parts were turned out per minute.

Shell Molding.   Powder molding of hollow parts is done by fusing a thin layer of powdered thermoplastic resin in a heated mold. This may be done by exposing the mold over a fluidized bed with particles charged at up to 80,000 V and thus strongly attracted to the mold. Unfused resin is dumped out of the mold. By another method, called *rotational molding*, the powder is placed in a mold that is heated while being rotated around two axes (at 90°) at the same time. This distributes the material uniformly, and fully closed shells may be produced. The mold is cooled, and the workpiece is removed. Another method, called *slush* or *dip molding*, employs a liquid dispersion, such as a vinyl plastisol, instead of a powder. Powder molding and the like produce thin-walled parts like toys, tanks, and other containers. Walls are stress free and crack resistant because there is no molding pressure and no flow of material. Wall thickness is uniformly controllable within about ±10%. Operation time is more but mold cost less than for injection molding. The break-even point is reported at somewhat less than 10,000 parts.

Blow molding is done in four steps as illustrated in Fig. 11-13. First a heated length of thermoplastic tube (called a *parison*) is placed on an air nozzle between the halves of the open mold. The parison is extruded in place on some automatic ma-

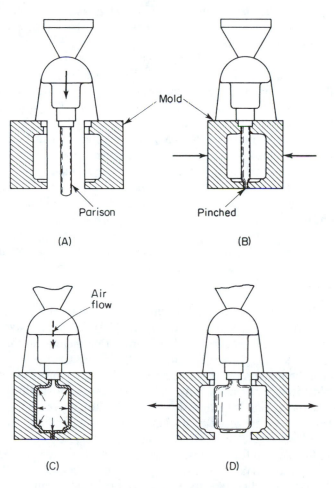

Figure 11-13 Steps in blow molding.

chines. Second, the mold closes and pinches shut the open end of the parison. Then air is blown in to expand the parison to the walls of the mold, which are usually cooled to set the plastic. Last, the mold is opened, and the finished product is ejected. Blow-up ratio may be as high as 6:1 but is commonly 3:1.

Among the best known products of blow molding are rigid plastic detergent bottles and flexible squeeze bottles. Most thermoplastics can be blow molded, and objects as large as 50-gal-drum liners have been produced. A major drawback is that walls cannot be held uniformly because different parts are stretched by different amounts. Also, walls cannot be thickened for ribs or bosses. Blown surfaces do not have a high gloss because pressure in the mold is not over about 700 kPa (100 psi). The process is readily automated and fast. Dies cost one-half to one-fifth of those for injection molding because they do not need cores, runners, gates, etc.

Joining Plastics.   The four basic methods of joining plastics are (1) cementing with solvent, (2) bonding with an adhesive, (3) thermal and ultrasonic welding, and (4) mechanical fastening.

Only certain soluble thermoplastic materials can be cemented with a solvent. The strength of the joint is comparable to that of the parent material. All plastics may be adhesive bonded to metals and other materials as well as to each other. A large number of solvents and adhesives are available, and the properties of the joint depend upon the material selected.

All except highly inflammable thermoplastics can be softened or melted for welding. Softened surfaces may be pressed together or staked, by mashing a projection, to interlock one part with another. Melted joints may have filler plastic added and coalesce on cooling and hardening. Common welding means are (1) hot gas or air, (2) a heated tool, (3) induction heating, and (4) friction (ultrasonic or other rubbing).

Plastic parts may be joined with other parts by means of screws, bolts, nuts, rivets, swaging or peening, press or shrink fitting, etc. Allowance must be made for the weakness and localized stress susceptibility of plastics in designing serviceable joints.

Machining Plastics.   Molding and forming are the usual ways of making plastic parts, but they require costly molds and forms. Machining from standard shapes may be cheaper for small and moderate quantities; the break-even point has been reported as high as 15,000 to 60,000 pieces with automated machining. Some parts can be made most economically by slicing them off of extruded shapes. Hard-to-mold forms, such as threads and dimensions with small tolerances, can often be obtained most cheaply by machining. Some cutting to remove excess material in flash, runners, sprues, flanges, etc., is done on almost all molded and formed plastic parts.

Most of the techniques and equipment described in this text for machining metal are applicable also for plastics. However, there are some principles of machining that apply to plastics alone because the properties of plastics are different from those of metals. Because there are many plastics, there are many specifications for cutting plastics. This is not the place to list them, but specifications for tool shapes, speeds, feeds, etc. for particular applications are given in reference books and handbooks. What are important are the principles that explain why and how plastics must be treated differently from metals when cut. These will be discussed.

The properties of plastics that determine their machinability are: (1) they do not readily conduct but are easily affected by heat, (2) some contain abrasive fillers, (3) they are mostly soft and yielding, and (4) some are quite brittle though soft.

Thermoplastics soften, lose shape, become gummy, and clog cutters; thermosetting plastics deteriorate and char at high temperatures. The heat generated is not conducted away rapidly by a plastic when it is cut, so good results depend upon practices conducive to cool cutting. This calls for tools with keen cutting edges and smooth polished faces. For sawing, a band saw is preferable to a circular saw because the teeth on a long band have more time to cool. Air, water, and oil coolants are commonly used for cutting plastics.

Plastics with abrasive or high-strength fillers (composites) wear tools rapidly and require cemented carbide, sintered oxide, or even diamond tools. Care is required to avoid breakout of the reinforcing fibers of composites.

Cutting tools stand high speeds well for most plastics because the materials are soft. As for tool shape, a relatively obtuse cutting angle usually is necessary to keep the tool from digging into the plastic, just as for brass and copper. In fact, a common practical rule is to set up to cut a plastic like brass or copper if specific information is not available. Then make adjustments by trial during the operation to reach optimum conditions.

Machine tools can work to as close tolerances in cutting plastics as with any material, but in most cases a small tolerance is futile because the plastic will not retain a size. Many plastics are yielding and change appreciably in size under cut; some absorb moisture and swell. In some cases plastic pieces are chilled to make them rigid for cutting.

Some plastics are brittle and chip readily when cut. For these, tools must be sharp and cuts light. Shearing is commonly done with sharp dinking dies or rule cutters. In some cases, plastics are heated before being cut.

Rubber Processing. Raw rubber is composed of long molecules of great molecular weight and is therefore quite springy and resistant to being worked. These molecules must be broken up so the rubber can be molded and formed. For that purpose crude rubber may be extruded in a *plasticator*, masticated by revolving beaters in a *Banbury mixer*, or plasticized between rolls in a *rubber mill*. The last may be done alone or after one or both of the other treatments. In the rubber mill, the rubber is squeezed between two rolls turning toward each other on the entering side. One revolves up to one-third faster than the other and induces a severe shearing as well as compressive action in the rubber. The sheet coming out of the rolls is commonly fed back for a time into the entering mixture for thorough blending. In the mixer and mill the rubber is impregnated with the substances added to it for the final product. Much the same processes are used also for some plastics, one example being the calendering of decorative vinyl sheets and films. Most synthetic elastomers do not respond to mastication or working and must be synthesized to an amenable state.

The second step is to mold or form the rubber as desired and vulcanize it. The sulfur in vulcanizing forms cross links between rubber molecules. This makes the rubber elastic, nonsticky, strong, and more resistant to heat and solvents. The structure of most of the synthetic elastomers is set up when they are polymerized, and they are not vulcanized. Actual forming and molding are done in a number of ways common to plastics. Rubbers are extruded, compression and injection molded, and formed. Rubbers and thermoplastics are calendered between rolls into films ($\frac{1}{4}$ mm or 10 mils and under) or sheets. Also the materials may be pressed or wiped into the voids of fabrics. Some rubber and thermoplastic products are made on forms by dipping into, spraying, or electrodepositing latex or gels.

Thermoplastic elastomers can be molded when heated but act as cross-linked elastomers on cooling. Such a material has short sections of stiff monomers in the long elastomeric chains. These sections become mobile at high temperatures.

DESIGN OF MOLDED PLASTIC PARTS

A molded plastic part should be designed to serve its purpose at the lowest possible cost. Many objects are made from plastics for appearance's sake, and art should have a place in their design. Still, the part must be serviceable and economical to make.

Many of the same rules and their reasons given for casting and molding of metal apply to the molding of plastics. Taper is essential to remove parts from molds; 3° is considered standard for plastics. Thick sections should be avoided because they take more material and cool slowly and retard molding. Instead, ribs, beads, and flanges should be used to add strength where needed. Transition should be gradual between thick and thin sections to promote uniform cooling and avoid stress. Adequate radii and fillets should be provided to eliminate sharp edges and corners wherever possible. This makes parts stronger and more durable, cuts mold cost, and helps the material to flow properly in the mold. One rule is that a radius or fillet should be at least 25% of wall thickness and never less than 0.8 mm ($\frac{1}{32}$ in.). Mold parting lines should be placed to assure low mold cost, simple flash removal, and easy part ejection.

Plastics are different from metals in some ways when molded. Thick and thin sections under one surface should be avoided because the thicker shrinks more and causes noticeable heat sinks or dimples. If these cannot be avoided over ribs or bosses, a pattern may have to be put on the surface to disguise the defects. Plastic walls must not be too thin or weak; generally not less than 1.5 to 2.5 mm ($\frac{1}{16}$ to $\frac{3}{32}$ in.). Holes should be cored wherever possible to avoid machining. A through hole is better than a blind hole because its core pin can be supported at both ends. Reference texts and handbooks give many pointers on the design of holes and openings, threads, knurling, lettering, inserts, and undercuts.

The surface finish and color specified for a plastic part influence all costs. First they enter into the selection of the material. Surface finish dictates the degree of finish and thus the cost of the mold. Combinations of materials and colors can be obtained by various techniques of mold design and operating procedure. Most plastic parts have flash, runners, or sprues that must be removed, usually by secondary operations. Much thought is given to designing parts so that this finishing can be done most easily without detracting from the appearance of the product. A typical solution is to mold a bead around a piece at the parting line. Flash can be trimmed from the bead, which serves as a guide, without marring large smooth areas of the piece. Where extra effects are required, masking, buffing, painting, and vapor metal coating operations may become necessary.

Practical tolerances for molded plastic parts depend largely upon size. Dimensions of 25 mm (1 in.) or less on small parts can be held within ± 50 μm (± 0.002 in.). For larger dimensions, say not over 200 mm (8 in.), realistic tolerances may be ± 10 to 20 μm/cm (± 0.001 to 0.002 in./in.), across die parting lines. In any event, no tolerances closer than really needed should be specified.

The design for production of plastic products is not a simple matter. Even the most experienced of plastics engineers commonly takes the precaution of first building a single-cavity experimental mold to perfect a process before putting a part into production with a multiple-cavity mold. Many viewpoints help, and the designer of plastic products can obtain valuable aid by consulting the supplier of the plastic material and the molder.

QUESTIONS

1. What advantages do plastics offer as a class?
2. Describe the differences in chemical composition and physical properties between thermoplastic and thermosetting resins.
3. What kinds of substances are added to plastic resins, and for what purposes?
4. Discuss the relative merits of the major thermosetting plastics.
5. Discuss the relative merits of the major thermoplastic materials.
6. How is rubber obtained and made serviceable?
7. Discuss the relative merits of the principal synthetic elastomers.
8. How do the silicones differ from organic materials, and what makes them useful?
9. What is the place of adhesives in metal fabrication?
10. Describe compression molding of plastics and the three basic types of molds used.
11. How is injection molding done, and what are its advantages and disadvantages?
12. How are plastics extruded?
13. What are plastic foams, and how are they made?
14. What are high-pressure laminates, and how are they made?
15. Describe the principal ways of making reinforced plastic moldings and their relative advantages.
16. What is filament winding, and what are its advantages?
17. How are parts made from plastic sheets, and when is it economical to do so?
18. Describe blow molding and state its advantages and limitations.

19. What are the common methods for joining plastics?
20. What are the properties of plastics that affect their machinability? What are some of the resulting practices?
21. How are rubber products made?
22. What are the major considerations in the design of plastic parts?

PROBLEMS

1. A case for an electrical instrument can be made from either an amino urea compound by compression molding or from cellulose acetate butyrate by injection molding. The volume of the article is 150 cm³ (9 in.³). The urea compound costs 0.12 cent/cm³ (1.97 cent/in.³). It takes 90 seconds to mold one piece in a mold that costs $1500. The cellulose compound costs 0.18 cent/cm³ (2.95 cents/in.³). A piece can be molded from it in 15 seconds, but the injection mold costs $4500. Time is worth $12/hr. When should each material and process be selected?

2. A rectangular plaque 76 × 127 mm (3 × 5 in.) is to be compression molded from a phenolic molding compound. A mean pressure is required. What force in kN (tons) should the press be able to exert to process four pieces in a gang mold?

3. A nylon gear may be injection molded or machined from bar stock. A die for injection molding costs $4800 and material costs $0.0656 and operation $0.0372/piece. The stock for machining costs $0.263 and operation time $1.14/piece. What is the cost for each method for the following numbers of pieces? **(a)** 1000; **(b)** 3000; **(c)** 6000.

4. An acetal flanged bushing made in different ways is subject to the following costs. Assume that only one lot is to be made. For what quantities should each method be used?

Factors	Injection mold	Conventional machining	Automatic machining
Die or special tools	$5400	—	$90
Setup	—	—	$22
Material/piece	0.033	0.204	0.1734
Labor/piece	0.030	1.043	0.036

REFERENCES

ADAMS, R. F., "Design Considerations: Thermoplastics vs. Die Casting Alloys," *Mechanical Engineering*, July 1970, p. 19.

Adhesives in Modern Manufacturing, Society of Manufacturing Engineers, Dearborn, Mich., 1970.

DWYER, J. J., JR., "What You Should Know about Composites," *American Machinist*, July 13, 1970, p. 87.

———, "Fillers: A Bigger Bargain for Improving Resins," *Modern Plastics*, Apr. 1980, p. 84.

FUNNER, R. E., and W. S. ZIMT, "Thermoplastics and Thermosets," *Machine Design*, July 22, 1971, p. 68.

HENRY, D. W., "Designing Molded Plastic Parts," *Machine Design*, Aug. 10, 1978, p. 114.

HUNTRESS, E. A., "Adhesive Assembly," *American Machinist*, Oct. 1979, p. 145.

KAMBOUR, R. P., and R. E. ROBERTSON, *The Mechanical Properties of Plastics*, Report 70-C-104, General Electric Co., Schenectady, N.Y., 1970

"Plastics/Elastomers Reference Issue," *Machine Design*, Feb. 15, 1973.

Plastics—Military Standardization Handbook, MIL-HDBK-700 A, U.S. Government Printing Office, Washington, D.C., 1975.

"Reinforced Plastics: The Composites Lead The Way," *Manufacturing Engineering*, July 1981, p. 56.

SNOGREN, R. C., "Adhesive Bonding," *Mechanical Engineering*, May 1970, p. 33.

SPI Plastics Engineering Handbook, 3rd ed., Reinhold, New York, 1960.

TRUCKS, H. E., *Designing for Economical Production*, Society of Manufacturing Engineers, Dearborn, Mich., 1974.

VACCARI, J. A., "Stamping Plastics Almost like Metal," *American Machinist*, June 1981, p. 131.

———, "Winding Plastics for New Jobs," *American Machinist*, May 1981, p. 125.

VASILASH, G. S., "Advanced Composites: Yesterday, Today, and Tomorrow," *Manufacturing Engineering*, Feb. 1978, p. 60.

WINSHIP, J., "Plastics—Your Future Feedstock," *American Machinist*, May 15, 1975, p. 53.

WOOD, A. S., "For Really Better Parts: New SCM Technologies," *Modern Plastics*, Jan. 1980, p. 56.

WROTEN, C. D., "A Guide to Estimating the Cost of Plastic Parts," *Machine Design*, May 18, 1972.

12

PRIMARY METAL WORKING PROCESSES

The processes described in this chapter produce what are known as the *wrought metals*. These are important engineering materials because of their strength and toughness. They are mandatory for many applications, such as critical structural members, for which cast metals do not suffice. Examples of the forms of these products are structural I-beams, channels, and angles; railroad rails; round, square, and hexagonal barstock; tubes and pipes; forgings; and extruded shapes.

Common primary metal-working processes included in this chapter are metal rolling, cold drawing, pipe and tube manufacture, forging, and extrusion. All squeeze metal. Although much of their output is in final form, such as rails, most of it goes to feed secondary processes that make finished products by cutting or forming as will be described later in this book.

Metals are worked by pressure in the primary processes for two reasons: (1) to form desired shapes, and (2) to improve physical properties. The results depend on whether the work is done *hot* or *cold*. Hot working is done above the recrystallization temperature. This is at or near room temperature for lead, tin, and zinc. It is above the critical temperature for steel, as depicted in Fig. 12-2. Comparisons of the effects of hot and cold working are made in Table 12-1. The principles will be illustrated mostly for steel in this discussion for the sake of brevity.

Hot Working. The properties of a metal are different when above and when below its recrystallization temperature. The strength of a metal decreases as temperature rises, and its grains can be distorted more easily. If a ductile crystal is distorted by working, it does not visibly come apart, but its lattice structure is

TABLE 12-1 COMPARISON BETWEEN PROPERTIES OF HOT- AND COLD-WORKED METALS

Alloy	Condition	Ultimate tensile strength		Yield strength		Hardness
		MPa	ksi	MPa	ksi	
Aluminum 1100	"O"	110	16	40	6	28 Bhn
	H18	200	29	175	25	55 Bhn
Electrolytic tough	Hot-rolled	235	34	70	10	45 R_F
pitch copper	Extra spring	395	57	365	53	95 R_F
Steel, SAE 1010	Hot-rolled	430	62	220	32	60 R_B
	Cold-rolled	560	81	345	50	90 R_B
Brass, yellow	Annealed	340	49	115	17	68 R_F
	Spring hard	630	91	430	62	90 R_B

fragmented. New and smaller crystals form out of the fragments. If the temperature is dropped soon, a fine structure results. However, if the metal is held above the recrystallization temperature and below the melting point, its crystals grow larger. Small crystals tend to combine, and large ones to absorb small ones. The higher the temperature, the faster the growth. The longer the time, the larger the grains become. These conditions help explain the following advantages of pressing or working hot metals.

1. True hot working does not change the hardness or ductility of the metal. Grains distorted and strained during the process soon change into new undeformed grains.
2. The metal is made tougher because the grains are reformed into smaller and more numerous crystals.
3. The metal is made tougher because its pores are closed and impurities segregated. Slag and other inclusions are squeezed into fibers with definite orientation. A typical wrought structure is shown in Fig. 12-1. Chains of crystals intertwined with the filaments of impurities make the metal particularly strong in one direction. Metal is hot worked to orient the flow lines as nearly as possible for strength in the direction of largest stress.
4. Less force is required, the process is faster, and smaller machines can be used for a given amount of hot as compared with cold working because the metal is weaker.
5. A metal can be pushed into extreme shapes when hot without ruptures and tears because the crystals are more pliable and continually reformed.

Hot working is done well above the critical temperature to gain most of the benefits of the process but not at a temperature high enough to promote extreme grain coarsening. This is exemplified in Fig. 12-2 which shows the range of working temperatures for carbon steels.

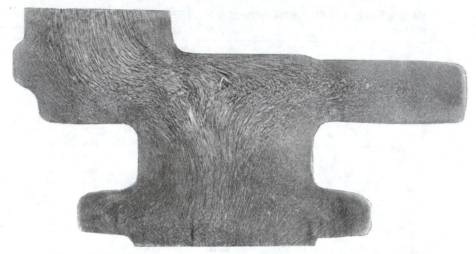

Figure 12-1   Cross section of a forging for a crankshaft. This shows the fine-grained structure resulting from hot working. (Courtesy Forging Industry Association.)

Ausforming is a semihot-working process done on certain high-alloy steels in the time they remain austenitic at temperatures around 550°C (1000°F). This occurs below the knee of the S-curve of Fig. 5-3. Strengths of over 6 GP (900,000 psi) have been obtained in this way.

Hot working has several major disadvantages. It requires heat-resistant tools which are relatively expensive. The high temperatures oxidize and form scale on the surface of the metal. Close tolerances cannot be held. Cold working is necessary to overcome these deficiencies.

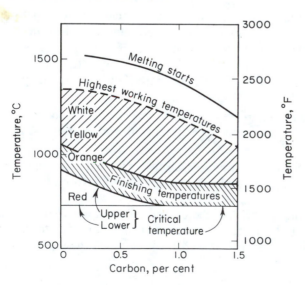

Figure 12-2   Range of rolling and forging temperatures for carbon steel.

Cold Working. Cold-worked metal is formed to shape by the application of pressure at temperatures below the critical and for the most part nominally at room temperature. It is preceded by hot working, removal of scale, and cleaning of the surface, usually by pickling. Cold working is done mostly to hold close tolerances and produce good surface finishes but also to enhance the physical properties of the material.

When a piece of metal is initially subjected to stress, it is strained in proportion in an elastic manner as depicted by the line *oy* in Fig. 12-3. More stress causes permanent or inelastic deformation, along the line *yl*, The point *y* is called the *yield point*. Stresses and strains beyond it are in the region where cold working must take place to change the shape of an object. What happens within the metal when it is cold worked is described in Chap. 4.

The stress-strain diagram of Fig. 12-3 may typify tension, compression, or shear and the resulting strain in any one direction in a material as a basis for illustration. How such a curve is derived is explained in Chap. 3. The diagram at the left is characteristic of a ductile material, one that can stand considerable straining between its yield point *y* and point of rupture *l*. That is the kind of material amenable to cold working. The diagram at the right is indicative of a brittle material that breaks before it is deformed appreciably, like cast iron.

Consider that cold working applies a stress to a ductile material and causes a plastic strain to point *y'* in Fig. 12-3. When the stress is released, the strain falls back slightly to point *o'* at zero stress. This constitutes an elastic return along path *y'o'*, which is parallel to *yo*, and accounts for the phenomenon called *springback* that always occurs when metal is cold worked. When a piece is released from the shaping tools, it returns slightly toward its original shape.

Now assume that a material has been cold worked and released to point *o'* in Fig. 12-3. If the material is again stressed in the same way, its yield point is then *y'*, and

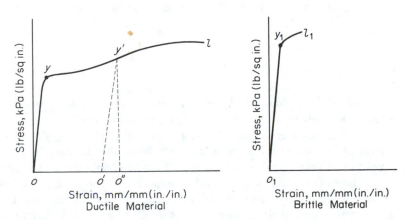

Figure 12-3 Effect of cold working a metal. Typical stress-strain relationships are depicted for room temperature.

further plastic stress takes place along the path $y'l$. In the cold-worked state, the material exhibits a new stress-strain relationship along $o'y'l$. Thus the material has a higher yield point, is harder, and has less ductility than before the original cold working. The material has become *strain hardened*. The more the material is cold worked, the closer its properties approach those of a brittle material illustrated on the right of Fig. 12-3.

The natural effect of most cold-working operations is to apply much more stress in one direction than in others. Thus in one direction the material may be strained to the equivalent of point o' with a yield point y' as in Fig. 12-3, but to points closer to o and yield points closer to y in other directions.

Strains that occur in different or opposite directions within the same piece often react upon each other when the applicable forces and stresses are released. That keeps the material from settling back to a completely unstressed condition and causes what are called *residual stresses*. For example, a sheet may be rolled in such a way that the material is compressed plastically near its surface but not throughout its thickness. After rolling, the outer layers are kept from expanding and are held in compression by tension exerted by the inner material which resists being stretched.

Strain hardening must be relieved in some cases. It is not a desirable property in many products. If a metal is cold worked along line oyl to a point close to l in Fig. 12-3, further cold working will lead to failure. What happens during strain hardening is that the crystals become distorted and disarrayed and resist further change. The metal can be returned to or near its original state, depicted by point o, by annealing or normalizing as described in Chap. 5. Those processes *heat* the metal above its recrystallization temperature and reform and relax the grains.

Relatively large forces must be exerted for cold working. That means that equipment must be proportionately rugged and powerful, particularly for rapid production. Even so, many products can be finished by cold working to close limits and with good finishes at lower cost than by other means. Cold-working processes have a major and basic role in most high-production industries.

ROLLING

Principles of Metal Rolling.   When metal is rolled, it passes and is squeezed between two revolving rolls in the manner indicated in Fig. 12-4. The crystals are elongated in the direction of rolling, and the material emerges at a faster rate than it enters. In hot rolling the crystals start to reform after leaving the zone of stress, but in cold rolling they retain substantially the shape given them by the action of the rolls.

The rolls make contact with the metal over a length of contact depicted by arc AB in Fig. 12-4. At some point of contact the surfaces of the material and roll move at the same speed. This is the no-slip point C, in Fig. 12-4. From C to the exit at A the metal is in effect being extruded and moves faster than the roll surface. In that

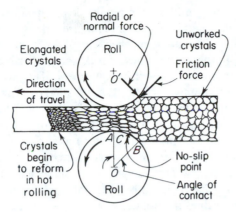

Figure 12-4 Sketch to show what happens when metal is rolled.

zone, friction between workpiece and rolls opposes the travel and hinders the reduction of the metal. Normal and friction forces at a point are depicted in Fig. 12-4. The metal is moving slower than the rolls between points C and B, and the resultant friction force over arc CB draws the metal between the rolls. The position of the no-slip point C in arc AB depends upon the amount of reduction, the diameters of the rolls, and the coefficient of friction. Point C tends to move to A as the amount of reduction and the angle of contact increase. When the angle of contact (called *angle of nip*) exceeds the angle of friction, the rolls cannot draw a fresh piece of material spontaneously into the space between them. When the angle of contact is more than twice the angle of friction between roll and work, point C coincides with A, and the metal cannot be drawn through by the rolls even if placed between them. That is because the horizontal component of the normal pressure of the rolls against the metal equals and nullifies the horizontal component of friction tending to draw the metal along.

As the metal is squeezed together between the rolls, it is elongated because it is incompressible. To accomplish this, the rolls have to apply both normal squeezing and frictional drawing pressures. Normal pressure of the rolls on the work is usually one to several times the amount of the yield stress of the metal. The pressure may rise to several hundred thousand pounds per square inch in severe operations. The frictional force between roll and work in the driving direction approaches the normal force times the coefficient of friction. This friction force times the surface speed of the rolls determines the power.

Both the frictional and normal pressures that the rolls must apply to stretch the work can be reduced appreciably if axial tension is applied to the work either fore or aft or both. For instance, it has been found with a metal having a yield strength of y psi that the maximum normal pressure of $3y$ without tension falls to y when axial tension of $\frac{1}{2}y$ is applied front and back to the strip. This is commonly done in cold rolling.

The forces and power increase with the amount a piece is reduced in thickness. Thus, the strength and power capacity of the equipment and the workability of the metal determine how much a workpiece may be reduced at any one time.

Rolling Mills.   A rolling mill is commonly designated by the number and arrangement of its rolls as indicated in Fig. 12-5. A nonreversing two high mill passes the work in one direction only. The stock may be passed back over the top of the rolls, but that is slow, or it may go through a series of rolls for successive reductions. The latter is faster but requires more investment in equipment. The work may be passed back and forth through a reversing two high mill, but that takes extra time and power. The work can be passed between the bottom two rolls of a three high mill and then raised by an elevator and passed back between the top two rolls. Large backing rolls support small working rolls in four high and cluster mills. Small rolls are weak by themselves but are cheaper to replace as they wear, make contact with the work over less area, tend to spread the work less sideways, are subject to smaller separating forces, and require less power than large rolls. Material can be reduced more in fewer passes if it is bent back and forth as it is rolled. These varieties of rolling mills are not all but illustrate alternatives engineers have in designing equipment. Each has a different price. They must pick the one that does the required job at lowest cost.

Plain rolls, as depicted in Fig. 12-5, serve for flat sections, and grooved rolls for bars and shapes. Mostly they are made of cast iron or cast or forged steel. Roll design is a challenging engineering problem. The dimensions and properties of each roll must be selected for optimum conditions of hardness, wear resistance, strength, rigidity, and shock resistance. Chilled or alloyed cast iron rolls can be made hard and low in cost. Mostly they lack strength for severe service, and their usage is somewhat limited. Relatively new nodular-iron rolls have replaced both steel and flake-graphite iron rolls in some applications. For the most part superior strength, rigidity, and toughness can

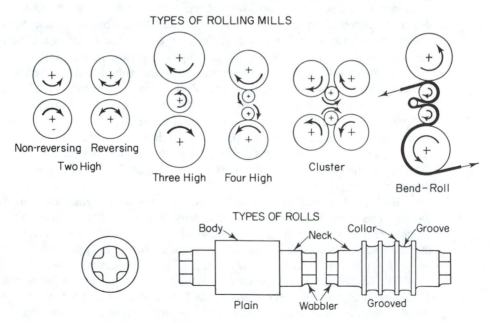

Figure 12-5   Types of rolls and rolling mills.

be attained in steel rolls, particularly alloy steel, at a price. Stronger materials make possible smaller rolls with their inherent advantages. The material in a roll must not have affinity for the work material. Hot rolls are commonly rough, even notched, to bite the work, but cold rolls are highly finished to impart good finish. A brief description of roll grinding is given in Chap. 28.

A set of rolls in their massive housing is called a *stand*. A number of stands may be arranged in a row in a continuous mill like the one in Fig. 12-6. In operation, the metal runs continuously through all the stands at once. For jobbing, the stands may be side by side. When the work is finished in one stand, it is moved to the next, etc. These arrangements have many variations to suit specific conditions. Each mill is designed and operated for a limited range of products. For instance, a huge mill for rolling chunks of steel with a cross-sectional area of almost 4 ft^2 is not economical for rolling small pieces of less than a square foot in area across. The small pieces can be rolled as well on a less powerful mill that costs only a fraction as much. On the other hand, each mill can take pieces only so big. Also, to change rolls, particularly in a large mill, is costly. For that reason, when a mill is set up for some particular shape or shapes, it is economical to keep it on the same work.

Most rolling mills today have a full complement of equipment to handle the work, particularly hot work, mechanically all along the line.

Figure 12-6 Steel bars travel up to 80 km/h (50 mph) through 22 stands of an electronically controlled 13-inch bar mill. (Courtesy Bethlehem Steel Corp.)

Hot-rolling Steels. After steel has been melted and refined as described in Chap. 4, traditional practice has been to cast it into a form called an *ingot*. Steel ingots are held and heated uniformly throughout to around the highest working temperature indicated by Fig. 12-2. This is done in a *soaking pit,* which is a large furnace lined with refractory silica brick, having a neutral or reducing atmosphere, and usually loaded from the top.

Ingots are rolled into blooms or slabs as indicated in Fig. 12-7. This is done rapidly before the metal cools below the working temperature. A typical performance is to reduce an ingot with a square section almost 0.6 m (2 ft) on a side down to a bloom 0.15 m (6 in.) square in about 2 minutes, all in about 17 passes through the rolls. Most blooming mills are two high reversible mills. The work is turned 90° between heavy reductions to work it uniformly on all sides. The ends of the blooms are sheared away to remove cavities or pipes carried over from the ingot. At the same time the bloom may be cut to convenient lengths for later operations.

A rising trend is to produce slabs, blooms, or billets directly by continuous casting, as described in Chap. 9. This is also called *concasting* and *strand casting*. It eliminates the expensive equipment and the steps for ingot casting and saves up to 25% in material lost in the scrap normally cropped from billets, etc., rolled from ingots.

The great bulk of flat plates, sheets, and strips are rolled in continuous mills from slabs or directly from ingots. For premium quality products, defects are removed from

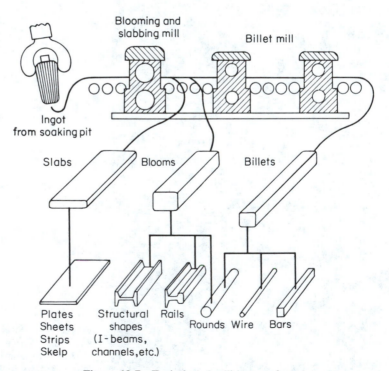

Figure 12-7 Typical steel-rolling procedure.

the surfaces of slabs by pneumatic chipping or flame machining (Chap. 14). Structural shapes are rolled from blooms. For bars, rods, or wire, the blooms are customarily reduced to billets. If the temperature drops too low during processing, the blooms may be reheated. Blooms, billets, and slabs are semifinished shapes with rectangular sections, rounded corners, and all dimensions over 38 mm ($1\frac{1}{2}$ in.).

Because of limitations in the equipment and workability of the metal, rolling is done in progressive steps. An illustration of this is given by the 15 steps required to reduce a 100×100 mm (4×4 in.) billet to a 20-mm ($\frac{3}{4}$-in.)-diameter bar as indicated in Fig. 12-8. From 8 to 10 steps are required to complete most commercial shapes, such as I-beams, channels, and rails from blooms.

Cold Rolling. Bars of all shapes, rods, sheets, and strips are commonly finished in all common metals by cold rolling. Foil is made of the softer metals in this way. Cold-rolled sheets and strips make up an important part of total steel production and are major raw materials for some high-production consumer goods industries, such as for household appliances.

Metals are cold rolled for improved physical properties, good surface finish, textured surfaces, dimensional control, and machinability. Sheet steel less than about 1.5 mm (0.05 in.) thick is cold rolled as a matter of course because it cools too rapidly for practical hot rolling. Cold rolling is a practical means of producing the degree of hardness wanted in material. Cold-rolled sheets and strips are classified commercially as skin rolled, quarter-hard, half-hard, and full hard to denote amounts of reduction up to 50% without annealing. If a bright finish but not hardness is desired, the metal may be annealed just before the final rolling pass. A large tonnage of sheet steel is precoated with an organic film, plain or figured, which becomes the ultimate finish on the final product. Various indented or raised textures or patterns are rolled into sheets of steel and other metals to increase rigidity, provide a surface that hides defects and is easier to coat, give variety in appearance, and reduce glare. Cold rolling produces uniform thicknesses and close tolerances in sheets and bars. Machinability of most steels is improved by cold working and for that reason cold-rolled or drawn stock is widely used in fast automatic machining operations.

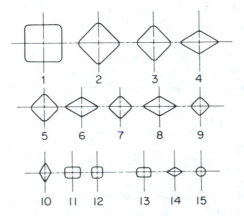

Figure 12-8 Steps taken to reduce a 100×100 mm (4×4 in.) billet to a 20 mm ($\frac{3}{4}$-in.) diam bar.

Steel is pickled prior to cold rolling to clean the surface and remove scale. Sheets or strips are often given a light cold rolling at first to establish a good surface finish and uniform thickness as a basis for good quality from later heavy cold rolling. Most work is done with small rolls in four high or cluster mills and frequently tension is applied at either end or both ends of the sheet or strip to minimize the effects of the high pressures of cold rolling.

Materials may need to be straightened at any stage of fabrication. Common practice is to pass barstock, rods, wire, sheets, or strip through a series of rollers as depicted in Fig. 12-9. This is called *roller leveling*. A mill that unrolls steel up to 13 mm ($\frac{1}{2}$ in.) thick by about 2 m (84 in.) wide from coils and straightens it through rollers represents an investment of about $750,000. Sheets are *stretcher leveled* or straightened by pulling them between jaws to induce a tensile stress throughout slightly in excess of the yield strength.

Quality and Cost.   Steel shapes have been traditionally rolled in the United States in standard inch sizes, but in recent years mills have also been offering products in "standard metric sizes." These conform to the preferred sizes prescribed by the ANSI standards listed at the end of this chapter and do not command premium prices.

Steel shapes are rolled to definite tolerances, varying with size, shape, and composition, tabulated in handbooks and mill catalogs. Inch sizes commonly have bilateral tolerances. As an example, thickness tolerances for cold-rolled carbon steel sheets or strips 20 in. wide are ±0.002, ±0.005, and ±0.006 in. for thicknesses of 0.015, 0.060, and 0.180 in., respectively. Wider sheets are given more tolerance, and narrower ones less. Pickled hot-rolled sheets have tolerances of about ±0.001 in. more for each size. A different practice is to specify a 0.3 minus tolerance for all "metric steel plates" with a variable plus tolerance depending upon thickness and width. Alloy steel and aluminum sheet and strip tolerances are about the same as for carbon steel.

Cold-rolled sheets and strips are given surface finishes varying all the way from smooth and bright as a base for chrome plating to a rough matted finish for enameling.

Little consistency is found in tolerances from one shape to another. Hot-rolled round bars commonly have bilateral tolerances depending on size and carbon and alloy content, but cold-finished bars a negative unilateral tolerance. As a rule cold-drawn bars have better precision and finish than cold-rolled bars, but ground bars are the highest quality.

The values added by working steel into commercial shapes are indicated by the following average market prices on one day. Pig iron was $234 ($213) and No. 1 steel scrap $70/metric ton ($64/ton). Plain-carbon steel rerolling billets were $394 ($358),

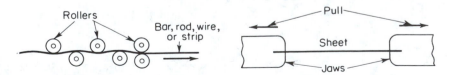

Figure 12-9   Principles of operation of typical straightening devices.

plates \$534 (\$485), hot-rolled strips \$458 (\$416), cold-rolled strips \$655 (\$595), structurals \$504 (\$458), hot-rolled merchant bars \$373 (\$339), and cold-finished bars \$688/metric ton (\$625/ton). For comparison, the prices of alloy steel forging billets were \$459 (\$418), plates \$704 (\$641), hot-rolled strips \$542 (\$493), hot-rolled bars \$563 (\$512), and cold-finished bars \$752/metric ton (\$684/ton). These were base prices for large quantities f.o.b. mill. Any size, composition, or requirements other than standard add to the price. Cost may be twice as much for small quantities from a distributor.

COLD DRAWING

Round, rectangular, square, hexagonal and other shapes of bars up to about 100 mm (4 in.) across or in diameter, wire of all sizes, and tubes are commonly finished by cold drawing. Wire cannot be hot rolled economically smaller than about 5 mm (0.2 in.) in diameter and is reduced to smaller sizes by cold drawing. Steel, aluminum, and copper and its alloys are cold drawn in large quantities.

Cold-drawing Operations.   Hot-rolled stock is descaled, cleaned, and pre-pared for drawing. A common way of treating steel is to immerse it in hot sulfuric acid, rinse, coat with lime, and bake. The leading end of a piece is tapered for insertion through the die. The action as the work is pulled through the die is illustrated in Fig. 12-10. A piece is pulled through a hole of smaller size and emerges correspondingly reduced in size. Drawing pressure against a die must exceed the yield strength of the work material and commonly is as much as 0.7 to over 2 GPa (100,000 to 300,000 psi) for steel. Steel is only able to slide through a die if coated by a lubricant that stands up under such tremendous pressures. Soap, at times with moly disulfide, is commonly applied and is fixed to the surface by the lime coating which in turn is anchored by a soft oxide coating, called the *sull,* left by pickling. A thin copper or tin and copper plate also provides a good bearing surface on steel. It has been aptly said that what actually is drawn is a tenuous cylinder of copper or soap-lime-sull inside of which a steel core is squeezed to a new shape.

Dies must be hard and wear resistant as well as strong. They are made of chilled iron, hardened alloy steel, cemented carbide, and diamonds. The harder materials last longer but cost more.

The force to pull a wire or bar through a die is transmitted by tensile stress in the material that has just left the die. This stress increases more than proportionately with the amount the area of the wire is reduced by the draw. The stress in the material leaving the die may not exceed the yield stress. Theoretically, the yield stress is approached with a reduction in area of 50%. In practice, a reduction in area of less than 40% for each pass usually is found desirable. If the wire must be reduced more, it is passed through several dies. After a number of draws, a work-hardening material like steel becomes so brittle it must be annealed if it is to be drawn further.

Coarse low-carbon steel wire for fences, bolts, etc., may be drawn just once; hard bright wire is produced by several draws after annealing. Soft wire is annealed

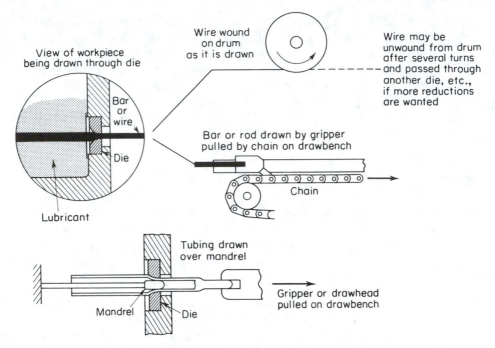

Figure 12-10 Methods of cold drawing.

after being drawn. A soft bright wire is annealed and then given a final mild draw. Heat-treated steel with a carbon content of 0.3 to 1.2% is made into stiff and high-strength music wire, spring wire, wire for brushes, etc.

Bars are reduced from 0.5 to 3 mm ($\frac{1}{64}$ to $\frac{1}{8}$ in.) by cold drawing from the hot-rolled size. The amount depends on the size and composition of the bar and the extent to which it is desired to change the physical properties.

MANUFACTURE OF PIPE AND TUBING

Butt-welded Pipe.   Pipe is formed and butt welded in several ways. In one way, pipe is made from a strip, originally flat, called the *skelp*. Its edges are beveled enough to butt together when the skelp is rounded. The skelp is heated to welding temperature and is gripped at one end by tongs pulled by a draw chain. This pulls the skelp through a welding bell which forces it into a circular shape as depicted in Fig. 12-11(A). The edges of the hot skelp are pressed and welded together.

For continuous butt welding of pipe, the skelp is used in coils, and the ends of the coils are welded together to make a continuous strip. Flames are directed to the edges to heat them to welding temperature as the skelp passes through a furnace. From the furnace, the skelp passes through a series of grooved rolls and is formed into pipe as illustrated in Fig. 12-11(B). Pipe as large as 75 mm (3 in.) in diameter is made in this way.

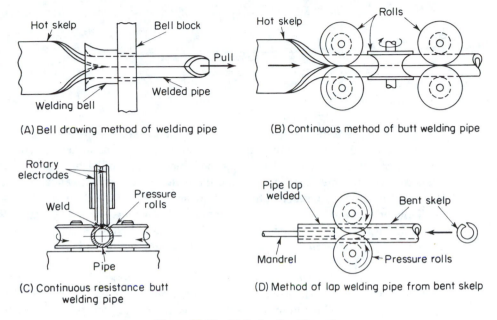

(A) Bell drawing method of welding pipe

(B) Continuous method of butt welding pipe

(C) Continuous resistance butt welding pipe

(D) Method of lap welding pipe from bent skelp

Figure 12-11 Methods of welding pipe.

Continuous steel strip is roll formed to a circular shape to prepare it for electric-resistance butt welding. The principles of roll forming are described in Chap. 13. After being roll formed, the pipe passes between pressure rolls that hold the edges together and electrode rolls that supply current to create welding heat at the joint. This arrangement, indicated in Fig. 12-11(C), is used for pipe up to 400 mm (16 in.) in diameter and wall thickness of about 3 to 15 mm ($\frac{1}{8}$ to $\frac{1}{2}$ in.). Larger pipes are commonly formed in large presses and butt welded by the submerged-arc method.

After being formed and welded, pipe is normally passed through sizing and finishing rolls that make it round, bring it to size, and help remove scale. Continuously made pipe is cut to desired lengths. Cutters remove the extruded flash metal from both inside and outside of the larger sizes of pipes.

Lap-welded Pipe. The edges are beveled as the skelp comes from the furnace to make lap-welded pipe. The skelp is then rounded in one of the ways previously described but with the edges overlapping. It is then reheated and passed over a mandrel between two rolls as illustrated in Fig. 12-11(D) to press and weld the lapped edges together. Lap-welded pipe ranges in size from about 50 to 400 mm (2 to 16 in.) in diameter.

Seamless Tubing. Seamless steel tubing is pierced from heated billets passed between tapered rolls and over a mandrel in the manner depicted in Fig. 12-12. The rolls are shaped so that their surfaces converge on the entering end to a minimum distance apart called the *gorge*. From there the surfaces diverge to the exit end. The billet may have a small center hole drilled in the end. It is pushed and guided between

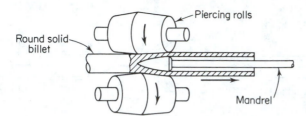

Figure 12-12 Mannesmann process of tube piercing.

the rolls, which are set to grip it in the entering taper. The rolls revolve with a surface speed of about 5 m/s (1000 fpm) in the direction shown. Their axes are crossed, and so they impart axial as well as rolling movement to the billet and force it over the mandrel. The mandrel can revolve, and the material is in effect helically rolled over the mandrel and not extruded. Shells as long as 12 m (40 ft) and up to 150 mm (6 in.) in diameter are produced in 10 to 30 seconds in this way. A second piercing operation is applied for sizes up to about 360 mm (14 in.), and a third of similar kind for still larger sizes. The pierced shells are given subsequent rolling and sizing operations to make finished tubes.

Seamless steel tubing is available in almost all compositions and alloys of steel and in common nonferrous metals such as aluminum, brass, copper, etc. It is the natural form from which to make many thin-walled round objects. Seamless tubing is a popular and economical raw stock for machining because it saves drilling and boring of many parts.

Tubes from some hard-to-work steel alloys and nonferrous metals are not easily pierced and are produced by other methods. One way is to draw and redraw cups from hot plates in the manner described for drawing in Chap. 13. The bottom of a long cup may be cut off to make a tube. Tubes also are extruded as described later.

FORGING

Forging is the forming of metal, mostly hot, by individual and intermittent applications of pressure instead of applying continuous pressure as in rolling. The products generally are discontinuous also, treated and turned out as discrete pieces rather than as a flowing mass. The forging process may work metal by compressing its cross section and making it longer, by squeezing it lengthwise and increasing its cross section, or by squeezing it within and making it conform to the shape of a cavity.

Forging may be done in open or closed dies. Open die forgings are nominally struck between two flat surfaces, but in practice the dies are sometimes vee shaped, half round, or half oval. (Fig. 12-16 shows an open die operation.) Closed die forgings are formed in die cavities. All forging takes skill, but more is required with open than with closed dies. Faster output and smaller tolerances are obtained with a closed die. Open dies are, of course, much less costly than closed dies and more economical for a few parts. Either open or closed die forging may be done on most hammers and presses.

The high order of skill required for forging is becoming scarce. Various systems exist in which the hammer and an automated manipulator are controlled by a computer program to execute an operation.

Heating the Work.   It is important that a piece of material be heated uniformly throughout and to the proper temperature for forging. The proper temperature range for steel has been indicated in Fig. 12-2. Heating is done in furnaces of various sizes to suit specific needs and in forms from the open forge fire to refractory-lined furnaces with precise atmospheric and temperature controls and conveyors and rotary hearths. An average furnace or forge costs about $20,000. Automated lines for large-quantity forging commonly employ induction or electric resistance heaters.

Hammer Forging.   A blacksmith does a simple form of open die hammer forging when he strikes a hot workpiece on an anvil. That work is done mostly by machines today. The blows must be heavy to penetrate and knead the metal deeply, uniformly, and completely. Light blows affect only material near the surface. On cooling, the inner structure then differs from the outer, and the part lacks the flow lines, homogeneity, and impurity dispersion of a quality forging.

A mechanical hammer raises a heavy weight and drops it on an anvil. Various means have been employed. The *helve hammer* is used for light work, particularly to strike blows rapidly. It has a beam with a fulcrum at the middle, a heavy hammer at one end, and a revolving cam applied to the other end to raise and release the hammer repeatedly.

The most common forging hammers are steam or air operated. A single-frame steam forging hammer that gives access to the anvil from three directions is illustrated in Fig. 12-13. A double frame is stronger and is in the form of an arch around the hammer and anvil, but the work space can be reached only from two directions. Most steam hammers today are double acting; the hammer is driven down by the steam pressure as well as by gravity. To keep down vibration, the anvil for open die work is mounted on its own foundation separate from the frame. The effective work done by the hammer depends on the weight of the anvil. Ratios of 20:1 or more between anvil and hammer weights are found in standard hammers.

The ability of a hammer to deform metal depends on the energy it is able to deliver on impact. The energy from falling is augmented by the work derived from the steam in a double-acting hammer. Steam pressures are commonly from 500 to 850 kPa (75 to 125 psi). As an example, a hammer has a falling weight of 9 kN (2000 lb) and a steam cylinder bore d equal to 305 mm (12 in.). Mean effective steam pressure p is assumed to be 550 kPa (80 psi), and the stroke is 760 mm (30 in.):

$$\text{steam force} = \frac{\pi d^2}{4} \times p = \frac{\pi \times \overline{0.305}^2}{4} \times 550 = 40 \text{ kN} \quad \left(\frac{\pi \times 12^2}{4} \times 80 = 9050 \text{ lb} \right)$$

$$\text{total downward force} = 40 + 9 = 49 \text{ kN} \quad (9050 + 2000 = 11{,}050 \text{ lb})$$

$$\text{energy in blow} = 49 \times 0.76 = 37 \text{ kJ} \quad (11{,}050 \times 30 = 331{,}500 \text{ in.-lb})$$

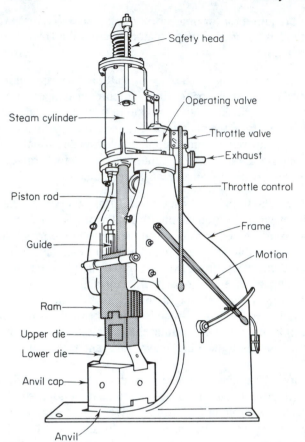

- Safety head
- Operating valve
- Steam cylinder
- Throttle valve
- Exhaust
- Throttle control
- Piston rod
- Frame
- Guide
- Motion
- Ram
- Upper die
- Lower die
- Anvil cap
- Anvil

Figure 12-13 Single-frame steam forging hammer. (Courtesy Forging Industry Association).

If the hammer travels 3.175 mm ($\frac{1}{8}$ in.) after striking the metal, the average force exerted is

$$\frac{37.2 \times 10^3}{10^{-3} \times 3.175} = 11.7 \text{ MN} \quad \left(\frac{331,500}{0.125} = 2,652,000 \text{ lb} = 1326 \text{ tons}\right)$$

The amount of energy and force needed for a particular job is a matter of economics. A large hammer is expensive but can concentrate the energy to work the metal deeply and quickly. A small hammer may do the job but works lightly and takes the time for many blows. A starting rule is that a hammer should have at least 50 lb of falling weight for every square inch of cross-sectional area to be worked in the metal.

Drop Forging.   Drop forging is the name given to the operation of forming parts hot on a drop hammer with impression or cavity dies. The products are known as *drop forgings, closed die forgings,* or *impression die forgings.* They are made from carbon and alloy steels and alloys of aluminum, copper, magnesium, nickel, and other metals.

Stock in the form of the heated end of a bar, slug, preform, or individual billet is placed in a cavity in the bottom half of a forging die on the anvil of a drop hammer. An example of a die is shown in Fig. 12-14. The upper half is attached to the hammer or ram and falls on the stock. Generally, a finished forging cannot be formed in one blow because the directions and extent to which the metal can be forced at any one time are limited. Thus most dies have several impressions, each a step toward the final shape. The workpiece is transferred from one impression to another between blows.

Figure 12-14 Set of forging dies and illustrations of the successive steps for forging a connecting rod. (Courtesy Forging Industry Association).

The main steps in forging a connecting rod are set forth at the bottom of Fig. 12-14. First the *tonghold* is formed at the right front corner of the die block. Then the stock is rolled between a number of blows and elongated at the corner and on the left side of the block. This is called *fullering*. The piece may be flattened between the surface of the die before it is *blocked* or rough shaped in the right-hand cavity. Finally, the preformed metal is pounded into the final shape of the left-hand cavity in the *finishing* operation. Excess metal is squeezed into a thin flange around the forging called the *flash*. This is sheared from the forging in a subsequent trimming operation. Actually, flash is waste metal and increases forging forces 5 to 10 times. Efforts have been made to eliminate it, but then filling the die requires close control of the raw stock, and that is usually more costly.

Most forging is done with unheated dies, but some has had dies heated to 870°C (1600°F). The work is chilled less and remains plastic longer. Thus it can be forged to closer tolerances and with thinner sections. Flange depths have been reported increased 800%.

The die establishes the efficiency of an operation, and its design requires a high order of skill. Some dies are cast, but more are made of heavy blocks of forged alloy steel heat treated to less than maximum hardness but to a toughness to resist shock. The cavities are cut or *sunk* to allow for shrinkage in the workpiece when it cools. In addition to size, a die is designed to produce a forging with a minimum of residual stress and the most benefit from the original grain fibers of the bar. This requires enough but not too many stations, as dictated by a careful study of each case. The die is provided with draft to release the workpiece readily and with generous fillets, radii, and ribs to prolong die life. At times locking surfaces or pins are provided to make the two halves of a die match the same way each time they come together. Multiple die impressions may be provided at each station to forge several pieces in each operation for large-quantity production.

Drop Hammers. A drop hammer has a guided falling hammer or ram but differs from a forging hammer by having the anvil attached to the frame. This is to keep the upper and lower halves of a die aligned.

The board drop hammer illustrated in Fig. 12-15 is suitable for small and moderate-size forgings. The ram is fastened to the lower ends of vertical hardwood boards. These pass between powered friction rolls that press from opposite sides against the boards when the ram is down. The revolving rolls raise the boards, which become latched in their uppermost position. Tripping the press releases the boards and allows the ram to drop. Maintenance and downtime cost are relatively high. One study showed that boards had to be replaced every week, and about 14% of the work time was lost each year.

The ram is lifted by compressed air acting on a piston in an overhead cylinder on another type of drop hammer. The ram is clamped in the top position but is released and drops when the press is tripped. It takes more energy for a power drop hammer, but repair and downtime costs are negligible, and total operating cost is less than for a board drop hammer.

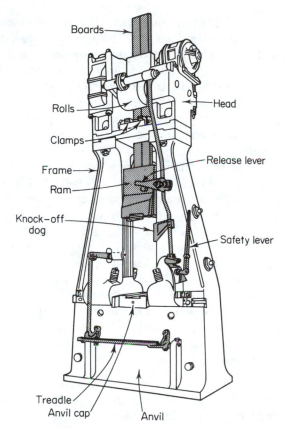

Figure 12-15 Board drop hammer. (Courtesy Forging Industry Association).

Most drop hammers are manually controlled and require considerable skill for fast and efficient operation. Some hammer systems have electronic controls that govern the number, intensity, and timing of blows in a preset cycle to produce a forging. An unskilled operator needs only to shift the stock from station to station in a routine manner.

The same factors as explained for forging hammers determine the energy and force delivered by a drop hammer. The formula $E = KA$ gives an estimate of the energy needed for a forging. A stands for the plan area in m^2 (in.^{2}) including flash. Flash may be 25 mm (1 in.) on a side for a workpiece 200 mm (8 in.) or less in diameter or width and in proportion up to 50 mm (2 in.) for a part 600 mm (24 in.) or more in diameter or width. Some values for factor K are:

E	Aluminum alloy	Carbon steel	Alloy steel	Stainless steel	Titanium alloys
kJ	475–680	525–735	735–1050	840–1470	1260–1890
ft-lb	225–325	250–350	350–500	400–700	600–900

A hammer is rated by the weight of its falling ram. The die adds about 25% to the falling weight. Board drop hammers are usually of 22 kN (5000 lb) capacity or less because larger sizes are not efficient. One line of air drop hammers ranges in size to 45 kN (10,000 lb). A 4000-lb model with a 1.3-m (50-in.) effective stroke and 28 kJ (20,000 ft-lb) capacity, including a 4.5-kN (1000-lb) die, sells for about $200,000, but the cost of a massive foundation, furnaces, and air compressor equipment must be added. A 1.35-Mg/h (3000-lb/hr)-capacity furnace for a forge shop recently sold for $140,000 including the latest energy-saving and pollution controls. A 150-kW (200-hp) compressor to deliver 0.5 m³/s (1060 cfm) costs about $50,000. Double-action air or steam hammers, called power drop hammers, are also used for closed die forging. A 3000-lb model capable of 46.6 kJ/stroke (34,400 ft-lb/stroke) costs about $250,000 plus foundation, furnace, and air or steam equipment. *Counterblow hammers* have rams driven together at the same time from the sides, or from top and bottom, to expend their combined energies in the workpiece instead of on an anvil. They may be set to strike single or repeated blows. The horizontal arrangement is easily automated in a production line because of clear space above the dies, and faster production rates can be achieved. A leading make is called an *Impacter System*. Equipment cost is high; a model capable of delivering 54 kJ/stroke (40,000 ft-lb/stroke) costs about three times that of a comparable power drop hammer. Even so, in the case of a typical connecting rod forging, the output is 536 pieces/hr on a drop hammer and 972 on the two-ram Impacter, with the cost per piece on the hammer about $1\frac{1}{2}$ times that on the Impacter.

Press Forging.   The main feature of forging in presses is that the metal is finish formed in most cases in two or three squeezes. Preforming is usually done in other operations, such as by casting, powder metallurgy methods, rolling, and upsetting. In press forging, pressure is sustained momentarily to penetrate the metal fully and give it time to fill out the die cavity. Dies may have a minimum of or no draft, and the closest tolerances are held in press forging. By careful control of material, flash is eliminated in some operations with appreciable savings in material, energy, and trimming time. A class of work called *precision forging* is done on presses, turning out such products as gears that need almost no machining, only a little on their teeth. An *Autoforge* is an automatic machine that casts preforms from molten metal in one station, cools and moves them when solid but still hot to another station for press forging, and finally trims the forgings and returns the scraps to the melting pot.

Most press forging is done on upright hydraulic presses (Fig. 12-16) or mechanical presses with eccentric, toggle, or screw drives like those described in Chap. 13. A press is rated on the basis of the force in tons it can deliver near the bottom of a stroke. Pressures in MPa (tons/in.²) of projected area on the parting plane have been found to be 70 to 275 (5 to 20) for brass, 275 (20) for aluminum, 205 to 415 (15 to 30) for steel, and 275 to 550 (20 to 40) for titanium. These values are for conventional forgings with adequate draft, fillets, etc. Precision forgings made in dies that confine the metal almost completely may require twice as much pressure. The force the press must deliver is equal to the unit pressure times the projected area.

Mechanical presses are favored over hammers for high-volume production be-

Figure 12-16 Ingot being shaped on a 10,000-ton forging press. (Courtesy Bethlehem Steel Corp.)

cause they are faster and require less operator skill. A press (and its tooling) may cost four to six times as much as a hammer that will do the same work, and thus the press is not justified for low production and frequent idle periods for die changes. It is reported that about two-thirds of all forgings are made on hammers.

Some unusual forging presses have multiple vertical and horizontal actions and can do operations like that of Fig. 12-17(A).

Incremental forging makes it possible to forge large pieces that could not be formed all at one time because a press large enough to do so is not available. First the part may be preformed in open dies as indicated on the left of Fig. 12-17(B), in which the portion on the right is being forged to final shape. Finally, the remainder of the part is forged as illustrated in Fig. 12-17(C). This method requires care because time lost in a number of steps may allow some portions to get too cool for forging. In some cases the hot billet is covered with insulation to keep it hot and pliable longer.

High-energy-rate Forging. Although most presses do not run at high speeds, forging is done at high impact rates on some. This is different from hammer forging because the blows are not repeated. One type of machine for high-energy-rate forging (HERF), also called controlled-energy flow forming (CEFF), is illustrated in Fig. 12-18. In the ready position the ram has been lifted to the top of its stroke by the elevating pistons. The high-pressure cylinder is filled with air or gas at around 1.5 MPa (200 psi). The ram piston is pressed against a seal ring at the top. Enough high-pressure gas is admitted to the area inside the seal ring to dislodge the piston. The

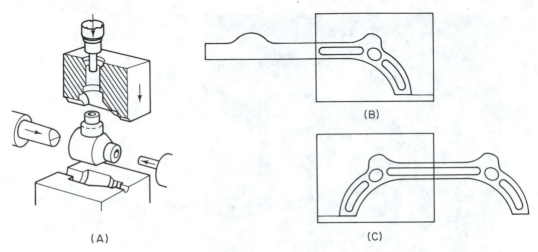

(A)   (B)

                                                       (C)

Figure 12-17 (A) Sketch of a split-die forging operation. The workpiece in the center is forged in an 11,000-ton press (main ram rating) from a sheared length of billet stock. After the die closes, the upper piercing ram with over 25 MN (ca. 3000 ton) force and the side rams with over 50 MN (ca. 6000 tons) each push the punches into the material to fill the die. (B) and (C) Steps in incremental forging.

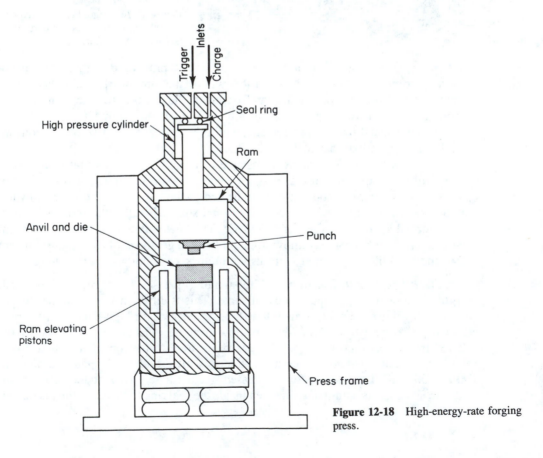

Figure 12-18 High-energy-rate forging press.

gas in the high-pressure cylinder then acts over the whole piston and drives the ram down at a speed up to 20 m/s (ca. 60 fps) and over on the impact. Most of the energy is expended on the work and not lost in the foundation.

High-energy-rate forging does not give the metal time to cool much in contact with the die. In fact, the temperature is raised because the heat from the work done does not have time to escape. The metal can be worked more at higher temperatures and forced into intricate shapes and thin sections not possible in other ways. Thus, some parts can be made in one blow instead of in several steps by other means, and finer detail obtained. The process is limited mostly to symmetrical parts of small to medium size. Dies must be designed and built carefully to withstand high impact. A CEFF press with facilities to supply high-pressure air or gas costs about the same as or less than a mechanical press of comparable capacity, but operating cost is higher. Time to reset the press, etc., for each cycle makes the operation rate slow, about the same as for a forging hammer. Thus, the CEFF process is not competitive unless it gives a definite benefit in workpiece quality.

Upset Forging. Upset forging, also called *hot heading* and *machine forging,* consists of applying lengthwise pressure to a hot bar gripped in a die to enlarge some section or sections usually on the end. Piercing can be done, too. The bar stock may have any uniform cross section but is mostly round and may be steel, aluminum, copper, bronze, or other metal. Upset forgings range in weight from a few grams (ounces) to several hundred kilograms (pounds). Examples are automobile mushroom valves, gear blanks with stems, and shafts and levers with knobs or forks on their ends.

Upset forging is done on a machine designed particularly for the purpose. The action may be illustrated by the example of Fig. 12-19. The cluster gear blank shown there requires four steps. A piece of hot barstock sheared to length is placed in the top cavity in one half of the die. The machine is tripped and closes the die to clamp the stock. A ram pushes the punches in a horizontal direction into the die to upset the stock. Then the punches are retracted, and the die is opened. The stock is moved to the next station, and the cycle is repeated until the part is finished.

If too much stock extends from the die, it can buckle and jam between the punch and die. That can cause a serious wreck. Thus the amount of stock that can be worked in one stage is limited. Figure 12-20 shows the basic limitations found by experience. More stock can be gathered by repeated steps at more cost. Large amounts of material can be gathered by continuous upsetting on electrohydraulic machines as indicated in Fig. 12-21.

Although used for many other parts, an upset forging machine is rated by the largest bolt it can head. Some take bolts to 200 mm (8 in.) diameter and exert 18 MN (2000 tons) of force. A machine for bolts 15 to 40 mm ($\frac{1}{2}$ to $1\frac{1}{2}$ in.) in diameter has a 11-kW (15-hp) motor, weighs 13.8 Mg (30,500 lb), and with tooling may cost over $200,000.

Forging with Rolls. Plain rolling is done on work of uniform cross section. Forging by rolling is the production of discrete pieces or lengths of varying cross section by rollers.

Roll forging is done with two half rolls on parallel shafts as depicted in Fig.

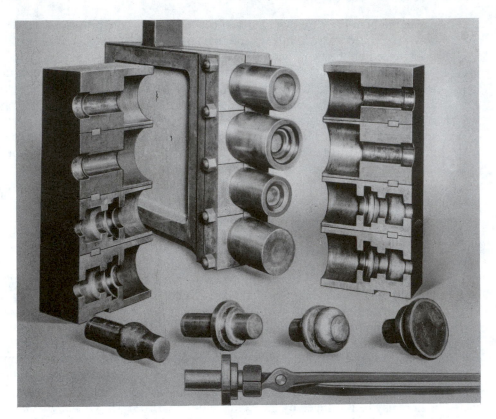

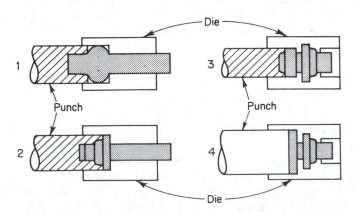

Figure 12-19 A photo of the tools used for a four-position upset forging operation. The die halves are shown on each side of the punches. At the bottom of the photo are examples of the work done at each position to forge a cluster of gear blanks. Also shown is the workpiece held by tongs in the third position. Below the photo is a sketch of the work done at each station. (Photo courtesy Ajax Manufacturing Co.)

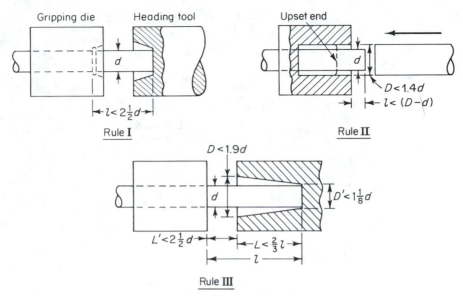

Figure 12-20 Rules for upset forging.

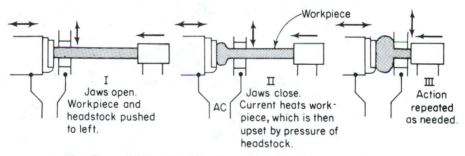

Figure 12-21 Principle of operation of continuous upsetting.

12-22(A). These roll segments have one or more sets of grooves. A piece of stock is placed between the rolls, which then turn and squeeze the stock in one set of grooves. The stock is transferred to a second set of grooves, the rolls turn again, and so on until the piece is finished. Each set of grooved segments is made to do a specific job. By this method bar stock can be increased in length, reduced in diameter, and changed in section as desired. Because it is rapid, roll forging is of advantage in preparing some shapes for forging machines and hammers and also for completely forging parts like levers, leaf springs, and axles.

Unidirectional or *die rolling* consists of passing stock continuously between one or more pairs of rollers with die sunk imprints around their peripheries. One form is indicated in Fig. 12-22(B). Some versions of the process are known by trade names. Parts like shafts, axles, levers, and ball blanks are produced.

Ring rolling, shown in Fig. 12-22(C), starts with a small ring blank and deforms

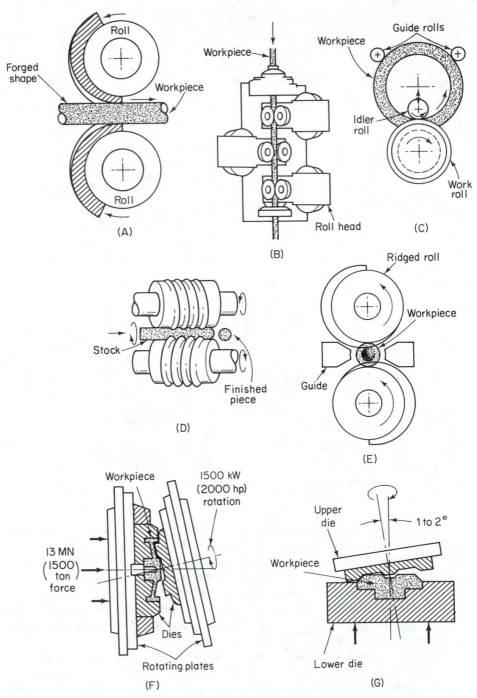

Figure 12-22 Principles of (A) roll forging; (B) unidirectional rolling; (C) ring rolling; (D) skew rolling; (E) cross rolling; (F) circular forging; (G) orbital forging.

it between one or two work rolls and an idler. The ring is increased in diameter and decreased and shaped in cross section. The blank may be prepared by forging or punching. Pieces finished by this method range from small roller-bearing races to rings about 9 m (30 ft) in diameter.

Skew rolling is done with two rolls on cross axes as indicated in Fig. 12-22(D). Each roll has an outside helical pattern that carries the stock along and progressively shapes it as the rolls turn. Such diverse products as steel balls (up to 400 per minute) and railway car axles are forged by skew rolling.

Cross rolling or *wedge rolling* sketched in Fig. 12-22(E) uses two synchronized rolls with a rising spiral ridge around each. Their axes are slightly crossed. A typical operation is to place a heated bar between the rolls. Then, as the rolls turn, a groove or neck is forged in the workpiece. In through-feed cross rolling successive formed pieces can be cut off from a bar as it is fed between them. Production time is 300 small balls per minute to 4 to 6 seconds each for larger pieces.

Circular forging is done in a Slick Mill, named after its designer, Edwin E. Slick, in the manner shown in Fig. 12-22(F). A heated slug is placed between two dies on face plates that are pressed together as they turn on crossed axes. Round forgings up to 1.4 m (55 in.) in diameter are made in 55 seconds.

In *orbital forging,* Fig. 12-22(G), a workpiece in a lower fixed die is pressed against an upper die inclined at 1 to 2°. The upper die is rolled substantially in line contact around the workpiece surface and may be rocked as it goes for certain effects. The action is not fast but is quiet and easy on dies. Available equipment forges flanged parts, disks, rings, gears, and even symmetrical parts within a 100-mm (4-in.) diameter.

Quality and Cost.   The dimensions of a series of forgings from a die vary because of differences in the behavior of the material, temperatures, closing of the die, mismatch of the die halves, and enlargement of the cavities as they wear. A tolerance of ± 0.8 mm ($\pm \frac{1}{32}$ in.) is considered good for small carbon steel forgings and may be as large as 7 mm ($\frac{1}{4}$ in.) in all directions for large pieces. Tolerances of 0.25 mm (0.010 in.) and less have been held on precision press forgings, but at higher cost. Tolerances are larger for less workable space-age materials. Tables of commercial tolerances for various sizes and kinds of forgings are available in reference books and handbooks.

Many forgings are finished by machining to close tolerances and must have enough stock on the surfaces to be machined. The least stock is about 1.5 mm (0.06 in.) per surface on small forgings, and may be as much as 7 mm ($\frac{1}{4}$ in.) or more on large ones.

Parts made from forgings may be made also as castings, cut from standard shapes, fabricated by welding pieces together, or made in other ways. A forging can be made stronger, more shock and fatigue resistant, and more durable than other forms. This is because it can be made of fine grain size and fibrous structure with highest strength in the direction needed as was shown in Fig. 12-1. A forging may provide required properties with less weight. Other forms are selected only when they serve as well at lower cost. Even so, forgings are cheaper in some cases, as illustrated in the following paragraphs.

Forgings are economical in some cases because less material has to be removed from them than from bar stock. An example is given by a brass compression fitting originally machined from $1\frac{3}{4}$-in.-diameter hexagonal rod. Each lot of 5000 pieces requires 717 kg (1580 lb) of brass at \$1.72/kg (\$0.78/lb), a total of \$1230. A forging made from round stock costs \$1.61/kg (\$0.73/lb). Each lot requires 423 kg (932 lb) at a total cost of \$680. In addition to the material saving of \$550 or \$0.11/piece, shortening of machining time raises the total savings to about \$0.15/piece. A forging die costing about \$2000 is paid for by three lots.

Dies are expensive and usually rule out forgings for small quantities. This is illustrated by Fig. 12-23, which shows a casting to be cheaper for less than about 300 pieces in one case. In this instance the forging dies cost about $3\frac{1}{2}$ times as much as the temporary pattern equipment and 15% more than the permanent pattern equipment. The scrap loss is much less for the forging, which is more economical in large quantities.

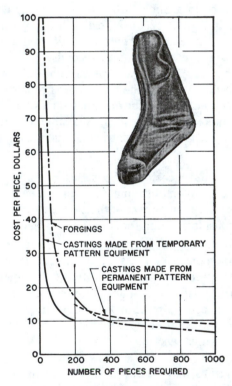

Figure 12-23 Unit cost of a 1.6-kg ($3\frac{1}{2}$-lb) brace for various quantities and two methods of manufacture. (From "Design of Closed Die Forgings," *Metals Handbook 1955 Supplement*, Taylor Lyman, ed., American Society for Metals, p. 71.)

EXTRUSION

Principles.   When metal is extruded, it is compressed above its elastic limit in a chamber and is forced to flow through and take on the shape of an opening. An everyday analogy is the dispensing of paste from a collapsible tube. Metal is extruded in a number of basic ways, as depicted in Fig. 12-24. The metal is normally com-

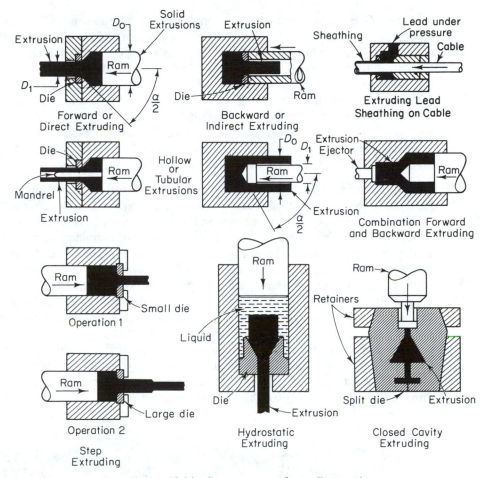

Figure 12-24 Common ways of extruding metal.

pressed by a ram and may be pushed forward or backward. The product may be solid or hollow. The process may be done hot or cold. The problems and results of hot and cold extrusion are somewhat different, and the two methods will be discussed separately.

Hot Extrusion. Forward hot extrusion of solid or hollow shapes enables the metal to be easily supported, handled, and freed from the equipment. When a piece is forward extruded, it is cut off, and the butt end is removed from the chamber.

Preservation of the equipment subjected to high temperatures, as it is, is the major problem of hot extruding. Temperatures are 340 to 425°C (650 to 800°F) for magnesium, 340 to 480°C (650 to 900°F) for aluminum, 650 to 1100°C (1200 to 2000°F) for copper alloys, and 1200 to 1325°C (2200 to 2400°F) for steel. Pressures range from as low as 35 MPa (5 ksi) for magnesium to over 700 MPa (100 ksi) for steel. Lubrication and protection of the chamber, ram, and die are necessary. Mopping these parts with an oil and graphite mixture may be sufficient at the lower temperatures. Glass, which becomes a molten lubricant, has made possible the extrusion of steel at high temperatures. Components like the ram and mandrel may be sprayed with cooling water while idle. A dummy block is used between the ram and hot metal. For extruding steel, the die is changed and allowed to cool for each piece. The best safeguard for equipment is to extrude the metal as rapidly as possible. A steel tube 150 mm (6 in.) in diameter and 15 m (50 ft) long is extruded in 9 seconds.

Most hot extrusion is done on horizontal hydraulic presses especially constructed for the purpose. Common sizes are rated from 2 to 50 MN (250 to 5500 tons), but some designs in recent years have reached as high as 220 MN (25,000 tons). One with a 100-MN (12,000-ton) capacity is illustrated in Fig. 12-25.

Applications of Hot Extrusion.   Most hot extrusions are long pieces of uniform cross section, but tapered and stepped pieces are also producible. Examples of commercial extruded products are trim and molding strips of aluminum and brass and structural shapes, rods, bars, and tubes of all forms of aluminum and steel. A few aluminum sections are shown in Fig. 12-26. Sections that can be contained within a 760-mm (30-in.)-diameter circle are available for aluminum and within a 165-mm ($6\frac{1}{2}$-in.)-diameter circle for steel. Usual lengths are about 6 m (20 ft), but some are as long as 20 m (64 ft). Not as many shapes are available for steel as for aluminum. Examples of other kinds of hot extrusions are poppet valves, gear blanks, projector shells, piling connectors, and propeller and turbine blades.

A common tolerance for extrusions of soft metals like aluminum is ±125 μm (±0.005 in.). Tolerances for steel extrusions range from ±0.75 mm (±0.030 in.) under 25 mm (1 in.) to ±3 mm (±0.12 in.) and more for the largest crosswise dimensions. Surfaces are like those of hot-rolled stock.

Figure 12-25   A 12,000-ton extrusion press for seamless steel tubing. The press is about 38 m (126 ft) long and 6.7 m (22 ft) high. Estimated cost today over $25,000,000 installed. It is capable of producing alloy and stainless steel tubes up to 500 mm (20 in.) in diameter and 15 m (50 ft) long. (Courtesy Curtiss Wright Corp., Buffalo Facility.)

Figure 12-26 A few cross sections of extrusions.

Shapes that can be rolled are more expensive to extrude, but extrusion can produce many shapes, such those with reentrant angles, that cannot be rolled or produced in other ways. In some cases, extrusion offers an economical way to make large parts that replace an assembly of many individual parts and fasteners, such as a ribbed section of a bomber wing. At the other extreme is extruding to produce small parts in large quantities. A simple pump gear is an example. A long gear is extruded and then sliced into a number of individual gears. In other cases, extrusion may be the cheapest way of making parts even in small quantities. Extrusion dies are not expensive; for most shapes they average about $500, and tools for other processes often cost much more.

Cold Extrusion. Cold extrusion, also called *cold forming, cold forging,* and *extrusion pressing,* is normally done at room temperature. Its forms are like those of hot extrusion illustrated in Fig. 12-24. Cold extrusion is done quickly, at ram speeds of $\frac{1}{4}$ to $1\frac{1}{2}$ m/s (50 to 300 fpm), generates heat that raises the temperature several hundred degrees, and takes less force than if done slowly. Some parts are formed in one pressing in a single die; others in two or more stages in a series of dies, sometimes in conjunction with cold heading. Presses mostly used are the same as for sheet metal forming (Chap. 13).

Several makes of continuous extruders have been developed to produce wire, rods, and various shapes from powders, ground-up scrap, or larger-diameter stock. They utilize one or more grooved wheels that take and compress the feedstock as they revolve and force it into the die through which the metal is extruded.

Warm-extrusion or *warm-forming* attempts to gain still better metal flow without changes in microstructure and surface damage of high forging temperatures. It is typically done below the recrystallization temperature at 425 to 650°C (800 to 1200°F) but is otherwise a variation of cold forming. Energy may be reduced 35 to 40% below cold forming, but extra induction or resistance heating equipment may cost $50,000 to $100,000.

An old and until recent years the main cold extrusion operation was the manufacture of collapsible tubes from soft aluminum, lead, tin, and zinc. To perform this operation, a slug of metal is placed at the bottom of a closed cavity. A punch strikes it sharply, and the metal squirts up around the punch to form the tube. The tube is blown off as the punch retracts. Production rates of 40 to 80 tubes/min are reported. Copper tubes are forward extruded by similar operation. Because of the fast impulsive action, operations like these are called *impact extrusion*. Such work is done mostly on vertical mechanical and hydraulic presses like those described in Chap. 13.

Cold extrusion pressures range from one to three times the finished yield strength of the metal. Over 20 formulas are reported for calculating pressures, and some are quite complex. Empirical relationships developed at General Motors Institute for carbon steels have been found accurate to a few percent. For forward extrusion with dimensions defined in Fig. 12-24, the pressure in psi is $P = 0.45k \times [(D_0^2 - D_1^2)/D_0^2]^{0.787}\alpha^{0.375}$. For backward extrusion, also shown in Fig. 12-24, $P = 0.62k[D_1^2/D_0^2]^{0.855}\alpha^{0.355}$. The factor k is the true stress at a true strain $= 1$ as explained on page 31, and is 81,050 for AISI 1008, 91,800 for 1020, 132,500 for 1035, and 142,100 for 1050 steel. $P_m(\text{kPa}) = 6.89P(\text{psi})$. In spite of high pressures, the metal volume is not changed.

Adequate lubrication is mandatory for flow at the high pressures of cold extrusion. Oils, waxes, greases, some saponified, are the main lubricants. Solids like graphite, MoS_2, ZnO, and PTFE polymer add to boundary lubrication. To extrude steel, a zinc phosphate or copper coating is necessary to help hold the lubricant to the surface.

Cold extrusion work hardens metals. For example, an aluminum alloy with a yield strength of 40 MPa (6000 psi) and tensile strength of 110 MPa (16,000 psi) may acquire on cold extrusion a yield strength of 210 MPa (30,000 psi) and a tensile strength of 270 MPa (39,000 psi). This can be an advantage if the product can be used in the work-hardened condition with lowered ductility.

Applications of Cold Extrusion. Aluminum, copper, steel, lead, magnesium, tin, titanium, and zinc and their alloys are cold extruded. Examples of products are cans, fire extinguisher cases, trimmer condensers, aircraft shear tie fittings and brackets and automotive pistons from aluminum, and projectile shells, rocket motors and heads, hydraulic and shock absorber cylinders, wrist pins, and gear blanks from steel. Stock may be solid slugs or powder metal preforms.

Advantages of cold extrusion are that it is fast, may improve physical properties and save heat treatment, wastes little or no material, can make parts with small radii and no draft, and can produce to small tolerances and save machining. Tolerances can be as close as ± 25 μm (± 0.001 in.), but larger tolerances are much cheaper. Walls are commonly held to ± 0.25 mm (± 0.01 in.) tolerance when about 3 mm ($\frac{1}{8}$ in.) thick and ± 0.5 mm (± 0.02 in.) when thicker. Diameter tolerances normally are ± 0.25 mm (± 0.01 in.) and length tolerances ± 5 mm ($\pm \frac{3}{16}$ in.). Surface finishes of 0.25 μm (10 μin.) are obtainable, but 0.5 μm (20 μin.) or rougher are more practical.

A cold-extruded part must be one with a uniform wall thickness all around and with ribs, flutes, or fins symmetrical with the part axis. The main limitation of cold extrusion is in the size of equipment to exert the tremendous pressures required. For the most part, the process is confined to small- and medium-size pieces.

Cold extrusion is competitive with deep drawing from sheet metal, described in Chap. 13, for making cups and deep shells. Extrusion has the advantage of requiring fewer steps thus saving tooling. For example, a round can of 50 mm (2 in.) diameter and 400 mm (16 in.) deep can be extruded in one operation but must be drawn in more than six operations. Tooling for this extrusion was estimated to cost one third as much as for drawing, even though an individual compressive die costs upward of 50% more than a drawing die. Other advantages over drawing are that shells may be extruded with thick bottoms or flanges and walls may be stepped. However, cold extrusion is not competitive with drawing of shallow cups.

Cold extrusion is competitive with casting and forging for some parts. Extrusions are usually lighter and stronger than castings. They need have no draft or flash to trim. They are not porous or brittle as castings may be. Tolerances are closer and less machining is required for extruded parts. Cheaper metals can sometimes be put in extrusions because the process improves the physical properties.

An illustration of the competitive situation of cold extrusion for making an aircraft aileron nose rib is given by Fig. 12-27. Little tooling investment was required to machine the part from barstock, and the cost per piece was the lowest by that method when few pieces were to be made. A forging required a little less tooling but more machining than an extrusion, which proved to be cheapest for more than 70 pieces. Break-even quantities are commonly much higher for less costly parts—over 10,000 parts/month in the high-production industries.

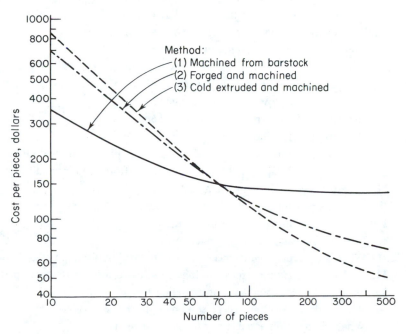

Figure 12-27 Relative costs for three methods of making an aircraft part in various quantities.

QUESTIONS

1. How does a metal act above its recrystallization temperature?
2. What are five advantages of hot working metal?
3. What are the disadvantages of hot working metal?
4. Why is metal cold worked?
5. Explain what happens to a metal when it is cold worked.
6. What are residual stresses, and why do they occur?
7. Why is cold-worked metal annealed?
8. Describe what occurs in metal when it is rolled.
9. What advantage is gained by applying lengthwise tension to a piece of metal being rolled?
10. Describe and specify the merits of the different kinds of rolling mills.
11. What are the forms through which steel goes when rolled into sheets or plates, structural shapes, and bars or rods?
12. Why are a number of passes required to roll a steel bar?
13. What benefits are obtained from cold rolling metal?
14. How are metal wires or sheets straightened?
15. How is cold rolling done?
16. How is metal cold drawn? Why is it done?
17. What determines how much the area of a bar may be reduced when drawn through a single die and how much altogether when drawn through a series of dies?
18. Describe three ways of making butt-welded pipe.
19. How is seamless tubing pierced?
20. What is important in heating the work for forging and how is it accomplished?
21. Compare open and closed die forging.
22. Why are heavy blows necessary for good forgings?
23. Describe the common kinds of forging hammers.
24. How are drop forgings made?
25. How are a forging hammer and drop hammer alike, and how do they differ?
26. What is press forging, and how does it differ from drop forging?
27. Describe a press for high-energy-rate forging.
28. What is upset forging, and how is it done?
29. What are the limitations of upset forging?
30. Describe six ways of forging with rolls.
31. What is the order of tolerances that can be held by forging?
32. Under what conditions may forgings be selected for manufactured parts?
33. Describe the common ways of extruding metals.
34. What is done to help preserve equipment for hot extrusion?
35. What are the main applications for hot extrusion?
36. What is impact extrusion?
37. What are some of the applications of cold extrusion?

PROBLEMS

1. A 25 × 925 mm (1 × 36 in.) slab enters a hot-rolling mill at 2.5 m/s (500 fpm). It passes through seven stands and emerges as a strip 6 × 925 mm ($\frac{1}{4}$ × 36 in.). What is the exit speed of the strip from the last set of rolls?

2. Draw a diagram of the resultant forces of a set of rolls on an entering bar of metal and show the state of equilibrium that is reached when the rolls are not able to draw the metal spontaneously into the space between them. That is when the angle of contact is approximately equal to the angle of friction. Show why that is so. Depict the limiting conditions after the bar has been fully introduced between the rolls.

3. A hot steel bar 76 × 400 mm (3 × 16 in.) is to be reduced in one pass to 63.5 mm (2$\frac{1}{2}$ in.) thick. It is assumed the 400 mm (16 in.) width does not change appreciably. Rolls are 635 mm (25 in.) in diameter. The yield stress of the hot steel is 140 MPa (ca. 20,000 psi), and the average pressure between the rolls and work is 1$\frac{1}{2}$ times the yield stress. The coefficient of friction is 0.50. What is the force tending to spread the rolls apart? How much torque must be applied to drive the rolls? What power must be delivered to the stand for a rolling speed of 127 mm/s (25 fpm)?

4. A carbon steel wire has a yield strength of 550 MPa (80,000 psi). It is to be drawn from 5.54 mm (0.218 in.) in diameter to 4.80 mm (0.189 in.) in diameter, which is expected to stress the small size near its yield point. What is the percent reduction in area? What is the expected drawing force? What power must be applied to draw the wire at a speed of 400 mm/s (80 fpm)?

5. A low-carbon steel has a yield strength of 415 MPa (60,000 psi). What is the maximum force that may be exerted to cold draw a bar to 38 mm (1$\frac{1}{2}$ in.) in diameter? What horsepower is required for a drawing speed of 100 mm/s (20 fpm)?

6. Wire of 1.60 mm (0.063 in.) diameter is to be drawn from stock of 5.54 mm (0.218 in.) diameter. The material will stand a 60% reduction in area between annealing operations. It can be reduced 30% in area in any one draw. How many drawing operations and how many annealing operations are necessary? When must annealing be done?

7. A forging can be made in 15 minutes by means of standard open dies and smith tools. The skilled operator's rate is $13.00/hr. A set of closed dies to make the same forging costs $2800. The operator using these dies has a rate of $9.00/hr and can turn out a piece every 3 minutes. Overhead is the same in both cases. Interest and related charges on the dies may be neglected. For how many pieces is a set of closed dies justified?

8. The actual falling mass of a steam hammer is 550 kg (1200 lb), the cylinder is 250 mm (10 in.) in diameter, and the stroke is 685 mm (27 in.). The mean average steam pressure is 550 kPa (80 psi).
   (a) What is the energy of the hammer blow?
   (b) What is the average work force exerted by the hammer if it travels 3.2 mm ($\frac{1}{8}$ in.) after striking the workpiece?

9. A free-falling drop hammer weighs 680 kg (1500 lb) and drops 0.9 m (36 in.).
   (a) With what velocity does it strike?
   (b) What is the energy of the blow?
   (c) What average force is exerted if the ram travels 1.6 mm ($\frac{1}{16}$ in.) after striking the workpiece?
   (d) What diameter of cylinder for steam at an average pressure of 700 kPa (100 psi) is required to quadruple the working capacity of this hammer?

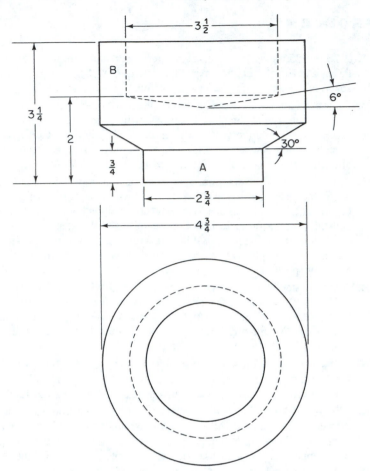

Figure 12-28   Cold-extruded workpiece.

10. A forging has a face projected area of 150 cm² (23 in.²). What energy must a drop hammer be able to deliver if the material is **(a)** alloy steel? **(b)** aluminum? **(c)** carbon steel?

11. A steel cluster gear 95 mm (3¾ in.) on the largest diameter and 180 mm (7 in.) long can be machined from barstock of 100 mm (4 in.) diameter by 185 mm (7¼ in.) long. Machining time by this method is 26 minutes. An upset forging can be made from round barstock 45 mm (1⅞ in.) in diameter by 230 mm (9 in.) long, and 17 minutes is required to machine the forging. The material costs $0.99/kg ($0.45/lb), forging costs $0.66/kg ($0.30/lb), and machining costs $12/hr. The forging die can be made for $1500.
(a) Which method would you select for 100 pieces? Why?
(b) For how many pieces is the forging warranted?

12. A high-energy-rate forging machine like the one depicted in Fig. 12-18 has a 230-mm (9-in.)-diameter piston in a 330-mm (13-in.)-diameter cylinder and a ram stroke of 500 mm (20 in.). The ram weighs 1.36 Mg (3000 lb), and the anvil and frame weigh 13.6 Mg (30,000 lb). The gas pressure in the cylinder is 14 MPa (2000 psi) when the press is fired and decreases adiabatically as the volume increases upon the piston leaving the cylinder.

No gas can be added during the short time of the stroke. The reaction of the gas pressure raises the frame and anvil freely mounted on springs. The springs are assumed completely relaxed when the anvil reaches its highest position.

(a) What is the velocity of the ram when it strikes the workpiece?

(b) What is the velocity of the anvil at the same time?

(c) What energy is there in the ram when it strikes the workpiece?

(d) How much energy is there in the anvil and frame at the same time?

(e) From what height would a 1.36-Mg (3000-lb) ram have to fall to deliver the same energy as available in this press?

13. The piece shown in Fig. 12-28 is to be forward extruded at A and backward extruded at B. The material is AISI 1020 steel. Rough size is 120 mm ($4\frac{3}{4}$ in.) in diameter by 46 mm ($1\frac{53}{64}$ in.) long.

(a) What force in meganewtons is required for the forward extrusion? In tons?

(b) What force in meganewtons is required for the backward extrusion? In pounds?

REFERENCES

ASA B32.1-1952, *Preferred Thicknesses for Uncoated Thin Flat Metals;* USASI B32.2-1969, *Preferred Diameters for Round Wire-0.50 in. and Under;* ANSI B32.3a-1978, *Preferred Metric Sizes for Flat Metal Products;* ANSI B32.4M-1980, *Preferred Metric Sizes for Round, Square, Rectangle and Hexagon Metal Products,* American Society of Mechanical Engineers, New York.

BLICKWEDE, D. J., "Cold Extruding Steel," *Metal Progress,* May 1980, p. 76.

COHEN, A., "Metric Material Standards," *Metal Progress,* June 1978, p. 33.

DRAKE, R. J., and J. W. THROUP, "How to Predict Cold Extrusion Forces," *Metal Progress,* May 1971, p. 72.

DWYER, J. J., JR., "Sheet Steel Today, Special Report 687," *American Machinist,* May 1976, p. S-1.

KULKARNI, K. M., "Hybrid Processes Combine Casting and Forging," *Machine Design,* May 2, 1974, p. 125.

"Lubricants for Extrusion," *American Machinist,* Aug. 10, 1970, p. 107.

Metals Handbook, 8th ed., Vol. 4: *Forming,* 1969, Vol. 5: *Forging and Casting,* 1970, American Society for Metals, Metals Park, Ohio.

SEMIATIN, S. L., and G. D. LAHOTI, "The Forging of Metals," *Scientific American,* Aug. 1981, p. 98.

SHERIDAN, S. A., and P. M. UNTERWEISER, *Forging Design Handbook,* American Society for Metals, Metals Park, Ohio, 1972.

SPROW, E. E., "Cold Forming," *Machine Design,* Aug. 10, 1972, p. 90.

SUZUKI, Y., "The Case for Warm and Cold Forging," *American Machinist,* Feb. 1979, p. 100.

———, "The Push towards Orbital Forging," *American Machinist,* Nov. 1982, p. 142.

THIEME, J. C., and S. AMMARELLER, *Rolling Mill Rolls,* Climax Molybdenum Co., New York.

WINSHIP, J. T., "Fundamentals of Forging," *American Machinist,* July 1978, p. 101.

———, "Flashless Forging Is Here," *American Machinist,* June 1981, p. 138.

———, "Ready to Roll Big Rings," *American Machinist,* Aug. 1981, p. 105.

13

METAL SHEARING AND FORMING

A large proportion of the products of industry are manufactured by processes that shear and form standard shapes, largely sheet metal, into finished parts. The common forms of these processes and their principles of operation will be described in this chapter. A few examples of products from these processes are pots and pans, metal cabinets, door and window hardware, and automobile bodies. Other examples can be seen in almost any manufactured product because these processes are versatile, fast, and naturally adaptable to large-quantity production. These processes mostly work metal cold and produce the effects of cold working described in Chap. 12.

Cold working and forming processes take less energy and material as a rule than the metal removal processes to produce finished products. This is becoming more and more important in a world where energy and metals are growing more costly and less available.

The operations that make up the processes being considered may be classified as those for shearing, bending, drawing and stretching, and squeezing and will be described under those headings. The machines and tools used for most of those operations are presses and dies. They will be taken up in the last sections of this chapter.

METAL SHEARING OPERATIONS

Types of Operations. Operations that cut sheet metal, and even barstock and other shapes, have various purposes. Common operations and the work they do are depicted in Fig. 13-1. *Shearing* is a general name for most sheet metal cutting but in

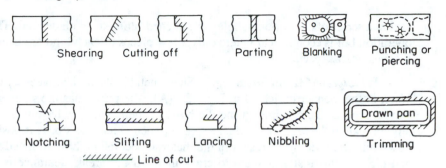

Shearing   Cutting off   Parting   Blanking   Punching or piercing

Notching   Slitting   Lancing   Nibbling   Trimming

⁄⁄⁄⁄⁄⁄⁄⁄ Line of cut

Figure 13-1 Typical patterns of common sheet metal cutting operations.

a specific sense designates a cut in a straight line completely across a strip, sheet, or bar. *Cutting off* means severing a piece from a strip with a cut along a single line. *Parting* signifies that scrap is removed between the two pieces to separate them.

    Blanking cuts a whole piece from sheet metal. Just enough scrap is left all around the opening to assure that the punch has metal to cut along its entire edge. If the object is to cut a hole and the material removed is scrap, the operation is called *punching* or *piercing*. *Slotting* refers to the cutting of elongated holes. *Perforating* designates the cutting of a group of holes, by implication small and evenly spaced in a regular pattern. *Notching* removes material from the side of a sheet or strip. *Lancing* makes a cut part way across a strip. *Trimming* is cutting away of excess metal in a flange or flash from a piece.

    Coiled thin metal stock from the rolling mill may be utilized directly in dies for large parts like automobile body panels or may be cut up for use. One way is to shear the stock into sheets. Another is by *slitting,* which is cutting the original stock lengthwise by passing it through spaced and continuous rolls as indicated in Fig. 13-2. Wider sheet metal is available, but most that is slit is rolled in widths of 1.5 m (60 in.) or less. Widths are held to within 1.5 mm (ca. $\frac{1}{16}$ in.) tolerance. Such strips are run through dies to make small and medium size pieces.

    Nibbling is an operation for cutting any shape from sheet metal without special tools. It is done on a *nibbler,* which is a machine that has a small round or triangular punch that oscillates rapidly in and out of a mating die. The sheet of metal is guided

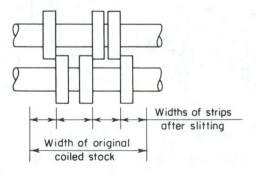

Widths of strips after slitting

Width of original coiled stock

Figure 13-2 Slitting rolls.

so that a series of overlapping holes is punched along the path desired. This is a slow operation but is economical where only a few pieces of each kind are needed because it saves costly special dies.

Principles of Metal Shearing.   Sheet metal is sheared between a *punch* and *die block* in the manner indicated in Fig. 13-3(A). The punch has the same shape all the way around as the opening in the die block, except it is smaller on each side by an amount called the *break clearance*. As the punch enters the stock, it pushes material down into the opening. Stresses in the material become highest at the edges of punch and die, and the material starts to crack there. If the break clearance is correct, the cracks meet and the break is complete. If the clearance is too large or too small, the cracks do not meet, further work must be done to cut the metal between them, and a jagged break results. The proper amount of break clearance depends on the kind, hardness, and thickness of the material. For steel it usually is from 5 to 8% of the thickness of the stock.

As the punch in its downward course enters the material, the force exerted builds up as indicated in Fig. 13-4. If the clearance is correct, the material breaks suddenly

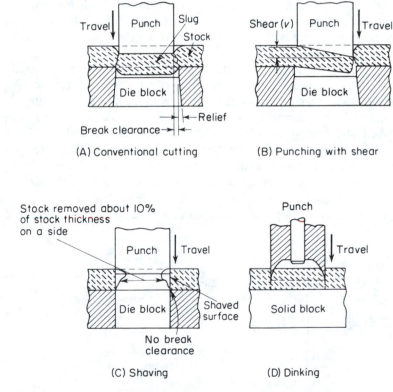

Figure 13-3 Methods of die cutting.

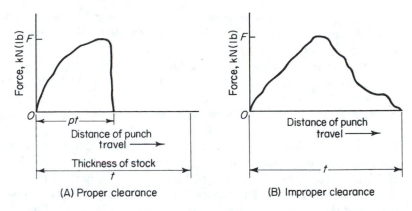

Figure 13-4 Indicator diagrams of the force exerted by a punch penetrating sheet
metal.

when the punch reaches a definite penetration, and the force vanishes as shown in Fig.
13-4(A). This distance is the percent penetration p times the thickness of the stock t
in mm (in.). The maximum force F in newtons (pounds) is equal to the product of the
length of cut in mm (in.) times the thickness of the stock in mm (in.) times the shearing
strength S in MPa (psi). If the piece is round and has a diameter D in mm (in.),
$F = \pi D t S$. The shearing strength and percent penetration are properties of the material and are 55 MPa (8000 psi) and 60% for soft aluminum, 330 MPa (48,000 psi) and
38% for 0.15% carbon steel annealed, and 490 MPa (71,000 psi) and 24% for 0.5%
carbon steel annealed. Values for other metals are given in reference books and
handbooks.

   If the break clearance is not correct, the force does not fall off suddenly, and the
curve is something like that of Fig. 13-4(B). In any case, the theoretical amount of
energy needed for the operation is represented by the area under the curve. In practice,
the situation is not always ideal, and energy is also needed to overcome friction. A
conservative estimate of energy in joules is $E_J = 0.00116F \times p \times t$ in the SI units
specified above. Power in watts is $P_W = (E_J \times N)/60$ on a press running at N strokes
per minute. For energy in ft-lb, $E = 1.16 \times F \times p \times t/12$, in English units, and
horsepower is $P = E \times N/33,000$.

   It has been assumed in the discussion so far that the end of the punch and the
top of the die block lie in substantially parallel planes. If they do not, they are said
to have *shear*, which can be put on either the punch or die block in a number of ways.
One way of putting shear on the punch is shown in Fig. 13-3(B). With shear, only part
of the cut is made at any one instant, and the maximum force is much less. The energy
expended to take a cut is not changed. Shear distorts the material being cut and
consequently cannot be applied in many cases. An effect similar to shear can be
obtained by *staggering* two or more punches that all work in one stroke. For staggering, no shear is put on the individual punches, but they are arranged so that one
does not enter the material until the one before it has broken through. Then the most
force that must be exerted during the stroke is that needed for the largest punch.

Practical tolerances in punching range from ±50 μm (±0.002 in.) for the smallest parts to ±0.40 mm (±0.015 in.) for dimensions over 150 mm (6 in.). Tolerances as small as desired can be held at extra cost.

When sheet metal is sheared as shown in Fig. 13-3(A), the edge is more or less jagged and not square with the large surface of the stock. Surfaces in holes may be improved by *shaving*. This is a light cut in a second operation, as illustrated in Fig. 13-3(C). Edges of blanks may be improved by milling in a costly second operation. However, a square and smooth edge may be obtained in one stroke for thick pieces by *straight edge blanking,* also known by other names, such as *fine edge blanking* or just *fine blanking*. Punch and die are fitted closely, typically with 5 μm (0.0002 in.) clearance, and high pressure is applied by an outer punch all around the edge being sheared. A much more rigid and costly press is required, and dies cost about twice as much and last about half as long as for conventional blanking. Fine blanking can only be justified where it saves enough by eliminating machining or secondary press operations.

Paper, rubber, and other soft and fibrous materials are cut with a sharp-edged punch against a wood or soft metal block in a *dinking* operation, as illustrated in Fig. 13-3(D).

BENDING

Punch and Die Bending.   Bars, rods, wire, tubing, and structural shapes as well as sheet metal are bent to many shapes in dies. Several common kinds of sheet metal bends are shown in Fig. 13-5. All metal bending is characterized by the condition depicted in Fig. 13-6, with the metal stressed beyond the elastic limit in tension on the outside and in compression on the inside of the bend. Stretching of the metal on the outside makes the stock thinner.

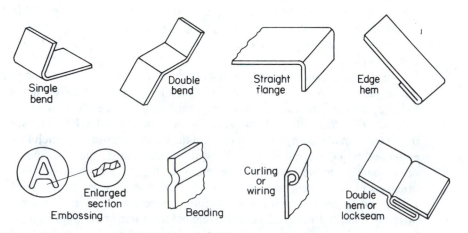

Figure 13-5 Some kinds of sheet metal bends.

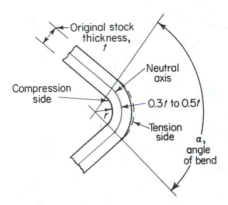

Figure 13-6 Nature of a bend in metal.

The stretching of a bend causes the neutral axis along which the stock is not strained to move to a distance of $0.3t$ to $0.5t$ from the inside of the bend in most cases. An average figure of $0.4t$ is often used for calculations. If the inside radius of the bend is r, the original length of the stock in the bend is estimated to be $L = 2 \times \pi(r + 0.4t) \times (\alpha/360)$, where α is the angle of the bend in degrees and t is the original stock thickness in millimeters (inches).

As has been explained, even metal that has been stressed beyond the elastic limit is prone to a certain amount of elastic recovery. If a bend is made to a certain angle, it can be expected to spring back to a slightly smaller angle when released. This *springback* is larger for smaller bend radii, thicker stock, larger bend angles, and hardened materials. Average values are 1 to 2° for low- and 3 to 4° for medium-carbon soft steels. The usual remedy for springback is to bend beyond the angle desired.

Certain limitations must be observed to avoid breaking metal when bending it. In general, soft metal can be bent 180° with a bend radius equal to the stock thickness or less. The radius must be larger and the angle less for metals of hard temper. The amount depends upon the metal and its condition. Working values are given in handbooks. A bend should be made not less than 45° and as close as possible to 90° with the grain direction of rolled sheet metal because it cracks most easily along the grain. A bend should not be closer to an edge than $1\frac{1}{2}$ times the metal thickness plus the bend radius.

The derivation of a formula for the force F in pounds to make a bend will be explained for the case of a single bend in a vee die illustrated in Fig. 13-7. A basic formula of mechanics of materials for the stress in the outer fibers of a beam of thickness $2c$ and moment of inertia I, subjected to a moment M, is $S = Mc/I$. This applies when the stress in the beam nowhere exceeds the elastic limit. For the case illustrated by Fig. 13-7, $M = F_E l/4$; $c = t/2$; and $I = wt^3/12$. If the formula has these values substituted in it and is rearranged, it becomes $F_E = 0.67Swt^2/l$ for elastic deformation. Experiments have shown that for plastic bending the maximum force is about twice as much as indicated for elastic flexure by the formula. On this basis, $F = 1.33Swt^2/l$, in which S is the ultimate tensile strength of the material. For SI units, linear dimensions must b. in meters to satisfy this formula. The same approach

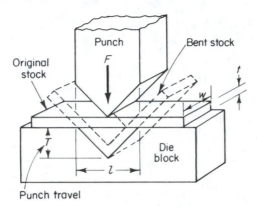

Figure 13-7   Vee die bending operation.

leads to variations of this formula for other types of bending operations, such as single flange bending and for dies with pressure pads. Such formulas are given in texts devoted to a detailed treatment of bending.

Tube and Structural Shape Bending.   Tubes, pipes, and structural shapes of all kinds are bent by methods that keep them from collapsing or distorting. Pipes and shapes may be joined at corners by fittings or by welding or brazing, but bending is cheaper and more dependable. Examples are automobile exhaust and tail pipes, aircraft hydraulic lines, and structural frames. Tubes and shapes are usually supported in grooves and bent around form blocks. Bends are made in production to well within 0.5° and with the inside radius of the bend as small as the tube diameter. Common bending methods are illustrated in Fig. 13-8.

The workpiece is pulled at both ends while being bent over a form block in *stretch bending* or *forming*. The method is slow but almost eliminates springback. It is used to make large irregular and noncircular bends without mandrels. A custom machine for stretch forming truck bumpers costs almost $400,000. One that makes eight bends in 15 seconds on mobile home window frames, two at a time, costs about the same amount.

Draw bending is done with the workpiece clamped against a form block, which rotates and pulls the metal around the bend. The work going into the bend is supported by a pressure bar. A mandrel may be inserted in a tube to restrain flattening. Flexible ball, laminated, or cable mandrels, depicted in Fig. 13-8, provide support around the bend length for delicate work. Draw bending is best for small radii and thin walls and is most versatile. A basic rotary bending machine for tubing up to 75 mm (3 in.) in diameter with wall thickness to about 2.75 mm (0.109 in.) in steel produces up to 200 bends per hour and costs about $40,000 equipped for manual operation; about $100,000 with numerical control (Chap. 35), and as much as $200,000 with numerical control and automatic loading for unattended operation.

The workpiece is clamped to and wrapped around a fixed form block by a wiper shoe in *compression bending* or *forming*. Flat sheet metal is commonly bent in the same way on ungrooved blocks in an operation called *wing* or *tangent bending*.

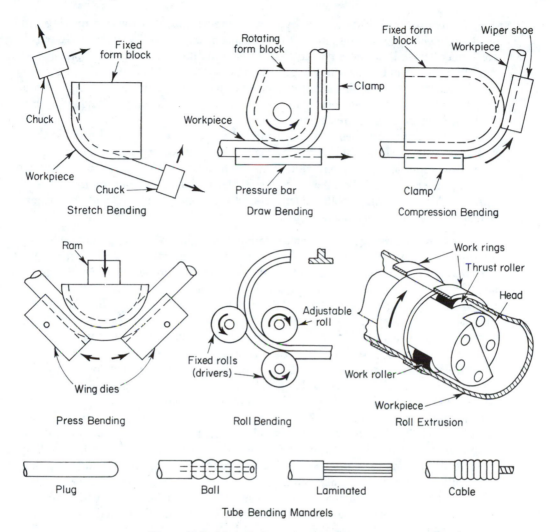

Figure 13-8 Methods for bending pipes, tubes, and structural shapes.

Bending radius may be very small. Compression bending can make series of bends with almost no spaces between them. A combination of stretch and compression forming is called *radial draw forming* and is advantageous for difficult curved parts.

Roll extrusion bending is for pipes over 130 mm (5 in.) OD and walls to 16 mm ($\frac{5}{8}$ in.) thick. A head is rotated inside the pipe with wide thrust rollers on one side and a narrow work roller on the other. The pipe is enclosed by work rings outside of the head. The work roller is cammed in and out as the head rotates to apply pressure to extrude metal in the pipe wall on the side to make it bend. As the material is worked, the pipe is advanced past the head. This method is reported 10 times faster than others for large pipes.

Ram or *press bending* is done by pressing the workpiece between a moving ram block and two swinging pressure dies as indicated in Fig. 13-8. A fixed stroke punch press may be used, but an adjustable stroke bending press is better. Equipment cost is a little more than for draw bending, and angles are limited to about 165°, but press bending is three to four times faster than other methods. A different press setup is required for each different bend, so the process is suitable only for quantity production, such as in furniture factories.

Roll bending of plates, bars, structural shapes, and thick-walled tubes is done with three rolls as shown in Fig. 13-8. One roll is adjusted between the other two for the desired radius of bend. Continuous coils can be made in this way. Bend radius can be changed easily, and the operation is suitable for job work, but angle control is difficult. A medium-sized roll bender for steel plates to 3 m (10 ft) wide by 16 mm ($\frac{5}{8}$ in.) thick is quoted at over \$50,000.

Cold-roll Forming.   Cold-roll forming is a high-production process whereby a flat strip of metal is passed through a series of rolls and is progressively formed to a desired uniform shape in cross section. Among its many products are metal window and screen frame members, bicycle wheel rims, furnace jacket rings, garage door trolley rails, metal molding, trim, and siding. A set of rolls is made for each job and mounted on a standard machine of adequate size. A setup is shown in Fig. 13-9. Each pair of rolls can only bend the metal properly a certain amount, so the number of rolls needed for a job depends on how much bending must be done altogether.

Rotary roll forming for parts like auto and bicycle wheel rims is done by placing one side of a straight cylindrical hoop between two parallel formed rolls. The rolls rotate and close together to impress their form on the continuous ribbon as it passes around and around between them. The process is readily automated with production rates up to 1200 pieces per hour. In a similar manner, rings of thick sections may be squeezed and progressively formed between rolls in what is called *cold ring rolling*.

Roll forming in a production line is depicted in Fig. 34-4. Both hot- and cold-rolled sheet metal, mostly thinner than 1.5 mm (0.06 in.) but as thick as about 20 mm ($\frac{3}{4}$ in.) for soft materials and 10 mm ($\frac{3}{8}$ in.) for steel and with polished, galvanized, electroplated, and even painted finishes, can be roll formed. Stock generally comes in rolls from less than 0.6 m (24 in.) to as much as 2.5 m (96 in.) wide to suit the product. Common speeds through the rolls are from 15 to 35 m/min (45 to 120 fpm), but sometimes as high as 60 m/min (200 fpm). In even a few months out of a year, millions of meters or feet of a shape can be cold-roll formed, and that can be quite profitable alone. Then it can be changed over to other jobs if needed. A typical small machine has seven stations, is driven by a 1.5-kW (2-hp) motor and costs about \$5000. A set of rolls may cost \$10,000 more or less. A representative job is the production of channel forms for the tripod leg assembly of motion picture screens. A large machine has two parallel lines with 16 pairs of rolls in each, is driven by a 11-kW (15-hp) motor and may cost \$60,000, with a set of rolls at almost \$100,000 more. It can take stock as wide as 1.2 m (48 in.), and a representative job is to roll-form tag molding shelving from prepainted sheet metal for storage racks. Automatic feeding and control equipment may add \$50,000 to \$100,000 to machine cost.

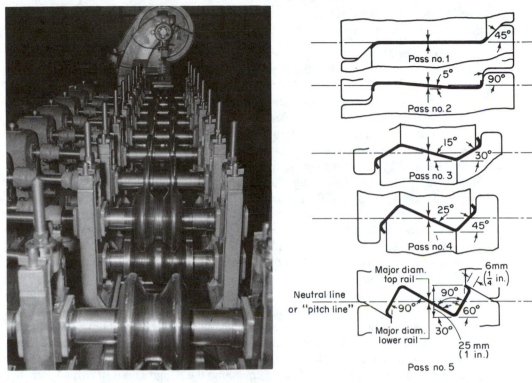

Figure 13-9 Left, view of a cold-roll forming machine, with rolls in place for a job; right, drawings to show how a shape is evolved from a strip passing through a series of rolls. (Courtesy The Yoder Division, Intercole Bolling Corporation.)

Cold-roll forming is competitive with two major types of operations. One is the hot rolling and extrusion group described in Chap. 12. The equipment costs much less for cold-roll forming, but the raw material is more expensive. The other type of operation is the bending of shapes in discrete lengths on presses or press brakes. That equipment cost is much less but the operation is much slower than cold-roll forming. A molding, for example, would be bent in press brake dies for quantities up to thousands of linear meters (feet). Cold-roll forming would be desirable for millions of meters (feet), but extrusion might be economical for even larger quantities.

DRAWING AND STRETCHING

The operations in this category produce thin-walled hollow or vessel-shaped parts from sheet metal. Examples are seamless pots, pans, tubs, cans, and covers; automobile panels, fenders, tops, and hoods; cartridge and shell cases; and parabolic reflectors. The sheet metal is stretched in at least one direction but is often compressed also in other directions in these operations. The work is mostly done cold but some-times is done hot.

Rigid Die Drawing.   A great variety of shapes are drawn from sheet metal. The action basic to all is found in the drawing of a round cup, and that will be posed to illustrate the principles. The cup depicted in Fig. 13-10 is formed by being drawn from the blank shown next to it. Shaded segments of the blank and cup indicate what is done to the metal. A trapezoid in the blank is stretched in one direction by tension and compressed in another direction into a rectangle. Metal must be stressed above the elastic limit to form the cup wall, but not the bottom.

The wall of the cup may be thinned at the radius by bending and thickened elsewhere by drawing. The changes in thickness are usually negligible. If $t = t_1 \simeq t_2$ and r is ignored in Fig. 13-10, then $D = \sqrt{d^2 + 4dh}$ is obtained by equating outside areas of the blank and cup. This is enough for practical estimates. Longer equations can be derived to take into account the radius in the cup and changes in wall thickness.

A cup with an even edge is an ideal. In most cases the edge comes out uneven because of the anisotropy of the metal, and the cup is made higher than needed. The excess is trimmed away.

The way a cup is drawn is shown in Fig. 13-11. The blank is placed on the top of a die block. The punch pushes the bottom of the cup into the hole in the block and draws the remaining metal over the edge of the hole to form the sides. The edges of punch and die must be rounded to avoid cutting or tearing the metal. The clearance between punch and die block is a little larger than the stock thickness. As has been explained, compressive stresses are set up around the flange as it is drawn into smaller and smaller circles. If the flange is thin (less than about 2% of the cup diameter), it can be expected to buckle like any thin piece of metal compressed in its weakest direction. To avoid wrinkling, pressure is applied to the flange by a *pressure pad* or *blank holder*. In practice, pressure is obtained from springs, rubber pads, compressed air cylinders, or an auxiliary ram on a double-action press. The force required is

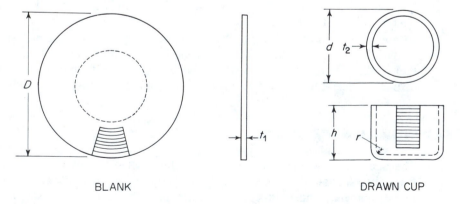

BLANK   DRAWN CUP

Figure 13-10   Example of a cup drawn from a round blank.

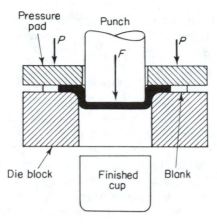

Figure 13-11   How a cup is drawn.

normally less than 40% of the drawing force. Usually the blank is lubricated to help it slide under the pressure pad and over the edge of the die.

The force applied by the punch is transmitted solely through the tensile stress in the wall of the cup to draw the metal against friction over the edge of the hole from under the pressure pad and set up the necessary stresses in the flange. Only as much force can be applied as the wall of the cup can support. Otherwise the cup will be torn. This limits the amount of stress that can be set up in the flange and the amount of reduction possible. Theoretically it can be shown that from a blank of diameter D mm (in.) to a cup of diameter d mm (in.), a reduction $(D - d)/D$ of 50 to 70% is possible, depending upon the behavior of the material. Actually friction from the hold-down pressure and bending forces detract from this, and in practice a reduction in diameter of only 35 to 47% is feasible for an initial draw. Generally thinner blanks require more hold-down pressure to prevent wrinkling and can be reduced less than thicker blanks. Results of exhaustive tests that show how much various materials may be formed in various ways are given in the references at the end of this chapter.

A drawn cup may be redrawn in another operation into a longer cup of smaller diameter. Practical reductions in diameter for first, second, third, or fourth redraws are reported by E. V. Crane to be 30, 25, 16, and 13%. Metal becomes work hardened as it is drawn and redrawn and must be annealed to prevent failure before it reaches its limit. The reduction in area during a tensile test is an indication of the total reduction in diameter to which a metal can be subjected before it must be annealed. For instance, if a metal shows a reduction in area of 60% in tensile tests, indications are that a blank of diameter D mm (in.) can be reduced to a cup of diameter d mm (in.), such that $(D - d)/D = 0.6$. This probably will have to be done in several operations in single rigid dies. Exceptional amounts of reduction (up to 14:1 length-to-diameter ratios) have been obtained by *multiple-stage drawing* in one stroke. Benefit is probably obtained from the heat of work done in consecutive steps. One method employs a telescoping punch whose parts draw the sheet metal through progressively smaller die openings.

The most force that can be applied to draw a cup is $F = \pi d t S_t$, where S_t is the tensile strength, d the diameter, and t the wall thickness of the cup. More exact formulas have been derived, but this one always specifies enough force. The necessary force may be appreciably less for small reductions in diameters. The energy for a draw is estimated from the formula $E = CFh$, where h is the height of the cup and C is a constant with an average value of 0.7.

Several hypothetical parts drawn from sheet metal are sketched in Fig. 13-12 to point out some of the considerations in drawing parts more complex than round cups. Often two or more basic actions occur at once. In the case of the rectangular pan at A, the sides and ends are formed mostly by bending while the corners are drawn. Parts like B and C represent problems in control of parts which do not take the same shape as the punch until just about done. That means the punch and die cannot hold contact with enough of the metal during most of the operation to have full control. Out of control metal tends to wrinkle or become misshapen. A part like B may have to be formed in steps as indicated by the dashed lines before the final shape is struck. In some cases blanks must be preformed before drawing. A flange is required on some drawn parts, like C, to hold the metal while it is stretched to its final shape. The flange may ultimately be trimmed away as indicated in Fig. 13-1.

The fastest production rates are achieved by rigid die drawing, from 100 or more small cups a minute to four auto fenders a minute with automated equipment.

Flexible Die Drawing and Forming.   Some drawing and forming methods use either a punch or die but not both. The workpiece is forced into the die or wrapped over the punch by uniform hydraulic or rubber pad pressure. Several typical processes are illustrated in Fig. 13-13.

Rubber pad forming, also known as the *Guerin process,* forms the work over an inverted punch by the action of a pad of rubber in a container attached to the ram of a standard hydraulic press as indicated in Fig. 13-13(A). The operation is limited to shallow drawing, simple bending and forming, and shearing of sheet metal against sharp edges because there are no pressure pads around the punch. Typical jobs are forming flanges around flat pieces, raising ridges, and beads to add rigidity to flat pieces, embossing, and trimming. Tolerances are not close.

In rubber forming, several punches and pieces may be placed under one pad. Loading tables that can be filled alternately are helpful to keep a press fully occupied.

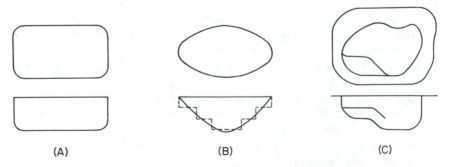

(A)   (B)   (C)

Figure 13-12 Some parts drawn from sheet metal.

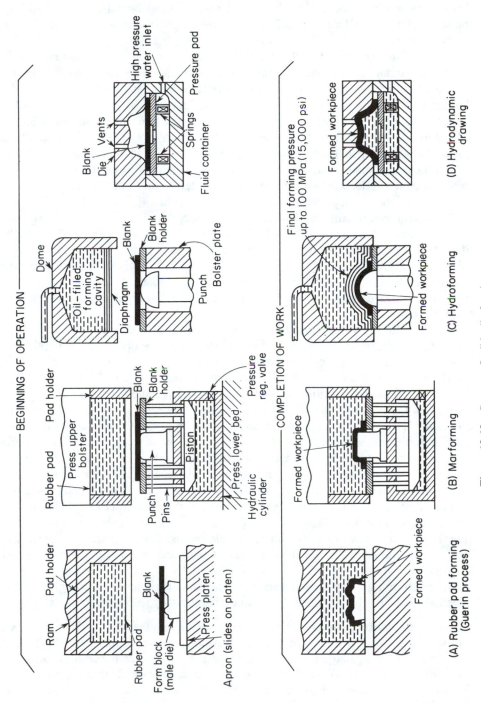

BEGINNING OF OPERATION

COMPLETION OF WORK

High pressure water inlet
Pressure pad
Blank
Vents
Die
Springs
Fluid container

Dome
Blank
Oil-filled forming cavity
Blank holder
Diaphragm
Punch
Bolster plate

Pad holder
Blank
Blank holder
Press upper bolster
Rubber pad
Punch
Pins
Piston
Press. lower bed
Pressure reg. valve
Hydraulic cylinder

Ram
Pad holder
Rubber pad
Blank
Form block (male die)
Press platen
Apron (slides on platen)

Final forming pressure up to 100 MPa (15,000 psi)
Formed workpiece

(D) Hydrodynamic drawing

Formed workpiece
Formed workpiece

(C) Hydroforming

Formed workpiece

(B) Marforming

Formed workpiece

(A) Rubber pad forming (Guerin process)

Figure 13-13 Common flexible die-forming processes.

295

Lubricants are commonly used. The force applied must be sufficient to build up a pressure of 5 to 15 MPa (1000 to 2000 psi) over the entire bottom face of the pad, not just on the workpiece.

The *Marform process* utilizes a rubber pad to envelop the part and also a blank holder or pressure pad around the punch. A blank is laid on the punch and blank holder as shown in Fig. 13-13(B). The blank is drawn from between the rubber pad and blank holder as it is wrapped around the punch while the press closes. The blank holder is pushed down against hydraulic pressure. Forming pressures are mostly from 35 to 55 MPa (5000 to 8000 psi) but sometimes as high as 85 MPa (12,000 psi). Typical parts produced are flanged cups, spherical domes, conical and rectangular shells, and unsymmetrical shapes with embossed or recessed area. Marforming is slower but is more suitable for deep drawing and gives better definition to shallow forms than does rubber pad forming. Operation rates range from 60 to 240 cycles/hr.

Hydroforming employs a punch and a flexible die in the form of a diaphragm backed up by oil pressure. The piece is laid on a blank holder and over the punch as depicted in Fig. 13-13(C). First the dome is lowered until the diaphragm covers the blank, and initial oil pressure is applied. Then the punch is raised, and the oil pressure augmented to draw and form the metal to the desired shape. Hydroforming produces the same kinds of parts as Marforming with a little sharper detail particularly in external radii.

Hydroform presses and equipment are available in 200 to 800 mm (8 to 32 in.) sizes which designate the diameter of the blank that can be drawn. Draw depths range from 125 to 300 mm (5 to 12 in.) and operating rates from 90 to 200 cycles/hr. The small presses are fastest. A complete outfit may cost as much as $500,000.

Flexible punch forming is exemplified by the patented *Hydrodynamic process* illustrated in Fig. 13-13(D). The blank is pressed between the die and a spring-loaded pressure plate. Water or oil admitted under pressure passes through an opening in the plate and pushes the work into conformity with the die cavity. The process is limited to forming shallow pieces with inclined rather than vertical sides but is able to finish in one operation some pieces that require several steps by other methods.

Thermoforming (p. 235) or *blow molding* (p. 237) as done with plastics are applicable to some superplastic metallic alloys, usually hot. An example is Zn 22 Al. Pressures are reported 0.6 to 1.2 MPa (90 to 175 psi) over male molds or at atmospheric pressure drawn by a vacuum in female molds. Complex and intricately styled parts with smooth surfaces can be produced with low-cost tooling and equipment. However, forming rates are low (3 or 4 minutes for a medium-sized part) and conventional forming of ordinary material or die casting is preferable for large quantities. The material may be stretched and thinned appreciably over certain areas.

Applications of Flexible Die Forming.   As a rule the flexible die processes are not nearly as fast and cannot compete with rigid steel dies in mechanical presses for drawing or forming large quantities of pieces. Flexible dies have an advantage for quantities up to several hundreds or thousands of pieces, depending on the part, because their tool costs are low and lead times short. Only one member is needed, and it generally can be made from easily machined material such as a plastic, soft metal, or wood because the service is not harsh. Tooling costs run from 30 to 80% of those for hard steel dies, with savings of several hundred to thousands of dollars for each job. The mild forming action keeps maintenance costs low and does not mar the work material, not even prepainted sheets.

In Marforming and Hydroforming, the stresses in the material being formed are low. The pressure locks the metal to the punch and prevents stress concentrations. When the metal is drawn off the blank onto the punch, the rubber does not force it to bend sharply. Because of the easier action, reductions in diameters up to and sometimes over 60% are feasible, almost twice as much as with steel dies. Many jobs can be done in fewer operations than with rigid dies, and that sometimes gives the flexible die methods the advantage for large quantities.

Equipment costs for Marforming and Hydroforming especially are high and considerable work in small quantities must be available to justify the investment. A number of jobbing shops have come into being to do work on these forms of equipment for manufacturers who cannot justify the investments individually. Stock as thick as $\frac{1}{4}$ to $\frac{3}{8}$ in. is commonly worked, and even much thicker material has been formed from aluminum alloys. Tolerances of ± 50 μm (0.002 in.) are possible and ± 130 μm (0.005 in.) are practical. These are comparable to performances with the best quality rigid dies.

Hydrostatic Forming.   Hydrostatic pressure is uniform from all directions like that on a body immersed deep in water. Metal under hydrostatic pressure of the order of 3.5 GPa (500,000 psi) becomes extra ductile and can be ultraformed. An example of an operation in that state is hydrostatic extruding as illustrated in Fig. 12-24. Cups are drawn under hydrostatic pressure with a reduction of 75% in diameter.

A commercial hydrostatic stretching operation is the bulging of a 9.5-mm ($\frac{3}{8}$-in.) diameter copper tube to make a 19.20-mm (0.756-in.) diameter coaxial cable connector in the manner shown in Fig. 13-14. The tube is filled with and surrounded by fluid between two plungers in a sleeve. The boost pressure keeps the die parts together. The ram force creates the pressure in the tube. As the tube expands, the fluid around it cannot escape until its pressure is high enough to expand the sleeve. The resultant hydrostatic pressure makes it possible to increase the tube diameter 100%; this is more than can be done by any other method. The production rate is 3 parts/min.

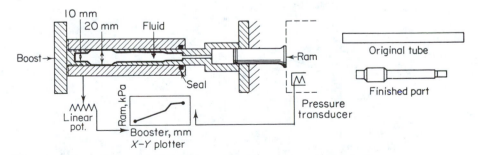

Figure 13-14   Example of a hydrostatic forming operation.

Metal Spinning. Parts that have circular cross sections can be made by spinning them from sheet metal (Fig. 13-15). A blank of sheet metal is clamped on center against a chuck or form block. This block may be plaster, wood, or metal and is revolved on the spindle of a lathe. A rounded stick or roller is pressed against the revolving piece and moved in a series of sweeps. This displaces the metal in several steps to conform to the shape of the chuck. The pressure may be applied by hand or mechanically. The latter requires less skill and gives more uniform results.

In addition to flaring parts like reflectors, re-entrant shapes required in such products as kettles and pitchers can be spun as indicated in Fig. 13-15. These are spun on sectional chucks or with internal rollers in hollow chucks. Pieces may be as small as 6 mm ($\frac{1}{4}$ in.) in diameter to as large as 6 m (20 ft) in diameter and 50 to 75 mm (2 to 3 in.) thick. Spinning is done both hot and cold. Metal thickness usually is not changed substantially, but it can be if desired. A practical tolerance on dimensions of hand-spun articles is ±0.8 mm ($\pm\frac{1}{32}$ in.); about half as much is quoted for mechanical spinning, and even less at extra cost. All ductile metals that can be drawn can be spun. Metal can be trimmed, curled, beaded, and burnished in the spinning operation.

Spinning is both supplementary and competitive with drawing in presses. For straightforward parts, spinning is usually slower but offers a lower tool cost and is economical for small quantities. In one case press tools cost about $10,000 for drawing, redrawing, ironing, trimming, and beading operations to make a pan. These produced 200 pieces/hr in presses at a unit cost of $0.12/piece, not including tool cost. Tools for spinning in two operations cost $1500; output was 18 pieces/hr; and unit cost $1.78/piece. Spinning was more economical up to about 5100 pieces. For any amount over that, the lower unit cost of drawing more than offset the extra cost of tools. In this case the spinning tools could be obtained in 2 weeks, but the press tools in 7 weeks. After getting started, the press output could overtake the spinning in about half a week, at about 4000 pieces. Thus, spinning has an advantage in getting production under way in a short time and sometimes is done while preparations are made for drawing.

Spinning may be just about as fast as drawing for some parts. As an example, a conical shell required eight drawing operations as against one operation on an automatic spinning machine. Some shapes can most economically be made partly by

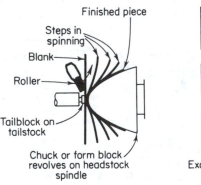

Finished piece
Steps in spinning
Blank
Roller
Tailblock on tailstock
Chuck or form block revolves on headstock spindle

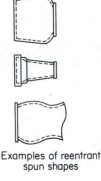

Examples of reentrant spun shapes

Figure 13-15 Principles of metal spinning.

spinning and partly by drawing. Parts that are too large for available presses can be spun.

Roll Turning. Roll turning, also called *roll forming, Hydrospinning, Flo-turning, flow forming, power spinning,* and *power roll forming,* uses some of the techniques of spinning but is a more drastic squeezing and extruding process. Three recognized kinds are illustrated in Fig. 13-16.

Shear forming basically extends a thick blank into a cone in such proportion that $t_2 = t_1 \sin \alpha$, as designated in Fig. 13-16(A). *Tube forming* continuously extrudes a thin-walled tube along a mandrel from a short and thick-walled ring. Reductions in thickness up to 90% in low-carbon alloy steel have been accomplished. *Contour forming* acts like the other two kinds but produces parts with curved instead of straight profiles.

Roll-turning operations are also done inside of externally confined rings and cylinders to make them longer and thinner. A less penetrating operation with longer rolls that act on the surface only to improve finish is called *roller burnishing.* It is done mostly in holes but on outer surfaces as well.

Roll turning is done on machines like lathes and vertical boring machines designed to be extra rigid for the work. Sections as thick as 50 mm (2 in.) have been reported worked. Reductions in thickness may be substantial with consequent cold working and changing of some properties of the metal. Parts with shapes favored by the process can be produced more rapidly than by other means. Parts that have been made in this way are television cones, cream separator bowls, missile noses, thin-walled seamless tubing, and pressure vessel components. Ductile metals may be roll turned cold, but others must be heated. Accuracy and finish are equivalent to that obtained by grinding.

If flow turning is done severely enough, it can peel away the surface. Equipment for such *Flo-peeling* is available to remove up to 6 mm ($\frac{1}{4}$ in.) stock per pass.

Stretching and Shrinking. Several common operations in which sheet metal is formed by being stretched or shrunk are depicted in Fig. 13-17. Although straight

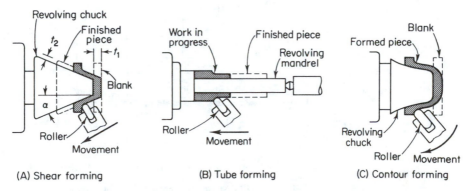

(A) Shear forming   (B) Tube forming   (C) Contour forming

Figure 13-16 Three kinds of roll turning.

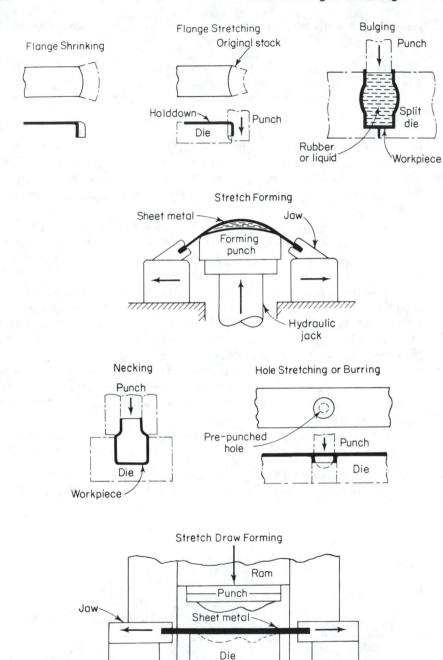

Figure 13-17   Stretching and shrinking operations.

flanging is bending, the forming of curved flanges involves drawing. That may be done with solid or rubber dies.

Bulging is done by placing a cup in a die cavity of the desired shape and filling the cup with rubber or liquid. A punch is applied to create hydrostatic pressure to bulge the walls of the cup to the limits of the die cavity. The die must be split so it can be opened to remove the finished piece.

Ardforming is a process of stretch forming austenitic stainless steel pressure vessels and rocket cases at $-196°C$ ($-320°F$) in liquid nitrogen to raise yield strength above 2 GPa (300,000 psi). It also increases creep strength and toughness. The fabricated vessel is enclosed in and expanded to the walls of a die by gaseous nitrogen at high pressure.

Shallow shapes of large areas are difficult to draw from thin sheet metal. The amount the sheet must be depressed is not enough to raise stresses all over the area beyond the elastic limit and cause permanent set. Enough localized stretching is obtained in conventional dies, such as for auto body panels, by tightly restraining the metal flange around the area drawn. Even better, *stretch forming,* in Fig. 13-17, stretches the metal sheet uniformly to near the yield point initially, and a punch forces the work into the desired shape and readily tips the stresses into the plastic range to cause permanent set. *Stretch draw forming* is another version of the process. A sheet is gripped by rams on each side and stretched over a forming die in a press. The punch is then brought down to impress the shape in the sheet. Stretching is commonly done to form aircraft panels. A large stretch-forming press for aluminum panels 2.5 m (100 in.) wide by 12 m (40 ft) long to produce fuselage panels for commercial airlines costs about $2 million. The process aids particularly in forming hard-to-work space-age materials. The metal is strengthened uniformly. Dies are less costly because less force is needed than with conventional methods. It is reported that a job usually requiring a 11 MN (1200 ton) double-action press can be done on a single-action stretch-forming press rated at 3.6 MN (400 tons). The advantages of stretch forming have not been found sufficient to offset its relative slowness in the automobile and other high production industries.

Expanding is an operation to increase the size of round parts; an example is forming a bell at the end of a pipe. One type of machine called an *expander* carries a circle of shoes guided in radial slots on a face plate and driven outward by wedges to expand the work. An expander for parts up to 1.5 m (5 ft) in diameter with a wall thickness of 13 mm ($\frac{1}{2}$ in.) exerts 220 kN (25 tons) of radial force and costs around $550,000. Dies for a specific job cost about $1000 per set. It takes about 5 minutes to form a part of this size. Another type of machine uses a rubber bladder with oil up to 35 MPa (5000 psi) to expand and set thin-walled shells such as washing machine tubs. *Shrinking* is the converse of expanding. A ring of even or varying cross section is completely surrounded by shoes tapered on their outer surfaces. Wedges act upon the shoes simultaneously to drive them inward to shrink the workpiece. The outside diameter of a wheel rim, for instance, can be sized accurately in this way.

Large sheets, such as 2 by 26 m (7 by 85 ft), wing panels, or difficult-to-form sections for aircraft are gently curved by *peen* or *ball forming*. Steel balls are slung or dropped on the work surface and induce stresses in the skin layer to deform the material. Patterns of impingement, sizes of balls, etc., can be controlled to produce shapes within close limits. Machines and tool are simple and cheap.

   High-energy-rate Forming.   Forces applied at high velocities and over short periods of time to cut or form metal give exceptional results in some cases. A number of processes do high-energy-rate forming (HERF). A description of one type, called high-energy-rate forging, accompanies Fig. 12-18. Operations mainly for forming sheet metal are *explosive forming, electrospark* or *electrohydraulic forming,* and *magnetic forming*. Examples of these operations are shown in Fig. 13-18.

   The relationship of high-energy-rate forming to other methods can be seen from the fact that the energy applied to form a piece of material is $E = Fd = WV^2/2g = MV^2/2$. Energy of 68 kJ (50,000 ft-lb) may be supplied by a massive press delivering an average force F of 450 kN (50 tons) over a distance d of 150 mm (6 in.).

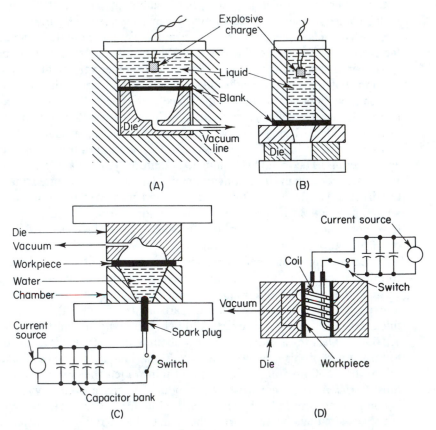

Figure 13-18   Some methods of high-energy-rate metal forming: (A) and (B) explosive; (C) electrohydraulic; (D) electromagnetic forming.

The same results may be obtained from a falling drop hammer with a mass of 4.5 Mg (10,000 lb) which strikes the workpiece with a velocity V of 5.5 m/s (18 fps). The same effect is found in explosive forming with a moving water front of 27 N (6 lb) and an impact velocity V of about 223 m/s (730 fps). Velocity is even much higher in some operations.

The timing of the operations just cited tells even more about them. Assume that each method is forming a 152-mm (6-in.)-deep cup. The press at 0.3 m/s (1 fps) does its work in 0.5 second and delivers energy at the rate of about 135 kW (180 hp). The drop hammer comes to rest in 0.06 second and gives up energy at an average of about 1.2 MW (1600 hp). The explosive operation takes place in about 0.0014 second with an output of around 48 MW (65,000 hp). Metals are deformed at high strain rates (commonly over 100 mm/mm/s or in./in./sec) by HERF. Yield strength is increased appreciably at high strain rates because dislocations resist rapid movement. Thus somewhat more energy usually must be applied to a HERF operation than to an ordinary one.

Many metals can be worked more fully by HERF than by other methods. Previously intractable space-age alloys are formed successfully at high velocities. Energy may be applied uniformly rather than at high spots as is done by a punch, and the metal does not thin out and fail locally.

Explosive forming is done with low and high explosives and gas mixtures. The charge may be set off in direct contact with the workpiece. In that way pressures in the GPa range (millions of psi) are developed but must be carefully controlled to avoid damage. Usually, the charge is placed at a *standoff distance* from the workpiece, as shown in Fig. 13-18(A) and (B), and the shock wave is transmitted through water. In that way pressures of the order of 350 MPa (50,000 psi) and speeds of less than 300 m/s (1000 fps) are obtained. In forming, sheet metal is blown into and takes the shape of a die.

The main advantage of explosive forming is that it is a means of working difficult materials and large area or thick pieces with relatively cheap equipment (no huge presses) and a low-cost energy source. Only a punch or die is needed (not both), and it may be of cheap and easy-to-machine material for a few pieces. There is no limit to size, and tolerances equal those of other methods. The process is especially suitable for unusual and intricate shapes because pressure can be distributed over an entire surface and is not concentrated in a few spots as with punch and die. However, explosive forming takes exceptional care, skill, isolation, and time and cannot compete with press forming for ordinary work.

Explosive hardening is an offshoot of explosive forming. Metals are work hardened when subjected to high enough pressures. As an example, an annealed mild steel (0.17% C) exposed to contact explosive pressure of around 20 GPa (3,000,000 psi) had its yield strength increased from 240 to 800 MPa (35,000 to 115,000 psi) and tensile strength from 400 to 860 MPa (58,000 to 125,000 psi) and elongation decreased from 25% to 7%. Although results are like those of cold working, the crystals are not distorted in the same way by explosive hardening. After recovery, the grains of a metal hardened by an explosion are distorted less than 5% as compared to 80% by cold rolling for the same increase in strength.

Electrohydraulic forming (EHF), also called *electrospark forming,* is done with shock waves like explosive forming but with smaller amounts of energy. The waves may be created by one or a series of spark discharges in a liquid as indicated in Fig. 13-18(C). Another way is to discharge a large current through a wire in the liquid. The wire explodes under the heavy load and sends forth a shock wave. EHF has most of the advantages of explosive forming.

EHF is not competitive with mechanical forming except for difficult materials and shapes, mostly in small and moderate quantities. The time to form a piece is only a few seconds per shot, but the number of shots depends on the energy available. As an example, a steel dome of 220 MPa (32,000 psi) yield strength, 635 mm (25 in.) in diameter, 6.6 mm (0.26 in.) in thickness, and 225 mm (8.875 in.) in depth required 18 shots of about 70 kJ each. That amount of energy costs only a few cents, but the time is relatively long, and the total production cost is high. Equipment of up to 100 kJ capacity may cost as much as $150,000. Some machines can take parts up to about 1.5 m (5 ft) in diameter. An EHF machine can form almost any shape in its capacity range.

Electromagnetic or *magnetic pulse forming* is done in a sudden and intense magnetic field around a coil next to or inside the workpiece. Eddy currents are induced in the metal part. The wall of the piece is strongly repelled by the magnetic field, like any conductor of current, and is driven into the shape of a restraining die of dielectric material, as depicted in Fig. 13-18(D). A poor conductor is formed more easily if coated with a thin layer of copper. Metal can be formed to its limit because nothing but the die need contact the workpiece, and the forces can be distributed uniformly over the part. A major use for this process is to join parts by swaging one tightly around or into grooves or recesses in another. Tubes are natural shapes for the process, but forming often is done on flat pieces. Most equipment has a capacity of less than 15,000 J and work is confined to small and moderate-size parts and areas. Operations include expanding, bulging, swaging, blanking, perforating, flanging, dimpling, and corrugating.

Electromagnetic forming is competitive for parts in moderate and large quantities. Cycle time is only a few seconds, but tooling may cost thousands of dollars. The process is easily automated. Machines cost upward of $50,000 for one of 6000-J capacity.

Ultrasonic Aid to Forming.   Ultrasonic radiation reduces forces and increases the amount metal can be deformed in conventional operations. It is thought that the acoustic energy is taken up mainly at the lattice defects and grain boundaries instead of uniformly throughout the crystals. That is why the effect of macrosound is even more than that of heat for the same amount of energy. As an example of *ultrasonic forming,* a copper cup was ironed (see Fig. 13-21) to about twice its original length between a steel die and punch. Macrosound was applied with an intensity of about 70 W/cm^2 (450 $W/in.^2$). The force was about 300 N (70 lb) compared to 900 N (200 lb) without macrosound.

SQUEEZING

Squeezing is a quick and widely used way of forming ductile metals. Its applications in primary metal working in the processes of rolling, forging, wire drawing, and extrusion are described in Chap. 12. Other applications are cited in thread rolling in Chap. 32 and gear burnishing in Chap. 33. The squeezing operations of cold heading, swaging, sizing, coining, ironing, riveting, staking, and hobbing discussed in this section come under the heading of presswork.

Cold Heading.   Cold heading is a method of forcing metal to flow cold into enlarged sections by endwise squeezing. It is similar to upset forging, which does much the same work hot. Typical cold-headed parts are standard tacks, nails, rivets, screws, and bolts up to about 40 mm ($1\frac{5}{8}$ in.) diameter and a large variety of machine parts, such as small gears with stems.

Cold heading is done from wire in machines specifically designed for the process. A typical series of operations is depicted in Fig. 13-19. The stock is cut off at one station and transferred by mechanical fingers to the die holder, where it is struck by one or more punches as needed to give it the shape desired. Some parts are expanded in the middle in addition to or instead of the end. In the case of nails, the points are formed at cutoff. The base price for a machine for 5-mm ($\frac{1}{4}$-in.) stock is about $50,000.

For common steel alloys, cold heading is considered severe if a length $2\frac{1}{2}$ times the original diameter is deformed in one stroke, and the limit is usually $4\frac{1}{2}$ to 5 diameters in two strokes and eight diameters in three strokes. Heat treatment may be necessary between strokes. Stainless steel and other metals that work harden quickly are *warm headed* by being heated to 300 to 550°C (600 to 1000°F) to improve workability and avoid cracking.

Cold-headed parts may be heat treated, but otherwise have a bright and finished appearance. As a rule, shank diameters are held to ±75 μm (±0.003 in.), head

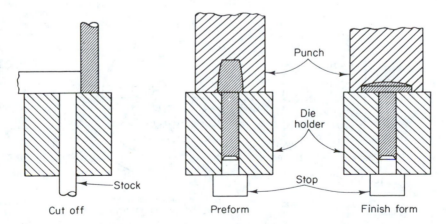

Figure 13-19   Method of cold heading a part.

diameters to ± 125 μm (± 0.005 in.), and lengths to ± 0.8 mm ($\frac{1}{32}$ in.). Subsequent operations such as thread rolling may be done to complete the parts. The strength of cold-headed parts is improved by the cold working and the directional flow of the metal. Little or no material is wasted. The process is fast, with outputs of perhaps 50 pieces/min for large sizes to several hundred per minute of small sizes.

Swaging. The term swaging is used quite loosely to designate many kinds of forming operations, often any squeezing operation in which the material is free to flow perpendicularly to the applied force. This discussion will be confined to one type of operation. This is sometimes more exactly called *rotary swaging* and consists of reducing the size of the diameter, usually over part of the length, of a rod, bar, or tube. One way that rotary swaging is done is by a pair of tapered dies as indicated by Fig. 13-20(A). The dies are opened and shut rapidly. This may be done in a press, while the workpiece is rotated and fed lengthwise. One type of swaging machine makes use of the mechanical device illustrated in Fig. 13-20(B). The jaws are inserted in slots in a spindle, rotated, and forced together repeatedly by the rollers around the periphery, as much as several thousand times a minute. The workpiece can be fed into the jaws mechanically or by hand. All is shielded, so there is no danger. The dies only hammer in and out while the outer race and rollers revolve on some machines. Square, fluted, and other shapes of tubes may be swaged in that way.

Another form of rotary swaging is depicted in Fig. 13-20(C). The tubing is pushed into a bushing, as either one revolves. A ring of balls in a cage may be used in place of a bushing. Tubes may be swaged on a mandrel for support or to form an internal shape like a spline.

Rotary swaging is usually done cold but may be performed on hot metal. When cold, the metal is work hardened and may have to be annealed after several passes. Reduction in diameter usually should not exceed 30% in one pass; too much causes flaking and cracking of the work. The angle of taper between the large and small

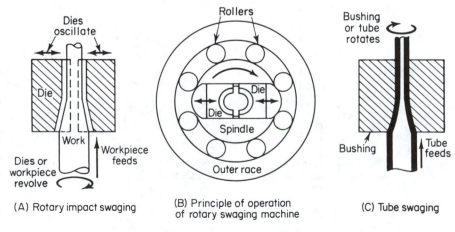

(A) Rotary impact swaging   (B) Principle of operation of rotary swaging machine   (C) Tube swaging

Figure 13-20   Methods of rotary swaging.

diameter on a piece should not be over 10 or 12°. Tolerances from ± 125 μm for a 25-mm-diameter (± 0.005 in. for a 1 in. diameter) piece to as little as ± 12.5 μm (0.0005 in.) for small sizes have been held. A piece elongates as it is swaged to keep its volume unchanged. The elongation is only about 10% for tubing because the walls thicken. Common feed rates are 25 to 75 mm/s (1 to 3 in./s). The force in newtons necessary to cold swage a bar to an average diameter of D mm and with a length of contact in the swaging die of L mm is $F = 1.75DLS$, where S is the compressive strength of the material in MPa. The same formula applies for a force F in lb, a diameter D in in., a length of contact L in in., and a compressive stress of S in psi.

Sizing, Coining, and Hobbing. Parts of malleable iron, forged steel, powdered metals, aluminum, and other ductile nonferrous metals are commonly finished to thickness by squeezing in an operation called *sizing*. An example is given by the sizing of the bosses of a connecting rod depicted in Fig. 13-21(A). Dimensions x and y can be held between hardened blocks with a tolerance of ± 25 μm (± 0.001 in.). Surface finish is comparable to that of milling. About 0.8 mm ($\frac{1}{32}$ in.) of stock is provided for sizing. A special die is needed for almost every job, but each piece can be sized in a fraction of the time of machining. Thus, sizing is economical wherever applicable in high-production industries.

Operations like sizing have been called coining, but *coining* more truly involves the impression and raising of images or characters from a punch and die into metal. This is illustrated in Fig. 13-21(B). The metal is made to flow, and the designs on opposite sides of a coined piece are not necessarily related as in embossing. Hard money is probably the best known product of coining.

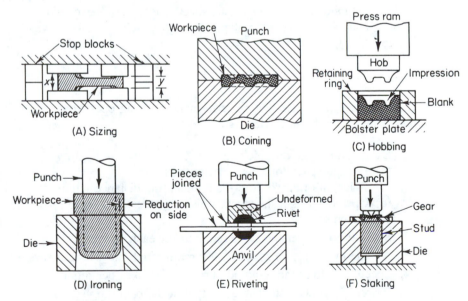

Figure 13-21 Some common metal-squeezing operations.

Hobbing or *hubbing* is a method of making molds for the plastic and die-casting industries. A punch called the *hob* or *hub* is machined from tool steel to the shape of the cavity, heat treated for hardness, and polished. It is then pressed into a blank of soft steel to form the mold; this is done slowly and carefully and sometimes in several stages between annealing operations for the blank. A retaining ring keeps the mold from spreading out of shape. A prime advantage of this method is that one hob properly applied can make a number of cavities in one mold or in a series of molds.

Ironing.   Ironing is a name given to an operation for sizing and thinning the walls of drawn cups. As indicated in Fig. 13-21(D), the cup is squeezed between a punch and hole in a die as it is pushed through the hole. This is sometimes done at the same time as a redrawing operation. The action is similar to that of wire drawing. The maximum possible theoretical reduction in wall thickness in one pass is 50%, but more has been reported in some cases.

Riveting, Staking, and Stitching.   A rivet is like a bolt without threads. A basic way to rivet two parts is depicted in Fig. 13-21(E). A rivet is put through a hole or forced through thin material, and its head is placed on an anvil. A punch with a hollowed end mashes the stem. Some rivets are hollow, and their edges are pushed outward.

Staking is not done with a separate fastener, but a projection on one of the mating pieces is mashed, curled over, or indented and spread by a punch with sharp edges or points as illustrated in Fig. 13-21(F).

One way to join metal sheets by stitching is to pierce one or more holes through both sheets. Stock is not removed but is pushed through in tabs that are bent over to clinch the sheets together. Another way is to use staples like in paper stapling. Stitching is limited to fairly thin metal sheets but is fast. A general rule is that a staple is strong enough to hold any material through which it can be driven.

PRESSES

Presses are the machines that perform metal-forming operations. The capacity of a press depends on the following factors.

1. Dimensional size that includes:
   (a) Enough space to accommodate the tools
   (b) A length of stroke to drive a punch the distance required
   (c) Openings to get the stock, finished pieces, and scrap readily in and out of the press
2. Strength to deliver the force required for each stroke
3. An energy supply to sustain the force through the working stroke
4. Speed to deliver the required number of strokes per minute
5. Power to maintain the energy output at the operating speed

6. Strength and stamina to maintain alignments, hold tolerances, and produce economically for a long time

Every press is made up of certain basic units, as indicated in Fig. 13-22. These are a frame and bed, a ram or slide (or rams or slides), a drive for the ram, and a power source and transmission. Each unit can be made in a number of forms, and each form has certain advantages and some disadvantages. By combining various kinds and sizes of units, a large variety of presses are constructed to suit many purposes. Each unit determines part of the physical capacity of the press. Typical units and ways of putting them together will be described and their principles explained to give a comprehensive picture of presses.

Frame and Bed. The lower part of a press frame on which the die is placed is called the *bed*. The bed is heavily ribbed for strength and hollow to accommodate accessories such as scrap chutes and pressure springs. A thick *bolster plate* on top of the bed gives full support to the die which is bolted to it. Important dimensions of the bed are the distances front to back and right to left available to contain a die.

The frame contains the drive mechanism and ways to guide the reciprocating ram in a fixed path. Press frames are made of both iron and steel. They must be strong and rigid to hold true alignment between punches and dies. Common types of press frames are shown in Fig. 13-23. A press is rated first in tons of force it is able to exert without undue strain. To keep deflections small, some authorities always choose a press rated 50 to 100% higher than the force to be exerted in an operation.

Most presses up to 1.8 MN (200 tons) capacity have C-type frames. This type of frame allows full access to the die space from three sides. This speeds production because dies can be positioned and stock fed in many ways; in each case in the fastest way. The back also has an opening as a rule. An inherent disadvantage is that the top and bottom of a C-frame swing apart under load. This impairs alignment of the press and is detrimental to work accuracy and tool life. Of course, tie rods can be fastened

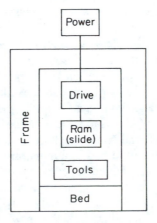

Figure 13-22 Elements of a press.

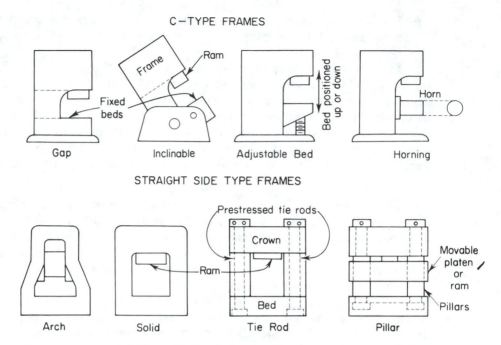

Figure 13-23 Common types of press frames.

to the front to reduce deflection, but they hinder access to the die area and nullify the main advantage of the press.

The most common press in industry is the *open back inclinable C-type frame press,* commonly OBI press, illustrated in several sizes in Fig. 13-24. It is inclined backward to discharge scrap or parts by gravity through the open back. One rated as a 55-ton press has a single crank, an air clutch and disk brake, a nominal 460 × 710 mm (18 × 28 in.) bed area and lists at around $15,000.

The *gap type* of press in a fixed vertical position on an integral base is somewhat more rigid than an inclinable press. Gap-type presses often have wider beds and rams.

An *adjustable bed press* or *knee press* has the lower projection of the C-type frame in the form of an adjustable bed, table, or knee. This press can be adjusted for different sizes of dies and work but loses some in rigidity. A *horning press* has a large round post, called a *horn,* projecting out front to support round pieces.

Press frames that have two or more columns like the straight-sided types in Fig. 13-23 are more balanced and rigid than C-type frames. The design is appropriate for wide beds and long strokes. Access to the die on the bed may be somewhat restricted. Straight-sided frames are found on the medium to largest sizes of presses. The larger sizes of mechanical presses have bed, columns, and crown as separate units but are keyed to hold alignment and bound together by tie rods. The rods are heated and shrunk in place to minimize stretching under load.

The *pillar* or *open frame press* is usually a hydraulic press and has four pillars like the one in Fig. 12-16. The pillars hold the crown to the bed but are not prestressed

Figure 13-24   Group of inclinable presses with capacities of, from right to left, 22, 35, 45, and 60 tons. (Courtesy E. W. Bliss Co.)

like tie rods. Extension under load does not matter appreciably for a hydraulic press which does not work to a fixed stop. The pillars ordinarily act as guides or ways for the ram.

Press Ram.   The ram of a press drives the punch in an operation. Most mechanical presses have a fixed length of stroke. The position of the stroke can be varied by an adjusting nut and screw just above the ram.

The alignment of the ram in its slides determines how precisely punches and dies can be set to each other in the press. A definite and often minute clearance must be held between each punch and the die opening it enters. Otherwise, cutting or forming action is not uniform all around, and product quality is not good. Also, the tools are damaged if they touch even a little, and tool life is shortened. Commonly, the vertical travel of the ram is made square with the bed within 13 μm (0.0005 in.). The bottom of the ram should be parallel with the top of the bed within 40 μm/m (0.0005 in./ft).

Shut height is an important dimension of a press because it limits the height of the punch and die that can be used in it. *Shut height* of a mechanical press is defined as *the distance from the top of the bed to the bottom of the ram when the ram is at the bottom of its stroke and the position adjustment is all the way up.*

The *action* of a press refers to the number of rams. A single-action press has one ram, like those in Figs. 13-24 and 13-26. A double-action press has one ram inside another. The outer ram is used to apply pressure to the flange of a piece drawn by the inner ram. A triple-action press has a double action above and a third ram that moves upward in the bed soon after the upper rams descend. This may be used to combine drawing and redrawing operations.

A 200-ton single-action, double-crank straight-sided mechanical press with a 1.2 × 2.0 m (48 × 78 in.) bed area is quoted at about $65,000.

Press Drives.   The *drive* of a press as meant here is the means of applying force to the ram. Two kinds of drives are mechanical and hydraulic. The mechanical devices in use today are the crank, eccentric, cam, toggle, knuckle joint, screw, and rack and pinion as depicted in Fig. 13-25.

Most mechanical presses derive the movement of the ram from the throw of a crank or eccentric. These may be on a crankshaft or eccentric shaft running from right to left or from front to back in the press, usually at the top. An eccentric provides more bearing area but has to be excessively large for long strokes. A press may have one crank, as do those in Fig. 13-24, and is said to have a single point of connection or suspension. Better backing is given to large rams by two points of connection from a double crank, as on the press in Fig. 13-26, and even by four points from a pair of double cranks for the largest rams.

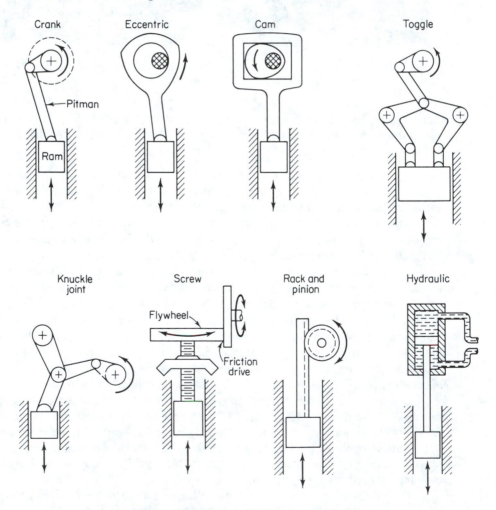

Figure 13-25   Principal kinds of press drives.

Figure 13-26 A 200-ton single-action straight-sided press with two-point suspension. (Courtesy Danly Machine Corp.)

Cam and toggle mechanisms are used to drive the outer rams of double-action presses. The purpose is to make the outer ram dwell to hold the stock during part of the stroke. A *knuckle joint press* is used for a forceful squeezing operation over a short distance, like in a sizing operation.

Mechanical presses are rated in tons exerted at or near the bottom of the stroke. This is an important consideration for operations such as drawing in which a near maximum force must be applied during a large part of the stroke. With a given rating at the bottom, the actual capacity at higher points of the stroke is less. Press manufacturers specify these capacities in tables and charts in their catalogs. A double-action press is rated on the basis of the capacity of the inner ram. The outer ram usually has a corresponding capacity, and its amount is specified in the press catalog.

With a crank or eccentric drive, the ram speed is highest at midstroke and zero at the bottom. A formula for ram speed is given in Fig. 13-27. This may not be important for short working distances like in blanking but is important for work like deep drawing that starts well above the bottom. Too fast a draw makes the metal stick to the die. The proper speed depends upon the condition of the metal, lubrication, the dies, and the severity of the draw. As a rule, speeds should not be more than about 15 to 28 m/min (50 to 90 fpm) for mild steel, 20 to 45 m/min (75 to 150 fpm) for aluminum, and 45 to 60 m/min (150 to 200 fpm) for brass. These limitations are met in some modern presses with two-speed drives that are fast for the approach to and return from the work and slow down for the actual drawing. Presses of this kind are making 40 strokes/min (spm) without harm to the work as against 12 spm for older types.

A press should have as short a stroke as possible. In an operation where pieces must be put in or taken out of a die, the length of stroke should be at least twice the height of a piece. Where a press is used for many jobs, as most are, it should have capacity for the largest even though that is more than is needed for the majority.

Hydraulic Presses.   A hydraulic press ram is actuated by oil pressure on a piston in a cylinder. The principles of hydraulic circuits discussed in Chap. 21 are applicable to presses. Hydraulic presses are more versatile and easier to operate than mechanical presses. A hydraulic press usually has a long stroke and can deliver full rated force over the entire length of stroke. The length of stroke and the force can be quickly changed. The force and speed can be held uniform or varied readily throughout the stroke. For example, a rapid approach and return can be combined with a slow steady working stroke. Pressure and distances can be recorded and readily repeated

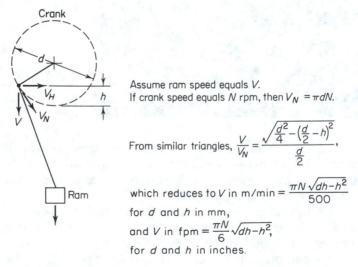

Assume ram speed equals V.
If crank speed equals N rpm, then $V_N = \pi d N$.

From similar triangles, $\dfrac{V}{V_N} = \dfrac{\sqrt{\dfrac{d^2}{4} - \left(\dfrac{d}{2} - h\right)^2}}{\dfrac{d}{2}}$,

which reduces to V in m/min $= \dfrac{\pi N \sqrt{dh - h^2}}{500}$

for d and h in mm,

and V in fpm $= \dfrac{\pi N}{6} \sqrt{dh - h^2}$,

for d and h in inches.

Figure 13-27   Formula for the speed of a crank-driven ram.

when a job is rerun. A hydraulic press is safer because it will stop at a pressure setting, whereas a mechanical press must plunge through its stroke, even to destruction if it has no safety release.

The main disadvantage of hydraulic presses is that to make them as speedy as mechanical presses is costly. Short stroke mechanical presses are running in production at speeds up to 2000 spm. Hydraulic presses of that sort have not been found generally feasible. For slow and long stroke work, like deep drawing with a 9-MN (1000-ton) press and a 840-mm (33-in.) stroke at 14 spm, hydraulic presses are available that operate as fast as mechanical presses and are more fully controllable, but they are more costly. For one thing, a hydraulic press must have a motor about twice as large because it cannot store energy in a flywheel during part of a stroke as does a mechanical press. As a result, most presses for quantity production are mechanical. An exact comparison is difficult, but it has been said that a mechanical press for $100,000 is comparable for many production purposes to a hydraulic press costing $160,000. The extra cost is justified in some cases because the advantages offered by the hydraulic press are needed. On the other hand, if speed is not necessary, a hydraulic press can be built for many purposes more cheaply than a mechanical press.

Power Transmission. A crank or other mechanical means of driving a press ram is actuated by a flywheel through a clutch that is engaged by tripping the starting lever. If the lever is released during the stroke, the clutch is disengaged, and the crankshaft is grabbed at its uppermost position by a brake. The brake is often on the opposite end of the crankshaft from the flywheel as on the large press of Fig. 13-24.

Many small presses have positive mechanical clutches, but some small presses and all of over about 900 kN (100 ton) have friction clutches. Some quite large presses have electric eddy-current clutches. A typical form of mechanical clutch has one pin, sometimes more, in a collar on the crankshaft. The pin is made to engage a hole or slot in the hub of the flywheel. Friction clutches are of the disk type and usually are air operated.

A mechanical clutch acts with a sudden shock that becomes more unendurable the larger the drive; a friction clutch is smoother. Once engaged, a positive clutch cannot be released until the end of the stroke, but a friction clutch promotes safety because it can be disengaged at any time. A friction clutch can be set to slip under overload. A friction clutch costs more to make, to operate (because it uses compressed air), and to maintain.

The flywheel runs all the time a press is in operation and slows down to furnish the energy for each stroke. A flywheel running with a velocity of V m/s (fps) at its radius of gyration and having a mass M in kg or weight W in lb has a kinetic energy in joules of $E = MV^2/2$. For energy in ft-lb, $E = WV^2/2a$, where a is the gravitational constant 32.2 ft/sec/sec. The more the flywheel slows down, the more energy it gives up, but more time is lost in the stroke. An economic balance must be found between the cost of the press and rapid production. Experience has indicated that this is realized if the flywheel slows down less than 10% during continuous operation, with a press stroke for every revolution, and as much as 20% for intermittent operation, with the operator loading each piece and then tripping the press.

For 10% slowdown, the energy given up by the flywheel is $E_{10} = 0.19MV^2/2 = 0.19WV^2/2a$, and for 20% slowdown, $E_{20} = 0.36MV^2/2 = 0.36WV^2/2a$. Most of the mass of an ordinary flywheel is in a heavy rim, and for practical purposes V may be taken as the speed at the mean radius of the rim. It is necessary when selecting a press to ascertain whether it will supply sufficient energy without slowing down excessively. That may have to be calculated in some cases. In other cases, the energy capacity is tied to the rating of the press. For instance, some manufacturers design their presses for an energy capacity in inch-tons for 15% slow-down to be approximately equal to the tonnage rating. Thus, such a 500-ton press is able to deliver a little over 500 in.-tons of energy in 15% slowdown.

Modern presses have individual motor drives. Standard motors made for constant speed applications such as most machine tools, pumps, and generators resist slowdown over about 5% by increasing torque and are called *stiff motors*. Such a motor is satisfactory for a press running continuously at over say 40 spm but is likely to be badly overloaded on a press operated intermittently with a slowdown of as much as 20%. *Soft motors* are made for such purposes. They permit the flywheel to do most of the work and restore energy to the wheel in the relatively long period between strokes. A stiff motor would have to have a much higher rating to supply a major part of the work in part of one stroke. Space does not permit a discussion of motor design, but this points out some basic problems.

Various forms of power transmission between motor and crank- or eccentric-shaft are used on presses. The flywheel is usually mounted on the crankshaft of a small high-speed press and driven directly by the motor through gear teeth or belts. This is called a *direct drive* or *flywheel drive*. A large and slow press ordinarily has gear reductions between flywheel and crankshaft. A *single-geared press* has one reduction; a *double-geared press* has two. A short crankshaft may have one drive gear on it, and that is called a *single drive*. A long crankshaft has a drive gear at both ends to reduce twist, and that is a *double drive*.

Applications of Presses.   Most presses are mechanical because such drives are simple, durable, and fast but certain applications require other types. Hydraulic presses provide long strokes for drawing and easy action for rubber pad forming and difficult forming and drawing. Drawing and forming have been done as a makeshift on drop hammers when presses have not been available, but that is too crude and slow for production.

Some squeezing operations, such as forging, are done on drop hammers, but mostly eccentric, knuckle joint, screw, and hydraulic presses are used. The last are finding favor because through control of speeds a large part of the time cycle of an operation can be devoted to the actual squeezing. This gives the metal time to flow.

Faster presses and automation of press lines have made presswork faster and faster. Presses that turn out from hundreds to tens of thousands of pieces per hour can produce large lots in short periods of time. They must, therefore, be changed over from job to job often, and the cost for set-up is important. The trend is to provide means to shorten the die-change time of modern presses. One system for small- and medium-size stamping presses has permanent fixtures attached to the ram and bolster plate of each press. The punches, die blocks, and other members are not mounted on die sets but on standard upper and lower die plates. These plates are precisely located from pins in the fixtures and are held by air clamps. Systems like this have made even quite short runs feasible. It is reported that as many as six die setups with 10 pieces in each run have been made in 10 minutes. Movable and alternating bolster plates on small, medium-size, and large presses make it possible to set up a die on one plate while another is in operation in the press. Change over is then mainly a matter of rolling one set out while the other goes into place. Quick acting air clamps may attach the punch to the ram. Change over is also aided by semi- or fully automatic slide positioners and feed length setters. Times for die changes on large presses have been reduced from 2 to 3 hours to 10 to 15 minutes.

Specialized Presses.   Some presses have features for certain kinds of work but operate on the same principles as other presses. One of these is a *trimming press* that is a crank-operated single-action press for dies to trim forgings and die castings. It has an auxiliary ram on the side of the frame for light punching, sprue cutting, etc.

Some huge presses have the power transmission and drive mechanism under the bed where it is more accessible than on top. The ram on top is pulled from below. Such an *underdrive press* is mounted in a factory with the top of the bed near floor level and the mechanism extending into the basement.

A *dieing machine* is a small to medium-size press with most of its mechanism below the die surface. The ram is above the working surface, is carried on four posts, and is pulled rather than pushed down. That helps to stabilize the ram under load, maintain alignments, and preserve the tools. Access to the working area can be had from all four directions. A low center of gravity is favorable to high-speed operation.

A *forcing press* is usually a hydraulic press capable of exerting large forces to press car wheels, gears, bushings, etc., on or off of mating parts. Some are horizontal, others vertical.

Press Brakes and Shears.   A press brake is a wide press with a relatively thin bed and ram as shown in Fig. 13-28. It can handle wide sheets and plates or accommodate several dies to bend a number of small pieces at once. Almost any kind of bend can be made with suitable dies.

Among other parts, lengths of uniform sections, such as channel, Z, U, S, and I shapes, are commonly bent on press brakes. This method is only economical for a total length up to several hundred feet. An aircraft manufacturer has found that when 300 to 600 m (1000 to 2000 ft) or more of such sections are needed, they can more economically be drawn through dies on a drawbench, in the manner described in Chap. 12 for making pipe. For larger quantities continuous cold-roll forming is most economical.

Some press brakes are rated in terms of the widest and thickest plate or sheet that can be bent, such as *8 ft–10 gage (0.135 in.).* Others are rated by the number of meganewtons (tons) that can be delivered; in some cases at midstroke and others near the bottom of stroke. A 100-ton (near bottom) press brake, with 3.15 m (124 in.)

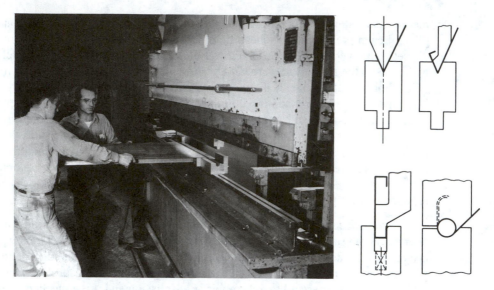

Figure 13-28 Press brake corrugating sheet metal, and a few of the many bending operations done on a press brake. (Courtesy Verson AllSteel Press Co.)

between housings and a 75-mm (3-in.) stroke, weighs 7.7 Mg (17,000 lb) and costs about $30,000.

A *shearing press* or *squaring shear* is like a press brake but cuts wide sheets with a long blade or knife on its ram or slide. This upper blade is inclined at an angle to make a gradual cut through a sheet of metal across a lower blade on the bed. A plate with hold-down fingers alongside the blades presses down on the work as it is cut.

Hole Punching Machines.   All the holes in a workpiece are punched at the same time on a conventional press with a punch and die set for the particular job. This tooling is quite expensive, and many pieces must be produced to pay for it, but the press time per piece is very small. In contrast, on a hole punching machine, all the holes in one piece are punched in sequence one at a time, and line shearing is done by punching a series of overlapping slots. Thus, press time per piece can be appreciable, but tool cost is low. A punch and die module unit is required for each size and shape of hole, but these are relatively inexpensive and can often be used over and over again for many jobs. To locate the holes accurately accounts for much of the high cost of a multi-hole die, whereas the spacing is taken care of by the movements on a hole punching machine. Hole punching machine operations are economical for small and moderate quantities of pieces.

Typically on a hole punching machine the workpiece (a sheet of metal) is moved about on a large table and positioned as required under the punch for each hole. For this purpose, the workpiece is commonly held by mechanical fingers from a cross slide mounted on a crossbar that slides along the table as shown on the machines of Fig. 13-29. On the older manual machine of Fig. 13-29(A), the workpiece is positioned under the punch by means of a stylus handle, in the right hand of the operator, affixed to the cross slide. The stylus is inserted in a hole in a template in front of the operator

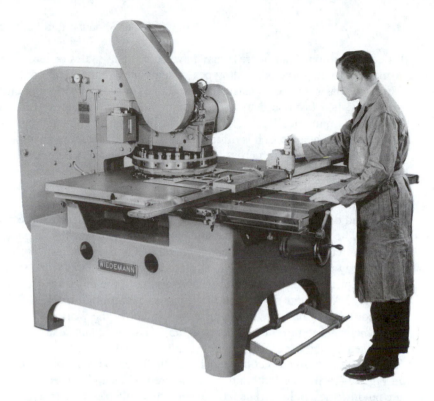

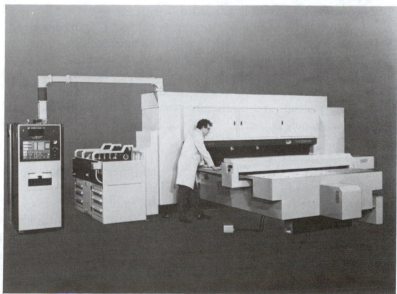

Figure 13-29 Two hole punching machines. (A) A manually operated turret punch press with a workpiece between punch and die. An operator is positioning the piece from a template. (B) A Quantum 2000 NC press with two punching heads on a bridge, next to the operator, over the table. Tool units in pallets are loaded into the machine at the end of the bridge. (Courtesy Bendix Wiedemann Division.)

for each position. Such a press may have coordinate scales or leadscrews to position workpieces when making prototypes or templates. Numerical control, described in Chap. 35, has been found particularly suitable for work positioning on hole punching machines. It is fast and does away with the need for templates. The machine of Fig. 13-29(B) is numerically controlled, with a program to run each operation.

A different approach is offered by one press maker. The positions of holes to be punched are marked with cross lines on the workpiece. An electronic optical system senses the hole-center marks and aligns each in turn under the punch, again by numerical control.

Since a number of holes need to be punched in each workpiece and a different punch and die unit is required for each hole size and shape, an appreciable amount of time may be spent in changing the tool units. Various types of hole punching machines are made with different tool changing means. On the simplest types, the workpiece is withdrawn and each tool unit is placed by hand in the work station as needed. Various quick change devices to receive and hold the units are used to speed up tool changing. A popular type is the *turret press,* exemplified in Fig. 13-29 (A). It holds an assortment of punches in the turret shown above the workpiece and matching dies in a synchronized turret under the worktable. The punch nearest the operator is the one depressed by the ram when the press is tripped. The operator turns a handwheel to index the turrets and select the punch and die for each hole. On the machine illustrated in Fig. 13-29(B), the tool units for a job are preloaded into rectangular pallets which are put into the machine. The tools are automatically selected and placed into position, under numerical control, as needed.

Most single station and turret presses have C-frames with a single work station. The machine of Fig. 13-29(B) carries the punches in a bridge over the table. Thus workpieces can be unloaded at the rear while others are fed in from the front. That machine has two punching heads, so two pieces can be fabricated at one time.

Punching rates are from 50 to 500 holes/min. To this must be added time for changing punches and positioning work. Tool changing may be done during workpiece positioning, especially with numerical control, but otherwise may take 5 to 15 seconds.

For typical machines of 220 kN (24 tons) capacity, the price of a manual single station model is about $25,000, a manual turret press about $60,000, and a numerically controlled turret press around $160,000.

A most advanced 300-kN (35-ton) 18 station turret press with numerical control has an auxiliary 475-W carbon dioxide (CO_2)-type laser (described in Chap. 14) to enable it to cut any material. Any shape can be cut in a sheet guided by the numerical control system. The total equipment cost is about $400,000.

High-production Presses. Certain gap-type and straight-sided presses are known as *high-productivity presses.* They look like ordinary presses but have features that enable them to produce faster and they cost about 50% more. Typically their stroke is short and speed high. Ordinary presses operate up to about 200 spm; above that speed dynamic balancing is necessary. Presses rated from about 200 to 3500 kN (25 to 400 tons) are available to deliver 200 to 600 spm. Presses with speeds over 600 spm are not common but do exist.

High-productivity presses are made with exceptional rigidity and alignment to yield long die lives, especially with multiple station dies. They commonly have variable speed drives that can be set to the right speed for best die life and part quality. They are fitted with automatic controls and quick-acting safety controls, and often one can do the work of two or three standard presses.

Small sheet metal and wire objects such as clips, lugs, brackets, eyelets, fasteners, and bottle caps are turned out in large quantities on presses that look somewhat different from the ordinary kinds. All embody one or both of two principles. One is that there is a series of stations, each an individual press unit with one or more slides. Each station is tooled to perform one or more operations on the work, which is carried automatically from station to station. In some presses the pieces go through individually; in other presses they are kept in a strip and cut off at the end. The other principle is to provide several slides at one station. The slides converge in timed order on a workpiece to make intricate bends or forms.

The *Verti-slide press* in Fig. 13-30 utilizes both principles just cited to form strip

Figure 13-30 High-production Verti-slide automatic press (without covers) for stock up to 76 mm (3 in.) wide by 1.57 mm (0.062 in.) thick. Output is 40 to 160 pieces per minute. The machine has a 3.7-kW (5-hp) motor and weighs 31 Mg (14,000 lb). A special welding attachment is swung out of the way on the right. (Courtesy Torin Machine Division, Clevepak Corporation.)

Figure 13-31   Close-up view of the die area of a 300-ton Transmat press tooled with
eight stations for forming 14-in. automobile wheels. About 900 complete wheels are
produced each hour. (Courtesy Verson AllSteel Press Co.)

and wire. At the left where the stock enters is a feeding mechanism. To the left of
center are two small press units. To the right of center is a station with three main
slides and a total of six actions. Capacity in a single station is 220 kN (25 tons).
Among other makes are those called *four-slide* and *multislide* presses.

Transfer presses for products like ice cube and refrigerator trays, metal shelves,
oil pans and headlight housings for automobiles, and stove pans have capacities from
0.25 to 90 MN (30 to 10,000 tons). Such parts require a series of shearing, bending,
drawing, and even squeezing operations. Typical operations performed at successive
stations on an automobile wheel like the one made in the press of Fig. 13-31 might
be (1) blank, (2) preform, (3) rough form and trim, (4) pierce holes, (5) enlarge and
extrude center hole, (6) finish form, (7) coin to set shape, and (8) finish trim. All the
punches are carried on a single ram and descend at once to work on the parts in the
stations. On the upstroke, a synchronized mechanism transfers each part to its next
position, and so on. The press runs continuously. Transfer presses produce up to 1500
pieces/hr but are economical only if production requirements are high. One manufacturer has found transfer presses justified only for parts with five or more operations
and outputs of over 4000 pieces/day.

A nine-station transfer press rated at 1.5 MN (170 tons) with a bolster area 450 mm (17.7 in.) wide by 1640 mm (64.6 in.) long is quoted at about $250,000.

PRESS TOOLS AND ACCESSORIES

Dies.   Sheet metal cutting and forming are done to the shape of a punch (external) or die block (internal) or with a mating punch and die block. They may be made of soft metal, plaster, or plastic, particularly for forming, to produce only a few pieces but are of hardened tool steel and even cemented carbides for larger quantities.

A punch may be fastened to the ram, and a die block to the bolster plate of a press and used that way. In fact, that is commonly done to save die cost when very few pieces are to be made, but it is slow to set up and operate. Additional details are added for production to facilitate operations. The assembly of all the details is called a *die,* and the same name is also given to the die block at times.

Production dies have the punches and die block mounted in a *die set,* as in Fig. 13-32. The die set consists of a *punch holder* on top and a *die shoe* on the bottom for attachment to the press. Heavy *leader pins* between top and bottom maintain alignment between punches and die block.

When sheet metal is blanked or pierced, it grips the punch after the breakthrough. Pieces drawn or bent also tend to cling to punches and stick in die openings. One variety of details added to dies has the purpose of stripping pieces from punches or knocking pieces from die openings to help remove work and scrap and speed up operations. They are called by descriptive names of stripper plate, knockout pad, etc. Also, pressure plates or pads of similar construction are found in drawing dies to prevent wrinkling. Details in dies for locating workpieces may be in forms of stops, nests, pins, etc.

Most dies are special tools, made specifically for one job. Many standard details such as die sets, stops, and punches for common shapes are available and widely used

Figure 13-32 Die for piercing six holes in the ends of the piece shown. This simple die costs about $1000 and is of little use except for the specific job for which it was built. If the job is discontinued, the major items that might be salvaged are the die set that originally cost about $200 and punches worth perhaps $75. (Courtesy Unipunch Products, Inc., Buffalo, N.Y.)

for economical construction. Even so costs are high and run from several hundred dollars for even a simple die to tens of thousands of dollars for large automobile body dies. Several commercial systems are available for constructing dies from standard reusable units for blanking, piercing, and notching simple common shapes. One of these is illustrated in Fig. 13-33.

Many dies are made to do single operations. Such a die may be designated as a blanking die, piercing die, drawing die, etc. according to its purpose. When the quantity of pieces to be made warrants the cost, a die is constructed to perform a number of operations on a piece. One such type is called a *progressive die,* like the one illustrated in Fig. 13-34. A progressive die has a series of stations, each performing an operation on a piece during a stroke of the press. Between strokes, the pieces, usually in a strip, are transferred to their next stations, and one piece is finished for each stroke. Combination and compound dies do two or more operations in a single station. A *combination die,* like the one in Fig. 13-35, does simultaneous operations

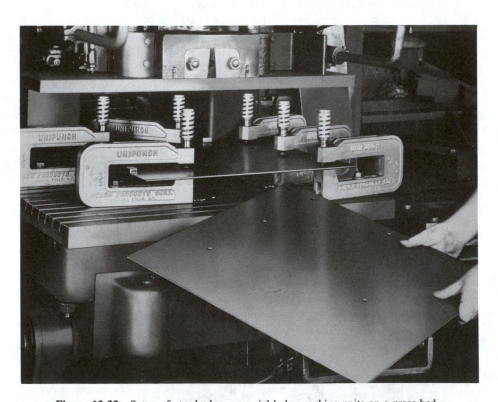

Figure 13-33 Setup of standard commercial hole-punching units on a press bed. These are quickly positioned from the template shown and then fastened in place. The punching units are actuated by the press ram when it descends. The template is estimated to cost about $200 and the punching units about $100 each. The punching units can be reused on a variety of jobs for holes in many locations. (Courtesy Unipunch Products, Inc., Buffalo, N.Y.)

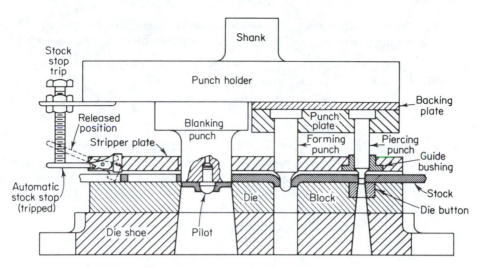

Figure 13-34 Sketch of a progressive die for blanking, piercing, and forming a piece made in a strip.

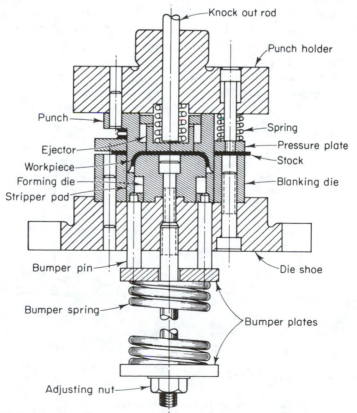

Figure 13-35 Combination blanking and drawing die.

of different kinds, such as cutting and drawing. A *compound die* is like a combination die but does operations of the same kind, such as blanking and piercing.

Stock Feeding Devices.   A variety of commercial devices are available for feeding presses. A stock feeder usually is economical on any job of more than a few thousand pieces. Two general classes are devices for feeding strips and devices for feeding individual pieces.

A typical attachment for feeding strips and coiled stock is the *roller feed unit* typified in Fig. 13-36. The rolls are actuated through a linkage from an eccentric on the crankshaft. They release the stock when the ram descends but grip and draw the stock along as the ram rises. Adjustments can be made for the amount of feed and length and thickness of stock. Sometimes two sets of rolls are used: one to push the stock into and the other to pull it out of the die. Coiled stock is held in reels or cradles and may be passed through a straightener. Another device is the *hitch feed,* which grips the stock between blocks or shoes and pulls it along and then releases it to return to start the next step.

A device for feeding pieces one at a time is the *dial station feed*. A round table with several equally spaced stations around it is indexed through an eccentric on the crankshaft. For each stroke, a station holding a piece is positioned under the punch. The stations are unloaded and loaded on the side away from the punch. A few among many other devices are mechanical hands, arms with suction cups, and magazines from which one piece at a time is pushed mechanically into the die.

For multiple operations small parts are moved from one station to another in a transfer press or progressive die. Large parts such as automobile body panels are transferred from press to press. This is done manually for small quantities and by synchronized walking-beam devices, mechanical hands, conveyors, and robots

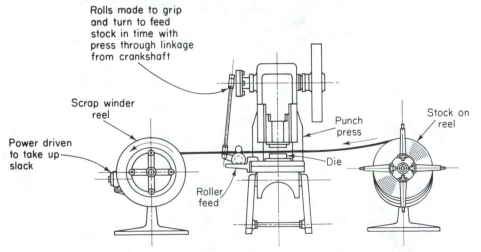

Figure 13-36   Roller feed device pulling stripstock off a stock reel and through a die. The scrap is wound on a power scrap winder. The parts being made are punched out of the strip as it passes through the die.

(Chap. 34). Such devices can be integrated with presses into fully automated straight-line transfer machines (Chap. 34) for large quantities. A manual press line putting out 12 to 20 pieces per minute can be made to yield 30 pieces per minute by automation. A line of four presses to produce appliance panels might cost $1,000,000 alone and fully automated as much as $1,500,000 plus another $400,000 for dies. One authority has stated that such an automated line must turn out at least 1,000,000 pieces per year to be justified.

Safety Devices.   A noted authority once said that: "When one considers that 97% of all press accidents can be traced to man failure and only 3% can be attributed to any mechanical failure, it is evident that by eliminating the human element you have gone a long way towards a solution of the problem." That places the responsibility on the engineer to provide the means to make notoriously dangerous press operations as safe as possible.

One of the best safeguards is to take the operator from the dangerous task, and that is an important benefit from the use of automatic feeding devices just described. However, many operations must have an operator, and two types of devices are used to protect him or her. One type keeps the operator out of the danger zone; the other assures that he or she is out of the way before the press can be tripped.

The barrier guard of Fig. 13-37 is a typical means of keeping a human being out of the danger zone. It is interlocked with the starting lever so that the press becomes inoperative if the guard is not in place. Other guards swing in front of the die to sweep

Figure 13-37   Stationary barrier guard on a punch press.

the arms of a person out of the way and prevent the press from starting if the path is not clear. Among the devices that assure that the operator is out of the way are two hand starting buttons, a harness attached to the operator's wrists to jerk them back when the ram descends, electronic eyes and light beams, and a sliding die that is loaded away from the punch and slid through a barrier into working position under the punch.

A complete and far-reaching mandate for the safety of press work as well as all other industrial operations was given by the passage of the Federal Williams-Steiger Act (Public Law 91-596) of 1970, which cited detailed and exacting safety standards and set up the Occupational Safety and Health Administration (OSHA) to enforce the law. This act brought forth no new knowledge about safety; its severe penalties more likely assured strict adherence to the principles of safety that were too often disregarded in the past. Anyone responsible for industrial operations must be familiar with this law.

QUESTIONS

1. Name and describe 10 common sheet metal cutting operations.
2. What is slitting, and why is it done?
3. What is nibbling, and what is its advantage?
4. Describe what happens when sheet metal is sheared.
5. What is shear on a punch or die? What are its disadvantages?
6. What is metal shaving?
7. What happens to metal when it is bent? Why does it spring back?
8. What limitations must be observed to avoid cracking sheet metal when bending it?
9. Describe and compare stretch, draw, compression, press, roll extrusion, and roll bending.
10. What is cold-roll forming and when is it profitable?
11. What takes place when a cup is drawn from sheet metal?
12. What is the purpose of a pressure pad in drawing a cup?
13. What limits the amount a cup can be drawn in one operation and altogether before annealing? What is the difference between these two circumstances?
14. Describe rubber pad forming and its limitations.
15. Describe the Marform process and its advantages.
16. Describe the Hydroform process and its advantages.
17. Compare the major flexible die forming processes with each other and with rigid die forming.
18. What is hydrostatic forming, and what is its advantage?
19. How is metal spinning done? How does it compare with drawing?
20. Describe three kinds of roll turning.
21. What are stretch forming and stretch draw forming, and what are their advantages?
22. What is high-energy-rate forming, and how is it done? What are its advantages?

23. What is cold heading? What are its uses and advantages?

24. Tell how rotary swaging is done.

25. What does hubbing do?

26. When is ironing done?

27. Describe riveting, staking, and stitching of metal.

28. What are the features of a press that determine its capacity?

29. What are the basic units of a press, and what does each do?

30. What is the most common press frame type, and what are its advantages and disadvantages?

31. What are the design principles and advantages of straight-sided frames for presses?

32. What is the difference between a double-crank and a double-action press, and what is the purpose of each?

33. What is the difference between a knuckle joint and a toggle press, and what is the purpose of each?

34. What determines the actual tonnage capacity of a press?

35. How should a press be selected to obtain the most production from a drawing operation? Why?

36. How do hydraulic drives compare with mechanical drives for presses?

37. Explain quantitatively how the energy is obtained during a stroke of a mechanical press.

38. What kinds of motors are used on presses, and why?

39. What are the features of a trimming press, underdrive press, and dieing machine?

40. In what way does a press brake compete with other machines able to do bending?

41. Describe a turret press and state its advantages.

42. What are the principles of operation of high-production presses?

43. What kinds of details do dies have, and what is the purpose of each kind?

44. How can standard details be used for economy in die construction?

45. Describe a progressive, a combination, and a compound die.

46. Describe the common ways of feeding stock mechanically into presses.

47. What two types of devices protect press operations?

PROBLEMS

1. A round disk 150 mm (6 in.) in diameter is to be blanked without shear from 1.5-mm (0.06-in.)-thick stock of annealed 0.15% carbon steel. What blanking force and energy are required per stroke?

2. A blank has a perimeter of 317.5 mm (12.5 in.). The metal is 0.96 mm (0.038 in.) thick cold-worked 0.15% carbon steel with a shear strength of 415 MPa (60,000 psi) and percent penetration of 25%. Two holes of 12.7 mm ($\frac{1}{2}$ in.) diameter each are to be pierced during the same stroke when the piece is blanked. What are the forces required for blanking and for piercing? What is the maximum force the press must exert at any one time without shear? What energy is required per stroke?

3. (a) Explain why the force in newtons (pounds) required to punch with shear is $F_s = F \times p \times t/(pt + v)$, where F is the force required without shear, p is percent penetration, t is thickness of stock, and v is amount of shear as designated in Fig. 13-3(B).
   (b) What force is required to blank the disk described in Prob. 1 with 3.05 mm (0.12 in.) shear?

4. A piece of stock 2.36 mm (0.093 in.) thick is bent to an angle $\alpha = 120°$ (Fig. 13-6) with an inside radius of 6.35 mm ($\frac{1}{4}$ in.). What is the original length of the stock that goes into the bend?

5. How much should a medium-carbon soft-steel piece be bent for a finished 90° angle bend?

6. A section has been bent in experimental quantities on a press brake. Each piece is 1.8 m (6 ft) long. It takes 1 minute to bend each length, at a charge of $2/hr for use of the brake and $8.50/hr for labor. The section is going into production, and purchase of a roll-forming machine costing $35,000 plus tooling at $9000 is being considered. This must be paid off in one year with a 25% charge for interest, insurance, and taxes. Labor on the roll-forming machine costs $8.50/hr. The machine will produce the section at the rate of 18 m/min (60 ft/min) but is not expected to have any other use. What must be the least expected amount of production in linear feet of section to justify purchase of the roll-forming machine and equipment? How many working days of 8 hours each does this represent?

7. The thickness of the wall of a cup is assumed to be the same as that of the blank in Fig. 13-10. Thus $t_1 = t_2 = t$.
   (a) If the bottom radius r of the cup is ignored, and the outside surface of the cup is assumed to have the same area as the blank, show that $D = \sqrt{d^2 + 4dh}$.
   (b) In the case where the radius r in Fig. 13-10 is large, t is small in comparison and may be neglected. Thus the area of the outside corner at the bottom of the cup is a part of a toroid of minor radius r and may be approximated as $A_t = \pi^2 r(d - 0.7r)/2$. If the outside area of the cup is assumed to have the same area as the blank, show that

$$D = \sqrt{(d - 2r)^2 + 4d(h - r) + 2\pi r(d - 0.7r)}$$

8. A cup 50 mm (2 in.) in diameter and 75 mm (3 in.) deep is to be drawn from 1.5-mm (0.06-in.)-thick drawing steel with a tensile strength of 310 MPa (45,000 psi). The corner radius is negligible.
   (a) What must be the diameter of the blank?
   (b) What must be the least number of drawing operations?
   (c) What force and energy must be applied for the first draw with a 40% reduction?
   (d) The reduction in area in a tensile test is 70%. Is an annealing operation necessary?

9. A fluted cup 70 mm ($2\frac{3}{4}$ in.) in diameter by 57 mm ($2\frac{1}{4}$ in.) deep is to be drawn from 1.0-mm (0.04-in.)-thick soft aluminum. It can be drawn in one operation by Marforming at the rate of 0.40 min/piece. Marform tooling with a soft steel punch costs $450 and with a hardened steel punch $1300. Two operations are needed with conventional steel dies, but each can produce 10 pieces/min. Soft-steel dies cost $2000 and hardened steel dies $2500. Soft-steel tools are not expected to last for more than about 5000 pieces, but the hardened steel tools will serve for as many as will be needed. Setup time is about the same for either alternative. Manufacturing time costs $21.50 per hour. Which type of operation should be selected for each of the following quantities of pieces? (a) 1000; (b) 5000; (c) 10,000; (d) 25,000; (e) 100,000.

10. A bar of carbon steel with a compressive strength of 620 MPa (90,000 psi) and a diameter of 25 mm (1 in.) is to be rotary cold swaged to a diameter of 13 mm ($\frac{1}{2}$ in.). The overall length of the finished piece is 250 mm (10 in.), and the length from the 25-mm (1-in.) diameter to the small end is 75 mm (3 in.). The average feed rate is 75 mm/s (3 in./sec). The dies contact the workpiece over the 10° taper and 13 mm ($\frac{1}{2}$ in.) beyond.
    (a) How long must the original piece of stock be?
    (b) How many passes are needed?
    (c) What is the maximum force required?
    (d) How much machining time is required for each piece?

11. The disk described in Prob. 1 is to be blanked and then drawn into a cup 57 mm ($2\frac{1}{4}$ in.) deep in one stroke on a single-action mechanical press with a 150-mm (6-in.) stroke. If the blanking is done 57 mm ($2\frac{1}{4}$ in.) from the bottom of the stroke, what is the highest speed at which the crankshaft may turn and what power is required for continuous operation?

12. For the conditions given by Prob. 8, specify the kind of press needed, its tonnage requirements, stroke, speed, and power.

13. Show that the energy given up by a press flywheel (a) for 10% slowdown is $E_{10} = 0.19MV^2/2 = 0.19WV^2/2a$, (b) for 20% slowdown is $E_{20} = 0.36MV^2/2 = 0.36WV^2/2a$, as stated in the text.

14. A 60-ton open-back inclinable press has a 550-kg (1210-lb) flywheel that revolves at 90 rpm. The wheel has a 1.0 m (39 in.) OD and a rim thickness of 150 mm (6 in.). What energy is it able to furnish when it slows down (a) 10%? (b) 20%?

REFERENCES

BAXTER, D. F., JR., "Cold Forming Steel Parts to Greater Advantage," *Metal Progress,* Oct.–Nov. 1972.

BECK, W. A., "Explosive Forming: Scaling Down the Costs," *The Tool and Manufacturing Engineer,* July 1969.

BRANDEL, W. W., and L. S. KLASS, "Ball Forming Solves Contouring Problems," *Metal Progress,* Mar. 1971.

BRAUER, E. H., "Contouring Parts by Stretch and Compression Forming," *Machine Design,* Oct. 18, 1973, p. 160.

CHEPKO, F. E., "Designing Formed Wire Parts," *Machine Design,* Apr. 16, 1970, p. 127.

CRANE, E. V., *Plastic Working in Presses,* Wiley, New York, 1944.

DALLAS, D. B., "Press Working: The Punching Machines Have Arrived," *Manufacturing Engineering and Management,* Feb. 1973.

EARY, D. F., and E. A. REED, *Techniques of Pressworking Sheet Metal,* Prentice-Hall, Englewood Cliffs, N.J., 1974.

High Velocity Forming of Metals, ASTME, Prentice-Hall, Englewood Cliffs, N.J., 1964.

Metals Handbook, Vol. 4: *Forming,* American Society for Metals, Metals Park, Ohio, 1969.

WICK, C., "Metal Spinning—A Review and Update," *Manufacturing Engineering,* Jan. 1978.

WINSHIP, J. T., "A Fresh Look at OSHA," *American Machinist,* May 29, 1972, p. 53.

———,"Pressworking Equipment, Special Report 696," *American Machinist*, Apr. 1977, p. 89.

———,"Fundamentals of Fineblanking," *American Machinist*, July 1976, p. 104.

———,"A New Era in NC Punching," *American Machinist*, Nov. 1979, p. 139.

———,"How Metal Containers Are Made," *American Machinist*, Apr. 1980, p. 155.

WOODS, W. W., et al., *Final Report on Sheet Forming Technology*, AD416412, 1963, and *Theoretical Formability*, Vol. I, PB181098, and Vol. II, PB181099, 1961, U.S. Government Printing Office, Washington, D.C.

14

WELDING AND ALLIED PROCESSES

Welding is a means of joining metals by concentrating heat or pressure or both at the joint to cause coalescence of the adjoining areas. A good weld is as strong as the parent metal. Welding is done in a number of ways. The common processes of commercial importance are listed in Fig. 14-1. In one major class of processes, metal is melted at the joint, and filler may be added. *Fusion* takes place, and no pressure is needed. For a homogeneous joint, the metal added is the same as the base metal. For a heterogeneous joint, the base metal is not melted. Another class of processes depends only on pressing the pieces together at the joint. The metal is usually heated locally to a plastic state, but adherence of metal can be enforced with pressure alone under favorable conditions.

Electric-arc, gas torch, energy-ray, and Thermit welding are fusion processes wherein the filler metal is essentially the same as the parent metal in the parts being joined. Braze welding, brazing, and soldering use filler metals different from and melting at lower temperatures than the base metal, which is not melted. The main types of plastic metal joining processes are resistance, pressure, and forge welding.

Welding is done in manual, semiautomatic, or automatic operations depending largely upon the quantity and variety of work. Automation may consist of mechanical handling and positioning of parts, feeding of filler metal and flux, or manipulation and control of the welding device. All these are done by the operator in manual welding.

Although known and practiced in some forms before then, welding has mostly grown to its present vast importance in industry since World War I. It has supplanted riveting almost entirely for boilers, pressure vessels, tanks, and structural members of bridges and buildings; it is the chief means of fastening panels and members together into automobile bodies; it has taken the place of castings for a large proportion of

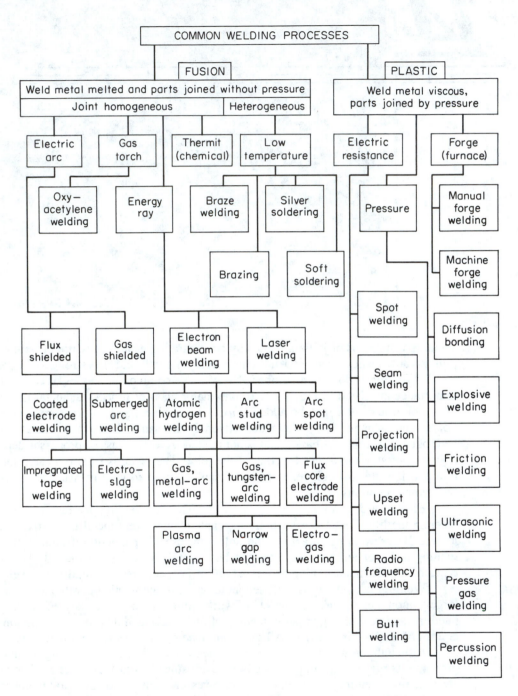

Figure 14-1 Common welding operations and their relationships.

machine, jig, and fixture bases, bodies, and frames; and it has become the means of joining at least some of the parts in most products manufactured today. A survey showed that among metalworking plants, 99% did some sort of welding.

ELECTRIC-ARC WELDING

Principles.   The basis for electric-arc welding is an electric arc between an electrode and the workpiece or between two electrodes. The arc is a sustained electrical discharge through a path of ionized particles called a *plasma*. The temperature may be from about 2800°C (5000°F) to 28,000°C (50,000°F) at different parts of an arc under various conditions.

Applications are classified as to whether the electrode is *nonconsumable*, for *carbon-arc* and *tungsten-arc welding*, or *consumable*, for *metal-arc welding*. Of these, carbon-arc welding is seldom used; the others will be discussed in detail later.

The metal electrode in metal-arc welding is melted progressively by the arc and is advanced to maintain the arc length. The molten metal must be shielded from the air. Coated electrodes furnish a protective gaseous cloud around and slag that floats on top of the melt as shown in Fig. 14-2. Other methods of weld protection are to pour slag forming flux or inject inert gas around the arc and molten metal when using a bare electrode. Parent metal is melted under the arc, and filler metal is added to the pool as the electrode melts.

The Main Factors of Arc Welding.   The *rate* that energy is delivered is expressed by I^2R with a current of I amperes and a resistance of R ohms. Resistance in an arc-welding operation consists of that of the electrodes, a phase between each electrode and the arc, and the resistance in the arc column. Each of these is independent of the other and may vary differently as current, voltage, shielding, and other conditions are changed. Apparent overall resistance may decrease as current is increased to around 100 A but generally assumes a fairly constant value for currents of several hundred or more amperes commonly employed for welding. The rate at which

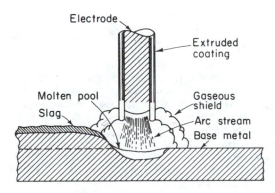

Figure 14-2 Shielded metal-arc electrode, arc stream and its shield, deposited metal, and protective slag.

metal is melted depends upon the energy delivered and may be expressed approximately in kg/min (lb/min) as

$$M = k_1 I^2 \qquad (14\text{-}1)$$

The k_i in this discussion are constant factors; k_1 here takes into account average values for the heat capacity of the metal, resistance, and heat losses.

The rate at which metal is melted determines the size of and the speed of laying a weld like the one depicted in Fig. 14-3. In such a case

$$M = \delta A V \qquad (14\text{-}2)$$

where A is the vertical cross-sectional area of the bead in mm^2 (in.^{2}), including melted filler and parent metal, V is the rate of traverse, in mm/min (in./min), of the electrode along the weld, and δ is the density in kg/mm^3 (lb/in.^{3}).

The depth to which metal is deposited and melted is called the penetration P of a joint. It determines the size and thus the strength of the bead that holds the workpiece

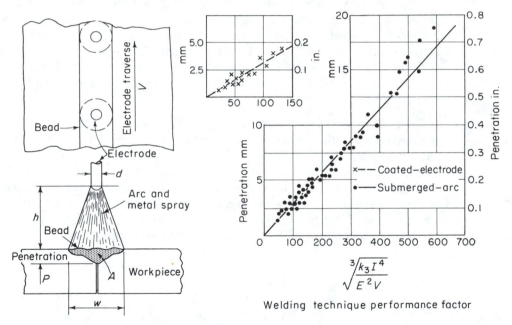

Figure 14-3 Left, an idealized model of metal-arc welding. Right, experimental and theoretical effects of welding current, voltage, and traverse rate on penetration. (As reported by Clarence E. Jackson in "The Science of Arc Welding," *The Welding Journal,* 1959.) Ranges of welding conditions for coated-electrode process: $K_3 = 0.0330$ for V in mm/min (0.0013 for ipm), current (I) = 85 to 350 A, travel (V) = 152 to 457 mm/min (6 to 18 ipm), voltage (E) = 23 to 25 V, and electrode diameter (d) = 3.2 to 5.6 mm ($\frac{1}{8}$ to $\frac{7}{32}$ in.). For submerged-arc process: $K_3 = 0.02921$ for V in mm/min (0.00115 for ipm), current (I) = 250 to 1200 A ac, travel (V) = 144.8 to 1099.8 mm/min (5.7 to 43.3 ipm), voltage (E) = 28 to 45 V, and electrode diam (d) = 4 to 6.4 mm ($\frac{5}{32}$ to $\frac{1}{4}$ in.).

together. The amount of penetration depends upon the cross-sectional area A of the bead, the current, and the voltage. As the distance h between electrode and weld is increased, the arc flares out more and the width of bead w increases. Less penetration ensues. The arc voltage E increases with electrode separation; an average relationship is $E = 20 + 1.2h$ for h in mm ($E = 20 + 30h$ for h in in.). Also, as the current is increased, the more intense arc drives the penetration deeper. Experimental and analytical results indicate a fair value of

$$P = \sqrt[3]{k_2 \frac{I^2 A}{E^2}} \qquad (14\text{-}3)$$

If Eqs. (14-1), (14-2), and (14-3) are combined, the result is

$$P = \sqrt[3]{\frac{k_3 I^4}{E^2 V}} \qquad (14\text{-}4)$$

The experimental results displayed in Fig. 14-3 show that this is a realistic relationship of the factors that affect the depth of penetration and thus the effectiveness of a weld. Various investigators have shown that this applies to common materials and operations. The right-hand part of Eq. (14-4) is called the *welding technique performance factor*. Its terms stand for current, voltage, and rate of traverse; these factors can be varied most readily to control a welding operation.

Criteria of Arc-Welding Performance. Arc welding is done most efficiently by utilizing as much current as the work and equipment allow. As shown by Eqs. (14-1) and (14-3), a large current means metal is melted faster, penetration is deeper, and fewer passes are required. Deep penetration is obtained from a short arc giving a low voltage drop. A common rule is that the arc length should not exceed the electrode wire diameter. With a large I and small E, a fast V is permissable, and even desirable, to avoid buildup of filler metal. All this results in a higher rate of production. Limitations are imposed by the workpiece, capacity of the welding equipment, and electrode. A common example of workpiece limitation is that thin sheets cannot be welded with too intense an arc or they will be burned through and damaged.

Equipment capacity is selected upon the basis of cost and utilization. A power source costing several hundred dollars and providing 200 to 300 A current may be adequate for intermittent use for maintenance. One worth thousands of dollars and capable of delivering 1000 A or more is justified for continuous production of heavy work. More current can be used profitably for some operations than for others. Average ranges for some arc-welding processes are indicated in Fig. 14-12.

There is a proper-size electrode for each type of work, and an ideal current range for each electrode. Penetration and fusion are poor when too little current is passed through a thick electrode, and thin electrodes should be used for small currents for fine work. On the other hand, if too much current is passed through a coated electrode of a certain size, resistive heating spalls the coating. A large diameter electrode must be used for a heavy current. Even so, manual-arc welding with coated electrodes is not practiced generally with currents of more than about 400 A. Bare wire fed continuously as an electrode in an automatic welding is not subject to the same limitations. In fact, up to 70% more metal may be deposited by an electrode, which is a long free length of fine wire fed fast than by a heavy wire because the fine wire is preheated by its electrical resistance. The submerged-arc and gas-shielded welding operations of Table 14-1 on page 349 utilize bare wire electrodes and carry larger currents and are faster than the operations with coated electrodes.

The radiation from a welding arc is harmful to the eyes. Anyone within 15 m (50 ft) should wear a protective shield over face and eyes. Spatter makes protective clothing necessary. To protect others in the vicinity, welding is commonly done in booths or behind opaque screens.

Electric Current for Welding. If direct current (dc) is used for arc welding, a positive workpiece (anode) and a negative electrode (cathode) constitute *straight polarity*. Electrons flow from the negative to the positive terminal of an arc. With straight polarity, they strike the workpiece at great speeds, and the material is heated faster than the electrode. This is of advantage in welding massive pieces because it puts the heat where needed. *Reverse polarity*, with opposite connections to straight polarity, limits the current that can be put through an electrode but is preferable for welding thin sections. It also has an inherent ability to scour the oxide film from the surface of aluminum, magnesium, etc.

Much welding is done with dc because it can handle all situations and jobs, usually provides a stable arc, is known to most operators, and is preferred for difficult tasks like overhead welding. Sometimes a distorted magnetic field will deflect a dc arc and degrade the work. This is called *arc blow* and can be minimized with alternating current (ac). Although all work cannot be done, about 90% of all jobs can be handled by ac, which has been growing in favor because its equipment is simpler and costs only about 60% as much as for dc.

Open circuit potential is usually from 50 to 90 V. The electrode tip is touched to the base metal and withdrawn slightly to *strike* the arc. As the electrode melts, it must be adjusted toward the workpiece to maintain the arc. Voltage increases with the arc length. The arc is extinguished when its length exceeds the capacity of the available voltage. Metal-arc voltages range from almost zero on short circuit to a minimum of 17 V to sustain an arc and to around 40 V for a usable long arc.

Shielded Electrodes. Practically all stick electrodes used by hand are of the shielded type, having an extruded coating over the wire. The coating may contain ingredients like SiO_2, TiO_2, FeO, MgO, Al_2O_3, and cellulose in various proportions. Over 100 formulations of electrode coatings are made. The ingredients are intended to perform all or a number of the following functions in various degrees to suit different purposes.

1. Help stabilize and direct the arc for effective penetration.
2. Provide a gaseous shield to prevent atmospheric contamination.
3. Control surface tension in the pool to influence the shape of the bead formed when the metal freezes.

4. Act as scavengers to reduce oxides.

5. Add alloying elements to the weld.

6. Form a slag to carry off impurities, protect the hot metal, and slow the cooling rate.

7. Electrically insulate the electrode.

8. Minimize splatter of weld metal.

9. Form a plasma to conduct current across the arc.

One type of electrode has a thick coating containing a substantial amount of iron powder. The coating forms a shell around and helps concentrate the arc. The iron powder adds extra metal to the weld and increases the speed of welding.

A coating with more ionizing capacity than the electrode metal is usually favored to avoid losing the arc. Coatings on *drag* or *contact electrodes* melt more slowly than the metal so that the electrode can be positioned in touch with the workpiece without a short circuit. The proper arc length is maintained, and welding is easier.

The core of a typical electrode for welding steel is rimmed steel with about 0.1% carbon and small amounts of other elements. Some cores are killed steel, and some are alloy steel, although it is cheaper to add alloying elements through the coating. Core sizes range from 1.6 mm ($\frac{1}{16}$ in.) to 8 mm ($\frac{5}{16}$ in.) in diameter.

A standard classification for electrodes, known as the AWS–ASTM classification, designates the characteristics of steel electrodes by a letter and series of numbers such as E 6010, E 7016, E 9030. The prefix "E" indicates the filler material to be a conducting electrode. The *first two*, sometimes *three*, *digits* specify the minimum tensile strength in 1000-psi units as welded. The examples stand for 60,000, 70,000, and 90,000 psi. Strengths range from 400 MPa (60,000 psi) in the low-carbon steel class to 800 MPa (120,000 psi) in the alloy steel class. The *third digit* indicates the welding position for which the electrode is suited: (1) all positions, (2) horizontal and flat, and (3) flat positions only. The position is determined by ingredients that control the surface tension of the molten metal. The *fourth digit* indicates the type of coating and conditions for which the electrode is intended, including the kind of current and polarity. In addition, the description of a low-alloy electrode carries a suffix, such as A1, B2, etc., that designates the type and amount of alloy. For example, E 8018-B2 designates steel alloyed with 0.40 to 0.65 Mo and 1.00 to 1.50 Cr. Full specifications of the properties and applications of standard electrodes are tabulated in reference books and handbooks. Some electrodes are identified by brand names.

Plain carbon electrodes cost less than \$2.00/kg (\$0.90/lb) in large quantities to \$4.50/kg (\$2.00/lb) and more at retail. Special and alloy types may cost several times as much.

Applications of Arc Welding.   Arc welding has the advantages of being quite versatile and able to make welds under many conditions, of producing high quality welds, of depositing metal rapidly, and of being competitive costwise for many situations. As a result it is used more than any other welding process. Examples of structures arc welded are tanks, bridges, boilers, buildings, piping, machinery, furniture, and ships. Almost all metals can be welded by one or more of the forms of arc welding.

Manual Metal-Arc Welding Equipment. The basic units for manual metal-arc welding (formally called **shielded metal-arc welding—SMAW**) are (1) a source of current called a *welder* or *welding machine*; (2) conductor cords, wires, or leads (one to the ground and one to the electrode); (3) an electrode holder; (4) an electrode; and (5) a workpiece. A typical outfit is shown in Fig. 14-4. A complete outfit for general-purpose work can be obtained for less than $1000.

Welding is commonly done on a metal table to which the ground lead is attached and on which the workpieces are laid or fastened. The operator manipulates the electrode. Tables or holding fixtures that tilt and turn to present joints to be welded in the most accessible and advantageous positions are called *welding positioners*. They make welding much faster. For instance, downhand welding in the most convenient position can be four times or more as fast as welding in vertical or overhead positions. The positioner in Fig. 14-5 is manually adjusted, and ones like it may cost only a few

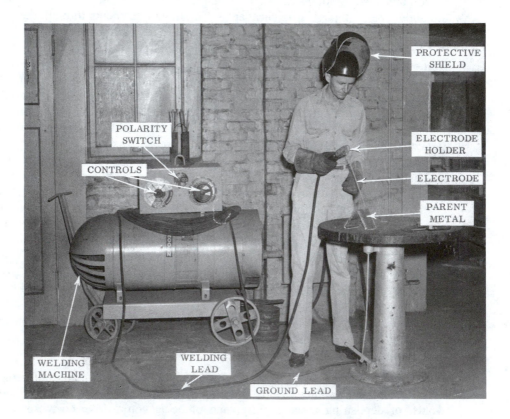

Figure 14-4   Manual metal-arc welding equipment.

Figure 14-5 A 1200-lb-capacity, manually adjusted, weld positioner. (Courtesy Cullen Friestedt Co., Chicago.)

hundred dollars. Some are motor operated for big work and easy adjustments and may cost many thousands of dollars.

Automatic-Arc Welding. A bare wire electrode is fed continuously through motor-driven rollers with semi- or fully automatic equipment. The wire may be solid or hollow and filled with flux for benefits like those from coated electrodes; the latter is called *flux-cored arc welding*. The molten metal is surrounded by gas or flux in the protective processes described later. A semiautomatic gun or torch is moved along the weld by hand. Some have integral smoke collectors. Either the welding head or work table is traversed mechanically. A traveling head for submerged-arc welding is shown in Fig. 14-6.

Special-purpose welding machines are common in the high-production industries. One example is a large fully automatic machine to produce box section frame cross members from stock 3 to 4 mm ($\frac{1}{8}$ to $\frac{5}{32}$ in.) thick for automobiles. An operator puts two halves of a section in the first station, where they are pressed together and tacked by resistance spot welding. A walking beam transfers the section to the welding station where automatic clamps square the flanges, ensure fit-up, and position it. Four welding heads, feeding 2-mm ($\frac{5}{64}$-in.)-diameter wire and guided along the curved profiles, complete 2 m (80 in.) of welds in less than 8 seconds. Special fixtures to position and hold components to be joined are necessary for mechanized welding in quantity production.

Among machines for positioning and moving work for repetitive production welding is a Weld-Lathe for round pieces such as tubing. An assembly to be joined is rotated and traversed between headstock and tailstock (Chap. 18) to enable one or more welding torches to move along the seams in a preset program. The price is about $30,000. Another system rotates relatively flat work around a vertical axis for welding circular joints automatically.

Figure 14-6   Automatic machine for submerged-arc welding. (Courtesy Linde Division, Union Carbide Corp.)

Sources of Welding Current.   An electrical generator was long the only source and is still a major source of dc for welding. It may be driven by an electric motor or by an internal combustion engine for portability. Another means is to reduce the voltage of ac through a transformer and convert it to dc through a selenium or silicon rectifier. Ac is obtained directly from a transformer. Combination sources that supply both ac and dc are popular. A transformer source has no moving parts but a fan. Thus it operates with less maintenance cost and a higher operating efficiency than a generator. One study with a 60% duty cycle and a welding current of 300 A for a 9-hour shift showed electric power cost at 3 cents/kWh to be $3.42 for a dc motor generator, $2.56 for a dc rectifier, and $2.10 for an ac transformer unit.

Arc welder sizes are designated in amperes (see Fig. 14-12). A 100- to 200-A machine is small but portable and satisfactory for light manual welding. A 300- or 400-A size is suitable for manual welding of average work like ships, structures, and piping. Automatic welding requires capacities between 800 and 3000 A either in a single unit or a number of smaller units in parallel. Controls are provided on the best machine for varying both open-circuit voltage and welding current in amperes. Some have adjustments only for current. Some machines have an *arc booster* that provides a momentary surge of current to give an arc a good start when it is struck.

The *duty cycle* of a welder specifies the part of a 10-minute period in percent that the rated current can be drawn from the machine without overheating. For example, if a welder is rated at 300 A at a 60% duty cycle, the machine can be operated safely at 300 A welding current for 6 out of 10 minutes. A welder must be operated for a smaller portion of time at a higher than rated current, and the current output must be reduced if the rated duty cycle is exceeded.

A *constant-current* or *drooping power source* with characteristics typified by the solid curves of Fig. 14-7 is necessary for all manual-arc welding. For any one setting of the welder, the current varies little over a wide range of voltages resulting from variations in the arc lengths. Thus, although the operator cannot hold a constant arc length by hand, he or she is given the benefit of stable melting of the electrode and easy control of the arc. The settings on the welder for the volts and amperes give the effect of a large number of curves, some steep and some flatter, to meet a variety of situations. Thus a uniformly low current is desirable for a small electrode to weld thin sheet metal without burn-through. A flatter curve would be desirable for overhead welding. In that case the electrode is brought close to the work to control the metal, the voltage decreases, and a heavy current is beneficial to melt and drive an adequate amount of metal into the weld.

Automatic equipment may be powered by a constant current source. The electrode wire is fed by an adjustable speed motor. If the melting rate is too fast and tends to stretch the arc, a control circuit responds to an increase in voltage and speeds up the wire feed motor, and vice versa. Simpler control is possible with a *constant arc voltage* (CAV or CV) or a slightly *rising arc voltage* (RAV) source. A voltage for the conditions of the job and the rate of feed of the wire is selected from the controls and maintained by the source. Current is delivered from the source as needed to melt the electrode and maintain a constant arc length.

Gas-Shielded Arc Welding. The arc and metal pool in welding may be protected by an envelope of inert or semi-inert gas. This gas may be contained in an enclosed chamber in which the welding is done but commonly is injected in the open around the point of welding. Gas shielding adds cost but affords a clean and clear operation. It must be protected from strong drafts. Gas-shielded arc welding is done mostly with direct current. Thin, particularly nonferrous, sheet metal can be welded better and faster with a power supply that pulses the current at a set rate of 20 to 120

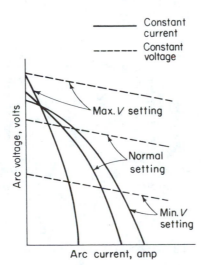

Figure 14-7 Characteristics of constant-current and constant-voltage power sources for arc welding.

times per second. Equipment for *pulsed-arc welding* may be four to five times as expensive as a conventional power supply.

One gas-shielded arc process is *gas, tungsten-arc welding*, GTAW, also called *Tig* for tungsten inert-gas-shielded arc welding, depicted in Fig. 14-8. It utilizes a tungsten alloy electrode that does not waste away in an inert-gas atmosphere. Filler metal is put in by a separate rod or wire as needed. Helium and argon alone, together, or mixed with other gas form the shield. The process requires care and skill but makes clean and reliable welds and is important in aerospace and other critical applications. It is better suited for sheet metal than for thick sections. No foreign substance need touch the weld. The arc may be initiated by a high-frequency and high-voltage pulsed discharge to obviate even touching the electrode to the workpiece.

Atomic hydrogen arc welding is similar to gas, tungsten-arc welding but is done with an arc between two tungsten electrodes in a stream of hydrogen gas. The hydrogen gives protection from the atmosphere and enhances heat transfer from arc to workpiece. The process gives exceptionally clean welds but is expensive and not used much except for deep welds, as in die blocks, and for high-temperature alloys, particularly for surfacing.

Gas, metal-arc welding, called GMAW or Mig for metal inert-gas shielded arc welding, is done with a wire fed through the welding head to act as the electrode and supply filler metal as depicted in Fig. 14-8. Inert gases are used for critical jobs, but cheaper carbon dioxide has become quite popular for a large variety of production operations. Carbon dioxide does not support an arc well. One remedy is to maintain a short arc with provisions to automatically limit the current during frequent periods of short circuiting. The carbon dioxide also dissociates into carbon monoxide and oxygen, and deoxidizers must be added to protect the weld. One form of the process

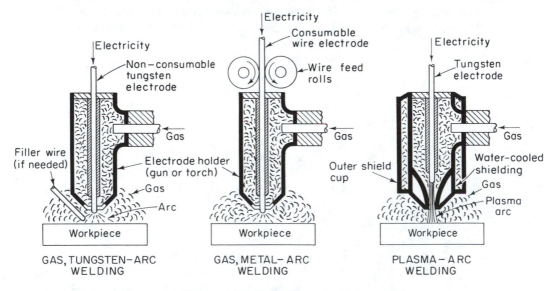

Figure 14-8 Types of gas-shielded arc welding.

utilizes a *flux-cored wire* containing arc stabilizers and deoxidizers. Another variant of the process is called *micro-wire welding* and feeds wires as small as 0.75 mm (0.030 in.) in diameter at high speeds. With high current densities, up to 23,000 A/cm^2 (150,000 A/in.^{2}), the wire is well preheated and the current is concentrated at the weld. GMAW is fast, versatile, and applicable for semiautomatic welding in all positions.

Arc-spot welding is done by Tig or Mig welding in one spot at a time through two or more lapped or butted sheets or plates. An advantage is that it can be done entirely from one side without high pressure. It can weld thicker sections, and equipment costs are less than half as much as for resistance spot welding, but the latter still is faster and more suitable for most production operations. Arc-spot welding is mostly confined to mild and stainless steel and leaves a visible lump on the surface. A way to pierce metal is to burn through a piece with a shielded electrode and blow out the molten metal. A process for quantity production utilizes a string of electrodes along a straight or curved joint. The electrodes are fired in rapid succession and produce a series of overlapping spot welds. Some joints are reported made faster in this way than by traversing electrodes. This is called PIGME welding for *programmed inert-gas multielectrode welding*.

Plasma-Arc Welding.   Plasma is high-temperature ionized gas and occurs in any electric arc. If a stream of injected gas and the arc are made to flow through a restriction (a water-cooled copper orifice as in Fig. 14-8), the current density of the arc and the velocity of the gas are raised. In that way the ionization and temperature of the gas are greatly increased. The excited particles give up large amounts of energy when they reform into atoms, some at the workpiece surface.

Most materials can be melted, many even vaporized, by the plasma-arc process and thus become subject to welding. Penetration is deep and thorough. The process can be operated at currents from less than 1 A to over 500 A and close control can be achieved; stainless steel foil as thin as 25 μm (0.001 in.) is easily welded. Results are clean. The process is two to five times as fast, but equipment cost is twice as much (or more) as for Tig welding.

Submerged-Arc Welding.   In submerged-arc welding granular flux is poured on the weld area in advance of the moving arc. The electrode is bare wire automatically fed into the flux blanket. Flux around the arc is melted, protects the arc and weld, and is deposited as slag on top of the weld on freezing. The effect is shown in Fig. 14-9. The flux may be neutral or contain alloying elements to enrich the weld. The protection affords a good quality weld and eliminates arc spatter. An operator cannot see the arc and may have trouble following a joint but does not need an eye shield. The method operates with alternating or direct current but is confined to flat or horizontal positions. Unmelted flux may be put back for reuse, slag must be removed from each pass, and this all adds work to the operation.

The submerged-arc method is used for semi- and fully automatic welding mostly of steel and is capable of the largest deposition rates. For example, heavy steel plates, such as for ships, are welded through from one side in one pass with the addition of

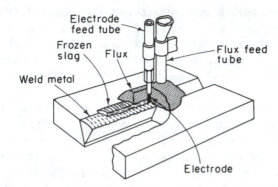

Figure 14-9 Cutaway view of a submerged-metal arc weld.

powder metal to the flux or into the gap before the flux. Two or more electrodes travel in a row with 1500 A or more on the lead arc and 1000 A or more on the trailing arcs for welding rates to 635 mm/min (25 ipm) on plates 25 mm (1 in.) thick or more.

Flux is applied to welding in other ways. *Magnetic flux welding* utilizes a flux that is attracted magnetically to and coats the electrode wire carrying a heavy current. *Impregnated-tape metal-arc welding* is done with a machine that winds a fluxing tape around the electrode as it is fed to the arc. Also, *flux-cored electrode-arc welding (FCAW)* with or without gas provides flux neatly with high productivity.

Vertical Welding.   *Electroslag welding* (ESW), illustrated in Fig. 14-10, is a form of vertical welding used particularly for joining steel sections more than 25 mm (1 in.) or so thick, such as for crusher bodies, large press frames, and pressure vessels. Welding is initiated by an arc on the bottom of the vertically positioned joint. Flux poured around the electrode is fused to slag that floats on the molten metal. After the start, there is no arc, and heat comes from the electrical resistance of the slag. Metal is added as the wire filler is fed in, melted, and solidified. This continues from the bottom to the top of the joint. The molten metal and slag are kept in the joint by dams on the sides which may be fixed or slide upward with the progress of the operation. They usually are water cooled. More than one electrode may be fed at a time into quite thick joints. Simple equipment for plates as thick as 50 mm (2 in.) is available below $10,000; more elaborate systems cost up to $25,000.

Electrogas welding (EGW), depicted in Fig. 14-10, is suitable for welding sections about 15 to 40 mm ($\frac{1}{2}$ to $1\frac{1}{2}$ in.) thick in one pass. The consumable wire electrode may be solid or flux cored, but most or all of the shielding is provided by an argon and carbon dioxide gas mixture injected into the gap. *Narrow gap welding* utilizes specific techniques to weld joints less than 15 mm ($\frac{1}{2}$ in.) wide. A narrower gap requires less filler metal and time and minimizes the heat-affected zone. Vertical welding is most natural and easy for many applications. It is economical for welding sections in one pass that require several passes by other means, in some cases 10 to 50 times as fast.

Preparation is simple for vertical welding because elaborate scarf preparation and accurate fit-up are not necessary as for conventional arc welding. Heating and cooling are inherently slow so there is no need for preheating or controlled cooling.

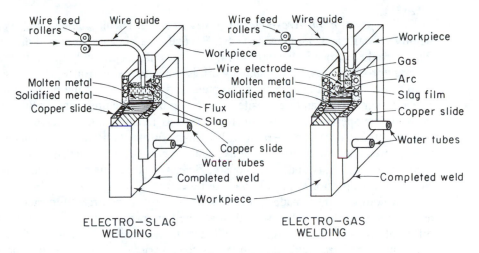

Figure 14-10   Two forms of vertical welding.

However, the heat-affected zone is large, and heat treatment to obtain acceptable fatigue properties may be desirable.

Stud Welding.   The *arc stud-welding process* utilizes a gun that automatically controls an electric arc and attaches a stud in place. The scheme of the initial set-up is shown in Fig. 14-11(A). A current is turned on, and the stud withdraws from the workpiece to strike an arc inside the ceramic ferrule. After a predetermined time the current is turned off, and the stud is pushed into the molten pool. After the metal solidifies, the equipment is withdrawn to leave the stud welded to the workpiece as illlustrated in Fig. 14-11(B). A variation of the process particularly suited for attaching small studs to thin sheets is *capacitor-discharge welding*. For this, the stud is made with a thin tip on the end as depicted in Fig. 14-11(C). A heavy current discharge melts the projection and sets up an arc in the gap. The stud is then pushed against the workpiece to complete the weld.

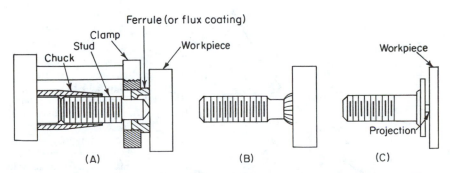

Figure 14-11   Procedures for stud welding: (A) setup for arc stud welding; (B) arc-welded stud; (C) stud for capacitor-discharge welding.

Comparison of Arc-Welding Processes. Manual shielded-arc welding is wholly versatile and has a low first cost. For one-of-a-kind assemblies of diverse work, the covered electrode in the hands of a skilled welder is probably the fastest and most efficient process. However, manual work is inherently slow for repetition; stick ends need to be discarded and work interrupted, and there is a definite human limit to the rate at which metal can be deposited. Semiautomatic machines that mechanize part of the welding operation cost two to four times as much as stick shielded-arc welding equipment. However, an operator with semi- or fully automatic equipment can control molten metal and the arc more readily, can make use of more current, and can deposit metal more uniformly and continuously. He or she is capable of welding 2 to 10 times as fast as an operator with only a coated electrode.

A comparison is made in Fig. 14-12 of performance rates reported for several arc-welding processes. The record might be somewhat different in other shops for different kinds of work. Semiautomatic gas, metal-arc welding is often faster overall than submerged-arc welding, particularly for a variety of work, because the operator can see the weld, and there is no slag to chip away, and no flux to clean up. Submerged-arc welding has some advantage in that it has no loss from spatter, whereas the loss of metal may be as much as 10% for gas, metal-arc welding. For fully automatic operation with complete continuous control, submerged-arc welding offers the means for utilizing heavy currents to lay down metal at the fastest rates, particularly with strip electrodes, multiple electrodes, and vertical welding techniques.

Relative costs for doing a job by several common methods are given in Table 14-1. Common for all processes are a labor cost of $12/hr, overhead cost of $16/hr, a weld deposit amount of 0.17 kg/m (0.11 lb/lin. ft) of weld, a power cost of $0.05/kWh, and a power source efficiency of 50%. For the submerged-arc process the flux usage ratio is 1.5 kg/kg (lb/lb) of flux to metal and the flux cost is $0.88/kg

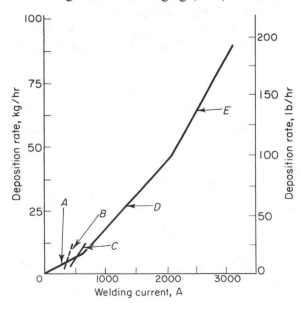

Figure 14-12 Average performance with several arc-welding processes: (A) manual shielded-arc welding with $\frac{3}{16}$-in. electrode; (B) semiautomatic gas, metal-arc welding; (C) semiautomatic submerged-arc welding; (D) fully automatic submerged-arc welding with single electrode; (E) fully automatic submerged-arc welding with multiple electrodes.

TABLE 14-1 RELATIVE UNIT WELDING COSTS FOR SEVERAL COMMON PROCESSES

Factor of cost	Type of operation			
	Conventional metal-arc with coated electrode	Metal-arc with powder-metal electrode	Semi-automatic submerged-arc	Semi-automatic gas-shielded
Electrode diameter [mm (in.)]	4.8 ($\frac{3}{16}$)	4.0 ($\frac{5}{32}$)	2.0 ($\frac{5}{64}$)	1.2 ($\frac{3}{64}$)
Travel speed [mm/min (ipm)]	510 (20)	635 (25)	890 (35)	890 (35)
Duty cycle (%)	30	35	45	60
Electrode cost [$/kg ($/lb)]	1.75 (0.80)	2.20 (1.00)	1.50 (0.68)	2.65 (1.20)
Deposition eff (%)	68	70	100	92
Welding current (A)	300	350	500	450
Nominal arc potential (V)	30	30	35	32
Unit weld cost [$/m ($/ft)]	3.52 (1.07)	2.66 (0.81)	1.68 (0.51)	1.41 (0.43)

($0.40/lb). For the CO_2 gas process, the gas flow is 0.85 m³/h (30 ft³/h) and the gas cost is $1.40/m³ ($0.04/ft³).

In Table 14-1, the *duty cycle* is the percentage that arc time is of the total operation time. Other than arc or active welding time is that required to change electrodes, chip slag, handle flux, and make adjustments, and for personal needs, fit-up, etc. The manual CO_2 gas-shielded process has the least lost time largely because it has no flux or slag to handle. The *deposition efficiency* is the percentage that the usable metal deposited in the weld is of the total weight of electrode used. Some of the loss is from stub ends with stick electrodes.

Table 14-1 applies to a particular situation and is presented to show how costs are compared. Under other circumstances the data might very well show the conventional metal-arc process with coated electrode or with iron powder electrode to be most economical. Such a case could occur in a job shop where the costs of adapting the semiautomatic methods to a large variety of jobs would be excessive. Another case could be that of welding the framework of a high structure on which the semiautomatic equipment would be too difficult if not impossible to manipulate.

ENERGY-RAY WELDING

Electron-Beam Welding. Energy may be supplied for welding and cutting by directing a concentrated beam of electrons to bombard the work in the manner depicted in Fig. 14-13. The beam is created in a high vacuum. If the work is done in a vacuum of around 10^{-4} torr, no electrodes, gases, or filler metal need contaminate it, and pure

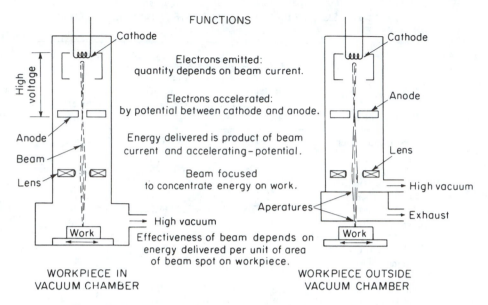

FUNCTIONS

Electrons emitted:
quantity depends on beam current.

Electrons accelerated:
by potential between cathode and anode.

Energy delivered is product of beam
current and accelerating-potential.

Beam focused
to concentrate energy on work.

Effectiveness of beam depends on
energy delivered per unit of area
of beam spot on workpiece.

WORKPIECE IN   WORKPIECE OUTSIDE
VACUUM CHAMBER   VACUUM CHAMBER

Figure 14-13 Schematic diagram of an electron-beam welding operation.

welds can be made. Electron-beam (EB) welding can do the same jobs as Tig and plasma-arc welding; in some respects it is better. The beam of energy can be highly concentrated (up to 50 times as much as in arc-welding) with power densities to 3 MW/cm² (20 MW/in.²) to melt and even vaporize ferrous and nonferrous refractory, dissimilar, and even reactive metals. Welds can be confined to shallow depth or extended to as much as 200 mm (8 in.) deep with a depth-to-width ratio as high as 100 to 1 (compared with 1 to 1 for other fusion techniques). This means that melting can be confined to quite narrow limits and done fast so that the heat-affected zone is small. Welding traverse rates may be high; grain size remains small, and welds are essentially straight sided. A notable application for cutting is producing very small diameter holes, particularly in hard materials.

If welding is done in a high vacuum, considerable time may be lost if the chambers must be pumped down for each new piece (from 1 minute or less for small chambers to 20 minutes or so for large ones). One machine has twin chambers in which work is done alternately. Air locks and seals have been utilized for slipping piece after piece into position or passing long pieces through a chamber. Another approach is to pass the beam through two or more chambers with the welding done in a soft vacuum (10^{-1} to 10^{-3} torr) or even in the atmosphere, as illustrated in Fig. 14-13. Total operation time may be reduced to seconds, but some of the advantages of the process are lost. An electron beam is dispersed in a gas in proportion to the density of the medium; for example, about three times as much energy as in a high vacuum is required for a given penetration after an electron beam has passed through 10 mm ($\frac{3}{8}$ in.) of gas at atmospheric pressure. Thus the weld is wide and not as deep, and contamination occurs.

Electron-beam welding can be justified when it can produce results not obtainable by other means, i.e., reduction or elimination of filler metal and contamination, less joint preparation, access to hard-to-reach places, and least heat affect on the parent metal with little distortion. In some cases electron-beam welding is economical because it is faster. In any case, the advantages must be enough to make up for a high first cost. Medium-size systems range in prices from about $200,000 to $400,000; the largest and most advanced costs over $1,000,000. A leading maker offers models ranging in rated sizes from 6 to 35 kW for high vacuum, 10 to 15 kW for partial vacuum, and 12 to 25 kW for nonvacuum welders. Equipment cost depends to a large extent upon the rate and amount of vacuum that must be drawn. High potentials require lead shielding to protect the operator from X-rays.

Heat treating is done by soft-focusing an electron beam and under computer direction making it impinge as an array of dots over the surface to control temperature. As an example, in this way rocker arm pads are hardened over an area of about 500 mm² ($\frac{3}{4}$ in.²) in 2.2 seconds at a cost of 0.365 cent with power at 5 cents/kWh. Heating is so rapid and closely controlled that adjacent metal stays cool and serves as a quencher.

The Laser. A high-energy light beam capable of welding, cutting, and heat treating metal and other materials is produced by a laser (an acronym of "light amplification by stimulated emission of radiation"). A suitable medium, such as a crystal (e.g., ruby) or gas mixture (mainly CO_2), is stimulated, a crystal by a bright flash of light in the manner depicted in Fig. 14-14 or a gas by an electrical discharge. Ions in the substance are raised to an unsteady energy level. Then they fall back and release an intense burst of a single monochromatic light. The wavelength depends upon the medium; some are better than others for various purposes. The light is amplified by reflection from one end, and the surge of light from the other end of the laser is focused by a conventional optical system.

Solid-state laser equipment is compact but less than 2% efficient, and the heat generated limits it to a pulsed output of low capacity. One system of that kind is rated at 400 W, can deliver 29 J/pulse with duration of 0.65 ms, up to 100 pulses per second, and costs about $40,000. With three to five axes, part manipulator, and computer

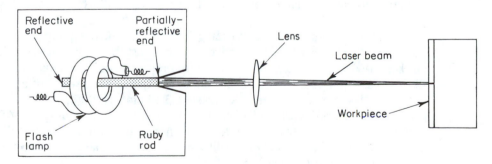

Figure 14-14   Laser system.

numerical control (Chap. 35), the cost is about \$175,000. Gas lasers are 15% or so efficient, and gases can be circulated for effective cooling. Such systems may be pulsed but usually are lased continuously. A drawback is that CO_2 lasers do not work well on aluminum and some other materials because the wavelength is not absorbed efficiently. A machine that employs an 800-W continuous laser that is traversed by numerical control and applied anywhere over a 1.6 m (63 in.) by 2 m (79 in.) work surface with facilities for oxygen-assisted cutting is quoted at around \$350,000. A large 15-kW CO_2 laser unit has a price of \$1,000,000. High equipment cost limits lasers to applications not quickly or readily done by more conventional methods.

Laser welding may be done in a number of ways and has several advantages. A seam may be welded by a series of overlapping fused spots with a pulsed laser or continuously by a powerful gas laser. Gas lasers are twice as fast or more than solid-state lasers. A laser beam can be precisely controlled and directed almost anywhere and concentrated as needed, even on minute spots on microelectronic devices. Welds can be made inside transparent enclosures, such as in vacuum tubes, or to join fine wires inside their insulation. Otherwise inaccessible areas can be welded by means of mirrors. The process is ideal for automated operation because the weightless beam is easy to manipulate.

Normally, a small puddle is melted and frozen in milliseconds by a laser, and the heat-affected zone is confined to 0.25 mm (0.010 in.) or less. The time in the molten state is too short for appreciable chemical reaction, and little or no protection is needed from the atmosphere. The beam does not add foreign substances to the weld.

Tremendous amounts of energy can be delivered when needed by a laser. Laser beams have been concentrated to small spots of light with densities up to almost 5 GW/cm^2 (30 $GW/in.^2$), enough to vaporize almost any metal in an instant. It takes from 1 to 150 MW/cm^2 (10 to 100 $MW/in.^2$) for normal melting and cutting operations. The length of time that an intense beam impinges on any one spot is limited so that only the amount of energy needed is delivered over the area processed.

In addition to welding, lasers have many applications in surface hardening of metals and cutting operations such as drilling of tiny holes and slicing, trimming, and scribing of ceramics, semiconductors, films, cloth, wood, and plastics and metal sheets. A laser can do a variety of work because the light beam can easily be focused by optics and moved about as needed. Laser action is illustrated below by several typical operations.

In heat treatment the metal is heated far below the melting point. A concentrated light beam may be oscillated to produce a raster to distribute the heat over a large area and keep the temperature within the required range. Cast iron is surface treated by 5 kW of laser power traversed at 1.5 m/min (60 ipm) over a width of about 15 mm (0.6 in.). This puts in an average of about 1.3 kJ/cm^2 (8 $Btu/in.^2$).

Enough energy must be delivered to melt the metal in welding. A 5456 aluminum alloy 6 mm ($\frac{1}{4}$ in.) thick is welded at 2.3 m/min (90 ipm) rate with 8 kW of laser power. Average width of weld is about 2 mm (0.08 in.), and average surface energy input is 10.4 kJ/cm^2 (64 $Btu/in.^2$).

In cutting steel, much of the heat in the kerf is obtained by injecting oxygen to burn the metal, as in flame and electric-arc cutting (pp. 382–388). Carbon steel 6 mm ($\frac{1}{4}$ in.) thick is reported cut at the rate of 1.0 m/min (39.4 ipm) by an 800-W laser. Typical for cutting is a kerf of 1 mm (0.04 in.). Average surface energy input is 4.8 kJ/cm² (30 Btu/in.²). Holes from 0.25 to 1.25 mm (0.01 to 0.05 in.) diameter are drilled to depths up to 15 mm (0.6 in.) in most alloys by pulsed lasers that generate 50-J pulses. The average surface energy input is 11.3 kJ/cm² (69 Btu/in.²) per pulse.

Laser and electron-beam systems can do many chores alike but in effect seem to supplement each other. Both can be concentrated to melt any metal, but energy transfer is more efficient with the electron beam, and laser penetration takes more power. For laser heat treatment the work surface needs to have a dark coating to absorb light, and that adds cost. On the other hand, a laser does not need a vacuum; the beam can travel to almost any length in air, and is not deflected by magnetic fields.

RESISTANCE WELDING

Principles.   Resistance welding is done by passing an electric current through two pieces of metal pressed together. The pieces coalesce at the surfaces of contact because more resistance and heat are concentrated there. The heat is localized where needed, the action is rapid, no filler metal is needed, the operation requires little skill and can easily be automated, and these advantages make the process suitable for large-quantity production. All the common metals and dissimilar metals can be re-sistance welded although special precautions are necessary for some. The parent metal is normally not harmed, and none is lost. Many difficult shapes and sections can be processed.

The main disadvantage of resistance welding is that equipment cost is high. Ample work must be ready to justify the investment. Some jobs call for special equipment, such as fixtures, which add appreciably to the investment. A high order of skill is required to set up and maintain the apparatus.

Resistance welding is usually done with ac from the line stepped down through a transformer and applied for a length of time controlled by a timer. A typical circuit is depicted in Fig. 14-15. The heat generated in a circuit is $H = I^2RTK$, where I is the current in amperes, R the resistance in ohms, T the time of duration of the current flow in seconds, and K a conversion factor from kW to the unit of heat desired.

The electrodes that carry the electricity to the work also press the pieces together. The current meets resistance in the metal but more so at the surfaces of contact. The most heat is generated where the resistance is highest. Thus the aim is to put the most resistance and heat at the *faying surfaces* between the workpieces to make a sure weld without harming the electrodes. Under pressure, melting of the metal is not always necessary for coalescence. The heat distribution that occurs in a satisfactory operation is indicated by the diagram of Fig. 14-15.

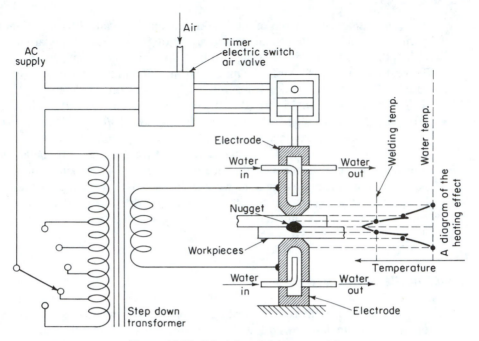

Figure 14-15   Principles of resistance welding.

Outside the zone to be welded the temperature should be low to conserve the electrodes. This is done by conducting away as much heat as possible and generating as little heat as possible where it is not needed. The electrodes are normally water-cooled to carry away heat. The heat generated at any point is proportional to the resistance. Electrodes are made of copper to conduct electricity and heat well but are alloyed and faced with other elements for good bearing strength and endurance. Clean and smooth workpiece surfaces promote low resistance and help preserve electrodes.

When the work and electrode materials have nearly the same resistance, they tend to weld together. Low-resistance metals like copper and silver are hard to weld. Aluminum with a conductivity about two-thirds that of copper requires a high current of short duration so that the weld zone is brought to welding temperature before the heat spreads. Special copper-tungsten alloy electrodes are recommended for aluminum.

Metals of medium and high resistance, such as steel, stainless steel, Monel metal, and silicon bronze, are easy to weld. When heat-treatable steel is welded, heat sinks rapidly into the surrounding metal mass, and the weld is more or less quenched to a hard and brittle state. This can be corrected by annealing or tempering in a separate furnace or on the welding machine. In the latter case, a second surge of metered current is put through the workpiece to reheat it to a drawing temperature before it is released.

High-frequency resistance welding is done with 400 to 450 kHz current commonly supplied by an oscillator. The high-frequency current readily breaks through oxide film barriers and produces a thin heat-affected zone because it travels on the surface of the material. It is applicable to joining metals from 0.1 to 20 mm (0.004 to 0.75 in.) thick into structural shapes, pipes, or tubes in the manner depicted in Fig. 12-11(C).

The principles that have been discussed are applied in several processes to suit various purposes. These are spot, projection, seam, upset- and flash-butt, and percussion welding. The features of each will be discussed.

Resistance Welding Equipment. There is no universal machine to do all kinds of resistance welding, but several basic features are common to the various forms of equipment. Common to all machines are a power supply, a system of controls, a mechanical drive, and a structure.

Most resistance welders operate on ac from a single-phase transformer as indicated in Fig. 14-15. This causes a low power factor and a serious unbalance in three-phase power systems. Better circuits are available, particularly on large machines, to utilize a three-phase system efficiently and reduce the load on the power source.

One capacity of a resistance welding machine is designated in kilovolt-amperes (kVA). The rating is based on a 50% duty cycle and means the welder will carry that kVA at 50% duty cycle and not exceed a safe specified temperature rise. The kVA rating is the product of the welding current times the secondary voltage. Actually, a machine can do a job with a higher kVA demand than its rating but at a lower duty cycle, or vice versa.

Any resistance welding machine must have means to adjust the amount and duration of current flow to suit various jobs and conditions. Early machines had manual or mechanical controls, as do some low cost ones today, but these do not give accurate results and are not adequate for large currents. A simple control for the amount of current consists of taps on the transformer primary. Another is an auto-transformer that varies the voltage impressed on the primary of the welding transformer. A common method that gives current adjustment in infinite steps is phase-shift control. This is done by altering the magnitude and wave shape of the current to the transformer primary by means of tubes or solid-state devices. By still another method, called slope control, the starting current is allowed to rise gradually to reach a peak in 3 to 25 cycles as desired.

Modern high-grade controls for switching the current on and off are electronic. They start or stop the current to the welding transformer at or just after the power factor angle in the phase relationship when the voltage is low. This eliminates transient currents which may occur when the current is switched at random in relation to its cycle. Such transients could reach several times the size of the steady current and burn electrodes and work.

Welding currents must be switched on and off in very short lengths of time and often repeatedly for modern applications. Pulsating currents with definite on and off time are often needed. A typical welding schedule might be 6 cycles on and 4 cycles off, repeated 10 times. Complex electronic controls are used to provide a large variety of pulsation schedules with times of $\frac{1}{2}$ cycle ($\frac{1}{120}$ second) or less to as long as desired with exact duplication over any time period desired.

Small resistance welders may be foot operated to hold the pieces together. Mechanical devices such as a power cam, air cylinders, magnetic solenoids, and hydraulic operation are all utilized. A common need is for delivery of the force in steps. A typical condition is to apply a moderate force during passage of the welding current to assure proper contact resistance. Then when welding temperature is attained and the current shut off, the force is increased considerably to complete the weld and forge the metal to help refine the grain structure. On most modern welders, the mechanical schedule is automatically controlled and synchronized with the electrical program.

Many welding machines have their electrodes on the ends of two long arms or horns to accommodate the work. The leads to the electrodes constitute a loop of the secondary circuit in which a heavy current flows. A metal workpiece in the throat between the horns may add considerably to the impedance of the loop and reduce appreciably the ac that can flow at a given voltage. The loss goes into heat generated throughout the workpiece by induction. The amount of impedance increase depends upon the magnetic properties of the material and how much of the workpiece extends into the loop.

Spot Welding.   Spot welding is the most common form of resistance welding and the simplest. It is commonly done on sheet metal up to about 3 mm ($\frac{1}{8}$ in.) thick, but sometimes even on thicker metals. The essentials are shown in Fig. 14-16. Electrodes with reduced ends are pressed against the work, the current is turned on and off, and the pressure is held or increased to forge the weld while it solidifies. This is commonly repeated in a series of spots along a joint.

If a welded spot between two sheets is sectioned, a small mass or nugget of metal is found embedded in and joining the sheets together as indicated by Fig. 14-16(C). If a good weld is pulled apart, the nugget remains intact, and the sheets tear around it.

If an attempt is made to weld several thicknesses of metal, the current tends to spread out between the electrodes as indicated by Fig. 14-16(D). Thus the current

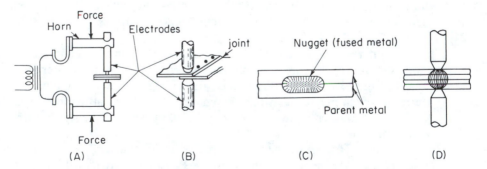

Figure 14-16   (A) Typical spot welding circuit; (B) spot-welded joint; (C) enlarged cross section through a spot weld; (D) indication of the way the current spreads out when passed through several sheets.

density is less at the inner than at the outer faying surfaces, and specific provisions have to be made to assure enough heat to get good welds at the inner surfaces without burning near and at the electrodes.

Sound welds are obtained consistently by applying the proper current density, timing, and electrode pressure uniformly in each case to clean surfaces. The results of tests are given in Fig. 14-17 to show the effects, in terms of weld strength, of the variables. One factor was varied at a time, and all other conditions were held constant. Welds were made with time values of 1 to 12 cycles at 60 Hz. No coalescence took place at less than 4 cycles with an 8900-A current; that is, the peak of the temperature curve depicted in Fig. 14-15 did not rise above the welding temperature. Weld incipience would occur in less time with higher currents; later with lower current. For time periods longer than the minimum for coalescence, the size and strength of the weld increase with time but at a descending rate. Little additional benefit can be expected from still longer time periods, and long time periods give the heat a chance to spread and harm the workpiece and electrodes.

As welding current was increased above 3100 A with other conditions constant, the size and strength of the weld rose and then fell (Fig. 14-17). The two high tests at 10,600 and 11,800 A showed considerable electrode indentation into the work-pieces and squeezing of the metal out of the weld at the electrode pressure applied. Under a given set of conditions, usable current is limited.

The tests of Fig. 14-17 indicate that there is an optimum electrode pressure for a given set of conditions. At this pressure, strength is highest and indentation low. It is commonly held that one sign of a good spot weld is little or no indentation from the electrode tip. Here are the reasons for optimum performance. As the electrode force is increased, the resistance decreases at the faying surfaces between the metal sheets. The heat generated is proportional to the resistance. In these tests, large amounts of metal melted and were squeezed out of the weld at low pressures because the re-

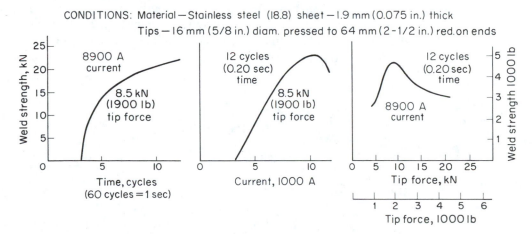

Figure 14-17   Curves showing how the strength of a spot weld varies with time, current, and tip force. (After Herbert Van Sciver.)

sistance and heat were high. The workpiece showed large indentations below but not above 4.5 kN (1000 lb) tip force. A maximum strength was reached with 8.5 kN (1900 lb) tip force. For larger forces, the resistance at the faying faces was less, the heat less, the weld smaller, and the weld strength less.

The test results of Fig. 14-17 illustrate that there is an optimum balance of current, time, and force in a resistance welding operation, and they depend on the material and its size. Too much current causes excessive indentation in a given operation. Typical values for a conventional system are indicated in Fig. 14-17. However, a newer system utilizes much higher currents over time periods of a few milliseconds. It is reported to give a minimum heat effect without marring finished or painted surfaces, but the equipment costs several times as much as the conventional kind. In any case, the ideal condition is for the temperature to be low at the electrodes (Fig. 14-15) and to rise sharply to a suitable peak at the interface of the workpieces. Both current and time are increased to spot weld thicker pieces because more heat is needed. Electrode size is also increased to carry the heavier current. The electrode force is increased even more. Operating specifications for various materials and sizes are given in handbooks and are usually adjusted to find the best conditions for any particular operation. Adaptive control of spot welding is described in Chap. 35.

Fatigue life of spot welds is low. Sometimes spots are coined (p. 307) after welding to increase fatigue life. Spot welding has not been favored for aircraft because of low fatigue life, but some combinations of spot welding with adhesive bonding have been found satisfactory.

Heat Balance.   Two pieces to be resistance welded together should be heated the same amount so the weld becomes attached equally well to both. The principles will be explained for the simple case of spot welding but apply to other forms, too. If a thin and thick piece of the same metal are welded between electrodes as indicated in Fig. 14-18, the thick one has more resistance and receives more heat. One solution is to make the electrode tip on the thinner piece of smaller diameter than the other. This raises the current density in the thin piece. Another solution is to face one electrode with a highly resistant material such as tungsten or molybdenum. The same problem exists for two metals of different conductivity. The one of higher conductivity may be made thicker to realize a heat balance.

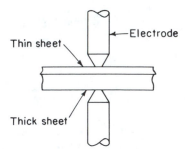

Figure 14-18 Illustration of the problem of heat balance.

Spot Welding Machines.   Spot welders may be classified as standard stationary machines, special multiple-electrode machines, and portable welders.

Portable spot welders are needed for large assemblies or spots hard to reach,
e.g., rail-freight cars. A *welding gun* consists of a pair of caliper arms carrying
electrodes with means for clamping them together. The transformer may be attached
for low impedance or may be a separate unit. The gun is normally suspended from a
spring-loaded cable on an overhead trolley. Controls are in a separate cabinet. One line
of spot welding guns ranges from manually operated models rated at about 3 kVA and
weighing 14 kg (30 lb) to air-operated, water-cooled models rated from 15 to 85 kVA
and weighing as much as 116 kg (256 lb).

A standard stationary spot welding machine, like the one in Fig. 14-19, has an
upper and lower horn carrying the electrodes and extending from an upright frame.
Two types are the rocker arm spot welders and the press-type spot or projection
welders. The upper horn on the rocker arm type is pivoted in the frame and is tilted
upward to open the gap and downward to apply the electrodes. The press type has a
ram on the end of the upper horn that moves the electrode straight up and down. The
various kinds of power sources, electrical circuits, controls, and mechanical drives
described for resistance welders in general are found in spot welders.

Figure 14-19   View of a spot welding machine in operation. (Courtesy Sciaky
Bros., Inc.)

Common sizes of standard stationary spot welders are 5 to 500 kVA. They are also rated by depth of throat, which designates the largest size of workpiece accommodated, commonly 200 to 900 mm (8 to 36 in.). Single-phase 150-kVA spot welders are quoted at $12,000 to $20,000, depending on features. A three-phase spot welder delivers more power for the same kVA rating and is advantageous for some work, such as welding aircraft aluminum alloys and high-heat resistant, gas turbine engine alloys. A 125-kVA three-phase spot welder has a price of $50,000.

Special spot welding machines with many combinations of electrodes are found on high-production jobs. Special care is needed to make multiple welds by using two or more electrodes in parallel on a welding machine to get equal current distribution to the welds. One system used one common welding transformer and a hydraulic cylinder for each electrode pair. The electrodes are brought in contact with the work one pair at a time. In another system, all electrodes are pressed against the work at one time, and the current from the transformer secondary is commutated to one electrode pair at a time. Some machines have a separate transformer and controls for each electrode set. Special machines are built in many sizes and shapes, each to suit its own job. Some have been built to weld hundreds of spots in a single operation. They are rapid, obviate handling the work between welds, and are economical for large-quantity production. Some of the largest special spot welders, such as one to weld the panels and top of an automobile body together, may cost $1 million, and more.

Projection Welding.   Projection welding is done like spot welding, but the current is concentrated at the spots to be welded by projections preformed on the work as indicated in Fig. 14-20. The electrodes are relatively large and are subject to a low current density, so they stand up well. The process is fast because a number of spots can be welded in one closure of the press.

Projections for welding may be made on sheet metal, cast, forged, or machined parts. A variation is called *stud welding*. A stud with its ends rounded is held in one electrode and pressed against its mating part while current flows to heat the weld. The

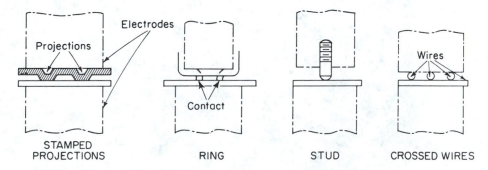

Figure 14-20   Types of projection welds.

effect of projection welding is obtained with crossed wires, such as might be welded together into a grill.

A metal must have sufficient hot strength to be projection welded successfully. For this reason aluminum is seldom welded by this process, and copper and some brasses not at all. Free-cutting steels high in phosphorus and sulfur must not be projection welded because the welds are porous and brittle. Most other steels are readily projection welded. The projections should be in the heavier of two mating parts so they will not be burned off before the weld is completed.

Spot welding machines may be used for projection welding with the proper electrodes. Machines specifically for projection welding are like press type spot welders and are rigidly built to hold parts in alignment during an operation. Projection welds usually require more current over shorter lengths of time and more pressure than spot welds.

Seam Welding.   A *seam weld* is a series of spot welds either overlapping or spaced at short intervals. The latter is called a *roll spot weld* or *stitch weld*. Seam welding is done by passing the work between revolving roller electrodes as shown in Fig. 14-21 or between a fixed bar and welding electrodes. A coolant is applied to conserve the electrodes and cool the work rapidly to speed the operation. Commonly, the rollers run continuously along a seam, and the current is interrupted. Another method utilizes a steady current with intermittent motion of the rollers or with notched rollers. Surfaces to be seam welded must be thoroughly cleaned, descaled, and deoxidized for satisfactory results. Pickling is a preferred method of preparing surfaces.

Both lap and butt joints may be seam welded. Continuous seams are gas and liquid tight. Seam welding is done on metal sheets and plates from 0.075 to 4.75 mm (0.003 to 0.187 in.) thick with standard equipment and up to 9.5 mm ($\frac{3}{8}$ in.) thick with special machines. Seam welding is done mostly on low-carbon, alloy, and stainless steels but also on many other metals including aluminum, brass, titanium, and tantalum. Typical seam welded products are mufflers, barrels, and tanks. Specifications for proper seam proportions and designs for various materials and applications are tabulated in handbooks. A good seam is stronger than the parent metal.

A seam welding machine may be made to do either flat (horizontal) or circular work or both. Seam welders have much the same elements as spot welding machines and also are classed as rocker arm and press types. In addition, a seam welder must have a drive for turning the rollers and be able to supply heavy currents and forces. Current must be strong because much of it is lost through spots near the weld of the moment. An ordinary duty cycle for seam welding may be as high as 80% while spot welding is seldom over 10%. A recommended pressure for low-carbon steel is 100 MPa (15,000 psi). Sturdy construction is necessary for the heavy forces. Good-quality controls are necessary for precise timing. Accordingly, a fully equipped seam welder may cost $1\frac{1}{2}$ or more times as much as a spot welder with the same kVA rating and other features.

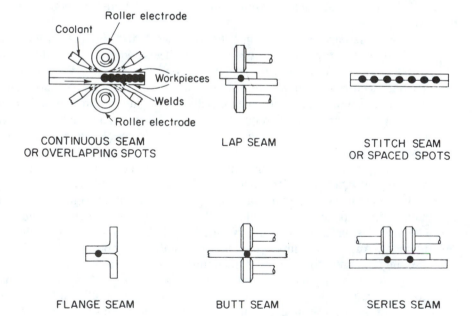

Figure 14-21   Seam welder and sketches of common types of welded seams. (Photo Courtesy Taylor-Winfield Corp.)

Upset-Butt Welding. Upset-butt welding consists of pressing two pieces of metal together end to end and passing a current through them. Current densities range from about 300 to 800 A/cm^2 (2000 to 5000 A/in.^{2}). The resistance of the contiguous surfaces under light pressure heats the joint. Then the pressure is increased. This helps metal from the two parts to coalesce and squeezes some metal out into a *flash* or *upset* as depicted in Fig. 14-22. The current may be interrupted one or more times for large areas. Final pressures range from about 15 to 55 MPa (2500 to 8000 psi) depending on the material. Too little pressure leaves a porous and low-strength joint; too much squeezes out an excess of plastic metal and makes a joint of low impact strength.

Metal is not melted when upset-butt welded, and there is no spatter. The upset is smooth, symmetrical, and not ragged, but the ends of the pieces usually must be machined before welding. Most metals can be upset welded. Common applications are the joining of wires and bars end to end, welding of a projection to a piece, and welding together the ends of a loop to make a wheel rim.

Flash-Butt Welding. Two pieces to be flash welded are clamped with their ends not quite touching. A current with a density of 300 to 800 A/cm^2 (2000 to 5000 A/in.^{2}) is applied to a piece and arcs across the joint in a flash that melts the metal at the ends of the pieces as indicated in Fig. 14-23. A pressure of about 35 to 140 MPa (5000 to 20,000 psi) is applied suddenly to close the joint, clear out voids, and extrude impurities. On upsetting, the current density may rise as high as 8000 A/cm^2 (50,000 A/in.^{2}). Flying particles of molten metal expelled from the joint are detrimental to equipment and personnel and present a fire hazard.

Most commercial metals may be flash welded. Pieces welded together in this way should each have about the same area at the joint. Common applications are the end welding of sheets, strips, and bars. An example is flash welding the end of one coil of stock to the next for uninterrupted passage of material through a continuous rolling mill. A flash weld has a small amount of sharp and ragged upset material around the joint. Because the metal is melted, a weld of full strength may be obtained

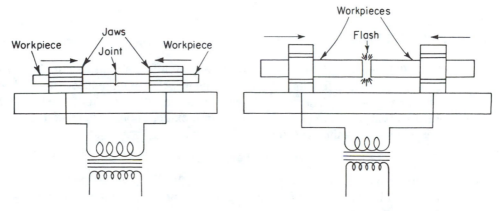

Figure 14-22 Upset-butt welding.   **Figure 14-23** Flash-butt welding.

even with dissimilar metals. The ends of the pieces need no preparation. Flash welding requires less power, is faster, and heats the whole piece less than upset welding.

Magnetarc welding is a form of flash-butt welding to join steel tubes with a minimum wall of thickness of 3 mm ($\frac{1}{8}$ in.) and a maximum outside dimension of 50 mm (2 in.). A magnetic coil energized by an alternating current is placed around the joint between two workpieces held as in Fig. 14-23. A shielding gas is injected. An arc is struck between the pieces and rotates around the joint under the influence of the magnetic field. When the ends of the pieces are heated to forging temperature, they are forced together to complete the weld. This process is reported to take less current and time, require less force, and to produce less flash than any of the others for joining tubing.

Both upset- and flash-butt welding have the advantages over other joining operations of giving reliable joints, being fast and of low cost, handling dissimilar metals and shapes not suitable for other processes, and requiring little operating skill on readily available equipment. Extruded metal generally must be removed from around the joints.

Percussion or Percussive Welding. Two parts to be percussion welded are clamped end to end but some distance apart. One is on a spring-loaded slide. When the machine is tripped, the one part is hurled into contact with the other. The parts are connected to the terminals of a high-voltage charged condenser that flashes an arc between them for about 0.001 second before they touch. The arc fuses a layer about 80 μm (0.003 in.) thick on the end of each part. The molten and softened metal is forged into a weld as the parts slam together.

Percussion welding is a fast method of joining and gives very little splatter, flash, and heat-affected zone. It can handle dissimilar metals. The process is limited to welding areas of less than 3 cm^2 ($\frac{1}{2}$ in.^{2}). For connecting small wires to electrical components, percussive welding has been found to give strong and more reliable joints than crimping or soldering but to be more expensive for making less than millions of joints because equipment is relatively expensive.

THERMIT WELDING

Principles. Thermit welding is done by filling a joint with molten metal that is obtained by reducing its oxide by aluminum. Aluminum reduces any oxide but that of magnesium, but Thermit welding is done mostly with iron, steel, and copper. Finely divided aluminum and magnetic iron oxide, in proportions of 1:3 by weight, are mixed and ignited and react as follows:

$$8Al + 3Fe_3O_4 \longrightarrow 9Fe + 4Al_2O_3$$

The reaction raises the temperature to 2500 to 2800°C (ca. 4500 to 5000°F). The metal produced is about one-half of the original mixture by weight or one-third by volume.

Procedure. The first step in making a Thermit weld is to prepare a mold for the metal. The pieces to be welded are positioned and fastened in place. A wax pattern of the weld desired is made around the joint, and a sand mold is rammed around the zone to be welded. A typical setup is illustrated in Fig. 14-24. A torch is inserted into the mold to melt out the wax and heat the workpieces to cherry red.

The Thermit mixture is placed in a crucible and ignited by a welding torch or by the addition of a small amount of barium peroxide and magnesium ribbon. The reaction takes about 30 seconds to produce up to a ton or more of metal, which flows into the mold around the parts to be welded. The superheated weld metal fuses appreciable amounts of the parent metal, and all solidifies on cooling into a strong and homogeneous weld. Later the mold is torn down, gates and risers are removed, and the weld is chipped and cleaned.

Applications. Thermit welding is largely, but not entirely, applied to joining heavy sections. It is able to supply a large quantity of heat rapidly to parts that have large heat capacities. Typical jobs are the joining of cables, conductors, rails, shafts, and broken machinery frames and rebuilding of large gears. Forgings and flame cut sections may be joined in this way to make huge parts. Sometimes this is the only feasible method and often it is the fastest method of welding large pieces. The composition of the weld metal may be controlled by the addition of steel scrap or

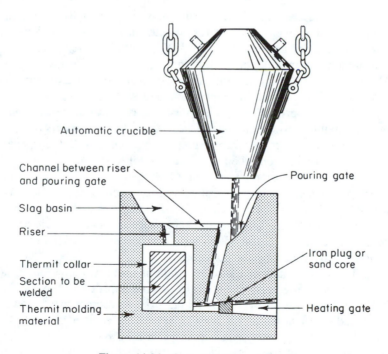

Figure 14-24 Thermit welding process.

various alloys in oxide form in the original mixture. Tensile strengths from 340 to 760 MPa (50,000-110,000 psi) and elongations of 20 to 40% in 50 mm (2 in.) are commonly obtained. Thermit welds are considered better than cast steel, and test specimens can be bent flat on themselves. Complete deoxidation occurs, slag has ample egress, and air is excluded from the weld. Slow cooling relieves stresses.

GAS WELDING

Gas welding is done by burning a combustible gas with air or oxygen in a concentrated flame of high temperature. As with other welding methods, the purpose of the flame is to heat and melt the parent and filler metal of a joint. Much gas welding has been replaced by faster electric-arc and resistance welding but gas welding still has important uses. Its temperatures are lower and controllable, which is necessary for delicate work, such as for sheet metal and tubing. It can weld most common materials. Equipment is inexpensive, versatile, usually portable, and serves adequately in many job and general repair shops. Probably of more importance is that gas heating is the means for pre- and postheating, flame cutting, metal spraying, braze welding, brazing, and soldering. The processes are described later but what is said here about the fuels applies to them.

Fuel Gases.   Acetylene is the most important hydrocarbon in the welding industry. Newer stabilized mixtures of methylacetylene-propadiene, known as MAPP, have been gaining favor. Other commercial fuel gases are hydrogen, propane, butane, and natural and manufactured illuminating gas, and chlorine burned with hydrogen. The properties that explain the advantage of acetylene are compared with those of propane (as an example of other kinds of gases) in Table 14-2.

Acetylene produces higher temperatures than other gases because it contains more available carbon and releases heat when its components (C and H) dissociate to combine with oxygen and burn. Most other fuel gases, like propane, absorb some of the heat of combustion when their elements dissociate.

Acetylene is colorless and has a sweetish but to many an obnoxious odor. It is generated industrially by a controlled reaction of calcium carbide in water; the formula is $CaC_2 + 2H_2O = C_2H_2 + Ca(OH)_2$. The calcium carbide is a gray stone-like substance made by fusing limestone and coke together in an electric furnace. The gas may be generated in a central plant and compressed into cylinders for distribution or generated as needed by the customer.

The main disadvantage of acetylene is that it is dangerous if not handled carefully. By law, free acetylene is limited to pressures of 100 to 140 kPa (15 to 20 psi) because it explodes at over 170 kPa (25 psi), and sometimes below. However, it can be stored safely at about 1.4 MPa (200 psi) if dissolved in acetone. A steel tank or cylinder for storing acetylene is packed with 80% porous material such as asbestos, balsa wood, charcoal, infusorial earth, silk fiber, or kapok. The packing is saturated thoroughly with acetone which is capable of absorbing acetylene to the extent of 25

TABLE 14-2 SOME PROPERTIES OF GASES FOR WELDING AND CUTTING

Property	Units	Acetylene, C_2H_2	MAPP C_3H_4	Propane, C_3H_8
Gross heat of combustion	MJ/kg (Btu/lb)	50.0 (21,500)	49.0 (21,100)	50.4 (21,700)
Heat released	MJ/kg (Btu/lb)	8.6 (3720)	4.7 (2020)	
Heat absorbed	MJ/kg (Btu/lb)			2.4 (1020)
Oxygen required	kg/kg (lb/lb)	3.1	3.2	7.3
Heat in combustion products	MJ/kg (Btu/lb)	13.56 (5830)	11.70 (5030)	8.02 (3450)
Maximum flame temperature (burned in O_2)	°C (°F)	3087 (5589)	2927 (5301)	2526 (4579)
Cost for flame cutting[a]		$5.42	$5.18	$5.96

[a]Relative costs to cut 30.5 m (100 ft) of 25-m (1-in.)-thick low-carbon steel plate with oxygen at $0.18/m³ ($0.50/100 ft³) as reported in *Metals Handbook*, Vol. 4, American Society for Metals, Metals Park, Ohio, p. 284.

times its volume per atmosphere of pressure. Gas is forced in to charge the cylinder and withdrawn for use through a valve on top of the cylinder. Safety fuse plugs are provided to relieve the pressure upon exposure to fire. As a safety measure, tanks are emptied in use at a rate not exceeding $\frac{1}{3}$ tank/hr.

MAPP is comparable to acetylene in performance and cost as indicated in Table 14-2 but can be stabilized by additives. Thus MAPP as available commercially can be handled and subjected to shocks without danger. It can be stored at pressures of 1.4 MPa (200 psi) and over in simple tanks and used in high-pressure streams for faster operations, such as in metal spraying.

Fuel gases are burned with commercially pure oxygen for higher temperatures. For industrial purposes, oxygen is extracted by liquefaction of air and distributed in steel cylinders at about 14 MPa (2000 psi) pressure.

Hydrogen is burned with oxygen for low flame temperatures, below 1980°C (3600°F), advantageous for thin sheets and materials that must not be overheated. The flame can be made slightly reducing for good-quality welds free of oxides. The hydrogen is stored in cylinders at up to 14 MPa (2000 psi) pressure.

Oxyacetylene Gas Welding. Much oxyacetylene gas welding is done manually in the manner illustrated in Fig. 14-25. Gas coming from either the acetylene or oxygen tank is first reduced in pressure through a *regulator*. This is a diaphragm-operated valve that can be adjusted to let only enough gas out of the tank to maintain a desired pressure on the outlet side. Gages on each regulator show the tank and the hose pressures.

Hoses conduct the gases to the torch or blowpipe held by the operator. The torch mixes the two gases properly and emits them into the flame. It consists basically of

Figure 14-25   Oxyacetylene welding operation. (Courtesy Air Reduction Sales Co.)

regulating valves, body, mixing head, and a tip. A number of sizes of tips are available to give different sizes and intensities of flames for various purposes.

Torches are classified as *low-pressure* or *injector* and *medium-pressure*, also called *equal-* or *positive-pressure* types. Low-pressure torches operate at up to 35 kPa (5 psi), and medium-pressure torches in the range 7 to 100 kPa (1 to 15 psi) acetylene pressure. In the low-pressure type, high-pressure oxygen is injected through a venturi and draws the necessary amount of acetylene along through the mixing chamber and out through the tip. Both gases pass through the medium-pressure torch at about the same pressure.

Three distinct types of flames (Fig. 14-26) can be obtained from different mixtures of the gases. The *neutral flame* has no tendency to react with materials being welded. The highest temperature is at the tip of the inner cone and is capable of melting all commercial metals and many refractories. The *carburizing flame* is distinguished by a reddish feather at the tip of the inner cone. It is capable of reducing oxides. Steel will take up carbon deposited on the surface and start melting at a lower temperature. An *oxidizing flame* assures complete combustion and the highest temperature but has a strong tendency to oxidize metals being welded, which may be detrimental. Actually, heating is done with the inner cone, and the envelope of a flame shields and protects the weld zone from the atmosphere.

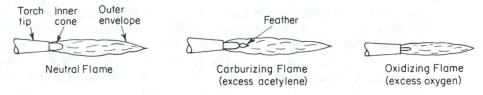

Figure 14-26 Types of oxyacetylene flames.

The operator in Fig. 14-25 is applying a welding rod to the weld with his right hand. Such rods supply filler metal, help control the impact of the flame, and restore elements lost from the parent metal. Flux is also employed in the welding of such metals as cast iron, some alloy steels, and nonferrous metals to dissolve and remove impurities, control surface tension, and give protection from the atmosphere. It is usually a paste in which the rod is dipped.

Three hundred dollars will provide the manual equipment for gas welding and flame-cutting operations. Automatic oxyacetylene welding machines are used for some production operations, but they operate on the same principles discussed for manual welding. They may cost several thousand dollars or more. Generally, they employ a number of small flames to obtain large amounts of heat.

Butt welding of steel can be done by oxyacetylene pressure welding. By one method called *closed-gap welding*, two pieces to be joined are pressed together, and the joint is heated by a torch or ring of torches until plastic. More pressure may then be applied, and heating is stopped to allow the joint to solidify. By a second method, the ends of two pieces are heated separately and then pressed quickly together. Applications of these methods include welding a piece of alloy steel to the end of a tool and joining pipeline sections and rails. This process is slower than electrofusion methods, but since metal is not melted, a cast structure is not formed at the joint, flash is not extruded, and cracking is minimized because the temperature gradient is not steep.

SOLID-STATE WELDING

Metals are held together by bonds between their atoms and crystals. Therefore, the atoms and crystals of two pieces must be brought into actual contact over their entire common area for a joint as strong as the parent material. Normally, even the smoothest surfaces touch only on a relatively few high spots when placed together. Also, metallic surfaces are covered with films of oxides and adsorbed gases and water vapor and are kept appreciable distances apart at the closest spots. Fusion welding overcomes the barriers between pieces because the atoms of molten metal flow together. If cold metal pieces are pressed together hard enough, the projections can be mashed down, to spread contact over wide areas, and oxides can be squeezed out. With some heat, the oxides become more fluent, and the metal more plastic, and less pressure is needed for welding. This is done to a certain extent in the electrical resistance welding operation and is the basis for *forge welding*, one of the oldest forms of welding, practiced from ancient times by armor makers and blacksmiths. It consists of heating two pieces to red heat, applying a flux such as borax, and completing the weld by hammering the metal on an anvil to press the joint together. Practice of the manual art is rare today, but some of the mechanical methods described here are counterparts. The processes described in this section are done by application of pressure with or without heat.

Friction Welding.   In friction welding, the ends of two pieces are pressed together while one is held still and the other revolved. Often the one piece is revolved in a spindle driven by a flywheel from which energy is drained, and so some people call the process *inertia welding*. Friction force between the abutting and sliding surfaces generates heat for welding and adds a forging component to that of pressure found alone in other butt-welding operations.

Common and unusual metals in similar and dissimilar pairs can be joined by friction welding for essentially round sections up to solid 100 mm (4 in.) in diameter (much larger for tubing) on standard machines. The process is attractive for small and large quantities; operation time is short, from 0.2 to 2 seconds. Pieces are shortened less than 0.5 mm (0.02 in.) as a rule, and there is little flash and waste. Under proper control of energy and pressure, the metal is worked thoroughly, the bond is clean and usually as strong as the base metal, and results are uniform from piece to piece. The workpiece must be able to stand a large torque. The operation emits no bright light, sparks, fumes, or loud noises. A friction welding machine for rod diameters from 15 to 60 mm ($\frac{5}{8}$ to $2\frac{1}{4}$ in.) or tubing from 25 to 90 mm (1 to $3\frac{1}{2}$ in.) diameter has a 30-kW (40-hp) drive motor and a base price of $125,000.

Ultrasonic Welding.   Two pieces may be bonded if pressed together and vibrated at ultrasonic frequency, one on the other, parallel to the contact interface. The ultrasonic transducer may be like the one in Fig. 29-5 but acting perpendicular to the direction of pressure. The vibrations shatter surface oxides and films and can tear right through dirt and surface coatings to establish intermingling of nascent metals. The surfaces become hot and plastic, and a solid metallurgical bond is produced. Welds may be made in spots or around rings in a second or less, or along seams at up to 120 m/min (ca. 400 fpm). The process is of advantage for thin wires, foils, and sheets of soft metals because no fusion occurs. There is no heat-affected zone, and dissimilar metals of similar hardness can be joined. No precleaning or filler metal is needed, and no contamination is introduced. The weld is as strong as the base metal. Even plastics of similar molecular structure are commonly joined by ultrasonic welding. Equipment is expensive; a small 2-kW unit may cost over $50,000.

Explosive Welding.   Surfaces may be joined by driving two pieces together with explosive force. Applications include cladding of sheets [up to 3 by 9 m (10 by 30 ft) in size] and simple forgings, lining and joining of tubes, and combining dissimilar metals into billets and various parts. Two pieces to be joined are placed a small distance apart, usually at an angle to each other, so that they collide along an advancing line when hit by the explosion. Under proper conditions, high pressures expel thin layers from impinging surfaces and crush the freshly exposed metal surfaces into intimate contact for a uniform bond. Heat is generated only incidentally, and no melting occurs. Thus quite dissimilar metals may be joined without thermal interaction. The equipment is simple, but explosive shocks require some isolation.

Diffusion Bonding.   Diffusion bonding is done by pressing pieces together while they are heated to below their melting temperatures, commonly in a vacuum or inert gas. Bonding takes place after a time because the base metals coalesce through interatomic diffusion. Surfaces to be joined must be machined flat and thoroughly cleaned to assure close contact over the entire area. Various metal interlayers (bonding aids) may be added (some are melted in the process) to reduce temperature and pressure needed, provide closer contact, obviate oxide films, fill voids, hasten diffusion, or serve as stop-off layers in selective bonding.

Heating and pressing are done in a variety of ways for diffusion bonding. Individual assemblies may be pressed in a die with heater elements in a hydraulic press, or subjected to a dead weight load in a furnace to apply forces in one direction. They may be processed in a heated pressure or vacuum chamber or autoclave for isostatic pressure. In a new method, called *thermomagnetic* or *electromagnetic* forming, the pieces to be joined are placed inside an induction coil and heated by eddy currents. Then a large capacitor bank is discharged through the coil, which induces currents of 40,000 to 100,000 A in the parts and sets up pressure at the joint reported up to around 350 MPa (50,000 psi). A series of such pulses completes a solid-state weld in less than 10 seconds, whereas older methods take minutes or hours. Continuous strips or sheets may be heated and then rolled together in *roll bonding*. In *continuous seam diffusion bonding*, a heavy current is passed between the rolls through the work to heat the narrow zone under pressure. Roll bonding exerts high pressure under the rolls and effectively disperses surface oxides and impurities. Thus no protective atmosphere is needed for some metals.

No fusion takes place and no filler metal is needed for diffusion bonding. Thus no weight is added, and the joint is as strong and temperature resistant as the base metal. No residual stress, excessive deformation, contamination, or crystal changes are introduced except by the severe rolling methods. The process is applicable to reactive and refractory metals, and for joining similar and many dissimilar metals and thick and quite thin pieces. The process is relatively costly and not competitive except for work difficult to join by other means, such as for joining heat-sensitive or brittle materials as well as thin plate or foil. Important uses include welding metals that cannot be fused readily such as zirconium and beryllium for nuclear reactor components and tungsten for aerospace parts, alternate layers of dissimilar metals for high strength at high temperatures, and thin honeycomb structures.

FUNDAMENTALS OF WELDING

Welded Joints and Symbols.   Common welded joints are illustrated in Fig. 14-27; each has several elements. These are the type of joint, the type of weld, and the preparation for the weld. The elements can be put together in various ways. For

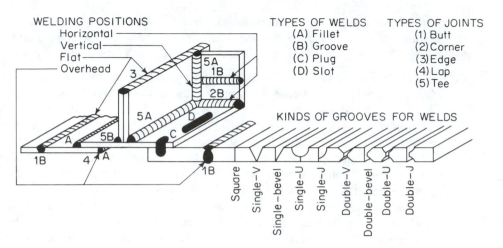

WELDING POSITIONS   TYPES OF WELDS   TYPES OF JOINTS
  Horizontal   (A) Fillet   (1) Butt
  Vertical   (B) Groove   (2) Corner
  Flat   (C) Plug   (3) Edge
  Overhead   (D) Slot   (4) Lap
                                                 (5) Tee

KINDS OF GROOVES FOR WELDS

Square   Single–V   Single–bevel   Single–U   Single–J   Double–V   Double–bevel   Double–U   Double–J

Figure 14-27   Types of welded joints.

example, a lap joint may be held by a fillet, plug, or slot weld, and a tee joint by a fillet or groove weld. The nature of the joint depends upon the kind and size of material, the process, and the strength required. Material less than 0.25 mm (0.010 in.) thick is usually lapped; thicker material is commonly butted. Butt joints are prepared for high-strength steels because they are more easily inspected and involve simpler stress patterns than lap joints. Lap joints are best for most pressure and resistance welding of sheets and for electron beam welding where no filler metal is added. A joint may be given no particular preparation, such as a square butt joint. That joint requires no filler metal and may be as much as 80% faster to weld than one that does, but a square butt joint depends on penetration into the edges of the piece and is not strong except for thin material. On the other hand, a grooved joint leads to a stronger weld but requires preparation, and that adds cost. A joint is selected in each case to fulfill requirements at lowest cost.

Proportions of welded joints have been standardized. Preferred sizes, dimensions, and charts for calculating the strengths of and amounts of filler metal required for welded joints are given in reference texts and handbooks.

Position, as defined in Fig. 14-27, is an important consideration for any welded joint. Gravity aids in putting down the weld metal into a flat position, which is the easiest and fastest to execute.

Precise instructions for any welded joint can be given on a drawing by a system of symbols and conventions. This is a special language and is governed by definite rules, like the rules of grammar. A full list of symbols and their meanings is given in reference books. Several illustrations are presented in Fig. 14-28.

Metallurgy of Welding.   The heat of welding affects the microstructure and composition of weld and base metal, causes expansion and contraction, and leaves stresses in the metal. A knowledge of what happens in metal when it is welded is necessary for an understanding of the welding operation, and will be explained here.

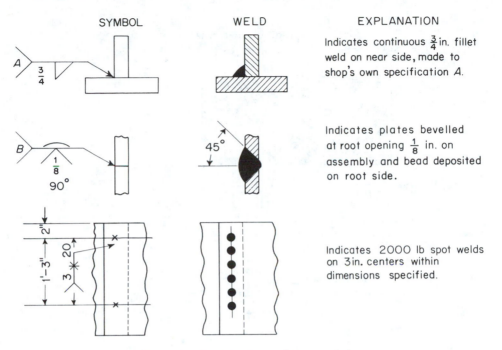

SYMBOL	WELD	EXPLANATION

Indicates continuous $\frac{3}{4}$ in. fillet weld on near side, made to shop's own specification A.

Indicates plates bevelled at root opening $\frac{1}{8}$ in. on assembly and bead deposited on root side.

Indicates 2000 lb spot welds on 3 in. centers within dimensions specified.

Figure 14-28 Examples of welding symbols.

For the sake of brevity the discussion will be directed mainly to steel, but some important considerations for other metals will be included.

A cross section of a typical cooled weld is shown in Fig. 14-29. The central mass, designated by *A*, represents metal that has been melted. It has the characteristic dendritic structure of a casting, which it essentially is. When the metal solidifies, it cools from the outside inward, and the crystals grow toward the center. Some segregation of constituents occurs with an alloy. The juncture of the dendrites in the center is weak, not so much in a ductile metal like steel as in a brittle one like cast iron. Slow cooling or subsequent annealing improves homogeneity and strength.

Parent metal adjacent to the molten metal in a weld is heated above the critical temperature. This is in zone *B* of Fig. 14-29. Steel so heated recrystallizes to austenite around many nuclei to form small grains. The grains grow at higher temperatures, and the structure becomes coarse. The metal nearest the molten pool almost reaches the melting point and becomes quite coarse. Farther from the center the structure is finer. Beyond that, in zone *C*, the parent metal is unchanged.

Coarse-grained steel hardens more readily than a finer structure of the same composition. A fine structure is tougher and stronger than a coarse one in most nonferrous metals because fine grains offer more points of resistance to slip.

Welding tends to harden high-carbon and alloy steels. The principles of hardening of steel have been explained in Chap. 5, and their role in welding will be elaborated upon here. With thick pieces the welding zone is normally a small spot within a large mass of cooler metal. Heat flows off rapidly into the surrounding metal.

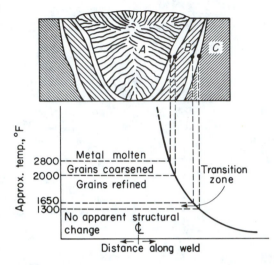

A, Weld metal
B, Heat–affected zone
C, Unaffected zone

Figure 14-19 Temperatures attained and the resulting structure in a typical weld in steel.

When the heat source is removed, what is called a *mass quench* results. This causes hard martensite to form in hardenable steel in part or all of the zone heated above the critical temperature. Formation of martensite causes cracking and must be avoided. The more hardenable the steel, the slower must be the cooling rate. The rate that heat is drawn off depends upon the mass of the surrounding metal and the difference in temperature between the weld zone and workpiece. Thin sections with little mass do not give trouble from rapid cooling. A proper cooling rate for a thick section can be estimated from the time–temperature diagram for the material, like that illustrated in Fig. 5-3. The workpiece temperature can be raised to retard cooling by preheating the work and by a mild but pervading heat input during welding. A workpiece may be heated all over or locally; in either case preheating adds substantially to the cost of the operation. One authority prescribes that all steel sections that are over 40 mm (1.5 in.) thick must be preheated. As for heat input during arc welding, it is increased by heavier currents and slower traverse rates, as explained in the discussion of Eqs. (14-1) and (14-3). Figure 14-12 indicates welding methods capable of large heat inputs. Care must be taken to avoid overheating and excessive penetration. Gas welding heats more slowly but more pervasively and causes less hardening than arc welding.

Chilling of welded pieces must be avoided with hardenable metals but otherwise has benefits. The metal is exposed for a shorter time to gas contamination, the heat-affected zone is smaller, the grain structure is finer, and a higher strength weld often results.

Some aluminum and other nonferrous alloys are hardened by keying agents that are dissolved on heating. The structure of such metal may be altered in the vicinity of a weld, and subsequent heat treatment may be necessary to obtain properties desired throughout the material.

Control of Welding Quality. What has been shown to happen in a weld explains the faults the weld may have and their remedies. These faults are distortion and shrinkage, cracks, voids and inclusions, undercuts and craters, and corrosion. Their natures and remedies are discussed in the following sections.

Heating and cooling cause expansion and contraction in various and different places as a weld is made along a joint. The metal in the joint is hotter and tends to shrink more on cooling than the bulk of the pieces on either side. However, lengthwise shrinkage is restrained by the metal adjacent to the joint, and that induces a residual tensile stress along the joint that may exceed the yield point of the material. This pulls some parallel fibers of base metal into light compression. If pieces being welded are restrained in a fixture or by the structure to which they are attached, stresses may be induced in any direction by contraction of the metal in the welded zone when it cools, and thus cause cracking. Even if cracking does not occur, residual stresses may impair fatigue strength significantly and commonly do cause warpage, especially when they are unbalanced by later machining.

Annealing, called *post heating*, is a means of relieving stresses but is not always desirable because it affects the properties of the base metal of the parts. Shot or hammer peening has been found to increase the fatigue strength of welds more than heat treatment. In that way fatigue life may be restored to the life of the unwelded material. A typical cost is $2.00/m ($0.60/ft) of weld.

Much can be done by design and welding practice to enable components of a weldment to yield and move slightly to alleviate stresses and warping. Effective ways are to use as thin material and as little filler metal as possible, to preheat to minimize temperature differences between the weld and base material, and to weld from the inside or confined portion of a structure to the outside or points of most freedom. Manual welding is inherently variable; automatic welding provides a better control of quality.

Cracks, Voids, Undercuts, and Craters. A cracked weld is a defective weld and usually is rejected. Cracks may occur in the weld metal or in the parent metal, lengthwise or normal to the weld. They may occur during or after welding.

Martensite formed in welding steel is a leading cause of cracking. The martensite is brittle and does not yield but breaks when the stresses in the weld become high enough. Moreover, the martensite adds to the strains and resulting stresses. It has a lower density and occupies more volume than the softer steel from which it is formed. Measures previously described to prevent hardening and minimize stresses are effective to prevent cracking.

As a weld cools, it shrinks. If the members joined are restrained from moving, high stresses are induced across the weld. A concave bead has higher stresses, particularly at the surface, and is less desirable than a convex bead. An excessively deep and narrow weld also becomes highly stressed. If the stresses are high, they impair fatigue strength and cause cracking. A bead may be weakened by use of filler metal different from the base metal if there is a difference in expansion rates. This is prone to happen, for instance, if steel filler is used to weld cast iron.

Some alloys weaken and crack at welding temperatures. As an example, magnesium alloys with more than about 0.15% calcium have a grain boundary constituent with a low melting point. This causes frequent cracking upon welding. The remedy is to change and control the raw material. The formation of intermediate alloys may promote cracking if dissimilar metals are welded together.

Hydrogen is a major cause of cracking in steel. It is highly soluble in hot steel but is largely expelled on cooling. If the gas cannot escape, it exerts pressure to crack the metal. This is likely to happen under the same conditions that form brittle martensite and aggravate the cracking of the martensite. Low-hydrogen electrodes and flux, cleanliness, preheating, and slow cooling to allow the hydrogen to escape help eliminate hydrogen cracking.

Tests have shown that voids up to about 7% of cross section do not materially change the tensile or impact strength and ductility of a weld. In excess of that amount, inclusions of foreign matter and blow holes or gas pockets weaken welds appreciably and act as stress risers from which cracks spread. Inclusions are usually slag but may be scale and dirt. Grease, oil, or paint left on surfaces liberate gases when heated. Surfaces must be clean before welding to avoid contamination. Most welding is done shielded from the atmospheric gases. Much can be done with welding techniques that keep the welding pool at sufficient temperature for a long enough time to liberate gases and float out slag and other contaminations. Freecutting sulfur steels are particularly difficult to weld because of the copious release of hydrogen sulfide and sulfur dioxide gases.

An *undercut* is a groove melted in the base metal alongside a bead. A *crater* is a depression left at the end of a bead. These may be weak points in highly stressed weldments. They may be prevented by proper welding procedures.

Corrosion.   Welding makes metals more susceptible to corrosion in a number of ways. Actually, corrosion occurs from the attack of the air on the hot metal in the welding operation if shielding is not adequate. The intense heat of welding effaces conversion and other protective coatings from metal surfaces. Clad metals should be welded with the same composition as the surface metal, at least on top of the weld. From the standpoint of design, the inner surfaces of a lap joint are difficult to protect from corrosion. Notches and cracks that come from welding are foci for corrosion.

The heat of welding causes changes in some metals to make them more susceptible to corrosion. Welding can make stainless steel lose its corrosion resistance. The reason and remedies for this are explained in Chap. 6. When some aluminum alloys are heated by welding, parts become overaged and subject to corrosion.

Design for Welding.   A product to be fabricated by welding must meet two requirements. First it must have adequate strength, rigidity, endurance, etc. Second, it must be producible at the lowest possible cost. The first of these considerations is in the realm of mechanics of materials and is largely outside the scope of this book. For the second, the designer must understand the principles and practices of welding to utilize them most effectively. Several such points will be reviewed here to indicate how they influence welded designs.

Some of the main principles of designing for welding are illustrated in Fig. 14-30. The bent enclosure welded on two ends in view (A) is easy to fit to the assembly and provides welding grooves without preparation of the edges. An inaccessible enclosure in a weldment should be completely sealed to inhibit corrosion. View (B) illustrates the rules that sections welded together should be about the same size for the least amount of heat distortion and that thin sections should be joined rather than thick ones. As indicated also, provision must be made for shrinkage and machining after welding. View (C) shows a weld between thin sections. If a standard shape without a flange were available for a hub, it might be most economical even if some extra care in welding were necessary, but if a hub must be machined anyway, the flange should be added to match the spokes. View (D) illustrates how a joint should be welded if subsequent machining is to be done on one of the pieces. With the weld in the position shown, there is no need to machine it. Hard spots in the weld can damage the cutting tools.

With the nature of the process in mind, a designer specifies welds in the easiest positions and provides ample accessibility to them. The principles of welding explain why high-carbon and alloy steel and cast iron are hard to weld. Low-carbon steel is used for welding wherever possible. For each weldment, thought should be given to choosing the most suitable welding process. Often several may be selected for one product for the best results. As an example, a bicycle frame is made with seven resistance welds, four spot welds, four electric-arc welds, and four oxyacetylene brazed joints, each where it serves most economically.

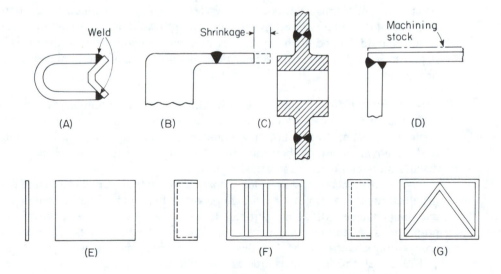

Figure 14-30 Weldment design principles.

Welding can be a means to use material most efficiently but must be applied properly to be efficient. A flat plate of about the proportions of Fig. 14-30(E) was fixed at one end and twisted 10° at the other end under a given torque. A box section like that of Fig. 14-30(F) was little more rigid than the plate and twisted 9°. Under the same conditions a box with diagonal braces, as in Fig. 14-30(G), twisted only one-fourth of one degree. It proved 36 times as rigid as the cross braced box with 6% less material. Many weldments are designed to replace castings for machine frames or bases, jig and fixture bodies, etc. A proven rule is that such a design should not just follow the lines of the castings but should be a complete revision to take full advantage of the benefits of welding.

Normally no effort is made to hold small tolerances on raw weldments. The tolerances that can be held depend upon those of the component pieces, the errors in fabrication and fitting, and the distortions from welding and heat treatment. Tolerances on weldments are commonly broad; 1.5 mm (ca. $\frac{1}{16}$ in.) is feasible in many cases. Surfaces that need to be held to smaller tolerances are left with stock and are machined after welding and annealing.

Inspection of Welded Joints. Welded joints may be subjected to destructive or nondestructive testing by the methods described in Chap. 3. Destructive testing may be on a sampling or specimen basis. Visual inspection is often the only way welds are checked. Much can be judged in this way because good workmanship shows itself in uniform, properly shaped and filled, and attractive welds and is often the best assurance of quality. Inspection should start on the welding floor to detect faulty methods and procedures that cause defects. Inspection is aided if weldments are designed so that welds are as accessible as possible for inspection.

Various systems have been set up to specify how welds should be inspected and what flaws are permissible, but no one code is universally recognized. An underlying idea is that the amount of effort and time put into welding a piece and inspecting the results should depend upon the severity of service to which the product is subjected. A part to be highly stressed under critical conditions should be of higher quality than one in light service.

Welding Costs. The cost of a weldment includes a number of items. Among these may be the costs of material, machining before and after welding, forging, forming, finishing, fitting up, positioning, welding, inspecting, heat treatment, and flash removal. Most of these are treated elsewhere in this book, and the present discussion is confined to the actual welding costs.

The elements of cost in welding operations are those for (1) labor and overhead; (2) electrodes, flux or gas, or rods; (3) power or fuel; and (4) equipment depreciation and maintenance. All are not pertinent to all operations, and they appear in different proportions. A leading equipment manufacturer has estimated that for manual metal-arc welding about 80 to 86% of the cost is for labor and overhead, something like 8 to 15% for electrodes, and as little as 2% for power and equipment costs. In contrast, the cost of a projection welding operation may be mostly for power and equipment and little for labor and none for consumable electrodes.

A welder's pay rate is usually based on the position in which he or she can make a satisfactory weld. For instance, one who can do overhead welding properly receives more pay than another who can do only flat welding. Thus the labor rate as well as the speed of doing a job depends upon the position of the weld and the kind of weld.

The curves in Fig. 14-31 show typical amounts of unit electrode and power

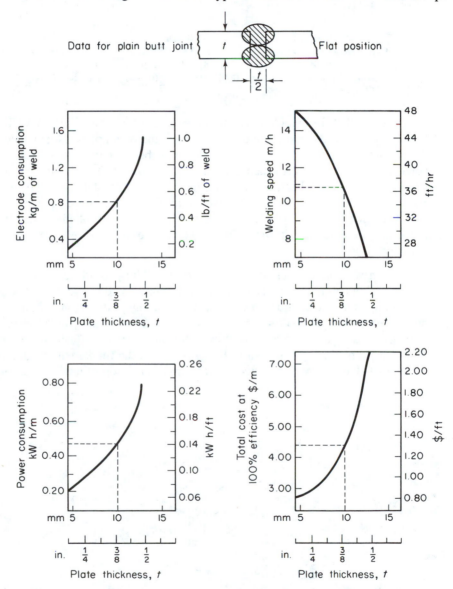

Figure 14-31   Chart of manual-arc welding performance. The total welding cost at 100% efficiency assumes power cost of $0.06/kWh, electrode cost of $2.00/kg ($0.90/lb), labor at $12.00/hr, and overhead of $18.00/hr.

consumption, welding speeds, and costs for several sizes of plain butt joints. Basic data of this sort have been compiled for many kinds of welding under various conditions and are given in charts and tables in reference books and handbooks.

The following are the detailed calculations for the cost of a plain butt weld in a nominal 10 mm ($\frac{3}{8}$ in.) thick plate to illustrate how the total cost curve is obtained in Fig. 14-31.

Thickness of plate, t	10 mm	$\frac{3}{8}$ in.
Cost of labor and overhead	30/10.9 = $2.75/m	30/36 = $0.83/ft
Cost of electrodes	0.8 × 2 = 1.60/m	0.55 × 0.9 = 0.50/ft
Cost of electricity	0.48 × 0.06 = 0.03/m	0.14 × 0.06 = 0.01/ft
Total cost	$4.38/m	$1.34/ft

Notice that the calculations and the chart are for 100% efficiency. The cost of labor and overhead does not allow for the time the operator is not engaged in laying down metal on the weld. The lost time may be as much as 80% and must be determined from the performance in each shop. If a 40% efficiency is assumed to apply, the cost of overhead and labor for the 10-mm-thick plate is 30/(10.9 × 0.4) = $6.88/m, and the total cost is $8.51/m of weld. For the $\frac{3}{8}$-in. plate, 30/(36 × 0.40) = $2.08/ft, and total cost is $2.59/ft. The unit cost is multiplied by the length of a particular weld to find its cost. The cost of electricity is relatively small and is commonly ignored.

Comparison of Welding with Casting. Many products, such as machine frames and other members, can be either cast or fabricated by welding. The advantage of welding is that steel structures can be made stronger, stiffer, and lighter than those of cast iron. As a general rule, machine steel can safely be subjected to stresses about four times as high as those for cast iron. Stiffness may be illustrated by the deflection of a simple beam as shown in Fig. 14-32 with the fundamental equation for the amount of deflection. The deflection d is inversely proportional to the modulus of

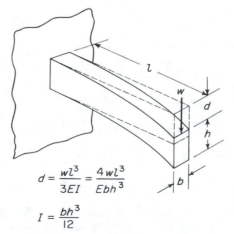

$$d = \frac{wl^3}{3EI} = \frac{4wl^3}{Ebh^3}$$

$$I = \frac{bh^3}{12}$$

Figure 14-32 Deflection of a cantilever beam.

elasticity E of the material, which is 12,000,000 for cast iron and 30,000,000 for steel. For the same deflection, the width b of a steel beam needs to be only 40% of that of a cast iron beam. Approximately the same ratio applies for all kinds of bending and torsion. Good welded steel designs have about half the weight of cast iron structures that are no stronger or stiffer.

Cast iron is considered better than steel for damping vibrations in some cases. This is discussed in connection with machine tool design in Chap. 21.

Steel costs about one-half to two-thirds as much per kilogram or pound as does cast iron. In a well-designed steel weldment that weighs about half as much, the material cost is about one-fourth to one-third as much as for cast iron. In addition, the steel must be cut, shaped, fitted, and welded, and the structure annealed. The casting needs only to be cleaned and chipped, but each different casting needs a pattern, which is expensive. In practically all cases a single unit, and particularly large units, can be made by welding more cheaply than by casting. In some cases welding is cheaper no matter how many units are made; in other cases castings are cheaper for larger quantities. Casting is well adapted to automatic production of large quantities, especially of complex pieces. For example, a number of attempts have been made to fabricate automobile engine blocks by welding, but none has ever displaced casting generally.

An example of costs for a cast versus welded base for a machine tool is illustrated by Fig. 14-33. The casting weighs 360 kg (ca. 800 lb) and can be obtained for \$1.06/kg (\$0.48/lb) for one unit and at a declining rate to \$0.79/kg (\$0.36/lb) for 100 units. Cleaning costs \$45 for each unit. A pattern costs \$1350 and serves for any number of units from 1 to 100. The total cost for one casting is \$1777. If a lot of 20 is made, the distributed pattern cost is \$67.50/unit, the cast iron costs \$1.01/kg (\$0.46/lb), and each unit costs \$476. A welded base for the same machine weighs 170/kg (375 lb). Steel costs \$0.51/kg (\$0.23/lb) and heat treatment \$0.18/kg (\$0.08/lb), making the total material cost \$117/unit. Fabrication takes 25 hours at \$18/hr, but initial preparation and set up amount to 10 hours at the same rate. By welding, one unit costs \$747. The setup charge can be distributed over a lot of 20 units, and the cost per unit then is \$576. As seen from Fig. 14-33, casting is cheaper for eight or more units; welding for seven or less.

Welding has several practical advantages. Thin and thick sections and unlike materials may be joined together, and sections may be made thin more easily in a weldment than in a casting. Holes may be prepunched in welded sections. Patterns for castings are costly to alter for design changes and to store; templates for welding are usually simpler and less bulky.

Comparison of Welding and Riveting. An analysis of a joint made by 19-mm ($\frac{3}{4}$-in.)-diameter rivets showed a cost of \$0.37 for each joint of 45 kN (ca. 10,000 lb) capacity as against \$0.07 for a welded joint of equal capacity. At one time all joints in structural steel buildings, boilers, tanks, automobile chassis, etc., were riveted. Welding has largely replaced riveting for such applications, especially where strength is important and joints permanent.

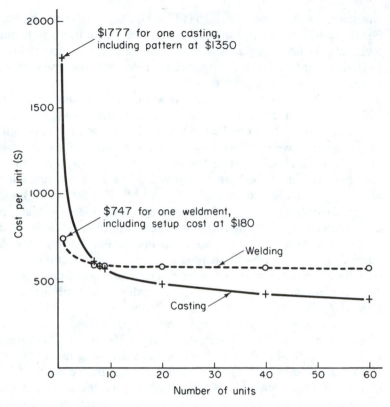

Figure 14-33 Cost versus quantity for a machine tool base made by casting or welding.

Riveting always requires lap joints. The holes and the rivets subtract from strength, and a riveted joint at best can only be about 85% as strong, whereas a good welded joint is fully as strong as the parent metal. Joints can be made gas- and liquid-tight by welding but must be caulked when riveted. Welded joints are easier to inspect because it is difficult to ascertain whether a rivet has been drawn up fully. The inspector must depend on the ability and integrity of the maker of manually riveted joints.

GAS AND ELECTRIC-ARC CUTTING

Principles of Gas Cutting. *Gas* or *flame cutting* is done by preheating a spot on ferrous metal to its ignition temperature and then burning it with a stream of oxygen in the manner illustrated in Fig. 14-34. The reaction that takes place at about 870°C (1600°F) is

$$3Fe + 2O_2 \longrightarrow Fe_3O_4 + 50 \text{ MJ/mol (48,000 Btu/mol)}$$

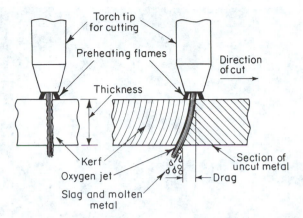

Figure 14-34 Principles of flame cutting.

Theoretically, 1 m³ of oxygen is required to oxidize about 430 cm³ (1 ft³ of O_2 for about $\frac{3}{4}$ in.³) of Fe. Actually, about 30 to 40% of the metal is melted and blown away without being oxidized, and removal of 600 cm³ or more of iron per 1 m³ of oxygen (1 in.³ or more of Fe per cubic foot of O_2) is not uncommon performance.

An oxygen jet spurts out of a hole in the center of the tip of the cutting torch depicted in Fig. 14-34. Around that, gas-with-oxygen flames issue from several holes and heat the top of the metal piece to keep it at the ignition temperature. Acetylene (or MAPP) is widely used as fuel because of its hot and adjustable flame, but among other fuels are hydrogen and illuminating gas. As the metal is burnt and eroded away, the torch is moved steadily along the path of cut. A uniformly wide slot, called the *kerf*, is cut by the jet of oxygen. The faster the rate of traverse, the more the bottom lags behind the top of the cut. The amount is called the *drag* and is evidenced by a series of curved lines on the sides of the kerf. Fine lines characterize a quality cut; coarse ones a fast or heavy cut. The drag must be kept small to cut a surface with a straight side around a curve.

Flame-Cutting Equipment and Procedures. Flame cutting may be done by a manual torch, like gas welding, but for production and more precise results one or more torches are mounted on a mechanical guide. Each torch is moved over a path determined by a tracer on a sheet metal template, by an optical scanner following the lines on a drawing, or by numerical control (Chap. 35). Other production features are automatic ignition and torch height control. In the automated mode the operation is sometimes called *thermal machining*. The work is commonly clamped on a series of disposable bars forming an open table. A production machine with four torches on an arm controlled from a tracer and template is shown in Fig. 14-35. This is called *multiple-torch cutting*. A six-torch tracer-controlled flame-cutting machine with a 3-m (10-ft) work span is quoted at about $25,000. With numerical control, a comparable machine costs about $100,000.

A high degree of skill is required to get best performance in flame cutting. The gas and oxygen pressure, position of torch, intensity of preheat, cutting speed, and type of tip must all be selected and regulated to suit the kind of material cut, the

Figure 14-35   Multiple flame cutting of die shoes from 2-in.-thick steel plate from a master template. (Courtesy Danly Machine Specialties, Inc.)

thickness of the work, the shape of the path of the cut, and the finish and accuracy required at the lowest possible cost for gases and time. Initial preheat tends to burn a hole in metal, so a cut is started away from the line of cut and usually at an outside edge of the plate where ignition is quick.

A principal use of flame cutting is to cut off and prepare plates and other shapes for welding. As an example, a plate may be cut off and beveled at the same time by means of two torches, one vertical and the other inclined at the bevel angle, traversed along the cut together.

Flame cutting usually implies cutting all the way through a piece, but a groove, cavity, hole, or even the entire top to a certain depth may be removed or cut from a piece. This is called *flame machining*, and specific applications of it are termed flame-planing, -milling, -turning, -drilling, and -boring, like the analogous machining operations. In flame machining, a cutting torch is inclined at an angle and adjustments are made so that the stream of oxygen does not penetrate through the piece but curves around and returns to the top. The torch is then moved to generate the shape desired.

One variation of flame cutting, called *oxygen-lance cutting*, is done with a long iron pipe of small diameter with oxygen flowing through it. The end of the pipe is set aflame and furnishes preheat for the oxygen stream. This torch is able to pierce holes in all kinds of metal. One example of its use is to burn holes in a hunk of metal frozen in a ladle. Dynamite is then put in the holes to break up the chunk and remove it.

Applications of Flame Cutting. Most ferrous metals are flame cut. Thicknesses up to 1.5 m (60 in.) can be cut in the ordinary way, and virtually any thickness by the oxygen-lance method. A number of plates may be piled on top of each other and cut at one time in what is called *stack cutting*.

In addition to cutting out sections for weldments and parts, such as gears, sprockets, and cams, from steel plates, flame cutting is used to cut off structural shapes and barstock, cut up steel scrap, cut off rivet heads, and remove butt ends and seamed, cracked, or defective sections from billets, slabs, and rounds, and for many other purposes. Rough flame cutting is done just to cut off pieces; precision flame cutting to produce fairly accurate shapes.

The metal on the sides of the kerf is heated above its critical temperature but the effect seldom penetrates more than 3 mm ($\frac{1}{8}$ in.) below the surface. In steel of less than about 0.3% carbon and little alloy content, the result is normally confined to changes in grain size and structure near the surface. That may improve surface strength and toughness. A thin layer is likely to be hardened on high-carbon and alloy steel surfaces and cause high internal stresses and cracks. Heating before or annealing after cutting or both are often done to relieve this situation.

Flame cutting can be done at moderate cost and still leave negligible drag lines, with edges sharp, kerf uniform in thickness, and surfaces square with tolerances satisfactory for many purposes. Good flame cut surfaces compare favorably with machined surfaces. Thick pieces do not warp as a rule, but plates 13 mm ($\frac{1}{2}$ in.) or less thick may require careful treatment, such as staggering of cuts, to avoid excessive warpage.

Ordinarily, a tolerance of ± 1.5 mm (ca. $\pm \frac{1}{16}$ in.) is considered practical in cutting plate up to 15 mm (ca. $\frac{1}{2}$ in.) thick, or about ± 0.8 mm ($\pm \frac{1}{32}$ in.) more for each additional 25 mm (1 in.) of thickness. Closer tolerances are held but at higher than usual commercial costs. In one case of cutting gears about 2.4 m (8 ft) in diameter in segments from 127-mm (5-in.)-thick steel plate, the tooth contours were reported held to ± 150 μm (± 0.006 in.). In precision work, cross-sectional squareness is held from 75 μm (0.003 in.) for 25-mm (1-in.)-thick sections to 760 μm (0.030 in.) for 150-mm (6-in.)-thick sections. For the most precise results, a piece may be flame cut oversize to remove most of the stock and finish machined to the degree of accuracy required.

Costs of Flame Cutting.   The main elements of operating cost for flame cutting are (1) for labor and overhead, and (2) for gas. Labor and overhead costs are based upon the time required to do a job. This usually includes time for preparation, setup, and teardown. The cutting time is calculated by dividing the length of cut by the cutting speed. Typical values for cutting speeds and rates of gas consumption, which vary with plate thickness, are given by the curves of Fig. 14-36. Ranges of values apply for any one thickness depending on the skill of the operator, the operating conditions, and the results required. For instance, the cutting speed must be slow to hold small tolerances. Similar tables and charts for various conditions can be found in reference texts and handbooks as a guide for cost estimating. In addition to operating cost, the cutting of a shape may call for a special template chargeable to the job.

An example for estimating the cost of a flame-cutting operation is furnished by a job that requires a cut 6 m (236 in.) long in 76-mm (3-in.)-thick mild steel. No special template is needed. Setup time is 35 minutes. The labor and overhead rate in the shop is \$20/hr, oxygen costs \$2.80/m^3 (\$0.08/ft^3) and acetylene \$6.35/m^3 (\$0.18/ft^3). The conditions are those given by Fig. 14-36.

$$
\begin{aligned}
\text{Cost of labor} \\
\text{and overhead} \quad &= (35 + 6/0.3)20/60 = \$18.33 \approx (35 + 236/12)20/60 \\
\text{Cost of oxygen} \quad &= \quad\; 0.6 \times 6 \times 2.80 = \quad 10.08 \approx (6 \times 236/12)0.08 \\
\text{Cost of acetylene} &= \quad 0.05 \times 6 \times 6.35 = \quad\;\; \underline{1.91} \approx (0.5 \times 236/12)0.18 \\
\text{Total} \quad &\qquad\qquad\qquad\qquad\quad \overline{\$30.32}
\end{aligned}
$$

The calculations are made for SI units, and those for in.-lb units are indicated on the right. Because the chart obviously must be an approximation, precise factors are not justified, and the final numbers differ somewhat for the two systems.

Comparison with Other Methods.   Flame cutting is directly competitive with shearing for cutting off plates, bars, rails, and other shapes. Straight shearing is much faster; one comparison showed it cost 0.049 cent/m (0.015 cent/ft) to shear plates as against 0.673 cent/m (0.205 cent/ft) for flame cutting. However, flame cutting is more practical for quite thick materials or a wide variety of work. Big shears are needed for thick sections and do exist but are not available nor justified in all plants. Single-torch flame-cutting equipment is relatively cheap (like gas-welding equipment), adaptable to all sizes of work, and portable to work not easily moved.

Friction sawing is more economical than flame cutting but not as versatile. For instance, rails are cut to desired length by friction sawing when they come out of a rolling mill. Occasionally a rail going through the mill runs afoul and becomes tangled in the mechanism. Flame-cutting equipment is then brought up to slice the rail into pieces to free it from the mill.

Irregular shapes may be cut from stock 13 mm ($\frac{1}{2}$ in.) or less in thickness by nibbling at relative reported cost of 0.105 cent/m (0.032 cent/ft) and accuracy of 0.4 mm ($\frac{1}{64}$ in.) or by sawing at 0.394 cent/m (0.12 cent/ft) and accuracy of 0.25 mm (0.010 in.) for small quantities and by die cutting large quantities. Intermediate quantities are sometimes more economically done by flame cutting, particularly by

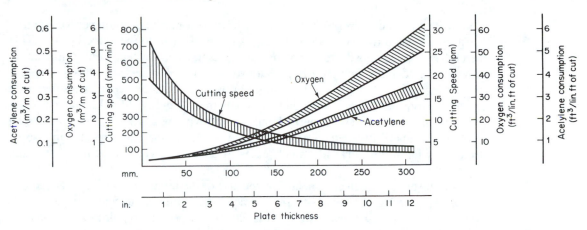

Figure 14-36   Performance data for machine flame cutting of mild steel not preheated.

means of multiple-torch cutting with templates and stacking of workpieces. Thick irregular pieces may be sawed from plates but flame cutting is commonly more economical and utilized.

Powder Cutting of High Alloys.   Flame cutting of some high-alloy steels, such as stainless steel, and many nonferrous alloys is difficult because the alloying elements, such as chromium and nickel, oxidize along with the base metal. Many of these oxides do not melt at attainable temperatures and form an insulating coating on the work that hinders progress of the cut. Free carbon forms a like barrier in cast iron. Also the combustion of alloys does not add enough heat to the operation.

The same kind of work done on low-carbon steel by flame cutting can be done successfully on stainless steel, cast iron, copper, Monel metal, and others by the *powder-cutting and scarfing process*. In addition to the usual procedure of flame cutting, a fine iron-rich powder is injected into the flame and oxygen stream. This burns, and the added heat aids melting. Aluminum powder may be added to cut copper, glass, and even concrete.

A somewhat larger torch tip to pass the extra ingredient must be used for powder cutting, and the cut is rougher and wider than for straight flame cutting. Otherwise the results are comparable. Stainless steel can be powder cut about as fast as low-carbon steel can be flame cut but at about twice the cost. Most of the additional cost is for powder.

In *flux injection*, also called *chemical-flux cutting*, a fine stream of flux powder is injected into the oxygen stream to increase the fluidity of refractory oxides so that they can be blown easily from the kerf.

Electric-Arc Cutting.   Although most of the electric-arc welding operations can be adapted for cutting metals, the only three of commercial importance are air carbon-arc, oxygen-arc, and plasma-arc cutting. *Air carbon-arc cutting* is a method of melting metal by an arc from a graphite electrode and blowing away the molten metal with a jet of compressed air. This may be done for through cutting or for gouging out grooves when the electrode and airstream are inclined to the work surface. This method is applied mostly to removing gates, risers, and defects from castings, removing weld defects, and preparing plates for welding. *Oxygen-arc cutting* or *metal-arc cutting* uses a flux covered steel tube for an electrode. The coating insulates the electrode from the sides of a cut and augments metal fluidity. Metal is melted by an arc from the electrode and is burned and blown away by a stream of oxygen blown through the tube. This method was developed for underwater cutting but can also be used in air for almost any metal thicknesses. It does not give good surface finish and accuracy.

A plasma-arc torch cuts metal fast because of the high temperatures it generates. *Plasma-arc cutting* of 6-mm ($\frac{1}{4}$-in.)-thick metal is reported up to 5 m/min (200 ipm), up to 10 times as fast as gas cutting. It is capable of penetrating almost any material that conducts electricity, and is used especially for those metals difficult for flame cutting. Surface finish is better than for gas cutting in some cases, and in some cases not, but accuracy is generally not as good. Power demands are high, and production machines are generally limited to one, or at most two, plasma arc torches each. Arc radiation is intense. Equipment is expensive. A numerically controlled 30-ton hole-punching and plasma-arc contour cutting machine has a base price of $275,000.

METAL SPRAYING

Principles and Methods.   Metals and nonmetals are sprayed by being melted or softened and then swept away at high speed and atomized in a jet of air or gas. The material is fed into some spray guns as wire and into others as powder. Tiny plastic or fluid particles are hurled against a workpiece surface; they spread around and interlock with projections, embed in pits, and freeze quickly upon contact with the cool surface. Separate particles overlap and intertwine with one another to form a coherent structure. Equipment utilizing a gas flame as depicted in Fig. 14-37 is obtainable for $1000 to $2000 and is satisfactory for many metals. An electric-arc spray gun that atomizes droplets from two continuously fed wire electrodes is also depicted in Fig. 14-37. A gun of this type costs about $10,000 but is reported to operate at one-third the cost and three to five times faster than oxyacetylene equipment. As a rule, plasma-arc, the third type shown in Fig. 14-37, is the most costly spray equipment to buy and operate, but it is an economical way to spray materials that melt above 2200°C (4000°F) and ceramics; one report was of a cost per pound of material deposited about one-third that for the oxyacetylene method. By a method called *flame plating* or *Detonation-Gun coating*, heated particles are shot in bursts from a gun barrel by rapidly successive oxyacetylene explosions and are impacted into the workpiece surface. Excellent bonding and density are obtained without excessively heating the part. Equipment costs are quite high, particularly because elaborate isolation measures are necessary to reduce high noise levels.

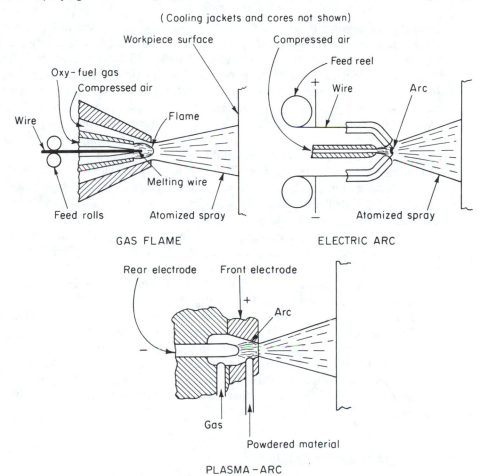

Figure 14-37 Several types of metal spray guns.

A metal spray gun may be directed by hand or mounted on a machine. A typical application is to spray a round piece turning between centers on a lathe with the gun mounted on the carriage for a uniform feed. Most sprayed metals adhere to a surface essentially through mechanical bonding, so the surface must be roughened first and be free of dirt, oil, and grease. Surfaces are prepared by rough machining or grinding, knurling, blasting with sand or steel grit, inserting screws or studs, tack welding, or undercoating and painting. One method is to spray first with a high melting point metal that fuses and sticks to the surface.

Applications. All commercial metals are sprayed (in fact, the process is sometimes called *metallizing*) as well as nonmetals like oxides and ceramics. Spraying may be done on metallic or nonmetallic surfaces such as fabrics, ceramics, and plastics. Spraying may be done to replace material cut away by mistake or worn away or to confer some physical property on a surface. An example of rebuilding is a 460-mm (18-in.)-diameter axle worn to 420 mm ($16\frac{1}{2}$ in.) diameter. Metal spraying is not alone a precision process, so the axle was sprayed with a 13% chromium steel at the rate of 12 kg/hr (26 lb/hr) with 63.5 kg/journal (140 lb/journal) and reground to original size. The cost was about half that of a new part. Other uses for spraying are to impart corrosion resistance by a coat of stainless steel, heat resistance by a coat of zirconium oxide in the combustion chamber of a jet engine, and wear resistance by a coat of aluminum oxide in an extrusion die or tungsten carbide on a new metal-forming die. Sprayed surfaces are porous and hold lubricant well. The appearance of cast surfaces can be improved by metal spraying. Sprayed metal can be decorative, like aluminum or bronze on cast iron. Thin-walled parts can be made in shapes or of materials that cannot be fabricated easily by other means by spraying a coating on a formed mandrel and then removing the mandrel.

Sprayed metal can be expected to oxidize somewhat, be up to 15% less dense, and be weaker than parent material on a part. Because oxyacetylene flame spraying is done at lower temperatures and is slower than the other methods, it results in two to three times as much oxidation and less interfusion of the particles and surface. Bond strengths of 10 to 20 MPa (1500 to 3000 psi) are achieved in flame spraying, 20 to 70 MPa (3000 to 10,000 psi) in electric-arc and plasma-arc spraying, and 55 to over 175 MPa (8000 to 25,000 psi) for Detonation-Gun coating. Partial welding between particles and surface appears to occur with the higher-temperature methods. Sprayed coatings serve best in compression and may be made quite hard. When hardenable steel is sprayed, it is quenched rapidly on contact. A coating may be as thin as 50 to 80 μm (0.002 to 0.003 in.) and there is no upper limit to its thickness if properly applied.

SURFACING AND HARD FACING

Principles. Hard facing or surfacing is a process of welding wear- or corrosion-resistant metal on a part to make it serviceable or to rebuild or repair it. It is commonly done on metal-working dies and tools, oil well drilling tools, parts of earth-moving and excavation equipment, rolling mill rolls, and tractor parts. As an example, it has been found that parts for heavy tractors can be rebuilt by surfacing at about 40% of the cost of replacement parts and last about 50% longer. On the other hand, new forming dies for sheet metal are commonly hard faced at critical spots to make them run longer before they have to be repaired.

All but a few hard-facing materials consist of hard particles of carbides of chromium, tungsten, molybdenum, etc., uniformly distributed in a soft matrix. The hardness of an alloy depends on the types and amounts of carbides it contains. No one surfacing material can serve all purposes. The many materials used may be classified in groups. For the ferrous alloys, *group A* contains those with less than 20% and *group B* those with more than 20% alloy content. The lower alloys are generally tougher and more shock resistant but not as wear resistant as the higher alloys. The nonferrous alloys in *group C* are highly resistant to wear and corrosion. They include the cobalt-chromium-tungsten alloys, such as stellite, and the nickel-base alloys like Hastelloy. *Group D*, known as the diamond substitutes, are bits of cemented carbides or sintered oxides welded or brazed to oil well drilling or metal-cutting tools. *Group E* consists of metal strips, tubes, or rods as electrodes containing crushed carbide particles.

Procedures. Low- and high-carbon, low-alloy, stainless, and manganese steels and cast iron can be hard faced with some difference in methods for each. Except for those attached as bits, surfacing metals are available commercially as electrodes or rods and are laid down as molten filler metal on workpiece surface metal in a conventional welding operation. All forms of gas and arc welding are utilized to suit various materials and applications. Much surfacing is done manually on diverse repair, rebuilding, and maintenance jobs. Rapid area coverage on production jobs is achieved with submerged-arc welding using wide ribbon electrodes with large amounts of current. Another production method is *bulk-process welding* in which granular metal and flux are spread on the surface and melted along with the surface by an imposed arc. This gives higher deposition rates than other methods.

A process for surfacing with a tungsten carbide electrode utilizes dc arc discharge at the rate of 8000 pulses/sec. Steel surfaces are impregnated in this way with a layer of tungsten carbide 50 to 75 μm (0.002 to 0.003 in.) thick having a hardness of 72 to 74 R_C to improve wear resistance of dies and cutting tools.

BRAZE WELDING, BRAZING, AND SOLDERING

Braze Welding. Braze welding, also called *bronze welding*, is like fusion welding, in that a filler is melted and deposited in a groove, fillet, plug, or slot between two pieces to make a joint. In this case the filler metal is a copper alloy with a melting point below that of the base metal but above 425°C (800°F). The filler metal is puddled into and not distributed in the joint by capillarity, as in plain brazing described later.

Metals with high melting points, such as steel, cast iron, copper, brass, and bronze, are braze welded. The base metal does not melt, but a bond is formed, sometimes stronger than the base metal alone. Studies of the bonds between copper alloys and cast iron have shown three sources of the forces that bind braze-welded joints. One is in the atomic forces between metals at their interfaces in close contact. A second is alloying which arises from diffusion of the metals in a narrow zone at the interface. The third is intergranular penetration.

Braze welding may be done by oxyacetylene, metallic-arc, or carbon-arc welding. The filler metal is applied by a rod or electrode together with a suitable flux. Most metals require little, if any, preheat, with the exception of cast iron, in which localized heating may set up enough stresses to cause cracking.

The main advantages of braze welding result from the low temperature of the operation. Less heat is needed and a joint can be made faster than by fusion welding. The filler metal yields substantially on cooling to 260°C (500°F) and even some below, without weakening, and residual stresses are small. Dissimilar metals not amenable to fusion welding may be joined by braze welding.

Braze-welded joints are not satisfactory for service at over about 260°C (500°F) nor for dynamic loads of 100 MPa (15,000 psi) or more.

Brazing.   Brazing is the name given a group of welding operations in which a nonferrous filler metal melts at a temperature below that of the metal joined but is heated above 425°C (800°F). The molten filler metal flows by capillarity between the heated but unmelted adjacent or overlapping joint members or is melted in place between those members. Examples of the kinds of joints made in this way are shown in Fig. 14-38.

Two classes of filler metals for most work are copper alloys and silver alloys. An exception is aluminum that is brazed by aluminum alloys that melt just before the parent metal. There are a number of different alloys in each class. Some are considered general-purpose alloys and are satisfactory for a range of jobs. References and treatises prescribe proper alloys, fluxes, joint designs, and methods of operation for best results in specific cases.

Copper alone or alloyed with other metals is applied in brazing at 700 to 1175°C (1300 to 2150°F). Some of the alloys withstand temperatures to 425°C (800°F) in service, but most are not considered serviceable above 260°C (500°F).

Brazing done with silver alloys is called *silver brazing* or *silver soldering*. Silver alone or alloyed with other metals is applied at 635 to 850°C (1175 to 1550°F). Some metals and parts must be joined at these lower temperatures to avoid overheating or warping. Service temperatures should usually not be over 260°C (500°F). Silver brazed joints are about as strong as and sometimes stronger than copper brazed joints, but the silver alloys are relatively expensive.

Aluminum alloy brazing is done from 565 to 615°C (1050 to 1140°F). Up to 100% joint efficiency in tension is obtainable. For economical operation, parts are commonly fabricated from brazing sheet, which consists of a layer of brazing alloy bonded to one or both surfaces of a core alloy.

The bond between a brazing metal and the clean metal of the parts joined is due to some diffusion of the brazing metal into the hot base metal and to some surface alloying of the metals. A good joint is at least as strong as the filler metal. If the base metal is weaker than the filler metal, failure occurs outside the joint. If the base metal is stronger, the joint fails but at a stress much higher than the strength of the filler metal. A good joint can only be obtained with a minute clearance between the surfaces being joined and by the practice of proper brazing techniques that assure full penetration of the joint by the filler metal. Misfits that cause voids too large to be filled naturally, as suggested in Fig. 14-38, result in joints of less than full strength. Tests of stainless steel with a tensile strength of 1.1 GPa (160,000 psi) joined in a butt joint by means of a silver alloy of 480 MPa (70,000 psi) strength showed a maximum joint strength of 900 MPa (130,000 psi) with a clearance of 40 μm (0.0015 in.) in the joint. The strength dropped off almost proportionately to about 275 MPa (40,000 psi) as the clearance was increased to 0.6 mm (0.024 in.). In addition to strength, good brazed joints are ductile and resistant to fatigue and corrosion.

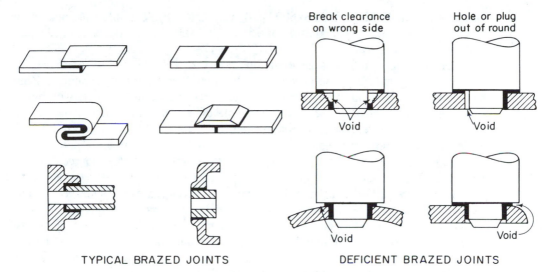

Figure 14-38 Brazed joints.

Surfaces must be thoroughly cleaned before brazing and then usually are covered with a flux to break down and prevent further formation of oxides. Borax is a widely used flux, but many proprietary brands are available. Parts should be tightly held together in process; they may be staked or crimped together or held in a fixture for production. The filler metal may be in the form of wire, preformed shapes, or alloy paste and may be applied before or during heating. The actual heating may be done in a number of ways. Torch brazing is popular because it is convenient and adaptable. Furnace, electrical resistance, and induction heating serve in various ways in production. Parts may be dipped in molten salt or flux for preheating or final heating. With or without preheating, parts may be dipped in molten filler metal; this is particularly of advantage when brazing or soldering a number of joints simultaneously and uniformly in one assembly. Equipment costs are highest for dipping. Brazing and soldering operations are readily and commonly automated for production from 40 to 20,000 assemblies/hr.

Steel, copper, brass, bronze, aluminum, and many less common metals are brazed together and to each other. Hardened steel and some aluminum alloys cannot be brazed satisfactorily. The strengths, operating temperatures, and costs of brazed joints are less than those for fusion welding but more than those for soft soldering.

Soldering. *Soldering* or *soft soldering* is the process of joining metals by means of alloys that melt between 175 and 370°C (350 and 700°F). They are generally lead and tin alloys. The metals mostly joined by soldering are iron, copper, nickel, lead, tin, zinc, and many of their alloys. Aluminum can be soldered by special means.

The strength of a soldered joint depends on surface alloying and upon mechanical bonding, such as crimping, between the joined parts. The solder alone has a low unit strength, little resistance to fatigue, and is limited to service temperatures below 150°C (300°F). Tests on various soldered copper sleeve joints showed shear strengths from about 20 to 40 MPa (3000 to 6000 psi) at 29°C (85°F). Thin films are necessary for the strongest joints. Thicknesses of 75 μm (0.003 in.) on copper and 125 μm (0.005 in.) on steel are desirable.

For soldering, a flux is generally necessary to rid the surface of oxides to promote wetting and obtain intimate contact between the solder and base metal. Zinc chloride is most efficient but corrosive as a flux. Rosin does not clean as well but is noncorrosive, and must be used for dependable electrical connections. There are a number of soldering techniques, some for particular materials. In general the flux is applied first, the parts are heated at the joint to just above the melting point of the solder, and then the solder is touched to and flows into the joint. Any source of clean heat is satisfactory. A heated copper soldering iron or soldering copper is widely used for general-purpose work. An open flame from an alcohol, gasoline, hydrogen, or gas torch may be played directly on the joint. A heated neutral gas, like nitrogen, may be necessary for some extremely fussy work. Induction or resistance heating or immersion of the workpieces in a solder bath are fast methods and adapted to production.

Soldering produces liquid- and gas-tight joints quickly at low cost. Temperatures are not high, equipment is simple, and the method is the most convenient and feasible means of making joints in the workshop, laboratory, or home where often the equipment for other processes is not available. Soldering provides positive and dependable electrical connections. If a soldered joint is strong and durable enough for a particular purpose, it is usually the most economical.

QUESTIONS

1. What is the principle of operation of electric-arc welding?
2. What factors affect the depth of penetration in arc welding? What are their effects?
3. What is the optimum amount of current to expend in metal-arc welding?
4. What determines how large an electrode should be for manual-arc welding?
5. How do dc and ac compare for arc welding?
6. What are the functions of coatings on shielded electrodes?
7. What are the advantages of each of the several sources of current for arc welding?
8. How are arc welder sizes designated, and under what conditions?
9. What are the necessary current characteristics of a power source for manual-arc welding, and why?
10. What two kinds of power sources are used for automatic welding, and what are their principles of operation?
11. Explain the Tig and Mig systems of arc welding.
12. Describe plasma-arc welding. What is its main advantage?
13. What is submerged-arc welding, and where does it serve best?
14. Describe electroslag and electrogas welding and their uses.
15. How do the main automatic-arc welding methods compare with each other?
16. What is electron-beam welding, and when is it practicable?

17. What is a laser beam, how may it be produced, and how may it be used?

18. What are the principles of operation of resistance welding?

19. What are the relative and optimum conditions of time, current, and tip force in a spot welding operation?

20. Describe and compare spot, seam, and projection welding.

21. What is heat balance?

22. Compare upset-butt welding, flash-butt welding, and percussion welding as to the ways they are done and their relative merits and limitations.

23. What is the principle of Thermit welding? What can it do better than other processes?

24. What properties make acetylene the favorite for gas welding?

25. Describe the features of a gas welding operation.

26. What are the advantages of gas welding?

27. Describe friction or inertia welding and its uses.

28. What is ultrasonic welding, and what are its advantages?

29. Describe explosive welding.

30. What is diffusion bonding or solid-state welding, and where does it serve to advantage?

31. What are the elements of common arc- or gas-welded joints?

32. What are welding symbols, and what do they do?

33. How does welding affect grain size and structure of a metal?

34. To what extent does steel harden in welding? Why? What effect does it have on the weldment?

35. What causes weldments to crack, and what are the remedies? Explain the reasons for the events.

36. What causes inclusions and voids in a weld, and how can they be prevented?

37. Why is hydrogen detrimental to welds?

38. How does welding make metals susceptible to corrosion?

39. What are the main principles of designing for welding?

40. What are the elements of cost of welding, and how are they estimated?

41. How do weldments compare with castings?

42. How does an oxygen jet cut steel?

43. What is the difference between flame cutting and flame machining?

44. What is oxygen-lance cutting, and for what is it used?

45. How does flame cutting compare with metal shearing? With friction sawing? With machining?

46. Why is it difficult to flame cut some materials, and what can be done for them?

47. How is electric-arc cutting done and what are its limitations? How does it excel?

48. How is metal sprayed? Describe three kinds of equipment.

49. For what purpose are metals and other materials sprayed?

50. What is surfacing or hard facing, and why is it done?

51. How do brazing and braze welding differ, and how are they alike? How do they differ from welding and soldering? What are their advantages?

52. What are the fundamental requirements of a good brazed joint?

PROBLEMS

1. Show how the weld cost in $/m ($/ft) is computed from the data given in Table 14-1 and accompanying text:
   (a) For conventional metal-arc with coated electrode.
   (b) For metal-arc with powder metal electrode.
   (c) For manual submerged-arc process.
   (d) For manual CO_2 gas-shielded process.

2. Arc welding to lay down 5.5 kg/h (12 lb/hr) is to be done with automatic machines that are capable of welding at that rate while the arc is on. Labor costs $10.00/hr. Overhead is not thought to be much different for either case and is neglected. For the submerged-arc welding process, flux costs $0.73/kg ($0.33/lb) and is used at the rate of 1.5 kg/kg (lb/lb) of electrode wire consumed. The wire costs $1.65/kg ($0.75/lb), and the deposition efficiency is 100%. The duty cycle is 60%. For the CO_2 gas-shielded welding process, gas costs $1.17/m³ (3 cents/ft³) and is used at the rate of 0.85 m³/h (30 ft³/hr) of welding time. The wire costs $2.40/kg ($1.10/lb), and the deposition efficiency is 90%. The duty cycle is 80%.
   (a) Which process appears more economical for this job?
   (b) Why are the deposition efficiency and the duty cycle different for the two processes?

3. Conventional welding equipment costs $1250, and equipment for manual CO_2 gas-shielded welding costs $4200. For the conditions shown in Table 14-1, how much welding must be done to justify the more expensive equipment? Interest and taxes on the investment need not be considered.

4. An end dome 25 mm (1 in.) thick by 600 mm (24 in.) in diameter may be welded on the end of a cylinder 600 mm (24 in.) in diameter by 900 mm (35 in.) long by electron-beam, gas tungsten-arc, or gas metal-arc welding. The following costs have been assembled for each of these methods.

Cost item	EB	GTA	GMA
Labor ($/hr)	7.00	6.00	6.00
Overhead ($/hr)	22.40	11.24	11.24
Welding speed [m/min (ipm)]	1.0 (40)	0.1 (4)	0.25 (10)
Number passes	1	19	10
Set up, prepare, and clean (min)	47	205	205
Inspection ($/piece)	20	40	40
Filler metal ($/piece)	—	150	170
Gas flow [m³/h (ft³/hr)]	—	1.7 (60)	1.4 (50)
Power cost ($/piece)	0.48	0.64	0.48

Preparation for arc welding includes machining of a single-U-groove in joint. Labor and overhead rate for setup, preparation, and cleaning is $15/hr. Perishable EB elements cost $1.00/piece, and gas $3.50/m³ ($0.10/ft³). What is the cost to weld an end dome in place by each method?

5. **(a)** A single phase resistance welding machine has a rating of X kVA with a 50% duty cycle. The impedance of the secondary circuit of the transformer is Z ohms, the power factor is p, and the voltage is E volts. How much heat H_1 is generated in the secondary circuit during an appreciable period of time T in minutes?

   (b) If the machine is operated to deliver Y kVA, and other conditions remain the same except that the duty cycle is changed to a value C, how much heat H_2 is generated in a time period T?

   (c) Set up an expression for C in terms of X and Y for operating the machine at maximum output without overheating.

   (d) A resistance welder is rated at 50 kVA at 50% duty cycle. Secondary voltage is 5 V and does not change. A job is put on the machine to draw 15,000 A. What is the most the duty cycle may be for 15,000 A?

6. A spot-welding machine has a throat depth of 300 mm (12 in.) with 200 mm (8 in.) between horns. The secondary loop impedance is 165×10^{-6} Ω. If the throat depth is changed to 760 mm (30 in.), the impedance is increased to 340×10^{-6} Ω. The secondary voltage is 6 V. How much does the secondary current decrease with the change in throat depth?

7. A single-groove butt weld is to be made between two pieces of steel plate.

   (a) What kind of steel is least likely to crack from the welding? Why?

   (b) If a steel of 0.5% carbon content and medium hardenability is selected, which welding process is least likely to crack it? Why?

   (c) If arc welding is used for the steel specified in part (b), what can be done to lessen the chances of cracking?

8. Estimate the cost of a plain-butt joint weld 460 mm (18 in.) long on a 6-mm ($\frac{1}{4}$-in.)-thick plate at 70% efficiency. Power costs $0.04/kWh, labor and overhead $24/hr, and electrodes $2.20/kg ($1.00/lb).

9. It is found in a certain shop that welding speed for a square butt joint in the vertical position is 80% of that for the flat position as given in Fig. 14-31. The welder is paid $12/hr and overhead is $10/hr. Welding efficiency is 50%. Electrodes cost $2.65/kg ($1.20/lb), and electricity $0.04/kWh. What is the cost per meter (foot) of vertical square butt welds in each of the following sizes of plates? **(a)** $\frac{1}{4}$ in.; **(b)** $\frac{3}{8}$ in.; **(c)** $\frac{1}{2}$ in.; **(d)** 5 mm; **(e)** 10 mm; **(f)** 15 mm.

10. A cast base for a machine tool weighs 2200 kg (4900 lb). The pattern costs $1000 and cast iron $1.10/kg ($0.50/lb). The cost to clean a casting is $50. A welded design for the base weighs 1130 kg (2500 lb). Steel costs $0.62/kg ($0.28/lb). Fabrication requires 65 hours at $28/hr for labor and overhead. Setup and preparation take 15 hours for a lot. Templates for cutting the steel cost $100.

    (a) For how many pieces is the cost of a casting the same as the cost of a weldment?

    (b) Which process would be cheaper for 25 pieces? How much? Why might this not be the deciding factor?

11. A welding shop that needs work is willing to cut its rate for labor and overhead to $23.00/hr. If all other conditions stated in Prob. 10 are the same, what effect does the new rate have upon the choice of process?

12. A lot of 40 gear segments are to be rough-flame cut by machine and then finished by machining. The length of cut for each segment is 3.3 m (130 in.). Four segments can be

cut at one time from a template that costs $200. Oxygen costs $2.65/m^3$ ($7.50/100 ft^3), and acetylene $5.80/m^3$ ($16.50/100 ft^3). The labor and overhead rate in the shop is $15/hr. An hour is required to set up and tear down the job. What is the cost per piece for flame cutting? The material is 25 mm (1 in.) thick.

REFERENCES

ALM, G. V., "Diffusion Bonding," *Mechanical Engineering*, May 1970, p. 24.

BOLIN, S., "Lasers Light the Way to Low-Cost Drilling and Cutting," *Manufacturing Engineering*, Dec. 1981, p. 63.

COLLOPY, W. F., "Powders Add Flexibility to Hardfacing, Cut Costs," *Metal Progress*, May 1982, p. 47.

ENGEL, S. L., "Heat Treating with Lasers," *American Machinist*, May 1976, p. 107.

GONSER, T. R., "Computer Sharpens EB Hardening," *American Machinist*, Nov. 1981, p. 139.

HINES, W. G., JR., "Selecting the Most Economical Welding Process," *Metal Progress*, Nov. 1972, p. 42.

HORWITZ, H., *Welding: Principles and Practice*, Houghton Mifflin, Boston, 1979.

LESNEWICH, A., "The Real Cost of Depositing a Pound of Weld Metal," *Metal Progress*, Apr. 1982, p. 52.

Metals Handbook, 8th ed. Vol. 4: *Forming*, 1969, Vol. 6: *Welding and Brazing*, 1971, American Society for Metals, Metals Park, Ohio.

OSBORN, M. R., "Magnetically Controlled Arc Joins Tubular Components," *Metal Progress*, Nov. 1974, p. 79.

Procedure Handbook of Arc Welding Design and Practice (and many other publications on arc welding), Lincoln Electric Co., Cleveland, Ohio.

READY, J. F., *Industrial Applications of Lasers*, Academic Press, New York, 1978.

SCHAFFER, G., "Lasers in Metalworking," *American Machinist*, July 1, 1975, p. 41.

———, "Welding, Special Report 698," *American Machinist*, Sept. 1977, p. 83.

———, "Fundamentals of Brazing, Special Report 732," *American Machinist*, Apr. 1981, p. 147.

SCHWARTZ, M. M., *Metals Joining Manual*, McGraw-Hill, New York, 1979.

"Subarc Welding with Powder Filler," *American Machinist*, Feb. 1, 1975, p. 43.

TAMASCHKE, W., "Sheet Metal Cutting by Laser," *NC Commline*, May–June 1981, p. 17.

Welding Handbook, American Welding Society, New York.

"What Automation Can Do in Arc Welding," *Metal Progress*, Feb. 1970, p. 67.

ZERNOW, L., "Explosive Bonding," *Mechanical Engineering*, May 1970, p. 39.

15

MEASUREMENT AND INSPECTION

When you can measure what you are speaking about you know something about it.

Lord Kelvin

The basic purpose of manufacturing is to produce engineering materials and products with specified shapes, sizes, and finishes. These shapes, sizes, and finish specifications are generally found on the part drawing or the manufacturing drawing, and they are often referred to as *quality characteristics*.

INTERCHANGEABLE MANUFACTURE

Our modern mass-production systems, based on the concepts of interchangeable manufacture, require that each part or assembly going into a final product be made to definite size, shape, and finish specifications. The mass production of both consumer and producer goods relies on interchangeability, and interchangeability requires fabrication to exacting dimensions and close tolerances. Compressor pistons, for example, must be machined within limits so that a piston selected at random will fit and function properly in the compressor model for which it was designed. This interchangeable manufacturing system is to a large degree responsible for the high standard of living enjoyed today by the people of the United States. It makes possible the standardization of products and methods of manufacturing and provides for ease of assembly and repair of products.

QUALITY ASSURANCE

The quality of a product may be stated in terms of a measure of the degree to which it conforms to specifications and standards of workmanship. These specifications and standards should reflect the degree to which the product satisfies the wants of a particular customer or user. The *quality assurance* function is charged with the responsibility of maintaining product quality consistent with those requirements and it involves the following four basic activities:

1. Quality specification
2. Inspection
3. Quality analysis
4. Quality control

Quality Specification. The product design engineer provides the basic specifications of product quality by means of the various dimensions, tolerances, and other requirements cited on the engineering drawings. These basic specifications are further refined and elaborated upon on the manufacturing drawings which are used by the methods engineering personnel to specify the manufacturing and fabrication procedures. In many cases, the quality assurance group will provide a further interpretation of those specifications as a basis for specifying inspection procedures.

Inspection. The mass production of interchangeable products is not altogether effective without some means of appraising and controlling product quality. Production operators are required, for example, to machine a given number of parts to the specifications shown on a drawing. There are often many factors that cause the parts to deviate from specifications during the various manufacturing operations. A few of these factors are variations in raw materials, deficiencies in machines and tools, poor methods, excessive production rates, and human errors.

Provisions must be made to detect errors so that the production of faulty parts can be stopped. The inspection department is usually charged with this responsibility, and its job is to interpret the specifications properly, inspect for conformance to those specifications, and then convey the information obtained to the production people, who can make any necessary corrections to the process. Inspection operations are performed on raw materials and purchased parts at "receiving inspection." "In-process inspection" is performed on products during the various stages of their manufacture, and finished products may be subjected to "final inspection."

Quality Analysis. During the various inspection processes a variety of quality information is recorded for review by representatives from both manufacturing and quality assurance. In essence, this information provides a basis for analyzing the quality of the product as it relates to the capability of the manufacturing process and to the quality specifications initially prescribed for the product. Generally, it is not possible to mass produce products that are 100% free of defects except at considerable expense. The quality analysis will determine the level of defectivity of the product so that a decision can be made whether or not that level is tolerable. If a given level of defectivity is not tolerable, decisions must be made relative to (1) what to do with the process, and (2) what to do with the product.

Quality Control. The word "control" implies regulation, and of course, regulation implies observation and manipulation. Thus a pilot flying an aircraft from one city to another must first set it on the proper course heading and then must continue to observe the progress of the craft and manipulate the controls so as to maintain its flight path in the proper direction. *Quality control* in manufacture is an analogous situation. It is simply a means by which management can be assured that the quality of product manufactured is consistent with the quality-economy standards that have been established. The word "quality" does not necessarily mean "the best" when applied to manufactured products. It should imply "the best for the money."

STATISTICAL QUALITY CONTROL

Increasing demands for higher quality of product often result in increased cost of inspection and surveillance of processes and product. The old philosophy of attempting to inspect quality into a product is time consuming and costly. It is, of course, more sensible to control the process and make the product correctly rather than rely on having to sort out defective product from good product. Certain statistical techniques have been developed which provide economical means of maintaining continual analysis and control of processes and product. These are known as *statistical quality control methods*, and many of them are formulated on the following basic statistical concepts:

1. A *population* or *universe* is the complete collection of objects or measurements of the type in which we are interested at a particular time. The population may be finite or infinite.

2. A *sample* is a finite group or set of objects taken from a population.

3. The *average* is a point or value about which a population or a sample set of measurements tends to cluster. It is a measure of the ordinariness or central tendency of a group of measurements.

4. *Variation* is the tendency for the measurements or observations in a population or a sample to scatter or disperse themselves about the average value.

In many cases the sizes observed from the inspection of a dimension of a group of pieces have been found to be distributed as shown in Fig. 15-1. If the pins represented in Fig. 15-1 include all the existing pins of a particular type, then this would be referred to as a *population distribution*. If those pins represent only a portion of a larger batch of the same type pins, then it would be called a *sample distribution*.

The pattern of variation shown in Fig. 15-1 is typical of that obtained from data taken from many natural and artificial processes. It is referred to as a *normal distribution*, and the smooth curve formed by this distribution is called the *normal curve*. This, like other distributions, can be described by its arithmetic average (measure of central tendency), called $\overline{X}$, and its standard deviation (measure of variation or dispersion),

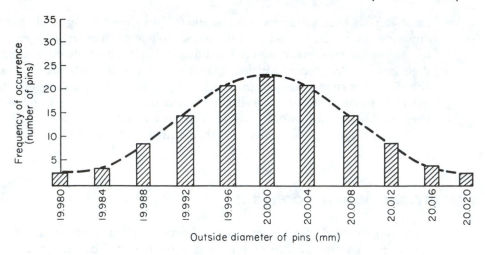

Figure 15-1   Frequency distribution of outside diameters of ground pins.

called σ. The formulas for these factors are:

$$\bar{X} = \frac{\sum\limits_{1}^{n} X_i}{n} \tag{15-1}$$

$$\sigma = \sqrt{\frac{\sum\limits_{1}^{n}(X_i - \bar{X})^2}{n}} \tag{15-2}$$

If $\bar{X}$ and σ are calculated from a population distribution they are called population *parameters*. If they are calculated from the data of a sample they are called sample *statistics*.

The range value R is often used as a measure of variation or dispersion for small samples. The range is the difference between the largest and smallest observed values in a sample set of values: $R = X_{\text{max}} - X_{\text{min}}$.

The greater portion of the area under the normal curve is included between the limits $\bar{X} \pm 3\sigma$. The curve actually continues out to plus and minus infinity, but the area under it beyond plus and minus three standard deviations from the mean is practically negligible.

The areas under intervals of the normal curve commonly used in statistical quality control practice are shown in Fig. 15-2. These mean that if a population of values is normally distributed, 99.73% of the values from that population will probably appear with the limits of $\bar{X} \pm 3\sigma$. Only 0.27% are expected to fall beyond those limits. Similarly, 95.46% of the values normally fall within the limits $\bar{X} \pm 2\sigma$, and 68.26% within $\bar{X} \pm 1\sigma$.

If the manufacturing specification on the pins shown in Fig. 15-1 was 20.00 ± 0.02 mm (0.7874 ± 0.0008 in.) and if the limiting dimensions of that specification 19.98 to 20.02 mm (0.7866 to 0.7882 in.) corresponded to plus or minus

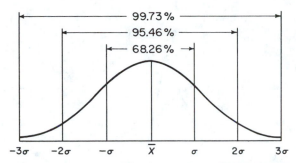

Figure 15-2 Areas under the normal curve.

three standard deviations from the mean, 99.73% of the pins from that population would be expected to be within specifications. Only 0.27% would be expected not to conform to specifications. Most distributions encountered in industrial inspection activities are not exactly normal, but many approach normality. As a distribution approaches normality, its properties approximate those given. Tables of areas under the normal curve for various values of standard deviations from the mean are given in texts on statistical quality control.

Process Control Charts.   One of the statistical tools that is commonly used in quality control work to evaluate the process is the control chart. A control chart is simply a frequency distribution with the observed values plotted as points joined by lines in the order of occurrence so that each value retains identity relative to time. The chart is provided with limit lines, called *control limits,* within which the points fall if influenced only by chance causes.

Two of the most common charts used in process control are the chart for averages, *X̄-chart,* and the chart for ranges, *R-chart.* Figure 15-3 shows an example of such charts for a rough turning operation on the outside diameter of steel shafts. The first point on the $\bar{X}$-chart of Fig. 15-3 was determined by measuring the diameters of five shafts and then calculating the average of those measured values. Each succeeding point is also an average of the measured diameters of five shafts. Average values are plotted instead of individual values because sample averages tend to be more normally distributed than single values. The central line of the $\bar{X}$-chart represents the grand average of the subgroup averages and is

$$\bar{\bar{X}} = \frac{\sum_{1}^{k} \bar{X}}{k}$$

where k is the number of subgroups of 5 shafts each. The control limits are set at three standard deviations of the sample averages from the grand average, and are called *upper control limit* (UCL $= \bar{\bar{X}} + 3\sigma_{\bar{x}}$) and *lower control limit* (LCL $= \bar{\bar{X}} - 3\sigma_{\bar{x}}$). From formula (15-2),

$$\sigma_{\bar{x}} = \sqrt{\frac{\sum_{1}^{k} (\bar{\bar{X}} - \bar{X})^2}{k}}$$

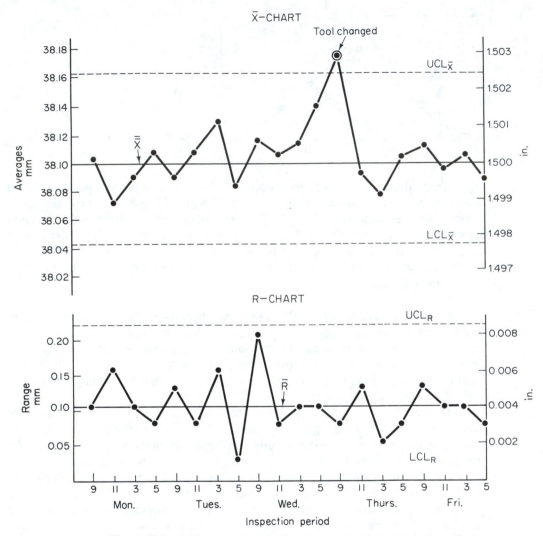

Figure 15-3   Quality control chart, showing averages and ranges of samples.

Theoretically, chances are that less than 3 out of 1000 points will fall outside the limits as long as no change is made in the system producing the values.

The range of values of the R-chart of Fig. 15-3 is obtained from the same subgroups of five samples each as were the $\overline{X}$ values. The central line $\overline{R}$ represents the average of the subgroup ranges. Control limits on range charts are calculated by multiplying the average range by a factor which may be obtained from texts on statistical quality control.

The $\overline{X}$-chart of Fig. 15-3 indicates that the process average remained in a state of statistical control until the nine o'clock inspection period on Thursday, at which time a point exceeded the upper control limit. In this case, the out of control point was found to be caused by a worn cutting tool. Replacement of the tool caused the subsequent points to fall well within the control limits. This illustrates how a major change in the production process is reflected by the chart. Points that fall outside the limits of either chart occur because of chance causes or because of actual changes in the process.

It must be emphasized that the control limits of a process control chart do not represent the performance limits of the process nor the specification limits of the dimension. The performance limits of the process are the limiting dimensions within which practically all the parts fall. These are the $\pm 3\sigma$ limits of the population distribution, if it is near normal. For a very large (theoretically infinite) population, $\sigma = \sigma_{\bar{x}}\sqrt{n}$, where n is the number of items in each sample. From this relationship it can be shown that the process represented by Fig. 15-3 is producing shafts from 37.97 to 38.23 mm (1.495 to 1.505 in.). For the sake of manufacturing economy, it is normally desired that the process be designed to perform within the specification limits.

Sampling Inspection. Inspection operations are costly and do not contribute directly to the value of the product. Therefore, the amount of inspection should be kept to a minimum consistent with the quality requirements of the product. In order to be assured that each and every part produced conforms to specifications it is usually necessary to perform *100% inspection* on them. However, if a few defective items can be tolerated among a large number of good items, then an inspection procedure known as *sampling* can be applied. In this procedure a given number of parts are chosen at random from a group or lot of parts and are inspected for conformance to certain specifications. According to previously determined acceptance criteria, the lot of parts is judged acceptable or rejectable on the basis of the sample results.

There are quite a number of published sampling plans available based on *single sampling, double sampling,* or some form of *sequential* or *group sequential sampling*. A typical single-sampling plan might require the inspection of 110 random samples from a lot of 1300 parts. If only three or less of the 110 were found to be defective, the lot would be accepted. The lot would be rejected if more than three defectives were detected in the sample of 110.

Sampling plans are selected on the basis of the amount of risk that can be tolerated in accepting defective material and rejecting acceptable material. Information about these risks is obtained from the *operating characteristic curve* of the sampling plan. Figure 15-4 shows an operating characteristic curve for the single-sampling plan described in the preceding paragraph. From this curve it is observed that with the quality of the material coming into inspection being 1% defective (point p_1 on the abscissa), the material would be accepted by the sampling plan about 97% of the time. If the material coming in were 6% defective (point p_2 on the abscissa), it would be accepted only about 11% of the time. Thus, a sampling plan should be selected that will satisfy the demands of both the producer and the consumer of the material being manufactured, so that each party will be aware of the risks inherent in sampling.

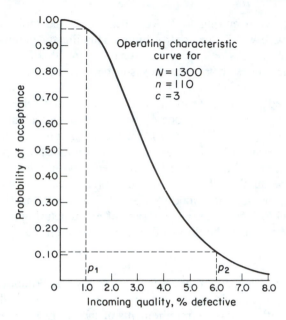

Figure 15-4   Operating characteristic curve for a single-sampling plan.

MANUFACTURING SPECIFICATIONS

Effective interchangeability relies upon complete specifications of the dimensions of a part or group of parts making up a product. Modern mass manufacturing systems are so complex that it is usually not economical for one skilled worker to machine and fabricate all of the individual parts that go into an assembly. Rather, it is necessary that the various parts be worked upon by numerous people who are responsible for only one or perhaps a few operations on one of the component parts of a product. Thus, exacting specifications relative to the dimensions of these parts must be supplied to the workers so that they may produce articles that can be assembled with a minimum of costly hand fitting and reworking.

Tolerances.   Ideally, it would be desirable to manufacture parts to an exact size, but this is not physically practical nor economically feasible. To grind a cylindrical shaft to exactly 25 mm (1 in.) diameter would require a grinding machine of ultimate perfection—perfect spindle bearings, perfect way surfaces, perfect balance of the grinding wheel, etc. Even though such a machine could possibly be built and maintained in such a state of perfection, it would be beyond the realm of practical measurements to determine whether or not the shafts ground on the machine were exactly 25 mm (1 in.) in diameter. For this reason and others cited previously, it is necessary that some deviation be allowed from the exact theoretically desired size of a part. This deviation is usually referred to as a *manufacturing* or *working tolerance* and may be defined as the *permissible variation in a dimension*.

Ways of Specifying Tolerance.   Manufacturing tolerances may be assigned according to three different systems as shown in Fig. 15-5. Part *A* is assigned a

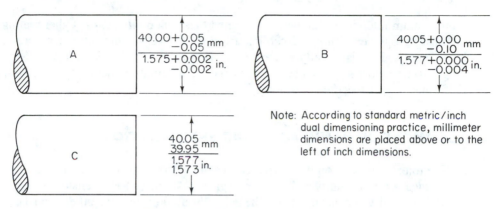

Figure 15-5 Methods of assigning tolerances.

bilateral tolerance; part *B* has a *unilateral tolerance;* and part *C* has the size specified in terms of *limiting dimensions* or *manufacturing limits*. Notice that all three parts have the same total amount of tolerance and the same limiting dimensions.

There are certain advantages to specifying tolerances according to one or the other of these systems. A unilateral tolerance often implies that it is more critical for a certain dimension to deviate in one direction than in another. Unilateral tolerances are also more realistically applied to certain machining processes where it is common knowledge that dimensions will most likely deviate in one direction. For example, in drilling a hole with a standard-size drill, the drill is more likely to produce an oversize rather than an undersize hole. Unilateral tolerances also facilitate the specification and application of standard tools and gages. The application of unilateral tolerances also permits easy revision of tolerances without affecting the allowance or clearance conditions between mating parts. Thus this system of tolerancing usually finds the greatest acceptance in industrial application.

More recently the trend has been to utilize the bilateral tolerance system as more desirable for manufacturing dimensions. This system vividly points out the theoretically desired size and indicates the possible and probable deviations that can be expected on each side of that theoretical size. Bilateral tolerances are easier to add together.

Clearance. One of the basic reasons for specifying precise limiting dimensions for machined objects is to be assured that component parts of an assembly will fit properly and function well under certain operating conditions. For example, a crankshaft must be free to rotate within the confines of the main bearings. Yet it must not fit so sloppily that excessive vibrations cause possible damage to the shaft or engine block. There must be a limited amount of free space between the shaft and the bore. This free space is usually referred to as *clearance,* and it may be defined as the *intentional difference in the sizes of mating parts.* In many cases it is necessary that mating parts be assembled more or less permanently; one part being pressed firmly into another. Thus, a given amount of what is termed *negative clearance* or *interference* must be assigned to this condition to assure a tight fit. The minimum clearance or maximum interference between mating parts is called *allowance*. Other mating parts must fit together with no perceptible freedom and yet require little or no pressure on assembly. This is usually termed a *metal-to-metal* or *transitional fit*. These three general categories of fits (clearance, transition, and interference) may be broken down further to suit specific conditions.

DEVELOPMENT OF MANUFACTURING SPECIFICATIONS

The tolerance that should be assigned to a dimension is that which gives an economic balance between quality and cost. For a given tolerance on a dimension some parts can be expected to be further from the most desirable size than others and be able to function less well or wear not as long. If a larger tolerance is assigned, more parts can be expected to be inferior, but still within limits, and the total value of the product will be less. In general, the value of the product in a hypothetical case is shown by the upper curve of Fig. 15-6 to decrease in some manner as tolerance is increased.

A large tolerance for a given dimension can be held more easily and is cheaper than a small tolerance. Each machine and process has a certain capability. Within that range more care and skill are required, the closer the limits that must be held. If smaller tolerances are demanded, resort must be made to other and usually more costly processes. Thus, in a typical case depicted by the lower curve of Fig. 15-6, cost increases as the tolerance decreases. The curve, of course, is different for every situation. Such a curve may represent grinding a diameter, or a similar composite curve may be true for turning, grinding, or even Superfinishing for the smallest tolerances.

If for a particular situation the value and cost curves are plotted on the same scale, the result is as shown in Fig. 15-6. The ideal tolerance is that which gives the largest difference between value and cost. It would be worthwhile to ascertain this ideal tolerance for large-quantity production because of the savings involved. Other-

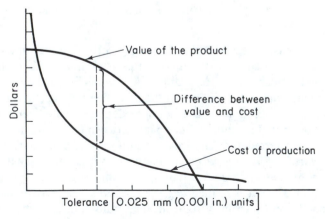

Figure 15-6 Curves of value and cost, showing location of ideal tolerance.

wise, it could be approximately set because tolerances within a range are close enough for practical purposes.

Certain dimensions of nonmating parts or products such as the length of a handle or diameter of a handwheel may not require very precise specifications because their functional effectiveness does not depend on whether or not their dimensions vary by as much as say ± 6 mm ($\pm \frac{1}{4}$ in.) However, for the sake of uniformity of method, stock usage, packing, etc., a nominal amount of tolerance ± 0.4 mm ($\pm \frac{1}{64}$ in.) or some other nominal amount of tolerance is usually specified.

Assembly Methods.   Basically, there are two methods of assembly for mass-produced components, random assembly and selective assembly. In random assembly, the mating parts must be made to a tolerance that will permit any component selected at random to fit properly with any randomly selected mating component. Normally in selective assembly, the components are put into groups according to size and then assembled with mating components also segregated by sizes. For example, a shaft diameter may be produced to a tolerance of 0.03 mm (0.0012 in.), with a nominal diameter of 25 mm (ca. 1 in.) and actual limits of 25.00 to 24.97 mm (ca. 1.0000 to 0.9988 in.) The bearing may likewise have a tolerance of 0.03 mm (0.0012 in.) with actual limits of 25.03 to 25.00 mm (ca. 1.0012 to 1.0000 in.) The clearance between parts assembled at random may be anywhere from 0 to 0.06 mm (0.0024 in.) In the event that the clearance must not be over 0.03 mm (0.0012 in.) without excessive losses in the product, two courses of action are open. One is to reduce the tolerance on each part, at greater cost. The other is to make and divide the shafts into two groups, one with limits from 24.985 to 25.000 mm (ca. 0.9994 to 1.0000 in.) and the other from 25.000 to 25.015 mm (ca. 1.0000 to 1.0006 in.), which still embraces a production tolerance of 0.03 mm (0.0012 in.). The bearings, made to the same tolerance as before, are divided into two groups with ranges of 25.000 to 25.015 mm (ca. 1.000 to 1.0006 in.) and 25.015 to 25.030 mm (ca. 1.0006 to 1.0012 in.). Now by assembling from proper groups, clearances can be held to 0.03 mm (0.0012 in.) or less. This is called selective assembly, and in some cases is more economical than manufacturing to small tolerances. A practice common in tool and job shop work but uncommon for production of quantities is to machine one part of a pair to a size and the mating part to a clearance with a specified range.

Tolerances on Linear Dimensions.   The exact theoretically desired size of a part is usually referred to as the *basic size,* and it is the size from which variation is permitted. A *standard size* is a commonly used integer or subdivision of a unit of length. Whole-number millimeters and common fractions of an inch are examples.

Tolerances are usually developed to conform to certain standardized design procedures. Two commonly used procedures are called *standard hole practice* and *standard shaft practice.* In standard hole practice the basic size of the hole is assigned a standard size, and a positive unilateral tolerance is applied. The basic size of the mating shaft is determined by subtracting the prescribed allowance from the standard size for a clearance fit, or adding the prescribed allowance to the standard size for an interference fit. A negative unilateral tolerance is assigned to the shaft. Notice that the holes and shafts of Fig. 15-8 are dimensioned according to standard hole practice. This system permits the use of standard reamers for finishing holes and standard limit plug gages for checking.

Standard shaft practice designates the maximum limiting size of commercial shafting as the standard size and applies a negative unilateral tolerance to it. The basic size of the hole is determined by adding the prescribed allowance to the standard size for a clearance fit, or subtracting the prescribed allowance from the standard size for an interference fit. The hole is assigned a positive unilateral tolerance.

Standards for Allowances and Tolerances.   One very common method for determining allowances and tolerances for mating parts is through the use of formulas or tables prepared by technical organizations. For example, the American National Standards Institute has published standard tables prepared by the American Society of Mechanical Engineers (ANSI B4.2-1978) on preferred metric limits and fits for mating parts in which hole and shaft limits are provided for three basic types of fits.

Table 2 of the standard, a portion of which is shown in Fig. 15-7, gives limits for clearance fits applicable to basic hole sizes ranging from 1 to 500 mm (0.0394 to 19.685 in.). Five subclasses of this type fit are provided ranging from *loose running fits,* intended for wide commercial tolerances or allowances on external members, to *locational clearance fits,* which provide a snug fit for locating stationary parts, but which can be freely assembled and disassembled. Other tables are given in the standard for both transition and interference types of fits. One of the transition types, the *location transition fit,* is a compromise between clearance and interference, and is used for accurate location of mating parts. Three subclasses of interference fits are given, ranging from *locational interference fits* to *force fits. Force fits* are suitable for parts which can be highly stressed or for shrink fits where heavy pressing forces are impractical.

Hole and shaft dimensions for a free running fit and a sliding fit are shown in Fig. 15-8. Basic hole size in each case is 40 mm (1.5748 in.)

Tolerances for 100% Interchangeability.   If the amount of clearance or interference required between mating parts is known, the tolerances for 100% interchangeability can be determined quite easily by simple addition. The shaft and bearing assembly of Fig. 15-9 illustrates this procedure. For this assembly it is assumed that nominal assembly size is 50 mm (ca. 2 in.) with a minimum total clearance of 0.05 mm (0.002 in.) and a maximum total clearance of 0.20 mm (0.008 in.) Tolerance is shown bilateral from basic size but could be specified in any way. For purposes of analysis, Fig. 15-9 shows the shaft resting on the bottom of the bearing so that maximum and minimum total clearances can be observed. Tolerances and basic sizes may be obtained by simply summing dimensions from a reference surface of the part under consideration. The tolerance on the shaft may be determined as follows: Starting at B,

$$\overline{BD} + \overline{DE} - \overline{EB} = 0$$

where $\overline{BD}$ = tolerance on the shaft, $\overline{DE}$ = half of the minimum clearance = 0.05

Basic size		Free running			Close running			Sliding		
		Hole H9	Shaft d9	Fit	Hole H8	Shaft f7	Fit	Hole H7	Shaft g6	Fit
40	Max.	40.062	39.920	0.204	40.039	39.975	0.089	40.025	39.991	0.050
	Min.	40.000	39.858	0.080	40.000	39.950	0.025	40.000	39.975	0.009
50	Max.	50.062	49.920	0.204	50.039	49.975	0.089	50.025	49.991	0.050
	Min.	50.000	49.858	0.080	50.000	49.950	0.025	50.000	49.975	0.009
60	Max.	60.074	59.900	0.248	60.046	59.970	0.106	60.030	59.990	0.059
	Min.	60.000	59.826	0.100	60.000	59.940	0.030	60.000	59.971	0.010
80	Max.	80.074	79.900	0.248	80.046	79.970	0.106	80.030	79.990	0.059
	Min.	80.000	79.826	0.100	80.000	79.940	0.030	80.000	79.971	0.010
100	Max.	100.087	99.880	0.294	100.054	99.964	0.125	100.035	99.988	0.069
	Min.	100.000	99.793	0.120	100.000	99.929	0.036	100.000	99.966	0.012
120	Max.	120.087	119.880	0.294	120.054	119.964	0.125	120.035	119.988	0.069
	Min.	120.000	119.793	0.120	120.000	119.929	0.036	120.000	119.966	0.012
160	Max.	160.100	159.855	0.345	160.063	159.957	0.146	160.040	159.986	0.079
	Min.	160.000	159.755	0.145	160.000	159.917	0.043	160.000	159.961	0.014
200	Max.	200.115	199.830	0.400	200.072	199.950	0.168	200.046	199.985	0.090
	Min.	200.000	199.715	0.170	200.000	199.904	0.050	200.000	199.956	0.015
250	Max.	250.115	249.830	0.400	250.072	249.950	0.168	250.046	249.985	0.090
	Min.	250.000	249.715	0.170	250.000	249.904	0.050	250.000	249.956	0.015
300	Max.	300.130	299.810	0.450	300.081	299.944	0.189	300.052	299.983	0.101
	Min.	300.000	299.680	0.190	300.000	299.892	0.056	300.000	299.951	0.017
400	Max.	400.140	399.790	0.490	400.089	399.938	0.208	400.057	399.982	0.111
	Min.	400.000	399.650	0.210	400.000	399.881	0.062	400.000	399.946	0.018
500	Max.	500.155	499.770	0.540	500.097	499.932	0.228	500.063	499.980	0.123
	Min.	500.000	499.615	0.230	500.000	499.869	0.068	500.000	499.940	0.020

Dimensions in mm.

Figure 15-7 Abbreviated table of clearance fits extracted from American National Standard *Preferred Metric Limits and Fits*, ANSI B4.2-1978, with the permission of the publisher, the American Society of Mechanical Engineers, United Engineering Center, 345 East 47th Street, New York, NY, 10017.

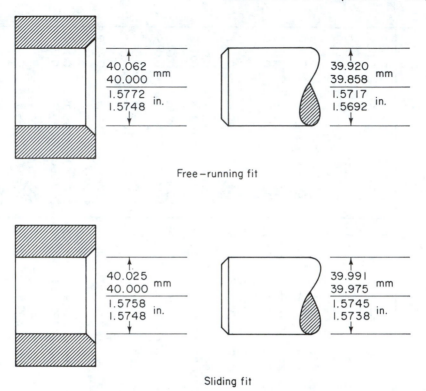

Free-running fit

Sliding fit

Figure 15-8 Dimensions of shaft and hole for a free running fit and a sliding fit.

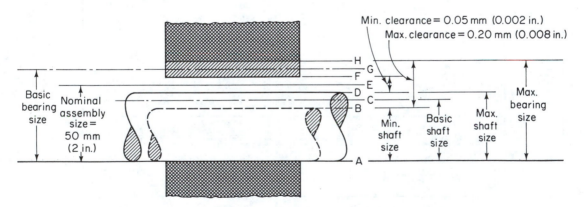

Figure 15-9 Extreme positions for a shaft and bearing.

mm/2 (0.002 in./2), and $\overline{EB}$ = half of the maximum clearance = 0.20 mm/2 (0.008 in./2). Thus

$$\overline{BD} + 0.05 \text{ mm}/2 \text{ (or 0.002 in.}/2) - 0.20 \text{ mm}/2 \text{ (or 0.008 in.}/2) = 0$$

or

$$\overline{BD} = 0.10 \text{ mm (or 0.004 in.)} - 0.025 \text{ mm (or 0.001 in.)}$$
$$= 0.075 \text{ mm (or 0.003 in.)}$$

Other dimensions may be determined by a similar process.

Determination of Tolerances for Statistical Average Interchangeability. Methods of statistical analysis may be applied to increase tolerances and effect manufacturing economies. The statistical concepts applicable to this problem are those of the normal distribution and its parameters $\overline{X}$ and σ defined by Eqs. (15-1) and (15-2). Theory and experience have shown that if the variations of the dimensions of the parts approximate a normal distribution, as they commonly do, and the parts are selected at random, the distribution of fits obtained is practically normal. Also, the mean value of the clearance is

$$\overline{X}_{\text{clearance}} = \overline{X}_{\text{bearings}} - \overline{X}_{\text{shafts}} \tag{15-3}$$

and the standard deviation of the variations in the clearance is

$$\sigma_{\text{clearance}} = \sqrt{\sigma^2_{\text{bearings}} + \sigma^2_{\text{shafts}}} \tag{15-4}$$

where the σ's for bearings and shafts are the standard deviations of the variations in sizes from the means.

In the case of the bearing and shaft assembly of Fig. 15-9, $6 \times \sigma_{\text{clearance}}$ = 0.20 − 0.05 = 0.15 mm (0.008 − 0.002 = 0.006 in.) and $\sigma_{\text{clearance}}$ = 0.025 mm (0.001 in.). If not specified otherwise, $\sigma_{\text{bearing}} = \sigma_{\text{shaft}} = \sigma_p$, and $\sqrt{\sigma^2_p + \sigma^2_p}$ = 0.025 mm (0.001 in.) from Eq. (15-4). Thus σ_p = 0.018 mm (0.0007 in.), and the tolerance for bearing or shaft is $6\sigma_p$ or 0.108 mm (0.0042 in.). This permits 40% more tolerance on the parts than is required for 100% interchangeability. Yet if the prescribed conditions are met, fewer than 3 assemblies out of 1000 can be expected to have clearances greater or less than specified.

Geometric Dimensions and Tolerances.   The limit dimensions of the simple cylindrical piece at the top of Fig. 15-10 define the maximum and minimum limits of a profile for the work. The form or shape of the part may vary as long as no portions of the part exceed the maximum profile limit or are inside the minimum profile limit. If a part is everywhere on its maximum material limit of size, it should be of perfect form. This is referred to as the *maximum material condition* and is at the low limit for a hole or slot but at the high limit for a shaft, bolt, pin, etc.

If it is desired to provide greater control on the form than is imposed by the limit dimensions, then certain tolerances of form must be applied. In most cases these

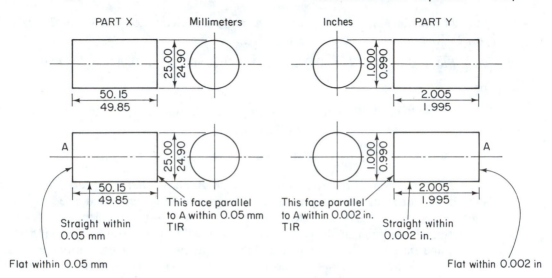

Figure 15-10 Part drawing with and without tolerances of form.

tolerances appear in the form of notations on the drawing as is illustrated at the bottom of Fig. 15-10.

Positional Tolerances.   Positional tolerancing is a system of specifying the true position, size, or form of a feature of a part and the amount the feature may vary from the ideal. The advantage of the system is that it allows the one responsible for making the part to divide tolerances between position and size as he or she finds best. The principles are illustrated for two simple mating parts in Fig. 15-11. The basic dimensions without tolerances are denoted by *BSC*. Beneath the size dimension for holes or posts is a box with the notations for positional tolerancing. Actually, a number of specifications are possible, but only one set is shown here as an example. The circle and cross in the first cell of the box is the convention that says the features are positionally toleranced.

Part I introduces the idea of the maximum material condition called MMC utilized in most positional tolerancing. This is designated by the letter M in a circle and means that the smallest hole (12.70 mm or 0.500 in.) determines the inner boundary for any hole. The "0.20 mm (0.008 in.) diam." notation specifies that the axis of any minimum-size hole must not be outside a theoretical cylinder of 0.20 mm (0.008 in.) diameter around the true position. A 12.50-mm (0.492-in.)-diameter plug in true position will fit in any 12.70-mm (0.500-in.)-diameter hole with its axis on the 0.20-mm (0.008-in.)-diameter cylinder. Any hole that passes over such a plug is acceptable provided that its diameter is within the high and low limits specified.

The letter A in the specification box designates that the theoretical cylinder bounding the hole axes must be perpendicular to the datum surface carrying the A flag. Features usually are referred to three coordinate datum surfaces, but for simplicity in this case the holes are related only to each other and surface A and not to the sides of the part.

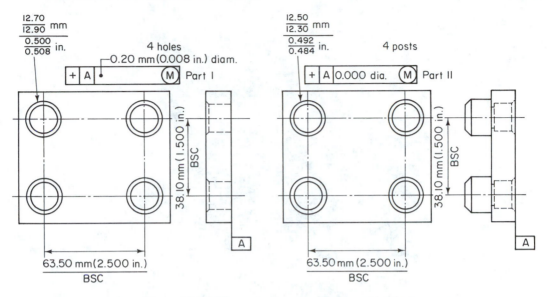

Figure 15-11 Two parts dimensioned with positional tolerances.

Part II introduces the idea of zero maximum material condition specified by 0.000 diameter before the MMC symbol. This means the axis of the largest-diameter post (12.50 mm or 0.492 in.) must be exactly in the true position, but smaller sizes of posts may vary in position as long as they do not lie outside the boundary set by the largest. Thus, if the posts are held to a tolerance smaller than the 0.20 mm (0.008 in.) specified, say to a tolerance of 0.05 mm (0.002 in.), the difference (0.15 mm or 0.006 in.) is then available for variations in post positions. The advantage of zero MMC is that only one limit of the feature, in this case the lower limit of the post diameter, needs to be checked along with position.

STANDARDS FOR MEASURING AND GAGING

If manufactured parts of a kind are to be interchangeable, all measurements must be based on a set of reliable standards. This is especially true when mating parts are made in different places in the nation or the world. The parts will not fit together unless each maker uses the same standards of measurement.

Length Standard. In September 1975 the U.S. Congress passed the Metric Conversion Act, which ended U.S. isolation in a metric world. This legislation called for a voluntary conversion to the international metric system, SI (from the French Système International d'Unités) and it was expected that transition to that system could be effected in an orderly manner within a 7-year period. SI consists of a foundation of seven base units from which all others are derived, and it represents a logical and comprehensive framework for all measurements in science, industry, and commerce. According to the American National Standards Institute publication ANSI

Figure 15-12 Set of precision gage blocks and accessories. (Courtesy Pratt and Whitney, Inc.)

2210.1-1976, the "meter" is the basic length standard under the metric system and the meter is defined as the length equal to 1,650,763.75 wavelengths in vacuum of the radiation corresponding to the transition between levels $2p_{10}$ and $5d_5$ of the krypton-86 atom.

End Standards.   Gage blocks are the practical length standards of industry. They are rectangular, square, or round blocks of steel or carbide, each with two faces flat, level, and parallel within approximately 30 to 160 nm (0.000001 to 0.000006 in.) depending upon length and accuracy grade. There are four basic classes of gage blocks which conform to specified federal accuracy standards. *Laboratory master blocks,* which conform to federal accuracy grade 0.5 (formerly AAA grade), must be accurate to about ±25 nm per 25 mm of length (±0.000001 in./in.) and are intended for use in checking other gage blocks or setting very precise laboratory equipment. Federal accuracy grade 1 blocks (formerly AA grade) are accurate to about ±50 nm per 25 mm of length (±0.000002 in./in.) and are used as reference blocks to calibrate measuring instruments, to set gages, and for very close layout work. Federal accuracy grade 2 and 3 blocks are normally used as working gage blocks in shop operations for layout inspection, and machine settings, with the more accurate grade 2 blocks being used where a higher level of accuracy is required. Grade 2 blocks through 25 mm (1 in.) length have a length accuracy of $+100$ or -50 nm ($+0.000004$ or -0.000002 in.), while grade 3 blocks of similar lengths have a length accuracy of $+160$ or -50 nm ($+0.000006$ or -0.000002 in.).

Gage blocks may be bought individually or in sets that can be put together to get various series of sizes. The blocks can be wrung together with a film of less than 8 nm (0.0000003 in.) between them. Many sets are available commercially; one is shown in Fig. 15-12. A set with 88 blocks can be combined to get any length from 3 mm to over 550 mm in steps of 0.0005 mm, and smaller dimensions in larger steps. Such a set is listed at almost $1200 in steel and over $3000 in cemented carbide. A comparable set of 81 blocks gives lengths from 0.200 in. to over 25 in. in steps of 0.0001 in., and as small as 0.050 in. in larger steps. Accessories are also provided for gaging external and internal dimensions, scribing lines, and marking centers directly from the blocks. The major source of error in gaging to submillimeter tolerances is temperature variation. When a gage is said to have a certain length, that is understood to be the length at the standard temperature of 20°C (68°F). Other necessary conditions for precise measurements are freedom from dust and low humidity to inhibit rust.

MEASURING AND GAGING INSTRUMENTS

The dimensions of manufactured parts have to be checked as they are made and after they are finished to assure quality. *Measuring* is done to find the actual size of a dimension while *gaging* merely shows whether a dimension is within specified limits. Parts made in large quantities are gaged because that takes the least time to sort the bad from the good. Less skill is needed for gaging, as a rule, than for measuring.

Measuring instruments and gages may be classified as precision and non-precision. The *precision of measurement* of an instrument is the smallest increment of size that it can reveal. Instruments capable of measuring to 0.02 mm (or 0.001 in.) or less are usually considered *precision measuring instruments*. The need for such devices arises from the fact that the tolerances on the dimensions of many parts manufactured today are less than 25 μm or 0.001 in. and not uncommonly as small as 25 nm or 0.000001 in.

Measuring instruments may be *direct reading* or of the *transfer type*. An ordinary steel rule such as is shown in Fig. 15-13(31) contains a graduated scale from which the size of a dimension being measured can be determined directly, while the spring caliper of Fig. 15-13(1) contains no scale graduations. It is adjusted to fit the size of a dimension being measured and then is compared to a direct reading scale so as to obtain the size of the dimension.

Most of the available measuring instruments may be grouped according to certain basic principles of operation. Many simple instruments use only a graduated

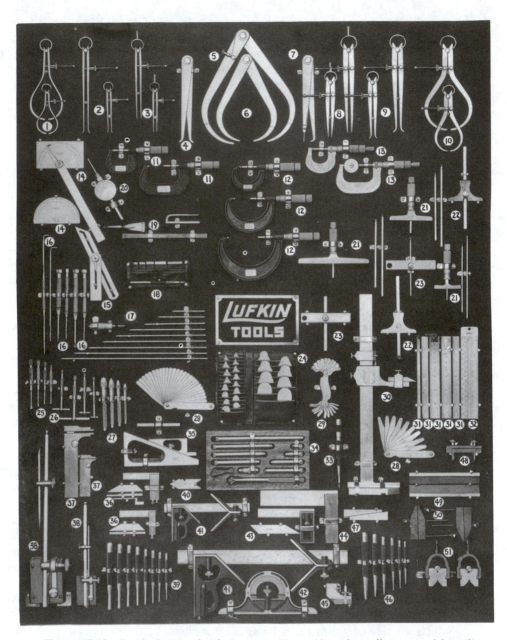

Figure 15-13 Standard measuring instruments: (1) outside spring calipers, round leg; (2) inside spring calipers; (3) spring dividers; (4) inside firm joint caliper; (5) outside firm joint caliper with adjusting screw; (6) outside firm joint caliper; (7) firm joint hermaphrodite caliper; (8) spring divider; (9) inside spring caliper; (10) outside spring caliper; (11) outside micrometer calipers, medium weight; (12) outside micrometer calipers, heavy duty; (13) outside micrometer

scale as a measurement basis, while others may have two related scales and use the vernier principle of measurement. In a number of instruments the movement of a precision screw is related to two or three graduated scales to form a basis for measurement. Many other instruments utilize some sort of mechanical, electrical, or optical linkage between the measuring element and the graduated scale so that a small movement of the measuring element produces an enlarged indication on the scale. Air pressure or metered airflow is used in a few instruments as a means of measurement. These operating principles will be more fully explained in the descriptions of a few of the instruments in which they are applied.

Basic Measuring Instruments and Gages. People in nearly every craft, whether they be television repairmen, automotive mechanics, or telephone installers, have a set of tools applicable to their work. Similarly, machinists, machine operators, toolmakers, etc., have a variety of basic measuring and gaging devices which they use in their daily work and which may be considered tools of their trade. Many of these are often referred to as *standard* or *general-purpose* tools, and for the most part they are relatively simple in construction. The results obtained from the use of these tools are considerably dependent upon the skill and dexterity of the person using them. For instance, the accuracy obtained in many cases depends upon the amount of pressure applied to the measuring elements. Thus the craftsman through training and experience acquires the sense of touch necessary to apply the tools properly. A group of basic instruments is shown in Fig. 15-13. The group includes direct reading and transfer-type linear measuring instruments, angular measuring devices, fixed and adjustable gaging devices, layout tools, and other miscellaneous metalworking accessories.

Basic Direct-Reading Measuring Instruments. Most of the basic or general-purpose linear measuring instruments are typified by the steel rule, the vernier caliper, or the micrometer caliper.

Steel rules are used effectively as *line measuring devices,* which means that the ends of a dimension being measured are aligned with the graduations of the scale from which the length is read directly. Steel rules are found in depth rules, Fig. 15-13(22 and 23), for measuring the depth of slots, holes, etc. They are also incorporated in slide calipers, Fig. 15-13(37), where they are adapted to *end measuring operations,* which are often more accurate and easier to apply than in line measuring.

---

calipers with lock nut and ratchet stop; (14) steel protractors; (15) universal bevel; (16) scribers; (17) inside micrometer set, solid rods; (18) steel rule set and holder; (19) universal indicator; (20) dial test indicator; (21) micrometer depth gages; (22) depth rules; (23) depth gage; (24) radius gage set; (25) small hole gages; (26) telescoping gages; (27) pin vises; (28) thickness gages; (29) screw pitch gage; (30) vernier height gage; (31) steel rules; (32) mechanics' reference table; (33) automatic center punch; (34) inside micrometer set, tubular; (35) planer and shaper gage; (36) diemakers' squares; (37) slide calipers; (38) universal surface gages; (39) drive pin punches; (40) center gage; (41) combination square; (42) bevel protractor; (43) double squares; (44) steel square; (45) right-angle rule clamps; (46) center punches; (47) tapered parallels; (48) rule clamps; (49) hold-down parallels; (50) toolmakers' parallel clamps; (51) V-blocks and clamps.

Verniers.   The *vernier caliper* shown in Fig. 15-14 typifies the type of instrument using the vernier principle of measurement. The main or beam scale on a typical metric vernier caliper is numbered in increments of 10 mm, with the smallest scale division being equivalent to 1 mm. The vernier scale slides along the edge of the main scale and is divided into 50 divisions, so that these 50 divisions are the same in total length as 49 divisions on the main scale. Each division on the vernier scale is then equal to $\frac{1}{50}$ of (49 × 1) or 0.98 mm, which is 0.02 mm less than each division of the main scale. Aligning the zero lines of both scales would cause the first lines on each scale to be 0.02 mm apart, the second lines 0.04 mm apart, etc. A measurement on a vernier is designated by the positions of the zero line of the vernier and the line on the vernier that coincides with a line on the main scale. For example, the metric scale (top scale) of the illustration included with Fig. 15-14 shows a reading of 12.42 mm. The zero index of the vernier is located just beyond the line at 12 mm on the main scale, and line 21 (after 0) on the vernier coincides with a line on the main scale indicating the zero index is 0.42 mm beyond the line at 12 mm. Thus 12.00 + 0.42 = 12.42 mm.

The vernier caliper illustrated in Fig. 15-14 also has an inch scale so that it can be used interchangeably for either inch or millimeter measurements. The smallest division on the main scale represents 0.025 in. and the vernier is divided into 0.001-in. increments. Thus the measurement illustrated is 0.475 from the main scale plus 0.014 from the vernier scale, for a total of 0.489 in.

A vernier may be designed to indicate practically any increment of length (within

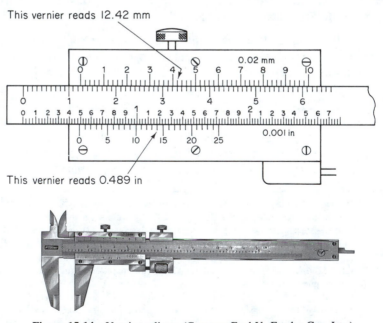

Figure 15-14   Vernier caliper. (Courtesy Fred V. Fowler Co., Inc.)

practical limits of visual perception) according to the relationship

$$\frac{d_m(d_s + 1)}{I} = 1 \qquad (15\text{-}5)$$

where d_m is the number of divisions in one unit of length on the main scale, d_s is the length of the secondary scale measured in divisions of the main scale, and $1/I$ is the smallest increment to be read with the vernier.

The vernier caliper shown in Fig. 15-14 consists of a steel rule with a pair of fixed jaws at one end and a pair of sliding jaws affixed to a vernier. Outside dimensions are measured between the lower jaws; inside dimensions over the tips of the upper jaws. It costs about $100.

The *digital reading caliper* shown in Fig. 15-15 provides LCD readouts in either millimeters or inches and operates on a microprocessor-based system. The caliper has a measuring range of 0 to 150 mm or 0 to 6 in. with readings in increments of 0.01 mm or 0.0005 in. The unit is capable of retaining a reading in the display when the tool is used in an area where visibility is restricted. It is powered by long-life disposable batteries or rechargeable batteries. It costs about $250.

The *vernier height gage* of Fig. 15-13(30) is similar to a vernier caliper except that the fixed jaw has been replaced by a fixed base, and the sliding jaw may have a scriber attached to it for layout work or a dial indicator for measuring or comparing operations. A more sophisticated version of the vernier height gage is represented by the microprocessor-based digital height gage shown in Fig. 15-16. That instrument is a multifunction gage that can measure external, internal depth, and distance

Figure 15-15 Digital-reading caliper. (Courtesy Fred V. Fowler Co., Inc.)

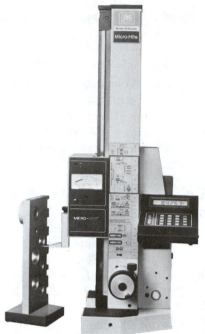

Figure 15-16 Digital-reading microprocessor-based height gage. (Courtesy Brown and Sharpe Mfg. Co.)

dimensions—plus perpendicularity, flatness, straightness, slots, centers, and diameters. Vertical measurements are made in either metric or inch units to a resolution of 0.001 mm or 0.0001 in. by an optoelectronic sensor moving over a precision glass scale. The microprocessor system permits the operator to select 13 function programs, singly or in a variety of combinations, which will cause the gage to automatically calculate deviations from preset dimensions, center-to-center distances, and a number of other feature relationships.

Micrometer.   The *micrometer caliper* illustrated in Fig. 15-17 is representative of the type of instrument using a precision screw as a basis for measuring. The measuring elements consist of a fixed anvil and a spindle that moves lengthwise as it is turned.

The thread on the spindle of a typical metric micrometer has a lead of $\frac{1}{2}$ or 0.5 mm, so that one complete revolution of the thimble produces a spindle movement of this amount. The graduated scale on the sleeve of the instrument has major divisions of 1.0 mm and minor divisions of 0.5 mm. Thus one revolution of the spindle causes the beveled edge of the thimble to move through one small division on the sleeve scale. The periphery of the beveled edge of the thimble is graduated into 50 equal divisions, each space representing $\frac{1}{50}$ of a complete rotation of the thimble, or a movement of the spindle of 0.01 mm. Micrometers with scales in inch units operate in a similar fashion. Typically, the spindle thread has a lead of 0.025 in. and the smallest division on the sleeve represents 0.025 in. The periphery of the beveled edge of the thimble is

Figure 15-17 A 0–25-mm micrometer caliper. (Courtesy Fred V. Fowler Co., Inc.)

graduated into 25 equal divisions, each space representing $\frac{1}{25}$ of a complete rotation of the thimble or a movement of the spindle of 0.001 in.

A reading on a micrometer is made by adding the thimble division which is aligned with the longitudinal sleeve line to the largest reading exposed on the sleeve scale. For example, in Fig. 15-18 the thimble has exposed the number 10, representing 10.00 mm, and one small division worth 0.50 mm. The thimble division 16 is aligned with the longitudinal sleeve line, indicating that the thimble has moved 0.16 mm beyond the last small division on sleeve. Thus the final reading is obtained by summing the three components, $10.00 + 0.50 + 0.16 = 10.66$ mm.

A *vernier micrometer caliper* such as that represented by the scales shown in Fig. 15-19 has a vernier scale on the sleeve permitting measurements to 0.001 mm. The vernier scale shown has ten divisions over a length equivalent to nineteen divisions around the periphery of the thimble. Thus the difference in length of a division on the vernier scale and two divisions on the thimble is $0.02 - (1/10)(19 \times 0.01) = 0.001$ mm. Thus the reading illustrated in Fig. 15-19 is $10.00 + 0.50 + 0.16 + 0.006 = 10.666$ mm.

Digital Micrometers.   Micrometers with digital readouts are also available so as to make readings faster and easier for inspection personnel regardless of their degree of experience. The digital micrometer shown in Fig. 15-17 represents one instrument

READING TO 0.01 mm

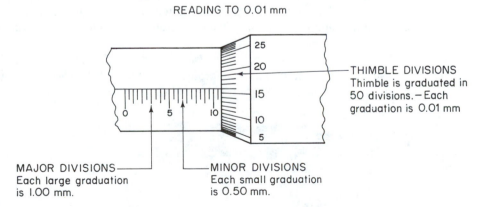

THIMBLE DIVISIONS
Thimble is graduated in 50 divisions.—Each graduation is 0.01 mm

MAJOR DIVISIONS—
Each large graduation is 1.00 mm.

MINOR DIVISIONS
Each small graduation is 0.50 mm.

Figure 15-18   Micrometer reading of 10.66 mm.

READING TO 0.001 mm

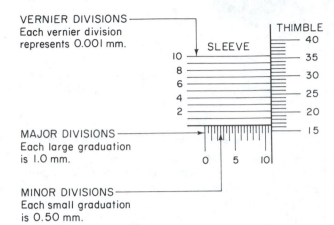

VERNIER DIVISIONS
Each vernier division
represents 0.001 mm.

SLEEVE

THIMBLE

MAJOR DIVISIONS
Each large graduation
is 1.0 mm.

MINOR DIVISIONS
Each small graduation
is 0.50 mm.

Figure 15-19   Scales of a vernier micrometer showing a reading of 10.666 mm.

of this type for use in measuring to a resolution of 0.01 mm. The instrument shown in Fig. 15-20 has a digital readout with a resolution to 0.001 in. When equipped with vernier scales, the resolution may be increased to 0.001 mm (commonly 0.0001 in. in the case of an inch-reading device).

Micrometer Caliper.   The micrometer caliper, or *mike* as it is often called, is an end measuring instrument for use in measuring outside dimensions. Although the mike is fairly easy to apply, the accuracy it gives depends upon the application of the proper amount of torque to the thimble. Too much torque is likely to spring the frame and cause error. Thus it is important that personnel using these instruments be trained in their use, and also that they be required periodically to check their measurements against a standard so as to minimize measurement errors. The indicating micrometer of Fig. 15-21 has a built-in dial indicator to provide a positive indication of measuring pressure applied. The instrument can also be used like an indicating snap gage.

A standard metric micrometer is limited to a range of 25 mm (1 in. for a micrometer reading in inch units). Thus different micrometers are needed to measure a wide range of dimensions.

The precision screw principle is also applied directly in other measuring instruments such as the type of inside micrometer shown in Fig. 15-13(17 and 34), the micrometer depth gage, Fig. 15-13(21), and the internal micrometer plug. It is also

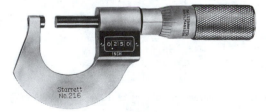

Figure 15-20   Digital-reading micrometer. (Courtesy L. S. Starrett Co.)

Figure 15-21 Indicating micrometer. (Courtesy Federal Products Corp.)

used as a device to provide precise calibrated linear movement to staging devices and other moving components of toolmakers' microscopes and optical projecting comparators.

Basic Transfer-Type Linear Measuring Devices. Transfer-type linear measuring devices are typified by the spring caliper, spring divider, firm joint caliper, telescoping gage, and small hole gage. Examples of each of these are shown in Fig. 15-13.

The outside caliper is used as an end measure to measure or compare outside dimensions, while the inside caliper is used for inside diameters, slot and groove widths, and other internal dimensions. They are quite versatile, but due to the construction and method of application their accuracy is somewhat limited.

ANGULAR MEASURING DEVICES

The unit standard of angular measurement is the degree. The measurement and inspection of angular dimensions are somewhat more difficult than linear measurement and may require instruments of some complexity if a great deal of angular precision is required.

Simple Angle Measuring Tools. The *combination set* consists of a center head, protractor, and square with a 45° surface, all of which are used individually in conjunction with a steel rule. The heads are mounted on the rule and clamped in any position along its length by means of a lock screw. The parts of such a set are shown in Fig. 15-13(41 and 42). The center head is used to scribe bisecting diameters on the end of a cylindrical piece to locate the center of the piece. The protractor reads directly in degrees. Both the square head and the protractor may contain a small spirit level. A *bevel protractor* utilizes a vernier scale to show angles as small as five minutes.

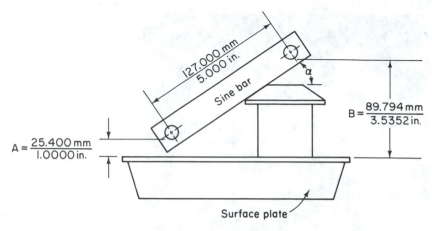

Figure 15-22   Application of a sine bar.

Sine Bar.   The sine bar is a relatively simple device for precision measuring and checking of angles. It consists of an accurately ground flat steel straight edge with precisely affixed round buttons, a definite distance apart, and of identical diameters.

Figure 15-22 illustrates one method of applying a sine bar in the determination of the angle α on the conical surface of the part located on the surface plate. For precise results, a sine bar must be used on true surfaces. In Fig. 15-22 the center-to-center distance of the sine bar buttons is 127 mm (5 in.) and the distances A and B are determined by means of gage blocks or a vernier height gage to be 25.400 mm (1.0000 in.) and 89.794 mm (3.5352 in.), respectively. Thus the sine α equals $(89.794 - 25.400)/127.00 = 0.50704$ and from trigonometric tables the angle α is $30°28'$.

Dividing Heads.   Mechanical and optical dividing heads are often employed in the circular measurement of angular spacing. The mechanical dividing head is described in Chap. 24. The optical dividing head performs the same function but more precisely. One make has a disk around its main spindle with graduations in fine increments inscribed around its circumference. These are viewed through a microscope.

LAYOUT INSTRUMENTS AND LOCATING DEVICES

Considerable metal and wood working, particularly in job shop work, pattern building, model building, and tool and die work, is done to lay out lines, circles, center locations, etc., scribed on the workpiece itself. Chalk or dye is often applied to the work surface before scribing so that the lines can be readily seen.

A *surface plate* provides a true reference plane from which measurement can be made. A cast-iron surface plate is a heavy ribbed box-like casting that stands on three points (that establishes a plane) and has a thick and well-supported flat top plate. The method by which a true surface is obtained is described in Chap. 21. New plates

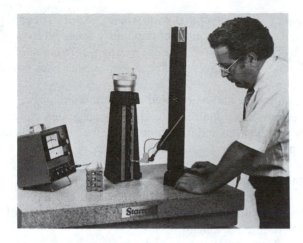

Figure 15-23 Application of a granite surface plate. (Courtesy L. S. Starrett Co.)

generally have an average of 18 bearing spots on an area of 6.5 cm^2 (ca. 1 in.^{2}) that do not vary from a true plane by more than 0.005 mm (0.0002 in.). The use of natural stones for surface plates is becoming increasingly popular because of their hardness, resistance to corrosion, minimum response to temperature change, and nonmagnetic qualities. Figure 15-23 shows a granite surface plate used in inspection work. Reference surfaces may also be obtained by the use of bar parallels, angle irons, V-blocks, and toolmakers' flats.

A variety of hand marking tools such as the scriber, spring divider, and center punch are employed by the layout person. These tools are shown in Fig. 15-13. The *surface gage,* Fig. 15-13(38), consists of a base, an adjustable spindle, and a scriber, and may be used as a layout instrument. The scriber is first adjusted to the desired height by reference to a steel rule or gage blocks and then the gage is moved to the workpiece and a line is scratched on it at the desired location. The vernier height gage may be employed in a similar manner.

GAGES

Classes of Gages. In mass-manufacturing operations it is often uneconomical to attempt to obtain absolute sizes during each inspection operation. In many cases it is only necessary to determine whether one or more dimensions of a mass-produced part are within specified limits. For this purpose a variety of inspection instruments referred to as *gages* are employed. However, the distinction between gaging and measuring devices is not always clear as there are some instruments referred to as gages that do give definite measurements.

To promote consistency in manufacturing and inspection, gages may be classified as working, inspection, and reference or master gages. *Working gages* are used by the machine operator or shop inspector to check the dimensions of parts as they are being produced. Working gages usually have limits within those of the piece being inspected. *Inspection gages* are used by the inspection personnel to inspect purchased parts when received or manufactured parts when finished. These gages are designed and made so as not to reject any product previously accepted by a properly designed and functioning working gage. *Reference* or *master gages* are used only for checking the size or condition of other gages, and represent as exactly as possible the physical dimensions of the product.

A gage may have a single size and be referred to as a *nonlimit gage,* or it may have two sizes and be referred to as a *limit gage.* A limit gage, often called a "go" and "not go" gage, establishes the high and low limits prescribed by the tolerance on a dimension. A limit gage may be either *double end* or *progressive.* A double end gage has the "go" member at one end and the "not go" member at the other end. Each end of the gage is applied to the workpiece so as to determine its acceptability. The "go" member must pass into or over an acceptable piece, but the "not go" member should not. A progressive gage has both the "go" and "not go" members at the same end so that a part may be gaged with one movement.

Some gages are *fixed* in size while others are *adjustable* over certain size ranges. Fixed gages are usually less expensive initially, but they have the disadvantage of not permitting adjustment to compensate for wear.

Most gages are subjected to considerable abrasion during their application and must therefore be made of materials which are resistant to wear. High-carbon and alloy steels have been used as gage materials for many years because of their relatively high hardenability and abrasion resistance. Further increased surface hardness and abrasion resistance may be obtained from the use of chrome plating or cemented carbides as surface material on gages. Some gages are made entirely of cemented carbides or they have cemented carbide inserts at certain wear points. Chrome plating is also used as a means of rebuilding and salvaging worn gages.

Common Gages. Some typical gages are shown in Fig. 15-24. They include *ring* and *snap gages* for outside dimensions, *plug gages* for holes, and *thread, form,* and *taper gages.* Some are fixed for size [Fig. 15-24(A), (D), (E), and (W)], and others can be adjusted over small ranges [Fig. 15-24(B), (J), and (S)]. Some fit only one size [Fig. 15-24(A), (C), and (I)], but others check dimension limits [Fig. 15-24(B), (D), (E), (H), (L), (O), (P), (S), and (W)]. Limit gages may be of the double-end type [Fig. 15-24(L), (N), (O), (P), and (W)] so that the "go" and "not go" members can be applied independently. Progressive-type gages [Fig. 15-24(B), (D), (S), and (U)] are quicker to use. Progressive plug gages are not applicable for blind holes. The size of a tapered piece determines how far it enters a tapered hole. Thus *tapered plug* and *ring gages* [Fig. 15-24(F), (R), and (V)] are marked to show the limits that they should go into or over the parts they gage. A *form gage* may also be called a profile or template gage and checks a contour or profile of a workpiece [Fig. 15-24(G) and (T)]. A set of standard *radius form gages* is shown in Fig. 15-13(24).

A *flush pin gage* like that in Fig. 15-24(M) checks the limits of a dimension between two surfaces in the manner illustrated in Fig. 15-25. The step on pin B is the same size as the tolerance of the dimension and must straddle the top of collar A to be within limits. An inspector can compare the surfaces quickly and reliably by feeling them with a finger or nail.

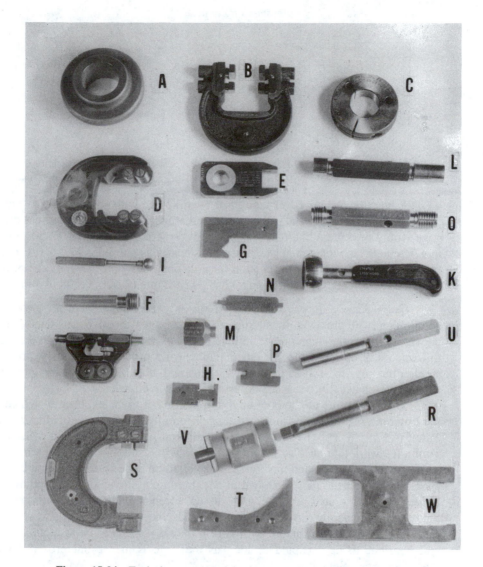

Figure 15-24 Typical gages: (A) plain ring gage; (B) adjustable limit progressive thread snap gage; (C) adjustable thread ring gage; (D) fixed-limit progressive thread snap gage; (E) fixed-limit ring-snap gage; (F) tapered thread plug gage; (G) form gage; (H) fixed-limit snap gage; (I) single end ball plug gage; (J) adjustable limit inside diameter or length gage; (K) single-end spherical plug gage; (L) cylindrical double-end plug gage; (M) flush pin gage; (N) double-end slot-width gage; (O) double-end thread plug gage; (P) double-end step gage; (R) taper plug gage; (S) adjustable-limit progressive snap gage; (T) form gage; (U) cylindrical progressive plug gage; (V) tapered ring gage; (W) fixed-limit double-end snap gage.

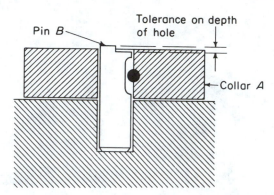

Figure 15-25 Typical flush pin gage for gaging the depth of a hole.

A *functional gage* checks the fit of a workpiece with a mating part. It normally just simulates the pertinent features of the mating part. An example of a functional gage would be a plate like part II of Fig. 15-11 with four plugs of 12.50 mm (0.492 in.) diameter each located in true position as nearly as possible. Any part I that would fit on that gage would pass inspection for hole positions. The sizes of the holes would also need to be checked with a plug 12.70/12.90 mm (0.500/0.508 in.) in diameter.

Gage Sizes. In gage making, as in any other manufacturing process, it is economically impractical to attempt to make gages to an exact size. Thus it is necessary that some tolerance be applied to gages. It is desirable, however, that some tolerance still be available for the manufacturing process. Obviously, though, the smaller the *gage tolerance,* the more the gage will cost. Along with the gage makers' tolerance it is usually necessary to provide a *wear allowance*.

There are three methods of applying tolerances to gages, each of which affects the outcome of the inspection operation differently. These three methods are illustrated in Fig. 15-26. The first is to use unilateral gage tolerance and make the gage within the work tolerance as shown at A. This will result in some acceptable products being rejected. The second method is to use bilateral gage tolerance about the limiting specifications on the part as shown at B. This might allow some acceptable parts to be rejected or some rejectable parts to be accepted. The third method is to use unilateral tolerance and make the gage outside the work tolerance, as in C. Gages made according to this method will permit defective parts to be accepted at the start and continue to be accepted as long as the gage is in use but provides the most manufacturing tolerance.

There is no universally accepted policy for the amount of gage tolerance. A number of industries where part tolerances are relatively large use 20% of the part tolerance for working gages and 10% for inspection gages. For each of these gages, one-half of the amount is used for wear on the "go" member and one-half for the gage makers' tolerance on both the "go" and "not go" members. This method has been used to determine the tolerances for the plug gages shown in Fig. 15-27 for checking a hole with a diameter of $40.00 \begin{array}{c} + \ 0.10 \\ - \ 0.00 \end{array}$ mm $\left(1.575 \begin{array}{c} + \ 0.004 \\ - \ 0.000 \end{array} \text{in.} \right)$. The total part tolerance is 0.10 mm (0.004 in.). Thus 20% of 0.10 mm (0.004 in.) gives 0.020 mm

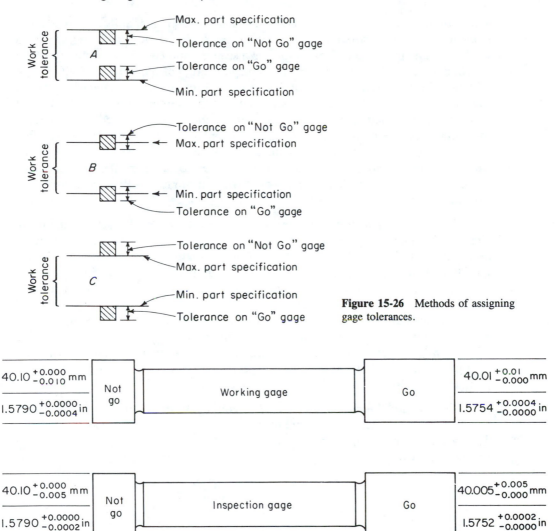

Figure 15-26 Methods of assigning gage tolerances.

Figure 15-27 Specifications on working and inspection limit plug gages.

(0.0008 in.) for the work gage, and 10% of 0.10 mm (0.004 in.) gives 0.010 mm (0.0004 in.) for the inspection gage, applied unilaterally.

INDICATING GAGES AND COMPARATORS

Indicating gages and comparators magnify the amount a dimension deviates above or below a standard to which the gage is set. Most indicate in terms of actual units of measurement, but some show only whether a tolerance is within a given range. The ability to measure to 25 nm or 0.000001 in. depends upon magnification, readability (sometimes called resolution), accuracy of the setting gages, and staging of the workpiece and instrument. Graduations on a scale should be 1.5 to 2.5 mm (0.060 to 0.100 in.) apart to be clear. This requires magnification of 60,000× to 100,000× for a 25-nm or 0.000001-in. increment; less is needed, of course, for larger increments. Mechanical, air, electronic, and optical sensors and circuits are available for any magnification needed and will be described in the following sections. However, measurements have meaning and are repeatable only if based upon reliable standards, like gage blocks, and if the support of the workpiece and instrument is stable. An example is that of equipment to trace the roundness of cylindrical parts. Either the probe or part must be rotated on a spindle that must run true with an error much less than the increment to be measured.

Mechanical Indicating Gages and Comparators.   Mechanical indicating gages and comparators employ a variety of devices. One type is the dial indicator depicted in Fig. 15-28. Movement of stem A is transmitted from the rack to compound gear train B and C to pointer D, which moves around a dial face. Springs exert a constant force on the mechanism and return the pointer to its original position after the object being measured is removed.

Dial indicators are used for many kinds of measuring and gage operations. One example is that of checking the runout of the hole in a round piece as illustrated in Fig. 15-29. They also serve to check machines and tools, alignments, and cutter runout. Dial indicators are often incorporated in special gages and in measuring instruments, as exemplified by the indicating micrometer of Fig. 15-21.

Electric and Electronic Gages.   Certain gages are called *electric limit gages* because they have the added feature of a rack stem that actuates precision switches. The switches connect lights or buzzers to show limits and also may energize sorting and corrective devices.

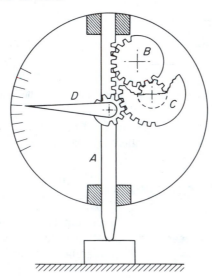

Figure 15-28 Simple dial indicator mechanism.

Figure 15-29 Dial indicator with an attachment for checking the runout of the bore of a piece held in a chuck. (Courtesy Brown and Sharpe Mfg. Co.)

An *electronic gage* gives a reading in proportion to the amount a stylus is displaced. It may also actuate switches electronically to control various functions. An example of an electronic gage and diagrams of the most common kinds of gage heads are shown in Fig. 15-30. The *variable inductance* or *inductance-bridge* transducer has an alternating current fed into two coils connected into a bridge circuit. The reactance of each coil is changed as the position of the magnetic core is changed. That changes the output of the bridge circuit. The *variable transformer* of LVDT (linear variable displacement transformer) transducer has two opposed coils into which currents are induced from a primary coil. The net output depends on the displacement of the magnetic core. The deflection of a *strain gage* transducer is sensed by the changes in length and resistance of strain gages on its surface. This is also a means for measuring forces. Displacement of a *variable capacitance* head changes the air gap between plates of a condenser connected in a bridge circuit. In every case an alternating current is fed into the gage as depicted in Fig. 15-30(E). The output of the gage head circuit is amplified electronically and displayed on a dial, or digital readout. In some cases the information from the gage may be recorded on tape or stored in a computer.

Depending upon capacity, range, resolution, quality, accessories, etc., electronic gages are priced from a little under $1000 to many thousands of dollars. An electronic height gage like the one being used in Fig. 15-23 lists for $6000. The height gage is being set to a height reference gage that contains a stack of 25-mm (1-in.) gage blocks which can be adjusted to any desired height in the range of the instrument by the micrometer on top. A digital reading height reference gage like the one shown in Fig. 15-23 is accurate to within 2.5 μm (0.0001 in.) and costs about $1500.

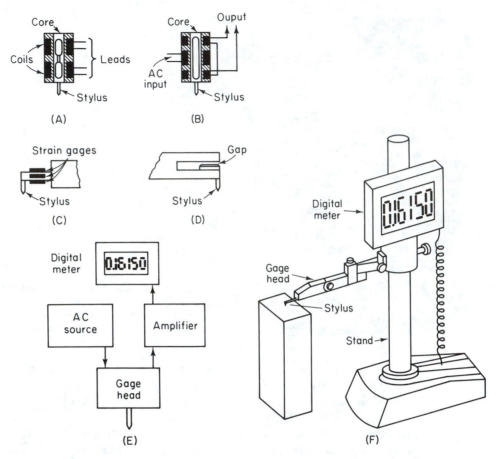

Figure 15-30   Elements of electronic gages. Types of gage heads: (A) variable inductance; (B) variable transformer; (C) strain gage; (D) variable capacitance; (E) block diagram of typical electronic gage circuit; (F) one model of electronic gage.

Electronic gages have several advantages. They are quite sensitive (they commonly read to a few micrometers) because output can be amplified as much as desired, and a high-quality gage is quite stable. It can be used as an absolute measuring device for thin pieces up to the range of the instrument. The amount of amplification can be switched easily, and three or four ranges are common for one instrument. Two or more heads may be connected to one amplifier to obtain sums or differences of dimensions, as for checking thickness, parallelism, etc.

Air Gages.   An air gage is a means of measuring, comparing, or checking dimensions by sensing the flow of air through the space between a gage head and workpiece surface. The gage head is applied to each workpiece in the same way, and the clearance between the two varies with the size of the piece. The amount the airflow is restricted depends upon the clearance. There are four basic types of air gage sensors as shown in Fig. 15-31. All have a controlled constant-pressure air supply. The

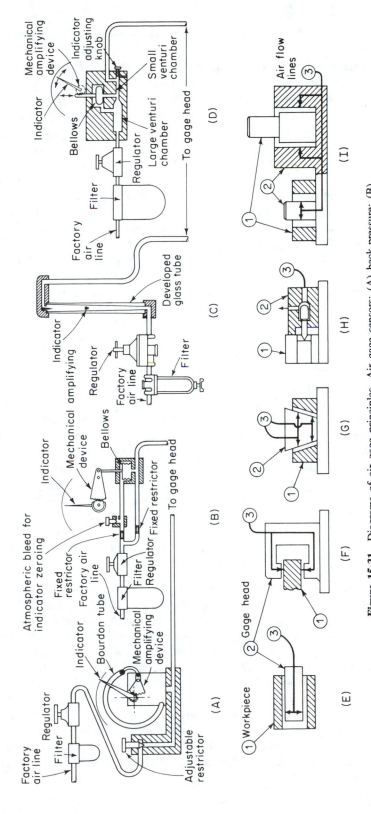

Figure 15-31 Diagrams of air gage principles. Air gage sensors: (A) back-pressure; (B) differential; (C) flow; (D) venturi. Sketches of some gage heads: (E) plug; (F) thickness; (G) taper; (H) cartridge or contact; (I) matching.

back-pressure gage responds to the increase in pressure when the airflow is reduced. It can magnify from 1000:1 to over 5000:1 depending on range but is somewhat slow because of the reaction of air to changing pressure. The *differential gage* is more sensitive. Air passes through this gage in one line to the gage head and in a parallel line to the atmosphere through a setting valve. The pressure between the two lines is measured. There is no time lag in the *flow gage,* where rate of airflow raises an indicator in a tapered tube. The dimension is read from the position of the indicating float. This gage is simple and does not have a mechanism to wear, is free from hysteresis, and can amplify over 500,000:1 without accessories. The *venturi gage* measures the drop in pressure of the air flowing through a venturi tube. It combines the elements of the back-pressure and flow gages and is fast but sacrifices simplicity.

A few of the many kinds of gage heads and applications are shown in Fig. 15-31. An air gage is basically a comparator and must be set to a master for dimension or to two masters for limits. The common single gage head is the plug. Practically all inside and outside linear and geometric dimensions can be checked by air gaging. Air *match gaging,* depicted in Fig. 15-31(I), measures the clearance between two mating parts. This provides a means of controlling an operation to machine one part to a specified fit with the other. A *multidimension gage* has a set of cartridge or contact gage heads [Fig. 15-31(H)] to check several dimensions on a part at the same time. The basic gage sensor can be used for a large variety of jobs, but a different gage head and setting master are needed for almost every job and size.

A major advantage of an air gage is that the gage head does not have to fit the part tightly. A clearance of up to 0.08 mm (0.003 in.) between the gage head and workpiece is permissible, and more in some cases. Thus no pressure is needed between the two to cause wear, and the gage head may have a large allowance for such wear as does occur. The flowing air helps keep surfaces clean. The lack of contact makes air gaging particularly suitable for checking against highly finished and soft surfaces. Because of its loose fit, an air gage is easy and quick to use. An inexperienced worker can measure the diameter of a hole to 25 nm (0.000001 in.) in a few seconds with an air gage; the same measurement to 25 μm (0.001 in.) with a vernier caliper by a skilled inspector may take up to a minute. The faster types of air gages are adequate for high-rate automatic gaging in production.

Optical Comparators. Many industrial products and component parts are so small and of such complex configuration as to require magnification for accurate discernment. For this purpose a number of measuring and gaging instruments using various optical systems, such as the toolmakers' microscope, the binocular microscope, and the optical projecting comparator, find wide application in the inspection of small parts and tools.

The optical projecting comparator projects a magnified image of the object being measured onto a screen. A workpiece is staged on a table to cast a shadow in a beam of light in *diascopic projection,* as shown in Fig. 15-32. The outline of the part is magnified and displayed on a screen. In *episcopic projection* the light rays are directed against the side of the object and then reflected back through the projection lens.

Optical projection provides means to check complex parts quickly to small

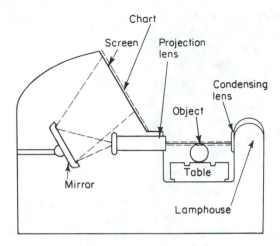

Figure 15-32 Optical comparator system.

tolerances. Commonly, a translucent drawing is placed over the screen with lines drawn to scale on it of the contour of the part, the limits of the outline, or critical features such as angles. For instance, the outline of a part can be compared with a drawing on the screen and deviations in the whole contour quickly seen. A fixture or stage may be supplied for a part to mount all pieces in the same way in rapid succession. The table can be adjusted in coordinate directions by micrometer screws to 2 μm for tables with metric micrometers or 0.0001 in. for tables with inch micrometers. Thus a part can be displaced to measure precisely how far a line is from a specified position. The screen can be rotated to a vernier scale to measure angular deviations to a minute. Magnifications of commercial comparators range from 10× to 250×. At 250×, 0.002 mm on a part becomes 0.500 mm on the screen, which is readily discernible.

A self-programmed computerized optical comparator system is shown in Fig. 15-33. The entire system is operated and programmed from the control panel with visual aid from the magnified image on the comparator screen and a discrete measurement section displayed on a cathode ray tube (CRT). Self-programming is accomplished by running a test part through the X, Y coordinate motions to physically view all dimensions to be inspected. Final dimensions are automatically encoded and entered into the memory of the microprocessor control system, with readout in increments to 1 μm (0.00005 in.). In addition, menu-type software subroutines are available to permit the operator to determine the center of a circle, centroid, center of radius, intersect point, angular measurements, mean and standard deviation of successive measurements, and other features.

Coordinate and Roundness Measurement. Many parts have surfaces and holes dimensioned from coordinate axes and from each other. One example is shown in Fig. 22-25. Such a part is commonly machined and may be checked by coordinate location methods as described in Chap. 22. One way is to move the part from point to point while it is fastened on a table positioned by precision lead screws under a fixed reference such as a probe or indicator on the machine spindle. This may be done

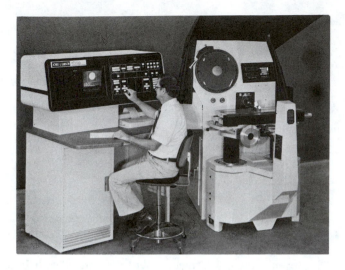

Figure 15-33   Self-programmed computerized optical comparator system. (Courtesy Jones and Lamson Co., Division of Textron Inc.)

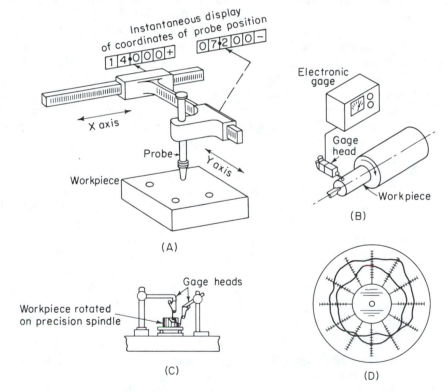

Figure 15-34   (A) Elements of one kind of coordinate measuring machine; (B) electronic gage checking the roundness of a workpiece; (C) inside and outside of a cylinder being checked for roundness; (D) example of the charted record obtained from a test like that at (C).

automatically as described in the section of Chap. 35 on NC inspection and measuring machines. The elements of a popular kind of *coordinate measuring machine* (CMM) are shown in Fig. 15-34(A). A probe is positioned by brackets slid along two arms. Coordinate distances from one point to another are measured in effect by counting electronically the lines in gratings ruled along each arm. Any point in each direction can be set to zero, and count is made in a plus or minus direction from there. Direct readout of position is displayed in digital form to about 25 μm (0.001 in.), and on some machines less. A machine of this type to cover an area of 460 $\times$ 610 mm (18 $\times$ 24 in.) costs about $20,000.

Curved surfaces are measured in the basic ways depicted in Fig. 15-34(B) and (C). Round surfaces must merely be revolved around true centers. Deviations may be read on a meter or recorded to an enlarged scale on a polar chart like the one in Fig. 15-34(D). Other curved surfaces, such as spheres or impeller blades, are measured by moving the probe or workpiece linearly as the piece is revolved to simulate a series of true paths on the surface.

Automatic Gaging Systems. As industrial processes are automated, gaging must keep pace. Automated gaging is done in two general ways. One is in-process or on-the-machine control by continuous gaging of the work. An example is given in the section on automatic tool compensation in Chap. 34. The second way is post-process or after-the-machine gaging control. Here the parts coming off the machine are passed through an automatic gage. A control unit responds to the gage to sort pieces by size and to adjust or stop the machine if parts are found out of limits.

MEASURING WITH LIGHT RAYS

Interferometry. Light waves of any one kind are of invariable length and are the standards for ultimate measures of distance. Basically, all interferometers divide a light beam and send it along two or more paths. Then the beams are recombined and always show interference in some proportion to the differences between the lengths of the paths. One of the simplest illustrations of the phenomenon is the optical flat and a monochromatic light source of known wavelength.

The optical flat is a plane lens usually a clear fused quartz disk from about 50 to 250 mm (2 to 10 in.) in diameter and 10 to 25 mm ($\frac{1}{2}$ to 1 in.) thick. The faces of a flat are accurately polished to nearly true planes; some have surfaces within 25 nm (0.000001 in.) of true flatness.

Helium is commonly used in industry as a source of monochromatic or single-wavelength light because of its convenience. Although helium radiates a number of wavelengths of light, that portion which is emitted with a wavelength of 587.5 nm (0.00002313 in.) is so much stronger than the rest that the other wavelengths are practically unnoticeable.

The principle of light-wave interference and the operation of the optical flat are illustrated in Fig. 15-35(A), wherein an optical flat is shown resting at a slight angle on a workpiece surface. Energy in the form of light waves is transmitted from a

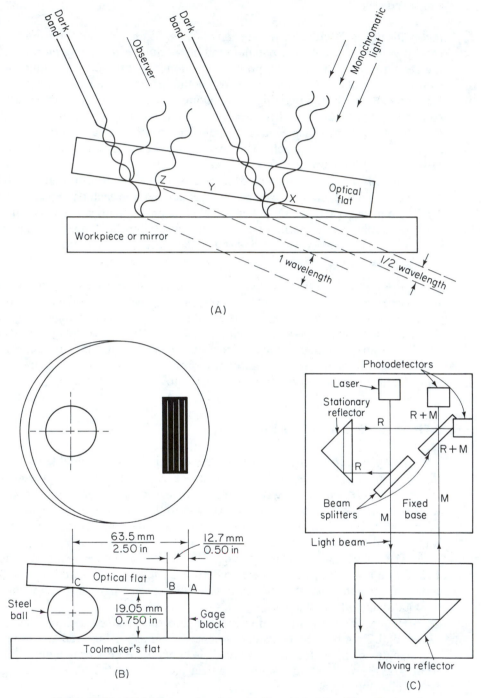

Figure 15-35 (A) Light-wave interference with an optical flat; (B) application of an optical flat; (C) diagram of an interferometer.

monochromatic light source to the optical flat. When a ray of light reaches the bottom surface of the flat, it is divided into two rays. One ray is reflected from the bottom of the flat toward the eye of the observer, while the other continues on downward and is reflected and loses one-half wavelength on striking the top of the workpiece. If the rays are in phase when they re-form, their energies reinforce each other, and they appear bright. If they are out of phase, their energies cancel, and they are dark. This phenomenon produces a series of light and dark fringes or bands along the workpiece surface and the bottom of the flat, as illustrated in Fig. 15-35(B). The distance between the workpiece and the bottom surface of the optical flat at any point determines which effect takes place. If the distance is equivalent to some whole number of half wavelengths of the monochromatic light, the reflected rays will be out of phase, thus producing dark bands. This condition exists at positions X and Z of Fig. 15-35(A). If the distance is equivalent to some odd number of quarter wavelengths of the light, the reflected rays will be in phase with each other and produce light bands. The light bands would be centered between the dark bands. Thus a light band would appear at position Y in Fig. 15-35(A).

Since each dark band indicates a change of one-half wavelength in distance separating the work surface and flat, measurements are made very simply by counting the number of these bands and multiplying that number by one-half the wavelength of the light source. This procedure may be illustrated by the use of Fig. 15-35(B). There the diameter of a steel ball is compared with a gage block of known height. Assume a monochromatic light source with a wavelength of 0.5875 μm (23.13 μin.). From the four interference bands on the surface of the gage block, it is obvious that the difference in elevations of positions A and B on the flat is equal to $4 \times 0.5875/2$ or 1.175 μm ($4 \times 23.13/2$ or 46.26 μin.). By simple proportion the difference in elevations between points A and C is equal to $(1.175 \times 63.5)/12.7 = 5.875$ μm [$(46.26 \times 2.5)/0.5 = 231.3$ μin.]. Thus the diameter of the ball is 19.05 + 0.005875 = 19.055875 mm (0.750 + 0.0002313 = 0.7502313 in.).

Optical flats are often used to test the flatness of surfaces. The presence of interference bands between the flat and the surface being tested is an indication that the surface is not parallel with the surface of the flat.

The way dimensions are measured by interferometry can be explained by moving the optical flat of Fig. 15-35(A) in a direction perpendicular to the face of the workpiece or mirror. It is assumed that the mirror is rigidly attached to a base, and the optical flat is firmly held on a true slide. As the optical flat moves, the distance between the flat and mirror changes along the line of traverse, and the fringes appear to glide across the face of the flat or mirror. The amount of movement is measured by counting the number of fringes and fraction of a fringe that pass a mark. It is difficult to superimpose a real optical flat precisely on a mirror or the end of a piece to establish the end points of a dimension to be measured. This difficulty is overcome in sophisticated instruments by placing the flat elsewhere and by optical means reflecting its image in the position relative to the mirror in Fig. 15-35(A). This creates interference bands that appear to lie on the face of and move with the workpiece or mirror. The image of the optical flat can be merged into the planes of workpiece surfaces to establish beginning and end points of dimensions.

A simple interferometer for measuring movements of a machine tool slide to nanometers (millionths of an inch) is depicted in Fig. 15-35(C). A strong light beam from a laser (described in Chap. 14) is split by a half-mirror. One component becomes the reference R and is reflected solely over the fixed machine base. The other part, M, travels to a reflector on the machine slide and is directed back to merge with ray R at the second beam splitter. Their resultant is split and directed to two photodetectors. The rays pass in and out of phase as the slide moves. The undulations are converted to pulses by an electronic circuit; each pulse stands for a slide movement equal to one-half the wavelength of the laser light. The signal at one photodetector leads the other according to the direction of movement.

When measurements are made to nanometers or to millionths of an inch by an interferometer, they are meaningful only if all causes of error are closely controlled. Among these are temperature, humidity, air pressure, oil films, impurities, and gravity. Consequently, a real interferometer is necessarily a highly refined and complex instrument; only its elements have been described here.

Optical Tooling. Telescopes and accessories to establish precisely straight, parallel, perpendicular, or angled lines are called *optical tooling*. Two of many applications are shown in Fig. 15-36(A) and (B). One is to check the straightness and truth of the ways of a machine tool bed at various places along the length. The other is to establish reference planes for measurements on a major aircraft or missile component. Such methods are especially necessary for large structures. Accuracy of 1 part in 200,000 is regularly realized; this means that a point at a distance 2.5 m (100 in.) can be located within 13 μm (0.0005 in.). Common optical tooling procedures, described below, are autocollimation, autoreflection, planizing, leveling, and plumbing.

Autocollimation is done with a telescope having an internal light that projects a beam through the cross hairs to a target mirror as indicated in Fig. 15-36(A). If the mirror face is truly perpendicular to the line of sight, the cross-hair image will be reflected back on itself. The amount the reflected image deviates from the actual reticle image is an indication of the tilt in the target. A target may have a crossline pattern for alignment with the line of sight. An autocollimated image is not clear for distances over 15 m or 50 ft and then a somewhat less accurate method must be used. This is *autoreflection,* with an optical flat containing a crossline pattern mounted on the end of the illuminated telescope which is focused to twice the distance to the target mirror. Then if the mirror is perpendicular to the line of sight, the pattern of the flat is reflected in coincidence with the cross hairs in the telescope.

Planizing is fixing planes at 90° with other planes or with a line of sight. This may be done from accurately placed rails on which transits are mounted in a tooling dock as indicated in Fig. 15-36(B). A transit is a telescope mounted to swing in a plane perpendicular to a horizontal axis. Square lines may also be established with an optical square or planizing prism mounted on or in front of a telescope as depicted in Fig. 15-36(C). Angles may be set precisely by autocollimating on the precisely located faces of an optical polygon as in Fig. 15-36(D).

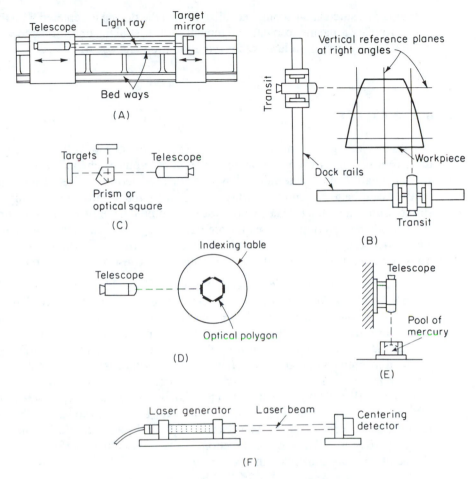

Figure 15-36 Optical tooling: (A) autocollimation, or autoreflection, for checking the straightness of the ways on a machine tool bed; (B) scheme for establishing reference planes in a tooling dock; (C) establishing a line at right angles to a line of sight by means of an optical square; (D) collimating the faces of an optical polygon to check angles on an index table; (E) example of a plumbing operation to establish a vertical line; (F) use of a centering detector to establish alignment with the center of a laser beam.

Leveling establishes a horizontal line of sight or plane. This may be done with a telescope fitted with a precision spirit level to fix a horizontal line of sight. A transit or sight level so set may be swiveled around a vertical axis to generate a horizontal plane. *Plumbing*, sketched in Fig. 15-36(E), consists of autocollimating a telescope from the surface of a pool of mercury to establish a vertical axis.

An advanced step in optical tooling is the use of the intense light beam of a laser, described in Chap. 14. A centering detector, shown in Fig. 15-36(F), has four photocells equally spaced (top and bottom and on each side) around a point. Their output is measured and becomes equalized when the device is centered with the beam. This provides a means to obtain alignment with a straight line. Squareness may be established by passing a laser beam through an optical square.

SURFACE QUALITY

The quality of surface finish is commonly specified along with linear and geometric dimensions. This is becoming more common as product demands increase because surface quality often determines how well a part performs. Heat-exchanger tubes transfer heat better when their surfaces are slightly rough rather than highly finished. Brake drums and clutch plates work best with some degree of surface roughness. On the other hand, bearing surfaces for high-speed engines wear in excessively and fail sooner if not highly finished but still need certain surface textures to hold lubricants. Thus the need is to control all surface features, not just roughness alone.

Surface Characteristics.   The American National Standards Institute has provided a set of standard terms and symbols to define such basic surface characteristics as profile, roughness, waviness, flaws, and lay. *Profile* is defined as the contour of any section through a surface. *Roughness* refers to relatively finely spaced surface irregularities such as might be produced by the action of a cutting tool or grinding wheel during a machining operation. *Waviness* consists of those surface irregularities which are of greater spacing than roughness. Waviness may be caused by vibrations, machine or work deflections, warping, etc. *Flaws* are surface irregularities or imperfections which occur at infrequent intervals and at random locations. Such imperfections as scratches, ridges, holes, cracks, pits, checks, etc., are included in this category. *Lay* is defined as the direction of the predominant surface pattern. These characteristics are illustrated in Fig. 15-37.

Surface Quality Specifications.   Standard symbols to specify surface quality are included in Fig. 15-37. Roughness is most commonly specified and is expressed in units of micrometers (μm), nanometers (nm) or microinches (μin.). According to the American National Standard ANSI B46.1-1978, the standard measure of surface roughness adopted by the United States and approximately 25 other countries around the world is the arithmetic average roughness, R_a (formerly AA or CLA). R_a represents the arithmetic average deviation of the ordinates of profile height increments of the surface from the centerline of that surface. Thus

$$R_a = \frac{1}{L} \int_{x=0}^{x=L} |y| \, dx \qquad (15\text{-}6)$$

where R_a = arithmetic average deviation from the centerline

$\quad\quad y$ = ordinate of the curve of the profile

$\quad\quad L$ = sampling length

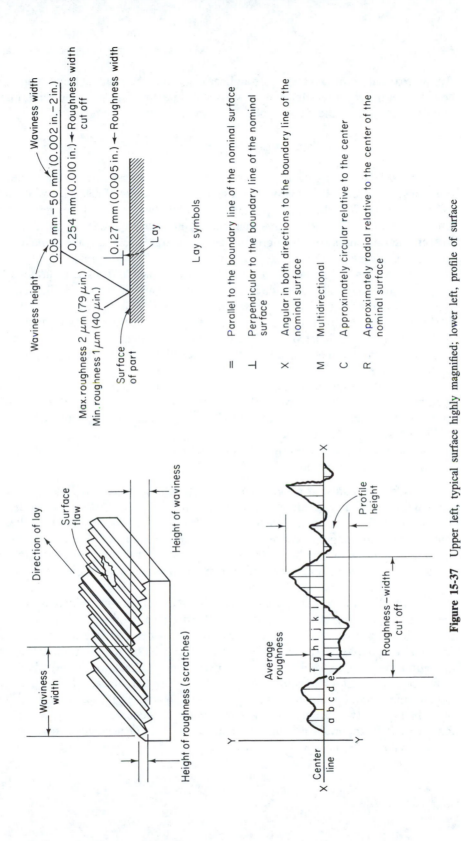

Figure 15-37 Upper left, typical surface highly magnified; lower left, profile of surface roughness; right, specifications of surface quality.

Waviness height

Waviness width

0.05 mm – 50 mm (0.002 in.–2 in.)

0.254 mm (0.010 in.) ← Roughness width cut off

0.127 mm (0.005 in.) ← Roughness width

Max. roughness 2 μm (79 μin.)
Min. roughness 1 μm (40 μin.)

Surface of part

Lay

Lay symbols

= Parallel to the boundary line of the nominal surface

⊥ Perpendicular to the boundary line of the nominal surface

X Angular in both directions to the boundary line of the nominal surface

M Multidirectional

C Approximately circular relative to the center

R Approximately radial relative to the center of the nominal surface

Direction of lay

Surface flaw

Height of waviness

Waviness width

Height of roughness (scratches)

Average roughness

Profile height

Roughness – width cut off

Center line

445

An approximation of the average roughness, R_a, may be obtained by summing the deviation of the absolute values of the surface profile ordinates from the centerline and dividing the sum by the number of sample measurements, i.e.,

$$R_a \text{ (approx.)} = \frac{y_a + y_b + y_c + \cdots + y_n}{n}$$

The longest length along the centerline over which the measurements are made is the roughness-width cutoff. In many cases the maximum height of a surface is about four to five times the R_a value in μm, nm, or μin. Thus two such surfaces may not have a total roughness value (R_a) greater than one-eighth of the tolerance on the dimension. In fact, the roughness specification must be considerably less to leave some tolerance for other sources of errors.

Prior to 1955, the root mean square (rms) was used to designate surface roughness. If n measurements are made (plus or minus) from the centerline like the one in Fig. 15-37 and are called y_i, the rms average is $[(\Sigma y_i^2)/n]^{1/2}$. Rms values are about 11% larger than R_a figures. Some surface roughness measuring instruments have a scale with numbers labeled "rms" and a scale calibrated in R_a values. On such instruments, the numbers called "rms" are root-mean-square values only when the profile is sinusoidal.

Waviness height alone may be specified, or it may be accompanied by a width specification. Thus, in Fig. 15-37, the specification 0.05 mm-50 mm (0.002 in.-2 in.) means that no waves over 0.05 mm (0.002 in.) high are allowed in any 50 mm (2 in.) of length. If no width specification is given, it is usually implied that the waviness height specified must be held over the full length of the work. Other specifications in Fig. 15-37 are less common.

Surface Finish and Cost. Each manufacturing process ordinarily produces surface finishes in a certain range, as indicated in Fig. 15-38. Some may overlap with others, but each has its own surface pattern. Turning and shaping leave parallel feed lines, and face milling puts curved or crossed lines on a surface. The large number of small cutting edges acting at random in grinding give a directional pattern of small scratches that vary in length and often overlap. Honing and lapping may produce multidirectional or crisscross patterns.

Generally, improved surface finish quality requirements incur increased machining costs. A principal reason is that methods that give good surface finishes cannot remove stock rapidly. Therefore, two or more steps often are necessary to get a good finish. For example, rough and finish turning followed by rough and finish grinding operations are normal to obtain a 0.5 μm (20 μin.) R_a finish on a steel shaft where 8 mm or $\frac{5}{16}$ in. of stock must be removed. These steps are usually less costly than a number of turning operations, with special care, to achieve the same results. On the other hand, just two turning passes should be quite adequate for a 3 μm (125 μin.) R_a finish. It is important that no better finish than really needed be specified for a surface. Otherwise, cost will be excessive.

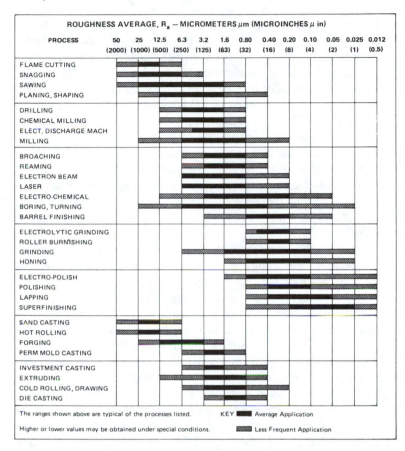

Figure 15-38 Typical ranges of surface finish from common production processes. Higher or lower values may be obtained under various conditions. (Basic chart extracted from *Surface Texture* (ANSI B46.1-1978), with the permission of the publisher, The American Society of Mechanical Engineers, United Engineering Center, 345 East 47th Street, New York, NY 10017.)

Measurement of Surface Finish.   Waviness and roughness are measured separately. Waviness may be measured by sensitive dial indicators. A method of detecting gross waviness is to coat a surface with a high-gloss film, such as mineral oil, and then reflect in it a regular pattern, such as a wire grid. Waviness is revealed by irregularities or discontinuities in the reflected lines.

Many optical methods have been developed to evaluate surface roughness. Some are based on interferometry. One method of interference contrast makes different levels stand out from each other by lighting the surface with two out-of-phase rays. Another method projects a thin ribbon of light at 45° onto a surface. This appears in a microscope as a wavy line depicting the surface irregularities. For a method of replication, a plastic film is pressed against a surface to take its imprint. The film then may be plated with a thin silver deposit for microscopic examination or may be sectioned and magnified. These are laboratory methods and only economical in manufacturing where other means are not feasible, as on a surface inaccessible to a probe.

Instruments that trace a profile are used mostly in the shop to measure surface roughness. Rugged commercial models are available that stand hard usage, and they require only moderate skill and express roughness by a number or in a record, one of which is adequate for most cases. In general, a pointed-diamond stylus in a head is moved at a constant rate across a surface as depicted in Fig. 15-39. The stylus rises and falls and moves a coil in a field to generate a current in proportion to the irregularities. The current is amplified and averaged (R_a or rms as desired). The results are shown on a meter or recorded as a profile line on a paper tape. Prices range from under $1500 for simple hand-held models to $10,000 and more for recording models for gage rooms, etc.

The *SurfEx* surface finish measuring instrument is a capacitance-based system for measuring the texture of surface finish on conductive and most semiconductive materials. A probe with an area typically of about 40 mm^2 ($\frac{1}{16}$ in.^{2}) is placed on the work surface and held still momentarily. The system measures the capacitance of the air space in the surface voids and electronically converts the quantity to a figure for average surface roughness in micrometers or microinches, which is displayed on a digital readout. The probe does not have to be positioned with respect to the surface lay and can be applied from any direction, and the workpiece does not have to be set up in any particular position. Surfaces without definite lay (such as from ECM and EDM) can be measured more significantly than with a sliding stylus. Since the probe does not have to be moved, scratching of soft surfaces can be avoided. A different probe is required for each kind of surface; different probes may cover more or less area than others. Typical probes are the flat universal probe, the one-up probe for outside diameters of 1 in. and larger, low-profile probe for contoured surfaces, the side or groove sidewall probe, the inside diameter probe, and many others. The price of the basic hand-held system is $2800.

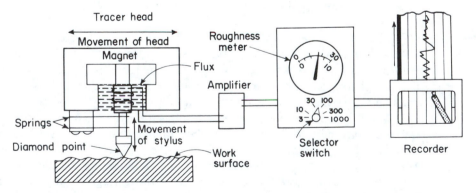

Figure 15-39   How surface roughness is measured by a stylus moved over a profile.

QUESTIONS

1. What is meant by the term "interchangeable manufacture"?
2. Name and describe the four basic activities commonly involved in the quality assurance function.
3. Why is the inspection process necessary in most mass-production activities?
4. During what stages in the manufacturing process are inspection operations commonly performed?
5. What are a statistic, a sample, and a population?
6. Why are average values ($\overline{X}$) plotted instead of individual values (X) on a control chart?
7. Explain the difference between the statistical control limits and the performance limits of a process.
8. Name five industrial products and the characteristics of each which would make sampling mandatory.
9. Define tolerance, allowance, and clearance.
10. Give three different ways of specifying tolerance and cite advantages or disadvantages of each.
11. Give the three general classifications of fits between mating parts.
12. Define basic size, standard size, and nominal size.
13. Explain the difference between 100% interchangeability and statistical average interchangeability.
14. Explain the concept of positional tolerance and maximum material condition.
15. What are gage blocks, and why are several federal accuracy grades required?
16. What is the difference between measuring and gaging?
17. What is the precision of measurement of a measuring instrument?
18. Explain the principle of operation of a vernier scale on a measuring instrument.
19. Give one of the major sources of measurement error in the use of a micrometer caliper and indicate how this might be controlled.
20. What is a sine bar used for?
21. Indicate which of the three methods of applying tolerances to gages should be used if adequate customer satisfaction is the primary criterion.
22. Explain the principle of operation of four types of electronic gages.
23. Give three advantages that air gaging provides over other gaging processes.
24. Describe the principle and application of interferometry.
25. Why is surface finish important to the functional performance of mating parts?

PROBLEMS

1. If the distribution of a particular dimension of a population of manufactured parts can be represented by the normal curve, what proportion of those parts could be expected to meet specifications if the specification limits were set to plus and minus two standard deviations

from the mean, i.e., upper specification limit (USL) = $\bar{X} + 2\sigma_x$, and lower specification limit (LSL) = $\bar{X} - 2\sigma_x$?

2. The 25-mm outside diameter of a bushing was measured at intervals in subgroups of five pieces coming from an automatic turning machine with the following results. Each unit in the table stands for 0.01 mm, and 25.00 = 0.

1	2	3	4	5	6	7	8	9	10	11	12	13	14	15
+1	0	0	−1	0	−2	+1	−2	+1	0	+2	−1	−1	+2	+1
0	+2	−1	−1	0	+2	−3	−1	+1	−2	+1	+2	0	−1	0
−1	0	+2	0	−1	+4	0	−1	−1	+2	0	+1	+2	0	−3
+1	0	0	0	+3	+1	0	−1	−1	+1	+1	+1	−2	0	−1
−1	−3	+1	0	+2	0	−3	0	0	+5	+1	+2	+1	0	−2

16	17	18	19	20	21	22	23	24	25	26	27	28	29	30
0	+1	0	0	+5	+1	−2	+3	+1	+3	0	0	+2	0	−1
+3	−2	−1	+1	0	−1	−1	0	0	0	−2	0	−1	+1	−1
+1	−2	+2	−1	+1	0	+2	0	+1	−2	+3	+2	−1	+2	0
−1	+3	+2	−3	+1	+1	0	−1	−3	0	+2	0	0	0	0
−1	+3	−2	0	+1	+3	0	+1	−2	0	−2	−1	+4	+3	+2

(a) Compute $\bar{\bar{X}}$, $\sigma_{\bar{x}}$, and $\bar{R}$.

(b) Construct $\bar{X}$ and R charts. Determine and show UCL and LCL for $\bar{X}$. (UCL for R) = 2.114 × $\bar{R}$.

(c) Estimate the tolerance limits of the process.

3. A hole and mating shaft are to have a nominal assembly size of 38 mm (1.496 in.). The assembly is to have a maximum total clearance of 0.16 mm (0.006 in.) and a minimum total clearance of 0.05 mm (0.002 in.). Determine the specifications of the parts

(a) For 100% interchangeability.

(b) For statistical average interchangeability.

4. (a) Specify the features of a functional gage to be used to check the positions of the posts of part II in Fig. 15-11. What gages would be necessary to check the sizes of the posts?

(b) Redimension part I of Fig. 15-11 for zero MMC and an upper limit of 12.90 mm (0.508 in.) for hole diameter.

(c) Specify the dimensions of a set of gages to be used to check the part redimensioned according to part (b).

5. A hole and mating shaft are to be machined to provide a close running fit. The basic hole size is 50 mm (1.969 in.). Using standard hole practice and unilateral tolerance, determine the manufacturing specifications for the hole and shaft according to the standards given in Fig. 15-7.

6. Make a sketch of the graduated scales of a vernier caliper with a reading of 93.68 mm (3.688 in.).

7. Make a sketch of the graduated scales of a vernier micrometer caliper with a reading of 18.732 mm (0.7375 in.).

8. Determine the angle α of the conical part in Fig. 15-22 if the distance B were given as 76.200 mm (3.000 in.).

9. Determine the specifications for the "go" and "not go" ends of a set of manufacturing and inspection plug gages to be used in checking a hole with a diameter specification of 40.000 $^{+\ 0.025}_{-\ 0.000}$ mm $\left(1.5748 \ ^{+\ 0.0010}_{-\ 0.0000} \ \text{in.} \right)$.

10. An optical flat is used to check a workpiece under a monochromatic light having a wavelength of 0.5875 μm (23.13 μin.) in the manner shown in Fig. 15-35. The distance between the center of one band to the center of the next is 5.08 mm (0.200 in.). What is the angle between the surfaces of the optical flat and workpiece expressed in μm/m (μin./in.)?

REFERENCES

ANSI B4.3-1978, *General Tolerances for Metric Dimensioned Products;* ANSI B46.1-1978, *Surface Texture, Surface Roughness, Waviness and Lay,* American Society of Mechanical Engineers, New York.

FARAGO, F. T., *Handbook of Dimensional Measurement,* Industrial Press, New York, 1968.

HARTWIG, G. C., "Electro-optics Inspection—Choosing the Right Light for the Job," *Manufacturing Engineering,* May 1981, p. 64.

SCHAFFER, G., "A New Look at Inspection," *American Machinist,* Aug. 1979, p. 103.

———, "Taking the Measure of the CMMs, Special Report 749," *American Machinist,* Oct. 1982, p. 145.

SPOTTS, M. F., "Simple Guide to TP Dimensioning," *Machine Design,* Sept. 13, 1975, p. 132.

"Surface Technology," *Machining Data Handbook,"* 3d ed., Metcut Research Associates, Cincinnati, Ohio, 1980.

"3D Vision Inspects Incoming Parts," *American Machinist,* Sept. 1981, p. 168.

16

HOW METALS ARE CUT

Most materials can be and are cut to desired sizes and shapes, but in engineering practice the chief concern is with metal cutting.

Why Metal Is Cut.   It has been said that the loss of a few ounces of metal on the working surfaces of an automobile engine weighing hundreds of pounds is enough to make the engine useless. In a good engine the functional surfaces of the parts must have definite shapes and sizes so they fit and work together perfectly. The purpose of metal cutting for all products is to finish surfaces more closely to specified dimensions than can be done by other methods. Parts formed roughly by other processes, like founding and forging, normally have some or all of their surfaces refined by cutting. For instance, most engine blocks are cast and then their cylinders, faces, and bearing surfaces are cut to size. By various cutting processes, metal surfaces can be refined to any discernible degree of accuracy, truth, or smoothness desired. The greater the degree of refinement, the more the cost.

Metal cutting is a convenient way of making one or a few pieces of almost any shape from an available chunk of raw material. Large amounts of material can be cut away when necessary. But metal cutting is not limited to making parts in small quantities. It can readily be adapted to fast, automatic, and accurate production. Certain metal removal processes, such as grinding, are capable of finishing very hard substances.

How Cutting Is Done.   In all metal-cutting operations an edged tool is driven through material to remove chips from the parent body and leave geometrically true surfaces. All else that occurs merely contributes to that action. The kind of surface produced by the operation depends on the shape of the tool and the path it traverses through the material. If a workpiece is rotated about an axis and a tool is traversed in a definite path relative to the axis, a surface of revolution is generated. If the tool path is parallel to the axis, the surface is a cylinder as indicated by Fig. 16-1(A). This is called *straight turning* or just *turning*. An inside cylindrical surface is generated in the same way by *boring*, as depicted in Fig. 16-1(B). If the tool path is straight but not parallel to the workpiece axis, a conical surface is generated. This is called *taper turning*, as in Fig. 16-1(C). Both outside and inside tapers can be generated. If the tool is directed in a curved path as shown in Fig. 16-1(D), a profile of varying diameter is generated by *contour turning*. In the foregoing examples, the shape of the surface generated depends more upon the path than the form of the tool. A surface of revolution may also be machined by plunging a tool into a revolving workpiece. The profile cut in that way corresponds to the form of the cutting edge of the tool. *Contour forming* done in that way is illustrated in Fig. 16-1(E). Straight and tapered surfaces may be formed in a similar manner.

A plane surface on the end or shoulder of a workpiece may be generated by revolving the piece and feeding a tool at a right angle to the axis as shown in Fig. 16-2(A). This is called *facing*. Planes may also be generated by a series of straight cuts, without turning the workpieces, as illustrated in Fig. 16-2(B). If the tool is reciprocated and the workpiece is moved a crosswise increment at each stroke, the operation is called *shaping*. *Planing* is done by reciprocating the workpiece and moving the tool a little for each stroke. Formed contours can be cut by these methods by varying the depth of cut or by using a formed tool as indicated in Fig. 16-2(C).

Surfaces may be machined by tools having a number of edges that can cut successively through the material. Drills for opening holes are of this type. A drill may turn and be fed into the workpiece, or the piece may revolve while the drill is fed into it. Boring also is often done with tools having several edges. Drilling and boring are treated in Chap. 22. Plane and contour surfaces are machined by milling cutters. A milling cutter has a number of teeth on its periphery. The cutter revolves and moves over the workpiece as illustrated in Fig. 24-1.

The act of metal cutting is in some ways like cutting a slice of bread. There the knife is moved rapidly back and forth and at each stroke penetrates the bread a certain amount. When metal is cut, the workpiece surface is driven with respect to the tool,

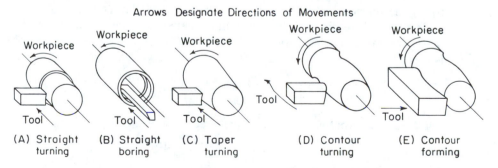

Arrows Designate Directions of Movements

(A) Straight turning (B) Straight boring (C) Taper turning (D) Contour turning (E) Contour forming

Figure 16-1 How surfaces of revolution are generated and formed.

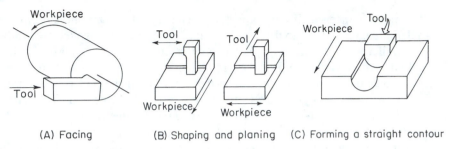

(A) Facing   (B) Shaping and planing   (C) Forming a straight contour

Figure 16-2   How plane surfaces are generated and formed.

or the tool with respect to the surface, at a relatively high rate of speed. This is called the *cutting speed* or *speed*. Mostly, the tool or workpiece revolves. Almost all such machine tools are calibrated in revolutions per minute (rpm). The cutting speed is related to the rpm and thus is conveniently expressed in m/min or in feet per min (fpm) or in surface feet per minute (sfpm). Speed in m/min must be converted to m/s for calculating other quantities in SI units, such as power. Cutting speed is commonly in the range of 30 to 300 m/min (100 to 1000 fpm). At the same time, the tool is advanced comparatively slowly in a direction generally perpendicular to the speed. This motion is called the *feed* and is defined as *the distance the tool advances into or along the workpiece each time the tool point passes a certain position in its travel over the surface*. Feed is expressed in mm/rev or in a fraction or thousandths of an inch per revolution for turning; per stroke for shaping; or per tooth for milling.

   The depth of cut is the normal distance from the surface being removed to the surface exposed by a cutting tool. It is measured in millimeters or inches.

   In turning, the rate of travel of the surface of the workpiece is the speed; the distance the tool advances per revolution at a right angle to the speed is the feed, and half the amount the diameter is changed by the action is the depth of cut. In milling, the peripheral rate of travel of the cutter is the speed; the distance the workpiece advances between the time one tooth makes contact and the time the next tooth starts to cut is the basic feed; and the normal distance from the original surface to the surface left by the cutter is the depth of cut.

   A workpiece or cutter must be revolved at the number of revolutions per minute (rpm), designated by N, that will give the required surface speed of V_m in m/min (V in fpm). If the diameter is d_m in mm (d inches), in one revolution a point on the periphery travels a distance of $\pi d_m/1000$ m ($\pi d/12$ ft). The necessary rate of rotation is then

$$N = \frac{1000V_m}{\pi d_m} = \frac{V}{\pi d/12} = \frac{12V}{\pi d} \qquad\qquad (16\text{-}1)$$

For practical purposes, π can be considered to be 3, and

$$N = \frac{333V_m}{d_m} = \frac{4V}{d} \qquad\qquad (16\text{-}2)$$

The rate of metal removal during turning or boring is

$$Q_m = V_m \times f_m \times c_m \quad \text{or} \quad Q = 12 \times V \times f \times c \qquad (16\text{-}3)$$

Q_m is in cm³/min if f_m is mm/rev, and c_m is in mm. Q is in cubic inches per minute if f = the width of uncut chip in inches, equivalent to the feed in ipr, and c = the depth of cut in inches.

Machine Tools. Metal may be cut by simple hand tools such as hammer and chisel, file, saw, or stone. These are used today to remove metal in small amounts or as makeshifts. At one time such tools were about the only means available for cutting metals. Obviously, the articles cut from metal solely by hand tools were few and quite expensive.

With the advent of the industrial revolution, the invention and development of devices like the steam engine and textile machinery called for faster and more accurate methods of cutting metals. Machines were devised to apply power to metal cutting and cut with consistent precision. These superior tools were given the name of *machine tools*, in contrast to hand tools, and the work done by them is called *machining*.

Machines for turning, drilling, boring, and planing came into being early. At first it was considered quite an accomplishment just to make a few articles of metal precisely; later the demand arose for varieties of products and in quantities. Machining methods were applied to making firearms and clocks, the reaper and sewing machines, and a multitude of new inventions still coming along. Other machine tools like the milling machine, turret lathe, and grinding machine were developed to cut metal faster, reduce labor, and increase precision. To meet the demands of the present century for production in large quantities, highly specialized and automatic machine tools have been developed. The basic types of machine tools and the principles of their operation will be described in connection with the processes for which they are used.

THE MECHANICS OF METAL CUTTING

How a Tool Penetrates Metal. The most important part of a metal machining operation is the spot where the cutting tool meets the workpiece and pries away chips. An understanding of what happens in the cutting zone is necessary to appreciate what makes a good cutting tool and how it should be operated. The basic action is the same whether a single edge is cutting or several edges in a multiple tooth tool are cutting at the same time or in succession.

When a tool cuts metal, it is driven by a force necessary to overcome friction and the forces that hold the metal together. The metal that the tool first meets is compressed and caused to flow up the face of the tool. The pressure against the face of the tool and the friction force opposing the metal flow build up to large amounts. Figure 16-3 is a diagram of the action in a single plane of a cutting tool forming a chip. At point A the material may be sheared by the advancing tool or torn by the bending of the chip to start a crack. The stress in the material ahead of the advancing tool

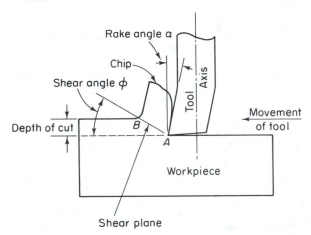

Figure 16-3 Cutting tool action.

reaches a maximum value in a band that becomes narrow at high cutting speeds and looks like a plane approximately perpendicular to the tool face. That plane is known as the *shear plane*, and one edge is depicted by the line *AB* of Fig. 16-3. When the strength of the metal is exceeded, rupture or slippage occurs along the shear plane. With further movement, new material is compressed by the tool, and the cycle is repeated again and again. As it travels along, the cutting edge scrapes and helps clean up the surface.

Types of Chips. When a brittle material like cast iron or bronze is cut, it is broken along the shear plane. The same may happen if the material is ductile and the friction between chip and tool is very high. The chips come off in small pieces or segments and are pushed away by the tool as illustrated in the highly magnified view of Fig. 16-4. A chip formed in this way is called a *Type I* or *segmental chip*.

A ductile material, cut optimally, is not broken up but comes off like a ribbon as shown by the highly magnified section of Fig. 16-5. This is known as a *Type II* or *continous chip*. An evident line of demarcation separates the highly distorted crystals in the chip from the undistorted parent material. That line is the edge of the shear plane at one instant and corresponds to the line of *AB* of Fig. 16-3. As the material slips along one plane, it is work hardened and resists further distortion. The stresses build up on the next plane to bring about slippage in new material, and so on.

When steel is cut, a continuous chip usually is formed, but the pressure against

Figure 16-4 Photomicrograph showing how a chip is formed and ruptured from a brittle material. Successive positions of the advancing tool are depicted from left to right. (Courtesy Cincinnati Milacron, Inc.)

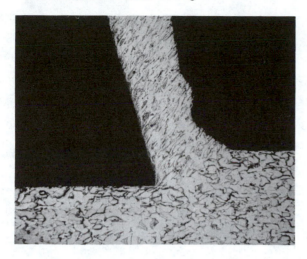

Figure 16-5 Photomicrograph of the formation of a continuous chip. (Courtesy Cincinnati Milacron, Inc.)

the tool is high, and the severe action of the chip quickly rubs the natural film from the tool face. The freshly cut chip and the newly exposed material on the face of the tool have an affinity for each other, and a layer of highly compressed material adheres to the face of the tool. Such formation is illustrated in Fig. 16-6 and is called a *built-up edge*. The chip is a *Type III* or *continuous chip with built-up edge*. As the cut progresses, the pile on the face of the tool becomes large and unstable. At frequent intervals pieces topple from the pile and adhere to the work surface or pass off with the chip. The fragments of built-up edge are a main cause of roughness of a cut surface. The built-up edge pushes on ahead of the tool and to some extent protects the edge and changes the effective rake angle.

Cutting Theory.   Figure 16-7 depicts the formation of a Type II chip with the single cutting edge of the tool at right angles to the direction of movement, and the surface cut parallel to the original. This is called *orthogonal cutting* and is idealized and easy to understand, and the principles it reveals are true for all forms of metal cutting. The tool exerts a force R on the chip with a normal component F_n and a friction component F_f that opposes the flow of the chip up the tool face. For equilibrium, the chip must be subjected to a substantially equal and opposite reaction R' from the workpiece at the shear plane with a normal component F_N and a shearing force F_S along the shear plane. For convenience, the force R applied to the tool is resolved into a component F_C in the direction of movement of the tool and a normal component F_L. To illustrate the relationship, all the forces may be represented by the force R acting at the edge of the tool with the components in their respective positions as in Fig. 16-8.

The shear plane angle can be calculated from the change in size of the chip that is deformed along the shear plane. The precut chip thickness t_1 and rake angle α are known. The chip thickness t_2 is measured normal to the rake face of the tool along a line that makes an angle of $\phi - \alpha$ with the shear plane. The length of the shear plane is $t_2/\cos(\phi - \alpha)$, and $\sin\phi = (t_1/t_2)\cos(\phi - \alpha)$. This is reduced by trigonometry

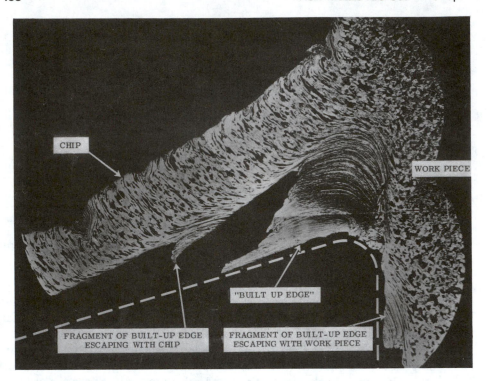

Figure 16-6   Composite photograph of a highly magnified chip and a built-up edge. (Courtesy Cincinnati Milacron, Inc.)

identity to

$$\tan \phi = \frac{r_t \cos \alpha}{1 - r_t \sin \alpha} \qquad (16\text{-}4)$$

where $r_t = t_1/t_2$ and is called the *chip thickness ratio*.

The strain that takes place in chip formation can be depicted ideally as a displacement of thin parallel plates as in Fig. 16-9. Displacement occurs for one plate at a time sliding the distance AC along the shear plane. Shear strain is the displacement

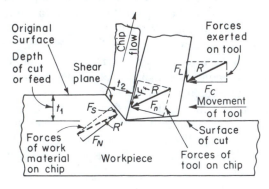

Figure 16-7   Forces exerted by a cutting tool.

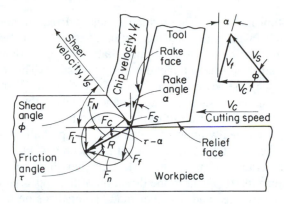

Figure 16-8 Force and velocity system of a cut.

divided by the thickness of a plate. This can be expressed in terms of the angles of movement from the right triangles ADB and CDB, and the strain

$$\epsilon = \frac{\Delta s}{\Delta x} = \cot\phi + \tan(\phi - \alpha) \tag{16-5}$$

Secondary strain occurs from friction on the chip face sliding along the tool. The result is seen in the smooth face on one side of a Type II chip. In contrast the other side is rough and jagged as indicated in Figs. 16-5 and 16-9.

All the components of force as arranged in Fig. 16-8 are sides of right triangles with a common hypotenuse R, the diameter of the force circle, and can readily be related by simple trigonometry. The components of force, F_C and F_L, applied to the tool can be measured by means of a dynamometer. Cutting speed is known. With α and ϕ already ascertained, all the other forces and velocities can be calculated. From the forces, velocities, and strains already identified, energy rates of shear and friction and their sum can be determined. As an additional technique, use is made of the fact that the dissimilar tool and workpiece material form a thermocouple to measure the

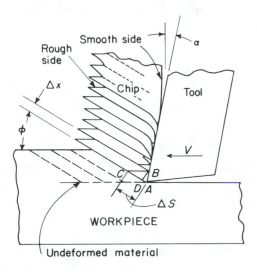

Figure 16-9 Simplified concept of chip strain and deformation.

temperature at the work–tool interface. These calculations and measurements have been performed by research investigators and are reported in detail in treatises on metal cutting. What is important here is to recognize that such calculations make it possible to express what really happens in a metal-cutting operation. This we will do later when we tell how and why the power, forces, tool life, productivity, and surface finish vary as speed, feed, and other variables are changed. If we know why results occur, we then understand what we can do to optimize operations.

The act of metal cutting is really quite complex and only partially understood. The direction of shear can be ascertained after a metal has been cut, but no one can predict without previous experience what the shear plane angle will be before the first trial. Merchant derived a formula for shear in the direction of the apparent maximum shearing stress and least energy. Lee and Schaefer made an analysis on the basis of the theory of ideal plasticity. Other investigators have proposed ingenious and some intricate solutions. Most formulas are of the form $\phi = C_1 - C_2(\tau - \alpha)$, for the angles identified in Fig. 16-8. Each theory derives certain values for the constants C_1 and C_2, but no one solution applies to all tool-work material combinations and other conditions, and no one has been able to explain fully why the shear angle is different for different materials. There may be no really unique solution because too many factors are involved: anisotropy, work hardening, variation and distribution of coefficient of friction, thermal effects, etc. However, the fact remains that for a given work–tool combination, the shear plane angle and, thus, the shearing force are related to the angles of friction and rake on the tool.

Oblique Cutting.   Most cutting action takes place in three dimensions and along more than one edge. The simple two-dimensional picture already presented applies basically in normal planes but must be broadened for a full view. The next stage is *oblique cutting* with the cutting edge set at an angle θ from the y direction in Fig. 16-10. The workpiece is identified in the horizontal x-y and vertical z directions. The normal rake angle of the tool α_n is in a vertical plane normal to the cutting edge *MN*. A *velocity rake angle* α_v is in the X-Z plane (containing the cutting velocity V_c

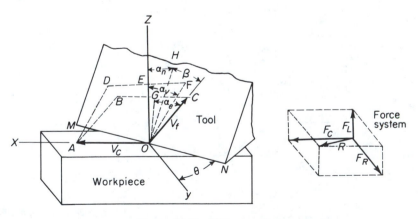

Figure 16-10   Oblique cutting.

and points *ADEFO*). The chip goes off in a direction V_f in a plane *ABCO*, in which *OG* is perpendicular to V_c. The rake angle between *OG* and V_f is called the *effective rake* α_e. The chip flow in the direction V_f is at an angle β with the normal *OH* on the tool face.

The conditions in a normal plane through *OZ* and *OH* are like those in orthogonal cutting. The shear plane angle in this plane can be determined by Eq. (16-4) with α_n substituted for α. Armarego and Brown have found that the size of the power or cutting force F_C in the direction of the cutting velocity V_C is determined by the normal rake angle. The angle of inclination, and thus the effective rake angle, have an influence upon the other components of force and the size and direction of the resultant cutting force R. The main benefit of oblique cutting is that it is a means of controlling chip flow. A curling chip takes the form of a helical spring. Stabler found that $\beta = \theta$ as a first approximation. It can be shown that under that condition

$$\sin \alpha_e = \sin^2 \theta + \cos^2 \theta \sin \alpha_n \qquad (16\text{-}6)$$

and the effective rake is always larger than the nominal rake angle of the tool.

THE CONDITIONS OF METAL CUTTING

At production rates, metal is cut under extreme conditions. The tool exerts a tremendous pressure upon the chip, normally of the order of around 1 to 5 GPa (several hundred thousand pounds per square inch). The temperature at the interface may reach 760°C (1400°F) in cutting steel at 90 to 120 m/min (300 to 400 fpm). The frictional resistance to the flow of the chip up the face of the tool is high. The coefficient of friction is usually over 0.5 and often over 1, as compared with a coefficient of less than 0.2 normally experienced in mechanical devices. Rubbing and temperatures near to those on the rake face occur on the relief faces behind the cutting edge. The high temperatures in metal cutting are sustained by the heat derived from the work done in sliding and shearing. About 80% or more of the heat passes off in the chips; most of the remainder goes into and contributes largely to deterioration of the tool. The forces, pressures, stresses, and temperatures determine how precisely the tool cuts and how long it lasts; these factors depend in turn upon the speed, feed, depth of cut, and tool materials and angles. We will now look at the ways these are related.

Effect of Cutting Speed.   At low speeds tool wear takes place largely by abrasion and interaction of surface asperities, edge deterioration under high pressures, and the formation and breakup of cold pressure welds. Temperature becomes an important cause of tool wear at high cutting speeds. When a typical steel is cut at a speed under 30 m/min (100 fpm), the temperature of the tool face is around 540°C (1000°F). As the cut speed is increased, more work is done in a unit of time in shearing the chip and sliding it over the face, and more heat is produced. The temperature increases at a declining rate; doubling the speed in cutting steel increases the temperature an average of 120°C (250°F). Tool materials soften at higher temperatures, some sooner than others, but really serious breakdown comes from chemical activity.

Above a certain *critical temperature* for each workpiece–tool combination, the two materials interfuse and weld together. A softer layer is formed on the tool surface as atoms intermingle. Chip particles welded to the surface of the tool are swept away and tear out minute chunks of adulterated tool material. This action diminishes somewhat as the work material becomes softer at still higher temperatures. The ploughing action of the workpiece and chip naturally proceeds at a higher rate at faster speeds and is even more harmful on the debased surface of the tool. An approximate picture of the influences of the various causes of tool wear is given in Fig. 16-11. Critical temperatures are reported around 620°C (1150°F) for high-speed steel (H.S.S.), 870°C (1600°F) for cemented carbide, and over 1200°C (2200°F) for sintered oxide cutting AISI 4142 steel, as examples. Tool wear rises sharply above the critical temperature.

As speed increases and temperature rises, the chip material next to the tool face becomes weaker and shears more easily in friction. Both the coefficient of friction and the friction force decrease. Whereas the friction conditions for cutting steel at speeds below 30 m/min (100 fpm) may be such as to cause the formation of a built-up edge, their change with increased speed leads to the diminution and eventual disappearance of the built-up edge. The surface finish produced is correspondingly improved.

The angle ϕ of the shear plane increases with speed. It should be recognized that the force of R of the tool on the chip sets up stresses throughout the base of the chip and adjacent workpiece material. In a quasiplastic material such as metal these stresses occur in all directions with a definite intensity in each direction. The shear plane represents that direction along which the stresses have a magnitude sufficient to cause plastic deformations in the material. As the force applied to the material changes in

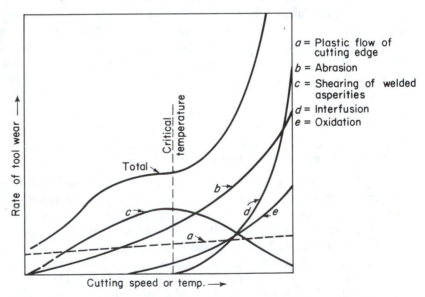

Figure 16-11   Indication of the influences of the causes of tool wear. (After L.V. Colwell, in *IRPE*, 1963, p. 140.)

size and direction, the pattern of the stresses changes likewise. When the speed is increased, the friction force and the friction angle (τ) both decrease. This means the resultant R of Fig. 16-8 must rotate clockwise. The pattern of stresses rotates correspondingly and the angle ϕ of the shear plane becomes larger.

As the shear angle ϕ increases, the distance along the shear plane from the tool point to the original surface decreases. That means the area of the shear plane is reduced. For a substantially constant shearing strength of the material, the shearing force F_S required to cause deformation of the material is smaller. As a result, the force R needed to cause formation of the chip can and does decrease, as do its components F_C and F_L. This phenomenon usually does not appear until the cut speed rises to around 30 m/min (100 fpm). Then the cutting force falls off rapidly at first but at a less rapid rate as the speed is increased further. Although decreases in cutting forces of as much as 50% have been found in some cases, the reduction is generally less than 15%.

The power, in kW, required for a cut is $P = F_c V_c /60$, where F_c is in kN and V_c is in m/min. In hp, $P = F_c V_c /33,000$, with F_c in lb and V_c in fpm. If the speed is increased, the power does not increase as much because the force decreases at ordinary cutting rates. The unit power is $P_u = P/Q$, where Q is the rate of metal removal, which may be in m³/s with P in kW for P_u in kW/m³/s or kJ/m³. If Q is in in.³/min and P is in hp, P_u is in the commonly used units of hp/in.³/min, or with P in kW and Q in cm³/min, the analogous P_u is in kW/cm³/min. Since Q increases proportionately with speed and P does not, P_u decreases slightly as speed is increased.

Effect of Feed.   The depth of cut designated by t_1 in Fig. 16-7 is equivalent to the feed in turning and most other operations and will be referred to as feed in this discussion. As the feed is increased, the tool presses against more material, more work is done, and the temperature at the interface increases. However, an increase in feed causes a smaller rise in temperature than does a corresponding increase in speed. In turning steel, doubling the feed causes an average increase of around 30°C (90°F) in temperature. Thus rate of metal removal may be increased by increasing the feed with less temperature rise and consequently less wear on the tool than by increasing the speed.

As feed is increased with other factors held constant, temperature increases, and the coefficient of friction decreases. Friction force and related cutting force increase but not in proportion to the increased rate of metal removal. In a typical case the cutting force was found to increase from 670 N to 1780 N (150 lb to 400 lb) when the feed was increased from 75 μm/rev to 250 μm/rev (0.003 in./rev to 0.010 in./rev). If feed is increased and speed is kept constant, the increase in power is less and the reduction in unit power is more than if speed is increased with constant feed.

Effect of Rake Angle.   The rake angle (α) shown in Fig. 16-8 is considered positive to the right of the vertical and negative to the left. Any change in the angle changes the direction of the resultant force applied by the tool to the chip and changes the stress pattern. An increase in the rake angle increases the shear angle and decreases the forces required to deform the work material but at the same time decreases the mass and strength of the tool point.

Hot Machining.   Cutting becomes easier when a workpiece is heated just in front of the tool to raise the temperature and decrease the material strength on the shear plane. The improved machinability is more than offset by the deleterious effects upon some materials, particularly refractory metals. The heating has been done by r.f. induction currents and plasma arc or inert tungsten arc torches. Equipment is costly and not easy to apply to all operations, and the process has received only limited acceptance.

Tool Wear.   After a tool has been cutting for some time, depending upon conditions, its cutting edge breaks down. The chip rubbing over the rake face may wear a crater that grows until it undermines the edge. The relief face of Fig. 16-8 rubbing over the cut surface and abraded by the chip particles may wear away just behind the edge. Too high a temperature may soften the tool, and the edge may be wiped away. The cutting edge may chip or crumble or the tool may break from high pressure, mechanical or thermal shock, or vibration. Often a combination of factors leads to tool failure. For instance, a crater on the rake face and wear land on the relief face may grow to the stage where the edge is weakened and breaks away. When the cutting edge breaks down, surface finish becomes poor and cutting forces and power consumption rise rapidly.

Deterioration of the faces of a tool may be retarded by use of a cutting fluid, a sharp and smooth tool, and the choice of work and tool materials with low natural coefficients of friction. Chipping or breaking can be avoided by selection of a tough tool material and a rigid tool, careful sharpening, uniform rather than intermittent cooling, and a rigid machine.

The length of time a tool cuts before it has to be resharpened is called the *tool life*. The amount of metal removed in this time is sometimes made the measure of tool life. A tool should be removed and reground before it wears to where an excessive and uneconomical amount of material must be ground from its faces to recondition it. A practical criterion for judging when a tool should be resharpened is the amount of wear on the relief face or *flank*. The criterion may be average or maximum wear because the amount of wear behind the cutting edge (the width of the land) is not always uniform across the face. There are a number of standards, but a common rule is to allow a cemented carbide cutting tool to have a wear land width of 0.4 to 0.8 mm ($\frac{1}{64}$ to $\frac{1}{32}$ in.) and a H.S.S. tool about 1.5 mm ($\frac{1}{16}$ in.). After a tool has been reground a number of times, it must be reworked or replaced. Tool material and the labor for sharpening, resetting, readjusting, and reworking tools make up a definite part of the cost of any machining operation. Throwaway tools that are not reground may be run to imminent destruction.

Vibration and Chatter.   Metal cutting is inherently cyclic. Cutting forces build up as the tool penetrates the material and deflect the tool, even if slightly. When rupture or shear occurs to form the chip and the forces momentarily drop, the tool springs back. Vibrations increase when the cutting forces get out of phase with the tool forces. Even in a seemingly continuous cut fluctuations can occur because of the change in the cutting force with the relative velocity of the tool and the workpiece.

The body of the tool is being driven through the material at a constant velocity. As it penetrates, the tip of the tool is sprung backwards by the increasing resistance it meets, and the relative velocity between the cutting edge and workpiece decreases accordingly. At the lower velocity the forces rise, and the tool is stressed still more. When the bending moment in the tool becomes large enough, it begins to move the tool back to its original shape. That increases the relative speed between the cutting edge and workpiece, and the cutting forces drop. The tool springs back until equilibrium is reached, the relative velocity decreases, the cutting forces start to rise, and another cycle begins. Actually, cyclic variations in other factors, such as depth of cut, material properties, friction forces, and rubbing of the tool nose, affect vibrations.

The actions described in the foregoing paragraph are called *self-excited vibration*. In addition, *force vibrations* may be induced by nonbalanced rotating parts, by intermittent cutter impacts (as in milling), from other machines, etc.

Strong vibration in metal cutting is called *chatter*. It may become quite noisy and obnoxious, can damage tools and machines, and defaces work surfaces with patterns called *chatter marks*. The tendency to chatter depends upon the type of operation and the workpiece–tooling–machine system. The chatter proneness of a work material is measured by a factor known as its *cutting stiffness*. Some values are 1.1 to 1.8 (159,000 to 258,000) for B1112 steel, 3.13 (453,000) for 2340 steel, and 0.6 to 0.8 GPa (88,000 to 112,000 lb/in.^{2}) for 2024-T4 aluminum, depending on operating conditions; detailed tables are given in reference texts and handbooks. The higher the value of cutting stiffness in an operation, the more the tendency to chatter. To eliminate chatter, the dynamic stiffness of the machine tool (discussed in Chap. 21) must be at least twice as much as the cutting stiffness. Remedies to decrease chatter are to reduce speed, raise feed, and increase dampening capacity and rigidity of tooling and machine.

METAL-CUTTING TOOLS

Metal-cutting tools may be classified as single-point and multiple-point tools. The latter are in effect, and act like, combinations of single-point tools. Thus the factors that give single-point tools their characteristics also are basic to multiple-point tools. In this chapter the elements of cutting tools will be discussed in detail in connection with single-point tools. Later the features of multiple-point tools, such as drills and milling cutters, will be described along with the processes for which they are used.

The factors that determine how a cutting tool performs are (1) the tool material, (2) the shape of the tool point, and (3) the form of the tool.

Cutting-Tool Material. Hardness is the first requisite of a cutting-tool material because it must be able to penetrate other materials. Toughness is also desirable to withstand shock. Cutting tools must work upon many kinds of metals and under a variety of conditions. No one cutting material is best for all purposes. The principal cutting tool materials are (1) carbon tool steel, (2) high-speed steel, (3) cast nonferrous alloys, (4) cemented carbides, (5) sintered oxides, (6) hard crystalline materials like diamonds, and (7) artificial abrasives. The last will be described in connection with the grinding processes in Chap. 27.

Carbon Tool Steel.   Carbon tool steel is the oldest kind of cutting material but is little used today. It contains from 0.90 to 1.2% carbon and sometimes appreciable amounts of alloying elements. Its chief disadvantage is that it softens at temperatures above 200°C (400°F) and therefore is limited to very slow cutting speeds and light duty. At low temperatures carbon tool steel is hard, wear resistant, and as serviceable as more expensive materials for some applications. It is comparatively inexpensive and suitable for special tools, like odd sizes of drills, that are infrequently and lightly used and do not warrant much investment. It is easy to fabricate and simple to harden.

High-Speed Steel.   High-speed steel is so named because it cuts at higher speeds than other steels. Even so, it is limited to speeds and conditions that do not give rise to temperatures above about 600°C (1100°F). It is moderate in cost, workable, and tough, which makes it preferable in many cases to harder but more brittle and expensive materials. For instance, high-speed steel is able to withstand interrupted cuts better than do harder materials. It can be more readily made into complex tools and is preferred for such tools as twist drills, reamers, taps, and form tools.

High-speed steel, commonly abbreviated H.S.S., is composed of alloyed elements that form hard, wear-resistant carbides (about 10 to 20% of the volume) dispersed in a matrix of steel. There are a number of types offering different degrees of hardness and toughness. One of the oldest is known as 18-4-1; it contains about 0.7% carbon, 18% tungsten, 4% chromium, and 1% vanadium. Molybdenum is used in some types to replace tungsten partially or wholly with comparable performance at a saving of about one-third in cost. A popular general-purpose "moly" H.S.S. contains 8% molybdenum, 4% chromium, $1\frac{1}{2}$% tungsten, and 1% vanadium. Each type of high-speed steel is designated by a number with a letter prefix to designate the principal alloying element, e.g., T for tungsten and M for molybdenum, such as T1 or M43. Some alloys have 1% and more of carbon to increase hardness and some up to 12% cobalt for superior red hardness and abrasion resistance. Powder metal techniques are used to obtain H.S.S. with exceptionally fine and well-dispersed carbides and higher alloy content. Some tools are given surface treatments (coatings) that improve performance. The more refined tools cost 50 to 100% as much as conventional grades.

Cast Nonferrous Alloys.   Cast nonferrous alloys contain no iron and cannot be softened by heat treatment so as to be machined easily. They must be cast to shape and ground to size. One type of alloy has the trade name *Tantung* and consists mainly of chromium, tungsten, columbium, and carbon in a cobalt matrix. This material is not quite as hard or tough as H.S.S. at room temperatures but retains hardness and resists wear up to red-heat temperatures. It serves best in the speed range 30 to 60 m/min (100 to 200 fpm) between H.S.S. and cemented carbides. An application is turning a large diameter with a cemented carbide tool while turning a smaller diameter on the same piece with a Tantung tool so that each tool runs at its optimum speed.

Nonferrous alloys at the high end of the speed range are given outside coatings for high surface hardness. One has the trade name *Ucon* and contains 50% columbium, 30% titanium, and 20% tungsten. After the tool surface receives a nitriding treatment, it attains a hardness up to 25% more than sintered oxide and 50% more than cemented carbide. Initial tool cost is high, but the alloy is quite competitive for heavy cuts at high speeds in common steels, where it resists chip welding. It has not been found practical for many materials and for interrupted cuts.

Carbides.   *Cemented carbides* or *sintered carbides* are the most popular cutting tool materials for production operations. They are composed of hard metallic particles (about 75 to 95% by volume) bonded together in a metallic matrix. The materials are processed by powder metal techniques. Sintering causes intergrowth of the hard particles to build a skeleton in the surrounding matrix. Carbides are for the most part not as strong as steel tools. Good wear resistance and cutting ability come from the high proportion of hard particles. The main ingredients of most commercial tools are tungsten carbide (WC) and a cobalt binder. Titanium carbide (TiC) or tungsten titanium carbide (WTiC) and, to a lesser extent, tantalum and columbium carbides (TaC and CbC) suffer less cratering and wear in cutting steel because of lower friction forces and temperatures and less chip welding. For such advantages, TiC tools with nickel-molybdenum binder are popular, although not as strong and as resistant to chipping and breaking as are WC tools.

Cemented carbides are made in many grades to suit many purposes by varying the kinds, sizes, and proportions of the carbide particles and the amount of binder. At one extreme are the hardest but most brittle carbides with high resistance to abrasion and wear. In the other grades (with more soft binder) hardness is sacrificed in various degrees for strength and shock resistance. Exceptionally small-grained cemented carbides have been developed with superior strength and wear resistance at high cost. Carbides are classified into two areas of usage: for cutting and for noncutting applications. For cutting, they may be classified according to the types and properties of the materials they cut best; i.e., steels, cast iron, high alloys, nonferrous, etc. Most carbide makers have their own classification and identification systems to accommodate their own grades. Several general classification systems have been proposed, but none covers all ramifications and has been universally accepted. Cemented carbides are made and sold under a number of trade names, such as *Kenametal* and *Carboloy*.

Cemented carbide tools are coated for some applications, giving them the advantages of composite materials. As a leading example, the benefits of TiC (also TiN and HfN) for high-speed cutting is obtained by bonding a layer of such materials 5 to 8 μm (0.0002 to 0.0003 in.) thick on a higher-strength WC body. Chemical vapor deposition (CVD) for such coatings is described in Chap. 30. Thin coatings are practical only on throwaway inserts that are not ground.

Cast carbide (not sintered) consists of a dispersion of hard W-Ti-C alloy in a high-strength refractory binder. It has high hot-hardness and hot-strength and is particularly suited for rough and heavy cuts in low-alloy and stainless steels at high speeds. In many other applications it has not performed well, and its use has been limited.

Sintered Oxides.   *Sintered oxides, cemented oxides,* or *ceramics* are compressed and sintered aluminum oxide powder with small to moderate additions of other metallic compounds. With metallic additives, such as TiC among many, the materials may be called *cermets*. Ceramic tool material is harder than most carbides, retains its hardness and strength up to about 1100°C (2000°F) and has a low coefficient of heat conductivity and a low coefficient of friction in cutting common metals. It performs best at 150 to 600 m/min (500 to 2000 fpm) but has been applied successfully up to 5500 m/min (18,000 fpm). This material is brittle and has a low rupture strength with little resistance to mechanical and thermal shock. As a result, sintered oxide tools have earned a poor reputation for roughing and have not stood up to interrupted cuts, for the most part, but improvements are being made slowly. Some shops do not have the skill or equipment or take the care necessary to operate these tools properly. Still there have been many reports of remarkable performance when the tools have been properly applied in cuts up to 10 mm (ca. $\frac{3}{8}$ in.) deep. Oxides have made their best marks with light cuts for good finishes at high speeds and are best suited for long, steady dry cuts. They are at most advantage in machining hard and abrasive ferrous materials, of little advantage for soft materials that can be cut easily by other tool materials, and are not practical for some alloys, such as certain stainless steels and high-temperature alloys. Oxides must be used on machines that have adequate speed and power and are rigid and do not vibrate. Cutting edges must be fully supported.

Cemented carbide tools with an aluminum oxide coating 8 to 10 μm (0.0003 to 0.0004 in.) thick are available, often with other coatings added. They offer the high cutting speeds of the oxides and the greater strength of the carbides. They are of no advantage where solid oxide or carbide tools work well but extend the high-speed capabilities of ceramics into areas not fully served otherwise.

Hard Crystalline Materials.   Whole diamonds have had limited applications for many years as cutting tools for some hard, nonferrous, and abrasive materials and to produce fine finishes at high cutting speeds. In recent years polycrystalline cutting materials of compacted and sintered diamond particles and also cubic boron nitride have been developed.

One polycrystalline brand, *Megadiamond*, is produced as all-diamond inserts. Another, *Compax*, has a 0.5-mm (0.020-in.) polycrystalline diamond layer on a substrate of cemented carbide about 2.5 mm (0.1 in.) thick. Boron nitride inserts are also deposited on carbide in the brand *Borazon*. Because diamonds react with iron, nickel, and some other metals, they are limited to specific areas, such as for hard cemented carbides and abrasive and difficult-to-machine nonferrous alloys, such as silicon aluminum castings, and nonmetals, such as reinforced or filled plastics and high-alumina ceramics. Generally, speeds can be raised as high as the machine can go, and still the diamond tools last many times as long as other tools, in a typical case four times as long as carbide tools. Boron nitride is almost as hard and not as reactive as diamond and has found acceptance for machining high-alloy space-age materials difficult to cut with other materials. As an example, Borazon is reported to cut at around 215 m/min (700 fpm) on Inconel 718 on which cemented carbides are limited to about 45 m/min (150 fpm). The main disadvantage of these tool materials is their high cost; a Borazon insert sells for about 50 to 100 times as much as a cemented carbide tip.

Comparison of Cutting-Tool Materials. An approximate comparison is made in Fig. 16-12 of typical cutting-tool materials. The stronger the material, the deeper the cuts and the more shocks and abuse it can take. The speed ranges given cover most practices, but other speeds are at times used for any of the tool materials, especially with uncommon operations and work materials. Relative costs may vary with market conditions, quantities, and tool shapes. Of the sintered tool materials used, about 60 to 70% are straight tungsten carbides, 25% coated, 5% titanium carbides, and 2% sintered oxides.

A comparison is made in Table 16-1 of the costs to turn a particular material with three common tool materials under a given set of conditions (feed, depth of cut, tool life, etc.). Under these conditions sintered oxide is the most economical, but in other cases it might not be so. Even at a lower theoretical cost, sintered oxide might not be practical for the job, such as if the tool would not stand up if the cut were interrupted or if the machine available did not have enough power or enough rigidity to prevent vibration.

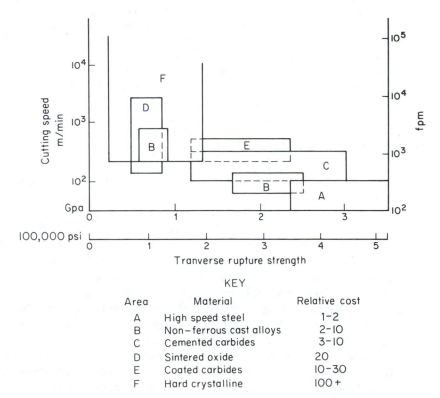

Figure 16-12 Relative areas of strength, common cutting speeds, and cost of tool materials.

TABLE 16-1   DETAILED COMPARISON OF THE COST OF TURNING AISI 4340 STEEL OF 300 BHN HARDNESS WITH THREE COMMON CUTTING-TOOL MATERIALS AT 3.81 MM (0.150 IN.) DEPTH OF CUT

Tool material	High-speed steel	Cemented carbide	Sintered oxide
Speed [m/min (fpm)]	20 (65)	143 (470)	244 (800)
Feed [mm/rev (ipr)]	0.38 (0.015)	0.38 (0.015)	0.25 (0.010)
Tool life (min)	30	15	15
Sharpening time (min)	3		
Total time per edge, (min)[a]	35	17	17
Cutting rate [cm^3/min (in.^{3}/min.)][b]	29.0 (1.755)	208.0 (12.69)	236.0 (14.4)
Unit time [min/cm^3 (min/in.^{3})][c]	0.04 (0.665)	0.0055 (0.089)	0.0048 (0.079)
Operating cost at $20/hr [$/cm^3 ($/in.^{3})]	0.013 (0.222)	0.0018 (0.030)	0.0016 (0.026)
Tool cost ($/edge)	0.02	0.25	0.50
Tool cost [$/cm^3 ($/in.^{3})]	0.00002 (0.0003)	0.00008 (0.001)	0.0001 (0.002)
Total cost [$/cm^3 ($/in.^{3})]	0.01 (0.22)	0.0019 (0.031)	0.0017 (0.028)
Power [kW (hp)][d]	2 (3)	15 (20)	17 (23)

Note: A detailed discussion of tool cost comparison and computer programs for that purpose are contained in *Determination and Analysis of Machining Costs and Production Rates Using Computer Techniques*, *AFMDC 68-1*, Air Force Machinability Data Center, Cincinnati, Ohio 45209.

[a]Time to change or index insert is 2 minutes.

[b]Cutting rate = speed × feed × depth of cut × factor for units.

[c]Unit time = 1/(cutting rate × tool life/total time per edge).

[d]P_u = 0.07kW/cm^3/min (1.6 hp/in.^{3}/min).

CUTTING-TOOL SHAPES AND FORMS

Tool Angles.   The *point* is that part of a cutting tool where cutting edges are found. It is on the end of the *shank* or *body*. The surfaces on the point bear definite relationships to each other and are defined by angles. The angles of a single-point cutting tool of a type used on a lathe, shaper, or planer are sketched in Fig. 16-13. The main elements that define the shape of a tool point are the back rake, side rake, end relief, side relief, end-cutting edge, and side-cutting edge angles, and nose radius. The angles are measured in degrees and the radius in inches. The shape of the tool may be described by a series of numbers specifying the values of the angles and radius in the order just listed. Thus a tool with a shape specified as 8-14-6-6-6-15-$\frac{3}{64}$ has 8° back rake, 14° side rake, 6° end relief, 6° side relief, 6° end-cutting edge, and 15° side-cutting edge angles, and a $\frac{3}{64}$-in. nose radius.

The positions of the angles on a tool are determined by the way the tool acts. One kind of lathe tool, depicted by Fig. 16-13, is designed to enter the material top first and the rake angles are on the top face. The sizes of the angles largely affect tool performance.

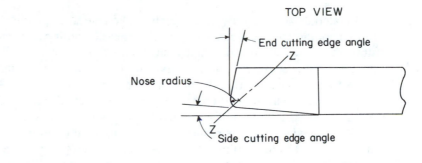

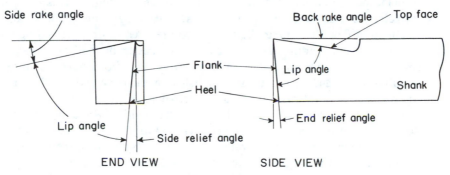

Figure 16-13   Conventional cutting tool angles. Figure 16-1(A) shows how a tool like this cuts.

Relief Angles.   The purpose of a relief angle, as the name implies, is to enable the side of the tool to clear the work and not rub. The least amount of relief needed for this purpose depends on the kind of cut. As an example, a turning tool is fed sideways into the work, and the side relief must be greater than the helix angle of the cut. Investigations have shown that the larger the relief angle, the lower the rate of wear on the flank. On the other hand the cutting edge is weakened and crumbles if the relief angle is too large. Thus, for most purposes, the relief angle should be as large as possible and still give enough support to the cutting edge. The angle may be larger for tough H.S.S. (5 to 12°) than for a brittle tool material like carbide or ceramic (5 to 8°). It may be larger for cutting soft materials or for a continuous cut than for cutting a hard material or for an interrupted cut. Often a secondary relief angle, called a *clearance angle*, is ground on the shank below the insert of a carbide or ceramic tool. A shaper or planer tool is subjected to repeated shocks as it enters the material at the start of its stroke and is given relief angles as small as 4°. As long as a relief angle is large enough to avoid rubbing, it has no effect upon forces, power, or surface finish.

Rake Angles.   The rake angle of a tool affects the angle of shear during the formation of a chip. The larger the rake angle, the larger the shear angle and the lower the cutting force and power. A large rake angle is conducive to good surface finish. However, increasing the rake angle decreases the cutting angle and leaves less metal at the point of the tool to support the cutting edge and conduct away the heat. Harder

tool materials are generally given smaller rake angles. A practical rake angle represents a compromise between a large angle for easier cutting and a small angle for tool
strength. In general, the rake angle is small for cutting hard materials and large for soft
ductile materials. An exception is brass which is cut with a small or negative rake
angle to keep the tool from digging into the work.

The two conventional components of rake are back rake and side rake, designated by the rake angles of Fig. 16-13. The tool shown is designed to cut on the
side-cutting edge, the nose radius, and to some extent on the front-cutting edge. The
chip separated by the cutting edges flows along a line Z-Z, and the *true rake angle* in
a plane perpendicular to the base of the tool and through Z-Z is comparable to the
effective rake angle α_e of Fig. 16-10. Back rake on a turning tool is like the angle of
inclination θ and side rake like the velocity rake α_v of oblique cutting. A difference
is that in turning, cutting takes place along two edges, on the front and side of the tool,
instead of along one edge as in oblique cutting. In effect though, the directions of the
resultant force and chip flow are established by the back and side rake angles ground
on the tool. Typical rake angles are given in Table 16-2.

The rake angles shown in Fig. 16-13 are positive. Rake angles measured counterclockwise from zero are called *negative rake angles*. They have been found to give
good results on carbide and ceramic tools particularly where the tools is subjected to
shocks. A tool with negative rake receives initial impact behind the cutting edge when
it starts to cut, and its edge has added material for support. A negative rake angle does
increase the cutting forces at lower speeds and gives a poor finish, but carbide tools
with negative rake can be run at high speeds where cutting forces drop off and surface
finish improves. Tests have shown that at such operating speeds, a 7° negative rake
angle on carbide tools results in cutting forces and power requirements only 8.4%
higher than with zero rake angle.

TABLE 16-2   RAKE ANGLE RECOMMENDATIONS (IN DEGREES)

| Work material | | High-speed steel and cast alloys | | Cemented carbide | | | |
| | | | | Brazed | | Throwaway | |
Class	Hardness (Bhn)	Back rake	Side rake	Back rake	Side rake	Back rake	Side rake
Aluminum alloys	30–150 (500 kg)	20	15	3	15	0	5
Cast iron	110–200	5	10	0	−6	−5	−5
	300–400	5	5	−5	−5	−5	−5
Copper alloys	40–200 (500 kg)	5	10	0	8	0	5
Steel	85–225	10	12	0	6	0	5
	325–425	0	10	0	6	−5	−5

Source: Based on tool geometry recommendations in *Machining Data Handbook*, 3d. ed., Metcut
Research Associates, Inc., Cincinnati, Ohio, 1980.

Cutting Edge Angles. An end-cutting edge angle gives clearance to the trailing end of the cutting edge and reduces drag that tends to cause chatter. Too large an end-cutting edge angle takes away material that supports the point and conducts away heat. An angle of 8 to 15° has been found satisfactory in most cases for side-cutting tools, like turning and boring tools. Sometimes a flat 1.5 to 8 mm ($\frac{1}{16}$ to $\frac{5}{16}$ in.) long is ground on the front edge next to the nose radius so that the edge can get in a wiping action to help produce a good finish. End-cutting tools, like cutoff and necking tools, often have no end-cutting edge angle.

A *side-cutting edge* or *lead angle* affects tool life and surface finish. It enables a tool that is fed sideways into a cut to contact the work first behind the tip. A side-cutting edge at an angle has more of its length in action for a definite depth of cut than it would without the angle, and the edge lasts longer. On the other hand, the larger the angle, the greater the component of force tending to separate the work and tool. This promotes chatter. The most satisfactory side-cutting edge angle is generally 15°, although advantage is found in angles as large as 30 to 45° for heavy cuts. No side-cutting edge angle is desirable when cutting castings or forgings with hard and scaly skins because then the least amount of tool edge should be exposed to the destructive action of the skin.

The actual effect of the cutting edge angles in practice depends upon the angle to which the shank of the tool is set with respect to the workpiece, as indicated by Fig. 16-14. The entering angle is 180° minus the sum of the side-cutting edge and setting angles.

A *nose radius* is favorable to long tool life and good surface finish. A sharp point on the end of a tool is highly stressed, short lived, and leaves a groove in the path of cut. As the nose radius is increased from zero, the improvements in surface finish and permissible cutting speed in representative tests are indicated by Fig. 16-15.

The amount of nose radius that can be put on a tool is limited because too large a radius is conducive to chatter. Radii 0.4 to 6.4 mm ($\frac{1}{64}$ to $\frac{1}{4}$ in.) are common but 0.8 to 3.2 mm ($\frac{1}{32}$ to $\frac{1}{8}$ in.) are most often used. The size of a nose radius may be prescribed by the fillet that must be left in the corner at the end of a cut.

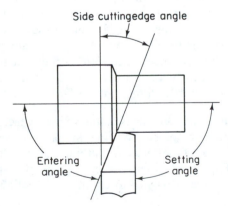

Side cuttingedge angle

Entering angle

Setting angle

Figure 16-14 Positioning angles of a tool.

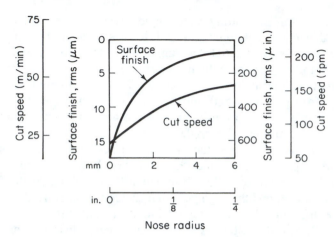

Figure 16-15 Variations of surface finish and tool life with nose radius of a turning tool.

The physical condition of the cutting edge and face of a tool has a considerable effect upon performance. A tool that is ground so that the cutting edge is jagged will break down quickly. Also, a keen cutting edge and a good finish on the tool face are helpful in minimizing the formation of a built-up edge and promote good surface finish on the workpiece. A good practice is to stone a high-speed steel tool after it is ground to whet the cutting edge and improve the finish of the face. Carbide and ceramic tools are usually finish ground with fine grit diamond wheels. A carbide or ceramic tool for cutting steel may have its edge chamfered or "dubbed" 50 to 130 μm (0.002 to 0.005 in.) at 45° by means of a hand hone to remove weak irregularities along the edge for heavy cuts.

Chip Breakers.   A continuous type chip from a long cut can be quite troublesome. Such chips become tangled around the workpiece, tool, and machine members and are dangerous to the operator because they are hot and sharp. At high speeds chips come off fast, often out of control, and do not tend to curl. Chip breakers are features of cutting tools for curling and breaking up chips for easy disposal.

Common chip breakers are shown in Fig. 16-16. The gullet type is a groove, and the stepped type an offset; both are ground or formed into the rake face of the tool. The groove weakens the cutting edge somewhat and is suitable only for moderate feeds. The mechanical type is a block of hard tool material clamped on the face of the tool and is adjustable for different feeds. The form of the land angle type is pressed into tool inserts. It does not present an obstruction to the chip and is reported to give good chip control with much smaller forces and less power than that of other types.

Tool Shapes.   Although the elements that have been described are found in all single-point cutting tools, they are put together in many ways to satisfy various requirements. Common shapes of tools used for turning, facing, shaping, planing, and boring are illustrated in Fig. 16-17. These are only a few of many varieties.

Some side-cutting tools are designed to cut in one direction, others in another.

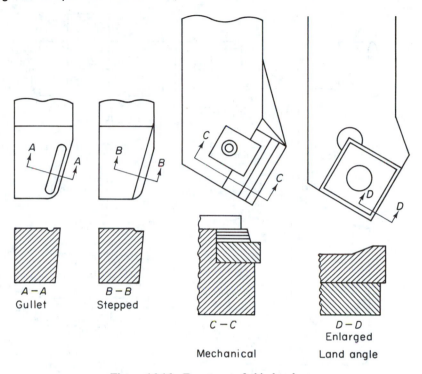

Figure 16-16 Four types of chip breakers.

They are called right-hand or left-hand tools. The hand is revealed when the tool is placed with its nose pointing at an observer. If the cutting edge is on his right side, the tool is a right-hand tool, and vice-versa.

Single-Point Tools. Single-point tools are formed in a number of ways to suit the various kinds of cutting materials. Small pieces of tool material, called *bits*, are ground on their ends and fastened in toolholders like those in Fig. 16-18. To make a large solid tool, a piece of high-speed steel may be welded on the end of an inexpensive soft steel shank.

Small pieces of expensive cutting materials are commonly brazed, cemented, strapped, or clamped onto heavy shanks of soft steel. Tools made in this way are said to be *tipped*. Some typical commercial tools suitable for cemented carbides, ceramics, etc., are shown in Fig. 16-19. View (A) depicts an insert brazed into a pocket on the end of the tool shank. Tips brazed or cemented in this way are securely held, but as a result of brazing and the different coefficients of expansion of the adjacent materials, inherent stresses may be set up that weaken or crack the tip. In view (B) a sandwich consisting of a carbide chip breaker, tool bit, and support is held by a mechanical clamp. The support at the bottom is made of cemented carbide because it has a high modulus of elasticity, about 7×10^7, and deflects less than half as much as steel under

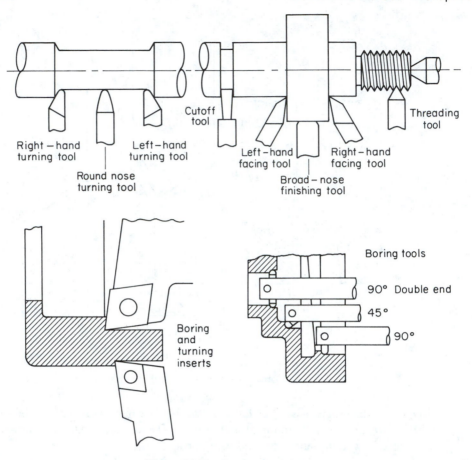

Figure 16-17 Common tool shapes.

a load. The insert of Fig. 16-19(B) is positioned with a negative rake angle so both sides can be used with clearance under each edge. Thus eight corners of the insert can be indexed into position and used before the insert needs to be resharpened or discarded. In many cases it is more economical to throw away such inserts than to sharpen them. A triangular insert is held by a central screw in view (C). Other common shapes are diamond and circular.

The tool in view (D) has a positive rake angle; its top is flat and its sides are relieved, so it cannot be turned over to obtain the use of eight edges, and only four are serviceable. Tool inserts with positive rake angles formed in both faces, like the one sketched in view (E), offer eight cutting edges. As has been explained, positive rake angles give lower cutting forces and temperatures, and are better for many operations, even though more expensive. In one case, tough Inconel 718 was cut at 30 m/min (100 fpm) with a cemented carbide tool having a 5° negative rake angle.

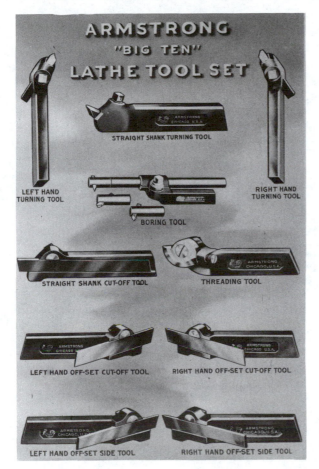

Figure 16-18 Forged toolholders and bits. (Courtesy Armstrong Bros. Tool Co.)

Tool life was 1.3 minutes. The same tool material with a 15° positive rake angle permitted an increase in cutting speed to 56 m/min (185 fpm) with the same tool life for an increase in productivity of 85%.

Styles, shapes, and sizes of cutting tools have been standardized through the American National Standards Institute (ANSI) to the extent that most tools can be described by a series of letters and numbers. For example, the shape of a general-purpose carbide-tipped tool is designated by a letter; designating straight-shank tools, A specifies a 0° side-cutting edge angle (SCEA), B a 15° SCEA, C a square end, D a centrally located 80° nose angle, and E either a central or offset 60° nose angle. Designating 0° offset tools, F specifies end cutting, and G side cutting. A second letter, applicable to styles A, B, F, and G, is R for right-hand and L for left-hand. The letter or letters are followed by one or two numbers. For square shanks, the number represents the number of sixteenths of an inch of width and height. For a rectangular

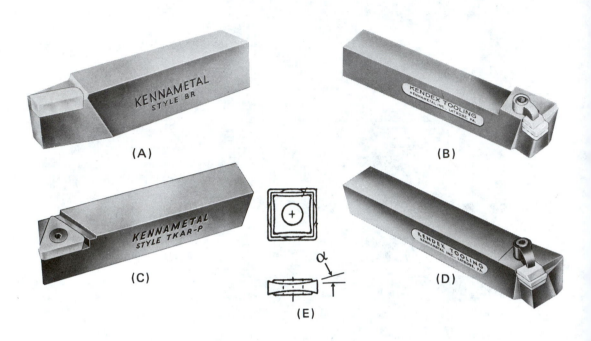

Figure 16-19   Typical cemented carbide-tipped tools. (Courtesy Kennametal, Inc.)

shank, two numbers designate the number of eighths of an inch of width and the number of fourths of an inch of height, in that order. If the tool shown in Fig. 16-19(A) has a shank $\frac{3}{4}$ in. wide by $\frac{3}{4}$ in. high, it is designated by BR-12. Such a tool with a shank 1 in. wide by $1\frac{1}{4}$ in. high is designated by BR-85.

Similar standards and coding systems have been compiled for cemented carbide and other kinds of inserts, seats, chip breakers, and holders. The source for the bulletins describing the standards is referenced at the end of this chapter.

Form Tools.   A form tool has a cutting edge with a definite profile or contour that produces a desired form on the workpiece in the manner indicated in Fig. 16-1(E). A form tool may be made by grinding a profile on the end of an ordinary single-point tool or bit. That is done for small and simple profiles like circular arcs. Two common types for production work are flat and circular form tools (Fig. 16-20). Form tools are sharpened by grinding the rake face behind the cutting edge. Because of the angles at which a form tool must be ground and positioned, it usually must be designed with a form somewhat different from that desired on the workpiece.

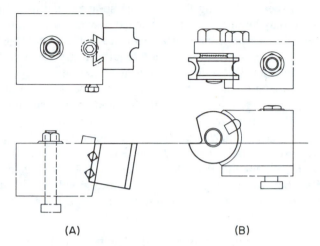

(A)   (B)

Figure 16-20   Examples of form tools:
(A) flat form tool held by a dovetail;
(B) circular form tool.

CUTTING FLUIDS

Purpose.   Fluids are commonly applied to metal-cutting operations, chiefly to cool the tool and workpiece and to provide lubrication. In some cases little benefit is derived from a cutting fluid, but in most cases increases of 20 to 50%, and sometimes more, in cutting speed are possible with the same tool life when a cutting fluid is used as compared with dry cutting.

A cutting fluid is often called a *coolant*, and cooling is an important function at all cutting speeds. High temperatures are the chief cause of tool wear. An overheated workpiece may warp. Coolants help correct these conditions.

Cutting fluids may serve to lubricate the chip sliding over the tool face. The evidence is that capillary action tends to draw the fluid in through the natural grinding scratches on the face of the tool. Lubrication reduces friction forces acting on the tool, improving tool life and decreasing power consumption. The tendency to form a built-up edge is decreased by lubrication, and surface finish is improved, but speed is much more effective than cutting fluid in improving finish.

The lubricating action of cutting fluids is effective only at low speeds; it is already poor at 30 m/min (100 fpm) and totally absent at 120 m/min (400 fpm) and above. At high speeds the fluid does not have time to reach the tool face where it can lubricate; external cooling is all that can be done.

A cutting fluid is useful in cooling and washing away the chips formed in an operation. A fluid also should be capable of lubricating exposed machine elements, prevent corrosion, and not be harmful to the operator.

A cutting fluid is usually flowed in a copious stream on top of the chip and tool. The flow must be uninterrupted with carbides because they crack easily from sudden temperature changes. Some advantage is obtained by directing the flood upward between the relief face of the tool and workpiece. Fluid may be flung away from the cut and create a mess at high speeds. Cutting fluid may be sprayed as a mist from above or below. A jet of fluid may be injected into the space between the relief face of the tool and the workpiece. Under some circumstances it reaches the cutting edge and appreciably increases tool life. However, the method requires fairly costly equipment and extra care from the operator, and is not widely used. Flooding is as effective as any other method at low temperature and costs the least. At higher temperature, a layer of steam is trapped by flooding, thus preventing the fluid from reaching and cooling the surfaces. A mist blows away the steam layer and cools effectively. This helps only for a limited range because a thick cloud of steam is generated at still higher temperatures and keeps away even the mist or spray. In one test at 90 m/min (300 fpm) mist cooling showed 68% more tool life than flooding and 150% more than dry cutting. At 180 m/min (590 fpm) dry cutting was as efficient as flooding with mist cooling showing a 41% longer tool life, but dry cutting became as efficient as mist spraying at 275 m/min (900 fpm).

Kinds of Cutting Fluids.   Cutting fluids may be classified as (1) gases, (2) water solutions, (3) oils, and (4) waxes.

Gases have inferior cooling capacity and are relatively unimportant cutting fluids. Compressed air is sometimes blown on cast iron being cut. Carbon dioxide at low temperatures may be directed to cool a tool without quenching the work material. This has limited application in machining ultrahigh-strength alloys to keep them from hardening while being cut and from damaging the tool.

Water is the best cooling medium and the most effective fluid for high-speed cutting but has little lubricating value, does not spread well over a surface to wet it because of high surface tension, and causes rust and corrosion. It is mixed with chemicals and oils to improve it as a cutting fluid.

Chemical or *synthetic cutting fluids* contain primarily water modifiers without oils. They may be pure coolants containing just water softeners and rust inhibitors or may be lubricating coolants with wetting agents and/or extreme pressure (EP) agents such as iodine, chlorine, sulfur, and phosphorus. Other chemicals for cutting fluids include blending agents and germicides. Chemicals enhance the penetrating and cooling abilities of water even more than oils, reduce corrosion, and add lubricity approaching that of oils. However, when lubrication is of prime importance, oils are usually recommended. Chemical fluids have long useful lives, high detergency and cleanliness, and do not require degreasing after use. They are not usable on some machines where they can get into ways and bearings, and some substances leave abrasive residues upon evaporation, which may be harmful to slides.

Popular cutting fluids, known as *soluble* or *dispersible oils*, are emulsions of mineral oil with emulsifiers (such as soap in water) and sometimes with EP agents also. Mixtures vary from 5 to over 100 parts of water to 1 of oil. Other compounds are added to give various properties, such as extreme pressure resistance when needed. The mixtures vary in character from heavy solutions with high lubricity and cushioning suitable for heavy turning, milling, broaching, and similar operations to light solutions with little lubricity but high detergency suitable for fine grit grinding and other high-speed operations. The cost of the soluble oil solutions is low.

Straight cutting oils are those not mixed with water; they are classified as inactive and active, according to whether or not they are mixed with chemicals.

Inactive *straight mineral oils* are not widely used but serve satisfactorily for inherently free-cutting materials. They have a specific heat about half that of water and a low degree of adhesion or oiliness but are quite stable and do not develop disagreeable odors. They range in viscosity from kerosene used on magnesium and aluminum to light paraffins for free-cutting brass. Inactive *fatty oils* at one time were quite popular but are little used today. They are expensive. Fatty oils have better wetting and penetrating properties than mineral oils, and the two are chiefly blended together or with small amounts of chemicals to serve nearly as well as active oils with less tendency to stain the work surface.

Sulfur and, to a lesser degree, chlorine and phosphorus are mixed with both mineral and fatty oils to make *active cutting oil compounds* for high antiweld properties and lubrication under extreme pressures. The active ingredients combine with metallic surfaces to form tenacious but slippery films. These compounds play an important part in modern metal-cutting practice, being used extensively for heavy turning, gear cutting, broaching, etc., of tough, stringy, and unusually soft materials. Such agents are not advantageous for light cuts.

Certain *waxes* are adsorbed strongly to metallic surfaces and augment the actions of other ingredients to form cutting fluids having high-pressure and high-temperature lubrication properties. It is not easy to incorporate wax successfully in a cutting fluid, and indiscriminate attempts to apply it have failed and have given wax a bad reputation as a cutting fluid ingredient in some quarters. Where successful, the results with wax have been rather spectacular, but the applications are limited.

QUESTIONS

1. Why is metal cut?

2. How is a surface generated? How is a surface formed?

3. Describe the actions of drilling and milling.

4. What is meant by the cutting speed of an operation? The feed? The depth of cut?

5. Describe what takes place when metal is cut.

6. Name and describe three kinds of chips.

7. Draw a diagram of the forces acting on a chip during its formation.

8. What are the conditions of pressure, friction, and temperature in a cutting zone?

9. Why do cutting tools wear faster at higher speeds?

10. What happens to the forces in the cutting zone as the speed is increased? Why do they change as they do?

11. What happens to the temperature and forces as the feed is increased?

12. In approximately what direction does the chip flow in oblique cutting?

13. What is a major benefit from oblique cutting?

14. How do the shear plane angle and the shearing force vary with the rake angle and coefficient of friction?

15. In what ways may a tool wear?

16. What is chatter? Why is it harmful?

17. Name and describe the principal cutting-tool materials.

18. What determines which cutting-tool material is best for an operation?

19. Name in conventional order and describe the angles of a cutting tool.

20. What is the purpose of relief angles?

21. What does the rake angle of a cutting tool do?

22. What is the purpose of the front-cutting edge angle? The side-cutting edge angle?

23. Specify the effect upon forces, power consumption, and tool life of each angle and the nose radius of a cutting tool.

24. What is a chip breaker, and what purpose does it serve?

25. Describe four types of chip breakers.

26. What are the common shapes of single-point tools?

27. What is a form tool? Describe two kinds.

28. What are the purposes of cutting fluids?

29. What are the principal kinds of cutting fluids?

30. How are cutting fluids applied to metal-cutting operations?

PROBLEMS

1. Calculate the number of revolutions per minute for each of the following diameters to get the specified cutting speeds.

	(a)	(b)	(c)	(d)	(e)	(f)
Diameter [mm (in.)]	102 (4)	305 (12)	178 (7)	457 (18)	25 (1)	229 (9)
Cut speed [m/min (fpm)]	18 (60)	23 (75)	27 (90)	30 (100)	60 (200)	90 (300)

2. If each of the following diameters is rotated at the number of revolutions per minute specified for it, what is its surface speed in m/min (fpm)?

	(a)	(b)	(c)	(d)	(e)	(f)
Diameter [mm (in.)]	76 (3)	457 (18)	254 (10)	127 (5)	178 (7)	305 (12)
Revolutions/min	230	70	20	160	200	160

3. What is the rate of metal removal for each of the following situations?

	(a)	(b)	(c)
Cut speed [m/min (fpm)]	60 (200)	15 (50)	107 (350)
Feed [mm/rev (ipr)]	0.25 (0.010)	0.75 (0.030)	0.20 (0.008)
Depth of cut [mm (in.)]	6.5 ($\frac{1}{4}$)	9.5 ($\frac{3}{8}$)	1.5 (0.06)

4. In a cutting operation like that depicted in Figs. 16-7 and 16-8, the feed t_1 is 100 μm (0.004 in.) and the chip is found to have a thickness t_2 of 0.25 mm (0.010 in.). The cutting force F_c is 1330 N (300 lb) and the normal force F_L is 775 N (170 lb). The rake angle of the tool

is $+10°$. Find:
(a) The shear angle ϕ.
(b) The size of the force R exerted by the tool on the chip.
(c) The coefficient of friction on the face of the tool.
(d) The sizes of the friction force F_f and the normal force F_n.
(e) The sizes of the shearing force F_s and the normal force F_N.

5. An orthogonal cut 2.5 mm (0.100 in.) wide is made at a speed of 30 m/min (100 fpm) and feed of 0.25 mm/rev (0.010 ipr) with a high-speed steel tool having a 20° rake angle. The chip thickness ratio r_t is found to be 0.58, the cutting force F_c is 1380 N (310 lb), and the normal force F_L is 355 N (80 lb).
(a) How thick is the chip?
(b) What is the shear plane angle?
(c) What is the size of the resultant force R?
(d) What is the coefficient of friction on the face of the tool?
(e) Calculate the sizes of the friction force F_f and normal force F_n.
(f) Calculate the sizes of the shearing forces F_S and the normal force F_N.
(g) What is the specific energy in J/cm^3 (in.-lb/in.^{3})?

6. In a cutting operation like that depicted in Figs. 16-7 and 16-8, the feed t_1 is 0.13 mm (0.005 in.) and the depth of cut normal to the plane of the paper is 2.5 mm (0.100 in.). The cutting speed is 245 m/min (800 fpm). The cutting force F_c is found to be 1780 N (400 lb) and the normal force F_L is 890 N (200 lb). The rake angle of the tool is $+8°$. Find:
(a) The power required for the cut in kW (hp).
(b) The rate of metal removal in cm^3/min (in.^{3}/min).
(c) The unit power in kW/cm^3/min (hp/in.^{3}/min).

7. A workpiece is being cut at 76 m/min (250 fpm), and the power is found to be 2.0 kW (2.7 hp). The feed is 0.25 mm/rev (0.010 in./rev) and the depth of cut is 5.0 mm (0.200 in.).
(a) What is the cutting force in newtons (pounds)?
(b) What is the unit power consumption in kW/cm^3/min (hp/in.^{3}/min)?

8. A tool making an orthogonal cut has a $-10°$ rake angle. The feed t_1 is 100 μm (0.004 in.), the width of cut 6.5 mm (0.25 in.), the speed 165 m/min (540 fpm), and a dynamometer measures the cutting force F_c to be 1780 N (400 lb) and the normal force F_L to be 1510 N (340 lb). A high-speed photograph shows a shear plane angle of 20°.
(a) What should the thickness of the chip be?
(b) Compute the coefficient of friction.
(c) Calculate the shearing and normal stresses on the shear plane.
(d) What is the shearing strain?
(e) What power is expended in shearing the metal and altogether in making the cut?

9. An oblique cut is 6.5 mm (0.25 in.) wide. The tool has a 5° normal rake α_n and is inclined at $\theta = 10°$.
(a) What is the angle β on the tool face between the directions of the normal and effective rake angles?
(b) Calculate the effective rake angle.

10. A cutting tool has a normal rake of 10°. How large an inclination angle is required for an effective rake angle of 15°?

11. A shaft 1.6 m (64 in.) long and 100 mm (4 in.) in diameter is turned from tough steel having a hardness of 22 to 26 R_C. With a high-speed steel tool the speed is 24 m/min (78

fpm), the feed 0.50 mm/rev (0.020 ipr), and the depth of cut 1.3 mm (0.050 in.). The tool must be ground four times before it finishes one shaft and can be ground 40 times before being discarded. The cost of a tool bit is $2.50. It takes 10 minutes to grind and replace the tool bit. A sintered oxide tool bit with six edges and costing $3.90 is put on the job. After all six edges are dull, this bit is not sharpened but is thrown away. It cuts with a speed of 90 m/min (295 fpm), a feed of 0.50 mm/rev (0.020 ipr), and a depth of cut of 1.3 mm (0.050 in.). Two edges must be used to cut one shaft. The time to index the tool is 1/2 minute. The cost for labor and overhead in the shop is $26/hr. Which tool is more economical?

12. A workpiece of SAE 4340 steel (300 Bhn) is rough turned for a distance of 460 mm (18 in.) with a stock removal of 11 mm (0.435 in.) on a side of a 140 mm ($5\frac{1}{2}$ in.) diameter. With high-speed steel tools, the speed is 25 m/min (80 fpm) and feed 0.30 mm/rev (0.012 ipr). The tool must be resharpened for each piece. The tool costs $2.60 and can be reground 40 times. Time for sharpening and resetting the tool is 2 minutes for each piece. A cemented carbide tool costs $5.48 and can be ground 10 times. It is operated at 100 m/min (330 fpm) with a feed of 0.60 mm/rev (0.024 ipr). It can turn 10 pieces before having to be sharpened, but the time to sharpen and reset it is 10 minutes. The labor and overhead rate is $26/hr. Which tool is more economical for the job?

13. A workpiece has a hardness of 34 to 36 R_C and is turned on the end to a diameter of 46 mm (1.810 in.) from a diameter of 64 mm ($2\frac{1}{2}$ in.) for a length of 140.5 mm (5.530 in.). A brazed carbide insert tool has been making the cut on production at 65.5 m/min (215 fpm) with a feed of 0.28 mm/rev (0.011 ipr). Fifty pieces are obtained between tool grinds. The tool can be reground four times and costs $8.26 new. Each grind costs $2. A throwaway replaceable insert tool is tried on the job. Because the tip is free from brazing strains, this tool can be operated at 92 m/min (300 fpm) with a 0.38 mm/rev (0.015 ipr) feed and completes 60 pieces per cutting edge. Three edges are available. Each insert costs $3.30, and the holder, which lasts for 1000 inserts, costs $21.50. Can the use of throwaway replaceable inserts be justified on this operation where the labor and overhead rate is $15/hr?

REFERENCES

AMAREGO, E. J. A., and R. H. BROWN, *The Machining of Metals*, Prentice-Hall, Englewood Cliffs, N.J., 1969.

"Applying New Carbide Technology," *American Machinist*, Jan. 1, 1975, p. 37.

DALLAS, D. B., ed., *Tool and Manufacturing Engineers Handbook*, Society of Manufacturing Engineers, Dearborn, Mich., 1976.

FEINBERG, B., "Cutting Tools: Meeting the Challenge of the 70's," *Manufacturing Engineering and Management*, Feb. 1975, p. 40.

HATSCHEK, R. L., "What's New at the Cutting Edge, Special Report 654," *American Machinist*, Mar. 5, 1973, p. 65.

———,"Turning with Inserts, Special Report 707," *American Machinist*, Oct. 10, 1978, p. 119.

———,"High Speed Machining, Special Report 710," *American Machinist*, Mar. 1973.

————,"Take a New Look at Ceramics/Cermets, Special Report 733," *American Machinist*, May 1981, p. 165.

Howe, R. E., ed., *Producibility/Machinability of Space-Age and Conventional Materials*, Society of Manufacturing Engineers, Dearborn, Mich., 1968.

Kalish, H. S.,"Carbide Grade Classifications—What They Mean," *Manufacturing Engineering and Management*, Jan. 1976, p. 49.

————,"An Update on New Developments in Cutting Tools," *Manufacturing Engineering*, Sept. 1978, p. 58.

Kuderko, M. J., and J. Kral,"Machining the Problem Alloys," *American Machinist*, Jan. 11, 1971, p. 57.

Metals Handbook, Vol. 3: *Machining*, American Society For Metals, Metals Park, Ohio, 1967.

"Metalworking Fluids," *Manufacturing Engineering*, Nov. 1975, p. 31.

Prodab, M.,"CVD Hard Coatings Lengthen Tool Life," *Metal Progress*, May 1962, p. 50.

Sanders, E. H.,"Choosing the Right Carbide Insert," *American Machinist*, Apr. 1982, p. 139.

Standards: cutting tools, inserts, holders, etc. Complete list available from the American Society of Mechanical Engineers, 345 East 47th Street, New York, NY 10017.

17

ECONOMICS OF METAL CUTTING

The efficiency of a metal-cutting operation can be judged from the main criteria of (1) the life of the cutting tool, (2) forces and power, (3) surface finish and dimensional accuracy, and (4) the rate of material removal. The first two considerations determine costs; the last two measure the output. Economy is achieved when the required finish and accuracy are obtained at the lowest unit cost.

The factors within an operation that may be varied to change the costs and results are (1) speed, (2) feed and depth of cut, (3) work material, (4) tool material, (5) tool form and shape, and (6) cutting fluid. The nature and effects of the last three of these have been discussed in Chap. 16. The first three will be dealt with in the following pages.

CUTTING SPEED

Speed and Tool Life. Tests with many materials under many conditions have shown that tool life is shorter, the higher the cutting speed. In most cases this follows the relationship that

$$VT^n = C \qquad (17\text{-}1)$$

In this expression, V stands for the cutting speed in m/min (fpm) and T for the tool life in minutes. C is a constant that is different for each change in work material, tool material, tool form and shape, size and shape of cut, and cutting fluid. The exponent *n* also varies with the same changes, but for any tool and work material combination *n* has a value that does not vary much with changes in the other factors.

Expression (17-1) is a straight line when plotted on log-log coordinates, as shown for several typical cases in Fig. 17-1. The exponent *n* is the slope of the line. Approximate values of *n* for several average conditions are tabulated. The constant *C* has the same value as the cutting speed for a one minute tool life in each case. Each line in Fig. 17-1 represents a specific set of conditions. If any of the conditions changes, the situation would be represented by a new line. These are empirical curves that have been found to apply within the usual range of cutting speeds, but at times the trend is in a different direction at low or high speeds for a tool material, as indicated by the broken line at one end of the curve for cemented carbide. Values for *C* and *n* have been determined for many specific conditions and are given in reference books and handbooks. If such information is not available for a specific operation, tool life can be measured at several cutting speeds and the points plotted and connected by a line to obtain the necessary data. Such a curve should not be extrapolated beyond observed points.

Optimum Tool Life.   The tool life versus speed relationship does not alone tell what the best speed is for an operation. What speed is best depends upon the other conditions, such as feed, depth of cut, material, etc., and the criterion for optimizing the operation. A common criterion is that of lowest cost. For a given set of other conditions that are held constant, there is only one speed that results in the lowest total cost for the operation. This is illustrated in Fig. 17-2. When the cutting speed is low, tools last a long time, and tool cost is low. At the same time metal removal is slow,

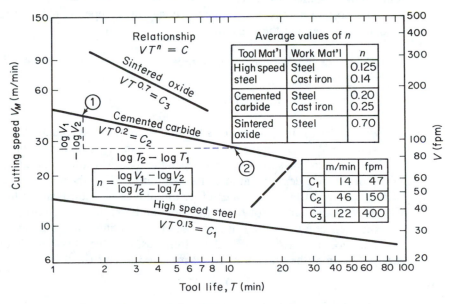

Figure 17-1 Typical tool-life curves, based on cutting speeds.

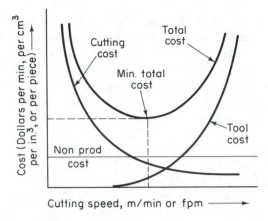

Figure 17-2 Cost elements for a metal-cutting operation.

and the cutting cost and total cost are high. On the other hand, cutting cost is low at high speeds, but tool cost is high because tool life is short, and the net result is that the total cost is high. At some intermediate cutting speed, the total cost is at a minimum. The tool life corresponding to this cutting speed is called the *economical tool life*.

The costs that need to be considered are the tool costs and the cutting costs. Others, such as costs for loading and unloading and setup, are not affected by cutting speed and need not be included. Unit cost is most significant and may be cost per piece, per cubic centimeter, per cubic inch, etc. The relevant costs will be reduced to $/cm³ ($/in.³) in this discussion.

The cost to supply a cutting-tool edge for an operation is C_t and has three components. They are the costs to:

1. Change or index the tool, $c_1 = t_1 \times R_c$
2. Grind or sharpen the tool as necessary, $c_2 = t_2 \times R_s/N_1$
3. Pay for the tool, $c_3 = C_T/(N_1 \times N_2)$

Thus $C_t = c_1 + c_2 + c_3$. Here, t_1 is the time in minutes to change the tool, R_c is the labor and overhead rate applied to the metal-cutting operation in dollars per minute, t_2 is the time in minutes to grind or sharpen the tool, R_s is the labor and overhead rate in the tool grinding department in dollars per minute, N_1 is the number of cutting edges obtained per grind or the number of cutting edges on a throwaway tool that is not ground, N_2 is the number of times the tool can be ground (including once when the tool is made), and C_T is the original cost of the cutting tool in dollars.

For a tool life of T minutes, the cutting cost over the life of the tool is $C_c = R_cT$. During this time, the amount of metal removed in cm³ (in.³) is

$$Q_T = V_mTfc = 12VTfc \qquad (17\text{-}2)$$

where f = feed equivalent to width of cut in mm (in.), c = depth of cut in mm (in.),

V_m is in m/min, and V in fpm. If C/T^n is substituted for V_m or V in Eq. (17-2) and the several constants are combined into one constant C_G, $Q_T = C_G/T^{n-1}$.

The total unit cost in \$/cm³ (\$/in.³) is

$$C_u = \frac{C_c + C_t}{Q_T} = \frac{T^{n-1}(R_cT + C_t)}{C_G} \tag{17-3}$$

If C_u is differentiated with respect to T and set equal to zero to find the minimum, the expression for the economical tool life becomes

$$T_e = \left(\frac{1}{n} - 1\right) \frac{C_t}{R_c} \tag{17-4}$$

The cutting speed that corresponds to the economical tool life can be found from Eq. (17-1). That is the speed at which the operation should be run for lowest total cost.

A second criterion is to achieve a maximum rate of production. For this goal it is assumed that adequate spare tools are available so that the operation is never held up for tool grinding and the tool cost is disregarded. The only tool factor that affects the rate of production is the time, t_1, to change or index the tool. This cannot be done while the tool is cutting, and the shorter the tool life, the more often the cutting must be interrupted. The average rate of production, $R_p = Q_T/(T + t_1) = C_GT^{(1-n)}/(T + t_1)$. If $dR_p/dT = 0$, the tool life for maximum rate of production is

$$T_M = \left(\frac{1}{n} - 1\right) t_1 \tag{17-5}$$

Since $t_1 < C_t/R_c$, the tool life for maximum production is always less than the economical tool life for a given operation. Thus the cutting speed for maximum production is always higher than that for lowest cost; the interval between the two has been called the *Hi-E Range*.

A third criterion is for maximum profit, which seldom coincides with lowest cost or maximum production. No simple expression has been found for tool life or cutting speed to yield maximum profit. However, it has been shown that the cut speed for maximum profit always lies within the Hi-E Range. Profit is near maximum anywhere in that range.

As an example, the labor and overhead rate for an operation is \$0.24/min. Tool changing time is $\frac{1}{2}$ min; labor and overhead rate for tool grinding is \$0.27/min; time to grind a tool is 15 minutes; a tool costs \$10.46 and can be ground eight times, and eight cutting edges are obtained from each grind. The tool is a steel-cutting grade of cemented carbide; the work material SAE 4340 steel; and $V_mT^{0.2} = 166$ ($VT^{0.2} = 544$) applies. At what speed should the operation be run for economical tool life? What tool life and speed will give the maximum rate of production? The total tool cost per cutting edge is

$$C_T = \frac{0.24}{2} + 15 \times \frac{0.27}{8} + \frac{10.46}{8 \times 8} = \$0.79$$

Economical tool life is

$$T_e = \left(\frac{1}{0.2} - 1\right) \frac{0.79}{0.24} = 13 \text{ minutes}$$

$$V_e = \frac{166}{13^{0.2}} = 99 \text{ m/min}$$

$$= \frac{544}{13^{0.2}} = 326 \text{ fpm}$$

$$T_M = \left(\frac{1}{0.2} - 1\right) 0.5 = 2 \text{ minutes}$$

$$V_M = \frac{166}{2^{0.2}} = 145 \text{ m/min}$$

$$= \frac{544}{2^{0.2}} = 474 \text{ fpm}$$

Speed versus Forces, Power, and Surface Finish. The three components of force acting on a turning tool are shown in Fig. 17-3. The cutting force F_C acts in the direction of the speed V at the tool point and the resulting power accounts for over 95% of that normally consumed in the cut. The feed movement in the direction of F_L is small and there is no motion in the direction of F_R in this case.

The cutting force F_C generally decreases as speed is raised above about 30 m/min (100 fpm), and power increases less than proportionately, but the decrease in force is usually less than 15% within ordinary operating speed ranges.

As speed is increased, the built-up edge on the face of a cutting tool gets smaller and at a sufficiently high speed disappears, improving surface finish. The actual improvement in any case depends upon the material and other conditions of the cut. An indication of the trend in the case of several tests is given in Fig. 17-4. Because good surface finish is one of the aims of finishing cuts, such cuts generally are taken at higher speeds than heavier roughing cuts. In the case of a finishing cut, the surface finish obtained may be a more important consideration than the very lowest cost.

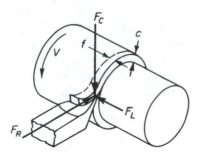

Figure 17-3 Forces acting on a turning tool.

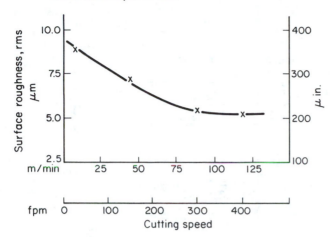

Figure 17-4 **Figure 17-4** Average values of surface finish for five materials at various cutting speeds.

Practical Operating Speeds.   For ordinary turning operations the economical tool life generally is $\frac{1}{4}$ to $1\frac{1}{2}$ hr. The economical cutting speed for any operation depends upon a number of factors, as has been shown, and is not likely to be identical for any two operations. Only when production is high is it worthwhile to make a study to ascertain the economical cutting speed for an operation. If only a few pieces of a kind are to be produced, a study might well cost more than could be saved on the job. As a rule, speeds within a reasonable range will give results close to those of the most economical cutting speed because total cost curves like the one in Fig. 17-2 are rather flat and broad at the bottom. For general practice, tables in reference texts and handbooks are used. They specify cutting speeds that have been found optimum under various conditions and can be used to estimate the best speed for similar conditions. The operator then may try higher or lower speeds as the job progresses to see if he or she gets better results. Typical recommendations are given in Table 17-1.

FEED AND DEPTH OF CUT

Effect on Tool Life.   Experiments with some materials have shown that as feed is increased with a constant speed, tool life increases to a maximum and then decreases as shown for 8640 steel in Fig. 17-5. The feed for maximum tool life generally is not important because it is well below feed rates that are economical and used in practice. As an example, if the material of Fig. 17-5 is turned at 90 m/min (300 fpm) under typical conditions, the cost is $0.003/cm^3 ($0.05/in.^{3}) of metal removal at 0.25 mm/rev (0.010 ipr) feed and about $0.002/cm^3 ($0.03/in.^{3}) at 0.5 mm/rev (0.020 ipr) feed. Although the tool does not last as long at the higher feed, the faster rate of metal removal more than offsets the extra tool cost.

The most efficient feed and depth of cut for an operation depend also upon the cutting speed. Numerous investigations have reported a relationship for most materials

TABLE 17-1 TYPICAL RECOMMENDATIONS OF CUTTING SPEEDS FOR TURNING

Material	Hardness (Bhn)		H.S.S.		Cut speed, [m/min (fpm)] according to tool material (see notes A, B, C, or D for depth of cut and feed)					
					Uncoated cemented carbide brazed		Uncoated cemented carbide indexable		Coated cemented carbide	
Aluminum, cold drawn	30–80 (500 kg)	A	275 (900)	550 (1800)	C	Max.	C	—	A
		B	305 (1000)	610 (2000)	D	Max.	D	—	B
Copper alloys, wrought	60–100 R_B	A	145 (480)	290 (950)	C	335 (1100)	C	—	A
		B	175 (575)	345 (1125)	B	395 (1300)	B	—	B
Gray iron (as cast) (ASTM Class 50)	220–260	A	17 (55)	69 (225)	A	81 (265)	A	105 (350)	A
		B	26 (85)	84 (275)	B	100 (325)	B	130 (425)	B
Steel (H.R. or C.D.) 1005 through 1025	175–225	A	35 (115)	115 (385)	C	135 (450)	C	170 (850)	A
		B	44 (145)	140 (460)	B	175 (570)	B	260 (850)	B
Steel (H.R. or C.D.) 1030 through 1527	225–275	A	27 (90)	90 (300)	C	115 (380)	C	150 (500)	A
		B	35 (115)	115 (380)	B	150 (490)	B	230 (750)	B
Steel (H.R. or Ann.) 1213–1215	100–150	A	69 (225)	170 (550)	C	200 (650)	C	260 (850)	A
		B	90 (295)	220 (725)	B	260 (860)	B	395 (1300)	B
Alloy steel (H.T.) 1330 through 94B30	275–325	A	23 (75)	79 (260)	A	100 (330)	A	130 (425)	A
		B	29 (95)	105 (340)	B	130 (420)	B	170 (550)	B

Note:

	A	B	C	D
depth of cut [mm (in.)]	4 (0.150)	1 (0.040)	4 (0.150)	1 (0.040)
feed [mm/rev (ipm)]	0.4 (0.015)	0.18 (0.007)	0.5 (0.020)	0.25 (0.010)

Source: Data were extracted from the *Machining Data Handbook*, 3d. ed., Machinability Data Center, © 1980, by permission of Metcut Research Associates, Inc., Cincinnati, Ohio.

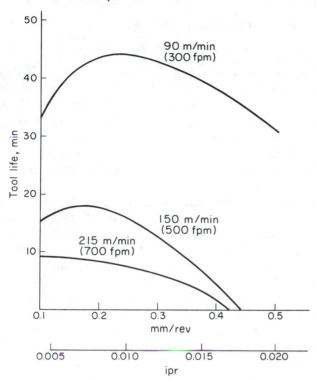

Figure 17-5 How the tool life varies with feed in turning 8640 steel of 190 Bhn at several speeds.

between cutting speed, feed, and depth of cut at a constant tool life to be

$$V_c = \frac{C_1}{f^x c^y} \tag{17-6}$$

The constant C_1 depends mainly upon the work–tool material combination. Exponents x and y vary somewhat with work–tool combination, but each exponent is always between 0 and 1. O.W. Boston has found $x = 0.77$ and $y = 0.37$ for low-alloy steel and

$$V_c = \frac{C_1}{f^{0.77} c^{0.37}} \tag{17-7}$$

will be used here to illustrate the principles. Values of C_1, x, and y are given in reference texts and handbooks for specific conditions.

The economical or maximum production tool life, as preferred, should be maintained in an operation for most efficient results. As has been shown, the economical or maximum production tool life depends upon the constant n and the tool cost and does not change appreciably as f and c are changed. Equations (17-6) and (17-7) reveal that the cutting speed must be decreased as f or c is increased, and vice versa, to maintain the desired tool life.

The effect that changes in the feed and depth of cut have upon the efficiency of metal removal in an operation can be appraised from Eq. (17-2), with T as part of a constant K_2, and Eq. (17-7) substituted for V, which is

$$Q_T = K_2 Vfc = K_3 f^{0.23} c^{0.63} \tag{17-8}$$

This relationship reveals a basic law of metal machining, that *as feed or depth of cut (f or c), or both, are increased and the cutting speed is decreased to keep the tool life substantially constant, the amount of material removed during the life of the tool and consequently the amount of material cut during each productive minute goes up.* Furthermore, since the exponent for c is larger, an increase in the depth of cut will produce a larger increase of material removal than the same proportionate increase in feed. Thus deep cuts with light feeds are more efficient than shallow cuts with heavy feeds, from the standpoint of tool life.

Practical considerations limit the actual amount of feed or depth of cut in an operation. The depth of cut cannot exceed the stock to be removed. Heavy cuts set up large tool forces, and these are limited by what the workpiece, tool, and material can stand. Heavier cuts call for more power, which can only be supplied up to the capacity of the machine. Heavy cuts cause poor surface finish, and cannot be tolerated if the surface finish must be good, as usually it must be in a final cut.

The rule for efficient operation is to take as heavy a depth of cut and feed as the tool, workpiece, and machine will stand, and adjust the speed for economical or maximum production tool life. If the machine is old, or power or speed and feed ranges are not available to operate at recommended speeds and feeds, it is more economical to cut back the speed rather than the feed or depth of cut.

Forces and Power. A number of formulas have been developed for calculating cutting force, which acts in the direction of the speed. As the basis for an empirical expression, the cutting force is measured on a dynamometer for a given set of conditions. This has been done for many conditions and for all components of force. It has been found that the cutting force depends mainly on the work material, feed f, and depth of cut c. A simple empirical formula for the cutting force in turning is

$$F_c = C_f f^a c^b \tag{17-9}$$

Average value found for a is around 0.8, and for b about 0.9. Some average values reported for C_f are given in Table 17-2. For f and c in mm and corresponding C_f, F_c is in kN. For f and c in in. and corresponding C_f, F_c is in pounds force.

Formulas are available that are more detailed and more accurate than Eq. (17-9). They take into account more factors, such as chip shape, tool shape, and variations in work materials. Similar formulas exist for various kinds of operations, such as drilling, milling, broaching, etc., and for forces in all coordinate directions. Factors for Eq. (17-9) and other formulas to suit specific conditions are given in reference books and handbooks.

How power requirements are affected by changes in feed and depth of cut can now be shown. Substantially all the mechanical power in cutting metal ensues from the cutting force in the direction of the speed because velocities in other directions are so relatively small. Typical expressions for speed and cutting force are given by Eqs.

TABLE 17-2 AVERAGE VALUES OF C_f IN EQ. (17-9)

Material	Bhn	C_f for f and c in: mm	C_f for f and c in: in.
Low-carbon steel	100	2.18	120,000
Medium-alloy steel	207	4.00	220,000
Cast iron	126	0.53	29,000
	181	1.00	55,000
	241	1.16	64,000
Yellow brass		1.51	83,000
Leaded brass		0.62	34,000

(17-7) and (17-9). These may be substituted into the basic equation for power,

$$P = K_p F_c V = \frac{K_p (C_f f^{0.8} c^{0.9}) C_1}{f^{0.77} c^{0.37}} = C_2 f^{0.03} c^{0.53} \qquad (17\text{-}10)$$

The constant C_2 is a collection of constants K_p, C_f, and C_1 and includes tool life assumed held at its optimum value as f or c is varied.

Unit power, introduced on page 463, is $P_u = P/Q$. For this discussion, the numerator is Eq. (17-10), and the denominator is Eq. (17-8). Thus

$$P_u = \frac{C_2 f^{0.03} c^{0.53}}{K_3 f^{0.23} c^{0.63}} = \frac{C_3}{f^{0.2} c^{0.1}} \qquad (17\text{-}11)$$

The effects of changes in feed and depth of cut can now be seen from Eqs. (17-9), (17-10), and (17-11). The cutting force increases with feed or depth of cut, more with depth of cut than with feed, but less than proportionately. For a constant tool life, power increases moderately with increases in depth of cut but almost not at all with increase in feed. The unit power decreases moderately as either feed or depth of cut, or both, are increased. It must be remembered that these stipulations are based upon the premise that cutting speed is adjusted always to maintain economical tool life when other factors are varied. Thus, the general rule is that heavy cuts are more efficient than light cuts from a power as well as a tool life standpoint but require adequate strength in workpiece and tools, and rigidity and power in the machine.

The cutting-force equations that have been given are not always used in practice. Cutting force and power are probably most often estimated by multiplying the rate of metal removal by the unit power. The power is divided by the cut speed to obtain an estimate of the cutting force. Average values of unit power are given in Table 17-3. Some tables take more factors into consideration. Data like these are compiled from experiments. Power consumed in an operation may be measured by a wattmeter in the motor circuit. The power required at the cutter can be estimated by subtracting the idle power from the power under load. Another approach is to measure cutting force using a dynamometer, and multiply the amount of the force by the cut speed. Tabulated data are commonly based on experiments conducted under ideal conditions with sharp tools. Not only do tools become dull, but higher-than-expected feeds may be used, and

TABLE 17-3 AVERAGE UNIT POWER FOR SOME COMMON MATERIALS AND MACHINING OPERATIONS

Material	Hardness (Bhn)	Unit power [W/cm³/min (hp/in.³/min)]		
		Turning shaping	Drilling	Milling
Aluminum alloys	30–150 (500 kg)	11 (0.25)	7 (0.16)	15 (0.32)
Copper alloys (brass)	80–100 R_B	46 (1.0)	36 (0.8)	46 (1.0)
Cast iron (gray, ductile,	110–190	32 (0.7)	46 (1.0)	27 (0.6)
and malleable)	190–320	64 (1.4)	73 (1.6)	50 (1.1)
High-temperature alloys				
(nickel and cobalt base)	200–360	114 (2.5)	91 (2.0)	91 (2.0)
Nickel alloys	80–360	91 (2.0)	82 (1.8)	86 (1.9)
Steels—wrought	85–200	50 (1.1)	46 (1.0)	50 (1.1)
and cast	35–40 R_C	64 (1.4)	64 (1.4)	68 (1.5)
(Plain carbon,	40–50 R_C	68 (1.5)	77 (1.7)	82 (1.8)
alloy, and tool	50–55 R_C	91 (2.0)	96 (2.1)	96 (2.1)
steels)	55–58 R_C	155 (3.4)	118 (2.6)	118 (2.6)
Stainless steel	135–275	59 (1.3)	50 (1.1)	64 (1.4)
	30–45 R_C	64 (1.4)	55 (1.2)	68 (1.5)
feed [mm/rev or mm/tooth (ipr or ipt)]		0.15–0.50 (0.005–0.020)	0.05–0.20 (0.002–0.008)	0.12–0.30 (0.005–0.012)

Notes:

1. Equation (17-11) can be applied to estimate unit power at smaller or larger feeds.

2. Estimates are for power at the spindle drive motor with sharp tools. Spindle drive efficiency is 80%. Dull tools are expected to add 20 to 30% to power requirements.

Source: Data extracted from *Machining Data Handbook,* 3d ed., Machinability Data Center, © 1980, by permission of Metcut Research Associates, Inc., Cincinnati, Ohio.

materials may vary in hardness and stock allowance. Thus in practice power and forces may well be 50 to 100% and even more than those determined experimentally.

As an example of a typical calculation, let a piece of steel of 200 Bhn hardness be turned at 115 m/min (375 fpm) and depth of cut of 6.35 mm ($\frac{1}{4}$ in.) on a machine with a 7.5-kW(10-hp) motor and an efficiency of 80%. If the full motor capacity is to be used, estimate the cutting force. How much may the feed be?

$$F_c = 0.8 \times 7.5 \times \frac{60}{115} = 3.13 \text{ kN} \quad \text{or} \quad 8 \times \frac{33,000}{375} = 704 \text{ lb}$$

$$f = \frac{7500}{1.25 \times 50 \times 115 \times 6.35} = 0.16 \text{ mm/rev}$$

$$\text{or} \quad \frac{10 \times 4}{1.25 \times 12 \times 375 \times 1.1} = 0.006 \text{ ipr}$$

Surface Finish. A heavy feed is conducive to formation of a built-up edge and a rough surface finish. Figure 17-6 shows the surface roughness reported for several

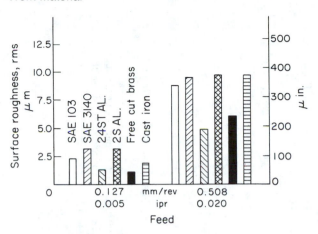

Figure 17-6 Changes, with feed, in surface roughness.

materials cut at a light and heavy feed. In the same tests, each feed was taken at three depths of cut: 0.25, 1.6, and 3.2 mm (0.01, $\frac{1}{16}$, and $\frac{1}{8}$ in.). At the light feed there was little difference in surface roughness at the three depths, but at the heavier feed, the surface roughness measured about 25% more at a depth of cut of 3.2 mm ($\frac{1}{8}$ in.) than at one of 0.25 mm (0.01 in.). Feed seems to affect surface quality much more than depth of cut. Fine feeds and light cuts are necessary for the best surface finishes.

Practical Feeds and Depths of Cut. As has been shown, the proper feed and depth of cut for an operation depend upon a number of factors and no recommendation can be made to cover all cases, but some indication of starting points can be given for turning, boring, and related operations. The depth of cut for finishing is generally 0.25 to 0.75 mm (0.01 to 0.03 in.), but for roughing may be as much as 15 mm (ca. $\frac{1}{2}$ in.) and even more up to the limit of the tool and stock available. Feeds from 0.1 to 0.4 mm/rev (0.005 to 0.015 ipr) are generally used for finishing, but they may be larger with broad-nose tools. Feeds for roughing are usually as coarse as the work-piece, tool, and machine will stand. When the depth of cut does not exceed 6 mm (ca. $\frac{1}{4}$ in.), a feed of 0.4 to 1.0 mm/rev (0.015 to 0.040 ipr) may be selected. For greater depths, a feed of 0.25 to 0.50 mm/rev (0.010 to 0.020 ipr) may be used.

WORK MATERIAL

A measure of how easily and how well a material can be cut is called its *machinability*. Under various circumstances it includes the criteria of productivity, tool life (some-times termed *abrasiveness*), surface finish (or *finishability*), size control, and sensi-tivity to changes in speed, feed, or tool angles. In practice the machinability of a material is rated by comparing its performance with that of another material consid-ered to be standard. Each material is given a number designating its rating. One example of a listing of machinability ratings is given in Table 17-4. There are many published machinability tables, and they do not all agree because they are based on different criteria. Appreciable disagreement has also been found in the ratings of the

TABLE 17.4 MACHINABILITY RATINGS OF A NUMBER OF METALS

Class I, Ferrous, rating over 70%

Material specs.	C1110	C1117	C1120	C1137	C1016	B1112	A4023	A4119
Hardness (Bhn)	137–166	143–179	143–179	187–229	137–174	179–229	156–207	170–217
Rating	85	85	80	70	70	100	70	70

Class II, Ferrous, rating 50 to 65%

Material specs.	C1141	C1020	C1040	A3120	A4032	A5120	NE8024
Hardness (Bhn)	183–241	137–174	179–229	163–207	170–229	170–212	174–217
Rating	65	65	60	60	65	65	60

Class III, Ferrous, rating 40 to 50%; Class IV, Ferrous, rating under 40%

Material specs.	A1320	A2330	A6120	A2515	Stainless 18-8	H.S.S.
Hardness (Bhn)	170–229	179–229	179–217	179–229		
Rating	50	50	50	30	25	30

Class V, Nonferrous, rating over 100%; Class VI, Nonferrous, rating under 100%

Material specs.	Mg. Alloys	2S Al.	Yellow brass	Mng. bronze	Monel cast metal	Inconel
Rating	500–2000	300–1500	200	40	35	45

Source: This table condensed from the complete *Machinability Rating Tables* of the Independent Research Committee on Cutting Fluids. Machinability to the nearest 5% rating is based on 100% rating for AISI steel B1112, cold-rolled or cold-drawn Bessemer screw stock, machined with suitable cutting fluid at 55 m/min (180 fpm) under normal conditions as to tool life and surface finish. Hardness values indicate a desirable range.

same work material with different tool materials and kinds of operations. It has been recommended that any machinability index be applied with care to specific situations where it has been found to have meaning and value.

There are three common ways of rating materials by accelerated tests to save time. One is to run at a high speed with short tool life and extrapolate to the cutting speed that gives a 60-minute tool life for each material. The rating may be the ratio of the cutting speed of the material to that of the standard material or may be merely the speed itself in some listings. Another test is for the rate of tool wear under standard conditions without running to tool failure. Then tool wear rates are compared. A third test is to measure the cutting forces and take the ratio of the force for each material to that of the base material, commonly B1112 or C1212 steel. These tests do not correlate well with production experience, and the best kind of test has been found to be the machining of long runs of one part from different materials, all held to the same specifications of surface finish and size. Speeds, feeds, and tool angles are varied to find the fastest rate of production with 6 to 8 hours of tool life for each material. The resulting rating is the ratio of hourly output with one material to that of the standard.

Machinability ratings from cutting force or tool life tests generally decrease as material hardness and strength increase. On the other hand, productivity ratings for steel increase with tensile strength to a broad maximum around 600 MPa (85,000 psi) (with a corresponding hardness around 180 Bhn) and decrease for stronger and harder steels. The reason is that steel cuts cleaner and finishes more easily at higher rates as it is made harder (up to a point). Production tests are based upon maintenance of a good surface finish at a rapid rate of production. However, above a certain hardness, tools are impaired and the production rate declines, as does the machinability rating. A good correlation has been found between practicable cutting speeds, V_p, and the thermal properties of materials. For face milling, the relationship is given as $V_p = K_m k/d$, and for drilling $V_p = K_d ks$, where K_m and K_d are constants, k is the conductivity, d the density, and s is the specific heat of a material.

The sizes of the metallic grains, the structure, and the proportions of constituents of a metal are important in determining tool life, forces, and surface finish. An illustration is given in Fig. 17-7 of the effect of various structures in steel upon tool life-cutting speed curves.

The properties wanted in the material of a finished article often are not those desirable for good machinability. A finished part may be expected to have high strength or be quite hard. Common practice is to anneal or normalize alloy steel parts in the rough, remove most of the stock by machining, heat treat again to get the desired properties for the finished product, and finish the surfaces by grinding when required.

Various elements are added to metals specifically to make them easy to machine. Such compositions are said to be *free machining* or *free cutting*. They permit high cutting speeds with long tool life, well-broken-up chips, and smooth and accurate finishes. Small to moderate amounts of sulfur, phosphorus, lead, selenium, telerium, and/or bismuth (separately or in different combinations for various grades) are added to steels to help reduce friction and form inclusions that make the chips break up more easily. Such additives may weaken the final product somewhat. They may add $1 or

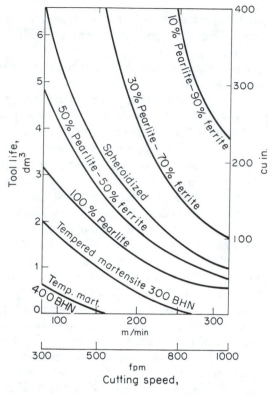

Figure 17-7 Affect on tool life of various structures in steel as the result of various kinds of heat treatment. The basic forms of heat treatment and their effects are described in Chapter 5. (This chart indicates results from a study of machinability prepared by Curtiss-Wright Corp. for the U.S. Air Force.)

more per 50 kg (ca. 100 lb) to the cost of steel and are not justified unless more is saved in machining. A rule of thumb is that at least 10%, and preferably over 20%, of a bar should be removed in machining to warrant such additives. Nickel and molybdenum are added to cast iron, lead to brass and bronze, and copper-lead and bismuth to aluminum to improve machinability.

COMPUTING METAL-CUTTING PARAMETERS

A type of empirical formula for cutting speed in fpm that takes into account the effects of some of the more important of the many variables in a metal-cutting operation is

$$V = \frac{A \times B \times C \times D \times E \times F \times G \times P \times Q^{0.2}}{H^{1.72} \times R^{0.16} \times T^n \times f^{0.58} \times c^{0.2}} \qquad (17\text{-}12)$$

A accounts for tool material: 180,000 for H.S.S., 300,000 for cemented carbides, and 1,500,000 for sintered oxides. *B* provides for the effect of cutting fluid: 1.0 for dry cutting, 1.15 for cutting oils, and 1.25 for soluble oil and water solutions. *C* represents the type of work material: typical values are 0.8 for carbon steel, 1.05 for free-cutting steel, 1.1 for alloy steel, 0.75 for cast iron, 2.0 for free-cutting brass, 0.85 for aluminum alloys, and 0.90 for magnesium alloys. *D* furnishes an allowance for different microstructures ranging from 0.7 for austenitic stainless steels to 1.0 for commercial hot-rolled, cold-drawn, quenched and tempered, normalized, or annealed stock to 1.4 for coarse spheroidized structures. E accounts for the rough workpiece surface: 0.7 for a sand cast surface, 0.75 for sand cast and shot blasted, 0.80 to 0.95 with heat treatment scale, and 1.0 for a clean surface. F covers the type of tool: 1.0 for single-point turning, facing, and boring tools, and most milling cutters, 0.7 for drills and form cutters, and 0.8 or less for reamers. G is determined by the tool proportions and varies from less than 1.0 for a sharp pointed tool with no entering angle to around 1.50 with a large nose radius and entering angle. G is given values of 1.14 for drills, 0.8 to 1.3 for face mills, 1.0 for slab mills, and 0.8 for slot milling. H is the Brinell hardness number of the workpiece material. P provides for differences in tool materials: 1.0 for H.S.S., an average of 5.0 for carbides (although it ranges from 4.0 to 8.0 for various grades of carbides), and 8.0 for sintered oxides. Q is the decimal amount of flank wear allowed on the tool. R is the number of teeth on the cutting tool. T stands for the tool life in min, f for the feed in ipr, and c for the depth of cut in inches. Average values of n are 0.125 for H.S.S, 0.25 for cemented carbides, and 0.7 for sintered oxides.

Values for the factors and exponents in a formula like Eq. (17-12) are selected to fit a large number of tests points. This may be done by standard mathematical curve fitting and regression techniques. Some such formulas are designed for a limited set of conditions; some are based upon one set of tests, and others on different tests. For these reasons, differences appear among various formulas in the values assigned to the factors and exponents, although they all are constructed to approximate actual performance. Equation (17-12) is somewhat simplified.

A formula like Eq. (17-12) but designed for steel alone is the basis for the chart of Fig. 17-8. Many such charts are available in reference texts and handbooks for the specification of speeds and feeds and other conditions for metal-cutting operations. A popular industrial analog computer depicted in Fig. 17-9 is based upon a formulation like Eq. (17-12). Dials on the panel of the computer operate rheostats representing the logarithmic values of the factors in the formula. The resistors are balanced in a bridge circuit to make the meter read zero and arrive at a proper combination.

A number of digital computer programs have been written to calculate and specify metal-cutting parameters to satisfy input describing operation conditions. A few are described here. One type of program uses a mathematical model like Eq. (17-12) to calculate cutting speed. A prominent program of this type is the G. E.-Carboloy Systems Department Computerized Machinability Program. Another approach is that of the IBM Work Measurement Aids, which is based on relating each machining operation to a standard operation for which optimum speeds and feeds have been determined. Speed and feed adjustment factors have been ascertained, experimentally and from shop performance, for deviations from the standard conditions. These factors are tabulated, and suitable ones are selected and applied to calculate the speeds and feeds for each new operation of the same kind. The program is arranged to update the factors from continuing feedback of performance results. This program has an even broader capability; it selects the best machine from those available to carry

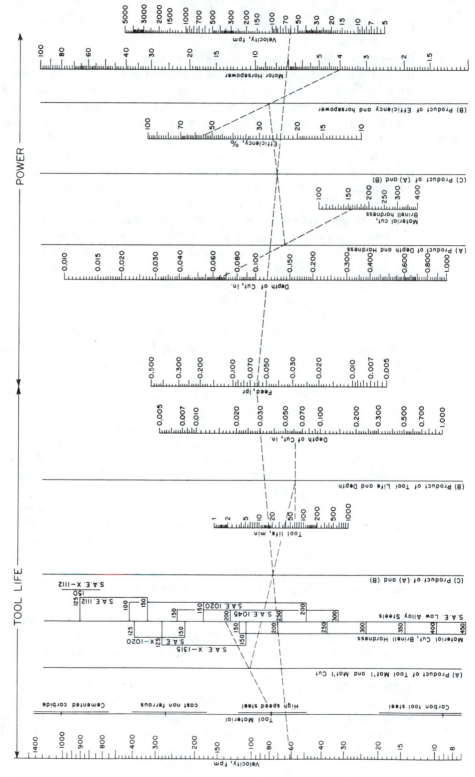

SAMPLE CALCULATIONS: TOOL LIFE

GIVEN:

Tool material.... High Speed Steel
Material cut ....160 Bhn—S.A.E.
                     1020 steel
Desired tool life.. 60 minutes
Depth of cut.... 0.0625 inch
Feed ....0.0625 inch per rev.

READ FROM CHART:

Velocity = 60.5 feet per minute

MAXIMUM OUTPUT

GIVEN:

Tool material
Material cut
Tool life
Depth of cut
  (deepest cuts most efficient)
Machine efficiency
Motor horsepower
  (use rated horsepower)

The feed should be varied until the velocity on the tool life side is equal to the velocity on the power side. This feed and speed will give the maximum metal removal for the given conditions.

SAMPLE CALCULATIONS: POWER

GIVEN:

Feed ....0.0625 inch per rev.
Velocity ....60.5 feet per minute
Depth of cut ....0.0625 inch
Material cut ....160 Bhn—S.A.E.
                        1020 steel
Machine efficiency ....60 percent

READ FROM CHART:

Motor Horsepower = 3.75

Figure 17-8 Nomograph of the variables in turning with single point tools. This chart is based upon the assumption of cutting steel dry. Cutting speeds may be increased 15 to 30% by means of soluble cutting oils and 10 to 25% by straight cutting oils. The chart is drawn for a single point tool of shape 8-14-6-6-15-$\frac{3}{64}$. If the best tool is used for each type of material, performance can be expected to be better than that calculated from the chart. Economical feeds specified by the chart may be too heavy for the workpiece, tool, or machine and may have to be reduced. (After W. W. Gilbert and W. C. Truckenmiller, "Metal Cutting Nomograph," *Mechanical Engineering*, Vol. 65, Dec. 1943, p. 893.)

Figure 17-9 Carboloy Machinability Computer. (Courtesy Carboloy Systems Department, General Electric Co.)

out the operation specified and determines job standards and sets standard operation time. The Metcut Computerized System starts with the input of a number of cutting speed–tool life points determined experimentally for workpiece–tool combinations (even for various feeds) suitable for an operation. Operation costs are calculated for each point based upon input of economic and operation conditions. The point or points of lowest cost may then be selected.

The main reason for presenting Eq. (17-12) is to show in general how the principal factors affect cutting speed. Many other variables like the shape and size of the workpiece, the condition of the machine and tools, and the conduct of the operation influence performance more or less in various cases. Actually no one formula can account for all possibilities with the present state of knowledge of metal cutting. The same operation may show as much as 40% difference in tool life from one machine to another; different lots of steel of one kind may require 40% or more difference in cutting speed for the same tool life. One investigator reported that ordinary differences in grinding tools in the shop resulted in variations of about 15% in cutting speed for a 60-minute tool life, and variations in the microstructure in the same bar may cause the cutting speed for the same tool life to vary more than 30%.

Where formulas are used in the shop, as they are, to determine cutting speeds, it is good practice to have a procedure to compare the results continuously with performance and modify the factors to suit current conditions.

PROBLEMS

1. A bar of SAE 1035 steel is being turned on a lathe with a H.S.S. tool of the shape of 8-14-6-6-6-6-1/32 at a feed of 0.32 mm/rev (0.0127 ipr) and a depth of cut of 1.25 mm (0.050 in.). It was found experimentally that a tool life of 30 minutes resulted at a cutting speed of 27 m/min (90 fpm), 90 minutes at 24 m/min (79 fpm), and 150 minutes at 23 m/min (75 fpm). What should be the cutting speeds for tool lives of 60 and 120 minutes?

2. When the tool taking the cut described in Prob. 1 reaches the end of its life, the operator takes it from the machine, sharpens it, and resets it. This takes 5 minutes. The tool costs $1.60 new and can be ground altogether 20 times. The labor and overhead rate is $26/hr. What is the economical tool life for the tool, and at what speed should it be run?

3. To facilitate production, an arrangement is made for spare tools to be sharpened in the tool room for the operation described in Probs. 1 and 2. It takes 1 minute for the operator to replace a tool on the machine.
   (a) At what speed should the operation be run for a maximum rate of production?
   (b) What increase in the rate of production may be expected from the arrangement described in this problem as compared to that of Prob. 2?

4. Two cemented carbide tools are tried for an operation. One has a brazed insert and is designated as tool A. The other has a replaceable clamped insert and is called tool B. Tool A costs $5.30 new and can be ground a total of six times. Each grind gives one cutting edge and takes $5\frac{1}{2}$ minutes at $0.27/min. To change tools on the machine takes 2 minutes at $0.25/min. The clamped insert of tool B has eight cutting edges and can be put in place and rotated to a new edge in $\frac{1}{2}$ minute at $0.25/min. Each grind restores the eight edges and takes 15 minutes at $0.27/min. The insert costs $6.53 new and can be ground eight times altogether. The tool life–speed characteristics of both tools are represented by the formula, $V_m T^{0.2} = 152$ (or in fpm, $VT^{0.2} = 500$). Find the economic tool life and corresponding cutting speed for each. When each tool is run at its economic speed, which does the job more cheaply?

5. A cemented carbide tool is turning a cylinder of alloy steel 50 mm (2 in.) by 150 mm (6 in.) long under the conditions that depth of cut is 3 mm ($\frac{1}{8}$ in.), feed is 0.38 mm /rev (0.015 ipr), and $V_m T^{0.2} = 152$ or ($VT^{0.2} = 500$). The time to change the tool is 1 minute. The cost to grind a tool is $2.20, including the original cost of the tool. Labor and overhead total $26.00/hr or $0.43/min. The time to load and unload the workpiece is 1 minute?
   (a) What is the minimum cost per piece?
   (b) This is a production operation in which many pieces of the same kind are machined. How many pieces can be produced in an hour at 100% efficiency?

6. A 108-mm ($4\frac{1}{4}$-in.)-diameter bar of SAE 1020 steel is being turned on an engine lathe with a high-speed steel tool at a speed of 30 m/min (100 fpm). At a feed of 0.8 mm/rev (1/30 ipr) and a depth of cut of 3 mm ($\frac{1}{8}$ in.), the cutting force was found to be 3.25 kN (730 lb). What horsepower is needed for this cut?

7. When the feed rate for the cut described in Prob. 6 was changed to 0.2 mm/rev ($\frac{1}{120}$ ipr) and all other conditions remained the same, the cutting force was found to be 1.6 kN (360 lb). What power should be needed for a feed of 0.25 mm/rev (0.010 ipr)?

8. To make a cut, feeds of 0.25, 0.40, 0.50, 0.75, and 1.0 mm/rev (0.010, 0.015, 0.020, 0.030, and 0.040 ipr) are available. The material is carbon steel of 200 Bhn hardness. The diameter of the 100-mm (4-in.)-diameter workpiece is to be reduced to 75 mm (3 in.). Cutting speed will be 27 m/min (90 fpm). The machine has a 15-kW (20-hp) motor and a 75% efficiency. What should be the depth of cut, and how many cuts are required?

9. Given the following conditions for an operation:
   (1) Cemented carbide tool.
   (2) Work material, SAE low-alloy steel with Bhn 300.
   (3) Desired tool life 30 minutes
   (4) Depth of cut $\frac{3}{8}$ in.
   (5) Machine efficiency 75%.
   (6) Motor horsepower 15 hp.
   Find the proper speed and feed at which to operate from the nomograph of Fig. 17-8.

10. If in the operation described in Prob. 9 it is desired to raise the feed to 0.025 ipr and keep all other conditions except the power and speed constant, what motor horsepower would then be required? At what work surface speed?

11. A tool used for a metal-cutting operation shows a tool life–speed relationship of $V_m T^{0.125} = 44.5$ ($VT^{0.125} = 146$). Originally, 15 minutes was required to remove a dull tool, but a new tool holder has made it possible to reduce the time to 5 minutes. What increase in cutting speed does this permit to obtain the maximum rate of production from the operation?

REFERENCES

ALBRECHT, J. R., and L. MAIR, "Understanding Free-Machining Steels," *American Machinist*, Oct. 4, 1971, p. 47.

Determination and Analysis of Machining Costs and Production Rates Using Computer Techniques, AFMDC 68-1, Air Force Machinability Data Center, Cincinnati, Ohio, 1968.

DOYLE, L. E., "Principles for Programming Manufacturing Operations for Maximum Profit," *SME Technical Paper MM72-101*.

———, "Optimum Cutting Speed and Tool Replacement Policy with Variable Tool Life," *SME Technical Paper MR73-913*.

ELGOMAYEL, Y. I., "Predicting Ceramic Cutting Tool Life," *Manufacturing Engineering and Management*, May 1970, p. 45.

KRONENBERG, M., *Machining Science and Application*, Pergamon Press, Elmsford, N.Y., 1966.

LORENZ, G., "The Effect of Dispersed Phases on the Machinability of Metals," *CSIRO*, National Standards Lab., Sydney, Australia.

Machining Data Handbook, 3d ed., Metcut Research Associates, Inc., Cincinnati, Ohio, 1980.

Metals Handbook Vol 3: *Machining*, American Society of Metals, Metals Park, Ohio, 1967.

RUFF, K. E., "Computer Aided Selection of Feeds and Speeds," *Manufacturing Engineering*, May 1979, p. 53.

WALTOU, C. F., "Machining Cast Iron, Special Report 730," *American Machinist*, Feb. 1981, p. 137.

WELLER, E. J., and C. A. REITZ, *Optimizing Machinability Parameters with a Computer*, G. E. Carboloy Systems Dept., Detroit, Mich.

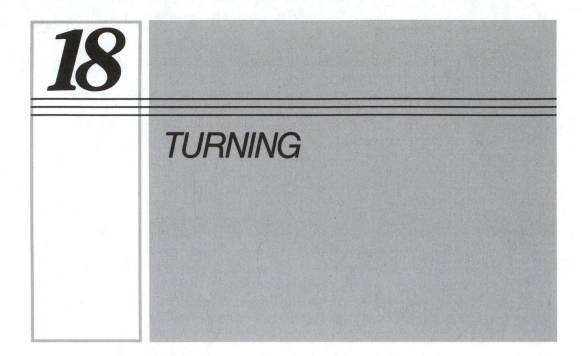

TURNING

TURNING OPERATIONS

Small and medium-size workpieces usually are turned around a horizontal axis. Turning operations may be divided into two classes: those done with the workpiece between centers and those done with the workpiece chucked or gripped at one end with or without support at the outer end.

Plain or Straight Turning. The principal kinds of operations done on work between centers are indicated in Fig. 18-1. The workpiece is driven by a dog clamped on one end. If work is to be done on both ends, the dog is clamped on each in turn, and the workpiece is reversed in position.

A workpiece held between centers deflects less under a given force than if held at only one end. Also, a workpiece runs true on good centers, and several diameters cut at the same or at different times are the most likely to be concentric if turned on centers.

To be turned on centers, a workpiece must have a center hole at each end. These holes have 60° conical bearing surfaces and are cut with a combination center drill and countersink, as in Fig. 18-2. This may be done with the workpiece chucked on a lathe or on a center drilling machine like a horizontal drill press.

Chuck Work. When a workpiece is chucked, the same operation can be done on it as between centers. In addition, parting or cut off and internal operations can be done, like those illustrated in Fig. 18-3. The types of tools described in Chap. 22 for drilling and related operations are used to machine holes in chuck work.

508

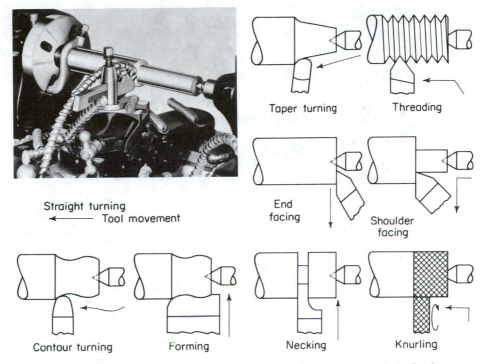

Figure 18-1 Turning operations between centers. (Photo courtesy South Bend Lathe, Inc.)

Figure 18-2 Combination center drill and countersink. (Courtesy Chicago-Latrobe Twist Drill Works.)

Taper Turning and Boring. As illustrated in Figs. 18-1 and 18-3, turning produces not only straight, but also tapered outside and inside surfaces. A taper may be designated by the angle between opposite sides or by the increase in diameter along the length, in mm/m (in./ft). Certain tapers are standard. The *Morse taper* found on drilling machines and some lathes is approximately 52 mm/m ($\frac{5}{8}$ in./ft). Sizes, designated by whole numbers from 0 through 7 (the largest), are given in handbooks. Other tapers used on lathes are the *Reed* and *Jarno tapers,* each of 50 mm/m (0.600 in./ft).

Three methods of generating tapers by offsetting the tailstock, swiveling the compound rest, and use of a taper attachment will be described when the equipment is discussed. Tapers may also be form cut, but the length of cut must be kept small so the force between tool and work does not become excessive.

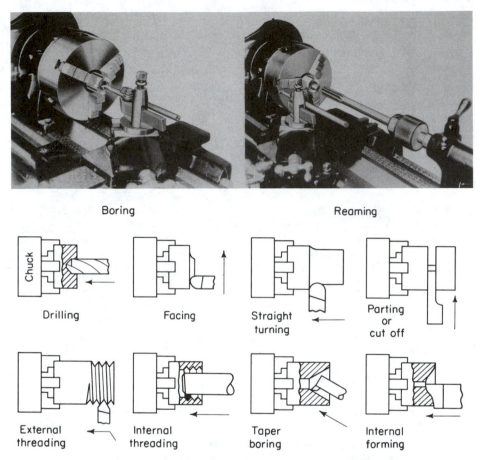

Boring   Reaming

Figure 18-3   Chucking operations in turning. (Photo courtesy South Bend Lathe, Inc.)

THE LATHE

The basic machine tool on which turning operations are done is the lathe, typified by the engine lathe in Fig. 18-4. The diagram of Fig. 18-5 delineates the principal parts and movements of the engine lathe.

Principal Parts of Lathes.   A lathe is built around a *bed,* made massive and rigid to resist deflection and vibration. On top of the bed at the left is the *headstock* that carries a revolving *spindle.* A lathe spindle is hollow to take long barstock, and the diameter of the hole determines the largest size barstock that can be passed through the spindle for chucking. The spindle hole has a definite taper at the front end to receive tapered center and tool shanks. The *nose* or end of the spindle has true locating surfaces for positioning and means for fastening a chuck, as shown in Fig. 18-3, a face plate, or a dog plate as in Fig. 18-1.

The workpiece is driven by the headstock spindle. Present-day lathes have

Figure 18-4 A 20-in. engine lathe turning a piece chucked at the headstock end and supported by the tailstock center. (Courtesy Monarch Machine Tool Co.)

individual motor drives, usually of constant speed. Most of them have geared head-stocks like the one in Fig. 18-4. The drive from the motor to the spindle goes through several gear combinations that are shifted by means of levers or dials on the outside of the headstock to change spindle speeds. On some small lathes, the drive from the motor to the spindle is through a belt and step pulleys to get several spindle speeds. In addition, a set of reduction gears may be engaged to get a lower series of speeds.

The *tailstock* is on the other end of the bed from the headstock. Its spindle does not revolve but can be moved a few inches lengthwise and clamped as desired. Drills, reamers, taps, and other end-cutting tools are held and fed to the workpiece by the tailstock spindle, which is hollow with a taper to take the shanks of centers, drill chucks, drills, reamers, etc. The whole tailstock can be moved to and clamped in any position along the bed where it can best serve its purpose.

The body or top of the tailstock can be adjusted crosswise on its base. This may serve to align the tailstock with the headstock so work can be turned straight. On the other hand, the tailstock may be offset intentionally to hold a piece between centers at an angle for turning it tapered.

Between the headstock and tailstock is the *carriage* that has several parts that serve to support, move, and control the cutting tool. Of these parts, the *saddle* slides on ways on top of the bed. On top of the saddle is a *cross-slide* that is adjusted and

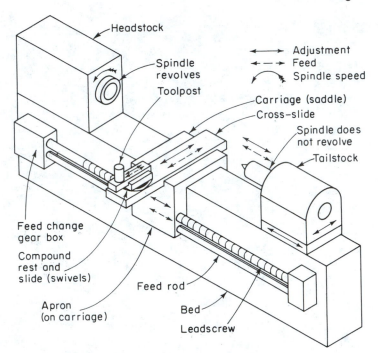

Figure 18-5 Principal parts and movements of a lathe.

fed at right angles to the length of the bed by a crank and graduated dial on the front of the saddle. Adjustments can be made to 25 μm (0.001 in.) in positioning a tool.

The commonest device for clamping the tool or toolholder to a lathe is a simple toolpost, shown in Fig. 18-1. It is normally mounted on a *compound rest* on top of the cross-slide. The compound rest has a graduated base and can be swiveled around a vertical axis. In this way, its slide can be set at any angle with the axis of a workpiece. The slide can be adjusted or fed by hand through a screw and nut controlled by a crank and graduated dial. The slide can travel only a few inches but is useful for feeding tools at an angle, such as for generating short and steep tapers.

The bracket that hangs from the front of the saddle is the *apron*. It contains the mechanism for moving the carriage along the bed. Turning the handwheel on the front of the apron turns a small pinion extending from the other side of the apron. The pinion is engaged with a rack attached to the bed and pulls the carriage along.

Power Feed.   Power comes to the apron for feeding the carriage through the leadscrew and feed rod along the front of the bed in Fig. 18-4. The leadscrew is used to move the carriage along at a precise rate for cutting a thread. The leadscrew passes through a split or half nut attached to the apron. This nut is normally spread apart but can be closed and engaged with the leadscrew by throwing a lever on the front of the apron.

The feed rod is used to save the leadscrew when other than threading operations are done. It drives a train of gears in the apron. Clutches in this gear train are engaged to apply the power either to moving the carriage along the bed or the cross-slide across the bed.

The power feed drive on a lathe is always taken off the headstock spindle. In that way the feed, whether for turning or thread cutting, is always related to the speed of the spindle. The drive goes through a set of reversible gears for setting the direction of feed and through a set of change gears for setting the amount of feed. With a definite setting of the feed change gears, the carriage travels a definite distance in inches for each revolution of the headstock spindle no matter how fast the spindle turns.

The feed change gears are in a sliding transmission gear box on the left of the bed below the headstock, as shown in Fig. 18-4 and indicated in Fig. 18-5. A chart on the box tells the operator how to shift the levers to select the available feeds, and changes can be made quickly. On some lathes the changes are made by means of pick-off gears. Most lathes have a large range of feeds. For example, a general-purpose 15-in. lathe cuts 48 different threads from 0.1 to 6 mm pitch (equivalent to 4 to 224 threads/in.) and has 48 feed rates from 0.05 to 3 mm/rev (0.002 to 0.120 ipr).

Types of Lathes.   There are many kinds of lathes. Two broad classes are the manual one-tool-at-a-time lathes like those described in this chapter and automatic or automated and generally multitooled lathes for production, which will be presented in Chap. 19.

The most common name given the general-purpose manually controlled lathe is *engine lathe*. It has the principal parts already described and depicted in Fig. 18-5. Swing capacities generally range from 230 to 1270 mm (9 to 50 in.), and bed sizes from around 1 to 5 m (3 to 16 ft), although lengths up to 15 m (50 ft) and more are available. A heavy-duty 400-mm (16-in.) swing engine lathe offers 25 speeds from 14 to 1800 rpm. One with 1.3 m (52 in.) of swing has a speed range of 2.3 to 185 rpm in 27 steps.

Some in the engine lathe family are given names that describe particular features, such as *bench lathe, toolroom lathe* (exceptionally accurate), and *gap lathe* (with a removable section in the bed to increase swing). *Wheel lathes* are made for finishing the journals and turning the treads of railroad car and locomotive wheels mounted in sets. *Oil country lathes* are used to make and maintain oil-well-drilling equipment and have holes from 178 to 406 mm (7 to 16 in.) through their spindles to pass long pieces.

Sizes of Lathes.   The rated size of a lathe indicates the largest diameter and length of workpiece it will handle. Thus a 14-in. lathe will swing a piece 356 mm (14 in.) in diameter over the bed ways. Some manufacturers designate the swing by four digits, such as 1610. The first two designate the largest diameter that can be swung over the bed ways, the last two the diameter over the cross-slide (16 and 10 in., respectively, in the example). For length, some lathe makers specify the maximum distance between centers, in inches; others, the overall bed length in feet. Thus one lathe designated to take 760 mm (30 in.) between centers may be the equivalent of another specified as 1.8m (6 ft) long.

More than the swing size needs to be considered in selecting a lathe. Complete specifications are given in manufacturers' catalogs. Lathes of the same nominal workpiece size capacity may differ considerably in ruggedness, strength, and power.

A bench lathe capable of swinging pieces 310 mm ($12\frac{1}{4}$ in.) in diameter by 915 mm (36 in.) long has a 0.37-kW ($\frac{1}{2}$-hp) motor, weighs 225 kg (500 lb), and can be bought for $2000. A 432 × 1016 mm (17 × 40 in.) lathe has a 5.6-kW ($7\frac{1}{2}$-hp) motor and costs about $12,000. This larger lathe may be expected to remove metal about 15 times as fast as the cheaper but costs only about six times as much. Yet the extra power and rigidity may not be of any value if the lathe is not going to be used most of the time or is needed only for light work that the smaller lathe can handle as well as the larger. On the other hand, power is a necessity to get the most from the better cutting materials described in Chap. 16, especially for production, and medium-size lathes with motors of 20 and 40 kW (25 and 50 hp), and strength and rigidity to suit, are not uncommon. A few are powered to over 75 kW (100 hp). A 19-kW (25-hp) lathe with a nominal 635 mm (25 in.) of swing and 2 m (80 in.) between centers costs about $50,000.

Large workpieces must be turned on big lathes. As an example, steel mill rolls up to 1.7 m (66 in.) in diameter by 8 m (26 ft) long are turned on a 300-kW (400-hp) lathe with a cut as deep as 50 mm (2 in.) and feed of 13 mm/rev (0.5 ipr). Such a machine costs about $1 million.

Tracer Lathe. A *tracer* or *duplicating lathe* is one with an attachment that enables the machine to turn, bore, face, and generate all kinds of contours from templates. The cutting tool is made to follow a path that duplicates the path of a stylus or tracer finger moving along the template. With two-axis control on the lathe, one direction is that of traverse and is called the *tracing axis*. That would be the lengthwise feed in turning. The other axis provides the in-feed and is called the *feeding axis*.

There are a number of models of tracer attachments. Those that utilize a machine movement along a tracing axis are called *motor tracers* as depicted in Fig. 18-6. A

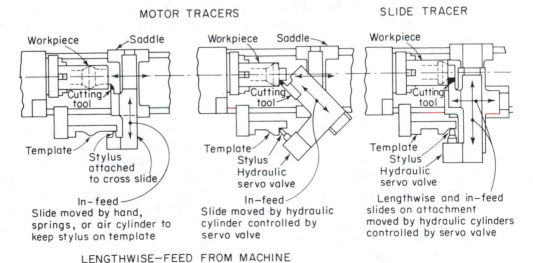

Figure 18-6 Details of the main types of tracer or duplicating attachments.

simple form has the stylus rigidly connected to the tool and held in contact with the template. Attachments of this type are available for a few hundred dollars but are limited to work on simple shapes and broad tolerances. Better control and accuracy are obtained through servovalve control of the tool. The stylus is on the end of a hydraulic valve that is spring loaded to pass oil to a hydraulic cylinder to drive the tool slide to the work. When the stylus, also driven by the slide, makes contact with the template, the valve is closed or reversed and changes the in-feed accordingly. Steep slopes may be traversed along a workpiece by setting the in-feed slide at an angle.

Slide tracer attachments have both axes controlled by a hydraulic servovalve as depicted in Fig. 18-6. This arrangement facilitates cutting steps, back tapers, and shoulders with a constant feed along all parts of the path traversed, which is necessary for the best finishes and smaller tolerances. One manufacturer guarantees part-to-template accuracy within 25 μm (0.001 in.) and part-to-part accuracy of 13 μm (0.0005 in.) Tracer attachments of this type cost several thousand dollars.

A tracer lathe is generally faster than a manually operated lathe for two or more diameters, shoulders, or faces on a part because the time to adjust the machine from one surface to another is eliminated. The more complex the part, the more the advantage. One authority advocates a rule of thumb that the tracer lathe is superior if one-third or more of the time is manipulating time on the engine lathe. Of course, an initial cost is incurred in making and setting the template, so the advantage of tracer control only makes it economical for a number of pieces of one kind. As an added benefit, modification of the profile and adjustment of the template can be made to compensate for inherent inaccuracies in a machine.

Tracer control has much the same advantages as numerical control described in Chap. 35; the two often are equally fast and easy to operate. It is more expensive and takes more lead time to obtain a tracer template for many parts, particularly the more complex ones, than to prepare a numerical control program, but the initial cost of the tracer control system is of the order of one-fifth (or less) of the cost of numerical control.

Faster cutting than with a tracer can be done on automatic and turret lathes where several tools can be made to cut a workpiece at the same time. However, more expensive tooling and setup and a more powerful machine are required, and these other methods are not more economical except for relatively large quantities.

ACCESSORIES AND ATTACHMENTS

Lathe accessories are common work holders and tool holders and supports such as chucks, collets, centers, drivers, rests, fixtures, and mandrels. Attachments are devices to facilitate specific operations. They incluce stops, thread chasing dials, taper attachments, and devices that enable milling, grinding, gear cutting, and cutter relieving to be done on the lathe.

Chucks.   A *universal* or *scroll chuck* has three jaws engaged and moved in unison by a scroll plate as shown in Fig. 18-7. A wrench inserted in any one of three

Figure 18-7 Cutaway view of the mechanism of a three-jaw universal self-centering chuck. (Courtesy Cushman Industries, Inc.)

pinions around the chuck body rotates the scroll plate, and the chuck is fast to operate. The jaws can grip outside or inside surfaces. Hardened serrated jaws are used on rough workpieces, and soft jaws that may be trued in place are applied to finished surfaces.

Loss of gripping force at high speeds becomes a serious problem with ordinary lathe chucks. It is not unusual to run over 1000 rpm with modern cutting tools, and centrifugal forces become appreciable. A random survey was made on 24-in. chucks in one plant and found "jaw force losses at high speeds ranging from 22 to 77 percent." *Counter-centrifugal chucks* have pivoted weights that act to offset the lost gripping force, but each chuck works best for one specific jaw weight and workpiece diameter, and such devices are not panaceas.

An *adjustable chuck* is a universal chuck mounted on an adapter that attaches to the spindle nose of a lathe. A good universal chuck can be expected to run out 50 μm, (0.002 in.) when new, and the error increases with age. An adjustable chuck can be adjusted on the adapter to run as true as 13 μm (0.0005 in.).

As shown in Fig. 18-8, a *four jaw independent chuck* has jaws that are moved

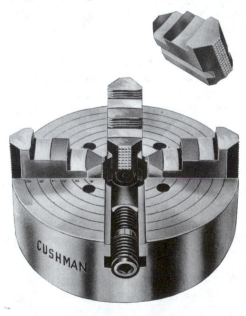

Figure 18-8 Four-jaw independent chuck. One jaw has been removed to show an operating screw. (Courtesy Cushman Industries, Inc.)

separately, each by a screw. The jaws will grip almost any shape of piece and can be adjusted to run as true as desired, but the chuck is slow to operate.

A *combination chuck* has jaws that can be moved together through a scroll plate or adjusted separately.

Two jaw chucks are adapted to hold workpieces of irregular shapes by means of slip jaws added to the permanent jaws. Each piece can be chucked in less time than with a four jaw chuck, but sufficient production is necessary to justify the special jaws.

Air- and *hydraulic-operated chucks* are quick, grip the work strongly, and are economical for production. A cylinder is carried on the rear of and revolves with the spindle of the machine. The piston actuates a rod lengthwise through the spindle and through levers opens and closes the jaws of the chuck. Manufacturers of chucks of this kind guarantee runout of less than 13 μm (0.0005 in.).

A *wrenchless chuck* is operated by a lever on a ring on the rear of the chuck body. The lever does not revolve with the chuck and can be actuated before the chuck body comes to rest. The action is fast, and wrenchless chucks often are used on production.

A *drill chuck* may be used on either the headstock or tailstock spindle of a lathe to hold straight shank drills, reamers, taps, or small-diameter workpieces. The jaws of the drill chuck of Fig. 18-9 are wedged by the inside taper of the shell to grip a piece. The shell is fastened to the body that is screwed up or down on the shank to close or open the chuck.

Collets. A collet is a thin steel or brass bushing with lengthwise slots and an outside taper. When it is forced into the tapered sleeve of a collet chuck, the collet is sprung together slightly to grip a workpiece securely and accurately. The simple *collet chuck* of Fig. 18-10 is operated by turning the hand wheel on the left end of the spindle. Air and hydraulic cylinders are used to operate collet chucks for rapid production.

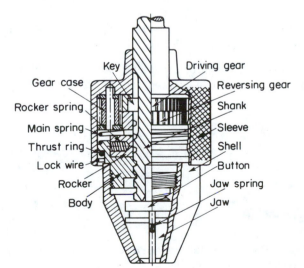

Figure 18-9 Sectional view of a drill chuck. (Courtesy Wahlstrom Tool Division, American Machine and Foundry Co.)

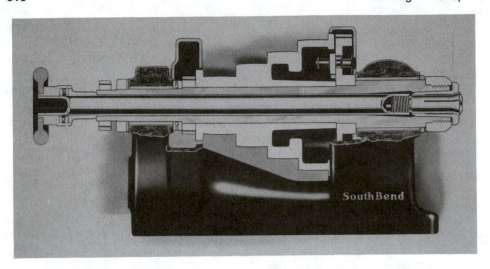

Figure 18-10   Cross section of a lathe headstock, showing a draw-in collet chuck. (Courtesy South Bend Lathe, Inc.)

Centers and Drivers.   A lathe center has a 60° included angle taper at one end and a sticking taper at the other end to fit a machine spindle. Typical centers are shown in Fig. 18-11. A live center mounted on the tailstock wears less but is more expensive and not as accurate as a solid center.

A *dog plate* on the spindle nose is shown in Fig. 18-1. A *face plate* is larger than a dog plate and has a number of radial slots for bolts. Workpieces are bolted on the front of the face plate.

A *fixture* is a special device fastened directly to the spindle nose or bolted on a face plate to hold and locate a specific piece or pieces. Fixtures are commonly used for quantity production of pieces on production, turret, and automatic lathes rather than engine lathes.

A *mandrel* locates a workpiece from a hole. Common types are depicted in Fig. 18-12. A tapered mandrel is pressed into the workpiece hole.

Rests.   A *center* or *steady rest* has three shoes that are brought up to contact and support a slender workpiece that would otherwise deflect too much under its

Figure 18-11   Left, solid center (courtesy Chicago-Latrobe Twist Drill Works); right, ball-bearing live center (courtesy Ready Tool Co.).

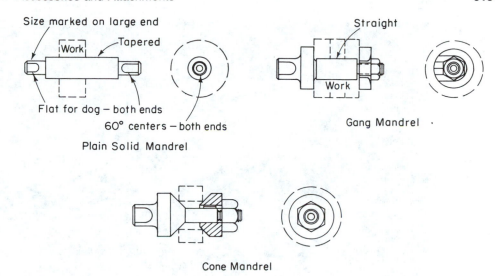

Figure 18-12   Common mandrels.

weight or from the cutting forces. The shoes are carried in a bracket clamped on top of the bed. A *follower rest* is fastened to and moves along with the carriage with shoes that support the workpiece at the cutting tool position.

Attachments.   A *taper attachment* shown fastened to the rear of the lathe in Fig. 18-13 has a slide on top that is swiveled to the angle of the taper desired. A block riding on the slide is clamped to the rear extension of the cross-slide and causes the tool to cut along the angular path as the carriage is traversed along the bed.

As has been pointed out, outside tapers can be turned without an attachment by offsetting the tailstock, but the adjustments required make that method slow. Inside or outside steep tapers can be generated by swiveling the compound rest, but the length of taper must be short. Short or long and inside or outside tapers may be generated with the taper attachment, but steepness is limited. The attachment is easy to adjust, and the lathe may be reset easily for straight work.

A *relieving attachment* is a device for moving the cutting tool in and out in relation to the revolving workpiece to back off the teeth of multiple-point tools such as milling cutters and reamers.

Stops of various kinds can be attached to the bed to position the carriage accurately and quickly for spacing grooves, facing shoulders, etc.

A variety of attachments are available for adapting the lathe to do milling, gear cutting, grinding, shaping, and fluting. Such work can be done more efficiently on machines especially designed for it, and the lathe is justified only as an expedient where more suitable equipment is not available.

Lathe manufacturers have developed and are able to furnish many other ingenious attachments to enable lathes to perform special operations economically at moderate and large-scale production rates. Examples of these are attachments for turning crankshafts and pieces with unusual shapes.

Figure 18-13 Taper-turning with a taper attachment. (Courtesy South Bend Lathe, Inc.)

LATHE OPERATIONS

Practical Limits. Lengthwise dimensions on a piece faced in a lathe are normally given a tolerance of ± 0.5 mm (ca. $\pm\frac{1}{64}$ in.). To hold closer tolerances requires time-consuming cut-and-try adjustments unless carriage stops are used, and they do not save much unless several pieces are to be made.

Under average conditions, reasonable tolerances for rough turning and boring range from 0.15 mm (ca. 0.005 in.) for diameters under 15 mm (ca. $\frac{1}{2}$ in.) to 0.40 mm (ca. 0.015 in.) for diameters over 50 mm (2 in.). For finished surfaces, tolerances from 50 μm (0.002 in.) for diameters below 15 mm (ca. $\frac{1}{2}$ in.) to 0.180 mm (0.007 in.) for diameters above 50 mm (2 in.) are usual. A fluted reamer properly used will produce holes within 25 μm (0.001 in.) of nominal size. Smaller tolerances than these can be and are held on lathes, but the cost rises rapidly as the tolerance is reduced. From single-point turning and boring, surface roughness can be expected to range from 15 μm (ca. 500 μin.) R_a to as fine as 1 μm (40 μin.) R_a. Holes may be finished by reaming to as smooth as 0.5 μm (20 μin.) R_a. Grinding, described in Chaps. 27 and 28, usually is more economical for smaller tolerances and finer finishes.

Because the simple lathe is versatile and flexible, it is not generally a fast producer. The tools can be arranged in many ways, but for the most part the tools can be used only one at a time; and for each piece and every different cut tools must be changed, set, and adjusted. This takes up an appreciable part of the time to make a part. If a quantity of pieces must be made, the time soon adds up to a large amount. A skilled machinist is required to operate a lathe properly, labor is expensive, and a sizeable part of the time is spent just waiting while the machine is cutting. It is not feasible for one person to operate more than one engine lathe at a time as a rule.

Where only a single cut is needed on a part, many pieces of that kind might well be produced on an engine lathe as economically as on any other machine tool. However, most parts require more treatment, and for them the ordinary lathe is suitable for making only one or a few pieces, except in cases where extra equipment, such as an indexing turret or a tracer attachment, is added. Other machine tools of the lathe family that are more efficient for producing work in quantities are described in Chap. 19.

Calculating Cutting Time.   The time in an operation during which a machine is making a cut can be calculated. The cutting time in minutes is

$$T = \frac{L}{fN} \tag{18-1}$$

where f is the feed and N is the number of rpm. The length of cut L includes the length of surface cut plus the distance the tool is fed to enter and clear the cut, usually 1.5 to 6.5 mm ($\frac{1}{16}$ to $\frac{1}{4}$ in.) for turning. As an example, a piece 25 mm (1 in.) in diameter by 50 mm (2 in.) long is to be cut at 30 m/min (100 fpm) with a feed of 0.25 mm/rev (0.010 ipr). The number of revolutions per minute $N \approx 333 \times 30/25 = 4 \times 100/1 = 400$ rpm. The time $T = 51.5/(0.25 \times 400) = 2.06/(0.010 \times 400) = 0.52$ minute. In this case the approach and overtravel is assumed to be 1.5 mm (0.06 in.).

QUESTIONS

1. Name and describe the major units of lathes.
2. What movements does the tool have on a lathe? How are they obtained?
3. From where does the power feed come on a lathe? How is it varied?
4. How is the carriage moved for cutting threads on a lathe? For other operations?
5. How is the size of a lathe designated?
6. What is an engine lathe?
7. How does a toolroom lathe differ from an engine lathe?
8. Describe three types of tracer attachments and state their relative advantages.
9. For what kind of work is a tracer lathe efficient?
10. What are lathe accessories and attachments?
11. Name and describe eight kinds of chucks and specify the uses of each.
12. Describe four ways to cut tapers on a lathe.

13. What is plain or straight turning? What is chuck work?

14. For what kinds and quantities of work is the ordinary lathe best suited?

15. What are typical tolerances attainable with a lathe, and why is work usually not done to smaller tolerances?

PROBLEMS

1. A taper 150 mm (6 in.) long has a large diameter of 52.000 mm (2.050 in.) and a small diameter of 38.100 mm (1.500 in.). What should be the setting of the taper attachment in mm/m (in./ft) to machine this taper?

2. The large diameter of a piece measures 23.8125 mm (0.9375 in.); the small diameter, 11.1125 mm (0.4375 in.). The taper is 420 mm/m (5 in./ft). What is the length of the taper?

3. A taper of 26 mm/m ($\frac{5}{16}$ in./ft) is to be cut on a piece 460 mm (18 in.) long. How much should the tailstock be set over if that method is to be used?

4. What is the nominal diameter at the small end of a No. 0 Morse taper? Of a No. 7 Morse taper?

5. A piece of aluminum is to be cut at 90 m/min (300 fpm). Stock totaling 3.2 mm ($\frac{1}{8}$ in.) is to be removed, to leave a finished surface of 125 mm (5 in.) diameter. The length of cut is 100 mm (4 in.) and the feed is 0.65 mm/rev (0.025 ipr). What is the cutting time?

6. A finish cut for a length of 250 mm (10 in.) on a diameter of 50 mm (2 in.) is to be taken in cast iron with a speed of 45 m/min (150 fpm) and a feed of 0.2 mm/rev (0.008 ipr). What is the cutting time?

7. A piece 100 mm (4 in.) in diameter is to be cut off by a tool fed at 0.125 mm/rev (0.005 ipr). The lathe is set at 100 rpm. How long should the cut take?

8. A workpiece 250 mm (10 in.) in diameter is to be faced down to a diameter of 100 mm (4 in.) on the end. The lathe is equipped with an electronic device that controls the spindle speed and maintains the cutting speed at 60m/min (200 fpm) for the diameter the tool is cutting at any instant. The feed is 0.38 mm/rev (0.015 ipr). What should be the time for the cut?

9. If the spindle speed for the workpiece described in Prob. 8 is set to give a speed of 60 m/min (200 fpm) at 250 mm (10 in.) diameter and is not changed during the cut, what is the time required for the cut?

10. A lathe has a 1.5-kW (2-hp) motor and costs $6000. It is to be depreciated in 10 years, and 10% of its cost is charged each year to cover interest, insurance, and taxes. Thus the annual charge for this machine is $1200. If the shop works 300 days a year, the machine must show a return above other expenses of $4 a day to pay for itself. Another lathe that will take workpieces of the same size has a 7.5-kW (10-hp) motor and costs $12,000. On the same basis as for the other machine, what must the daily return be to pay for this one? Each machine is 75% efficient, so the first is able to deliver 1.1 kW (1.5 hp) to the tool point and the second 4.6 kW (7.5 hp). For the material to be cut, 1 kW is required at the tool point to remove 22 cm^3/min (1 hp to remove 1 in.^{3}/min). Labor and applicable overhead costs are $20/hr. Mostly light work is done that does not require over 1.1 kW (1.5 hp), but some heavy cutting is required on which can be expended an average of 3.4 kW (4.5 hp) if available. If that power is not available, the work will have to be done more

slowly. What amount of the heavy cutting, in cm^3 (in.^{3}) of stock removal per day, will justify the investment in the larger lathe? What does this mean in cutting time on the two lathes?

REFERENCES

BERG, R. T., "Fundamentals of Turning, 1," *American Machinist,* Apr. 26, 1965, p. 79.

DALLAS, D. B., ed., *Tool and Manufacturing Engineers Handbook,* 3rd ed., Society of Manufacturing Engineers, Dearborn, Mich., 1976.

How to Run a Lathe, South Bend Lathe, Inc., South Bend, Ind.

Metals Handbook, Vol. 3: *Machining,* 8th ed., American Society for Metals, Metals Park, Ohio, 1967.

19

PRODUCTION TURNING MACHINES

Simple lathes like those described in Chap. 18 are efficient for turning one or a few pieces of a kind of large variety. However, more complex machines have evolved that are faster and take less labor and skill than the engine lathe to produce duplicate parts in quantities. A basic feature of such machines is that once they are set up, the tools can be applied quickly to the work repeatedly and stopped precisely when they reach the ends of their cuts. On some machines a number of or all tools cut at once. More skill is needed to set up than to run the machines after setup. Sometimes a setup worker at a higher pay rate attends to several machines, and operators at a lower rate keep the machines going.

Typical examples of production turning machines and their principles of operation are covered in this chapter. The simplest are the manual turret lathes that require constant operator attention. Beyond these are the machines that go automatically through every step of the operation and require little attendance after they have been set up.

TURRET LATHES

A turret lathe is a manual lathe and has a hexagonal tool-holding turret in place of the tailstock of an engine lathe. Some turret lathes are designed and equipped for working on barstock and are called *bar-type machines*. The name of *screw machine* or *hand screw machine* has been used for such machines, particularly in the smaller sizes. Other turret lathes are equipped for chuck work.

The name "turret lathe" alone ordinarily implies a horizontal spindle machine.

Vertical turret lathes are described in a separate section. The two main types of horizontal turret lathes are the ram type and saddle type.

A *ram-type turret lathe* carries its turret on a ram as shown in Figs. 19-1 and 19-2. The ram slides longitudinally on a saddle positioned and clamped on the ways of the bed. Tools in their holders are mounted on the faces of the turret, and the tools on the face toward the headstock are fed to the work when the ram is moved to the left. When the ram is withdrawn, the turret indexes, and the next face, called a *station,* is positioned to face the headstock.

A ram is lighter and can be moved more quickly than a saddle but lacks some rigidity. Because of convenience and speed, the ram-type construction is favored for small and medium-sized turret lathes where the ram does not have to overhang too far.

Gears are shifted manually to change speeds on some turret lathes; others have automatic shifts. Typical machines offer 8, 12, or 16 speeds over wide ranges.

A *reach over* or *bridge type carriage* across the entire bed is commonly found between the saddle and headstock on a ram-type turret lathe. On the carriage is the cross-slide with a quick hand-indexed four-station turret tool holder on the front end and a holder for one or more tools at the rear. Heavy single-point tools are clamped in these holders and fed to the work by movement of the carriage along the bed and the cross movement of the slide.

A *plain* cross-slide is entirely hand operated, but the *universal* kind is power fed also and is more common. The ram usually has power feed in addition to hand feed. Eight feeds from 0.075 to 0.75 mm/rev (0.003 to 0.030 ipr) are typical.

The cross-slide can be positioned accurately by means of a cross-screw and micrometer dial. Individual stops for each tool station can be set to throw out the power feed and limit the longitudinal movement of the ram or carriage. In this way the movement of any tool along the workpiece can be precisely controlled and repeated readily for as many workpieces as desired.

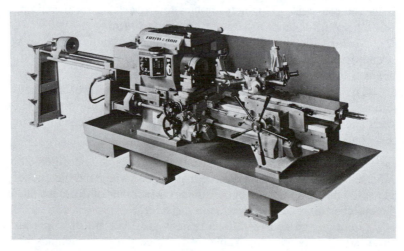

Figure 19-1   View of a ram-type turret lathe tooled for a bar job. (Courtesy Bardons and Oliver, Inc.)

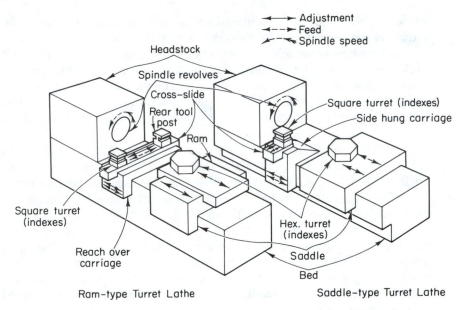

Figure 19-2 Principal parts and movements of horizontal turret lathes.

The hexagonal turret of a *saddle-type turret lathe* is carried directly on a saddle that slides lengthwise on the bed as depicted in Figs. 19-2 and 19-3. This construction is favored for large turret lathes because it provides good support for the tools and the means to move the tools a long way when necessary. The saddle is moved toward the headstock by hand or power to feed the tools to the work, and is withdrawn to index the turret.

The turret is fixed in the center of the saddle on some machines. On others it may be moved crosswise. This helps reduce tool overhang for machining large diameters and is helpful for taper or contour boring and turning.

Most saddle-type turret lathes have the *side hung type* of carriage that does not extend across the entire top of the bed and allows larger pieces to be swung. This means the rear tool station on the cross-slide is lost.

The cross-slide and carriage usually are both power and hand fed. The cross-slide is adjusted by a micrometer dial and screw. Stops are provided to throw out the feeds and position the tools longitudinally for any of the stations of either square or hexagonal turret.

Turret Lathe Sizes. The size of a turret lathe is designated by a number that indicates the diameter of workpiece that can be swung and the diameter of bar that can be passed through the hole in the spindle. Machines of different makes with the same size number may vary somewhat in capacity.

Some of the considerations besides size that are of importance in selecting a turret lathe are indicated in Table 19-1. Three sizes of machines were considered for the production of a steel shaft in moderate quantities. The largest and most powerful machine could remove the stock the fastest and was found able to turn out a piece in

Figure 19-3 Saddle-type turret lathe taking cuts on a large workpiece with tools on both the square turret on the cross-slide and the hexagonal turret on the saddle. (Courtesy Warner and Swasey Co.)

TABLE 19-1 SPECIFICATIONS AND PERFORMANCE RECORD OF THREE MODELS OF TURRET LATHES

Size and type	Capacity[a] [mm (in.)]	Weight [Mg (lb)]	Power [kW (hp)]	Best time per piece (min)	Actual production per 8-hr day (pieces)	Price	Net annual savings
No. 4 ram type	50–241–470 $(2–9\frac{1}{2}–18\frac{1}{2})$	2.8 (6200)	11.2 (15)	2.96	143	$70,000	$2700
No. 3 ram type	38–178–390 $(1\frac{1}{2}–7–15\frac{3}{8})$	2.4 (5200)	7.5 (10)	3.18	137	54,000	3184
No. 3 Electro-Cycle	38–178–390 $(1\frac{1}{2}–7–15\frac{3}{8})$	2.4 (5200)	7.5 (10)	3.20	147	62,000	2808

[a]Bar diameter—swing over cross-slide—swing over bed.

the shortest time, 2.96 minutes. That alone was not enough, because the No. 3 Electro-Cycle machine was able to turn out the most pieces in an 8-hour day. Although the Electro-Cycle machine is basically a ram-type turret lathe, it is arranged for partial automatic operation and causes less operator fatigue during the day. Even so, the largest daily production did not designate the best choice. The job had previously been run on a machine that was due for replacement. The annual labor savings for each of the machines of Table 19-1 compared with the old machine were calculated. The biggest producer of course showed the biggest labor savings. Then the net savings were ascertained by subtracting the annual charges on the investment from the labor savings, and the result was that the machine with the least daily production promised the largest annual net savings ($3184/yr) because it cost the least.

Tools and Attachments.   Collets and collet chucks are commonly used for barstock, and hand and power chucks for individual pieces, on turret lathes. Essentially the same kinds of single-point tools, form tools, and multiple-point tools such as drills, reamers, and taps are used on turret lathes as on engine lathes. Single-point tools generally are heavier.

Convenient devices are made specifically for holding and adjusting cutting tools singly and in groups on the hexagonal turrets. This equipment is available commercially in many standard forms and sizes and is fully described in manufacturers' catalogs. A few typical kinds are presented here. Some equipment is intended for bar work, other for chucking work, but much is suited for both kinds of service.

Barstock generally is supported by the tailstock center on an engine lathe but that usually is not feasible on a turret lathe, especially when cuts are taken from the hexagonal turret. *Box tools* support overhanging bars that are being turned, faced, chamfered, or centered from the hexagonal turret. Rollers or a crotch bear against and back up the work surface opposite the cutting tool. The *bar turner* of Fig. 19-4(A) is an example of a box tool. Other models may carry several turning bits, a facing tool, or a center drill.

The *quick-acting slide tool* of Fig. 19-4(B) is designed to hold round shank single-point tools and boring bars for fast recessing and facing cuts on both bar and chuck work. The slide that carries the cutting tools moves 12.5 mm ($\frac{1}{2}$ in.) with a quarter turn of the handle. The *adjustable knee tool* of Fig. 19-4(C) can be set up quickly for turning combined with drilling, boring, or centering on short pieces. The *combination stock stop and starting drill* is a two-purpose tool that saves one turret face and one index. A typical set of bar equipment is illustrated in Fig. 19-1.

Chucking work often involves a greater range of diameters and more tool overhang than bar work. The chucking setup of Fig. 19-3 contains several characteristic tools. *Multiple turning heads* carry *cutter holders* and *boring bars* on the turret faces in line with the machine spindle. A *stationary pilot bar,* like the one in Fig. 19-3, is attached to the headstock and slips into the bushings and gives extra support to the turning heads. It can be heavy and strong because it does not add to the load on the turret. *Piloted boring bars* slip into and are guided and reinforced by an *internal* or *center pilot* in the machine spindle.

Planning Turret Lathe Operations.   Time is the major item of cost in a turret lathe operation. This includes the time to set up the machine and make the actual cuts. The following principles are guides to obtaining low costs. They apply also to other kinds of operations and machine tools.

A large part of setup time is that spent in mounting and adjusting the cutting

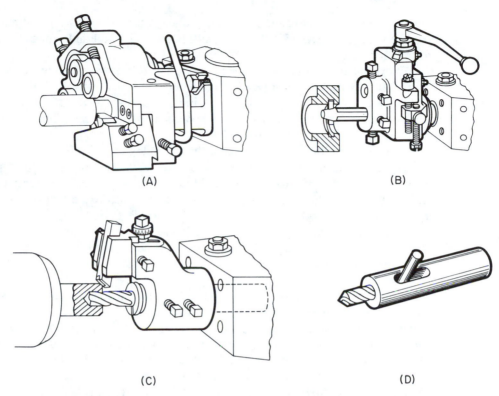

(A)   (B)

(C)   (D)

Figure 19-4 Examples of tooling for turret lathes: (A) bar turner on the hexagonal turret; (B) quick-acting slide tool arranged for cutting an inside groove; (C) adjustable knee tool set-up turning the outside and drilling a hole in a piece; (D) combination stock stop and center drill. (Courtesy Warner and Swasey Co.)

tools. These costs may be minimized by using universal tooling and maintaining a permanent setup on a turret lathe. To do this, large and heavy tools that perform basic functions on most operations are permanently mounted in their logical order on the turret. All these tools are not needed for every job, but then the turret may be back- or skipped-indexed. In most cases the extra indexing time is less than would be taken to remove the tools and change them around on the turret. The lighter tools are rearranged in various combinations on the heavy toolholders for various jobs. Recommendations for proven permanent setups for various classes of work and sizes and types of machines are available from turret lathe manufacturers.

Work handling time depends partly upon the raw material, but its selection is based upon several factors. Barstock is easily held and pieces can often be completed and cut off in one operation. A casting or forging may require that less stock be removed but calls for the cost of a pattern or die and the founding or forging operations. As an example, a part can be cut from barstock at a cost of $10/piece. The cost of 5 pieces is $50 and for 25 pieces is $250. If the part is cast, a pattern must be made at a cost of $25. Molds can be made and the pieces cast for $2 each. The machining charge to finish the castings is $5 each. To make 5 pieces by casting and machining costs $60; for 25 pieces, $200. Obviously, barstock is preferable for 5 pieces, and castings for 25 pieces.

Work handling time also depends upon the selection of collets, chucks, and fixtures. For average work in small or moderate quantities, standard holding devices are best with special jaws, arbors, and simple fixtures added as justified. Special fixtures can pay for themselves on jobs where the parts are otherwise hard to hold and are made in fairly large quantities.

Machine handling time consists of time to index and position the tools and set the speeds and feeds. More time is required to advance from step to step in an operation and it is harder to keep up a fast pace on a large machine than on a small one because of the heavier masses that must be moved. The effect of this on one operation is illustrated by the case described by Table 19-1.

Parts like collars, spacers, and gear blanks can be machined in groups with turning, drilling, boring, reaming, and cutting off done on all pieces in one group at each setting. In that way the machine movements per piece are less than if the pieces are done individually.

Machine handling time is reduced by taking combined and multiple cuts to save indexing. Cutting time is also reduced. A *combined cut* is one where tools in both the hexagonal turret and square cross-slide turret are made to cut at the same time. A *multiple cut* is one where two or more tools are applied at the same time from one turret station. An example of combined and multiple cuts is given in Fig. 19-3.

Internal cuts are almost always made by tools in the hexagonal turret and are planned and set up first for an operation. Provision must be made for the proper order of internal cuts, for instance for drilling before boring and boring before reaming a hole.

Tolerance down to 10 μm/cm (0.001 in./in.) and finishes as fine as 1.5 μm (60 μin.) R_a are practicable on turret lathes, but the more exacting the requirements, the more the cost. One cut may suffice to hold a tolerance of 0.25 mm (0.010 in.), but as a rule two cuts are needed for a tolerance between 0.15 and 0.25 mm (ca. 0.005 and 0.010 in.), and three cuts for tolerance less than 0.15 mm (ca. 0.005 in.), with corresponding surface requirements.

Economics of Tooling.   Machines are like people in that without tools they can do nothing; but the better their tools, the more efficiently they work. On the other hand, tools cost money, and money can be spent for them only if they earn a profit. These principles apply to all processes, all kinds of machine tools, and all tools, but they will be illustrated and applied for turret lathe tooling, the case at hand, by Fig. 19-5 and Table 19-2.

Three methods are shown for tooling the cast iron flywheel in Fig. 19-5 on a turret lathe. Method A is the simplest and requires only standard tools but two operations. Method B also calls for two operations but is faster. It requires more tools and setup time. Method C produces the part in one operation with the highest cost for tooling and setup time but is the fastest producer after setup.

The analysis of the costs in Table 19-2 shows that for low production or a small

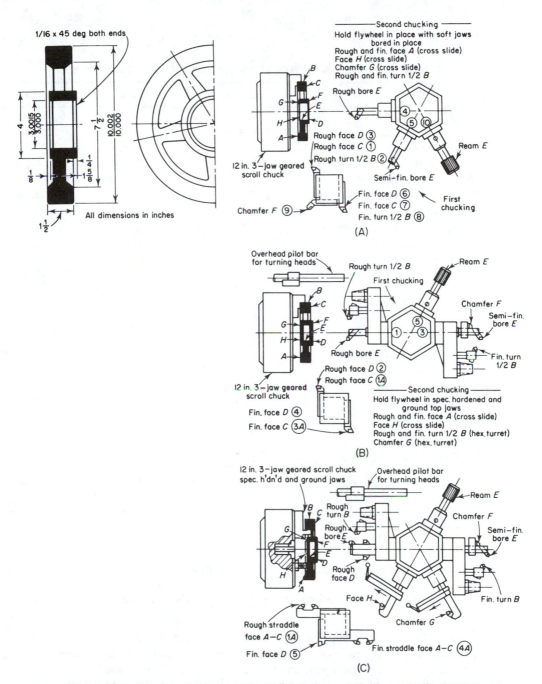

Figure 19-5 Three turret lathe methods of increasing complexity for machining the illustrated cast iron flywheel: (A) simple method with a minimum of special tools for producing the piece in two chuckings; (B) requires two chuckings but represents a method suitable for most turret lathe operations for parts of this kind; (C) requires only one chucking and represents tooling that is an extension and refinement of that proposed for method (B). Tool layouts like these are helpful in planning and depicting operations. (From *How to Get the Most Out of Your Turret Lathe*, Warner and Swasey Co.)

TABLE 19-2 COMPARISON OF THREE TURRET LATHE TOOLING METHODS

Cost item	Method A	Method B	Method C
Tooling cost			
Standard tools ($)	2685	3735	6354
Special tools ($)	285	699	4704
Time to machine one piece (min)	13.6	9.0	6.5
Setup time per lot (hr)	2.6	3.2	3.4
Hourly cost (setup or prod.) ($/hr)[a]	12.79	12.92	13.24
Setup cost per lot ($)	33.25	41.34	45.02
Production per 48-min hour (pcs/hr)	3.5	5.3	7.4
Cost per piece ($/pc)[b]	3.65	2.44	1.79
For total of 300 pieces[c]			
Cost of special tools ($/pc)	0.95	2.33	15.68
Cost of production ($/pc)	4.60	4.77	17.47
For total of 3000 pieces[c]			
Cost of special tools ($/pc)	0.10	0.23	1.57
Cost of production ($/pc)	3.75	2.67	3.36
For total of 9000 pieces[c]			
Cost of special tools ($/pc)	0.03	0.08	0.52
Cost of production ($/pc)	3.68	2.52	2.31
For lot size of 5 pieces[d]			
Total of 300 pieces ($/pc)	11.25	13.04	26.47
Total of 3000 pieces ($/pc)	10.40	10.94	12.36
For lot size of 50 pieces[d]			
Total of 300 pieces ($/pc)	5.27	5.60	18.37
Total of 3000 pieces ($/pc)	4.42	3.50	4.26
For lot size of 500 pieces[d]			
Total of 3000 pieces ($/pc)	3.82	2.75	3.45
Total of 9000 pieces ($/pc)	3.75	2.60	2.40

[a]Standard tools written off over 8000 hours. Overhead rate $4.50/hr for all methods. Hourly labor rate $7.95/hr.

[b]Not including cost of special tools or setup cost.

[c]Not including setup cost. For simplicity, charges for interest, insurance, taxes, and maintenance not included.

[d]Includes setup cost. For simplicity, charges for interest, insurance, taxes, and maintenance not included.

lot size, the simple tooling at least cost is the most economical. As lot size and production increase, more complex tooling is justified. In many cases, several proven ways are available to do a job, and a given rate of production and a specific lot size are required. One way to solve the problem is to calculate the cost for each alternative for the required conditions, as is done for the cases in Table 19-2. The alternative that shows the lowest total cost is the best for the purpose. Only the factors that actually change from one alternative to another should be included in a comparison. Many overhead costs do not change, and only a part of overhead is included.

Two alternatives can be compared by a simple formula. For two methods or tools for a specified production rate or lot size, the cost factors that must be taken into account are the number of pieces (N) to be made; the direct savings (s) in dollars per piece of one method over the other; the relevant overhead rate (t) in dollars invested in tools; the capital charges, (A) for interest, (B) for insurance and taxes, (D) for depreciation, (M) for maintenance, all as annual percentage rates of the investment; and the extra setup cost (Y) in dollars per year of one method over the other. This last factor (Y) is the product of the number of lots run per year times the extra setup cost per lot.

The principle which is the basis for comparing any two tooling methods can be stated in common sense terms as follows: a tool or tooling method that requires a larger investment should be selected instead of one requiring a smaller investment only if the annual amount saved by the more costly tooling is at least equal to the annual cost of the extra investment and any extra setup charges. This principle may be written as a mathematical formula in the following form:

$$Ns(1 + t) = I(A + B + D + M) + Y \qquad (19\text{-}1)$$

This formula may be applied to the data of Table 19-2 to show how it is used. The question may be asked, what is the lowest production requirement that justifies the more expensive tooling for method C instead of method B, for 10 set-ups per year? The answer is obtained by solving for N in Eq. (19-1). The overhead rate (t) is already included in the hourly rate of Table 19-2.

For the first solution, it will be assumed that the interest, insurance, tax, and maintenance rate may be ignored. Special tools are normally depreciated in a year. Standard tools are charged to overhead. The figures for Eq. (19-1) from Table 19-2 are

$$s = \frac{12.92}{5.3} - \frac{13.24}{7.4} = 2.44 - 1.79;$$

$$N(2.44 - 1.79) = (4704 - 699) \times 1 + 10(45.02 - 41.34)$$

and

$$N = \frac{4005 + 36.80}{0.65} = 6218 \text{ pieces/yr}$$

to justify method C over method B.

Now let it be assumed that the interest rate is 10%, insurance and tax rate 5%, and maintenance rate 10% per year. Then

$$N \times 0.65 = 4005(0.10 + 0.05 + 1.0 + 0.10) + 36.80$$

and

$$N = \frac{4005 \times 1.25 + 36.80}{0.65} = 7759 \text{ pieces/yr}$$

Vertical Turret Lathes.   Vertical turret lathes like the one in Fig. 19-6 are more convenient for short pieces over about 500 mm (ca. 18. in.) diameter because the work can be laid upon the table and fastened more easily than hung on the end of the spindle of a horizontal turret lathe. A turret on a vertical turret lathe is carried on a ram on a cross-rail above the worktable and can be fed up or down and crosswise. There is also a side head, essentially a carriage and cross-slide, alongside the table with a square turret that can be fed radially and parallel to the axis of the table.

The line of machines of one leading manufacturer is typical; indexing turrets are available with table capacities to 3.7 m (12 ft) diameter. Larger sizes, and smaller sizes, too, if desired, have single tool rams; there are normally two rams on the cross-rail. These larger machines are called *vertical boring mills,* in sizes up to 18 m (60 ft) diameter. They do turning, facing, boring, and grooving of huge, fairly round and symmetrical pieces like reduction gear housings and turbine casings.

A vertical turret lathe with 1.4 m (55 in.) diameter swing and 65 kW (87 hp) drive is quoted at $180,000, over $350,000 with numerical control. A vertical boring mill rated at 2.3 m (90 in.) diameter capacity, maximum work height 1.7 m (67 in.), workpiece weight up to 15 Mg (33,000 lb), and power of 90 kW (120 hp) costs over $400,000.

Figure 19-6   A 36-in. vertical turret lathe taking cuts with the turret and side head. (Courtesy The Bullard Co.)

AUTOMATIC TURNING MACHINES

A machine that moves the work and tools at the proper rates and sequences through a cycle to perform an operation on one piece without the attention of an operator is commonly called an *automatic*. Strictly speaking, the machine is a semiautomatic if an operator is required to unload and load the machine and start each cycle. Often an operator can do this for several machines in a group. Workpieces may come to a fully automatic machine on a conveyor or an operator may load a magazine or hopper at intervals. Automatic machines are widely used for drilling, boring, milling, broaching, grinding, and other operations, and examples of them are given in later chapters.

Automatic turning machines are made massive, rigid, and powerful to drive cutting tools at their utmost and get the most from gangs of tools and multiple and combined tooling. Tool setups are planned and tools are designed carefully to get as many tools cutting at once and do the work as fast as possible.

Automatic machines intended for large lots of pieces and infrequent changeover usually are not designed for quick setup. For instance, speeds and feeds are not changed by sliding levers or turning dials, as on an engine lathe, but by removing and replacing pick-off gears. The multiplicity of tools must be set with respect to each other as well as to the machine. In some cases, practice is to preset the tools in blocks off the machine. Then the blocks go into definite positions quickly on the machine at setup time, and machine downtime is saved. Setup time may be less than an hour in favorable cases where not much has to be changed from one job to another, but normally is several hours, and not infrequently may be up to a day or more as compared to a few minutes on an engine lathe. Careful scheduling to run similar jobs in succession can save changeover time. Although setup time is long, an automatic machine is at an advantage when cutting because it is fast and often able to make up for the time lost in setup in less than 100 pieces.

An automatic machine follows a definite program for work positioning, movements of tool slides, and spindle speeds to perform an operation. Programming is done in various ways on different makes and models of automatic turning machines. A basic mechanical device for driving tool slides and other units is the cam. Some machines require a set of cams for each job. The shape of each cam programs one or more movements. That is costly and is warranted only to produce many pieces of the same kind, but each set of cams can be made to do the job in the shortest time. Other machines do not require cam changes for each job and are called *camless automatics*. One kind has a permanent set of cams that act through adjustable linkages. Without cams, activities are carried out through adjustable electro- and hydromechanical devices. Suitable settings or adjustments are made to program each job. Camless machines are more versatile but more complicated, cost $1\frac{1}{2}$ to 3 times as much, and are not as popular as cam machines. A different kind of automatic operation is numerical control, wherein the program is expressed in numbers that are fed into the controller to make the machine go through the steps of a desired operation.

Leading kinds of automatic turning machines are presented here under the classifications of automatic lathes, numerical control (NC) lathes, and single-spindle and multiple-spindle automatic bar and chucking machines.

Automatic Lathes.   Automatic lathes have the basic units of simple lathes: bed, headstock, tool slides, and sometimes a tailstock. In addition, an automatic lathe drives the tools through all the steps of a cycle without operator attention once the machine has been set up. A view of the working zone of a horizontal automatic lathe is given in Fig. 19-7. The workpiece is rotated between centers. The tools are carried on blocks on the front and rear slides. The front slide is traversed along the bed, and the tools in this case make straight cuts along the workpiece, retract at the end of the cut, and are withdrawn to the starting position. The rear tool slide typically feeds the tools toward the center of the workpiece for facing, necking, grooving, and forming but can be given a sideways movement to relieve the tools at the end of a cut.

Automatic lathes perform basically similar functions but appear in a variety of forms. Many have no tailstock; some models have one slide, and others have two or three. Some slides move in one direction only; others in two. Some machines have level tool slide ways; others have sloping ways, and some have overhead slides for additional tools. Some slides are fed by screws, others by hydraulic or air-hydraulic means, and still others entirely by cams and templates. There are horizontal and vertical models according to spindle position. Some automatic lathes have two or three work spindles; two or three sets of tools perform the same cuts on two or three workpieces at once.

Automatic lathes, particularly vertical machines, without tailstocks are commonly called *chucking machines* or *chuckers*. The same name is given to other types

Figure 19-7   View of a job on an automatic lathe. The inset shows how the tools cut. (Courtesy White-Sundstrand Machine Tool Co.)

of machines described later. The distinguishing feature of the automatic lathe type is that all the tools cut the workpiece substantially at the same time. On the other types also called *chucking machines* a series of groups of tools or single tools are applied to each workpiece. On the other hand, a line called *precision production boring machines* makes a number of cuts at one time like automatic lathes. The distinction there generally is that their movements are in one direction, while the movements on the automatic lathes are in two or more directions independently.

Numerically Controlled Lathes. A typical numerically controlled lathe has the same basic elements as an engine lathe or turret lathe plus the numerical control system. As shown in Fig. 19-8, a carriage, that moves longitudinally between headstock and tailstock, carries a cross-slide. Commonly one or more tool turrets may be indexed into position for different cuts under numerical control. On some machines, the turrets are on different slides so combined cuts may be taken. In addition to basic lathes, numerical control is also applied to horizontal and vertical turret lathes and other types of turning machines. Many, but not all, numerically controlled lathes (and some automatic chuckers) are built with slanted beds (as in Fig. 19-8). Conventional lathes have flat beds to put the controls where convenient for the operator, but numerically controlled lathes have no manual controls on the front of the bed.

Numerical control (NC) systems for lathes operate on the same principles as for other machines, as described in detail in Chaps. 35 and 36. Programming starts with

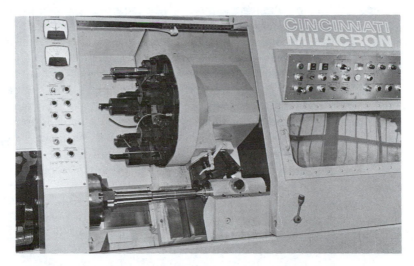

Figure 19-8 View of the working area of a numerically controlled lathe. A workpiece is shown held between a chuck in the headstock and a center in the tailstock. Just above the tailstock is a turret with a tilted vertical axis for single point turning tools. Higher on the cross slide is a turret with a horizontal axis. It carries tools typically for chuck work and can be brought down to working position for a piece held solely in a chuck when the tailstock is slid out of the way. The turrets and tools are positioned and fed as programmed by numerical control. (Courtesy Cincinnati Milacron, Inc.)

a list of statements describing the steps in an operation. A simple example is the following:

011	X−013000	Z−000800	F0300	S08	T04	M03
012		Z−049480	F0115			
013	X+000500		F0030			
014		Z+043480	F1200			
015		Z+006000	F0200			

These are a few lines taken from a long program. Each line, called a block, gives instructions for a step in the operation. The first line calls for tool 04 to move crosswise (toward the centerline) a distance of 1.3 units (u.) and lengthwise (toward the spindle) a distance of 0.08 u. at a feed rate 0300 with spindle speed 08. The M03 function calls for the coolant. For the next step, the tool stays at the same diameter setting (no change in the X dimension) and is fed toward the spindle for 4.948 u. Next, the tool is moved crosswise away from centerline a distance 0.05 u. at feed rate 0030. Then it is returned lengthwise a distance of 4.348 u. at feed rate 1200. The feed and speed specifications are commonly coded. There are many program formats for NC, as explained in Chap. 36.

The NC program is fed into and interpreted by the machine control unit (MCU) that issues electrical impulses, corresponding to the numbers, to the drive units. Sensors on the activated units return signals to the MCU reporting the results. The reports are compared to the orders. If there is any discrepancy, further orders are issued until the requirements are met. Then the MCU goes on to the next step.

A major advantage of an NC lathe is fast changeover, with little lost time for setup. Thus the machine can be cutting most of the time. This can be realized by doing programming away from the machine, presetting tools to suit the program, and utilization of universal tooling. When one or a very few pieces of a kind are to be turned, a manual engine lathe or turret lathe may be more economical; it is simpler and cheaper and requires no extra programming. For more than a few pieces, the NC lathe is commonly more economical. As a rule, the NC lathe is preferable for smaller numbers of pieces than can be justified on other kinds of automatic turning machines. However, for large quantities (thousands and tens of thousands of pieces or more), automatic machines that can utilize gangs or groups of tools acting optimally are usually at an advantage.

An NC lathe of the type illustrated in Fig. 19-8 can do work chucked or between centers, can swing 552 mm (21.75 in.) diameter over bed ways and accommodate a 203-mm (8-in.)-diameter chuck. It has a single turret that can take 12 tools. The lathe has a 15-kW (20-hp) motor and a price of about $100,000.

AUTOMATIC BAR AND CHUCKING MACHINES

Automatic machines for internal and external operations on barstock have been called *automatic screw machines* for years but the name of *automatic bar machines* is now preferable because screws are seldom made on them any more. Their counterparts for individual pieces are *automatic chucking machines*.

Automatic bar and chucking machines may be classified as single spindle or multiple spindle, with a number of variations in each class. Several typical kinds will be described.

Single-Spindle Automatic Bar Machines. The single-spindle automatic bar machine depicted in Fig. 19-9 is made in several sizes for bar work from 10 to 60 mm ($\frac{3}{8}$ to $2\frac{3}{8}$ in.) diameter. A similar cam-controlled machine with a barstock capacity of about 40 mm (ca. $1\frac{9}{16}$ in.), a mass of 2.5 Mg (5500 lb), and a 5.6-kW ($7\frac{1}{2}$-hp) drive motor, has a base price of about $30,000. Machines of like specifications plus complete tooling and accessories may cost over twice as much.

Barstock is fed through the revolving spindle in the center of Fig. 19-9 at the start of each cycle of operation. The stock is located by butting against a swing stop, which saves a tool station or turret stop, and is gripped by a collet. Cutting tools needed can be mounted on the horizontal cross-slides and on the six- or eight-station round turret as well as on the overhead slides. Disk cams on shafts driven off the work spindle move the tool slides and turret slide. Disks, also on the shafts, carry trip dogs or tabs set to engage switches and clutches to change or reverse spindle speeds, feed stock, index the turret, and control attachments. Each function is fast; for instance, $\frac{1}{2}$ second

Figure 19-9 Working area of a single-spindle automatic bar machine. (Courtesy Brown and Sharpe Mfg. Co.)

is needed to index the turret. Tools can act independently or together, and noncutting movements can be overlapped to minimize operation time. A large number of standard tools and holders (as for a turret lathe) are available. A variety of standard and special attachments enable the machine to do such auxiliary operations as screw slotting, burring, cross drilling, and milling.

Various other single-spindle automatics are available to handle work from minute parts like watch staffs to bars about 200 mm ($7\frac{3}{4}$ in.) in diameter and chuck work up to over 300 mm (12 in.) in diameter. These automatics have essentially the same movements and do work similar to that described, but the actual mechanisms vary somewhat with each make of machine.

Swiss-Type Automatic.   The Swiss-type automatic works somewhat differently from other bar machines as shown in Fig. 19-10. This machine is intended for stock from 0.5 to 11 mm (0.020 to 0.44 in.) in diameter. The barstock is held and rotated by the headstock spindle behind the tool head. The headstock is made to slide lengthwise by a cam and feeds the rotating barstock through a hard bushing in the center of the toolhead. Synchronized cams actuate adjustable linkages that bring the tools in as needed to turn, face, form, and cut off the workpiece from the bar as it emerges from the bushing.

The cutting action on the Swiss type of machine is confined close to the support bushing, so that small tolerances can be held and good finishes obtained. Tolerances of 5 to 15 μm (0.0002 to 0.0005 in.) are common. The machine does step, straight, taper, back, and form cutting and with an attachment can perform centering, drilling, and reaming. Tools are simple and adjustments easy. All tools that can, work at once, and a piece is finished in one pass, making the time short for most work.

Single-Spindle Automatic Chucking Machines.   An *automatic turret lathe* has a headstock, turret, and cross-slide on a bed and in its major features looks like a hand turret lathe. However, hand wheels and levers are absent, and operation is

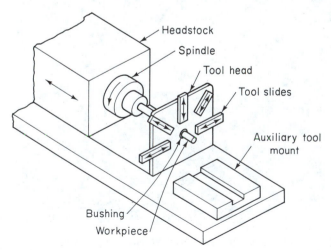

Figure 19-10 Parts and movements of a Swiss-type automatic turning machine.

automatic in a preset cycle. The turret is indexed, advanced, and fed as needed; cross-slides feed to and from the work, and speeds and feeds are changed for each step as desired; all this is done automatically.

The working end of a different design of single-spindle automatic chucking machine with chip guard removed is shown in Fig. 19-11. The main tool turret on this machine above the work spindle has five faces for toolholders and tools. Each face is indexed in turn to working position. The turret then moves lengthwise to feed the tools at the station to and from the workpiece. The two cross-slides below the work spindle can be made to feed at the same time as any turret station. The tool turret is carried on one end of a large round slide. On the other end is a drum from which adjustable dogs set stroke lengths and select speeds and feeds. The machine can also be controlled manually from pushbuttons and switches on a control panel. Other models are completely numerically controlled. A medium-size automatic chucking machine like the one in Fig. 19-11 with a 300-mm (12-in.)-diameter chuck and a 19-kW (25-hp) motor is quoted at about $150,000, and a comparable NC model (Chap. 35) at $200,000.

Multiple-Spindle Automatics.   Automatic bar and chucking machines are built with four, five, six, and eight spindles. Bar-type machines are rated by the largest diameter of stock that can be fed through the spindles. Some take bars up to 150 mm (6 in.) in diameter. The capacity of a chucking machine is the diameter of work that can be swung over the tool slides. As an example, a 32-mm ($1\frac{1}{4}$-in.)-capacity six-spindle bar automatic has a 19-kW (25-hp) motor and costs over $200,000 equipped, plus more than $50,000 for numerical control.

Figure 19-11   Working area of a single-spindle automatic chucking machine tooled for a job. (Courtesy Warner and Swasey Co.)

A cutaway view of a six-spindle automatic bar machine is shown in Fig. 19-12. The opening in the center of the machine is where the tools and work go. The workpiece spindles are arranged on a circle in a large drum or spindle carrier on the right of the opening. Each work spindle carries a bar of stock, revolves continuously, and is moved from station to station as the carrier indexes. The spindle carrier is indexed smoothly by a modified Geneva mechanism and is locked in position between indexing periods. Each piece is machined in stages as it proceeds from station to station, and one piece is finished and cut off at each index.

End-working tools are mounted on the end tool slide in the middle of the opening. The end tool slide does not index but moves lengthwise to feed its tools to and from the workpieces. The end-working tools are carried on separate slides on some machines and can be fed at different rates.

Side- or cross-slides for forming and cutoff tools are mounted next to the spindle stations and move radially to and from the workpieces. Cross-slides on some machines have a longitudinal as well as radial motion with respect to the work for relieving, contour turning, and grooving.

On most machines the spindles are indexed only one station at a time, and a bar is fed forward or pieces are loaded at only one station. Some six- and eight-spindle machines double index, and two pieces are completed at each index.

Automatic chucking machines take individual castings, forgings, and second-

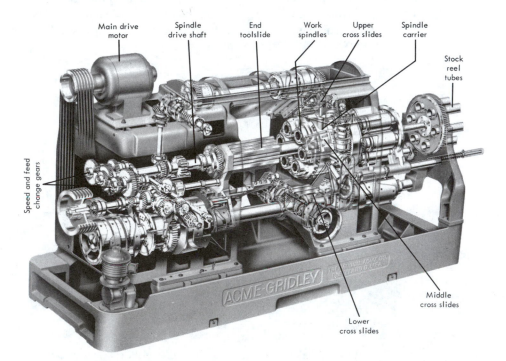

Figure 19-12 Cutaway view of a six-spindle automatic bar machine. (Courtesy National Acme Div. of Acme-Cleveland Corp.)

operation pieces cut from bars. A *horizontal multiple-spindle automatic chucking machine* is like the bar machine of Fig. 19-12 without the bar reel and tubes on one end. Chucks instead of collets often hold pieces at the ends of the spindles. End-cutting tools are fed on a common slide, but the cross-slides may feed independently. Horizontal machines commonly handle pieces under 250 mm (10 in.) in diameter, and vertical machines larger sizes. A *vertical multiple-spindle automatic chucking machine,* as depicted in Fig. 19-13, occupies a minimum of floor space for its capacity and has each station readily accessible to facilitate setup and adjustments. The tools are carried and fed on slides around a central column. Slides are available for vertical, horizontal, angular, and combination movements, and each slide feeds independently of the other stations.

Some models of multiple-spindle automatic machines are numerically controlled for feeds, speeds, and tool positions and travel. This shortens time for setup and makes the machines more competitive for short runs.

Tooling and Operation. An example of tooling for a multiple-spindle automatic bar machine is given in Fig. 19-14. Combined and multiple cuts are taken wherever feasible. The machine actually operates on several pieces at once. The time

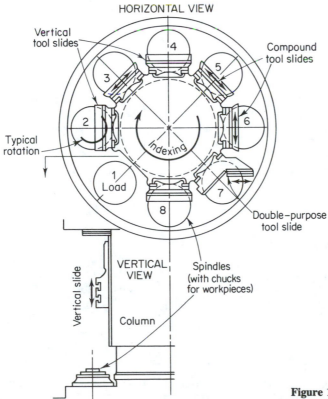

Figure 19-13 Working stations of an eight-spindle vertical chucking machine.

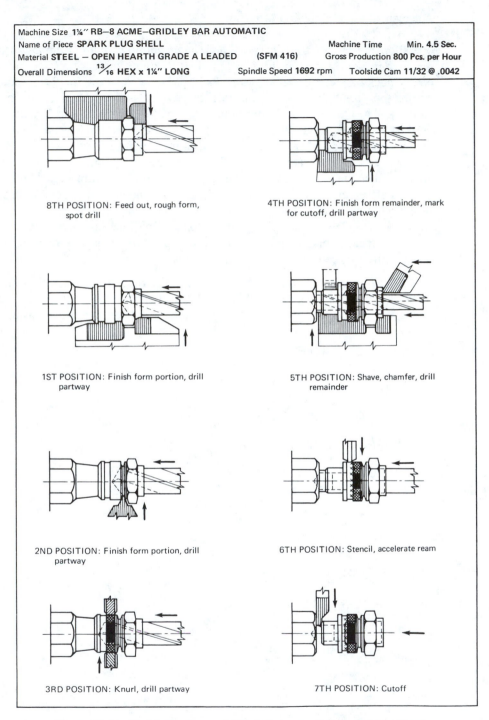

8TH POSITION: Feed out, rough form, spot drill

4TH POSITION: Finish form remainder, mark for cutoff, drill partway

1ST POSITION: Finish form portion, drill partway

5TH POSITION: Shave, chamfer, drill remainder

2ND POSITION: Finish form portion, drill partway

6TH POSITION: Stencil, accelerate ream

3RD POSITION: Knurl, drill partway

7TH POSITION: Cutoff

Figure 19-14 Tool layout for an eight-spindle automatic bar machine. (Courtesy National Acme Div. of Acme-Cleveland Corp.)

to make one piece on a single indexing machine is the time for the longest cut plus the idle time. The idle time is that taken to move the tools rapidly to and from the work and index the spindles. Typical idle times are 2 seconds for a 1-in. machine, 2.25 seconds for $1\frac{5}{8}$ in., and 2.3 seconds for $1\frac{3}{4}$- and $2\frac{1}{4}$-in. machines.

Every effort is made to shorten the long cuts and minimize the cutting time on a multiple-spindle automatic. This may be done by dividing parts of a long cut among two or more spindles. For instance, a length of 50 mm (2 in.) may be turned for a distance of 25 mm (1 in.) at one station and the rest of the way at a second station. The drilling of deep holes may be divided in the same way. The disadvantage of dividing cuts is that the cuts cannot be made exactly to match each other when made at different spindle positions.

Tooling attachments and accessories increase the area of application and productivity of automatic turning machines. Attachments are added to revolve drills, reamers, or taps to increase or decrease the relative speeds between the tools and work and accelerate operations. Attachments are available for such auxiliary operations as milling, slotting, and cross drilling, right on the machine. Quick mounting and preset tool blocks and toolholders can do much to save on setup and down time for changing tools. As has been shown, if the time for mounting and replacing tools can be shortened, a shorter tool life is economical. With a shorter tool life, cutting speeds can be increased with a corresponding increase in production.

Tolerances considered economical for multiple-spindle automatics are of the order of 50 to 100 μm (0.002 to 0.004 in.) for turning or forming a diameter; 130 to 250 μm (0.005 to 0.010 in.) between two shoulders; 250 μm (0.010 in.) on an overall length directly from a stock stop or 130 μm (0.005 in.) by facing at cutoff; and 25 μm (0.001 in.) for size of a reamed hole. Typical attainable runout tolerances are 50 μm (0.002 in.) total indicator reading (TIR) between diameters machined at the same station; 150 μm (0.006 in.) TIR between surfaces machined at different stations, and 130 μm (0.005 in.) TIR between a machine surface and the original stock surface. Closer tolerances than those quoted can be and are held, even to 15 μm (ca. 0.0005 in.), but the smaller the tolerance, the slower and more expensive the operation.

This is particularly important with multiple-spindle automatic operations, where the investment is large and the equipment must be kept producing at the highest possible rate to be economical. For that reason, it generally is preferable to do small tolerance jobs on single-spindle rather than on multiple-spindle machines.

If run at the same speed, a multiple-spindle automatic is a faster producer than a single-spindle automatic because all its tools work at once. However, the mechanism necessary for a multiple-spindle machine may hinder it from turning as fast as a single-spindle machine can with small pieces or soft materials like brass. Single-spindle automatics can be indexed faster, and that is an advantage when few cuts are taken and cutting time is short as compared to idle time. Single-spindle automatics are available for larger work than can be done on multiple-spindle machines.

A multiple-spindle automatic is economical only when it can turn out parts faster than a single-spindle automatic, and enough parts must be produced to justify the larger investment and longer setup time of the multiple-spindle equipment. A rule of thumb is that a multiple-spindle automatic is not justified for a job unless it can be kept busy for 4 or more days.

QUESTIONS

1. Why are there different kinds of automatic turning machines?
2. Describe a typical automatic lathe and how it works.
3. What are the competitive advantages and disadvantages of automatic lathes?
4. What can be done to make automatic lathe operations economical?
5. What are the two main types of horizontal turret lathes? Describe each and tell how they differ.
6. What can be done to achieve low costs in a turret lathe operation?
7. What are combined and multiple cuts?
8. What basic principles determine what tool should be selected for a job?
9. Describe briefly how an NC turning system operates.
10. In what areas are NC lathes economical?
11. What basic principle determines whether a tool should be selected for a job?
12. Describe a typical single-spindle automatic bar machine and what it does.
13. Describe a Swiss-type automatic and tell how it differs from other single-spindle automatics.
14. Describe a typical single-spindle automatic chucking machine.
15. Describe a multiple-spindle automatic and tell how it operates.
16. What are the relative advantages and disadvantages of single-spindle and multiple-spindle automatics?

PROBLEMS

1. The workpiece sketched in Fig. 19-15 is to be turned from barstock 75 mm (3 in.) in diameter. Each diameter is turned in one cut. 50 W is required to remove 1 cm^3 of material per minute (1.1 hp to remove 1 in.^{3}/min).

   Two machines are available for doing the job. Each has excess capacity, so overhead charges will be the same on whichever machine the job is done. Labor rate is $8/hr. All but setup and cutting time will be the same on both machines. One machine is an engine lathe with a tracer attachment and a 7.5-kW (10-hp) motor. A template costs $50 and setup time takes 10 minutes. The other machine is an automatic lathe with a 15-kW (20-hp) motor. A tooling setup for this job costs $150 and setup time is 30 minutes. Each machine is 80% efficient and is capable of removing material at a rate equivalent to its power capacity. Find:
   (a) Which machine should be selected for one lot of 5 pieces.
   (b) Which machine should be selected for one lot of 1000 pieces.
   (c) The least number of pieces that should be run on the automatic lathe in 10 lots during a year. Ignore charges for interest, insurance, taxes, and maintenance.

Millimeters   Inches

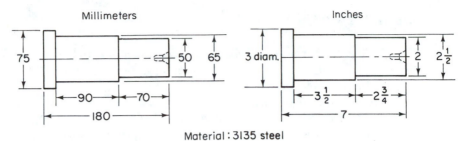

Material : 3135 steel

Figure 19-15 Sketches of a workpiece.

2. A piece can be turned on an NC lathe utilizing one tool at a time in 4 minutes. Programming costs $50, setup time is 10 minutes, and labor and overhead on the machine is $45/hr. Special tooling costs $250 for gang cutting the piece in 2.5 minutes on an automatic lathe, on which setup time is 30 minutes and the labor and overhead rate is $20/hr. The rate for interest is 10%, for insurance and taxes 5%, and for maintenance 15%, applicable for tools and for NC programs.
    (a) If only one lot of parts is to be made, how large a lot should be run on the NC lathe?
    (b) If five lots are to be run during a year, what is the lowest annual amount of production that justifies the use of the automatic lathe?

3. A workpiece can be held in a chuck on a turret lathe, but if a special fixture that costs $50 is provided, loading time is shortened by $\frac{1}{2}$ min/piece. The composite rate for interest, insurance, taxes, and maintenance is 20%. Setup time is not changed. The rate for labor and overhead is $18/hr. For how many pieces is the fixture justified?

4. Ten thousand of the flywheels of Fig. 19-5 are to be machined in lots of 1000 pieces during one year. Disregard interest, insurance and tax, and maintenance charges. Should tooling method B or C be selected? How much is saved?

5. Four thousand pieces at 500 pieces to the lot are to be run to make the flywheel of Fig. 19-5. Interest is 10%, insurance and taxes 5%, and maintenance negligible. Apply only a single charge for interest, insurance, and taxes against the full amount for standard and special tools. What tooling method should be selected? How do the results compare with those obtained when interest, insurance, and taxes are neglected?

6. The labor and overhead rate on an automatic bar machine is $0.40/min. For the tool taking the major cut in an operation, the tool life–speed relationship is $VT^{0.125} = 146$. Fifteen minutes is required to regrind the tool, which cost $32 new and can be ground 50 times. Originally 20 minutes was required to change the tool when dull, but this time was reduced to $\frac{1}{2}$ minute by means of a quick-change toolholder that enabled the tool to be preset off the machine. The machine has ample power to allow the speed to be increased to any extent justified. What increase in production can be expected from the use of the quick-change holder?

7. The times taken for operations at the stations of a six-spindle vertical chucking machine are (1) unload and load 10 seconds, (2) 9 seconds, (3) 12 seconds, (4) 13 seconds, (5) 11 seconds, and (6) 8 seconds. Indexing time is 3 seconds. What is the output in a 50-minute hour?

REFERENCES

BERG, R. T., "Fundamentals of Turning, 2," *American Machinist,* Dec. 6, 1965, p. 103.

DALLAS, D. B., ed., *Tool and Manufacturing Engineers Handbook,* 3rd ed., Society of Manufacturing Engineers, Dearborn, Mich., 1976.

Handbook for Single Spindle Bar and Chucking Automatics, How to Machine Parts on Turret Lathes. Production Handbook for Turret Lathes, Warner and Swasey Co., Cleveland, Ohio.

LABARR, R. F., "Changes in Chuckers: From Flat Belts to CNC," *Manufacturing Engineering,* Nov. 1981, p. 76.

WICK, C., "Advances in NC Turning," *Manufacturing Engineering,* Sept. 1978, p. 40.

20

ECONOMICS OF PROCESS PLANNING

The choice of a method or process for machining a part largely determines the machine tool needed. On the other hand, the selection of a machine tool for an operation determines within limits how the operation is to be done. A decision to machine a flat face by revolving a workpiece points to the use of a turning type of machine. Conversely, if a person decides to machine a face by putting a piece on a lathe, he or she probably intends to revolve the workpiece. Thus, in effect, the principles that govern machine tool selection also are basic to machining process selection. These principles are discussed in this chapter and illustrated mostly by reference to machines of the lathe family because those have been described. However, the principles apply just as much to all other kinds of machine tools, machines, and processes, and as the other types of machines are described, the factors that concern their selection are included.

The choice of a machine tool must take into account (1) the size and shape of the workpiece, (2) the work material, (3) the accuracy and surface quality required, (4) personal preferences, and (5) the quantity of parts and the sizes of lots required. Usually, a number of machine tools can do a job, but the one that will do the job at the lowest cost when required is the one to be chosen.

Cost is a matter of dollars and cents and in the final analysis must be estimated and calculated. Of the number of machine tools that might conceivably do a job, most can be eliminated without detailed estimates of their costs, since they are too small or too large, too weak, or in some other ways obviously deficient. The costs of the remaining few can then be ascertained to determine which tool is the best for the job. First, in the following discussion, the general considerations of dimensional size, strength and power, and performance characteristics that lead to the initial selection will be discussed. Then the principles of estimating and comparing actual costs will be presented.

GENERAL CONSIDERATIONS IN MACHINE TOOL SELECTION

Size and Capacity.   The dimensions that designate the size of a machine tool generally specify the size of the largest workpiece that can be handled. If enough pieces of one kind are to be produced to keep a machine busy practically all the time, a size just able to take the part might well be chosen. For instance, for pieces to be made from 40-mm (ca. $1\frac{1}{2}$-in.)-diameter barstock, an automatic bar machine with a collet capacity of 40 mm (ca. $1\frac{1}{2}$ in.) or a little larger would be favored. On the other hand, if only a few pieces of a particular size are to be made, the general-purpose machine selected for them would probably be larger so that it would be adaptable to other jobs as well. Thus pieces from 40-mm (ca. $1\frac{1}{2}$-in.)-diameter barstock would probably be turned on lathes with 300 mm (ca. 12 in.) or larger swing, because lathes of that size would be found in a job shop for the run of medium-sized parts.

Workpiece size and dimensions may dictate particular features that a machine tool must have. As an example, small and medium-size parts are turned on horizontal lathes, but short pieces of large diameters are commonly machined on vertical lathes.

Other dimensions of a machine that may have to be considered are the directions and lengths of movements of tools to assure that the surfaces to be cut can be covered; the clearances for the tools that must be used; and the provisions for the holding device.

The dimensions of the various sizes of a machine suitable for a particular job may be ascertained from the manufacturer's catalog. By comparison with the requirements of the job, the proper size can be selected.

Strength and Power.   The rigidity and strength of a machine tool are not easy to calculate but for reputable machine tools are in keeping with the rated power capacity. Thus a light machine usually has a smaller motor than a heavier one. In general, a machine tool is designed to resist the forces arising from cuts at rated power. Thus the power required in an operation must be a major consideration in selecting a machine tool. The machine must have enough power, but too much is wasteful.

Ways of calculating forces and power at the cutting zone were explained in Chap. 17. A convenient way of estimating power is to multiply the rate of metal removal in cm^3/min (in.^{3}/min) by the unit power in W/cm^3/min (hp/in.^{3}/min). The unit power varies with the work material, type of operation, rake angle of the cutting tool, size of cut, and speed, but mostly with the first two. Accordingly, average values of unit power, like those given in Table 17-3, may be used to estimate the power requirements of common operations.

Some loss in power can be expected in any machine tool, so the power at the motor must be more than that at the cutting zone. An efficiency of 80% is a fair estimate for average conditions.

As an example, a 16-mm ($\frac{5}{8}$-in.)-diameter hole drilled in steel of $35R_C$ at 550 rpm and 0.15 mm/rev (0.006 ipr) requires power

$$P_D = 16^2 \times \frac{\pi}{4} \times 0.15 \times 550 \times 64 \times \frac{1.3}{10^6} = 1.4 \text{ kW}$$

$$= (\tfrac{5}{8})^2 \times \frac{\pi}{4} \times 0.006 \times 550 \times 1.4 \times 1.3 = 1.8 \text{ hp}$$

The factor of 1.3 is to provide enough power as the drill gets dull. The motor power should be $1.4/0.8 = 1.8$ kW or $1.8/0.8 = 2.3$ hp.

In actual production tools may be run until extremely dull, the operator may choose to run at higher speeds and feeds than anticipated, and the work material may vary in hardness and stock allowance. This means that if a machine tool is loaded to capacity on a job for maximum economy under ideal conditions, it may be as much as 50% or more overloaded at other times. Actually, that is a common experience, and good machine tools are built intentionally to stand overloads. As an example, one leading machine tool manufacturer has recommended:

Rated capacity for continuous operation.

25% over the rated capacity for normal operation.

50% over the rated capacity for intermittent operation, 5-minute maximum period. Minimum idle time between cuts should equal one-fifth of the cutting time.

75% over the rated capacity for intermittent operation, 1-minute maximum period. Minimum idle time between cuts should equal the cutting time.

Frequently the situation is that a machine meets all other requirements or happens to be available but has a limited power rating. The problem then is to determine the speed and feed at which the job may be run. As an example, a depth of cut of 3 mm (0.118 in.) is required to reduce a diameter of 40 mm (1.575 in.) to 34 mm (1.339 in.) at 60 m/min (197 fpm) in $40R_c$ steel. The lathe has a $7\frac{1}{2}$-kW (10-hp) motor and is 80% efficient. The permissible rate of metal removal is

$$Q = 7500 \times \frac{0.8}{64} = 93.75 \text{ cm}^3/\text{min} = f \times 3 \times 60$$

$$= 10 \times \frac{0.8}{1.4} = 5.71 \text{ in.}^3/\text{min} = f \times 0.118 \times 197 \times 12$$

The feed rate should be $f = 0.5$ mm/rev $= 0.020$ ipr.

Other Considerations. Among other factors that need to be considered in machine tool selection are the accuracy and surface finishes which a machine is capable of producing, the removal of hard material or large amounts of stock, the skill available and required to operate the machine, personal likes and dislikes, and availability. Most of these factors are not as basic as others but in some cases may be decisive. A few examples will be given. If fine surface finishes and small tolerances must be held, they often are obtainable only on grinding equipment. Grinding also is the only means of cutting some hard substances but is not well suited to remove large amounts of stock from any substance. In a situation where skill to set up automatic machines is not available, operations might have to be simplified and spread over the other simpler types of machines. Often in a shop, a machine that is available will be selected for a job rather than buying another or waiting for one that is already overloaded.

HOW COSTS ARE ESTIMATED AND COMPARED

As the result of the general considerations just described, a person may be able to eliminate all but one size of two or more types of machines from consideration for an operation. It then becomes necessary to estimate and compare the costs.

All costs that vary must be considered and for convenience may be divided into direct costs, indirect or overhead costs, and capital costs. The direct cost that varies most from machine to machine is labor, which is usually calculated by multiplying the time required for an operation by a labor rate. Thus the time to set up and perform an operation must be estimated to find its direct cost. Other direct costs such as for power and material do not vary much for the same job when done in one way or another and are not included as a rule. Overhead costs are commonly calculated by multiplying the operation time by an overhead rate. Such a rate is obtained by dividing the total indirect costs applicable to a production unit (such as a machine center or department) for a period of time (say a month) by the total number of hours of direct labor in the same period. Capital costs are determined by distributing the major machine and tool costs on an hourly basis or among the pieces produced.

The Parts of Productive Time. The total time required to perform an operation may be divided into four parts. They are:

1. *Setup time*. This is the time required to prepare for the operation and may include time to get tools from the crib and do paperwork as well as to arrange the tools on the machine.
2. *Worker or handling time*. This is the time the operator spends loading and unloading the work, manipulating the machine and tools, and making measurements during each cycle of the operation.
3. *Machine time*. This is the time during each cycle of the operation that the machine is working or the tools are cutting.
4. *Down or lost time*. This is the unavoidable time lost by the operator because of breakdowns, waiting for the tools and materials, etc.

Setup, Worker, and Down Time. Setup time is performed usually once for each lot of parts. It should therefore be listed separately from the other parts of the operation time. If 30 minutes is required for a setup and only 10 pieces are made, an average of 3 minutes of setup time must be charged against each piece. On the other hand, if 60 pieces are made from the same setup, only $\frac{1}{2}$ minute is charged per piece. Thus a prorated setup time may be very misleading because it depends so much on lot size.

Both setup and worker time are estimated from previous performance on similar operations. All work on a particular type of machine tool consists of a limited number of elements. These elements may be standardized, measured, and recorded. That is the essence of time study, a large field in itself. Space does not permit a detailed treatment of that subject here. An example of time standards for lathes is given in Fig. 20-1. The time to perform an operation also includes time for personal needs of the operator, time to change tools, etc.

The actual amount of downtime that will occur in a specific operation can scarcely be predicted. Some operations will run smoothly; others will be beset by troubles. The best estimate that can be made is based upon the average amount currently lost in the plant. For a comparison between two operations, the assumption is that both will be subject to the same downtime, so that part of the cost is not included as a rule.

Machine Time.   The way to calculate machine or cutting time for turning operations was explained in Chap. 18. The basic relationship for any operation is that the cutting time in minutes is equal to the distance the tool is fed in mm (in.) divided by the feed in mm/min (ipm).

The distance a tool is fed to make a cut is the sum of the distance the tool travels while cutting to full depth plus its approach distance plus its overtravel. The *approach* is the distance a tool is fed from the time it touches the workpiece until it is cutting to full depth. Approach distance for a drill is the length of its point, which is about one-fourth the diameter of a standard drill. The approach of most single-point tools is negligible. *Overtravel* is the distance the tool is fed while it is not cutting. It is the space over which the tool idles before it enters and after it leaves the cut. Overtravel may be less than 1 to over 6 mm (about $\frac{1}{32}$ to $\frac{1}{4}$ in.).

How Operation Time Is Estimated.   The workpiece in Fig. 20-2 may be made on an engine lathe or on a turret lathe with the tool layout shown. To illustrate the details of estimating operation time and as a basis for further comparison, Table 20-1 contains figures compiled for both engine lathe and turret lathe operations. The speeds and feeds selected are customary ones for the operations and tools. A check of the heaviest cut, that of element 7, shows power required of $66 \times 0.46 \times 2.75 \times 50 \times 1.3/1000 = 5.4$ kW ($12 \times 216 \times 0.018 \times 0.109 \times 1.1 \times 1.3 = 7.3$ hp) at the tool point. The values for standard time for the engine lathe were taken from Fig. 20-1 and for the turret lathe from a similar table for that machine tool.

Comparison of Engine Lathe and Turret Lathe.   The operating differences between engine lathes and turret lathes are illustrated in Table 20-1. To produce 5 pieces of the part shown in Fig. 20-2 takes a total of 41.70 minutes or 8.34 minutes per piece on the engine lathe as compared with 93.40 total minutes or 18.68 minutes per piece on the turret lathe. For 100 pieces the total time is 454 minutes or 4.54

THE MONARCH MACHINE TOOL COMPANY
SIDNEY, OHIO, U. S. A.

TURNING DATA SHEET No. 104

HANDLING TIME

RECHUCK OR PLACE BETWEEN CENTERS — LENGTH IN INCHES

TIME IN MINUTES

Avg. Diam. In Inches	2	4	6	8	10	12	14	16	18	20	24	28	32	36	40	44	48	52	56	60	72	84	96	108
3/4	.10	.10	.10	.10	.10	.12	.14	.14	.16	.16	.18	.18	.20	.20	.24	.28	.32	.36	.40	.45	.58	.71	.84	.97
1	.10	.11	.12	.15	.18	.21	.24	.25	.28	.29	.32	.33	.36	.37	.42	.47	.52	.57	.62	.68	.81	.94	1.07	1.20
1¼	.14	.16	.18	.22	.26	.30	.34	.36	.40	.42	.46	.48	.52	.54	.60	.66	.72	.78	.84	.91	1.12	1.33	1.54	1.75
1½	.18	.21	.24	.29	.34	.39	.44	.47	.52	.55	.60	.63	.68	.71	.78	.85	.92	.99	1.06	1.14	1.38	1.66	1.94	2.22
2	.22	.26	.30	.36	.42	.48	.54	.58	.64	.68	.74	.78	.84	.88	.96	1.04	1.12	1.20	1.28	1.37	1.64	1.91	2.18	2.45
2¼	.26	.31	.36	.43	.50	.57	.64	.69	.76	.81	.88	.93	1.00	1.05	1.14	1.23	1.32	1.41	1.50	1.60	1.90	2.20	2.50	2.80
2½	.30	.36	.42	.50	.58	.66	.74	.80	.88	.94	1.02	1.08	1.16	1.22	1.32	1.42	1.52	1.62	1.72	1.93	2.53	3.13	3.73	4.33
2¾	.34	.41	.48	.57	.66	.75	.84	.91	1.00	1.07	1.16	1.23	1.32	1.39	1.50	1.61	1.72	1.83	1.94	2.16	2.76	3.36	3.96	4.56
3	.38	.46	.54	.64	.74	.84	.94	1.02	1.12	1.20	1.30	1.38	1.48	1.56	1.68	1.80	1.92	2.04	2.16	2.39	2.99	3.59	4.19	4.79
3½	.42	.51	.60	.71	.82	.93	1.04	1.13	1.24	1.33	1.44	1.53	1.64	1.73	1.86	1.99	2.12	2.25	2.38	2.52	3.12	3.72	4.32	4.92
4	.44	.56	.66	.78	.90	1.02	1.14	1.24	1.36	1.46	1.58	1.68	1.80	1.90	2.04	2.18	2.32	2.46	2.60	2.75	3.35	3.98	4.55	5.15
4½	.48	.61	.72	.85	.98	1.11	1.24	1.35	1.48	1.59	1.72	1.83	1.96	2.07	2.22	2.37	2.52	2.67	2.82	2.98	3.58	4.18	4.78	5.38

PLACE AND REMOVE - HAND - ELECTRIC - AIR - 3 OR 4-JAW CHUCK—LENGTH IN INCHES

TIME IN MINUTES

	2	4	6	8	10	12	14	16	18	20	22	24	26	28	30	32	34
5	.52	.66	.80	.94	1.08	1.22	1.36	1.50	1.64	1.78	1.92	2.06	2.20	2.34	2.48	2.62	2.76
5½	.56	.71	.86	1.01	1.16	1.31	1.46	1.61	1.76	1.91	2.06	2.21	2.36	2.51	2.66	2.81	2.96
6	.60	.76	.92	1.08	1.24	1.40	1.56	1.72	1.88	2.04	2.20	2.36	2.52	2.68	2.84	3.00	3.16
6½	.64	.81	.98	1.15	1.32	1.49	1.66	1.83	2.00	2.17	2.34	2.51	2.68	2.85	3.02	3.19	3.36
7	.68	.86	1.04	1.22	1.40	1.58	1.76	1.94	2.12	2.30	2.48	2.66	2.84	3.02	3.20	3.38	3.56
7½	.72	.91	1.10	1.29	1.48	1.67	1.86	2.05	2.24	2.43	2.62	2.81	3.00	3.19	3.38	3.57	3.76
8	.76	.96	1.16	1.36	1.56	1.76	1.96	2.16	2.36	2.56	2.76	2.96	3.16	3.36	3.56	3.76	3.96
8½	.80	1.01	1.22	1.43	1.64	1.85	2.06	2.27	2.48	2.69	2.90	3.11	3.32	3.53	3.74	3.95	4.16
9	.84	1.06	1.28	1.50	1.72	1.94	2.16	2.38	2.60	2.82	3.04	3.26	3.48	3.70	3.92	4.14	
9½	.88	1.11	1.34	1.57	1.80	2.03	2.26	2.49	2.72	2.95	3.18	3.41	3.64	3.87	4.10		
10	.92	1.16	1.40	1.64	1.88	2.12	2.36	2.60	2.84	3.08	3.32	3.56	3.80	4.04			
10½	.96	1.21	1.46	1.71	1.96	2.21	2.46	2.71	2.96	3.21	3.46	3.71	3.96				

Use Place & Remove Time & Factor

	Factor
Face Plate and Centers with Dog	.8
Face Plate and Centers with Driver	.7
Chuck and Center	1.2
Chuck and Steady Rest	1.5
Chuck and Steady Rest and Center	1.7
Air Arbor—Thread or Stud	1.0
	Min.
Pcs. On and Off Thread Arbor—Long	.50
Tighten & Loosen Headstock Center	.20
Split Bushings use in P.& R.—Add	.05
Minimum Time to P. & R. Work Between Centers	.20
Arbor Press In & Out, Add to P.& R.	.30
Pcs. In & Out of Fixtures—On or Off Table—Small	.15

11	1.00	1.26	1.52	1.78	2.04	2.30	2.56	2.82	3.06	3.34	3.60	3.86	4.12
11½	1.04	1.31	1.58	1.85	2.12	2.39	2.66	2.93	3.18	3.47	3.74	4.01	
12	1.08	1.36	1.64	1.92	2.20	2.48	2.76	3.04	3.30	3.60	3.88		
13	1.12	1.41	1.70	1.99	2.28	2.57	2.86	3.15	3.42	3.73	4.02		
14	1.16	1.46	1.76	2.06	2.36	2.66	2.96	3.26	3.54	3.86			
15	1.20	1.51	1.82	2.13	2.44	2.75	3.06	3.37	3.66	3.99			
16	1.24	1.56	1.88	2.20	2.52	2.84	3.16	3.48	3.78	4.12			
17	1.28	1.61	1.94	2.27	2.60	2.93	3.26	3.59	3.90				
18	1.32	1.66	2.00	2.34	2.68	3.02	3.36	3.70	4.02				
19	1.36	1.71	2.06	2.41	2.76	3.11	3.46	3.81					
20	1.40	1.76	2.12	2.48	2.84	3.20	3.56	3.92					
21	1.44	1.81	2.18	2.55	2.92	3.29	3.66	4.03					
22	1.48	1.86	2.24	2.62	3.00	3.38	3.76						
23	1.52	1.91	2.30	2.69	3.08	3.47	3.86						
24	1.56	1.96	2.36	2.76	3.16	3.56	3.96						
Over	1.60	2.01	2.40	2.83	3.24	3.65	4.06						

Medium	.30
Large	.50
Extra Large	.80
Tighten Nut and Bolt	.20
Tighten Clamp 1 Nut or Bolt	.25
Tighten Clamp 2 Nut or Bolt	.40
Clamp On & Off 1 Nut or Bolt	.50
Clamp On & Off 2 Nut or Bolt	.70
Jack Moved to P. & R. Piece	.60
Clean Chips Off Job	.30
Adjust Set Screw	.10
Place & Remove Shim in Fixture	.05
Nut Arbor—Add to P. & R.	.50

Add one (1) minute for hoist on piece over 35 pounds.

(lbs.=D³ × length × .22)—Solid piece.

Tubing or like pieces—Factor .5

Double above times for Independent 4-Jaw Chuck—Includes ordinary indicating.

TOOL ADJUST—MEASURING—SPECIAL ALLOWANCES

Short Operations by Stock Diameter	¾"	1¼"	2"	3"	4"	5"	7"	10"	15"	Over
Spot Drill or Center	.10	.15	.20	.25	.30	.35	.40	.45	.50	.55
Chamfer—Bevel—Radius—Neck—Recess	.05	.10	.15	.20	.25	.30	.35	.40	.60	.80

Use these Material Factors with above operations, S A E 1020, 1112, Cast Iron, Brass - 1.00 — Machine Steel, Bronze, Tubing - 1.50 — Tool Steel - 2.00

Measuring Times by Outside-Inside Diameters or Lengths	½"	1"	2"	3"	4"	5"	7"	10"	15"	Over
Scale Short Length by O. D.	.10	.10	.15	.15	.15	.20	.20	.25	.30	.35
Scale Long Length (over 4 feet) by O. D.	.35	.35	.40	.40	.50	.50	.60	.70	.80	.90
V-Gauge—Calipers by O. D.	.20	.25	.25	.25	.30	.30	.40	.50	.60	.70
Thread Gauge Male by O. D. Female by O. D.	.10	.15	.20	.25	.35	.45	.65			
Plug Gauge by I. D.	.05	.05	.10	.20	.30	.30	.40	.50	.60	.70
Taper Gauge Male by I. D. Female by O. D.	.20	.25	.30	.35	.40	.45	.50	.60	.70	.80
Bevel Protractor	.20	.20	.20	.30	.30	.30	.40	.50	.60	.70
Depth Micrometers by Length of Depth	.15	.20	.25	.30	.35	.40				
Micrometrs and Verniers (X2 on inside mikes)	.05	.10	.15	.20	.25	.30	.40	.50	.75	1.00
Height Gauge	.10	.10	.15	.15	.20	.20	.25	.25	.30	.30

Tool Adjust — By Stock Diameters	¾"	1¼"	2"	3"	4"	5"	7"	10"	15"	Over
Hexagon Turret or Cross Slide	.10	.15	.17	.20	.25	.27	.30	.35	.40	.45
Tailstock (Hole Diameter)	.20	.30	.40	.50	.60					

Tool Adjust on Work Supported on Both Ends—By Length	6"	12"	18"	24"	30"	36"	48"	60"	72"	Over
Cross Slide	.10	.15	.20	.25	.30	.35	.40	.45	.50	.55

Figure 20-1 Standard elements for handling time for lathes. (Courtesy Monarch Machine Tool Co.)

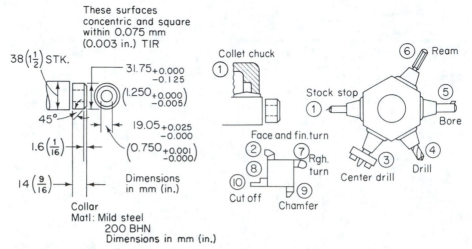

Figure 20-2 Workpiece and a turret-lathe tool layout for making it.

TABLE 20-1 COMPARISON OF ELEMENTAL TIMES ON 14-IN. ENGINE LATHE AND
NO. 4 TURRET LATHE

						Minutes standard time	
	Element	m/min	Cutting time			Engine	Turret
No.	Designation	(fpm)	(rpm)	[mm/rev (ipr)]	(min)	lathe	lathe
1.	Advance and position bar					0.20	0.12
2.	Face end—set tool[a]					0.16	0.12
	0.8 mm (1/32 in.) deep cut	66 (216)	550	0.25 (0.010)	0.16		
3.	Center drill—set tool[b]					0.20	0.12
	Cut to 5 mm (3/16 in.) diameter		1200	hand	0.15		
4.	Drill—set tool[b]					0.20	0.13
	16 mm (5/8 in.) diameter × 17.5 mm (11/16 in.) deep cut	27 (90)	550	0.18 (0.007)	0.23		
5.	Bore—set tool[c]					0.36	0.13
	18.85/19.0 mm (0.742/0.747 in.) diameter × 16 mm (5/8 in.) deep cut	42 (138)	700	0.18 (0.007)	0.14		
6.	Ream—set tool[b]					0.20	0.13
	19.05/19.075 mm (0.750/0.751 in.) diameter × 16 mm (5/8 in.) deep cut	12 (39)	200	0.79 (0.031)	0.11		
7.	Rough turn—set tool[a]					0.26	(with No. 4)
	32.5 mm ($1\frac{9}{32}$ in.) diameter × 19 mm (3/4 in.) long cut	66 (216)	550	0.46 (0.018)	0.09		
8.	Finish turn—set tool[a]					0.25	(with No. 5)
	31.75/31.625 mm (1.250/1.245 in.) diameter × 16 mm (5/8 in.) long cut	84 (275)	700	0.25 (0.010)	0.13		
9.	Chamfer—set tool[a]					0.15	0.13
	1.5 mm (1/16 in.) × 45°	70 (230)	700	hand	0.10		

10. Cut off—set tool[a]					0.25	0.13
Cut to 14 mm (9/16 in.) thick	20 (65)	200	0.10 (0.004)	0.35		
11. Break edges					0.25	0.20
12. Check (every piece on lathe, every fifth piece on turret lathe)					0.40	0.10

Handling time	2.88	1.31
Applicable cutting time	1.46	1.37
Cycle time	4.34	2.68
Setup time	15.	75.
Teardown and cleanup	5	5
Total per lot	20	80

Notes:

	On engine lathe	On turret lathe
a	Place and adjust tool on cross-slide (includes 0.10 minute to measure if dimensional)	Index square turret and position tool
b	Place tool in tailstock and adjust	Index hex. turret, advance tool to work, and start feed
c	Place and adjust tool on cross-slide	Index hex. turret, advance tool to work, and start feed

For element 5, bore, the standard time for the lathe of 0.36 minute includes "tool adjust 0.16 minute" and "measure ID 0.20 minute." The tool is preset to cut to size on the turret lathe, and the standard elemental time for that machine is only 0.13 minute to "index hexagonal turret, advance tool to work, and engage feed." The total length of cut includes 1.5 mm (1/16 in.) overtravel, and the cutting time = $17.5/(700 \times 0.18)$ = 0.14 minute = $0.69/(700 \times 0.007)$.

On a 7.5-kW (10-hp) turret lathe, element 7 has a total time of 0.22 minute and can be performed entirely within the cutting time of 0.23 minute of element 4. The value of 0.09 minute for cutting time in element 7 is therefore not applied to total cutting time on the turret lathe.

For element 8, the handling time on the turret lathe of 0.13 minute can be performed during the cutting time of 0.14 minute for element 5.

For element 3, center drill, feed is by hand and machine time is not calculated. Instead, a value is obtained for "spot drill or center 0.15 minute" from Fig. 20-1.

The setup time on the lathe was calculated from the following elements:

Check-in on job	1.00 min
Study blueprint	1.00
Trip to tool crib	5.00
Handle 8 tools at 0.4 min	3.20
Handle 4 measuring instruments at 0.4 minute	1.60
Install chuck	3.00
Total	14.80 min

Teardown and cleanup consists of these elements:

Sign out	1.00 min
Remove and clean 8 tools at 0.3 min	2.40
Clean 4 measuring instruments at 0.4 min	1.60
Total	5.00 min

The setup time on the turret lathe is estimated in the same way but is larger than for the lathe because elements must be included to mount the tools, adjust them, and set the stops to get the cuts to size.

This estimate does not include time for personal needs of the operator, changing tools, delays, etc. In a comparison between machines, the time for such items usually can be expected to be about the same for both machines and often is ignored. One way to include it is to allow a fixed amount for each hour. Thus the productive hour may be considered to consist of only 50 minutes, for example.

minutes per piece on the engine lathe but only 348 total minutes or 3.48 minutes per piece on the turret lathe. If the labor and overhead rates and capital costs are nearly the same on both machines, and they usually are for two machines like these, the comparison of the operation times tells which machine is more economical for a required number of pieces. This comparison bears out the principle that the engine lathe is usually economical for a few pieces, but for larger numbers the turret lathe shows lower costs.

Finding the Lowest Cost for an Operation.   Commonly, an operation can be done on two or more machines. One calls for a smaller investment; another may do the job faster. Often the problem is to find which alternative promises the lowest cost to make a definite quantity of pieces. In that case, the amounts of direct costs, applicable indirect costs, and fixed or capital cost are computed for each alternative for the quantity of parts required.

Some of the fixed costs for an operation are for standard machines and tools that can be used fully for other work as well. Those costs are charged to each job in proportion to the amount of use of the assets on the job. Other fixed costs are for special machines and tools that have no use other than for the one job; they must be charged entirely to that job.

The costs of interest, insurance, and taxes are neglected in this presentation. This simplifies calculations and does not cause appreciable difference in relative costs. Some methods of analysis that are more refined take these factors into account and are recommended for advanced study.

An example of calculations for a job that can be done satisfactorily in four ways is given by Table 20-2. The single-spindle automatic machine offers the lowest total cost for the required quantity of 1000 pieces in 10 lots. It is assumed that no more than 1000 pieces will be made, and thus all the special tools are charged to this one job. If there were prospects of repeating the job, the special tooling cost might be prorated in some other way. The cost of the standard machines and tools is distributed on an hourly basis over the life of the equipment and 2000 hr/yr during which the facilities are expected to be engaged with other work as well as this. The computed hourly rate for use of the standard equipment is added to the rates for labor and applicable overhead to make up the composite hourly rate.

Equal Cost Point.   In the comparison of two machine tools, the equal cost or break-even point for an operation is at the quantity at which the total and unit costs are the same for both machines. The machine with the smaller fixed cost is the more economical for a smaller quantity, and the other for a larger quantity. A typical situation of this sort is shown in Fig. 20-3.

An equal cost or break-even point analysis is useful for appraising prospects in many cases. If a preliminary study is being made, the demand for the product may not be known exactly. The equal cost point may be compared with various possible quantities of output to ascertain which machine is preferable for each quantity. Even if a definite production quantity is specified, it may be compared with the equal cost

TABLE 20-2 COMPARISON OF MACHINE COSTS

	Ram-type turret lathe		Single-spindle automatic with proper tooling	Multispindle automatic with proper tooling
	With standard tools	With special tooling		
Cost of machine ($)	19,000.00	19,000.00	41,500.00	54,650.00
Cost of standard tools ($)	4,469.50	319.00	3,500.00	3,500.00
Total cost of standard items ($)	23,469.50	19,319.00	45,000.00	58,150.00
Setup time, estimated (hr)	2.5	2.5	3.5	6.0
Cost of special tools ($)	1,190.00	10,850.00	1,650.00	3,000.00
Operation time per piece, estimated (min)	6.5	4.0	3.0	1.0
Production per 50-minute hour (pcs/hr)	7.69	12.5	16.67	50.0
Annual depreciation on 15-yr basis of standard items ($/yr)	1,564.63	1,287.93	3,000.00	3,876.67
Over 2000 hr/yr—depreciation ($/hr)	0.782	0.644	1.500	1.938
Composite rate ($/hr)[a]	17.28	17.14	14.25	14.69
Total setup cost per lot ($)[b]	43.20	42.85	63.00	110.64
Cost per piece, without setup and special tools ($/pc)	2.25	1.37	0.86	0.29
Analysis for 1000 pieces in 10 lots of 100 pieces per lot				
Direct costs ($)	2,250.00	1,370.00	860.00	290.00
Setup for 10 lots ($)	432.00	428.50	630.00	1,106.40
Special tools ($)	1,190.00	10,850.00	1,650.00	3,000.00
Total cost for 1000 pieces ($)	3,872.00	12,648.50	3,140.00	4,396.40

Note: For simplicity, interest, insurance, and taxes are not included.

[a]Labor rate is $7.50/hr on hand turret lathe but is $3.75/hr on automatic where one person attends to two machines. Overhead rate (not including depreciation) is $9.00/hr.

[b]Labor rate is $7.50/hr for setup time on all machines.

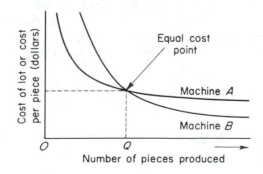

Figure 20-3 Typical equal cost situation.

quantity to find out how much change in the quantity of output will change the advantage from one machine to the other.

Let Q stand for the number of pieces produced at the equal cost point for two machine tools, A and B. Subscripts A and B indicate the following factors applicable to each machine.

P_A or P_B = number of pieces produced per hour.
S_A or S_B = number of hours of setup and tear down.
L_A or L_B = labor rate, in \$/hr.
O_A or O_B = overhead rate, in \$/hr (not including machine depreciation).
E_A or E_B = cost of special tools and equipment chargeable to the job, in dollars.
D_A or D_B = depreciation rate on standard items, in \$/hr.
R_A or R_B = composite rate = $L + O + D$.

For the equal cost quantity,

$$\left(\frac{Q}{P_A} + S_A\right)(L_A + O_A + D_A) + E_A = \left(\frac{Q}{P_B} + S_B\right)(L_B + O_B + D_B) + E_B$$

or

$$\left(\frac{Q}{P_A} + S_A\right)R_A + E_A = \left(\frac{Q}{P_B} + S_B\right)R_B + E_B$$

The left side is the cost of producing Q pieces on machine A, which for the equal cost quantity must equal the cost for Q pieces on machine B, represented by the right side. The solution for the equal cost quantity is

$$Q = \frac{P_A P_B (S_B R_B + E_B - S_A R_A - E_A)}{P_B R_A - P_A R_B} \tag{20-1}$$

It must be emphasized that only the costs that actually do change from one machine to the other should be included in the overhead rates O_A and O_B. For instance, it is not likely that there is going to be any difference in the salaries of the officers of the company whether one machine or another is used for an operation, and the cost is irrelevant.

As an example, Eq. (20-1) may be applied to the case described in Table 20-1, for which the rate of production is 11.52 pieces per 50-minute hour on the engine lathe and 18.69 pieces on the turret lathe. Assume the composite rate to be \$18/hr on the engine lathe and \$20/hr on the turret lathe. No special equipment is required for either machine. Then

$$Q = \frac{11.52 \times 18.69(1.33 \times 20 - 0.33 \times 18)}{18.69 \times 18 - 11.52 \times 20} = 42 \text{ pieces}$$

Thus the engine lathe is the more economical for lots of up to 42 pieces, and the turret lathe for larger lots.

The operation described by Table 20-2 may also be studied by an equal cost point analysis. The single-spindle automatic in this case is more economical than the turret lathe with special tooling at any level of production. That is because the single-spindle automatic not only produces faster but also has a lower composite rate and tooling cost than the special tooling setup on the turret lathe. On the other hand, the single-spindle automatic produces faster but requires more tooling and setup cost than the turret lathe with standard tools. Accordingly, when tooled simply, the turret lathe is the more economical for a few pieces.

Equation (20-1) tells the number of pieces for the equal cost point for the turret lathe with standard tools and the single-spindle automatic. At this level

$$Q = \frac{7.69 \times 16.67(3.5 \times 18 + 1650 - 2.5 \times 17.28 - 1190)}{16.67 \times 17.28 - 7.69 \times 14.25} = 345 \text{ pieces}$$

Thus 345 pieces will justify the extra special tool cost of the single-spindle automatic with one lot. For more pieces in a lot, the single-spindle automatic is preferred. The equal cost point for the multiple- and single-spindle automatic is

$$Q = \frac{50 \times 16.67(6.0 \times 18.44 + 3000 - 3.5 \times 18 - 1650)}{50 \times 14.25 - 16.67 \times 14.69} = 2491 \text{ pieces}$$

The multiple-spindle automatic should be chosen for more than 2491 pieces.

Special Considerations. Equation (20-1) may be used to find the equal cost quantity when a special machine is involved, but care must be exercised to assign the factors their correct values. This may be illustrated by assuming that machine B can be utilized to make the part under consideration, but that there is no other work that can be put on it.

One case arises when machine A is the turret lathe with standard tools and can be kept busy when not on this job. Machine B is the single-spindle automatic and has no use other than for this job. In that case, the value of the special tools and equipment E_B includes $45,000 + $1650 = $46,650. The composite rate is $12.75 instead of $14.25 because it includes only labor and overhead without any depreciation. The setup rate may be considered the same or even neglected because no changeover is required and setup time is small. In this case

$$Q = \frac{7.69 \times 16.67(3.5 \times 16.50 + 46650 - 2.5 \times 17.28 - 1190)}{16.67 \times 17.28 - 7.69 \times 12.75}$$

$$= 30{,}680 \text{ pieces}$$

Another comparison is that of the standard turret lathe with special tools and the single-spindle automatic that can be used only for this job. For that case

$$Q = \frac{12.5 \times 16.67(3.5 \times 16.50 + 46650 - 2.5 \times 17.14 - 10850)}{16.67 \times 17.14 - 12.5 \times 12.75}$$

$$= 59{,}066 \text{ pieces}$$

A comparison of the turret lathe with special tooling and the multiple-spindle automatic, also considered a special machine, shows an equal cost quantity

$$Q = \frac{12.5 \times 50(6 \times 16.50 + 61150 = 2.5 \times 17.14 - 10850)}{50 \times 17.14 - 12.5 \times 12.75}$$

$$= 45,114 \text{ pieces}$$

These comparisons indicate that under the circumstances the turret lathe with standard tools is the economical choice for a small quantity, the turret lathe with special tools is economical for moderate quantities, and the multiple-spindle automatic is preferable for any quantity over 45,114 pieces. The single-spindle automatic does not seem to have a place in this situation. Before, when all the machines were considered standard, the turret lathe with special tooling was not found to be economical, and the single-spindle automatic was the choice for medium lot sizes.

A Rule of Thumb.   A leading manufacturer of both manual turret lathes and automatics has proposed simplifying assumptions for Eq. (20-1) for average conditions based upon extensive experience. They are that factory overhead except for machine depreciation is really not appreciably different for the two types of machines and should be omitted, the cost of special tools and equipment is the same for either type, setup time of the automatic averages three times as long as that of the hand operated turret lathe, and hourly production is on the average three times as much on the automatic as on the turret lathes. On the basis of these assumptions, with a labor rate for setup and operation of $10.00/hr for both types of machines and hourly depreciation of $2.80 for hand turret lathes and $8.00 for automatics, the equal cost quantity is

$$\frac{3P_A^2(3S_s \times 18 - S_A \times 12.80)}{3P_A \times 12.80 - P_A \times 18} = 6S_A P_A$$

A turret lathe should be selected for any lot size up to this amount, and an automatic for any larger quantity when the conditions are applicable.

QUESTIONS

1. Is the general-purpose machine tool with a size capacity just large enough usually selected for a workpiece? Why?
2. What should the size capacity of a special- or single-purpose machine tool be in relation to the size of part it is intended to handle?
3. What kinds of pieces are machined on vertical lathes or boring mills?
4. What is one method of estimating the power required for an operation?
5. Why is the power at the motor of a machine tool likely to be considerably higher than that estimated at the tool point?
6. Is it permissible to overload a machine tool?
7. What are some particular considerations important in machine tool selection?

8. How are labor and overhead costs usually calculated?

9. Into what four parts may the time to perform an operation be divided? Describe these parts.

10. What is the basic relationship for calculating cutting time?

11. How do the engine lathe and turret lathe compare as far as quantity of production is concerned? Why?

12. What does an equal cost point show in the comparison of two machine tools?

PROBLEMS

1. Calculate the cutting time for the starter pinion gear blank shown in Fig. 20-4. Assume a cutting speed of 60 m/min (200 fpm) for cemented carbide tools and 18 m/min (60 fpm) for high-speed steel tools (except for reaming). Barstock size is 65 mm ($2\frac{1}{2}$ in.).

2. Estimate the total cycle time to turn out of the gear blanks of Fig. 20-4 on a 14-in. engine lathe with a 5.6-kW ($7\frac{1}{2}$-hp) motor.

3. Estimate the total cycle time to turn out one of the gear blanks of Fig. 20-4 on a No. 5 ram-type turret lathe with a 7.5-kW (10-hp) motor.

4. It is estimated that it takes 21 minutes to set up and tear down and 10 minutes for each piece like Fig. 20-4 on a 14-in. engine lathe. Setup and teardown is estimated to be 85 minutes, and each piece takes 6 minutes on a No. 5 turret lathe. The rate for labor and overhead is $16/hr on both machines. No special tools are required.
   (a) What is the equal cost quantity for the two machines?
   (b) Calculate the cost for each machine to produce (1) 5 pieces; (2) 10 pieces; (3) 25 pieces; (4) 50 pieces.

5. For the operation of the ram-type turret lathe with standard tools and the same machine with special tooling described in Table 20-2, calculate the following.
   (a) The equal cost quantity for the two machines.
   (b) The cost for each machine to produce (1) 1000 pieces in one lot; (2) 5000 pieces total in 25 lots; (3) 10,000 pieces total in 10 lots; (4) 15,000 pieces total in 150 lots.

6. If the part shown in Fig. 20-4 is made on a No. 5 ram-type turret lathe with standard tools, setup time is 85 minutes and the cycle time 6 minutes per piece. The machine costs $30,000 and tools $5000, depreciated over a 15-yr period and 2000 hr/yr. Labor rate is $8/hr and overhead (not including depreciation) is $8/hr. If $4000 of special tools are applied to the job, the cost of standard tools is reduced to $2500, and the time per piece to 5 minutes. Setup time is not changed.
   (a) Calculate the equal cost quantity for the two options on the basis of a 50-minute hour.
   (b) Calculate the cost for each option to produce (1) 1000 pieces total in 10 lots; (2) 5000 pieces total in 25 lots; (3) 10,000 pieces total in 10 lots; (4) 15,000 pieces total in 100 lots.

7. The part shown in Fig. 20-4 can be made on a $2\frac{1}{2}$-in.-capacity single-spindle automatic bar machine in 4.5 minutes, at the rate of 11.1 pieces in a 50-minute hour. The machine costs $40,000 and standard tools $2700, depreciated over a 15-yr period and 2000 hr/yr. Special tools cost $1200. Setup time is 3 hours. The labor rate on setup is $8/hr, but otherwise is $4/hr because one operator attends more than one machine. The overhead rate except for depreciation is $8/hr. This machine can be used for other work whenever it is not busy with the job.

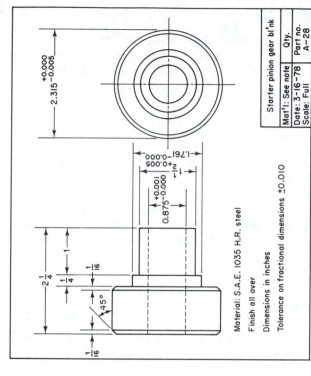

Material: S.A.E. 1035 H.R. steel

Finish all over

Dimensions in inches

Tolerance on fractional dimensions ±0.010

Starter pinion gear bl'nk	
Mat'l: See note	Qty.
Date: 3-16-78	Part no.
Scale: Full	A-28

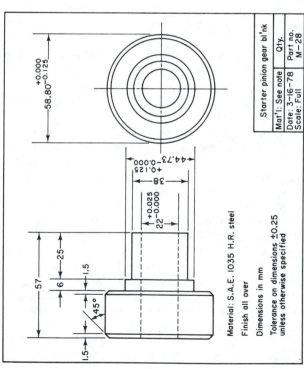

Material: S.A.E. 1035 H.R. steel

Finish all over

Dimensions in mm

Tolerance on dimensions ±0.25
unless otherwise specified

Starter pinion gear bl'nk	
Mat'l: See note	Qty.
Date: 3-16-78	Part no.
Scale: Full	M-28

Figure 20-4 Starter pinion-gear blank.

564

(a) Calculate the cost of the operation on this machine for a quantity of (1) 500 pieces total in 10 lots; (2) 1000 pieces total in 2 lots; (3) 1500 pieces total in 15 lots; (4) 3000 pieces total in 100 lots.

(b) What is the equal cost quantity for the single-spindle automatic and the turret lathe with standard tooling for which costs are given in Prob. 6?

(c) What is the equal cost quantity for the single-spindle automatic and the turret lathe with special tooling for which costs are given in Prob. 6?

8. If the single-spindle automatic bar machine described in Prob. 7 has no use other than for this part,

(a) What is the equal cost quantity to justify use of the single-spindle automatic in preference to the hand-operated turret lathe with standard tooling of Prob. 6?

(b) What is the equal cost quantity to justify the use of the single-spindle automatic in preference to the hand turret lathe with special tooling of Prob. 6?

9. The part shown in Fig. 20-4 can be made on a 67-mm ($2\frac{5}{8}$-in.) capacity six-spindle automatic bar machine in 1.5 minutes. The machine costs $85,000 and standard tools $10,000, depreciated over a 15-year period and 2000 hr/yr. Special tools cost $7200. Setup time is 7 hours. The labor rate for set up is $8/hr, but otherwise is $4/hr because one operator attends more than one machine. The overhead rate, except for depreciation, is $8/hr. The machine can be used for other work when it is not busy with this job.

(a) What is the equal cost quantity for the six-spindle automatic and the turret lathe with special tooling for which costs are given in Prob. 6?

(b) What is the equal cost quantity for the six-spindle automatic and the single-spindle automatic described in Prob. 7?

10. If the six-spindle automatic bar machine described in Prob. 9 cannot be used for other work, what quantity must be produced on it to justify its selection?

REFERENCES

ASTME, *Manufacturing Planning and Estimating Handbook*, McGraw-Hill, New York, 1963.

EARY, D. F., and G. E. JOHNSON, *Process Engineering for Manufacturing*, Prentice-Hall, Englewood Cliffs, N.J., 1962.

IRESON, W. G., and E. L. GRANT, eds., *Handbook of Industrial Engineering and Management*, Prentice-Hall, Englewood Cliffs, N.J., 1971.

21

PRINCIPLES OF MACHINE TOOL DESIGN

All machine tools serve a common purpose, to cut and form materials, and all are dependent upon certain principles. These principles govern the designs that enable the machine tools to:

1. Produce precise results repeatedly
2. Apply forces and power as required
3. Do their work in an economical manner

The principles in each of these areas and the ways they are applied are discussed in this chapter. All of the practical designs that carry out the principles cannot be illustrated in the space available, but typical and basic ones will be described. Readers will then be in a position to recognize the applications of the principles as they observe and study various types of machine tools. The principles and applications cited here are common to most machine tools. Others of more limited scope will be brought out in connection with the machine to which they pertain.

PRECISION

Modern machine tools are marvels of near perfection. Consider a lathe producing round pieces to a tolerance of 50 μm (0.002 in.). That is expected performance; yet it means that the machine maintains a relationship between a whirling workpiece and gliding tool within 25 μm (0.001 in.) on a side and does it over and over again. That dimension is less than half the thickness of a human hair.

To turn to a tolerance of 25 μm (0.001 in.) on a side, the tool first must be adjusted to within 12.5 μm (0.0005 in.) of exact size. Such a minute amount can scarcely be seen, and the machine has to magnify it to reveal it to the crude vision of the operator. Then as metal is slashed away with tremendous force at varying depth, the machine must guide the tool along a firm course and hold the workpiece steady so that neither deviates from the other by more than 12.5 μm (0.0005 in.)—and this is not close work. Tolerances smaller than 2.5 μm (0.0001 in.) are held in some operations.

Errors in the work done by a machine tool are caused by (1) inaccuracy in its construction, (2) deflection, (3) wear, (4) thermal expansion, (5) dirt, and (6) human laxity. Good design and operation of a machine tool depend upon observing principles that keep errors small. Evidences of these principles are found in the structural members, the bearings and guideways for straight and rotary motions, the measuring devices, and the standards of construction of all good machine tools.

Design for control of errors is especially important for automated machine tools, such as for numerical control, than for simpler manual machines, where the operator can compensate for errors.

Structural Members. An evident feature of all major machine tool members is rigidity. This is illustrated by the view of the base or bed for a planer in Fig. 21-1. The same general characteristics of deep and well-braced sections are found in other

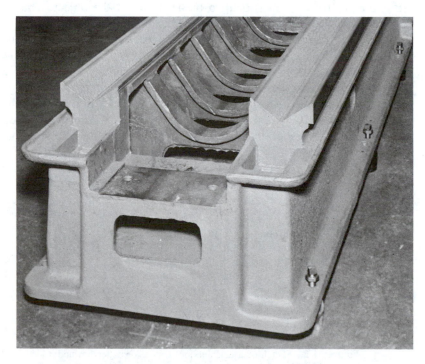

Figure 21-1 Planer bed. (Courtesy Ex-Cell-O Manufacturing Systems Co.)

units. The components of standard machine tools made in lots are most often cast, but some, and especially special units, are built up by welding steel plates and sections together.

One purpose of rigidity in machine tool design is to keep deflections small and maintain true alignments. The principles of mechanics show that deflection of a machine member is inversely proportional to the cube of its depth in the direction of an applied load. For that reason, a machine tool section is deep in the direction of the main force and heavily ribbed and wide to take other forces and moments. Ribs and walls must be properly placed and proportioned. A series of tests on a machine tool base like the one in Fig. 21-2 revealed that deflections for the full depth ribbed base were one-third of those for the partially ribbed base. In other words, rigidity increased three times. Furthermore, a plate affixed to the bottom along with full-depth ribs increased total rigidity about tenfold.

Machine tool components are designed not only to be rigid, but to have the most rigidity with the least possible weight. One obvious reason is that a machine has to be moved, at least from where it is made to where it is used. A second reason is that rigidity with small mass avoids vibration, and raises machine productivity. A third reason is that moving components are more easily and thus accurately controlled with less inertia, of particular importance in automatic control.

For a simple case, any object with a single degree of freedom has a natural frequency in cycles per second of $W_n = \sqrt{k/m}$. The factor m is the mass of the structure, and k is proportional to the stiffness of the object. Thus the stiffer the member and the less its mass, the higher is its natural frequency.

A high natural frequency is desirable because it is less excited by the usual disturbances. As has been pointed out (page 464), metal cutting is inherently cyclic and vibratory. It tends to induce vibrations in machine tools and to cause chatter. Vibrations may also be set up by other actions, such as the running of gears and external disturbances. The further the natural frequency of a machine member is from the exciting frequency, the smaller the intensity is of the vibration induced in the member. For the best effect, the natural frequency should be higher than the induced

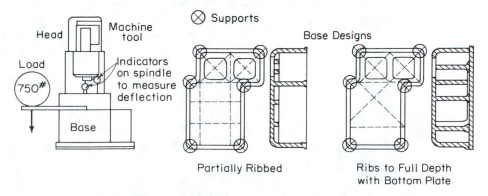

Figure 21-2 Sketch of a machine tool tested for deflection under load, with two designs of different rigidity for its base.

frequency. Thus if a machine member is to be least susceptible to vibration, its structure should be as rigid and as light in weight as possible. This explains why machine tool members are designed like the bed of Fig. 21-1 with thin deep sections, adequate cross ribbing, and many hollow spaces.

Stiffness can be increased and natural frequency raised by making a member shorter, supporting it more fully, or making it from stiffer material. The first two means are illustrated by the gap and straight-side types of press frames in Fig. 13-23. Similar shapes are found in drill presses, lathes, jig borers, etc. The C-type frame provides accessibility but tends to open when operating forces are applied in the gap. Closed-type frames are more rigid because top and bottom members are connected at both sides. As for the third factor, gray cast iron traditionally has been the material used for most machine tool members. However, steel is stronger and stiffer and can be fabricated in thinner and deeper sections for the same weight.

Dampening capacity is important in a machine tool because it absorbs the energy and reduces the amplitude of vibrations. Cast iron has good dampening qualities; the interactions of its constituents absorb vibrational energy. Steel must be loaded to high stresses to have equal or better dampening capacity, but it can sustain the necessary stresses. Kronenberg reported tests of a cast-iron lathe bed that showed excessive vibrations between 60 and 180 Hz at machine spindle speeds from 20 to 600 rpm. A comparable steel bed vibrated excessively only between 90 and 120 Hz, corresponding to speeds of 300 to 400 rpm. Thus when it is not possible to raise the natural frequency of the machine above induced frequencies, proper steel construction can narrow the range.

Much more dampening capacity (even 10 times as much) can be obtained from tight joints, large surfaces between components firmly bolted or edge-welded together, than from the internal structure of material. When such surfaces in joints rub together, they absorb vibrational energy. As an example, a beam fabricated of two bars, one on top of the other, fastened tightly at the ends showed 64 times as much dampening capacity as a solid beam of the same size.

Bearings and Guideways.   Straight-line motion in a true path is obtained from most machine tools by having precisely finished guideways of one member slide along those of another member. A way may be flat or vee shaped; the latter acts as a guide in two directions. A table will slide on the two vee ways on top of the planer bed of Fig. 21-1. End views of vee and flat ways are shown at (A) and (B) in Fig. 21-3. A vee has the advantage of not becoming loose as wear takes place but may ride up a little on the side with a large side thrust. The ways so far described are limited to horizontal movements. Two types suited for vertical mounting are shown at (C) and (D) in Fig. 21-3. Looseness is taken up in a slide of that sort by tapered adjustable inserts called *gibs*. Most ways have been cut in cast iron, but in recent years the trend has been toward hardened steel inserts or flame hardening of alloy cast iron or cast steel. A few heavy machine tools have plastic inserts for ways. Chips embed in these and do not cause severe scoring.

Machine tools slide at low speeds and lack hydrodynamic oil films. As a result, slides are subject to wear and a stick-slip condition that makes accurate control

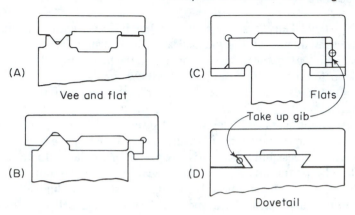

(A)

Vee and flat

(B)

(C)

Flats

Take up gib

(D)

Dovetail

Figure 21-3   End views of several types of ways or slides.

difficult. Antifriction ball and roller and hydrostatic bearing ways (for high rigidity under heavy loads) are put on many machines, particularly for numerical control. Such ways are costly.

Movements along precise paths are obtained from machine tool ways because the ways themselves are true. Hardened ways are ground. Soft-cast-iron ways are machined and then hand scraped to desired straightness, alignment, and bearing by comparing and matching them with master surfaces and fitting them to each other.

True plane surfaces are painstakingly developed. Two pieces B and C in Fig. 21-4 may have surfaces matching piece A, but will not match each other unless all three surfaces are true planes. Straight edges and surface plates are made originally on this principle in sets of three. They are compared, after being machined, by coating them lightly with red lead or Prussian blue and rubbing them together. High spots that show contact are removed by selectively hand scraping away minute amounts of metal. This leaves other high spots. This process is repeated until enough high spots are obtained on each surface to simulate true planes. Stone plates are ground and lapped together. Surfaces precisely at right angle may be obtained in a similar way. Master surfaces made in these ways are the references for making true machine slides.

Machine Tool Looseness.   Because of the looseness that must exist between sliding members, more than elastic deflection takes place in machine tools. If a force in the positive direction of Fig. 21-5 is applied to a machine tool member in a neutral position, a movement is found to take place as represented by line OA. When the force

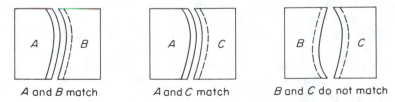

A and B match   A and C match   B and C do not match

Figure 21-4   Two surfaces that match a third will not match each other unless they are all true flat planes.

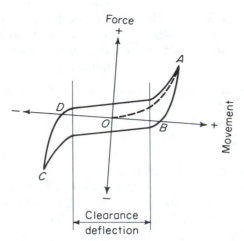

Figure 21-5 Representation of deflection of machine tool members.

is released, the member does not return to point O, but rather to point B. A negative force can be expected to cause a negative movement to point C, and so on. With slides free enough for feeding and adjusting a member, deflection movements under normal loads may amount to a fraction of a thousandth to several thousandths of an inch. Comparable movements in the form of vibrations and chatter can be expected to occur from varying applied forces.

Universal and general-purpose machine tools usually have many slides and adjustable members. As a result they lack some rigidity and are not capable of taking cuts as heavy and fast as special-purpose and high-production machines, which are designed with as few connections as possible for sturdiness but are limited in flexibility and are harder to adjust.

Even though the ways on the base or bed of a machine tool are made straight and parallel, they will become untrue if the structure is placed on an uneven foundation and allowed to sag. This is particularly true of large and long machines like planers, but all machines need to be well supported. The bed of Fig. 21-1 has leveling jack screws at intervals along each side at the bottom, which is typical. The bed is intended to stand on these leveling screws. Leveling is done with a precision spirit level applied to finished surfaces along and across the ways. The straightness of a long bed may be checked by stretching a wire lengthwise and sighting along the wire with a microscope mounted on a bracket guided by the ways. Alignments may be checked most precisely by optical tooling, as described in Chap. 15.

Spindles.   The members that revolve workpieces or cutters on machine tools are called *spindles*. They have to be sturdy and well supported in true bearings to avoid deflection and runout as much as possible. In recent years the trend has been away from sleeve-type sliding bearings except in heavy service where the highest degree of accuracy is required. Thus, large grinding wheel spindles mostly run in sliding bearings, although they usually are some form of rocker shoe type rather than plain sleeve bearings. Most machine tool spindles today run in antifriction bearings. Roller bearings, usually tapered, are used for heavy service at low and moderate speeds. A typical spindle design is shown in Fig. 21-6. Ball bearings run freely, stand up at high speeds, and are favored for light service. For the highest precision, ball bearings are preloaded and selected in matched sets to minimize runout. Pressurized gas journal bearings of high rigidity with low friction are used for high spindle speeds.

Accurate Measurement. A simple and common way of precisely setting the position of a slide on a machine tool is through a screw and nut. A plain cross screw for a lathe is illustrated in Fig. 21-7. This screw is attached to the carriage and restrained from moving lengthwise but is free to turn in bearings. The nut shown on the screw is fastened to the cross-slide and moves along as the screw is turned. On the left end of the screw is the hand wheel and the micrometer dial, normally graduated to indicate 25-μm or 0.001-in. increments. The screw is also the means to feed the cross-slide by power, as evidenced by the pinion in the middle of the shaft. An improved device is the circulating ball screw and nut (with balls engaging threads of both screw and nut); a typical set may have an accumulated error of less than 8 μm/m (0.0001 in./ft) and a power transmission efficiency of 85 to 95%.

When in good condition and properly used, a micrometer lead screw on a good quality machine tool can be expected to indicate increments of movement corresponding to the dial graduations. However, necessary clearance between screw and nut, wear, and deflection can cause a reading on a micrometer dial to differ appreciably from an actual movement. To correct for the looseness, or *backlash* as it is called, an operator always makes sure that the dial is turned in the same direction at the end of an adjustment as it was turned to reach the starting point. It is not so easy to compensate for backlash in automatic machines, such as with numerical control. A common but expensive way to eliminate backlash is to preload two nuts (usually

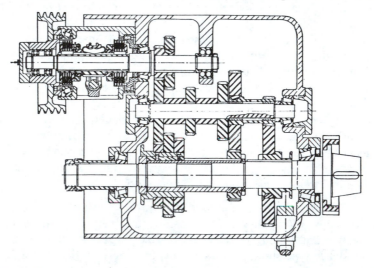

Figure 21-6 Layout of an all-geared headstock for a lathe. The sliding gears on the spindle, at bottom, and pulley shaft are shifted by three levers on the outside of the headstock to give 12 spindle speeds. (Courtesy Ex-Cell-O Manufacturing Systems Co.)

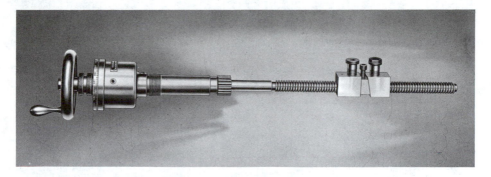

Figure 21-7 Cross screw with nut and micrometer dial for a lathe. (Courtesy American Tool, subsidiary of White Cons. Ind.)

circulating ball nuts to reduce friction and binding) acting in unison to maintain contact with both sides of the thread of the leadscrew.

Scales are also used to measure machine movements. Older machines had directly read vernier scales, sometimes through microscopes. A growing trend is to read scales electronically and display the movement digitally or utilize the reading as feedback in numerical control. A digital readout system (DRO) for a machine tool is activated by the fringes that occur as one fine scale passes over another, with light rays cast through the scales. The principle has been explained for the coordinate measuring system of Fig. 15-34(A). Each fringe creates an electronic pulse for a certain increment of movement, and the pulses are counted. Also, interferometry, described in Chap. 15, is used for the finest measurements of machine tool movements.

Thermal Distortion. Machine tool members get hot during operation, and the temperature rise is not uniform as a rule. This means that some members expand more than others, and alignments and settings change. This is most noticeable during the first two hours of operation of a machine tool, and usually conditions become stable after equilibria of temperatures are reached. An example is cited by Kronenberg of a turret lathe running at 1000 rpm. During the first hour the temperature rose about 17°C (30°F) in the headstock, and the spindle moved 50 μm (0.002 in.) upward and 180 μm (0.007 in.) sideward. During the second hour, spindle movements were 10 μm (0.0004 in.) up and 2.5 μm (0.0001 in.) to the side. Room temperature change also has an affect; a day-to-night temperature difference of 4.5°C (8°F) is reported to have caused a large vertical tracer lathe to drift by 80 μm (0.003 in.). A skilled operator can do much to compensate for temperature changes, but the problem is more difficult with automatic systems.

Heat sources that cause distortion may be in the environment, the fabricating or cutting process and in the machine elements, such as bearings, motors, etc. An obvious remedy is air-conditioning the room, or chilling coolant and oil, and flooding the work area. Machines for precision operations may be turned on well before starting time in a plant and kept running during breaks and lunch periods. A heat source, such as a motor, may be moved from inside to outside of a machine. Good machine design takes heat distortion into account, in such ways as providing adequately for heat

TEST — RECOMMENDED STANDARDS

TEST	Tool Room Lathes	12" to 18" incl. Engine Lathes	20" to 36" incl. Engine Lathes
1 — BED LEVEL – TRANSVERSE DIRECTION	WHEN USING PRECISION LEVEL, BOTH READINGS TO BE WITHIN .0005 IN 12 INCHES	WHEN USING PRECISION LEVEL, BOTH READINGS TO BE WITHIN .0005 IN 12 INCHES	WHEN USING PRECISION LEVEL, BOTH READINGS TO BE WITHIN .001 IN 12 INCHES
2 — BED LEVEL – LONGITUDINAL DIRECTION	WHEN USING PRECISION LEVEL ALONG BED MAXIMUM READING TO BE WITHIN .0005 IN 12 INCHES	WHEN USING PRECISION LEVEL ALONG BED MAXIMUM READING TO BE WITHIN .0005 IN 12 INCHES	WHEN USING PRECISION LEVEL ALONG BED MAXIMUM READING TO BE WITHIN .001 IN 12 INCHES
3 — TAILSTOCK WAY ALIGNMENT	MAXIMUM READING ALONG LENGTH OF BED .0005 IN 48 INCHES	MAXIMUM READING ALONG LENGTH OF BED .00075 IN 48 INCHES	MAXIMUM READING ALONG LENGTH OF BED .001 IN 48 INCHES
4 — SPINDLE CENTER RUNOUT	TOTAL INDICATOR READING 0 TO .0004	TOTAL INDICATOR READING 0 TO .0005	TOTAL INDICATOR READING 0 TO .00075
5 — SPINDLE NOSE RUNOUT	TOTAL INDICATOR READING 0 TO .0003	TOTAL INDICATOR READING 0 TO .0004	TOTAL INDICATOR READING 0 TO .0006
6 — CAM ACTION OF SPINDLE	TOTAL INDICATOR READING WITH INDICATOR ON REAR SIDE OF TEST PLATE 0 TO .0003	TOTAL INDICATOR READING WITH INDICATOR ON REAR SIDE OF TEST PLATE 0 TO .0005	TOTAL INDICATOR READING WITH INDICATOR ON REAR SIDE OF TEST PLATE 0 TO .00075

TEST — RECOMMENDED STANDARDS

TEST	Tool Room Lathes	12" to 18" incl. Engine Lathes	20" to 36" incl. Engine Lathes
7 — SPINDLE TAPER RUNOUT	TOTAL INDICATOR READING AT END OF 12 INCH TEST BAR 0 TO .0006 AT END OF SPINDLE NOSE 0 TO .0003	TOTAL INDICATOR READING AT END OF 12 INCH TEST BAR 0 TO .0008 AT END OF SPINDLE NOSE 0 TO .0004	TOTAL INDICATOR READING AT END OF 12 INCH TEST BAR 0 TO .00125 AT END OF SPINDLE NOSE 0 TO .0006
8 — HEADSTOCK ALIGNMENT – VERTICAL	HIGH AT END OF 12 INCH TEST BAR 0 TO .0005	HIGH AT END OF 12 INCH TEST BAR 0 TO .001	HIGH AT END OF 12 INCH TEST BAR 0 TO .001
9 — HEADSTOCK ALIGNMENT – HORIZONTAL	AT END OF 12 INCH TEST BAR 0 TO ±.0003	AT END OF 12 INCH TEST BAR 0 TO ±.0005	AT END OF 12 INCH TEST BAR 0 TO ±.0008
10 — TAILSTOCK SPINDLE ALIGNMENT – HORIZONTAL	FORWARD AT END OF SPINDLE WHEN FULLY EXTENDED 0 TO .0005	FORWARD AT END OF SPINDLE WHEN FULLY EXTENDED 0 TO .0005	FORWARD AT END OF SPINDLE WHEN FULLY EXTENDED 0 TO .0005
11 — TAILSTOCK SPINDLE ALIGNMENT – VERTICAL	HIGH AT END OF SPINDLE WHEN FULLY EXTENDED 0 TO .0005	HIGH AT END OF SPINDLE WHEN FULLY EXTENDED 0 TO .0008	HIGH AT END OF SPINDLE WHEN FULLY EXTENDED 0 TO .0015
12 — TAILSTOCK TAPER ALIGNMENT – HORIZONTAL	END OF 12 INCH TEST BAR 0 TO ±.0005	END OF 12 INCH TEST BAR 0 TO ±.0008	END OF 12 INCH TEST BAR 0 TO ±.0015

TEST — RECOMMENDED STANDARDS

TEST	Tool Room Lathes	12" to 18" incl. Engine Lathes	20" to 36" incl. Engine Lathes
13 — TAILSTOCK TAPER ALIGNMENT – VERTICAL	HIGH AT END OF 12 INCH TEST BAR 0 TO .0005	HIGH AT END OF 12 INCH TEST BAR 0 TO .0008	HIGH AT END OF 12 INCH TEST BAR 0 TO .0015
14 — VERTICAL ALIGNMENT OF HEAD & TAIL CTRS.	HIGH AT TAILSTOCK 0 TO .0008	HIGH AT TAILSTOCK 0 TO .001	HIGH AT TAILSTOCK 0 TO .0015
15 — LEAD SCREW ALIGNMENT (READINGS FOR BASE LENGTH BED TAKEN WITH LEAD SCREW STATIONARY. ADD .001 INCH FOR EACH ADDITIONAL 4 FEET OF BED LENGTH)	PARALLEL WITH WAYS 0 TO .004 HORIZONTAL 0 TO .004 VERTICAL; ALIGNMENT OF HALF NUT HORIZONTAL OR VERTICAL 0 TO .006	PARALLEL WITH WAYS 0 TO .004 HORIZONTAL 0 TO .004 VERTICAL; ALIGNMENT OF HALF NUT HORIZONTAL OR VERTICAL 0 TO .006	PARALLEL WITH WAYS 0 TO .006 HORIZONTAL 0 TO .006 VERTICAL; ALIGNMENT OF HALF NUT HORIZONTAL OR VERTICAL 0 TO .008
16 — LEAD SCREW CAM ACTION	MAX. .0003	MAX. .0004	MAX. .0005
17 — CROSS SLIDE ALIGNMENT	TO FACE HOLLOW OR CONCAVE ONLY ON 12 INCH DIAMETER 0 TO .0005	TO FACE HOLLOW OR CONCAVE ONLY ON 12 INCH DIAMETER 0 TO .001	TO FACE HOLLOW OR CONCAVE ONLY ON 12 INCH DIAMETER 0 TO .001
18 — FACE PLATE RUN OUT	ON DIAMETER 0 TO .0005 ON FACE AT NOMINAL DIAMETER 0 TO .001	ON DIAMETER 0 TO .0015 ON FACE AT NOMINAL DIAMETER 0 TO .0015	ON DIAMETER 0 TO .0015 ON FACE AT NOMINAL DIAMETER 0 TO .002

TEST — RECOMMENDED STANDARDS

TEST	Tool Room Lathes	12" to 18" incl. Engine Lathes	20" to 36" incl. Engine Lathes
19 — CHUCK – RUN OUT	FACE AND PERIPHERY .003; FACE OF STEPS .003; BAR TEST 3" FROM END OF JAW, BAR DIA. SAME AS HOLE .003	FACE AND PERIPHERY .003; FACE OF STEPS .003; BAR TEST 3" FROM END OF JAW, BAR DIA. SAME AS HOLE .003	FACE AND PERIPHERY .004; FACE OF STEPS .004; BAR TEST 3" FROM END OF JAW, BAR DIA. SAME AS HOLE .004
20 — COLLET CHUCK – RUN OUT	ONE INCH FROM SPINDLE 0 TO .001	ONE INCH FROM SPINDLE 0 TO .001	ONE INCH FROM SPINDLE 0 TO .001
21 — LATHE MUST TURN ROUND WITH WORK MOUNTED IN CHUCK	.0003	.0004	.0008
22 — LATHE MUST TURN CYLINDRICAL WITH WORK MOUNTED IN CHUCK	.0008	.0015	.002
23 — LATHE MUST TURN CYLINDRICAL WITH WORK MOUNTED BETWEEN CENTERS	.0004	.0008	.001
24 — LEAD SCREW – LEAD PER FT. / LEAD IN ANY 4"	±.001 / ±.0004	±.0015 / ±.0005	±.002 / ±.0007
25 — BACK LASH ON CROSS FEED SCREW / ON COMPOUND REST SCREW	.004 / .004	.004 / .004	.005 / .005

Figure 21-8 Standards of accuracy as recommended by the Lathe Group of the National Machine Tool Builders Association.

dissipation, heater elements to maintain working temperatures, and use of low-expansion alloys.

Standards of Construction. The standards of accuracy for engine lathes recognized by most manufacturers are shown in Fig. 21-8. A study of these standards will reveal the alignments and limits held in the construction of good-quality machine tools. The accuracy of a machine tool cannot be represented by one or a few numbers but depends on many measurements. Sheets of test standards like those illustrated are prepared by reputable manufacturers of all kinds of machine tools, and each machine is tested against the standards.

Machine capability tests are run by actually cutting workpieces and measuring the dimensions held. Accuracy may be ascertained by means of process control charts as described in Chap. 15. An important test is for the ability of a machine to put forth full power without chatter and too much deformation.

POWER DRIVES

A primary function of a modern machine tool is to deliver the required power to the metal cutting zone with little or no exertion on the part of an operator. Most modern machines are driven by individual electric motors run at 1200, 1800, or 3600 nominal rpm. Multiple vee belt drives from the motor to the first drive shaft of the machine predominate, although chain drives are found on some heavy equipment.

Two general types of power transmissions to give the speeds and feeds desired in machine tools are (1) mechanical, and (2) hydraulic or pneumatic.

Mechanical Drives. Rotary motion is transmitted predominately by mechanical means for economy and reliability. This is generally through hardened and ground gears for more than fractional horsepower drives, as typified by the lathe headstock design of Fig. 21-6. The gears in that headstock slide into mesh. Another common design has pairs of gears, usually helical, already in mesh and engaged by clutches. The simplest arrangement is to shift gears or engage clutches directly through levers on the outside of the gear case. A faster and more convenient means found on some machines is to select speeds or feeds by setting a single dial or pointer. This shifts the gears or changes motor speeds through hydraulic or electromagnetic means. Also, while the machine is cutting at one speed, the next speed can be preselected.

Speeds are commonly varied in geometrical progression; each speed is multiplied by a constant to get the value of the next higher one. For example, if the lowest speed is 12 rpm and the constant ratio is 1.5, the next speed is $12 \times 1.5 = 18$ rpm, the third speed is 27 rpm, and so on. Thus speeds are always proportional and have small numerical differences in the low ranges. A change-gear speed range may be doubled by using a two-speed motor, etc.

Belts and stepped pulleys are popular for fractional-horsepower drives because they are simple and cheap. Belts are preferred for precision and high-speed drives,

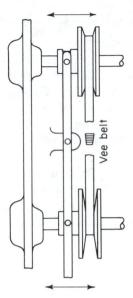

Lever moved to vary pulley widths   **Figure 21-9** Stepless variable-speed
and belt positions   device.

such as in a grinding machine workhead and wheelhead, because they run smoothly, and the slightly uneven action of gears tends to leave marks on fine finished surfaces.

Continuously variable speed or feed rather than adjustments in steps allows the user to discriminate more closely. This may be done mechanically, as illustrated by the stepless variable-speed drive of Fig. 21-9. For electrical means, there is a trend toward dc servo drive motors with silicon-controlled rectifiers (SCR) on such machines as small- to medium-horsepower lathes and machining centers. This gives less noise and maintenance and more power efficiency. By adding gears or belts in the drive, one continuous speed range may be increased to several with a large total range (well over 100 to 1 in some cases).

Three principal types of mechanical devices are used commonly to transform rotary motion to straight line or reciprocating motion. One is the pinion and rack that has been described for the lathe; another is the screw and nut described earlier in this chapter; and the third is the crank that will be described in connection with the mechanical shaper.

Hydraulic Drives.   The advantages offered by hydraulic drives for certain applications are:

1. A hydraulic drive is smooth and reverses without shock. Thus hydraulic drives are found on most reciprocating grinding machine tables because they contribute to good surface finish.
2. A hydraulic drive stops when pressure reaches a preset maximum and tool breakage is less likely than with a mechanical device that surges relentlessly to

the end of its stroke. This is one reason hydraulic drives are preferred for fragile and expensive broaching tools.

3. A hydraulic drive is infinitely variable for speed and feed within its range, and the length and position of stroke it gives are easily adjusted.

4. Faster reverse and acceleration rates are possible with hydraulic drives because of less inertia and the cushioning effect of the fluid. On the other hand, a mechanical drive is easier to reverse accurately, particularly at high and varying speeds and loads.

5. A hydraulic drive can deliver a large amount of power for its size and can be operated continuously at maximum output; this is not as feasible with electric drives. Variable speed or feed is a primary requisite for most machine tools with something near full driving force desirable over the full range.

As a rule, however, hydraulic drives are more expensive to make, operate, and service than mechanical and some electrical drives.

Pumps and Motors. *Positive* and *variable displacement pumps* are the two main types. Positive displacement pumps may be divided into gear, vane or roller, and plunger pumps. The first two are essentially like the gear and vane type motors depicted in Fig. 21-10. A plunger pump consists of one or more pistons reciprocating in cylinders. Variable displacement or delivery pumps may be subdivided into swash plate and radial types similar to the same types of motors in Fig. 21-10 but with means to vary the amount of eccentricity, and thus the displacement.

Rotary hydraulic motors were rather uncommon for machine tool drives until the advent of numerical control for which they provide quicker response and higher gains for leadscrew and spindle drives. The types of hydraulic motors are the turbine, gear, vane, and plunger types. The turbine is widely used for converting water power but has practically no machine tool application. The principles of the other types are illustrated in Fig. 21-10. Each form has many refinements, such as pressure balancing to ease operation, and many variations in actual commercial products.

Linear Drive Systems. Essentially, there are two basic forms of linear hydraulic drives; each has many variations. One is the *throttle type* with a positive-displacement pump, and the other utilizes a variable-displacement pump.

The circuit diagram of Fig. 21-11 is for a system with a pump that delivers a constant volume of oil. As much of the fluid as is needed flows through a reversing valve to one end of the machine table cylinder. The rest of the oil is passed back to the oil tank through the relief valve. As the oil under pressure pushes the piston along to move the table, it forces oil out of the other end of the cylinder through the reversing valve and throttle valve to the tank. The resistance of the variable throttle valve determines the rate of oil flow and the feed rate of the machine table. A combination of two pumps may be used, a large one for rapid rates and a small one for slow feeds.

The circuit in Fig. 21-11 is set for the machine table to move to the right. When the left-hand dog reverses the pilot valve, oil will be admitted to the left end of the reversing valve and will push the plunger of that valve to the right. The oil flow to the

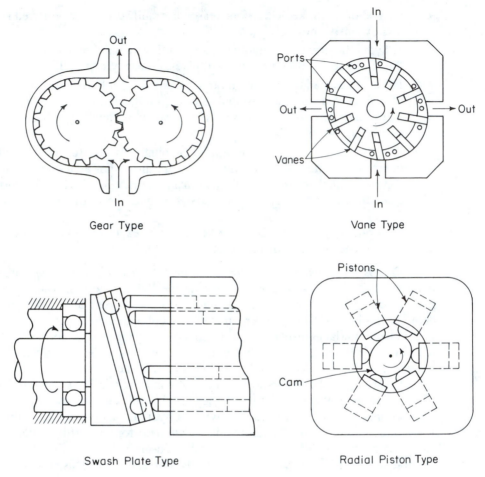

Gear Type

Vane Type

Swash Plate Type

Radial Piston Type

Figure 21-10   Principles of operation for the main types of hydraulic motors.

cylinder will be reversed, and the table will feed to the left. To stop the action altogether, the start-stop valve is opened to allow all the oil from the pump to discharge freely to the tank.

    If the proper components are selected, a circuit of the type shown in Fig. 21-11 can be made to maintain a preset feed rate over most of the range of loads for which it is designed. For light loads, such as driving a grinding machine table, a circuit like that of Fig. 21-11 is adequate and normally used, but it is inefficient from a power standpoint. At other than maximum feed rate, part of the oil is being pumped under pressure through the relief valve, and that energy is wasted.

    A typical circuit utilizing a variable delivery pump is depicted in Fig. 21-12. The amount of oil delivered and the rate of feed are varied by adjusting the pumps. No excess oil is pumped, except for a small amount of slippage and leakage, and this

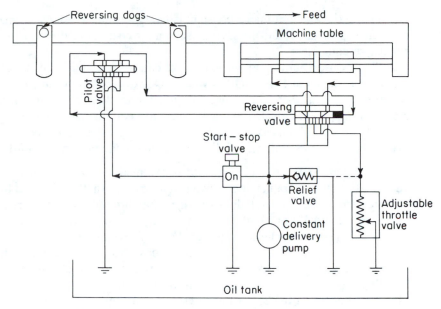

Figure 21-11   Elementary constant-delivery hydraulic system.

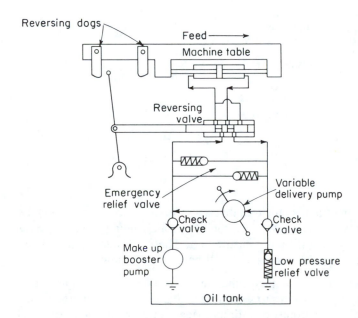

Figure 21-12   Variable-delivery circuit.

system is more efficient than a constant delivery system. Even so, in many cases the difference is not large, and the saving in operating costs alone does not justify the more expensive equipment.

The booster pump puts oil into the circuit to make up for that lost by leakage. The circuit shown in Fig. 21-12 is what is called a *locked circuit,* because the table will feed at the rate set no matter what direction the load is acting on the table. The circuit of Fig. 21-11 can also be made locked to a certain extent, but not as completely under the heaviest loads as the circuit of Fig. 21-12. A fully locked circuit is needed to control heavy cuts and is normally used for hydraulic planers and milling machines.

Pneumatic Drives.   Compressed air is already available in most plants and can be put to work with rather inexpensive equipment. Air flow is fast, but the use of compressed air has several disadvantages that limit it to light service. Pressures available are usually not high. A compressed air system by itself is hard to control because of the compressibility of the air. Feeds or speeds are inclined to vary too much as the load changes and the equipment may not stop and reverse within desired limits.

Air is widely used for work clamping devices and feeding small machines such as drill presses. In the latter capacity, an air-driven but hydraulically controlled circuit like that shown in Fig. 21-13 mitigates some of the shortcomings of air. With the reversing valve in the position shown, air is admitted behind the piston. The spindle advances first at fast rate with the choke valve open. When the cam closes the choke valve, the oil flow from the right cylinder is throttled, and then a slow feed rate is maintained. With the reversing valve plunger moved to the left, the pistons return at a rapid rate because the oil is bypassed through the check valve.

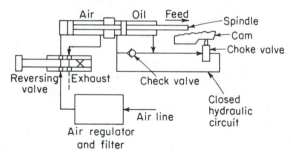

Figure 21-13   Air-hydraulic circuit.

MACHINE TOOL ECONOMY

Major aspects of the design of a machine tool that determines its economy are (1) the operating controls, (2) provisions for safety, (3) facilities for changing jobs, (4) means of maintenance of accuracy, and (5) unit construction. These considerations explain important features of many machine tools and will be discussed now.

Machine Tool Controls.   Essentially, the means for controlling and adjusting a machine tool must enable the operator to work fast with a minimum of fatigue. One way is to eliminate the operator partially or entirely. Means of doing that are explained in connection with automatic machines. However, automatic operation is not warranted for much work, and most machine tools require the full attention of an operator. Even so most machines have power feeds and movements to save effort. Fast movement, called *rapid traverse,* is commonly provided to save time between cuts.

The controls on a well-designed machine tool are arranged so the operator does not have to move or exert himself any more than absolutely necessary. All unnecessary motions are eliminated; the need to move the body about is minimized; necessary motions are kept as short and simple as possible; both hands are kept busy and moving; and motions of the eyes are minimized. The diagram on the left of Fig. 21-14 illustrates that an operator in a fixed position can conveniently make motions within a certain space. The boundaries of the work space have been determined for normal people and are specified in reference texts and handbooks. As indicated by the composite photograph on the right of Fig. 21-14, the controls of a well-designed machine tool are placed within the maximum normal working area.

Short motions are easier and faster than long ones. Thus finger movements are preferable to hand movements, and so on. Accordingly, machine controls should require as short movements as possible consistent with adequate leverage. Sufficient mechanical advantage must be provided because controls must not be hard to move and tiring. Handles should be proportioned to the natural grasp of the operator.

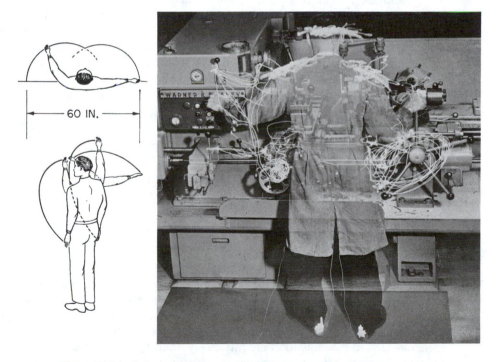

Figure 21-14 Left, a persons's normal working area; right, operator's movements on a well-designed turret lathe are delineated by light paths on a time exposure. (Photo courtesy Warner and Swasey Co.)

The machine operation depicted in Fig. 21-14 requires the continuous use of both hands with only limited body and practically no foot movements. The dial that is set to select speeds is on the headstock near eye level for ready vision.

On some machine tools it is convenient for the operator to take different stations for different kinds of work, and duplicate sets of controls may be provided for convenience. An example of this is seen in general-purpose milling machines that often have controls at the front and on one side behind the table. Limitations in present-day designs make it necessary for the operators to stand when attending most machine tools, although less fatigue is experienced when sitting.

Unfortunately the principles that have been pointed out have been disregarded in machine tool design in too many cases. An understanding of the principles should help a person evaluate and understand the arrangement of controls on any particular machine.

Safety.   Safety is provided on machine tools by:

1. *Safeguarding the point of operation*. If possible, provision should be made so the operators do not need to put their hands into the working areas of tools. For that purpose, mechanical loading devices often are justified for high-production operations. Guards or cages are commonly built around a danger zone (Fig. 13-37). For low production, the operator commonly must reach into the working zone to load workpieces and make adjustments when tools are not cutting. To reduce the danger, provisions may be made so that the machine cannot be started until both hands are withdrawn. One way is to require the operator to depress two buttons or levers at the same time, one with each hand.

2. *Safeguarding controls and machine mechanisms*. Starting levers may be placed up out of the way of ordinary motions or covered by guards so they are not tripped by falling objects. Gear case covers or working area guards may be interlocked with the power source of the machine so the machine will not start when the cover guards are off.

3. *Guarding moving parts and power transmissions*. An evident feature of present-day machines is that covers and guards completely enclose all shafts, belts, gears, etc., largely as a safety precaution.

Changing of Jobs.   In connection with the machine tools of the lathe family, features were described that made engine lathes and even turret lathes easy to change over from one job to another. As an example, speeds and feeds are easy to change. In contrast, it was pointed out that to change speed or feed on an automatic turning machine commonly requires that a cover be removed from a gear case and pick-off gears be changed. This illustrates a basic principle for all types of machine tools. General-purpose machine tools are made easy to change from one job to another, not only in changing speeds and feeds but also in making all necessary adjustments. However, the construction necessary for this restricts the general-purpose machine to being a slower producer than a corresponding special-purpose machine after a set-up has been made.

One reason a general-purpose machine is slow has already been explained. That is because it has more components, is not as rigid, and cannot cut as fast. Another reason a general-purpose machine is a slow producer is that the operator must spend time manipulating the controls and adjustments for each piece. In contrast, an automatic machine may have dogs or cams to govern the actions. Time is required for setup, but once that is done, the machine can get along without the operator's attention.

Accessories and attachments are important adjuncts to adapt machine tools to various jobs and reflect an extension of the design of each machine. Typical adjuncts of this kind are described along with the basic machines.

The tools are normally set to cut to size on a general-purpose machine by making adjustments by means of micrometer dials. Quite commonly with the equipment furnished, on a special-purpose or automatic machine the tools must be set by a cut-and-try procedure, which is slow. Adjustable tool adapters and special presetting gages help to change tools faster. An example of one is given in Fig. 21-15. The drill and adapter are placed in the gage, and the stop collar on the adapter is adjusted to the setting dimension. Then when the drill and adapter are placed on the holder on the machine tool, the stop collar positions the drill to cut to the correct depth with no need to adjust the machine.

Maintenance of Accuracy.   The chief value of a machine tool lies in its accuracy. To preserve this, protection and lubrication of the bearings and guideways are important.

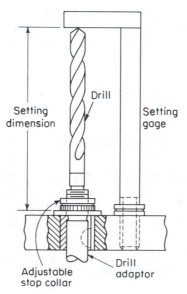

Setting dimension

Drill

Setting gage

Adjustable stop collar

Drill adaptor

Figure 21-15 Gage for presetting a drill in its adapter.

The type of lubrication system used for a machine tool depends upon the need, and often different systems may be used on different parts of a machine. The four most common types of systems are:

1. A fully automatic system, usually a pump continually forcing oil through tubes or holes to the bearings. This is an expensive system but efficient for heavy duty. Examples of its application are in the lubrication of plain sleeve bearings for large grinding wheel spindles and the ways under heavy reciprocating tables. Often such a system is interlocked with the power supply so that the main drive motor will not start until ample lubricating oil is assured to the bearings.

2. Semiautomatic and intermittent systems such as splash, oil ring, and metering arrangements. These generally are moderate in cost and satisfactory for all but severe services.

3. Manual single-shot system, conventionally a hand operated plunger that forces a shot of oil from a reservoir through tubes or holes to desired bearing areas. This is a popular means of distributing lubrication to miscellaneous bearing areas requiring only periodic attention.

4. Various single-shot devices such as sight feed oilers, oil cups, etc. These are the traditional and cheapest means but require individual attention, and some may be overlooked.

Lubrication may help wash away dirt and chips that damage bearings and ways, but the best protection in that respect is a cover or enclosure. As has been pointed out, modern machine tools are well covered for operator safety, but covers are important also to protect the bearings. Covers for ways range from spring steel to impregnated fabric strips and from telescopic metal guards to fabric bellows. Instead of covers, wipers of plastic, leather, bronze, or other materials may be used to clear off the ways as a table is traversed along them.

Unit Construction.   When typical machine tools are described in this text, reference is made to the major components or units such as the base, headstock, or saddle. This is intentional because machine tools are normally made up of such distinct units and are designed on that basis. Aside from other considerations, unit construction is particularly economical for building special-purpose machine tools. A large proportion of machine tools are made for specific purposes by modifying standard machines to a larger or smaller extent. This can be done by adding, substituting, or altering one or a few components instead of building an entirely special machine for each purpose, which would be more expensive. For example, a tracer lathe is commonly constructed by substituting a tracer attachment for the regular saddle of a standard engine lathe. An example of a special-purpose machine made largely from drill press components is shown in Fig. 21-16.

Figure 21-16 Special machine made from units of a small drill press on a special base for the specific task of facing the ends of a die-cast aluminum motor housing. (Courtesy New Jersey Zinc Co.)

QUESTIONS

1. What are the causes of errors in metal machining?
2. What dimension is most important to the rigidity of a machine tool member?
3. Why is it desirable that a machine tool member have a high natural frequency?
4. What makes the frequency of a member high?
5. What are the desirable proportions of machine tool members, and why?
6. What are the relative advantages of iron and steel for major machine tool components?
7. How is accurate straight line motion obtained on a machine tool?
8. How are truly flat and straight surfaces obtained?
9. Describe how a machine tool member deflects under varying and reversing loads.
10. Why must machine tools be kept level?
11. What types of spindle bearings are used for machine tools, and in what type of service is each used?
12. How are precise adjustments made on a machine tool?
13. What effect does heat have on a machine tool, and what can be done about it?
14. Describe a common drive for rotary motion.
15. In what steps are machine tool speeds usually provided?
16. Describe the main types of hydraulic motors.
17. Why are hydraulic drives popular for straight-line or reciprocating motion?
18. Describe the two basic types of reciprocating hydraulic drives and explain their advantages and disadvantages.

19. What are the advantages and disadvantages of pneumatic drives?
20. What principles apply to the arrangement of controls on a machine tool?
21. How is safety provided on machine tools?
22. Why is a general-purpose machine a slow producer?
23. What provision may be made to change tools faster?
24. Describe four common types of lubrication systems found on machine tools and explain for what type of service each is used.
25. What is unit construction and what are its advantages?

PROBLEMS

1. A design for a machine tool member calls for a depth of 150 mm (6 in.). Under a given load the deflection is 25 μm (0.001 in.). If everything else remains the same and the depth is increased to 610 mm (24 in.), what should the deflection be under the same load?

2. When the gibs on a milling machine were fully tightened and a force of 4.45 kN (1000 lb) was applied, the table moved 7.6 μm (0.0003 in.) but returned to its original position when the force was released. Then the gib tightening screws were loosened one turn as recommended by the manufacturer for normal operation. Upon application of a 4.45-kN (1000-lb) load in one direction and then the opposite, the total displacement was found to be 38 μm (0.0015 in.). Draw a deflection-force loop for this situation, showing the approximate points for various conditions.

3. A setting gage like the one shown in Fig. 21-15 costs $186. It must be paid for in a year's operation plus a charge for interest, insurance, and taxes of 15%. Maintenance on the device is negligible. A drill on an automatic machine must be removed and replaced by a sharp one for every 500 pieces. With the setting gage, the time to make the change is $\frac{1}{4}$ minute. Without the gage, 1 minute is needed for the change. The direct labor rate on the machine is $8/hr and overhead is $12/hr.
    (a) What quantity of production justifies purchase of the setting gage?
    (b) Should a setting gage be ordered if only 50,000 pieces are to be made?
    (c) Should a setting gage be ordered for a lot of 500,000 pieces?

REFERENCES

BRYAN, J. B., and J. W. PEARSON, "Reduce Thermal Errors in Precision Machining," *The Tool and Manufacturing Engineer,* Mar. 1969, p. 38.

DONALDSON, R. R., "Repeatability, a Key to Accuracy," *American Machinist,* Jan. 8, 1973, p. 57.

DWYER, J. J., Jr., "Effective Lubrication," *American Machinist,* Aug. 1976, p. 69.

HASZ, J. R., T. C. AGGARWAL, W. M. GILDMEISTER, and C. T. CALIRI, "Trends in Machine Tool Design," *American Machinist,* Sept. 2, 1974, p. 53.

KOENIGSBERGER, F., "Modular Design of Machine Tools," *International Conference of Manufacturing Technology,* ASME, 1967.

MADDUX, K., D. BROWN, and F. SCHIERLOH, *Design of Chatter Free Machine Tools,* ASME Paper 75-DET-5.

RIEGER, N., "Machine Tool Vibration," *American Machinist,* Aug. 11, 1969, p. 65.

TLUSTY, J., "Specifying the Characteristics of Machine Tools," *International Conference of Manufacturing Technology,* ASME, 1967.

22

DRILLING AND ALLIED OPERATIONS

The kinds of operations to be considered at this time are those concerned mostly with the opening, enlarging, and finish cutting of holes from a small fraction of a millimeter to hundreds of millimeters in diameter. The tools, and not the workpieces, are revolved and fed into the material in most of the operations discussed in this chapter.

The common types of operations under consideration are illustrated in Fig. 22-1. *Drilling* is the easiest way to cut a hole into solid metal. It is also done to enlarge holes and then may be called *core drilling* or *counter drilling*. When a hole of two or more diameters is cut by one drill, the operation is called *step drilling*.

Boring is the enlarging of a hole, sometimes with the implication of producing a more accurate hole than by drilling. Enlarging a hole for a limited depth is called *counterboring*. If the depth is shallow so the cut leaves in effect a finished face around

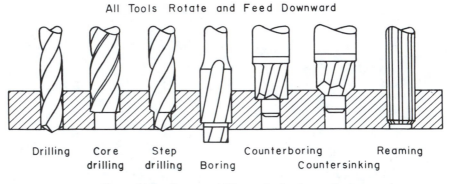

Figure 22-1 Common drilling and related operations.

the original hole, it is called *spot-facing*. The cutting of an angular opening into the end of a hole is *countersinking,* also loosely termed *chamfering. Reaming* is also a hole enlarging process but its specific purpose is to produce a hole of accurate size and good surface finish, and stock removal is small.

Tapping is often done with other operations in a hole, but it will be discussed with other thread-cutting operations in Chap. 32.

DRILLS, BORING TOOLS, AND REAMERS

Common Drills.   The most common form of metalworking drill is the *twist drill* with helical grooves or *flutes* as shown in Fig. 22-2. Those with three or more flutes cannot start holes but can only enlarge holes previously drilled or cored. They are called *core drills,* sometimes *spiral reamers* or *core reamers*.

Drills with cemented carbide inserts, like the one in Fig. 22-2(E) are in wide usage, particularly for large-quantity production. Larger sizes may have four or more inserts along the two cutting edges.

A *multicut drill* makes holes of two or more diameters as in step drilling in Fig. 22-1. It can also drill, counterbore, and countersink within limits. A standard drill ground in that way is called a *step drill*. Drills specifically made for the purpose are named *subland drills* (Fig. 22-2(D)). Since a multicut drill gives two or more surfaces

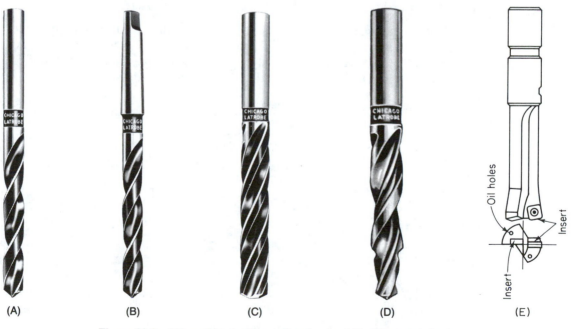

(A)   (B)   (C)   (D)   (E)

Figure 22-2   (A) straight-shank, two-lipped twist drill; (B) tapered shank, two-lipped twist drill; (C) four-flute core drill; (D) subland drill (courtesy Chicago-Latrobe Twist Drill Works); (E) drawing of a two-flute drill with carbide inserts.

in one pass, it is desirable for quantity production, although it costs more than a standard drill. Large-diameter flat drills without helical flutes are called *spade drills*.

The fluted portion of a drill is its *body*. The *point* is the cutting end. The drill is held and driven at the *shank* on the other end. The shank may have a Morse taper and driver tang or may be straight.

Drill Sizes and Materials.   The size of a drill designates the nominal diameter of its body and the hole it is intended to produce. Standard drills are available in *numbered, lettered,* and *fractional inch* and *millimeter* sizes.

Fractional-size drills come in $\frac{1}{64}$-in. steps up to $1\frac{3}{4}$ in. and larger steps above that to over 75 mm (3 in.) diameter. Spade drills are usually cheaper for over 38 mm ($1\frac{1}{2}$ in.) diameter and some are reported used for diameters up to 380 mm (15 in.). Numbered and lettered size drills run from 0.0135 to 0.413 in. in diameter in between the fractional sizes, so there is only a few thousandths of an inch difference between one drill size and the next in that range. A leading maker offers carbide insert drills in sizes upward from $\frac{3}{4}$ in. diameter. Metric-size drills are made in preferred sizes with as little as 0.05 mm between diameters in smaller sizes. The size of a drill is generally stamped on the shank just behind the flutes. Drill lengths vary with diameter and many sizes are available in short, medium, and long lengths.

Carbon tool steel drills have a low first cost and have a place for occasional usage but must be run slowly. High-speed steel drills are the most popular and have good strength. Drills tipped with cemented carbide are economical for high production but are expensive and must be handled carefully to avoid breakage.

Drill Angles and Edges.   The body and point of a drill must have certain components for efficient performance. These are designated for the common form of twist drill in Fig 22-3. A twist drill cuts only at the point, not along the sides of the body. Both the chisel edge and the cutting lips are cutting edges.

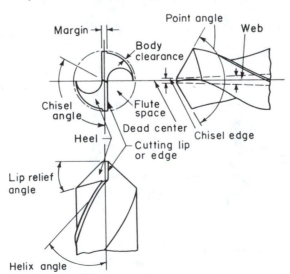

Figure 22-3   Twist drill elements.

SECTIONS THROUGH DRILL POINT EDGES

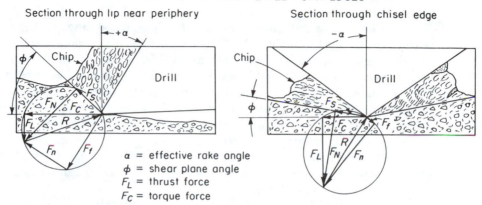

α = effective rake angle
φ = shear plane angle
F_L = thrust force
F_C = torque force

Figure 22-4 Sketches made from photomicrographs of chip formation at the two cutting zones of a twist drill. Force circles like that of Fig. 16-8 are superimposed to illustrate differences in actions.

The *chisel edge* of an ordinary drill indents as it is forced into the metal and, as it turns, partially cuts like a cutting tool with a large negative rake angle as depicted in Fig. 22-4. The chisel edge also does not penetrate like a sharp point and tends to make a drill start off center. Some drills are ground to reduce or eliminate the chisel edge; several among a number of forms are the thinned point, the crankshaft grind, and the spiral point of Fig. 22-5. Too much compensation may weaken the point, but optimum amounts have been found to reduce thrust force by one-third, increase tool life by as much as three times, and improve hole location precision as compared to the full chisel edge. Guidelines for grinding various points are given in reference texts and handbooks.

The *cutting lips* or *edges* illustrated in Fig. 22-3 correspond to the cutting edges of a single-point tool. The rake angle depicted on the left of Fig. 22-4 results primarily from the *helix angle* of the flutes. An average value for the helix angle is 30°, but angles from about 18° for hard materials to 45° for soft materials are used. The effective rake angle at the lip is larger at the periphery than toward the center of the

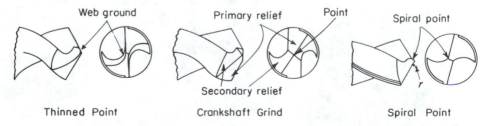

Figure 22-5 Several ways of reducing the ill effects of the chisel edge at the point of a drill.

drill. Some users grind drills at the end of the flutes to create a uniform rake angle along the lips.

The heel of the drill point is backed off when ground to give relief behind the cutting lips, as depicted in Fig. 22-3, like the relief on a single-point tool. The cutting lip relief angle is ordinarily 12 to 15° at the outside diameter. Too much relief weakens the cutting edges and shortens drill life, but the relief angle must always be larger than the lead angle of the path of the cutting edge to prevent rubbing. The lead angle (the complement of the helix angle) of the path, increases for smaller diameters, and therefore the relief angle is made larger toward the center on a properly ground drill.

The point angle between the cutting edges corresponds to the side cutting edge angle of a single-point tool. It is 118° for average work but has different values for specific purposes. For example, a point of 136° is suitable for hard manganese steel, but only 60° for wood and fiber.

Chip breakers help drills, like other tools, cut stringy chip materials more efficiently. Notches are sometimes ground in the cutting lips as chip breakers. One make of drill has a step along each flute to curl and break chips.

It is particularly important that the cutting edges or lips be of equal length and lie at equal angles from the axis of the drill. Otherwise the drill cuts erratically and has a short life. Obvious results of unequalized drill sharpening are shown in the oversize and misshapen holes of Fig. 22-6. This is merely an exaggeration of what may be expected from ordinary errors in drill grinding and helps explain why most drills in practice cut oversize holes. Landberg found that drills carefully ground in the laboratory had lives up to three times as long as when sharpened under usual shop conditions.

The *body clearance* on all but very small drills leaves a narrow *margin* or strip at full nominal diameter along the edge of each flute. This reduces rubbing between drill and hole and allows cutting fluid to reach the point of the drill. Also, the body decreases a few thousandths of an inch in diameter from the point to the shank to reduce rubbing. Drill rigidity is needed for stamina and depends on web and body thickness and flute length. Long drills have been shown to have short lives. One rule

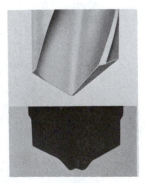

Figure 22-6   Bad holes resulting from unequal drill lip lengths or angles. (Courtesy Cleveland Twist Drill Co.)

is to keep the flute length less than 10 times the diameter. The longer its unsupported length, the more a drill tends to wander off center, particularly when starting a hole.

A twist drill is sharpened by grinding the heel behind the cutting edge on the point—never the outside diameter. Skilled mechanics may grind chisel point drills off hand with passable results, but generally machine ground drills cut faster, last longer, and produce more accurate holes. Machines definitely are needed for grinding particular forms precisely, such as the spiral point. In principle, a drill grinder is a grinding stand with an attachment or fixture to hold the drill at a certain angle and swing it in a particular path with respect to the grinding wheel, or vice versa. A means is also provided to true the wheel.

Deep Hole Drills. Deep holes (over about 10 diameters in depth) are difficult to drill. Chips are difficult to get out of the hole; it is not easy to get the fluid to the point of the drill, and the drill tends to run out too much. These conditions must be corrected in drilling such parts as gun barrels, crankshafts, camshafts, and hollow spindles. Certain procedures help, such as revolving both workpiece and drill and withdrawing the drill often, but specific drills for the purpose are often necessary.

For a diameter over about 20 mm ($\frac{3}{4}$ in.), a drill with oil holes between the flutes and a supply of high-pressure oil helps wash out chips and cool the drill point. Cutting fluid forced through the holes under constant pressure has been found to increase drill life severalfold, and under pulsating pressure even more.

A *crankshaft drill* is a special twist drill for deep holes smaller than 10 mm ($\frac{3}{8}$ in.) diameter, such as oil holes in crankshafts. It has a thick web for strength but a crankshaft grind (Fig. 22-5) and a high helix angle to minimize thrust and clear out chips.

Deep holes requiring smooth finish and minimum runout are drilled with single flute–single edge *gun drills* like that depicted in Fig. 22-7. These are operated at relatively high speeds and low feeds for good accuracy and finish. The workpiece preferably is revolved, and oil is forced through a hole and emerges from the end of the drill to wash out chips and provide cutting fluid. Gun drilling is mostly done on horizontal drilling machines specifically designed to accommodate the long drills and workpieces.

An *ejector drill* has a hollow cylindrical head with carbide tips that cut in overlapping paths. The head is mounted on two concentric tubes. Fluid is forced to the head, between the inner and outer tubes, cools the tip, and washes the chips out

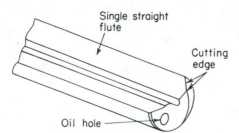

Figure 22-7 Elements of a gun drill.

through the inner tube. The multiple cutting edges can remove metal faster than the single edge of a gun drill.

Boring Tools.   A boring tool meant to revolve has several cutting edges or blades to balance the cutting forces. Typical boring tools, commonly called *counterbores* or *counterboring tools,* are shown in Fig. 22-8. The same kinds of tools are also used for spotfacing and in that role are called *spotfacers.*

An example of a special boring tool, one for machining eight surfaces in one operation, is also shown in Fig. 22-8. The blades for the different cuts are staggered to facilitate grinding to resharpen the edges.

Countersinking tools or *countersinks* are similar to counterboring tools except that their blades are ground at an angle to do countersinking as illustrated in Fig. 22-1. Included angles of 45°, 60°, 82°, and 90° are common.

Usually, a counterboring or countersinking tool has a pilot on one end to guide the tool in the hole previously drilled.

Reamers.   Reamers mainly finish holes and are made in a number of styles. They may be hand or machine driven, for roughing or for finishing work, have integral shanks or be attached to holders, be solid or have inserted blades that may be expanded or adjusted, have straight or helical flutes, and have straight, tapered, or other shapes.

A *hand reamer* has a straight shank with a square tang for a wrench, as shown in Fig. 22-9. It is expected to remove only a small part of a millimeter of metal at most from a hole. Its teeth are ground with relief behind the cutting edges and taper slightly from each end to a straight portion in the middle.

Machine or *chucking reamers* are made with or without relief, with straight or spiral flutes, and solid or with inserted blades. Common forms are described in the paragraphs that follow.

A *rose chucking reamer,* like the one in Fig. 22-9, is cylindrically ground and has no relief behind the outer edges of the teeth. It cuts on the end chamfer of the teeth. Rose reamers are used for heavy roughing cuts, particularly for clearing out cored holes, and not for especially smooth holes.

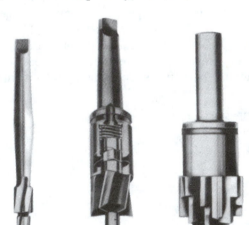

Figure 22-8 Typical boring, counterboring, and spotfacing tools. Left, solid, taper-shank counterbore with integral pilot. Middle, interchangeable counterbore or spotfacer and pilot; the cutter can be removed easily from the driver and replaced with another (courtesy Ex-Cell-O Corp.). Right, special multi-diameter boring cutter for machining eight surfaces in one operation (courtesy Eclipse Counterbore Co.).

Figure 22-9 Typical reamers with integral shanks: top, straight-flute hand reamer (courtesy Chicago-Latrobe Twist Drill Works.); middle, rose chucking reamer with tapered shank (courtesy Cleveland Twist Drill Co.); bottom, cutaway view of a straight-flute expansion chucking reamer (courtesy Cleveland Twist Drill Co.).

Two kinds of machine reamers with relief behind the outside edges of their teeth as well as chamfer on the front of the teeth are the *jobbers' reamer* with long flutes and the *fluted chucking reamer* with shorter flutes. The latter is designed for light finishing cuts.

A reamer over about 20 mm ($\frac{3}{4}$ in.) in diameter is usually made as a shell that fits over an arbor and is called a *shell reamer*. When a shell is worn out, another one can be put on the same arbor.

An *expansion reamer* can be enlarged to remove an extra fraction of a millimeter (few thousandths of an inch) from a hole or to compensate for wear. One design is shown in Fig. 22-9. The blades are part of or, if tipped, brazed to the body, which is hollow and has several slots running part way along the flutes. A tapered thread pin expands the body.

An *adjustable reamer,* as depicted in Fig. 22-10, has inserted and replaceable blades locked to the body. The blade seats are tapered so the diameter of the reamer is increased by moving the blades forward.

As shown by Fig. 22-11, the teeth of a reamer have angles corresponding to and

Figure 22-10 Adjustable shell reamer. (Courtesy Cleveland Twist Drill Co.)

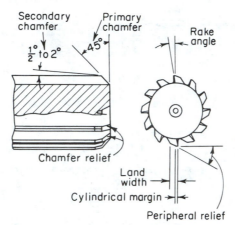

Figure 22-11   Machine reamer angles.

Figure 22-12   Adjustable blade hollow mill. (Courtesy Gairing Tool Co.)

governed by the same factors as those of single-point tools which are described in Chap. 16. A machine reamer does most of its cutting on the end.

Hollow Mill.   Short diameters, like a boss, can be turned by a revolving tool called a *hollow mill*. One is illustrated in Fig. 22-12. Hollow mills are also used with the stock revolving on machines of the lathe family. The blades are pitched and sharpened so that they cut on their inner corners and front edges. The work enters the hollow space in the body of the tool.

DRILLING MACHINES

Drilling machines are made in many forms and sizes. Portable or hand drills are well known. The drilling machines commonly used for precision metal working are known as drill presses. Representative types will be described.

Vertical Drill Presses.   The main features of *standard upright drill presses* are depicted in Fig. 22-13. A column on a base carries a table for the workpiece and a spindle head. The table is raised or lowered manually, often by an elevating screw, and can be clamped to the column for rigidity. Some tables are round and can be swiveled. On vertical drill presses with round columns, the tables generally can be swung out from under the spindle so workpieces can be mounted on the base.

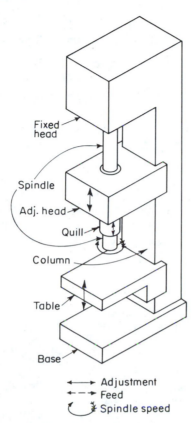

Fixed head

Spindle

Adj. head

Quill

Column

Table

Base

⟶ Adjustment
⟵ - ⟶ Feed
Spindle speed

Figure 22-13 Principal parts and movements of a single-spindle upright drill press.

The spindle that drives the cutting tool revolves in the nonrevolving quill that is fed up or down. Some machines have only hand feed; others have power feeds. Machines of this kind may be equipped with a positive leadscrew for tapping and a spindle reversing mechanism. As a rule an adjustable stop is provided to limit the depth of travel of the quill and, with power feed, to disengage the feed or reverse a tapping spindle at a definite depth. Most machines have a Morse taper hole in the end of the spindle, but small machines often have a drill chuck attached to the end of the spindle. The spindles of fractional horsepower drill presses are usually driven by vee belts; larger ones have gear transmissions, and some have multiple-speed motors. Numerical control is also utilized (Chap. 35).

A *bench-type drill press* is a light machine for small work. Light drill presses, bench and upright, that are hand fed so the operator can feel the resistance met by the drill are called *sensitive drill presses*. They are advantageous for feeding small drills to avoid breakage.

Very small holes must be drilled on highly sensitive presses with spindles running quite true at high speeds, in one design in vee bearings. The action of the drill is watched through a microscope. Holes less than 25 μm (0.001 in.) in diameter have been drilled, and diameters around 125 μm (0.005 in.) are common in the instrument and watch industries.

Production drill presses are sturdily built for heavy work and simple in design, but in overall appearance look like other upright drill presses.

Multispindle Drill Presses.   A single-spindle drill press is not as a rule efficient when a number of pieces are to be machined and several different holes are required in each piece or several cuts (such as drilling, counterboring, and tapping) are to be performed on each hole. In such cases tools, speeds, feeds, and positions must be changed over and over again for each piece or each hole. More efficient results can be obtained in a number of ways from multispindle drill presses, each of which has advantages for certain applications.

A *gang drill press* is the equivalent of two, three, four, or more upright or production drill presses in a row with a common base or table. A production job under spindles of a gang drill press is shown in Fig. 22-14. A gang drill can be set up so that work can be passed from spindle to spindle to undergo two or more operations. In another mode, the same operation may be performed at all spindles; the operator unloads and loads the jig at each spindle in turn while the other spindles are cutting with automatic feed.

Figure 22-14   Production job on a two-spindle gang drill press has a jig clamped to the table under each spindle. Quick-change chucks are mounted on the spindles, and the tools are held in quick-change collets. An air line is arranged with a nozzle to blow the chips away from each jig. (Courtesy Consolidated Machine Tool Corp.)

For an example of a *turret drill press* see Fig. 36-3. Machines of this type are popular for numerical control, but many are hand operated also. A variety of tools can be held on the turret, and each indexed quickly into cutting position on the end of the spindle.

A *multiple-spindle drill press* has a cluster of spindles on one or more heads for a part having a number of holes and produced in large quantities. These machines range in size from small ones powered by a few horsepower to massive ones driven by as much as 37 kW (50 hp). The one in Fig. 22-15 has a 21 kW (28 hp) drive, drills 50 holes in each part, and produces 20 parts/hr. Some of the more elaborate machines have heads and spindles in more than one position to operate on a workpiece from several directions or upon several stations, each holding a workpiece.

Radial Drill Presses. Radial drills are convenient for heavy workpieces that cannot be moved around easily or are too large for other kinds of drill presses. A *plain radial drill,* like the one in Fig. 22-16, has a base and column that carries an arm. The arm can be raised or lowered and swung around the column. The head can be moved along the arm, and the spindle it carries can thus be positioned in a circle with a radius

Figure 22-15   Multiple-spindle drilling machine for drilling 50 holes in a gear case.

Figure 22-16 Operation on a large workpiece on a radial drill press. (Courtesy Giddings and Lewis Machine Tool Co.)

TABLE 22-1 TYPICAL DRILLING MACHINE SPECIFICATIONS

Type	Workpiece diameter [mm (in.)]	Drill diameter [mm (in.)]	Morse taper (no.)	Number of speeds	Power [kw (hp)]	Weight [kg (lb)]	Cost
Hand feed	400 ($15\frac{1}{2}$)	13 ($\frac{1}{2}$)	Chuck	12	0.4 ($\frac{1}{2}$)	100 (220)	$ 250
Upright power feed	660 (26)	50 (2)	5	4	3.7 (5)	950 (2100)	9,000
Upright four-spindle gang type	660 (26)		2	8	Each spindle 1.5 (2)	2200 (4800)	20,000
(12) Multiple-spindle	300 × 500 (12 × 20) work area				5.6 ($7\frac{1}{2}$)		35,000
Programmable multi-spindle	600 × 1170 (24 × 46) area			Inf. var.	18.75 (25)		107,000
Radial 330 mm (13 in.)	1.2 m (4 ft) arm		5	16	4.5 (6)	2720 (6000)	19,000

about as large as the length of the arm. All adjustments can be locked once the spindle is positioned. The drill spindle is fed up and down by hand or power.

Sizes of Drilling Machines. The sizes of drilling machines are designated in several ways. The most common designation for a vertical drill press is the diameter in millimeters (inches) of the largest disk or workpiece in which a hole can be drilled at the center on the press. Other designations are the diameter of the largest drill the press is designed to drive in cast iron or steel and the Morse taper size in the spindle hole. The size of a radial drill press is given in meters (feet) and designates the radius of the largest disk in which a center hole can be drilled with the head at its outermost position on the arm. Some makes also specify the diameter of the column in millimeters (inches) (see Table 22-1).

DRILLING MACHINE ACCESSORIES AND ATTACHMENTS

Toolholders and Drivers. The essential purpose of all toolholders for drilling machines is to make the tool run true with the tapered hole in the machine spindle. Straight shank tools may be held by a drill chuck, as on a lathe, or by a split collet. If of the right size, the tapered shank of a tool may be placed directly in the tapered hole of the machine spindle. If the tapered shank is smaller than the tapered hole, a *taper shank socket,* with inside and outside tapers, is used. A short socket is shown in Fig. 22-17. The cross slot takes the tang of the tapered shank tool and allows a wedge (called a *drift*) to be used to push the tool out of the socket when the two are to be separated.

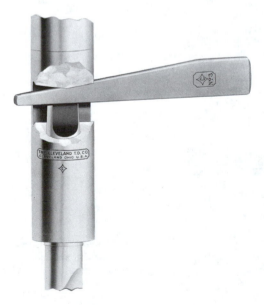

Figure 22-17 Taper shank sleeve or shell socket. (Courtesy Cleveland Twist Drill Co.)

A *floating driver* is a toolholder with its two ends somewhat loosely coupled to allow a reamer or tap to follow a previously drilled or bored hole. An *adjustable extension assembly* is a form of taper socket adapter that can be adjusted for length. It is the means whereby drills of different lengths can be used together on a multiple-spindle head.

A *quick-change chuck* and *quick-change collets* allow tools to be taken off and put on the spindle of a drill press while it is running. Two are shown in Fig. 22-14.

Multiple-Spindle Drill Heads.   A standard single-spindle drill press can be converted to a multiple-spindle machine, within limits, by attaching a multiple-spindle head to the machine spindle. Some of these heads are made for specific purposes and have their spindles in fixed positions. On others, like the one in Fig. 22-18, the locations of the spindles can be changed.

Work-Holding Devices.   If a drill or other tool catches in a hole, it can twirl a workpiece not properly fastened, and that is dangerous with all but small drills. A workpiece may be kept from turning by an obstruction placed in its way, or it may be clamped to the table by bolts and straps.

Vee blocks make good casual supports and locators for round pieces. A workpiece may be clamped to an angle plate. A universal angle plate has a T-slotted surface that can be tilted and swiveled and then secured.

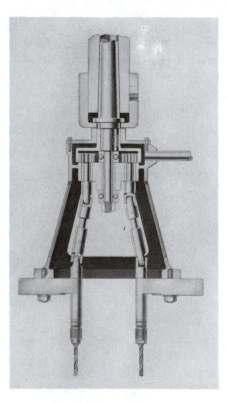

Figure 22-18 Cross section of a portable and adjustable multiple-spindle drill head. (Courtesy Baush Machine Tool Co.)

A typical vise of the kind commonly used to hold work on drill presses is shown in Fig. 22-19. Its open construction allows a drill to pass through the work. Many vises are actuated by cams or toggles and are quicker.

A three jaw chuck, like the one used on lathes, may be mounted on a base with the jaws up to hold pieces for drilling. The base often contains an indexing mechanism so that holes can be spaced and drilled at equal intervals on a circle.

Positioning Tables. Sometimes a table on a saddle on a base is added to a drill press or radial drill to position workpieces under the spindle with respect to two coordinate directions. Thus holes may be located as specified for the pieces. The table and saddle may be positioned by leadscrews and dials, against preset stops, or by a numerical control system as described in Chap. 35.

Fixtures and Jigs. A fixture is a device that holds and locates a workpiece. Strictly speaking, conventional work-holding devices such as chucks and vises are fixtures, but mostly the name is given to single-purpose holding devices. Fixtures are mostly associated with lathes, shapers, planers, millers, broaches, and grinders.

A jig not only holds and locates a workpiece but also guides the cutting tool. That is particularly desirable in drilling because the point of the drill tends to wander unless it is guided when a hole is started. Multiple-point boring tools and sometimes reamers need to be guided.

Workpiece location has a particular meaning. A free body in space has six degrees of freedom; three represented by coordinate axes of translation and three by rotation about those axes. A piece is fully located when definitely restricted in all six degrees of freedom. This occurs only if the piece is held against three points in one plane, two in a second plane, and one in a third plane, with the planes preferably perpendicular to each other. Full restriction is not always desirable, as for instance when a piece must be left free to rotate between centers. Thus fewer than six locating points are supplied in some cases. A basic feature of any jig or fixture is that it provides the locating surfaces or points against which all pieces of one kind can be precisely located.

The simplest kind of jig is a template that fits a part and has holes to guide one or more drills. More elaborate jigs have locating and clamping details to hold the workpiece in relation to the jig plate. The jig plate is the essence of the jig, is made

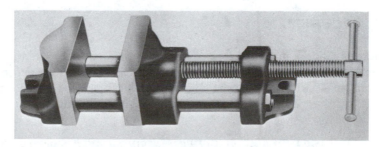

Figure 22-19 Typical drill vise. (Courtesy Atlas Press Co.)

Figure 22-20 Jig to line-bore six holes in a master rod for an aircraft engine. (Courtesy Swartz Tool Products Co.)

of soft steel, and has accurately located holes bored in it. Hardened bushings, inserted in the plate to withstand wear, do the actual guiding of the drills, reamers, etc. *Slip* or *removable bushings* are convenient where tools of different sizes are to be used in one hole.

Jigs have many forms. Two are illustrated in Figs. 22-14 and 22-20. Economical fixtures and jigs for small quantities are made by putting special jaws on standard vises and chucks. Jigs are economical for locating holes to be machined in parts made in quantities.

Whether the layout method, a positioning table, or a jig should be used in any particular case depends upon the factors related by Eq. (19-1), the same as for any other tooling problem. For instance, suppose 10 holes are to be drilled, bored, reamed, tapped, etc., in a piece and the work takes 1 hour. A jig costs $450 and will be depreciated in 1 year with a combined rate of 25% for interest, insurance, taxes, and maintenance. It costs $3 to set up a positioning table and after that the charge for its use is $1/hr. Overhead costs do not change. For how many pieces in one lot is it economical to make a jig and release the positioning table for other work? In this case

$$N \times 1 = 450 \times 1.25 - 3 = 559.5 \text{ pieces}$$

A jig should be provided for 560 pieces or more.

BORING MACHINES

Several kinds of machines tools are called boring machines. Vertical boring machines are really vertical lathes and do much the same work and are described in Chap. 19. Horizontal boring machines are like milling machines and are described in Chap. 24. The types treated here are precision production boring machines and jig boring machines.

Precision Production Boring Machines. Precision production boring machines use mostly single-point tools to machine surfaces rapidly, precisely, and repetitively. They are capable consistently of holding tolerances of a few micrometers (a few ten-thousandths of an inch) and finishing surfaces of 0.2 to 0.4 μm (ca. 10 to 20 μin.) R_a or better. As their name implies, they are used basically for boring, but also are arranged for facing, turning, grooving, and chamfering. The work they do can also be done on general-purpose machines, such as the lathe, but the precision boring machines are more efficient where large quantities of parts are produced because they operate semiautomatically.

A popular type of standard precision production boring machine that is simple but can be adapted for many jobs with special tooling for each job is depicted in Fig. 22-21. The table in the center moves lengthwise and can be made to traverse, dwell, or reverse at any point in its stroke. Some machines have a bridge at one end; this one has bridges at both ends spanning the table and carrying the boring heads.

For some jobs, the boring bars are mounted on the table, and the workpieces are revolved by chucks or fixtures on the boring heads. The fixture on the table in Fig. 22-21 holds two workpieces. When the preset operation cycle is started, the table advances to the left for boring and facing. When that is done, the table traverses to the right. The heads on the right-hand bridge bore and face both pieces. Then the table returns rapidly to its original position and stops.

Various forms of precision production boring machines of many kinds are

Figure 22-21   View of the workstation of a double-end horizontal precision production boring machine with tooling for machining ten surfaces on a pump body. (Courtesy Heald Machine Div. of Cincinnati Milacron, Inc.)

constructed for particular purposes. Some are entirely special; others have special tooling applied to standard basic structures. An example of a popular vertical type is shown in Fig. 22-22.

Jig Boring Machines.   Some jig boring machines resemble in form the horizontal milling machines described in Chap. 24. A popular type in the United States is of vertical openside construction as depicted in Fig. 22-23. The vertical spindle revolves and moves up and down with its quill in a bracket clamped to the front of the column and adjustable for height. The table is mounted on a saddle on the bed and can be moved lengthwise or crosswise. Large pieces on the table can extend out on the sides or front, and the operator has ready access to the work.

Another style of jig borer has its table sliding lengthwise directly on the bed. Two columns, one at each side in the middle of the bed, support a cross rail that carries the vertical spindle head. The head is moved across the table and the spindle is fed vertically.

A basic jig boring machine of high quality with manual controls and about

Figure 22-22 Vertical four-spindle production boring machine. Semifinish boring of four cast-iron cylinder liners is done simultaneously. Stock removal is 6 mm ($\frac{1}{4}$ in.) on the diameter at a rate of 40.5 pieces/hr at 75% efficiency. (Courtesy Heald Machine Div. of Cincinnati Milacron, Inc.)

Figure 22-23 Open-side jig boring machine with direct dimension measuring and automatic positioning. (Courtesy Fosdick Machine Tool Co.)

500 × 1000 mm (20 × 40 in.) table capacity costs around $100,000. A comparable capacity vertical milling machine of good quality costs about half as much. Jig boring machines are costly because they are built to ensure the utmost accuracy through extra rigidity, low thermal expansion, ultratrue geometry, and refined means for measurement. The spindles of most machines run in preloaded antifriction bearings. Structural members are massive and well reinforced against deflection. The spindle housing may be cast of Invar iron with a low coefficient of expansion. A wide range of available speeds helps to optimize cutting and control heating. As an example of true geometry, one maker requires the table top to be flat and parallel with the ways and to move in true paths through its full travel in X and Y directions with no deviation more than 0.5 μm (0.00002 in.). The basic measuring devices on jig boring machines are micrometer leadscrews, optical and electronic systems, end measuring and gaging, and electromechanical gaging.

Most jig borers have leadscrews and graduated dials for moving their tables.

These are the only means for accurate positioning on some machines. As an example of what is feasible, one manufacturer of machines with hardened, ground, and lapped ways and leadscrews guarantees positioning within 0.8 μm (0.00003 in.) in 25 mm (1 in.) and 2.3 μm in 460 mm (0.00009 in. in 18 in.) when new, and added error from wear not to exceed 1.3 μm (0.00005 in.) in 10 years. Further refinement is offered by compensated leadscrews on some machines. These have a cam along the table with a profile representing measured deviations in the leadscrew. The cam causes displacement of the leadscrew nut or dial during table movement to compensate for errors. Adjustments for wear can be made by modifying the cam. Other devices have advantages, such as optical systems for longer distances or more accuracy and end measures for simplicity, and are described in the following paragraphs.

One optical measuring system has an accurate scale (commonly a vernier scale) on each slide. Each scale is read through a microscope or from an enlarged image on a screen to 2.5 or 1.25 μm (0.0001 or 0.00005 in.). Coordinate readout systems like that described for Fig. 15-34(A) are becoming quite popular for jig boring machines because of fast operation. Interferometer systems like that illustrated in Fig. 15-35(C) are used for the most accurate jig boring, especially for calibrating machines. Numerical control as described in Chap. 35 is applied to many jig boring machines at a cost of two or more times as much as for manual controls.

The basic end-measuring system uses rods of even inch lengths made to gage block accuracy. An inside micrometer is adjusted for decimal parts of an inch. The end measures and micrometer are placed in a trough between an adjustable stop on the table and a 0.0001 in. dial indicator at the other end of the trough as depicted in Fig. 22-24. The procedure is to position the table for the first hole or surface, insert measuring instruments and a micrometer set to the required dimension, and adjust the table stop to set the dial indicator to zero. The measuring instruments are changed to the value of the next dimension, and the table is moved until the dial indicator again reads zero. The same procedure is followed for the cross movement of the saddle on which the table rides. On some machines the end measures can be put in place and the slide positioned automatically to suit dialed-in dimensions. End measures are

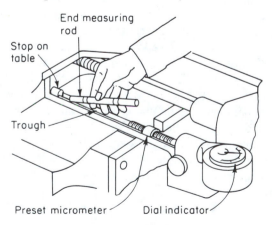

Figure 22-24 Scheme of an end-measuring system for a jig borer.

simple, inexpensive, and minimally affected by deflection and wear, but the system is not fast.

An electromechanical system utilizes a row of permanent magnetic poles accurately positioned 1 in. apart. An electromagnetic pole on the table is aligned with a permanent pole for the nearest inch desired, and the remaining decimal part of the inch is measured by a short but quite accurate micrometer screw.

Jig boring machines are used for accurate toolmaking, manufacturing of exacting parts in small and moderate quantities, and for close limit inspection. Many makes and models exist to meet the wide range of uses. They vary from machines designed for quite precise boring and light milling of toolroom work to those with up to 15-kW (20-hp) drives for production boring and milling but still with a high degree of precision.

Jig Grinding Machines.   A jig grinder is like a jig borer except that the spindle head of the machine carries a high-speed grinding spindle that revolves in a planetary fashion. Jig grinders are capable of finishing holes in hard materials, such as hardened steel, to a degree of accuracy equal to that of jig boring machines in soft materials and are used for finishing operations.

Jig Boring Operations.   A jig boring machine and its accessories represent a large investment and a well-paid operator is essential to get the best out of the machine. Even so, the machine is capable of producing results usually attainable only by buttoning or from using other machines, such as millers, with expensive extra equipment. Also, the jig boring machine achieves these results at the lowest cost when enough work is available to keep the machine busy. To get the most out of the machine, several principles that will be discussed must be observed.

A variety of work is usually done on a jig boring machine, and much more time is consumed for setup and changeover than for cutting. Thus, important savings in time can be realized from tools and accessories that make manipulation of the machine quick and easy. These include brackets for quick attachment of indicators, a spindle centering microscope, proving bars, and auxiliary rotating and tilting tables.

Generally adjustments in workpiece position can be made more easily than the tools can be changed on a jig borer. Also changing of tools adds a certain amount of error. Consequently a desirable procedure is first to make all roughing cuts and then the finishing cuts on all holes of the same size in a workpiece.

Jig boring is done from coordinate location, and a workpiece drawing should be dimensioned the same way, like the example of Fig. 22-25. The coordinate basic dimensions enclosed by rectangles are those the operator uses to set the measuring instruments.

Temperature changes are important in working to small tolerances on a jig borer. These may result from the handling of measuring instruments, the actions of cutting tools, or heat from motors, pumps, and moving parts. Care must be taken constantly to control temperatures, by allowing for heat dissipation and maintaining constant room temperature.

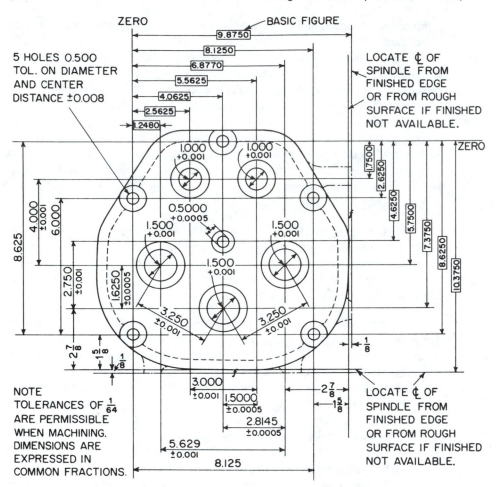

Figure 22-25 Dimensioning of a part for jig boring. (Courtesy Pratt and Whitney Inc.)

DRILLING AND BORING OPERATIONS

Accuracy. The accuracy of a hole involves both size and location. Accuracy of hole size depends largely upon the tools and the way they are used. Under average conditions it may be said that practical drilling tolerances range from 50 μm (0.002 in.) for 4.75 mm ($\frac{3}{16}$ in.) diameter to 0.25 mm (0.01 in.) for 25 to 50 mm (1 to 2 in.) diameter. Boring generally gives appreciably better results. A multiblade boring tool will produce a large number of holes within 25 to 50 μm (0.001 to 0.002 in.) of a specified size. A fluted reamer properly used with limited stock removal (often achieved by prior boring) is a quick way to produce holes within 25 μm (0.001 in.). Where a truly positioned and round hole with an accuracy of less than

15 µm (0.0005 in.) is required, finishing by several cuts with a single-point boring tool or by grinding, lapping, or honing are the only means of assuring results. The surface finishes obtainable from drilling and related operations are indicated in Fig. 15-38.

The accuracy required for the location of holes varies from 0.8 mm ($\frac{1}{32}$ in.) commonly needed for clearance holes to a few thousandths of a millimeter (ten-thousandth of an inch) for holes in exacting production parts, such as those for aircraft engines, and many jigs, fixtures, dies, and gages. The method selected to locate a hole or holes depends upon the accuracy required and the number of pieces to be made.

The accurate location of holes calls for three steps. The first is to establish the positions of the holes, the second is to cut the holes, and the third is to check the results. The position of holes may be established by layout, transfer, buttoning, and coordinate location; these methods and their merits will be discussed. What has been said about cutting holes for size applies also to location. Of the abrasive methods, grinding alone is a way of appreciably correcting positional errors.

Layout consists of drawing lines on a workpiece and center punching for the locations of holes in the manner indicated in Fig. 22-26. A drill, usually one of small diameter, is started in the centerpunch marks. A skilled machinist can evaluate how true a drill is cutting and make compensations to centralize the hole with the scribed circle. Even so, location within 0.15 to 0.25 mm (0.005 to 0.010 in.) is all that can be expected. The method is slow and suited only for rough work in small quantities.

One form of the *transfer method* is to drill, and even ream, through the holes already in a part into a mating part. In this way holes between two parts can be matched as precisely as in any other way. This is practical for some production assemblies and for making dies, fixtures, jigs, and gages. An extension of this method is in the use of jigs, but their cost can be justified only for producing parts in quantities.

Buttoning is the name of a method using toolmakers' buttons. These are accurately sized hollow cylinders with squared ends. A button is clamped by a screw to the workpiece and adjusted with precision measuring tools to the position desired for a hole. The workpiece is then mounted on the face plate of a lathe with the button protruding. The workpiece is shifted until a dial indicator shows the button running true. The workpiece is secured, the button removed, and the hole is bored in the same spot. Holes may be located by this method to within 15 to 25 µm (0.0005 to 0.001 in.) of true location. No expensive equipment is needed, but the method is time consuming and not practical in modern shops.

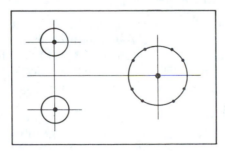

Figure 22-26 Layout for drilling three holes.

Coordinate location is done by moving a workpiece from a reference point through measured distances along perpendicular axes. Movements are commonly made through cross- or leadscrews and graduated dials by means of a positioning table on a drill press or on a milling machine (Chap. 24), manually or numerically controlled (Chap. 35). Holes can be located within 25 to 125 μm (0.001 to 0.005 in.) on such machines without extra attachments. Coordinate location is ordinarily done on jig boring machines by the refined methods already described for positioning within 2 to 15 μm (0.0001 to 0.0005 in.) and closer at premium cost.

Feeds and Speeds.   The speed at which a drill, boring tool, or reamer should be run depends upon the same considerations as for other tools, as explained in Chap. 17. In general, the proper peripheral cutting speed of a drill is about the same as for a single-point tool under comparable circumstances.

The feed of a drill is the distance it advances in one revolution. Feeds depend mostly upon what the drill will stand, determined by its size and the work material. As a general guide, the Cleveland Twist Drill Co. recommends "a feed of 0.001 to 0.002 in./rev for drills $\frac{1}{8}$ to $\frac{1}{4}$ in., 0.004 to 0.007 for drills $\frac{1}{4}$ to $\frac{1}{2}$ in., 0.007 to 0.015 for drills $\frac{1}{2}$ to 1 in., and 0.015 to 0.025 for drills larger than 1 in." This corresponds to 0.025 to 0.05 mm/rev for drills 3 to 7 mm, 0.10 to 0.20 for drills 7 to 13 mm, 0.20 to 0.40 for drills 13 to 25 mm, and 0.40 to 0.65 for drills over 25 mm in diameter. Alloy and hard steel should generally be drilled at a lighter feed than given above, while cast iron, brass, and aluminum may usually be drilled with a heavier feed than given above.

Boring and similar tools are run at about the same speeds and feeds as drills, sometimes slightly less. As a rule, reaming must be done at low speeds and high feeds for best results. Speeds of 50 to 75% of drilling speeds and feeds of 200 to 300% of drilling feeds for rose reamers and 300 to 500% for fluted reamers are recommended.

Cutting Forces, Power, and Time.   The two components of force in drilling and boring operations are the thrust T in kN (lb) in the axial direction of the tool and the torque or moment M in Nm (lb-in.). Investigations have shown that these depend upon the feed f in mm/rev (ipr), the drill diameter d in mm (in.), the chisel edge length c, the material, and the number of teeth. Simplified formulas for two flute drills with a normal c/d ratio of 0.18 have been given by Oxford as

$$T = 2Kf^{0.8}d^{0.8} + Ld^2 \quad \text{and} \quad M = Kf^{0.8}d^{1.8} \tag{22-1}$$

The factor K is 0.6035 (24,000) for 200 Bhn steel, 0.7795 (31,000) for 300 Bhn steel, 0.8549 (34,000) for 400 Bhn steel, 0.1760 (7000) for aluminum and leaded brass, 0.1006 (4000) for most magnesium alloys, and 0.3520 (14,000) for most brasses. The value of L is 4.309×10^{-3}(625). The factors for SI units are given first, and those for English units are in parentheses. Similar expressions are given in reference books and handbooks for hole-enlarging tools.

The horsepower for a drilling operation may be estimated on the basis of $P = MR/63{,}025$, where R is the drill speed in rpm. The power in kW is $MR/9549$, with M in Nm. An insignificant portion of the power is related to the thrust because the feed is slow compared to the speed. Power may also be estimated on the basis of the rate of stock removal as explained for Table 17-3.

The basic relationship that cutting time is equal to the distance the tool is fed in mm (in.) divided by the rate of feed in mm/min (ipm) applies to drilling and boring. This may be illustrated by an example. A hole 25 mm (1 in.) in diameter is drilled through a cast-iron piece 76 mm (3 in.) thick by a H.S.S. drill with a surface speed of 15 m/min (50 fpm). The drill rotates at 190 rpm. With an advance of 0.4 mm/rev (0.016 ipr), the rate of feed is $0.4 \times 190 = 76$ mm/min ($0.016 \times 190 = 3$ ipm). The distance the drill is fed in this case is 76 mm (3 in.) plus an assumed overtravel of 3 mm ($\frac{1}{8}$ in.) plus an approach of 6.5 mm ($\frac{1}{4}$ in.) (one-fourth of the diameter of a standard drill). Thus the total travel is 85.5 mm ($3\frac{3}{8}$ in.). The time for the cut is $85.5/76 = 1.13$ minutes ($3.375/3 = 1.13$ minutes).

Drilling and Boring Operations Compared with Others. Drilling machines are best for many jobs, particularly for small holes, because they are simple, of low cost, easy to set up and manipulate, and can be tooled at moderate cost. Drilling, boring, and reaming are usually done on other machines, such as lathes or milling machines, for particular advantages. For instance, a hole may be machined more economically and accurately on a lathe in the same setup with outside surfaces, especially when concentric or square. The need to locate holes accurately is often a prime factor; the selection of machines for that purpose has been discussed in the section on accuracy.

When feasible, punching generally is cheaper than any other way of producing holes. As demonstrated in Fig. 22-27, more accuracy is achieved only from the use of several tools or operations in succession. If punching is not practicable, drilling

Method	Normal tolerance		Comparative cost	
	mm	in.	Total cost (%)	Direct labor cost (%)
Punch (template)	+100 −50	+0.004 −0.002	100	100
Drill (jig)	+180 −50	+0.007 −0.002	175	300
Drill and ream (jig and bushings)	+15 −000	+0.0006 −0.0000	225	400
Bore (fixture), including punch, or rough and finish bore on borematic	+10 −000	+0.0004 −0.0000	540	700
Hone or lap (fixture) including punch and bore	+5 −000	+0.0002 −0.0000	730	1100

The setup costs, based on 200 plate quantity (0.180–in.–thick brass plate 3.50 x 5.00 size) have been included in direct labor costs.

Figure 22-27 Comparative direct and tool costs for various ways of producing holes. (As reported by Richard C. Johnson, "The Cost of Finishes and Tolerances," *Journal of the American Society of Naval Engineers*, Nov. 1958.)

alone is cheapest, but either must be followed by other operations for smaller tolerances. However, direct and tool costs increase with the number of operations, and no more precision than necessary should be specified or attempted.

QUESTIONS

1. Define drilling, core drilling, counter drilling, and step drilling.
2. Define boring, counterboring, spot-facing, and countersinking.
3. What does reaming entail?
4. Sketch a twist drill and name its principal parts.
5. Why is it desirable to minimize the length of the chisel edge of a drill? How can it be done?
6. What angles of a drill correspond to the rake and relief angles of a single-point tool?
7. What determines the proper amount of relief angle on a drill?
8. Why should drills be carefully ground? What precautions should be taken?
9. What means are used to drill deep holes?
10. Name and describe the principal kinds of reamers.
11. Describe and designate the principal units of a vertical drill press.
12. What is the difference between a gang drill press and a multiple-spindle drill press? For what are they of value?
13. Describe a radial drill press. For what is it used?
14. Describe and compare the four methods for establishing the positions of holes.
15. Describe a typical jig boring machine. Why is it expensive?
16. Describe and compare the four basic positioning systems of jig boring machines.
17. What determines how accurately a hole can be cut?
18. What tolerances should be specified for the size and position of a hole, and why?

PROBLEMS

1. A bearing cap must have four holes of 13 mm ($\frac{1}{2}$ in.) diameter drilled in it. If these holes are drilled one at a time, each piece takes 3 minutes. The labor rate is $10/hr and overhead on the machine $10/hr. A four-spindle drill head for the job costs $1000 and will do each piece in 1 minute but has no other use. The labor rate is $10/hr, but overhead on the heavier machine required is $12/hr. A composite rate of 25% is required for interest, insurance, taxes, and maintenance of special tools. The depreciation period is one year. Setup cost is negligible. For how many pieces is it economical to get a four-spindle drill head?

2. A workpiece must have 10 holes finished in it. Layout time is $\frac{1}{2}$ hr/piece. One-half hour is required to set up a positioning table for a whole lot. To finish the holes requires 1 hour for each piece, not counting layout or setup. The labor rate is $10/hr, the machine rate is $10/hr, and the use of a positioning table costs $2/hr. If the table is used, the labor cost to lay out each piece can be saved. Both methods give the same-quality product. How large a lot justifies the use of the positioning table?

3. A part may have a hole located for drilling by layout. If a jig is provided, $\frac{1}{2}$ minute is saved for each piece. The labor rate is \$9.60/hr, which means a savings of \$0.08/piece. The overhead rate on the labor saved is 100%. Setup time is no more with than without the jig. The combined rate for interest, insurance, taxes, and maintenance is 35%. The cost of the jig is \$1000.
 (a) How many pieces must be made in one lot to make the jig worthwhile?
 (b) How many pieces must be made on the jig in one lot each month to earn the cost of the jig in 2 years?
 (c) How many pieces must be made on the jig in one lot each year to save its cost in 2 years?

4. If one lot of 3000 pieces is to be made under the conditions described in Prob. 3, how much is it justified to spend for a jig?

5. A part with seven holes can be machined on a numerically controlled turret drill press in 15 minutes. The rate on the machine for labor and overhead is \$24/hr. The part can be machined on a gang drill press with a special jig in 17 minutes per piece. The jig costs \$250, and the combined rate for depreciation, interest, insurance, and taxes is 135%. The hourly rate for the machine and operator is \$16. Setup time is the same for both machines. For how many pieces is it economical to make a jig?

6. A jig for machining a part with three holes costs \$200 and with it the operation takes 12 minutes. The operation can be done without a jig on a numerically controlled drill press in 10 minutes. The other conditions are the same as in Prob. 5. For how many pieces is it economical to make a jig?

7. Write a list of the steps or unit operations required to machine all the holes in one piece shown in Fig. 22-28. Specify the machine and tools to use.

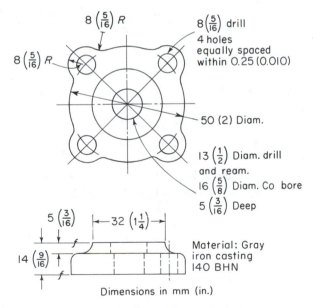

Figure 22-28   Workpiece.

8. Write a list of the steps or unit operations required to machine 5000 pieces shown in Fig. 22-28. A four-spindle drill head is available. Specify the machines and tools required.

9. Estimate the cutting time for the operation and the power of the machine for Prob. 7.

10. Estimate the cutting time for the operation and the power of the machine for Prob. 8.

11. A jig is to be made for drilling a 20-mm (ca. $\frac{3}{4}$-in.)-diameter hole in 300 Bhn steel with a high-speed steel drill at 25 m/min (80 fpm) speed and 0.25 mm/rev (0.010 ipr) feed. What drilling thrust must the jig be designed to sustain? What power must the drill press be able to deliver?

12. To be justified in a certain plant, a jig boring machine must show a savings of $8000/yr. It is estimated that on the average, about one-fourth of the time now spent in locating holes by other methods can be saved by jig boring. Labor and overhead are considered worth $26/hr. How many hours of work per year should be available for this jig boring machine to justify its purchase?

13. A jig for a job will cost $900. The operation can be done with the jig in 4 minutes and on a jig borer without a jig in 12 minutes for each piece. Setup time is the same either way. The labor and overhead rate on the drill press with the jig is $12/hr and on the jig boring machine $16/hr. A composite rate for interest, insurance, taxes, and maintenance is 20%. For how many pieces is the jig justified?

REFERENCES

BAKER, A., "The Use and Care of Reamers," *American Machinist,* Mar. 15, 1975, p. 71.

BUTRICK, F. M., "Spade Drill or Twist Drill?" *Machinery,* June 1971, p. 47.

DALLAS, D. B., ed., *Tool and Manufacturing Engineers Handbook,* 3d. ed., Society of Manufacturing Engineers, Dearborn, Mich., 1976, Chap. 3.

Gundrilling, Eldorado Tool and Mfg. Co., Milford, Conn., 1968.

HATSCHEK, R. L., "Fundamentals of Drilling, Special Report 709," *American Machinist,* Feb. 1979.

McKAY, D. M., "Using Standard Small Drills," *American Machinist,* Apr. 19, 1971, p. 118.

OXFORD, C. J., JR., and M. C. SHAW, "On the Drilling of Metals: II. The Torque and Thrust in Drilling," *Trans. ASME,* Vol. 79, 1957, p. 139.

———— and M. C. SHAW, "On the Drilling of Metals: II. The Torque and Thrust in Drilling," *Trans. ASME,* Vol. 79, 1957, p. 139.

"Twist Drilling or Gun Drilling," *Machinery,* Aug. 1968, p. 56.

USASI B5.12-1958, *Twist Drills,* U.S. American Standards Institute, New York.

23

SHAPING
AND PLANING

Both shaping and planing are intended primarily for flat surfaces, horizontal, vertical, or at an angle as indicated in Fig. 23-1, but can be arranged for machining curved surfaces and slots. Short internal surfaces like square or splined holes can also be shaped.

Shaping and planing differ with respect to action and workpiece size. In shaping, the tool is reciprocated over the workpiece surface, while in planing, the workpiece is moved past the tool, in both cases at cutting speeds. In shaping a horizontal surface the workpiece is fed, but for shaping vertical and inclined surfaces and in all planing, the tool is fed an increment for each stroke in a direction perpendicular to the cutting speed.

Because of the necessary structure of the machine, shaping is limited to small and moderate-size workpieces.

In most shaping and planing operations, cutting is done in one direction only. The return stroke represents lost time. Thus these processes are slower than milling and broaching, which cut continuously. On the other hand, shaping and planing use single-point tools that are less expensive, are easier to sharpen, and are conducive to quicker setups than the multiple-point tools of milling and broaching. This makes shaping or planing often economical to machine one or a few pieces of a kind.

SHAPING

Horizontal Shapers. A horizontal shaper depicted in Fig. 23-2 (left) has a horizontal ram that reciprocates at cutting speed. A cutting tool is carried on the toolhead on the front of the ram. The length and position of the stroke of the ram are

617

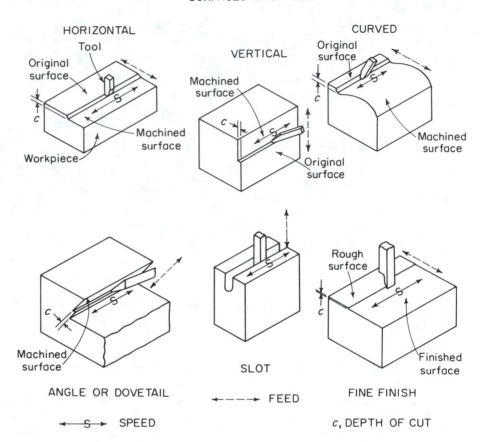

SURFACES MACHINED

Figure 23-1   Typical surfaces machined by shaping or planing.

adjustable so that the tool can be set to cover any part of the maximum stroke of the shaper and need not travel any more than necessary for each job. The slide that carries the tool on the toolhead can be swiveled to and clamped at any angle in a vertical plane on the front of the ram. An application of the adjustment is illustrated in Fig. 23-2 (right). The slide can be adjusted by a micrometer dial or fed by hand or automatically in the direction to which is it swiveled. The available movement is limited because the slide is short. The cutting tool, normally in a tool post, is fastened to a clapper box on the front of the tool slide. The clapper box is pivoted and swings to allow the tool to lift and ride loosely over the work on the return stroke. This eases the pressure on the tool and prevents marring the work surface.

A cross-rail mounted on ways on the front of the column of a horizontal shaper is adjustable up or down. The work table rides crosswise on the rail and can be adjusted or fed manually or automatically. Feed takes place just before the beginning of each stroke. The power feed is activated by the ram driving mechanism.

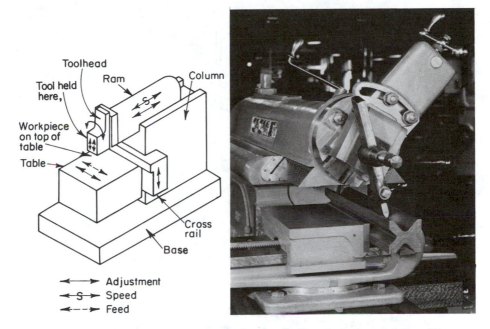

Figure 23-2 (A) Left, principal parts and movements of a horizontal shaper; (B) right, shaper operation. The slide on the front of the ram is inclined for cutting the surface at an angle on the V-block held in a vise. The toolholder and clapper box are swiveled to swing the tool away from the surface on the return stroke. (Courtesy Cincinnati Shaper Co.)

Bench shapers run at high speeds for small work. Others are floor mounted. A *plain, utility,* or *tool room shaper* is a light shaper. *Standard industrial, heavy-duty,* or *production shapers* are heavy and rugged for large pieces and fast and deep cuts. A *universal shaper* has a table that can be swiveled around two horizontal axes in addition to horizontal and vertical adjustments. In addition, special shapers have been made with such features as two or more heads on one ram for multiple cuts and two tables for loading and cutting alternately.

All the shapers described so far push the tool away from the column to cut. In contrast, a *draw cut shaper* cuts towards the column. It can be built with a long stroke and take heavy cuts and is made in the larger sizes. Draw cut shapers are intended for heavy duty and are correspondingly expensive.

Vertical Shapers. A vertical shaper or *slotter* has a vertical ram and normally a rotary table as depicted in Fig. 23-3. On some machines the ram is inclinable up to 10° from the vertical, which is useful for cutting inclined surfaces. The rotary table can be indexed accurately or rotated continuously by hand or power. It moves on a saddle that slides on the bed and has horizontal adjustments and feeds in two directions.

The horizontal table of the vertical shaper is easy to load. The circular plus the two straight line motions of the table permit easy machining of circular, convex,

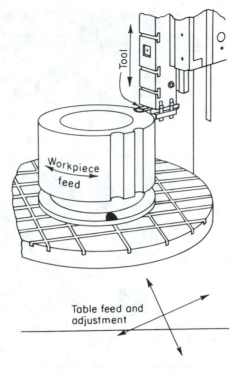

Figure 23-3 Operation on a vertical shaper or slotter.

concave, and other curved surfaces. Slots or grooves can be accurately spaced around a workpiece.

The vertical design of this shaper requires a minimum of floor space and makes possible a convenient grouping of controls. The operator can readily control and observe the work being done. The tool enters the work from the top and can be guided to a line thereon with relative ease.

Shaper Drives.   Several types of drives are built for shaper rams, and the name given to a shaper frequently denotes the kind of drive it has. One kind is through a *mechanical crank,* another is *hydraulic.*

The mechanism of a typical crank-operated shaper is shown in Fig. 23-4. Power goes from the motor to a pulley through vee belts and passes through a clutch and gear transmission to the pinion that drives the large bull gear in the middle of the column. The bull gear's speed is varied by shifting gears in the transmission.

The bull gear in the middle of the column in Fig. 23-4 rotates clockwise at a uniform rate. A block on a crankpin that travels in a circle on the bull gear slides in a slot in the crank and causes it to reciprocate. The crank may be identified by its near elliptical shape. It is pivoted at the bottom and is connected at the top to the ram through a link.

As depicted by the diagram on the right in Fig. 23-4, the direction of movement of the crank changes when the centerline of the crank is tangent to the circular path of the crankpin on the bull gear. The crankpin is positioned in or out radially on the

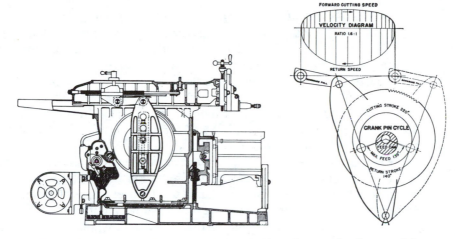

Figure 23-4   Cross section views of a crank-driven shaper and a diagram of the crank mechanism. (Courtesy Cincinnati Shaper Co.)

bull gear from an external control to change the length of stroke. For a constant bull gear speed, the ram speed changes with the radial setting of the crankpin. When the ram moves forward on the cutting stroke, the driving pin moves through an arc of 220°. On the return stroke, the pin travels through only 140° of arc. Thus the ram travels much faster and takes less time on the return stroke than on the forward or cutting stroke. This *quick return motion* saves time when the tool is not cutting.

The features of mechanical and hydraulic drives in general are explained in Chap. 21. Mechanical shapers are most popular, especially for heavy cutting. The drive inertia furnishes a reserve for heavy and varying cuts. On the other hand, hydraulic shapers offer more constant cutting speeds for uniform cuts, easier adjustments for ram position and stroke length, and infinitely variable feeds and speeds. A comparison was made to show the benefit of a constant cutting speed with a 250-mm (10-in.) stroke and a maximum speed of 12 m/min (40 fpm). Under those conditions a hydraulic shaper was reported able to make 31 strokes/min, and a mechanical shaper 18.7 strokes/min. Actually, a choice in most cases seems to be based upon personal preference rather than the result of outstanding advantage of either type of drive.

Sizes of Shapers.   The size of a shaper designates its longest nominal cutting stroke. Thus, a 24 in. shaper has ram travel enough to drive a tool across a 610-mm (24-in.)-long surface, sometimes a little more. On most horizontal shapers, the table can be fed crosswise a distance at least as large as the stroke. That means that a 24-in. shaper usually is capable of machining a plane surface at least 610 × 610 mm (24 × 24 in.) square. Horizontal shapers range from bench models with strokes of 180 to 200 mm (7 to 8 in.), through industrial shapers to 915 mm (36 in.), to draw cut shapers with strokes as long as 1.8 m (72 in.). Shapers with longer rams are not practical. One with a stroke to 250 mm (10 in.) and a 1-hp motor for tool and model making is quoted at $2300.

Shaper Tools and Attachments. The single-point tools used on horizontal shapers are much like lathe tools, except that shaper rake angles may be slightly less, particularly for hard materials. High-speed steel is the most common cutting tool material for shaping, but shockproof grade carbides are in wide use, especially for hard materials. A *tool lifter* is a device that automatically raises the tool to clear the work on the return stroke. It is particularly desirable for use with carbide tools.

Index centers like those that will be described for milling machines are used for spacing shaper cuts around workpieces. *Universal tables* are available for most shapers to tilt and swivel workpieces.

Profiling and duplicating tracer attachments are added to shapers to make them capable of reproducing surfaces of curvature. A finger or follower is arranged on a bracket attached to the toolhead so that it travels over a master-surface as the tool passes over the workpiece. As the finger rises and falls in tracing the master surface, the tool is raised and lowered in unison by hydraulic means and reproduces the master profile on the workpiece.

Shaping Operations. Workpieces are commonly clamped to the table or held in a vise on a shaper. Small quantities normally do not justify fixtures. Forces are preferably directed against the fixed jaws of a vise for rigidity. A tool should travel lengthwise over a surface if possible. In that way fewer strokes are needed, and less time is lost in return strokes.

Copper, brass, or lead strips called *false jaws* are inserted at the sides of a rough piece as in Fig. 23-5(A) to protect the vise jaws. A surface can be shaped square with another by locating against the fixed jaw as in Fig. 23.5(B). To machine the top parallel with the bottom, a workpiece is held down firmly by *hold-downs,* as in Fig. 23-5(C). These are thin tapered strips tilted at an angle.

A common practice is to scribe the outline of a surface along its edges on a workpiece and adjust the shaper tool to the line to machine the desired surface. The tool is adjusted to cut an irregular surface by the operator manipulating the controls.

Very small tolerances can be held on a shaper if sufficient skill and care are exercised by the operator. These may be of the order of 25 μm (0.001 in.) or less on dimensions and 25 μm in 150 mm (0.001 in. in 6 in.) for squareness and parallelism. However, more usual and economical tolerances are 75 to 125 μm (0.003 to

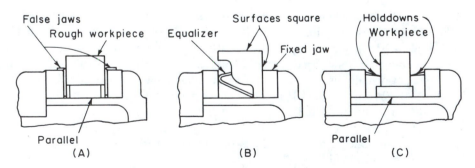

Figure 23-5 Ways of holding work in a vise.

0.005 in.) on dimensions and 50 to 75 μm in 150 mm (0.002 to 0.003 in. in 6 in.) for squareness and parallelism.

Estimating Shaping Time and Power. The time for each cutting stroke is found from the following reasoning. The cutting stroke occupies only a part of each full stroke. The proportion varies with different shapers, but a common ratio shown in Fig. 23-4 of 1.6:1 for duration of cutting stroke to return stroke will be used as an example. With that ratio, the tool moves at the average cut speed during $(1.6 \times 100)/(1.6 + 1) = 61.5\%$ of the full stroke. For N strokes per minute (spm), the time for a full stroke is $1/N$ minute and for the cutting stroke $0.615/N$ minute.

For length of stroke l_m in millimeters and cut speed V_m in m/min, $N = 615V_m/l_m$. As an example, a machine steel surface 250 mm (10 in.) long is to be shaped with a H.S.S. tool at 24 m/min (80 fpm). The shaper should be set as near as feasible to $615 \times (24/250) = 59$ spm. The length of stroke l in in. is equal to cut speed V in fpm (converted to 12V ipm) multiplied by time in minutes, or $l = 12V \times 0.615/N$, and $N = 7.4V/l$. Thus, $7.4 \times (80/10) = 59$ spm. The cut speed (in m/min or fpm) of a single-point tool on a shaper should be about the same as that on a lathe under comparable conditions.

It is well to remember that long strokes and high speeds together impose a strain on a shaper because of the large forces of reversal and must be avoided. For example, a 610-mm (24-in.) stroke at 100 spm gives an average cutting speed of 99 m/min (324 fpm). That is common for turning softer materials such as aluminum and even for steel with cemented carbide tools but is unattainable on the shaper because it requires ram accelerations of thousands of g's. Thus the shaper cannot be a rapid-cutting machine tool.

The feed on a shaper should be as heavy as the machine, workpiece, or tool will stand and as will not give too rough a surface. Table 23-1 shows average feeds for cast iron and machine steel as a guide. Higher or lower feeds may be selected to suit particular situations. The feed may be reduced to one-half or one-third for irregular surfaces, grooves, and cutting off. The finer the feed, the better the finish. Softer materials allow high feeds, and harder materials require lower feeds. A rigid setup permits a heavier cut than a weak one. A feed as high as 6 mm/stroke (1/4 in./stroke) may be desirable for a broad-nose finishing tool, and one as fine as 125 μm/stroke (0.005 in./stroke) for a sharp-point tool.

For an example of estimating the cutting time, a machine steel surface 250 mm

TABLE 23-1

Type of cut	Roughing				Finishing	
Depth or manner of cut						
mm	1.5	3	6	Toolhead feed	0.8	Toolhead feed
in.	1/16	1/8	1/4		1/32	
Feed						
mm/stroke	1.5	1.0	0.8	0.5	0.5	0.25
in./stroke	0.06	0.04	0.03	0.02	0.02	0.01

(ca. 10 in.) long and 125 mm (ca. 5 in.) wide is to be shaped at 60 strokes/min. The depth of cut is 3.2 mm (ca. $\frac{1}{8}$ in.) and the feed 1.0 mm/stroke (0.04 in./stroke). The feed rate is $1.0 \times 60 = 60$ mm/min ($0.04 \times 60 = 2.4$ ipm). If 5 mm (ca. $\frac{1}{4}$ in.) overtravel is assumed, the distance the work is fed is 130 mm (ca. $5\frac{1}{4}$ in.) and the machine time is $130/60 = 5.25/2.4 = 2.2$ minutes.

In the foregoing example, the average cutting speed for a 260-mm ($10\frac{1}{4}$-in.) stroke is $60 \times 260/615 = 25$ m/min ($60 \times 10.25/7.4 = 83$ fpm). The average rate of metal removal is $1.0 \times 3.2 \times 25 = 80$ cm^3/min ($0.04 \times 1/8 \times 83 \times 12 = 5.0$ in.^{3}/min). For a unit power consumption of 50 W/cm^3/min at the drive motor indicated in Table 17-3, 4 kW is needed. For 1.1 hp/in.^{3}/min, 5.5 hp is required.

Shaping Compared with Other Operations.   Other machine tools are able to cut and remove stock faster than shapers, but shapers are favored for many short-run jobs because of several advantages they offer. A shaper can be put to many uses in a toolroom or job shop and can easily be changed from one job to another. Setup time for many jobs is less on a shaper than on other machines. Practically all work can be done with simple and inexpensive tools. This is exemplified by a curved surface that would require a special form tool if machined by another method such as milling but can be shaped by a single-point tool. Even if a form tool is used on a shaper it can be made and sharpened more easily than a multiple-tooth milling cutter or broach.

A shaper is convenient for cutting inclined surfaces. On the other machines, such as the milling machine, fixtures and attachments often are needed to machine inclined surfaces. Frail workpieces can sometimes be shaped with ordinary setups because the cutting forces are not large, whereas extra supports would be needed on other machine tools.

PLANING

The Planer.   The *planer* or *planing machine* carries the work on a massive table, fully supported by a heavy bed, like the one in Fig. 21-1, and capable of sustaining heavy loads. The table slides on ways on the bed. Most planers cut in one; some, in both directions. Tee slots and holes are provided for bolts, keys, and pins for holding and locating workpieces on the finished table top.

The common type of planer illustrated in Fig. 23-6 has two heavy *housings,* also called *columns* and *uprights,* at about the middle of the bed, with one on each side of the table. These carry the horizontal cross-rail that can be raised or lowered and then clamped in place. The columns and rail carry the toolheads. Those on the side slide up and down; those on the cross-rail slide horizontally.

A planer toolhead normally can be swiveled on its base, called the *saddle,* up to about 60° of each side of its neutral position. The plate that swivels carries a slide that has a clapper box on the end for mounting the tool. The clapper allows the tool to rise from the workpiece on the back stroke like on a shaper. The clapper box can usually be swiveled about 20° in each direction to place the tool in advantageous

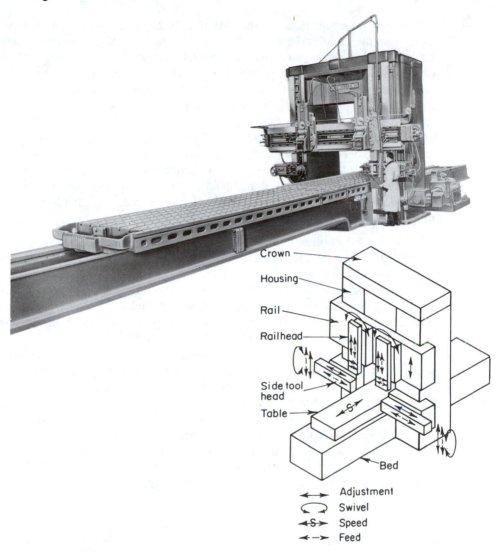

Crown
Housing
Rail
Railhead
Side tool head
Table
Bed

↔ Adjustment
↻ Swivel
◄S► Speed
◄-► Feed

Figure 23-6 A 48 in. × 48 in. double-housing planer. The diagram shows the principal parts and movements of the machine. (Photo courtesy Giddings and Lewis Machine Tool Co.)

positions as needed. Many planers have air or hydraulic tool lifters that automatically swing the clapper block out for each return stroke to save the tools.

Some planers have hydraulic drives, with locked variable-delivery circuits. Others have mechanical drives, commonly with variable-speed, reversing dc motors. The power is carried from the motor through a set of reduction gears. The last gear in the series meshes with a rack fastened to the underside of the table. Table speeds range from 15 or less to as much as 90 m/min (50 to 300 fpm).

Adjustable dogs bolted to the side of a planer table trip a switch or control valve to reverse the table at the end of the desired stroke. If not reversed as intended, a heavily loaded planer table might very well run off the end of the bed and cause considerable damage. Most planers have a safety device to take care of just such an emergency. Among these devices are hydraulic bumpers. Another form has cutting tools bolted to the underside of the table to bite into replaceable stop blocks fastened to the bed.

Feed on a planer is intermittent and is the distance in inches the tool is moved for each stroke of the workpiece. One means is through a ratchet mechanism actuated by table reversal. Each toolhead can be fed horizontally or vertically as shown in Fig. 23-6. The tool may also be fed at an angle by swiveling the toolhead and feeding the tool slide. The feeds to the various heads are independent of each other. A typical feed range is 0.25 to 25 mm/stroke (0.01 to 1 in./stroke).

Types of Planers. The *standard* or *double housing planer* that has been described is capable of heavy service. An *openside planer* has a housing only on one side of the bed. The other side is open so that extra wide work can hang over the side of the bed sometimes supported on an auxiliary rolling table alongside. Small sizes of openside planers are also called *shaper planers*. A *divided* or *latching table planer* has a table in two sections. They may be coupled together for long work or separated so the work on one table may be set up while that on the other is machined.

The *planer-type milling machine* is a cross between the planer and milling machine and is described in Chap. 24. A *planer-type grinder* has a grinding head in place of one or more of the conventional toolheads on the rail.

A *plate planer* is a special-purpose machine for squaring and beveling the edges of steel plates for armor, ships, or pressure vessels. One edge of the plate is held down and machined by a tool traversed on a carriage along the front of a machine.

When workpieces are too heavy or bulky, the tools may be moved more readily than the work. That is the basis for the design of the *pit planer* on which the workpiece is mounted on a stationary table. Columns carrying the cross-rail and toolheads ride on long ways on both sides of the table.

Sizes of Planers. The size of a standard planer is designated by the distance between the vertical housings in inches, the height from the top of the table to the rail in its uppermost position in inches, and the maximum length of table travel in feet. The length of travel is often the length of the working area of the table. The size of an openside planer is designated by comparable figures, but the first specifies the distance from the column to the tool in its outmost positions. Sometimes when the first two figures are the same, they are expressed by one quantity, such as 42 in. × 10 ft for 42 in. × 42 in. × 10 ft. Planers range in size from 24 in. with 42 in. stroke to 16 ft × 16 ft by 60 ft long.

Planer Tools and Attachments. Single-point cutting tools of the same general shapes, materials, and angles as lathe and shaper tools are used on planers but for the most part are heavier and larger because the planer normally takes deep cuts at heavy feeds. Round nose tools are favored for roughing, but sharp point tools are necessary to get into corners, such as in dovetails. Various arrangements of gangs of tool bits in a holder are widely used. Finishing tools may have cutting edges up to about 40 mm ($1\frac{1}{2}$ in.) wide set carefully parallel to the surface cut.

Most workpieces are clamped directly to the table on a planer. Some typical arrangements are depicted in Fig. 23-7. Sometimes work is held in a vise or vises fastened to the table top. Occasionally fixtures may be justified by the quantity of pieces to be machined. Setup time can be saved by loading one set of fixtures while a duplicate set holds pieces being planned. *Setup plates* fit the table top, and one is loaded off the machine while another is on the table with work being machined.

Planing Operations. Efficient setup practice is probably the most important phase of planer operation. It has been said that a planer is more difficult to set up than any other machine tool, in spite of the fact that is is a relatively simple machine in itself. Large and intermittent forces varying in direction must be forestalled. Workpieces are bulky and heavy but must be precisely and safely located and fastened, and each job is almost a new problem.

To get most out of a planer, as many tools as possible are set to cutting at the same time, and each tool must be held securely with a minimum of overhang. As an example, top and side surfaces of a large piece may be cut simultaneously by tools held in two or more rail and side-heads. A single surface can be rough cut by one tool and semifinished by another tool set slightly lower and alongside the first tool. A number of workpieces may be placed side by side or in rows to utilize the toolheads fully.

The large work commonly done on planers is not expected to be machined as closely as smaller work done on other machines, such as shapers. Tolerances of 0.13 to 0.25 mm (0.005 to 0.010 in.) are considered practicable, although smaller tolerances are realizable with care and skill.

Estimating Planing Time and Power. A planer tool is usually set to rough a surface to about 125 μm (0.005 in.) in size. The depth of cut depends upon the amount of stock to be removed and frequently is as much as 30 mm (ca. $1\frac{1}{4}$ in.) and more. An average feed is 3 to 6 mm (ca. $\frac{1}{8}$ to $\frac{1}{4}$ in.) for roughing, but may be more or less to suit conditions.

For fair finishes, only two cuts may be taken. For fine finishes, three cuts are customary, with 25 to 50 μm (0.001 to 0.002 in.) of stock taken off by the final cut. Broad-nose finishing tools for cast iron are fed 6 to 25 mm/stroke (ca. $\frac{1}{4}$ to 1 in./stroke) at speeds of about 12 m/min (40 fpm) for high-speed steel and 60 m/min (200 fpm)

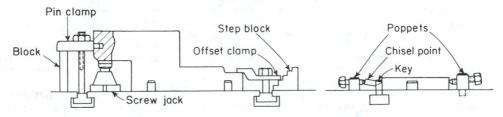

Figure 23-7 Typical work-holding methods for a planer.

for carbides. Feeds up to 6 mm/stroke (ca. $\frac{1}{4}$ in./stroke) are recommended for finishing steel.

Planing tools are governed by the same factors and economically can stand the same speeds as other single-point tools but the actual speeds and feeds in planing operations are often limited by sizes of the workpieces and machines. The strength of the workpieces or the pull of the machines may limit the feed. However, cuts are generally heavy in planing, and for a large cut, the speed must be decreased to maintain an economical tool life. Thus operating speeds tend to be lower for planing than some other operations. The speed may be limited for a heavy cut by the power of the machine especially with several tools cutting at once. In general, both cutting and return speeds should be lower for heavy workpieces because of their inertia. On the other hand, full advantage should be taken of the capacities of the tools and machine when the workpiece or cut, or both, are light. Speeds and feeds used in practice are given in Table 23-2 to serve as a guide. For iron and steel, the table recognizes higher speeds with lower feeds, and vice versa.

The return stroke speed on a planer may be from one to four times as high as the cutting speed. For an average ratio of $2\frac{1}{2}:1$, and following the same reasoning as for the shaper, $N = 714 \, V/l$ for V in m/min and l in mm. $N = 8.6 \, V/l$ for V in fpm and l in inches.

The cutting time for planing is calculated from the number of strokes per minute (N), the feed, and the distance the tool is fed, in the same way as described for shaping. The unit power consumption may be comparable to that required on a shaper for light cuts. Metal removal is more efficient for heavy cuts usually taken on a planer. One leading manufacturer uses the constants of 11.5 W/cm^3/min (0.25 hp/in.^{3}/min) for cast iron, 23 (0.5) for machine steel, and 7 (0.15) for bronze.

Planing Compared with Other Operations.   Planers generally are capable of performing the same basic operations as shapers and milling machines. Because they offer full support, planers can be made to take large, bulky, and heavy workpieces or numbers of pieces at one time. Although the planer is not as suitable as the shaper for small and medium-size parts done one or a few at a time, it often is better when enough parts are required so that a number can be done at one time or when heavy cuts can be taken. The components of a planer are massive and rigid, and heavy cuts and feeds are feasible.

TABLE 23-2 RECOMMENDED SPEEDS AND FEEDS FOR PLANING

| | Speed [m/min (fpm)] | | | |
Material	H.S.S.	Nonferrous alloys	Cemented carbide	Feed [mm/stroke (ips)]
Aluminum	30–60 (100–200)			0.75–2.25 (0.03–0.09)
Brass and bronze	15–45 (50–150)	At maximum table speed		0.75–2.25 (0.03–0.09)
Cast iron	15–30 (50–100)	30–45 (100–150)	45–90 (150–300)	0.75–3.0 (0.03–0.12)
Steel	10–20 (30–60)	25–40 (75–125)	30–60 (100–200)	3–25 (0.12–1.00)

Planing with single-point tools generally is conceded to be a slower cutting operation than milling with multipoint tools. The main advantage of planing is low tool cost and maintenance. For a typical operation, enough planer tool bits can be ground in about an hour for a 24-hour operation. Several hours may be spent in grinding milling cutters for the same operation. Even so, milling is preferred for most work, and few new planers are built and sold today, but many older machines are regularly in use throughout the world.

QUESTIONS

1. How are shaping and planing alike, and how do they differ?
2. What are the advantages and disadvantages of shaping and planing compared to other operations?
3. Describe a horizontal shaper.
4. What is a draw cut shaper?
5. Describe a vertical shaper.
6. What are the common kinds of shaper drives?
7. Discuss the relative advantages and disadvantages of hydraulic and mechanical shaper drives.
8. What does the size of a shaper designate?
9. What are false jaws, and why are they used?
10. What are hold-downs, and what purpose do they serve?
11. Describe a double housing planer; an open-side planer.
12. How is the size of a planer designated?
13. How is work held on a planer?
14. In what ways are planers economical?

PROBLEMS

1. List the steps and describe the setups and tools needed to shape one piece depicted in Fig. 23-8. The rough casting has 3-mm ($\frac{1}{8}$ in.) stock on all surfaces. Normal operation tolerances are satisfactory.
2. For an average cutting speed of 30 m/min (100 fpm), what should be the theoretical number of strokes per minute on a shaper with a cutting to idle stroke ratio of 1.8 : 1 and a length of stroke of (a) 3 in.? (b) 5 in.? (c) 8 in.? (d) 15 in.? (e) 75 mm? (f) 125 mm? (g) 200 mm? (h) 400 mm?
   Would it be likely that you would be able to get a cutting speed of 30 m/min (100 fpm) for all these lengths of stroke on a 24-in. shaper?
3. For a 305 mm (12 in.) length of stroke on a shaper with a cutting to idle stroke ratio of 1.8 : 1, how many strokes per minute are required for a cutting speed of (a) 25 fpm? (b) 50 fpm? (c) 75 fpm? (d) 100 fpm? (e) 7.5 m/min? (f) 15 m/min? (g) 25 m/min? (h) 30 m/min?

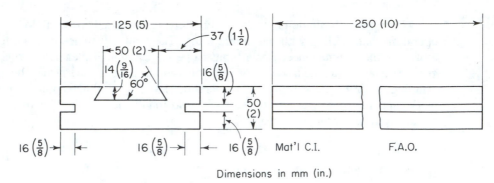

Dimensions in mm (in.)

Figure 23-8 Slide block.

4. A cast-iron surface 40 × 250 mm ($1\frac{1}{2}$ × 10 in.) is to be rough shaped with a depth of cut of 3 mm ($\frac{1}{8}$ in.). The shaper ratio is 1.6 : 1. Estimate the cutting time and power required for the cut.

5. The top of a mild steel plate 40 × 250 mm ($1\frac{1}{2}$ × 10 in.) is to be finish shaped with the removal of 0.8 mm ($\frac{1}{32}$ in.) of metal. The shaper ratio is 1.6 : 1. Cutting speed is 30 m/min (100 fpm) with a H.S.S. tool. Estimate the cutting time and power required for the cut.

6. What is the relationship between cut speed, length of cut, and number of strokes per minute on a shaper when the forward-to-return stroke ratio is (a) 2 : 1? (b) 3 : 1? (c) 4 : 1?

7. A cast-iron machine tool bed weighing 9 Mg (10 tons) is to be machined on a planer. As much as 19 mm ($\frac{3}{4}$ in.) of stock must be removed on the largest surface that is 3.65 m (12 ft) long and 200 mm (8 in.) wide. Two other surfaces of the same length and with the same stock removal may be machined at the same time, but are not as wide. Cemented carbide tools are to be used. The planer can deliver 56 kW (75 hp) to the cut.
   (a) What cutting speed and feed should be used?
   (b) For what return stroke and what number of strokes per minute should the planer be set?
   (c) Estimate the cutting time for the roughing operation.
   (d) Estimate the cutting time for the finishing operation.

8. A mild-steel plate has a top surface 0.6 × 1.4 m (24 × 55 in.) to be planed with a stock removal of 3 mm ($\frac{1}{8}$ in.). Two cemented carbide tools are to be used. Specify the number of strokes per minute. The machine has a 37-kW (50-hp) motor. Cut speed is 60 m/min (200 fpm) and machine efficiency 75%. Estimate the time to remove all the stock under each of the following conditions.
   (a) The planer cuts in one direction and is returned at 98 m/min (320 fpm) idle. The two tools both cut on the forward stroke.
   (b) The table returns at 60 m/min (200 fpm). One tool cuts on the forward stroke, and one tool on the return stroke.

9. Six millimeters ($\frac{1}{4}$ in.) of stock is to be removed from a cast-iron surface 1.07 × 1.22 m (42 × 48 in.) in two passes. Two roughing tools will be used at once. All tools are cemented carbide. A speed of 12 spm and feed of 6 mm ($\frac{1}{4}$ in.) for both roughing and finishing have been selected. Estimate the cutting time for the operation.

10. Twenty slide blocks like the one shown in Fig. 23-8 are to be machined on a planer. Specify the size of planer suitable for the job. Describe the steps and arrangements needed to machine these pieces.

REFERENCES

DALLAS, D. B., ed., *Tool and Manufacturing Engineers Handbook,* 3rd ed., Society of Manufacturing Engineers, Dearborn, Mich., 1976.

Set-ups on Cincinnati Rigid Shapers, The Cincinnati Shaper Co., Cincinnati, Ohio.

"Shapers and Planers," *Metalworking,* Oct. 1964, p. 33.

24

MILLING

Flat or curved surfaces, inside or outside, of almost all shapes and sizes can be machined by milling. Common milling operations are depicted in Fig. 24-1. As a rule the workpiece is fed into or past a revolving milling cutter that usually has a number of teeth all taking intermittent cuts in succession. Also, the rotating cutter may be fed into the workpiece.

As indicated in Fig. 24-1, the same kind of a surface can often be milled in several ways. For instance, plane surfaces may be machined by slab milling, side milling, or face milling. The method for any specific job may be determined by the kind of milling machine used, the cutter, or the shape of the workpiece and the position of the surface.

MILLING CUTTERS AND DRIVERS

Kinds of Milling Cutters. Many kinds and sizes of cutters are needed for the large variety of work that can be done by milling. Many standard cutters are available, but when they are not adequate, special cutters are made. The principal types of standard cutters are identified in Fig. 24-2. A cutter is often named for the kind of milling operation it does.

Milling cutters are made of various diameters, lengths, widths, and numbers of teeth. Milling cutters may be of the *solid, tipped,* or *inserted tooth* types with the same materials as for single-point tools. Large cutters commonly have teeth of expensive material inserted and locked in place in a soft-steel or cast-iron body, like the face milling cutter of Fig. 24-2.

632

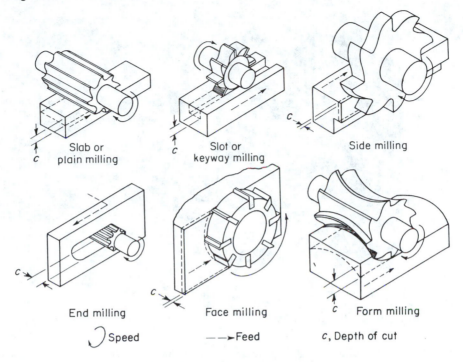

Slab or
plain milling

Slot or
keyway milling

Side milling

End milling

Face milling

Form milling

Speed — — ► Feed c, Depth of cut

Figure 24-1 Some milling operations.

The simplest type of special milling cutter is a *fly cutter*. It consists of a bit held in an arbor as in Fig. 24-3 or in a heavy disk that acts like a flywheel. Such a cutter is easy to form and can be made to do accurate work but is slow in operation. Fly cutters are used chiefly for form milling where only a few pieces are to be made. For milling larger quantities of a particular form, a special multitooth cutter is made.

Teeth of Milling Cutters. The teeth of a milling cutter have cutting edges and angles related to the edges like other cutting tools. In effect, each tooth acts like a single-point tool. The teeth are evenly spaced on most milling cutters, but uneven spacing helps to reduce chatter. The names of the surfaces or elements and angles of a plain milling cutter given in Fig. 24-4 are typical.

A *shaped* or *formed profile cutter,* also called a *profile ground cutter,* has a cutting edge of the desired form on each tooth with a narrow land behind the edge as in Fig. 24-4. Straight cutters are mostly of this kind, like the plain milling cutters in Fig. 24-2. This land is ground to sharpen the cutter, and it may be difficult to reproduce the original contour on a form cutter, although some form cutters are of this kind and machines are available for grinding them.

A *form* or *cam relieved cutter,* also called a *face ground cutter,* has a cutting edge around each tooth of the same shape as the surface to be cut and also has the same profile in radial or parallel planes behind the cutting edge. Examples shown in Fig. 24-2 are the concave, convex, involute gear, and corner-rounding cutters. The cutter is sharpened by grinding the same amount from the faces of all its teeth. Form relieved

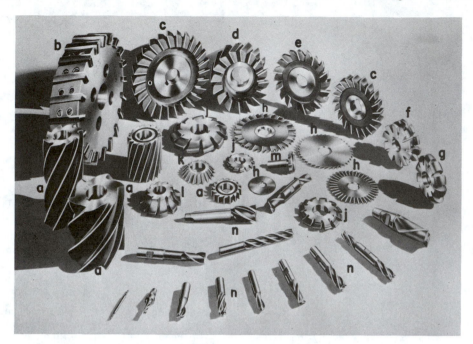

Figure 24-2 Principal types of standard milling cutters: (a) plain milling cutters (slab mills); (b) face milling cutter; (c) side milling cutters; (d) shell end mill; (e) staggered-tooth side milling cutter; (f) concave cutter; (g) convex cutter; (h) metal slitting saws; (j) involute gear cutters; (k) angular cutter; (1) corner rounding cutter; (m) Woodruff keyseat cutter; (n) end mills of various types. (Courtesy Brown and Sharpe Mfg. Co.)

cutters are relatively easy to sharpen, and their teeth may be reground until they become too frail to withstand the cutting load.

Cutters with inserted teeth are exemplified by Fig. 24-5 for a typical face mill. The teeth cut mostly on the nose chamfer edge. Both axial and radial rake determine the *true rake angle* in a plane perpendicular to the cutting edge. Cutters with both rake angles negative are common for cemented carbides and oxides because they help reduce shock at the edge but produce large forces that may be harmful to weak workpieces. With both rake angles positive, forces and power may be minimized, but teeth are weaker. Positive axial and negative radial rake cutters, called *shear angle*

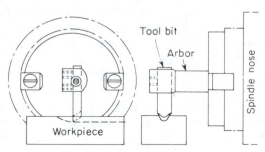

Figure 24-3 Sketch of a fly cutter.

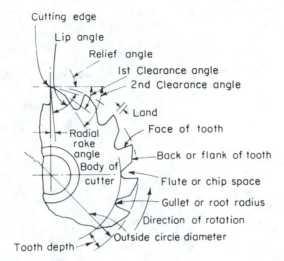

Cutting edge
Lip angle
Relief angle
1st Clearance angle
2nd Clearance angle
Land
Radial rake angle
Face of tooth
Back or flank of tooth
Body of cutter
Flute or chip space
Gullet or root radius
Direction of rotation
Outside circle diameter
Tooth depth

Figure 24-4 Elements and angles of the teeth of a plain milling cutter.

cutters, combine the best features of the others, but cannot cut squarely when close to a shoulder.

Detailed recommendations for milling cutter tooth angles for various applications are given in reference books and handbooks. Many different milling cutters exist; one manufacturer of inserted tooth cutters offers 850 styles and sizes.

Arbors, Collets, and Adapters. A variety of holders and drivers is needed to accommodate the many sizes and types of milling cutters. These are known as milling machine arbors, collets, and adapters.

The hole in the spindle of a modern milling machine has a taper of $3\frac{1}{2}$ in./ft at

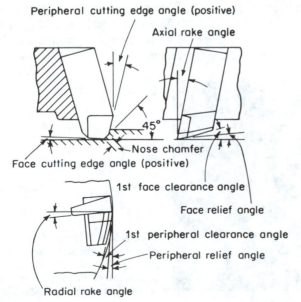

Peripheral cutting edge angle (positive)
Axial rake angle
45°
Nose chamfer
Face cutting edge angle (positive)
1st face clearance angle
Face relief angle
1st peripheral clearance angle
Peripheral relief angle
Radial rake angle

Figure 24-5 Angles of a typical face mill.

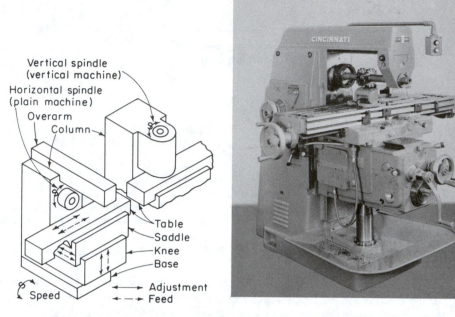

Vertical spindle
(vertical machine)
Horizontal spindle
(plain machine)
Overarm
Column
Table
Saddle
Knee
Base
Speed
Adjustment
Feed

Figure 24-6 Diagram of movements and a picture of a No. 2 plain knee and column-type general-purpose milling machine setup for an operation. (Courtesy Cincinnati Milacron, Inc.)

the cutter end. This is known as a National Machine Tool Builders Association taper and exists in several standard sizes.

Milling cutters are held in several ways. Face milling cutters are usually bolted on the spindle nose of the machine. A cutter with a center hole is held by a *milling machine arbor* like those illustrated in Figs. 24-6 and 24-7. The cutters are clamped and keyed on the straight portion, and the tapered end of the arbor is held in the hole

Figure 24-7 Universal knee and column milling machine with the table swiveled and carrying a dividing head and helical milling attachment. (Courtesy Brown and Sharpe Mfg. Co.)

of the machine spindle. A short arbor is available for shell end and small face milling cutters held close to the machine spindle. It is sometimes called a *shell end mill arbor*.

Collets and *adapters* serve to adapt taper shank cutters or drivers to the taper in the end of the hole of a milling machine spindle. An adapter usually has an outside NMTBA standard taper and a smaller inside taper. Collets usually but not always have sticking tapers, such as Brown and Sharpe ($\frac{1}{2}$ in./ft) or Morse ($\frac{5}{8}$ in./ft) tapers, inside and outside. A quick-change adapter engages a cutter shank or driver by a quick cam action.

A *spring chuck* or *collet holder* may be mounted on a milling machine spindle to hold wire, rods, and straight shank tools.

MILLING MACHINES

Many types of milling machines serve in various ways in industry. Some kinds are best for general-purpose work, others are suited for repetitive manufacturing, and some are ideally arranged for special jobs. In general, milling machines may be classified as general-purpose, production, planer-type, and specialized millers. Horizontal boring, drilling, and milling machines are included in this section because they also do milling. General-purpose milling machines and boring mills are commonly hand operated, and production machines run in automatic cycles, but numerical control (Chap. 35) is also applied to all sizes and models.

General-Purpose Milling Machines.   The *knee and column milling machine* for general-purpose work has the characteristics designated by Fig. 24-6. This type of machine is capable not only of doing straight milling of plane and curved surfaces but also gear and thread cutting, drilling, boring, and slotting when suitably equipped.

The *plain* knee and column-type milling machine of Fig. 24-6 has a horizontal hollow spindle in the column to drive cutters. Arbors and adapters are held by a quick-change clamping sleeve on the nose of this spindle, but on many machines a draw bar from the rear is screwed into arbors to hold them in the spindle. The overarm extending from the top of the column carries supports for cutter arbors. Braces are available to tie the arbor supports and overarm to the knee for added rigidity. The knee, saddle, and table are positioned and fed, by hand or power, in the three coordinate directions shown by the diagram of Fig. 24-6. One model of a general-purpose milling machine has the saddle and the table on a fixed base instead of a knee with the cutter spindle in a housing sliding on vertical ways on the column. That design provides rigid support for heavy workpieces and still retains the flexibililty needed for general-purpose milling.

A *universal* knee and column milling machine is like a plain type except that the table can be swiveled in a horizontal plane. This is especially helpful for milling a helix as shown in Fig. 24-7. The saddle is made in two parts. The upper part swivels on the lower and carries the table with it, to a limit of about 45°. The leadscrew that feeds the table is arranged so that a geared drive can be taken from it to drive a dividing head on the table. Some universal type machines have additional features. On one the knee can be swiveled to tilt the table end over end and an auxiliary spindle head on the side of the column can be swiveled to almost any angle.

A *vertical* knee and column milling machine has a vertical head and spindle as indicated in Fig. 24-6 but the same feeds and adjustments as the plain machine. On some models the head can be moved up and down, and on others it can be swiveled around a horizontal axis.

Knee and column-type milling machines can be arranged to do any kind of milling and are relatively easy to change from one job to another. However, these general-purpose milling machines have a certain amount of unavoidable looseness in the necessary joints between units and weakness from overhanging members. An operator must attend to a number of controls needed to govern all the available movements, adjustments, and arrangements. Production milling machines are simpler, more rigid, powerful, and automatic, and faster for machining parts in quantities.

Production Milling Machines.   Production or *manufacturing milling machines* are designed to remove metal rapidly and to require a minimum of attention from the operator. They are not as easy to adapt to various jobs as knee and column millers. For instance, adjustments are provided in three coordinate directions, but feeds are often available in only one direction and seldom in more than two directions. As a result, each workpiece must be held in a particular position to be milled. Versatility is not so important because production millers are intended for long runs where setup changes are not frequent and special fixtures and cutters are often justified to hold workpieces and adapt the machine to specific jobs.

Production milling machines are made in several styles. Some small models have knees, but the most common construction is on a heavy bed that forms a base for the major units and by which the table is fully supported. They are sometimes called *bed-type milling machines*. As many units as possible are securely tied together. The construction is rigid to withstand heavy cuts. The operator is aided because the controls are simple and the action often automatic.

Simple hand-operated millers are common among the smaller production machines. They are suited for light cuts, like slotting the heads of screws. As the name implies, the table is fed by hand through a hand wheel or lever, but the cutter is driven by a motor.

The characteristics of a typical medium-size bed-type production milling machine are illustrated in Fig. 24-8. The only feed movement is the lengthwise feed of the table. Dogs on the front of the table are set to trip plungers to direct the table through each cycle of the operation. The table may be fed in either or both directions. In a typical cycle, the table carries the work rapidly to the cutter, proceeds at slow feed, reverses at the end of the cut, and withdraws quickly. The spindle is started at the beginning and stopped at the end of each cut automatically. Once the machine has been set up, all the operator has to do to control it is to start each cycle by pushing a lever on the front of the bed. Production millers are available that can be programmed through complex operation cycles by the insertion of pegs in a control panel.

The spindle of the machine illustrated in Fig. 24-8 is carried in a quill in the spindle carrier and is adjustable crosswise over the table. The spindle carrier is

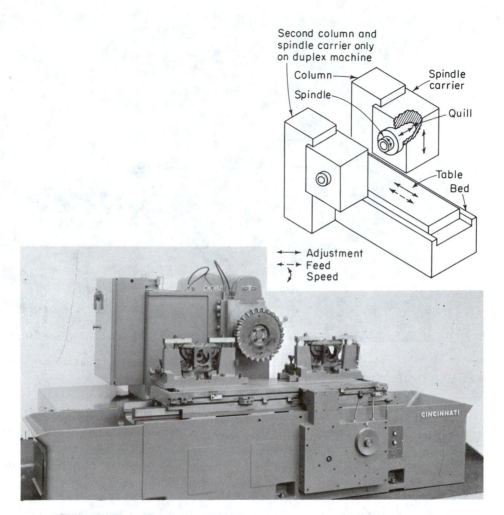

Figure 24-8 Diagram of the principal parts and movements of a bed-type production milling machine and a photo of a plain bed-type production milling machine with a setup for reciprocating facemilling. (Courtesy Cincinnati Milacron, Inc.)

adjustable vertically on a column attached to the bed. After adjustment, these units are clamped in position. Some machines of this kind are built with spindle carriers having controlled up and down movements; some have three axes of movement.

A production miller with one spindle carrier is called a *plain* machine. A *duplex* machine has two opposed spindle carriers as indicated in the diagram of Fig. 24-8. A rail may be placed across the columns and a third or fourth spindle carrier mounted vertically on it over the table. This type of machine is considered a special type.

Tracer-controlled profiling or contouring milling machines reproduce curved and irregular surfaces in moderate to large quantities. A typical job is shown in Fig. 24-9. A tracer is moved across the template surface, or the surface is moved in contact

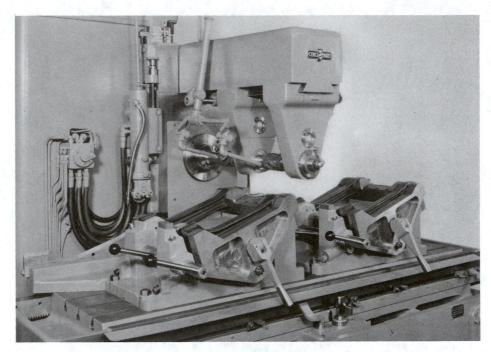

Figure 24-9   Plain production-type milling machine equipped with tracer control for milling profiles. (Courtesy Cincinnati Milacron, Inc.)

with the tracer. Through a servomechanism, the cutter spindle is made to move up and down as it traverses the workpiece the same way that the tracer moves, and the cutter reproduces the surface or form covered by the tracer finger.

Not all production millers have reciprocating tables. *Continuous millers* have rotary tables, some horizontal, others vertical. Their use is described in the section on planning for economical milling.

In addition to the common machines described to define the specific types, other models are available with various characteristics of both general-purpose and production millers.

Milling Machine Sizes.   Important factors of capacity of milling machines are table size, length of movements, and power. The more common sizes of machines have been standardized in ANSI B5.45 (see the references at the end of the chapter). Horizontal knee and column type millers are designated by size numbers 2, 3, 4, and 5. Minimum dimensions are specified for each size. Horizontal bed-type machines are designated by sizes 10, 14, 18, 22, and 30. Each size may have a range of dimensions. Commonly, for each dimensional size, machines are made for light, medium, and heavy duty, with corresponding strength and power. Some manufacturers use their own symbols to designate sizes. A few typical specifications are given in Table 24-1.

TABLE 24-1 SPECIFICATIONS FOR SEVERAL MILLING MACHINES

Type	Table size $L \times W$ [m (in.)]	Size number	Motor power [kW (hp)]	Weight [Mg (lb)]	Price
Knee and column swivel head	1.1 × 0.254 (44 × 10)	1	1.5 (2.0)	0.9 (2,000)	$ 6,000
Knee and column horizontal	1.37 × 0.305 (54 × 12)	2	5.5 (1.5)	2.4 (5,200)	25,000
Bed-type horizontal	2.54 × 0.635 (100 × 25)	20xx[a]	26 (35)	9.5 (21,000)	120,000
Knee and column numerical control	0.965 × 0.381 (38 × 15)	3	5.5 (7.5)		100,000
Bed-type horizontal programmable	Travel 1.2 to 2.4 × 0.6 or 1.2 (47 to 94 × 23 or 47)	700[a]	22.5 (30)		230,000

[a]Manufacturer's designation.

Standard milling machines provide wide ranges of speeds and feeds. For example, a No. 2 general-purpose miller has 24 speeds from 18 to 1800 rpm and 32 feeds from 10 to 2300 mm/min ($\frac{3}{8}$ to 90 ipm).

Planer-Type Milling Machines. A planer-type milling machine looks like and has comparable movements to a double housing planer, except that the table customarily feeds at a slow rate and spindle carriers for rotating cutters take the places of the planer toolheads. These machines are designed to handle large workpieces.

Horizontal Boring, Drilling, and Milling Machines. Horizontal boring mill is a common name for this machine because it is typically fitted with a backrest or end support for boring with long bars as illustrated at the top in Fig. 24-10. The bar in that picture is driven on the left by the spindle in the headstock or spindle head, which can be moved up or down on ways on a column. The end support on the right end of the bar is raised or lowered by a screw in unison with the headstock. Stub boring bars are also used without end support. Horizontal boring, drilling, and milling machines do milling as well as boring, usually with a face mill on the end of the spindle as shown at the bottom in Fig. 24-10.

Horizontal boring, drilling, and milling machines are built to provide support and rigidity to machine, with precision, large castings, forgings, and weldments for such products as diesel engines, turbines, and machine tool columns. The work table on a *table-type* machine, like the ones in Fig. 24-10, is mounted and moves lengthwise and crosswise over a saddle and bed. Other types offer still more rigidity. A *floor-type boring mill* has a headstock on a column that slides on runways. Workpieces are placed on floor plates alongside the runways. A *planer-type horizontal boring mill* has a table that moves and is directly supported on a bed as on a planer. The headstock

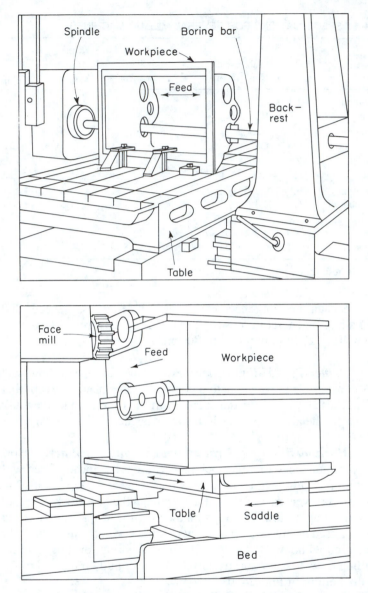

Figure 24-10 Operation being done on horizontal boring, drilling, and milling machines: top; boring a casting with a long boring bar supported in a back rest; bottom; face milling a pad on a welded structure.

and its column and the end support, or another headstock in its place, are movable on runways crosswise to and from the table.

The size of a horizontal boring mill is designated by the diameter of its spindle, customarily from 75 to 350 mm (3 to 14 in.). A 90-mm ($3\frac{1}{2}$-in.)-diameter bar machine with vertical travel of 1.12m (44 in.), horizontal travel of 1.4m (55 in.), and cross travel of 1.25m (49 in.) has a 7.5-kW (10-hp) motor and costs about $95,000. A numerically controlled table-type horizontal boring mill with a 130-mm ($5\frac{1}{3}$ in.)-diameter bar and 20-kW (27-hp) motor costs more than $400,000.

Special-Purpose Milling Machines. Milling machines are made for particular kinds of work such as duplicating of forms, milling of cams, and machining specific parts in large quantities.

Duplicating machines are commonly used to make forging dies, molds, forming dies, etc. and often are called *die sinking machines*. *Profilers* are capable of reproducing external and internal profiles from templates in two dimensions like the tracer-controlled milling machine of Fig. 24-9. *Duplicators* reproduce in three dimensions. The duplicator, also called a *copy milling machine,* of Fig. 24-11 is producing a die from a plaster model. As the table is fed lengthwise and crosswise, the tracer finger on the right traverses the surface of the model. Through servo control, the cutter spindle on the left moves as directed by the tracer to make the cutter reproduce the same surface on the workpiece. Some machines have several spindles and can reproduce a surface on several workpieces at one time.

Cam millers produce disk cams. The profile of the cam is cut on a slowly revolving workpiece by an end mill positioned by a master cam revolving in unison with the workpiece.

Special milling machines are often built to do specific jobs quickly and efficiently when production is large enough to justify the initial cost. Quite often these are essentially modifications of standard machines. For example, a duplex production milling machine may have special spindle carriers to hold and drive several face mills at the necessary angles to machine all the surfaces along a V-8 engine block at the same time.

Figure 24-11 High-speed duplicator or copy milling machine cutting a three-dimensional die from solid steel. The tracer on the right makes the cutter rise and fall to duplicate the model in the die block as the table is fed lengthwise and crosswise. (Courtesy Quality Machines, Inc.)

MILLING MACHINE ATTACHMENTS

Many standard attachments are available to make milling machines easier and faster to operate and increase the variety of jobs that can be done. They may be divided into two general classes. One class includes those for positioning and driving cutters. The other includes attachments for positioning and holding work.

Cutter Driving Attachments. Attachments are commonly put on horizontal spindle milling machines to hold and drive cutters with their axes inclined or swiveled from the conventional position. This puts the cutters into positions for milling helical gear teeth, racks, cams, and surfaces, grooves, or holes at all angles in workpieces that cannot conveniently be reached otherwise. A popular type is the universal high-speed milling attachment of Fig. 24-12 that can be swiveled 360° in a plane parallel to and 45° either way in a plane normal to the machine column face. The attachment shown is driven by the machine spindle as are many others, but some have their own driving motors.

Work-Holding Devices. Work must be held securely for milling. When one or a few pieces are to be milled, a workpiece may be fastened and located on the table

Figure 24-12 Universal high-speed milling attachment on a plain knee and column-type milling machine for end milling a cam track. (Courtesy Cincinnati Milacron, Inc.)

by tee bolts, strap clamps, blocks, etc., as is done on shapers, planers, and drill presses. Setup in this way is slow and not even feasible for many kinds of work such as gear cutting. Devices used to make work positioning easy are vises, chucks, fixtures, index bases, circular tables, and index and dividing heads.

A *vise* is the most common holding device found on milling machines. A *plain vise* is depicted in Fig. 24-13. Other kinds can be swiveled or tilted but are not as rigid.

Many vises are opened and closed by a screw like that in Fig. 24-13, but faster acting cam and toggle devices are often used. Air- or hydraulic-operated vises are economical for quantity production.

The vise jaws that make contact with the work are held on by screws and are removable. Standard jaws for general-purpose work have flat faces. Special jaws of various shapes are often made and applied to hold specific workpieces milled in quantities. This is illustrated in Fig. 24-13. Special jaws on a standard vise are cheaper than a whole special fixture.

Universal chucks like those used on lathes are employed to hold work either on the table or spindle of a milling machine.

Fixtures were introduced and defined along with jigs in Chap. 22. They are widely used to hold and locate parts milled in moderate to large quantities. Fixtures are mounted on the table of the machines in Figs. 24-8 and 24-9. A fixture may save

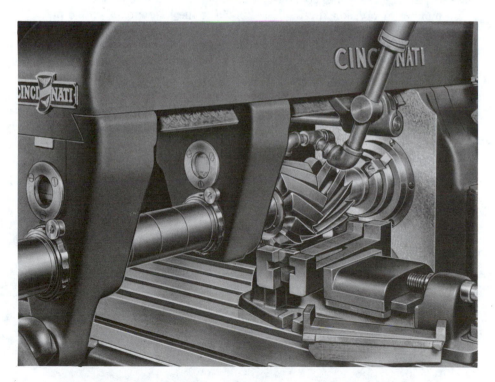

Figure 24-13 Plain milling vise with special jaws for holding an irregular workpiece. (Courtesy Cincinnati Milacron, Inc.)

time and money in an operation by holding a workpiece in a desired position to make attachments or a difficult setup unnecessary, by providing full support to a workpiece so that heavy cuts can be taken (better pieces and less scrap are made because deflection and distortion are eliminated), and by making unloading and loading the workpieces easier and quicker. A fixture usually is good for only one operation and is justified only when it can save enough on that operation to pay for its cost. The worth of a fixture may be estimated by Eq. (19-1).

A *circular milling attachment* or *rotary table* is a round table that can be turned about its axis on a base. It is set down on the reciprocating table of a conventional milling machine. Some rotary tables are turned or indexed by hand; others are power driven from the feed drive of the machine. Cuts may be made at desired intervals around a workpiece on the table by indexing. Circular arcs may be milled, and other curves obtained by combining the circular motion with the linear machine feeds.

Dividing Heads. A *dividing* or *index head* is a mechanical device for dividing a circle accurately into equal parts. This is called *indexing*. A common indexing device for milling machines is the *universal dividing head* shown in Figs. 24-7 and 24-12, priced at $1,500 and more.

Direct indexing is done by means of a plate on the front of the spindle of the head. The plate has equally spaced notches or holes in one or more circles. The number of divisions available is limited to the hole circles on the plate.

Plain or *simple indexing* is done through a single train of gears. The sections of a universal dividing head of Fig. 24-14 show a worm turned by gears and a crank on the side of the head. The worm is engaged with a worm wheel around the spindle. Forty turns of the crank are needed to turn the work spindle of this head one full revolution; five turns are needed on some heads. A pin in the crank handle registers in holes in a plate fixed to the side of the head. The plate and crank can be seen in Fig. 24-12. The holes are arranged in circles, and a different number is equally spaced

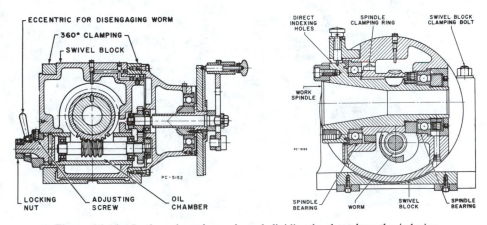

Figure 24-14 Sections through a universal dividing head to show the indexing mechanism. (Courtesy Cincinnati Milacron, Inc.)

in each circle. Standard plates on one make of dividing head have holes that make it possible to index all numbers up to and including 60 and many higher numbers.

The number of turns of the crank of a dividing head required to index the work one division is equal to the ratio of the dividing head (40, for example) divided by the number of equally spaced divisions required for one full turn of the workpiece.

As an example, a dividing head with a 40:1 ratio is to be used to cut a gear having 36 teeth. The crank must be turned $40 \div 36 = 1\frac{4}{36} = 1\frac{1}{9}$ turns to index from one tooth space to the next on the gear. If the index plate has a circle with 18 holes, the crank must be advanced $18 \times \frac{1}{9} = 2$ spaces after each full turn.

The dividing head has been called a jewel among machine tools because of its precision. Plain indexing is commonly done on standard heads with an error from setting to setting on the work of less than 1 minute of arc. This is equivalent to 37.5 μm (0.0015 in.) on the circumference of a circle of 300 mm (12 in.) diameter, or 1 part in 25,000.

Several means are available for indexing numbers not obtainable with standard plain indexing, especially large numbers. One of these is *differential indexing,* an arrangement whereby a suitable train of gears is installed between the spindle of the dividing head and a jackshaft that turns the side indexing plate. Thus when the crank is turned and causes the spindle to turn, the plate is rotated and the actual distance the crank is moved from one hole to another depends upon the displacement of the plate. A *wide range divider* has two sideplates and cranks, one that turns the spindle with a 40:1 ratio and another that furnishes an additional 100:1 ratio. This provides indexing from 2 to 400,000 divisions. An *astronomical dividing head attachment* has three plates and cranks arranged to divide a circle into degrees, minutes, and seconds.

A *helical milling* or *lead attachment* is mounted on the end of a milling machine table, as in Figs. 24-7 and 24-12, to provide a drive from the table leadscrew to the dividing head to cut helical gears, worms, threads, twist drills, etc. The attachment drives the jackshaft that causes the index plate to turn. The crank, engaged with the plate, turns and causes the spindle of the dividing head to revolve. The lead of a helix cut on a milling machine is equivalent to the distance the table advances while the dividing head spindle makes one full revolution. The lead is varied by means of change gears in the driving attachment.

Linear indexing may be done on a general-purpose milling machine for such jobs as cutting rack teeth by means of the table leadscrew dial or a *rack indexing attachment.* That unit consists of a gear or slotted plate connected to the leadscrew through change gears and indexed by a pin.

MILLING OPERATIONS

Performance.   Two styles of peripheral milling are depicted in Fig. 24-15. *Conventional* or *up milling* is the more common because the cutter is opposed by the feed of the work and the effect on the machine is more even. It is harder on cutters because each tooth tends to rub rather than to take a bite as it enters the cut; pronounced feed marks are left on the work surface; and forces tending to lift the work

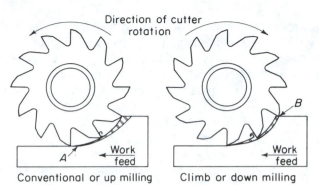

Conventional or up milling   Climb or down milling

Figure 24-15 Difference between conventional and climb milling.

are high when the depth of cut is over about 3 mm ($\frac{1}{8}$ in.). In contrast, each tooth enters the work with a substantial bite in *climb* or *down milling*. The cut is cooler, cutters last longer, feed marks are smaller, and the work is held down. However, the cutter tends to pull the workpiece along. The average milling machine has too much backlash in the leadscrew and nut and allows the cutter to draw the workpiece ahead and take bites that are too large. Damage is likely to result unless the workpiece and fixture are strong and backlash is eliminated as it is on hydraulic and some mechanical machines.

Tolerances of less than 25 μm (0.001 in.) can be held when milling a few pieces at a time with sufficient care and skill. However, tolerances of 50 to 130 μm (0.002 to 0.005 in.) are more practicable and economic for production milling.

Planning for Economical Milling.   Setup often accounts for most of the time to mill one or a few pieces of a kind. Time can be saved where a variety of work is milled by planning and scheduling the jobs so that similar parts are milled in succession.

It is shown in Chap. 19 that a turret lathe is tooled in different ways to get the lowest cost with different quantities of pieces. This same principle applies to milling operations as well as to most others. Some common milling arrangements are sketched in Fig. 24-16.

Plain or *simple milling* involves the loading and milling of one piece at a time and is the usual arrangement for one or a few pieces. Cutting time is saved in *string* or *line milling* with two or more pieces in a row because the cutter can be entering one piece as it leaves another. Efficiency is achieved by arranging for the operator to load at one station while the cut is taken at another, as in *reciprocating milling,* illustrated in Fig. 24-8. There the cutter cuts upward in one direction and downward in the other. If that is undesirable, it may be eliminated by *index base milling.* An index base consists of two plates mounted one above the other on the machine table. The upper plate carries a fixture on each end and is indexed 180° when retracted from the cutters. Then one fixture is advanced to the cut while the other is unloaded and loaded. Fixtures on a rotating round table are loaded with pieces and fed continuously to the cutter or cutters in *circular or rotary milling.* This may be done on a continuous miller with an integral rotary table or on an auxiliary circular table mounted on a conventional milling machine.

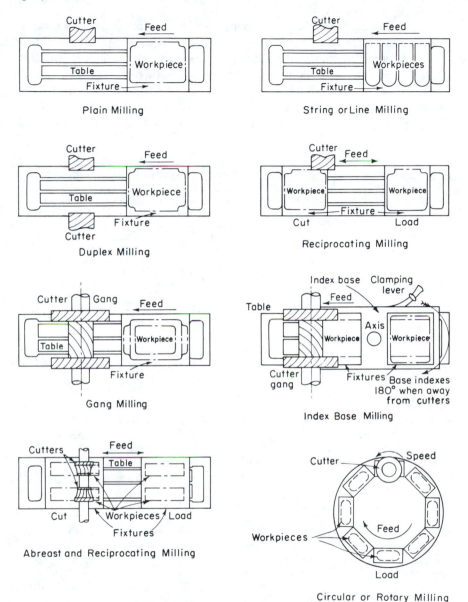

Figure 24-16 Some common forms of production milling operations.

Cutting time is saved when two or more cutters are put to work at the same time. Common examples are given in Fig. 24-16. *Duplex milling* is done on a duplex miller constructed as indicated in Fig. 24-8. *Gang milling* utilizes two or more cutters on one arbor. If side milling cutters machine two sides of a workpiece at the same time, the operation is called *straddle milling*. If the purpose is to machine two or more parts side by side, the term is *abreast milling*.

Tooling for milling operations may be as complex as the amount of production warrants. The basic forms may be combined, as suggested by abreast and reciprocating milling in one operation in Fig. 24-16. Special indexing attachments, some arranged for automatic unloading and loading of a number of pieces at a time, are examples of devices for quite large quantity production. In any event, each production arrangement requires a certain investment in tooling, and the principle exemplified by Eq. (19-1) applies here: that the amount saved per piece times the number of pieces

TABLE 24-2 TYPICAL RECOMMENDATIONS OF CUTTING SPEEDS AND FEEDS FOR MILLING

| | | | Face mill | | | | Plain or slab mill | |
| | | | H.S.S. | | Uncoated cemented carbide | | H.S.S. | |
Material	(Bhn)	Depth of cut [mm (in.)]	Feed [mm/tooth (ipt)]	Speed [m/min (fpm)]	Feed [mm/tooth (ipt)]	Speed[a] [m/min (fpm)]	Feed [mm/tooth (ipt)]	Speed [m/min (fpm)]
Aluminum	30–80	8	0.50	200	0.65	365	0.40	260
alloys	(500 kg)	(0.300)	(0.020)	(650)	(0.025)	(1200)	(0.016)	(850)
cold drawn		1	0.25	365	0.25	610	0.30	365
		(0.040)	(0.010)	(1200)	(0.010)	(2000)	(0.012)	(1200)
Copper	50–100R_B	8	0.45	120	0.50	215	0.45	120
alloys		(0.300)	(0.018)	(400)	(0.020)	(700)	(0.018)	(400)
cold drawn		1	0.25	185	0.25	395	0.36	190
145 to 782		(0.040)	(0.010)	(600)	(0.010)	(1300)	(0.014)	(625)
Gray cast	220–260	8	0.36	15	0.36	62	0.25	14
iron		(0.300)	(0.014)	(50)	(0.014)	(205)	(0.010)	(45)
as cast Cl.		1	0.15	26	0.18	120	0.15	24
45 and 50		(0.040)	(0.006)	(85)	(0.007)	(400)	(0.006)	(80)
Steel	175–225	8	0.40	34	0.40	95	0.25	34
H.R. OR		(0.300)	(0.016)	(110)	(0.016)	(310)	(0.010)	(110)
C.D.		1	0.20	58	0.20	170	0.15	56
1005–1025		(0.040)	(0.008)	(190)	(0.008)	(550)	(0.006)	(185)
Steel	225–275	8	0.36	24	0.36	81	0.23	21
H.R. OR C.D.		(0.300)	(0.014)	(80)	(0.014)	(265)	(0.009)	(70)
1030–1055		1	0.15	38	0.18	135	0.13	37
1525–1527		(0.040)	(0.006)	(125)	(0.007)	(450)	(0.005)	(120)
Steel	275–325	8	0.30	18	0.25	72	0.18	15
Heat treated		(0.300)	(0.012)	(60)	(0.010)	(235)	(0.007)	(50)
1330–4130		1	0.15	30	0.15	115	0.13	27
5130–8630	(0.040)	(0.040)	(0.006)	(100)	(0.006)	(375)	(0.005)	(90)

Notes: [a] Speeds given are for brazed carbide teeth. For throwaway or indexable uncoated inserts, speeds may be 10 to 20% higher, and for coated inserts 30 to 50% higher. These are relatively large and strong cutters. Feeds may be less for smaller and weaker cutters such as end mills, form cutters, and saws.

Source: Data extracted from the *Machining Data Handbook,* 3d. ed., Machinability Data Center, ©, 1980, by permission of Metcut Research Associates, Inc., Cincinnati, Ohio.

must at least equal the tooling cost and incidental charges, including any extra setup cost.

Speed, Feed, and Depth of Cut. Substantially the same factors determine economical speeds for milling cutters as for single-point tools. Typical recommendations for speeds and feeds are given in Table 24-2. The cutting speed is the speed at the periphery of the cutter. The cutter rpm is calculated in the same way as for the workpiece in turning.

Basic milling feed is the distance the workpiece advances in the time between engagements by two successive teeth. This is called feed per tooth in units of mm/tooth, μm/tooth, or in./tooth (ipt). However, the machine feed rate is given in mm/min or in./min and is equal to the feed in mm/tooth (ipt) times the number of teeth in the cutter times the number of rpm of the cutter.

The actual feed or maximum chip thickness in milling is considerably less than the nominal feed per tooth for shallow cuts as indicated by Fig. 24-17. The two components of feed are equal only when the depth of cut is at least equal to the radius of the cutter. Thus for the same tooth load a heavier feed can be taken with a shallow cut than with a deep cut.

Feed per tooth should be as high as possible for fast cutting, but the heavier the feed per tooth, the greater the load on the cutter teeth, workpiece, holding device, and machine. A large face mill will withstand a greater feed per tooth than a small end mill. A light feed may have to be chosen for a fragile workpiece. The rigidity and power of a milling machine may limit the rate at which stock can be removed. A heavier feed is possible in soft materials than in hard or tough metal. A good finish calls for a light feed.

One cut is enough for most jobs, but rough and finish cuts are required to produce the best surface finishes and hold small tolerances. The depth of a roughing cut should be as much as the cutter, machine, and work will stand, and in most cases is the full amount of stock on a surface minus that needed for finishing. 1.5 mm (ca. $\frac{1}{16}$ in.) or less is normally left for finishing.

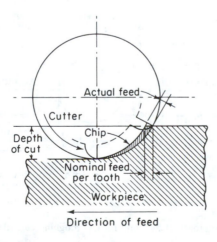

Figure 24-17 Relationship between actual and nominal milling feed.

Estimating Milling Time and Power. The approach of a milling cutter may be an appreciable part of the length of cut. A face mill taking a roughing cut is normally stopped when it has just cleaned the surface as indicated by Fig. 24-18(A). The approach shown at the beginning of the cut can be calculated from the right triangle having sides $(d/2) - A$, $w/2$, and $d/2$. It is $A = (d/2) - \sqrt{(d^2 - w^2)/4}$. However, if the diameter of the cutter is only a little larger than the width of the surface, the approach is $d/2$ for practical purposes. For a finishing cut, a face mill is passed entirely over a surface so that its trailing edge can get in a full wiping action. Thus the approach for finishing is equal to d.

The approach of a cutter with its surface offset from the center of the section or surface cut is depicted in Fig. 24-19. This might be a slab mill cleaning the top of a piece, a side milling cutter opening a slot, or a face mill forming a step. From the right triangle shown, $A = \sqrt{cd - c^2}$.

The cutting time in minutes is the quotient of the total length of cutter travel in mm (in.) divided by the feed in mm/min (ipm).

The rate of metal removal in cubic inches per minute for milling is the product of the width of cut in inches times the depth of cut in inches times the feed in inches per minute. An empirical formula proposed by Cincinnati Milacron, Inc., that takes into account the effect of the rate of metal removal Q in cubic inches per minute upon power consumption in milling is that horsepower

$$P = P_u Q^{3/4} \tag{24-1}$$

The factor P_u is the unit horsepower per cubic inch per minute. Some average values are given in Table 17-3. They apply mostly to face milling. Power may be about 25 to 50% higher for cutters that cut mostly on their peripheries, such as plain milling cutters.

For depth of cut C_m and width W_m in mm, and feed F_m, in mm/min, the rate of metal removal in cm³/min is $Q_m = C_m \times W_m \times F_m/1000$. For the specific power, P_{um}, in W/cm³/min from Table 17-3, which is predicated upon a metal removal rate of

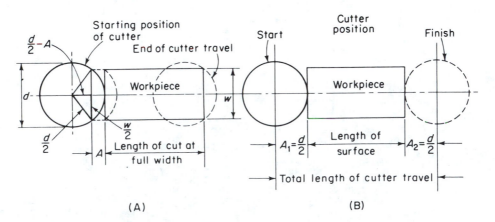

(A)   (B)

Figure 24-18   Approach of face mill for (A) roughing cut; (B) finishing cut.

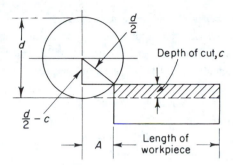

Depth of cut, c

Length of workpiece

A

Figure 24-19 Approach of plain or slot milling cutter.

about 16 cm³/min, the power in kW is

$$P_m \simeq 2 \times 10^{-3} P_{um} Q_m^{3/4} \tag{24-2}$$

Milling Compared with Other Operations.   Any surface that is accessible can be milled. This means that milling machines are to some extent competitive with all other machine tools. However, when the work is to be revolved, a milling machine can be used but is seldom selected for the job because machines of the lathe family are inherently more efficient for such purposes.

Milling machines are capable of machining holes and locating them with a fair degree of accuracy, to tolerances of 25 to 50 μm (0.001 to 0.002 in.). A milling machine is economical for doing such work in small quantities without extra equipment. If the holes do not need to be located accurately, a drill press will do the job more quickly and easily. For large quantities, the milling machine is usually slower and not able to compete with the use of jigs on drilling machines or with production boring machines. Jig boring machines are necessary where holes must be located more precisely than can be done with milling machines. Really large pieces require the capacity and range of horizontal boring machines, beyond that of most milling machines.

Flat, straight, and many curved and irregular surfaces can be shaped, planed, or broached as well as milled. The advantages of shapers and planers, particularly for one or a few pieces, were pointed out in Chap. 23. Broaching is more economical than milling in many cases for large quantities but is at a disadvantage in other cases as explained in Chap. 25. Milling often is best for moderate quantities.

Grinding is capable of producing to closer tolerances and finer finishes and can remove harder materials than milling. Some grinding is done entirely from rough stock in what is called *abrasive machining* (described in Chap. 28), but many parts are milled before grinding.

QUESTIONS

1. What kind of work can be done by metal milling?
2. Name and describe the principal kinds of milling cutters.
3. What is a fly cuttter, and what is its purpose?

4. Sketch a typical milling cutter tooth and name its elements.

5. Name and describe the common cutter holding devices on milling machines.

6. Describe the principal characteristics of general-purpose milling machines.

7. What are the relative advantages and disadvantages of knee and column and of bed-type milling machines?

8. Describe a typical production-type milling machine.

9. Describe a planer-type milling machine.

10. How is the size of a standard milling machine designated?

11. What are profilers and duplicators?

12. Describe a table-type horizontal boring, drilling, and milling machine and its usage.

13. Describe a typical cutter driving attachment.

14. How are workpieces held on milling machines?

15. What is plain or simple indexing, and how is it done?

16. What means are available to index higher numbers than possible with standard plain indexing?

17. How can a helix be milled?

18. Define conventional and climb milling and state the advantages of each.

19. Define and state the reasons for gang milling, straddle milling, simple milling, string milling, index base milling, rotary milling, and reciprocating milling.

20. When is a milling machine more economical than a shaper, planer, or broaching machine?

PROBLEMS

1. A form for which standard cutters are not available must be milled on the top of a workpiece 150 mm (6in.) long. A fly form cutter can be ground in 1 hour from a piece of high-speed steel worth $2.00. With it the workpiece can be fed at 12.5 mm/min ($\frac{1}{2}$ ipm). A special form cutter having 12 teeth costs $250. With it the feed is 150 mm/min (6 ipm). Overtravel and approach are 25 mm (1 in.) in both cases. Labor and overhead is worth $26/hr. Assume that either cutter will mill as many pieces as will be needed without having to be resharpened. Neither will have any other use. For how many pieces can the special form cutter with 12 teeth be justified?

2. If a fixture is made for a milling operation, in which pieces are now held in a vise, $\frac{1}{4}$ minute can be saved for each piece made. The fixture will cost $200, and the cost of interest, insurance, taxes, and maintenance is 25% altogether. No extra setup time is required for the fixture. The hourly rate for labor and overhead in the plant is $26. For how many pieces is the fixture justified?

3. An operation takes 3 minutes of floor to floor time. The need for a vertical milling attachment can be eliminated by the use of a fixture that costs $250. The cost of the fixture must be recovered in one lot plus 25% for interest, insurance, taxes, and maintenance. The cost of this attachment is $2.00/hr, and the device can be put to work elsewhere if not needed on this operation. The hourly rate for labor and overhead is $26. Under these circumstances, how many pieces justify the cost of a fixture? What is the most that should be paid for a fixture if only 1000 pieces are to be run?

4. Specify the number of turns, the number of holes in the circle, and the number of spaces to index the following divisions on a universal dividing head with a 40:1 ratio: **(a)** 120; **(b)** 100; **(c)** 96; **(d)** 75; **(e)** 48; **(f)** 34; **(g)** 30; **(h)** 26; **(i)** 24; **(j)** 18; **(k)** 15; **(l)** 13; **(m)** 9.

5. The table leadscrew of a milling machine has a lead of 6.35 mm (0.250 in.). Thus that is the amount the table advances each time the screw makes one revolution. The ratio between the jackshaft and spindle of a dividing head placed on the table is 40:1. That means the jackshaft must turn 40 times to turn the dividing head spindle once.

   It is desired to cut a helix with a lead of L inches with the equipment just described. Derive an expression for the gear ratio R that must be provided between the table leadscrew and dividing head jackshaft.

   What should the gear ratio be for an L of **(a)** 1 in.? **(b)** 5 in.? **(c)** 10 in.? **(d)** 25 in.? **(e)** 25 mm? **(f)** 125 mm? **(g)** 250 mm? **(h)** 650 mm?

6. A surface 115 mm ($4\frac{1}{2}$ in.) wide by 255 mm (10 in.) long is to be rough milled with a depth of cut of 8 mm (0.30 in.) by a 16-tooth cemented carbide face mill 150 mm (6 in.) in diameter. The material is medium-hard cast iron (220 to 260 Bhn). Estimate the cutting time and the power required at the cut.

7. The cutter described in Prob. 6 is used for a finishing cut of 1 mm (0.04 in.) depth on the surface described. What is the time required for the finishing cut? How much power is needed at the cutter?

8. A high-speed helical milling cutter (slab mill) with 12 teeth is 100 mm (4 in.) in diameter and 125 mm (5 in.) long. It is used to mill a soft-steel surface (175 to 225 Bhn) 75 mm (3 in.) wide by 230 mm (9 in.) long with a depth of cut of 20 mm ($\frac{3}{4}$ in.). A cutting speed of 30 m/min (100 fpm) and feed of 0.25 mm/tooth (0.010 ipt) are selected. What is the cutting time, and how much power is required?

9. If the cutter described in Prob. 8 takes a finishing cut 1 mm (0.04 in.) deep, what time is required, and what power is consumed?

10. A slot 15 mm (ca. $\frac{1}{2}$ in.) wide by 100 mm (4 in.) long through a piece of medium steel 25 mm (1 in.) thick is to be widened to 20 mm ($\frac{3}{4}$ in.). Its other dimensions are to remain the same, and radii are allowed at the ends. What time is required to do the operation with a 20-mm ($\frac{3}{4}$-in.)-diameter H.S.S. end mill having eight teeth? The cutting speed is 25 m/min (80 fpm) and the feed 50 μm/tooth (0.002 ipt). How much power is required?

11. A piece shown in Fig. 23-8 is to be milled from a rough casting having 3 mm ($\frac{1}{8}$ in.) of stock on all surfaces. Normal operation tolerances are satisfactory. List the steps that must be taken to mill one piece. For each step, specify the machine and cutter to be used and how the workpiece is to be held.

12. A lot of 100 pieces like the one shown in Fig. 23-8 is to be milled from rough castings having 3 mm ($\frac{1}{8}$ in.) of stock on all surfaces. Describe the operations necessary to do the work. For each operation specify how the work is to be held and the machine and cutter are to be used.

13. An operation is to be performed to machine the sides and bottom of the dovetail grooves on a number of parts of the kind shown in Fig. 23-8. Setup time is 20 minutes on a shaper and 30 minutes on a milling machine. The direct time to machine each piece on the shaper is 14 minutes and on the miller is 11 minutes. Labor costs $8.00/hr. The charge for the use of the shaper is $10.00/hr and for the milling machine $11.00/hr.

    (a) What is the quantity below which the shaper is more economical and above which the miller is more economical?

    (b) Which machine would you choose for 5 pieces? For 25 pieces?

14. A machine shop has two machines available for a job. One is a 48 × 48 × 10 double housing planer that originally cost $50,000, is depreciated over a 20-year period, and is operated about 6000 hr/yr. The charge for the use of the machine is $1.85/hr, and labor and overhead in addition are charged at $18.00/hr. The other machine is a 48 × 48 × 10 double housing planer milling machine that cost $105,000. The charge for the use of the planer milling machine is $3.97/hr, and labor and overhead in addition are charged at $18.00/hr. To machine the workpiece under consideration takes 10 hours on the planer and 8.5 hours on the milling machine. The cutting tools consumed cost $5.00/piece for the planer and $21.00/piece for the miller.
    (a) Which machine should be selected to machine 1 piece?
    (b) Which machine should be selected for 10 pieces?

15. The surface described in Prob. 6 is to be milled on a number of identical pieces. The time to unload and load a piece in a fixture is 0.30 minute, and to rapid traverse a piece to or away from the cutter is 0.10 minute. Estimate operation time per piece for the following arrangements depicted in Fig. 24-16.
    (a) Plain milling.
    (b) String milling with three pieces 15 mm (0.6 in.) apart in a fixture.
    (c) Reciprocating milling.
    (d) Duplex milling (two pieces at a time).
    (e) Index base milling (0.15 minute required to index the base) on a single-spindle miller.
    (f) Rotary milling with the mean distance between pieces 75 mm (3 in.).

REFERENCES

ANSI B5.18-1972, *Spindle Noses and Tool Shanks for Milling Machines;* ANSI B5.45-1972, *Milling Machines;* ANSI B5.47-1972, *Milling Machine Arbor Assemblies;* ANSI B94.8-1967, *Inserted Blade Milling Cutter Bodies;* ANSI B94.19-1968, *Milling Cutters and End Mills;* American Society of Mechanical Engineers, New York.

HALL, F., "Choosing a Milling Machine," *Machinery,* Sept. 1971, p. 57.

Handbook for Horizontal Boring, Drilling and Milling Machines, Giddings and Lewis Machine Tool Co., Fond du Lac, Wis., 1947.

HUNTRESS, E. A., "Diesinking Today," *American Machinist,* May 1980, p. 151.

JABLONOWSKI, J., "*Fundamentals of Milling, Special Report 701,*" *American Machinist,* Feb. 1976.

MILEWSKI, V., SR., "Milling Cutters," *Manufacturing Engineering,* Part 1: Oct. 1977; Part 2: Nov. 1977.

A Treatise on Milling and Milling Machines, Cincinnati Milacron, Inc., Cincinnati, Ohio, 1951.

25

BROACHING

In broaching, a tool with a series of teeth called a *broach* is pushed or pulled over a surface on a workpiece as depicted in Fig. 25-1. Each tooth takes a thin slice from the surface. Broaching of inside surfaces is called *internal* or *hole broaching;* of most outside surfaces, *surface broaching*. Typical internal broaching operations are the sizing of holes and cutting of serrations, straight or helical splines, gun rifling, and keyways.

BROACHES

Types of Broaches.   Almost every broach is designed to do a specific job in a certain way. Typical forms are shown in Fig. 25-2. Some are intended to be pulled, others pushed, and still others to be held, either on a movable ram or in a fixed position. A broach may be made in one piece, called *solid,* or assembled or *built up* from *shells, replaceable sections,* or *inserted teeth.* Replaceable sections, teeth, or shells make a broach easier to repair and, in some cases, easier to make initially.

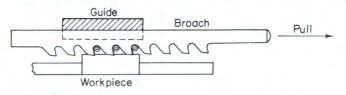

Figure 25-1   The way a broach works.

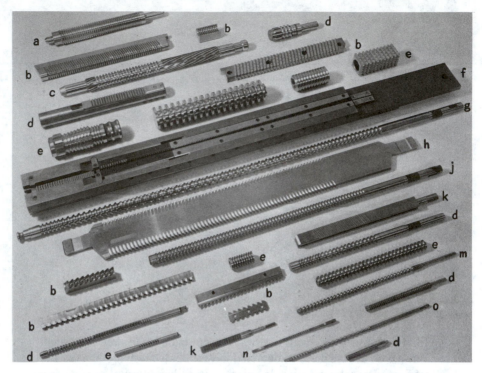

Figure 25-2   Typical broaches: (a) combination hole-sizing and involute spline push broach; (b) broach sections; (c) spiral spline hard-gear pull broach; (d) push broaches; (e) broach shells; (f) broach inserts assembled in holder; (g) rotary cut pull broach for round hole; (h) slotting broach; (j) hole-sizing and spline-cutting pull broach; (k) flat broaches; (m) spline pull broaches; (n) keyway broach; (o) combination hole-cutting and burnishing broach. (Courtesy Continental Tool Works.)

A *burnishing broach* makes a glazed surface in a steel, cast iron, or nonferrous hole. Burnishing teeth are rounded and do not cut but compress and rub the surface metal.

A *pot broach* is a hollow cylinder with teeth inside. A common usage is to cut all the teeth of an external gear at one time, while the workpiece is pushed or pulled through the broach.

Details of Broaches.   A hole broach depicted in Fig. 25-3 is gripped by a puller at the *shank* end. The *front pilot* centers the broach in the hole before the teeth begin to cut. The first group of teeth remove most of the stock and are called *roughing teeth*. The *finishing teeth* of a new broach are all substantially the same size and have the shape of the finished hole. As the first finishing teeth become worn, those behind take up the function of sizing. The *rear pilot* supports the broach after the last tooth leaves the hole. A broach handled automatically has a *tail*.

The enlarged section of broach teeth in Fig. 25-3 reveals features like those of other cutting tools. The *back-off angle* corresponds to the relief angle of a single-point

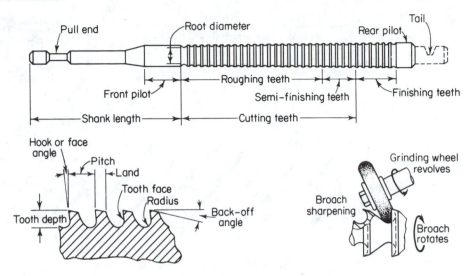

Figure 25-3 Broach details.

tool, and the *hook* or *face angle* to the rake angle. A hole broach is sharpened by grinding the tooth face. Surface broaches with curved shapes may be sharpened the same way, but others are ground on the back-off angle land.

The teeth of broaches are staggered, offset, relieved, and arrayed in various ways to break up chips, reduce chip load, and enable teeth to take deep cuts under scale. One way this is done is illustrated in Fig. 25-4.

Most broaches are made from high-speed steel, ground after hardening. Cemented carbide is used, especially for surface broaches, mostly for cast iron and high production. Throwaway inserts have been found economical in some cases.

Broach Pullers and Fixtures. Many surface broaches are mounted on holders bolted to the face of a ram, but some surface broaches and all pull broaches must be connected to the end of a ram by a *puller* or *puller head*. Several common pullers and broach shanks to fit them are shown in Fig. 25-5.

The *threaded puller* of Fig. 25-5(A) and the *key-type puller* in Fig. 25-5(B) are simple and inexpensive but relatively slow. The *automatic puller* of Fig. 25-5(C) is

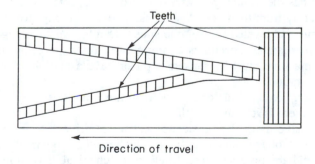

Direction of travel

Figure 25-4 Arrangement of a progressive surface broach.

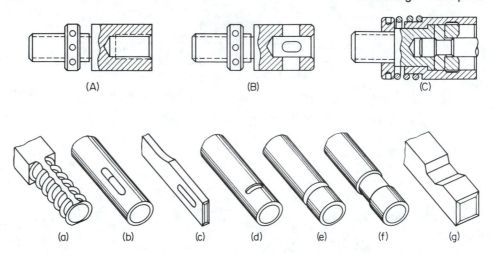

Figure 25-5   Broach pullers and shanks.

favored for production, especially on machines with broach elevators and automatic handling equipment. When the sleeve on this puller is pushed backward by hand or by striking a stop, the puller accepts or releases the broach shanks.

Fixtures generally are justified for holding workpieces being broached because production is large. Broaching fixtures are simple in comparison with those of other processes; one may even be just a plate to bear the part and with a hole to pass the broach. Broaching forces generally tend to stabilize the part in the fixture but are large, and fixtures must be strong.

BROACHING MACHINES

Broaching machines may be classified as (1) push broaching machines, (2) pull broaching machines, (3) surface broaching machines, and (4) continuous broaching machines. Some manufacturers offer a basic model that can be arranged for two or more purposes, for instance for pull broaching or for surface broaching.

Broaching machines are constructed in horizontal and vertical models. A *horizontal broaching machine* has the advantage that any part of it, especially the workstation, can be reached readily from the floor. Also a machine with a long stroke can be supported at many points and leveled to keep the slides straight. An advantage of a *vertical broaching machine* is that it occupies a minimum of floor space, but if its stroke is long, a vertical machine must be sunk in a pit or have a platform for the operator to reach the workstation.

Internal broaches last up to twice as long on vertical machines because cutting fluid is utilized better and there is less drag of the tools.

Broaching machines have hydraulic or electromechanical drives. A hydraulic machine exerts force by means of a piston and cylinder. Such machines generally cost less, give smooth action, and are more popular. An electromechanical drive employs a screw engaged with a recirculating ball nut. This type of drive is preferred for longer-stroke and high-speed machines. It is more energy efficient and avoids hydraulic system maintenance. Most drives have infinitely variable speeds within their ranges. The size of a broaching machine is commercially designated by the force in tons that can be applied to the broach and by the length of the stroke in inches. Thus a 10-54 machine can exert 10 tons of force and has a maximum stroke of 54 in.

Push Broaching Machines. Arbor presses are often used for internal push broaching such as hole sizing and keyway cutting. Push broaches must be short, and each cannot remove much stock. On the other hand, machines and tools are simple and inexpensive, and operations can be set up and changed over easily. On a hydraulic arbor-type press, like the one in Fig. 25-6, the workpiece is placed on the table or bolster, sometimes in a simple fixture under the vertical ram that pushes a short broach through a hole. Such presses can readily be used for other operations, such as assembling, bending, and staking. Presses are available in capacities from about 20 to 300 kN ($\frac{1}{4}$ to 35 tons), stroke lengths to 0.9 m (36 in.), and speeds to 12 m/min

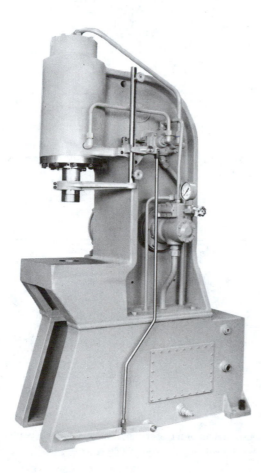

Figure 25-6 A 15-ton hydraulic arbor press with guided ram and a controlled ram speed for broaching. (Courtesy Greenerd Press and Machine Co.)

(40 fpm). A medium-size press rated to deliver 70 kN (8 tons) with a 400-mm (16-in.) stroke costs about $9000.

Pot broaching machines are arranged for machining outside surfaces such as gear teeth all in one pass by means of cutter teeth inside a hollow broach. Most push the work upward as indicated by Fig. 25-7 because such movement allows the chips to escape most easily and the arrangement is amenable to automatic loading and unloading. However, if the workpiece is small or the stroke must be long, the push

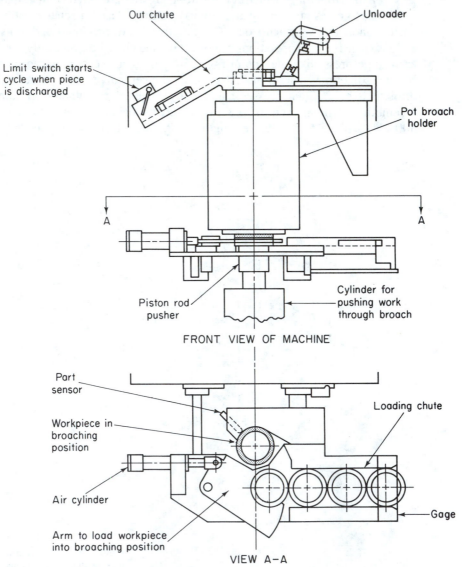

Figure 25-7 Schematic diagram of the operating zone of a push-up pot broaching machine with a typical automatic loading and unloading system.

rod would be slender and subject to buckling. For such cases, pull-up pot broaching machines are available.

   Pull Broaching Machines.   Pull broaching machines are used mostly for internal broaching but do some surface broaching. The working zone of a horizontal pull broaching machine is shown in Fig. 25-8. The shank of the broach is passed through the prepared opening in the workpiece and attached to the puller that draws it completely through the opening. The workpiece is located in and pressed against a cup centered in the machine's face plate at the back of the picture.

   Commonly, vertical broaching machines are arranged to pull broaches either downward or upward, although some do both. The action of a *vertical pull-down broaching machine* is depicted in Fig. 25-9. The broaches are grasped and pulled from below the table. Large and irregular pieces can be loaded somewhat more easily than on pull-up machines. Fixtures can be used to hold the locations of broached holes in relationship with external surfaces of parts. Application of cutting fluid is natural and effective. Vertical pull broaching machines range in size from 17 to 450 kN (2 to 50 tons) with strokes of 0.38 to 2.30 m (15 to 90 in.) and speeds up to 30 m/min (100 fpm). A 6-36 single-station pull-down broaching machine is quoted at $25,000. A large 36-120 two-station pull-down broaching machine is priced at $300,000.

   The broaches on a *vertical pull-up broaching machine* start from below the table and, as they are pulled upward through the parts, press the workpieces against the

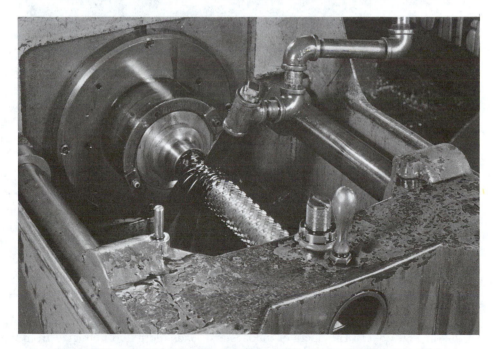

Figure 25-8   Internal helical spline being broached on a horizontal pull-type broaching machine. (Courtesy Colonial Broach Co.)

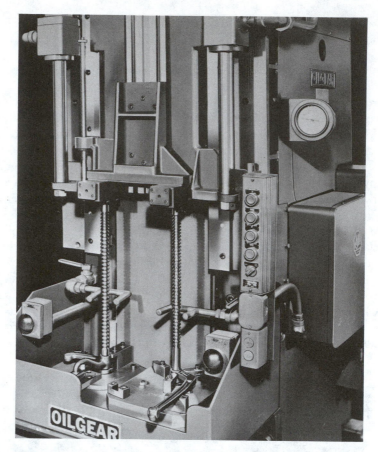

Figure 25-9 View of a setup on a vertical pull-down broaching machine. (Courtesy Oilgear Co.)

underside of the table. At the end of the stroke the parts are freed to fall down a chute, and motions are saved for the operator.

Surface Broaching Machines. Some *horizontal surface broaching machines* are single acting and their tools cut only in one direction. Others, like the one in Fig. 25-10, have two sets of broaches on the ram and are double acting; that is, a cut is taken as the ram moves in either direction. In the example two fixtures are integrated with a roller conveyer and are loaded and sustain the work in the cut alternately. Horizontal-surface broaching machines are common in capacities to 360 kN (40 tons) with strokes up to 10.7 m (420 in.) and speeds of 30 m/min (100 fpm). Cost may be in excess of $250,000.

The working zone of a *vertical single-ram surface broaching machine* is shown in Fig. 25-11. The operator unloads and loads the fixture retracted from the broach while the ram ascends. When the operator pushes two buttons, the fixture advances

Figure 25-10 A 25-ton horizontal double-acting surface broaching machine for finishing surfaces of an automobile cylinder head. (Courtesy Cincinnati Milacron, Inc.)

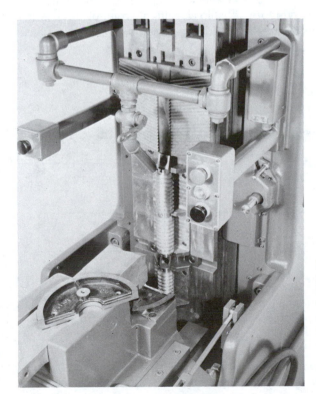

Figure 25-11 Workstation for broaching the diametral parting face and half-bore of cams, one of which is sitting on top of the fixture. Interchangeable fixture elements accommodate 90 sizes and shapes of cams, all requiring the same operation. Stock removal is 2.5 mm ($\frac{3}{32}$ in.) of cast iron at a production rate of 140 pieces/hr. (Courtesy Cincinnati Milacron, Inc.)

and the ram carries the broach down to the cut. After the ram reaches the bottom of its stroke, the fixture retracts and another cycle begins.

Single-ram broaching machines range in capacity from 26 to 450 kN (3 to 50 tons) with strokes up to 3 m (120 in.) and speeds to 36 m/min (120 fpm). A 5-48 single-ram vertical surface broaching machine is quoted at $66,000.

A *vertical double-ram surface broaching machine* carries two broach and fixture sets side by side. One ram carries its broach down with the fixture in cutting position. At the same time, the other returns to the top while its fixture is unloaded and loaded in a retracted position. The time to broach a piece is either the unloading and loading or cutting time, whichever is longer, plus the time to index the fixtures. Operation can be practically continuous. A small 3-36 double-ram vertical broaching machine is priced at $39,000, and a 10-54 machine at $167,000 without tooling.

Continuous Broaching Machine.   A *horizontal continuous broaching machine* is different from the machines previously described because the broaching cutters on it remain stationary while the workpiece held in fixtures (on carriers) are forced past the cutters. This is illustrated in Fig. 25-12. Parts are loaded manually or automatically at one end and may be discharged down a chute at the other end. Work can be broached as rapidly as it can be loaded.

One type of *rotary continuous broaching machine* is somewhat like a rotary miller. It has a slowly revolving round table carrying a group of fixtures in a circle. Workpieces loaded in the fixtures are carried past stationary broaches and may be ejected automatically thereafter.

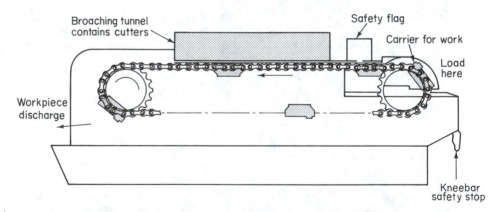

Figure 25-12   Scheme of a horizontal continuous broaching machine.

BROACHING OPERATIONS

Planning for Economical Broaching.   The skill in broaching is built into the tools and is exercised in setting up the equipment. After that the operation of the machine is mere routine.

   The cutting time in a broaching operation is short, and the loading and unloading time takes an appreciable part of the total time. Thus labor saving and motion economy are important considerations. For production of large quantities of pieces, the machines often have several workstations or pull a number of broaches at once, broach handling is done automatically, and fixtures are made quick acting to save operation time.

   Surfaces that run in the same direction on a workpiece, especially if they are contiguous, can generally be broached at the same time. As many surfaces on a part as possible should be broached in one operation.

   Although most broaching operations are completed in one pass, some are arranged for repeated cuts to simplify tooling and save cost where only small or moderate quantities are needed. For instance, the teeth of a gear or spline may be broached all together or indexed and cut one or a few at a time.

   Free-cutting material of 25 to 30 R_C hardness is considered best for broaching, but an acceptable range is from 10 to 35 R_C, and metal as hard as 45 R_C has been broached. Material that is too hard wears broach teeth rapidly, and too soft a material is difficult to cut cleanly.

   A well-designed broach should last for 10 to 30 or so sharpenings. A small simple broach may require less than an hour to resharpen, a large one several hours. The amount of service between grinds depends upon the length of cut and the number of times the broach is subject to the shock of entering the cut. Probable average numbers of pieces per grind at conventional speeds have been reported by Chas. O. Lofgren as 25,000 for brass and aluminum, 15,000 for bronze and SAE 1020 steel, 6000 for alloy steel, and 800 for high-temperature alloys. Thus broaches are operated to have long lives and produce many pieces.

   The principle of economical tool life expressed by Eq. (17-4) dictates that broaches should have long lives because they are expensive to make and sharpen. A long life means a slow speed. For years, broaching has been done with high-speed steel tools mostly at 3 to 12 m/min (10 to 40 fpm), but in recent years cases of up to 30 m/min (100 fpm) and more have been reported. Carbide broaching speeds range from 30 to 90 m/min (100 to 300 fpm). Broaching speeds are still well below conventional speeds for turning and milling.

   Tolerances within 25 μm (0.001 in.) can be held between surfaces and from locating surfaces with rigid workpieces in surface broaching. Less than half as much tolerance can be held to locating surfaces if the tooling is adjustable. Hole-position tolerances are quite difficult to hold in internal broaching, but 25 μm/25 mm (0.001 in./in.) of hole diameter is feasible for size if sections, and deflections, are uniform along the workpiece. Smaller tolerances have been reached by trial and error grinding of broaches during tryout.

   Estimating Broaching Time.   The cutting time in a broaching operation is the quotient of the length of stroke divided by the cutting speed in compatible units. For example, a stroke of 1.2 m (48 in.) at 7 m/min (24 fpm) is required. The cutting time is 1.2/7 = 0.17 min = 10 sec [48/(24 × 12) = $\frac{1}{6}$ min = 10 sec]. The return stroke may be calculated in the same way from the return speed of the broach, which may be 12 m/min (40 fpm) or more. Other elements of time are for stopping and starting, commonly 2 seconds, and unloading and loading, which depend upon the nature of workpiece and fixture.

Broaching, Compared with Other Operations.   The work done by broaching can also be done in other ways. Under certain conditions, broaching is preferable to other operations, but under other conditions broaching is either unfeasible or disadvantageous.

The main advantage of broaching is that it is fast; it commonly takes seconds to do a job that requires minutes in any other way. Little skill is needed to run a broaching machine (all the skill is built in the tooling), and automation is easily arranged. Good finish and accuracy are obtainable over the life of a broach because roughing and finishing are done by separate teeth.

The main handicap of broaching is that broaches are costly to make and sharpen. Standard broaches are available, but most broaches are made especially for and can do one job only. A standard H.S.S. broach for a 6-mm ($\frac{1}{4}$-in.) keyway costs about $50 and for a 25-mm (1-in.) internal hexagon around $400. Specials vary in price from a few hundred dollars for a fractional-inch internal spline broach to many thousands of dollars for a surface broach 1.8 m (6 ft) long or more.

Special precautions may be necessary in founding or forging to control variations in stock, or extra operations to remove excess stock may have to be added before broaching to protect the broach. These add to the overall cost of manufacturing.

Some of the limitations of broaching are enough to make it impracticable for certain work. A surface cannot be broached if it has an obstruction across the path of broach travel. For instance, blind holes and pockets normally are not broached. Frail workpieces are not good subjects for broaching because they are not able to withstand the large forces imposed by the process without distortion or breaking. For example, automobile engines have been redesigned drastically to reduce weight and save fuel. The engine blocks had previously been broached, but it has been found that the thinner walls of some cannot stand the broaching forces, and more costly milling is necessary. Surfaces that run in the same general direction often can be broached at the same time, but surfaces not so related must be broached separately as a rule. For instance, a hole and a perpendicular face may be machined in one operation on a lathe or boring machine but require two passes in broaching. The lines left on a surface lie in the direction of broach travel. For instance, broaching is not capable of producing a circular pattern in a hole if such a finish is required.

When broaching can be done, it is selected if the amount it saves as compared to other operations is more than enough to pay for the cost of the tools. This may not require a very large output where the job is hard to do otherwise. The cutting of an internal spline is one case, for example, a 6 D.P. spline, 50 to 100 mm (2 to 4 in.) long, in AISI 8620 steel. One piece could be cut with a single-point formed tool (costing several dollars) on a standard shaper, with a dividing head, in several hours. The job could be done with a gear shaper cutter, worth about $200, in 4 to 5 minutes. That cutter could produce 100 pieces/grind and stand sharpening about 50 times. It could be resharpened in 15 minutes. The cost for a broach for the splined hole is

$2,300. It cuts a piece in 20 seconds. On a vertical pull-down broaching machine it lasts for about 1000 pieces untill dull and can be resharpened 26 times. Each sharpening takes $1\frac{3}{4}$ hours. At $25/hr in the shop, the broach is economical for any quantity of more than about 1500 pieces. However, savings per piece are not large for some operations, and many pieces must be produced to justify broaching. To broach a surface on a cast-iron cylinder block may be only a half-minute faster than milling with cemented carbide cutters. The tooling for broaching may well cost $30,000 more than for milling. If the labor and overhead rate is $25/hr, the tooling is depreciated in 2 years, the annual charge for interest, insurance, property taxes, and maintenance is 25%, and setup time is ignored, an analysis based on Eq. (19-1) shows $25N/(2 \times 60) = 30,000(0.75)$, and $N = 108,000$ pieces/year. This is the smallest quantity of production that justifies broaching for such a case.

QUESTIONS

1. What is broaching?
2. Describe a hole broach and name its principal elements.
3. How is a broach pulled?
4. What are the main types of broaching machines?
5. What is a broaching press, and how is it used?
6. What is pot broaching?
7. What are the different kinds of pull broaching machines, and what are their relative advantages?
8. Describe the various kinds of surface broaching machines and the advantages of each.
9. How does a continuous broaching machine operate?
10. How is the size of a broaching machine designated?
11. By what means is economy achieved in broaching?
12. What determines the length of stroke and pull required in a broaching operation?
13. When is broaching economical, and when is it not feasible?

PROBLEMS

1. With an assumed 80% efficiency, how much power is required at the motor when the broaching machines with ratings specified are operated at the given speeds?
   (a) An 8 × 16 broaching press at 30 fpm.
   (b) A 10 × 54 vertical broaching machine at 40 fpm.
   (c) A 50 × 72 horizontal broaching machine at 80 fpm.
   (d) A 25-kN pull at 10 m/min.
   (e) A 225-kN pull at 15 m/min.
2. The roughing section of a broach is to remove stock 3.2 mm ($\frac{1}{8}$ in.) deep from a steel surface

200 mm (8 in.) long and 50 mm (2 in.) wide. Each tooth takes a cut 0.13 mm (0.005 in.) deep. The pitch of the teeth is given by the formula

$$\text{pitch (mm)} = 1.75\sqrt{\text{length of surface (mm)}}$$

or

$$\text{pitch (in.)} = 0.35\sqrt{\text{length of surface (in.)}}$$

How long should the roughing section be? What pull must the broaching machine exert if the chip pressure is 4 GPa (ca. 600,000 lb/in.^{2}) of chip area? What power is required for a broaching speed of 7 m/min (24 fpm)?

3. A 1.4-m (54-in.) stroke is required for the operation described in Prob. 2. The time to unload and load a fixture is 0.10 minute and to index the machine 0.03 minute. What is the cycle time per piece on
   (a) A single-ram surface broach with a return speed of 12 m/min (40 fpm)?
   (b) A double-ram surface broach?

4. A 24/48-pitch internal involute spline with 36 teeth and pitch diameter of 38 mm (1.500 in.) is to be cut in steel in a hole 50 mm (2 in.) long. This can be done on a gear shaper in 5 min/piece. Tooling costs $400. The spline can be broached with an operation time of $\frac{1}{2}$ minute, and the cost of tooling is $1000, including the broach. Setup time is negligible. Time saved is considered worth $12/hr. The rate for interest, insurance, taxes, and maintenance of tooling is 25%. For what quantity of pieces should each process be used?

5. A cast-iron housing has a surface 115 mm ($4\frac{1}{2}$ in.) in width by 150 mm (6 in.) long from which 3 mm ($\frac{1}{8}$ in.) of stock is to be removed. On a milling machine the feed is 1.2 m/min (48 in./min) and the time per piece is 0.30 minute complete. The surface can be broached in 0.25 min/piece on a double-ram surface broaching machine. The cost for the machine, overhead, and labor is $16/hr on either machine. Setup time is the same on both. Tooling for milling costs $700, and for broaching $5000. Tooling cost must be recovered in one run without interest. What annual rate of production justifies the use of the broaching machine?

6. In the design of a broach, common practice is to multiply the maximum cross-sectional area of chips taken at one time by a factor, C, to determine the pull required. The factor C is in GPa (lb/in.^{2}) of chip cross-sectional area and depends mostly on the material. A broach is to be designed for a material for which C has not been determined and a value of 4.14 GPa (600,000 lb/in.^{2}) is selected to be safe. The broach is to machine a round hole nominally 50 mm (2 in.) in diameter by 75 mm (3 in.) long. The pitch or spacing of the teeth is 11 mm ($\frac{7}{16}$ in.), and each roughing tooth is 50 μm (0.002 in.) larger in diameter than the one that cuts just before it.
   (a) After the broach has been put in service, the true value of the constant C is to be ascertained as a basis for designing other broaches for the same material. It is run on a hydraulic broaching machine with a cylinder pressure of 6.9 MPa (1000 psi) when pulling at 270 kN (30 tons) rated capacity. The pressure to move the ram under no load is negligible; a gage shows a pressure of 4.8 MPa (700 psi) in the cylinder when the broach is cutting to its full capacity. What is the actual value of the constant C?
   (b) The material from which the broach is made is considered to have a working strength of 345 MPa (50,000 psi). What should be the minimum diameter of the space between the teeth for the broach described herein?

REFERENCES

COTTRELL, R. P., "Fundamentals of Broaching, Special Report 638," *American Machinist,* Dec. 15, 1969, p. 85.

LENTZ, R. A., "Continuous Broaching; What It Is and What It Can Do," *Manufacturing Engineering and Management,* May 1971, p. 32.

LINDGREN, D. C., "Broaching Encroaching on Milling," *Machinery,* July 1971, p. 44.

LOFGREN, C. O., "What You Should Know about Broaching," *American Machinist,* Aug. 2, 1965, p. 101.

PSENKA, J. A., "Pot Broaching," *Manufacturing Engineering,* July 1977, p. 55.

26

SAWING AND FILING

Metal is removed in sawing and filing by the action of many small teeth. Saw teeth act in a narrow line, and a saw can sever a sizable chunk of material with a minimum of cutting. If a piece of metal is removed by milling, for instance, a large part or all of it may have to be reduced to chips. The same piece may be cut off or out by a saw acting on only a small part of the material. Thus in many cases work can be done faster and with less power by sawing than by other methods of metal cutting, and material can be saved.

The teeth of a file act over a wide surface and progress slowly. Their cutting effect can be watched and controlled. Thus filing is suited for finishing irregular surfaces and surfaces hard to reach with other kinds of cutting tools. Filing is limited to removing small amounts of soft materials.

Saws and files have been used as hand tools since ancient times because they require little force and power, but they also are machine driven today. Power driven hack saws, circular saws, and band saws are employed to cut off pieces of bar stock, plates, sheets, and other shapes of metal. Versatile band saw machines have been developed for cutting out cavities or pieces of intricate shapes with a minimum waste of material and time. Reciprocating and continuous filing machines are available for rapid and accurate finishing of plain and irregular surfaces in small quantities.

SAWS AND FILES

Saws.   Three common kinds of metal-cutting saws are hack saws, circular cold saws, and band saws. Although different in overall form, they all contain a series of

672

cutting teeth that operate in the same basic way. The important features of a saw are: (1) material, (2) tooth form, (3) tooth set, (4) tooth spacing, and (5) size.

Saws are made from low alloy high-carbon steel, special alloy steels, high-speed steel, and cemented carbide. Most saws are solid; some have teeth of a hard material backed by flexible steel; many have tipped or inserted teeth.

Saw teeth have rake and clearance angles corresponding to single-point tools as shown by the typical profiles in Fig. 26-1. The teeth of most band saws for metal cutting are like those of other saws, but other forms are available for specific materials and operations. Among these are scallop-edge band saw blades for cloth, special saw blades for paper, and diamond tooth blades for ceramic and vitreous materials.

Saw teeth are offset to the side to make the cut wider than the thickness of the back of the blade to prevent rubbing. The width of the saw cut is called the *kerf*. Three common types of saw settings are shown in Fig. 26-2. The wave tooth is suited to fine tooth spacing. Circular saws, and sometimes other kinds, have varying tooth heights and shapes such as the ones in Fig. 26-1. These forms help break up the chips, distribute the load, reduce chatter, and allow some teeth to take fine cuts to leave good finishes.

Tooth spacing or pitch has an important influence upon saw performance, as explained in Fig. 26-3. At least two or three teeth must bear at one time to avoid snagging of the teeth. On the other hand, enough space is needed between the teeth to take care of the chips. Straight saws are available with as many as 13 teeth per centimeter to less than 1 tooth per centimeter (from about 32 teeth per inch to 2 teeth per inch). The pitch of circular saws may run from 5 to 50 mm (0.20 to 2 in.).

Saws are commercially available in many sizes. Dimensions are given in suppliers' catalogs. A thin saw removes less material, but a thick blade makes a truer

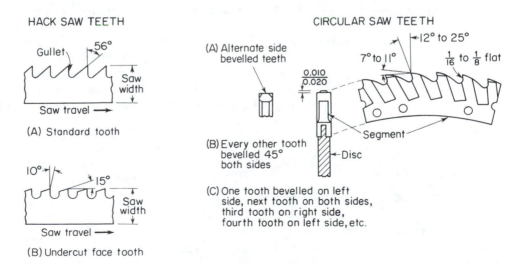

Figure 26-1   Typical saw-tooth profiles.

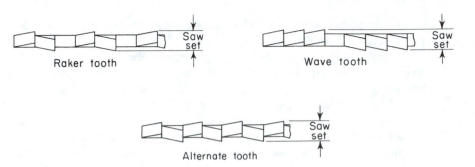

Raker tooth   Saw set   Wave tooth   Saw set

Alternate tooth   Saw set

Figure 26-2 Types of saw-tooth sets.

cut. Commonly, a circular saw cuts wider than a hack saw, and a hack saw cuts wider than a band saw.

Some band saws are as little as 3 mm ($\frac{1}{8}$ in.) wide to cut around curves. Some band and hack saws are as much as 25 to 100 mm (1 to 4 in.) wide for backup strength for heavy cuts. Circular saws are from about 200 mm to 2 m (8 to 80 in.) in diameter to accommodate various depths of cuts.

Files.   Files may be identified by (1) type, (2) class, (3) cut, (4) pitch, and (5) size.

The common hand file has a tang for a wooden handle. The file ordinarily is reciprocated across the work under pressure on the forward stroke. *Mill* files are used for sharpening saws, lathe work, and general smooth finishing. *Machinists'* files are popular in factories and shops; *foundry* files are similar but sturdier for rough castings. *Rasps* are suitable for wood and other soft substances. *Swiss pattern* files are made for fine finishing and precision work such as is done by instrument, tool, and die makers. *Curved tooth* files are favored for aluminum and other soft metals, particularly in auto body works.

Continuous filing is done with a band file, which is made up of a series of short file segments. Each segment is fastened near its leading end by a clip to a flexible steel band so that it can pass freely over the wheels on which the band runs. Each file segment is interlinked with the segment behind it so that the cutting action is not interrupted. The ends of the band are connected by a latch so they can be fastened together to make a continuous loop.

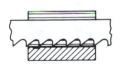

Coarse teeth for wide surfaces allows fast cut with space for chips

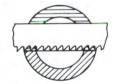

Fine teeth for narrow surfaces at least two teeth on thin wall at one time to prevent stripping teeth

Figure 26-3 Significance of saw-tooth spacing.

The class or kind of file is determined by its shape; a *tapered* file is somewhat reduced in size towards its end; a *blunt* file is about the same size throughout its length. The principal cross-sectional shapes are flat (rectangular), pillar (nearly square), square, round, half round (really one-third circular), oval, and triangular (three-cornered).

The cut of a file designates the way the teeth are formed. A *single-cut* file has a single row of parallel teeth across its face at an angle with its axis; this is the cut of a mill file. A *double-cut* file has two rows of teeth crossing each other, as on most machinists' files. Each tooth of a *rasp cut* file is formed by itself by a single punch mark. A *vixen cut* is a milled cut with large knife-like teeth, often *curved cut* across the face of the file.

Files are graded according to the pitch or spacing of the teeth. Descriptive terms that refer to the pitch, from wide spacing to close spacing, are rough, coarse, bastard, second cut, smooth, and dead smooth. Swiss pattern files are graded by numbers from the coarsest, Nos. 00, 0, and 1, through 8, the finest. No relationship between the descriptive name or number and the number of teeth per inch applies to all files. Several typical band file segments of various shapes, cuts, and pitches are shown in Fig. 26-4.

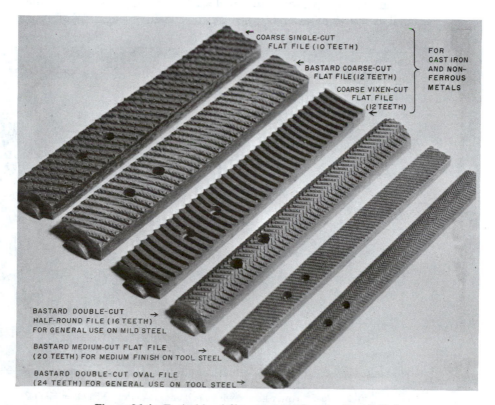

Figure 26-4 Typical band file segments. (Courtesy Do All Co.)

Coarse files remove metal rapidly, fine files give good finishes, and medium files are a compromise. *Safe edge* files have no side teeth, so they can cut up to but not damage a shoulder. Files most commonly used for ferrous metals are flat or half round double or single cut, in bastard, second cut, and smooth grades. Files for nonferrous metals and nonmetals should have deeply cut teeth for chip space.

SAWING AND FILING MACHINES

Power Hack Sawing Machines. A power-driven hack sawing machine drives a blade back and forth through a workpiece, pressing down on the cutting stroke and releasing the pressure on the return, much as a person does in sawing by hand. The blade in the typical operation of Fig. 26-5 is stretched in a C-frame guided by an overarm. In addition to tension, a saw may be fully backed up for heavy cuts. The saw is fed downward a positive preset amount on some machines; a preset uniform pressure is applied on other machines, and the amount of feed depends upon the resistance the saw meets. Still other machines utilize both systems to feed the saw as much as it can stand at each stroke.

Hack sawing operations are simple but can be adapted to production. Tolerances as small as ± 0.15 mm (± 0.005 in.) are considered practical. Work is usually held in

Figure 26-5   Power hack sawing operation. (Courtesy Nicholson File Co.)

a vise, and the machine stops at the end of a cut. The saw frames of some machines can be swiveled for angular cuts. Production-type machines are arranged to feed, measure, and cut off a series of pieces automatically from one or more bars.

Because the cutting is intermittent, hack sawing is not fast, but the machines are simple and not costly, easy to change from job to job, and easy to operate and to maintain. A general-purpose machine like the one in Fig. 26-5 costs only a few thousand dollars. A heavy-duty hack sawing machine of 250 by 250 mm (10 by 10 in.) capacity with a 3-hp motor, suitable for production with work track and automatic material feed for duplicate or multiple cutting, may be had for about $15,000. It uses throwaway blades that cost about $10 and have long lives. For the heaviest work, machines are available that are three to four times as powerful. On an average job, a continuous circular or band saw may be one-third or more faster than a hack saw, but the overall cost of hack sawing may be as low as one-half or less.

Circular Saw Machines. Circular saws are of three kinds. One has teeth as illustrated in Fig. 26-1 for *cold sawing;* another has a smooth or nicked outer edge for *hot sawing,* and the third is a thin abrasive wheel for *abrasive sawing.*

A cold saw is commonly fed horizontally through a workpiece as depicted in Fig. 26-6, particularly for heavy work. Other machines may feed the saw vertically or around a pivot with a chop stroke, shown in Fig. 26-7, particularly for light work. Workpieces are usually clamped in a vise, one or more at a time. The stock is pushed against a stop and clamped, and the saw is fed by hand on manual model machines. Other models are semi- and fully automatic in operation. Some also chamfer or center the pieces that are cut off.

Cold sawing is a continuous and fast method of cutting off and leaves a smooth and accurate milled surface with few or no burrs, which may save work in subsequent operations. A 150 mm (6 in.) diameter steel bar can easily be cut off in a minute. The typical experience of one plant is that pieces of bar stock can be cut off with a tolerance of 75 μm (0.003 in.) and a finish equal to or better than that obtained from a cutoff tool on a lathe.

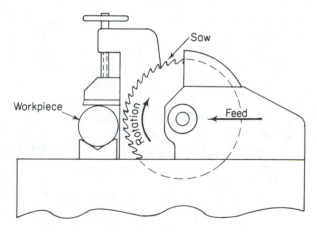

Figure 26-6 Cold circular sawing operation.

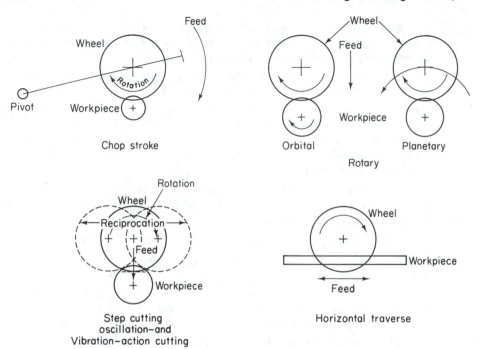

Figure 26-7   Basic types of abrasive cutoff machines.

Production cold sawing equipment is expensive. An automatic machine with a 250-mm (10-in.)-diameter capacity in steel and a 7.5-kW (10-hp) motor costs about $50,000. A segmental 710-mm (28-in.)-diameter blade for the machine has a price of about $500. It may be sharpened about 35 times for about $50 each sharpening. Light machines for small work, 50 mm (2 in.) or so in diameter, may cost a few thousand dollars, and saws less than $50.

Hot sawing is done at 10,000 to 25,000 fpm. The heat of friction softens the metal in contact with the disk, and the soft metal is rubbed away. Sharp saw teeth are not needed for cutting. Only a small portion of the saw is in contact at any instant, and the rest is cooled as it travels around to enter the cut again. Friction sawing is fast but leaves a heavier burr and a less accurate surface than tooth cutting does. Typical performance: 35 seconds for a 250-mm (10-in.) I-beam, and 18 seconds for a bar 300 mm (12 in.) in diameter.

In one form of hot sawing, a current (1000 to 4000 A at 30 to 55 V) is passed to maintain an arc between the disk and the workpiece. Molten metal is swept away by the high peripheral speed of the saw. The cutting rate is reported faster than for any other method. Such equipment with a 1.8-m (72-in.)-diameter blade to cut 760-mm (30-in.) steel billets costs over $100,000.

Abrasive sawing is done at speeds up to 18,000 sfpm with wheels a foot or less in diameter for small work and up to over 6 ft in diameter for large billets. Common forms of abrasive sawing operations are depicted in Fig. 26-7. A chop-stroke is quick and popular for general work, usually small. The rotary methods are advantageous for large diameters, particularly for tubing where feed through the wall only is necessary. For step cutting and also for oscillation- and vibration-action cutting, the wheel is reciprocated to minimize contact area, which allows high pressure and feed rate. The difference between these actions is that for step cutting the wheel is reciprocated over the width of the work, but for oscillation-action only over about a third of the width, and for vibration-action, reciprocation is quite short but rapid. A horizontal traverse action is suitable for long cuts on sheets, slabs, etc.

Abrasive sawing is advantageous for hard materials, even in large sections. On the other hand, cutting pressure can be kept small, and thin sections in hard or soft material can be cut easily without distortion. A thin abrasive disk removes a minimum of stock and saves expensive material, as illustrated by the results of a study presented in Table 26-1.

Band Saw Machines. A continuous saw blade or band runs over the rims of two shrouded wheels on a band saw machine. Horizontal band saw machines, like the one in Fig. 26-8, do cutoff work. The saw is carried on a frame and is fed downward through the workpiece clamped in a vise on the bed. A medium-duty general-purpose machine like the one shown with a 2.2-kW (3-hp) motor costs about $10,000. Blades cost $10 to $15 and have long lives. A heavy-duty automatic production machine with a 3.7-kW (5-hp) motor may cost $25,000.

Vertical band saw machines are used for cutting off pieces but in addition are widely used for cutting outside and inside shapes of all kinds for tool, jig, fixture, die, and gage making and the production of small intricate parts. For inside cutting, the band is cut, passed through a drilled hole, and butt welded together. An example of sawing an opening inside a piece is given in Fig. 26-9. Machines are available for manual operation, automatic cutting from templates, and numerical control. A machine with hydraulic table feed but essentially for manual operation, with a clearance

TABLE 26-1 COSTS IN CUTTING 380-MM (15-IN.)-DIAMETER HARD REFRACTORY ALLOY

	Method			
	Powder burning	Hacksaw	Cold saw	Abrasive saw
Operating and tool costs ($)	17.12	29.61	70.38	16.38
Cost of lost material ($)	66.20	11.55	62.50	16.18
Condition of surface	Uneven and oxidized	Clean	Clean and square	Straight and smoothest

Note: Estimated present-day cost based on actual performance.

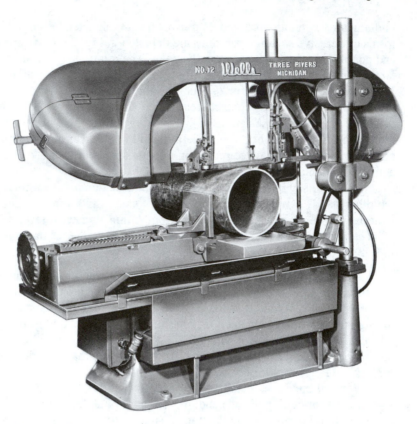

Figure 26-8   A 300 × 400 mm (12 × 16 in.) capacity horizontal metal-cutting band saw. (Courtesy Wells Manufacturing Corp.)

of 610 mm (24 in.) between saw and frame and a 2-kW (3-hp) motor costs about $6000.

Contour band sawing machines are adaptable to other operations. A continuous band of file segments or stones may be put in place of the band saw. Friction sawing is done on high-speed machines with bands having dull teeth. Hard crystalline materials, particularly thin sections and single crystals, are cut with wire charged with diamonds. Some machines are made especially for wire cutting.

Band sawing is steady and continuous and may be faster than hack sawing, and as fast as cold sawing within its limitations, especially through thin sections and weak workpieces. Thin band saws waste only a modicum of stock. An inherent limiting factor in band sawing is the relatively thin blade which may diverge from a true path in a heavy cut. One manufacturer guarantees a tolerance of 0.002 mm/mm (in./in.) of width of cutoff distance if proper limits are observed. Contour sawing is normally done to a tolerance of ±0.25 mm (±0.010 in.) but if carefully and skillfully done, ±40 μm (±0.0015 in.) can be held.

Figure 26-9 Openings in a die block being sawed on a contour band sawing machine. (Courtesy Grob Bros.)

SAWING OPERATIONS

Sawing and filing are governed by the same considerations as other cutting operations. Saw speeds range from 15 m/min (50 fpm) for hard and tough alloys to 900 m/min (3000 fpm) and more for soft materials. The speed of a hack saw is specified in strokes per minute; 60 to 150 represents the usual range from hard to soft materials. The rate a saw penetrates material depends upon the feeding force. Large forces tend to tear out teeth and deflect the blade from a true path. The feed rate for hack saws and cold saws is limited by what the teeth can stand. With band saws, unacceptable accuracy usually is reached before the teeth are hurt. As an example, in sawing mild steel bars 75 to 125 mm (3 to 5 in.) in diameter, typical rates of cutting in cm^2/min (in.^{2}/min) and tool cost in $/cm^2$ ($/in.^{2}) are for a hack saw 65 and 0.0003 (10 and 0.002), a band saw 90 and 0.0005 (14 and 0.003), and a cold saw 160 and 0.0009 (25 and 0.006). As has been shown, machine costs increase in about the same order. Thus if enough sawing can be done, a high cutting rate and low unit cost can be achieved, but at extra cost for machine and tools. Hack, horizontal band, and cold sawing are best for ordinary cutoff work, and other methods are advantageous for particular applications, such as for extra hard materials or unusual shapes and sizes. The method that should be selected for a job depends upon the amount of sawing and kind of work to be done.

QUESTIONS

1. What economy does sawing give?
2. For what is filing used and why?
3. Describe the important features of the three types of saws.
4. Describe the important features of files.
5. How does a power hack saw operate, and what are its advantages and disadvantages?
6. Describe cold sawing and its merits.
7. What is friction sawing, and what does it offer?
8. Describe abrasive disk sawing and its uses.
9. Describe the two types of band sawing machines and the work they do.
10. How do band sawing machines compare with other types of sawing machines?

PROBLEMS

1. The pitch of the teeth is 5.8 mm (0.23 in.) on a 460-mm (18-in.)-diameter circular cold saw. It is fed at a rate of 0.05 mm/t (0.002 ipt) and revolves at 18 m/min (60 fpm). How long will it take to cut through a 125-mm (ca. 5-in.)-diameter steel bar? What is the maximum power consumption at 0.05 kW/cm^3/min (1 hp/in.^{3}/min) of stock removal? The kerf of the saw is 6 mm ($\frac{1}{4}$ in.).

2. The cold sawing machine to do the operation described in Prob. 1 has an overhead rate of $4/hr. A hack saw will cut off the same piece in 5 minutes and has an overhead rate of $1.00/hr. Each machine stands idle for 1 minute while the operator gets the stock and loads it. Which machine would you select for the job, and why?

3. A cold circular saw is needed for general ferrous work that should keep it busy for the full 2000 hr/yr that the plant operates. It is estimated that the saw will be cutting 80% of the time and removing material at an average rate of 82 cm^3/min (5 in.^{3}/min) with a kerf 5 mm (ca. $\frac{3}{16}$ in.) wide. The machine costs $10,000, and $1000 a year is needed to amortize its cost. To do the same work on a horizontal band saw will require about 25% more cutting time, and therefore two machines are needed. Each costs about $6000, and the annual cost of two is $1200. Labor and overhead cost will be the same for either kind of saw. The band saw cuts up about only half as much material in making each cut, and the stock saved is considered worth $0.22kg ($0.10/lb). Which sawing machine would you recommend, and why?

REFERENCES

ANSI-B94.51-1976, *Specifications for Band Saw Blades*. ANSI-B94.52-1977, *Hack Saw Blades*, The American Society of Mechanical Engineers, New York.

AVERY, R., "Big Wheels Cut Off Tough Alloys," *American Machinist*, Jan. 10, 1972, p. 50.

DALLAS, D. B., ed., *Tool and Manufacturing Engineers Handbook*, 3rd ed., Society of Manufacturing Engineers, Dearborn, Mich., 1976.

FARMER, D. A., "High Speeds, New Equipment, Extend Abrasive Cut Off's Capabilities," *Machinery,* July 1971, p. 25.

JABLONOWSKI, J., "Fundamentals of Sawing, Special Report 676," *American Machinist,* Apr. 15, 1975, p. 53.

———, "Those Unconventional Saw Blades," *American Machinist,* Aug. 1976, p. 196.

SCHARFF, R., *Getting the Most of Your Band Saw,* Reston Publishing Co., Reston, Va., 1981.

27

ABRASIVES, GRINDING WHEELS, AND GRINDING OPERATIONS

ABRASIVES

Abrasives are hard substances used in various forms as tools for grinding and other surface finishing operations. They are able to cut materials too hard for other tools and give better finishes and hold closer tolerances than can be obtained economically by other means on most materials.

Abrasives may be used as loose grains, in grinding wheels, in stones and sticks, and as coated abrasives. When applied most efficiently, abrasives remove metal by cutting it into chips just like other metal-cutting tools, but the chips generally are so small that they must be magnified to be seen.

Common Abrasives. The principal abrasive substances are:

1. Aluminum oxide, basically Al_2O_3, known by such trade names as *Alundum* and *Aloxite*. Various substances may be added and methods of its manufacture may be varied to enhance hardness, toughness, friability, etc. Plain Al_2O_3 is white, but the additives color the grains, such as gray, pink, or green. Two common additives are zirconium and vanadium compounds. Aluminum oxide abrasive grains are shown in Fig. 27-1.

2. Silicon carbide, SiC, known by such trade names as *Carborundum* and *Crystolon*, shown in Fig. 27-1.

3. Boron nitride in the forms of single-crystal cubic boron nitride (CBN) and microcrystalline cubic boron nitride (MCBN) under trade names such as *Bor-*

684

azon and *Borpax* with suffixes to denote grade in the United States. In Europe it is ABN, for amber boron nitride.

4. Diamond, a pure form of carbon, both natural and artificial, in friable or blocky shapes.

The important properties of an abrasive material are (1) hardness, (2) toughness, (3) resistance to attrition, and (4) friability.

Hardness is the ability of a substance to resist penetration. An abrasive must be hard to penetrate and scratch the material on which it works. The greater the difference in hardness between an abrasive and the work material, the more efficient the abrasive. The diamond is the hardest known substance. If its hardness is designated by 70, then the hardness of CBN may be about 50, silicon carbide 25, aluminum oxide 20, cemented carbide 18, hard steel 8, and common glass 4. The super abrasives, diamond and CBN, cost many times as much as aluminum oxide and silicon carbide (CBN 10 to 15 times as much as Al_2O_3) but perform considerably better in particular applications, such as grinding hardened H.S.S., cemented carbides, and space-age materials. The total cost of grinding such materials with the hardest abrasives is a fraction of what it is with common abrasives. Although not as hard as diamond, CBN grinds some hard materials better because it is more inert and stands higher temperatures. Aluminum oxide and silicon carbide are still harder than most materials and therefore adequate and more economical than the harder abrasives for most work.

Abrasive grains deteriorate in service by the loss of fine particles, which flattens and dulls the edges, and by relatively large pieces of the crystal breaking away. The first action is called *attrition,* the second *fracture*. Toughness or body strength is necessary for an abrasive grain to stand the original shocks of the cut. How long it remains sharp depends upon its resistance to attrition. The latter is partly related to hardness but also to the chemical affinity between the abrasive and the material it penetrates under high pressures and temperatures. An abrasive may have a high attrition resistance with one material and a low resistance with another material of

Figure 27-1   Left, aluminum oxide abrasive grains; right, silicon carbide abrasive grains. (Courtesy Norton Co.)

about the same hardness. After attrition takes place, a grain must be friable to break apart in chunks to form new sharp edges.

Manufacture of Abrasives.   Natural abrasives were all that were available until about the beginning of this century. Impure aluminum oxide occurs naturally as corundum and emery. However, such natural abrasives lack uniformity and reliability and have been replaced largely by manufactured abrasives.

Silicon carbide does not appear in nature but is made from sand, coke, sawdust, and salt, mixed together and piled around a carbon electrical conductor. A wall of uncemented bricks is built around the mass, and a heavy current is passed through the electrode. A temperature around 2300°C (4200°F) is reached to make the silicon of the sand combine with the carbon of the coke to form SiC. The sawdust burns and leaves pores to let the gas escape. The salt helps remove impurities. After the process has run its course, the furnace is cooled, and the outside removed. The core of loosely knit silicon carbide crystals is broken into individual grains.

Aluminum oxide abrasive is derived from an ore called bauxite, which is mainly aluminum hydroxide. The ore is calcined to drive off excess water and then exposed to high temperatures in an arc-type furnace. Iron chips and coke are added to combine with and remove impurities, and other additives are put in as desired. Aluminum oxide comes out of the furnace in a large lump called a *pig*. It is crushed and rolled into small grains, treated magnetically to remove ferrous impurities, and washed.

Both natural and artificial diamonds are used as abrasives; cubic boron nitride does not appear in nature. These hard abrasives are made by subjecting the ingredients to very high temperature and pressures. The processes are largely proprietary. The grains are commonly clad with nickel or copper.

Grain Size.   Abrasive grains are sorted into various sizes for a uniform and dependable product. This is done by passing the grains through screens in mechanical sieving machines. Grain sizes are designated by numbers as indicated in Fig. 27-5. Each grain size passes through a screen of a certain size but not through smaller screens. Screen size openings in millimeters and their relation to grain sizes are given in tables in Standards Bulletin ANSI B74.12-1976, *Specifications for the Size of Abrasive Grains for Grinding Wheels, Polishing and General Industrial Uses*. The finest sizes, called *flours*, are segregated by flotation methods.

GRINDING WHEELS

Properties of Grinding Wheels.   A grinding wheel is made of abrasive grains held together by a *bond* (Fig. 27-2). These grains cut like teeth when the wheel is revolved at high speed and is brought to bear against a workpiece. The properties of a wheel that determine how it acts are the kind and size of abrasive, how closely the grains are packed together, and the kind and amount of bonding material.

To get the wide range of properties needed in grinding wheels, some are bonded by mixing abrasive grains with inorganic materials and others with organic materials.

Inorganic bonds are vitrified, silicate, and metallic. A *vitrified bond* is a clay bond melted to a porcelain- or glass-like consistency. It can be made strong and porous for heavy grinding and is not affected by water, oils, acids, or other than extreme temperatures. Most grinding wheels have vitrified bonds. Their strength and rigidity help to control size and finish. A silicate bond is essentially water glass hardened by baking. It holds the grains more loosely than a vitrified bond and gives a cooler cut. Large wheels can be made more easily with a silicate bond. Cubic boron nitride and diamond abrasives are usually but not always embedded in *metallic bonds* (by electroplating or electroforming) for the utmost in strength and tenacity to hold the costly and long-wearing grains.

Wheels with organic bonds are held together by such materials as phenolic resins (*resinoid*), *rubber,* and *shellac*. They tend to be somewhat more flexible and resilient than inorganic bonds, and the wheels can stand more bumping and side forces. They release abrasives readily when dull. They are cool cutting and give lustrous finishes. Thin cutoff wheels have resinoid or rubber bonds. Some CBN and diamond wheels have resin bonds.

Some grinding wheels are reinforced with such materials as steel, nylon, and fiberglass for added strength, particularly at ultrahigh speeds. Organic bonds mix well with reinforcement.

The *grade* of a grinding wheel is a measure of how strongly the grains are held by the bond. The bonding material in a wheel surrounds the individual grains and links them together by connectors called *posts,* as illustrated in Fig. 27-3. The sizes and strengths of the posts depend upon the kind and amount of bonding material in a wheel. The ability to hold its abrasive grains is called the *hardness* of a grinding wheel. A hard wheel holds its grains more tenaciously than a soft wheel. A wheel that is too hard for a job keeps its grains after they have become dull. A wheel that is too soft loses grains before they have done full duty. Hardness of the wheel should not be confused with hardness of the abrasive grains themselves.

Figure 27-2 Grinding wheels. (Courtesy Carborundum Co.)

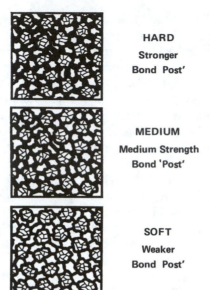

HARD
Stronger
Bond Post'

MEDIUM
Medium Strength
Bond 'Post'

SOFT
Weaker
Bond Post'

Figure 27-3 Explanation of the meaning of wheel grade. (Courtesy Carborundum Co.)

The *structure* or *spacing* of a grinding wheel refers to the relationship of abrasive grains to bonding materials and of those two elements to the voids between them. The meaning of structure is illustrated in Fig. 27-4. The spaces in a grinding wheel provide room for chips to escape during a cut and for cutting fluid to be carried into a cut.

Grinding wheels are marked with symbols that designate their properties. A typical wheel marking and an explanation of its meaning are shown in Fig. 27-5. Each letter or number in a certain position in the sequence designates a particular property.

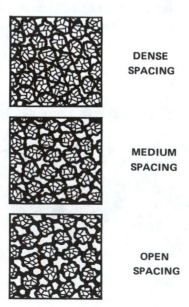

**DENSE
SPACING**

**MEDIUM
SPACING**

**OPEN
SPACING**

Figure 27-4 Explanation of the meaning of wheel structure. (Courtesy Carborundum Co.)

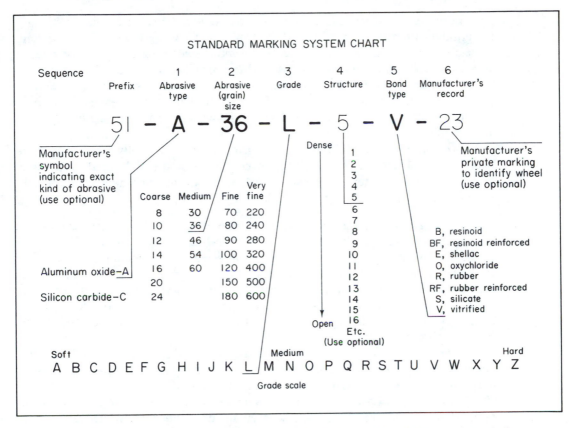

Figure 27-5 Standard marking system chart for aluminum oxide and silicon carbide grinding wheels. A similar chart exists for diamond and cubic boron nitride wheels. (This material is reproduced with permission from ANSI B74.13-1977, *Markings for Identifying Grinding Wheels and Other Abrasives*, copyright 1977, by the American National Standards Institute, copies of which may be purchased from the American National Standards Institute, 1430 Broadway, New York, NY, 10018.)

All grinding wheel manufacturers use substantially the same standard wheel marking system. However, properties of wheels are determined to a large extent by the ways the wheels are made. The processes vary from one plant to another, and wheels carrying the same symbols but made by different manufacturers are not necessarily identical.

   Wheel Shapes and Sizes.   A few typical grinding wheel shapes are shown in Fig. 27-2. The nine grinding wheel shapes recognized as standard include straight cylinders, with or without recesses in their sides, and others described as tapered two sides, straight cup, flaring cup, dish, and saucer. Other shapes may be obtained as specials.

   The principal dimensions that designate the size of a grinding wheel are the outside diameter, width, and hole diameter. Standard wheel shapes are made in certain sizes only, but the variety is large.

Disk wheels are abrasive disks cemented or bolted to steel disks and are stronger for grinding from the side of the wheel than straight wheels alone. Side grinding wheels known as *built-up, segmental,* or *sectored wheels* are composed of bonded abrasive blocks held in a chuck or fastened to a metal disk by wedges, steel bands, wire, or bolts. They are easier to make than solid wheels for diameters over 1 m (ca. 36 in.) and cut coolly because they cut intermittently. Segmental wheels adequately held can be run at higher speeds than solid wheels for peripheral grinding, such as on rough castings at surface speeds over 6 km/min (ca. 20,000 fpm).

Mounted wheels and points are small grinding wheels, usually a few millimeters in diameter, with attached shanks. They are commonly used at high speeds on portable grinders for burring, removing excess material from dies and molds, grinding in recesses and crevices, and for small holes.

Manufacture of Grinding Wheels.   Vitrified grinding wheels may be made by the puddling, tamping, or pressing processes. Pressed wheels are the most dense and puddled wheels the least dense. First clay and abrasive are machine-mixed thoroughly. In the puddling process, water is added, and the mixture is poured into molds. For pressed wheels, the dry or semidry mixture is placed in molds and squeezed in hydraulic presses. The same type of mixture is compressed less but still firmly in the tamping process. At this stage, the wheels are baked and dried. The puddled wheels must be trimmed to size.

Grinding wheels are vitrified by being fired for several days at high temperatures, like pottery. When hard, the wheels are trued, their arbor holes are bushed with babbitt metal or lead, and large wheels are balanced.

Other kinds of wheels are made by processes associated with the particular bonding agents. In general, the ingredients are mixed, molded, and heated as required. The finished wheels are sized, balanced, and graded.

OTHER ABRASIVE PRODUCTS

Silicon carbide and aluminum oxide abrasive grains are bonded into *sticks* and *stones* of various types and sizes. They are used for honing, touching up edges of cutting tools, and cleaning, polishing, and finishing dies, molds, and jigs.

Coated Abrasives.   Coated abrasives are made of abrasive grains, adhesive, and backing. The adhesive may be glue or resin and holds the grains together and to the backing of paper, cloth, or plastic. For a closed coating, the abrasive grains completely cover the surface; in an open coat they are uniformly distributed over 50 to 70% of the surface. Coated abrasives are available in sheets, strips, rolls, cones, and disks of various sizes but belts prevail for stock removal.

Polishing Wheels.   Flexible wheel bodies of cloth, leather, or wood, depending upon the work, are coated with adhesive and rolled in abrasive grains of uniform sizes, coarse for roughing and fine for finishing. After the adhesive, glue or

Figure 27-6 Polishing wheels. (Courtesy Norton Co.)

cold cement, has dried, the abrasive layer is cracked by pounding to make it resilient. The resulting polishing wheels, like those in Fig. 27-6, are revolved at surface speeds around 2.3 km/min (7500 fpm). After its grains have become dull and worn off, a polishing wheel is stripped and recoated.

GRINDING OPERATIONS

Work Done by Grinding. Grinding is done on surfaces of almost all conceivable shapes and materials of all kinds. Grinding may be classified as nonprecision or precision, according to purpose and procedure. *Nonprecision grinding,* common forms of which are *snagging* and *off-hand grinding,* is done primarily to remove stock that cannot be taken off as conveniently by other methods from castings, forgings, billets, and other rough pieces. The work is pressed hard against the wheel, or vice versa. The accuracy and surface finish obtained are of secondary importance. *Precision grinding* is concerned with producing good surface finishes and accurate dimensions. The wheel or work or both are guided in precise paths.

Any grinding is a high-energy operation and potentially quite dangerous. The code that prescribes mandatory safety measures and is the basis for most state standards and laws is the American National Standards Institute standard listed among the references at the end of this chapter.

The three basic kinds of precision grinding shown in Fig. 27-7 are *external cylindrical grinding, internal cylindrical grinding,* and *surface grinding.* Variations of each of these will be described in connection with grinding machines.

Grinding is able to produce accurate and fine surfaces because it works through small abrasive cutting edges, each of which takes a tiny bite. On the other hand, appreciable quantities of material can be removed by grinding because a large number of cutting edges are applied at high frequency. For instance, about 39,000,000 cutting points act in a minute when a 46-grit wheel, 450 mm (18 in.) in diameter and 50 mm (2 in.) wide, is revolved with a surface speed of 1500 m/min (5000 fpm).

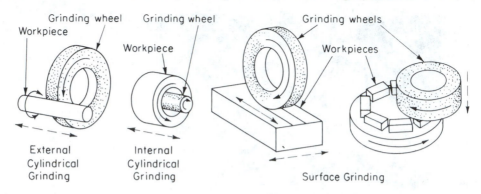

Figure 27-7 Basic precision grinding operations.

The Factors of Cost.   The major costs of a grinding operation are the time cost, for labor and overhead, and the wheel cost, for abrasive used. What these are depends upon (1) the grinding wheel and its selection, (2) the equipment and its operation (including such items as wheel speed, work speed, feed, depth of cut, cutting fluid, and wheel dressing), and (3) the workpiece and its material. How these factors affect costs and how they should be controlled for best results will be explained in the remainder of this chapter.

The Selection of the Grinding Wheel.   A grinding wheel may be needed to remove stock rapidly, give a high finish, or hold small tolerances. Each function calls for different properties in the wheel, and no wheel can do all best. The extent to which a wheel is suited for a job is called its *grinding quality*. A compromise may be made for a general-purpose wheel. A wheel suited just for the job is chosen for a production operation (quite often one for roughing and another for finishing). The following discussion is intended to provide a basic understanding of what is involved in grinding wheel selection. In practice, experts should be consulted to select wheels for important jobs.

Selection of Abrasive and Grain Size.   The resistance to fracture seems about the same for silicon carbide and aluminum oxide. Silicon carbide has a low resistance to attrition when cutting steel or malleable iron, and its grains dull quickly, so aluminum oxide is preferred for that purpose. Silicon carbide performs better as a rule for grinding cast iron, brass, copper, soft bronze. aluminum, stone, rubber, leather, and cemented carbides. The reason is that silicon carbide fractures more satisfactorily in relation to the dulling of its grains, and its cutting edges are renewed as needed. However, various kinds of aluminum oxide are made, and the crystals of some kinds are highly friable and desirable for some soft ductile materials.

If a fine finish rather than stock removal is desired, the positions of the abrasives may be reversed. A rapid dulling of the grains is desirable in some cases to produce fine finishes. Thus, silicon carbide wheels are used to get a mirror finish on hardened steel rolls, and aluminum oxide for a high finish on glass.

Diamond abrasive has physical properties for grinding far superior to other abrasives, but its cost and the cost of wheels made from it are high. Diamond wheels are used for rapidly cutting and finishing gems, ceramics, stone, and cemented carbides.

Soft materials are rough-ground with coarse grains, and hard materials with fine grains. Coarse grains take big bites in and rapidly remove soft materials. Only small bites can be taken in quite hard materials in any event, and consequently small grains are advantageous because more of them can be brought to bear on the material in a given time.

The curves of Fig. 27-8 for vertical rotary surface grinding show that surface finish is improved but metal removal rate decreases for abrasive sizes finer than No. 24. Larger grains were found to be held more securely, became duller before being torn out, and showed a lower metal removal rate than the No. 24 grit. Similar relationships prevail for other kinds of grinding operations. This means that as coarse an abrasive as will give the required surface finish should be selected for a grinding operation to obtain the highest rate of metal removal.

Fine-grain wheels can be trued to thin sections and hold up better at corners and edges than coarse-grain wheels. An example is found in thread grinding, where fine-grain wheels are desirable to hold the shapes required for the roots of thread.

Selection of Wheel Bond, Grade, and Spacing. Hard, tough materials dull abrasives rapidly and require soft grinding wheels that release the grains readily when they become dull. Hard wheels are suitable for soft material. On the other hand, hard wheels exert high pressure and tend to chatter, which is detrimental to good surface finish.

A common measure of wheel performance is the *efficiency ratio, grinding ratio,*

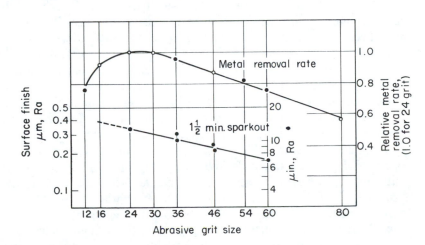

Figure 27-8 Curves showing that surface finish impoves but metal removal rate generally decreases with finer abrasive grains. (Data from *Grits and Grinds*, Vol. 57, No. 1, Jan. 1966.)

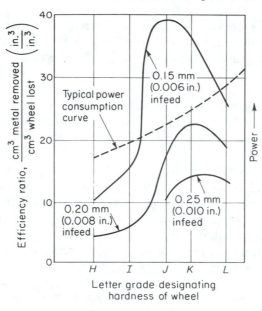

Figure 27-9 Example of the influence of grinding wheel hardness on the efficiency ratio and power consumption in a centerless grinding operation.

or *volume ratio,* which is the number of kg or cm³ (pounds or cubic inches) of metal removed in a given time divided by the kg or cm³ (pounds or cubic inches) of wheel loss. This may be plotted for a series of wheels of the same type but of different grades for a specific operation, as in Fig. 27-9. For any one wheel, the grinding ratio decreases as infeed is increased. This is generally the case for heavy feeds, although the grinding ratio may rise to a peak at low feeds as infeed is increased.

For a given set of conditions in an operation, one wheel grade generally shows the highest ratio, as indicated in Fig. 27-9. If wheel wear alone is to be considered, the best wheel is the one at the highest point. Wheel wear is important because of wheel cost. Also, in precision grinding, wheel wear affects wheel shape, and a wheel that wears rapidly and nonuniformly must be retrued often. This takes time, interrupts production, and is expensive. On the other hand, a wheel that does not have the highest volume ratio may be faster and can show a total cost less than the wheel at the top of the curve. Power consumption and the heat generated increase with grade hardness, and that may be harmful to the work. Experts recommend that the best wheel to use for a job is the softest grade that performs satisfactorily.

Grain spacing provides the openings for chips between grains during a cut. An open spacing or structure is desirable for a large area of contact and heavy roughing cuts in soft materials because it permits the grains to work at their fullest depths and provides good chip clearance space. If the face of a wheel tends to become loaded with metal, its structure is too dense for the work it is doing.

When the grains cannot bite deeply, as in grinding hard materials, chip clearance is secondary and a dense spacing is desirable so that many grains can act at once. Dense spacing is also necessary to produce scratches close together for fine finishes. A wheel with dense spacing holds its shape well and contributes to dimensional control.

Balancing the Grinding Wheel. Grinding wheels, particularly large high-speed ones, must be balanced to produce good finishes. A wheel is mounted on the machine and trued before it is balanced. A conventional wheel mount for a straight wheel fits into the hole of the wheel and has two flanges that clamp against blotting paper rings against the sides or in the recesses of the wheel. Weights attached to one flange can be adjusted manually for static balancing, which is the most common method for large wheels. Grinding wheel mounts are available with weights that tend to move to seek a balanced state while the wheel runs. One system for fine-balancing measures vibrations electronically and actuates a tool to abrade the side of the wheel to restore balance.

Dressing and Truing the Grinding Wheel. A grinding wheel retains its true form and resharpens itself fully as it breaks down in an ideal grinding operation. The condition is only approached in most operations, and the sharpness and form of the wheel must be restored from time to time by dressing and truing as indicated in Fig. 27-10. How often a wheel must be dressed or trued depends upon the type of work, the fitness of the wheel, and the skill of the operator. For internal grinding, the wheel is not uncommonly trued for each piece. For some high-production precision external cylindrical grinding jobs, the wheels may run for days without being dressed.

When metal particles become embedded and fill the spaces around the surface grains, the wheel face is said to be *loaded*. Ductile materials and dense wheel structure particularly engender that condition. When the abrasive grains become dull and cease to cut efficiently because their edges are rubbed off, the wheel face becomes *glazed*. Dressing is done to restore the cutting action of the wheel by fracturing and tearing away the dull grains to expose fresh cutting edges or clear away the embedded

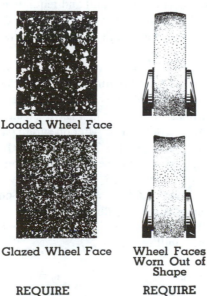

Loaded Wheel Face

Glazed Wheel Face   Wheel Faces
                          Worn Out of
                          Shape

REQUIRE   REQUIRE   **Figure 27-10** Meaning of dressing and
DRESSING   TRUING   truing. (Courtesy Carborundum Co.)

material. *Truing* is done to create a true surface on a wheel. The act of truing a wheel dresses it also. Most wheels are trued and dressed at usual grinding speeds.

Steel cutters, abrasive sticks, and small abrasive wheels are relatively inexpensive and are popular tools for dressing grinding wheels. They may be pushed against and wiped across the face of the wheel by hand or attached to holders on the machine.

Diamonds unsuited for gems are mostly used for truing wheels for precision grinding. A single large stone, a group of small ones in a setting, sintered polycrystalline compacts, or a diamond impregnated wheel may be used. Light cuts of less than 25 μm (0.001 in.) must be taken with a coolant to avoid overheating and damaging the stone. Continued use of a dull diamond makes for dull grains and a poor cutting wheel. Diamond tools are accurately fed and traversed for precision truing, in most cases by means of the normal movements of the machines. For that purpose a standard grinder usually has an attached diamond toolholder, like the one in Fig. 28-8. Truing attachments for straight surfaces, angles, radii, and almost any other form are available for addition to any grinding machine.

Crush dressing is a method of truing and dressing a grinding wheel by means of a hard roller, sometimes diamond impregnated, pressed against the slowly revolving grinding wheel. The reverse of the form desired on the wheel is given to the roller, which displaces and crushes the surface grains and imprints the form on the wheel.

Crush dressing is often more economical than diamond truing, especially for intricate forms. Sharper crystals are left by crush dressing, and that means cleaner and cooler cutting. Diamond truing is generally more accurate and can be made to produce better surface finishes.

Reactive dressing is a routine followed in grinding operations to restore wheel cutting efficiency. When the wheel becomes dull and requires more power, the work speed is increased automatically; this causes the wheel to break down and resharpen itself because of an increase in the grain depth of cut as explained in the next section.

The Theory of Grinding.   The effects of the principal variables in a grinding operation can be seen by analyzing the grinding action depicted in Fig. 27-11. The grinding wheel rotating in the direction shown with a surface speed of V m/min. is assumed to have n grains per linear millimeter in a narrow band around its periphery. The average spacing from grain to grain is $1/n$. After one grain passes point A, the time until the next grain reaches the same point is $T = 1/(1000Vn)$ minutes. During that time the workpiece is revolving with a surface speed of v m/min, and a point on its periphery advances from A to B, a distance $AB = 1000vT = v/Vn$. The chip removed in that time is represented by the area $CEAB$. The maximum chip thickness $t = \overline{EB}$ largely determines what happens to the grinding wheel. The area EAB is small and may be closely approximated by a triangle EAB with the angle $EAB = \alpha + \beta$. Then the maximum chip thickness in millimeters is

$$\overline{EB} = t = AB \sin(\alpha + \beta) = \frac{v}{Vn} \sin(\alpha + \beta) \qquad (27\text{-}1)$$

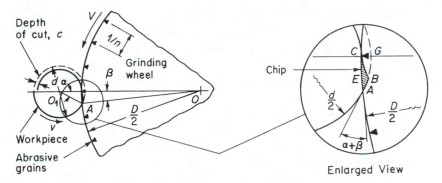

Figure 27-11 Grinding wheel action.

The triangle O_1OA in Fig. 27-11 has one side $D/2 + d/2 - c$, a second side $D/2$, and a third side $d/2$. By the law of cosines,

$$\left(\frac{D}{2} + \frac{d}{2} - c\right)^2 = \left(\frac{D}{2}\right)^2 + \left(\frac{d}{2}\right)^2 - 2\left(\frac{D}{2}\right)\left(\frac{d}{2}\right)\cos[\pi - (\alpha + \beta)] \qquad (27\text{-}2)$$

also

$$\sin(\alpha + \beta) = \sqrt{1 - \cos^2(\alpha + \beta)} = \sqrt{1 - \cos^2[\pi - (\alpha + \beta)]} \qquad (27\text{-}3)$$

If Eqs. (27-2) and (27-3) are combined and solved, and terms containing c^2 are neglected because c is quite small, it is found that

$$\sin(\alpha + \beta) = 2\sqrt{c[(1/d) + (1/D)]} \qquad (27\text{-}4)$$

If this result is substituted in Eq. (27-1),

$$t = \frac{2v}{Vn}\sqrt{c}\sqrt{(1/D) + (1/d)} \qquad (27\text{-}5)$$

This relationship is based on several approximations but is substantially the same as the exact expression that can be obtained for t for each type of grinding. Experience and experiments have shown that the force acting on a grain increases or decreases with the grain depth of cut t, although not necessarily in proportion. An increase in the grain depth of cut causes the forces to increase and the grains to fracture or break away sooner, and the wheel acts softer. Conversely, a decrease in the grain depth of cut makes the wheel act harder. Thus Eq. (27-5) reveals at least qualitatively how the variables in a grinding operation should be arranged for efficient performance.

The grain depth of cut must be small in precision grinding to make light scratches and leave a fine finish. Even in nonprecision grinding, the grain depth of cut cannot be excessive. From Eq. (27-5) it is evident that the wheel speed must be high for a small t. As wheel speed is increased and other parameters are held the same, grinding forces and wheel wear decrease, and the wheel produces a better finish over a longer time. On the other hand, production may be increased by increasing work speed and/or infeed rate along with increasing wheel speed; power rises, and more heat is generated. Low wheel speeds are desirable for some materials, particularly for heat-sensitive metals, but as a rule grinding wheels are run as fast as they safely can be; ordinary vitrified wheels up to 2600 m/min (8500 fpm) and resinoid, rubber, shellac, and segmental and reinforced (even vitrified) wheels up to 5500 m/min (18,000 fpm) and even more.

For a small grain depth of cut, the workpiece velocity v in Eq. (27-5) should not be high and the depth of cut c should be shallow, especially for fine surface finishes. For external cylindrical grinding, work speeds vary from 9 m/min (30 fpm) for hardened steel, which abrasives cannot cut deeply, 15 to 30 m/min (50 to 100 fpm) for average work, to as high as 60 m/min (200 fpm). For average internal grinding, work speeds of 45 to 60 m/min (150 to 200 fpm) are advocated. Table traverse speeds on surface grinders generally are less than 30 m/min (100 fpm). A depth of cut of 25 to 100 μm (0.001 to 0.004 in.) is satisfactory for roughing when precision grinding, but less than 25 μm (0.001 in.) for finishing. The work speeds and feeds cited are for conventional grinding, but for high-speed grinding at wheel speeds of 3500 to 5500 m/min (ca. 12,000 to 18,000 fpm) or more, a like increase in productivity may be obtained by increasing the work speed and/or feed proportionately without changing the grain depth of cut.

It would not be reasonable to expect that exactly the best wheel would be readily available for every grinding job. Equation (27-5) reveals in which direction each variable can be changed to modify the action of the wheel. As a wheel wears to a smaller diameter and its surface speed decreases with the same number of revolutions per minute, the wheel acts softer. The surface speed of the workpiece is increased to make the wheel act softer, and decreased for harder action. A deeper cut causes a wheel to act softer, and a lighter cut harder. Deep cuts and rapid stock removal call for hard wheels.

A small value of n in Eq. (27-5) corresponds to a wheel with an open structure or with its surface dressed coarsely. Such a wheel can be expected to have a soft action. This explains accepted practice of using a wheel for finishing that is of the same grade as for roughing but has finer grains more closely spaced, or the alternative of a softer wheel with the same grain size and spacing as for roughing. The first is a wheel that cuts finely; the second can break down readily and stays sharp and cuts cleanly.

Wheel dressing has a pronounced affect upon wheel action. A deep dressing cut or a long lead in the path of the dressing tool (such as a single-point diamond) across the wheel produces a relatively coarse wheel face that removes stock efficiently but leaves a poorer surface finish on the workpiece than if dressed more finely.

Forces and Power in Grinding.   A grinding wheel exerts two components of force on a workpiece, a normal F_n and tangential F in the manner shown in Fig. 27-12. The ratio $C = F/F_n$ is called the *coefficient of grinding pull* and varies from 0.1 to 0.3 for snagging to 0.4 to 0.5 for wet precision grinding. The normal force F_n determines the rate of stock removal in nonprecision grinding. As it is increased with the same wheel speed, the force F and the power increase with the stock removal. Approxi-

Grinding
wheel

Workpiece

Figure 27-12   Forces exerted by a grinding wheel.

mately 0.9 kN (200 lb) is the heaviest load for manual application with weights. Mechanical and hydraulic means are utilized for larger forces.

An empirical formula for estimating the power needed for grinding iron and steel with a wheel running at normal grinding speed is

$$\text{in kilowatts, } P_s = K_s\sqrt{Q_s} \qquad \text{or} \qquad \text{in horsepower, } P = K\sqrt{Q} \qquad (27\text{-}6)$$

The rate of stock removal in cm³/min is Q_s and in in.³/min is Q. The following are typical values of K:

	Kind of grinding operation				
	Snagging		Precision grinding with wheels about 25 mm (1 in.) wide		
	Floor stand	Swing frame	Surface	Internal	Cylindrical
Value of K_s	1.1	1.3	1.6	1.75	1.8
Value of K	6	7	8.5	9.5	10.0

Power is one of the least costly items in most grinding operations. However, the energy released when power is applied is important because most of it becomes heat which can crack, check, or soften the ground surface under severe conditions.

The Area of Contact.   An expression approximating the length of path of an abrasive grain through a workpiece is $l = \sqrt{cD}/[1 + (D/d)]$. This is really the length of the circular arc *CEA* in Fig. 27-11. It shows the same thing as Fig. 27-13, that the arc is shortest for external grinding, longer for surface grinding, and longest for internal grinding. Surface grinding with the side of a wheel gives still more contact. A large wheel has a longer arc of contact than a small wheel. A deep cut results in more contact than a shallow cut. The longer the path through the material, the longer each grain is exposed to the high temperatures and pressures of grinding, and the more the grains are subject to attrition, and the harder the wheel acts. For this reason, internal grinding calls for softer wheels than external grinding under comparable conditions.

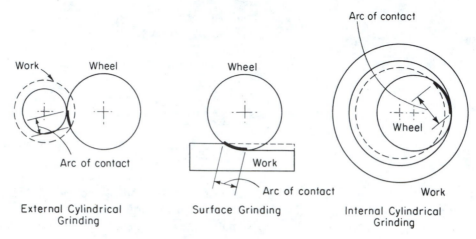

Figure 27-13 Relation between the type of operation and area of contact in grinding with the periphery of a wheel.

The area of contact is the product of the arc length times the width of contact. As the area of contact increases, the number of grains in contact with the work increases with a uniform grain spacing, and the force tending to separate the wheel from the work is increased. This affects dimensional accuracy and finish in precision grinding and indicates the need for a more open spacing.

Size Effect in Grinding.   Three stages have been discerned in the action of abrasives in grinding. When an abrasive grain first makes contact, it distorts and may displace material slightly, but if it penetrates no more deeply, it, in effect, merely *rubs* as it continues on its course. With somewhat deeper penetration, metal is plastically extruded around the grain in a *ploughing* action, and debris is scattered alongside the scratch. If a grain bites deeply enough to fracture metal before it, it cleaves a chip in a true *cutting* action. All three stages may exist with differently placed grains at one time, and a single grain may go through one, two, or all three stages as it is driven through the work material. The degree of penetration determines the forces and energy required to remove material. Plowing predominates for chips less than about 0.8 μm (30 μin.) thick with a uniformly high specific energy of cut as evidenced by the plateau on the curve of Fig. 27-14. The upturn at the top of the curve is evidence of rubbing. In grinding, the specific energy decreases as the size of cut increases as in other cutting operations.

Thermal Effects of Grinding.   Most of the energy of grinding becomes heat. The bulk of the heat passes off with the chips, but some goes into the abrasive grains, and some into the workpiece, and it affects both. Indications are that the instantaneous temperature on a surface being ground and on the contact area of a grain is normally 1100 to 1650°C (2000 to 3000°F). This may cause workpiece temperatures to reach heights around 425°C (800°F) at 25μm (0.001 in.) and 315°C (600°F) at depths of 125 μm (0.005 in.) in normal operations.

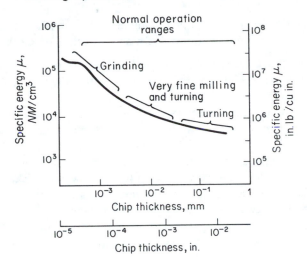

Figure 27-14 Trend of increase in specific energy as chip thickness decreases in metal cutting or grinding.

High temperatures are among the chief causes of both attrition and fracturing of abrasive grains. The high surface temperatures speed up chemical reactions between abrasive and work materials. For instance, titanium is notoriously difficult to grind because it combines with the surface layer of any common abrasive, dulling the grains quickly. In all grinding operations, sudden heating and then quenching, particularly with coolant, cause thermal shock and fracture of abrasive grains. If surface crumbling alone occurs, attrition results; if the effect is deeper, appreciable chunks are broken off and leave new sharp edges on a grain. The thermal stresses induced in a grain are dependent upon the heat injected, which Hahn has shown is $Q = ClA^{3/4}/V^{1/2}$, where C is a constant proportional to the ratio of specific heats of abrasive and work material, l is the length of grain path, A the area of contact of the grain, and V the wheel speed. This explains why wheel life is better at high speeds.

The heat of grinding may cause thermal stresses in the material and change its microstructure. In some cases, such as in snagging rough castings, the effects of heat are unimportant. In other cases, such as grinding hardened steel, excessive temperature may ruin the workpiece by softening, burning, rehardening, or cracking the surface material. To correct such situations, an understanding of the factors that cause high temperatures is necessary. Investigations have shown that surface temperature is a direct function of the depth of cut, wheel speed, and area of contact between grains and workpiece, all of which increase the rate of energy input. Slow wheel speeds are desirable for heat-sensitive materials. An increase in work speed reduces wheel-work contact time and temperature. Surface temperature is also an inverse function of chip thickness and thermal conductivity of the work material. A material with a high thermal conductivity to carry away heat, like low-alloy steel, can be expected to have a lower surface temperature than one like stainless steel with a low thermal conductivity. A thick chip requires less energy for each unit of material removed, and a light cut removes little material. Thus a light cut and thick chip are favorable to low grinding temperatures. In contrast, a thin chip is desirable for good surface finish, as has been noted. Consequently, some conditions favorable for fine surface finish are opposed to those necessary to keep temperatures down and prevent surface damage.

The Material and the Workpiece.   Three considerations are necessary to describe how hard or easy a material is to grind. These have been called grindability, finishability, and grinding sensitivity.

Grindability is a measure of the relative ease of removing material. The rate of wheel wear as indicated by the volume ratio is considered a satisfactory index of grindability because it generally agrees with the evaluations made in practice. Power consumption might also be considered an index because it is an indication of the amount of heat involved, but it does not correlate with the volume ratio. The grindability of hardened tool steels has been found to decrease to a great extent with an increase in the amount of hard carbide particles present in them. Sulfur in steel, particularly in tool and stainless steels, improves grindability as much as ten times. The most difficult steels to grind have been reported to cause wheels to wear 200 times faster than the easiest.

Finishability is related to the relative cost of putting a fine finish on a material. In general, materials of medium grindability have been found to have the poorest finishability. Hard materials with low grindability seem to have good finishability as a rule because they dull the grains and prevent deep scratches.

Grinding sensitivity is the propensity of a material to crack or lose its surface hardness when ground. Untempered martensite in high-speed steel, excessively high carbon content in the outermost layers of carburized steels, and retained austenite in medium- and high-alloy steels are conditions that have been shown to cause hypersensitivity. Even sensitive steels can be ground if the work is done slowly and carefully enough, but that is expensive. Corrective measures in heat treatment generally can eliminate causes of ultrasensitivity and keep costs down. Where some sensitivity still exists, control of the conditions that keep grinding temperatures down is necessary.

The condition of the rough workpiece determines much of the success of a grinding operation. Too much stock requires an unnecessary amount of time and wheel wear for grinding; too little stock may mean that a piece will not clean up before finished size is reached. A case-hardened piece may be left with a soft surface if too much material is removed. Warpage and runout determine to a large extent the amount of stock that must be provided for grinding. The better the control of these factors, the more efficient a grinding operation. Typical practice is to allow stock of 0.25 to 0.40 mm (0.010 to 0.016 in.) for rough and 0.05 to 0.15 mm (0.002 to 0.006 in.) on the diameter for finish cylindrical grinding, depending on the size of the workpiece. About half as much is left on a side for surface grinding.

Cutting Fluids for Grinding.   Water solutions are widely used for grinding because they cool well. Water alone markedly increases wheel wear, but chemical additives to deter or alter reactions may materially reduce wear. Oils may lubricate chips and abrasive grains, mitigate wheel loading, and inhibit chemical reactions, thus retarding attrition. Combinations of additives to oils are beneficial; one series of tests showed that combinations of soapy fats, sulfur, and chlorine increased grinding ratio tenfold.

Efficient use of cutting fluids presents unique problems in grinding. High wheel speed tends to eject fluid at the grinding zone, and the higher the speed, the worse the problem. In most cases the zone is flooded copiously, but other remedies, such as high-pressure nozzles and special guards to contain the fluid, are used. All fluids are helpful in removing particles but tend to hold them in suspension, and care must be taken to filter or settle out the particles so they are not recirculated and cause scratches.

Economics of Grinding. Operating cost goes down but wheel cost rises per unit of material removed as grinding is done at a faster rate, as shown in Fig. 27-15. Total cost is the sum of operating and wheel costs and generally falls to a minimum and then rises as the grinding rate is increased. However, dimensional accuracy and surface finish become poorer as the grinding rate is increased, and the production rate in many precision grinding operations cannot be set high enough for minimum cost if accuracy and finish requirements are to be met. In such cases, the rate of stock removal should be as high as the required quality of output permits. On the other hand, accuracy and finish are not the limiting factors in many abrasive machining, roughing, and nonprecision grinding operations, and the aim then is to operate at the lowest cost.

The components of cost are measured at several points to find the minimum for an operation. The volume ratio G decreases as the rate of metal removal Y increases and for many operations can be approximated by the empirical relationship

$$GY^n = C_0 \qquad (27\text{-}7)$$

For the operation depicted by Fig. 27-15, the exponent n was found to be 4.4, and $C_0 = 8.83 \times 10^8$ for Y in cm³/min and 4×10^3 for in.³/min. Those factors can be expected to be different for any other operation. The unit cost in dollars per unit volume removed is

$$C_u = C_M + C_W = \frac{R_H}{Y} + \frac{A}{G} = \frac{R_H}{Y} + \frac{AY^n}{C_0} \qquad (27\text{-}8)$$

The term R_H is the cost of labor and overhead in dollars per hour, and A is the wheel cost in dollars per unit volume. If the expression is differentiated with respect to Y, and the derivative is set equal to zero, the rate of metal removal for minimum cost is found to be

$$Y_{\min} = \left(\frac{C_0 R_H}{nA}\right)^{1/(n+1)} \qquad (27\text{-}9)$$

This occurs when the machine cost equals n times the abrasive cost expressed as

$$\frac{R_H}{Y} = n\frac{AY^n}{C_0} \qquad (27\text{-}10)$$

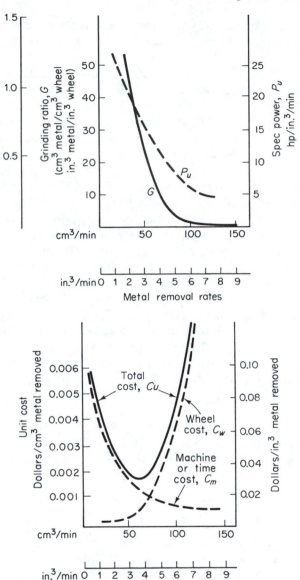

Figure 27-15 Variations of volume ratio, unit power, and components of cost with the rate of metal removal for surface grinding 1020 steel. (After Charles Pollock, "Try Abrasive Machining at Low Power," *Grits and Grinds*, Vol. 56, No.1, Jan. 1965.)

An example of a cost comparison is furnished by the grinding of stainless steel billets. The best type of grinding wheel for the job performs to the relationship $G_1 Y_1 = C$, which is Eq. (27-7) with $n = 1$. In this case G_1 is in Mg/cm^3 (tons/in.^{3}), and Y_1 in Mg/hr (tons/hr). Equation (27-10) can be written as $R_H/Y_1 = A/C/Y_1 = A/G_1$ for $n = 1$. Unit wheel cost A is estimated to be \$0.0168/cm^3 (\$0.275/in.^{3}), and the labor and overhead rate $R_H = $11/hr$. Only affected overhead costs are included. Trials with wheels of two grades showed the following results:

Wheel grade	Production rate, Y_1 [Mg/h (tons/hr)]	Volume ratio, G_1 [Mg/cm³ (tons/in.³)]	Machine cost, R_H/Y_1 [$/Mg ($/ton)]	Wheel cost, A/G_1 [$/Mg ($/ton)]	Total cost, C_u [$/Mg ($/ton)]
Y	0.1818 (0.200)	0.00044 (0.008)	60.51 (55.00)	38.18 (34.38)	98.69 (89.38)
Z	0.2291 (0.252)	0.00035 (0.00635)	48.01 (43.65)	48.00 (43.31)	96.01 (86.96)

The grade Z wheel removes stock at a higher rate but with more wheel cost than grade Y, but the machine cost and total cost are less for grade Z. Its machine cost is practically equal to the wheel cost, which indicates the wheel grade Z to be the most economical obtainable.

QUESTIONS

1. What are the principal abrasive materials, and what are their properties?
2. Describe how aluminum oxide and silicon carbide abrasives are made.
3. How is the size of an abrasive grain designated?
4. Name and describe the principal bonds for grinding wheels.
5. What is meant by the grade of a grinding wheel?
6. What is meant by the structure or spacing of a grinding wheel?
7. Describe common types and shapes of grinding wheels.
8. How are grinding wheels manufactured?
9. What are sticks, stones, coated abrasives, and polishing wheels, and how are they used?
10. Describe nonprecision and precision grinding.
11. Discuss the costs that are present in a grinding operation.
12. What considerations enter into the selection of a grinding wheel?
13. What considerations influence the selection of an abrasive?
14. When are coarse grains and when are fine grains preferred?
15. What is the efficiency, grinding, or volume ratio, and what bearing does it have on the selection of the wheel grade?
16. What considerations determine what grain spacing a grinding wheel should have?
17. How and why are grinding wheels balanced?
18. What are truing and dressing of grinding wheels, and how are they done?
19. Explain how the grain depth of cut, surface finish, and rate of wheel wear are affected by the work speed, wheel speed, wheel depth of cut, wheel diameter, and work diameter.
20. How does the length of contact between wheel and workpiece influence a grinding operation?
21. What is "size effect" and what does it mean in grinding?

22. What conditions are favorable to a low surface temperature in grinding, and why?
23. How do the conditions favorable to a low surface temperature compare with those favorable to a good surface finish?
24. What is meant by grindability, finishability, and grinding sensitivity?
25. How may grinding sensitivity be corrected?
26. What determines the proper amount of grinding stock on a workpiece?
27. What is meant by the grinding quality of a wheel?
28. How do the wheel cost and time cost vary with the grinding rate?
29. What should the rate of production be in a precision grinding operation, and why?
30. What is the economical rate of production for a snagging operation?

PROBLEMS

1. 4.5 kg (10 lb) of metal are being removed per hour with a power consumption of 4 kW (5.4 hp) at the wheel in a snagging operation on a swing frame grinder. The wheel has a surface speed of 1830 m/min (6000 fpm) and is pushed against the work with a force of 800 N (180 lb). To what amount must the normal force be raised to increase the metal removal rate to 7 kg/hr (ca. 15 lb/hr)?

2. A motor on a floor-stand grinder is delivering 4 kW (5.4 hp) to drive a vitrified grinding wheel at 1830 m/min (6000 fpm) to remove 16.4 cm³ of metal per minute (1 in.³/min) The drive efficiency is 80%. If a resinoid wheel is put on the stand and driven at 2740 m/min (9000 fpm) and the same normal and tangential forces are maintained at the point of contact, what power must the motor deliver at the same efficiency? If the K factor of Eq. (27-6) for the resinoid wheel is 6.6 (K_s = 1.22), what rate of metal removal may be expected from that wheel?

3. Estimate the normal force that must be applied for grinding steel to:
   (a) Remove 9 kg (20 lb) of metal per hour on a swing frame grinder with a resinoid wheel running at 2750 m/min (9000 fpm).
   (b) Grind wet at the rate of 8 cm³/min ($\frac{1}{2}$ cu.in./min) of metal removal on an external cylindrical grinder with a vitrified wheel having a surface speed of 1830 m/min (6000 fpm).

4. A 250-mm (10-in.)-diameter soft-carbon steel shaft is to be traverse ground with coolant and a wheel 50 mm (2 in.) wide running at 1830 m/min (6000 fpm) on a cylindrical grinder. The motor is rated at 11 kW (15 hp) and the machine efficiency is 80%. Machine rigidity allows a work-wheel normal force of 890 N (200 lb.). What is the traverse rate permitted with a depth of cut of 50 μm/pass (0.002 in./pass)?

5. What change in each of the following variables in a grinding operation will tend to give a finer surface finish (a) wheel speed? (b) work speed? (c) grain size? (d) depth of cut? (e) wheel size?

6. What should be the approximate properties of a grinding wheel with respect to abrasive, grain size, bond, grade, and structure for each of the following typical applications?
   (a) To commercially grind a mild-steel shaft.
   (b) For snagging cast iron.
   (c) To sharpen a high-speed steel milling cutter.

(d) To grind a 75-mm (3-in.)-diameter hole in a case-hardened steel bushing.

(e) To grind the top and bottom surfaces of a water hardening tool steel die block.

(f) To cut off aluminum bar stock.

7. Derive the expression for the length of arc *CEA* in Fig. 27-11 as $l = \sqrt{cD}/[1 + (D/d)]$. Show that the length of grain path really is $l_a = l[1 + (v/V)]$.

8. What is the error that may result from estimating the grain path as the length of arc $CEA = l$ in Fig. 27-11 if $v = 30$ and $V = 1500$?

9. Two wheels of a certain type are tried for a swing frame grinding operation. Grade A has a life of 13.11 hours with a production rate of 0.152 Mg/hr (0.168 ton/hr). Grade B has a life of 10.17 hours with a production rate of 0.173 Mg/hr (0.191 ton/hr). The cost of either wheel is $130.80, and the labor and overhead rate is $13.00/hr. $GY = C$ for this type of operation. Which wheel is more economical? Is there any indication that either is the most economical available?

10. Meehanite GC class 40 gray iron bars 75 × 75 × 300 mm (3 × 3 × 12 in.) in size were surface ground with a segmented wheel 450 mm (18 in.) in diameter. The relationship $GY^{3.33} = 40,000$ was found for the grinding ratio for Y in in.^{3}/min, $GY_s^{3.33} = 4.4 \times 10^8$ for Y_s in cm^3/min. Abrasive cost was estimated at 1.26 cents/cm^3 (20.6 cents/in.^{3}), and labor and overhead rate $14.00/hr. What rate of metal removal gives the lowest cost, and what is the cost?

11. Five wheels 900 mm diameter by 100 mm wide (nominally 36 in. diameter by 4 in. wide) tried for a precision grinding operation perform as follows:

	Wheel				
	A	B	C	D	E
Rate of production					
(cm^3 in 8 hr)	14,900	8,620	17,370	11,300	13,600
(in.^{3} in 8 hr)	910	526	1,060	690	830
Volume ratio	4.74	3.35	2.45	6.31	5.5
(cm^3 stock/cm^3 wheel);					
(in.^{3} stock/in.^{3} wheel)					

Wheel cost is $0.01/cm^3 ($0.16/in.^{3}) and the labor and overhead rate is $16/hr. Which would you recommend for use?

REFERENCES

ALDEN, G. I., *Operation of Grinding Wheels in Machine Grinding*, Norton Co., Worcester, Mass.

ANSI B7.1-1978, *Safety Requirements for the Use, Care and Protection of Abrasive Wheels; ANSI B74.13-1977, Markings for Identifying Grinding Wheels and Other Bonded Abrasives*, American National Standards Institute, New York.

ARMAREGO, E. J. A., and R. H. BROWN, *The Machining of Metals*, Prentice-Hall, Englewood Cliffs, N.J., 1969.

BHATEJA, C., and R. LINDSEY, eds., *Grinding Theory, Techniques, and Troubleshooting,* Society of Manufacturing Engineers, Dearborn, Mich., 1981.

GILES, M. T., "New Generation of Superabrasives," *Manufacturing Engineering,* June 1982, p. 60.

HAHN, R. S., and R. P. LINDSAY, "Principles of Grinding," *Machinery,* July–Nov. 1971.

"High Speed Plunge Grinding," *Manufacturing Engineering,* June 1979, p. 67.

JABLONOWSKI, J., "Fundamentals of Grinding," *American Machinist,* Feb. 1976, p. 61.

———, "Machining with Coated Abrasives," *American Machinist,* Aug. 1980, p. 149.

KRAFFT, F. G., and P. GRIEB, "Grinding with Plated CBN Wheels," *American Machinist,* Apr. 1982, p. 122.

LEWIS, K. R., and W. F. SCHLEICHER, *The Grinding Wheel,* Grinding Wheel Institute, Cleveland, Ohio, 1978.

MARTI, H., "Fine-Balancing—A Key to Precision Grinding," *Machine and Tool Blue Book,* Jan. 1976, p. 74.

MERRITT, R. H., "Wheel Selection for Better Grinding Operation," *Machine and Tool Blue Book,* June 1978, p. 121.

PIOTROWSKI, L., "Understanding Wheel-Dress," *American Machinist,* Feb. 24, 1969, p. 98.

SMITH, R. L., "Energy Adaptive Grinding," *American Machinist,* July 1977, p. 116.

28

GRINDING MACHINES AND METHODS

Grinding machines utilize grinding wheels and may be classified according to the types of operations described in Chap. 27. Thus the broad classes are precision and nonprecision grinders. The main types of precision grinding machines are external and internal cylindrical grinding machines and surface grinding machines. Certain types have been developed to do specific operations and are classified accordingly.

Space is available to describe only the basic grinding machines. Most types are available in simple hand-operated models and in various semi- and fully automatic models, as are other machine tools.

PRECISION GRINDERS

Cylindrical Center-Type Grinders. Cylindrical center-type grinders are used for grinding straight and tapered round pieces, round parts with curved lengthwise profiles, fillets, shoulders, and faces. A simple and the original form of cylindrical grinder is a head that revolves a grinding wheel and is mounted on the cross-slide or compound rest of a lathe. These *toolpost grinders* are made to deliver from a small fraction to about 7.5 kW (10 hp) at costs from under $1000 to several thousand dollars. They are expedient when regular grinding machines are not available.

A workpiece is usually held between dead centers and rotated by a dog and driver on the faceplate on a *plain cylindrical center-type grinder* as depicted in Fig. 28-1. The centers are held in the headstock and footstock of the machine, as shown in Fig. 28-2, and do not revolve because that provides the most rigid work support and accuracy between centers. The headstock and footstock are carried on an upper or

A. Grinding Wheel
B. Grinding Face
C. Wheel Spindle
D. Work Piece
E. Work Centers

Typical Cylindrical Grinder

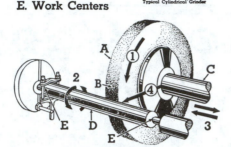

MOVEMENTS

1. Wheel   2. Work
3. Traverse   4. Infeed

Figure 28-1 Movements of an external cylindrical grinding machine. (Courtesy Carborundum Co.)

swivel table and can be positioned to suit the length of the workpiece. The upper table can be swiveled and clamped on a lower table to adjust for grinding straight or tapered work as desired. The amount of taper that can be ground in this way is normally less than 10° because the table bumps the wheelhead if swiveled too far. The lower table slides on ways on the bed of the machine to traverse the work past the grinding wheel and can be moved by hand or power.

The grinding wheel revolves in the direction shown in Fig. 28-1 on a heavy spindle—running in close fitting bearings to prevent flutter. The grinding force is directed downward for stability. The wheelhead carries the wheel to and away from the work. The movement is called in-feed and normally can be controlled to 5 μm (0.0002 in.) or less on manually controlled grinders and to as little as 0.7 μm (ca. 25 μin.) on some automatic grinders.

Cylindrical grinding may be done by the plunge cut or traversing methods. Similar methods are found in surface grinding. In *plunge cut grinding,* a wheel somewhat wider than the work surface is fed in as the workpiece revolves. With other factors constant, the depth of cut and rate of stock removal depend upon the rate of infeed. A work surface wider than the wheel is *traverse ground* by traversing the revolving workpiece lengthwise with respect to the wheel, or vice versa. The rate of traverse becomes one of the conditions determining the length of grain path. The radial depth of cut is determined by the amount the wheel is fed in at each reversal of the traverse. An advance along the workpiece of $\frac{1}{4}$ to $\frac{1}{2}$ of the width of the wheel per revolution of the work in cylindrical grinding or per stroke in surface grinding is common. The leading portion of the wheel removes most of the stock, and the remainder cleans up the surface.

The necessary steps in a precision grinding operation include bringing the wheel at a rapid rate to the workpiece (or vice versa) and then at feedrate to grind to size. The feed is continuous for a plunge cut but incremental (for each pass) for traverse grinding. The wheel is allowed to dwell momentarily at the end of the cut for cleanup

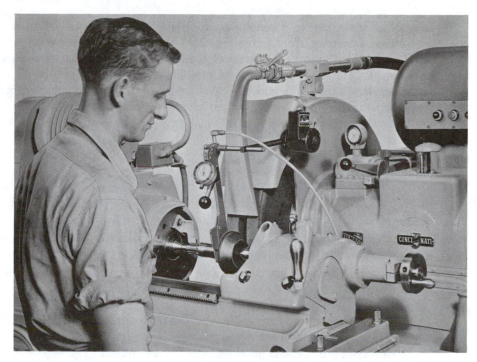

Figure 28-2   Setup on a plain cylindrical center-type grinder with wheels for grinding two diameters and a gage for automatic sizing. (Courtesy Cincinnati Milacron, Inc.)

and is then withdrawn at rapid rate. The usual treatment for one piece of a kind is to rough and finish grind it completely in one operation, with the wheel trued at least once for the final finishing pass or passes. One the other hand, a lot of pieces of the same kind may be all rough ground in one operation (leaving a small amount of stock) and then finish ground in another operation with a different feed rate and dressing and even a different wheel. In job shops and toolrooms, the operator may control all the steps. He moves the wheel in and out by turning a leadscrew with a graduated handwheel. He may measure the size when nearly finished and then adjust to grind to the desired size. He compensates for wheel wear, truing, and machine errors by skillful manipulation. One helpful device is a caliper indicator for measuring and displaying workpiece size continuously during grinding as shown in Fig. 28-2. Similar electronic devices display size in illuminated numbers and can control the machine. Automatic grinders are available with various degrees of refinement. Some feed the wheel to preset position and others compensate for wheel truing and wear. Once set to a reference, they can grind to a specified size dialed into the controls. One model can even grind up to 10 different diameters, one after another, on each workpiece.

Grinding wheels may be arranged in a number of ways. The wheelheads on some plain grinders are set at an angle, so the periphery of a wheel can grind workpiece shoulders and faces as well as diameters. One or several wheels may be mounted on a machine and trued to a certain shape or shapes for a workpiece ground in large quantities. Examples are given in Fig. 28-3.

Cylindrical center-type grinders capable of swinging diameters in excess of 500 mm (ca. 20 in.), particularly for grinding rolls for rolling mills, are called *roll grinders*. Roll grinders commonly have cambering attachments that enable them to grind accurate and reproducible curved lengthwise profiles on rolls. Rolls are ground in that way so they become straight when deformed by high temperatures and pressures in operation.

A *universal cylindrical center-type grinder* has all the units and movements of a plain grinder, but in addition:

1. Its headstock spindle may be used alive or dead (rotated or not), so that work can be held and revolved by a chuck as well as between centers.
2. Its headstock can be swiveled in a horizontal plane so that any angle, even a flat plane, can be ground on a workpiece chucked on the headstock spindle.
3. Its wheelhead and slide can be swiveled and traversed at any angle in the manner indicated in Fig. 28-4 so that any taper can be ground on work between centers.

Most universal grinders can be arranged for internal grinding by the addition of an auxiliary wheelhead to revolve small wheels at high speeds.

Universal grinders can grind surfaces like steep tapers and holes not accommodated on plain grinders, but they sacrifice rigidity, power, and rapid output because of their flexibility. They are found in toolrooms and jobbing shops and sometimes on production jobs for shapes hard to grind on plane grinders.

The size of a cylindrical center-type grinder usually is designated by the diameter in millimeters or inches and length in millimeters or inches of the largest workpiece the machine can nominally take between centers. Thus a 300 × 1000 mm (ca. 12 × 40 in.) center-type grinder can swing a workpiece 300 mm in diameter over the table and grind it with a new wheel. A workpiece up to 1000 mm long can be mounted between centers. Specifications of several types and sizes of center-type grinders are given in Table 28-1.

Chucking Grinders. Chucking grinders are designed for grinding small- and medium-diameter short parts automatically and in large quantities. Typical applica-

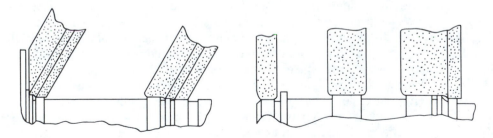

Figure 28-3 Typical multiwheel arrangements for production grinding.

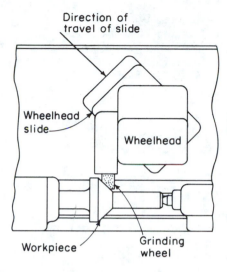

Direction of
travel of slide

Wheelhead
slide

Wheelhead

Workpiece

Grinding
wheel

Figure 28-4 Universal center-type grinder arranged for grinding a steep taper.

tions are the grinding of tapered roller bearing cone races, valve tappets, and small bevel gear shoulders and stems. The workpiece is held in a chuck, collet, or fixture.

Centerless Grinders. An external cylindrical centerless grinding machine revolves a workpiece on top of a workrest blade between two abrasive wheels as shown in Fig. 28-5. The grinding wheel removes material from the workpiece. The workpiece has a greater affinity for and is driven at the same surface speed as the regulating wheel, which is normally a rubber bonded abrasive wheel that turns at a surface speed of 15 to 60 m/min (50 to 200 fpm).

Thrufeed centerless grinding is done by passing the workpiece completely through the space between the grinding and regulating wheel, usually with guides at both ends, as indicated in Fig. 28-6(A). The regulating wheel is tilted a few degrees about a horizontal axis perpendicular to its own axis. This feeds the workpieces

TABLE 28-1 TYPICAL SPECIFICATIONS OF CENTER-TYPE CYLINDRICAL GRINDERS

Type	Nominal size [mm (in.)]	Main motor [kW (hp)]	Weight [Mg (lb)]	Cost
Universal— manual	320 × 1000 (12.6 × 39)	3.7 (5)	3.1 (6,800)	$ 38,000
Plain— manual	450 × 2200 (17.5 × 86.5)	11.2 (15)	6.5 (14,300)	76,000
Universal— automatic cycle	840 × 3050 (33 × 120)	37.5 (50)	15 (33,000)	130,000
Profile and step grinder— numerical control (external and internal)	406 × 812 (16 × 32)	3.7 (5)	5.9 (13,000)	150,000

Typical Centerless Grinder

A. Grinding Wheel
B. Grinding Face
C. Regulating Wheel
D. Work Piece
E. Work Rest Blade

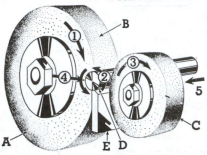

MOVEMENTS

1. Grinding Wheel	2. Work
3. Regulating Wheel	4. Infeed
	5. Traverse

Figure 28-5 Action of an external cylindrical centerless grinding machine. (Courtesy Carborundum Co.)

lengthwise. The rate of feed in mm/min (in./min) depends upon the angle of inclination and speed of the regulating wheel as expressed by the relation

$$F = \pi DN \sin \alpha \qquad (28\text{-}1)$$

D is the diameter in mm (in.), N is the speed in rpm, and α is the angle of tilt of the regulating wheel, which may be from 0 to 8°. A slow feed is necessary to remove relatively large amounts of stock within the power capacity of the machine and to produce accuracy and good surface finish. Most thrufeed work is ground in two passes with a total stock removal of 0.25 to 0.40 mm (0.010 to 0.015 in.)

In-feed centerless grinding is slower than thrufeed grinding but is necessary for

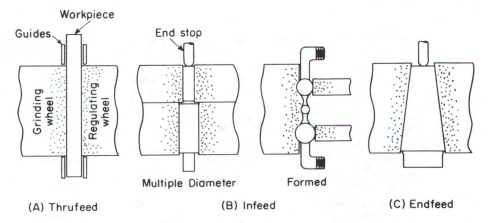

(A) Thrufeed   (B) Infeed   (C) Endfeed

Figure 28-6 Centerless grinding operations.

a workpiece with a shoulder, head, or obstruction that prevents its passing completely through the throat between the wheels. Two examples of in-feed grinding are given in Fig. 28-6(B). The workrest and regulating wheel are withdrawn from the grinding wheel to receive a workpiece. They are then moved toward the grinding wheel to grind the work to size. A variation of infeed grinding utilizes a *cam regulating wheel* that is recessed and relieved over a part of its periphery. Work is unloaded, loaded, and fed in as the cutaway side of the wheel passes the workrest (at about 16 rpm). In that way the workrest and regulating wheel need not be slid to and from the cut, and one piece is ground in each revolution of the regulating wheel.

End-feed centerless grinding is for tapered work, as shown in Fig. 28-6(C). Either the grinding wheel or regulating wheel or both are trued to a taper. The work is fed lengthwise between the wheels and is ground as it advances until it reaches the end stop.

A medium-size centerless grinder that takes workpieces up to 125 mm (ca. 5 in.) in diameter is driven by a 12.7-kW (15-hp) motor and is quoted at $70,000 for manual operation, $90,000 with automatic infeed, and $350,000 with fully automatic numerical control.

Comparison of Center-Type and Centerless Grinding.   As a rule more time is needed to set up a centerless grinder, but the difference is not large for many simple parts. Also much can be done to minimize centerless setup time by scheduling similar parts in successive lots over the same machine. Parts with several diameters or curved or tapered profiles usually require special workrests, supports, wheel mounts, truing devices, or other equipment for centerless grinding. Those adjuncts may cost hundreds or thousands of dollars and take considerable setup time. Therefore, such parts are not centerless ground unless produced in quite large quantities.

Centerless grinding is faster and often cheaper than center-type grinding because:

1. It is almost continuous, especially for thrufeed grinding, with a minimum of machine time lost for loading and unloading.
2. The work is fully supported by the workrest blade and regulating wheel and can be subjected to cuts as heavy as it will take without overheating. Plunge cuts can often be made over the entire length of a workpiece. Although most centerless grinding wheels are 150 to 200 mm (6 to 8 in.) wide, machines are available with wheels up to 1 m (ca. 40 in.) wide, and power to 75 kW (100 hp) and can plunge grind correspondingly long and slender or frail work (such as thin-walled tubes).
3. With large grinding wheels, wheel wear is relatively small, and a minimum amount of adjustment is necessary to compensate for wear.
4. No axial thrust is present, as it is on work between centers. Long thin pieces are not so likely to be distorted.
5. The action of centerless grinding is such that each workpiece is cleaned up with the removal of the least possible amount of stock. Errors of centering are eliminated.

6. Adjustments for size are made directly on the diameter of the workpiece, and that contributes to accurate results. If the regulating wheel and workrest blade are moved 25 μm (0.001 in.) toward the grinding wheel, the workpiece diameter is reduced 25 μm (0.001 in.).

7. A low order of skill is needed to attend to centerless grinding much of the time.

8. Center holes are costly if needed for center-type grinding only.

For simple parts, the saving in grinding time for only a few pieces may make up for the longer setup time for centerless grinding. Centerless grinding has been found profitable in many places for lots less than 100 pieces, sometimes for a dozen or less. However, as a rule, center-type grinding is preferable where the work is varied, irregular in shape, or large in size, especially in small quantities.

Equation (20-1) is helpful in showing for what quantities of production a centerless grinder is economical for any particular product. As an example, an armature shaft for an electric motor is to be ground on four diameters with a stock removal of 0.25 to 0.40 mm (0.010 to 0.015 in.) on each diameter. The shafts can be finished on a plain cylindrical center-type grinder at the rate of 125 pieces/hr, with 30 minutes required for setup for each lot. A production rate of 150 pieces can be realized per hour with setup time of 1 hour per lot on the centerless grinder. That machine must have special equipment for the job that costs $2400 and must be paid for by the first lot. The labor, overhead, and depreciation rate is $18/hr for either machine. The equal cost quantity in this case is

$$Q = \frac{125 \times 150(1 \times 18 + 2400 - \frac{1}{2} \times 18 - 0)}{150 \times 18 - 125 \times 18} = 100,000 \text{ pieces}$$

The centerless grinder is economical for this job if about 100,000 or more pieces are to be produced.

Figure 28-6 indicates a principle of economical grinding for moderate and large quantities. That is to use a wide wheel or several wheels on one mount trued to take care of two or more surfaces at the same time. This is especially applicable to centerless grinding because the work is well supported for multiple cuts, but the principle is often applied profitably to all other forms of grinding, as suggested by Fig. 28-3.

Equation (19-1) provides the basis for ascertaining when it is economical to combine grinding operations. For example, three diameters may be ground one at a time on the stem of a bevel gear pinion, with an output of 35 pieces/hr. The combined operation produces 80 pieces/hr but requires a special wheel mount and cam for the truing attachment that cost $1200 and $1\frac{1}{2}$ hours more setup time for each lot. The labor rate in the plant is $10.50/hr with a labor dollar overhead rate of 1. A rate of 35% for interest, insurance, taxes, and maintenance is required. The number of pieces in one lot for which the combined operation is justified may be ascertained from

$$N(\tfrac{1}{35} - \tfrac{1}{80})(10.50)(1 + 1) = 1200 \times 1.35 + 1.5 \times 21$$

Thus $N = 4893$ pieces is the smallest quantity for which it is economical to invest in the special wheel mount. It is presumed that the machine has the power to sustain the faster rate of production.

Internal Grinders. A *chucking internal grinder* holds the workpiece on a faceplate or in a chuck or fixture and rotates it around the axis of the hole ground, as depicted in Fig. 28-7. The revolving grinding wheel is reciprocated lengthwise through the hole and is fed crosswise on a slide to engage the workpiece. The workhead, and sometimes the wheelhead, can be swiveled to adjust for straight and tapered holes and faces.

A production-type internal grinder with automatic cycling can grind holes up to 100 mm (4 in.) diameter by 200 mm (8 in.) long and has a 2.2-kW (3-hp) motor and a cost under $50,000. A universal manual toolroom type grinds holes to 300 mm (12 in.) diameter by 400 mm (16 in.) long and has a 3.7-kW (5-hp) motor and a price of $65,000. An internal grinder of similar size costs over $200,000 with numerical control for fully automatic grinding of round and flat surfaces, steps, profiles, lobes, etc.

A *centerless internal grinder* grinds the bore of a round workpiece concentric with the outside surface. The workpiece is held and revolved amidst three rolls in a roll-type centerless internal grinder as shown in Fig. 28-8. The large roll is the driver; the rolls provide rigid support for the workpiece. The movements of the grinding wheel are the same as shown in Fig. 28-7. On the shoe-type centerless grinder, the workpiece is revolved against two fixed and hard shoes by the action of the grinding wheel and a rotating end backing plate. The shoes contact more area than rolls and bridge irregularities and produce better average concentricity between hole and outside.

Straight, tapered, continuous, interrupted, open end, and blind holes and grooves are ground on centerless internal grinders. The wall thickness of a finished piece is quite uniform. The manner of holding the work lends itself well to automatic unloading and loading of pieces.

A *planetary internal grinder* is designed for parts too large or unwieldy to be rotated conveniently. The workpiece is not revolved. Instead, the grinding wheel is orbited around the axis of the hole being ground.

A *vertical internal grinder* takes large pieces that can be rotated on a table like on a vertical boring mill.

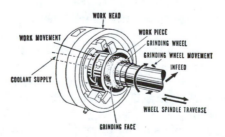

Figure 28-7 Action of a chucking internal grinding machine. (Courtesy Carborundum Co.)

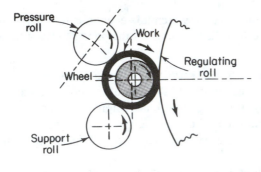

Roll–Type Centerless

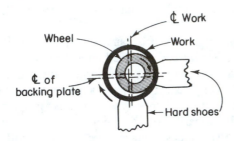

Shoe–Type Centerless

Figure 28-8　Left, the two kinds of internal centerless grinding. Right, view of a roll-type centerless internal grinder. An arm holding a diamond nib for truing the grinding wheel is shown in its retracted position in front of the large roller. The wheelhead is in the foreground in the position from which it is advanced to insert the grinding wheel into the hole to be ground. (Courtesy Heald Machine Div. of Cincinnati Milacron, Inc.)

Internal Grinding Operations.　Squareness between a hole and face or shoulder on a workpiece is achieved by grinding both surfaces in the same operation. This may be done with the periphery and end of one wheel, but some machines have two wheelheads on the same cross-slide, one with a small wheel for the hole and the other with a large wheel for the face.

In a long hole the wheel is reciprocated (traversed) over the length of the hole to cover all the surface. Even in a short hole the wheel may be reciprocated to distribute wear over its length.

A grinding wheel is commonly fed crosswise at a constant rate to grind a hole to size. Another way is to feed the wheel with a constant force; that is called *controlled force grinding*. Under a constant force, the grinding action is uniform, and better control of size and finish is obtained. Under constant force, the deflection of the grinding wheel spindle is constant and can be compensated for by swiveling the wheelhead slightly to produce quite straight or precisely tapered holes.

Accurate sizing is obtained in several ways. For one or a few pieces, an operator can grind a hole to size by controlling the in-feed through a handwheel and dial. This is a slow process because several measurements must be made on each hole and care is necessary. The small wheels needed to get into holes wear rapidly, and slender spindles deflect appreciably. One form of sizing device that shows an operator the size of a hole being ground is depicted in Fig. 28-9. It has a finger that rides in the hole and is connected to a dial indicator by a linkage. Air or electronic gaging is also used in some cases with electronic circuitry to control the machine and give digital readout of size and wheel slide position.

A *Size-matic* internal grinder is arranged to go through a routine to size each piece in production. The grinding wheel reciprocates through the hole and is fed automatically almost to size while it is roughing. In preparation for the finishing cut, the wheel is withdrawn, trued, and returned to the work. The trueing diamond is set to trim the wheel surface a definite distance from the final work surface. The wheel is then fed in a predetermined amount to account for wear and deflection and to grind to the desired size in the hole. This is the most common and least costly approach for large-quantity production.

A *Gage-matic* equipped internal grinder has a mechanism that tries to insert a round plug gage in the back of the hole each time the reciprocating wheel leaves the

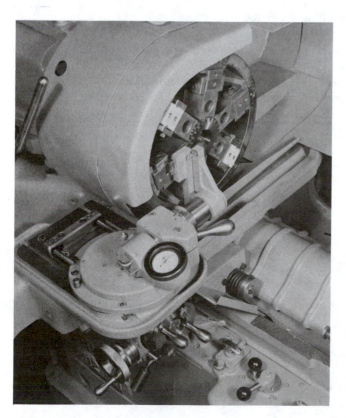

Figure 28-9 Manually operated sizing device on an internal grinder. The workpiece is a gear located on its pitch line by pins in a sliding jaw chuck. (Courtesy Bryant Grinder Div. of Ex-Cell-O Corp.)

front of the hole being ground. When the first part of the plug enters, the wheel is trued for finishing. When the whole plug enters, the correct size is indicated, the wheel is withdrawn, and the machine stops.

Surface Grinders. Surface grinding is concerned primarily with grinding plane or flat surfaces but also is capable of grinding irregular, curved, tapered, convex, and concave surfaces.

Conventional surface grinders may be divided into two classes. One class has reciprocating tables for work ground along straight lines. This type is particularly suited to pieces that are long or have stepped or curved profiles at right angles to the direction of grinding. The second class covers the machines with rotating work tables for continuous rapid grinding.

Surface grinders may also be classified according to whether they have horizontal or vertical grinding wheel spindles. Grinding is normally done on the periphery of the wheel with a horizontal spindle. The area of contact is small, and the speed is uniform over the grinding surface. Small-grain wheels can be used, and the finest finishes obtained. Grinding with a vertical spindle is done on the side of the wheel, which may be solid, sectored, or segmental. The area of contact may be large, and stock can be removed rapidly. A crisscross pattern of grinding scratches is left on the work surface.

The combinations resulting from the wheel and table arrangements just described for surface grinding are shown in Fig. 28-10.

Surface grinders with reciprocating tables and horizontal spindles, as depicted at the upper left in Fig. 28-10, are popular for toolroom work. Common practice is to reciprocate the workpiece lengthwise at 15 to 30 m/min (50 to 100 fpm) and feed it crosswise one-fourth to one-half the width of the wheel for each stroke. The wheel is moved down into the work incrementally each time the surface is covered, until size is reached. For roughing, increments may be 50 μm (0.002 in.) or more, and for finishing 25 μm (0.001 in.) or less.

Another method, called *creep grinding* or *creep-feed grinding,* is analogous to plunge cutting. Here the wheel is set to cut to full depth and the work is fed under it at a slow rate. This method is not common but has been found advantageous for high-temperature alloys.

Some surface grinders with reciprocating tables have wheelheads that can be tilted vertically; one variety is called a *combination way and surface grinder.* Examples of the kinds of surfaces that can be ground on such machines with reciprocating tables are presented in Fig. 28-11.

The wheelhead, rather than the table, is reciprocated on some machines. The table or magnetic chuck is fixed on a long bed. The wheel is mounted with no overhang in a carriage that bridges the table and is traversed on ways on the bed along the sides of the table. The wheel is moved in the carriage for vertical infeed and horizontal cross-feed.

Surface grinders with vertical spindles and rotary tables, as depicted at the bottom on the right of Fig. 28-10, are used for rapid production abrasive machining.

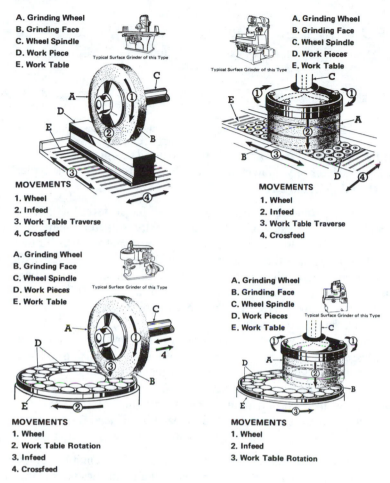

Figure 28-10 Principal kinds of surface grinders: top, reciprocating table grinders; bottom, rotary table grinders; left, horizontal spindles; right, vertical spindles. (Courtesy Carborundum Co.)

The rotary table is usually a magnetic chuck and can hold a large number of small pieces. Larger workpieces may also be ground. Machines of this type are relatively high powered; many have 75-kW (100-hp) and some as much as 375-kW (500-hp) motors. The *Williams Continuous Thru-Feed Production Surface Grinder* has a vertical spindle but no moving table. It feeds workpieces under the wheel on an endless belt over a magnetic chuck. The pieces ride against or between side guides that take the grinding forces. Production rates of tens of thousands of pieces per hour are achieved.

The capacity of a surface grinder with a reciprocating table is commonly designated by two numbers specifying the nominal width and length of the working surface of the table; a third figure may be given to specify the largest distance from the top

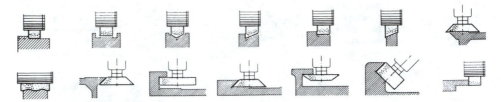

Figure 28-11   Examples of surfaces finished by grinders with reciprocating table.

of the table to the face of the wheel. The usual designation for a rotary surface grinder is the diameter of the chuck or table. Specifications for some typical surface grinders are listed in Table 28-2.

Disk Grinders.   Disk grinders finish flat surfaces and remove stock rapidly by grinding with the sides of disk wheels usually backed by metal plates and ranging in size from about 300 mm to almost 2 m (nominally 12 to 72 in.). The size of the machine designates the diameter of wheel it takes. Much disk grinding is done to large tolerances, but in other cases close tolerances are held. For ultimate precision work, flatness and parallelism are held to 1.5 μm (ca. 0.00005 in.), size to 3 μm (0.0001 in.), and surface finishes to 150 nm (6 μin.).

The horizontal single-spindle disk grinder of Fig. 28-12 has a wheel at each end of the spindle. A table at each wheel, often with a fixture added, supports work that is pressed and ground against the side of the wheel. Disk grinders also are made with horizontal disks, usually of large diameter.

Typical of many semi- or fully automatic disk grinders for large-quantity production is the opposed double-spindle machine of Fig. 28-13. Work is fed continuously between two disks, one on each wheelhead, and is ground on two sides at the same time. One such machine with tooling is quoted at $175,000.

Thread Grinders.   Threads are produced by a number of methods as described in Chap. 32. They are ground for accuracy and finishes not obtainable in other ways.

TABLE 28-2   SPECIFICATIONS FOR SEVERAL TYPICAL SURFACE GRINDERS

Type table–spindle	Size [mm (in.)]	Main motor [kW (hp)]	Weight [Mg (lb)]	Cost
Recip. horiz.	200 × 630 (8 × 25)	4 (5.5)	2.2 (4,840)	$ 15,000
	610 × 3050 (24 × 120)	150 (200)	18.6 (41,000)	110,000
(fixed table)	155 × 900 (6 × 36)	4.3 (5.8)		25,000
Rotary horiz.	610 (24)	15 (20)	5.6 (12,200)	60,000
Rotary vert.	915 (36)	26 (35)	6.4 (14,000)	40,000

Figure 28-12 A 26-in. single horizontal spindle disk grinder. (Courtesy Gardner Machine Co.)

Tolerances are held for size to ±0.0001 mm/mm of pitch diameter and for lead within 7.5 μm in 500 mm (0.0003 in. in 20 in.) of length. Hard materials can be threaded more economically by grinding than by other methods. Threads may be cut and then finish ground after heat treatment, or they may be ground from solid stock.

Thread grinding is done on center-type and centerless machines. They may utilize single-rib-type or multirib-type grinding wheels. The first is a thin wheel with its outer edge trued to the shape of the thread space. The second is a wide wheel with grooves and ridges formed on its periphery.

Center-type thread grinders grind external or internal threads, or both. A typical machine resembles a universal center-type cylindrical grinder but has features to enable it to do its intended work. A master leadscrew is geared to the work spindle, causes the table to traverse, and causes the workpiece to turn with the proper lead as it advances. The grinding wheel is tilted to the helix angle of the thread. An attachment trues the wheel to the thread form.

Tool and Cutter Grinders.   Grinders for finishing tools and sharpening cutters are available from simple grinding wheel stands for off hand work to complex single-purpose machines like automatic face mill grinders. Probably the most popular and versatile machine for precision sharpening of all kinds of tools is the *universal tool and cutter grinder*. It can sharpen multiple-tooth cutters like reamers, milling cutters, taps,

Figure 28-13 A 15-in. double horizontal spindle disk grinder equipped with a notched rotary carrier fed by an inclined chute. Small ball bearing inner races are conveyed continuously between the two wheels by the carrier and ground at the rate of 60 to 80 pieces/min. (Courtesy Gardner Machine Co.)

and hobs as well as single-point tools and also can do light surface, cylindrical, and internal grinding to finish such items as jig, fixture, die, and gage details. Prices range (with capacity) from about $1000 to $10,000.

The main parts of a typical tool and cutter grinder are visible in Fig. 28-14. An upper table can be swiveled on a lower table that slides longitudinally on a saddle that provides cross movement. The wheelhead can be raised or lowered and swiveled. Many attachments are available, such as radial truing devices, universal tilting workheads of various sizes, indexing devices, combination work holders, and form grinding equipment. Each cutter can be held so that proper angles can be ground on it; two examples are given in Fig. 28-14.

Profile or *contour grinders* are capable of reproducing a template form on a flat or round cutter. Some can grind metal surfaces to conform to outlines drawn on paper. An *optical profile grinder* is one on which a view of the zone of contact between wheel and workpiece is highly magnified (10, 20, or 50 times for example) and cast upon a screen. The form produced by the wheel can be seen as it is ground and compared with a large-scale drawing on the screen of the form desired. Machine movements may be simultaneously controlled by the operator.

A type of tool grinder adaptable to a large variety of tools, but particularly to spiral tools, as indicated in Fig. 28-15, is the *Monoset cutter and tool grinder*. The workhead spindle can be indexed and also synchronized with the table movement to grind helices. The major units are fully adjustable to enable much work to be done in one setting that otherwise would require several setups.

Figure 28-14   Two views of milling cutters being sharpened on a universal tool and cutter grinder: top, shell end mill; bottom, helical mill. (Courtesy Cincinnati Milacron, Inc.)

Miscellaneous Grinders. Cam and camshaft grinders are essentially modifications of center-type cylindrical grinders to finish various forms of round cams, camshafts, and pistons. The headstock and footstock are on a cradle and rock to and from the grinding wheel in response to a master cam that rotates in unison with the workpiece.

Crankshaft or *crank pin grinders* resemble cylindrical center-type grinders but are implemented to grind the offset pins in the throws of crankshafts.

Abrasive Belt Grinders.   Continuous coated abrasive belts of all widths are used for precision and nonprecision grinding of parts of all kinds, mainly to obtain good surface finishes with little stock removal. The same work may be done by grinding wheels, and the abrasive in belt form costs more, but other factors may make the cost of belt grinding less. For example, a belt on a flexible wheel can be readily adapted to an irregular or curved surface; a wheel would have to be trued carefully to the shape at considerable expense. Belts up to 2.5 m (ca. 8 ft) or so in width are applied over rollers to plunge cut steel slabs, steel and aluminum sheet, plywood panels, and rolls of metal, rubber, etc. This is faster than traversing a grinding wheel back and forth over the surface. Machines are available with abrasive belts instead of grinding wheels and with reciprocating or revolving tables. They do much the same work as surface grinders.

A belt grinder for rapid sanding of small and irregularly shaped work is shown in Fig. 28-16. It also has a spindle for abrasive rolls. Work may be applied, commonly by hand, against the open belt, sanding pulleys, platen, shaped forms, or rolls in succession to reach various curved and flat surfaces. Many special machines are in use in industry utilizing coated abrasives in belts, rolls, strips, etc., for automatically finishing pieces individually and for continuous products like wire.

Figure 28-15   Flutes of a twist drill being ground from the solid on a Monoset cutter and tool grinder. (Courtesy Cincinnati Milacron, Inc.)

Figure 28-16 Variety belt grinder. (Courtesy Mattison Machine Works.)

ROUGH OR NONPRECISION GRINDERS

Swing Frame Grinders. A swing frame grinder has a horizontal frame from $1\frac{1}{2}$ to 3 m (5 to 10 ft) long suspended at its center of gravity so as to move freely within the area of operation. The operator applies the wheel on one end of the frame to the work in the manner illustrated in Fig. 28-17.

Floor-Stand and Bench Grinders. A floor-stand grinder has a horizontal spindle with wheels usually at both ends and is mounted on a base or pedestal. Work is applied to the wheels in the manner shown in Fig. 28-18. A small size mounted on a bench is called a bench grinder. These machines are used for snagging and off-hand grinding of cutting tools and miscellaneous parts. Polishing wheels may be run on these grinders.

Portable and Flexible Shaft Grinders. The usual form of portable grinder resembles a portable or electric hand drill with a guard and grinding wheel mounted on the spindle. A similar purpose machine is the flexible shaft grinder that has the grinding wheel on the end of a long flexible shaft driven by a motor on a relatively stationary stand. Heavy tools of these kinds are used for roughing and snagging, and small ones for burring and die work.

GRINDING COMPARED WITH OTHER OPERATIONS

Grinding has always been considered mainly a finishing process to be preceded by other methods that remove the bulk of the stock from rough workpieces. For example, a shaft made from 25-mm (1-in.)-diameter barstock must have a 19.000/19.025 mm

Figure 28-17   Swing frame grinder in operation. (Courtesy Carborundum Co.)

(0.748/0.749 in.) diameter with a surface finish of 0.5 μm (20 μin.) for a length of 75 mm (ca. 3 in.) on one end. Grinding is the economical way of meeting the specifications, but ordinarily the piece is first turned to remove most of the stock. However, more and more parts are being ground completely from the rough. That is commonly called *abrasive machining*.

Abrasive machining is not a replacement for all other methods of metal removal but may be superior under certain conditions. Exceedingly hard and some space-age materials are difficult to machine by other methods, and for these abrasive machining from the solid may well be fastest. Even if grinding is slower than other means of removing a certain quantity of metal, the amount of metal that needs to be removed in grinding may really be much less. Usual practice is to provide thick stock on castings with hard and scaly skins so that cutting tools can get under and not be ruined by the scale. Abrasives are not deterred by the scale. Thus for grinding, 2 mm (ca. $\frac{1}{16}$ in.) or less of stock may be quite enough, whereas 3 to 5 mm ($\frac{1}{8}$ to $\frac{3}{16}$ in.) would be needed otherwise. Furthermore, the finished area may sometimes be less for grinding. For example, a surface may be completely finished except for openings, as in Fig. 28-19(A), to minimize interrupted cutting detrimental to cutting tools. A relieved surface, as depicted in Fig. 28-19(B), may serve the purpose just as well and can be

Figure 28-18   Snagging a casting on a floor-stand grinder. (Courtesy Carborundum Co.)

ground with no damage to the wheel from the interruptions. Stock saved may be of value in itself if the workpiece is made of a costly material.

Grinding forces are substantial, and the maximum rate of grinding depends upon the rigidity of the machine, wheel, and workpiece. This is important in abrasive machining, which must be done fast to be competitive. If the system is too flexible, chatter may occur, the grinding wheel may wear too rapidly, or spark out time for good finish and size is likely to be too long. Colding reported that when the rigidity of a particular system was increased 10 times, five times as many parts could be ground between wheel dressings, and spark-out time was reduced by a factor of 10 to 15, which resulted in a decrease of between 65 and 90% in operation cost.

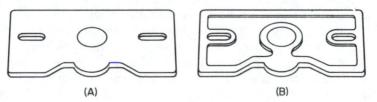

(A)   (B)

Figure 28-19   Motor base: (A) as originally designed for milling; (B) as redesigned for abrasive machining.

More power is consumed by grinding than by coarser methods, but relatively heavy abrasive machining consumes less unit power than fine grinding, as seen in Fig. 27-14. In a typical fine-grinding operation as much as 12 kW (16 hp) may be required to remove about 16 cm³/min (1 in.³/min) of steel. In an ordinary rough-grinding operation, the power consumed may be 7.5 kW (10 hp) for each 16 cm³/min (1 in.³/min) removed. With a rigid and powerful machine and proper grinding wheel, dressing technique, and operation procedure for abrasaive machining, the power expended may well be reduced to $1\frac{1}{2}$ to 3 kW (3 to 4 hp) for each 16 cm³/min (1 in.³/min). This is comparable to $\frac{3}{4}$ to $2\frac{1}{2}$ kW (1 to 3 hp) for rates of 16 cm³/min (1 in.³/min) for turning and milling steel. Powerful and rigid machines developed in recent years with capacities of 75 to 375 kW (100 to 500 hp) are able to grind at rates competitive with other methods. For one case reported, SAE 4140 steel forgings were milled at the rate of 33 pieces/hr and at a cost of $0.54/piece. On a surface grinder, 58.6 pieces were machined per hour at a cost of $0.11/piece.

New ideas are being explored to develop more efficient machines and methods for abrasive machining. Ways are being found to drive grinding wheels and work-pieces at higher speeds and cool them more efficiently. One proposal on which much work has been done involves a wheel 3 to 4.5 m (10 to 15 ft) in diameter on its side revolving with a surface speed of 11,000 m/min (36,000 fpm) with 6, 8, or 10 workstations around its periphery on which pieces are ground all at the same time.

Grinding has lagged other processes in automation. Almost no grinding operations are performed without the attention of an operator. A leading authority, Robert Hahn, has cited three essentials for unattended grinding. These are:

1. Automatic loading and unloading of work, which has been achieved.
2. A wheel that lasts without retruing for a full workshift. The new super abrasives, such as boron carbide, give promise in this direction and advantage is being taken of their durability to help automate abrasive machining.
3. Complete part gaging not only for size but also for waviness, chatter, surface quality, burning and deterioration, etc. This is an area in which much needs to be done.

Obvious savings can result from abrasive machining when it means two operations, cutting and grinding, are replaced by a single grinding operation. Even when grinding replaces only a cutting operation, the workpiece may be held more easily, on a magnetic chuck alone, with a saving in the cost of a fixture. Small parts are normally ground in a group while held by a magnetic chuck.

Fine finishes and tolerances less than 25 to 75 μm (0.001 to 0.003 in.) are more easily obtained by grinding than by nonabrasive methods in most cases. Even so, the cost of grinding increases for better finishes and smaller tolerances, as indicated by Fig. 28-20. Some grinding is done with tolerances as small as 0.5 μm (0.00002 in.) and surface finishes better than 50 nm (2 μin.) R_a but only at high cost. In many cases the smallest tolerances and finest finishes can better be obtained by lapping, honing, and superfinishing. As indicated by Fig. 15-38, these methods normally cover ranges only exceptionally reached by grinding. They are discussed in Chap. 29.

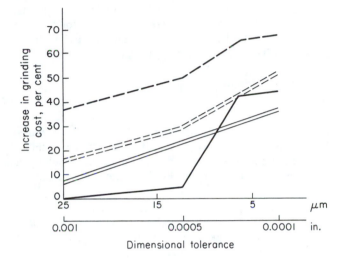

Surface roughness	0.6 (25)	1 (40)	μm (μin.)
Cylindrical grinding	– – – –	———	
Surface grinding	=======	====	

Figure 28-20 How precision grinding costs vary with tolerance and surface finish. (From *Guide to Tolerances and Finishes*, Martin Co., 1964.)

QUESTIONS

1. Describe a plain cylindrical center-type grinder and tell what it does.
2. Describe and distinguish between plunge cut and traverse grinding.
3. What is a roll grinder, and what does it do?
4. How does a universal cylindrical center-type grinder differ from a plain grinder?
5. How is the size of a cylindrical center-type grinder designated?
6. For what are chucking grinders used?
7. Describe the action of a centerless grinder. What are its advantages?
8. Describe thrufeed, in-feed and end-feed centerless grinding and their applications.
9. Make a comparison of the relative merits of center-type and centerless grinding.
10. Describe plain and universal internal grinders and the work they do.
11. Describe an internal centerless grinder and state its advantages.
12. What purpose does a planetary internal grinder serve and how?
13. What are several means for controlling workpiece size on an internal grinder?
14. Describe the four principal types of surface grinders.
15. What is the advantage of each kind of surface grinder?
16. What are disk grinders, and what do they do?
17. What are the advantages of thread grinding? How is it done?

18. How are cams ground?

19. Describe the machines used for snagging.

20. What is abrasive machining, and what are its advantages?

21. For what degree of accuracy and surface finish is grinding suitable?

1. A mild-steel workpiece, shown in Fig 28-21, is to be ground on a 75-mm (3-in.) diameter that is 250 mm (10 in.) long. It can be driven by a dog on the 50-mm (2-in.) diameter that is 50 mm (2 in.) long on one end. The machine is a 6 × 18 plain cylindrical grinder. It has a 7.5-kW (10-hp) motor and is 80% efficient. The workpiece is to be traversed past the 40-mm (ca. 1½-in.)-wide grinding wheel at a rate of 15 mm (ca. ½ in.) for each revolution. Total stock removal is 0.40 mm (ca. 0.015 in.) on the diameter, of which 0.08

PROBLEMS

mm (0.003 in.) is to be removed in four finishing passes of the wheel over the workpiece. 7.5 kW (10 hp) is required at the wheel to grind this material at a rate of about 16 cm³/min (1 in.³/min). Select a work speed and a suitable in-feed per pass for the roughing cuts within practical ranges and the capacity of the machine. How long should the grinding time be for this piece?

2. The workpiece described in Prob. 1 is to be ground on a centerless grinder with a 11-kW (15-hp) motor and 80% efficiency. Two passes will be taken with 0.25 mm (0.01 in.) of stock removed from the diameter in the first pass, and 0.15 mm (ca. 0.005 in.) in the second. 7.5 kW (10 hp) at the wheel is required to grind the material at a rate of about 16 cm³/min (1 in.³/min). Select regulating wheel speeds and tilt angles for best utilization of the machine. How long should the grinding time be per piece?

3. A workpiece has a 25-mm (1-in.) diameter for 75 mm (3 in.) of length from one end and a 50-mm (2-in.) diameter for the remainder of its total length of 180 mm (7 in.). A total of 0.40 mm (ca. 0.015 in.) of stock is removed to finish the 50-mm (2-in.) diameter. Three minutes is required per piece on a 6 × 12 plain cylindrical center-type grinder, and 1¾ minutes on a centerless grinder. Setup time is 20 min/lot on the plain grinder and 40 minutes on the centerless grinder. The labor, overhead, and depreciation rate is $26/hr on both machines. No special tools are needed. What is the equal cost quantity for this part?

4. A short shaft with three diameters to be ground is produced in 12 lots of 1000 pieces each during the year. The procedure has been to grind one diameter on all pieces in one lot, then a second, and finally the third. The production rate has been 37½ pieces/hr. It is proposed to mount three wheels on the machine to grind the three diameters on one piece at the same time. This is expected to produce 75 pieces/hr, but requires a special wheel mount and one

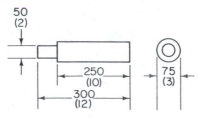

Dimensions [mm (in)]   **Figure 28-21** Workpiece.

hour extra setup time for each lot. The labor and overhead rate is $26/hr, and the rate for interest, insurance, taxes, and maintenance is 25%/yr. What is the most that can be justified for the cost of the wheel mount?

5. Three adjacent diameters and shoulders must be ground on a shaft. One hundred thousand pieces are to be produced within the coming year. A grinding machine available can be tooled with three wheels in the conventional positions to grind the surfaces. Better action can be obtained if the wheelhead can be turned to allow the wheels to make contact with the work at an angle. It is estimated the production rate can be increased from 80 pieces/hr to 100 pieces/hr in that way. However, for that improvement the machine must be rebuilt at a cost of $6500. The labor and overhead rate in the plant is $26/hr. Interest, insurance, taxes, and maintenance call for a rate of 35%/yr on an investment. Is is worthwhile to rebuild the machine for this job? It is assumed that it will not be impaired for any other work. The rebuilding cost must be recovered within a year.

6. The regulating wheel of a centerless grinding machine is turning with a surface speed of 15 m/min (50 fpm), and its axis is inclined at an angle of 6° with the horizontal. What is the rate of thrufeed of the work between the wheels?

7. A 20-hp milling machine and a 35-hp surface grinder have about the same costs per hour for labor, most overhead, and depreciation. The milling machine can remove stock about 20% faster than the grinder for a certain class of work. Power costs more on the grinder, but the difference is only around $0.06 for a typical piece. Still, the total grinding cost is less than for milling some workpieces. What factors would you expect to give the grinder the advantage?

REFERENCES

BUSH, J. F., "Some Hints on Designing for Grinding," *Machine and Tool Blue Book*, Nov. 1976, p. 97.

CARLSON, G. A., JR., "Advances in Abrasive Finishing," *Manufacturing Engineering*, Feb. 1979, p. 59.

COLDING, B., "How Stiffness Affects Grinding Performance," *Machinery*, Mar. 1970, p. 57.

GRIEB, P., "Putting CBN Wheels to Work," *Manufacturing Engineering*, June 1982, p. 53.

JABLONOWSKI, J., "Fundamentals of Grinding, Special Report 684," *American Machinist*, Feb. 1976, p. 61.

———, "Will Creep-Feed Grinding Catch On?," *American Machinist*, Dec. 1980, p. 106.

MUELLER, J. A., "How to Design for Abrasive Machining," *Machine Design*, June 1, 1972, p. 57.

STAUFFER, R. N., "Creep-Feed Grinding Cuts Cycle Time 60%," *Manufacturing Engineering*, June 1981, p. 68.

VASILASH, G. S., "The Advent of Superabrasive Machining," *Manufacturing Engineering*, Oct. 1981, p. 97.

WICK, C., "Switch to Centerless Grinding Boosts Productivity," *Manufacturing Engineering*, June 1978, p. 42.

———, "Advances in Double Disc Grinding," *Manufacturing Engineering*, June 1978, p. 46.

29

ULTRA-FINISHING OPERATIONS

Heavy cuts in a material leave rough and torn surfaces. The lighter and milder the cut, the better the surface and the smaller the tolerance. Good finishes can be obtained by operating cutting tools at light feeds, but that is slow. As has been explained, grinding is often faster for fine cutting because it removes material by the action of many grains taking small bites. Although grinding may be carried to the extreme to procure as fine finishes and as high a degree of precision as may be desired, other abrasive operations that have slower speeds and a milder action usually prove more economical for the best finishes. Such operations are lapping, honing, ultrasonic impact grinding, and Super-finishing.

The terms lapping and honing are often used interchangeably, and it is difficult always to make a clear distinction between them. In general, but not always, lapping uses a loose abrasive and is applied to external surfaces, while honing is done on internal surfaces with bonded abrasives.

When accuracy is not required, some of the costly aspects of grinding and other precision finishing operations may be eliminated, and abrasives applied in more economical ways to produce good surface finishes alone. This is done in the operations of polishing, buffing, brushing, tumbling, vibratory finishing, and shot- and sand-blasting. Specialty operations for burr removal include the thermal energy method and abrasive flow machining.

LAPPING

Purpose of Lapping. Lapping is an abrading process that leaves fine scratches arrayed at random. Its purpose is to improve surface quality by reducing roughness, waviness, and defects to produce accurate as well as smooth surfaces. Lapping pressure is light as compared to grinding, and the work is never overheated.

Lapping is done both by hand and by machines. Its range of usefulness is large. In some cases it may merely be an expedient to remove an occasional fault. It is a basic operation in job and tool shops where a typical application is to finish locating and wearing surfaces on precision tools and gages. Gage blocks, the standards of accuracy, are finished regularly by lapping. Machine lapping is common for production. Other typical lapping subjects are surfaces that must be liquid- or gastight without gaskets and those from which small errors must be removed, such as gear teeth.

How Lapping Is Done.   Only a small amount of stock normally is taken off by lapping, up to 1 mm (0.04 in.) or so, but usually only about 100 μm (0.004 in.) or less for roughing, and as little as 2 μm (ca. 0.0001 in.) for finishing. This is because the fine abrasive works slowly and the surface shape is hard to control if much stock is removed.

Fine loose abrasive mixed with a vehicle, bonded abrasive wheels, or coated abrasives are used for lapping. Wet lapping with clear or soapy water, oil, or grease may be as much as six times as fast as dry lapping.

Most lapping is done by spreading loose abrasive and vehicle on lapping shoes, plates, or quills, called *laps,* that are rubbed against the work. In *flat lapping,* the lap is made of soft close-grained cast iron, commonly with grooves across its face to collect excessive abrasive and dirt. Such a lap soon becomes charged with embedded abrasive particles. When a plate of hardened alloy steel is used, the process is called *free-abrasive machining.* A coarse abrasive can be used and washed away and replaced as needed, because it does not embed in the lap, and the stock-removal rate is rapid. Loose abrasive lapping is not often done on soft materials because the abrasive particles become embedded in the workpiece.

In lapping, the work and lap are not rigidly guided with respect to each other, and their relative movements are continually changed. In *equalizing lapping,* the work and lap mutually improve each other's surface as they slide together. This is done in seating mushroom valves, machine lapping gears, and hand lapping plug and ring gages. In *forming lapping,* the work acquires a definite shape from the lap. That is the case for most lapping done with abrasive wheels.

Lapping Machines.   The basics of a *vertical lapping machine* are illustrated in Fig. 29-1. Flat or round surfaces are lapped between two opposed laps on vertical spindles. The lower lap revolves at 95 to 65 rpm, and the upper one is lowered to float upon and adjusts itself to the work. Another type of vertical lapper uses coated abrasive cloth cemented to a horizontal vibrating disk. Workpieces may be applied to a lap by hand, but for production they generally are put in work holders. These are rings or cages around one or more workpieces and in some cases are made to recondition the lap continuously as they slide upon it. Work-holder motion spirals the workpieces around the lap for even action.

A *centerless lapping machine* is like a centerless grinder (described in Chap. 28) but has extra wide wheels. Lapping wheel speed may be 150 to 600 m/min (500 to

Figure 29-1   Vertical lapping machine with a two-piece work holder and adapters. The workpieces (like the one displayed near the center of the work holder) are placed in the adapters between the upper and lower lapping plates. The adaptors restrain the workpieces to produce relative motion with respect to the lapping plates.

2000 fpm), and work speed 45 to 150 m/min (150 to 500 fpm). Stock removal is usually 5 μm (0.0002 in.) or less, and fine surfaces 50 nm (2 μin.) R_a (or better) and close tolerances [1.5 μm (ca. 0.00005 in.) for size and half as much for straightness] are produced. The machines are designed for continuous production of round parts such as piston pins, bearing races and cups, valve tappets, and shafts. As an example of output, piston pins are produced at the rate of 40 pins/min.

HONING

Purpose of Honing.   Honing is an abrading operation mostly for finishing round holes but also to a lesser extent external flat and curved surfaces by means of bonded abrasive stones. Because the abrasive is not free to embed in the surface, soft metallic and nonmetallic as well as hard materials can be honed. Typical applications are the finishing of automobile engine cylinders, bearings, gun barrels, ring gages, piston pins, shafts, and flange faces.

In grinding with the periphery of a rigid wheel, there is near line contact with the work surface, whereas honing has a large area of contact and less pressure. Grinding is done at high speeds; honing at low speeds with a milder action.

Honing is a cutting operation and has been used to remove as much as 3 mm (ca. $\frac{1}{8}$ in.) of stock, but is normally confined to amounts less than 0.25 mm (0.01 in.). It normally is preceded by boring or reaming to establish surface shape and position. Then size and truth are typically refined to less than 10 μm (ca. 0.0005 in.) by honing. Surfaces can be finished to 25 nm (1 μin.) R_a, but 0.2 to 0.25 μm (8 to 10 μin.) R_a, and more are customary. A surface may be given a crosshatched finish by honing to aid lubrication.

How Honing Is Done. Honing stones are made from the common abrasive and bonding materials, often impregnated with sulfur, resin, or wax to improve cutting action and lengthen tool life. Grain sizes range from 80 grit for roughing to 320 for finishing hard materials to 500 for soft materials. A typical holder or toolhead to carry the stones is depicted in Fig. 29-2. The stones are expanded, when working, by a cone or wedge inside the holder. A flexible honing tool consists of a brush with abrasive nodules on the ends of the bristles. The tool or workpiece, or both, are rotated and reciprocated in relation to each other to hone a hole. The two movements are run purposely out of phase to cover all the surface without a regular pattern of scratches.

Hone forming simultaneously plates metal onto a base material and abrades the new surface to a desired dimension and finish. While a honing tool is revolved and reciprocated, electrolyte is circulated through the hole, and a current is passed between the tool and the workpiece. The operation is fast: for example, in one operation 50 μm (0.002 in.) of copper is deposited inside a steel cylinder, and the surface is cleaned and finished to size, all in less than a minute.

Honing Machines. Honing machines may be put into two general classes: vertical machines that avoid sagging of workpieces and tools, and horizontal machines that give ready access and are better for manual operations and long pieces.

A typical machine for easily held workpieces with short holes rotates the honing tool on the end of a spindle. The workpiece is reciprocated lengthwise over the hone or the hone is reciprocated within the work. This may be done expediently on lathes or drilling machines. Many honing machines are operated manually; the operator holds and reciprocates the work and expands the honing tool by means of a linkage from a foot treadle. A popular machine of that kind for holes from about 6 to 26 mm

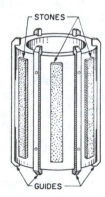

Figure 29-2 Sketch of a honing tool.

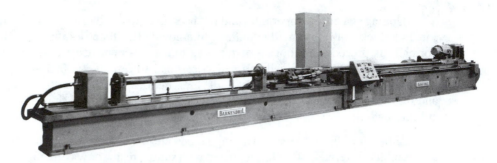

Figure 29-3 Single-stroke horizontal honing machine with a 3.7-m (12-ft) spindle travel for finishing 105-mm gun barrels. (Courtesy Barnes Drill Co.)

($\frac{1}{4}$ to $1\frac{1}{32}$ in.) in diameter has a price of about $5000 with tooling for a typical job at $600. On production machines the operation and sizing are done automatically with the work held in a fixture.

Typical for larger work, the tool is rotated and reciprocated by the head on the right end of the bed of the *horizontal hydraulic honing machine* of Fig. 29-3. Machines like this have been made with strokes up to about 25 m (ca. 80 ft) to hone holes over 1 m (39 in.) in diameter.

A *vertical spindle honing machine* resembles an upright drill press or boring machine. The machine normally incorporates a mechanism not only to rotate but also to reciprocate the honing tool or tools and expand the stones until size is reached. It may have a single spindle or a number of spindles for production like the vertical boring machine of Fig. 22-22. An example of performance is the removal of 0.1mm (0.004 in.) of stock in each of eight cylinders in 30 seconds to a tolerance of less than 12.5 μm (0.0005 in.).

SUPERFINISHING OR MICROSTONING

Purpose of Superfinishing. Superfinishing, also called *microstoning* and *microfinishing,* is done by scrubbing with a stone or stones pressed against a surface to produce a fine-quality metal finish. It is not basically a dimension-creating operation, although it can correct out-of-roundness as much as 75% and size to less than 30 μm (ca. 0.001 in.). Stock removal is limited to about 10 μm (0.0004 in.) and is often less. Substantial geometrical and dimensional accuracy must be created first, usually by grinding. Superfinishing is intended to correct minute surface defects like chatter marks and is also effective in removing amorphous, fuzzy, broken, and burned material, and leaves a true surface of parent base metal. Practically perfect surfaces with no apparent scratch pattern may be produced at one extreme, and at the other, surfaces with readings of 750 nm (30 μin.) R_a and more and a deliberate crosshatched scratch pattern for lubricating qualities.

How Superfinishing Is Done. A Superfinishing operation is done by rapidly reciprocating a fine grit stone with a soft bond and pressing it against a revolving round workpiece. The stone quickly wears to conform to the contour and to cover a large area of the workpiece. The motions are arranged so that a grit never follows the same path more than once around the workpiece. Spherical and flat surfaces may be superfinished by the edge of a cup wheel which is rotated during multidirection traversing over the work surface.

The workpiece and tool in Superfinishing are flooded with cutting fluid to carry away heat and particles of metal and abrasive. Although little force is imposed on the stone, the contact pressure is high at first because the stone touches only a few high spots, and the cutting action is rapid. The stone is able to bridge and equalize a number of surface defects at one time and corrects to the average of the rough profile. When the surface becomes smooth, the pressure decreases, and the stone rides on a film of fluid and ceases to cut. A short surface may be refined to better than 0.1 μm (4 μin.) in less than a minute.

Superfinishing and Microstoning Machines. The characteristic component of any Superfinishing machine is the head that reciprocates the stone (or turns the wheel) and presses it against the work, usually by means of air cylinders. The work may be held or driven in a number of ways. A piece may be swung between centers or chucked in a lathe, with the Superfinishing head mounted on the compound rest and traversed along the piece. Other setups utilize milling machines, planers, and boring mills. Machines are available specifically for Superfinishing. On some the work is held between centers or chucked. The scheme of a production machine of the center-less type is given in Fig. 29-4. Some such machines do plunge cutting; others are arranged for through-feeding work continuously and automatically, in some cases under a series of stones.

Ultrasonic Machining. *Ultrasonic impact grinding* is a means of cutting shapes of all kinds in hard materials of all kinds by rapid and forceful agitation of fine abrasive particles in a slurry between tool and workpiece. Figure 29-5 shows the elements of the operation. The tool is an image of the form to be cut, which may be a hole of almost any shape, a cavity, or figure in relief or intaglio. A sharp, pointed tool may be applied for engraving or die sinking. Vibrations of 15 to 30 kHz are generated by an electric driver, consisting of an oscillator and high output amplifier which supply high-frequency current to a coil around a laminated nickel core. This

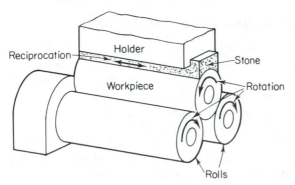

Figure 29-4 Scheme of centerless microstoning.

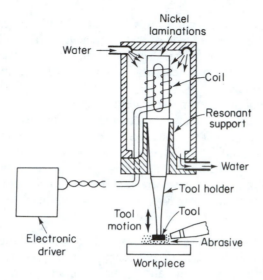

Figure 29-5 Ultrasonic transducer.

core has the property of expanding and shrinking under the influence of the alternating current.

The ratio of stock removed to tool wear is about 10:1, and tool life is tolerable. Because it is slow, ultrasonic grinding is practical only for substances harder than 64 R_c and shapes not amenable to regular grinding. In cemented carbide, stock removal is less than $\frac{1}{2}$ cm³/min (0.03 in.³/min). Ultrasonic grinding can do much the same work as EDM and ECM described in Chap. 31 (even though slower) and has the advantage that it works on nonmetallic substances while the others cannot. Typical jobs include dies for cemented carbide, slicing semiconductor materials, and engraving delicate patterns in glass. The action does not heat nor disturb the material below the workpiece surfaces. Practical finishes obtainable are around 0.25 μm (10 μin.) R_a, and tolerances 50 μm (0.002 in.) or less.

Another form of ultrasonic machining applies vibrations to a rotating diamond tool without abrasive slurry. Hard nonmetallic materials can be cut faster in this way than by conventional means.

NONPRECISION BURRING AND FINISHING OPERATIONS

Polishing.   Polishing is done to put a smooth finish on surfaces and may often involve removal of appreciable metal to take out scratches, tool marks, pits, and other defects from rough surfaces. Usually accuracy of size and shape of the finished surface is not important, but sometimes tolerances of 25 μm (0.001 in.) or less are held in machine polishing. Polishing wheels, described in Chap. 27, distribute cutting action and conform to curved surfaces on workpieces. The application of abrasives here follows much the same principles as in grinding. Commonly several steps are necessary, first to remove the defects and then to put the desired polish on the surface. Much polishing cost can be saved by adequate surface preparation.

The work may be applied to a wheel by hand for polishing on a floor-stand grinder like the one in Fig. 28-18. More production speed and consistency can be realized on semiautomatic polishing machines when there is enough work to justify the investment. The two general classes of such machines are (1) those that carry the work in a straight line past one or more wheels, and (2) those that revolve the pieces in contact with the wheels. The time needed by the operator to load a piece must be appreciably less than required to polish a piece by hand for a machine to be economical. Buffing and power brushing are done in similar ways.

Buffing.   Buffing gives a high luster to a surface. It is not intended to remove much metal and generally follows polishing. The work is pressed against cloth or felt wheels or belts on which fine abrasive in a lubricant binder is smeared from time to time.

Power Brushing.   High-speed revolving brushes are applied to improve surface appearance and remove sharp edges, burrs, fins, and particles. This tends to blend surface defects and irregularities and rounds edges without excessive removal of material. Surfaces may be refined to around 0.1 μm (4 μin.) R_a when desired. Brushing action helps avoid scratches that act as stress raisers.

Common power brushes are wire bristle, hard cord, and Tampico or tough fiber wheels. They are naturally flexible, able to conform to quite irregular surfaces, and can get into otherwise hard to reach places. Abrasive compounds are often put on brushes. Brushing is done by hand but is readily adaptable to semiautomatic machines, which are fast for production.

Tumbling and Vibratory Finishing.   The operation called tumbling, rolling, or barrel finishing consists of loading workpieces in a barrel about 60% full of abrasive grains, sawdust, wood chips, natural or artificial stones, cinders, sand, metal slugs, or other scouring agents, depending on the work and action desired. Water is usually added, often mixed with an acid, a detergent, a rust preventative, or a lubricant. The barrel is closed or tilted and rotated at a slow speed from 1 to more than 10 hours, according to the treatment required. With the right load and speed, the workpieces slide over each other, producing a scouring, trimming, and burnishing action as the barrel turns.

Vibratory finishing does the same work as barrel finishing, but it is done in an open rubber or plastic-lined tub or trough nearly filled with workpieces and media and vibrated at around 1000 to 2000 Hz with about 3 to 10 mm ($\frac{1}{8}$ to $\frac{3}{8}$ in.) amplitude. Various ways of inducing vibrations are employed; a common way is by means of eccentric weights on a revolving shaft. The action makes the entire load rotate slowly in a helical path, but the whole mass is agitated, and scouring, trimming, and burnishing take place throughout the mixture. Therefore, vibratory finishing is much faster (2 to 10 times and sometimes more) than tumbling where the action is confined to the pieces in the sliding zone at any one time as depicted in Fig. 29-6. Much vibratory finishing is done in batches, but the process is readily adaptable to continuous and automatic flow-through operation because of the steady movement of the mass.

Tumbling gives superior results on a few jobs, such as producing high finishes

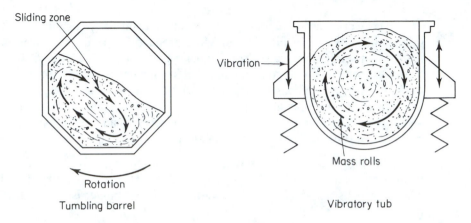

Figure 29-6 Principles of tumbling and vibratory finishing.

on some nonferrous metals. Tumbling is confined to finishing outside surfaces of pieces, but vibratory finishing under proper conditions also does well inside of pieces, in recesses, and upon shielded surfaces. Pieces that must be kept apart (such as quite large or soft ones) may be vibrated in batches in fixtures, whereas they must be tumbled in separate compartments.

Although slower, tumbling is often cheaper because of lower equipment costs. A rough rule of thumb is that tumbling equipment costs $60 to $80/L ($1700 to $2300/ft³) of total barrel capacity, and vibratory machines about $80 to $125/L (2300 to 3500/ft³) of machine capacity. Tumbling barrels have been found to serve many more hours with lower maintenence costs. One comparison showed depreciation cost (machine cost/operating hours) of $0.03/hr, maintenance cost $0.001/hr, and media, compound, and water costs of $0.15/hr for tumbling. The comparable costs for vibratory finishing were $0.40, $0.04, and $1.05/hr. Hourly labor and plant overhead costs are practically the same for the two processes.

Tumbling and vibratory finishing are applied to ferrous and nonferrous metals, plastics, rubber, and wood of small and large sizes. They clean castings, forgings, stampings, and screw machine products; remove burrs, fins, skin, scale, and sharp edges; take off paint and plating; improve surface finish and appearance; and have a tendency to relieve surface strains. Some reduction in size may be experienced but results are uniform in each lot.

A development of barrel finishing, called *Harperizing,* employs two equally loaded barrels on a turret, which revolves in a counterclockwise direction to generate centrifugal forces of 1 to 25g. The barrels revolve clockwise at the same time, and the parts and media therein convolute under high pressures. In this way, work may be done as much as 50 times as fast as by simple tumbling, but equipment is expensive and costly development and careful control are necessary for each job. A production machine that can handle a 320-kg (700-lb) load is priced at about $100,000. The process is not considered competitive with conventional tumbling or vibratory finishing for most work but has been found superior for certain jobs such as finishing and deburring precision parts, inducing high surface compressive stresses, and sizing steel balls.

Shot- and Sand-blasting. Shot- and sand-blasting are done by throwing particles at high velocity against the work. The particles may be metallic shot or grit; artificial or natural abrasive, including sand; agricultural products such as nut shells; glass beads, and ceramics, depending upon what is to be done and the condition of the workpiece. A primary reason for blasting is to clean surfaces. This may mean removing scale, rust, or burnt sand from castings by means of shot or sand, stripping paint by sand-blasting from objects to be redecorated, cleaning grease or oil from finished parts by means of nut shells, or any number of similar operations. A clean, uniform, and in many cases final surface finish is obtained by blasting. In addition, shot-blasting peens surfaces and leads to the advantages of appreciably increasing fatigue strength and stress corrosion resistance, reducing porosity in nonferrous castings, improving surface wearability as on gear teeth, and improving the oil retentivity of some surfaces.

Four common ways of blasting are by compressed air, centrifugal action, high-pressure water, and a mixture of compressed air and water. Compressed air equipment can be used with any type of abrasive, is easily controlled, is simple and relatively inexpensive, and gives ready access to inside surfaces. For centrifugal action, particles are fed to and slung by a rapidly revolving wheel. A high flow and a rapid production rate can be obtained in this way, and it is the most popular method. Water with or without a polymer additive and fine particles is applied in jets to produce smooth satin-like surface finishes and to cut thin and thick materials at fast rates. This is called *water jet machining* (WJM). A fine abrasive propelled by an air jet does what is called *abrasive-jet machining* (AJM). Typical uses include fine burring, drilling, and trimming of hard, brittle materials, particularly in thin sections such as silicon wafers. With soft particles, AJM is efficient for delicate cleaning.

Small lot blasting is commonly done in a cabinet where the operator from the outside manipulates a nozzle through safety gloves and sleeves. In high production, nozzles may be mounted in fixed positions in a large enclosure. Workpieces are carried past the nozzles on rotating tables, conveyors, etc.

Burr Removal. When cutters wear but are still able to yield required size and finish, burrs occur on the edges of machined surfaces. They are unsightly, dangerous, and impair proper fitting and functioning of parts. Burrs can be and are removed by the methods already described in this chapter and by manual trimming, but other methods are also important. One of these is ECM described in Chap. 31. Others are described in the following paragraphs.

The *thermal energy method* burns away burrs. Parts to be burred are placed in a chamber that is filled with gases (i.e., hydrogen and oxygen) that are spark ignited. Thin burrs and flash reach high temperatures and are burned by excess oxygen, but the main body of each part acts as a heat sink and is not affected.

Abrasive flow machining (AFM) or *extrude-honing* is done by forcing an abrasive-laden soft rubber or putty-like compound to flow over surfaces and edges and through holes, slots, and cavities of machined parts. The process can be controlled closely to act uniformly over a part to remove burrs, polish, and even help size surfaces, generate radii, and reach areas not adequately accessible with other methods.

Comparison and Selection of Methods.   Each finishing operation has certain areas in which it excels. Polishing may remove large defects and heavy stock around deep scratches and pits at less cost than to remove metal to the same depth over the whole piece. Buffing and brushing are quick ways of getting high luster where substantial stock need not be removed. Tumbling and vibratory finishing are economical for cleaning, improvement of appearance, and burring over the whole piece, especially for large-quantity production. Blasting is superior for heavy scale and stock removal as a rule. These are not the only applications of these operations; their provinces overlap, and often they work best together, such as in removal of the worst defects by polishing followed by vibration to form radii on edges and refine finish. When there is a question, any of these operations may be compared in the same way as for other operations.

As an example of a comparison, the time to polish and buff a part may be 3 minutes per piece. The same piece may be tumbled with satisfactory results. Loading and unloading time is 15 minutes, and tumbling time 4 hours. The labor and overhead rate is $12/hr, and the tumbling cost rate is $3/hr. The number of pieces for which the cost is the same by either method is N, and

$$\frac{3N \times 12}{60} = \frac{15 \times 12}{60} + (4 \times 3)$$

So $N = 25$ pieces. For a lot of fewer than 25 pieces, polishing is the more economical method. It is assumed that at least 25 pieces can be tumbled at once.

QUESTIONS

1. What are the purposes of lapping, honing, and Superfinishing?
2. How is lapping done?
3. Describe three common forms of lapping machines.
4. What is the difference between lapping and honing?
5. How is honing done?
6. Describe two general types of honing machines.
7. What does Superfinishing do, and what does it not do?
8. How is Superfinishing done?
9. How is ultrasonic impact grinding done?
10. When is ultrasonic impact grinding superior to, and when is it not competitive with, other methods?
11. Describe common ways of finishing surfaces when precision is not important.
12. Describe common ways of removing burrs from machine parts.
13. What determines the method best suited to finish a surface?

REFERENCES

"Another Look at AJM," *Manufacturing Engineering*, July, 1982.

DALLAS, D. B., ed., *Tool and Manufacturing Engineers Handbook*, 3rd ed., Society of Manufacturing Engineers, Dearborn, Mich., 1976.

DALY, J. J., "Boosting Gear Life through Shot Peening," *Machine Design*, Sept. 6, 1973.

EMERSON, C., "Deburring Metal Parts, Special Report 675," *American Machinist*, Apr. 1, 1975.

GILLESPIE, L. K., "How to Analyze Vibratory Deburring Costs," *Machine and Tool Bluebook*, May 1978.

———, "Barrel Tumbling: Is It Still Economical?" *Machine and Tool Bluebook*, Sept. 1978.

LAVOIE, F. J., "Abrasive Jet Machining," *Machine Design*, Sept. 6, 1973.

PATTERSON, M. M., "For I.D. Work—Honing or Grinding, Which Shall It Be?" *Machine and Tool Bluebook*, May 1975.

SHIRING, J. R., "AJM Cuts Brittle Parts," *American Machinist*, Aug. 7, 1972.

STAUFFER, R. N., "Cutting with Jets," *Manufacturing Engineering*, July 1976.

———, "What You Should Know about Vibratory Finishing," *Manufacturing Engineering*, July 1979.

30

SURFACE CLEANING AND COATING

Manufactured products naturally collect oil, dirt, chips, etc., during processing. This soil must be removed for certain operations, such as inspection and painting, for assembly, and especially for salability. Thus cleaning is an important part of many processes, and the principal ways it is done will be discussed.

Coatings are commonly applied to the surfaces of articles for decoration, texture, corrosion resistance, electrical insulation, lubricity, and protection against high temperatures. The common classes are conversion coatings formed by chemical reaction with the surface, organic coatings or paints, metallic platings, and inorganic or vitreous coatings. The chief forms of these and the methods of applying them are described.

CLEANING

Cleaners.   Cleaning is done by mechanical action and by washing with solvents, detergents, and other chemicals. Chunks and layers of sand, dirt, scale, rust, etc., may be removed by sand-blasting, tumbling, and other vigorous mechanical methods described in Chap. 29. Such rough cleaning must normally be followed by washing or degreasing prior to painting or plating. Washing and degreasing may be done by *mineral* or *organic solvents* or by *water solutions*. Solvents such as naphtha, kerosene, and chlorinated hydrocarbons (for low fire hazard) dissolve greases, oils, and waxes but not inorganic dirt. They are relatively expensive but are efficient degreasers and do not harm most surfaces. Water itself is not a good cleaner but is the universal solvent for cleaning agents and is used freely for rinsing, which must always

746

be done after washing for thorough cleanliness. Conditioners like softeners, inhibitors, wetting agents, and detergents make water solutions efficient. The three basic detergents are emulsified solvents and acidic and alkaline detergents. Water *emulsions* of organic solvents combine the advantages of a solvent with those of an agent that disperses soil. They work cold and are economical for light degreasing and for precleaning to save time and alleviate contamination in subsequent alkaline cleaning operations. Alkaline solutions, such as caustic soda or trisodium phosphate, often blended with colloidal materials, soap, and other wetting agents, are commonly available in strengths enough to remove any soil but attack some surfaces. They are the most widely used industrial detergents. Mild acids are used for materials attacked by alkalis to remove scale, oxides, and fluxes. Molten salt baths are able to strip tenacious deposits of sand, scale, etc., from forgings and castings.

Methods of Cleaning.   The best cleaning method for a product depends on how clean the surfaces must be, the kind of soil, the surface material, the size and shape of the part, and the number of pieces. Some washing is done cold, but much (particularly with alkaline detergents) must be done hot. The easiest way of cleaning and one that can be done with any fluid is *dipping* or *immersion*. This alone is not enough to dislodge clinging soil, and agitation, barrel tumbling, or rubbing may have to be added. A tank of fluid for washing becomes contaminated in time and thus less effective. Immersion of the work in a series of tanks helps some. All methods of cleaning may be done manually or may be highly automated for large-quantity production.

Electrolytic cleaning is a form of immersion in an alkaline solution with the workpiece as the cathode in an electrical circuit. Gas released on the surface helps dislodge foreign substances, and a thin protective layer of tin may be deposited.

Spraying of all kinds of fluids forcefully acts to dislodge solid dirt. The spray may be directed by hand or be part of an automated system as indicated in Fig. 30-1.

Vapor degreasing is a method of cleaning with solvents as depicted in Fig. 30-1. A nonflammable solvent (e.g., trichloroethylene) in the bottom of a tank is vaporized at 40 to 125°C (100 to 250°F). Cooling coils near the top condense the vapor and keep it in the tank. The vapor condenses on a relatively cool workpiece; the condensate

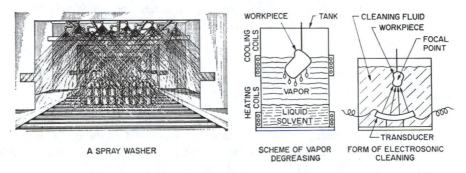

A SPRAY WASHER   SCHEME OF VAPOR   FORM OF ELECTROSONIC
                         DEGREASING   CLEANING

Figure 30-1   Methods of washing and degreasing.

dissolves grease and runs off, removing dirt and chips. Residue collects at the bottom and is not carried out with the work. Pieces are dry when they come out of the tank. The action is fairly rapid for removal of organic substances. Small light workpieces may become hot quickly and cease to condense vapor before they are cleaned; some parts have exceptionally heavy soil to be removed. These may be immersed in warm or violently boiling liquid or sprayed as well as dipped in vapor.

Volatile solvents are quite toxic and can be dangerous if used or handled improperly. Strict regulations for safety of workers, protection of the environment, and fire prevention have been enacted and must be closely followed by users.

In *electrosonic cleaning,* high-powered and high-frequency sound waves from one or more transducers are focused on a work piece immersed in a cleaning fluid as indicated in Fig. 30-1. This causes the rapid formation and collapse of minute bubbles or cavities in the liquid (called *cavitation*), giving a violent action on exposed surfaces. This is not widely used for removing heavy deposits or jelly-like substances, but is efficient for jarring loose tightly adherent smut and reaching inaccessible recesses. Deburring and rounding of edges can even be done at high power levels.

The individual operations just described are commonly combined into processes to suit specific situations. For example, a typical sequence is (1) preclean by dipping or spraying with an emulsifiable solvent to remove the bulk of the grease and dirt, (2) rinse by spraying with hot water, (3) dip and clean electrolytically to remove scale and oxide, (4) final hot rinse by dipping, and (5) dry in an air blast.

Pickling and Oxidizing.   *Pickling* is just the chemical removal of surface oxides and scale from metals by acid solutions. This is commonly done on rolled shapes, wire, sheets, heat-treated steel parts, wrought and cast aluminum parts, etc. In some applications, such as on aluminum, it is called *oxidizing.*

Common pickling solutions contain sulfuric or hydrochloric acids with water and sometimes inhibitors. Nitric and hydrofluoric acids are used for some applications. A solution may contain half acid for cold use but as little as 10% if intended for use at 95°C (200°F). Pickling is usually done by immersion for periods of several minutes or more.

In pickling, the acid cannot get to a surface that is covered with dirt. Thus, parts must be cleaned first. After pickling, the parts must be completely neutralized by an alkaline and then a clear rinse. Any residue of acid will harm paint or other subsequent coating.

SURFACE COATINGS

Conversion Coatings.   Conversion coatings are basically inorganic films formed by chemical reactions with metal surfaces but are often impregnated with organic substances. They are usually much less than 25 μm (0.001 in.) thick but are normally formed from the original surface and so are tightly bonded and cause no appreciable dimensional change. Common forms are phosphate, chromate, oxide, and anodic coatings described in the following paragraphs.

Phosphate coatings are essentially phosphate salts formed by dipping, spraying, or brushing with acidic solutions of metal phosphates. They are put on iron, steel, and zinc and to a lesser extent on aluminum, cadmium, titanium, and tin to resist corrosion (particularly under paint films), make paint adhere tightly, add lubrication, and resist abrasion. Some trade names are *Parkerizing, Granodizing,* and *Bonderizing*.

Chromate coatings are obtained by applying acidic solutions of chromium compounds to steel, zinc, cadmium, aluminum, copper, brass, silver, tin, and magnesium surfaces, occasionally with electrolytic assistance. The thin amorphous film resists abrasion, provides an excellent base for organic coatings, and may be dyed and serve alone as a decorative finish, although it is not lightfast.

Conventional *black oxide coatings* are put on steel by immersion in a boiling solution of sodium hydroxide and mixtures of nitrates and nitrites. Another black oxide process employs steam treatment for drills. Some proprietory processes utilize inorganic and organic substances in baths at room temperatures. Oxide coatings of various colors are put on aluminum and other nonferrous metals. Oxide coatings serve as paint bases and as final finishes. They are relatively cheap, and when impregnated with oil or wax, furnish good corrosion resistance.

Anodic coatings are applied to aluminum, zinc, beryllium, titanium, and magnesium alloys by electrolytic-chemical means. The workpiece is immersed in a solution (commonly sulfuric acid with or without organic additives for aluminum) and connected as the anode in an electrical circuit. Anodic coatings may be from about 2 to 250 μm (0.0001 to 0.010 in.) thick and are good protection against corrosion because they are in reality like but only more of the thin film that naturally protects the metal. Dense films over 25 μm (0.001 in.) thick are wear resistant. Anodic coatings may be colored in many hues with excellent permanency.

Conversion coatings may be impregnated with fluorocarbon resins, molybdenum disulfide, or graphite by further electrochemical and heat treatment. These are called *synergistic coatings* and can be made to have superior hardness, wear resistance, lubricity, and corrosion resistance. Originally developed for space-travel devices, these coatings are being applied to other demanding applications. Proprietory coatings of this kind include *Tufram, Nedox, Magnadize,* and *Canadizing*.

Organic Coatings.   Organic coatings in the form of thin plastic sheets or strips may be laminated to surfaces but are mostly applied as paints, enamels, or inks. A coating may be put on a finished product or precoated on the stock from which the product is made. Organic coatings go on almost all materials and offer unlimited color and gloss varieties. Thus they provide more decorative possibilities than other coatings. In durability, strength, and corrosion resistance, they generally are superior to conversion coatings but not as effective as some metallic coatings. Usually, they cost less than metallic coatings and thus are preferred if they serve satisfactorily.

Paint is the general term for an organic coating and consists of film forming materials and pigments for coloring, hiding power, and protection. Clear finishes lack pigments. Drying agents may also be added.

Oil paint is a dispersion of metallic pigments, such as white lead, in a vegetable drying oil, such as linseed oil, and solvent thinner and perhaps dryers. The thinner evaporates, and the oil oxidizes to form the film. Drying time depends on the oil used and drying agents added but is relatively long.

A *lacquer* is essentially a solution of plastic resins and plasticizers with or without pigments in a solvent. When the lacquer is applied, the solvent evaporates, and leaves a film that can be made quite attractive by polishing. Lacquer is relatively easy to apply and dries quickly, but the film is not as durable and resistant to some solvents as other coatings.

Varnishes and *enamels* of the older kinds are like oil paints in that they form a film by oxidation of a resin-oil vehicle. Newer synthetic types are based largely or entirely on plastic resins and elastomers and harden by polymerization. Almost all the principal substances described in Chap. 11 are used singly or compounded to obtain various degrees of corrosion, chemical, and environmental resistance, colorability, durability, and other properties. The synthetic resins can be compounded to be equal or superior to conventional enamels for any specific application. Extensive tables that show the relative properties and attributes of the common plastic compounds for coatings are given in reference books and handbooks.

Plastic resin and elastomer coatings come as liquids and as powders. Some of the liquids contain a large proportion of organic solvent that evaporates to leave a polymer film. The vapors can cause air and water pollution and require costly equipment to meet environmental standards, and the use of such liquid coatings has been greatly curtailed. Other liquid coatings with little or no solvent content have become more popular, although the changeover can be quite expensive because different equipment and techniques are usually required.

The newer liquids are *medium-* and *high-solid paints* and *water-base or water-borne paints*. Medium-solid paints have 50 to 60% solid content (by volume) compared to 30% for conventional paints; high-solid paints are available with much more. As an example of benefits, one user reported solvent emissions with 52% solids almost 60% less than with 30% solids, making it much easier to meet environmental requirements. Energy saving is also a factor. One user gained a 25% saving in the cost of fuel gas for drying with medium-solid paint. Water-base systems are water-soluble emulsion and colloidal dispersion types for different kinds of polymers. Water-base paints eliminate fire hazard.

Paints of another class are called two-component systems because they involve the combination of two substances at the time of painting to achieve polymerization of the film. Although these coatings are superior for some applications, in general their capital and operating costs are high and not competitive.

Total elimination of sacrificial solvent has been achieved by *powder coating*. Without solvent, thicker coats can be applied in one pass, and painting time decreased. Some materials, such as Nylon II, are not soluble and can only be used as powders. Powder coating requires heating the work to form a film from the powder.

Specialty finishes include those with metallic pigments, those with oils and dryers that give a crinkled surface, silicone additives for high temperature, and plastisols and organisols. The last listed are abrasion and chemical resistant vinyl coatings up to about 3 mm ($\frac{1}{8}$ in.) thick. A plastisol contains no solvent, while an organisol does.

Sometimes only one coat of paint is enough but usually two or more layers of different coatings are applied to obtain combinations of desirable properties. An undercoat may be applied to form a good base for a finish coat that provides color, luster, and appearance. Undercoatings include primers that form a bond and inhibit corrosion on the interface and intermediate coats that serve as fillers, smooth surfaces, or sealers. The composition of a paint depends largely upon its intended place in the layers on a surface. Powder coating usually does not need a primer.

Painting Methods.   Painting may be done by brush, knife, dip, roller, flow, tumble, silk screen, electrodeposition, fluid bed, or spray methods. Brushing is easily done but is slow, and other methods are used for production. Dipping demands little equipment and can be mechanized easily but requires paint that films out, stirring, and workpieces that can be immersed easily and are without pockets.

Flow coating, by pouring paint onto workpieces and recirculating the runoff, is gaining in popularity because it is applicable to many kinds of pieces of small to medium sizes and is fast, thorough, and economical of material.

Paint spraying is the most used method of industrial painting because it is fast, dependable, versatile, and uniform. It is based on the principle that a liquid stream atomizes when it exceeds a certain speed. The most common system is to introduce a liquid or powder into a high-velocity stream of compressed air released through a nozzle. In another system, the paint is heated and discharged in a high velocity stream through a small orifice at pressures up to about 35 MPa (5000 psi). In still another way, the paint may be slung off the edge of a rapidly revolving disk- or bell-shaped atomizer.

A spray gun or head may be directed by hand, but for continuous production is commonly automated to spray pieces as they pass by on a conveyor. Robots are being utilized more and more for automated paint spraying. Manual touch-up may be necessary at the end of a line, but the cost is normally less than if each piece were hand sprayed completely. An advantage of automated painting is that it can be done at up to 40°C (ca.100°F), which is ideal for paint but not for people.

Most industrial painting is done in segregated enclosures or booths that are well ventilated. This promotes cleanliness which is important for quality control. Enclosure is necessary because of toxicity and flammability of solvents and helps control air and water pollution. The recovery of excess material is aided by enclosures.

Much paint can be lost when sprayed. The loss is reduced by imposing an electrostatic charge on atomized liquid paint or powder. In one *electrostatic painting system* depicted on the left in Fig. 30-2, a potential of 80,000 to 150,000 V charges the paint slung from a disk- or bell-shaped atomizer. The droplets are drawn to and deposited uniformly, with almost no loss, on the grounded workpieces of opposite polarity.

When sprayed from an airgun, the particles can be charged inside or outside of the gun as indicated in the center of Fig. 30-2. The charged particles are propelled to the workpiece of opposite polarity. A "wraparound" effect occurs to deposit the coating material on all exposed surfaces (front and back, inside and outside), although restrictions may cause variations in film thickness. In another system, the particles are

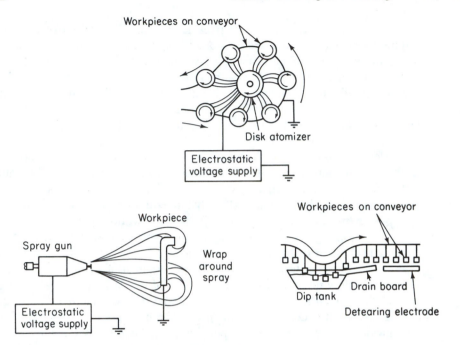

Figure 30-2   Electrostatic painting systems.

discharged into an electrostatic field set up between charged electrodes and the grounded workpiece. The paint particles pick up the electrical charge of the electrode as they pass near it first and are attracted to the work. Spray loss may be kept as low as 5 to 25% with an electrostatic painting system.

Drips and tears that collect at the bottoms of pieces that have been dipped can be drawn off electrostatically as on the right in Fig. 30-2. Another way to eliminate excess paint is to whirl the wet pieces in a centrifuge.

Electrodeposition under such names as *electrocoating, electropainting, paint plating,* and *E-coat* is done with a conductive workpiece at one potential dipped into a tank of specially formulated liquid paint of opposite charge (negative in some cases; positive in others). Colloidal particles of paint in solution in the tank are attracted to the work, become soluble on contact, and adhere firmly to the surface. Resistance increases on areas as they are coated, and buildup continues on other areas to deposit a uniform but thin film. Because of resistance, only one coat is feasible, and the process is mostly limited to priming. Prime coats are normally not more than about 20 μm (0.0008 in.) thick and show the slightest surface defects. Equipment is costly, and the process is economical only for large-quantity production.

Fluid bed coating is done by dipping a heated metal piece in an agitated swirling pool of fine powder suspended in a stream of air. The powder particles are a mixture of resin, catalyst, pigment, and stabilizer and melt upon the hot workpiece surface to form a uniform film. The workpiece then is usually oven heated to flow out and cure the coating. In an *electrostatic fluid bed,* a screen called a charging grid polarizes the powder pool, and particles are attracted to the oppositely charged workpiece. Coatings up to 1.5 mm (0.06 in.) thick can be obtained in one immersion by powder coating, but any less than 250 μm (0.01 in.) are difficult to achieve. Powder coatings are pore free, smooth, tightly held, and cover edges and corners well. However, a uniform coat is difficult to achieve on a part with thin and thick sections because the heating affect is different for different masses.

Paint may be baked in ovens heated by steam, gas, oil, or electricity. Infrared lamps in banks have become quite popular for baking and drying because the method is fast, clean, and easily changed about and adjusted. Attention has been given in recent years to curing of organic coatings by radiation, i.e., by ultraviolet rays, laser beam, and electron-beam methods. These methods have been reported to save fuel, reduce air pollution, and increase production speeds. For example, one project utilized a specially formulated coating cured by exposure to an electron beam in an inert gas atmosphere in 1 to 2 seconds per piece (as composed to many minutes or even hours in conventional processes). However, the electron beam gun cost several hundred thousand dollars, and the complete production installation over $1 million. Such a process is found economical only for curing 2 million square meters (ca. 20 million square feet) or more per year.

Precoated sheet metal strips with laminated, conversion, galvanized, and painted surfaces in rolls are popular because it is cheaper to coat the stock than the finished pieces. A large variety of coatings are available to withstand almost all fabrication operations and meet end use requirements.

Painting Costs. The first consideration in the selection of a paint is that it meets service requirements in regard to satisfactory corrosion protection, strength, durability, luster, color, etc. Often several kinds of paint can be found suitable for a particular application. The lowest cost is then the criterion: not the cost per liter or per gallon but the total cost of material, energy, labor, and equipment (including pollution control equipment). An analysis of the actual costs for four common paint materials considered for one plant is given in Table 30-1.

The following calculations for the conventional solvent paint in Table 30-1 explain how the analysis is made.

5. $[(5 \times 2.50) + (2 \times 0.5)]/7 = \$1.93/L$ or $[(5 \times 9.50) + (2 \times 2.00)]/7 = \$7.36/gal$

6. $5 \times 0.43/7 = 0.31 = 31\%$

7. $0.31 \times 10^{-3}/10^{-6} = 310\ m^2/L/\mu m$ or $0.31 \times 0.1337/0.001/12 = 497\ ft^2/gal/mil$

10. $310 \times 0.6/25.4 = 7.3\ m^2/L$ or $497 \times 0.6 = 298\ ft^2/gal$

11. $1.93/7.3 = \$0.2644/m^2$ or $7.36/298 = \$0.0247/ft^2$

13. $0.2644 \times 1,114,800 = \$295,000 \approx 0.0247 \times 12,000,000$

14. $187 \times 106 = \$19,800 \approx 6618 \times 3$

TABLE 30-1 COMPARISON OF FINISHING COSTS FOR COMMON PAINT MATERIALS

Cost items	Conventional solvent	Water borne	High solids	Polyester[a] powder
Material				
1. Commercial paint[a] [$/L ($/gal)]	2.50 (9.50)	2.90 (11.00)	4.10 (15.50)	4.40 (2.00)
2. Volume solids (%)	43	40	65	98
3. Reducing agent cost [$/L ($/gal)]	0.50 (2.00)	0	—	—
4. Mix ratio	5:2	10:3	—	—
5. Mixed coating cost [$/L ($/gal)]	1.93 (7.36)	2.23 (8.46)	4.10 (15.50)	4.40 (2.00)
6. Volume solids at spray viscosity (%)	31	31	65	98
7. Coverage at 100% efficiency [$m^2/L/\mu m$) (ft^2/gal/mil)]	310 (497)	310 (497)	650 (1043)	613 (118)
8. Dry film thickness [μm (mil)]	25 (1.0)	25 (1.0)	30 (1.2)	35.6 (1.4)
9. Utilization efficiency (%)	60	60	75	99
10. Actual coverage [m^2/L (ft^2/gal)]	7.3 (298)	7.3 (298)	16 (652)	17 (83)
11. Applied cost [$/m^2$ ($/ft^2$)]	0.2644 (0.0247)	0.3055 (0.0284)	0.2563 (0.0238)	0.2588 (0.0241)
Energy				
12. Annual volume of gas consumed [dam^3 (1000 ft^3)[b]	187 (6618)	200 (7066)	174 (6150)	101 (3568)
Total annual cost				
13. Material ($)[c]	295,000	341,000	286,000	289,000
14. Energy (gas) ($)[d]	19,800	21,200	18,400	10,700
15. Labor and maintenance ($)	131,000	131,000	129,000	74,890
16. Depreciation ($)[e]		9,500	9,000	14,500
17. Total ($)	445,800	502,700	442,400	389,090
18. VOC emissions[f]	C	B	B	A
19. Solid waste disposal[f]	C	C	C	A

[a]Commodity unit for powder is kg (lb) instead of L (gal). Thus powder cost is $4.40/kg ($2.00/lb), etc. The specific gravity of polyester powder is 1.6.

[b]Estimated amount of gas for 2000 hours per year of production time for spray booths and bake ovens. Pretreatment and other requirements assumed the same for all alternatives and not included.

[c]Production of painted surfaces is 1,114,800 m^2/yr (12,000,000 ft^3/yr).

[d]Gas costs $106/$dam^3$ ($3/1000 ft^3).

[e]This represents a study of the feasibility of replacing a conventional solvent system already in operation. No investment is needed if the present system is continued except for emission control equipment. The investments

Hot-Dip Plating. A low-cost way of putting a protective coating on metal pieces is to dip them into certain molten metals, mainly aluminum, zinc, tin, or lead. The same metals are also electrocoated. Steel mills supply sheets with more than ten kinds or combinations of dipped or electrocoatings.

Hot-dip galvanizing is done by dipping ferrous parts, such as outside hardware, into or passing strips, sheets, etc., continuously through a bath of molten zinc. The work is first cleaned and fluxed in a solution of zinc chloride and hydrochloric acid.

Zinc keeps iron from rusting even if the coating is broken because a galvanic action occurs in the presence of the moist carbon dioxide of the air. The zinc is the more active metal, and the iron does not rust until all the zinc is gone. Most other metals provide a barrier but do not give sacrificial protection. Dipping is an economical way of putting on a heavy and enduring coat of zinc, usually 100 to 500 μm (0.004 to 0.02 in.) thick.

Tin plating or *dipping* is done by immersing cleaned and fluxed steel sheets in a bath of molten tin. They then are passed through rolls in a palm oil bath to remove excess tin. Tinned sheet does not furnish as much outside protection as zinc but is adequate for some uses, such as the insides of food containers, for which it mostly is used. Tin-plated parts solder easily.

Terne plate is steel dipped in an alloy of lead and about 25% tin. It is cheaper than tin plate but has satisfactory corrosion resistance. *Lead* coatings protect automobile battery boxes and radiator fittings. The lubricating quality of the lead is beneficial on sheets and wire that are going to be drawn.

Electroplating. Electroplating is done on all the common metals and even on many nonmetals (particularly plastics) after their surfaces have been suitably prepared. Plating may be done for protection against corrosion or against wear and abrasion, for appearance, to rework worn parts by increase in size, to make pieces easy to solder, to provide a surface, usually of brass on steel, for bonding rubber, and to stop off areas on steel parts from being carburized during heat treatment. Most of these applications are evident in the articles about us every day. The common, but not the only, plating materials are aluminum, cadmium, zinc, silver, gold, tin, copper, nickel, chromium, and their alloys.

The principle of electroplating is illustrated in Fig. 30-3. The piece to be plated is immersed in a water solution of salts of the metal to be applied and made the cathode

---

in the other systems, if selected, are to be depreciated over 10 years on a straight-line basis. Thus the figures shown represent 10% of the investment required for each. Any investments required for hydrocarbon emission control and waste disposal systems are not included. It is expected that the solvent-borne systems will require such equipment to meet federal EPA guidelines, and the water-borne and powder systems may need such equipment to meet regulations in some areas. An indication of the relative merits of the systems with respect to environmental control is given in lines 18 and 19. Actual potential costs must be ascertained and taken into account for a final comparison.

[f]VOC stands for volatile organic compounds in the paint. From the standpoint of the disposal of pollutants, A designates least, B moderate, and C most cost.

Source: Data from H. W. Fishkin, "Finishing Systems Economic Overview," *Manufacturing Engineering,* Aug. 1981, p. 77; a detailed analysis of alternative systems for finishing formed sheet steel parts.

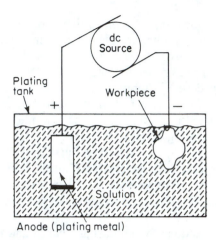

Figure 30-3 Scheme of electroplating.

in a direct current circuit. Anodes of the coating metal replenish the solution when the current is flowing, and ions of the metal are attracted to the workpiece to form the coating. Metals that cannot be electrodeposited from water solutions, such as the refractory metals, are deposited out of molten salts at high temperatures. The rate of deposition and the properties of the coating, such as hardness, uniformity, and porosity, depend upon getting a proper balance among the composition of the plating solution, current density, agitation, solution acidity, and temperature. For instance, the higher the current density, the faster the metal is deposited, but a rate above a critical level for a specific solution and temperature results in a rough and spongy plate.

The electroplating process presents several difficulties of concern to the designer. One of these is that a plating is not always deposited uniformly. It tends to be thick on projections, thin in recesses, and almost nonexistent in some corners. The designer must avoid irregularities as much as possible, but much can be done by good planning and control of the operation. Some solutions give better distribution of plating and are said to have better *throwing power* than others. The amount of plate deposited on a surface is related to the distance from an anode. Thus, anodes shaped to match the workpieces and suitably placed can help toward uniform plating.

Plating does not hide defects in the surface of the workpiece, and a surface must be fully finished if it is to be plated for appearance as well as corrosion resistance. Parts, such as automobile bumpers, nickel or chrome plated for durable appearance are commonly given an initial copper plating 5 to 15 μm (0.0002 to 0.0006 in.) thick. This adheres well to and effectively covers the steel, and its surface is easier to buff out than the steel. Decorative chrome plate is ordinarily only around a micrometer or less (a few hundred-thousandths of an inch) thick to maintain brightness over a protective intercoat of nickel. Various combinations of multiple layers are used to achieve best results at lowest costs for various purposes.

Hydrogen released at the cathode causes harmful embrittlement of hardened or cold-worked steel workpieces. The quantity of hydrogen can be kept at a minimum by proper control of the operation, and the embrittlement can be alleviated by heating the workpieces immediately after plating.

Electroplating Equipment. The basic unit for electroplating operations is the tank to hold the solutions. Tanks are constructed of various materials such as lead sheet, rubber, plastics, and tile to resist alkaline and acidic solutions. Large pieces are suspended individually. Small pieces may be mounted on racks but mostly are barrel plated or tumbled. A batch of pieces is put in a nonconducting perforated barrel and in touch with suitable contacts. The barrel is lowered into the plating solution and revolved several times each minute, and the pieces tumble around and are plated uniformly.

The electroplating process entails cleaning, washing, rinsing, and other treatment in addition to the actual deposition of metal. This means each workpiece or batch must be dipped into and transferred among a number of tanks, whether plated individually, on racks, or in barrels. That is commonly done manually for small lots, but labor is saved and quality controlled better by automatic and even numerically controlled plating machines for moderate- to large-quantity production. The three general types of machines are illustrated in Fig. 30-4. The transfer devices for these machines raise the work from one tank, move it to the next, and then lower it into place at preset intervals. The straight line and return types may be single- or double-line machines,

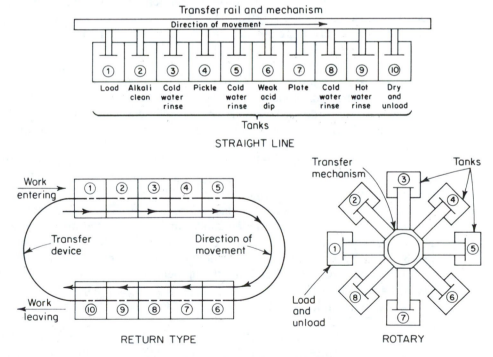

Figure 30-4 Typical plating machine layouts.

depending upon whether they have one or two rows of work carriers, one above the other. The rotary-type machine takes more floor space but can handle large parts. These machines can be tied in conveniently with conveyor systems. In certain industries, specialized machines have been developed for continuously plating sheet metal, a strip of parts, or wire as it is run through a series of baths.

High-speed plating techniques have been developed in recent years for large-quantity production. Instead of being immersed in a tank with current passing an average of about $\frac{1}{2}$ m ($1\frac{1}{2}$ ft) through relatively still electrolyte as in a conventional electroplating, the piece is positioned in a fixture cavity with wall contours matching the part surface, typically with a gap of about 2.5 mm (0.1 in.). Electrolyte is pumped through the cavity at around 100 dm^3/min (3.5 ft^3/min). The rapidly moving liquid overcomes ionic depletion in the layer adjacent to the work surface, and 20 or more times as much current can be passed effectively as in conventional plating, and metal can be deposited much faster. In one version, called *contour plating,* as much nickel is deposited on automobile bumpers in 1 minute as is put on in an hour in a tank.

Touch-up, small lot, and selective plating may be done by a brush or swab soaked with plating fluid and connected as the anode. The workpiece is the cathode. This is called *brush plating.*

Used fluids from electroplating tanks can be highly polluting. In recent years, stringent rules have been set down to control the levels of cyanide and metals in the effluent. A common remedy is to resort to chemical reactions to convert the waste to nontoxic substances. That way valuable materials may be lost, and in some cases evaporation and dialysis are used to concentrate and recover costly substances as well as eliminate pollution.

Costs of Electroplating.   Two major direct costs of electroplating are for the metal in the plate and for electricity. These and other costs which depend upon time can be calculated readily from data given in handbooks. For instance, a square meter of zinc plate 25 μm thick weighs 178.5 g (a square foot by 0.001 in. thick weighs 0.6 oz).

One faraday of electricity is equal to 96,540 coulombs (A-s) and deposits an equivalent weight in grams of any metal at 100% cathode efficiency. The equivalent weight of zinc is its atomic weight (65.38) divided by its valence (2), or 32.7 grams. An average cathode efficiency for zinc plating is 85%. That means that 85% of the current goes to deposit metal; the remainder into leakage, hydrogen generation, etc. The electricity to deposit 25 μm on 1 m^2 is (178.5/32.7) $\times$ (96,540/3600) $\times$ 1/0.85 = 172.2 Ah. At the usual potential of 6 V, the energy used is 172.2 $\times$ 6 = 1.03 kWh. For 0.001 in. over 1 ft^2, the amount is (17/32.7) $\times$ (96,540/3600) $\times$ 1/0.85 = 16.4 Ah. The energy then is 16.4 $\times$ 6 = 98.4 Wh.

At a permissible current density of 225 A/m^2, the time to deposit a thickness of 25 μm is 172.2/225 $\approx$ 0.8 hr.

In most cases electroplates of 25 to 50 μm (0.001 to 0.002 in.) and less thick are adequate for protection and finish. Certain applications call for thicker plates; as much as 0.2 mm (0.008 in.) of hard chrome plate may be put on tools and gages for wear resistance and even more where the purpose of the plate is to increase dimensions.

Electroforming.   Parts may be formed by electroplating metal on a mandrel, which may be collapsible, coated with a parting agent, dissolvable, or meltable for removal from the product. Copper, nickel, silver, and iron are commonly electroformed.

Electroforming is economical for making parts that have special features that are difficult to produce by more common methods. It is advantageous for complex (inside and outside) shapes with thin walls, for laminating metals without heat or pressure, for producing fine and precise details and openings (e.g., quite small holes), and for incorporating inserts and flanges (metallic and nonmetallic) difficult to attach otherwise. Walls can be made as thin as a few micrometers to 50 mm but seldom are over 15 mm (0.0001 to 2 in. but seldom over $\frac{1}{2}$ in.). Tolerances have been held to a fraction of the wavelength of light in electroforming diffraction gratings, and those of the order of 25 μm (0.001 in.) are commonplace, with surface finishes of 50 to 200 nm (2 to 8 μin.) R_a.

Vacuum Deposition.   Methods for thin coatings of metals and many compounds on metallic and nonmetallic (e.g., plastic, glass, and ceramic) materials are of two kinds: vapor deposition and plasma deposition.

The common vapor deposition process is *evaporated* or *vacuum metalizing* in which aluminum (most often) is flash heated in a high-vacuum chamber containing the work and condenses on all directly exposed surfaces. The film is relatively thin, from 25 to 125 nm (1 to 5 μin.) and closely reproduces the shape and finish of the original surface, which is commonly precoated with one or two layers of lacquer. A final lacquer or enamel coating may be applied after metalizing to protect and even to tint the light metallic film.

Most plasma deposition is called *sputtering,* but there are several forms of the process. Typically, the work is placed near the plating material (called the target) in a chamber that is first evacuated and then given a light backfill of inert gas. A negative potential is applied to the target, and the gas is ionized. The gas ions are attracted to the target with sufficient kinetic energy to knock metallic atoms from its surface. These atoms are driven to the work with enough energy to bind them to the surface, where they form a film as they collect. If a fraction of reactive gas is admitted to the chamber, metallic compounds can be formed and deposited on the work surface.

In a two-step operation called *ion plating,* the workpiece is reverse-sputtered in an inert-gas atmosphere. This means that the work is given a negative potential and is highly bombarded by gaseous ions, which clean its surface thoroughly. Then the plating material in the chamber is heated until atoms evaporate from its surface and are ionized and driven to plate the work surface.

Films may be deposited in a vacuum from a few angstroms to about 25 μm (0.001 in.) thick to serve as decorative surfaces on costume jewelry, automobile trim, toys, etc., as reflective and insulating layers on many products, for optical surfaces, and on electronic components. Coatings up to 150 μm (0.006 in.) thick give good corrosion and oxidation resistance. Solid film lubricants can be plasma deposited. Vacuum deposition methods can produce thinner films than usually are obtained by electroplating and use less material and energy. These methods do not create pollution problems.

All the vapor deposition methods can be applied to any nongasing surface, but ion plating is more difficult on nonconducting and heat-sensitive materials. If the part is complex or must be coated on more than one surface, it is usually rotated for complete and uniform coverage. Film adhesion is good on ordinary clean surfaces and excellent on sputter-cleaned surface; that is a normal part of the ion plating method.

Each vacuum deposition method has certain unique advantages. Vacuum metalizing is best suited to coating with pure metals with moderate melting points. Alloys require special techniques because their constituents evaporate at different temperatures. Vacuum metalizing is fast; a large batch of parts can be treated in a few seconds plus 5 to 15 minutes for drawing a vacuum, and continuous coating, such as on long strips, is done. However, equipment cost is high (an installation with a capacity of 10,000 or so parts per hour may cost $100,000 or more) but is justified for large-quantity production. Sputtering is only $\frac{1}{20}$ or so as fast as vacuum metalizing but is able to deposit almost any material, e.g., refractory metals, stainless steel, Pyrex, quartz, and Teflon. Film thickness can be held to $\pm 5\%$ for uniformity and to 10 nm (<0.5 μin.) for size tolerance. The workpiece is not heated, and its material integrity is upheld when subject to sputtering. On the other hand, the workpiece is heated when ion plated, and heat-sensitive materials cannot be so treated. Ion plating is suitable for applying elemental metals to surfaces and has a deposition rate between sputtering and vacuum metalizing.

Other Metal-Coating Processes. Metal-coating operations that utilize welding techniques are described in the sections on metal spraying and surfacing, and hard facing in Chap. 14.

Chemical reduction or *electroless plating* is the means of precipitating metal from a chemical solution to form bright films for mirrors and reflectors and as a basis for further electroplating. A variant of the process precipitates a nickel-phosphorus matrix impregnated with blocky-diamond powder to produce a highly wear resistant surface. In the process called *chemophoresis,* a latex film about 25 μm (0.001 in.) thick is chemically deposited on steel and cured by baking.

In *chemical vapor deposition* (CVD) or *gas plating,* a metal halide in an inert-gas or hydrogen stream is passed over a workpiece, heated to 500 to 2000°C (ca. 900 to 3600°F) and deposits the metal or compound on the surface. This process deposits metals and their compounds not readily suited to electroplating or mechanical working, such as the refractory metals, their compounds, and ceramics and is used for coating, plating, and electroless forming of such products as tubing, crucibles, cutting and forming tools, and electronic components. Common specific usage in industry is coating of alloy and tool steels, stainless and heat-resisting steels, and cemented carbide with super hard titanium carbide, titanium nitride, chromium carbide, and aluminum oxide singly or in various combinations. The process has good throwing power and can reproduce fine details faithfully. The substrate material must be capable of withstanding the process temperatures. It has a deposition rate about one-half that of vacuum metalizing but a relatively high cost for materials and equipment.

A *diffusion* or *cementation coating* is a hard and often brittle alloy-rich surface layer formed by heating a piece of metal in intimate contact with another metal in powder, liquid, or gaseous form. The purpose is to obtain corrosion resistance, in some cases against oxidation at high temperatures. Particular processes of this kind are *sherardizing* for zinc on steel, *chromizing* for chromium on steel, *calorizing* for aluminum on steel, *siliconizing* for hard iron surfaces, and *Nicrocoating* with a nickel chrome matrix containing other metals or ceramics.

Layers of corrosion-resistant metals may be added to base metals by heating and rolling and thus welding sheets together or applying a powder coating and heating to effect diffusion. This is known as *cladding*. Common examples are aluminum alloys *alclad* with soft aluminum, and steel clad with stainless steel, Monel, Inconel, aluminum, or copper in plates, sheets, strips, tubing, and wire.

Mechanical plating is done by depositing powdered zinc, cadmium, tin, or lead on a surface and consolidating it into a continuous uniform coating by the rolling action of glass beads in a vibrating and agitated mass or revolving barrel. Coatings from 2.5 to 50 μm (0.0001 to 0.002 in.) thick are obtainable with adhesion, corrosion resistance, and cost comparable to electroplated coatings. A particular advantage of mechanical plating is that there is no hydrogen absorption and embrittlement that weakens tough steels.

Vitreous Coatings.   Vitreous (porcelain or ceramic) enamel is a hard, glass-like, inorganic coating 75 to 250 μm (0.003 to 0.010 in.) thick fused to metal. The main ingredients are a finely ground frit of silicates, feldspar alumina for ceramics, fluxes like borax and soda ash, and various metallic oxides for coloring and other properties. They are applied commonly to certain grades of sheet steel called enameling irons but also to copper and bronze, stainless steel, refractory metals, cast iron, and aluminum. One process is to mix the ingredients with clay and water and apply the resulting *slip* by spraying, dipping, flow-coating, or brushing. The coat is fired at 500 to 900°C (ca. 900 to 1650°F) depending on the substrate. Ceramic coatings are also applied by flame spraying as described in Chap. 14.

Vitreous coatings are smooth, hard, lustrous, and resist high temperatures but are subject to chipping and cracking. They are used for food preparation and health service equipment, major appliances, containers to resist chemical attack, on surfaces to resist wear and abrasion, and jet engine combustion chambers and exhausts.

QUESTIONS

1. What are the principal cleaning fluids, and for what is each best suited?
2. What is the difference between electrolytic and electrosonic cleaning?
3. Why is spraying more effective than dipping for cleaning?
4. Describe vapor degreasing and state its advantages.

5. What is pickling, and what precautions must be taken with it?
6. What are conversion coatings? Describe the principal ones.
7. How do anodic coatings differ from other conversion coatings?
8. What are organic coatings, and why are they popular?
9. Describe four major types of paint and their uses.
10. Describe the important industrial painting methods.
11. What are the benefits of electrostatic painting, and how is it done?
12. On what basis should a paint be selected?
13. Why and how are ferrous articles galvanized?
14. Cite examples from your experience of at least four different applications of plating.
15. Describe the principle of electroplating and specify the factors that influence its operation.
16. What can be done to help put a uniform plate on an object?
17. Why are some articles plated with several metals?
18. How can plating cause embrittlement of steel, and how can it be alleviated?
19. Describe the common methods of plating.
20. What is electroforming, and what are its advantages?
21. Describe the process of vacuum metalizing and its uses.
22. Why is vacuum metalizing suitable only for large-quantity production?
23. Briefly describe chemical reduction, chemical vapor deposition, diffusion coating, cladding, and mechanical plating.
24. How are vitreous coatings applied, and what are their advantages?

PROBLEMS

1. A manufacturer is planning to produce an item at the rate of 50,000 pieces/yr. Each piece has an area of $\frac{1}{3}$ m^2 (3.6 ft^2) and will be painted with two coats. Paint loss is 15%. A baking enamel that meets requirements costs 32 cents/m^2 (3 cents/ft^2) for 25 μm (0.001 in.) thickness dry, and each coat is 38 μm (0.0015 in.) thick. A lacquer that is satisfactory costs 59 cents/m^2 (5.5¢/ft^2) per 25 μm (0.001 in.) thickness dry. A total thickness of 100 μm (0.004 in.) is needed for the lacquer. If the manufacturer chooses to use the enamel, how much can he afford to spend per year to bake the enamel? It is assumed that the cost of spraying either paint is the same.

2. Calculate the applied cost, line 11, from Table 30-1 for:
   (a) Waterborne paint in $/m^2.
   (b) High-solids paint in $/m^2.
   (c) Polyester powder paint in $/m^2.
   (d) Waterborne paint in $/ft^2.
   (e) High-solids paint in $/ft^2.
   (f) Polyester powder paint in $/ft^2.

3. An automobile bumper has an area of 1.4 m^2 (15 ft^2) and is to receive a copper plate 12 μm (0.0005 in.) thick. Copper has an atomic weight of 63.57, in this case a valence of 1, and a specific weight of 8.92 g/cm^3 (5.16 oz/in.^{3}). The cathode efficiency is 50%. The process

operates nominally at 6 V. How much copper and electrical energy are used for each bumper? How long should be the plating time for an allowable current density of 130 A/m^2 (12 A/ft^2)?

4. An automobile bumper has an area of 1.4 m^2 (15 ft^2) and is to receive a nickel plate 12.5 μm (0.0005 in.) thick. Nickel has an atomic weight of 58.69, a valence of 2, and a specific weight of 8.81 g/cm^3 (5.09 oz/in.^{3}). The cathode efficiency is 95%. The process operates nominally at 6 V. How much nickel and electrical energy are used for each bumper? How long should be the plating time for an allowable current density of 270 A/m^2 (ca. 25 A/ft^2)?

5. An automobile bumper has an area of 1.4 m^2 (15 ft^2) and is to receive a final chromium plate 0.5 μm (0.00002 in.) thick. Chromium has an atomic weight of 52.01, a valence of 6, and a specific weight of 6.9 g/cm^3 (4 oz/in.^{3}). The cathode efficiency is 15%. The process operates nominally at 6 V. How much chromium and electrical energy are used for each bumper? How long should be the plating time for an allowable current density of 1600 A/m^2 (ca. 150 A/ft^2)?

6. Instead of plating copper and nickel on a bumper as specified in Probs. 3 and 4, the requirements can be met by a single nickel plate 25 μm (0.001 in.) thick. In either case, a final chromium plate of 0.5 μm (0.00002 in.) must be applied. Copper costs $1.54/kg ($0.70/lb). Nickel costs $4.63/kg ($2.10/lb). Electricity costs 13 cents/kWh. Under what conditions would you recommend the single nickel plate rather than one of copper and one of nickel?

7. A system is being designed to cadmium-plate parts to a thickness of 12.5 μm (0.0005 in.) at a rate of 65 m^2/h (700 ft^2/hr). Cadmium has an atomic weight of 112.41, a valence of 2, and density of 8.64 g/cm^3 (5 oz/in.^{3}). The system operates with a cathode efficiency of 90%. What must be the minimum capacity rating in kWh of the dc generator at 6 V potential? If the current density must be 215 A/m^2 (20 A/ft^2), how many m^2 (ft^2) of work must the tank be able to accommodate at one time?

8. An electrostatic spray gun and accessories cost $4000 but save 30% of the paint used at $1.32/L ($5/gal).
   (a) If interest, taxes, etc., are neglected, how much paint must be sprayed to pay for the equipment?
   (b) If interest, insurance, and taxes are 20% per year, how much paint must be sprayed in 1 year to pay for the equipment?

REFERENCES

BONETTI, R., "Hard Coatings for Improved Tool Life," *Metal Progress,* June 1981, p. 44.

BREMER, R. C., "Mechanical Plating," *Machine Design,* Sept. 20, 1973, p. 162.

———, "Chlorinated Metal Cleaning Solvents: Metalworking's Two-Edged Sword," *American Machinist,* June 1977.

COVINO, C. P., "Slippery, Steel-Hard Coatings for Metals," *Machine Design,* Aug. 25, 1977, p. 75.

DALLAS, D. B., ed., *Tool and Manufacturing Engineers Handbook, 3d. ed.,* Society of Manufacturing Engineers, Dearborn, Mich., 1976.

DREGER, D. R. "Paints That Don't Pollute," *Machine Design,* Feb. 21, 1974.

———, "Diamond-Studded Coatings Improve Part Life," *Machine Design,* Nov. 24, 1977, p. 95.

EVANS, R. E., "Finishes for Aluminum," *Machine Design,* Oct. 4, 1973, p. 156.

KUEHNER, M. A., "Selecting Conversion Coatings," *Machine Design,* Mar. 5, 1970.

Metals Handbook, Vol.5; *Surface Cleaning, Finishing, and Coating,* 9th ed., American Society for Metals, Metals Park, Ohio, 1982.

"Preparing Metals for Paint," *American Machinist,* June 15, 1970.

ST. JOHN, W., "Powder Coating," *Mechanical Engineering,* Feb. 1974.

SPALVINS, T., "Sputtering—A Vacuum Deposition Method for Coating Material," *ASME Paper 72-DE-37.*

STAUFFER, R. N., "Surface Modified Metals," *Manufacturing Engineering,* Sept. 1981, p. 104.

"Using Electroless Nickel Plating, " *American Machinist,* Sept. 1977, p. 143.

VACCARI, J. A., "Changing Paints to Limit Emissions," *American Machinist,* July 1982, p. 119.

WHITE, J. M., "Plating with a Brush," *Machine Design,* Oct. 2, 1975, p. 72.

31

CHEMICAL AND ELECTRICAL METHODS OF REMOVING MATERIALS

Most of the processes for molding, forming, joining, and cutting materials have been around for many years. Newer techniques that have been developed are called *nontraditional, nonconventional, layless,* or *nonmechanical machining*. These include electron, plasma, and laser-beam cutting and welding described in Chap. 14 and abrasive flow, abrasive jet, water jet, and ultrasonic machining of Chap. 29. Among others is one group that is basically electrical, for hard materials that cannot be cut easily, if at all, by mechanical means. This group includes electrodischarge machining (EDM), electrodischarge wire cutting (EDWC), electrodischarge grinding (EDG), electrochemical machining (ECM), electrochemical grinding (ECG), electrochemical discharge machining (ECDM), and electrochemical honing (ECH). A second group removes metal by etching or eating it away chemically, in the photoetching and chemical milling operations.

OPERATIONS FOR CUTTING HARD MATERIALS

Electrodischarge Machining. EDM is a means of shaping hard metals and forming deep and complex shaped holes by arc erosion in all kinds of electro-conductive materials. Older EDM machines employed *resistance-capacitance (RC)* or relaxation circuits where energy is built up on a capacitor and discharged repeatedly across a gap. Solid-state circuitry depicted in Fig. 31-1 has proven to be more efficient and faster. The tool is brought close to the workpiece surface, e.g., 25 μm (0.001 in.), and the gap is filled with a dielectric fluid. When the transistor bank is triggered by the timing control, the potential polarizes a path over which direct current from the

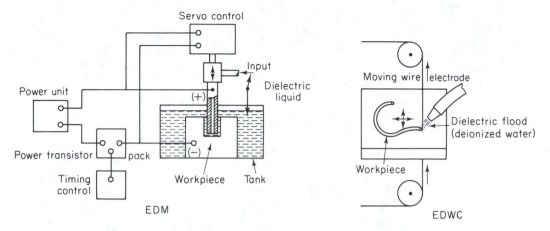

Figure 31-1   Elements of an EDM system.

power unit (such as a generator or rectifier) flows as a spark between the closest points of the electrode and workpiece. A minute amount of metal is melted and expelled where the spark strikes the workpiece, leaving a tiny crater, as evidenced by the pocked surface produced and the globular form of the debris. Wear also occurs on the electrode. The more the energy in a pulse (i.e., the more current supplied to the arc), the bigger the chunk torn from the workpiece; too much may create fissures and damage the piece and is inefficient. A good finish requires light sparking that leaves small craters. The amount of current depends upon the number of transistors activated in the bank (because each transistor carries only so much current) and the duration of pulse (spark) by the setting of the timer to turn the transistors on and off. When one pair of points (closest together) is blasted away by the arc, another pair becomes the closest and the next pulse sends a spark between them, and so on. Thus the arcing and material removal move around in the gap between the electrode and workpiece. The reverse polarity with the workpiece negative shown in Fig. 31-1 is commonly used for roughing, but straight polarity with the workpiece positive is favored for some applications, especially for finishing.

The timer of an EDM system acts to initiate a series of pulses through the course of an operation and regulates the length of each pulse and the time between pulses. These intervals and the amount of current are preset for most systems, but in some systems are varied during the operation to optimize performance through adaptive control circuitry. With time in microseconds, the pulses are quite short and occur at high frequencies. In one system, pulse lengths and time between pulses can be set separately in increments from 1 to 2999 microseconds; others have coarser controls. Fine settings provide close control for finishing. Some machines have means to group series of pulses into short trains with adjustable intervals between the groups. This gives the controls more time to correct for abnormal conditions such as excessive sparking or short circuiting when they happen.

The gap between tool and workpiece is maintained by a servo control device governed by the voltage across the gap at the time of spark discharge. In some systems the tool is given a pulsating motion to avoid dwell of the arc in one spot for too long and help flush away the fluid. This allows the use of more current and a higher metal removal rate; as much as four times is claimed in one case. Instead of being fed straight in as is common, the tool can be *orbited* on some machines; i.e., the tool is rotated about an eccentric axis under servo control to sweep a shape larger than itself, cut up or down tapers, undercuts, or other profiles. On some machines the tools can be moved in square or rectangular paths or straight lines as they are fed into the work. The workpiece, not the tool, is orbited in some systems. In addition to being able to form cavities of many shapes (some difficult by other means), orbiting helps the EDM action by stirring and flushing the electrolyte and helps distribute wear on the electrode, enhancing accuracy and finish. As a tool wears, size can be held by increasing the orbit.

The fluid bath around the tool and workpiece performs several functions. As a dielectric, it supports the voltage to assure a high buildup of energy for each discharge. Then the fluid and the impurities in it supply ions for the path of the arc. The heat of the spark instantaneously vaporizes and decomposes the fluid in its path. The fluid inertia resists rapid expansion and causes a high pressure in the discharge column that intensifies the arc, where temperatures are reported in tens of thousands of degrees, and expels the molten metal. The fluid then serves to chill and solidify and flush away the debris and cool the tool and workpiece. A copious flow of fluid is desirable; common practice is to immerse tool and workpiece in a bath and pump fluid through holes in the electrode. Light mineral oils, such as kerosene or lubricating oil, are satisfactory fluids for most cases. For particular applications, additives or water compounds have been found helpful. Some impurities are desirable, but filtering is necessary to prevent too much contamination.

Zinc-tin, copper, and tungsten alloys, cemented carbides, aluminum, steel, and graphite, and sometimes other materials are all used for electrodes to suit various conditions. One may perform better than others with a certain work material. Electrodes may be machined in conventional ways. A number of identical electrodes may be needed to make copies of a forging die, for instance, and zinc-tin alloys are economical for such a purpose because they can be cast and coined easily in a master die. Graphite is cheap and easily machined, provides fast metal removal, and is mostly used.

The factors that determine the performance of an EDM operation are the amount of electrical current supplied, I_s, the proportion of the time during which current flows, and the voltage across the gap at the arc. Let t_i be the time the current is on during any one pulse. Mostly this is a preset amount, t_p, but may be less than t_p in some pulses that are delayed, e.g., for slow ionization. Also, there is an idle time set for each cycle. Then the total time that the current, I_s, flows during a substantial period, p, is $\Sigma\ t_i$, and the effective average current is $I_e = I_s\ (\Sigma\ t_i/p)$. The rate of metal removal is large for a large effective current and smaller for a smaller effective current.

For any supplied voltage, there is a maximum gap beyond which the dielectric will not become sufficiently ionized and no discharge will occur. For example, if

100 V is applied to two points closest together but 25 μm (0.001 in.) apart, the dielectric ionizes between the points, and an arc ensues that transmits all the current that is supplied. (The numbers are likely to be different in another case.) For any smaller gap, the arc voltage is almost proportionately smaller, e.g., 40 V for 10 μm (0.0004 in.). These numbers are purely hypothetical for illustrations and what they would be in any case depends upon the circumstances. The operator adjusts the servo-feed device to seek a desired gap potential. In adhering to that potential, the servo maintains a constant gap as it feeds the electrode into the workpiece. Some of the pulses misfire because of impurities in the electrolyte and other factors; more when the gap is large than when it is small. Consequently, for a given input, the effective current increases and so does the rate of metal removal as the gap is held smaller, up to a peak, usually where I_e is about 90% of maximum. Any smaller gap appears to impede removal of debris, etc., and performance goes down. Empirical equations and charts have been derived for various electrode-workpiece material combinations and systems and are available to guide an operator to find optimum settings for the EDM machine. The most advanced systems include programmable controllers (Chap. 34) with memories for storing data on operation parameters and with the ability to apply these data as needed to optimize the action. An average stock removal rate is around 0.8 cm^3/Ah (0.05 in.^{3}/Ah) of nominal current for roughing. This means a removal rate of 16 cm^3/h (1 in.^{3}/hr) on a machine with a 20-A capacity. For finishing, the metal removal rate may be one-third to one-half as much.

The electrode is usually held at positive polarity for machining steel, aluminum, cast iron, and some super alloys and wears mostly from loss of ions during the initial stage of each cycle. This is a small part of the action during heavy but not excessive roughing cuts. Some metal removed from the workpiece can be made to adhere to the tool to compensate for wear. Thus under proper conditions and control in roughing, tool wear can be made so small that some machine makers claim practically "no wear," but it is seldom possible to achieve the ideal in production. On the other hand, tool wear is relatively severe for light finishing cuts but surface finishes are better. An EDM tool wears most at corners and edges, so these should be rounded, and small corners avoided as much as possible in the design of the workpiece.

Size can be held quite closely in EDM, but precision costs more. A hole sunk by conventional EDM has the same shape as the tool; a round tool makes a round hole, etc. An electrode with a sculptured cameo form produces an intaglio of the same form in the workpiece. With numerical control, a simple tool can be moved with respect to the work, or visa versa, to EDM a complex surface. The amount of gap between tool and workpiece, called the *overcut,* determines the size of the cut. The gap may range from about 5 μm (0.0002 in.) to 175 μm (0.007 in.) or so, but is usually between 25 μm (0.001 in.) and 75 μm (0.003 in.). The higher the rate of metal removal, the larger the overcut must be because the heavy spark discharges clear away more metal from the sides and space is needed to clear away large chips.

The accuracy obtained in EDM depends largely upon the accuracy of the tool, the wear it gets during operation, and control of the overcut. The more accurate the tool, the more its cost. If tool wear is to be kept small in finishing, the stock removal must be kept small. For a constant set of conditions, the overcut can be held uniformly to a tolerance within 5 μm (0.0002 in.) around the tool if the overcut is small. A common practice is to take roughing and finishing cuts with a series of fresh electrodes, just like several cuts for conventional machining. Typical tolerances held on forging dies are ±75 μm (±0.003 in.) with three consecutive electrodes to ±25 μm (±0.001 in.) with seven. In other work, as little as ±2.5 μm (±0.0001 in.) tolerance has been reported under carefully controlled conditions.

Another major consideration is surface finish, which depends upon how fast the work is done. Low-energy discharges that leave small craters are necessary for fine finishes. The rate of stock removal is then slow. Surfaces have been reported finished to less than 250 nm (10 μin.) R_a at removal rates of 50 mm³/h (0.003 in.³/hr), but 750 nm (30 μin.) to 4 μm (ca. 150 μin.) R_a may be expected at ordinary rates. However, an EDM surface has no *lay* like a mechanically cut surface, can hold lubricity, and for some purposes is better than a conventional surface with the same or less measured roughness.

Some serious shortcomings of EDM must be recognized and controlled. Surface porosity can result from EDM on sulfurized steel or from sulfurized cutting oils on the surface from previous operations. Of more importance, a carbon-enriched white layer from 2.5 μm (0.0001 in.) for light cuts to 125 μm (0.005 in.) for heavy cuts is left on hardenable steel by EDM. This is metal that has been melted and resolidified. Beneath that layer there is frequently a second layer of hardened or rehardened steel, usually deeper than the first. Below these two layers is a gradually tempered zone that may range in depth from 50 μm (0.002 in.) to 750 μm (ca. 0.030 in.). A too severe EDM operation may leave microcracks in the surface. Grinding an EDM surface may cause surface microcracks to develop and propagate under stress. EDM surfaces are quite hard and wear resistant but brittle, and fatigue strength may be cut more than in half. A surface may be improved by light and slow EDM after roughing. Stresses may be relieved by annealing, and impaired surfaces may be removed by careful grinding, lapping, or electrochemical milling.

A typical EDM machine looks like a vertical knee- and column-type milling machine with a ram or quill instead of a cutter spindle and with a tank on the table for the dielectric fluid. Many EDM machines have been made by converting vertical milling machines. Precision adjustments are provided in coordinate directions. On very large machines, the tool may be mounted on a platen on posts. Means are provided to circulate and filter the fluid. Most modern machines have solid-state power supplies and controls. Multiple-tool EDM machines for production have a variable number of separate electrodes, usually on a single machine head with one servo system and connected to a single power supply. Thus a number of parts (up to 50 are reported) can be machined at once for a low unit cost. Transfer machines (Chap. 34) are also built for EDM; one with five stations is used for drilling small holes in jet engine components. A small general-purpose EDM machine rated at 25 A is quoted at about $34,000. Power and control units with capacities up to hundreds of amperes are available, especially for production. Powerful numerically controlled EDM machines may cost hundreds of thousands of dollars.

EDM is at an advantage for cutting hard materials, internal shapes (particularly if hard to reach), shapes difficult to generate, and delicate pieces. It can reproduce any shape that can be cut into a tool, and mechanically making a tool and sinking a cavity by EDM may thus be easier than carving out the cavity. It is too slow to compete with conventional machining of common materials, particularly for simple shapes. On the other hand, EDM removes stock almost as fast as grinding from cemented carbide, and even faster than grinding from some of the space-age materials. Sinking and resinking of forging dies from hardened steel has become almost a monopoly for EDM. One forge shop reports the two halves of a crankshaft forging die took 122 hours by conventional machining but only 68.8 hours by EDM on a 200-A machine. Quantity production applications of EDM are growing, e.g., cutting fine and out-of-the-way slots and holes without burrs and to close tolerances in carburetors. With no physical contact and therefore no forces between tool and workpiece, frail pieces such as honeycomb structures can be machined without distortion. An example of a task particularly amenable to EDM is the cutting of 100 holes of 0.008 in. diam, 0.010 in. between centers, with 0.002 in. wall thickness between holes, to tolerances in ten-thousandths of an inch in molybdenum.

A variation of the process, called *electrodischarge grinding (EDG),* utilizes a graphite grinding wheel as an electrode for cutting carbide form tools, thin and closely spaced slots, and the like.

Electrodischarge wire cutting (EDWC) is a variation of EDM done in the manner indicated on the right of Fig. 31-1. A moving wire between spools and rolls is kept taut by a tensioning device, serves as an electrode, and passes in near contact with the workpiece. Conventionally, the wire is copper of 200, 150, or 100 μm (0.008, 0.006, or 0.004 in.) diameter or 50 μm (0.002 in.) diameter molybdenum. Since the wire is used only once, wear is not a factor. The workpiece is moved in the x and y directions perpendicular to the wire by numerical control (Chap. 35), and any path can be readily traversed. A third or "steering" axis may be provided to tilt the work with respect to the wire to cut, taper, draft, or relief. The rate of metal removal is governed by the same factors as in conventional EDM, and the rate of travel depends on the thickness of the workpiece. An EDWC machine rating in cm^2/h or in.^{2}/hr designates the area of one side of the cut made in a unit time. Thus, with a die block 25 mm thick, a rate of 15 cm^2/h is equivalent to feed along the path of cut of 60 mm/h.

Inside and outside shapes can be cut by EDWC. Common work includes blanking dies, prototype parts, and EDM electrodes. Carbide blanking or progressive dies previously had to be made in accurately ground sections and carefully fitted together but can be produced much more quickly as whole units by EDWC. Tolerances as small as 5 μm (0.0002 in.) are commonly held. Average surface finish obtained is estimated to be from 650 to 1150 nm (ca. 25 to 45 μin.) R_a.

EDWC can do some work better than other methods; tool cost is negligible and the process can be run for long periods without operator attention. Some shops let a machine run on a long cut for a whole weekend with reported good results. However, the machines are expensive; they combine EDM with numerical control. One with about a 25-A output and capacity of 26 cm²/h (4 in.²/hr) has a base price of $60,000. Another rated at 50 cm²/h (ca. $7\frac{1}{2}$ in.²/hr) costs $129,000.

Electrochemical Machining. ECM, also called *electrolytic machining*, removes metal essentially by deplating. Its commonest application is in the sinking of holes and cavities in the manner depicted in Fig. 31-2. Electrolyte is pumped through a gap from less than 25 μm (0.001 in.) to over 250 μm (0.010 in.) thick between the tool (the cathode) and the workpiece (the anode). The electrical current drains electrons from the workpiece surface and releases ions. In plating the metal, ions are carried to and deposited on the cathode, but in ECM those ions combine with hydroxil ions of the solution and form a sludge that is swept away by the flow of electrolyte. Hydrogen is liberated at the tool and no metal is removed or added there, so the tool does not change shape or size. The electrode (tool) is fed at a constant rate into the workpiece, and the hole or cavity is formed to the same shape as the tool. A hump may be left under the opening where the fluid is discharged into the gap and may have to be removed from a blind hole by a second operation but is eliminated ultimately from a through hole. The electrode is insulated to prevent electrolytic action and metal removal behind the tip and thus keep the hole straight, as indicated in Fig. 31-2. In some cases the electrode may be left bare and even given a particular profile to form draft or taper in a cavity.

The purposes of the electrolyte are to conduct electricity, chemically combine with the metal ions and remove them, carry away heat, and give off gas and prevent plating at the tool. The commonest is a saltwater solution but other substances are added to improve effectiveness with various work materials and in certain operations and to inhibit corrosion and intergranular attack. The fluid is pumped at the rate of 75

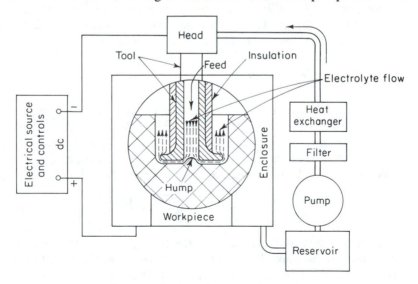

Figure 31-2 Elements of an ECM system.

to 375 liters/min (20 to 100 gal/min). To force it through passageways a fraction of a millimeter (a few thousandths of an inch) thick may take pressures of 1 to 2 MPa. (ca. 150 to 300 psi). Such pressures create large forces between tool and workpiece, which make sturdy tools and machines necessary. For example, a 150 × 150 mm (ca. 6 × 6 in.) projected area die cavity with a pressure of 1.5 MPa (217 psi) in the gap may create a force of 34 kN (ca. 7600 lb) between tool and work.

ECM performance can be estimated from Faraday's laws that the amount of metal removed is proportional to its equivalent weight and the current. Theoretically, 96,540 coulombs (A-s) takes off one equivalent weight, which is the atomic weight, N, divided by the valence, n. For a current of I amperes and material density of d g/cm^3, the rate of metal removal in cm^3/min is

$$M = \frac{60IN}{96,540nd} \tag{31-1}$$

As an example, the equivalent weight of iron (or steel) is $56/2$ and density 7.87 g/cm^3. If the current is 1000 A, the rate of metal removal $M = 60 \times 1000 \times 56/(96,540 \times 2 \times 7.87) = 2.2$ cm^3/min $= 0.13$ in.^{3}/min. Reports indicate efficiency between 70 and 90%. For most common metals, the attainable rate of metal removal is usually from 1.5 to 2.3 cm^3/min (0.1 to 0.14 in.^{3}/min) for each 1000 A of current. The lowest number is often used for conservative estimates. Exceptions include tungsten with a valence of 6 and magnesium with an atomic weight of 24.

The tool, workpiece, and electrolyte of ECM comprise an electrolytic cell governed by Ohm's law, and this determines the rate at which the work can be done. That means that for a given resistance of R ohms and potential E (usually 5 to 20 V) across the gap, $I = E/R$. Designate the gap thickness as γ cm, the area of cut as A cm^2, and the resistivity as $r\,\Omega$-cm. Then the resistance across the gap can be expressed as $R = \gamma r/A$. These two relationships combine to give

$$I = \frac{EA}{\gamma r} \tag{31-2}$$

The rate of metal removal $M = mA$, where m is the rate of recession (cm/min) of the work surface being removed. From Eq. (31-1), $M = CI$, in which the constant factors for a given operation are represented by C. Also, the rate of recession is assumed the same as the advance or feed of the tool, f in cm/min; i.e., $m = f$. Therefore, $m/C = f/C = I/A$. Substitute this relationship in Eq. (31-2) and solve for γ to get

$$\gamma = \frac{EA}{Ir} = \frac{EC}{fr} \tag{31-3}$$

This shows that as the feed is increased with all other factors constant, the gap decreases to maintain electrical and electrolytic equilibrium. It must be realized that actually there is not one uniform gap in an ECM operation. There are the frontal gap in the direction of feed, the side gap between the tool and cavity, and the normal gap between other surfaces. These gaps are not usually the same. The model for the ECM process being presented here assumes one uniform gap, which may be thought of as an average gap.

The question as to what is the best feed, f in mm/min or ipm, for the tool in an ECM operation does not have an exact answer. Experience has shown that the faster the feed, the better the accuracy and surface finish obtained and the higher the rate of production. There are two factors that limit the feed in any operation. One is the capacity of the electrolyte; the other is the capacity of the machine. Thus the best feed is the lower of the two feeds set by these limits.

The electrolyte limits the feed in an ECM operation when it no longer is able to conduct the current. Hydrogen is evolved at the cathode, and the electrolyte vaporizes in areas where it becomes hot enough to do so. Gases and vapors are not good conductors but normally are swept away, along with the sludge, where electrolyte flow is adequate. Equation (31-3) shows that the gap becomes smaller as the feed is increased. When the gap becomes so small that fluid flow is obstructed, current flow may be impeded by gases or vapors, potential is built up, and an arc ensues with likely catastrophic effects upon tool and workpiece. The feeds recommended in reference books and handbooks are those found to be on the safe side of electrolytic breakdown. Depending on size, shape, and configuration of cut and other factors, feeds generally are from 2.5 to 15 mm/min (0.1 to 0.6 ipm).

The current flow increases directly with the feed as shown by the relationship $f = CI/A$ in the derivation of Eq. (31-3). A machine can be set only to as much feed as the current it can deliver will support, to avoid overload. For example, consider a 50-mm-diameter hole to be cut by ECM in hardened steel. Experience indicates that the electrolyte can stand a feed of 10 mm/min in the system being used. To keep within the limit of the electrolyte, the rate of metal removal should be $25\pi/4 = 19.6\ \mathrm{cm^3/min}$. For a conservative estimating factor of 1.5 cm³/min/1000 A for current used, the current required is estimated to be $(19.6/1.5)1000 = 13,000$ A. If the machine is rated at 10,000 A, the feed must be reduced to $10/1.3 = 7.7$ mm/min to avoid overloading the system. The same considerations apply to estimating the time and energy required for an operation. The feed must first be ascertained as either that limited by electrolyte or that limited by machine capacity, whichever is lower. In the illustration, with a permissible feed of 7.7 mm/min and a hole depth of 2.5 cm, the time for the cut, $t = 2.5 \times 10/7.7 = 3.3$ min. If the voltage is to be set at 15 V, the energy for the cut at an overall efficiency of 75% is $W = [15 \times 10,000/(0.75 \times 1000)]3.3/60 = 11$ kWh.

Production of a good workpiece depends largely upon a uniform flow of electrolyte over all areas. If more electrolyte flows in one place, it removes more metal there than in another. Accurate results depend on proper design of the electrode and skillful control of the voltage, current, pressure, and other parameters of the operation. Copper and copper alloy electrodes are the most popular, for good conductivity, but other metals are used for specific purposes. Three common forms of tooling are shown in Fig. 31-3. Straight flow tooling is usually cheapest but does not provide enough fluid control for some jobs. Better surface finish and smaller tolerances are possible with reverse flow tooling. Mainly because of the need of dams and seals around the

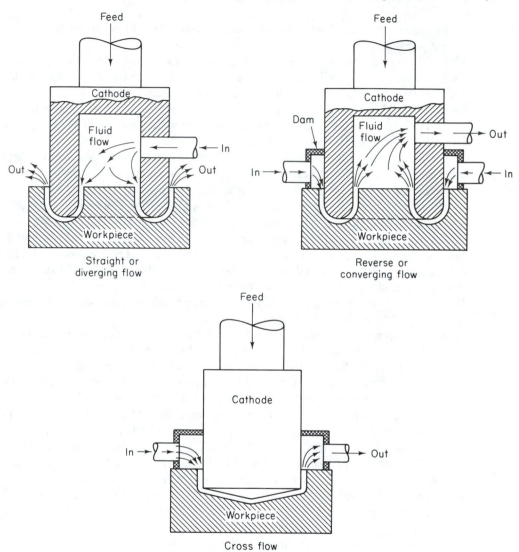

Figure 31-3 Typical ECM tooling.

work area, reverse flow tooling is more expensive to design and make. Cross-flow tooling is used on certain kinds of work, such as turbine blades. A fourth class of tooling, called compound or complex tooling, involves a combination of two or three of the basic types. Slots and holes for fluid must be carefully placed in a cathode for effective flow. For the most part electrode design and fabrication require special skills based on a thorough knowledge of ECM operations. There is no tool wear under normal conditions, and tool life is long.

A variation of ECM called *electroshaping* forms external surfaces in the manner depicted in Fig. 31-4. A tool ordinarily is made to encompass and machine a whole

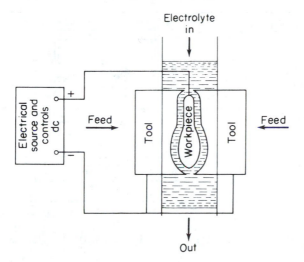

Electrolyte
in

+

Electrical
source and
controls
dc

Feed →

Tool

Workpiece

Tool

Feed ←

Out

Figure 31-4 Electroshaping system.

surface at one time. Another approach is to remove a slug of metal by cutting a groove around it with a thin-wall or bent tube electrode. *Wire cutting* is one name given to such an operation. In this role ECM may remove stock to reduce weight, produce thin sections [150 μm (0.006 in.) is common without distortion], and fabricate external stiffeners.

ECM accuracy depends upon control of several parameters of the operation, i.e., voltage, feed, fluid temperature and concentration, etc. Most important, these parameters must be kept constant during the operation. In any event, though, accuracy obtainable from ECM is limited. Distinction must be made between accuracy of tool frontal formed surfaces and side wall surfaces in an ECM cavity. Tolerances of ±7.5 μm (±0.0003 in.) have been reported under ideal conditions on tool frontal formed features, and sidewall tolerances of ±25 μm (±0.001 in.) in simple holes. However, ±25 to ±50 μm (±0.001 to ±0.002 in.) on surface substantially perpendicular to tool feed and ±125 μm (±0.005 in.) on wall dimensions, and up, are more usual tolerances. ECM naturally produces good surface finishes: better than 0.25 μm (10 μin.) R_a with care in many cases and seldom worse than 2 μm (80 μin.) R_a on frontal surfaces, but commonly as high as 6 μm (250 μin.) R_a on sidewalls. Much that can be done with ECM depends upon product design. Considerations to this end are suggested in Fig. 31-5.

ECM excells in some respects and is limited in others. It cuts most conductive materials well, no matter how hard they are, and can reproduce almost any shape inside or outside. Materials with many passive inclusions may not be amenable to the process; e.g., cast iron is not EC machined well because of the free graphite. A major advantage of ECM is that it does not damage the workpiece surface. The only affect ECM may have upon workpiece properties is that it may remove material previously stressed and thus cause distortion or detract from helpful compresive stresses. ECM leaves no burrs whatever and in modified forms is used to deburr parts machined by other methods. One form is called *electrochemical deburring* (ECD). Largely because of lack of burrs, ECM is popular for machining small-diameter and long holes,

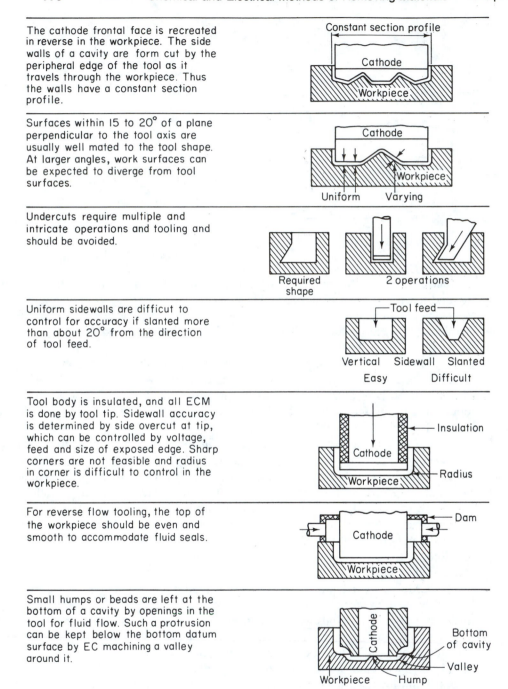

The cathode frontal face is recreated in reverse in the workpiece. The side walls of a cavity are form cut by the peripheral edge of the tool as it travels through the workpiece. Thus the walls have a constant section profile.

Surfaces within 15 to 20° of a plane perpendicular to the tool axis are usually well mated to the tool shape. At larger angles, work surfaces can be expected to diverge from tool surfaces.

Undercuts require multiple and intricate operations and tooling and should be avoided.

Uniform sidewalls are difficut to control for accuracy if slanted more than about 20° from the direction of tool feed.

Tool body is insulated, and all ECM is done by tool tip. Sidewall accuracy is determined by side overcut at tip, which can be controlled by voltage, feed and size of exposed edge. Sharp corners are not feasible and radius in corner is difficult to control in the workpiece.

For reverse flow tooling, the top of the workpiece should be even and smooth to accommodate fluid seals.

Small humps or beads are left at the bottom of a cavity by openings in the tool for fluid flow. Such a protrusion can be kept below the bottom datum surface by EC machining a valley around it.

Figure 31-5 Design considerations for ECM.

particularly in clusters. A variation of ECM for rather small holes, such as in turbine blades, is *shaped tube electrolytic machining* (STEM). Sludge formed by the salt electrolyte usual for ECM tends to clog small passages and impede the operation. STEM uses an acidic electrolyte that dissolves the metal, and the ions are easily carried away. For even smaller holes *electrostream machining* (ES) is a similar process with an acidic electrolyte but voltages 10 times or more than usual for ECM. It requires exceptionally close control. Hole diameters are reported to be 125 to 900 μm (0.005 to 0.035 in.) with depth-to-diameter ratios up to 40:1.

An ECM machine resembles a vertical press. Smaller machines have C-frames, some large ones two- or four-post frames to carry a vertical ram or quill for feeding the tool. Instead of a bolster or bed as on a press, an ECM machine has a table to carry the workpiece. An important part of the system is the means to deliver and contain the extremely corrosive electrolyte at high pressures. A tight compartment surrounds the work area; the slides and moving parts of the machine must be well protected, and pump and fittings are of stainless steel. The electrical equipment must supply heavy currents at constant voltage even under varying load with controls to prevent short circuits. All these factors make an ECM machine relatively expensive. A medium-size 10,000-A machine with power supply costs about $140,000.

Comparison of ECM with Other Processes.   ECM is not competitive with conventional methods for simple shapes, like round holes, in easily machinable materials. When either the shape or the material is hard to machine, ECM may have the advantage. It has been said that ECM can sink a hole in 450 Bhn steel as fast as a drill, and faster in harder material. When both shape and material are difficult to machine by conventional methods, ECM and EDM become likely contenders for the job.

EDM can hold tolerances too small for ECM, but in its range ECM is much faster. EDM works regularly in the tolerance range below 50 μm (0.002 in.) and ECM above that. On the other hand, what are ordinary surface finishes for ECM are obtainable only at the slowest EDM rates. If the accuracy it can deliver is acceptable, ECM equipment is commonly available for stock removal rates up to about 65 cm^3/min (4 in.^{3}/min), and average performance is around 15 cm^3/min (1 in.^{3}/min). In comparison, maximum EDM rates are less than 15 cm^3/min (1 in.^{3}/min.), and average performance only a small fraction as much. Even so, EDM is usually cheaper for a few pieces because the initial tool cost is high for ECM. A rule of thumb is that ECM is not economical for cavity work unless 20 or more identical pieces are needed.

Electrochemical Grinding.   Electrochemical grinding (ECG) or *electrolytic grinding* removes hard conductive materials partly by electrolytic attack, like ECM, and partly by conventional grinding. The proportion varies with the material and operation but is probably 90% or more by electrolytic action. The abrasive grains mainly scrape away weakened surface residue. With cemented carbide, for instance, the bonding material is dissolved, and the more resistant carbide skeleton is torn apart by the abrasive grains. The grinding wheel is the cathode and the workpiece the anode in a circuit like that in Fig. 31-6. Metal bonded diamond wheels are most common; aluminum oxide wheels with conductive bonds have been developed and are less costly. The abrasive grains support a gap of about 25 μm (0.001 in.) between the workpiece and wheel body. The electrolyte is usually poured on the point of operation, and a film is carried into the cut by the abrasive grains. One machine model with a 300-A power supply and rated to remove 0.3 cm^3/min (0.02 in.^{3}/min) of stock, costs about $20,000.

ECG may be as much as 80% faster than regular grinding but entails extra costs and normally is not economical unless either the workpiece or material, or both, is difficult to grind conventionally. In ECG, grinding force can be kept low, and frail and thin sections EC ground without distortion. Temperature is low and no metallurgical surface changes or residual stresses are induced by electrolytic grinding. Thus the process is faster (several times as fast for cemented carbides) and safer for grinding quite hard and sensitive materials that crack easily from conventional grinding. The process leaves no burrs. Wheel life is 10 times as long as without electrolysis, and tool cost is low because the wheel does little cutting. Much less wheel truing needs to be done, too.

In order to hold tolerances of less than about 25 μm (0.001 in.), ECG must be made to do essentially true grinding, and then all the advantages of the process are lost. In practice the aim is for tolerances of about $\pm$50 μm ($\pm$0.002 in.) or more. Surface finish from ECG is better than any other kind of grinding at the same stock removal rate; a satin finish (with little direction) of 125 to 250 nm (5 to 10 μin.) R_a is common.

Electrochemical discharge grinding (ECDG), also called *electrochemical discharge machining* (ECDM), is done with a nonabrasive and easily trued graphite wheel running adjacent to the workpiece in an electrolyte. The initial action is that of ECM but the residue is removed by electrical discharges (EDM) and not by abrasives as in ECG.

Electrochemical honing (ECH) for straight holes utilizes nonconducting abrasive stones like those shown in Fig. 29-2. The tool body is made the cathode and the workpiece the anode in an electrical circuit while a fine abrasive scrubs away film from the workpiece surface left by the electrochemical action. A similar but reversed process, called *Hone Forming* is described in Chap. 29.

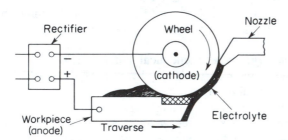

Figure 31-6 Electrolytic grinding system.

CHEMICAL MACHINING

Photo-Etching.   Photo-etching is known by a number of names, including photo-forming, photochemical machining (PCM), micro-milling, and chemical blanking, and utilizes photoengraving techniques practiced in printing for many years. Parts like those in Fig. 31-7 are made from flat 2.5 μm (0.0001 in.) foil up to sheets 3 mm (ca. $\frac{1}{8}$ in.) thick of some plastics and most metals, including alloys of aluminum, copper, and steel. The sheet is covered with a photosensitive resist on one or both sides and exposed in a camera to an image of the part or parts desired (commonly reduced as much as 20:1 for accuracy). The coating is developed to expose the lines or areas to be eaten away subsequently in an acid bath or high-pressure chemical spray. The resist may also be applied by printing. Pieces up to almost 2 m (ca. 6 ft) long have been made, but sizes less than about 100 $\times$ 150 mm (4 $\times$ 6 in.) are most common. Outlines may be laid down to less than 10 μm (0.0004 in.), but the edges eaten away are uneven and undercut, and tolerances from $\pm$10 to 50% of stock thickness, depending on material, shape, and size, are practicable.

For most parts, photo-etching is economical for quantities too large to be sheared out individually by hand but not large enough to justify the cost of a die. For instance, a radio manufacturer needed 100 small contactor leaves from sheet brass. They were made 25 to the sheet by photo-etching for a total cost of $75. A die alone could not have been made for that amount. A photo print master usually can be made for one-tenth of the cost of a die. The long lead time to make dies also can be saved. Changes in product design can be made easily because the photo-etching masters can be changed at little cost. Dies may be so expensive for parts that are quite complex or made from thin materials that electro-etching is justified for large quantities.

A complete set of equipment for batch photochemical machining of areas up to

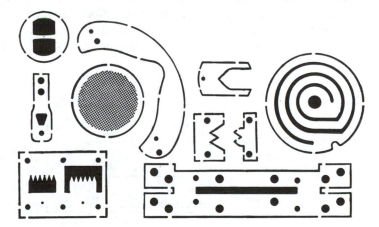

Figure 31-7   Examples of precision parts made from sheet metal by photo-etching. (Courtesy Buckbee Mears Co.)

0.6 m (2 ft) square, including all photographic, darkroom, developing, and etching needs, costs over $50,000.

Electrogel Machining (EGM).   EGM is an electrolytic process for removing metal in definite shapes by means of a formed tool made of a stiff gel consisting of cellulose acetate and acid. The molded gel is held against the workpiece as shown in Fig. 31-8 and as a current (about 8 A at 2.5 V) is passed through the stack, the pattern on the gel is etched in the workpiece at a rate of about 25 μm/min (0.001 in./min). Forces are negligible, and there is no effect on the structure of the metal; the mild operation is suited for frail pieces like those made from thin metal honeycomb structures. Steel and nickel alloys, titanium, and high-temperature heat-resistant alloys have been found amenable to the process.

Chemical Milling.   Chemical milling is the name given to a patented process for removing large amounts of stock by etching selected areas of complex workpieces. It was developed in the aircraft industry as one means of fabricating lightweight parts of large areas and thin sections but has been receiving attention in other industries. One kind of part chemically milled is the wing bulkhead depicted in Fig. 31-9. The large cavities are formed by removing metal from a thick slab.

Chemical milling entails four steps: cleaning, masking, etching, and demasking. Maskant of neoprene rubber or vinyl plastic is sprayed or flowed over all surfaces and baked. It is then slit to a template and stripped from the areas to be etched. Different surfaces can be milled to different depths by removing parts of the maskant at different times during the process.

The size of workpiece that can be treated is limited only by the size of the tank into which it is dipped for etching. Caustic soda is the usual etchant for aluminum, and acids for steel, magnesium, and titanium alloys. The action proceeds at the rate of about 25 μm/min (0.001 in./min) in the solution if proper concentration is maintained. A black smut that occurs may be removed by deoxidizing and rinsing. A variation of the process is to withdraw a long piece slowly from the etching tank to make a tapered or conical part.

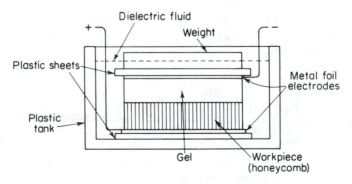

Figure 31-8   Electrogel machining operation.

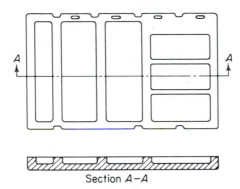

Figure 31-9 Aircraft wing bulkhead chemically milled.

Section A–A

Tolerances of ±25 μm (±0.001 in.) have been reported obtainable in chemical milling but ±1.5 mm (±0.060 in.) on length and width and +0.125 to 0.000 mm (+0.005 to 0.000 in.) on depth and thickness are more practical. Surface finish ranges from 0.8 to 3 μm (ca. 30 to 125 μin.) R_a. The deeper the cut, the rougher the finish, but finer-grain material etches more smoothly.

Chemical milling can be done on all kinds of parts: rolled sections, forgings, castings, and preformed pieces. It is not limited by shape, direction of cut, or cutter, and different sizes and shapes of cuts can be made at one time. Both sides of a sheet can be cut at one time to minimize warping and cost. There are no burrs. The evidence points to a higher fatigue strength after chemical milling because of lack of scratches and no residual stresses. Chemical milling is advantageous for complex cuts and parts and makes feasible the future design of many more such parts where needed but is not superior for simple straightforward work because that can usually be done more economically on regular machine tools. Scrap rates are low (less than 3% reported). There are some disadvantages. Only shallow cuts are practical, less than 15 mm (ca. 0.5 in.) usually. Handling and disposal of the chemicals may be a problem.

Chemical milling is simple and amenable to automatic operation. Equipment preparation time and costs are low. In one aircraft plant the usual period of three months to tool an average part for production has been reduced to less than one month where chemical milling is applicable. Masking costs may be high for each piece and chemicals add to the direct costs. Even so, chemical milling is economical in many cases. One manufacturer reported a cost of $9.36/piece for chemical milling as against $25/piece for machine milling in 60- to 150-piece lots.

QUESTIONS

1. How is electrodischarge machining done?
2. What are the advantages and disadvantages of electrodischarge machining?
3. Describe the ECM process.
4. How do EDM and ECM compare with each other?

5. Describe ECG.

6. When is ECG preferable to conventional grinding?

7. What is photo-etching, and how is it done?

8. When is photo-etching economical?

9. What is EGM, and for what is it used?

10. How is chemical milling done?

11. When is chemical milling advantageous, and when is it not?

PROBLEMS

1. How much average current is required to remove steel by EDM at the rate of 2 cm³/min (0.12 in.³/min)?

2. What power input to a 90% efficient EDM circuit is required to remove 2 cm³/min (0.12 in.³/min) from steel for an average gap voltage of 50 V?

3. Estimate the average time to sink a cavity with a hexagonal cross section and 10 mm (0.4 in.) depth on a 25 A capacity EDM machine. Each side of the hexagon is 15 mm (0.6 in.).

4. Estimate the time to sink a simple cavity 6 mm ($\frac{1}{4}$ in.) deep with cross-sectional area of 25 cm² (4 in.²) with a 20,000-A-capacity ECM machine in steel.

5. An ECM machine is to be designed for cavities with cross-sectional areas up to 260 cm² (40 in.²). Electrolyte will be supplied at 200 L/min (ca. 50 gal/min) at 1.7 MPa (ca. 250 psi) maximum pressure. What axial tool force must the machine be able to withstand?

6. A 20-mm (0.79-in.)-square blind hole is to be sunk by ECM in a block of tungsten. The potential across the gap is 15 V. Efficiency is 65%. Feed of 10 mm/min is adequate. How much power must be supplied? What is the minimum rating of the machine?

7. Cemented carbide cutting tools used in a certain plant must be ground on their rake faces to resharpen them. This can be done on an electrochemical grinding machine in the time of 2 minutes for each tool. The machine and equipment cost $20,000. Depreciation for 5 years, interest, and taxes amount to $6000/yr, or $24/day. The work can also be done in 4 minutes for each tool with a diamond wheel on a conventional grinder costing about $6000, prorated at $8/day. The extra cost of the diamond wheel amounts to $0.04 for each tool ground. Electricity costs $0.02 per tool more for the electrochemical method. Labor and related overhead costs amount to $24 for each hour of operation of either machine. Other costs are about the same for both machines. How many tools must be ground each day to justify using the electrochemical method?

8. For the situation described in Prob. 7, which method should be selected if 10 tools are to be ground each day? If 50 tools are needed every day?

9. In a manufacturing plant it costs $1.19 ($0.54) to remove a kilogram (pound) of metal by chemical milling based on a cost of $0.79/kg ($0.36/lb) of etchant. Any costs for masking must be added, including $1.08/m² ($0.10/ft²) to apply the maskant over the entire exposed surface, the prorated cost of the template, and $0.13/linear meter ($0.04/linear foot) of cut for slitting and removing the maskant. Machine milling costs $4.40/kg ($2.00/lb) of metal removed. Setup costs $10 for each lot. For each piece, let W = weight in kg (lb) of metal to be removed, A = the total surface area in m² (ft²), and L = the length in m (ft) of cuts

to be made in the maskant. Let T = the cost of the template to be used for all pieces. Set up and solve an expression for N, the number of parts in one lot for which the cost is the same by chemical or machine milling.

10. A part is to be milled under the conditions given in Prob. 9. Initially, it is a slab of aluminum 16 mm ($\frac{5}{8}$ in.) thick, 0.8 m (32 in.) wide, and 1.2 m (48 in.) long. Three pockets each 13 mm ($\frac{1}{2}$ in.) deep by 250 mm (ca. 10 in.) by 760 mm (ca. 30 in.) are to be cut from one side. If one part only is to be made, how much can be spent on a mask for chemical milling? How much if five parts are to be made?

11. A mask for the part described in Prob. 10 costs \$100. What process should be used if only two parts are to be made, both in one lot?

REFERENCES

BELLOWS, G., *Nontraditional Machining Guide*, 1976, and *Chemical Machining*, 1977, Machinability Data Center, Cincinnati, Ohio.

———, and J. B. KOHLS, "Drilling without Drills, Special Report 743," *American Machinist*, Mar. 1982, p. 173.

BOGUE, D., and R. HACH, "How to Cut Deburring Costs," *American Machinist*, June 1, 1970, p. 97.

BRECHTER, R. A., "Numerical Control Traveling Wire EDM," *NC Commline*, Nov.–Dec. 1981, p. 15.

BUDINSKI, K. G., "Photofabrication of Metal Parts," *Mechanical Engineering*, Nov. 1971, p. 19.

Chemical Machining: Production with Chemistry, MDC 77-102, Metcut Research Associates, Inc., Cincinnati, Ohio, 1977.

DALLAS, D. B., "Electrical Machining," *Manufacturing Engineering*, Mar. 1979, p. 54.

———, ed., *Tool and Manufacturing Engineers Handbook*, 3rd ed., Society of Manufacturing Engineers, Dearborn, Mich., 1976.

DINI, J. W., "Chemical Milling, Review 194," *International Metallurgical Reviews*, Vol. 20, 1975, p. 29.

ECM, ECD, ECG Simplified, Chemform, Pompano Beach, Fla.

HUNTRESS, E. A., "Electrical Discharge Machining, Special Report 706," *American Machinist*, Aug. 1978, p. 83.

———, "EDM Orbiters," *American Machinist*, July 1980, p. 105.

McGEOUGH, J. A., and H. RASMUSSEN, "Theoretical Analysis of the Electrochemical Machining Process," *ASME Paper 69-WA/PROD-10*.

"Non Traditional Machining," *Manufacturing Engineering*, Dec. 1981, p. 55.

32

SCREW THREADS AND THEIR MANUFACTURE

SCREW THREADS AND SCREWS

Nature of Screw Threads. A *screw thread* is a ridge of uniform section that lies in a helical or spiral path on the outside or inside of a cylinder or cone. The groove between the ridges is called the *space*. A *straight thread* lies on a cylinder; a *tapered thread* lies on a cone. A thread on an outside surface is an *external thread*. A screw has an external thread. An *internal thread* is found in a nut.

A *right-hand thread* is one that turns clockwise as it moves away from the observer. A *left-hand thread* turns counterclockwise from the same position. A thread is understood to be right-hand unless designated otherwise.

Features of a Screw Thread. The chief features of an external thread are illustrated in Fig. 32-1. Internal threads have corresponding features. They determine the size and shape of a thread. The important ones are described here.

The *pitch* is the distance parallel to the axis from any point on a screw thread to a corresponding point on the next ridge. The pitch is the reciprocal of the *number of threads* in a unit of length. Thus if a screw has a pitch of 2 mm, it has $\frac{1}{2}$ thread per millimeter. Another that has eight threads per in. has a pitch of $\frac{1}{8}$ in.

The *lead* is the distance a screw advances axially in one full turn. The lead is the reciprocal of the *number of turns* required to advance the screw axially a unit of length. Thus a drive screw that requires 100 turns to move forward 1 m has a lead of 10 mm.

A *single-thread screw* has only one continuous thread on its surface, as on most commercial screws, bolts, and nuts. A *multiple-thread screw* has two or more adjacent threads. A *double-thread screw* has two threads, a *triple-thread screw* has three, etc.

784

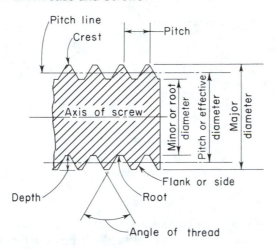

Figure 32-1   Features of a screw thread.

The lead of a single-thread screw is equal to its pitch, but the lead of a double-thread screw is twice the pitch, the lead of a triple-thread screw is three times the pitch, etc.

The *major diameter* of a straight thread is the diameter of a cylinder on which the crest of an external thread or the root of an internal thread lies. The *minor diameter* applies to the root of an external thread or the crest of an internal thread. The *pitch diameter* of a straight thread is the diameter of a cylinder that cuts the thread where the width of the thread is equal to the width of the space.

Screw Thread Forms.   Screw threads are made with a number of cross sections; one list showed 108. Common ones are illustrated in Fig. 32-2.

A *sharp V-thread* has an angle of 60° and is brought to a point at crest and root. The thread and space each have the same cross section of an equilateral triangle. This simple thread has little practical use.

Most screws produced in the United States to inch dimensions have the *Unified National Screw Thread Form* (Fig. 32-3). The crest of the external thread is truncated by $\frac{1}{8}$, and the root by $\frac{1}{6}$, of the depth of a full V-thread. Thus the crest has a width F_1 of $\frac{1}{8}$, and the root a width F_2 of $\frac{1}{6}$, of the pitch P. The basic depth of an external thread is $\frac{17}{24}$ of the depth of a V-thread, or depth $D = 0.6134P$. Tolerance is negative on both

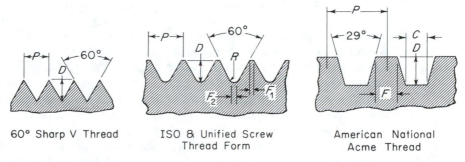

60° Sharp V Thread   ISO & Unified Screw Thread Form   American National Acme Thread

Figure 32-2   Cross sections of several forms of screw threads.

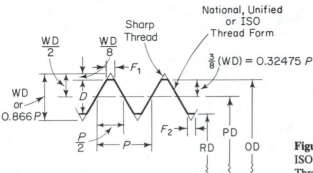

Figure 32-3 Basic profile of Metric or ISO M Thread and Unified National Thread Forms.

crest and root diameters. A flat or rounded root is specified for UN series of threads. The rounded root is partly to allow for wear of cutting tools because they deteriorate faster on the corners. Also, a rounded root increases fatigue strength and resistance to shock loads.

The *Metric* or *ISO Thread Form* (Basic M Thread) is like the UN Screw Thread Form but with dimensions in millimeters and other differences. The crest is truncated by $\frac{1}{8}$, and the root by $\frac{1}{4}$ of a V-thread depth. Thus the crest has a width of F_1 of $\frac{1}{8}$, and the root a width of F_2 of $\frac{1}{4}$ of the pitch P. The basic depth of an external thread is $\frac{5}{8}$ of the depth of a V-thread, or $D = 0.5413P$. The root may be rounded as for UN threads.

The *American National Acme Thread* has a 29° angle, which makes it easier to machine with uniform accuracy than a square thread. The basic Acme thread has a depth $D = P/2$, a crest width $F = 0.3707P$, and a width at the root C from 0.003 to 0.005 in. less than F. Acme threads can carry heavy loads and are used typically for jack screws and feed and operating screws for machine tools.

Threads developed on cones or tapers have specific applications, such as for pipe threads and wood screws. The *American National Taper Pipe Thread* has an angle of 60° between flanks of the thread. The crests and roots are cut to follow a taper of $\frac{3}{4}$ in./ft.

Screw Thread Standards. At one time screw threads lacked uniformity in size and shape. Each manufacturer produced screws according to his own system and standards. One product could not be interchanged with another. Standardization of sizes, shapes, and pitches was undertaken to create a condition of order.

A number of standards have prevailed over the years. An accord of the United States, Great Britain, and Canada in 1948 set up the Unified Screw Thread Form, which superseded previous standards for most screw threads produced in the United States. The purpose of this uniform thread system was to promote interchangeability of products, particularly war matériel. The standard designates a coarse thread series by UNC and a fine thread series by UNF, and there is a less often used extra fine thread series called UNEF and others. Each series specifies the threads per inch (tpi) and basic dimensions and tolerances for certain nominal inch sizes of diameters, like $\frac{1}{4}$, $\frac{5}{16}$, $\frac{3}{8}$, $\frac{7}{16}$, $\frac{1}{2}$, etc. As an example, the basic major diameter of a $\frac{3}{8}$-in. screw is 0.375 in., but the UNC series specifies 16 tpi and basic pitch diameter of 0.3344 in., and the UNF series 24 tpi and basic pitch diameter of 0.3479 in. for that size. For each nominal size, the coarse thread series has fewer threads per inch than the fine thread series. In each series, the number of threads per inch decreases as the size increases.

With the adoption of the SI (metric) system by all other countries and the commitment of the United States to convert to that system, metric threads are of increasing importance and are standardized by the American National Standards Institute (ANSI). Screw thread sizes are expressed in metric modules and are not just conversions of older inch standards. The ANSI tabulates preferred outside diameters from 1.6 to 300 mm with standard pitches for each size. Metric threads are designated by the letter M followed by the nominal outside diameter in millimeters, then by the symbol $\times$ and the pitch, e.g., M 20 $\times$ 2. This signifies a thread with a 20-mm nominal diameter and a pitch of 2 mm. The standard tables specify only one pitch for each coarse thread diameter; so the diameter alone may suffice after M for a coarse thread. A specification like M 20 $\times$ 2 is required for a fine thread. Other symbols are added when needed to designate thread tolerance classes, thread fits, modifications, special features, etc.

Complete specifications for the dimensions, allowances, and tolerances of the various thread forms and sizes are given in standards bulletins and handbooks.

Classes of Screw Threads.   Screw threads are divided into *classes* to designate the fits between internal and external mating threads. For some applications a nut may fit loosely on a screw; in other cases they must go together snugly. The different fits are obtained by assigning appropriate tolerances on the pitch, major, and minor diameters and allowances to the threads for each class.

The United Form Thread Standard recognizes several classes of threads. Those with A are for screws, B for nuts. Classes 1A and 1B are for a loose fit, where quick assembly and rapid production are important and shake or play is not objectionable. Classes 2A and 2B serve for most commercial screws, bolts, and nuts. Classes 3 through 5 provide for closer fits and for interference fits. Screws from one class may be used with nuts from another class for more fits.

The tolerance class of an external metric thread may be designated in the form 4g6g. Here 4g is the thread tolerance class for pitch diameter, and 6g for major diameter. The class of an internal thread might be shown by symbols like 6H. All classes are tabulated in the standards bulletins. A number of classes are available but there are two preferred classes of fits for general purposes and a third for close fits. The tolerance class may be specified in the thread specification following a dash after the pitch, e.g., M 20 $\times$ 2–4g6g.

MEASURING SCREW THREADS

The size of a screw or bolt is designated by its outside diameter. An M 10 ISO metric screw should fit a nut of the same nominal diameter, and a $\frac{1}{2}$-in. UNC screw should fit a nut with the same designation. However, other dimensions must also be measured to assure that the size and form of a screw thread are correct. The major and minor diameters of screw threads are dimensioned to clear the corresponding surfaces of mating threads. Threads make actual contact with each other on their flanks. Measurements must be made in the space against the flanks of a thread to find its true and effective size. The dimensions that need to be measured or gaged directly, indirectly, or compositely are the outside and root diameters, pitch diameter, thread angle, and pitch or lead.

The outside diameter and pitch specify a thread's size. The other dimensions are calculated from these. Ways of computing the thread depth for the common forms of threads have been explained. The root diameter for a screw is equal to the outside diameter minus twice the thread depth.

The outside diameter of ISO metric and Unified threads is specified over the thread crests truncated to a width equal to $\frac{1}{8}$ of the pitch. Accordingly, the basic pitch diameter, PD = OD (outside diameter) $- 0.6495P$. The basis for this formula is given in Fig. 32-3. As for actual dimensions, the OD and PD are given empirical allowances for clearance with mating threads and tolerances for manufacturing. These are specified in the tables of standards bulletins for the screw threads.

If the pitch cylinder of a thread were slit along an element parallel to the axis and unrolled into a plane, it would be a strip having a width equal to $\pi \times$ PD (pitch diameter). The pitch lines of the thread would lie at an angle across the strip. The angle between one of these lines and a normal to the sides of the strip is the lead angle of the thread, as shown in Fig. 32-4. This angle is $B = \tan^{-1}[L/(\pi \times \text{PD})]$.

The basic dimensions of a $\frac{3}{8}$ – 16 UNC external thread will be calculated as an example. The thread depth is $D = 0.6134 \times \frac{1}{16} = 0.0383$ in. The root diameter is RD $= 0.375 - 2 \times 0.0383 = 0.2984$ in. The pitch diameter, PD $= 0.375 - (0.6495/16) = 0.3344$ in. The lead angle, $B = \tan^{-1}[1/(16 \times \pi \times 0.3344)] = 3°24'$.

Screw Thread Micrometer Caliper.   A screw thread micrometer caliper is like a standard micrometer caliper described in Chap. 15 but has a spindle with a conical

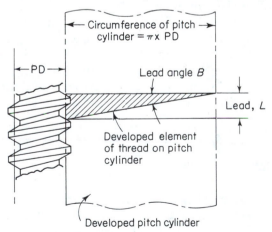

Figure 32-4 Basis for calculation of the lead angle of a screw thread.

point and an anvil with two V-shaped ridges. It makes contact on the sides of a screw thread and measures the pitch diameter directly. Any one anvil is limited to a small range of pitches. Even with the proper range, the readings are slightly distorted unless the micrometer is set to a standard thread plug and used to measure threads of the same diameter and pitch as the plug.

Measuring Screw Threads with Three Wires. The three wire method of measuring pitch diameters is more accurate but slower than the use of screw thread micrometer calipers. The arrangement of the wires is indicated in Fig. 32-5. Three wires of any one diameter that would fit within the space might be used, but the preferred diameter or *best wire* for each pitch makes contact on the flanks of the thread at the pitch diameter. A best wire has a diameter equal to $\frac{2}{3}$ of the depth of a full V-thread. That depth is equal to 0.866P. Thus $W = \frac{2}{3} \times 0.866P = 0.57733P$.

When a wire of diameter W touches a 60° thread, its center lies at a distance $W/4$ outside the points of contact as indicated in Fig. 32-5. Therefore, for a best wire size, the dimension over the wires is $A = PD + (\frac{3}{2})W$. The effect of the lead angle on the measurement usually is negligible for standard 60° single-thread screws. Sizes of best wires and measurements over wires are given in published tables.

Effect of Pitch, Lead, and Form Errors. The standards do not specify tolerances for thread pitch, lead, or angle. Some error can be expected in these elements, and it detracts from the pitch diameter tolerance, which is specified. For instance, an error of 25 μm (0.001 in.) axially in the lead between any two threads in the length of engagement of a screw adds 43 μm (0.0017 in.) to the effective pitch diameter in mating with another thread. Thus measuring or gaging the pitch diameter alone across one or two threads is not enough to verify the functional worth of a screw.

The lead of a thread may be checked separately from the pitch diameter, and that is done to check precision gages and thread rolls. For production purposes, it is more meaningful to gage the high limit of the pitch diameter of a screw over the normal length of engagement at one time because that indicates how well the screw will fit in a nut. On the other hand, the low limit is gaged over one or a few threads only at one time to minimize the effect that lead and form errors have in making the pitch diameter seem large.

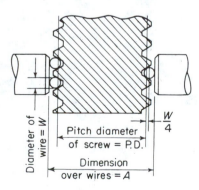

Figure 32-5 Measuring a screw with three wires.

A typical device checks thread lead by comparing the thread on the workpiece with a precise master and showing any difference between the two on a dial indicator.

A set of *screw thread pitch gages* is shown in Fig. 15-13(29). Such a gage is held up against a screw to check its pitch approximately.

Optical or projection comparators like the one in Fig. 15-32 are widely used for checking thread form and lead.

Thread Gages.   Typical plug, ring, and snap gages for threads are described in Chap. 15 in connection with Fig. 15-24. Such gages are made closely to theoretical sizes and forms of threads and check how screws and nuts will fit in service.

Thread snap gages like the one at the lower right of Fig. 32-6 are for rapid checking of screws. Two sets of rolls provide "go" and "not go" limits for the progressive type. A screw of correct size passes between the "go" threaded rolls but is stopped by the "not go" pair. The gages at the top of Fig. 32-6 are comparator types that are more sensitive. Their contacting members are threaded rolls or segments that bear against the workpiece, whose relative size is registered through a linkage on an indicator dial. "Go" rolls on gages like those in Fig. 32-6 each have a number of threads to indicate the effects of lead and form error over an appreciable length of screw. The "not go" rolls may have only one thread each.

Figure 32-6   Functional gages for checking screws. (Courtesy Standard Pressed Steel Co.)

WAYS OF MAKING SCREW THREADS

Screws may be cut or formed. They may be cut with single-point tools on a lathe or with multiple-tooth cutters that include dies, taps, and milling cutters on various types of machines.

Threads are formed on screws and bolts by rolling or pressing on thread rolling machines. Internal and external threads may be rolled in thin sheet metal and tubing, like those on a metal lid for a glass jar or the base of an electric light bulb.

The methods just named for cutting and forming threads will be described in more detail in the remainder of this chapter. Threads also are ground, as described in Chap. 28. They may be hobbed like gears, as indicated in Chap. 33. Parts with threads are also produced by die casting and plastic molding.

Thread Cutting on a Lathe. Thread cutting on a lathe is called *chasing* a thread (Fig. 32-7). The single-point tool is ground with its cutting edge of the same shape as the thread space and enough relief to clear the helical sides. Practically every engine and tool room lathe has an accurate leadscrew that drives the carriage, and the tool mounted on it, to chase the thread as the workpiece turns. The number of threads per inch cut on a lathe depends upon the relative rates of rotation of the work spindle and leadscrew, as well as the lead of the leadscrew. The necessary rate of rotation of the leadscrew for any job is obtained by driving it through a selective gear train from the spindle as described in Chap. 18.

A modern lathe with a sliding gear transmission in the leadscrew drive has a plate that tells how to shift the levers to cut any of the threads it can produce. The engineer who designs the lathe must select the gear ratios for each lever position. This is a typical problem in machine design and deserves attention. The same problem must be solved on those lathes, usually older ones, that have pick-off change gears between the spindle and leadscrew. With *simple gearing,* as shown in Fig. 32-8, the rate of

Figure 32-7 Cutting a screw thread on a lathe with the compound rest set at 29°. (Courtesy South Bend Lathe, Inc.)

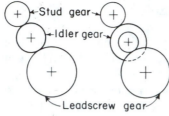

Simple gearing   Compound gearing

Figure 32-8 Change gears for driving the leadscrew on a lathe.

rotation of the leadscrew depends only upon the stud gear, driven at spindle speed, and the leadscrew gear. The idler gear may be any convenient size to connect the others together.

The proper ratio for simple gearing is found from the proportion that

$$\frac{\text{number of teeth on stud gear}}{\text{number of teeth on leadscrew gear}} = \frac{\text{pitch of thread to be cut}}{\text{pitch of leadscrew}}$$

$$= \frac{\text{lead of thread to be cut}}{\text{lead of lead screw}}$$

The last ratio applies if either thread is a multiple thread. As an example, a thread is to be chased with a pitch of 2.5 mm, and the leadscrew has a pitch of 6 mm. Both are single threads. Then

$$\frac{\text{stud gear}}{\text{leadscrew gear}} = \frac{2.5}{6} = \frac{10T}{24T} = \frac{15T}{36T} = \frac{20T}{48T}, \quad \text{etc.}$$

Sometimes simple gear ratios cannot be found to cut a desired thread. Then it is necessary to resort to *compound gearing*. One such arrangement is indicated in Fig. 32-8. Two idler or intermediate gears revolve together on one shaft. One is driven by the stud gear, and the other drives the leadscrew gear. The product of the ratios of the gear sets must equal the ratio between the pitches or leads of the workpiece and leadscrew.

A series of light cuts is taken to chase a thread accurately. The depth of the first cut or two may be as much as 125 μm (0.005 in.), but after that the tool is fed to only 50 to 75 μm (0.002 to 0.003 in.) for each cut, and finally 25 μm (0.001 in.) or less per pass for the last few finishing cuts. If the cuts are too heavy, the tool may be damaged, the workpiece distorted, or the threads torn. At the end of each pass the tool must be withdrawn and the feed stopped. The tool is then taken back to the beginning and set to depth, and the feed is engaged at the instant that starts the tool on the right path for the next pass. Most modern lathes have a *threading dial* on the front of the carriage. It is turned by a worm gear meshed with the leadscrew and shows the operator when to engage the half nut to start the tool in the right path.

Thread chasing is done at one-third to one-half of the surface speed of turning. This is partly to conserve the tool and partly to give the operator time to do all that is necessary. The steps to chase a thread have been described in some detail to explain why thread cutting on a lathe is slow, requires skill, and is expensive. Its merit is that it is versatile and calls for little special equipment. External and internal, right- and left-hand, straight and tapered, and practically all sizes and pitches of threads can be chased on screw-cutting engine lathes with regular equipment. Quite accurate threads can be produced on a good machine. Other methods are faster but usually require special equipment that is not justified unless a moderate or large quantity of threads of one kind is needed.

As was mentioned, the feed must be stopped and the tool withdrawn at the end of the cut. This is most easily done if a *relief groove* is first cut, as indicated in Fig. 32-9. A designer should always specify a groove, if at all possible, at the end of a thread, whether it is to be made on a lathe or in any other way, to provide relief for the tools. It is common practice to make the groove as wide as the pitch of the thread, but it may be wider. If a tool having several teeth is used, such as a die, the groove should be wide enough to take the lead teeth and the first full tooth.

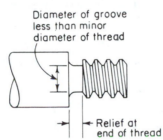

Diameter of groove less than minor diameter of thread

← Relief at end of thread

Figure 32-9   Relief needed at the end of a thread.

Thread Cutting Dies.   A threading die has an internal thread like a nut, but lengthwise grooves in the hole expose the cutting edges of the thread. The first few threads are on a taper to start on the workpiece. Dies are made of hardened carbon tool steel or high-speed steel. A *solid adjustable die,* shown in Fig. 32-10, is split on one side and can be adjusted for size slightly by a screw. Solid and adjustable dies are commonly sold for standard screw threads. A 1982 catalog lists high-speed steel adjustable round split dies at \$3.35 each for sizes up to $\frac{5}{16}$-in. diameter, \$4.15 to $\frac{1}{2}$-in. diameter, \$6.75 to $\frac{3}{4}$-in. diameter, and \$12.10 to 1-in. diameter. Outsizes may be much

Figure 32-10   Solid adjustable round split die and stock. (Courtesy Winter Brothers Co.)

higher, e.g., for a 3-in.-diameter right-hand thread as much as $276.25. Dies are used by hand in a holder called a *stock*.

Spring-adjustable dies and die heads are used on machines, mostly for production. A *spring adjustable screw threading die* resembles and can be sprung like a collet to cut to a desired size.

A *die head* has a body in which four or more serrated blades or chasers are mounted. The blades may be carbon tool steel, high-speed steel, or cemented carbide. They are removed when dull, reground, replaced, and adjusted to cut to a desired size. The chasers are mounted radially in some heads but positioned tangentially to the workpiece in other heads.

A *self-opening die head,* like the one in Fig. 32-11, is arranged so that it is tripped, and its chasers snap outward when a thread has been cut to a predetermined length. The workpiece does not then have to be screwed out of the die head. The chasers are returned to cutting position by pulling the handle on the head before another piece is cut. A self-opening die head for screws $\frac{1}{2}$ to $1\frac{1}{4}$ in. in diameter and a set of chasers costs about $650.

Threading Machines.   Dies and die heads are commonly used on lathes, turret lathes, and automatic bar and turning machines for cutting threads faster than they can be chased with single-point tools.

Universal threading machines like the one in Fig. 32-12 are used for threading bolts, studs, automotive parts, pipes, etc. They are made with one or two heads. Each head carries a revolving self-opening die head. Opposite each head is a carriage that slides on ways to carry the work to and from the dies. A standard vise is normally mounted on each carriage for holding work but may be replaced by a collet chuck or a special fixture. A leadscrew may be geared to the head to drive the carriage for cutting more accurate threads. The two carriages operate independently, and their operation cycles may be automatic or manually controlled. Cutting fluid is pumped to each head. An automatic bolt threading machine with capacity to about 25 mm (1 in.)

Figure 32-11   Self-opening die head. (Courtesy Geometric Tool Co.)

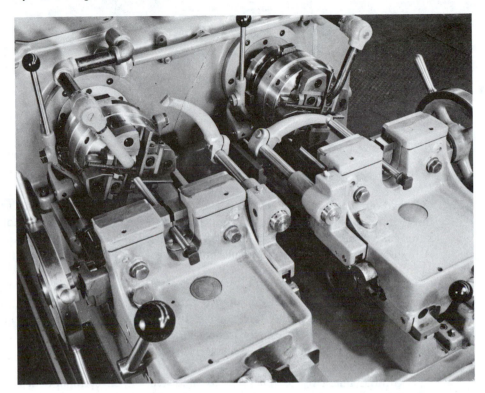

Figure 32-12 Working zone of a universal threading machine with two heads. (Courtesy Landis Machine Co.)

diameter weighs about 1.8 Mg (4000 lb) and costs about $21,000. For a capacity to about 65 mm (2.5 in.), the cost is about $50,000.

Taps.   Holes are usually threaded by taps. A *tap* has a shank and a round body with several radially placed chasers. Taps are made in many sizes and shapes to satisfy a number of purposes. They may be operated by hand or machine. They are made to cut all forms of threads. Small taps are solid; large taps may be solid or adjustable. A tap has two or more flutes that may be straight, helical or spiral, or spiral pointed. Taps are made of carbon tool steel for low first cost or high-speed steel for rapid production and endurance. Ground high-speed steel taps may be run up to drilling speeds. A tap works under strenuous conditions because it is buried in metal, where chips are hard to get out, and fed at an invariable rate. It must be kept supplied with a cutting fluid suitable for the work material to operate successfully. The principal kinds of taps are described in the paragraphs that follow.

Hand taps have short shanks with square ends and are made in sets of three for each size. The three are the *taper, plug,* and *bottoming* taps, shown in Fig. 32-13. As it cuts, a tap must be fed at a constant rate to suit the thread it is cutting. The only way to ease the load of a deep cut on the cutting teeth is to taper the tap so each tooth takes

Figure 32-13   Straight flute hand taps. From left to right: taper, plug, and bottoming tap. (Courtesy Standard Tool Co.)

only part of the load. Also, a taper tap is easier to start in a hole. It will cut a full thread through a hole, if advanced far enough, but not to the bottom of a blind hole. In the latter case, a taper tap must be followed by a plug tap and then by a bottoming tap. A high-speed steel tap with a ground thread for a $\frac{1}{2}$–13 NC thread costs \$3.30, but a $1\frac{1}{2}$-in.-diameter tap over \$50.00.

Hand taps are driven by machines as well as by hand. In either event, the tap must be started straight and kept aligned with the hole for true threads. The smaller a tap, the more fragile it is. A tap breaks if it meets too much resistance and too much torque is applied. This is a major trouble in some operations. Skill is needed to tap small holes by hand and avoid breakage. Torque limiting tap drivers are commonly used on machines.

Straight flute taps are easiest to make and sharpen, but spiral or helical flutes help to push chips out of a hole as depicted in Fig. 32-14.

Serial hand taps are made in sets of three. Two are undersize for roughing and are used first. A serial tap has one or more rings scribed around its shank to designate its place in the use sequence. Serial taps are used in tough metal, for threads like Acme threads that require a large stock removal, and to provide a light finishing cut for a smooth finish.

Pulley taps and *nut taps* have long shanks to reach into inaccessible places. *Tapper taps* are used for tapping nuts in large quantities on specialized nut tapping machines and are made in a number of lengths and shapes for specific applications.

A *collapsible tap* has internal thread chasers in a body; they are withdrawn inward from the thread when it is completed. Then the tap can be pulled out of the hole, and the time to reverse the machine is saved. Some such taps are reset by a hand lever; others by a trip mechanism on the machine.

Pipe taps are tapered and are used to cut internal pipe threads. One style carries a short drill in front of the tap to clean out the hole to be tapped.

Design for Tapping.   The larger a hole is drilled for tapping, the easier the thread is to cut. Less thread depth means fewer chips in the hole and less torque with less tap breakage. A typical illustration of how the torque increases with thread depth is given in Fig. 32-15. Theoretically a full thread is only 5% stronger than a 75%

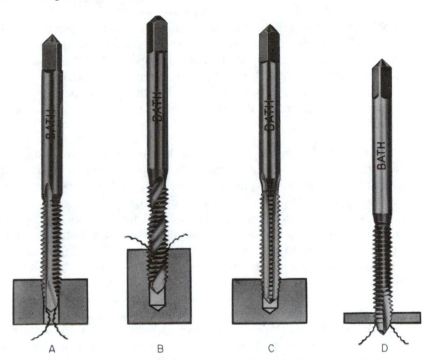

Figure 32-14 (A) Open hole threaded with a spiral-pointed tap that pushes the chips forward; (B) blind hole tapped with a long thread (longer than $1\frac{1}{2}$ times the hole diameter) by a helical-fluted tap that rejects the chips from a hole; (C) short, blind hole tapped by a straight-fluted tap; (D) short flute spiral-pointed tap for sheet metal and thin sections. (Courtesy John Bath and Co., Inc.)

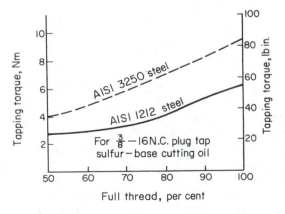

Figure 32-15 Typical torque versus percent of depth of thread curves. (From Stuart E. Sinclair, "What Horsepower for Tapping?" *American Machinist*, May 20, 1957, p. 132.)

thread and 20% stronger than a 50% thread. Common practice is to use, and the Unified Thread Standard is based on, a 75% thread, but in many cases even less is desirable. Experiments of M. L. Begeman and C. C. Chervenka showed that steel threads from about 6 to 20 mm ($\frac{1}{4}$ to $\frac{3}{4}$ in.) diameter and not over 40% full depth were as strong as the bolt for an engagement length equal to the diameter. This indicates that in many cases a 50% thread, to allow for tool runout and standard tap drill sizes, is adequate.

Tapping Machines.   Tapping is done on lathes, turret lathes, and automatics and on drill presses. Some machines called tapping machines are basically drill presses equipped with tap holders, reversing mechanisms, leadscrews, etc., to enhance their tapping ability. They may have one or more spindles.

A tapping attachment may be fastened to the spindle of a standard drilling machine that does not have built-in tapping accessories. Some attachments are of the speed-up type and revolve small taps at high speeds. Tapping attachments are arranged to rotate the tap in a forward direction when it is lowered into the hole and reverse the direction of rotation when the tap is withdrawn from the hole. This action may be obtained from opposed sensitive friction clutches in the tapping attachment head.

Multiple-spindle and gang-type machines are used for tapping nuts in large quantities. One kind employs straight shank tapper taps; the threaded portion is driven through nut after nut, and the nuts collect on the shank of the tap. When full, a tap is removed, and the nuts are stripped from it. Another type of machine cuts the thread and then reverses the tap to withdraw it. One such machine has 79 spindles, and turns out up to 75,000 nuts/hr. The blanks are loaded automatically from a hopper into holes in a circular indexing table to position them under the taps.

An illustration is given in Fig. 32-16 of the mechanism of an automatic nut tapper that uses a bent tap to produce nuts continuously. Blanks pass from a hopper down a chute and enter an ejector that feeds them onto the tap one at a time. The tap is revolved continuously and is moved forward into each blank. The nuts are held in guides to keep them from turning and are not pulled along by the tap while the threads are being cut, to prevent binding. After one nut has been tapped, the tap with the nut on it is moved back ready for the next blank. The tap is always filled with nuts, which support and hold the tap centrally in the revolving head. As each nut climbs onto the tap, it forces another off the bent end.

Thread Milling.   A conventional thread milling machine, shown in Fig. 32-17, is like a lathe with a headstock and tailstock mounted on a bed. A carriage slides between the two on ways and carries a cutter head. The work may be mounted between centers or chucked on the headstock spindle.

Multiple-thread form cutters, like the one in Fig. 32-17, are used for rapid thread cutting. The cutter does not have a thread or lead. Instead its teeth are arrayed on a series of closed circles. The axes of cutter and work are parallel. The revolving cutter is fed to depth in the work. It is longer than the thread. As the work revolves, the cutter is fed lengthwise to conform to the lead of the thread. The cutter is fed by a leadscrew

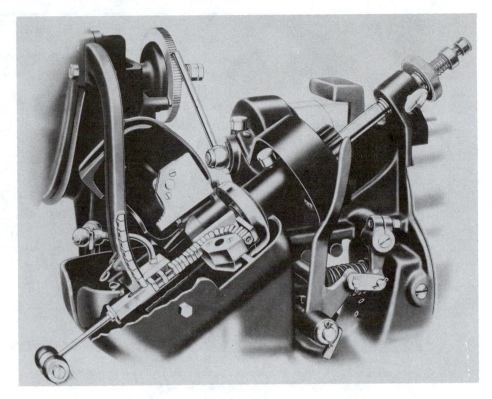

Figure 32-16 Sectional view of the head of an automatic tapper that uses a bent tap. (Courtesy National Machinery Co.)

through change gears to the work spindle. At the end of $1\frac{1}{10}$ revolutions of the work, the cutter is withdrawn from the completed thread. An internal thread may be milled in a similar manner. Milling with multiple-thread form cutters is often as fast as thread cutting with self-opening dies and collapsible taps and produces more accurate threads and better finishes. It is mostly confined to V-type threads (not necessarily sharp) because too much error is introduced in other threads.

Coarse threads, like those on feedscrews and leadscrews, are milled with single cutters on a *universal thread miller*. The cutter is tilted to match the lead angle of the thread. As the work revolves, the cutter head and carriage are moved longitudinally on the machine by a leadscrew or cam to produce the desired lead. The cutter thus traverses the entire thread, and the length of thread is limited only by the capacity of the machine. A large machine is capable of cutting threads from about 50 mm (2 in.) to 300 mm (12 in.) diameter and up to 3.65 m (12 ft) long in one setting. For accuracy and finish, thread milling is usually done in two or three passes, the same as other milling, but still is faster than single-point thread chasing for long threads.

Planetary millers do external and internal circular form and thread cutting. They are convenient for cumbersome pieces because the workpiece does not move. Instead,

Figure 32-17   View of an external thread milled with a multiple-thread form cutter on a thread miller. (Courtesy Pratt and Whitney Co.)

the cutter rotates about its axis and is also made to travel in a circular planetary orbit about the axis of the surface cut.

Thread Rolling.   Thread rolling is a cold forging rather than a cutting process. It produces external threads by subjecting a blank to pressure between dies in the form of grooved blocks or threaded rolls. The work material is depressed to open the root and raised to fill the crest of the thread. Threads are rolled on machines built especially for the purpose, on lathes and drill presses, or in combination with other operations on turret lathes and automatic bar machines. The principles of operation of the various methods are illustrated in Fig. 32-18.

Each type of thread rolling machine operates best in a certain range of sizes, but the ranges of different machines overlap. Where two or three types are acceptable for a certain size, one may be best for one kind of work, another for different work, etc. All types can be arranged with hoppers and automatic loading devices. The main advantages of each are the following. The *rotary-planetary die machine* has a continuous action and is fast for commercial screws of less than 13 mm ($\frac{1}{2}$ in.) diameter. It can turn out 6-mm ($\frac{1}{4}$-in.)-diameter screws at 400 to 1200 per minute. The *reciprocating die machine* rolls threads up to 25 mm (1 in.) diameter. Typical rates are 140 pieces/min for 8 mm ($\frac{5}{16}$ in.) diameter and 40 to 60 pieces/min for 19 mm ($\frac{3}{4}$ in.) diameter. It excels for precision threads, wide roots (like those on wood screws), and

TYPES OF THREAD ROLLING MACHINES

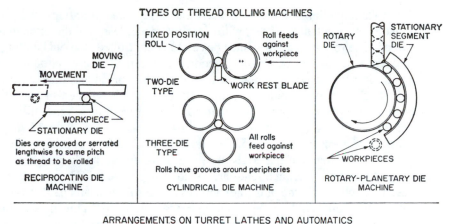

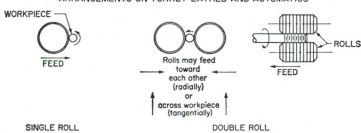

Figure 32-18 Methods of rolling threads.

gimlet point screws. The *cylindrical die machines* (two or three die types) are made in several sizes to handle diameters from about 3 mm ($\frac{1}{8}$ in.) to 150 mm (6 in.). They are relatively easy to set up and are preferred for hard materials, tapered and coarse threads, and tube threading. Cylindrical machines can thrufeed roll long threads; a $\frac{5}{8}$–11 UNC thread about 1 m (3 ft) long is rolled at the rate of 72/min. A basic cylindrical die machine for diameters from 3 mm ($\frac{1}{8}$ in.) to 50 mm (2 in.) and powered by a 5.6-kW ($7\frac{1}{2}$-hp)/motor weighs about 1.8 Mg (4000 lb) and costs about $50,000.

Thread rolling offers a number of advantages. It is capable of producing accurate, uniform, and smooth threads of all classes at high rates of production on all kinds of screws, bolts, and studs. Rolling speeds are equivalent to cutting speeds with high-speed steel. No material is cut away to form the spaces, and up to 27% of material may be saved unless the screw blank is cut from a large piece of stock anyway. The material is cold-worked; its grain pattern continuity is not cut away, and a smooth wearable surface is left on the thread flank. Rolling is superior to cutting for good surface finish. Wear life is lengthened; tensile strength may be increased 10%, and fatigue strength has been found raised as much as 5 to 10 times for hardened alloy bolts with rolled instead of cut threads. The dies roll rather than rub and retain their original sizes a long time, often for millions of pieces. Because the dies do not lose their true shape over a long time, the work is consistent, and inspection costs are low. Thread rolling is more convenient than die cutting for some setups on automatic bar machines, such as for cutting a thread behind a shoulder.

Thread rolling requires some care and has several limitations. A blank for rolling must have an initial diameter, with close tolerance, less than the pitch diameter of the thread. The rolling operation must be carefully controlled to avoid bending of the piece and seams, slivers, or other imperfections of the thread. A truncation must be expected on the last fraction of a turn at the end of a rolled thread and thus a thread cannot be rolled fully up to a shoulder. Rolling effectiveness is reduced in materials with less than 12% elongation, but some help can be had from heating. Rolling ceases to be practical if elongation is less than 5% or hardness is over about 32 R_C. Even above these approximate limits, some materials are difficult to roll. Specifications of the rollability of common materials are given in reference books and handbooks.

Almost all external threads are rolled in large quantities because that is up to 50% faster and cheaper. One of the advantages is that rolling is amenable to continuous and automatic work handling. Material saving is a big factor. Threads are both rolled and cut in moderate quantities on standard semiautomatic machines, and the total cost is not much different for either method. Commercial self-opening thread rolling heads and rolls for standard sizes of threads are somewhat higher in price than self-opening die heads and chasers. General-purpose threading in small quantities is seldom done by rolling because cutting is more adaptable and versatile for varieties of requirements and circumstances.

Formed Threads in Holes. A *forming* or *fluteless tap* has a tapered end but does not have grooves or flutes like an ordinary tap. It cold forms or swages threads in soft ductile material (even some steels) instead of cutting. The material is compacted and burnished. Grain fibers are distorted but not cut away. The thread is imperfectly formed as a rule but has about the same strength as a cut thread. No chips are made to clog the hole, and lead is easy to control. Torque is high, and a high-speed lubricant is better than a cutting fluid. Speeds up to twice those for cutting have been found practical. Holes must be tap drilled larger than for conventional tapping. There is a tendency to raise burrs at the end of holes so countersinking is desirable.

QUESTIONS

1. Define a screw thread, a right-hand thread, and a left-hand thread.
2. What is meant by the pitch and lead of a screw thread? How do the pitch and lead agree for a single-thread screw and for a multiple-thread screw?
3. Define the major, minor, and pitch diameters of a thread.
4. Make a sketch of an ISO Metric Screw Thread Form and name its parts.
5. Make a sketch of a Unified Screw Thread Form and name its parts.
6. Describe an Acme thread and its uses.
7. Why are screw threads divided into classes? What are common classes?
8. Describe four ways of measuring or checking screw threads.
9. What effect do pitch, lead, and form errors have on a screw thread?
10. In what ways can threads be cut or formed?

11. How is a lathe arranged to cut threads?
12. Why is thread cutting on a lathe slow and costly? When is it done?
13. Why should a groove be cut at the end of a thread?
14. Describe the principal types of dies. How are they used?
15. Describe the operation of a universal threading machine.
16. Describe the three styles of hand taps. How are they used?
17. What are serial hand taps, pulley taps, collapsible taps, and pipe taps?
18. Describe three types of tapping machines for threading nuts in large quantities.
19. In what two ways may threads be cut on thread milling machines?
20. How is thread rolling done? What are its advantages and disadvantages?

PROBLEMS

1. What is the nominal thread depth for each of the following threads:
   (a) M 6($P = 1$ mm)?
   (b) M 16($P = 2$)?
   (c) M 20 × 1.5?
   (d) No. 5(0.125)–40 UNC?
   (e) $\frac{5}{8}$–11 UNC?
   (f) $\frac{3}{4}$–16 UNF?

2. The basic addendum of a thread is the radial distance from the outside diameter to the pitch diameter. The basic dedendum is the radial distance from the pitch diameter to the root diameter. What are the basic addenda and dedenda of external threads with the specifications listed in Prob. 1?

3. Specify the basic outside diameter, root diameter, pitch diameter, and helix angle for each of the external threads listed in Prob. 1.

4. Calculate the basic minor diameters of external screw threads with the specifications listed in Prob. 1.

5. Show that the best wire size for a 60° thread has a diameter (W) = $\frac{2}{3}$ × the depth of a full V-thread of the same pitch, and thus that the best wire diameter (W) = 0.57735P.

6. Prove that the diameter over best wires on a 60° thread is $A = PD + (\frac{3}{2})W$.

7. Find the best wire size and measurement over three wires for a $\frac{5}{8}$–11 UNC thread.

8. What is the error in the answer to Prob. 7 from neglecting the lead angle?

9. Find the best wire size and diameter over three wires for an M 22 ($P = 2.5$ mm) thread.

10. Wires of 0.050 in. diameter are available for checking a $\frac{5}{8}$–11 UNC thread. The dimension measured over these wires is 0.6315 in. What does this indicate the pitch diameter to be?

11. The leadscrew on a lathe has four threads per inch. Specify the gear ratios required to cut each of the following numbers of threads per inch. (a) 4, (b) 5, (c) 6, (d) 7, (e) 8, (f) 12, (g) 16, (h) 18, (i) 20, (j) 25.

12. It is desired to cut a fine thread of 56 tpi on a lathe with pick-off gears and a leadscrew with 6 threads per inch. The smallest gear available has 20 teeth, and the largest 100 teeth, with all ratios available in between. How should the lathe be geared, and with what ratios?

13. What nominal size would you select for a tap drill for a $\frac{1}{2}$–13 UNC thread? For an M 14 ($P = 2$ mm) thread? Give your reason for your choices if the material is steel.

14. Six H.S.S. taps are to be driven at 18 m/min (60 fpm). They include (2) M 10 ($P = 1.5$ mm), (2) M 14 ($P = 2$ mm), and (2) M 20 × 1.5 thread taps. Maximum torque per tap is estimated to be 16, 25, and 26 Nm (140, 220, and 230 lb-in.), respectively. Machine efficiency is 70%. What size motor should be supplied?

REFERENCES

ANSI B1.1-1974, *Unified Inch Screw Threads (UN and UNR Thread Forms);* ANSI B1.2-1974, *Gages and Gaging Practice for "J" Series Metric Screw Threads;* ASA B1.5-1952, *Acme Screw Threads;* ASA B1.7-1965, *Nomenclature, Definitions and Letter Symbols for Screw Threads;* ANSI B1.13-1979, *Metric Screw Threads—M Profile;* ANSI B1.16-1972, *American Gaging Practice for Metric Screw Threads;* ANSI B1.22-1978, *Gages and Gaging Practice for "MJ" Series Metric Screw Threads,* American National Standards Institute, New York.

BEGEMAN, M. L. and C. C. CHERVENKA, "Increase Tap Drill Diameters and Save Money," *The Tool Engineer,* June 1954, p. 61.

DALLAS, D. B., ed., *Tool and Manufacturing Engineers Handbook,* 3rd ed. Society of Manufacturing Engineers, Dearborn, Mich., 1976.

"Machine Can Cut 12 ft. of Thread in One Set Up," *American Machinist,* Feb. 7, 1972, p. 51.

Metric Fasteners Standards, Industrial Fasteners Institute, Cleveland, Ohio.

Rollability of Materials, Laudis Machine Co., Waynesboro, Pa.

Screw Thread Standards for Federal Services–Handbook H28, U.S. Dept. of Commerce.

33

GEARS AND GEAR MANUFACTURE

A gear is a machine element that transmits motion in a positive manner through teeth around its periphery. The *spur gear* is the simplest form with teeth parallel to its axis as shown in Fig. 33-1. A *rack* is a gear with an infinite radius; it moves in a straight line.

    Gear Tooth Curves. The contact surfaces of gear teeth are curved to transmit motion uniformly as they roll and slide together. Most gear teeth today have or approximate an involute form because it is simple, easy to reproduce, and allows variations in center distances of mating gears. A gear tooth with the involute curve modified at the extremities is said to have a *composite* form.

Figure 33-1 Spur gear and rack. (Courtesy Foote Brothers Gear and Machine Co.)

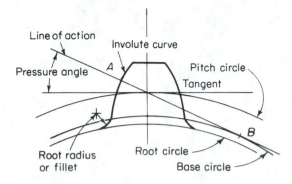

Figure 33-2 Involute gear tooth.

An *involute curve* is generated by a point on a straight line rolling on a *base circle*. The line *AB* in Fig. 33-2 is tangent to the base circle, and point *A* traces the involute profile of one side of the gear tooth as the line is rolled on the circle. In the position shown, the angle between the *line of action AB* and the tangent to the pitch circle is called the *pressure angle*. A *pitch circle* is an imaginary ring of the same diameter as a smooth disk that would transmit the same relative motion by friction as the gear does when meshed with another gear. The radius or fillet adds strength to the root of the tooth.

Elements of Gear Teeth. Gear teeth have been standardized so they mesh together. Two lengths of gear teeth have been common with inch dimensions. One is called the *full-depth tooth* and is longer than comparable sizes of the other, known as the *stub tooth*. Stub teeth are stronger but do not overlap as much as full-depth teeth. Only one length of tooth is common for standard gears with millimeter dimensions.

The important dimensions of gear teeth are called elements and are designated in Fig. 33-3. In the inch dimension systems, the elements are related to a factor called *diametral pitch, $P = N/D$*, where *N* stands for the number of teeth and *D* for the pitch diameter (in.). Any two standard gears of the same diametral pitch and tooth shape will mesh if mounted with the proper distance between their centers. In the millimeter system, the elements are related to a factor called the *module, $m = D/N$*. Here *D* is in mm. Again, gears of the same module and shape mesh together. Care must be taken

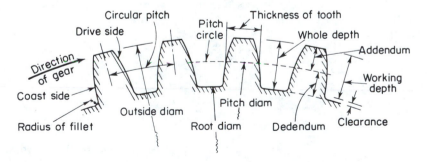

Figure 33-3 Elements of gear teeth.

not to confuse the symbol *m* with m for meter. *P* (in.) equals $25.4/m$ (mm). The module is commonly designated MOD, and the diametral pitch by DP.

Formulas for the main elements of spur gear teeth are given in Table 33-1. They show that the circular pitch and tooth thickness at the pitch line are the same for all gears of the same diametral pitch or the same module. Tooth size (length and thickness) decreases as diametral pitch increases and as module decreases. Helical and bevel gears have much the same basic elements as spur gears plus other elements given in reference books and handbooks.

Although gears in the inch diametral pitch and millimeter module systems have comparable elements, each system has adopted preferred standard values to suit whole number or common fraction tooth and center distance dimensions in each system. Thus standard gears of the two systems are not interchangeable. Generally, tools for one system are not applicable to the other. A set of gears must be designed in one system or the other. Conventional design formulas that determine the diametral pitch or module, number of teeth, and teeth width, as a basis for calculating the elements, may be used for any system with proper conversions. These are discussed in detail in gear design treatises and textbooks.

Types of Gears.   Spur gears are the easiest and cheapest kind to make. They must be mounted on parallel shafts. A *helical gear*, like the one in Fig. 33-4, has teeth along helices on a cylinder. The angle between a helix and an element of the pitch cylinder is called the *helix angle*. Helical gears are more expensive than spur gears but are stronger and quieter because the teeth engage gradually and more teeth are in mesh at the same time. They may be mounted on parallel shafts or on nonparallel and nonintersecting shafts.

A helical gear has a decided side thrust that is neutralized in a *herringbone gear,* like the one in Fig. 33-5, that has teeth on right- and left-hand helices.

A *worm* is like a screw and may have one or more threads, each a tooth. A high ratio can be obtained by engaging a worm with a *worm gear,* as shown in Fig. 33-6. Their axes are nonintersecting and usually at right angles. A worm gear with a small helix angle cannot drive the worm, which is an advantage for some applications.

Bevel gears operate on axes that intersect at any required angle but most commonly at right angles. A bevel gear is conical in form. A *straight bevel gear* has straight teeth. If all the lines along its teeth were extended, they would pass through a common point called the *apex*. This apex point coincides with the point of intersection of the axes of mating bevel gears. A pair of bevel gears with equal numbers of teeth and perpendicular axes are called *miter gears*.

A *crown gear* is a bevel gear with a plane instead of a conical pitch surface. A crown gear is in the form of a disk with teeth around one face and corresponds for bevel gears to the rack for spur gears.

A *Coniskoid gear* is a bevel gear with straight teeth inclined at a spiral angle for longer teeth and more overlap.

The teeth of a *spiral bevel gear* are curved and oblique. One is shown on the left of Fig. 33-7. Spiral bevel gears run smoothly and quietly and are strong because their teeth have what is known as spiral overlap. They are relatively easy to manufacture.

TABLE 33-1 FORMULAS FOR SOME MAJOR DIMENSIONS OF SPUR GEARS

Element name	Symbol	Inches		Millimeters with 20° pressure angle
		Full depth teeth with $14\frac{1}{2}°$ pressure angle	Stub teeth with 20° pressure angle	
Addendum	a	$a = \dfrac{1}{P}$	$a = \dfrac{0.8}{P}$	$a = m$
Circular pitch	p	$p = \dfrac{\pi}{P} = \dfrac{\pi D}{N}$	$p = \dfrac{\pi}{P} = \dfrac{\pi D}{N}$	$p = \pi m = \pi\dfrac{D}{N}$
Clearance	c	$c = \dfrac{0.157}{P}$	$c = \dfrac{0.2}{P}$	$c = 0.25m$
Dedendum	b	$b = a + c = \dfrac{1.157}{P}$	$b = a + c = \dfrac{1}{P}$	$b = 1.25m$
Number of teeth	N	$N = P \times D = \dfrac{\pi D}{p}$	$N = P \times D = \dfrac{\pi D}{p}$	$N = \dfrac{D}{m} = \dfrac{\pi D}{p}$
Outside diameter	D_o	$D_o = \dfrac{N + 2}{P} = D + 2a$	$D_o = \dfrac{N + 1.6}{P} = D + 2a$	$D_o = D + 2m = m(N + 2)$
Pitch diameter	D	$D = \dfrac{N}{P} = \dfrac{N \times p}{\pi}$	$D = \dfrac{N}{P} = \dfrac{N \times p}{\pi}$	$D = mN$
Tooth thickness	t	$t = \dfrac{\pi}{2P} = \dfrac{1.5708}{P}$	$t = \dfrac{\pi}{2P} = \dfrac{1.5708}{P}$	$t = \dfrac{\pi}{2}m$
Whole depth	b_t	$b_t = a + b = \dfrac{2.157}{P}$	$b_t = a + b = \dfrac{1.8}{P}$	$b_t = 2.25m$

Note: P is the symbol for diametral pitch, and m for module, in this table.

Figure 33-4 Helical gear and pinion, (Courtesy Foote Brothers Gear and Machine Co.)

Figure 33-5 Continuous-tooth herringbone gear. (Courtesy Foote Brothers Gear and Machine Co.)

Figure 33-6   Worm and worm gear. (Courtesy Foote Brothers Gear and Machine Co.)

Figure 33-7   Spiral bevel, hypoid, and Zerol bevel gear. (Courtesy Gleason Works.)

A *Zerol bevel gear* has curved teeth, but they lie in the same general direction as straight teeth, as shown on the right of Fig. 33-7.

Hypoid gears resemble bevel gears but their axes do not intersect, as indicated in the middle view of Fig. 33-7. They are quiet and strong. A common application is for automobile rear axle drives.

The gears described so far are the important *external gears*. An *internal gear* is one with teeth inside a cylinder or cone. Internal gears are used for clutches, speed train reducers, and planetary gear trains.

GEAR MANUFACTURING METHODS

Molding Gears.   Gears may be cast in sand or in permanent molds. Gray cast-iron gears are rough, inaccurate, and low in strength, but large sizes can be made at relatively low cost. Hypoid ring gears and pinions rough cast of nodular iron for ease of subsequent machining are found in some automobiles. Many small gears for light service are die cast of zinc, tin, aluminum, and copper alloys with a high degree of accuracy and finish. Gears are sometimes molded of plastic materials where quietness, insulating properties, and only moderate strength for light service are needed. Some gears are pressed and sintered from metallic powders.

Forming Gears.   Gears are made by several kinds of hot- and cold-forming operations. Gear stock of brass or aluminum is extruded and cut to desired lengths. Some gears are forged hot and finish coined when warm or cold. Even moderate-size steel gears are cold extruded, cold precision forged (Chap. 12), or formed by cold upsetting. One gearmaker reported the cost of a machined gear about $30, and the same gear forged for $12.

All types of gears and splines are rolled from soft steel in ways like those described for threads in Chap. 32. A form of rolling for finishing gears is called *burnishing*. The work is rolled as it is pressed between or under gear-shaped dies. Rolling is an important and fast process within the limits of size, tooth shape, and workable material for forming gears from solid stock or for finishing teeth already rough cut. A leading maker does not recommend rolling gears larger than 100 to 125 mm (4 or 5 in.) in diameter, with coarser than about 2 MOD (12 DP) teeth, and with fewer than 16 teeth. It is not considered practicable to roll pressure angles less than 20° or teeth with undercuts. There are exceptions to the rules, and gear teeth coarser than 5 MOD (5 DP), and up to around 300 mm (12 in.) diameter have been reported finish rolled. The gear material should contain little or no sulfur or lead to avoid flaking and should not exceed 28 R_C in hardness.

Good results are obtainable from rolling. The material is work hardened and given a desirable grain flow in the teeth and around the roots, which enhances strength. If residual stresses are excessive, heat treatment may be necessary and cause distortion for which corrections must be made. However, where feasible, rolling produces accurate gears with surface finishes to 100 nm (4 μin) R_a at rates up to 50 times and more than that of cutting. For example, involute splines on the ends of automobile axle shafts are cold rolled in soft steel at the rate of 6 seconds each in quantities of $2\frac{1}{2}$ million pieces per year. A major advantage of gear rolling is long die life; more than 1,000,000 pieces are common from one die in a finishing operation, with the last gear before failure identical to the first one checked.

Cold forming is a high-production process and involves risks. Process and tool development is largely an art and may be costly and time consuming. With one machine giving a huge production, a breakdown may be a catastrophe. Many gears (e.g., starter and transmission pinions) are cold formed or rolled in the automobile industry, but more accurate gears, such as for aircraft, must be machined. One luxury automobile manufacturer rolled transmission gears for several years but gave it up for gear cutting to improve quality.

Cutting Gears.   Large gears, such as the ring gear on the base of a revolving crane, are successfully made by flame cutting from thick steel plates. Tolerances reported held are ± 125 μm (± 0.005 in.) with plate up to 100 mm (4 in.) thick and ± 250 μm (± 0.010 in.) to 200 mm (8 in.) thickness.

Gears are cut from cast and forged blanks, bar stock, sheet metal, laminated plastic, and molded shapes. Sometimes machining is the most economical method for small quantities. Sometimes it is most economical for large quantities, such as for gears stamped from sheet metal for watches, clocks, toys, and appliances. Generally gears are machined because that is the only way of getting the degree of accuracy or processing the hard material required by modern exacting mechanisms like internal combustion engines, aircraft, machine tools, etc. Gear-cutting methods may be divided into three classes as follows:

1. The *forming* method, which uses a cutter having the same form as the space between the teeth being cut. The cutter may be a single-point tool on a planer or shaper, a rotating cutter on a milling machine, or a broach.
2. The *template* method, in which a reciprocating cutting tool is guided by a master former or template on a machine called a gear planer. This method is slow and has been displaced for all but quite large and coarse pitch gears.
3. The *generating* method, in which the cutting profile of the tool is like that of a mating gear or rack tooth. The cutter and work roll together as though in mesh to develop the tooth form.

FORM CUTTING

Cutting Gear Teeth on a Milling Machine.   Spur, helical, worm, and straight bevel gears may be cut on milling machines with standard dividing heads and arbors. Gear cutters are the only tools needed that are not used for other kinds of operations, and their cost is low, from \$25 to \$100 each depending on size. A cutter will cut many gears, if needed. Setup is easy. At one time most gears were form cut, but during the present century generating has proven to be a more efficient method of manufacturing gears. Milling machines are not used in modern gear manufacture except when one or a few gears are made at a time and when more efficient equipment is not available. That is because the cutting of gears on a milling machine is a relatively slow and inaccurate process.

When a gear is cut on a milling machine, it is mounted on a dividing head, usually but not always between centers, and the cutter is carried on an arbor. The table is swiveled as illustrated in Fig. 24-7 to align the teeth of a helical gear with the cutter but not for a spur gear. The dividing head is geared to the table for a helical gear but not for a spur gear, so that the helical gear revolves as it passes the cutter. One tooth space is cut at a time. After each cut on any gear, the dividing head is manipulated in the usual manner to index the gear to the next space, and so on.

Bevel gears with theoretically correct tooth forms cannot be cut with rotary cutters on a milling machine. Occasionally, a bevel gear may be gashed out on a milling machine in an emergency, but then the teeth must be filed by hand after being cut to make them perform satisfactorily.

Gear Tooth Form Cutters. Commercial form-relieved cutters for spur gears with a $14\frac{1}{2}°$ pressure angle and composite form are available in sets. Each set covers one diametral pitch. Each cutter in a set covers a range of certain numbers of teeth and is only an approximation for all but one of the gears in the range. Gear tooth cutters appear in Fig. 24-2. Those made particularly for heavy rough cuts are called *stocking cutters*.

Production Form Cutting. Gears sometimes are roughed out by form cutting and then finished by generating when manufactured in quantities. Form-cutting machines, commonly called *gashing machines,* are made for the specific purpose of roughing gears rapidly with inexpensive cutters. One type uses a circular form cutter and operates like a milling machine, but has a built-in indexing mechanism and roughs out gears automatically. The operator has only to unload and load the work. Such machines are also commonly used for cutting slots and grooves around parts other than gears. A fully tooled gashing machine for spur and bevel gears up to about 1.5 m (60 in.) diameter is quoted in excess of $200,000.

Internal gears and splines with no obstructions may be cut by normal internal broaching. External gears may be cut on surface broaching machines (Chap. 25), a few teeth at a time, indexing the gear for another few teeth, and so on all around. A faster method is to push or pull gear blanks (upward to let chips fall) through a *pot broach* or die containing a series of rings of internal teeth (or internal strips of broach teeth) that cut progressively along the length of the broach. A blank enters at the bottom and emerges at the top with a complete set of teeth (spur or helical). Production rates of more than 250 gears per hour are common for both cast iron and steel, and as many as 510 per hour for two at a time. Tool life may be well over 1 million gears, with 15,000 to 25,000 steel gears or 35,000 to 50,000 cast-iron gears per broaching tool grind. This is a large-quantity production process because a pot broach from 750 to 1500 mm (ca. 30 to 60 in.) long and usable for only one kind of gear may cost up to $10,000 and more, and a pot broaching machine about $200,000.

A *Shear-Speed gear shaper* form cuts internal and external spur gears, splines, clutch teeth, and many special shapes. Single-point tools, one for each tooth space, are arrayed in a circle and point radially. The cutters are mounted around a hollow head for an external gear. The gear blank is mounted on a fixture below and is reciprocated into the head. The tools are fed radially a predetermined amount each stroke and are retracted slightly on the return stroke for clearance. All tooth spaces are cut at the same time.

The Shear-Speed gear shaper is the fastest gear cutter for many cases and can turn out average gears in 15 to 50 seconds each. A high degree of accuracy is obtained because it depends mostly on the tooling, which is made up especially for each job.

The tooling for a job may cost several thousands of dollars, but the cutters can be resharpened easily many times. Because of the tooling cost, the process is economical only for large quantities of parts, but experience has been that tool costs per piece for large quantities are no more and may be less than for other methods.

Shear-Speed gear shaping machines are made in several sizes to take gears up to about 500 mm (20 in.) diameter. A model with a capacity for external gears up to around 175 mm (7 in.) diameter costs about $150,000.

GEAR GENERATING

Gear Hobs.   Hobbing is a generating process done with a cutter called a *hob* that revolves and cuts like a milling cutter. Its teeth lie on a helix like a worm. A typical hob is illustrated and its elements are designated in Fig. 33-8. Lengthwise gashes expose the cutting faces that have a contour simulating a rack. The teeth are form-relieved behind the cutting edges. As the hob revolves one turn, the effect is as though the simulated rack were to move lengthwise an amount equal to the lead of the thread on which the teeth lie. When a gear is cut, it is positioned and revolved as if it were in mesh with such a rack. The hob teeth take progressive cuts relative to each tooth space in the manner illustrated in Fig. 33-9. A hob cuts all gears having the same

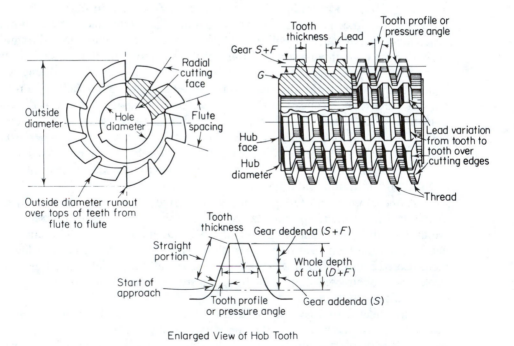

Enlarged View of Hob Tooth

Figure 33-8   Hob and its elements. (Courtesy Illinois Tool Works Co.)

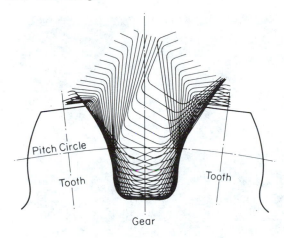

Figure 33-9 Action of a hob as its teeth progress through and cut the tooth space in a gear.

tooth form and pitch as the rack it represents regardless of number of teeth. When a hob becomes dull, all teeth are ground the same amount on the radial cutting face. Because of the way the teeth are relieved, the exposed tooth face after sharpening has substantially the same form as before.

A hob may have one, two, or more threads. When a spur gear with N teeth is being cut, it can turn only one revolution when a single-thread hob turns N times, once when a double-thread hob turns $N/2$ times, and so on. Thus a single-thread hob does not produce at as high a rate as a multiple-thread hob turning at the same speed but cuts a more accurate involute because more of its teeth act in each gear tooth space.

Hobs are made of high-speed steel or cemented carbide or with carbide-tipped teeth in several standard classes of accuracy. Hardened but unground hobs are satisfactory for average work, especially for roughing. High-speed steel hobs cost about $125 to $1100 for small to large sizes. Hobs finish ground all over for accuracy cost from $30 to $300 more. Solid cemented carbide hobs may cost 5 to 15 times as much as equivalent high-speed steel hobs. Hobs are made in several styles. The most common is the straight hob shown in Fig. 33-8.

Hobbing Machines. A gear is being hobbed on a hobbing machine in Fig. 33-10. The hob is set at an angle in a horizontal plane so its teeth line up with the tooth spaces of the gear. A motor drives the hob through speed change gears. Generally hob surface speeds are about the same as milling cutter speeds for comparable materials and other conditions and are governed by the same principles. When the hob is engaged with the gear, its teeth wear in a limited zone. When the teeth become dull there after cutting a number of gears, the hob is shifted lengthwise to bring sharp teeth into action. The hob is run in the new position until dull again, and the shifting is repeated until all the hob teeth are used. Then the hob is taken off, and all the teeth are resharpened.

The hob spindle and work spindle are connected through index change gears that are selected to make the work gear rotate at the proper speed in relation to the hob. Usually, the hob is set to cut to depth alongside the gear and then feed across the width

Figure 33-10   Gear being hobbed on a hobbing machine. (Courtesy Barber Colman Co.)

of the gear as the gear and hob rotate together. The feed is expressed in inches per revolution of the gear. Common feed rates are between 0.5 and 5.0 mm/rev (0.02 and 0.20 ipr). The feed can be obtained through feed change gears in a drive from the work spindle to a leadscrew that moves the hob carriage. Some machines have a hydraulic drive. Helical gears of limited width and angle may be cut by feeding the hob at the helix angle across the gear. However, on most machines the hob is fed only in a direction parallel to the work axis. The index and feed gears must then be selected in relation to each other to advance (or retard) the progression of the hob around the gear for each increment of feed parallel to the work axis to produce the required helix angle. Some machines have a differential between the feed and hob drives to advance (or retard) the progression of the hob. This makes index gear selection and setup easier.

For 200 years or so the motions of gear-cutting machines have been synchronized through gear drives, and that is the case for most hobbers today. However, hobbing machines have appeared in recent years with electronic and numerical controls on which the calculated rate and position of each motion to produce a given gear are digitally input, either by pushbuttons, dials, or tape control. The motions are kept in proper relationship by feedback (Chap. 35). Transducers constantly send back signals reporting the rates and positions of all the motions simultaneously, and any deviation from the input is corrected through the electronic circuitry. Electronic controlled machines are said to cost about 50% more than the older kinds, but save most of the setup time of 20 to 90 minutes for each different gear and thus offer an advantage for short-run production.

Hobbing machines are the most popular gear cutters and are made in many sizes, styles, and grades. Some have horizontal work axes, but most are vertical for stability.

Most are general-purpose machines, but some are specialized. For large-quantity production, hobbing machines are made with several workstations and often operate automatically. Sizes vary from small machines (may be bench mounted) for watch and instrument gears to huge ones for gears over 6 m (20 ft) in diameter. For a given nominal size, various grades are offered; e.g., in the medium-size range, the drive motor may be from about 3.7 kW (5 hp) to 19kW (25 hp) with corresponding machine strength and rigidity. The more powerful and stronger machines can cut coarser gear teeth, wider gears, more gears at one loading, faster, more accurately, etc. A medium-size general-purpose hobbing machine for gears up to 500 mm (19.6 in.) diameter, with up to 4 MOD (ca. 5 DP) teeth, and 240 mm (ca. 9.5 in.) wide can be purchased for less than $30,000, but heavier and more powerful models cost up to $200,000, and comparable CNC machines $250,000 and more.

Gear Shaping. A gear is shaped by a reciprocating cutter in the form of a single tooth, rack, or pinion. The gear blank and cutter move together as though in mesh, and a series of cuts are taken as depicted in Fig. 33-11.

The teeth of the typical pinion-type gear shaper cutter of Fig. 33-12 have a true involute form in any section normal to the axis and are form-relieved on the sides, outside, and root for clearance. The face of the cutter is dished to provide rake. As this face is ground to resharpen the cutter, the outside diameter becomes smaller, but the teeth retain their involute form and pitch. Cutters for helical gears have helical teeth. A spur gear cutter is capable of generating any gear of the same pitch in the same system, but a helical gear cutter can generate only gears having one pitch and helix angle. Disk-type cutters from stock run in price from about $200 to $900 depending on size and tooth form.

Gear Shapers. The cutter is mounted on the lower end of a reciprocating vertical spindle on most gear shapers, as shown in Fig. 33-13, and is revolved as it

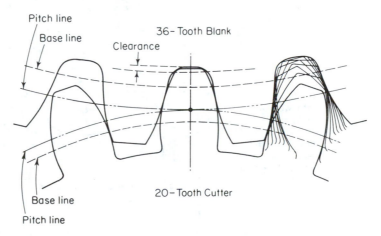

Figure 33-11 Generating action of a rotary-gear shaper cutter. (Courtesy Fellows Gear Shaper Co.)

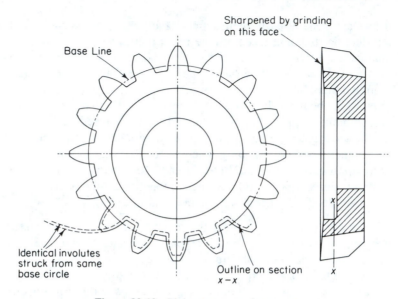

Figure 33-12 Pinion-type gear shaper cutter.

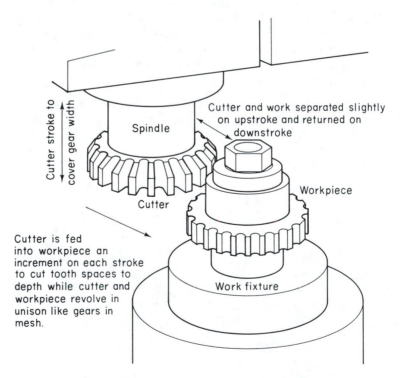

Figure 33-13 Operation zone of a gear shaper.

reciprocates up and down. The spindle is guided by a cam to move the cutter in a helical path to cut helical gears. The reciprocating drive of the cutter spindle may be mechanical or hydraulic. The workpiece is on a vertical spindle below the cutter, and the distance between the spindle axes is set to the required center distance of cutter and workpiece. The cutter and workpiece are made to revolve in unison as though in mesh. This relationship is arranged by change gears in the drive between cutter and work spindles on most machines. However, as with hobbing machines, electronic and numerical controlled gear shapers have appeared in recent years, and on such machines the necessary rates and positions for each spindle are specified digitally to an electronic circuitry that keeps the motions going and synchronized through feedback.

The cutter is fed inward to depth while revolving with the workpiece on a gear shaper. One or more cuts are taken in producing a gear depending upon material, design of gear and blank, work-holding fixture, and subsequent finishing operations if any. Sometimes economical results are obtained in production from rough cutting on one machine and finish cutting on another.

A mechanical gear shaper for gears up to about 250 mm (10 in.) diameter with 100 mm (4 in.) stroke and a 3.75-kW (5-hp) motor costs about $130,000 equipped. A numerically controlled gear shaper with about 450 mm (18 in.) diameter capacity has a price in the vicinity of $200,000.

Gear shaping can produce internal gears and splines, gears close to flanges, cluster gears, and continuous herringbone gears (all of which cannot be cut by rotating cutters like hobs), and also racks, cams, and pawls. A shaper in a factory for cutting forms for which it is best suited may well be kept busy in spare time with other gears. The length of stroke of a shaper may limit the width of gear it can cut, but on the other hand, short approach and overtravel distances make shaping fast for some narrow gears. Tooling costs about the same for gear shaping as for hobbing.

A number of varieties of gear shapers serve various purposes. Some are made with multiple work stations for large-quantity production. Some gear shapers use rack-type cutters which are relatively easy to make because the teeth have straight sides. However, a *rack shaper* is one that cuts racks but uses a pinion shaped cutter. The machine has a long table that feeds the work past the cutter.

Tangear Generator. Single-point cemented carbide cutting tools are rotated in opposite directions on the peripheries of two cutter heads with horizontal and parallel axes on the Tangear generator as shown in Fig. 33-14. The workpiece with its axis vertical is rotated as it is fed horizontally (typically a short distance of 8 mm) between the cutter heads. The motions are connected together and synchronized so that the cutters act as though in mesh with the gear and progressively generate the teeth and form cut the root fillets. The teeth are rough cut as the gear moves to the cutters and are finish cut on the back stroke. The relationship set between workpiece and cutter head velocities determines the helix angle.

Conventional and crowned helical gears can be cut with diameters from 20 to 100 mm (ca. $\frac{3}{4}$ to 4 in.), face widths up to 25 mm (1 in.), and helix angles from 10 to 40°. Gears can be generated at the rate of about 600 per hour, 6 to 10 times as fast

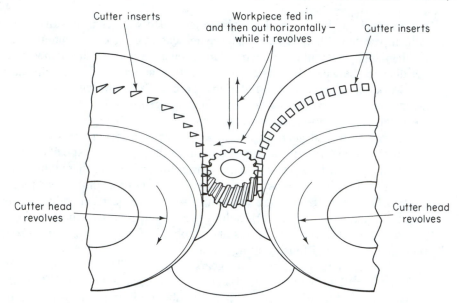

Figure 33-14 Scheme of operation of the Tangear gear cutter.

as hobbing. Time to change cutting tools is about 30 minutes but needs to be done only every 30 to 50 hours. A set of tooling is estimated to cost in excess of $15,000 and a Tangear generating machine $200,000 or so. Although fast, the process is only applicable for large-quantity production of a limited variety of gears.

G-Trac Gear Generators. Single-point high-speed cutting tools are carried on an endless chain of tool blocks on a G-Trac gear generator. One model for moderate quantities of gears has a single row of cutting tools partially shown in Fig. 33-15. As these are sped around the track, the work is fed into the cutters and rolled as though in mesh with a single tooth simulated by the cutters. Thus one tooth space is generated. Then the work is withdrawn, indexed to the next tooth space, fed in again, and so on around the gear.

Another G-Trac model for large quantities has a number of rows of teeth (typically 14) around the chain of blocks. The work is fed into the cutters and revolved continuously as though in mesh with a simulated rack, until all tooth spaces are finished. On both models spur and helical gears (up to 45° helix angle) as large as 356 mm (14 in.) in diameter can be cut and crowned and can be stacked to a height of 190 mm ($7\frac{1}{2}$ in.) times the cosine of the helix angle.

G-Trac generator cutter life is claimed to be six to 175 times as long as for hobs. Special machines are available for sharpening the cutters (one model at $150,000 and another at $300,000), and the cutters may also be sharpened all at one time in a special fixture ($2000) on a standard surface grinder. A G-Trac machine has a 25-hp motor. It is said to be 6 to 10 times as fast as hobbing, but the cost of a machine is high (over $600,000).

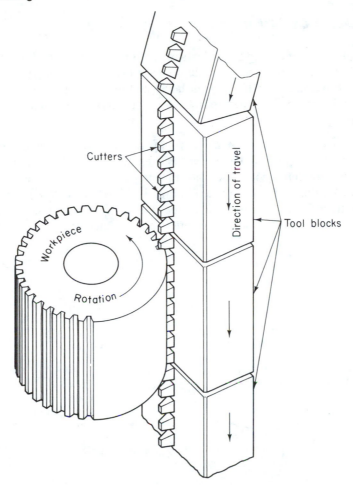

Cutters

Workpiece

Rotation

Direction of travel

Tool blocks

Figure 33-15   Method of operation of a Gleason G-Trac Gear Generator.

Comparison of Gear Manufacturing Methods.   The large majority of all gears are hobbed or shaped. Other methods all have some limitations, such as the range of sizes, kind of work, high tooling and equipment costs, etc. Each excels in certain applications, but none is as universal as hobbing and shaping. More gears are hobbed than manufactured in any other way. Shaping loses time on the backstroke, while hobbing is more continuous and in many cases is somewhat faster. For reasons already cited, shaping is more versatile. One authority concedes the advantage to hobbing with respect to tooth spacing and runout accuracy because of continuous indexing. Also, the heat generated in hobbing is dispersed uniformly over the workpiece and cutter. Shaping is considered better for accuracy of tooth profile because of the straight cut it takes along the tooth. Hobbing and shaping are considered about equal for lead accuracy. Many gears semifinished by hobbing and shaping and by other methods are finished by rolling and by shaving and grinding described later.

BEVEL GEAR CUTTING

Machines for cutting bevel gears may be divided into two classes: (1) for straight teeth, and (2) for curved teeth. The basic machines of universal type are the two-tool straight bevel generator and the spiral bevel and hypoid generator. Others are available for special or supplementary purposes, and the most important of them will be described briefly.

Machines and Methods for Straight Tooth Bevel Gears. A basic way of cutting straight tooth bevel gears is to employ two cutters reciprocating along the sides of one tooth (or tooth space) at a time in paths that impart the correct taper to the teeth. The cutting action is depicted in Fig. 33-16(A). The tools have straight cutting edges on their front ends and simulate the sides of teeth of an imaginary crown gear in mesh with the gear being cut. The cutters are mounted and reciprocated on a cradle that is

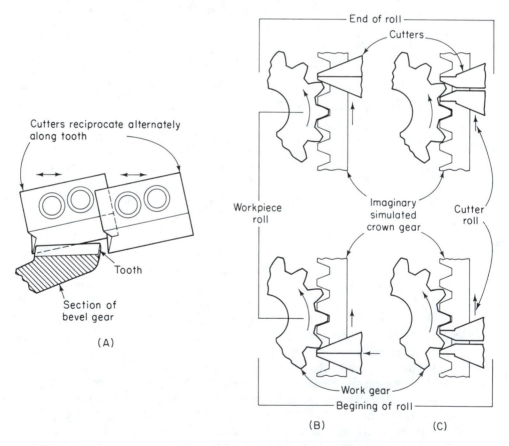

Figure 33-16 Actions of straight-tooth bevel gear generators: (A) reciprocating cutting action along each tooth; relative motions of workpiece and tools on (B) the completing generator; (C) two tool generator.

rocked in time with the roll of the gear to provide the generating action. To begin a cycle, a gear blank is chucked in the workhead of the machine, is advanced to the cutting position, and is then fed directly into the two reciprocating tools to cut a tooth almost to full depth. The workpiece and the cutters are rolled together as though in mesh. The initial roll is to the bottom of the generating cycle to rough shape the tooth. The workpiece is then fed to full depth, and a fast uproll generates the finished tooth. At the top of the roll, the workpiece is backed away and indexed while the cradle and workhead return to the roughing position for the next tooth. The cycle is repeated until all teeth in the gear are cut, and then the machine stops. A machine may be arranged to do only roughing or only finishing.

Two tool generators are economical for small and moderate quantities of gears. They can cut bevel gears with hubs or flanges that would interfere with rotary cutters. A typical 9 diametral pitch 30 tooth gear is completed at the rate of 7 gears/hr. A machine for small straight tooth bevel gears employs two disk-type milling cutters with interlocking teeth on a cradle that rolls with the workpiece to generate the teeth. That method is reported capable of rough and finish cutting 30 tooth gears at a rate of over 12 gears/hr.

Straight bevel gear generators are available in all sizes for gears from about 14 to 886 mm (actually 0.75 to 34.9 in.) in diameter. One with a capacity for gears up to 886 mm (34.9 in.) in diameter costs about $350,000 with tooling.

Teeth cut on newer straight bevel gear generators can be slightly crowned from end to end to localize contact and prevent damaging load concentration at the ends of the teeth. These are called *Coniflex* gears. The same effect is obtained from a difference in curvature of the mating surfaces of bevel gears with curved teeth.

Fine pitch straight bevel gears are commonly cut from the solid in one operation. Others may be rough cut in one operation and finished in another, particularly in large quantities for which machines and tools are available for rapid roughing without generation.

The *Revacycle Process* is the fastest way to produce straight bevel gears in large quantities. The rotating Revacycle cutter roughs and finishes a tooth space during each revolution it makes. The machine burrs each gear and automatically presents a new one to the cutter. A typical performance is finish cutting to a depth of 1 mm (ca. 0.04 in.) on a 10-tooth gear at a rate of 165 gears/hr. Such a machine for gears up to 150 mm (6 in.) diameter with a face width of 25 mm (1 in.) costs about $250,000. Automatic loading and handling devices are often added to enable one operator to take care of a number of machines.

Large straight bevel and spur gears are cut on the *gear planer*. This is the oldest type of machine capable of cutting bevel gears with teeth tapering in the correct manner. A single-point planing tool is reciprocated across the face of a gear and controlled by a template or former to produce the profile shapes of the teeth.

Machines for Curved Tooth Bevel and Hypoid Gears.   A *spiral bevel gear and hypoid generator* employs a special form of face mill like the one on the machine of Fig. 33-17. The cutter represents a tooth of a mating gear and is rolled with the gear or pinion being cut to generate the tooth profile. The machine can be arranged for

Figure 33-17   Spiral bevel gear, rotating cutter, and cradle on a Gleason hypoid generator. (Courtesy Gleason Works.)

spiral bevel, Zerol, and hypoid gears and pinions. Sometimes both sides of a tooth space are finish cut in one operation, and sometimes only one side, depending on the tools available or the quality and quantity of gears required. Machines and cutters are available for gears from about 7 mm to 2.2 m (actually 0.28 to 90 in.) diameter. A spiral bevel and hypoid generator for job cutting gears up to 406 mm (16 in.) diameter costs about $350,000; one to 864 mm (34 in.) diameter is $450,000, and for gears up to $1\frac{1}{4}$ m (50 in.) diameter is over $1,000,000 (over $1,500,000 with a full set of tooling).

The larger member of a pair of spiral bevel, Zerol, or hypoid gears is commonly cut complete without generation on a machine especially designed for this purpose. This reduces cutting time and cost, particularly for large quantities. This form cutting may be done in several ways. Of these, the *Formate* method utilizes a cutter with progressively larger teeth, so it is in effect a circular broach that finishes a tooth space in one revolution. A gap between the last tooth and first tooth permits the gear to be indexed to the next tooth space while the cutter turns. *Helix-form* gears are cut in much the same way, but the cutter is given an axial movement that produces form cut gears closer to theoretical shape. The pinion of the set is generated to match a form-cut gear.

Spiral bevel, Zerol, and hypoid gears too large for generating machines with rotating cutters are cut on a *planning generator*. It employs a single planing tool that is timed to take a cut on tooth after tooth on the continuously revolving blank. The tool is carried on a cradle that is rocked with respect to the workpiece to provide the generating action.

Spiral bevel and hypoid grinders are available in both generating and Formate types. They finish grind the teeth after the gears have been semifinished and hardened, using an abrasive cup wheel with the same effective shape and action as the face mill cutter (Fig. 33-17). This corrects hardening errors and makes the gears uniform. A Hypoid grinder for gears to 711 mm (28 in.) diameter costs about $500,000.

Gear Tooth Rounding and Chamfering. The ends of the teeth on a gear are commonly rounded or chamfered for strength, easy engagement, etc. Machines are available that use end milling and other types of cutters of suitable shapes for the cuts desired. Typically, the cutter is traversed under cam control around the profile at the end of a tooth as the gear revolves.

GEAR FINISHING

A gear tooth surface that is hobbed or shaped is composed of tiny flats. Such a surface is satisfactory for some purposes but is not good enough where a high degree of accuracy and stamina is required. The flats can be made very small by cutting at low feeds, but the operation then becomes slow and costly. Often the lowest net cost can be realized by cutting a gear fast with a less accurate and less expensive tool to tolerances of around 25 μm (0.001 in.). Then a finishing operation is added to obtain the necessary tooth straightness, size, concentricity, spacing, and involute form with small tolerances. Furthermore, gears often are heat treated for hardness and strength, and that tends to warp them and form scale. Finishing after hardening corrects these deficiencies.

Finishing operations are performed to make gears accurate, quiet, smooth running and long lasting. They include shaving and rolling (described on p. 811) for soft gears and grinding and lapping for gears harder than about 40 R_C. Only 100 μm (a few thousandths of an inch) or less of stock are left on gear teeth for finishing.

Gear Shaving. A gear is shaved by running it at around 120 m/min 400 fpm) in mesh with and pressed against a cutter in the form of a gear or rack with gashes or grooves on its tooth faces, as typified in Fig. 33-18. The edges of the grooves are sharp and actually scrape fine chips from the faces of the teeth of the workpiece. Cutting fluid is applied. Some sliding normally takes place between gear teeth in mesh, and this action is augmented in gear shaving by crossing the axes of the cutter and work gear, generally from 5 to 15°, and by reciprocating the workpiece as it is revolved in mesh with the shaving cutter. The workpiece may be fed radially or tangentially into the cutter. Shaving removes from 25 to 100 μm (0.001 to 0.004 in.) from tooth thickness and can correct from 65 to 80% of the errors on hobbed or shaped teeth. Shaving can be made to crown gear teeth slightly at their centers to localize tooth contact and keep it away from the ends of the teeth.

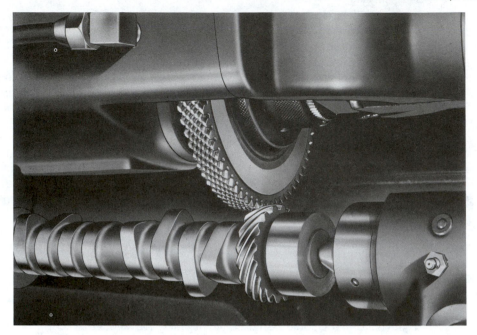

Figure 33-18   Camshaft gear being shaved on a rotary gear shaving machine. (Courtesy National Broach and Machine Co.)

The gear in Fig. 33-18 is being shaved by a gear-type shaving cutter on a *rotary shaving machine*. The workpiece is loaded between live centers, raised against the cutter, and reciprocated while being driven in one direction and then the other. Rotary gear shaving machines are made in many sizes for semi- and fully automatic operations to finish external and internal gears from the smallest to over 5 m (16 ft.) in diameter. A rotary gear shaving machine for gears up to 400 mm (ca. 16 in.) diameter by 150 mm (ca. 6 in.) wide costs about $125,000.

A shaving cutter in the form of a rack is reciprocated lengthwise at high speed in mesh with a workpiece on a *rack-type shaving machine*. At the same time the workpiece is reciprocated sideways and fed into the rack. A rack-type shaver produces uniformly precise gears because the rack form is easier to make accurately and has fuller contact with the work than a rotary shaver. The rack-type shaver cannot accommodate cluster or large gears. The cutters are large and expensive but have long lives and low cost per piece. They are more suitable for long runs, and circular-type tools are better for job lots.

Gear shaving is a low cost rapid production process. Many gears can be shaved in less than half a minute apiece, some in as short a time as five seconds. Each cutter is suitable only for a single pitch and tooth form, and a demand for many gears is necessary to warrant its cost. Average expected life with four regrinds for a rotary shaving cutter is reported to be 85,000 gears.

Gear Tooth Grinding.   Hardened gear teeth are ground by forming and by generating. Three variations of grinding gear teeth with formed wheels are depicted at the top of Fig. 33-19. The results depend upon the accuracy to which the wheel is trued. This is done by guiding the truing diamonds on the machine through a pantograph mechanism from templates typically six times the gear tooth size. A workpiece between centers is reciprocated under the grinding wheel which is fed down at each stroke until desired size is reached. Then the workpiece is cleared from the wheel and indexed to the next tooth space. Usual procedure is to rough grind around a gear in this way, and then finish grind with the trued wheel set to depth. Form grinding is done on external and internal spur and helical gears, splines, and similar parts.

When spur or helical gears are ground by generating, the wheel or wheels are trued to simulate a mating rack. On one type of machine that uses a single wheel, as at the lower left in Fig. 33-19, the workpiece is carried under a reciprocating wheel and rolled as though it were in mesh with the rack. A spur gear is ground with its axis in line with the wheel movement, and a helical gear is swiveled. When one tooth space has been ground, the gear is indexed to grind the next, and so on.

Another type of generating gear grinder has two wheels as indicated in Fig. 33-19. It operates on the same principle as just described, but the wheels are not

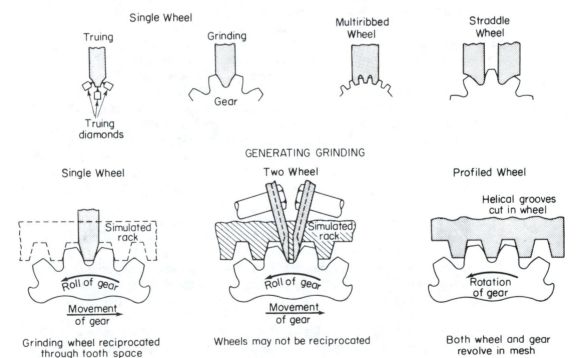

Figure 33-19   Methods of grinding gears.

reciprocated. They are large enough to cover an entire tooth working surface on gears not over about 32 mm ($1\frac{1}{4}$ in.) wide. It is faster than the one-wheel generator for narrow gears.

A third method of generating grinding employs a wide grinding wheel with a helical groove around its periphery. The grooved cross section simulates a basic rack form engaged with the gear as the grinding wheel and workpiece rotate in mesh with an action like that of hobbing. The gear is fed axially to carry the action fully across its teeth. An average of 40 to 60 gears are reported ground for one wheel dressing. This is the fastest generating method but requires much time to prepare a wheel for each pitch—an average of 4 hours to true and 20 minutes to retrue. Tooth spacing errors can be better controlled by a grooved wheel that covers several teeth at once as compared to grinding one space at a time.

Form grinding has been found faster in some cases, generating in others; but the differences are not large. The area of wheel contact is small for generating, and there is less likelihood of burning and cracking hardened steel, for which care must be exercised in form grinding. The root of a gear space can be finished and blended with the tooth profile better by forming than by generating. Generating leaves small flats on the teeth, and subsequent lapping is necessary if they must be removed.

Gear Lapping and Honing.   Hardened gears are commonly lapped or honed after heat treatment to remove scale, nicks, and burrs, improve surface finish, and correct small errors. Surfaces are finished to 0.5 μm (20 μin.) R_a and better. Occasionally, even ground gears may be given final touches by these methods to eliminate all wheel marks. Essentially, the workpiece is rotated in mesh with a gear form with crossed axes and reciprocated in the manner illustrated for shaving.

Internal and external spur and helical gears are lapped by running the workpiece with a mating gear or with one or more cast iron toothed laps under a flow of fine abrasive in oil. The work is turned first in one direction and then in the other to lap both sides of the teeth. Several methods are common; among them are *cramp lapping* or forcing the workpiece hard against the lap to speed the action, braking the workpiece against the driving lap, and running several laps at once at different pitch points to reduce tooth spacing errors. A gear lapping operation averages from one to several minutes. On average work, a lap can finish several thousand gears and then must be recut.

A flexible gear lapping tool (called a Poli-Tool) molded from a rubber-like porous material is run with a lapping compound to put a high polish on gear teeth. Surface finishes as fine as 150 nm (ca. 5 μin.) R_a have been obtained.

Bevel-type gears are commonly lapped (and kept) in sets by running gear and pinion together with abrasive slurry jet sprayed into the tooth mesh. Various axial, radial, and twisting motions with braking are added to speed the action and distribute it over the teeth.

Honing is done by helical gear or worm-shaped tools. They may be made of steel, for strength, with abrasive, cemented carbide, or diamond particles embedded in the tooth surfaces. However, most are made of plastic impregnated with abrasive. Their flexibility is advantageous and cost is lower than steel, mainly because each plastic hone can be retrued a number of times. The honing tool is pushed with constant force against the workpiece but must be allowed some float to prevent damage, in contrast to shaving done at constant center distance between the axes of workpiece and tool. Commonly, an axial vibratory motion is given to the hone in addition to other movements.

Internal and external spur and helical gears are honed to correct small errors in spacing, lead, or eccentricity and particularly to make them run quietly. Honing tools cost more, but honing is faster and is preferred to lapping for production.

Comparison of Finishing Operations.   Basically the finishing method for a gear is dictated by the degree of accuracy required and the available equipment. Invariably greater precision demands more costly operations for gears as illustrated in Fig. 33-20. In the case of an 8 DP gear cited in the example, the most that can be achieved in manufacturing is an involute accuracy of 1.5 μm (0.00006 in.) (AGMA 17). When limitations of measuring methods are also taken into account, a practical upper limit is 2.8 μm (0.00011 in.) (AGMA 15). At the extreme opposite end of the scale, for gears where accuracy is of no concern, there is little cost saving for a tolerance larger than 0.38 mm (0.015 in.) (AGMA 3 or 4). (See Gear Inspection for AGMA.)

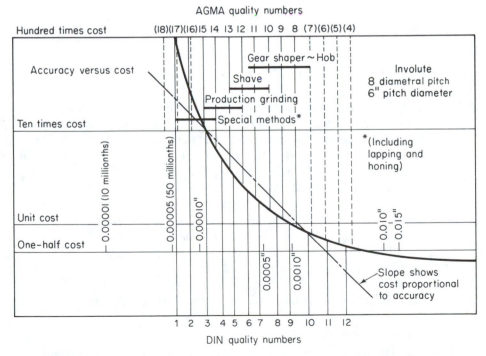

Figure 33-20   Typical comparison of gear quality versus manufacturing cost. (From Carl S. Rice, "Gear Accuracy versus Cost: Here Are the Trade-offs," *Manufacturing Engineering*, Apr. 1977, by permission of the publisher.)

It has been found that most good-quality machines perform well when errors in gear tooth form or spacing do not exceed 5 μm (0.0002 in.). Smaller tolerances are required for some products, but cost then rises rapidly. On the other hand, errors of 10 to 15 μm (0.0004 to 0.0006 in.) or larger cause a pronounced inferiority in the running qualities of hardened gears.

As an explanation of the differences in costs for different gear finishing methods, one authority has estimated the time to finish a 10 DP gear with 25 teeth and a 32° left-handed helix angle. He reported the gear was shaved or rolled in as little as 22 seconds, ground in 5 to 15 minutes (even longer with special care), and honed in 21 seconds. Thus shaving, cold rolling, or burnishing for finishing before heat treatment and honing afterwards is the cheapest way to finish hard spur and helical gears. That is usual treatment for most automotive, agricultural equipment, aircraft, and machine tool drive gears. Gears that cannot be shaved or rolled because of shape or small quantities, and spur and helical gears that require the highest degree of accuracy, must be ground after hardening. That is commonly done to make master gears and shaving cutters, for instance. Good-quality straight and spiral bevel and hypoid gears are lapped or ground for best results.

Care should be taken that gears are not made too much better than necessary. A machine tool manufacturer found that some gears case hardened to 60 R_C hardness and ground were not appreciably better for his purpose than others through-hardened to only 38 to 48 R_C. The softer but tougher and stronger gears could be finished by hobbing alone to tolerances around 10 μm (0.0004 in.) that were adequate.

GEAR INSPECTION

The American Gear Manufacturers Association (AGMA) has set up a practical gear-classification system for spur, helical, herringbone, bevel, and hypoid gears based on the broad experience of many manufacturers. Gears are classified in terms of tolerances commonly considered in manufacture and usage, and each class is given a number, e.g., AGMA Class No. 8. The larger the class number, the smaller the tolerance. In addition, the system codifies the more usual materials and heat treatments for gears. Thus a gear may be specified by its class number followed by symbols for specific backlash (tooth thinning), material, and heat treatment. Tables giving complete specifications are in the AGMA *Gear Handbook*.

The inspection and measurement of gears involve some techniques not common for other products. Gears are tested for:

1. The accuracy of linear dimensions such as outside and root diameters and tooth thickness and depth
2. Tooth profile
3. Positions of the teeth as reflected by tooth spacing, runout, radial position, backlash, and helix angle or lead

4. The bearing and finish of the tooth faces
5. Noise

Gear testing can be divided into two kinds: functional and analytical. Functional checking shows how errors affect the way the gears work together, as when they are rolled together to test them for freedom or noise. It is usually the easiest way of testing for acceptable gears. Analytical checking actually measures the important elements. That may be done by making absolute measurements or by finding how much a gear differs from a master. Analytical checking is usually required to adjust or correct gear cutting or finishing equipment in setting it up to produce. Usually but not always, functional checking is done on fine pitch gears, and analytical checking on coarse pitch gears. As a rule, a gear is inspected by one method or the other, not both. Examples of these forms of testing are given in the following descriptions of typical gear checking equipment and methods.

Checking the Sizes of Gears and Gear Teeth. A *gear tooth vernier caliper* measures the thickness of a gear tooth at the pitch line as is done in Fig. 33-21. A *gear tooth comparator* is a similar device that measures the addendum depth to a specified tooth thickness.

Ground rolls of precise diameter to make theoretical contact at the pitch line may be placed in opposite tooth spaces of a gear, and the distance across them measured

Figure 33-21 Application of a gear tooth vernier caliper. (Courtesy Brown and Sharpe Manufacturing Co.)

by a micrometer or comparator. This is like measuring threads across wires. Formulas and tables of proper roll sizes and measurements are given in handbooks.

Checking Gear Tooth Profile. An optical comparator like the ones in Figs. 15-32 and 15-33 offers one way of checking the profiles and positions of gear teeth by comparing their enlarged shadows on a screen with a large scale drawing. Fixtures are commonly used to position the gears.

The scheme of Fig. 33-22 for measuring gear tooth involute profiles utilizes a vertical spindle carrying the gear above a disk of the same diameter as the base circle of the involute to be checked. The disk bears against a bar on a slide on the front of the machine. As the bar moves in a straight line, friction makes the disk roll along it, and any point on the edge of the bar traces the locus of an involute with respect to the disk. A finger is mounted on the same slide with its top touching a gear tooth directly above a point on the edge of the bar. Thus, as the slide moves, the tip of the finger (if not disturbed) traverses an involute curve with respect to the base circle of the gear, in the same way as does the point below on the edge of the bar. Any deviation in the form of the tooth displaces the finger, and the amount of displacement is shown by an indicator. Some machines are arranged with an electrical recorder to trace the deviation on a chart.

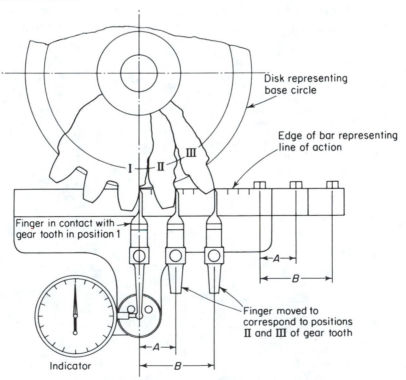

Figure 33-22 Operation scheme for an involute-profile measuring machine. (Courtesy Illinois Tool Works Co.)

Checking the Positions of Gear Teeth.   A typical device to check tooth spacing carries a gear freely between centers. A tapered block is brought in on a slide to locate a tooth space. An indicating finger previously set to a master makes contact with the face of the next tooth. Error in tooth spacing displaces the finger and is indicated on a dial.

The lead or helix angle of a helical gear may be compared with a master cam or the angle to which a sine bar is set (Chap. 15).

To check backlash, a work gear and master gear may be mounted on shafts at fixed center distances. The master gear is held still, and the slight movement or backlash of the engaged gear teeth is measured by an indicator.

Composite errors in tooth spacing, thickness, profile, runout, interference, and eccentricity are reflected in changes either in velocity or center distance when gears are run together. A common way of checking these errors is to run a gear with a quite accurate master gear as illustrated in Fig. 33-23. The work gear is held against the master gear which is rotated on a fixed center. The movements between the centers of the two gears caused by errors in the work gear are measured by a dial indicator

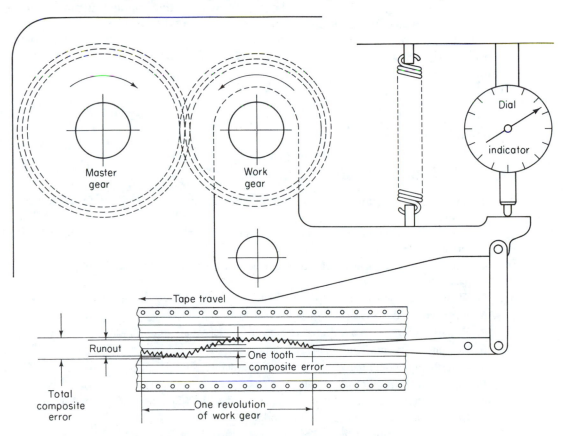

Figure 33-23   Sketch of the way a gear is rolled with a master gear to check composite errors.

and/or recorded on a moving tape or chart. The movements of the line on the chart indicate errors in the work gear.

Checking Gear Tooth Bearing and Surface Finish.   Bevel and hypoid gears commonly and other gears at times are inspected by running them together or with masters to determine where the teeth bear. Localized tooth bearing near the center of each face is desirable to avoid concentrating loads at the ends of teeth. The teeth are painted with marking compound that is rubbed away at contact to show bearing areas. Surface finish of tooth faces may be measured in the ways described in Chap. 15.

Checking for Noise.   Faulty gears are noisy and can be checked on machines in which they are run in a sound chamber together or with a master. Power is applied to one gear, and a brake loads the other. Characteristic sounds have such descriptive names as squeal, whine, growl, knocks, nicks, and marbles; each indicates certain kinds of gear errors to an experienced inspector.

Gear faults may also be detected by measuring frequencies and amplitudes of vibrations (sounds) while the finished product, such as a transmission, is run on a test stand. Careful analysis of the data obtained can point out the errors in gear production that cause the noises and lead to corrections. The matter of noisy gears has become particularly important with government regulation of noise levels in mechanical equipment.

QUESTIONS

1. What curve is found on most gear teeth, what are its advantages, and what are its characteristics?
2. Name the important elements of a gear tooth and specify the size of each for a full-depth tooth.
3. What are the main differences between gears in the diametral pitch system and those in the module system?
4. Define spur gear, helical gear, herringbone gear, worm, worm gear, bevel gear, crown gear, and hypoid gear.
5. What is gear form rolling, and when is it done?
6. What are the three classes of gear cutting methods?
7. How is a gear cut on a milling machine and under what circumstances?
8. How are gears form cut in large quantities?
9. Describe a hob and the way it generates gear teeth.
10. Describe the action of a vertical gear shaper and the pinion-type cutter used on it.
11. Compare gear hobbing and shaping with each other and with other methods of gear cutting.
12. Describe how a Tangear Generator works.
13. Describe the action of the G-Trac Gear Generator.

14. Describe the actions of the two basic machines of universal type for generating bevel gears.
15. Why are gear finishing methods used after gear cutting?
16. How are gears finished?
17. Describe the principle of gear shaving.
18. How and why are gear teeth ground?
19. Describe and compare honing and lapping of gear teeth.
20. What determines the methods used to finish a gear?
21. For what kinds of errors and in what basic ways are gears tested?
22. Describe the common methods of checking gear teeth.

PROBLEMS

1. Calculate the elements for:
   (a) A 12 diametral pitch gear of 36 teeth with full depth teeth and $14\frac{1}{2}°$ pressure angle.
   (b) A 12 diametral pitch gear of 36 teeth with stub teeth and 20° pressure angle.
   (c) A 36 teeth gear with a module of 2 mm.
2. Compute the important dimensions of a gear with a module of 4 mm, 32 teeth, and a width of 20 mm.
3. Compute the important dimensions for a 8 diametral pitch, $14\frac{1}{2}°$ pressure angle full-depth tooth gear that has 32 teeth and a width of $\frac{3}{4}$ in.
4. Compute the important dimensions for a 8 diametral pitch, 20° pressure angle stub tooth gear that has 32 teeth and a width of $\frac{3}{4}$ in.
5. A 1.187-in. diameter involute spline in SAE 1040 steel with a 20 R_C hardness can be form-rolled in 18 seconds. A set of forming dies costs $1050 but can turn out 200,000 pieces in its lifetime with no reconditioning necessary. The spline can be hobbed at a rate of 1 minute and 36 seconds per piece. A hobbing cutter costs $285, must be ground after cutting 200 pieces, and can be resharpened 50 times. The time to sharpen and replace the hob is 20 minutes. Capital charges are 50% for interest, insurance, taxes, and losses. Labor and overhead are worth a total of $27/hr. If machines are available in the plant for either method, what is the smallest number of pieces in a year's production that justifies the roll-forming method?
6. In the situation described in Prob. 5, hobbing machines are available with sufficient available time for the job, but machines must be purchased at a cost of $75,000 each if the parts are to be form-rolled. Each machine can be operated 1600 hr/yr. If 750,000 pieces are required per year, how long should it take to pay for the machine out of expected savings?
7. A 12 pitch gear with 36 teeth and $\frac{7}{8}$ in. wide can be cut on a Shear-Speed gear shaper at the rate of 2 gears in 55 seconds. The machine and tooling cost $169,000. On a hobbing machine that costs $43,000 best results are obtained from two cuts for each gear. Six gears are cut at a time, but the total time for each gear is 6 minutes. One worker operates four hobbing machines or two Shear-Speed shapers.

   Tool maintenance and overhead is assumed the same for either machine. Worker time costs \$15/hr. Twenty percent of the cost of a machine is charged each year for depreciation, interest, insurance, and taxes. A machine can be operated 2000 hr/yr.

(a) Which type of machine should be selected to produce 15,000 gears/yr if the machines are used for other work when not needed for this job?

(b) Which type of machine should be selected to produce 15,000 gears/yr if the machines have no other use and must be charged all to this job?

(c) Which type of machine should be selected to produce 100,000 gears/yr even if the machines cannot be used for other jobs?

8. A soft-steel spur gear with 40 teeth, 3.500 in. outside diameter, $14\frac{1}{2}°$ pressure angle, and 1 in. width is to be cut on a milling machine. What should be:

(a) The diametral pitch, addendum, tooth thickness, and whole depth?

(b) The specifications of the cutter?

(c) The number of turns of the dividing head crank to index each tooth?

(d) The cutting time with a feed rate of 0.003 ipt? Refer to a manufacturer's catalog for cutter specifications.

9. A spur gear with 30 teeth is to be hobbed with a 100-mm-diameter hob at 30 m/min. What should be the work speed in rpm if the hob has a single thread? A double thread?

10. A gear with 32 teeth and a module of 6 mm is made of mild steel. Two gears each 20 mm wide are put next to each other on a mandrel and cut in one pass by a single-thread hob having an outside diameter of 100 mm and run at 30 m/min. Calculate:

(a) The rpm of the hob.

(b) The rpm of the gears.

(c) The pitch diameter of the hob.

(d) The time to cut the gears with a feed of 1.5 mm/rev of the work and a distance for approach and overtravel of 40 mm.

11. A hardened 12 DP gear with 60 teeth and $1\frac{1}{4}$ in. width is shaved before heat treatment. After heat treatment it can be lapped in 3 minutes. A lap costs \$350 and is usable for 2000 gears. Honing takes 0.75 minutes; a hone costs \$975 and will finish 1000 gears before it must be discarded. Production time is worth \$30/hr. If satisfactory results can be obtained from either process, for what quantities should each be used?

REFERENCES

BRADLEY, W., "Noise Tells a Lot About Gears," *American Machinist*, July 26, 1971, p. 47.

CHIRONIS, N. P., *Gear Design and Application*, McGraw-Hill, New York, 1967.

CROCKETT, J. C., "Cold Rolling—Fast Way to Make Gears," *Machinery*, Mar. 1972, p. 33.

DALLAS, D. B., ed. *Tool and Manufacturing Engineers Handbook*, 3rd ed., Society of Manufacturing Engineers, Dearborn, Mich., 1976.

Gear Handbook, Vol. 1, AGMA 390.03, American Gear Manufacturers Association, Washington, D. C.,

"How Gearmaking Methods Compare," *Metal Progress*, Dec. 1973, p. 51.

HUNTRESS, E. A., "A New Way to Cut Gears," *American Machinist*, May 1979, p. 99.

JABLONOWSKI, J., "Fundamentals of Gear Cutting, Special Report 742," *American Machinist*, Feb. 1982, p. 139.

McCUE, J., "Rolling Splines—A Better Way," *American Machinist*, Aug. 1977, p. 87.

PFENNINGER, R., and E. BARTHOLET, "The Trend toward Gear Grinding," *Manufacturing Engineering*, June 1978, p. 57.

PSENKA, J. A., "Pot Broaching," *Manufacturing Engineering*, July 1977.

RICE, C. S., "Gear Production Update," *Manufacturing Engineering*, Apr. 1979, p. 83.

34

AUTOMATION

Automation is a word that has many meanings in industry today. The term was coined shortly after World War II at the Ford Motor Co. to describe the automatic handling of materials and parts between process operations. A concise definition is that automation represents "continuous automatic production"; in effect, the combination of automatic operations into integrated groups. This is said to be *fixed programming* and exists in molding lines in foundries, punch press lines, die casting, and for welding, assembling, and inspection operations as well as for chip-making machining. It is far advanced in the process industries, such as the petroleum and chemical industries, where production is high, processes are simple, not changed often, and straightforward, and the product is easy to move.

Automatic machines of all kinds existed long before the term "automation" was conceived. Some people consider automatic machines of all kinds within the realm of automation. Examples of automatic machines are given throughout this text; automatic bar and chucking machines and tracer lathes are examples. However, the discussion in this chapter is devoted to groups of machines in integrated manufacturing systems. The topics considered here are fixed program systems (synchronous and non-synchronous), flexible systems, fundamentals of system controls, automatic tool compensation, robotics, and automatic tracing.

Selectable or variable programming is another aspect of automation aimed at the output of a variety of parts or assemblies, each produced in small or moderate quantities, in one machine unit or system. This is carried out in *flexible manufacturing systems* described in this chapter and by numerical control of machines treated in Chaps. 35 and 36.

FIXED PROGRAMMING

Fixed Programming Systems.   Fixed program automation performs a certain specific operation or series of operations on a particular part or group of similar parts. Both the operations and the transfer of parts from station to station are automatic. Two forms are the *synchronous* and *nonsynchronous* systems depicted in Fig. 34-1.

A synchronous system, also called a dependent unit system, may have a series of machine or operation units in line, in a *transfer machine,* or around an indexing table, on a *rotary* or *circular index machine*. When the work is completed at all stations, all parts in the circuit are moved simultaneously to succeeding stations, and another cycle is started. The time for a cycle depends upon the slowest operation, and the highest efficiency is obtained when all operation times are made the same and minimal. For tool changes and breakdowns, all stations are shut down, and efficiency decreases as the number of stations increases. Examples of these systems and some variations will be described.

A nonsynchronous system, also called an independent unit system or power-free system, provides for a bank of parts to supply each machine and permits it to operate at its fastest rate. Any machine in the system may be shut down temporarily without stopping the others. Such a system has a high overall efficiency and can be planned

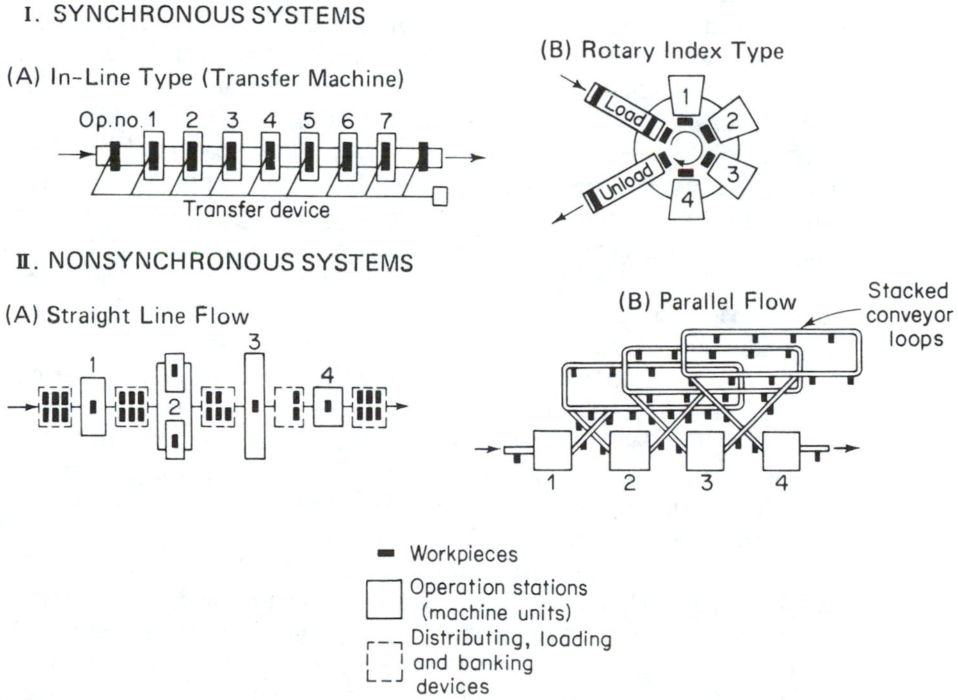

Figure 34-1   Diagrams of fixed-program systems of automation.

for the best combination of the machines. For *straight-line flow,* the banks of parts between machines may be contained in hoppers, magazines, elevators, etc. *Parallel flow* is an arrangement of conveyor stored banks between machines. The conveyors may be stacked one above the other in the least possible space adjacent to the line. Examples are described in more detail later.

Rotary Index Systems.   A moderate size rotary index machine is depicted in Fig. 34-2. The workpieces are carried on a circular table with a vertical axis. This type of system normally takes less floor space and is cheaper to construct than an equivalent in-line system but is limited to a few stations. One like that in Fig. 34-2 can be expected to cost several hundred thousand dollars. Typically, on machines with more stations (and for larger workpieces) on larger-diameter circles, the workpieces are carried on pallets that are moved from station to station on a circular track. An 11-station carousel rotary index machine for machining gate valve bodies is 34 ft in diameter and is priced at about $3 million. Another less common design has a small table, called a trunion, with a horizontal axis. The toolheads are arrayed on both sides, and the trunion indexes the work in a vertical plane from station to station.

Transfer Lines.   The common type of fixed program transfer line is the transfer machine (Fig. 34-3) consisting of a series of single-purpose machine tools through which a stream of parts is slid or lifted and carried from station to station. This system has been widely adopted for large-quantity production and even for moderate-quantity production with modifications because it has a number of favorable features. The straight-line workflow conforms naturally to continuous production and fits readily into desirable plant layouts. Considerable flexibility is permitted in planning for the number, kinds, and positions of stations with floor space and cost being the only limiting factors. Workpieces can be reoriented readily at desired stations in the line, and the least restriction is imposed upon approach of the tools to the part from any direction. Vibration, heat, and strain at any one station can be isolated from the others.

In addition to the unfavorable factors already cited for synchronous systems, transfer machines have some of their own. Some parts can be handled only on pallets or in individual fixtures for each piece, and that adds about 20% to cost. All pallets or parts moved from station to station need to be relocated and reclamped at each station. Usually, gaging and automatic tool compensation require extra stations, and that adds to cost. When a transfer machine is built to make one part, and after a period of time the part becomes obsolete, the machine must be scrapped or renovated. An auto manufacturer reports that on average the cost to changeover and retool for another part is about 90% of the original cost.

Transfer machines exist in sizes from those with only a few stations and costing less than $100,000 to some with several score stations and worth several millions of dollars. Each is designed and made especially for its job. A transfer machine with ten stations for processing 1000 connecting rods and caps per hour, 8 at a time, is illustrated in Fig. 34-3 along with a diagram explaining what is done at each station. Locators, guides, and strippers assure complete control of rods and caps at all times during transfer and machining cycles. The probe inspection at station 7 after drilling,

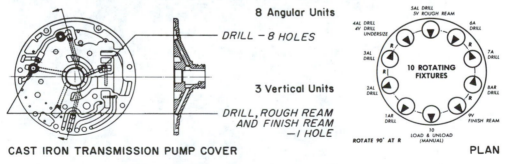

8 Angular Units

DRILL – 8 HOLES

3 Vertical Units

DRILL, ROUGH REAM
AND FINISH REAM
– I HOLE

CAST IRON TRANSMISSION PUMP COVER

5AL DRILL
5V ROUGH REAM

4AL DRILL
4V DRILL
UNDERSIZE

6A
DRILL

3AL
DRILL

7A
DRILL

**10 ROTATING
FIXTURES**

2AL
DRILL

8AR
DRILL

1AR
DRILL

9V
FINISH REAM

10
LOAD & UNLOAD
(MANUAL)

ROTATE 90° AT R

PLAN

Figure 34-2   Rotary, center column, indexing machine with vertical and angular heads. The workpiece shown is indexed from station to station and also indexed at each station to align it with the tools. (Courtesy Kingsbury Machine Tool Corp.)

milling, and spotfacing assures that all holes are ready for reaming in the final stations. Locating nests and bushing plates are removable readily so they may be checked and replaced as needed to maintain precision. The machine is arranged to machine two different lengths of connecting rods mating with the same caps.

A transfer machine or line is basically an integrated material handling device and is applicable to all kinds of operations besides machining. Transfer lines are widely used for such operations as welding, molding, assembly, and inspection. Typical of many sheet and strip metal stamping and forming lines is the one illustrated by Fig. 34-4 for producing bicycle rims.

Transfer machines are found in a number of forms. One type for large workpieces has toolheads moved sequentially to and from each workpiece while it is located and clamped in one position. One workpiece may be set up in its fixture while another is being machined.

Figure 34-3   Transfer machine to produce 1000 connecting rods per hour (shown by inset), eight at a time through the operations shown in the diagram on p. 843. An inspection operation at station 7 assures that the holes have been drilled before reaming. (Courtesy Greenlee Brothers and Co.)

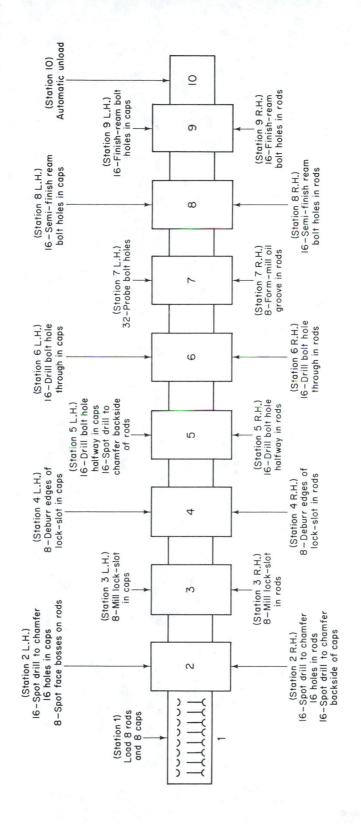

(Station 1)
Load 8 rods and 8 caps

(Station 2 L.H.)
16-Spot drill to chamfer 16 holes in caps
8-Spot face bosses on rods

(Station 2 R.H.)
16-Spot drill to chamfer 16 holes in rods
16-Spot drill to chamfer backside of caps

(Station 3 L.H.)
8-Mill lock-slot in caps

(Station 3 R.H.)
8-Mill lock-slot in rods

(Station 4 L.H.)
8-Deburr edges of lock-slot in caps

(Station 4 R.H.)
8-Deburr edges of lock-slot in rods

(Station 5 L.H.)
16-Drill bolt hole halfway in caps
16-Spot drill to chamfer backside of rods

(Station 5 R.H.)
16-Drill bolt hole halfway in rods

(Station 6 L.H.)
16-Drill bolt hole through in caps

(Station 6 R.H.)
16-Drill bolt hole through in rods

(Station 7 L.H.)
32-Probe bolt holes

(Station 7 R.H.)
8-Form-mill oil groove in rods

(Station 8 L.H.)
16-Semi-finish ream bolt holes in caps

(Station 8 R.H.)
16-Semi-finish ream bolt holes in rods

(Station 9 L.H.)
16-Finish-ream bolt holes in caps

(Station 9 R.H.)
16-Finish-ream bolt holes in rods

(Station 10)
Automatic unload

NONSTOP RIM LINE FOR BICYCLE WHEELS

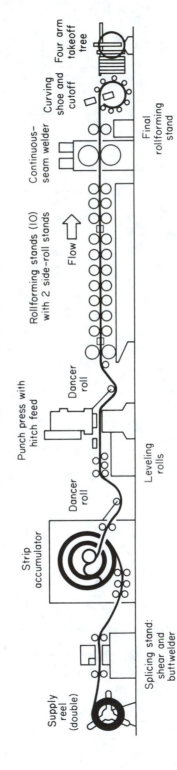

Figure 34-4 Continuous line for stamping, forming, and welding strip steel. (From "Advanced Line for Roll Formed Rims," *American Machinist*, June 1979, p. 103, by permission of the publisher.)

A common trend in transfer machine design is to make the systems more versatile so they can run varieties of parts and/or smaller batches economically. This may be done, for instance, by use of interchangeable toolheads for different parts. For example, a tractor manufacturer has installed a transfer line to machine (randomly and without shutdown for changeover) five different families of front- and rear-end axle housing components from about 225 to 375 kg (about 500 to 800 lb) mass. Even so, the versatility of transfer lines is limited, and for further capability, resort must be made to flexible manufacturing systems described later in this chapter.

The biggest saving from a transfer machine is in labor cost. Some prefer to turn the emphasis around and say that more output can be obtained from the same labor. The transfer machine of Fig. 34-3 needs only one operator; in contrast, a conventional line to do the same work would employ at least eight operators. Other savings may result from better quality, less scrap, less floor space, inspection on the machine, and scrap disposal through a conveyor.

The largest cost in transfer machine operation comes from the relatively heavy investment required. Even large savings can be more than eaten up by the heavy burden unless care is taken. One large user has found that no profit is returned unless a transfer machine is kept running 80 to 90% of the time, and even so it takes two to three years to recover the cost of a machine. The loss may very well be over $100 for every hour a $500,000 transfer machine is down. The engineer who plans and designs a transfer machine has much at stake and must provide for a minimum first cost, long enough life, and as little down time as possible. The main considerations to these ends are the following.

A transfer machine starts with the design of the product. The part or parts to be made must not be subject to change often and must be designed to be made in the easiest way with all needed surfaces for locating and handling. The machine must be as flexible as possible, should changes occur. Even so, an important disadvantage of the fixed program transfer system is that it usually is costly to make major workpiece design changes.

The extent of automation should always be subject to scrutiny. For example, hand loading of a transfer machine for machining automobile connecting rods was found more economical than a loading device that cost $90,000 when labor cost was around $10/hr.

Certain provisions may be made in the design of a transfer machine for efficiency. Every provision must be made for the safety of the equipment and personnel. This includes foolproofing and interlocking to prevent wrecks and personnel injuries, preinspection of rough workpieces, and means to stop the machine when it misses. The machine must take over everything done by an operator. This includes clearing and disposing of chips, rough checking and orienting of workpieces, and watching for trouble. Idle stations are commonly included for space to add operations if workpiece design changes occur or for unloading and loading so that entire sections may be cut out of the machine and workpieces routed partly over conventional machines if breakdowns occur. Some sections may be made replaceable so several sizes of workpieces may be processed. For example, the transfer devices between stations were changeable on a large transfer line for pressing sheet metal panels so that several sizes of panels could be accommodated.

Tool problems must be solved before a transfer machine is designed to assure as much dependability as possible. Even so, tools become dull and breakdowns do occur. To minimize interruptions, provisions are made to preset sharp tools before they are put on the machine, to mount them in quick-change holders, for tool racks to make the preset tools readily available when needed, for signals to alert the attendants to the times to change tools, and for schedules for changing the tools in batches. An example of preset tooling is given in Fig. 21-15. The best of components and adequate means for lubrication help prevent breakdowns.

Although each transfer machine is a special project, many of its units, such as tool heads, hydraulic drive units, controls, and slides can and should be standard items at considerable saving in construction cost and facility repair.

Nonsynchronous Systems.   An example of a nonsynchronous fixed program system is given in Fig. 34-5. In general, such a system altogether costs about 20% more than the total for the machines, which are mostly standard items. Because such

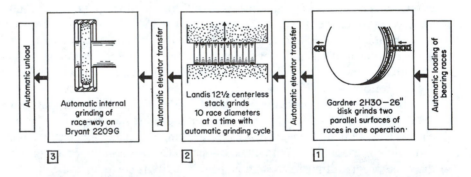

Figure 34-5   Nonsynchronous production system made up of three grinding machines to finish bearing races. (Courtesy Gardner Machine Co.)

a system utilizes standard components, even some of the conveyors and loading devices, it can be put together in the relatively short time of from 4 to 6 months. Because the machines are relatively independent, few interlocking controls are needed, and the units do not have to be precisely aligned with each other. Thus design and construction are simplified. The standard units are easy to service, and repair parts may be had off the shelf.

Other advantages of the independent unit systems are that parts can be positioned readily in the best way for each operation, there is plenty of room for chip removal, and with parts waiting at each station, loading time is minimal. Standard machines can be arranged to be operated manually if automatic controls fail. Independent stations are ideal for an assembly line where some operations may be manual and not easy to pace with automatic operations. Good scrap control can be had by including inspection units in the connecting devices between machines.

On the negative side, an independent unit system is not compact and some floor space is wasted. It is not suitable for some sizes and shapes of parts, such as large engine blocks.

A 19-station nonsynchronous line for machining two universal joint components cost about $2 million.

CONTROL OF FIXED SYSTEMS

Automatic Tool Compensation. As a cutting tool wears, the size that it cuts changes. In a manual operation, the operator checks the work from time to time and corrects the setting or changes the tool as needed. In many semi- or fully automatic operations, the tools are run for a predetermined period during which they normally do not go out of limits and then are preset or changed. This means that a few tools may break down too soon and spoil work, and others may be replaced before being fully worn. To get the most from the tools and minimize scrap, efficient automated systems are equipped with automatic tool compensation. A sensory device measures size after an operation, and if a limit is exceeded, it sends back a signal to adjust the tool to compensate for the error.

Fig. 34-6 offers an example of automatic tool compensation in a chamfering and turning operation. The cutting tool can be moved to the workpiece by a solenoid actuated cam a total distance of 50 μm (0.002 in.) in steps of 5 μm (0.0002 in.). The increments are small so that adjustment from one limit back into the tolerance zone through one step does not push the dimension outside the opposite limit. The tool can also be indexed around its axis in 100 steps to bring fresh bits of cutting edge into action. When the gage head senses a workpiece close to or over the high limit, it closes contacts to transmit an impulse to a storage relay system. If the next piece is well within size, the relay system returns to its starting position; but if the next piece is near but not over the high limit, the relay system energizes the solenoid that sets the tool in a notch. If the second piece is oversize, a chipped tool is indicated, the machine is shut off, and a signal is turned on to show trouble.

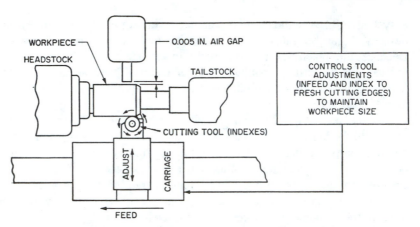

Figure 34-6   Automatic tool compensation system.

The workpiece of Fig. 34-6 is shown gaged on the machine. Quite often, pieces are gaged as they come off the machine. When gaging indicates out-of-limit performance, tool compensation can be made for the next piece, and so on.

For automatic tool compensation to be effective, the machine and tooling must be rugged and stable. Many other factors besides tool wear affect the results in an operation, and they must be kept small. If the machine were quite erratic, the regulating device would continually be activated, then tend to overcompensate, and soon compound the errors. Some consider it desirable that the machine be able to run at least 40 pieces without adjustment and still hold within one-half of the tolerance.

Control of Automatic Operations.   One kind of manufacturing operation consists of a sequence of steps each of which is started when the one before it is finished. Each step is timed by how long it takes to do its task and not by an external clock. This may be illustrated by the basic face milling operation of Fig. 34-7. For simplicity only the motions are considered; other functions, such as motor and coolant controls, are not included in this discussion. Each workpiece is located and clamped on a fixture platen before it comes to this operation. As one platen is transferred out of the station, a new one is moved in, located, and clamped in position. A limit switch (LS1) is closed when the platen is properly located and firmly clamped in place. Then the milling head with a revolving face mill is fed from left to right across the surface to be machined. After the cutter has cleared the workpiece at the end of the stroke, a limit switch (LS2) is tripped. The slide on which the milling head rides is retracted to back the cutter from the work, and the head is returned at rapid rate from right to left; when the cutter is out of the way, the platen is unclamped and raised from its locators and then can be transferred out of the station. Each sensor (limit switch) that sends a signal to the controller is designated by an input symbol in the tabulation of inputs and outputs from the controller. Each step is started by an output from the controller to energize an activator such as a solenoid valve, motor control, etc. Some control systems utilize air or hydraulic media, but most are electrical.

The logic of an operation like that illustrated in Fig. 34-7 is commonly expressed by either a *ladder diagram* or a set of *Boolean equations*. Both are shown for this case. In explanation, the first line of the Boolean equations states that when the sensor ($\overline{LS1}$) shows that the platen has been unclamped and raised from the locators and the milling cutter is fully retracted, the finished piece may be transferred out of the station (on its platen), and a new piece should be brought into position and its platen located and clamped. The second line specifies conditions that must exist to warrant advancing the cutter to starting position, and so on. The top rung of the ladder diagram corresponds to the first Boolean equation, the second rung to the second equation, and so on. The uprights on the side of the ladder represent two electrical lines with a voltage (V) between them. It may be 110 V. ac or dc, but for safety is often less. When the switches on a rung are all closed, the voltage V acts on a circuit that energizes necessary drivers to perform the step in the operation.

The output device (CR) of a controller may be an electrical-mechanical relay or equivalent solid-state device. These can be mounted on a panel and wired to the sensors to conform to the ladder diagram. This is called a hard-wired system and is common for small systems. One authority recommends hard-wiring up to about six relays. For large and complex systems, the preference is for a programmable controller, described later.

Another kind of manufacturing operation is one that is timed by an external clock. An example is given by the operations in the automatic plating processes illustrated in Fig. 30-4. There the time that a workpiece is in the washing, rinsing, plating, and other operations is determined by a programmed external clock that governs the transfer carriers. Some processes contain both timed and untimed operations. For example, an automatic die-casting machine starts a cycle with closing and locking the die. The next step of injecting a shot of metal is not started until sensors signal that the die is securely closed. Then when the die is filled, it is kept closed for a predetermined time to allow the metal to freeze. The next step is to free and eject the casting; a sensor signals when the workpiece is clear of the die and a new cycle may be started. A process like those just described may be controlled by a commercial timer and relays hard-wired into the machine. A common device is a rotating drum indexed by a timer or by signals from sensors. Pegs are inserted into rings of holes around the drum to trip switches at selected intervals. Drum-controllers are limited in scope, and programmable controllers are preferred for large and complex systems.

A *programmable controller* (PC), also known as a *programmable logic controller* (PLC), is a general-purpose control system that accepts input from such sources as pushbuttons, limit switches, and temperature, pressure, and flow sensors. It is capable of generating outputs to such devices as load relays, solenoid valves, motor starters, stepping motors, and even servo drives. There are many makes and they differ in detail but are based on the same principles. A diagram of a basic programmable controller is shown in Fig. 34-7. The program for a process is stored in the solid-state memory. The simplest is a read-only memory (ROM), not changeable in some systems but changeable in other systems by an auxiliary program or memory loader. As a rule, a program is not changed (except for corrections) while the controller is

DIAGRAM OF A FACE MILLING OPERATION

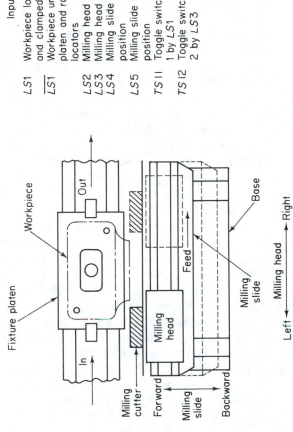

CONTROLLER

Input

LS1	Workpiece located on platen and clamped in place
$\overline{LS1}$	Workpiece unclamped on platen and raised above locators
LS2	Milling head in left position
LS3	Milling head in right position
LS4	Milling slide in forward position
LS5	Milling slide in backward position
TS I1	Toggle switch set to position 1 by LS1
TS I2	Toggle switch set to position 2 by LS3

Output

CR1	Transfer work and clamp in position
CR2	Advance milling slide and lock in forward position
CR3	Feed milling head left to right
CR4	Stop CR3 and retract milling slide to backward position
CR5	Stop CR4 and return milling head from right to left
CR6	Stop CR5 and unclamp and raise platen

BOOLEAN LOGIC EQUATIONS

$$\overline{LS1} \cdot LS2 \cdot LS5 \cdot \overline{CR1} = CR1$$
$$LS1 \cdot LS2 \cdot LS5 \cdot TS I1 = CR2$$
$$LS1 \cdot LS2 \cdot LS4 = CR3$$
$$LS3 \cdot LS4 = CR4$$
$$LS3 \cdot LS5 = CR5$$
$$LS2 \cdot LS5 \cdot TS I2 = CR6$$

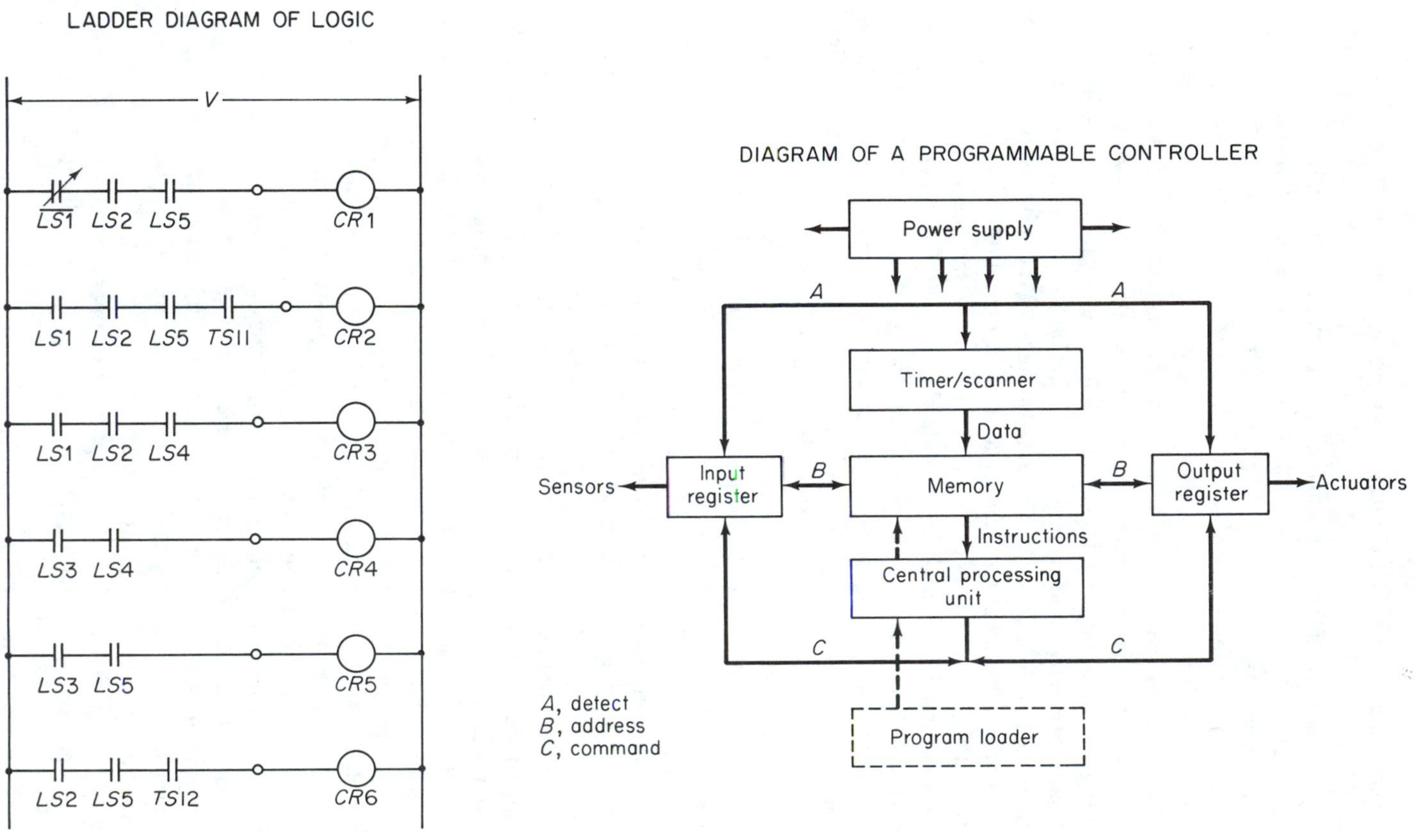

LADDER DIAGRAM OF LOGIC

DIAGRAM OF A PROGRAMMABLE CONTROLLER

A, detect
B, address
C, command

Figure 34-7 Simple manufacturing operation and its logic, and the elements of a programmable controller.

851

dedicated to a particular process. Input/output registers serve to convert signal levels from outside to inside (and vice versa) and to isolate the controller from outside transients. The scanner checks the input and output registers continuously and informs the memory and CPU of the status of input and output. It also serves to synchronize the activities of the controller. The central processing unit (CPU) or logic section makes all decisions based on the condition of inputs and outputs to conform to the program in memory and commands the output to change. All of this is executed repeatedly in milliseconds, which is much faster than most activities under control.

Most PCs have added features beyond the essential. One survey showed 95% of them with timing and counting functions. Many have read/write memories (RWM) that can be changed at any time by pushbutton, keyboard, or computer loading. RWMs are more volatile than ROM's. Cathode ray tube (CRT) display is available to show what is stored in the memory and the status of the operation. Memory capacity ranges in different makes from less than 1000 to tens of thousands of words of information. Almost all PCs accept logic or ladder formats for programming the memory, but a few utilize computer-like word programs. A sizable proportion of PCs have computer capabilities. A survey showed about one-third with arithmetic, comparison, and decision functions and over one-fourth with data handling capabilities. Such PCs can communicate and interrelate with computers and other PCs and can coordinate and monitor automated material handling and multilateral transfer lines. Fault diagnosis accessories are available. Prices range from under $500 for a basic controller for a dozen or so functions to tens of thousands of dollars for some able to control thousands of functions and provide full auxiliary services.

Programmable controllers lie between computers and hard-wired relays for controlling synchronous and nonsychronous systems in manufacturing and also for all kinds of processes. Without the power of computers, PCs are much cheaper than computers, and where more than a few functions are controlled, PCs are more compact and cheaper than hard-wired systems. The main advantage of PCs with respect to hard-wired systems is that the PC logic can be changed much more easily, quickly, and cheaply. This may be helpful to test a system, improve a system, or change a system for changes in part design, but most of all a PC need not become obsolete because if a machine is no longer needed, its PC may be easily reprogrammed for another. Common extras with PCs but not hard-wired controllers include scheduled tool change alarms, system diagnostics, real-time cycle analysis, machine utilization reports, and production control summaries. Solid-state devices on PCs without moving parts are more reliable than electromechanical relays on which contacts notoriously wear and corrode. On the other hand, PCs are not as sensitive as computers and can be designed to survive better in harsh and dirty industrial environments.

It is important to recognize the differences between PCs and numerical control (NC) systems. The purposes of the two systems are different. A PC is dedicated, at least for a significant period of time, to one process or operation and works to one program in that time. With a limited number of variables, little feedback is required. On the other hand, the task of an NC system is to accept and carry out ever-changing instructions continually. Thus the NC system is normally more complex and costly.

The PC operates only in on-off modes; it accepts signals and gives commands only for on and off. The NC system operates by numbers, although the numbers may be expressed in binary forms. Thus NC can recognize and work to any given dimension in its range, whereas PC cannot. The NC can do what the PC can, but costs much more.

FLEXIBLE AUTOMATION

Flexible Manufacturing Systems.   The fixed program manufacturing systems described so far are, as a rule, dedicated, each to the production of one or a few products, and thus suited only for large-quantity production. In contrast, automation for producing a few or a moderate quantity of parts at a time in large variety is found in what are called flexible or versatile manufacturing systems.

The scheme of one flexible manufacturing system for machining components of agricultural equipment is shown in Fig. 34-8. It was originally designed to machine 48 individual workpieces, and more may be added. The full array of machine tools includes six numerical controlled machining centers (described in Chap. 35), with one dedicated to milling, and four duplex multiple spindle head indexers. The latter are standard machines that carry special-purpose multiple-spindle heads for drilling, tapping, boring, reaming, milling, trepanning, and gaging. Some systems have only machining centers and gaging machines but not head indexers. The machining centers can do a number of operations (in this case drilling, boring, reaming, tapping, and milling), but each applies one tool at a time to the work. If a number of tools can work at the same time and produce the required results (such as a gang of milling cutters or a cluster of drills, taps, etc.), that is faster. In this case, each head on the duplex-head indexers carries tools dedicated to machining a pattern of surfaces on only one part run in the system. In some systems the tool heads are stored in racks and conveyed to a workstation as needed for a variety of parts.

Workpieces machined in the system of Fig. 34-8 are manually loaded on fixture pallets carried to the machine by carts on a towline. When a cart reaches an assigned station, the pallet is transferred onto rails and shuttled to the point of operation in its turn. Two computers program the routing of the workpieces and direct the machines (an example of DNC described in Chap. 35) in performing the required operations.

The example of Fig. 34-8 is typical of flexible manufacturing systems in that it is automated with some of the units tooled for specific operations, and the rest capable of random operation. Sequencing of operations can be varied as required. Thus the system is a hybrid between a fixed program system and an assembly of general-purposes stand-alone machines. It has advantages over both alternatives: more flexibility than the fixed program system, and less operation time than on the stand-alone machines. An indication of the place of the flexible manufacturing system in the realm of production is given by the chart of Fig. 34-8.

Robotics.   A large part of manufacturing involves the handling of materials, parts, and tools. This is done in transfer and other lines by special-purpose manipu-

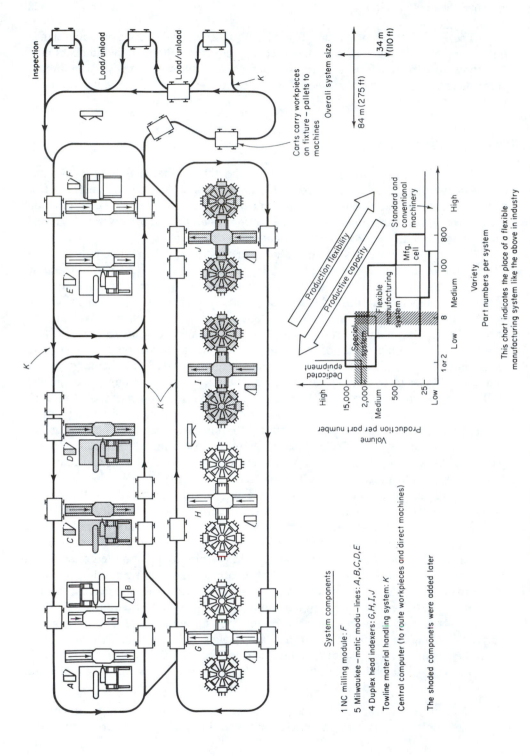

Figure 34-8 Flexible manufacturing system for components of agricultural equipment, and a chart that indicates the place for the flexible manufacturing system in the realm of production. (Courtesy Kearney and Trecker Corp.)

Inspection

Load/unload

Load/unload

Carts carry workpieces on fixture – pallets to machines

Overall system size

84 m (275 ft)

34 m (110 ft)

Production flexibility

Productive capacity

Dedicated equipment

Special system

Flexible manufacturing system

Mfg. cell

Standard and conventional machinery

Volume Production per part number

High
15,000
2,000
Medium
500
25
Low

Variety
Part numbers per system

1 or 2   Low   8   Medium   100   800   High

This chart indicates the place of a flexible manufacturing system like the above in industry

System components

1 NC milling module: F

5 Milwaukee – matic modu – lines: A,B,C,D,E

4 Duplex head indexers: G,H,I,J

Towline material handling system: K

Central computer (to route workpieces and direct machines)

The shaded componets were added later

854

lators, transfer mechanisms, conveyors, and positioners, each adapted to a particular purpose. Where parts or the work to be done are varied but the volume is still large, manual labor has been utilized. In recent years the use of robots has been growing to load and unload workpieces and to manipulate tools. In manufacturing, a *robot* has been defined as a programmable device capable of performing complex actions in a wide variety of operations. It is a manipulator that normally can be reprogrammed to do various repetitious actions without human intervention.

Three models of popular commercial robots are depicted in Fig. 34-9. Essentially, such a robot employs an arm that swivels on a base or pedestal through a total arc of 90° up to 360° depending upon the model. The arm also lifts or raises in a vertical plane. Some models have an elbow and others extend the arm to achieve their reach. Typical of medium size robots is a maximum reach of 2080 mm (82 in.) and a load capacity of 34 kg (75 lb) on the end of the arm. Large standard models boast a lift of 910 kg (2000 lb). A wrist on the end of the arm provides rotary motions for positioning the hand, which may grasp with finger-like grippers or have a tool fastened to it. The robot is directed by an information processer following instructions programmed in its memory. Robots are powered by air, hydraulic, electrical, or mechanical means, often by a combination of these in one unit. Some robots are mounted on wheels and can even be made to follow a course laid out by a wire in the floor.

Robots may be classified from the standpoint of capability as (1) pick and place, (2) point-to-point transfer, and (3) continuous-path robots. *Pick-and-place robots* are the simplest and typically are capable of picking up small loads and moving them rapidly from one point to another. Their movements are limited in number, and their control systems are rudimentary and may consist of as little as a series of switches or valves tripped by dogs. Length of movement may be determined by fixed stops. Programming may be done by placing tabs on a drum or pins in a plugboard, by making pneumatic connections as needed, or by pushbutton setting of binary controls. Reprogramming is slow and not expected to be done often.

A *point-to-point transfer robot* has the capability of moving to and from a number of points and not necessarily in the same sequence. This versatility and fast reprogrammability are imparted by a position servo at each joint. That feature aids in precise point location. Reprogramming is done by the operator leading the robot (usually from a console) through its routine initially. He or she presses a button to impress the memory with the location of the end points of each movement. Some robots are programmed off-line by input of coded instructions like NC machines (Chap. 36). An average robot may be able to store 100 or more program steps, some up to 1000. A subclass is the *tracking robot* that does its job, such as spot welding, while the work is moving along a line.

A *continuous-path robot* is the same as a point-to-point robot in general appearance but has much more memory storage and a processor capable of coordinating the movements of the joints and interpolating a given path between end points. When programmed, the robot is led not only from point to point but also along the paths between points. Such robots serve in such operations as spray painting and arc welding. The models sketched in Fig. 34-9 may be point-to point robots but with more sophisticated controls can serve as continuous-path robots.

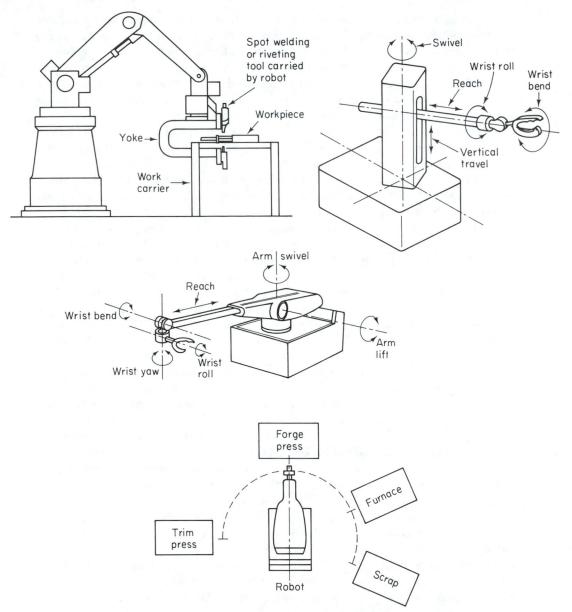

Figure 34-9 Three models of robots, and work they do.

Most robots go through a programmed routine on the assumption that the environment or conditions of the operation remain the same. Typical jobs are depicted in Fig. 34-9. At a basic level, a robot takes a hot billet out of a furnace and places it in a die on a forging press. Then it transfers the forging to a trimming press and the scrap to a bin. In the top view, a robot carries a gun on a yoke to rivet or spot weld assemblies as they pass on a conveyor. Through a camera or other means, the robot tracks the pieces and works on them as they pass. To take on operations more difficult than these, a new generation of robots is being developed. They have sensory capabilities to enable them to adapt to changing conditions in an operation. In this realm are robots for arc welding. A groove in which a weld is made between two pieces may vary in contour, width, and straightness. The welding torch must be traversed to adapt to these variations for best results. The problem is to get a robot to do this. As a first step, a robot may be guided by an operator in a dry run over the path to store its features in the robot's memory. The robot then retraces the path to lay down the weld. The environment of the arc is hostile to sensors that might guide the robot to adapt to variations as it proceeds along the groove. Sensors that have been used with some success include mechanical probes bearing on the sides of the groove, noncontacting induction coils that induce and sense eddy currents, camera discernment of a structured light beam reflected from the groove, and electronic sensing of the current as the arc approaches the sides of the groove. Another direction for expansion of capabilities is to make robots able to discriminate among different kinds of parts. One system can discriminate among several different parts passing on a conveyor, pick them off one by one, and deposit each at the station where it belongs. These are also called *adaptive* or *visionary* robots. Touch-sensitive fingers have been developed with an artificial skin made up of a grid of small electrode points. Feedback from the fingers enables a robot with programmed computer control to feel for spots to obtain a secure grip on quite irregular workpieces. In another direction, robots now exist to do rather complex assembly operations. For example, one is reported able to select and pick up an assortment of parts and arrange them into such assemblies as radio speakers and electric motors.

Human beings can do the same work as robots, often more economically, but there are conditions under which a robot is superior. Robots can work tirelessly in dirty, hot, tiring, monotonous, unhealthy, and unsafe circumstances. They can keep up a steady pace and make less scrap. Robots can lift heavy loads. They labor in foundries, die casting, plastic molding, forging, welding, machining, assembling, and many other operations.

Robots are expensive but a standard one may cost less and be available sooner than a special loader for a job. A robot can be reprogrammed and kept busy on many jobs and does not become obsolete. To reduce cost to basics, robot manufacturers claim that the average robot can be put to work for $6/hr. Pick and place robots may be obtained for a few thousand dollars (for small and simple ones) up to about $20,000. Point-to-point transfer robots are quoted in the range of $20,000 to $40,000, and most continuous-path robots at over $40,000. A robot that can be guided over a joint to be welded and then can traverse a welding torch over the path costs about $100,000. One with sensors to guide it over the course of a weld has a price of about $165,000.

Automatic Tracing. The tracing and duplicating machines that have been described so far in this text follow metal templates or forms to guide the cutters. A step beyond these are the machines that cut pieces to shapes in two dimensions directly from line drawings. They may operate on the mechanical pantograph principle or with electrical controls between the cutter and the scanner that follows the drawing. The drawings for one type of machine are made with a conductive ink. A tracer disk maintains contact with the line through control of a spark gap. Regular ink lines on clear plastic film are scanned by electric eyes on another type of machine. The scanner can follow a line as fast as 125 mm/min (5 ipm) with 25 μm (0.001 in.) traveling accuracy and 75 μm (0.003 in.) stopping accuracy. Drawings are made oversize, as large as 760 × 1270 mm (30 × 50 in.) and to a scale of as much as 10:1. These systems are suitable for cutting profiles where only one of each is required or for templates for tracing larger quantities.

ECONOMICS OF AUTOMATION

Selection of Automated Systems.   When an appreciable quantity of pieces is to be produced, the question usually is not whether to automate but rather how much is justified. An illustration is furnished by a case for blanking and then notching electric motor laminations. Seventeen different round blanks are needed in lots of 1300 to 8100 pieces, a total of 70,000 blanks a week. There may be anywhere from 18 to 58 notches required around the outside of a blank, in 50 different shapes and sizes.

One blanking press and four notching presses are capable of meeting production requirements. Several arrangements are possible, and all have been studied, but for simplicity only the two most feasible will be explained here and are indicated in Fig. 34-10. A detailed study shows that the following annual savings may be expected from the fully automated system as compared to no automation:

At blanking press (760 hr at $18.00/hr)	$ 13,680
Overhead saved at blanking press	2,430
At notching presses (8320 hr at $18.00/hr)	149,760
Overhead saved at notching presses	26,600
Total annual savings from full automation	$192,470

All four notching presses must process the same blanks being turned out by the blanking press at any one time. This necessitates three additional sets or 150 notching dies. The costs of equipment for the fully automated system are:

150 duplicate notching dies at $2500 each	$375,000
Automatic distribution mechanism	150,000
Automatic press loading, feeding, and stacking devices	298,000
Total cost of equipment for full automation	$823,000

A partially automated system, also depicted in Fig. 34-10, dispenses with the automatic distribution mechanism and requires handling and storing the blanks in lots by means of pallets and forklift trucks. With this system the blanking press can be run at its fastest speed because it is not held back by the notching presses when they are turning out laminations with large numbers of notches. Although handling costs are

I. FULLY AUTOMATED SYSTEM

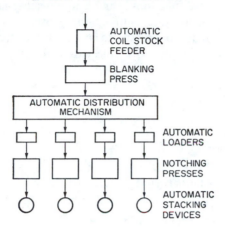

AUTOMATIC
COIL STOCK
FEEDER

BLANKING
PRESS

AUTOMATIC DISTRIBUTION
MECHANISM

AUTOMATIC
LOADERS

NOTCHING
PRESSES

AUTOMATIC
STACKING
DEVICES

II. PARTIALLY AUTOMATED SYSTEM

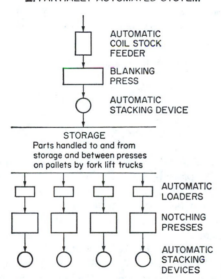

AUTOMATIC
COIL STOCK
FEEDER

BLANKING
PRESS

AUTOMATIC
STACKING DEVICE

STORAGE
Parts handled to and from
storage and between presses
on pallets by fork lift trucks

AUTOMATIC
LOADERS

NOTCHING
PRESSES

AUTOMATIC
STACKING
DEVICES

Figure 34-10 Two arrangements for producing motor laminations.

more, the annual saving for partial automation is not much less than for full automation and is estimated to be $176,360. The equipment costs are much less. The notching press can be run independently, and the 150 duplicate notching dies are not needed. Neither is the distribution mechanism required. Thus the total cost of equipment for partial automation is only $298,000 for automatic press loading, feeding, and stacking devices. The return on the investment (the total savings divided by the equipment cost times 100 for each alternative) is 23% for full automation but a handsome 59% for partial automation.

The complete manufacturing effort may be divided into handling of materials, fabrication of pieces, finishing, inspection, assembly, and packaging. The completely automated plant through all these functions is an ideal, but substantial savings may be realized by applying the principles of automation to each step of production as justified. The rule is that the areas that promise to be most profitable should be attacked first, and each area should be exploited to the extent that the return justifies the investment.

QUESTIONS

1. What does automation mean?
2. Describe the principal fixed program systems.
3. What are the advantages and disadvantages of transfer machines?
4. How can the costs of a transfer machine be minimized?
5. What are the advantages and disadvantages of a nonsynchronous system?
6. What is automatic tool compensation, and how is it accomplished?
7. Describe a typical programmable controller.
8. What are flexible manufacturing systems, and how do they differ from transfer lines?
9. What is a robot in manufacturing? Describe a typical robot. For what is it used?
10. How may automatic tracing be done?
11. How would you make an analysis to determine whether to automate an operation?

PROBLEM

A rotary index machine has three stations. Workpieces (one at a time) are unclamped, unloaded, loaded, and clamped by an operator in a jig at station 1. At the same time a six-spindle drill head at station 2 descends and six holes are drilled in a piece. Also at the same time, three holes are reamed in a piece by a three-spindle drill head at station 3. When both heads are finished and raised out of the way and the operator signifies that he or she is clear, each piece is indexed to the next station. Indexing time is 0.02 minute. It is estimated to take 0.20 minute to unload and load a workpiece, 0.25 minute to drill the six holes simultaneously, and 0.15 minute to ream three holes at the same time. The drilling and reaming heads are raised so that the tools clear each workpiece by at least 75 mm (3 in.). They descend at a rapid rate until the tools are within 5 mm (ca. 0.2 in.) of the pieces and then continue at feed rates.

(a) Write a set of Boolean equations to express the logic of this operation.
(b) Construct the ladder diagram to express the logic of this operation.
(c) Estimate the number of pieces that can be machined in 50 minutes of continuous operation.

REFERENCES

BEECHER, R. C., and R. DEWAR, "Robot Trends at General Motors," *American Machinist*, Aug. 1979, p. 71.

BRATKOVICH, A. M., "Auto Transfer Line: Some Basics," *American Machinist*, Feb. 1981, p. 104.

EMERSON, C., "Variations on Transfer Lines," *American Machinist,* Mar. 1980, p. 167.

ENGELBERGER, J. F. "Turning America around with Robotics," *Manufacturing Engineering,* Aug. 1982, p. 117.

FEINBERG, B., "Precision Payoff from Tool Point Control," *Manufacturing Engineering and Management,* Jan. 1973, p. 22.

GARCIA, G., "Status Report on Programmable Controllers," *Manufacturing Engineering,* May 1980, p. 49.

HARTWIG, G. C., "Machine Controls—PC Status Report," *Manufacturing Engineering*, Oct. 1981, p. 61.

HERZOG, R. E., "Programmable Controllers," *Machine Design,* May 2, 1974, p. 118.

Industrial Robots, Vol. 1: *Fundamentals,* Vol. 2: *Applications,* 2nd. ed. Society of Manufacturing Engineers, Dearborn, Mich., 1981.

JABLONOWSKI, J., "Aiming for Flexibility in Manufacturing Systems," *American Machinist,* Mar. 1980, p. 167.

———, "Robots That Assemble," *American Machinist,* Nov. 1981, p. 175.

———, "Robots: Looking over the Specifications, Special Report 745," *American Machinist,* May 1982, p. 163.

JONES, C. C., and L. THOMPSON, "Relays vs. Programmable Controllers," *American Machinist,* Mar. 1980, p. 167.

KENNICOTT, T. C., "Transfer Machines in the '80s," *Manufacturing Engineering,* Aug. 1982, p. 111.

KLAHORST, T., "Flexible Manufacturing Systems," *NC Commline,* Sept.–Oct. 1981, p. 16.

LOOMIS, R. M., "The Programmable Controller Today and Tomorrow," *Manufacturing Engineering,* Aug. 1982, p. 117.

SCHAFFER, G., "Programmable Controllers, Special Report 695," *American Machinist,* Feb. 1977, p. 66.

———, "Robot Builds Planes," *American Machinist,* Feb. 1980, p. 90.

STAUFFER, R. N., "Automating for Greater Gains in Productivity," *Manufacturing Engineering,* Nov. 1981, p. 59.

Understanding Manufacturing Systems, Kearney and Trecker Corp., Milwaukee, Wis.

WINSHIP, J., "Robots in Metalworking," *American Machinist,* Nov. 1975, p. 87.

35

NUMERICAL CONTROL

A numerical control (NC) system is one in which instructions for doing a job are given to a machine as numbers and are carried out automatically and precisely. The system is easily programmed for any job in its scope. When one job is finished, a new program is entered, and the system does the new job, and so on. Numerical control is thus called *variable programming,* in contrast to fixed programming described in Chap. 34. NC has mostly been applied to all kinds of machine tools: to engine and turret lathes, turret punch presses, drilling and boring machines, milling, broaching, and grinding machines. NC is also found in other areas; in arc welding and flame cutting, wiring of electronic apparatus, and in riveting and assembling operations. This is not even a complete list. NC machines are designed to meet each need most efficiently and economically, and therefore many types and sizes of NC machines exist, but all are based on certain underlying principles.

NC started out with punched-tape input, and has been called *tape control,* but other media are also used for input today. Punched cards and tapes have been applied to direct machines for over 150 years: in Jacquard looms and cloth-cutting machines and on the player pianos of a bygone era. The first modern NC machine, a milling machine, was developed and exhibited in 1953 at the Massachusetts Institute of Technology under the sponsorship of the U.S. Air Force. In the short period since then, NC machine tools have come to comprise an appreciable portion of all machine tools made and sold in the world.

NC has taken a prominent and secure place in industry but so far has not been able to replace all other methods. Along with its merits, NC has certain disadvantages, and these will be pointed out in the discussion of the system.

ELEMENTS OF NUMERICAL CONTROL

NC Input.   Instructions to an NC system for doing a job consist of a stream of numbers assembled into a program. Typical programs are displayed in Chap. 36. Programs are made up and fed into the unit that controls an NC machine in a number of ways, as illustrated in Fig. 35-1. It is necessary to show a number of different paths for the flow of information in NC programming, as in Fig. 35-1, because there are many systems and different procedures. Specifications for the product to be made generally are conveyed by an engineering or part drawing or print. A programmer lists the steps and operations (and the dimensions and conditions for each step) to produce the part on what is called a programming process sheet or like name. The instructions are then entered on a keyboard (in some cases by voice input) to a device that prepares tapes, cassettes, disks, or cards or directly into a general-purpose computer or into the control of the machine. Much of the drudgery of just repeating steps or making routine calculations may be done by a computer. A punched-tape preparation unit with keyboard and ability to duplicate and edit tapes costs from about $4000 to $6000. Some paper tapes are still used, but laminated Mylar tapes are preferred for durability. Flexible or floppy magnetic disks and magnetic tape are also popular.

In some advanced plants, particularly in the aerospace industry, product specifications are computer generated by the designers and transmitted directly to a computer that prepares the NC program. Drawings and program sheets for reference may be made up on automatic drafting machines instructed by the computers. At the other extreme are some NC systems wherein programming is done at the machine by the operator. The instructions for each step are entered by pushbuttons on a panel at the workstation. This is done one step at a time in turn. A system of this sort [sometimes called *digital control* or *manual data input* (MDI)] does not need a reader for tape or other medium and can cost 20% less than full NC. Most NC systems lie between these two extremes.

The route that a program takes to the control depends upon the kind of program written, the equipment available, and the input accepted by the control. The program that goes to the control must be quite detailed, as a rule, and such a program may be written by the programmer for a simple and short operation and thus bypass the computer. However, this is inefficient for long programs, and the programmer writes a "broad brush" program (as illustrated in Chap. 36) that is fed into a computer directly or through tape, cards, etc., depending upon the particular facilities. The computer is programmed to produce detailed instructions for the control. From the programmer or from the computer, programs are conveyed to the control in most systems by punched tape, flexible magnetic disk, or magnetic tape in cassettes.

Some systems have an external computer connected directly to the NC control. An NC machine is relatively slow because it must pace the process, and one computer can service a number of machines through their controls. This arrangement of a host computer and its NC satellites is called *direct numerical control (DNC)* or *distributed numerical control*. An application of DNC is in the flexible manufacturing system of

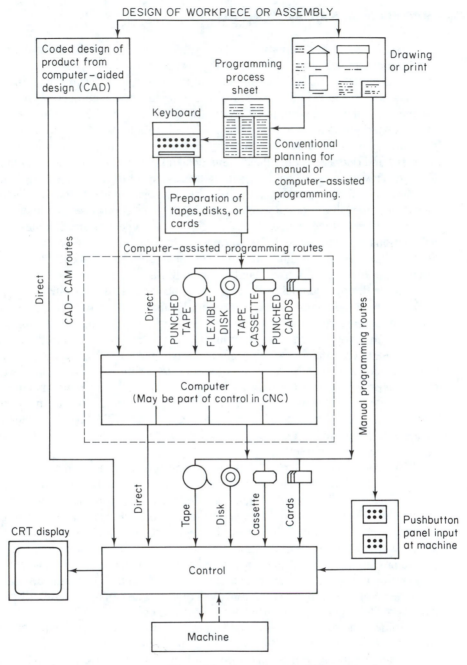

Figure 35-1 Procedures for NC programming.

Fig. 34-8. DNC systems range from small ones where one computer essentially supplies an expanded memory for a few machines to systems with over 100 machines directed and served by a hierarchy of computers. The external computers may not only prepare and store NC programs but also perform management reporting and production control functions, thus augmenting what is called *computer-aided manufacturing (CAM)*. DNC is efficient while working, but computer breakdown is a problem if it idles many machines. This problem is avoided by tape or disk or a small computer backup at each machine. DNC calls for a sizable investment, and a large number of DNC systems have not been built, but it is a step toward the ultimate automatic factory and is expected to grow.

Some controls offer output for a cathode ray tube (CRT) or other display. This may show the commands being executed on the machine at the moment or other information desired by the operator. Often, two-way communication is provided through a display and keyboard. Thus programs may be changed or optimized at will or troubles in the program or machine diagnosed and corrected through interaction. An NC control normally has a pushbutton station through which the operator may exert control; only a quick stop in some systems to many more options in others.

Figure 35-2 shows one kind of programming process sheet. Only one line is filled out for illustration but in practice as many lines would be written as required for the operation. Across the picture is a section of an NC punched tape: 1-in. wide, eight columns, perforated tape, and the code described below conform to the EIA (Electronic Institute of America) Standard, which is the usual NC input because of long usage. A newer code is the ASCIE (American Standard Code for Information Exchange), which is the same as the ISO (International Standards Organization) Code. It is the recognized standard in many areas, for instance for long-distance transmission of data. Many modern controls can take input in both codes.

The column of small holes along the EIA tape in Fig. 35-2 is for a drive sprocket and is not part of the coding. Each row across the tape represents a *character* (number, letter, or symbol). A number is given in *binary coded decimal* form by the first four positions of each row (read from the bottom upward in Fig. 35-2).

The binary code is the natural numbering system for digital computers and NC machines because it requires only two conditions to represent a number, such as a switch on or off in a circuit or a hole punched or unpunched in a tape at a particular position. A punched hole stands for one; an unpunched hole for zero. These are called *bits,* an abbreviation for binary digits. The value of a punched hole in position one is $1 \times 2^0 = 1$; in position two, $1 \times 2^1 = 2$; in position three, $1 \times 2^2 = 4$; and in position four, $1 \times 2^3 = 8$. An unpunched position is always zero. The values of the holes punched in the first four positions of any row are added to represent decimal digits one through nine. The numbers on the tape may be verified from the entries on the programming sheet in Fig. 35-2.

Each row across the standard tape is punched initially with an odd number of holes and is given a *parity check* for an odd number when read to guard against loss or addition of a hole and greatly reduce chance of error. If the number or symbol represented requires an even number of holes in a row, a hole is added in position five.

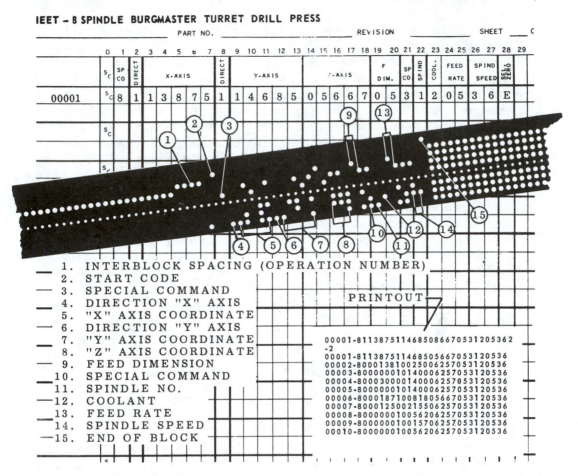

Figure 35-2 Block of information as it appears on a programming process sheet and on punched tape. (From R. H. Murray, "Tape Control Fabrication.")

Position six punched alone stands for zero, and seven for start. Those positions may be used in conjunction with the numbers to designate letters of the alphabet and symbols.

A group of characters constituting a normal unit of information makes up a *word*, such as the *x*-axis dimension of 13875 in Fig. 35-2. A group of words considered to be a unit is called a *block*, and is separated from other such units by a hole punched in column 8 and called the "end of block" character. A block, in effect, designates the disposition of all the controllable elements of an NC machine at each step of an operation. A block is essentially a line of the program. A number of blocks of a program are shown at the lower right of Fig. 35-2. The first block is the same as the first line of the process sheet. The other blocks would also appear as lines on the process sheet if it were complete. This illustration is for a punched tape, but the numbers would be the same for this particular job if the input were direct or on magnetic tape or disk.

The physical arrangement of the words in a block is called the *format,* and three standard forms are recognized. The one shown in Fig. 35-2 is called *fixed-sequential* format. Each word has a definite length and location in any one system. Words must be presented in a specific order, and all possible words preceding the last desired word must be present in the block. Each word in *tab-sequential* format is preceded by a *tab character* formed by holes punched in positions two through six in a row. Words must be in a specific order but may vary in length. In *word-address* format each word in a block starts with one or more characters which identify the meaning of the word. Each format in the order just given requires fewer characters for an average program but more complex circuitry in the translator.

The *one character per row code* that has just been described is standard for position and straight-cut control systems; it and a *one-word-per-track code* are both acceptable for continuous path systems. The latter code is also binary with one word along each column or track. The words for any one block are read in parallel along the tape, and end of block (EOB) characters separate the blocks.

NC Controls. Machine components that must be actuated to do a job normally cannot respond to numbers that people work with and put into NC controls. The numbers must be converted to timely signals of sufficient magnitudes to activate the machine components. Thus a control must perform certain functions to convert the numbers into adequate signals; all controls do not need to perform all the functions. The functions that are performed by controls are:

1. To read and verify each block.
2. To identify each word and assign it to a register or memory address for temporary storage. Common procedure is for a block of information to be read and put into storage while the preceding block is being processed. The numbers going in or being processed may be displayed on a CRT screen.
3. To convert each word into a signal. The commands for coolant, starting a spindle, etc., may initiate turning on or off an electric current to energize or deenergize a control valve, motor starter, etc. The position words, such as for the *x, y,* or *z* axis in Fig. 35-2, are commonly converted into a series of pulses. This is called a *digital signal.* In many systems, each pulse represents movement increment of 2.5 μm, (0.0001 in.).
4. To arrange the signals to carry out the commands for feed and speed rates. The feed rate for an increment of movement along an axis may be expressed by the rate at which pulses are emitted. A speed command for spindle speeds in steps may be translated into electric currents to the gear shifters in the spindle drive.
5. To interpolate from the point established by one block to the next. If a particular path must be traversed between two points, points in between can be calculated on a computer during programming so that movements between the interior points will not deviate from the prescribed curve by more than the tolerance allowed. This is not often necessary because many modern controls are able to synchronize the machine movements to produce slopes and common curves like circular and parabolic arcs. Some controls can interpolate over almost any path.

6. To coordinate the feed rates of the various axes if contouring is to be done.

7. To convert the digital signals into *analog signals* required to actuate many systems. An analog signal is a physical magnitude, such as the voltage of a direct current or a phase shift angle of an alternating current.

8. To amplify the signals into electric currents, pressures, forces, etc., required to drive the machine components.

9. To compare a response with each signal if the system employs feedback as most do. If there is a discrepancy between command and response, another signal must be given to correct the error.

Older controls and many still made and in use today are composed of a collection of electronic units, each with circuits to perform those functions described above as required in the particular system. These are called *hard-wired controls*. As a next step *computer numerical control (CNC)* was developed. Controls of this kind are like general-purpose computers, and software directs the control. A CNC has a central processing unit (CPU) that performs arithmetic and logic processes and can perform the functions required of the control. The CNC also has a memory in which is stored an executive program (software) that directs the CPU to carry out the control functions. The memory also stores the part programs, wholly or partially. Some CNCs can build up, refine, and do editing of part programs as would otherwise be done by external computers. A CNC also has input and output (IO) registers. CNC was first built on a macroelectronic basic, i.e., around a *minicomputer*. In recent years there has been a trend to large-scale integration (LSI) of the circuitry, and such controls with one or a few small chips for the CPU are called *microprocessors* and are based on *microcomputers*. Microprocessors have become cheaper and more reliable and take less space than the minicomputer forms. In some cases, a minicomputer may be faster, more flexible, and expandable and able to handle more peripheral accessories.

Software gives CNC a number of advantages. With a hard-wired control, the tape must be rerun each time the operation is repeated, but that is not necessary with the part program stored in the CNC memory. Also, the program in the CNC memory can be updated, revised, and edited more easily. Even the executive program can be revised in most cases to add new features. Subroutines may be incorporated in the executive program to provide such added features as a canned subroutine to carry out whole drilling, tapping, boring, etc., cycles from a single block of tape command; subroutine capability for family of parts programming from only one tape; built-in trouble diagnosis; and many others.

NUMERICAL CONTROL SYSTEMS

NC Machines.   Machines may be classified according to the number of axes of numerically controlled movements with respect to Cartesian *X-Y-Z* coordinates. There may be other movements not numerically controlled. A two-axis machine would have the table moved lengthwise and crosswise in a horizontal plane; a three-axis machine would have an additional vertical movement of the spindle, for example. Four-, five-, or six-axis machines provide additional linear or rotary movements.

Three classes of NC systems are commonly recognized. One of these is called *point-to-point* or *positioning* NC, where a cutting tool and workpiece are positioned with respect to each other before a cut is taken, as exemplified by an NC drill press. The path between points is of little concern and is not particularly controlled. Another class, known as a *straight-cut* NC system, involves movements between points like point-to-point NC but along straight or curved paths determined by the machine ways or slides. An NC turret lathe may be of the second class. A third class is *continuous-path* NC, or more formally *continuous tool path control,* which does contouring or profiling of lines, curves, or surfaces, of all shapes. One way of achieving continuous path NC is to move the workpiece or cutter from point to point along a straight line or curve (a parabolic path between points is used on some machines) with many points spaced closely enough together so that the composite path of the cut approximates a desired curve within limits required. Another way is to drive machine members, say a saddle and the table on it, along coordinate axes at varying velocities controlled so that the resultant motion is along a particular line or curve.

An NC machine may be controlled through an *open-loop* or a *closed-loop* circuit as depicted in Fig. 35-3. The open-loop system is the simplest and cheapest but does not assure accuracy. A signal that is an order for a certain action (such as to turn on the coolant, start the spindle, or move the table to a certain position) is issued by the control unit. This travels through the drive mechanism which imposes the action upon the controlled member of the machine. The basic drive mechanism for a table or other machine member in an open-loop system is a *stepping motor,* also called a *digital* or *pulse motor.* It has, for example, 49 poles around the armature inside of 50 poles around the stator. Two poles are always aligned. Poles are energized to align the next two poles and turn the armature through a definite small angle each time a pulse of electricity is received. The motor turns the leadscrew, which moves the table a corresponding distance. If, for example, a pulse stands for a 0.001-mm movement, and a movement of 0.05 mm is desired, the control unit issues 50 pulses; the motor turns through 50 steps and turns the leadscrew, and the table (or other member) is driven the 0.05 mm required. The rate at which the pulses are issued determines the rate of feed. The power of a stepping motor is limited, and if the resistance to movement is large, the motor may just stall and miss steps. There is no feedback to report the omission, and accuracy is lost. Direct drive with a stepping motor is confined to light service at fractional horsepower. For more power and heavy service, a stepping motor is matched with a hydraulic motor through a servovalve for table drives up to 7.5 kW (10 hp) and more.

It is common in closed-loop systems for the pulsed command signal for the movement of the table (or other member) of the machine to be converted to a steady analog signal. That signal turns on the power to the drive mechanism. Hydraulic and ac but mostly dc electric motors are all used for NC machine drives. The intensity of the signal is determined by the feed velocity ordered. For a higher feed, pulses are issued at a faster rate and/or the analog signal is larger, which turns on more power

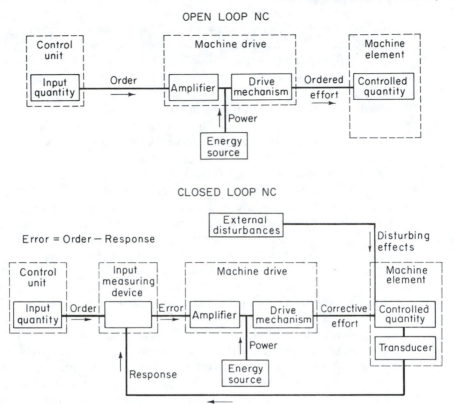

Figure 35-3 Schematics of open- and closed-loop NC systems.

to the motor to drive the table faster. A tachometer in the motor drive sends back a signal that is compared to the feed rate order to assure that the required feed rate is being delivered and to make corrections if it is not. Commonly, a resolver is driven by the leadscrew and returns a signal showing how far the table moves, as illustrated in Fig. 35-4. More accuracy for a longer period of time is obtained with the feedback device attached directly to the table (also shown), but such devices are more costly. The feedback signal is compared to the order, and where the feedback equals the order and signifies the required movement has been completed, the power is shut off, and the movement stops. Since they are controlled through separate channels, all movements may act at the same time. Indeed, it is necessary that they act simultaneously and be synchronized accurately for contouring.

    Machining Centers.   The NC principle was first applied to conventional types of machine tools, and most NC machines may still be classified as lathes or milling, drilling, or spot welding machines, etc. A view of an NC lathe is shown in Fig. 19-8. Further development has led to NC systems of more versatility, each capable of completely machining a wide variety of parts. These are called *machining centers*.

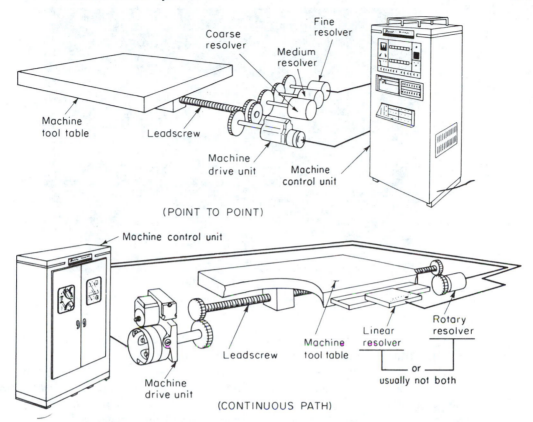

Figure 35-4 Sketches of typical closed-loop NC systems. (Courtesy Industrial Controls Section, Bendix Corporation.)

One of the most popular, shown in Fig. 35-5, is a three-axis machine with a range of 508 mm (20 in.) along each axis and an indexable table with 360 positions. The machine is capable of milling, drilling, boring, reaming, and tapping multiple faces in one setup. This model has a horizontal spindle, but others are available with vertical spindles.

The machining center of Fig. 35-5 carries up to 30 cutting tools (some have up to 60 tools), has a $7\frac{1}{2}$-kW (10-hp) spindle drive motor, weighs 5.7 Mg (12,500 lb), and costs about $180,000. One authority calls this the median price for machining centers. A 3-kW (4-hp) machining center with capacity for 24 tools has a price of about $75,000. One of the largest with a 38-kW (50-hp) motor costs over $1 million.

A machining center represents a large investment and must be kept working continuously and efficiently to be profitable. Each cutting tool is preset for diameter and depth in a quick-change holder so that when it is placed in the spindle, it cuts its programmed dimensions without any adjustment on the machine. Tools are placed in holes in a rotary drum on top of the machine column. When the program calls for a cutting tool, it is identified by a sensor, from coded rings around the tool shank, and

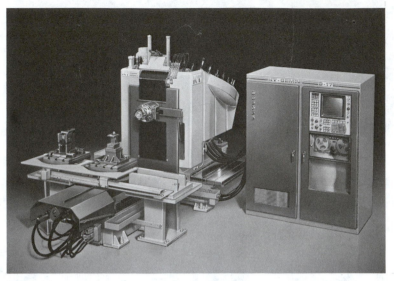

Figure 35-5   Milwaukee-Matic 180 NC machining center. (Courtesy Kearney and Trecker Corp.)

transferred by a mechanical tool changer in a few seconds to the machine spindle on the front of the column. The spindle has a speed range of 50 to 4000 rpm to accommodate many sizes of tools. A workpiece fixture is shown on a pallet in the workstation (on the machine table) in front of the machine spindle in Fig. 35-5. Alongside is another pallet on which work is set up while a piece is being machined in the workstation. Then when one piece is done, it is slid off mechanically, another is moved on its pallet into the workstation, and cutting is resumed at once, with no loss of machine time. A further step is the *unmanned machining center*. Fifteen or twenty or more parts are loaded on pallets in a repository next to the machine and are transferred into and from the workstation automatically in turn. The NC control has a memory large enough to store programs for all the work, and each program is called out to suit the part in the workstation. The machining center can be used conventionally and given maintenance and the pallets and programs can be loaded during the day, and then the machine may run all night or over a weekend with little or no supervision.

The typical machining center has one disadvantage for large-quantity production; it applies only one cutting tool at a time to a workpiece. Machining centers do have places in flexible manufacturing systems along with multiple-tool machines, like the one illustrated in Fig. 34-8. Efforts have been made to make machining centers more competitive for large-quantity production. A few have been built with two or more spindles. A major development has been the addition of multiple-toolhead storage and transfer devices to some machining centers. Multiple toolheads, such as drill heads, may be stored in a rack or on an endless conveyor and taken out on call by a tool changer and affixed to the machine spindle, even intermixed with single tools as required.

NC Accuracy.   The smallest increment of motion that can be specified by a signal in the system is the *resolution* of the NC system. Obviously, for a series of pulses, the value of one pulse is the resolution. Typical of high-quality NC systems is a resolution of 2.5 μm (0.0001 in.), but some have more and others less. *Accuracy* of the machine is a different matter because it depends on mechanical performance. It signifies how closely a machine member can be moved to any specified point. The advertised accuracy for any axis of the machining center of Fig. 35-5 is ± 13 μm within 300 mm and ± 20 μm over full range (± 0.0005 in. per foot and ± 0.0008 in. over full range). The accuracy of most NC machines lies in the range of ± 5 to 25 μm (± 0.0002 to 0.001 in.). Of equal importance is the *repeatability* or *precision* of an NC machine; that is how closely the table (or other member) can be returned to an initial position repeatedly. The repeatability of the machining center of Fig. 35-5 is ± 8 μm (± 0.0003 in.).

The ultimate accuracy of a machining operation is what the tools can do. For example, an NC jig boring machine was found accurate to 5 μm (0.0002 in.) in table positioning, but holes drilled on the machine were out of true position by as much as 81 μm (0.0032 in.) because of the tendency of drills to wander. An inexpensive NC drill press with table positioning accuracy estimated to be 25 to 50 μm (0.001 to 0.002 in.) consistently drilled holes to within 97 μm (0.0038 in.) of specified location. Experience has indicated that setup and tooling errors are commonly appreciably more than laxity of the machines.

An NC machine must have design features not always required for conventional machine tools. A skilled operator may be depended upon to compensate for the deficiencies of a machine tool, but all requisites must be programmed for or built into an NC machine. Much that a skilled operator would do can be planned for an NC operation, such as taking several boring cuts where hole location is important. An NC machine must be rigid, tight, accurate, and true because the operator cannot nurse it along as he or she might a manual machine. The drive system must be stiff to minimize windup and enhance stability of the servo drive. Low inertia is required for rapid response to changing command signals. Friction forces must be low and uniform for stability, rapid response, and positioning accuracy. This is achieved through the use of rolling contact bearings and hydrostatic bearings in many cases. Even so, NC machines are available at various levels of quality, and economy dictates that a machine be no more expensive than needed for the purposes intended.

NC Adjuncts.   An added feature of some NC systems is *adaptive control (AC)*, which is a means of continuously monitoring the critical parameters of an operation to maintain optimum conditions. AC has been applied largely but not solely to machining operations in manufacturing. One purpose is to detect faults, such as worn or broken cutting tools or hard spots in material, and correct for them. Another purpose is to periodically adjust speeds, feeds, and other variables for optimum performance. Sensors constantly measure critical parameters in an operation and report to a computer that is programmed to compare the current status to an ideal. If a difference persists for a predetermined period of time, the computer orders corrections to be made.

For AC of a metal-cutting operation, the common arrangement is to measure deflection, speed, and power at the machine tool spindle. Deflection is measured with strain gages or magnetic transducers around the spindle. Deflections can be translated into forces on the cutter by tests on the machine. The torque of the spindle may be calculated from power and speed. Other conditions, such as vibrations and work surface reflection, have also been monitored but not in many systems. An external computer may be used for AC with a hard-wired control, or the computer for AC may be part of a CNC control. Relationships among the parameters of speed, feed, depth of cut, type of cutter, material, forces, power, etc., are determined for each operation to be performed on the machine under AC, like the relationships discussed in Chap. 17 but in more detail. From these models and the capacities of the machine, working limits are set for the variables. This information is stored in the computer and called out by the AC program as needed. Thus, if no forces or power are detected during a cut, a broken tool is indicated, and the computer may order the tool replaced if the machine has a tool changer. Otherwise, it may stop the machine and signal the operator to change the tool. If deflections and torque of the spindle indicate cutting forces larger than the tool can stand, the computer orders an override of the originally programmed feed rate to reduce it to a tolerable level. As a cutter becomes dull, forces and power increase. The computer may be programmed to calculate the tool life to be expected under prevailing conditions and adjust the feed or speed to obtain optimum tool life. When the forces and power rise to the point that shows the tool is so dull that it must be removed for economical sharpening or to prevent catastrophic breakdown, the computer calls for a change. Where tool life or strength are not the limiting factors, the computer may regulate the feed to utilize the full capacity of the machine, but to prevent any harmful overload. Feed rate may be automatically raised in gaps between full cuts or when cutting resistance decreases.

In another area, acoustic type AC is used for production spot welding. Sounds that occur during deformation, melting, solidification, cracking, and other changes are measured. Sound intensity, current flow, and electrode forces are all taken into account to control the operation for optimum weld quality, electrode life, and productivity for the material welded. One system, called an expulsion limit controller (ELC), turns the current off when expulsion or splatter occurs to prevent overwelding and obtain maximum nugget size.

Tests have shown production increases of 23 to 90% with an average of 37% from AC fully utilized in metal cutting. Commercial AC systems are available at various levels of sophistication. The majority does not have all the capability that has been described as feasible for metal cutting; most are confined to reacting to tool failures and hazardous operating conditions. To do more is much more expensive. Even at the lowest level, AC is desirable for unmanned machining centers.

Verification and *correction* of NC programs is necessary, particularly when working with expensive materials, tools, and preprocessed pieces. As a minimum, an NC program should be examined carefully by a second person, just like an engineering drawing or project of any kind. Trial runs are commonly made on wood, aluminum, or foamed plastics. This is not really economical because it takes time on the machine tool and may upset production schedules for other parts. Because of corrections that must be made, the time to tryout a program is usually longer than to make a part afterward, and time on an NC machine may cost $20 to $120 per hour. It is reported that in one aerospace plant over a 12-month period, 3777 programs were verified by trial at a cost of over $1 million.

An NC program can be run on a computer with a plotter if the job is a point-to-point or plane contouring operation, but that is not feasible for three-dimensional cutting. Even so, an ordinary plot reveals only gross errors and may give some indication of the possibility of collisions but does not prove how well small tolerances are held. Groups in the aerospace industry are developing a system for verification of two- and three-dimensional NC programs by computer simulation. Specifications for the work, fixtures, and cutting tools together with the NC program are fed in as data. The verification program graphically simulates (with dynamic animation) the machining process on a CRT screen. It also displays relationships between cutter, workpiece, holding fixture, and machine tool. The cutter path is dynamically compared to models of the raw stock, part geometry, and holding fixture to verify part configuration and detect collisions, interferences, and unmachined conditions. Surfaces with excess stock or that are cut out of tolerance are shown in color.

Many modern NC systems have diagnostic capabilities to find the causes of troubles that arise and display instructions on a CRT screen to correct the faults. *Diagnostics* (so called) check the mechanical as well as the electrical parts of the system. Two kinds of diagnostic systems are in general use. One is resident diagnostics, which is programmed in the CNC control. The other is known as a diagnostic communication system, and its main program is contained in an outside computer, typically at the plant of the manufacturer of the NC machine, and is reached by telephone lines. Since experience has indicated that about 95% of the time in conventional troubleshooting is spent in finding the cause of the trouble, a diagnostic system saves considerable machine downtime. Less skill is also needed. In addition to breakdown emergencies, a diagnostic system can be a valuable service in routine preventive maintenance by detecting failing components before they collapse.

NC Inspection and Measuring Machines.   Coordinate and roundness measurement were discussed in Chap. 15; NC can do that work automatically. Some continuous-path control is found on measuring machines but is questionable because of the dynamic effects during machine movements. As a result, continuous-path measurements are made mostly along straight lines and circles. More precise results are obtainable from point-to-point measuring systems, where the apparatus and workpiece come to rest when readings are taken.

An NC measuring system touches a piece being measured through a probe that is displaced and emits a signal upon contact. There are two types of systems as indicated in Fig. 35-6. In *null probing* the signal from the probe is fed back to the control unit of the machine to position the workpiece to put the probe in a neutral position. The dimension to which the slide carrying the workpiece has moved from the reference zero position is then displayed on a screen or printed record. In *deviation*

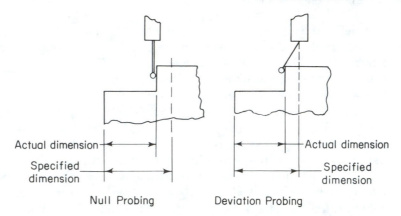

Figure 35-6 Two forms of NC measuring systems.

probing the workpiece is moved the amount of the specified dimension by the NC system as it would be in machining. The displacement of the probe when the final position is reached is shown on a scale, screen, or record and represents the difference between the actual and required dimensions. Most measuring systems with two or three axes employ both null and deviation probing so the user has either available as desired.

ECONOMICS OF NUMERICAL CONTROL

Comparison of NC with Other Methods.   The big drawback of NC is its initial cost. NC machines cost from around $1\frac{1}{2}$ to 5 times as much as conventional machines of like size, depending upon the capacity of the control and accessories. Maintenance of the NC equipment requires a high order of skill and trained personnel, although this is being alleviated by diagnostic systems and replaceable circuit boards for controls. Programmers are needed for most NC machines.

NC is not the best method for all jobs; it is more economical for certain kinds of work and quantities as indicated by Fig. 35-7. In many cases one or a few simple pieces (say to turn a diameter or mill a face) can be done by a skilled machinist in less time at a lower cost per hour on general-purpose conventional machines than is required to program and run the job on an NC machine. On the other hand, with more intricate parts even one piece may be made more economically by NC. Once the programming has been done, the time is often less per piece on the NC machine, which is then more economical for more than a few pieces.

Figure 35-8 indicates average savings and productivity gains from NC as compared to conventional machine tools. These results were found in a study at the University of Michigan of 356 companies employing 4648 NC machines. Productivity gains are more impressive than time savings. As an example, assume that the time to produce a part on an NC machine is 40% of the time required on a conventional machine; that is a saving of 60% in time. If the conventional machine takes 1 hour to

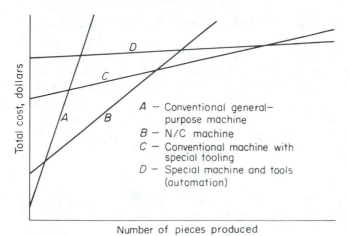

A — Conventional general-
    purpose machine
B — N/C machine
C — Conventional machine with
    special tooling
D — Special machine and tools
    (automation)

Figure 35-7 Typical comparison of the cost of NC with other methods.

make one part, the NC machine can make a part in 24 minutes and put out 2.5 parts per hour, which is an increase in productivity of 150%.

There are a number of reasons that NC machines can often work faster than manually operated machines and thus save time as indicated in Fig. 35-8. Idle time is a minimum (the machine does not demand a coffee break), fatigue is nonexistent, human mistakes are avoided, all planning must be done beforehand, rejects are fewer, and less time is needed for checking and inspection. A study by one manufacturer showed NC machines cutting 80% as against less than 25% of the time for conventional machine tools. Tool life may be better because speeds and feeds are set as

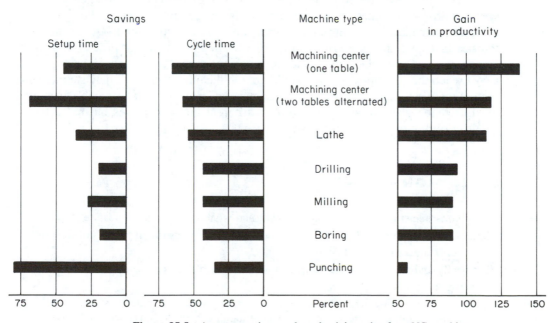

Figure 35-8 Average savings and productivity gains from NC machines.

planned and continuously maintained. Much setup can be done off the machine and in programming.

NC systems offer savings other than those reflected by reductions in operating time. Scrap and rework were reported reduced over 25%, material handling decreased 20 to 50%, and inspection cost was reduced by 30 to 40%. Since operator errors can be better controlled by NC, parts are produced more accurately, and assembly costs were reported reduced by 10 to 20%. An NC machining center may be able to do in one operation as much as several different conventional machines and thus save considerable floor space. Multiple control of machine tools and even remote control, say for dangerous material, is practical for NC. Tooling in the form of tapes or disks is easily stored and preserved.

Special tooling such as fixtures, jigs, or templates are commonly added to conventional machines for moderate to large quantities of pieces. Preparation or lead time is commonly long for special tools, and a job often can be started much sooner with NC that does not require as much or any special tooling. The tooling costs, tool storage charges, setup costs, and the costs of making changes are then much less for NC. In one case, the time to prepare tools was reported to be 240 hours for a conventional machine, but only 60 hours (including 22 hours of programming) for an NC machine. Even if the NC cycle time per piece is more after the job has been set up, and it is not always so, a moderate to large number of pieces must be run to make up for the difference in preparation cost, as indicated by Fig. 35-7. With NC flexibility setup cost is often less and smaller lot sizes are economical; less floor space is needed for materials in process and storage.

As indicated on the right of Fig. 35-7, NC cannot compete with fixed program special-purpose machines and tools to produce large quantities of pieces. For instance, automatic bar machines controlled by cams are simple, direct, and fast for turning; transfer machines are specialized in making certain products just as efficiently as any one knows how to produce them, and NC machines cannot do the same jobs at as low a cost when the quantities required are large. On the other hand, NC may supplement special machines in some aspects. For instance, NC may be part of a flexible machining line that machines large quantities of different kinds of pieces but not a large quantity of any one part at one time.

QUESTIONS

1. What is numerical control or tape control, and what are its principal features?
2. Draw a diagram of and describe the principal ways of preparing input to an NC system.
3. Describe direct numerical control.
4. Specify and explain nine functions that an NC control may perform.
5. What is a five-axis NC machine?
6. What are point-to-point, straight-cut, and continuous-path NC machines?
7. Explain the differences between plain or hard-wired NC, CNC, and an NC microprocessor.

8. What is meant in NC coding by character, bit, word, block, and parity check?

9. Explain the binary-coded decimal form of code.

10. Describe fixed- and tab-sequential and word-address formats.

11. What is the difference between an open-loop and a closed-loop NC system?

12. How does a typical closed-loop NC system operate? Explain by reference to Figs. 35-3 and 35-4.

13. What is a machining center, and to what factors does it owe its efficiency?

14. What are machine resolution, machine accuracy, machine repeatability, and the accuracy achieved in an operation, and why does the last differ from the others?

15. What is adaptive control, and how is it commonly done in NC systems?

16. How may NC programs be verified?

17. How may troubles be diagnosed quickly in NC systems?

18. What are null and deviation probing?

19. What are the advantages and disadvantages of NC compared to conventional methods?

20. What in general are the purposes for which NC is economical?

PROBLEMS

1. Rough and finish operations on a workpiece include boring a hole and profiling the front and two sides. For a conventional milling machine, 210 hours is required to design and make a jig, fixture, and template at a toolroom rate of $16/hr. Cycle time is $5\frac{1}{2}$ hr/piece at a rate of $30/hr.

For a numerically controlled machine 71 hours is required in the toolroom for a fixture, 46 hours at $20/hr for the drawing, process sheet, and punched tape, and 1 hour at $50/hr on an electronic computer. The cycle time is 3 hr/piece at $65/hr.

For how many pieces should the numerically controlled system be used?

2. A job can be set up on a standard jig boring machine in 1 hour. Each piece takes 6 hours for boring. If the job is done on a tape-controlled jig boring machine, 2 hours is needed for programming in the office. Then each piece can be bored in 5 hours. The shop rate is $24/hr on the standard jig borer and $28/hr on the numerically controlled jig borer. Office work costs $18/hr. When is the numerically controlled machine justified?

3. The following four machine tools are available.

(1)   An engine lathe at $16/hr. Setup time is 15 minutes for any job on this machine. To adjust for a rough cut on any diameter takes 0.2 minute, and for a finish cut 0.78 minute on this machine only but not on others. Adjustments must be made for each piece.

(2)   A tracer lathe at $16/hr for which a template must be made for each job at a cost of $50 plus $30 for each diameter turned. Setup time is 20 minutes.

(3)   An NC lathe at $20/hr on which the setup time is 10 minutes for any job. Programming for any job requires 30 minutes plus 15 minutes for each diameter at a rate of $12/hr.

(4)   An automatic lathe at $18/hr. Setup time is 30 minutes plus 15 minutes per diameter. Tools and cams cost $200 plus $50 for each diameter turned. All the diameters on one piece can be turned at once, so the time per piece is the time for the longest cut.

However, all pieces in a lot must be rough cut and then finish cut, so an extra time of 0.50 minute to unload and load each piece is required for this machine.

A workpiece 50 mm (2 in.) in diameter and 75 mm (3 in.) long is to be turned at 92 m/min (300 fpm) at a feed of 0.5 mm/rev (0.020 ipr) rough and 0.25 m/rev (0.010 ipr) finish. A 60-minute productive hour is assumed.

(a) For what quantities of pieces would each machine be economical?

(b) Which machine should be selected for one lot of (1) 1 piece? (2) 25 pieces? (3) 50 pieces? (4) 500 pieces? (5) 1500 pieces? (6) 2500 pieces?

4. The machines described in Prob. 3 are available for turning a workpiece with the following diameters and cutting times:

Diameter [mm (in.)]	Length [mm (in.)]	Cutting time (min)
50 (2.0)	75 (3.0)	0.78
57 (2.25)	13 (ca. 0.5)	0.15
80 (3.15)	50 (2.0)	0.82
110 (ca. 4.30)	38 (1.5)	0.88
120 (4.72)	20 (0.8)	0.49

The cutting time is the total for the rough and finishing cuts and includes time for approach and overtravel. A 60-minute productive hour is assumed. Only one setup is required.

(a) For what quantities should each machine be selected?

(b) Which machine should be selected for one lot of (1) 1 piece? (2) 10 pieces? (3) 25 pieces? (4) 100 pieces? (5) 1000 pieces? (6) 5000 pieces?

5. A cast-iron compressor body requires 152 operations consisting of 50 holes drilled, 12 bored, 38 co-sunk, 36 tapped, and 16 surfaces milled. These operations can be done on NC machining centers in 1 hr/piece at a rate of $40/hr. Programming and setup costs are negligible. Conventional machines may be tooled for the job at a cost of $300,000. The annual charge for the tools is $130,000, and the rate on the machines is $24/hr, including labor and overhead. It is estimated that about 1 hour will be required per piece by this method. A transfer machine to produce 188 pieces/hr will cost $1,800,000 with an annual charge of $800,000. Labor and overhead rate is $16/hr. For what quantities is each method suitable?

REFERENCES

Annual Proceedings, Numerical Control Society, Glenview, Ill.

CHILDS, J. L., *Principles of Numerical Control,* Society of Manufacturing Engineers, Dearborn, Mich., 1982.

GARCIA, G., "A New Generation of Computer Numerical Controls," *Manufacturing Engineering,* May 1980, p. 44.

————, "Control Systems for the '80's," *Manufacturing Engineering,* Jan. 1981, p. 80.

HATSCHEK, R. L., "Numerical Control Systems," *American Machinist,* Feb. 1977, p. SR-9.

MARTIN, J. M., "Voice Commands Produce NC Tapes," *American Machinist,* June 1980, p. 102.

MOOREHEAD, J., ed., *Numerical Control,* Vol. 1: *Fundamentals,* Vol. 2: *Applications,* Society of Manufacturing Engineers, Dearborn, Mich., 1980.

OLESTON, N. O., *Numerical Control,* Wiley-Interscience, New York, 1970.

PATTON, W. J., *Numerical Control: Practice and Application,* Reston, Reston, Va., 1972.

POLACEK, R., "Machining Centers: Today and Tomorrow," *Manufacturing Engineering,* Aug. 1982, p. 97.

SCHAFFER, G., "Stepping Up to CAM," *American Machinist,* Nov. 1978, p. 87.

SMITH, D. N., "NC for Profit and Productivity," *American Machinist,* Oct. 16, 1972, p. 68.

VASILASH, G. S., "Machining Centers on the Move," *Manufacturing Engineering,* Sept. 1980, p. 94.

WELCH, A., "Verification of NC Programs by Computer Simulation," *Manufacturing Engineering,* Sept. 1980, p. 77.

WILLETTE, E. J., "The Computer's Role in Numerical Control," *Manufacturing Engineering,* Sept. 1977, p. 36.

PROGRAMMING FOR NUMERICAL CONTROL

The detailed instructions for an NC operation may be listed by hand, but that can become long and tedious, particularly for continuous-path and involved point-to-point operations and can be done more quickly in many cases by digital computers. Compiler programs are available that enable digital computers to take simple statements of specifications and convert them into detailed instructions for NC machines. Compilers differ and may be classified as to whether the input must be in a restricted numerical form, in an English-like language describing the tool action or in words merely defining the conditions and areas for machining. A computer is able to translate input specifications into instructions because it can make decisions to pick the proper course of action for a situation and follow a routine to delineate the steps to be taken. Continuing development of NC is toward incorporating it into a total system of information processing through the stages of design and manufacture of products.

MANUAL PROGRAMMING

About half of the NC programming in the United States is manual. One way of programming an NC machine manually, as depicted in Fig. 35-1, is to write a programming process sheet or planning sheet from the part drawing or print. This process sheet contains all the instructions needed by the control for the operation and can be recorded on tape or disk to be read into the control as needed or entered directly into the memory of the control, depending on the system. The process sheet also commonly contains tool specifications and instructions to the operator. In another way, an operator composes one block at a time and enters it into the control through a pushbutton panel or keyboard for the operation at hand. The second procedure is typical for manual data imput (MDI).

A manually prepared programming process sheet is shown in Fig. 36-1 for machining the holes in the workpiece of Fig. 36-2 on the NC turret drill of Fig. 36-3. The tool chart near the top of the planning sheet specifies the cutting tool and the speed and feed assigned to each turret position when the job is set up. Every step to be taken in the operation is then listed. The first line, reading D1-00500 00500, prescribes that the turret indexes to position 1, the table positions the workpiece to coordinate points $X = 0.500$ in. and $Y = 0.500$ in. from the origin (previously established) at the lower left-hand corner of the piece, and the tool is advanced to, fed into, and retracted from the workpiece at the preset rates of speed and feed. The next line,--07938 00500, designates that the table repositions the workpiece to $X = 7.938$ in. and $Y = 0.500$ in., and a hole is spot drilled there still from turret position 1. The steps continue with spot drilling of all the holes and then completion of the work from the other turret positions.

Each line of coordinate data and machine function instructions in Fig. 36-1 is a block and is punched in tape between end-of-block symbols, like the illustration of Fig. 35-2, and the tape is all that is needed to actuate the control unit of the NC machine. After setup, the machine operator has little control over the operation; the machine only does precisely what it is told, and therefore the programmer must understand, anticipate, and specify explicitly what must be done.

Programming may be done directly from the part print (without a process sheet) through an input pad or keyboard into the NC control with an (MDI) system. Modern processors for such a system offer such auxiliary aids as canned cycles and linear, circular, parabolic, and even helical interpolation to simplify programming. MDI is practical mostly for simple jobs on less complex machines and for small lots that are not to be run again. The reason is that the machine is idle (an average estimated time of half an hour per job) while the operator is programming. A few systems allow programming while work is in progress, but that has not been widely adopted because operator attention is needed for much machining. Thus jobs that require even moderately long programs (over about 20 lines) and program editing, and can repeat parts of programs for similar work are more efficiently programmed off the machine (under circumstances more ideal than on the shop floor) so that costly NC time is minimized. MDI does have the advantages of requiring little or no tape-preparation equipment and only a simple organization and few steps for least chance of error. It gives a psychological benefit of full operator involvement.

All methods of NC programming must involve more than just listing steps in operations; planning starts in product design with the selection of parts most suitable for NC fabrication and design of the parts to utilize NC capabilities most fully. For instance, NC machines commonly operate on an *absolute system* in which all dimensions are referred to a zero point; optimum results are achieved if the workpiece is

Conventional Program

BROWN & SHARPE
TAPE CONTROLLED TURRET DRILLING MACHINE

PLANNING SHEET _____

COMPANY BROWN & SHARPE MFG. Co.

MATERIAL

PART NO. ZZ-8629

SFM

TOOL CHART

TURRET POSITION	TOOL	R.P.M.	FEED
1	Spot Drill	2000	.003
2	Drill .166 & Cha.	1900	.003
3	Tap 10-32	900	—
4	Comb Dr. 1/32 & 5/16	1345	.005
5	Comb Dr. 9/32 & 7/16	1233	.005
6	Drill .196	1800	.003

CONTROL SYSTEM DATA

MAKE	CODE
LONGITUDINAL (PLUS 5 DIGITS)*	X
TRANSVERSE (PLUS 5 DIGITS)*	Y
TURRET SELECTOR (PLUS 1 TO 6)	D
COOLANT ON	F
COOLANT OFF	G
CYCLE STOP	M

TURRET	AUX	COORDINATE DATA AND MACHINE FUNCTION	
		X	Y
D1		00500	00500
		07938	00500
		00500	03500
		07938	03500
		01125	00813
		04219	00813
		07312	00813
		01125	03188
		04219	03188
		07312	03188
		03563	02000
		04750	02000
		05438	02125
		06375	02125
		05438	02625
		06375	02625
D2		00500	00500
		07938	00500
		00500	03500
		07938	03500
D3		00500	00500
		07938	00500
		00500	03500
		07938	03500
D4		01125	00813
		04219	00813
		07312	00813
		01125	03188
		04219	03188
		07312	03188
D5		03563	02000
		04750	02000
D6		05438	02125
		06375	02125
		05438	02625
		06375	02625

Figure 36-1 Programming process sheet, manually prepared, for machining the holes in the workpiece of Fig. 36-2. (Courtesy Brown and Sharpe Mfg. Co.)

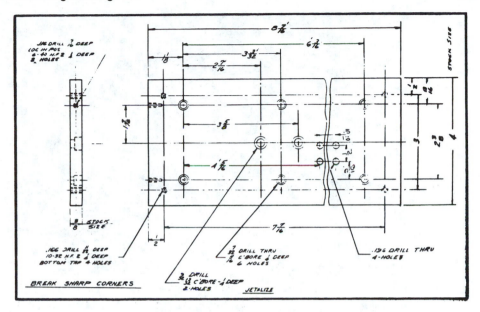

Figure 36-2 Print of a workpiece drawing. (Courtesy Brown and Sharpe Mfg. Co.)

dimensioned in the same way. As each part is programmed, it must be analyzed to ascertain the best orientation for it on the machine, the most efficient sequence of operations (such as mill, drill, rough bore, and finish bore for accurate hole location), the proper cutters to use, and the necessary fixtures or other holding means for security and reliability. For a point-to-point positioning operation the programmer normally takes three steps in resolving an operation. They are to (1) select the best zero point, (2) ascertain the order of positioning the coordinate points, and (3) determine what cuts are to be made at each point. Once these items have been determined, the programming is merely a matter of expressing them in the format required for the machine.

A point-to-point positioning program has been presented as an example of manual programming, but continuous-path contouring or profiling may be programmed in substantially the same way; only the task is likely to be longer and require more calculations. The instructions for profiling solely along straight lines and circles may have to include only the first and last points of each line or curve and the slope of a line or radius of a circle if the control of the NC machine is capable of interpolating between the ends, as many are. Still the points where lines and curves intersect must be calculated. Desk calculators may be used for simple cases and elaborate systems using tables are available to ease manual programming.

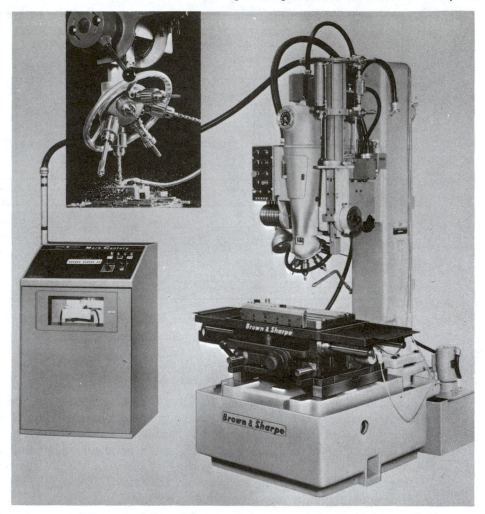

Figure 36-3   NC turret drilling machine. The inset shows how the tools are arranged on the turret, which is indexed to position each tool as required in operating position. (Courtesy Brown and Sharpe Mfg. Co.)

COMPUTER-ASSISTED NC PROGRAMMING

The need for a computer (either as part of the control or outside) is obvious for finding the coordinates of points on and at intersections of slopes, curves, and surfaces. Even so, manual programming of even simple point-to-point operations becomes tedious and time consuming when done for a continuous stream of jobs, and computer assistance gives fewer mistakes and lower costs. Figure 36-4 shows what is needed to prepare a *part program* for a computer to get the same results as shown in Fig. 36-1.

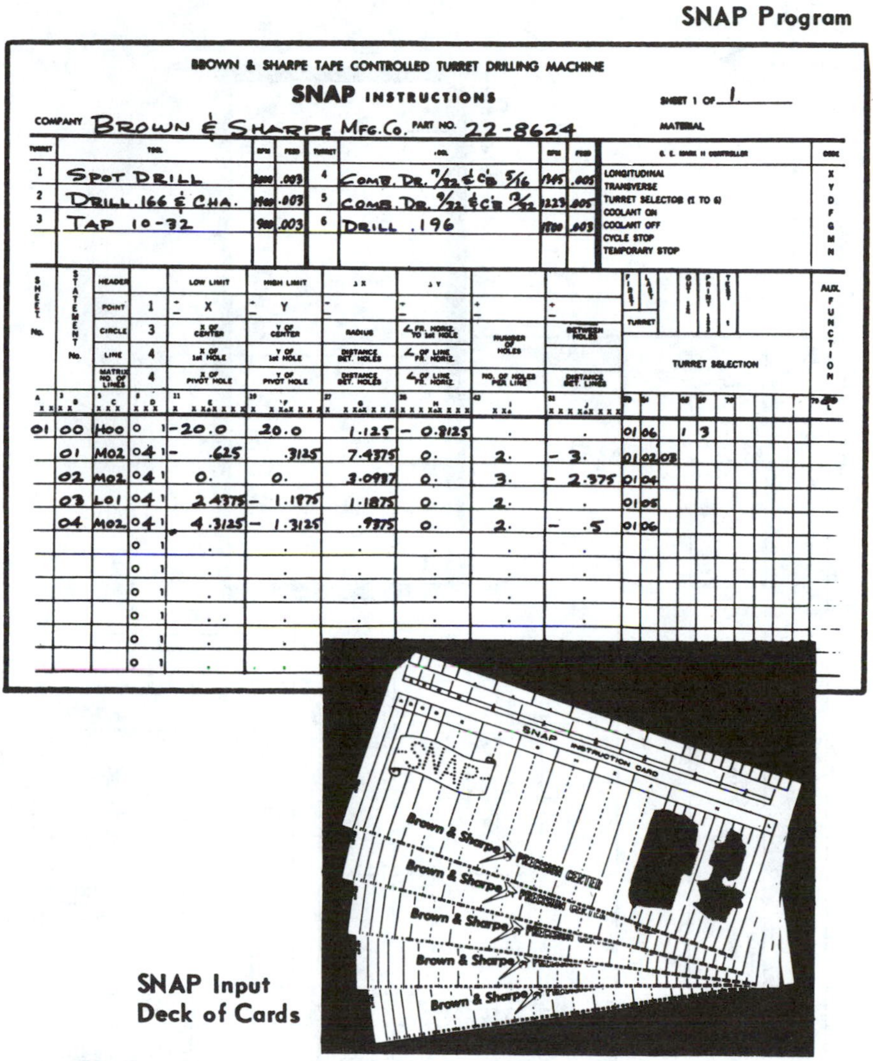

SNAP Program

BROWN & SHARPE TAPE CONTROLLED TURRET DRILLING MACHINE

SNAP INSTRUCTIONS

SHEET 1 OF _1_

COMPANY BROWN & SHARPE MFG.Co. PART NO. 22-8624   MATERIAL

TURRET	TOOL	RPM	FEED	TURRET	TOOL	RPM	FEED	G. E. MARK II CONTROLLER	CODE
1	SPOT DRILL	2000	.003	4	COMB. DR. 7/32 & C'B 5/16	1145	.005	LONGITUDINAL	X
2	DRILL .166 & CHA.	1900	.003	5	COMB. DR. 9/32 & C'B 3/32	1223	.005	TRANSVERSE	Y
3	TAP 10-32	900	.003	6	DRILL .196	1800	.003	TURRET SELECTORS (1 TO 6)	D
								COOLANT ON	F
								COOLANT OFF	G
								CYCLE STOP	M
								TEMPORARY STOP	N

	STATEMENT No.	HEADER		LOW LIMIT	HIGH LIMIT	Δ X	Δ Y				TURRET				AUX. FUNCTION
		POINT	1	X	Y										
		CIRCLE	3	X OF CENTER	Y OF CENTER	RADIUS	∠ FR. HORIZ. TO 1st HOLE	NUMBER OF HOLES	DISTANCE BETWEEN HOLES						
		LINE	4	X OF 1st HOLE	Y OF 1st HOLE	DISTANCE BET. HOLES	∠ OF LINE FR. HORIZ.	NO. OF HOLES PER LINE	DISTANCE BET. LINES			TURRET SELECTION			
		MATRIX NO. OF LINES	4	X OF PIVOT HOLE	Y OF PIVOT HOLE	DISTANCE BET. HOLES	∠ OF LINE FR. HORIZ.	NO. OF HOLES PER LINE	DISTANCE BET. LINES						

01	00	H00	0	1	-20.0	20.0	1.125	- 0.3125	.	.	01 06	1 3	
	01	M02	04	1	- .625	.3125	7.4375	0.	2.	- 3.	01 02 03		
	02	M02	04	1	0.	0.	3.0937	0.	3.	- 2.375	01 04		
	03	L01	04	1	2.4375	- 1.1875	1.1875	0.	2.	.	01 05		
	04	M02	04	1	4.3125	- 1.3125	.9375	0.	2.	- .5	01 06		

SNAP Input Deck of Cards

Figure 36-4 Input or part program for a computer to prepare the NC processing program for the workpiece of Fig. 36-2. The inset shows a set of cards on which the computer input instructions are punched. (Courtesy Brown and Sharpe Mfg. Co.)

Only five lines need to be written in this case for the computer, which is directed by a master program, called a *processor, compiler,* or *interpreter,* that tells the computer how to process the input statements to derive the necessary instructions for the NC machine. In the example given here, the output is on punched cards but more often it is on tape or disk. Also, a plot of the hole pattern is furnished for verification of the results as illustrated in Fig. 36-5. This may be displayed on a CRT screen by some

Listing of Input Data

PG	LN	ITM	EQU	PARAM 1	PARAM 2	PARAM 3	PARAM 4	PARAM 5	PARAM 6	MODE	MODE	MODE	MODE	MODE	AUXL
01	01	M02	041	- .625	.3125	7.4375	0.	2.	- 3.	01	02	03			
01	02	M02	041	0.	0.	3.0937	0.	3.	- 2.375	01	04				
01	03	L01	041	2.4375	- 1.1875	1.1875	0.	2.	.	01	05				
01	04	M02	041	4.3125	- 1.3125	.9375	0.	2.	- .5	01	06				
01	01	M02	041	- .625	.3125	7.4375	0.	2.	- 3.	01	02	03			
01	02	M02	041	0.	0.	3.0937	0.	3.	- 2.375	01	04				
01	03	L01	041	2.4375	- 1.1875	1.1875	0.	2.	.	01	05				
01	04	M02	041	4.3125	- 1.3125	.9375	0.	2.	- .5	01	06				
01	01	M02	041	- .625	.3125	7.4375	0.	2.	- 3.	01	02	03			
01	02	M02	041	0.	0.	3.0937	0.	3.	- 2.375	01	04				
01	03	L01	041	2.4375	- 1.1875	1.1875	0.	2.	.	01	05				
01	04	M02	041	4.3125	- 1.3125	.9375	0.	2.	- .5	01	06				
01	01	M02	041	- .625	.3125	7.4375	0.	2.	- 3.	01	02	03			
01	02	M02	041	0.	0.	3.0937	0.	3.	- 2.375	01	04				
01	03	L01	041	2.4375	- 1.1875	1.1875	0.	2.	.	01	05				
01	04	M02	041	4.3125	- 1.3125	.9375	0.	2.	- .5	01	06				
01	01	M02	041	- .625	.3125	7.4375	0.	2.	- 3.	01	02	03			
01	02	M02	041	0.	0.	3.0937	0.	3.	- 2.375	01	04				
01	03	L01	041	2.4375	- 1.1875	1.1875	0.	2.	.	01	05				
01	04	M02	041	4.3125	- 1.3125	.9375	0.	2.	- .5	01	06				
01	01	M02	041	- .625	.3125	7.4375	0.	2.	- 3.	01	02	03			
01	02	M02	041	0.	0.	3.0937	0.	3.	- 2.375	01	04				
01	03	L01	041	2.4375	- 1.1875	1.1875	0.	2.	.	01	05				
01	04	M02	041	4.3125	- 1.3125	.9375	0.	2.	- .5	01	06				

Computations

X	Y
.500	.500
7.938	.500
.500	3.500
7.938	3.500
1.125	.813
4.219	.813
7.312	.813
1.125	3.188
4.219	3.188
7.312	3.188
3.563	2.000
4.750	2.000
5.438	2.125
6.375	2.125
5.438	2.625
6.375	2.625

Plot of Hole Pattern

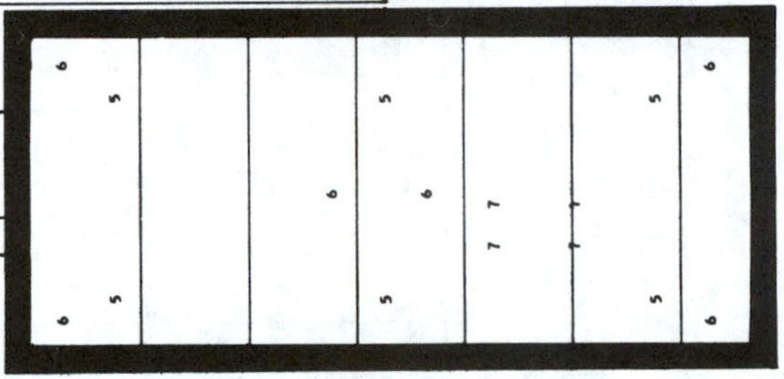

Listing of All Points

SEQUENCE	PAGE	LINE	ITEM	EQU	X	Y	TURR	AUXL
1	01	01	M02	041	.500	.500	1	-
2	01	01	M02	041	7.938	.500	1	-
3	01	01	M02	041	.500	3.500	1	-
4	01	01	M02	041	7.938	3.500	1	-
5	01	02	M02	041	1.125	.813	1	-
6	01	02	M02	041	4.219	.813	1	-
7	01	02	M02	041	7.312	.813	1	-
8	01	02	M02	041	1.125	3.188	1	-
9	01	02	M02	041	4.219	3.188	1	-
10	01	02	M02	041	7.312	3.188	1	-
11	01	03	L01	041	3.563	2.000	1	-
12	01	03	L01	041	4.750	2.000	1	-
13	01	04	M02	041	5.438	2.125	1	-
14	01	04	M02	041	6.375	2.125	1	-
15	01	04	M02	041	5.438	2.625	1	-
16	01	04	M02	041	6.375	2.625	1	-

Figure 36-5 NC program prepared by the computer from the input of Fig. 36-4. The computer output includes printed lists, a plot of the hole pattern, and a deck of cards giving coordinate data and machine data instructions, the same as listed in Fig. 36-1. (Courtesy Brown and Sharpe Mfg. Co.)

systems. The list of coordinates and turret positions in Fig. 36-5 is identical with that derived manually and shown in Fig. 36-1.

In the example given by Fig. 36-4 and 36-5, the program is processed in a computer external to the NC control. However, with a control that has computer capabilities, an abbreviated program like that of Fig. 36-4 may be sufficient for the control, which then generates the detailed instructions for the machine. The processor is an adjunct to the control.

A processor for NC programming performs several definite functions and commonly has sections to carry out each function. One section is the *translator* that converts the input into the computer code so that it can be processed into the series of basic commands required for the NC control. A *calculator* section performs the necessary computations to establish all points, tool center offsets, feed rates, etc. An *editorial and diagnostic* section detects errors and organizes the program. The result of this stage is what is called the *centerline* or *cutter location* (CL) file or tape. Overall, an *executive control* section supervises and coordinates all the other sections in the processor.

CL instructions must be converted to suit each NC machine control because almost every model of NC machine is different in some respects from all others. Thus for most, a control requires a final computer program called a *post-processor* to convert the CL data to suit the particular type of control. A processor like the one depicted by Figs. 36-4 and 36-5 may be dedicated to a particular machine, and its output is suitable to the specific controller, and a separate post-processor is not needed. This is called a *one-pass* system. Another may have a separate post-processor for each of a number of NC machines and is called a *two-pass* system. Some older machine controls have been changed, and new machines are being made with controls so that all accept a standardized single form of input called *CL Exchange Data,* which is derived from the CL file by a post-processor called a *CL Exchange Converter.* All such controls are compatible, and different post-processors are not needed for them.

Most NC language processors serve for a particular kind of operation, such as milling, turning, point-to-point drilling, electrodischarge wire cutting, etc. Whatever their purposes, NC processors may be divided into three groups in accordance with their format and complexity. Further explanation of these groups will be given in the following sections together with some examples. There are many program languages, and the examples given are merely typical and do not cover the details of all varieties.

Group I Programs. A group I program accepts the definition of the patterns of points, arrays, lines, curves, surfaces, etc. The input is largely, and in some cases entirely, numerical and in a fixed format. The kind of work to be done may be specified by a code, and the processor fills in the details of execution. Quite often the order of the instructions determines the final sequence of steps in an operation. The example given in the next paragraph is for a simple point-to-point drilling operation, but some group I programs have much more scope. A proprietary program of this type, called NUFORM, is described as a total system that can handle all kinds of NC operations from point-to-point to two-and-a-half axis continuous path through three-dimensional contouring with as much as a five-axis machine tool.

Figure 36-4 gives an example of the input format for a group I program. It requires a "header" line defining the ranges of dimensions in the program and provides for lines of information specifying hole center points individually, on circles, along straight lines, or arrayed in matrices. There may also be a set-up point statement describing the points for locating the workpiece on the machine. The programmer merely selects one of the available declarations and fills in the appropriate dimensions. The second line, as an illustration, says in effect that this is processing statement number 01, represents holes arrayed on a two line matrix, is in format four, the X coordinate of the first hole is −0.625 in., the Y coordinate 0.3125 in., the distance between holes in the X direction is 7.4375 in., the matrix is not at an angle with the X axis, there are two holes in each line and three inches between lines, and these holes are operated upon by the tools in turret stations 01, 02, and 03.

A computer is able to translate the specifications for a job into the detailed instructions for an NC machine because it can make prearranged decisions and follow prescribed routines. From the basic capability of adding positive or negative numbers, the computer can perform all the forms of arithmetic. The flowchart of Fig. 36-6 shows how these principles may be applied to specifications like those of Fig. 36-4 in constructing a program like that of Fig. 36-5. A flow chart is a conventional means of showing what takes place in a program that directs a computer to do a certain job. Symbols designate functions; a diamond depicts a point in the program where a decision must be made to proceed along one of two or more possible paths; a rectangle where general information processing, such as calculating, is done. There are many other symbols. The computer proceeds from step to step in the directions designated by the arrows, choosing its paths by the decisions it must make dependent upon the conditions encountered.

Each line of Fig. 36-4 is punched on a card that has holes in columns. The number and positions of the holes in a column stand for a character. The line just above the entries in the form of Fig. 36-4 contains letters to denominate the form columns; the numbers correspond to the card columns. The computer reads one card at a time.

As indicated by Fig. 36-6, a series of tests must be made by the computer to decide what to do with each card. To test for a header card, 001 is subtracted from the number in form column D (card columns 8, 9, and 10). If the difference is zero, which the computer can detect, the decision must be to proceed to the subroutine to process a header card. If the difference is other than zero, procession is to the next test—that for a point. Only the subroutine for calculating the coordinates of points on a line or matrix is given in Fig. 36-6. First the figures from form columns E and F are stored in the memory of the computer as the X and Y coordinates of the first or pivot hole. The coordinates are calculated and recorded for the next hole. The count for the number of holes N is increased each time new coordinates are stored, and a test is made by comparing N with I, the number of holes specified per line, to decide when there are enough holes in the line. When one line is complete, the number of lines is ascertained from card column 7. If more lines are needed to fill out a matrix, the points are calculated in the manner shown in Fig. 36-6. After calculations have been made for all the cards and the dimensions of the point coordinates and the numbers of the

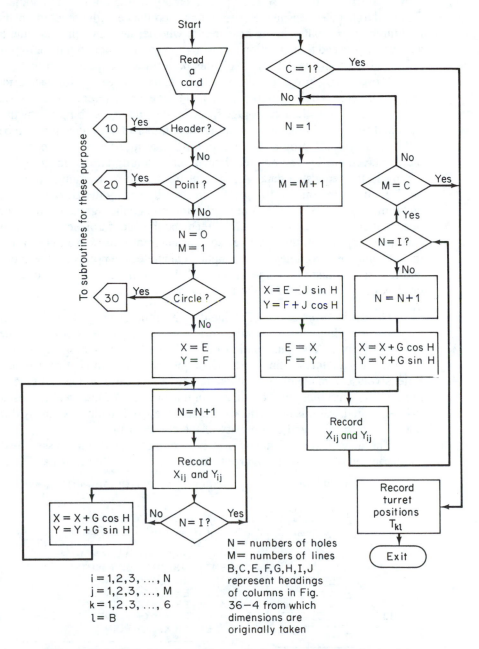

Figure 36-6 Flowchart of a routine to calculate the coordinates of points lying on lines and matrices as specified by the form of Fig. 36-4.

891

turret stations have been stored in the memory of the computer, another routine is followed to list the steps in the operation in accordance with predetermined rules. The programmer designates in the header card whether he wants the machine to index to a turret spindle and then position and work upon all pertinent points or to position each point and have all the pertinent spindles perform at one point at a time.

Most group I programs use separate routines in storage for each array of holes or type of curve (circle, parabola, etc.) and for each different use of the same curve. Consequently, considerable storage space is taken up in the computer by the program. That and the rigid format of input limit the number of situations that can be handled.

Some group I programs are tutorial, in that a series of statements or questions are displayed one by one on a CRT tube, and the programmer must reply to each by keying in the requested data. An excerpt from such a program is presented in Fig. 36-7. It covers the milling of a pocket in a workpiece by the zigzag movements of an end mill as depicted on the left in the illustration. To the right are shown some typical lines that are displayed on the CRT screen and the data furnished by the programmer. The latter appears on the screen as soon as entered in response to each query. When the information is complete, the computer calculates the points for the cutter locations and renders the instructions to the control, which may be punched in tape, recorded on disk or tape, or stored in the memory of a CNC.

Group II Programs.   The input of a group II program is in the form of an easy-to-learn, English-like, word description of tool positions or paths. The format is not rigidly fixed, and punctuation rather than position distinguishes and separates entries. The product is defined in terms of lines and circles and other geometric shapes. Extensive use is made of symbolic notations. Practically no manual precalculation is required. For instance, the coordinates of intersections of lines and curves do not have to be specified. All this makes it possible to write specifications for many different jobs but adds to the size and complexity of the compiler program.

The quasi-English languages of NC computer programs possess restricted vocabularies and formats. Recognized words consist of definitions like POINT, LINE,

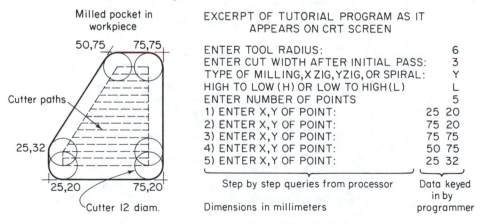

Figure 36-7   Example of a tutorial program for NC.

CIRCLE; action words like GO, STOP, CUT, GO BACK; modifiers like RIGHT, LEFT, TO, PAST; and punctuation marks. An abridged dictionary of terms based on actual languages is given in Table 36-1. As a rule, additional words or symbols may be defined and used throughout the program. A typical format is described in the next section.

The routines of group II programs are more generalized than those of group I programs. For instance, one procedure may calculate the points along any curve instead of a routine for each specific curve. This eliminates the need to store a large number of routines in the memory of the computer.

TABLE 36-1   ABRIDGED DICTIONARY OF AN NC LANGUAGE

Definitions

Points: SYMBOL = POINT/X, Y
Lines: SYMBOL = LINE/X_1, Y_1, X_2, Y_2
          SYMBOL = LINE/X, Y, ATANGL, A
Circles: SYMBOL = CIRCLE/CENTER, X, Y, RADIUS, R
X SMALL, Y SMALL = On the side of the small values of X or Y
X LARGE, Y LARGE = On the side of the large values of X or Y
TOLER/U = The maximum deviation permitted from a curve by approximation
TLRAD/U = Tool radius (in.)

Motions and Modifiers

TL LFT = Place the center of the tool on the left side of the line
TL RGT = Place the center of the tool on the right side of the line
TL ON = Place the center of the tool on the line
GO LFT = Go left on the next line or curve
GO RGT = Go right on the next line or curve
GO FWD = Go forward on the next line or curve
GO BAC = Go backward on the next line or curve
GO TO = Move the edge of the tool to the next line or curve
GO ON = The tool center is to be set on the next point, line, or curve
GO PAST = The trailing edge of the tool is to be tangent to the next line or curve
INDIR, VECTOR/X, Y = Move the tool in the direction of a vector with the specified components
GO DLTA/U, V = Move the tool by an amount $\Delta X = U$, $\Delta Y = V$
FROM/X, Y or FROM/SYMBOL = The first motion statement of the program
TAN = Directs the tool to move until it is tangent to a line or curve when used as a modifier
FAR = Directs the tool to be moved until it comes to the second intersection with the following curve
END = This part is done
FINI = All parts are done

Punctuation

/ Separates names or actions from modifiers
, Comma always used between every two words or symbols not separated by other punctuation
= Equal to or stands for
( ) Parentheses enclose a function
+ Means add, but is not needed to signify a positive number
− Means subtract and must always be placed before a negative number
All numbers must be expressed to the first decimal place like 3.0 or 4.2.
The letters X, Y, or U stand above in places of numbers.

APT.   One of the best known group II working programs is APT (Automated Programmed Tools), originated in the 1950s at MIT and developed over the years in several stages. It was first developed for milling and was used largely in the aerospace industry. Later additions were made for other kinds of operations. Overall responsibility for continued development was vested in IITRI, in Chicago, where in 1961 the version APT III was produced. Then about 1971, the development of APT was taken over by an organization known as Computer Aided Manufacturing International (CAMI). APT no longer represented the forefront of computerized manufacturing technology but has been developed since then as one of the important components of expanding management and manufacturing technology. In 1977 the American National Standards Institute (ANSI) published the Standards bulletin entitled *Programming Language APT, ANSI, X3.37* to establish the form for and the interpretation of programs expressed in the APT language. The purpose is to promote interchangeability of processing all APT systems on a wide variety of computers. To do this the standard establishes the syntax of the APT language, the rules governing the interpretation of the syntax, and the format of the tool positions in the output data file. The standard does not prescribe how APT programs are processed or implemented.

According to the ANSI standard, the APT language is composed of a hierarchy of five proper subsets. Each subset has the capability of all lower-level subsets. The simplest (subset 1) contains no geometric definitions; these are introduced in subset 2. Subsets 1 and 2 are suitable for point-to-point operations. Contouring in a plane begins with subset 3, three-dimensional contouring with subset 4, and multiaxis contouring with subset 5. With higher levels more and more comprehensive definitions and symbols are available, and lengthy routines (such as Do-loops) may be incorporated. Subsets 4 and 5 may be group III programs.

An APT system consists of an APT language and an APT processor which is available for a fee for anyone who does not have his or her own system. There is no one monolithic system. The early APT developed into a ponderous system, mainly for the aircraft industry, that required monstrous computers. It was beyond the needs and capabilities of most potential users, and consequently smaller and simpler versions were created. This is reflected in the present-day hierarchy set down in the ANSI standard previously described. Systems in the realms of the simpler subsets are commonly devoted to work on certain families of machine tools and can be processed on small to moderate-size computers. Well known and widely used of these are ADAPT and AUTOSPOT. A number of proprietary APT-based systems are available commercially. Prominent among these are COMPACT, SPLIT, UCC-APT, and UNI-APT. It is reported that some 15 different versions of APT exist in the United States, and probably as many more overseas. Of course, the APT family is not alone; it is estimated that there is a total of over 60 part programming languages of all kinds.

A sample program for plane contouring is displayed in Fig. 36-8 to give a basic view of the APT language. The program consists of a series of statements that include (1) geometric definitions (PT1 = POINT/5,4), (2) parameter definitions (FEDRAT/80), and (3) motion instructions (GO/TO, BASE). Items (1) and (3) may

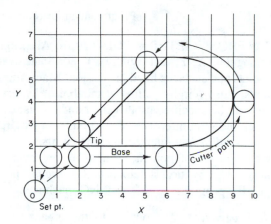

INPUT PROGRAM	EXPLANATION
CUTTER/I **$$** FLAT END	Use a 1 inch diameter cutter with a flat end.
TOLER/.OO5	All cuts must be within 0.005 inch of specifications.
FED RAT/80	The initial rate of feed (rapid traverse) is at 80 ipm
HEAD/I, MOD/I	Operate tool in mode No.1 in head No.1.
SPINDL/2800	Run spindle at 2800 rpm.
COOLNT/FLOOD	Apply flood of coolant.
PTI = POINT/5,4	Defines a reference point, called PTI, at coordinates (5,4).
FROM/(SETPT = POINT/O,O)	The tool is to start from the point called SETPT, which is defined as having coordinates (O,O).
INDIRP/(TIP = POINT/2,2)	Move the tool towards the point called TIP, which is a point with coordinates (2,2).
BASE = LINE/TIP, AT ANGL, O	A line called BASE is defined as passing through the point TIP at a zero angle with the horizontal.
FED RAT/5	The rate of feed is 5 ipm.
GO/TO, BASE	Move cutter to touch the line called BASE.
TLRGT, GORGT/BASE	Go right along the line called BASE with the tool on the right.
GO FWD/(ELLIPS/CENTER, PTI, 3,2,O)	Go forward along an ellipse with focus at PTI, semimajor axis 3 in., semiminor axis 2 in., and major axis at zero degrees with horizontal.
GO LFT/(LINE/6,6,2,2), PAST, BASE	Continue left along a line joining points (6,6) and (2,2) and past the line BASE.
FED RAT/8O	Return at rapid traverse rate.
GO TO/SETPT	Go straight to the point SETPT and stop.
COOLNT/OFF	Turn off the coolant.
SPINDL/OFF	Turn off the spindle.
END	This is the end of this part of the program.
FINI	This is the end of the whole program.

Figure 36-8   APT program for a hypothetical operation.

be combined, like FROM/(SETPT = POINT/0,0). All programming is in terms of a right-hand rectangular (X, Y, and usually Z) coordinate system. The cutter moves with respect to points and surfaces fixed in position. Many alternate ways are available for defining points, lines, circles, ellipses, parabolas, hyperbolas, and vectors. For instance, a circle may be specified by its center and radius, center and a tangent line, center and point on the circumference, three points on its circumference, center and a tangent circle, and radius and intersecting tangent lines. A mean curve may even be faired through a given set of points. In all there are over 1000 rules in the APT language defining words, syntax, statements, etc. Over 75 post-processors have been written to adapt APT programs to different NC machines.

Group III Programs.   In contrast to the others where tool paths must be specified, a group III program accepts a description of a shape to be machined and automatically generates all the tool paths to do the job most efficiently. The language is abridged English with symbolic notations and considerable flexibility. Programs in this class are rather long and logically complex and can be processed only on the largest computers.

A typical group III program recognizes and performs the calculations for any surface that can be expressed by an equation in three-dimensional analytic geometry. Common surfaces may be described in a number of ways and may be divided into parts for convenience. In addition, the program provides for a filleted surface to make a smooth transition between two intersecting analytical surfaces.

An example of a simple group III program is given in Fig. 36-9. The first set of statements defines the symbols arbitrarily assigned to pertinent surfaces in the operation: TOP for the upper surface of the workpiece, CLR for a plane above which the cutter may be moved without interference, and WORK for the surface to be machined. The next set of instructions sets forth the conditions of the operation: the idle tool position, the path over which the cutter moves to cutting position to clear the work, feed rate, radius of the ball end of the cutter, tolerated error of the machined surface, and coolant flowing. In the third set, REALM is an area that is to be machined in one pass of the tool—in this case one surface. The cutter is directed to start outside of the area at point (75, 0, 25) and proceed in the +Y direction. The region to be machined lies to the left. The external boundry of the cut is the intersection of WORK and TOP, and the cutter path is to be along a spiral. The last set of statements disposes of the tool and closes the operation.

Advanced Systems.   *Computer Graphics* systems are tutorial in nature for interactive NC programming between programmer and computer, commonly some versions of APT. With a typical system, the programmer picks part dimensions and angles off the part drawing in the order dictated by instructions that appear automatically on a CRT screen. These are entered into the system through a keyboard. With some systems, the programmer enters the proper commands (e.g., TL LFT, GOTO, etc.) to apply to the data; with other systems commands are issued automatically to suit the input data. The tool path is generated automatically in a simulated

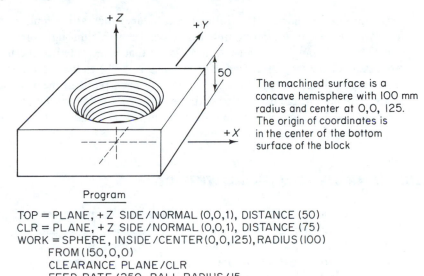

The machined surface is a concave hemisphere with 100 mm radius and center at 0,0, 125. The origin of coordinates is in the center of the bottom surface of the block

Program

```
TOP = PLANE, + Z  SIDE / NORMAL (0,0,1), DISTANCE (50)
CLR = PLANE, + Z  SIDE / NORMAL (0,0,1), DISTANCE (75)
WORK = SPHERE, INSIDE / CENTER (0,0,125), RADIUS (100)
        FROM (150,0,0)
        CLEARANCE PLANE / CLR
        FEED RATE / 250, BALL RADIUS / 15
        INSIDE TOLERANCE / 0.025, OUTSIDE TOLERANCE / 0.025
        ON COOLANT
REALM / WORK
EXTERNAL AT / (75,0,25), + Y DIRECTION, LEFT
EXTERNAL BOUNDARY / WORK (TOP)
SPIRAL
        GO TO / (150,0,0), OFF COOLANT
        STOP MACHINE TOOL, LAST
```

Figure 36-9 Sample of group III programs.

three-dimensional perspective (in some systems on a second CRT screen) to provide a visual check of the program created. Programming may be done for turning, milling, punching, and die-making operations. One computer graphics system is offered for less than $20,000.

A *preprocessor* is a program that prepares input statements for an NC processor from a series of point coordinates. Say, for instance, that a program is to be prepared to machine a mold to duplicate one already made by hand. The mold cavity is a surface of revolution, and a coordinate measuring machine is utilized to read out the coordinates of points along the profile. In another case, the designer of an object may define a profile by specifying the coordinates of the points establishing a series of lines, arcs, or curves. In any case, the preprocessor takes the statements giving the geometric and parameter definitions and motion instructions for a selected operation to enable a processor (e.g., an APT processor) to prepare the commands for the NC machine.

A worthwhile goal for NC programming, as well as for all computer programming, is to achieve voice input and thus eliminate the slower and tedious routine of typing or punching cards or tapes. *Voice programmning* for NC (VNC) is available but not widely used. It is most readily applicable to programming an English-like programming language with a limited vocabulary, such as a simple version of APT. In a typical system, the programmer delivers the words through a microphone into a translater that compiles them into a program that is executed in the usual way by a processor for the language used. The translator can be trained to recognize the voice of an operator simply by his or her repeating each word in the vocabulary 5 or 10 times. The parameters associated with the operator's voice are then stored in memory for later matching and identification. As each line is dictated, it is written on a CRT display so it can be checked for errors.

SELECTION OF PROGRAMMING METHOD

The first choice should be between manual and computer-assisted programming. Authorities recommend that a shop newly into NC should start with manual programming for at least 3 to 6 months. This provides closer hands-on experience with the NC system in the initial learning period and the opportunity to find out what manual programming costs really are in the shop. A survey of experts showed a profile for manual programming for up to four tapes a month; average preparation time not in excess of 15 minutes per block, and no more than 2 hours average debugging time per tape.

Computer-assisted programming is justified, of course, when its cost is shown to be lower compared to manual methods. True computer-assisted programming costs may not be easy to find for a plant without previous experience; costs from other plants or from system vendors may not be applicable. Factors to consider when selecting a particular language system are (1) the ability of the language to handle parts as complex as needed (now and in the future) without being too elaborate; (2) the dependability of the supplier of the system; (3) hardware requirements, including computer, terminals, peripheral equipment, etc.; (4) availability and cost of programmer training; (5) availability of technical assistance and support; and (6) actual unit programming costs.

Guidance in evaluating NC language systems is given by two studies that compare capabilities and costs for popular NC languages and explain how such comparisons can be made. The first is *Numerical Control Language Evaluation,* March 1974, and covers seven programming languages for boring, drilling, milling, and tapping operations. The languages were tried on 10 sample pieces of different complexity and all were not capable of programming all the pieces. APT was able to handle all 10 test parts, but its programming cost was higher with the simpler parts. The second study is *Numerical Control Lathe Language Study,* November 1979, which compares 15 languages for turning, as applied to 10 parts. Here, again, APT performed well for complex parts, but non-APT languages were more efficient on simpler parts. A definite conclusion is that "there is no one language or system which is superior to all others in all situations." These studies can be obtained from the Numerical Control Society, Glenview, IL 60025.

NC IN THE TOTAL MANUFACTURING SYSTEM

Figure 35-1 illustrates the conventional way of programming NC, manually or with computer assistance, from a description of a workpiece on a drawing. This is done because as the NC system has been developed, it has been attached to the existing industrial system of product design and manufacture. The ideal is to process information automatically from original design to fabrication. With such a refined system, only the functional specifications and economic conditions of a part (such as a drive housing to support certain loads, occupy certain space, and to be of minimum weight and cost) would be given by the designer. The system would automatically determine all the necessary dimensions, tolerances, and other details of the required part and proceed to generate instructions to make the product in the best way and provide a drawing if desired.

Progress toward the ideal in manufacturing systems is being made. The first step is to compile the product specifications in numerical form. This can come naturally because designers are more and more turning to computers to aid them in their work, i.e., computer-aided design (CAD). Some parts may be represented by mathematical models. An example is a functional cam, for which equations relating to follower displacement are all that are necessary. Many aerospace shapes may be defined mathematically. One system enables a designer to make a sketch with a light pen on a CRT screen. The lines may be altered, erased, corrected, rotated, etc., under the direction of the designer. The computer can also be called upon for calculations and file management. When the design is finished, its dimensions and other specifications are stored in an orderly program. Some shapes, like those of automobile bodies, are designed for appearance rather than mathematical considerations. Models of clay or other substances may be made of such products, and their dimensions determined at necessary points by photographic or mechanical methods. However obtained, the design data base can be stored and transmitted on tapes, disks, etc., for further use. Input from a CAD system for NC programming is shown in Fig. 35-1.

Design data are processed in a number of ways, more or less automatically, to plan production and program for NC. It has just been pointed out that interactive graphics on a CRT screen is one form of CAD. The same facilities may be employed with additions for NC programming. The programmer can trace cutter paths on the screen with a light pen and designate specific points for action. He or she can type on a keyboard the commands in APT or other language, and the computer fills in the dimensions and compiles the program. Such interactive systems used at some places in the aircraft industry are reported much faster than entirely manual programming. Computer-aided NC programming may be used to make tools, as well as parts. In the automobile industry, NC is not employed as a rule for actual production but is widely utilized to make the dies for shaping sheet metal and forgings.

The configuration of a workpiece is conventionally depicted by a drawing, which may be the basis for programming the NC operation to make the piece as illustrated in Fig. 35-1. Drawings can be made quickly from a computerized data base on an NC drafting machine. Authorities have estimated that NC drafting is on an average 10 times faster than manual. A typical automatic drafting machine has a pen or scriber on a head that slides along a bridge. The bridge is supported at each end on rails and moves along a table. Coordinate movements are made to conform to the data input to the NC control.

The initial step in manufacturing, once the design specifications have been finished, is to plan the processes. The process specifications include a list of operations, machines, tools, etc., required to make a part efficiently. These specifications together with the design specifications are passed on for material procurement, cost estimating, production scheduling and control, inspection, etc. At one time all these functions of manufacturing were done manually, but in recent years some or all have been automated in systems known as *computer-aided manufacturing* (CAM). It is reported that there are over 2500 stand-alone CAD/CAM installations worldwide. The initial step of a full CAM system is *computer-aided process planning* (CAPP).

NC programming is at least a sequel to process planning and in the ideal it is an integral part. CAPP and automatic NC programming start with a technique called *group technology* (GT) in which the parts made in a plant are coded and segregated into groups or families. All the parts in one family have common features or processing. Each new part is assigned to its proper family. For example, a family might be all shafts from 1 to 3 in. in diameter, 6 to 8 in. in length, and with no more than six diameters. An optimum routing is prepared specifying the operations, machines, and tools for any part in a family. The routing includes operations for permissible deviations such as threaded ends, cross holes, material differences, etc., in a family of shafts. These extra steps are eliminated to route any shaft that does not require them. Also, an optimum program is written for each NC operation on the routing. The routings and NC programs are stored in the memory of the computer without dimension and other specifics for any particular part. When a part is to be processed, the CAPP program identifies its family from its coding, retrieves the proper routing and NC programs, and inserts into them the necessary dimensions ascertained from the design data base. The CAPP also exercises subroutines to calculate and select cutting speeds and feeds, power requirements, etc., in the manner explained in Chap. 17. Detailed cutter paths may be calculated, if required, to conform to workpiece dimensions. In the end the computer issues routings for production control and other functions and NC programs on tape, disk, or directly into NC control storage.

QUESTIONS

1. Explain the difference between manual and computer-assisted NC programming.
2. Describe the characteristics of an MDI system and state its advantages and disadvantages.
3. What is a processor for computer-assisted NC, and what functions does it perform?

4. Describe briefly the three groups of computer-assisted NC programs and point out how they differ from each other.

5. What is a post-processor, and why is it used?

6. What is a flowchart?

7. Why is a computer able to translate specifications for a job into detailed instructions?

8. Describe briefly the APT programming system for NC.

9. What is the ideal concept of the totally automated industrial system, and how is it being approached?

PROBLEMS

1. Make up a flowchart to show how
   (a) A routine may enable a computer to calculate the coordinates of holes on a circle.
   (b) A computer may arrive at the final sequence of steps in an operation for machining the holes specified in Fig. 36-4.

2. Prepare a computer input program with format like that of Fig. 36-4 for machining all the holes in the part of Fig. 22-25.

3. Prepare a manual program like that of Fig. 36-1 for machining all the holes in the part of Fig. 22-25.

4. Write a program using the language of Table 36-1 to machine the contour around the workpiece of Fig. 22-25.

5. Simulate the program of Fig. 36-9 to construct a program for machining a partial cylindrical groove in the top of a block 4 in. × 6 in. × 2 in. high. The axis of the cylinder is parallel to and 5 in. above the bottom of the block, in the Z-Y plane depicted in Fig. 36-9. Its radius is 4 in. Specify the cutter path to be ZIGZAG.

REFERENCES

CHILDS, J. J., *Numerical Control Parts Programming,* Industrial Press, New York, 1973.

DINCAU, M. A., "Computer Graphics for NC Tapes," *American Machinist,* July 1974, p. 57.

DRAYTON, C., "Programming with APT", *NC Commline,* Nov. 1979–June 1980.

GRAHAM, C. J., "The Pre-processor," *NC Commline,* Feb.–Mar. 1975, p. 33.

GRINDSTATT, C. C., "Computer Graphics for CAM Applications," *NC Commline,* July–Aug. 1981, p. 12.

HATSCHEK, R. L., "NC Programming, Special Report 719," *American Machinist,* Feb. 1980, p. 119.

HERNDON, L. R., "CL Exchange Data as Common Input for NC Machines," *NC Commline,* July–Aug. 1982, p. 13.

JENKINS, L. J., et al., "Getting More out of NC, Special Report 738," *American Machinist,* Oct. 1981, p. 185.

SCHAFFER, G. H., "Implementing Computer Integrated Manufacturing (CIM), Special Report 736," *American Machinist,* Aug. 1981, p. 151.

SENKEIV, P. D., "A Final Report on Numerical Control Language Evaluation for Lathes," *NC Commline,* Jan.–Feb. 1980, p. 30.

SQUIER, B. H., "Automatic Numerical Control Processing," *Manufacturing Engineering,* Sept., 1981, p. 90.

WILLIAMS, J., "Evaluating Part Programming Languages," *NC Commline,* Nov.–Dec. 1976, p. 15.

ZWICA, T., "MDI Pros and Cons," *NC Commline,* Sept.–Oct. 1980, p. 15.

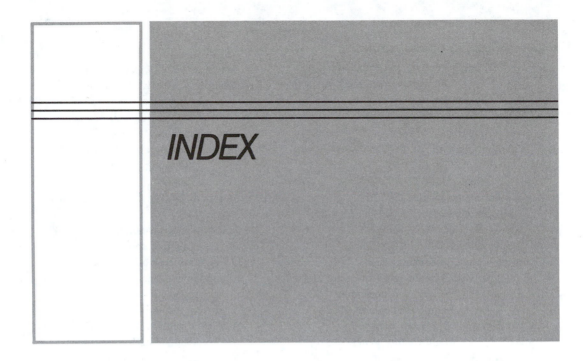

INDEX